FAMILY WORLD ATLAS

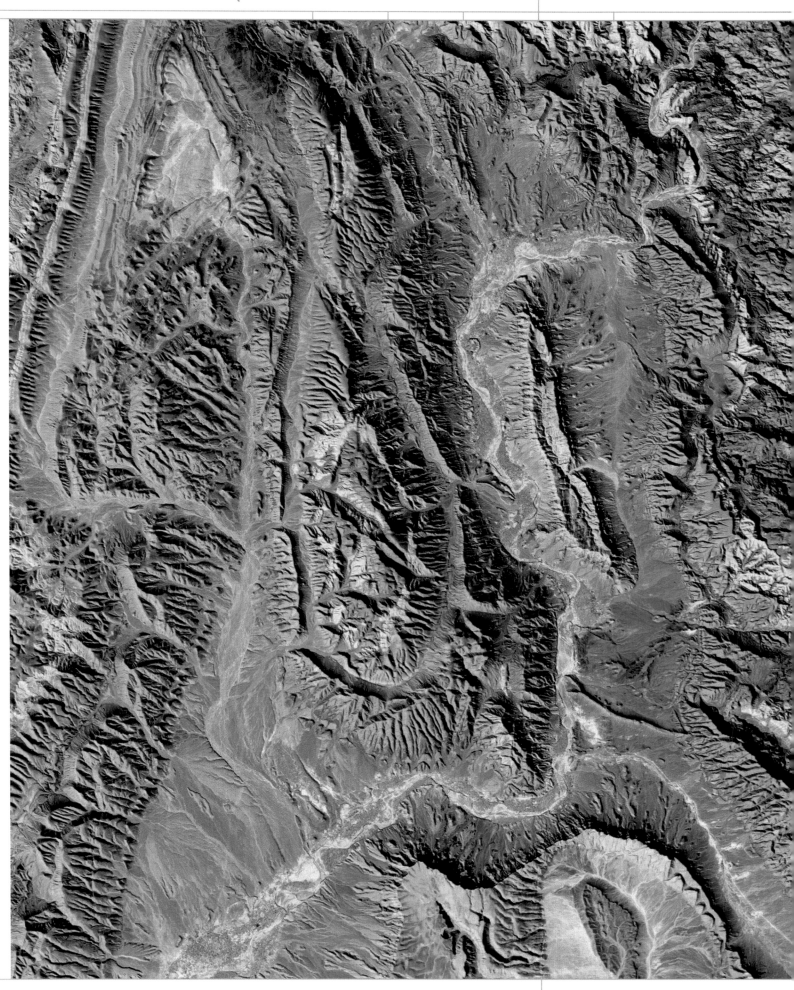

The satellite image shows the south-eastern section of the York Peninsula in the Australian state of Queensland. You can see part of the Barrier Reef lying off the coastline.

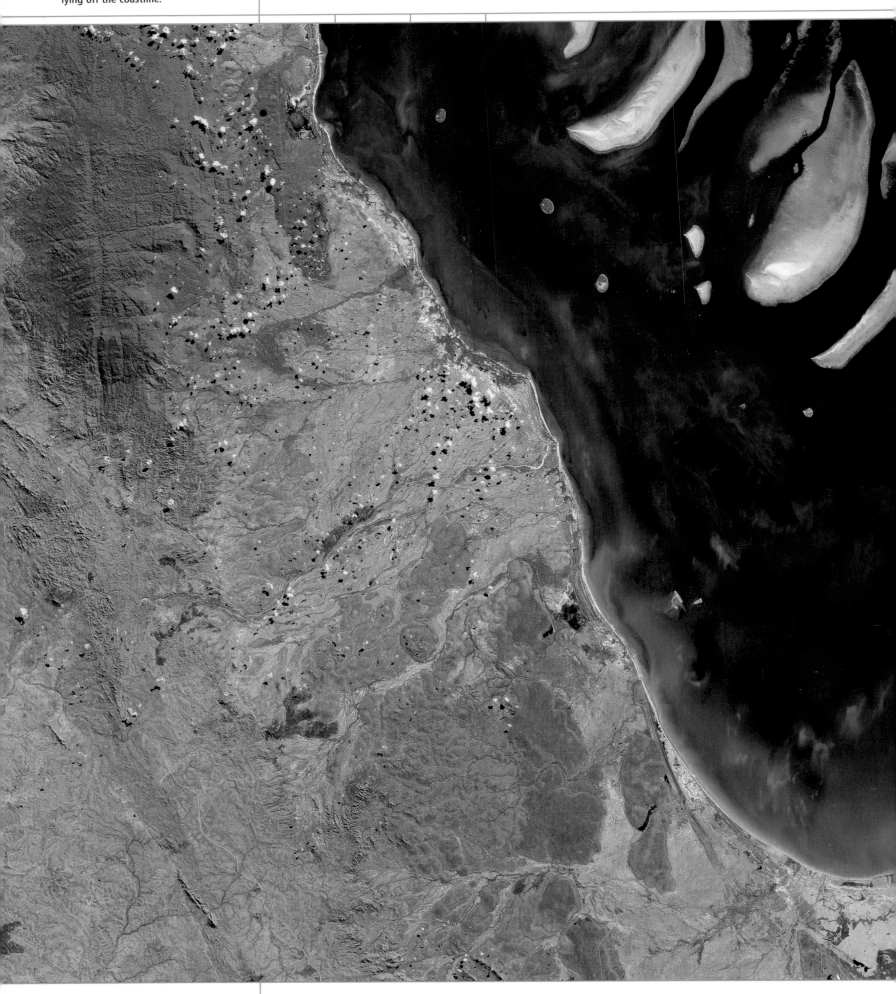

FAMILY WORLD ATLAS

"I wish to be a citizen of the world, at home everywhere...and everywhere a traveller."

Table of Contents

The world   14 – 23

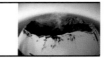

Europe   24 – 73

Asia   74 – 131

Australia / Oceania   132 – 159

Map locator

Europe

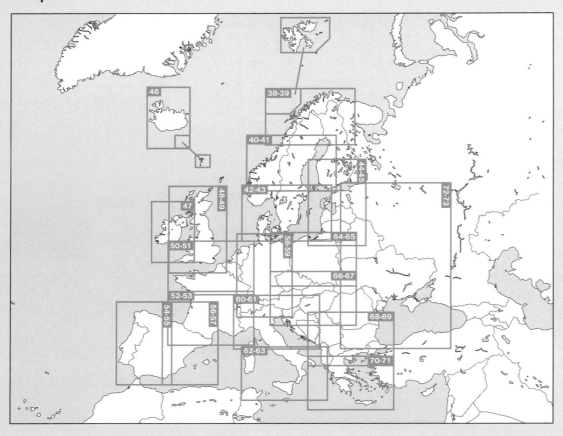

Southeastern Asia, Australia/Oceania

Near and Middle East, Northern Asia, Central Asia, Southern Asia

Africa

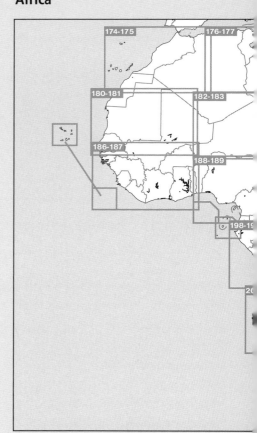

Map locator

The impressive modern skyline of Chicago, along the shores of Lake Michigan. The city is a leading commercial and financial center.

Easter Island was once home to an advanced civilization. The more than 300 stone sculptures (moai) scattered around the island are the most important remnants of this culture.

North and Central America

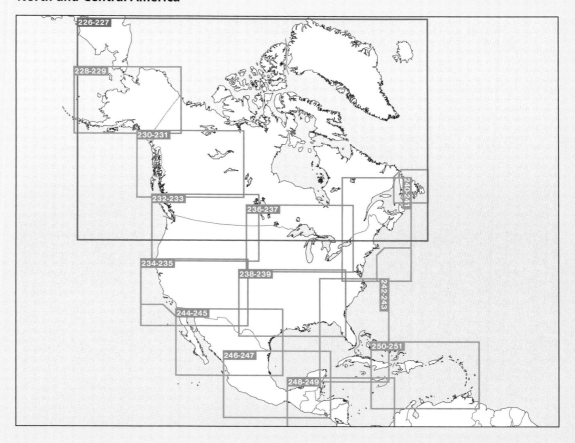

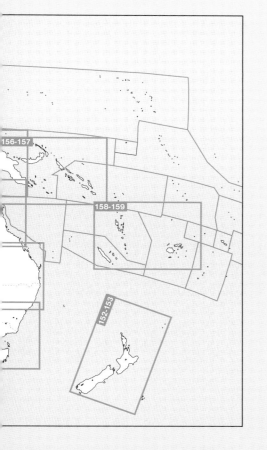

South America

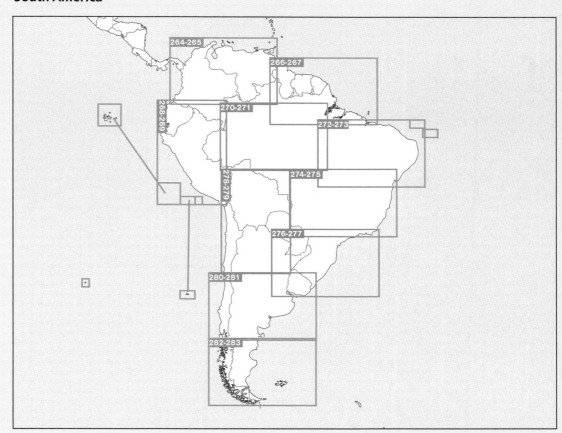

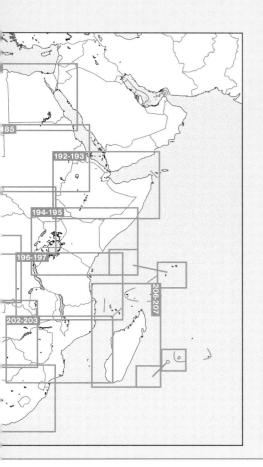

Legend • Natural geographical features

The Polynesian island of Moorea is the remnant of a massive volcano. The island, like so many in the Pacific Ocean, is surrounded by coral reefs.

The Scottish Highlands in the United Kingdom feature a variety of romantic and beautiful landscapes, including craggy mountains, pristine lakes, and rugged valleys.

Territorial waters

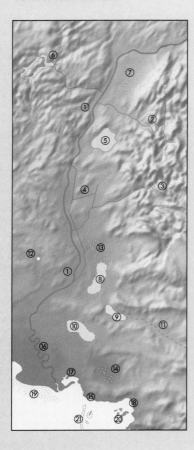

① Stream, river
② Tributary with headstreams
③ Waterfall, rapids
④ Canal
⑤ Lake
⑥ Reservoir with dam
⑦ Marsh, moor
⑧ Intermittent lake
⑨ Salt lake
⑩ Intermittent salt lake
⑪ Intermittent river (wadi)
⑫ Well, spring
⑬ Salt swamp
⑭ Salt pan
⑮ Shoreline
⑯ Meandering river
⑰ Lagoon
⑱ Ocean bay
⑲ Mud flats
⑳ Island, archipelago
㉑ Coral reef

High and low levels

Areas

① above – 5000 meters
② 4000 – 5000 meters
③ 3000 – 4000 meters
④ 2000 – 3000 meters
⑤ 1000 – 2000 meters
⑥ 500 – 1000 meters
⑦ 250 – 500 meters
⑧ 100 – 100 meters
⑨ 0 – 2000 meters
⑩ Depression

Depth tints

❶ 0 – 200 meters
❷ 200 – 2000 meters
❸ 2000 – 4000 meters
❹ 4000 – 6000 meters
❺ 6000 – 8000 meters
❻ below 8000 meters

Topography

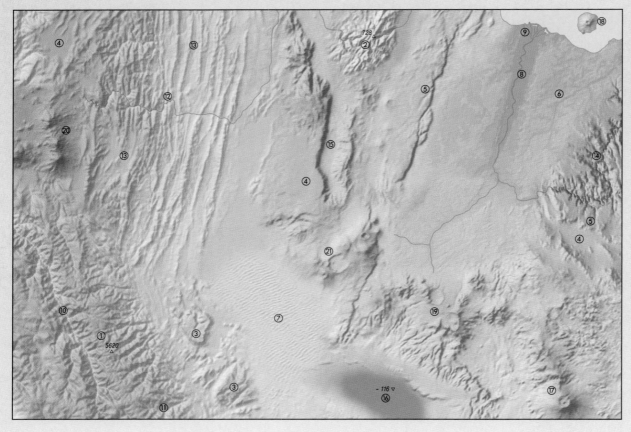

① High mountain region
② Highland with valleys
③ Table mountain
④ Plateaus
⑤ Water meadow on hilly ground
⑥ Escarpment
⑦ High dunes in arid areas
⑧ Lowland
⑨ Delta
⑩ V-shaped valley
⑪ U-shaped valley
⑫ Gorge
⑬ Cordilleras with high-lying valleys
⑭ Canyon
⑮ Rift Valley
⑯ Depression
⑰ Volcano
⑱ Volcanic island
⑲ Extinct volcanoes
⑳ High mountain volcanoes
㉑ Meteorite crater

Beijing's historic Forbidden City was the main residence of China's monarchs and the great imperial court for many centuries.

A full moon above the skyline of San Francisco in northern California. The city's beautiful Golden Gate Bridge is one of the world's longest suspension bridges.

Settlements and transportation routes

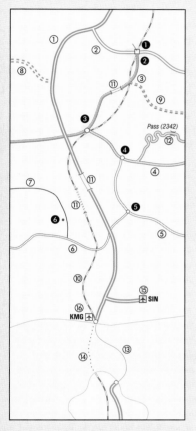

Transportation routes

① Interstate highway/motorway
② Multilane divided highway
③ Primary highway
④ Secondary highway
⑤ Main road
⑥ Secondary road
⑦ Unimproved road
⑧ Interstate highway/motorway under construction
⑨ Primary highway under construction
⑩ Railroad
⑪ Tunnel
⑫ Pass with elevation in meters
⑬ Ferry, shipping route
⑭ Railroad ferry
⑮ International Airport with IATA-code
⑯ Airport with IATA-code

Settlements

❶ Urban area
❷ City, over 1 million inhabitants
❸ City, 100,000 – 1 million inhabitants
❹ Town, 10,000 – 100,000 inhabitants
❺ Town, under 10,000 inhabitants
❻ Hamlet, research station

Typefaces of cities and towns

① □ **NEW YORK**
② ○ **Stuttgart**
③ ○ **Narvik**
④ ○ Porta Westfalica
⑤ ○ **Storuman**
⑥ ○ White Owl
⑦ • Glenayle
⑧ □ **BEIJING (PEKING)**
⑨ ○ **Firenze (Florence)**
⑩ Tikal
⑪ Grand Canyon du Verdon

① City, over 1 million inhabitants
② City, 100,000 – 1 million inhabitants
③ Significant city, 10,000 – 100,000 inhabitants
④ City, 10,000 – 100,000 inhabitants
⑤ Significant town, under 10,000 inhabitants
⑥ Town, under 10,000 inhabitants
⑦ Hamlet, research station
⑧ City, over 1 million inhabitants with translation
⑨ Town 100,000 – 1 million inhabitants with translation
⑩ Point of cultural interest
⑪ Point of natural interest

Political and other boundaries

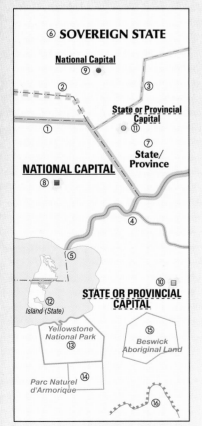

① International boundary
② Disputed international boundary
③ Administrative boundary
④ Boundary on rivers
⑤ Boundary in lake or sea
⑥ Country name
⑦ Administrative name
⑧ Capital with more than 1 million inhabitants
⑨ Capital below 1 million inhabitants
⑩ Administrative capital with more than 1 million inhabitants
⑪ Administrative capital with less than 1 million inhabitants
⑫ Dependent territory with administering country
⑬ National parks and biosphere reserves
⑭ Nature parks and other protected areas
⑮ Reservation
⑯ Walls (Great Wall of China, Hadrian's Wall)

Typefaces of topographic features

① *PACIFIC OCEAN*
② *GULF OF MEXICO*
    Gulf of Thailand
③ *Antalya Körfezi*
④ *Elbe   Rio Grande   Murray*
⑤ *White Nile   Suez Canal*
⑥ *H I M A L A Y A*
⑦ *Great Plains*
⑧ Mt. Olympus △ 2424
⑨ – 116 ▽ Danakil Depression
⑩ *Tahiti*
⑪ *Cape of Good Hope*
⑫ *325*
⑬ 5425
⑭ *Mexican Basin*
⑮ *Mariana Trench*

① Ocean
② Gulf, bay
③ Small bay, strait
④ River, lake, canal
⑤ River, lake, canal (translated)
⑥ Mountain name
⑦ Area name, landscape name
⑧ Mountain name with elevation above sea level in meters
⑨ Depression with depth below sea level in meters
⑩ Island name
⑪ Cape name
⑫ Elevation of lake above sea level
⑬ Depth in oceans and lakes
⑭ Undersea landscapes, mountains and trenches
⑮ Deepsea trench

Explanation of symbols

The passenger train services that pass through South Africa's Garden Route offer spectacular views of the Indian Ocean and the Karoo Mountains.

The landscapes of Los Glaciares National Park, including large glaciers and mountains, are among the most spectacular in the region of Patagonia. Photo: Fitz Roy Massif (3,128 m).

Principal travel routes

Remarkable landscapes and natural monuments

Beautiful natural landscapes, fascinating wildlife, historic architecture, and vibrant cities – our world is rich in wonders. The modern cartography and layout of the Family World Travel Atlas highlight many of the world's attractions – unspoiled wilderness areas, the most famous and significant historic sites, culturally diverse urban areas, holiday resorts, and sporting venues. The system of pictograms developed specifically for this atlas gives the reader a clear impression of the diverse attractions in the world's regions. All of the pictograms featured on each map are listed and labeled in a legend at the bottom of the respective page.

The following pages offer brief characterizations of the various pictograms used in the atlas. The pictograms are divided by color into two groups: green and blue pictograms represent natural attractions, while yellow pictograms represent cultural attractions and other manmade sites. The names of significant towns and cities are highlighted in yellow throughout the atlas. Blue pictograms represent sporting and recreational facilities. Important and well-known transportation routes, including highways and shipping routes, are also featured in the atlas. These routes are not only highlighted by pictograms but also by distinctly colored lines that identify each type of route.

Auto route
The maps display many of the world's most famous and historically significant roads and routes, such as the ancient Silk Road in Asia and historic Route 66 in the United States, The maps also feature important modern highways, including the Pan-American Highway that stretches through the Americas from Alaska to Tierra del Fuego, the highway stretching between Bangkok in Thailand and Singapore, and the Stuart Highway, which traverses the fascinating landscapes in Australia's sparsely populated interior.

Railroad
The age of the railroads started in 1804 when the world's first steam locomotive began operation in Wales. By the end of the 19th century it was possible to travel through most regions of Europe and North America and much of Asia and South America by train. The Orient Express, Europe's first long-distance luxury passenger line, began operation in 1883 and traveled between Paris. Bucharest, and Istanbul. The Trans-Siberian line was constructed between 1891 and 1916 with the goal of connecting Siberia to European Russia. The Trans-Siberian still runs between Moscow and Vladivostok on the Pacific Ocean almost 100 years after construction ended.

High speed train
The Eurostar trains travel at speeds up to 300 kilometers an hour and transport passengers between London and Brussels or Paris in less than three hours. Japan's Shinkansen line, also known as the "bullet train", connects several of the country's major cities. In Europe, France and Germany maintain the most extensive networks of high speed trains.

Shipping route
Millions of passengers travel on cruise ships every year and experience one of the most leisurely and comfortable forms of long-distance travel. Thousands of cruise ships traverse the oceans, seas, and rivers of the world. The Caribbean Sea, Mediterranean Sea, Scandinavia, and Alaska are among the most popular locations for cruises on the open seas. Modern cruise ships offer an astounding variety of attractions including casinos, entertainment, fine restaurants, and shops.

UNESCO World (Natural) Heritage
Since 1972, UNESCO, a body of the United Nations, has compiled a growing list of specially designated natural attractions and wonders that are deemed to be of outstanding importance and "universal" significance.

Mountain landscape
Mountain ranges are among the most scenic areas in the world. Many of the world's ancient low-mountain ranges, including the Appalachians and the Central Massif, feature heavily eroded and rounded peaks. Other, younger mountain ranges feature jagged and high peaks that are often covered by snow and glaciers.

Rock landscape
Many of the world's most interesting stone formations were shaped by wind and water erosion, including the natural attractions of Monument Valley National Park in the USA.

Ravine/canyon
Canyons and gorges are narrow and often deep valleys created by river and wind erosion. The Grand Canyon, in the American state of Arizona, is the most famous and one of the most spectacular canyons on the planet.

Extinct volcano
Volcanoes are formed when solid, liquid, or gas-like materials from the Earth's interior rise to the planet's surface. Magma passes through the structure of a volcano and leaves its crater as lava, often accompanied by plumes of hot ash. An extinct volcanoe is a volcano that has not experienced an eruption in the last 10,000 years.

Active volcano
Geologists consider any volcano that has erupted in the last 10,000 years to be an active volcano. Most of the world's active volcanoes are concentrated in geologically active regions, such as areas near the boundaries of the world's tectonic plates or mid-ocean ridges. The Pacific Ring of Fire is an area of relatively frequent volcanic activity.

Geyser
Active geysers are hot springs that occasionally release plumes of water into the air. Geysers are located in volcanically active regions.

Cave
Caves are formed during the creation of stone formations (mountains, underground layers of stone, etc.) or emerge later due to the eroding effects of water that seeps into stone and often carves out entire networks of large caves containing lakes and rivers.

Glacier
Glaciers are large fields or rivers of ice that often migrate through mountain valleys. Glaciers are formed above the snow line in mountainous areas such as the Alps or in regions with cold climates such as Alaska, northern Canada, and Greenland.

River landscape
The eroding power of flowing water formed many of the world's valleys and canyons. Many of the world's early civilizations emerged in fertile river valleys such as Mesopotamia or the Indus Valley. Many rivers in lowland areas have large branching deltas containing delicate ecosystems.

Waterfall/rapids
Waterfalls are formed when rivers flow over an area with a sudden drop in elevation. They come in a variety of heights and lengths. Waterfalls are among the most stunning natural attractions on the planet.

Lake country
Most of the world's major lakes were created by glaciers during the ice ages. Several regions have a large number of lakes, often interconnected and located near one another. In addition to glacial lakes, many lakes were created as a result of tectonic and geological activity.

Desert
Vast landscapes covered by sand dunes, sand fields, or stone with sparse rainfall, deserts are the most arid regions on the earth and only a few types of plants and animals can survive in these harsh environments. Most deserts have major differences between night and daytime temperatures. Most of the world's deserts remain sparsely populated.

Oasis
Oases are fertile islands surrounded by barren, arid deserts or steppes. They are supplied with water by rivers, springs or subterranean ground-water repositories.

Depression
Depressions are small basins located on land but at significant depths below sea level. Many depressions – including the Dead Sea – were created through tectonic activity.

Thick clouds above Mount Taranaki (2,158 m) on New Zealand's North Island, one of many active volcanoes in the Pacific Ring of Fire.

Dresden, the capital of the German state of Saxony, became a major cultural center in the 18th century. The city's waterfront along the Elbe River features many historic landmarks.

Remarkable cities and cultural monuments

Fossil site
Fossils are the ancient remnants and traces of animals and plants that have inhabited our planet during its long history.

Nature park
Conservation areas have been created to protect local flora and fauna. Most designated nature parks tend to be relatively small in size.

National park (landscape)
These large conservation areas protect areas of natural beauty and significant national or international importance. Development and industry are forbidden or heavily restricted in such area. Yellowstone National Park, in the US-State of Wyoming, is the world's oldest national park.

National park (flora)
This symbol designates national parks with interesting local flora.

National park (fauna)
This symbol designates national parks with unique local wildlife.

National park (culture)
National park with cultural attractions such as Native American historic sites.

Biosphere reserve
This symbol points out undeveloped conservation areas with pristine examples of distinct climate or vegetation zones. Many biosphere reserves exhibit high levels of biodiversity.

Wildlife reserve
These conservation areas have been created for the protection of endangered animals. Selous Game Reserve in Tanzania is home to herds of African elephants.

Whale watching
Boat tours providing the chance to observe whales or dolphins in their natural habitats.

Turtle conservation area
Several countries in the world have specially designated coastal areas where endangered sea turtle species live or lay their eggs.

Protected area for sea lions/seals
Some countries have coastal areas that have designated conservation sites to preserve the natural habitats of endangered seals and sea lions.

Protected area for penguins
These protected areas were created to preserve threatened penguin colonies and to observe these creatures in their habitats.

Zoo/safari park
Zoos are park-like areas that feature collections of animals, mostly from a variety of regions. Safari parks are large properties open to tourists that feature wildlife in open wilderness.

Crocodile farm
Most crocodile farms are commercial operations where the animals are bred. Many are open to the public.

Coastal landscape
Coastal areas often feature diverse landscapes including beaches, cliffs, tidal flats, and marshlands. Some coastal areas are flat with sand dunes, while others are lined by rock formations, stony beaches, and high cliffs. The beautiful fjords of Scandinavia are among the most stunning coastal areas in the world.

Beach
Beaches often offer diverse recreational activities. Sand beaches are common in flat areas. Many of the world's beaches are now heavily developed.

Coral reef
Coral reefs are formed by small animals called coral in warm saltwater. Many of the world's large coral reefs exhibit astonishing biodiversity and are accessible to divers. The world's largest coral reef is the Great Barrier Reef off the coast of Australia.

Island
Islands are land masses surrounded by water. Most islands are part of island groups. The islands on our planet have a combined land area of 10.5 million km². Many of the world's islands have become popular tourist destinations.

Underwater reserve
Underwater conservation areas have been created to protect local marine flora and fauna.

UNESCO World (Cultural) Heritage
Since 1972, UNESCO has compiled a list of specially designated cultural sites that are deemed to be of outstanding importance. The list now includes hundreds of cultural and historic sites around the world.

Remarkable city
Large and small cities of global importance or with an abundance of tourist attractions are highlighted in yellow on our maps.

Pre- and early history
Sites related to ancient human cultures and their ways of life during times before the emergence of written records. The most grandiose pre-historic sites include large megaliths created by different cultures, such as the circle of stone pillars at Stonehenge in the United Kingdom.

Prehistoric rockscape
Prehistoric paintings, carvings and reliefs created by nomadic peoples during ancient times. Such sites have been found on all of the world's inhabited continents and often provide scientists with valuable information about life in the times before the first civilizations emerged on our planet.

The Ancient Orient
Sites related to the ancient cultures that developed in the region comprising modern Anatolia (Asia Minor), Syria, Iraq, Israel, Lebanon, Iran, and in some cases Egypt, during the period between 7000 BC and the time of Alexander the Great (400 BC). The Sumerians developed one of the first urban civilizations on the planet. They also developed one of the first number systems. After 2000 BC, the first large empires emerged in the region including the kingdoms of the Babylonians, Assyrians, and Hittites. The region features temples, ziggurats, and palaces from ancient times.

Ancient Egypt
One of the greatest ancient civilizations developed on the banks of the Nile River in Egypt. Around 3000 BC, Egypt was unified under the reign of one ruler for the first time. Between this time and the period of Alexander the Great's conquests, Egypt was ruled by more than 31 dynasties. The all-powerful pharaohs were considered living gods in Ancient Egypt. The ancient Egyptians developed a writing system, a calendar, and eventually advanced building techniques. The greatest legacy of this fascinating culture is the spectacular pyramids. The arts of the ancient Egyptians were devoted primarily to religion and mythology.

Ancient Egyptian pyramids
The monumental pyramid tombs of Egyptian pharaohs were constructed during the Old Kingdom. The largest and most impressive pyramid is the 137-meter-high Great (Cheops) Pyramid at Giza.

Minoan culture
The advanced Bronze-Age culture of the Minoans flourished on the island Crete during ancient times. Minoan civilization first emerged during the 3rd millennium BC, after which the Minoans rapidly became the dominant power in the eastern Mediterranean. Modern Crete features the remnants of Minoan villas with impressive frescoes and interior design.

Phoenician culture
During ancient times the area encompassing modern Israel, Lebanon, and Palestine was once the center of Phoenician culture. The Phoenicians were the dominant trading power in the Mediterranean for several centuries and founded many colonies.

Early African culture
Ancient African civilizations include the cultures of the Kingdom of Ghana, Axum (Ethiopia), the Great Zimbabwe culture, and Kush, a complex and advanced society that developed south of Egypt.

Etruscan culture
The Etruscans probably originated in central Italy. During the 10th century BC, they conquered large sections of the Italian Peninsula before they were conquered by the Romans. Italy has numerous archeological and historic sites related to the culture of the ancient Etruscans.

Greek antiquity
No other civilization has had a greater influence on European culture than that of Ancient Greece. The city-state of Athens was one of the first basic democracies in history. The art, philosophy and architecture of Ancient Greece continue to inspire and shape our modern world. Ancient Greece was divided into city-states, many of which founded distant colonies in Southern Europe, the Middle East, and North Africa. Ancient Greek art dealt mostly with subjects related to Greek mythology. The Greek city-states constructed many great structures including impressive temples and amphitheaters. During the Hellenistic period – after the death of Alexander the Great – Greek-speaking cities outside the mainland, including Alexandria in Egypt, replaced the city-states as the centers of Greek civilization.

Explanation of symbols

Sunset above the Pyramids of Giza: the enormous pyramids were constructed as monumental tombs during the reign of ancient Egypt's pharaohs.

Borobudur: the Buddhist complex in Indonesia features numerous sculptures and reliefs. The site was buried beneath volcanic ash for centuries until it was rediscovered in the 19th century.

Remarkable cities and cultural monuments

Roman antiquity
Over a period of centuries the once small city of Rome emerged as the center of a powerful empire. The Roman Empire was at its largest under the reign of the Emperor Trajan (98–117 BC); during this period its borders extended from North Africa to Scotland and from Iberia to Mesopotamia. The Roman state that existed between 509 and 27 BC is referred to as the Roman Republic. The Roman state that was created after the reforms of Caesar Augustus is known as the Roman Empire. Roman art and culture was greatly influenced by Ancient Greek and other Mediterranean cultures. The Romans constructed impressive structures including amphitheaters, temples, and aqueducts.

Nabatean culture
The ancient city of Petra (in modern Jordan) was first settled by the Nabateans in the fifth century BC. By the 1st century BC, the Nabateans ruled a powerful trading empire. The monumental ruins of Petra are the greatest remnant of this ancient culture.

Vikings
Between the 9th and 11th centuries, Scandinavian Vikings conquered territories throughout Europe. During their centuries of conquest, the Vikings founded numerous settlements and trading posts in Russia, Western Europe, and in the British Isles.

Ancient India
India has a wealth of cultural and historic attractions. The Indus Valley civilization (2600–1400 BC) was one of the first urbanized civilizations to emerge on the planet. Indian culture reached one of its high points during the period between the 7th and 13th centuries. Many of India's greatest Buddhist and Hindu architectural masterpieces, as well as artworks, were created during these centuries. During the Mogul era (16th and 17th century), many impressive works of Islamic architecture were created throughout the country, including modern India's most famous structure, the Taj Mahal.

Ancient China
The oldest remnants of early Chinese culture date from the era between 5000–2000 BC. The Shang dynasty (1600–1000 BC) was the most influential and advanced bronze-age culture in China. Daoism and Confucian philosophy were both developed in China during the 5th century BC. The first great unified Chinese Empire was forged around 220 BC by Ying Zheng, the king of Qin. After the emergence of the first Chinese Empire, China was ruled by various dynasties and experienced many periods of cultural and technological advancement. The country's most impressive historic sites include the Great Wall of China, the tomb of Emperor Qin with its army of terracotta warriors in Xi'an, and the Forbidden City in the capital city Beijing.

Ancient Japan
The Yamato period of Japanese history began around AD 400. During this period, the country was ruled by an imperial court in Nara. During the 5th century the Japanese adopted the Chinese writing system and in the 6th century Buddhism arrived in Japan. The Fujiwara clan dominated the country for more than 500 years starting in the 7th century. During this period the country's imperial capital was moved from Nara to Kyoto. Between 1192 and 1868, Japan was ruled by a series of shoguns (military rulers). The Meiji Era (1868–1912) saw the restoration of imperial power and the emergence of modern Japan.

Mayan culture
The Maya are an Amerindian people in southern Mexico and Central America. During pre-Colombian times, the Maya developed an advanced and powerful civilization that ruled over a vast territory. Mayan civilization reached its cultural and technological peak around AD 300 and was eventually devastated by the arrival of the Spanish in the 16th century. Central America and Mexico have many impressive Mayan ruins.

Inca culture
The Inca culture emerged around Cusco during the 12th century. By the 15th century, the Inca ruled a vast empire that encompassed parts of modern Peru, Bolivia, Ecuador, Chile, and Argentina. Although their empire was shortlived, the Inca left behind impressive stone monuments and structures throughout western South America. The Inca city of Machu Picchu in Peru is one of the most impressive historic sites in South America.

Aztec culture
At some point during the second millennium BC, the Aztec people migrated into Mexico, where they eventually established a powerful empire. The Aztec capital, Tenochtitlan (modern Mexico City), was founded in 1325 and was once one of the world's largest cities. The Aztecs constructed many grand temples and pyramids throughout their empire and made important cultural advances, including the creation of a writing system and calendar. Central Mexico has numerous Aztec cultural sites.

Other ancient American cultures
Advanced Amerindian cultures appeared in both North America and the Andean regions of South America. Countless Amerindian historic sites, including the remnants of ancient settlements, can be found throughout the Americas.

Places of Jewish cultural interest
Judaism is the oldest of the world's major monotheist religions. The Jerusalem temple was a great achievement of early Jewish culture – now only a section of its walls remain (the Western Wall). Historic synagogues can be found throughout the world, a legacy of the Jewish Diaspora.

Places of Christian cultural interest
Christianity is the world's most practiced and widespread religion. Christianity is based on the teachings in the old and new testaments of the Bible, and emerged in western Asia during the first century AD. Christian religious sites, including churches, cathedrals, and monasteries, can be found in most regions of the world.

Places of Islamic cultural interest
Islam, one of the world's major religions, was founded by Mohammed (AD 570–632). The teachings of the Quran (Koran) are its basis. Muslims around the world pray in the direction of Mecca in Saudi Arabia, Islam's holiest city.

Places of Buddhist cultural interest
Buddhism is based on the teachings of Siddhartha Gautama (around 560–480 BC), also known as the Buddha. Most of the world's Buddhists live in East Asia. Important Buddhist sites include temples, pagodas, stupas, and monasteries.

Places of Hindu cultural interest
Most of the at least one billion followers of Hinduism, one of the world's most practiced religions, live on the Indian subcontinent. Hinduism encompasses a variety of beliefs and practices, many of which are thousands of years old.

Places of Jainist cultural interest
Most followers of Jainism live in India. It is based on the teachings of Mahavira, who lived in the 5th century BC. Jainist sites include temples and monasteries.

Places of Sikh cultural interest
The Sikh religious philosophy emerged in 16th-century northern India, as an attempt to merge the teachings of Islam and Hinduism. The "Golden Temple" in Amritsar is the most important Sikh religious center.

Places of Shinto cultural interest
Shinto, the indigenous religion of Japan, is based on the reverence of kami (nature spirits) and ancestral spirits. Historic Shinto shrines can be seen throughout Japan.

Sites of interest to other religions
Sites related to other religious and spiritual communities.

Places of cultural interest to indigenous peoples (native peoples)
Sites related to the culture or history of indigenous peoples around the world.

Aborigine land reserves
The almost 500,000 Aborigines form only a small portion of Australia's population. Many Aborigine communities administer large land reserves.

Places of Aboriginal cultural interest
Cultural sites of the Aborigines, including rock paintings, are among the interesting attractions in Australia.

Native American reservation
Most of the Native American reservations in North America were founded during the 19th century. Despite the history of low living standards on some reservations, many Native American communities have successfully protected their traditions.

Pueblo Indian culture
The Pueblo Indians are a group of Native American communities who have lived in the southwestern United States for centuries. Their traditional settlements – known as pueblos – consist of adobe buildings.

Places of Amerindian cultural interest
The different regions of North America feature hundreds of sites related to the history and cultures of Native Americans.

Amazonian Amerindians/ protected area
Land reserves have been created to protect the Amerindian cultures in the Amazon basin in South America.

Spanish settlers built Nuestra Senora church in Cholula, Mexico atop a series of ancient Amerindian pyramids. The historic church lies close to the snow-capped volcano Popocatepetl.

Las Vegas, the largest city in the American state of Nevada, is a popular tourist destination with numerous casinos, theme hotels, and amusement parks.

Sport and leisure destinations

Cultural landscape
Areas with landscapes that have been shaped by human settlement or cultivation.

Historical cities and towns
Historic cities and towns with well-preserved architectural attractions.

Impressive skyline
Cities featuring modern skylines, such as New York City, Chicago, and Hong Kong.

Castle/fortress/fort
Europe features the greatest concentration of these structures.

Caravansary
Historic inns along the ancient caravan routes of the Middle East, Central Asia, and North Africa.

Palace
Grand castles and palaces that once housed nobility and royalty can be found in many different regions.

Technical/industrial monument
Man-made attractions related to the achievements of industrialization and modern times.

Dam
The largest and most important dams and retaining walls on the planet.

Remarkable lighthouse
Many coastal areas feature beautiful or historic lighthouses.

Remarkable bridge
Many of the world's great bridges are considered engineering marvels.

Tomb/grave
Mausoleums, monuments, burial mounds, and other grave sites.

Theater of war/battlefield
Site where important battles occurred, including Waterloo in Belgium.

Monument
Sites dedicated to historic figures and important historical events.

Memorial
Site dedicated to the victims of wars and genocides.

Space mission launch site
Landing and launch sites of manned and unmanned space missions.

Space telescope
Radio, X-ray, and gamma-ray telescopes are important tools of modern astronomy.

Market
Important markets where people gather to trade and purchase goods.

Festivals
Large celebrations of music and culture including Rio de Janeiro's Carnaval.

Museum
Important collections of man-made works (art, technology, anthropology) and natural relics.

Theater
Famous theaters presenting opera, musicals, and other productions.

World exhibition
Cities that have hosted world expositions, including London in the United Kingdom.

Olympics
Cities and towns that have hosted the modern summer or winter Olympic Games.

Arena/stadium
The largest and most famous sporting venues in the world – including stadiums for football (soccer), baseball, rugby, hockey, and other popular sports.

Race track
Auto and motorbike racing are popular sports in many of the world's regions. The atlas highlights many of the most famous autoracing venues, including Formula 1 and NASCAR race tracks in Indianapolis, Melbourne, and numerous other cities.

Golf
Golf has become an increasingly popular sport around the world in recent years. The atlas highlights several of the most famous and beautiful golf courses as well as areas that host important golf tournaments.

Horse racing
Horse racing has a long history in many regions. Several well-known race tracks and events are highlighted in the book, including the Ascot racecourse in England, a major event for Britain's high society. The Kentucky Derby remains one of the most popular annual sporting events in the United States, while Hong Kong's Happy Valley draws thousands of visitors every week.

Skiing
The maps in the atlas point out the most important ski areas in the world, including Chamonix in the French Alps, St. Moritz in Switzerland, Aspen in the Rocky Mountains of Colorado, and Whistler in Canada. Many of these areas also offer facilities for other winter sports, including snowboarding.

Sailing
Once a sport for the wealthy, sailing is now enjoyed by millions of people. The atlas highlights areas with good conditions for recreational sailing.

Diving
Beautiful, colorful coral reefs, fascinating shipwrecks, and close encounters with wonderful marine life – this atlas presents popular and famous dive sites around the world.

Wind surfing
A mix of surfing and sailing, windsurfing is a popular aquatic sport. The atlas points out coastal areas well suited to the sport.

Surfing
Popular coastal areas with adequate waves for surfing are highlighted – including well-known beaches in Australia, California, Europe, and in Hawaii, the birthplace of surfing.

Canoeing/rafting
Travelers can enjoy both adventurous and relaxing journeys along many of the world's rivers and lakes in canoes or rafts.

Seaport
The largest and busiest harbors in the world are highlighted.

Deep-sea fishing
The atlas highlights several of the best and most well known locations on the world's seas and oceans for recreational fishing.

Waterskiing
Popular beaches, coastal areas, and lakes with ideal conditions for waterskiing.

Beach resort
Many of the world's beachside communities feature a laid-back atmosphere and excellent tourist facilities. The atlas highlights popular beaches and resorts.

Mineral/thermal spa
The atlas locates several historic and beautiful towns with spas that have attracted visitors for centuries.

Amusement/theme park
Modern amusement parks offer diverse attractions. The parks highlighted in the atlas include Walt Disney World in Orlando, Sea World in California, Disneyland Paris, and Tivoli in Copenhagen.

Casino
Well known casinos, including the historic casino of Monte Carlo and the resort-hotels of Las Vegas.

Hill resort
Exclusive resorts located in temperate highland areas. Mostly in Asia, hill resorts were once very popular destinations, especially for European colonial officials.

Lodge
Comfortable and luxurious camps or inns in pristine wilderness areas, mostly in Africa and North America.

The World

Romantic, bizarre, barren or majestic: the words that we use to describe the Earth's fascinating natural geography prove that we respond emotionally to mountains, plains, coastlines and river valleys. The landscape is in constant flux, as is everything else on our planet. Heat energy released by the sun and from the Earth's interior causes continuous change in nature. This energy powers tectonic plate displacement, volcanic eruptions, the winds and the flow of rivers. It defines and delineates climate and vegetation. Each continent has its own special features, from panoramic landscapes such as mountains to vast expanses of desert. Within

these areas is an almost boundless variety of natural landscapes unaltered by man, which sometimes develop their own personality. We make this concession to them: by giving names to certain distinctive beauty spots, we single them out, thus distinguishing them from the mass of peaks, rivers, lakes and rock formations.

The crater of Mount Saint Helens, an active vulcano that last erupted in 1980.

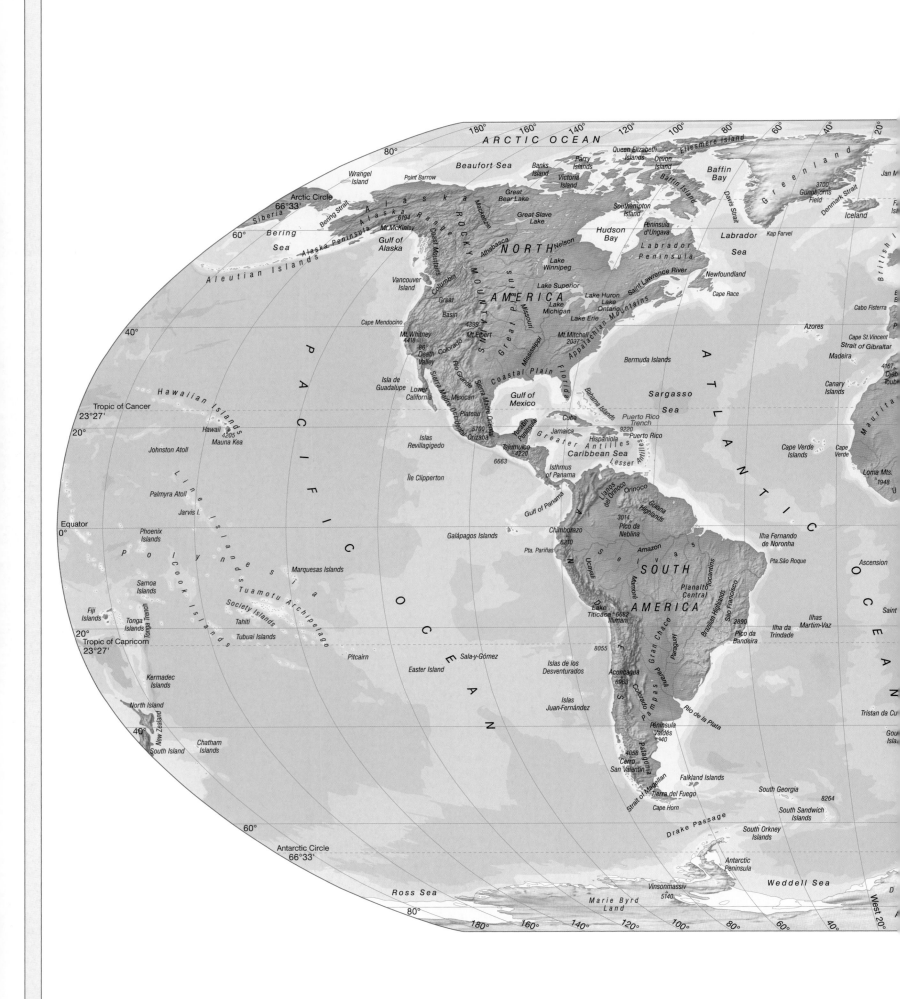

Scale 1:80,000,000

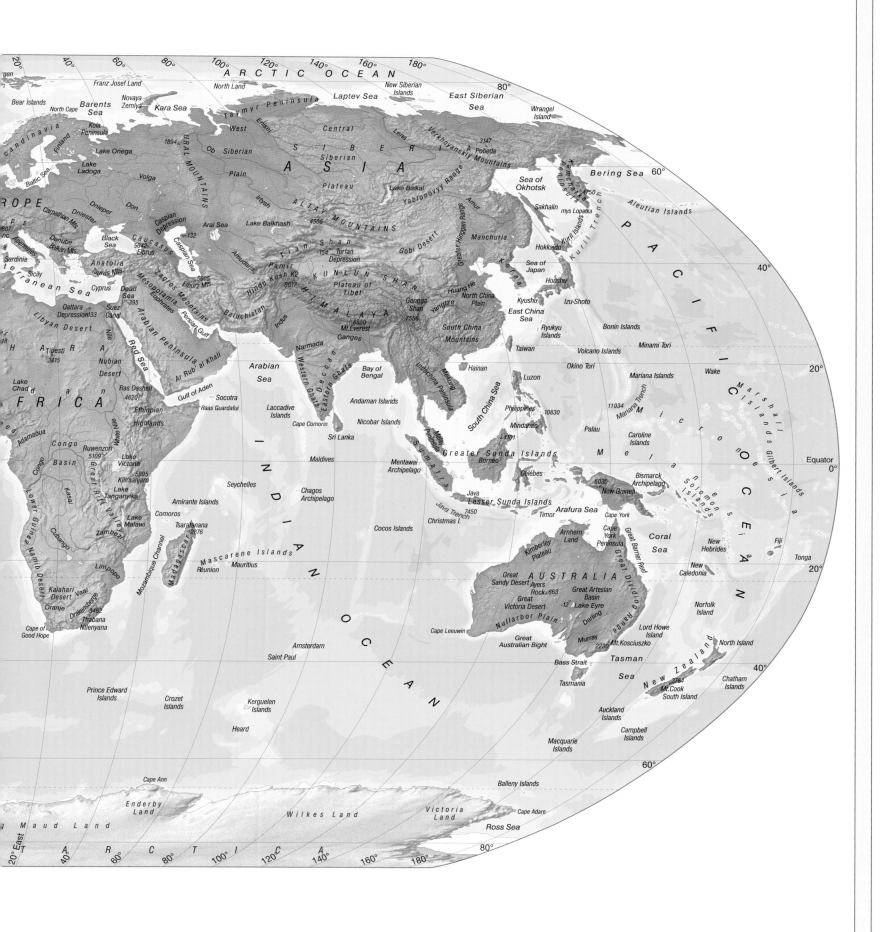

ARCTIC OCEAN

20° 40° 60° 80° 100° 120° 140° 160° 180° 80°

Franz Josef Land
North Land
New Siberian Islands
East Siberian Sea
Wrangel Island

Bear Islands
North Cape
Barents Sea
Novaya Zemlya
Kara Sea
Taymyr Peninsula
Laptev Sea

Scandinavia
Finland
Kola Peninsula
West
Yenisei
Central
Lena
Verkhoyanskiy Mountains
3147 Pobeda
Kamchatka Peninsula
Bering Sea 60°

Baltic Sea
Lake Onega
Lake Ladoga
1894
URAL MOUNTAINS
Ob
Siberian Plain
Irtysh
SIBERIA
Siberian Plateau
ALTAY MOUNTAINS
Lake Baikal
Yablonovyy Range
Amur
Sea of Okhotsk
4750
mys Lopatka
Kuril Trench
Aleutian Islands

EUROPE
Carpathian Mts.
Dnieper
Dniester
Don
Volga
Caspian Depression
Aral Sea
Lake Balkhash
4506
Manchuria
Sakhalin
Hokkaido
Korea
Kuril Islands

Alps
Danube
Balkan Mts.
Black Sea
Caucasus 5642
Elbrus
Caspian Sea
-132
Almaty
Tian Shan
154
Turfan Depression
Gobi Desert
Greater Hingan Range
Sea of Japan
Honshu
40°

Sardinia
Sicily
Anatolia
Taurus Mts.
Cyprus
Zagros Mountains
Mesopotamia
Euphrates
Pamir
Hindu Kush K2
6617
5605
Elburz Mts.
Baluchistan
KUNLUN SHAN
Plateau of Tibet
Huang He
North China Plain
Yangtze
Kyushu
Izu-Shoto
East China Sea
Ryukyu Islands
Bonin Islands

Mediterranean Sea
Dead Sea -395
Qattara Depression -133
Suez Canal
Arabian Peninsula
Persian Gulf
Indus
HIMALAYA
8850
Mt.Everest
Gongga Shan 7556
South China Mountains
Taiwan
Volcano Islands
Minami Tori

Libyan Desert
Nile
Red Sea
Narmada
Deccan
Western Ghats
Eastern Ghats
Bay of Bengal
Ganges
Indochina Peninsula
Mekong
Hainan
Okino Tori
Mariana Islands
Wake
20°

AFRICA
Tibesti 3415
Nubian Desert
Arabian Sea
Luzon
11034
Mariana Trench
Marshall Islands
Gilbert Islands

Lake Chad
Ar Rub al Khali
Gulf of Aden
Socotra
Raas Guardafui
Laccadive Islands
Cape Comorin
Andaman Islands
Nicobar Islands
South China Sea
Philippines 10830
Mindanao 4101
Palau
Caroline Islands
Micronesia

Adamaoua
Ras Dashan 4620
Ethiopian Highlands
Sri Lanka
Maldives
Mentawai Archipelago
Malay Peninsula
Greater Sunda Islands
Borneo
Celebes
Melanesia

Congo
Ruwenzori 5109
Lake Victoria
5895
Kilimanjaro
Seychelles
Chagos Archipelago
Java
Java Trench 7450
Lesser Sunda Islands
Bismarck Archipelago
New Guinea 5030
Solomon Islands

Congo Basin
Lake Tanganyika
Amirante Islands
Comoros
Cocos Islands
Timor
Christmas I.
Arafura Sea
Cape York
Coral Sea
New Hebrides
Fiji

Lower Guinea
Namib Desert
Kasai
Zambezi
Lake Malawi
Tsaratanana 2876
Madagascar
INDIAN
Mascarene Islands
Mauritius
Reunion
Kimberley Plateau
Arnhem Land
Cape York Peninsula
Great Barrier Reef
Great Dividing Range
New Caledonia
Tonga 20°

Limpopo
Kalahari Desert
Vaal
Oranje
Mozambique Channel
OCEAN
Great Sandy Desert
Ayers Rock 863
Great Victoria Desert
Great Artesian Basin
Lake Eyre -12
AUSTRALIA
Norfolk Island
Lord Howe Island

Drakensberge 3482
Thabana Ntlenyana
Cape of Good Hope
Amsterdam
Saint Paul
Cape Leeuwin
Nullarbor Plain
Great Australian Bight
Murray
Darling
Mt.Kosciuszko 2230
North Island
New Zealand

Prince Edward Islands
Crozet Islands
Kerguelen Islands
Heard
Bass Strait
Tasmania
Tasman Sea
Mt.Cook 3764
South Island
Chatham Islands 40°

Auckland Islands
Campbell Islands
Macquarie Islands

60°

Cape Ann
Balleny Islands

Enderby Land
Wilkes Land
Victoria Land
Cape Adare
Ross Sea

Queen Maud Land
20° East
40° 60° 80° 100° 120° 140° 160° 180°
ANTARCTICA 80°

PACIFIC OCEAN

0 1000 2000 3000 Kilometers
0 1000 2000 Miles

17

Endogenous forces involved in the earth's formation

Deep in the core of planet Earth, forces are created which have a substantial influence on its superficial shape. Mountain ranges which have folded upwards provide proof of the movement of continental plates, impelled by thermal energy from the Earth's core. Volcanic eruptions and earthquakes are further visible consequences of endogenous forces.

The shape of the Earth

The diverse forms and material of which the Earth's natural landscapes consist are the visible consequences of the forces prevailing at the core of the Earth. In order to understand how these forces control the processes that take place on the surface of the Blue Planet, it is necessary first to envisage a rough diagram of the composition of the globe.

Core and crust

The Earth has a round-shaped composition as a result of its cosmic formation over a period that lasted for several millions of years. The centre of the Earth consists of a hard, thick core made of iron, with a diameter of 2,440 km. The temperature is estimated to be as high as 5,000°C. A liquid outer core surrounds it, which is at an approximate distance of 2,890 km from the Earth's surface and is 5,150 km thick.
The Earth's mantle consists of rocks of medium thickness that surround the core, followed by the relatively thin crust which measures approximately 40 km in depth. The crust was formed by rocks that were lighter in weight and that rose to the Earth's surface and solidified during the formation of the planet.
The repeated fusion and solidification of these primaeval crusts eventually led to the formation of the continental core.

Plate tectonics

The entirety of all geological phenomena can now be explained by a single theory – the theory of plate tectonics. According to this theory, the Earth's crust is divided into various slabs which move towards each other, away from each other or past each other in a continuous, dynamic process.

Lithosphere and asthenosphere

The outer shell of our planet consists of two layers that can be distinguished from one another and that play a significant role in the shaping of the Earth's surface.
The hard, solid lithosphere surrounds not only the Earth's crust but also the solid parts of the Earth's outer mantle which lie directly beneath it. It floats on the malleable, viscous area of the mantle (the asthenosphere), which consists of fused rocks. These rocks are extremely hot and subject to extreme pressure.
Approximately a dozen larger and a few smaller plates have now been discovered. The actual motion of the continental plates is caused by the flows of currents of hot material that pour out from the Earth's core to the surface, cool down and drop back down again in a continuous cycle.

Plate boundaries

Perhaps the most important of all the geological processes can be observed at the boundaries of the great continental plates as this is where the mechanical movements of the plates move towards each other. Massive fold mountains are formed when plates drift on top of one another where plate boundaries overlap. This is known as subduction or uplift and it leads to the formation of volcanoes.
Ridges are torn open where plates drift away from one another. As a rule, these take the form of a mountain ridge in the sea and are therefore referred to as mid-oceanic ridges. Such a ridge has emerged on the surface of Iceland and is discernible as a crevice-shaped rift.
The zones in which the Earth's surface is pressurised by the force of two plates as they move past each other are called transform faults. The friction of the plates against one another only permits sporadic movement slide which expresses itself in frequent earthquakes.

Rock deformation

It is possible to deduce which massive forces are at play in the Earth's core through the movement of plates, if the shapes of mountain ranges are studied closely. Hard rocks and sediment will be bent, folded or slanted at an angle.
In this process, three types of tectonic force act upon the rocks, known as pressure, distention and dissection. Pressure and compression forces are at work when plates move on top of one another; distension forces are in play when they move away from each other. Dissection forces produce deformities in rocks when two plates glide past each other.

Folding and fault tectonics

Folds form in the Earth's crust when it is compressed horizontally. The extent of the folding – the shape and altitude of a fold mountain, for example – is fundamentally dependent on two factors: on the amount of time during which the rock is subjected to the forces that are distorting it and the composition of the rock which determines the resistance it can use to counter the compression forces acting upon it.
Distension forces do not produce folds at all, but rather expand and thin out the crust, thus forming basin landscapes.
Fault structures occur when tensions in the rock become too great. Fault structures include fissures, which may be formed locally within a plate in specific areas of tension and faults which may be caused by various forces producing distortions. When the broken edges of rock collide with one another they produce so-called 'faults'.
Tectonic forces are very strong, particularly at the plate boundaries. They not only act upon the outer plate boundaries – they can also produce faults in rock formations, even at a great distance from the actual boundary zones of the plates.

Volcanic activity and earthquakes

Life is dangerous at the plate boundaries. This is where tectonic forces distort the plates most strongly and their effects can be felt particularly intensely. Volcanoes make islands explode or smother vast landscapes in pyroclastic flows of lava, fire, ashes and smoke. Earthquakes can ravage entire regions or cause mountain ranges to collapse.

Volcanic activity

The majority of the Earth's crust is composed of fused rock which rose from the Earth's core to the surface and cooled down to form volcanic rock. This process, known as volcanic activity, is a phenomenon which is almost exclusively limited to the plate boundaries.
About 80 per cent of the Earth's approximately 500 volcanoes are located on the plate boundaries which are constantly colliding. This is particularly striking in what is known as the Pacific Ring of Fire which runs along the outer edges of the Pacific and Nazca Plates.

The San Andreas fault: the visible shift of the continental plates.

Earthquakes and volcanic eruptions

The strongest earthquakes in the last 100 years (magnitude based on Richter/Kanamori scale)	The most disastrous volcanic eruptions in human history (by number of victims)
Chile (22.5.1960) 9.5	Tambora, Sumbawa (1815) 90,000
Alaska (28.3.1964) 9.2	Miyi, Java (1793) 53,000
Indian Ocean (26.12.2006) 9.1	Pelé, Martinique (1902) 40,000
Russia (4.11.1952) 9.0	Krakatoa, Java (1883) 36,300
Ecuador (31.1.1906) 8.8	Nevado del Ruiz, Colombia
Alaska (4.2.1965) 8.7	(1985) 22,000
Sumatra (28.03.2005) 8.6	Etna, Siclly (1669) 20,000
Alaska (9.3.1957) 8.6	Laki Island (1783) 20,000
India (15.8.1950) 8.6	Unzen, Japan (1792) 15,000
China (16.12.1920) 8.6	Vesuvius, Italy (79 AD) 10,000

Volcanic sources: the water heated in the Earth's core is very rich in sulphur and minerals. The Grand Prismatic Spring in Yellowstone National Park owes its bright colours to the millions of micro-organisms that live in it. Champagne Pools is one of numerous hot springs on the North Island of New Zealand.

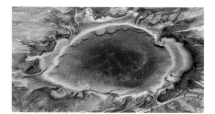

When an oceanic plate in the asthenosphere pushes up against a mainland plate and slides under it, the edges fuse in places. The molten rock, which is known as magma, now rises to the surface. The majority of the magma hardens within the Earth's crust. However, some magma vents rise as far as the Earth's surface. This produces volcanoes. The rising magma initially collects inside the volcano in what is known as a magma chamber until the pressure inside is so great that lava streams out or erupts from the volcanic crater in a massive explosion.

Volcanoes have determined the appearance of our natural landscapes in significant ways – not only where we can clearly identify them as volcanoes due to the lava fields, trails of smoke, basalt columns, remains of craters or the shape of the volcanic mountain, which usually forms a cone.

Earthquakes

The tectonic plates are subject to constant forces that cause them to distort. Where the plates push up against each other, the sort of faults occur that have been described above.

In the immediate proximity of these zones, the forces of distortion and deformation initially act upon the blocked, displaced rocky masses until resistance due to friction has been overcome. At this point, the rock either breaks or fissures, and parts of the crust are displaced with explosive force.

This spontaneous jolt jars the Earth's crust so strongly that it produces what we call an earthquake. If the earthquake is strong enough, the shape of the Earth's surface may change permanently. Rift valleys can emerge. Probably the largest rift valley of this kind that the Earth has ever experienced is the one that runs from the shores of the Dead Sea, right down through Africa. This is the Great Rift Valley,

Hawaii: the volcanoes lie over the so-called Hot Spot.

Crater Lake: the water filled caldera of a collapsed volcano.

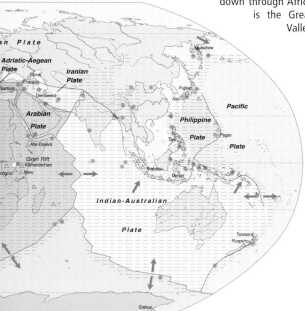

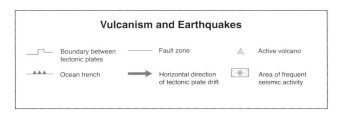

Vulcanism and Earthquakes

⌐⌐ Boundary between tectonic plates	——— Fault zone	△ Active volcano
▲▲▲ Ocean trench	➤ Horizontal direction of tectonic plate drift	Area of frequent seismic activity

Enormous eruptions which occurred several hundred thousands of years ago have produced vast landscapes of volcanic rocks, whose actual dimensions can only be calculated by using satellite pictures taken from space.

which produced the Dead Sea, the Red Sea and the Bitter Lakes of Egypt and Kenya.

There are other, smaller rifts of this kind and there may be yet more which are so old that they have eroded over time.

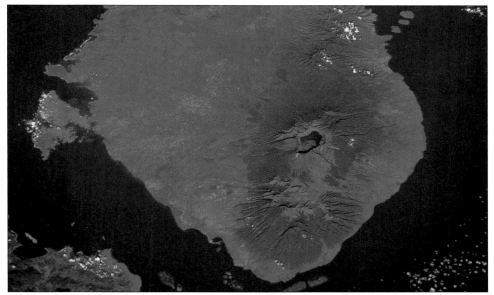

Sunda rift: volcanic activity created numerous islands in the area.

Exogenous forces involved in the Earth's formation

The constant movement of wind and water – the current of a river, glaciers, marine or ground water – shapes the Earth's natural landscapes through erosion. These exogenous forces are impelled by the thermal energy inherent in solar radiation. They determine the dynamic circulation of the atmosphere and oceans.

Numerous waterfalls in the Norwegian Fjords.

Annapurna massif: a mixture of endogenous and exogenous forces.

Coastal erosion: 'The Twelve Apostles' rock formation, Australia.

The 'building blocks' of Planet Earth

The extent to which exogenous forces form and alter the appearance of natural landscapes depends, above all, on the nature of the rocks upon which they act. The key to rock composition lies in the crystalline structures of the minerals of which they consist.

Minerals

Minerals are the basic building blocks of our planet. They determine the nature, i.e. the hardness, colour and shape of rocks. Few rocks consist of a single mineral. Notable exceptions are chalk and quartz. Most other rocks consist of several mineral ores.

Rocks

Rocks are the basis of the landscape; their nature and the history of their formation also determines how the appearance of a natural landscape comes about. There are three different groups of rocks: magmatic rocks which have been formed through volcanic activity; sedimentary rocks which can occur in loose or solid forms and are formed by erosion and weathering processes; and metamorphic rocks which have emerged through the transformation of pre-existing rocks, during the formation of a mountain range, for example.

Landscape development

Wind, water and even gravity are responsible for ensuring that the Earth's rocks remain in constant motion. That is why natural landscapes are constantly changing their appearance.

Mass movements

When great lumps of soil or rock detach themselves from outcrops due to the effect of gravity and move towards the valley, their long journey to the ocean begins. Rock falls and landslides are classed as mass movements, but streams of loose material may detach themselves almost imperceptibly from the substrate. Water which has been absorbed by the rock also plays an important role in these processes. It reduces resistance and weakens the structure of rock and soil so it breaks up more easily.

Rivers

Rivers are probably the most diverse landscape forms among the exogenous forces. They carry away outcrops, wash up sediments in a delta and sculpt deep grooves into underground rock. The course of a river follows the shape of the surface of the landscape as it searches for the easiest route to the ocean. This route determines whether the river runs relatively straight or flows towards the valley in torrents and waterfalls. These forms of current produce differences in the nature and volume of the method of absorption and transportation of eroded rock.

In the transverse section of a river, the volume of matter transported is not constant. Dissolved suspensions move at different speeds and have different effects on the landscape, depending on whether they are carried along near the surface or lie as silt on the river bed. Sediment in suspension is deposited differently. Smaller and lighter suspended particles remain in the stream longer than larger particles. They are whirled around and deposited periodically. The river bed is exposed to a constant two-way process of erosion and sedimentation. Rivers not only erode loose material, they can also erode hard rocks. The sediments which have been carried along have an important part to play, as they serve as an abrasive.

Meteor Crater in Arizona: 'alien' landscape formation.

The deepest canyons and ravines

Grand Canyon (USA) 1,800 m	Black Canyon/Colorado (USA) 700 m
Hell's Canyon/Snake River (USA) 1,700 m	Grand Canyon du Verdon (France) 700 m
Barranca del Cobre (Mexico) 1,400 m	Milford Sound (New Zealand) 600 m
Wu chasm at Yangtse (China) 900 m	Bryce Canyon (USA) 600 m
Vicos chasm (Greece) 900 m	Sanmen chasm at Huang He (China) 600 m
Neretva chasms (Bosnia-Herzegovina) 800 m	Visriviere Canyon (Namibia) 600 m
Canyon of the Black River (Vietnam) 800 m	Vaihiria lake (Tahiti) 550 m
Via Mala (Switzerland) 700 m	Wadi Dadès (Morocco) 400 m
	Wadi al-Kantara (Algeria) 400 m

While the forces shaping rivers on loose soil can easily be observed, where hard rock is concerned one can often only observe the sublime legacies created over several hundred thousand years by streams that may even have run completely dry by now. Deep canyons and gorges have remained as eloquent proof of the Earth's history.

The sea

The great ocean currents, the storms and the power of the tides shape not only the profile of the ocean floors, which are invisible to us, but even the coastline, especially at continental boundaries, which are strongly affected by the force of waves.

In the same way that rivers erode and deposit soil, the sea removes rock from the coastlines in order to redeposit it on the ocean floor or on other coastlines as sediment. The diversity of the natural landscapes which have been shaped by sea water seemingly knows no boundaries. Long sandy beaches have been formed to which the tides carry freshly ground sand; in other places blustering breakers sculpt strange formations into cliffs.

The ocean floor is also exposed to constant sedimentation. This can be observed when ocean floors are broken up due to endogenous processes. Then the solidified sediments are exposed to the same exogenous forces as the remaining rocks and fascinating landscapes can emerge from the weathered strata of rocks of different degrees of hardness.

Glaciers

Water is also a very important factor in the formation of the landscape in the cold regions of the world. There are two types of glacier – the inland ice sheets found in Greenland and the Antarctic, and the moving rivers of ice that form on mountains at high altitudes. Like ocean currents, these ice sheets push through valleys towards the ocean, though their movement is almost imperceptible to the human eye.

In order for us to calculate the immense force that is concealed in the movement of this glacier ice, we must take a look at the numerous landscapes that were formed in Europe, Asia and North America during the last Ice Ages.

Accumulated scree has cut deep gullies in the rocky sub-soil and sculpted vast U-shaped valleys. Where secondary glaciers have fused with a primary glacier after the ice has melted away, steep rocky cliffs have been created from which waterfalls cascade.

The large stones deposited by glaciers are known as rubble. They are left behind when the ice melts that once enclosed them. Moraines are masses of stony and sandy material that have been transported by the glacier.

Wind

Winds have similar powers of erosion to rivers through accumulated dust and sand. They play an important part in the formation of the deserts in particular.

The sand is transported by the wind in the same way as a river transports water. Larger stones are propelled directly along the surface of the ground, grains of sand and pebbles are whirled upwards and propelled in leaps. When the wind dies down, the wind-borne sand particles remain in situ as sediment.

If sand and silt particles are blown away, the subsoil is also gradually worn away. Enclosed basins emerge. Rocky outcrops are eroded by wind-borne sand. This can cause a rounding of sharp edges or an outcrop can even be worn away completely.

Meteorite craters

Meteorite strikes are an exception. Although they alter the shape of the surface of the Earth, they are 'external' effects which do not originate in the oceans and the Earth's atmosphere, unlike exogenous processes.

Large meteorites have altered the appearance of vast landscapes and even whole continents within seconds, in the course of the Earth's history. There have been two recent incidents of meteorites striking the earth. The first is known as the Tunguska Incident when a large meteorite fell in a remote part of Siberia in 1908 destroying 2,000 sq. km of forest. The earlier incident was only discovered when it was realised that a 'moon crater' formation in the Arizona desert had been left by a meteor that hit the earth 50,000 years ago.

Heavily eroded rocks can be used to read the history of the Earth layer by layer, like a book.

Ahaggar: the erosive forces in the Sahara are particularly strong, resulting in unusual rock formations.

'Totem pole' in Monument Valley: the reddish colour of the sandstone is due to erosion.

Climate and Vegetation Zones

The Earth is divided into several vegetation zones, each of which contains specific varieties and groups of plants. The vegetation zones run parallel to the lines of latitude, and are roughly similar to the climatic zones. Climate is affected by geographical factors, such as latitude, altitude, ocean currents, topography and vegetation.

Polar Regions

The Earth has two polar regions, the Arctic at the North Pole, and the Antarctic at the South Pole. Both regions are characterised by snow and ice and a six-monthly cycle of polar night and polar day. The South Pole, south of the 55th parallel, consists of Antarctica, scattered islands and ice-shelves and has a surface area of just under 14 million sq. km. The mainland is mountainous, with altitudes up to 5,140 m, and is covered with a thick ice-sheet (average thickness 2,000–2,500 m), which constitutes over 90 per cent of the world's total ice mass. The climate is extremely cold and dry. The only vegetation, found on a few sub-antarctic islands, are mosses, lichen, grasses and some flowering plants. The North Pole includes the Arctic Ocean and has a land area of 11 million sq.km. Most of the North Pole consists of a 12 million sq. km pack-ice layer. The climate is more temperate than in the Antarctic, due to the effect of the sea currents. Ice-free areas have sparse vegetation.

Tundra and Taiga

The tundra lies south of the Polar region and north of the tree-line. This belt of vegetation, covering parts of northern Asia, Europe and America, is typified by short but warm summers, long, severe winters and little precipitation. The climate only allows for the sparse growth of mosses and stunted shrubs. Temperatures range from -55°C to 25°C, but even in summer, the average temperature of 10°C is rarely exceeded. The taiga region, a belt of woodland (also called boreal woodland) consisting mainly of conifers lies south of the tundra. This terrain is found mostly in Siberia and north-west Russia. Both the tundra and the taiga are covered in permafrost, meaning that the sub-soil remains permanently frozen all year round.

Polar regions
Tundra
Forested tundra
Sub-arctic forests (taiga)
Mixed forests
Deciduous forests
Glasslands (prairies, steppes)

Deciduous and Mixed Woodland Zones

Deciduous and mixed woodland is found in cool, temperate zones and is characteristic of the landscape in the east and west of North America, East Asia and Central and Western Europe. Deciduous trees shed their leaves annually to protect them against the winter cold.

Prairies and Steppes

The temperate, open steppes of Eurasia from the Puszta to Mongolia, and the prairies of North America are characterised by dry vegetation, with broad expanses of grass, devoid of any shrubs. Herbs and herbaceous perennials bloom in spring, but disappear again in the heat of the summer. Scattered dwarf shrubs and bushes grow on dry steppe terrain. Nearer the North Pole, the grass becomes denser. Towards the deciduous and mixed woodland regions, it is possible to find tree steppes, in which there is sufficient precipitation to support the growth of a few trees. In the southern hemisphere, steppes are only found in Patagonia.

Humid and Dry Savannah

The savannah climate has a rainy season in summer, and a marked dry period in winter. This type of terrain is mainly found in South America and Africa, but also in northern Australia, Central America, India and southeast Asia. The amount of precipitation decreases the greater the distance north or south of the rainforest zone, and the dry periods become longer. Humid savannah can be found bordering tropical rainforest zones. Towards the poles, the length of the dry spells increases. In the equatorial regions, only the taller trees lose their leaves, and the undergrowth remains green year-round. In monsoon regions there is a severe wet-dry climate, and the whole forest loses its leaves. The dry savannah is closer to the poles than the humid savannah regions. It mainly covers large areas of Africa. This terrain is characterised by open grassland, interrupted by the odd tree, and occasional small woods. Main tree species are baobab, xerophile palms, ponytail palms and umbrella trees.

Semi-desert

Almost one third of the Earth's land surface is covered by desert or desertified areas. A large proportion of this is known as 'semi-desert'. This is the transitional region between the almost vegetation-free full deserts and the steppe regions. Semi-deserts have a low annual precipitation level, averaging from 100 to 200 mm. After the occasional shower, they can temporarily change in appearance and take on the character of steppe or savannah terrain, and for this reason they are also referred to as 'desert steppes' or 'desert savannahs'. Typical semi-desert vegetation includes thorn bushes, thorny trees, dry grasses and stunted bushes. These featureless wastes can be interrupted by oases, which appear wherever there is access to ground water. Freshwater pools or river water enables trees, such as date palms and poplars, to grow even in the desert.

Deserts

These regions of Earth have such dry or cold climates that only certain types of flora, such as cacti and succulents, can tolerate them, and they have no landscape-defining vegetation. A distinction can be made between cold deserts and dry or hot deserts. The latter are mainly found in sub-tropical regions with high atmospheric pressure, beside oceans with cold water currents and in enclosed mountain basins. Full deserts have almost no vegetation and their annual precipitation levels are below 100 mm. The aridity and the temperature differences between day and night cause heavy erosion. Temperature differences also produce large amounts of powerful air circulation, creating dust storms and sandstorms.

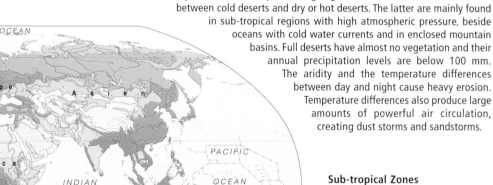

Sub-tropical Zones

The sub-tropical zone is a 2,000-km-wide band between the tropical and temperate zones, characterised by dry summers and mild winters. It is defined by a large number of smaller vegetation zones with alternating rainy and dry seasons. The sub-tropics contain deserts and steppes as well as moist woodland.

Rainforests

Tropical rainforests extend either side of the equator in the zone of the tropics, which is constantly wet. Precipitation falls all year round, with most rain falling during the rainy seasons in spring and autumn. Maximum temperatures can be as high as 35°C. Temperature variations are very small. Rainforests are characterised by large numbers of plant species and most commonly three canopy levels. In the centre of the forests, relative humidity is almost 100 per cent. Rainforests affect the carbon, oxygen and nitrogen cycles of the Earth, making them an important climate regulator.

Mountains

Mountains are divided into low ranges and high ranges, depending on altitude. They can also be classified according to the shape of the peaks (mountains ridges and mountain chains) and according to their origin (volcanic and eroded mountains). Low mountain ranges are much older and have more rounded hilltops and ridges, which are often wooded to their upper reaches. High mountains ranges were formed much nearer to the present time and were caused by folding of the Earth's crust. They are characterised by sheer faces, high summits, and deep valleys. The summits of high mountain ranges have no vegetation and the peaks are mainly covered in snow and ice. The highest and most imposing mountain range on Earth is the Himalayas, between the north Indian lowlands and the Tibetan plateau. The range forms an arc, 2,400 km long and between 150 km and 280 km wide. The highest peaks in the Himalayas are Mount Everest (8,850 m – the highest peak on Earth) and Kanchenjunga (8,586 m). Fold mountain ranges are continuously being formed by tectonic plate movement.

Legend (map):
- Desert
- Mediterranean vegetation
- Subtropical forests
- Tropical deserts
- Humid savannah
- Arid savannah
- Tropical rainforests

Europe

In geological terms, Europe is merely the western extension of the huge continent of Eurasia; however, the Ural and Caucasus mountain ranges, together with the Black Sea, form a well-defined, natural boundary between the two continents. The landscape of the European Continent is very disparate and uneven.

This means that this relatively small continent, covering a total area of just 10.5 million sq. km, has a wide range of different landscape features: mountain ranges and basins, ranges of hills and lowlands, craggy coastlines and numerous offshore islands, both large and small. The landscapes of northern Europe were

mainly formed during the Ice Age. This region is adjoined by Central Europe with its low mountain ranges. The Alps and the Pyrenees form the natural borders of countries in Western Europe. The southern European peninsulas are situated along the north coast of the Mediterranean Sea.

The steep, pyramid-shaped peak of the 4,478-m-high Matterhorn is made of hard crystalline rock. The mountain is one of the most imposing peaks of the Swiss Alps.

Europe

Greenland

Kong Christian X Land
Kong Frederik VIII Land
Greenland Sea
Nordaustlandet
1717
Svalbard
Edgøya
Novaya Zemlya
Gydanskiy P-ov
1547
Kara Sea
Yamal P-ov
West Siberian Plain

Kong Christian IX Land
Greenland Basin
380
Barents Sea
Pečorskoe more
1894
Ob

Arctic Circle
Denmark Strait
3069
Bear Islands
White Sea
Timanskiy Kryazh

Jan Mayen
North Cape
Murmansk
Kola Peninsula

Iceland
Norwegian Sea
3188
Lofoten
Lapland
Kola Peninsula
Syktyvkar
1569
YEKATERINBURG

Reykjavik
Grímsvötn 1719
Norwegian Basin
2111
Kebnekaise
Oulu
Karelia
PERM'
UFA

832
465
Iceland Basin
Jotunheimen 2472
Gulf of Bothnia
Umeå
Lake Onega
Severnye uvaly
KAZAN'

ATLANTIC
Rockall Plateau
Faroe Islands
Bergen
Helsinki Helsingfors
Lake Ladoga
NIŽNIJ NOVGOROD
Volga Upland
SAMARA

Shetland Islands
Oslo
Stockholm
ST.PETERSBURG
MOSCOW
volga
Oral

Hebrides
Orkney Islands
Ben Nevis 1343
Vänern
459
Gotland
Lake Peipus
Riga
Srednerusskaja vozvyšennost'
Orel
VOLGOGRAD
Caspian Depression

Rockall Trough
240
Göteborg
Baltic Sea
MINSK
Don
Caspian Sea

Ireland
OCEAN
Dublin
North Sea
Great Britain
Jutland
Copenhagen
Bornholm
Gdańsk
WARSAW
KIEV
Dnieper
ROSTOV-NA-DONU
Manych Depression

Cork
Pennines
BIRMINGHAM
Amsterdam
HAMBURG
BERLIN
Vistula
Cracow
L'viv
DNIPROPETROVS'K
g.Elbrus 5642

Celtic Sea
LONDON
BRUSSELS
COLOGNE
Elbe
Sudetes
PRAGUE
Béskid Mts.
Dniester
ODESSA
Crimea
CAUCASUS
TBILISI

Land's End
English Channel
Normandie
PARIS
Rhine
Burgundy
MUNICH
VIENNA
BUDAPEST
Carpathian Mts.
2100
Transylvanian Alps
2544
Black Sea
TBILISI
YEREVAN
Ararat 5137

Brittany
Loire
Berne
Alföld
BUCHAREST
Danube
Trabzon
Pontic Mountains
Van Gölü
Van

5465
Bay of Biscay
Massif Central 1885
Lyon
Mt.Blanc 4807
MILAN
3797
Zagreb
BELGRADE
Balkan Mts.
Varna
2180
İSTANBUL
Taurus Mts. 3524
Anatolia
AL-MAWSIL

La Coruña
Cabo Fisterra
Gijón
Bordeaux
Rhône
Provence
Po
Dinaric Alps
Dalmatia
SOFIA
Rhodope Mts.
Bosporus
ANKARA
Tuz Gölü
ADANA
ALEPPO

Porto
Cantabria Mountains
Pyrénées
Marseille
Apennines
Adriatic Sea
Tirane
Olymp 2917
Aegean Sea
İZMIR
Euphrates

LISBON
MADRID
Cordillera Central
Sistema Ibérico
Pico d'Aneto 3404
Corsica 2622
ROME
2914
Strait of Otranto
Pindos Mts.
ATHENS
Cyprus
BEIRUT
DAMASCUS
Al Widyan

Tagus
Sierra Morena
Ebro
BARCELONA
València
Palma d.M.
Sardinia
1834
NAPLES
Vesúvio 1281
Tyrrhenian Sea
Peloponnesus
Ionian Sea
Rhodes
2456
Crete
2427
JERUSALEM
AMMAN

Cabo de São Vicente
Sevilla
Cordillera Bética
Granada 3431
Balearic Islands
2784
Palermo
Etna 3323
1955
5054
MEDITERRANEAN SEA
Levantine Basin
Port Said
Suez Canal
El Aqaba
An Nafud

Tangier
RABAT
Oran
ALGIERS
2305
Constantine
TUNIS
Sicily
Gulf of Sirte
Benghazi
882
Tubruq
ALEXANDRIA
Sinai 2285
Hejaz
Red Sea

CASABLANCA
MARRAKECH
Haut Atlas
Atlas Tellien
Atlas Saharien
TUNIS
Sfax
Île de Jerba
Cyrenaica
Sahra Surt
Qattara Depression -134
CAIRO
1207

Béchar
Atlas Saharien
ATLAS MTS
Great Western Erg
TRIPOLI
Tripolitania
Libyan Desert
Great Sand Sea
Western Desert
Eastern Desert
Nile

Hamada du Drâa
El Ménia
Great Eastern Erg
Hamada de Tinrhert
Al Jufra Oasis
El Kufrah Oasis
Luxor
Aswân
Djebel Musbih 1445

Erg Iguidi
Plateau du Tademaït
Awbari Sahra
A F R I C A
Ras Banas

Chech
Erg
Tassili n'Ajjer
Fezzan
Ramlat Rabyanah
Aswân
Lake Nasser
2300

Taoudenni
Tanezrouft
Asedjrad
Adrar 2158
Tahat 2918
Hoggar
Sarir Tibesti
El Kufrah Oasis
1893
Djebel Al Awaynat
Nubian Desert
Port Sudan

Tropic of Cancer
Djebel Timétrine
Tassili du Hoggar
Ténéré du Tafassasset
Pic Touside 3376
3315
Tarso Emissi
Tibesti
Erdi
Nubia
Nile

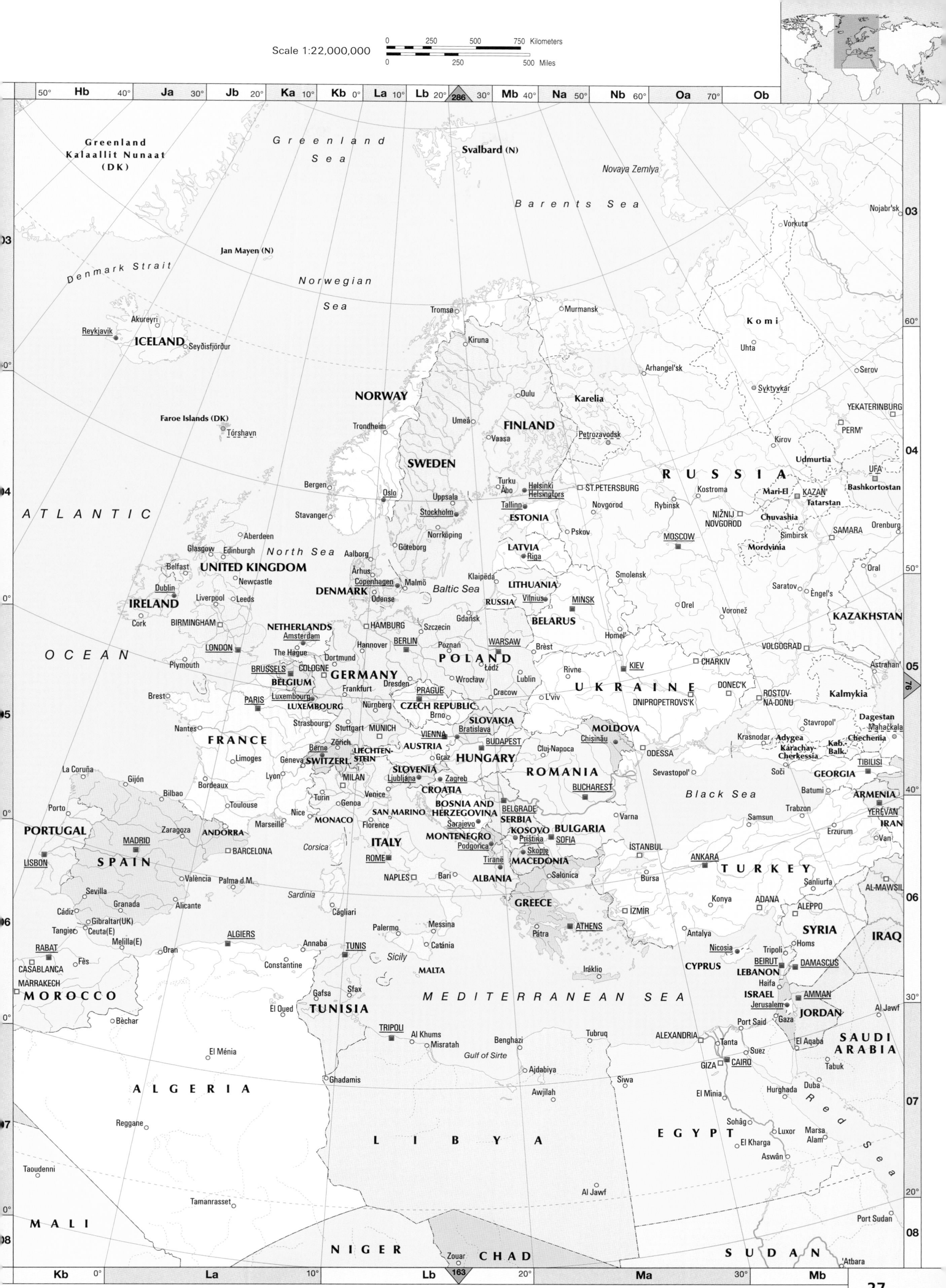

Hb 50° 40° Ja 30° Jb 20° Ka 10° Kb 0° La 10° Lb 20° 286 30° Mb 40° Na 50° Nb 60° Oa 70° Ob

Greenland
Kalaallit Nunaat
(DK)

Greenland
Sea

Svalbard (N)

Novaya Zemlya

Barents Sea

Nojabr'sk

Jan Mayen (N)

Denmark Strait

Norwegian
Sea

Tromsø

Murmansk

Vorkuta

60°

Akureyri

Reykjavik

ICELAND

Seyðisfjörður

Kiruna

K o m i

Uhta

Seroy

NORWAY

Oulu

Karelia

FINLAND

Petrozavodsk

R U S S I A

YEKATERINBURG

Faroe Islands (DK)

Tórshavn

Trondheim

Umeå

SWEDEN

Vaasa

Kirov

Udmurtia

PERM'

Bergen

Turku Åbo

Helsinki
Helsingfors

ST.PETERSBURG

Kostroma

Mari-El

KAZAN'

UFA

04

ATLANTIC

Stavanger

Oslo

Uppsala

Stockholm

Tallinn

ESTONIA

Novgorod

Rybinsk

NIŽNIJ
NOVGOROD

Chuvashia

Tatarstan

Bashkortostan

Aberdeen

Norrköping

Göteborg

LATVIA

Riga

Pskov

MOSCOW

Simbirsk

SAMARA

Orenburg

Glasgow Edinburgh

North Sea

Klaipėda

LITHUANIA

Smolensk

Mordvinia

Oral

Belfast

UNITED KINGDOM

Newcastle

Aalborg

Århus

Copenhagen Malmö

Vilnius

RUSSIA

MINSK

Orel

Voronež

Saratov

Èngel's

50°

Dublin

Liverpool Leeds

DENMARK

Odense

Gdańsk

BELARUS

Homel

KAZAKHSTAN

IRELAND

Cork

BIRMINGHAM

NETHERLANDS

Amsterdam

HAMBURG

Szczecin

Poznań

WARSAW

Brèst

Rivne

KIEV

CHARKIV

VOLGOGRAD

Astrahan'

OCEAN

LONDON

The Hague

Hannover

BERLIN

Łódź

Kalmykia

05

76

Plymouth

Brest

BRUSSELS

BELGIUM

COLOGNE

Dortmund

GERMANY

Dresden

POLAND

Wrocław

Cracow

Lublin

L'viv

UKRAINE

DONEC'K

ROSTOV-
NA-DONU

Frankfurt

PARIS

Luxembourg

LUXEMBOURG

Nürnberg

PRAGUE

Brno

CZECH REPUBLIC

DNIPROPETROVS'K

Dagestan

Nantes

Strasbourg

Stuttgart

MUNICH

SLOVAKIA

Bratislava

Krasnodar

Stavropol'

Adygea

Karachay-
Cherkessia

Kab.
Balk.

Chechenia

FRANCE

Zürich

VIENNA

AUSTRIA

BUDAPEST

Chişinău

ODESSA

TIBILISI

05

Limoges

Berne

SWITZERL.

LIECHTEN-
STEIN

Graz

HUNGARY

Cluj-Napoca

MOLDOVA

Soči

GEORGIA

Geneva

Lyon

SLOVENIA

Ljubljana

Zagreb

ROMANIA

Sevastopol'

Batumi

ARMENIA

40°

La Coruña

Gijón

Bilbao

Bordeaux

Turin

MILAN

Venice

Genoa

CROATIA

BOSNIA AND
HERZEGOVINA

Sarajevo

BELGRADE

BUCHAREST

Black Sea

Samsun

Trabzon

YERÉVAN

IRAN

Porto

Toulouse

Nice

SAN MARINO

SERBIA

Varna

Erzurum

Van

PORTUGAL

Zaragoza

MADRID

ANDORRA

Marseille

MONACO

Florence

MONTENEGRO

Podgorica

KOSOVO

Priština

BULGARIA

SOFIA

İSTANBUL

ANKARA

T U R K E Y

LISBON

SPAIN

BARCELONA

Corsica

ITALY

ROME

Skopje

Tiranë

MACEDONIA

Bursa

Şanlıurfa

AL-MAWSIL

València Palma d.M.

Sardinia

NAPLES

Bari

ALBANIA

Salonica

İZMİR

Konya

ADANA

06

Sevilla

Granada

Alicante

Cágliari

GREECE

Palermo

Messina

Catánia

ATHENS

Pátra

Antalya

ALEPPO

SYRIA

IRAQ

Cádiz

Gibraltar(UK)

Ceuta(E)

Melilla(E)

Oran

ALGIERS

Annaba

TUNIS

Sicily

MALTA

Nicosia

CYPRUS

Tripoli

Homs

BEIRUT

DAMASCUS

Tangier

Fès

CASABLANCA

Constantine

MALTA

Iráklio

LEBANON

Haifa

RABAT

Sfax

Jerusalem

ISRAEL

AMMAN

MARRAKECH

Gafsa

M E D I T E R R A N E A N   S E A

Port Said

Gaza

JORDAN

Al Jawf

MOROCCO

Bèchar

El Oued

TUNISIA

TRIPOLI

Al Khums

Benghazi

Tubruq

ALEXANDRIA

Tanta

Suez

El Aqaba

SAUDI
ARABIA

Tabuk

Misratah

Gulf of Sirte

Siwa

GIZA CAIRO

30°

El Ménia

Ghadamis

Ajdabiya

El Minia

Hurghada

Duba

A L G E R I A

L I B Y A

E G Y P T

El Kharga

Luxor

Marsa
Alam

07

Reggane

Sohâg

Aswân

Taoudenni

Tamanrasset

Al Jawf

Port Sudan

20°

M A L I

N I G E R

Zouar

C H A D

S U D A N

'Atbara

08

Kb 0° La 10° Lb 163 20° Ma 30° Mb

27

Europe

Iceland: Hveravellir lies between the enormous volcanic glaciers of Langjökull and Hofsjökull. In this region, the geothermal springs put on an impressive display. These hot springs are just one of the many indications of volcanic activity.

This island in the North Atlantic is of volcanic origin and has a fascinating natural landscape, including several active volcanoes, hot springs, fumaroles, glaciers and fjords. The island of Surtsey lies just south of the mainland.

Iceland

Iceland is the second largest island in Europe. It is located in the North Atlantic, just south of the Arctic Circle. The island is of volcanic origin and contains more than 140 volcanoes, some 30 of which are still active. Two such volcanoes are **Hekla** and **Askja**. Signs of continued volcanic activity include geysers and solfatara, which are particularly common on the western half of the island. Glaciers and melt-water flows have also played an important role in shaping Iceland's landscape. Glaciers still cover 11,800 sq. km of the island.

On the coasts in the west, north and north-east, immense basalt promontories rise out of the sea to heights of up to 1,000 m. In the south and south-east, the coast is largely flat. The gravel moraine adjoining this flat coastal land are also a result of glaciation during the Ice Age, as are the country's many fjords, trough valleys, cirques and outwash plains. The **Fjell Plateau** is between 300 and 1,200 m high and rises to form the Iceland Plateau, which is 1,200 to 2,000 m high. The uplands are dotted with sheer cliffs up to 500 m high. The highest point is **Hvannadalshnúkur** (2,119 m), and the largest glacier is **Vatnajökull** (8,410 sq. km).

Scandinavian Peninsula

This is the longest peninsula in Europe and covers 750,000 sq. km, including the countries of Sweden and Norway, and by extension Denmark and Finland. The North Sea coast of **Jutland** is flat with coastal lagoons and dunes in the north and mud flats and marshes in the south. To the north of the peninsula, the landscape is dominated by the **Scandinavian Mountains**. Several rivers cross the mountains of **Norland**. In **Sveåland** there are numerous large lakes. **Götaland** is a hilly region to the south, which also contains a large number of lakes. The region's countless **fjords** are a relic from the Ice Age.

The **Skerry coast** was formed during the Pleistocene glaciations. The Scandinavian Mountains, with their wide plateaus (fjells) and numerous glacial plateaus, run along the whole north coast of the peninsula and

drop into the North Sea in the west. **Lappland** lies north of the Arctic Circle. It is a plain containing isolated mountains which adjoins the hills of the **Central Finnish Ridge**, with its many lakes.

Lappland

Lappland, home of the Lappish people, covers eastern Sweden, eastern Norway, northern Finland and parts of the **Kola Peninsula**. The landscape is characterised by wide plateaus covered in tundra and bogs, interspersed with scattered, isolated mountain peaks.

Finnmark

In the extreme north-east of Norway, the snowline has been pushed back northwards due to the Gulf Stream. This means that

the region is able to support pine forests, such as those of the Stabbursdalen National Park at 70° N, the northernmost pine forest in the world.

Scandinavian Mountains

The **Scandinavian Mountains** extend over the whole of the Scandinavian Peninsula. Although some peaks reach a height of more than 2,000 m, such as Glittertind (2,472 m) and Kebnekaise (2,111 m), this is mainly a low mountain range. The etchplains in the west, which fall steeply into the sea and whose deep valleys form **fjords**, are typical features of the region.

Finnish Lake District

The **Finnish Lake District** contains approximately 55,000 lakes which date from the last Ice Age. The principle lakes are **Saimaa** and **Päijänne**.

British Isles

This island group sits on the northwest European continental shelf. It consists of the two main islands of **Great Britain** and **Ireland**, the **Shetlands** and **Orkneys**, the **Inner** and **Outer Hebrides**, the **Isle of Man**, **Anglesey**, the **Isle of Wight** and numerous other smaller islands.

Great Britain is divided into three geographical areas, the **Highlands** in the north and west, the **Midlands** and the **Lowlands** in the

Scandinavian mountains: Geirangerfjord in Norway

south. The Scottish Highlands are separated from the **Southern Uplands** by a deep rift, the Great Glen. The **Cheviot Hills** form the border between Scotland and England. The **Pennines** run in a north–south direction down the centre of England, and the **Cumbrian Mountains** are located in the west. The far south-west of the island consists of the granite, hilly peninsula of **Devon and Cornwall**. **Lowland Britain** consists of a flat cuesta landscape. The Midlands and Lowlands of Scotland mark the border between the Highlands and Lowland Britain. **Southern England** is characterised by ranges of hills, the Thames Valley and the Hampshire

Basin. **East Anglia** and **The Fens** in the east are flat and marshy, some parts lying below sea-level. Fjord-like inlets, such as the **Firth of Forth** and **Moray Firth** are characteristic of the Scottish coast. The high cliffs on the **south coast facing the English Channel** were formed by buckling of the layers of chalk. These are the famous White Cliffs of Dover.

Ireland

Most of the island is dominated by the Irish Lowlands that rise no higher than 100 m. This region contains numerous bogs and lakes. In the north-west, the landscape rises to form the low mountain range of the **Caledonian Mountains**. The highest points are **Nephin** (806 m) and **Mount Errigal** (752 m). In the south, the Irish Lowlands are bordered by

a range of mountains formed during the **Armorican period**. Ireland's highest mountain, the 1,038 m-high **Carrauntoohill**, is in this area. The **Wicklow Mountains** are up to 924 m high and form the central mass of the Leinster Mountains. The coasts consist mainly of deeply-fissured cliffs, with inlets that can extend far inland.

Shetland and Orkney Islands

There are more than 100 islands in the **Orkneys and Sheltlands**. The largest are Mainland, Sanday, Westray and Stronsay, Yell, Unst, Fetlar, Bressai and Whalsay. The **Pentland Firth** separates the

Scottish mainland from the 70 Orkney Islands. The coasts are characterised by a large number of bays and high cliffs.

Scottish Highlands

The Scottish **Highlands** are split in two by the 95-km-long **Glen More** to form the **Northern Highlands**, which are up to 1,183 m high, and the **Grampians**, which include Scotland's highest mountain, the 1,344-m-high **Ben Nevis**. This long valley also contains many lakes, including **Loch Ness**, which in places is 229 m deep. The western Highlands end in craggy cliffs. The largest lake in the British Isles is **Loch Lomond** (70 sq. km) south of the Grampians.

Pennines

This Palaeozoic low mountain range runs from north to south and is England's watershed. The highest point is the 893-m-high **Cross Fell**. West of the Pennines lie the **Cumbrian Mountains**, whose numerous ravines and lakes are known collectively as the **Lake District**.

Wales/Cambrian Mountains

Wales mainly comprises barren hills devoid of trees. The highest point in the **Cambrian Mountains** is the egg-shaped **Mount Snowdon**, which reaches a height of 1,085 m. The plateaus, which are covered in meadows, drop suddenly into the sea, forming spectacular 90-m-high cliffs.

Cornwall

The steep, vertical cliffs of **Cornwall** extend into the Atlantic in the far south-west of Great Britain. The rounded peaks of the land away from the coast are traversed by narrow valleys. The mountain ridges rise in stages and are covered in moorland and marshes.

European Lowlands

The European Lowlands stretch from the Atlantic, along the North Sea and the Baltic Sea coasts and into Russia. Much of the area is characterised by dry, sandy deposits of poor soil left over from the Ice Age. It was originally covered in mixed woodland, but is today partly covered by stunted shrubs and

The Giant's Causeway on the north coast of *Ireland* is the stuff of legends. It is up to 60 m wide in places and stretches for some 5 km. This tongue of land near the fishing village of Ballycastle consists of 40,000 symmetrical basalt columns which can be up to 6 m high. Most of the columns are regular hexagons. They were formed by crystallisation, when lava flowing into the sea cooled down very quickly. The formation continues under the water.

pine heathland. The terminal moraines of Lower Saxony have a dry, loamy-sandy soil, dotted with clumps of trees.

The impressive moraines from the Wolstonian glaciation period include **Lüneburg Heath**, the **Hamburg Mountains** and **Fläming**. The southern land ridge extends from Emsland over Fläming and into the Lower Silesian Mountains. The moraines of the **Baltic land ridge** surround the Baltic Sea from **North Jutland** to **East Prussia**. The **North Sea Coast** has a barrier of dunes and tidal shallows, extending north-east from Calais as far as North Schleswig. Away from the coast, the sandy plains are covered in marshes.

French Lowlands, Brittany and Normandy

The fertile cultivated land that forms the **Paris Basin** is interspersed with wooded areas and sandy soil. The Seine valley is bordered in the north-west by **Brittany** and **Normandy**. The crystalline rocks of the coast have been eroded by surf to form steep cliffs and numerous islands.

Brittany's landscape actually consists of a very ancient mountain range that has now been eroded to a maximum height of 384 m in the **Monts d'Arrée**. Vegetation in the region is characterised by heathland, moorland, woodland and clumps of tall trees.

The Paris Basin adjoins the **Garonne Basin**. The extensive pine forests south of Bordeaux dominate the landscape, along with the straight, flat coastline with its many coastal lagoons and an impressive belt of dunes. The **Rhône-Saône Basin**, lying between the **Cévennes** and the **Alps**, has a distinctly Mediterranean character. The flood plains of **Languedoc**, the **Rhône Delta**, the **Riviera** and **Provence** are all part of this region.

North Sea Coast/Mud-flats

The Belgian **North Sea Coast** is flat and has no off-shore islands. This coast is lined with a wall of dunes up to 30 m high and a series of dykes, behind which lies a stretch of treeless marshland, traversed by numerous drainage ditches. This area adjoins the dry, sandy plains of **Flanders**. The North Sea coast of the Netherlands is characterised by barrier beaches

and a belt of dunes that are only interrupted by the estuaries of the **Rhine** and **Meuse rivers**. The original moorland and silt landscapes have been transformed by the man-made polders (dykes) into broad, treeless stretches of pastureland, some of which is land reclaimed from the sea. The North Sea coast of Germany is flat and protected from flooding by dykes. The **North and East Frisian Islands** rise out of **tidal mudflats**. The **small, low islands off the coast of Schleswig-Holstein** are an interesting feature. These flat, marshy islands have manmade terps (sea-walls) to provide protection from storm surges for both humans and grazing animals.

Between these islands and the dykes lie mud-flats, which are dry when exposed at low tide.

Central European Low Mountain Range

The **Central European Low Mountain Range** is a chain of disparate rugged massifs, beginning in western Europe. The region is bordered to the south by the Alps and the Carpathian Mountains and in the east it joins the Lublin basin and gradually merges with the Russian plateau. These highly eroded mountains date from the Variscan Orogeny. The constituent massifs have both craggy folds and flat crests. Most of the low mountain range is covered in mountain forest, but in many places, the original trees have been replaced by plantations of spruce.

Vosges and the Black Forest

The **Vosges** to the west of the Rhine extend from the Belfort Gap

in the south to the Col de Saverne in the north. The **Southern Vosges** is a chain of mountains and ridges with craggy hills, covered in woodland. The **Northern Vosges** are also densely forested and consist of large red sandstone slabs. The highest elevation is Grosser Winterberg at a height of 581 m. The highest mountain in the

1 Dawn in the wild Scottish Highlands: Buachaille Etive Mór at an altitude of some 1,000 m.

2 Land's End is the extreme tip of Cornwall, the peninsula in the south-west of England. These rugged cliffs are the country's westernmost point.

3 Ireland: Galway Bay lies on the western coast of the island.

4 St. David's Head: the cliff-lined tongue of land in west Wales extends out into the Atlantic. The south coast is relatively calm, but the north is often battered by the surf.

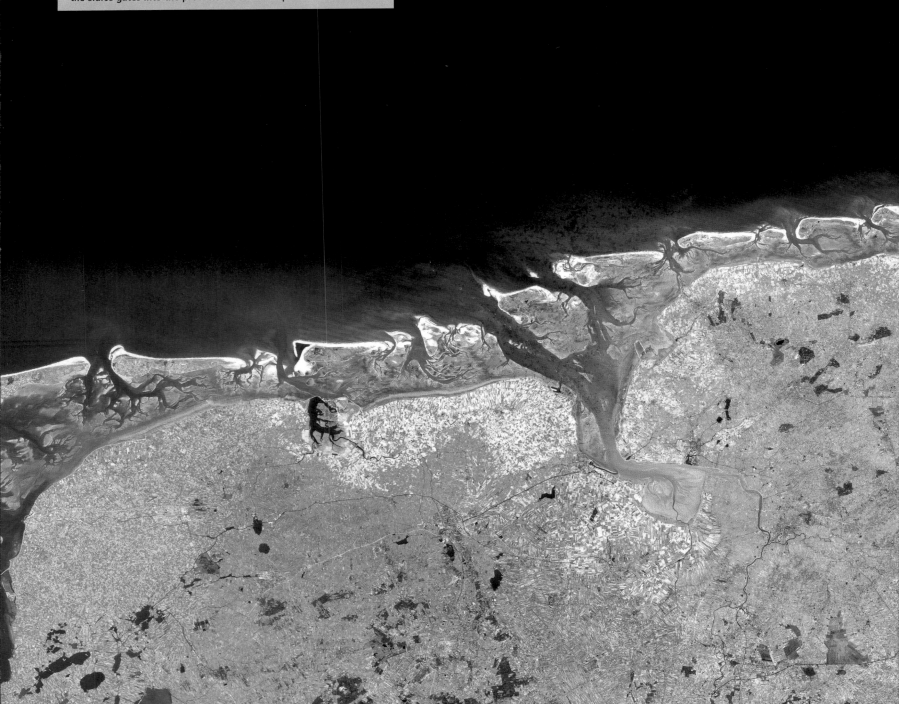

Along the Danish, German and Dutch North Sea coastline stretches a biotope as rich and diverse in forms of life as the tropical rainforest. The Wadden Sea, an area of water and wetland about 450 km long and 10 km wide, lies between Den Helder in the Netherlands and Ebsjerg in Denmark. This vast natural area – the largest of its kind in the world – has evolved over 10,000 years. When the mudflats first began to build up, the North Sea was relatively young and its shallow waters still prone to drying up. The uppermost layer of islands, sandbanks and mudflats was deposited by winds that predominantly blew in from over the land. Today with each tide the North Sea flows through the sluice gates into the protected area and deposits fine sediment.

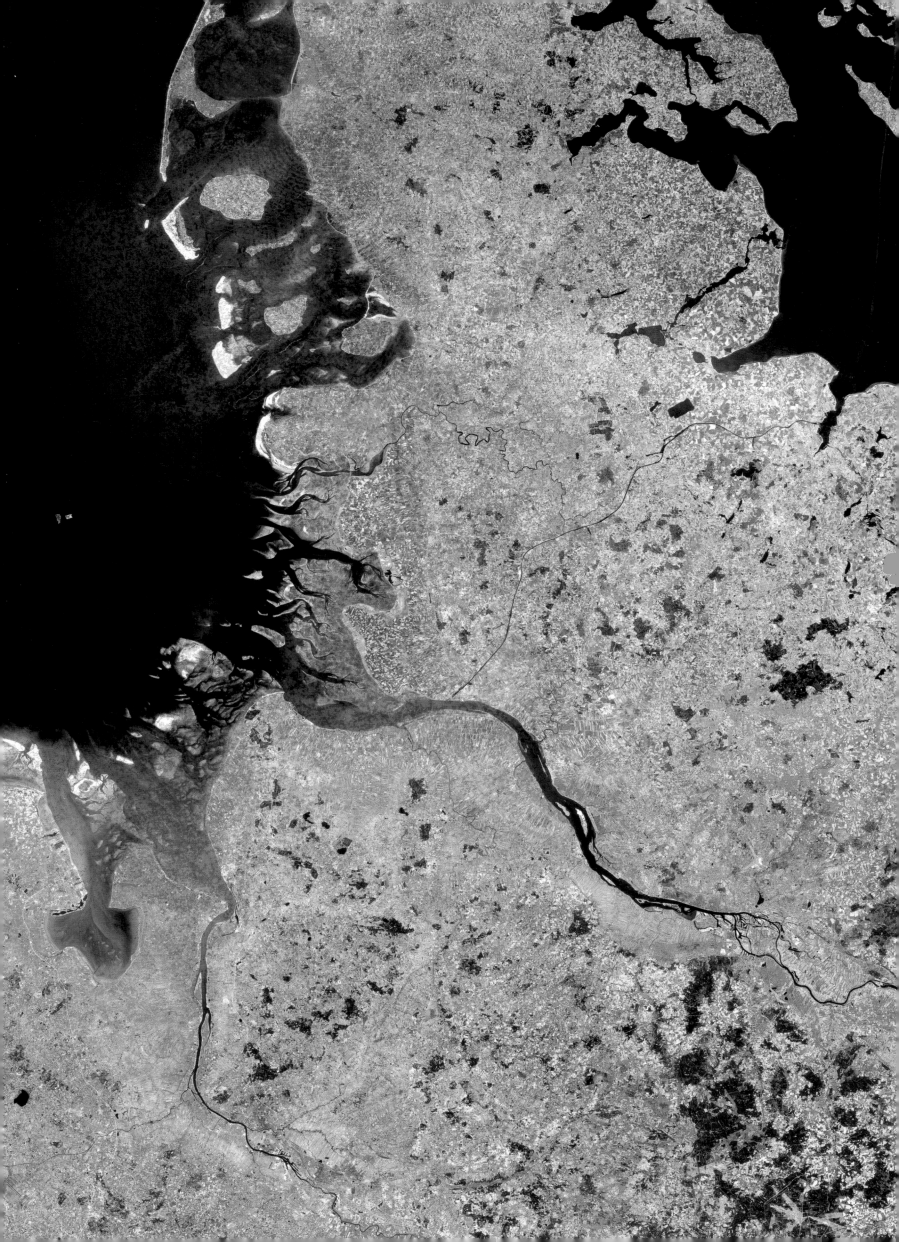

*The Strait of Bonifacio separates the Mediterranean islands **Sardinia** and **Corsica**. Both islands are mainly mountainous. Corsica has numerous peaks above 2,000 m, while the highest point on Sardinia reaches only 1,834 m.*

Vosges is Grand Ballon (1,423 m). To the east of the Rhine lies the **Black Forest**. It is 160 km long and between 22 and 60 km wide. Its romantic valleys and mountain lakes are particularly attractive. The region's numerous mineral and thermal springs, particularly around Baden-Baden, are signs of seismic activity.

The Black Forest also contains the highest cascade in Germany, the Triberg Waterfalls (162 m).

German Low Mountain Range

The **Rhenish Slate Mountains** are located to the west of this range of low mountains. To the west of the Rhine and north of the **Moselle** lies the volcanic **Eifel region** with its circular crater lakes. South of the Moselle is the **Hunsrück**, which is mirrored to the east of the Rhine by the **Taunus**.

The **Westerwald** mainly consists of areas of pastureland covering the basalt bedrock. To the north, **Bergisches Land** adjoins **Sauerland**. Further to the east lie the forest-covered red sandstone plateaus of the **Weserbergland** and **Leinebergland**. To the south lie the **hills of Hesse** and the **Vogelsberg Mountains**.

The **Harz Mountains** are 100 km long and 35 km wide, an isolated

Rhine

The Rhine is 1,320 km long and is one of Europe's most important transport routes. It originates in the Swiss canton of Graubünden (Grisons). The two upper branches of the river join to form the Alpine Rhine which opens out into a delta in Lake Constance. The river flows out of the lake and plummets over the 20 m falls at Schaffhausen. The Thur and Aare Rivers join from the west and the Wutach from the east. The Rhine flows through the lowlands of the Upper Rhine until Bingen, where it joins the Neckar and Main. In the Rhine Gorge, the river flows through slate mountains. The Mosel, Ahr, Lahn and Sieg rivers flow down deep valleys to join the Rhine. The Lower Rhine winds through the Lower Rhine Valley in the Netherlands, before its main estuary arms, the Waal and Lek Ijssel, spill out into the North Sea.

massif south-east of Hanover. The **Frankenwald** and **Thuringian forests** have lost some of their once impressive woodland. The **Fichtel Mountains**, on the other hand, still have dense woodland, and the region's granite hills form an undulating basin at a height of 600 m. Further east lie the **Ore Mountains, the Elbe Sandstone Mountains** and the **Lusatian Mountains**.

The hills around the fringes of the **Upper Rhine Valley, Spessart and Odenwald,** are covered by **the Palatine Forest** and the **Black Forest**. This is followed by the cuesta of southern Germany, with the **Swabian Mountains** and the **Frankish Alb**. To the east of these mountains, the Naab Valley extends to the mountains on the east Bavarian border, the **Bavarian Forest** and the **Bohemian Forest**.

Bavarian Forest, Bohemian Forest, Sudetenland

The **Bohemian Forest** is divided by the Cham-Further Lowland. In the south-east, a long, broad basin divides the **Bavarian Forest**, which lies between the Danube and Regen rivers and rises to a barren landscape at an altitude of about 1,121 m. The highest point is the **Great Arber** at 1,456 m.

The **Sudetenland** extends for a length of some 300 km and is between 30 km and 60 km wide. It lies between the Lusatian Mountains and the Moravian Gate. The **West Sudetenland** consists of the **Karkonosze**, the Jizera Mountains and the Bóbr-Kaczawa Mountains. It adjoins the Klodzko Valley and the Masyw Snieznika. The **East Sudetenland** consists of the Hruby Jeseník Mountains and the Nízky Jeseník. The highest peak in the range is **Snow Mountain** at a height of 1,602 m.

Danube

The second longest river in Europe (2,858 km) begins as the Breg and Brigach in the eastern Black Forest. It flows through the Bavarian Forest into the Vienna Basin and from there through the lowlands of Hungary. The river divides into several branches covering a wide delta before it drains into the Black Sea.

Massif Central

The French **Massif Central** covers some 85,000 sq. km, making this the largest connected mountain range in France. The mountains are bordered by the **Garonne Basin**, the **Paris Basin** and the **Rhône-Saône Basin**.

The **Auvergne** is the centre of the Massif and is one of Europe's most impressive volcanic regions. The highest point of the Massif Central is in the volcanic Chaîne des Puys. It is the 1,885-m-high **Puy de Nancy** in Mont Dore. In the karst plateaus of the **Causses** in the south, the Tarn, has carved out deep gorges.

Pyrenees

This high mountain range between the Mediterranean Sea and the Bay of Biscay divides the **Iberian Peninsula** from the rest of mainland Europe. The **Pyrenees** are 435 km long, but only have a maximum width of some 100 km. The highest point is **Aneto** at 3,408 m. Between the passes of **Col de Somport** in the west and the 1,915-m-high **Col de Puymorens** lie the Central Pyrenees, which reach heights of about 2,900 m in the region around Andorra, and can be over 3,355 m high in the Monte Perdido and Maldeta Massif.

The East Pyrenees adjoin the **Albères** near the Mediterranean. The highest point here is the **Pic Carlit** (2,921 m). The major high

valleys are Capcir, Cerdagne and Vallespir. Although **Pic d'Anie** is 2,504 m high, the West Pyrenees between the **Irati Valley** and the 1,632-m-high **Somport Pass** is more like a low mountain chain, and descends to the coast of the Basque Country.

Iberian Peninsula

The largest and westernmost of the three southern European peninsulas is bordered by the Pyrenees in the north, the Atlantic in the west and south-west, and by the Mediterranean in the east and south-east. The heart of the peninsula is an almost circular high plateau (**meseta**), which is traversed by a range of mountains running from west to east. The **Cordillera Central** divides the plateau into the smaller North Meseta, up to 800 m high, and the South Meseta, up to 600 m high. The edges of the plateau are surrounded by chains of high hills: in the north the **Cantabrian Mountains (Cordillera Cantábrica)**, in the east the **Sistema Ibérico** (highest point: 2,313 m) and in the south by the **Sierra Morena**. To the west, the plateau descends gradually over the **Estremadura** to the Atlantic. The **Ebro River** forms the Ebro Basin between the Pyrenees and the Sistema Ibérico, and the **Guadalquivir River** creates the **Andalusian Basin**, which opens out into a wide lowland area towards the Atlantic.

Cantabrian Mountains

The **Cantabrian Mountains** stretch to the north Spanish coast between the Pyrenees and the **Galician Hills**. Only 30 km from the coast, this range of hills reaches its highest point, the 2,648-m-high **Picos de Europa**.

Cordillera Central

The **Cordillera Central** crosses the whole of the Iberian Peninsula and divides Spain's central

Steep escarpments characterise the Rhine valley in Germany.

plateau. They are rolling hills that reach a height of 2,592 m in the **Sierra de Gredos**. These hills divide the meseta into the North Meseta, traversed by the **Douro River**, and the South Meseta, also known as **La Mancha**.

Cordillera Bética

The **Cordillera Bética** or Sistema Bética is an area of alpidic folds that run north-east from the **Straits of Gibraltar**, parallel to the coast and as far as **Cabo de la Nao**. The mountain system continues in the **Balearic Islands**. The main chain of the Cordillera Bética is the 90-km-long **Sierra Nevada** in Andalusia. One of its peaks, **Mulhacén**, is 3,481 m high, making it the highest mountain on the Iberian Peninsula.

Sierra Morena

The so-called 'brown mountains' form the southern edge of the plateau of inland Spain and receive a lot of rain. The plateaus

*The highest volcano in Europe is the 3,323-m-high **Etna** on the east coast of **Sicily**. The active volcano has a main crater and more than 200 smaller craters made of ash and clinker. The volcano has erupted more than 100 times in its history. Etna's plumes of smoke are a reminder of its continued activity – and unpredictable nature.*

rise so gradually that the incline is barely noticeable, but they reach heights of 1,323 m. The 400-km-long steep escarpment of the Guadalquivír Lowland is particularly impressive.

Balearic Islands

The **Balearic** island group lies in the western Mediterranean and consists of the main island **Mallorca**, the slightly smaller **Menorca**, the Pitiusas (**Ibiza and Formentera**) and several smaller islands. The islands are the continuation of the **Cordillera Bética**. The highest peak is the 1,445 m **Puig Mayor** on Mallorca.

Apennine Peninsula

The **Apennine Peninsula** is divided into three main areas. In the north, the **Alps** form a divide from the rest of Europe. South of the Alps, the **plain of the Po River** extends as far as the **Adriatic**. In the Ice Age, this former sea bay became choked with debris carried down by rivers from the Alps and the Apennines.

Vicenza and Padua are overshadowed by the extinct volcanoes of **Colli Berici** and **Colli Euganei**, where hot sulphurous springs, the Abano Terme, rise to the surface. In the north-west, the **Apennines** extend almost all the way to the coast, where the narrow coast of the **Riviera** can be found.

The mountains surround an area of hills in a broad arc that is open towards the west. These are the **hills of Tuscany** which are also part of the Umbrian Basin. South of Monte Amiata lies Latium with its forest-covered extinct volcanoes and beautiful crater lakes. Between the volcanic hills lie plateaus formed of tufa, a volcanic rock, with few trees, surrounded by extensive, but largely dry moors and marshes.

The **Adriatic coast** has few harbours and is flat, but the west coast has numerous coves, bays and off-shore islands.

Apennines

The **Apennines** extend across the peninsula from the Alps to the north of **Sicily,** covering 1,100 km. The highest peaks are in the central section, the karstified limestone hills of the **Abruzzi**. The highest point is

Gran Sasso d'Italia (2,912 m). The Southern Apennines are an uneven disconnected range of mountains. The crystalline massifs of **La Sila** and **Aspromonte** are in Calabria.

Corsica

The 8,680 sq. km Mediterranean island is 185 km long from north to south and is a maximum of 85 km wide. The mountainous interior is rugged and crossed by numerous valleys. The highest point is the 2,706-m-high **Monte Cinto**. The mountains in the west are granite and porphyry. In the east the mountains are younger and are made of slate.

The vegetation consists of maquis shrubland, beech and conifer woodland. The west coast has many natural harbours, but the east coast is lined with marshes and coastal lagoons.

Sardinia

The interior of the 23,813 sq. km island is a plateau-like mountain terrain, with craggy peaks in the north-east, covered in maquis shrubland. The **Campidano Basin**, is a wide graben in the southwest. The highest point is **Gennargentu** (1,834 m).

Sicily

The **Straits of Messina** divide Sicily, the largest island in the Mediterranean (25,426 sq. km), from the Italian mainland. In the west of the island, **Monti Peloritani** (1,279 m), **Monti Nebrodi** (1,847 m) and **Madonie** (1,979 m) are a continuation of the Apennine Mountains. The steep cliffs are

covered in maquis scrub and the remains of oak and beech woodland. South of Palermo lies a sedimentary ridge and plateau landscape, which extends into an area of hills and mountains, largely devoid of trees. On the east coast of Siciliy is Europe's largest active volcano, the 3,340-m-high **Mount Etna**.

1 Bizarre limestone walls and strangely-shaped peaks rise in the southern foothills of the Pyrenees.

2 A view over the east coast of Sicily to the gradual slopes of the 3,350-m-high Mount Etna, an almost constantly erupting volcano.

3 The Straits of Gibraltar on the south coast of the Iberian Peninsula: the cliff-lined tongue of land is connected to the mainland by alluvial plains.

4 The Dentelles de Montmirail in Provence, at the extremity of the arc of the Western Alps.

The Alps

The Alps emerged relatively recently in the earth's history, in the Cretaceous and Tertiary eras, but did not take their present form until the Quaternary. The longitudinal valleys run from Lake Constance in the north to Lake Como in the south, deep into the high mountains separating the Western from the Eastern Alps.

Ranging from France and Switzerland through Austria, Germany and Italy, the Alps – Europe's highest mountain range – are about 1,200 km long and 150–250 km wide. The Passo dei Giovi near Genoa is considered to be the border with the Apennines. The Alps extend to Lake Geneva in the north and break off in the west towards the Rhône valley. In the north-east they reach as far as the Danube near Vienna and in the south to the Plain of the Po.

The Western Alps, with many peaks over 4,000 m high, have a southern chain of crystalline and metamorphic rocks and a limestone northern chain, separated by a valley. The French limestone Alps change to crystalline from Mont Blanc (4,807 m). Near Nice, this crystalline zone begins with the oceanic Alpine chain, reaching 3,297 m in the Aiguille de l'Argen-

tière. To the north, the crystalline massifs extend to Mont Blanc and then continue along an east-west axis. Mont Blanc, Europe's highest mountain, has given its name to the whole glaciated massif rising between the longitudinal valleys of the Arve and the Dora Baltea. The Eastern Alps are twice as broad as the Western, but markedly lower, with peaks no more than 4,000 m high.

The Central Alps include the Walliser Alps, the Bernese Oberland, the Gotthard massif, the Bernina group, the Silvretta group, the Ötztal and Zillertal Alps, the Hohe and Niedere Tauern, and the Ortler and Adamello groups. The Matterhorn is the mightiest mountain in the Walliser Alps. This giant of crystalline plutonic rock tapers to a height of 4,478 m, more than 1,000 m higher than the glacier passes that surround it.

The crystalline Central Alps are flanked to the north and south by limestone areas. The mineral nature of the rock creates the particularly stark formation of this rocky landscape, such as the beautiful Dolomites on the south side and the impressive 2,962-m-high Zugspitze massif in the north. The limestone mountains in the marginal zones are on average only about 2,000 m high. The northern limestone Alps include the Dachstein massif in Austria, with typical karst rock formations.

The nature of the Alpine landscape, so rich in relief formations, was created by the variety of rock as well as by an upward thrust following the completion of folding and shifting processes in the Late Tertiary. Massive Ice Age reshaping also contributed to the creation of the relief. Huge primeval glaciers created the valleys and

mountain passes, the deep lakes (Constance, Geneva and Lucerne), and the northern Italian lakes. Typical features are the narrow gorges, wide valleys and stepped formation of the high passes, as well as waterfalls, cirques and smaller lakes in the summit region. The Königssee, near Berchtesgaden, is a typical alpine lake. Its clear waters reflect the evergreen forests and steeply towering rock faces that surround the lake.

Today only the highest regions lie above the snowline. These are the plateau glaciers of Mont Blanc, the Walliser Alps and Bernina. Some glaciers still flow down into the valleys. In the accumulation zones, less snow thaws in the course of a year than new snow falls. In the ablation zones, below the snowline, it is the exact opposite. Here, the glacier tongues thaw and turn into mountain streams.

which feed the many rivers that flow down the narrow Alpine gorges, such as the Rhine, Rhône, Po, Inn, Drau and Save.

The snowline varies in altitude from 2,500 m to 3,400 m, depending on latitude and longitude. The Alpine zone with its extensive meadows and pastures can reach an altitude of 1,600 m. Lower down is a band of dense coniferous forest, then deciduous trees, and finally the cultivated land at the foot of the mountains.

Big picture: the Ahornspitze in the Zillertal Alps.

Inset: view from the Jungfrau ridge over the Aletsch Glacier.

Opposite: satellite image of the Bernese Alps with the Aletsch Glacier, the three great 'firns' and the smaller Grüneggfirn.

*The island of **Pag** in the Adriatic Sea is 60 km long, with a area of 290 sq. km and elevations of up to 348 m. It is one of more than 600 islands that stretch along the Dalmatian Coast of the **Balkan Peninsula**. The islands are a series of parallel folds, which over time have been submerged by the sea.*

Dinaric Mountains: the Plitvice Lakes are connected by waterfalls.

Balkan Peninsula

The easternmost of the Mediterranean peninsulas begins in the north-west in the **Dinaric Alps**, which then extend along the coast of the **Adriatic Sea** to join the **Albanian Alps** in the south, with peaks reaching a height of up to 2,700 m. These are followed by a series of disconnected mountain ranges.

The high peaks drop steeply into the Adriatic, leaving just a narrow coastal area. The Adriatic coast is dotted with numerous offshore islands, all with mountainous karstified terrain. The northern edge of the Balkan Peninsula is defined by the **Danube** and **Sava Rivers**.

The '**Danube Lands**' of Bulgaria is the name given to a region of undulating plains that rise to form a steep escarpment 150 m above the Danube. Deep valleys

Volga

The Volga is the longest river in Europe, running a length of 3,530 km. It also has the largest volume of water. It originates in the Valdai Hills and initially flows north. Further downstream, the river turns south. Below Volzhskiy, the Volga branches to form the Achtuba, and the two rivers form a valley 25 km wide where they drain into the Caspian Sea.

with vertical cliffs traverse this loess-covered landscape. Here, the **foothills of the Balkans** begin to rise, slowly climbing to reach their full height.

Located parallel to the **Balkans** but lying slightly to the south is the **Sredna Gora**, a low mountain range in Bulgaria adjoining the **Balkan-Turkish lowlands and hills** and traversed by the **Maritsa River**. The **Thracian Massif** is divided into the **Rila, Pirin** and **Rhodope Mountains**.

In the southern half of the Balkan Peninsula, the coasts are lined with numerous bays and headlands, while the interior of the region is mountainous.

The karstified mountain region of **Epirus** is treeless, with few depressions. To the east lie the plains of **Thessaly**, which are dominated in the north-east by **Mount Olympus** at a height of 2,917 m. Greek Macedonia consists of impassable mountains with small, enclosed valleys.

The **Halkidiki Peninsula** is lined with cliffs and has three tongues of land that extend into the sea. East of this lie the undulating hills

Dnieper

The Dnieper is the third largest river in Europe (2,200 km). It rises in the north of the Central Russian Uplands, crosses the Ukraine in nine cataracts and drains into the Black Sea below Kherson.

of **Thrace**. In the heart of central Greece, the **Attica Peninsula** has mountains that extend right to the coast. This region has many fertile basins and depressions. The **Isthmus of Corinth** separates central Greece from the **Peloponnese**, which, along with the numerous **Aegean Islands**, constitute southern Greece.

Balkans and Rhodope Mountains

The **Balkan Mountains** extend for 600 km and are 21–50 km wide. They run in parallel chains from the **Danube** to the **Black Sea**. Only the **High Balkans** are as high as the Alps.

The **West Balkans** date from the Triassic and Jurassic periods and reach a height of 2,168 m. The **Balkans** become significantly lower to the east, and descend to **Cape Emine**. The **Rhodope Mountains** lie between the plains of the Maritsa to the north, the Aegean coast to the south, the Mesta valley in the west and the Bulgarian-Greek border in the east. The highest peak is the 2,191-m **Golyam Perelik**.

Pindus

The **Pindus** mountain range is part of the young Dinaric-Hellenic fold mountain system that runs parallel to the **Ionian Sea** coast. The craggy mountains reach heights ranging from 2,200 m to over 2,600m. The highest point is **Smolikas** at a height of 2,637 m.

Peloponnese

The peninsula is separated from the rest of the mainland by the Gulf of **Patras** and the Gulf of **Corinth**. The interior of the peninsula consists of jagged limestone mountains which rise to 2,407 m at Mount St. Elias in the **Taygetos Mountains**. **Arcadia** is a rough highland area with an average altitude of 1,000 m.

Aegean Islands, Crete

Thassos, Samothrace, Lemnos, Lesbos, Chios, Samos, the **Cyclades** and the **Sporades** are the major island groups in the **Aegean Sea**. The largest and southernmost of the islands is **Crete** which is mainly mountainous. The heavily karstified high ridges reach a height of 2,456 m at **Mount Ida**. The mountains fall steeply to the coast in the south, but in the north they descend to form an area of upland hills at an altitude of up to 1,500 m.

Carpathian Mountains

The **Carpathian Mountains** stretch over some 1,300 km in an arc around the north and east of the **Pannonian Plain**. Despite a maximum height of 2,655 m, the mountains have the characteristics of a low mountain chain. The Carpathian mountains are divided by basins and deep valleys to form the **Western Carpathians** extending to the valley of the Harnad River, the **Central Carpathians** which reach as far as the region around the source of the Tisza River, the heavily wooded **Eastern Carpathians** with their thermal springs that extend as far as the Romanian Plains and the **Southern Carpathians**.

Eastern European Lowlands

The **Eastern European Lowlands** lie east of the Central European Lowlands and are bordered by the **Caucasus** in the south and the **Urals** in the east.

Baltic Ridge, Eastern European Lowlands

The **Baltic Ridge** rises to the west and south of the **Baltic Sea**. It reaches a height of up to 329 m in Eastern Pomerania.

The **Russian Plain** extends to the east of the Central European Lowland seam, running as far as the **Carpathians**, the **Crimean Mountains** and the **Caucasus Mountains**. The whole area lies on a bedrock of gneiss, granite and crystalline schist, which extends under the Caspian Sea to a depth of up to 10,000 m. This bedrock comes to the surface in the **Donets Basin**, the **Podolian Upland** in Karelia and on the **Kola Peninsula**.

In Karelia and on Kola, glaciers have left behind bare hills and deep lakes. Further to the east and south-east lies a gently undulating young moraine landscape dotted with lakes.

The **Valdai Hills** and northern Belarus are characterised by terminal moraine plains and pine-covered sandy soil.

The Smolensk-Moscow Uplands and the **Siberian Uvali** are ancient moraine landscapes, which today take the form of flat-topped ridges. In the south lie moors and the extensive marshlands of the meandering rivers. The major rivers are the **Polesye**, which joins the **Pripyat** which in turn flows into the **Dnieper**. Broad marshy lowlands have also formed along the middle sections of the **Oka** and the tributaries of the **Desna**.

The numerous rivers flowing through the landscapes of southern and central Russia have eroded countless valleys. South of the plateaus there is a belt of steppe terrain, which borders the lowland regions of the **Caspian** and **Black Seas**.

Russian Plains

The plains of southern and central Russia form part of the Eastern European Lowlands and rarely rise to a height of more than 300 m. The higher plains, which run alongside the courses of the great rivers, have a regular relief. To the west, they rise gradually from a broad river plain, and fall steeply to the east. In between there is a series of high plateaus containing symmetrical hills.

The forks of the numerous river systems have formed large numbers of ravines and valleys on the edges of the plains. In the **Donets Basin** and the **Podolian Uplands**, a thick layer of bedrock rises to the surface, which forms the foundation of the entire Eastern European Lowlands.

The Greek Island of Santorini is the southernmost of the Cyclades group, formed by the remains of a volcanic peak which came into being almost 3,500 years ago after a violent explosion.

The beaches on this unique island are covered in grey-black laval sand, and the island's interior is also covered in volcanic rock. Santorini was devastated by an earthquake in 1956.

Urals

The **Urals** divide the Eastern European Lowlands from the West Siberian Plain and form the boundary between Europe and Asia. They are 40–150 km wide and stretch for 2,000 km along the 60th parallel from the tundra of the **Kara Sea coast** to the steppes of **Kazakhstan**.

The **Arctic** and **Sub-arctic Urals** lie between Mount Konstantinov (492 m) in the north and the Sablya (1,425 m) in the south. The north of the Urals consists of a series of massifs, whose rounded peaks reach a height of about 1,000 m. This region ends south of **Mount Isherim** (1,331 m).

The **Middle Urals** are a series of highly eroded low mountains which gently undulate at a height of 300–700 m. The highest point is **Konchakovski Kamen** (1,569 m). Mount Yurma (1,002 m) marks the border. Here the mountains spread out in a fan shape into several relatively high ridges, before giving way to treeless steppe terrain. The highest point in the Southern Urals is **Gora Yamantau** (1,638 m). South of the Byelaya river, an undulating plateau with a large number of valleys descends to the **Ural River**. The **Mugodzhar Hills** are even lower, and it is here that the Urals give way to the hills and plains of Kazakhstan.

Caspian Basin, Caspian Sea

The **Caspian Basin** is a lowland area north of the **Caspian Sea** covering an area of some 200,000 sq. km at altitudes of 28–149 m. The Caspian Sea is the largest inland sea on Earth, covering an area of 371,800 sq. km.

Black Sea, Crimea

The **Black Sea** is part of the **European Mediterranean Sea**. It covers a total area of 423,000 sq. km and has extensive shelves at a depth of below 100 m in Odessa Bay and in the western part of the sea. The Black Sea is believed to have been created when a narrow land bridge that separated a shallow lake from the Bosphorus was subjected to massive rainfall. The sea finally broke through the land bridge and poured into the lake. The event is said to have happened within human existence

and is the origin of the story of Noah's Flood and similar legends. The 25,600 sq. km **Crimean Peninsula** is connected to the mainland by the 8-km-wide Perekop Isthmus. In the west, the Crimea narrows to form the **Tarchankut Peninsula**, and in the east to form the **Kerch Peninsula**. The north is characterised by flat, dry steppes dotted with salt lakes. The **Crimean Mountains** rise in the south; Roman Kosh is the highest peak at a height of 1,545 m. The northern slopes are partially forested. The southern slopes leading to the Black Sea and the narrow coastal stretch are covered in typically Mediterranean lush vegetation.

Caucasian Mountains

The land connecting the Black Sea and the Caspian Sea is an extensive mountain region with varied topography. The steppes of the **Caucasian foothills** rise to form the **Greater Caucasus**, which extend over 1,500 km and are between 32 km and 180 km wide. The area is divided from west to east into five regions.

The **Pontic Mountains** have Mediterranean vegetation along the coastline and deciduous woodland at a higher altitude.

The **Abkhazian Mountains** reach heights of up to 4,046 m at Mount Dombay-Ulgen, which is partly glaciated.

The mountains reach their highest average elevation in the **Central Caucasus** region between the two extinct volcanoes of **Elbrus** (5,642 m) and **Kazbek** (5,033 m). A total of 15 peaks in this region rise to heights of more than 4,800 m.

In the **Caspian Caucasus**, the high mountains descend into

the Sumqayit (Sumgait) valley to form a gentle, wooded low mountain range. In the south, the Greater Caucasus terminate abruptly in the Transcaucasian Highlands. The **Lesser Caucasus** rise to the south of this divide. A lava plateau at an altitude of between 1,500 m and 2,000 m lies at the heart of these mountains.

1 The Meteora Monastery in Thessaly was constructed on the steep, craggy, weathered sandstone peaks of the Pindus Mountains.

2 Surf in the Bay of Kolpos Merembellou in the east of Crete, the largest of the Greek islands.

3 Naxos is the largest of the Cyclades: this mountainous island is steep in the east, but the western half is fertile.

4 The Black Drina River rises in Lake Ohrid. The surrounding limestone formations, south of the Albanian Alps, are divided by deep ravines.

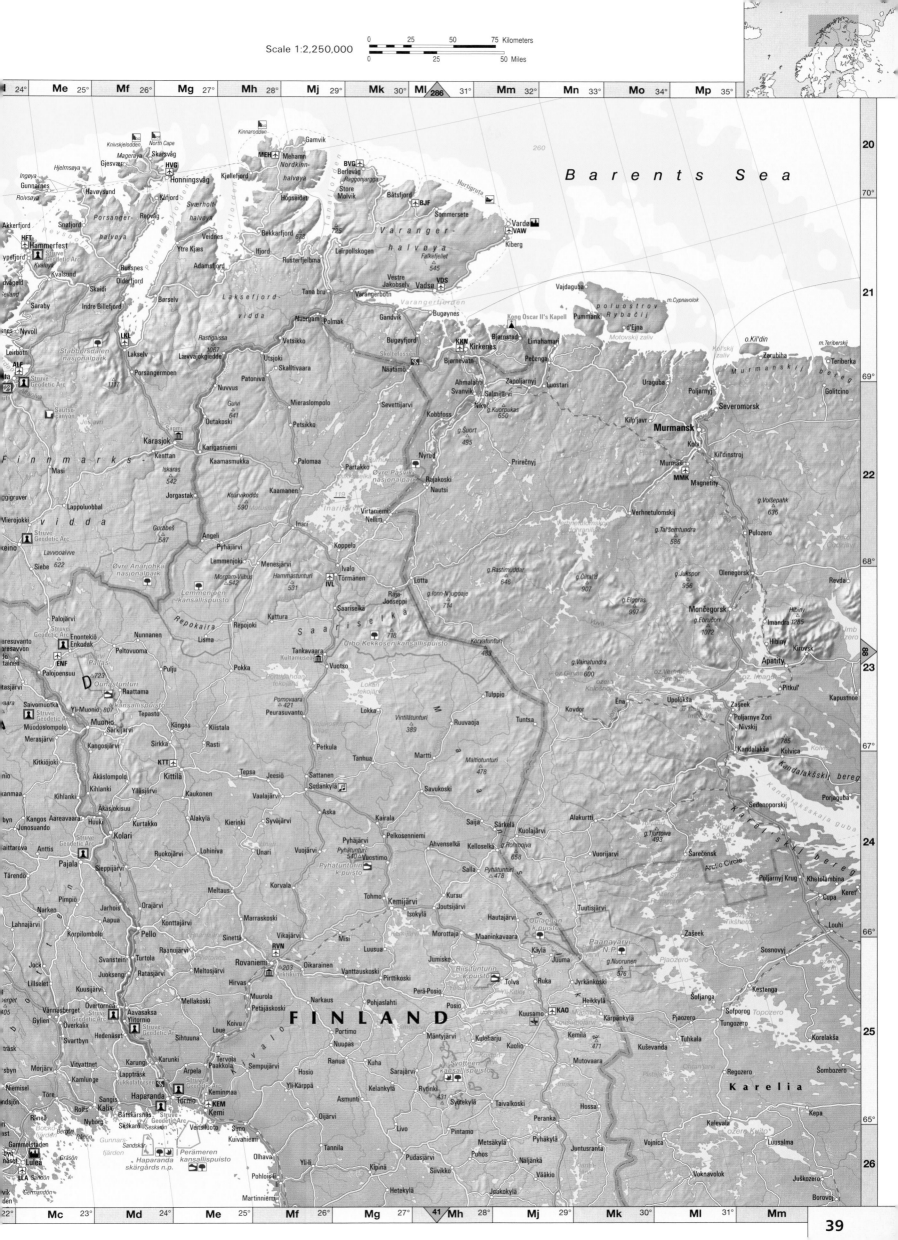

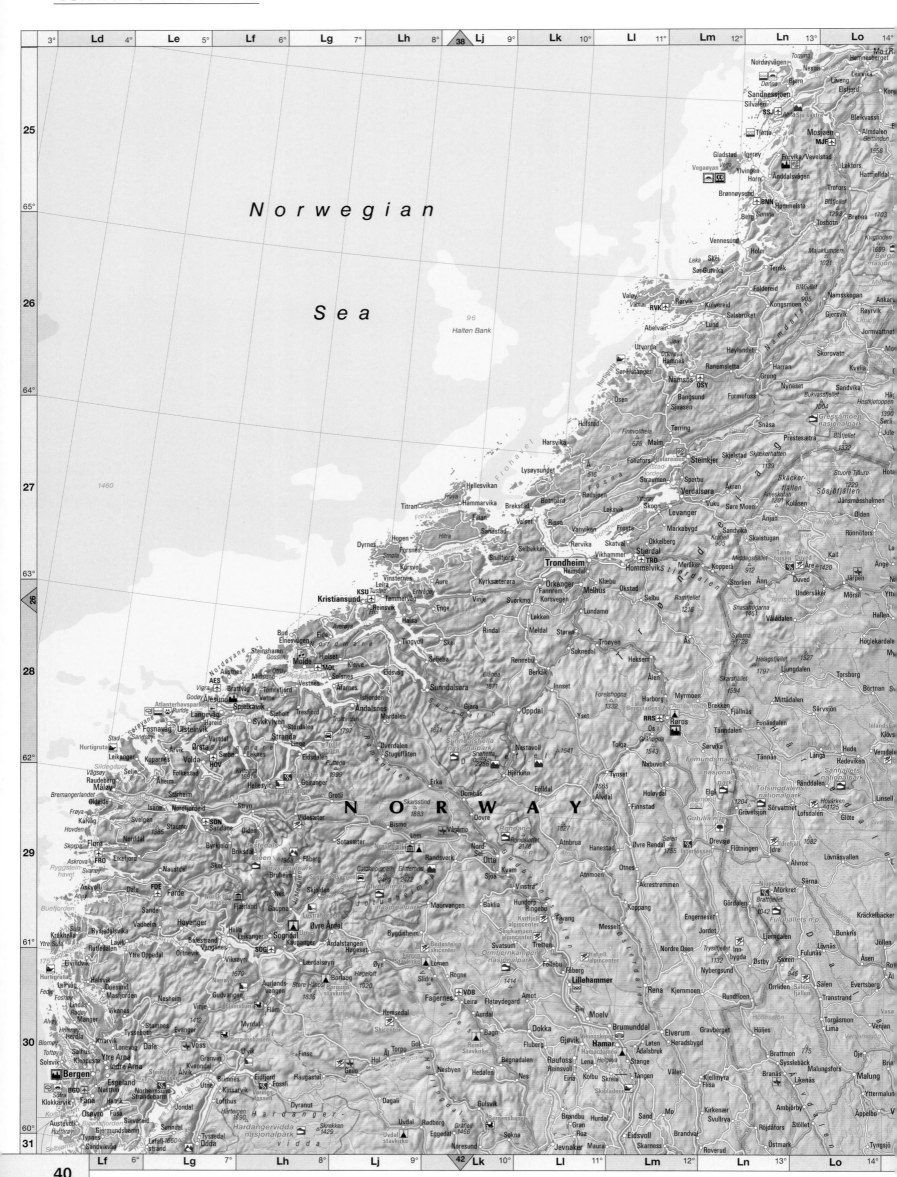

Norwegian

Sea

Halten Bank

NORWAY

Trondheim

Kristiansund

Molde

Ålesund

Åndalsnes

Bergen

Lillehammer

Hamar

Steinkjer

Namsos

Røros

Volda

Sogndal

Florø

Førde

Voss

Odda

Gjøvik

Fagernes

Dombås

Otta

Elverum

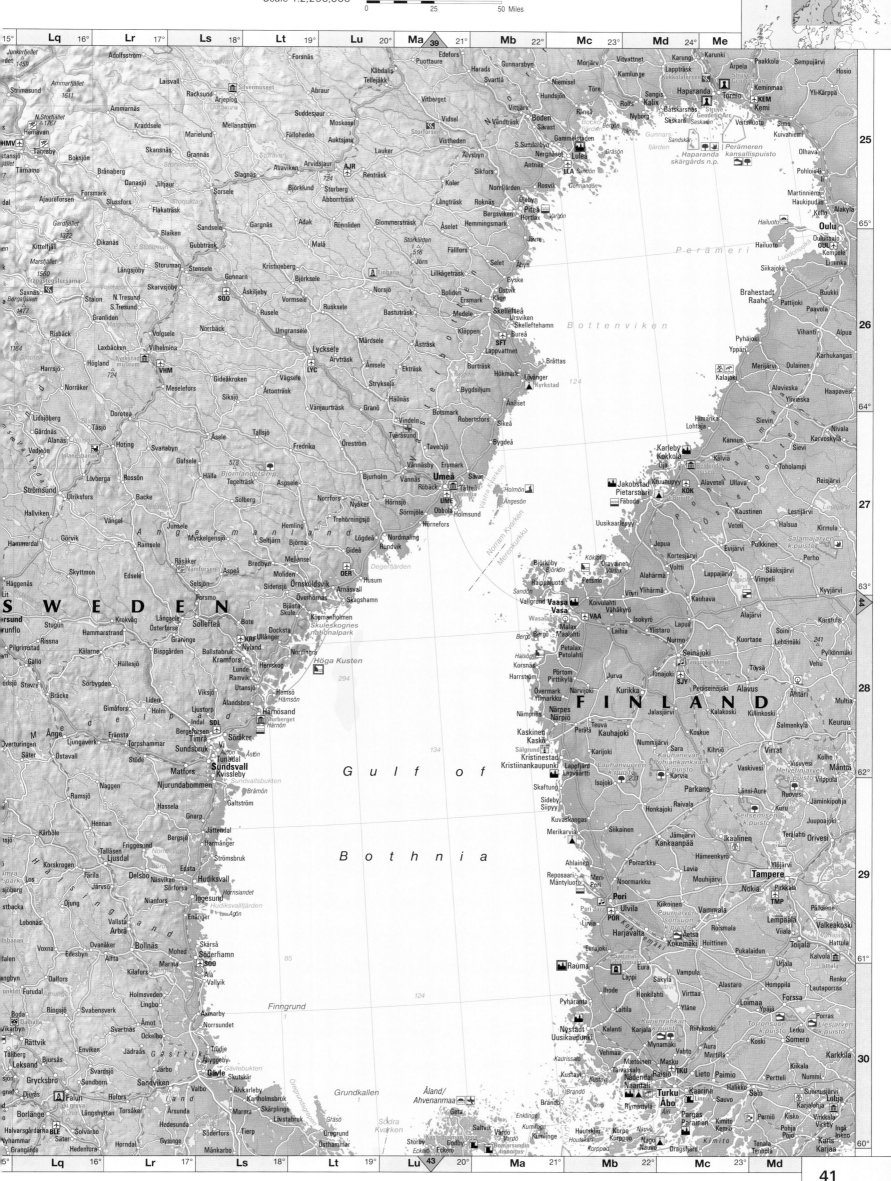

Scale 1:2,250,000

0 25 50 75 Kilometers
0 25 50 Miles

SWEDEN

FINLAND

Gulf of

Bothnia

Bottenviken

Perämeri

Oulu
OUL
Luleå
Piteå
Skellefteå
Umeå
UME
Vaasa
Vasa
VAA
Karleby
Kokkola
KOK
Jakobstad
Pietarsaari
Härnösand
Sundsvall
Hudiksvall
Söderhamn
Gävle
Tampere
TMP
Pori
POR
Rauma
Uusikaupunki
Turku
Åbo
TKU
Haparanda
Tornio
Kemi
KEM

Höga Kusten

Åland/
Ahvenanmaa

Scale 1:2,250,000

0 25 50 75 Kilometers
0   25   50 Miles

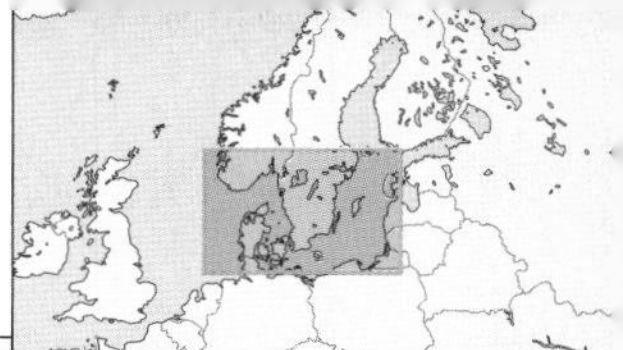

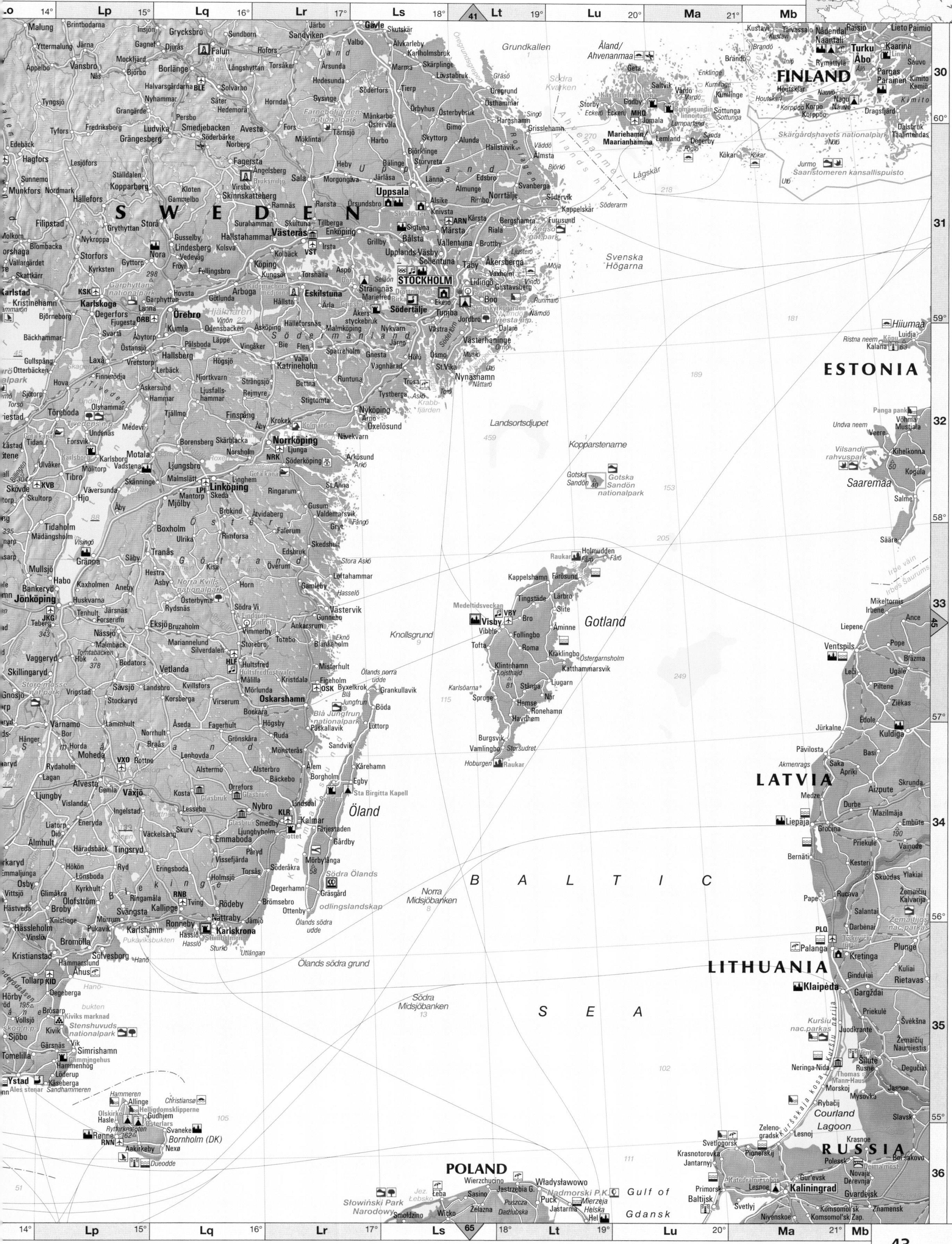

FINLAND

SWEDEN

ESTONIA

LATVIA

LITHUANIA

RUSSIA

POLAND

Grundkallen
Åland/Ahvenanmaa
Turku Åbo
Mariehamn Maarianhamina

Gävle
Falun
Borlänge
Uppsala
Västerås
STOCKHOLM
Eskilstuna
Södertälje
Örebro
Karlskoga
Norrköping
Linköping
Jönköping
Oskarshamn
Växjö
Kalmar
Öland
Karlskrona
Ystad

Gotland
Visby
Hiiumaa
Saaremaa
Ventspils
Liepāja
Palanga
Klaipėda

BALTIC SEA

Bornholm (DK)
Rönne

Gulf of Gdansk
Kaliningrad

45

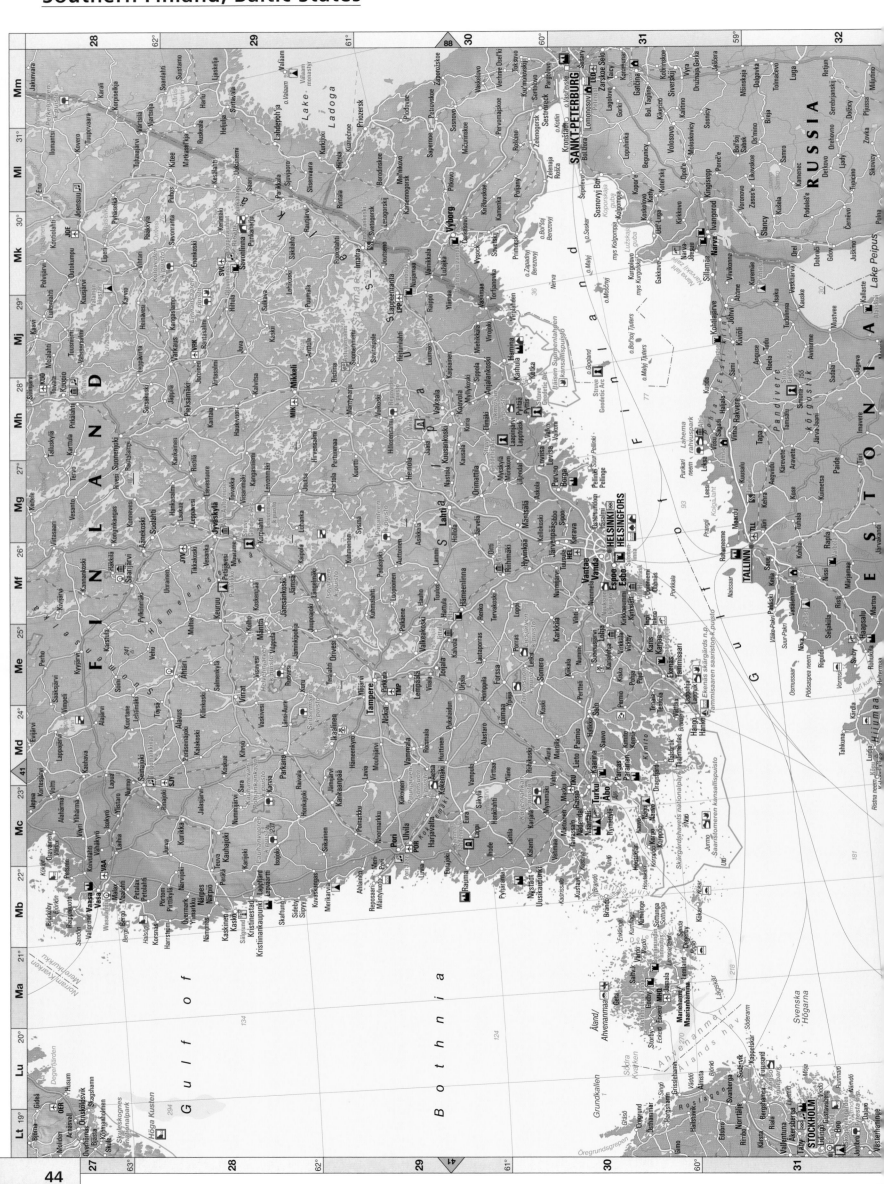

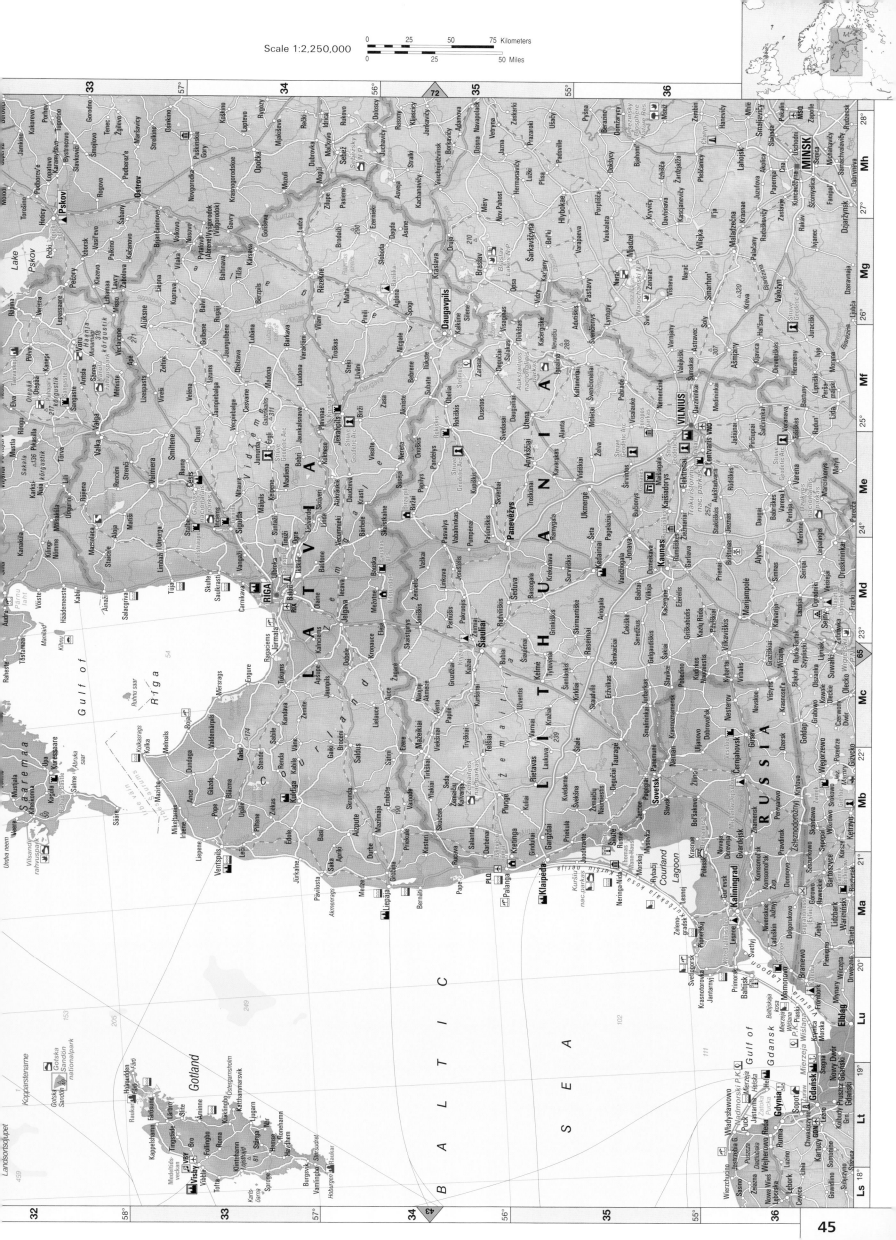

Scale 1:2,250,000

0 25 50 75 Kilometers
0 25 50 Miles

Rockall Trough

3244

A T L A N T I C

Stanton Bank
33

O C E A N

Sea of the Hebrides

2414

Sligo
Bay

97

IRELAND / ÉIRE

141

88

Connemara N.P.

Galway Bay

Irish Sea

Isle of Man (UK)
Isle of Man

180

130

Dublin/Baile Átha Cliath

St. George's Channel

Nymphe Bank
87

99

**UNITED
KINGDOM**

*Cardigan
Bay*

W a l e s

115

C e l t i c   S e a

55

Labadie Bank
62

Bristol Channel

Cardiff

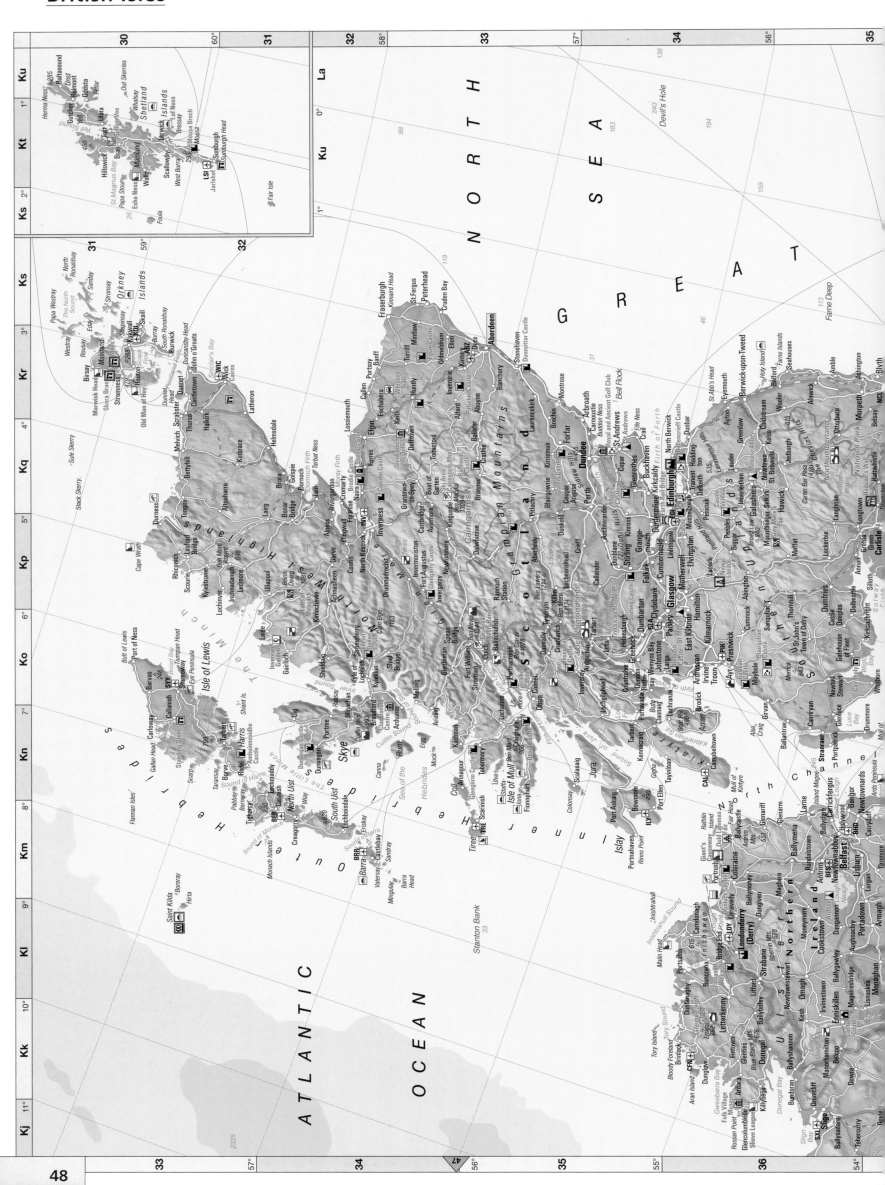

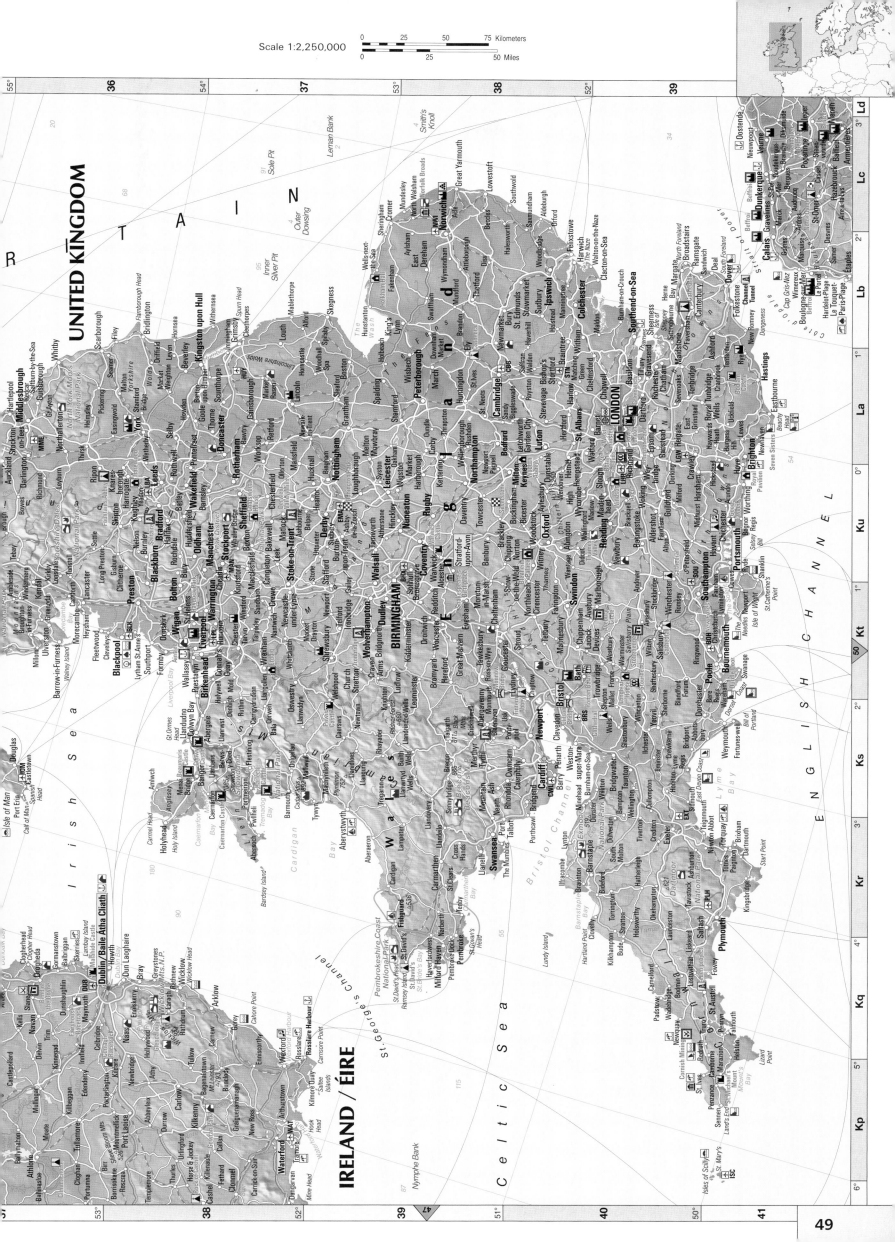

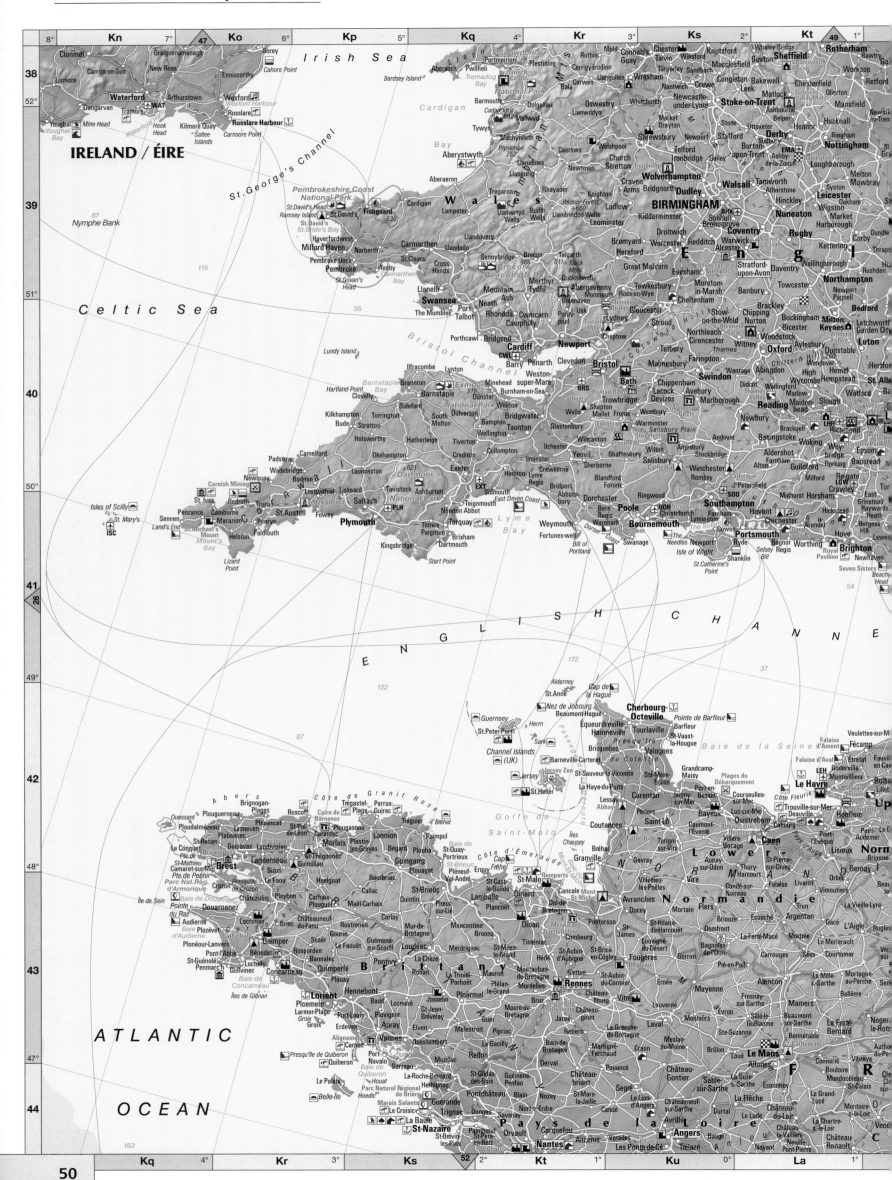

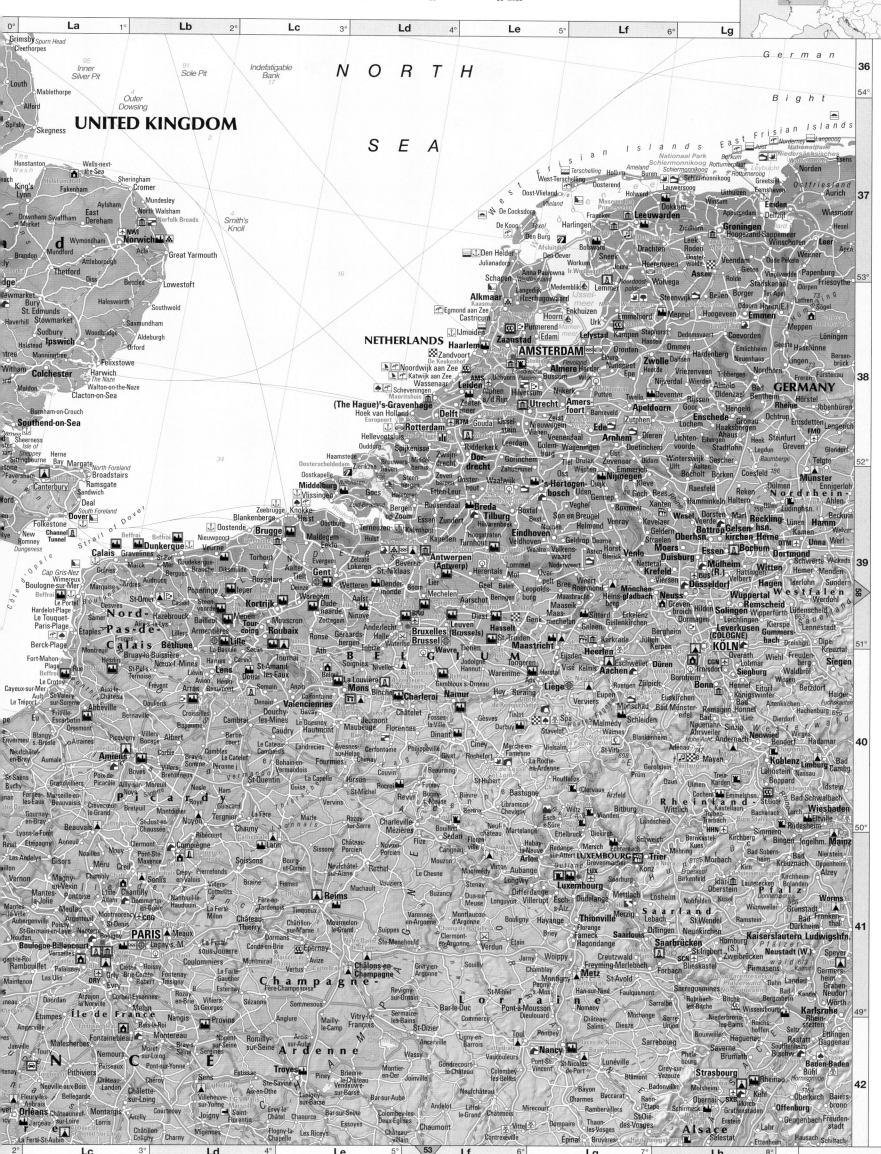

0   25   50   75 Kilometers

0   25   50 Miles

La 1° Lb 2° Lc 3° Ld 4° Le 5° Lf 6° Lg

N O R T H

S E A

UNITED KINGDOM

Inner Silver Pit   Sole Pit   Indefatigable Bank

Outer Dowsing

Smith's Knoll

German

Bight

West Frisian Islands   East Frisian Islands

NETHERLANDS

AMSTERDAM

GERMANY

Haarlem

(The Hague)'s-Gravenhage

Rotterdam

Utrecht

Arnhem

's-Hertogenbosch

Nijmegen

Münster

Middelburg

Breda

Tilburg

Eindhoven

Venlo

Nordrhein-

Duisburg

Essen

Dortmund

Antwerpen (Antwerp)

Gent

Brugge

Dunkerque

Calais

Düsseldorf

Westfalen

Wuppertal

Leverkusen (COLOGNE)

KÖLN

Brussel (Brussels)

B E L G I U M

Maastricht

Aachen

Liège

Charleroi

Namur

Bonn

Siegen

Koblenz

Nord-Pas-de-Calais

Lille

Roubaix

Valenciennes

Amiens

P i c a r d y

Wiesbaden

Mainz

LUXEMBOURG

Luxembourg

Trier

Pfalz

Saarland

Saarbrücken

Lorraine

Metz

Kaiserslautern Ludwigshn.

Worms

PARIS

Î l e   d e   F r a n c e

Reims

Champagne-

Châlons-en-Champagne

A r d e n n e

Troyes

Nancy

Strasbourg

Karlsruhe

Baden-Baden

Alsace

F R A N C E

51

Lc Ld Le Lf Lg Lh

France

Orléans · Montargis · Sens · Troyes · Chaumont · Langres · Épinal · Strasbourg · Alsace · Colmar · Mulhouse · Freiburg

Bourges · Dijon · **Burgundy** · Besançon · **Franche-Comté** · Belfort · Basel · Zürich

Nevers · Beaune · Chalon-s-Saône · Dole · Neuchâtel · Bern · **Switzerland**

Moulins · Mâcon · Bourg-en-Bresse · Lausanne · Lake Geneva · (Geneva) Genève

Vichy · Roanne · Villeurbanne · Lyon · Annecy · Chamonix-Mont-Blanc

Clermont-Ferrand · **Auvergne** · St-Étienne · Chambéry · Aosta · **Valle d'Aosta** · Torino (Turin)

Massif Central · **Rhône** · Grenoble · **Alpes** · Briançon · **Piemonte** · Novara

Le Puy-en-Velay · Valence · **Italy** · Alessandria

Mende · Montélimar · Gap · Cúneo

Millau · Nîmes · Avignon · Carpentras · **Provence** · Digne · Nice · Monaco · Ligúria · Génova (Genoa)

Montpellier · Arles · Aix-en-Provence · Cannes · San Remo

Languedoc- · Marseille · Toulon · **Alpes-Côte d'Azur** · Ste-Maxime · St-Tropez · **Riviera di Ponente**

Narbonne · **Golfe du Lion** · Îles d'Hyères · **Ligurian Sea**

MEDITERRANEAN SEA · Corsica · Calvi · St-Florent

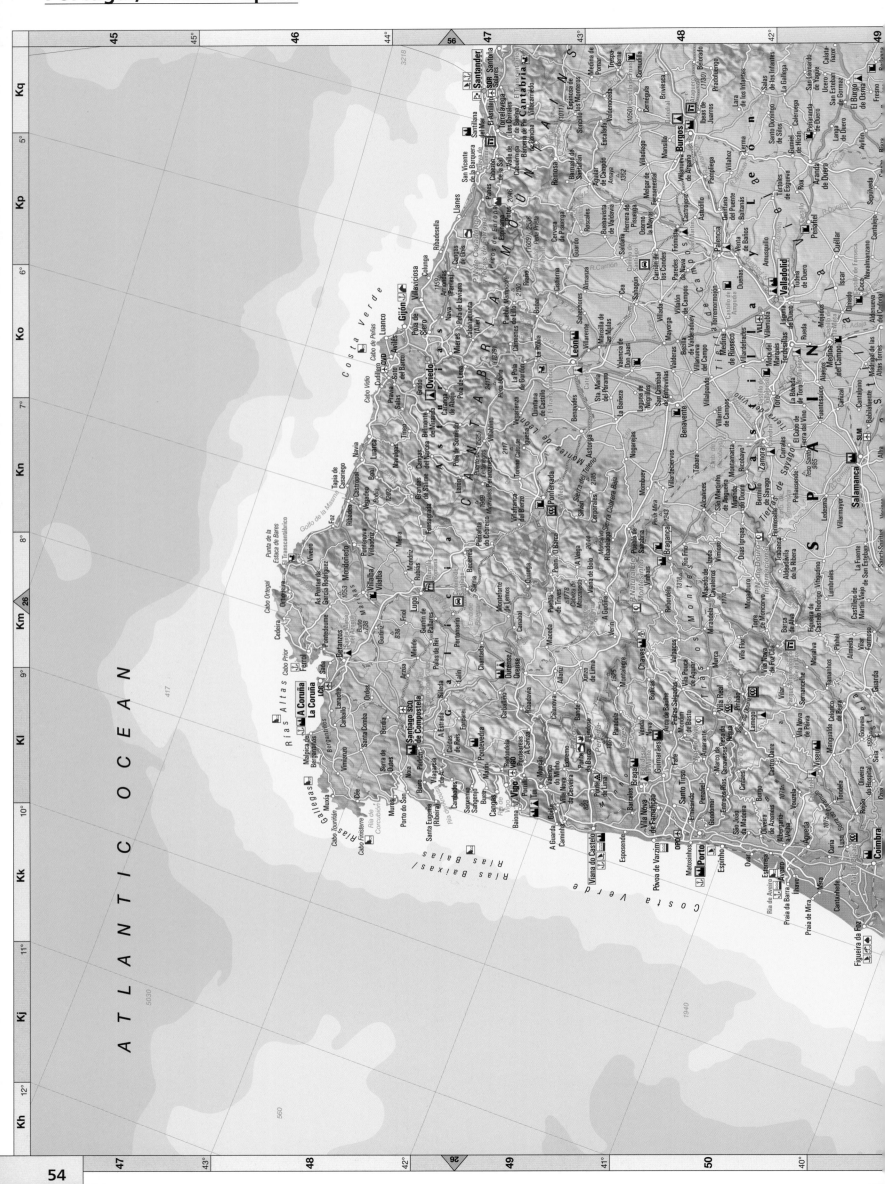

Scale 1:2,250,000

0 25 50 75 Kilometers

0 25 50 Miles

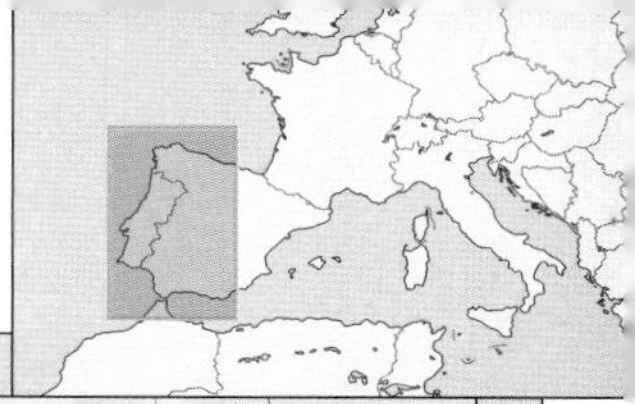

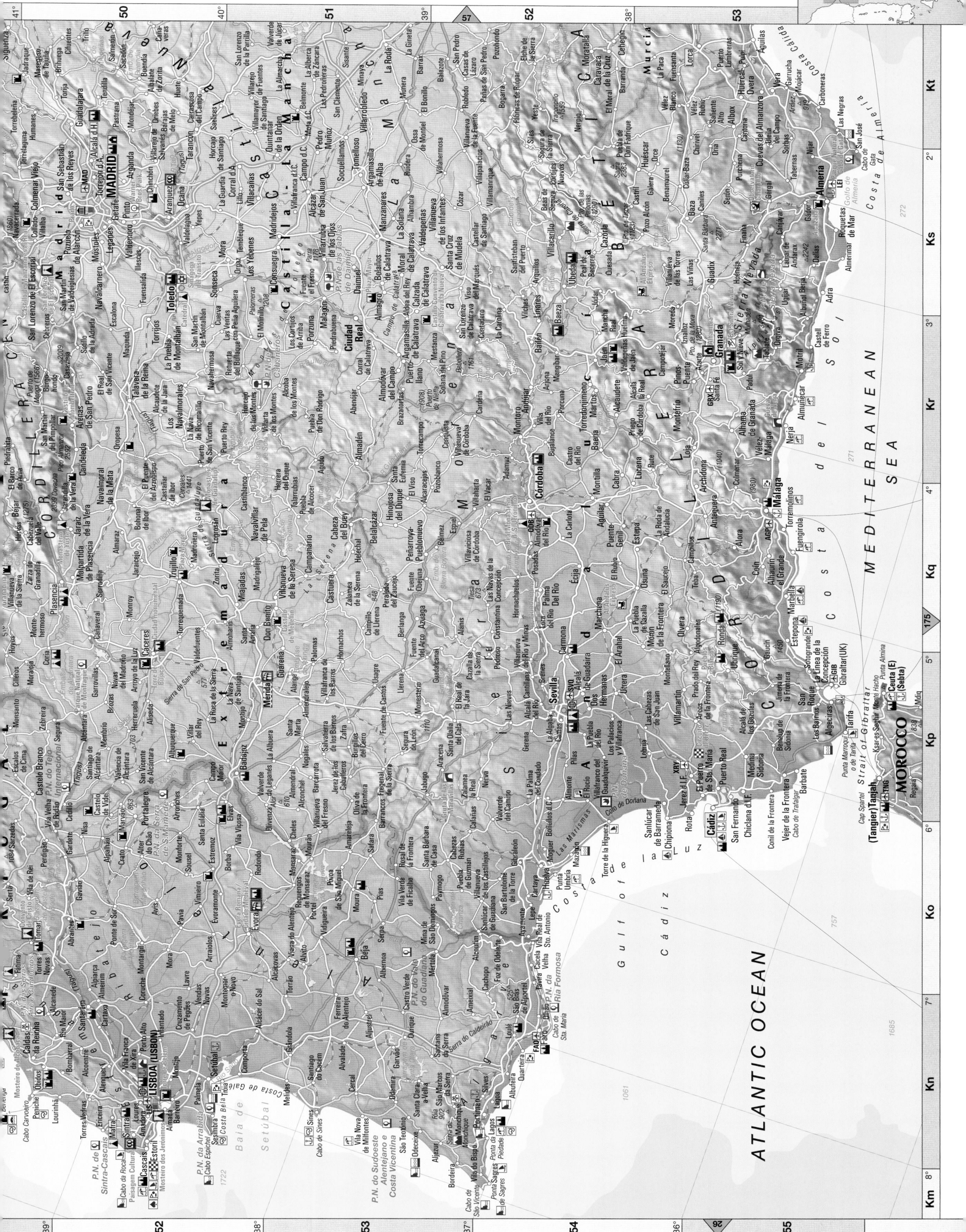

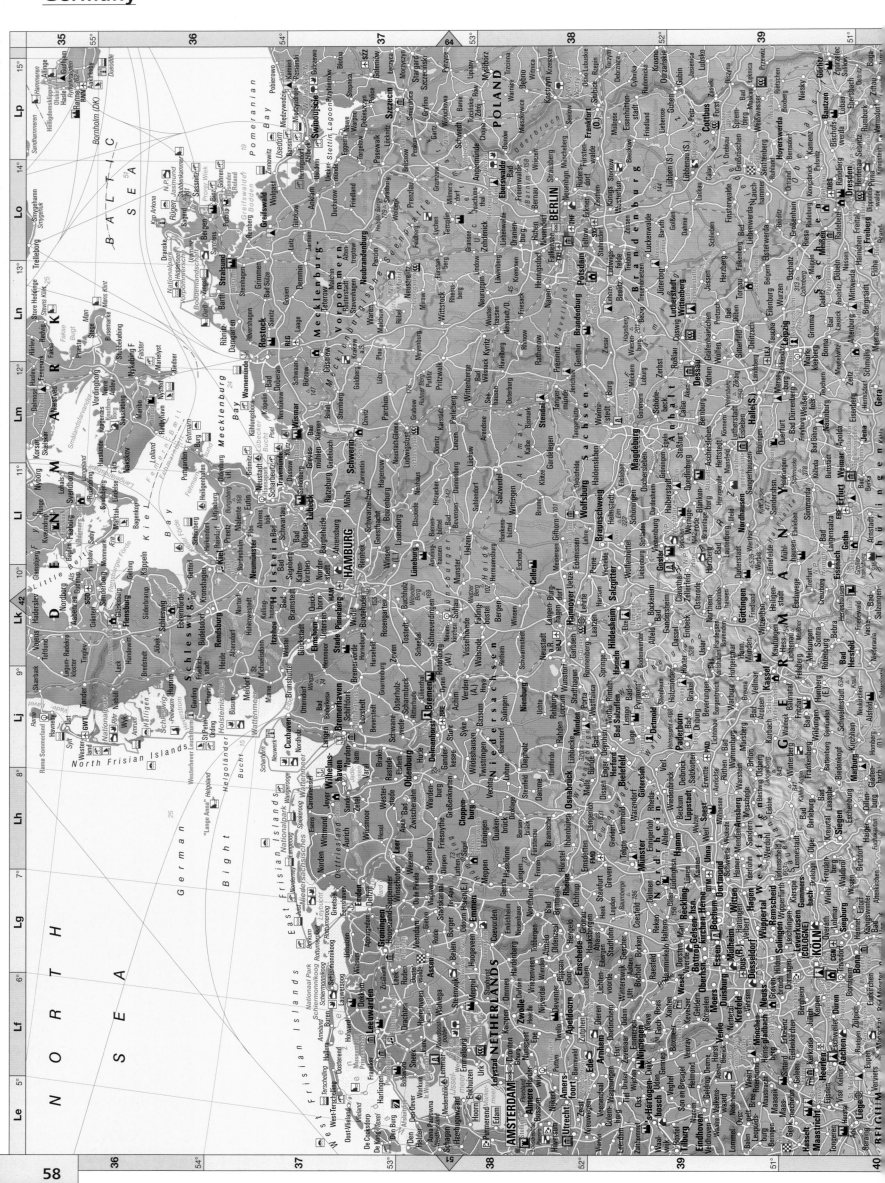

Scale 1:2,250,000

| 0 | 25 | 50 | 75 | Kilometers |

| 0 | 25 | | 50 | Miles |

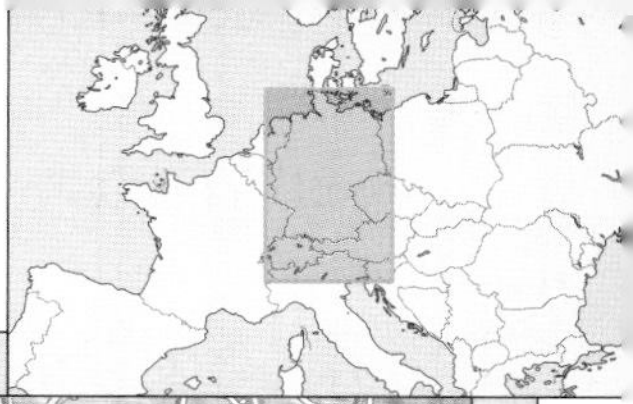

CZECH REP.

PRAHA (PRAGUE)

Plzeň

AUSTRIA

SLOVENIA

Ljubljana

Salzburg

Linz

Passau

München (MUNICH)

Regensburg

Nürnberg

Bayern

Würzburg

Bamberg

Bayreuth

Ingolstadt

Augsburg

Ulm

Baden-Württemberg

Stuttgart

Reutlingen

Karlsruhe

Heidelberg

Mannheim

Frankfurt

Wiesbaden

Mainz

Darmstadt

Worms

Ludwigshafen

Rheinland-Pfalz

Saarland

Saarbrücken

Luxembourg

Trier

Metz

Lorraine

France

Nancy

Strasbourg

Alsace

Mulhouse

Freiburg

Basel

SWITZERLAND

Zürich

Luzern

Bern (Berne)

Lausanne

Lake Geneva

LIECHTENSTEIN

Vaduz

Innsbruck

Bolzano/Bozen

Trento

Trentino

Alto Adige/Südtirol

ITALY

Udine

Venezia Giulia

Friuli

Klagenfurt

59

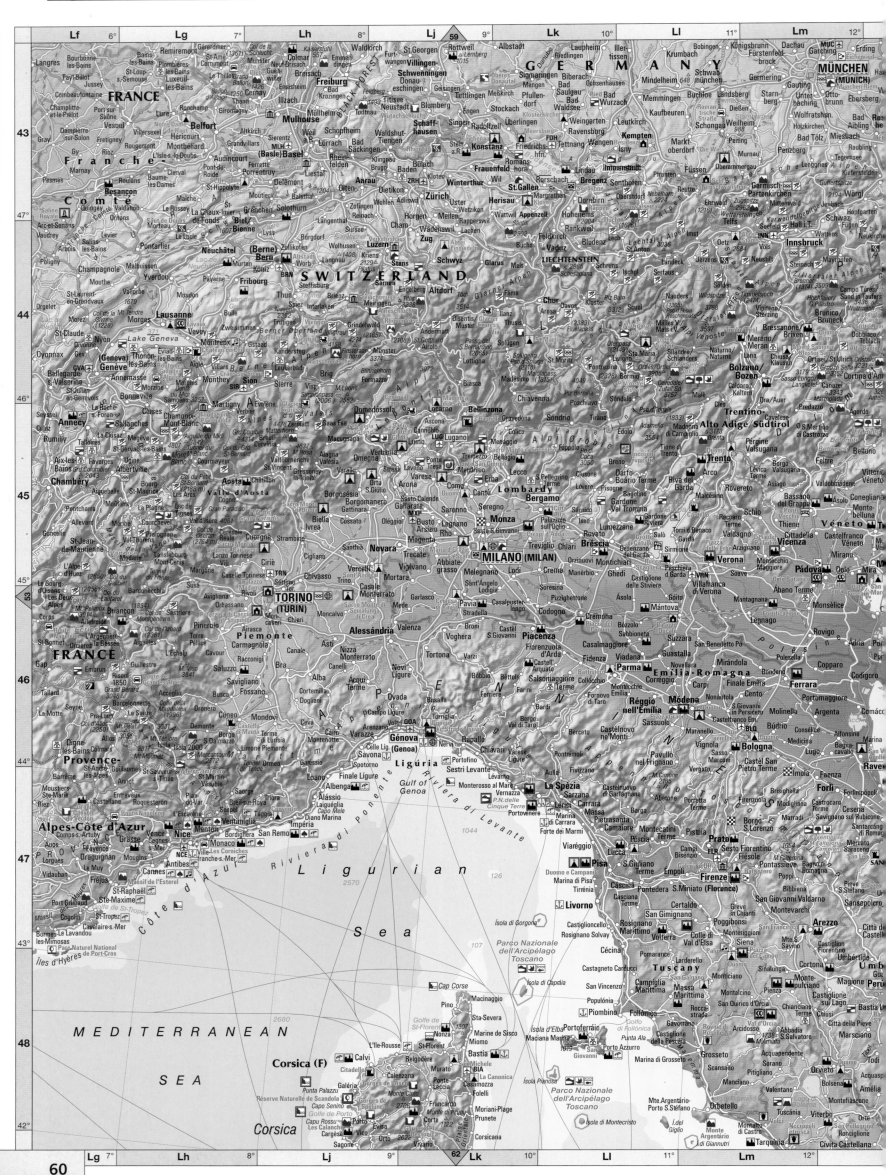

0   25   50   75 Kilometers

0   25   50 Miles

66

SLOVAKIA

WIEN (VIENNA)

Bratislava

AUSTRIA

Linz

Salzburg

Graz

Klagenfurt

HUNGARY

BUDAPEST

Győr

Székesfehérvár

Pécs

SLOVENIA

Ljubljana

Maribor

Zagreb

Trieste

Rijeka

Pula

CROATIA

Zadar

Šibenik

Split

Mostar

BOSNIA AND

HERZEGOVINA

Banja Luka

Bihać

Zenica

Sarajevo

Tuzla

Osijek

ITALY

Ancona

Pescara

L'Aquila

Adriatic Sea

Gulf of Venice

MONTENEGRO

Dubrovnik

Kotor

Nikšić

Cetinje

61

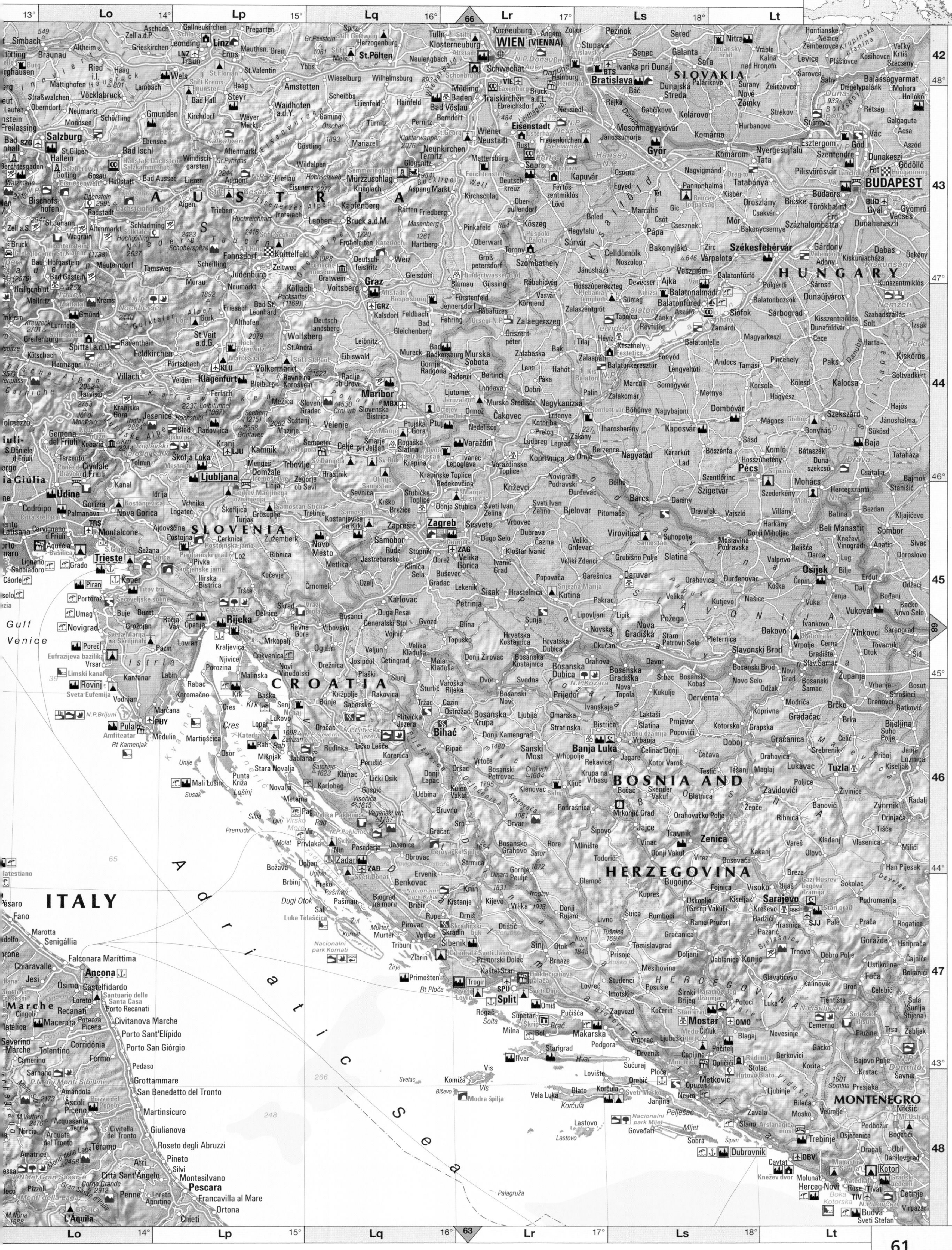

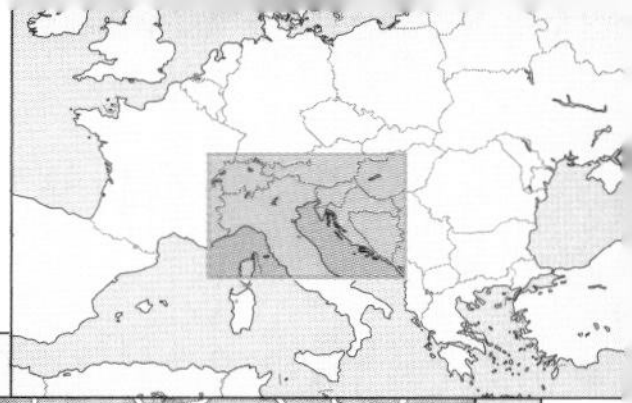

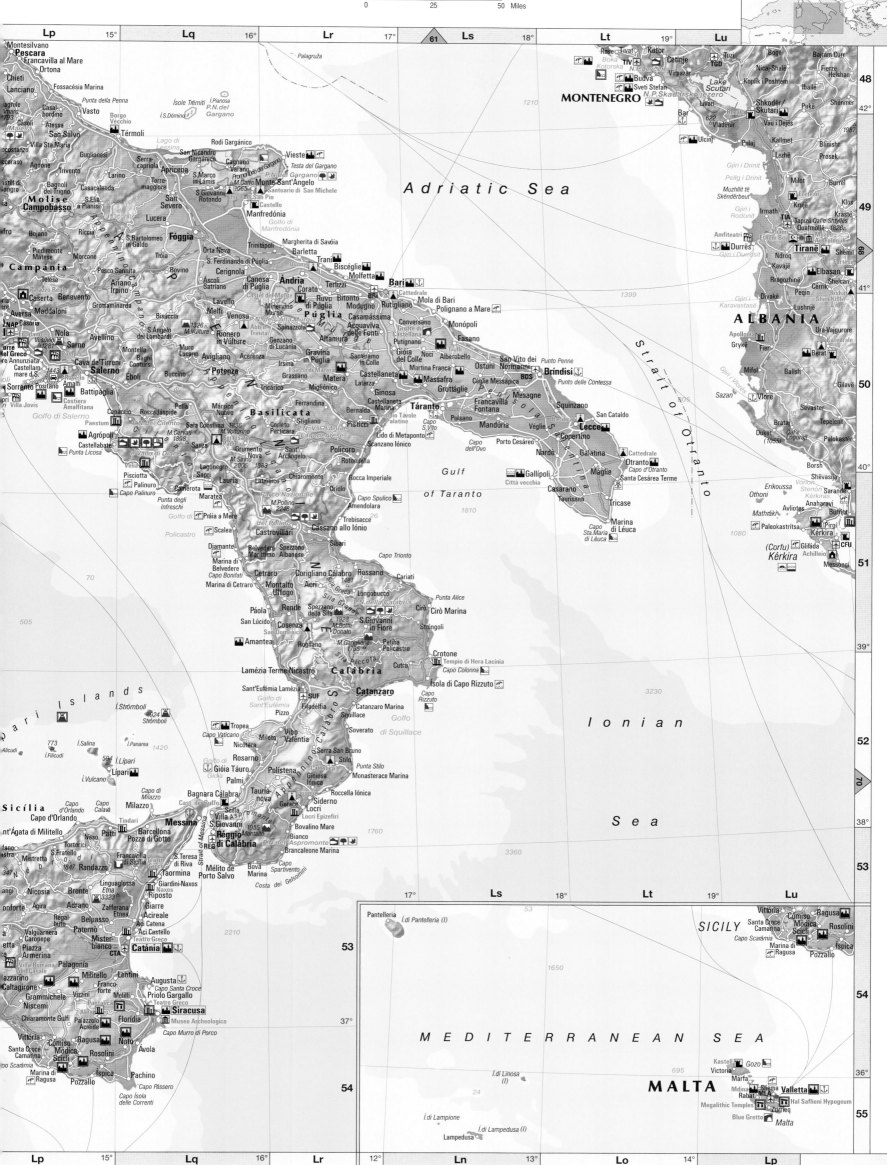

0   25   50   75 Kilometers
0   25   50 Miles

Lp   15°   Lq   16°   Lr   17°   61 Ls   18°   Lt   19°   Lu

A d r i a t i c   S e a

MONTENEGRO

ALBANIA

Tiranë

Campánia

Molise
Campobasso

Púglia

Bari

Brindisi

Basilicata

Táranto

Lecce

Potenza

Salerno

Gulf
of Taranto

Otranto

Strait of Otranto

Kérkira
(Corfu)

Calábria

Catanzaro

I o n i a n

S e a

Cosenza

Reggio
di Calábria

Messina

Sicília

Catánia

Siracusa

17°   Ls   18°   Lt   19°   Lu

SICILY

53

54

Pantelleria

M E D I T E R R A N E A N   S E A

MALTA

Valletta

Malta

Lp   15°   Lq   16°   Lr   12°   Ln   13°   Lo   14°   Lp

63

Poland

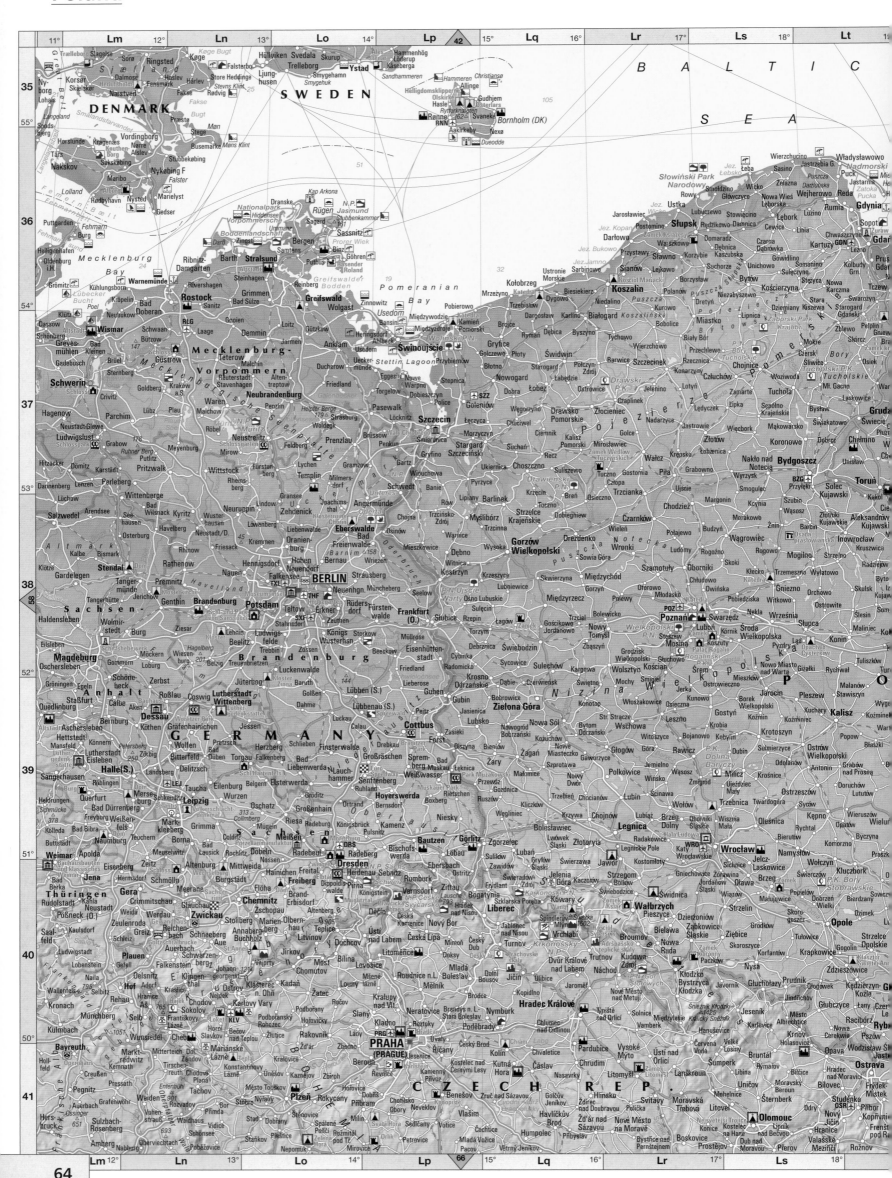

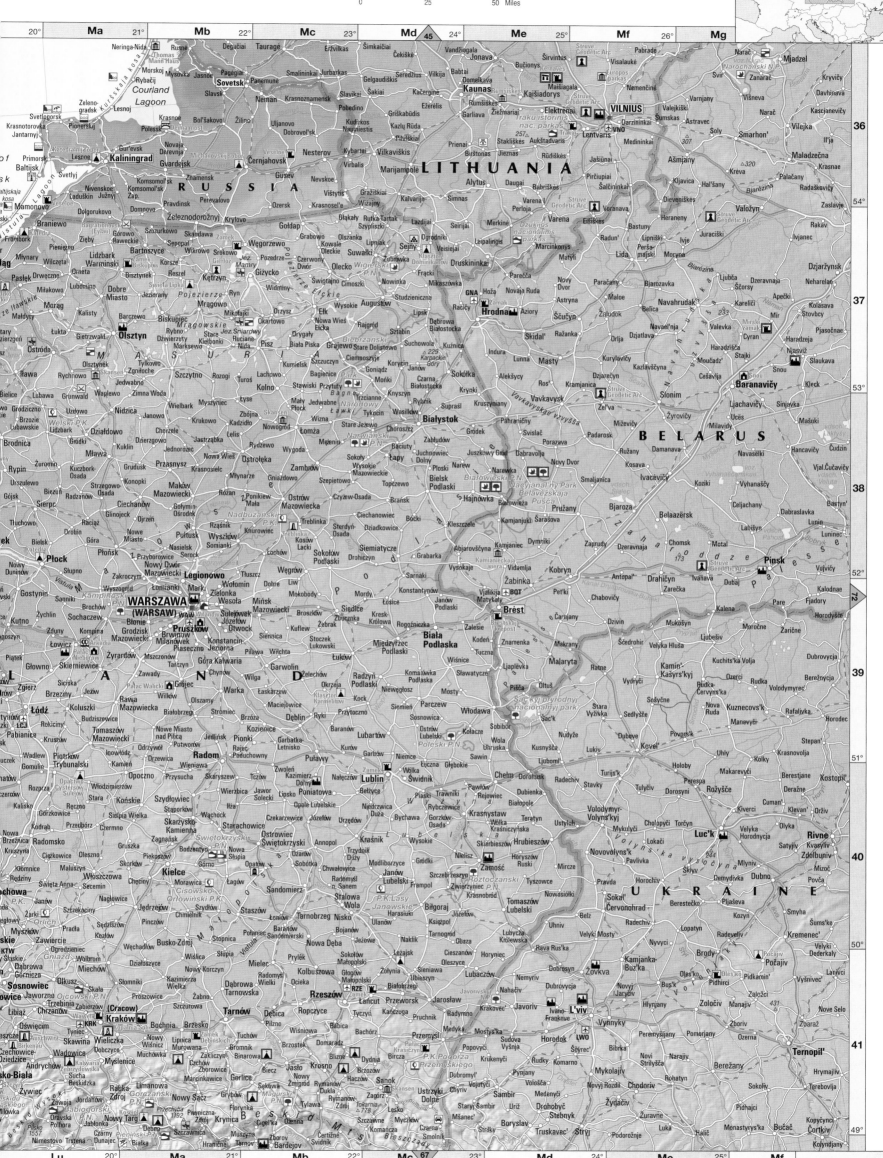

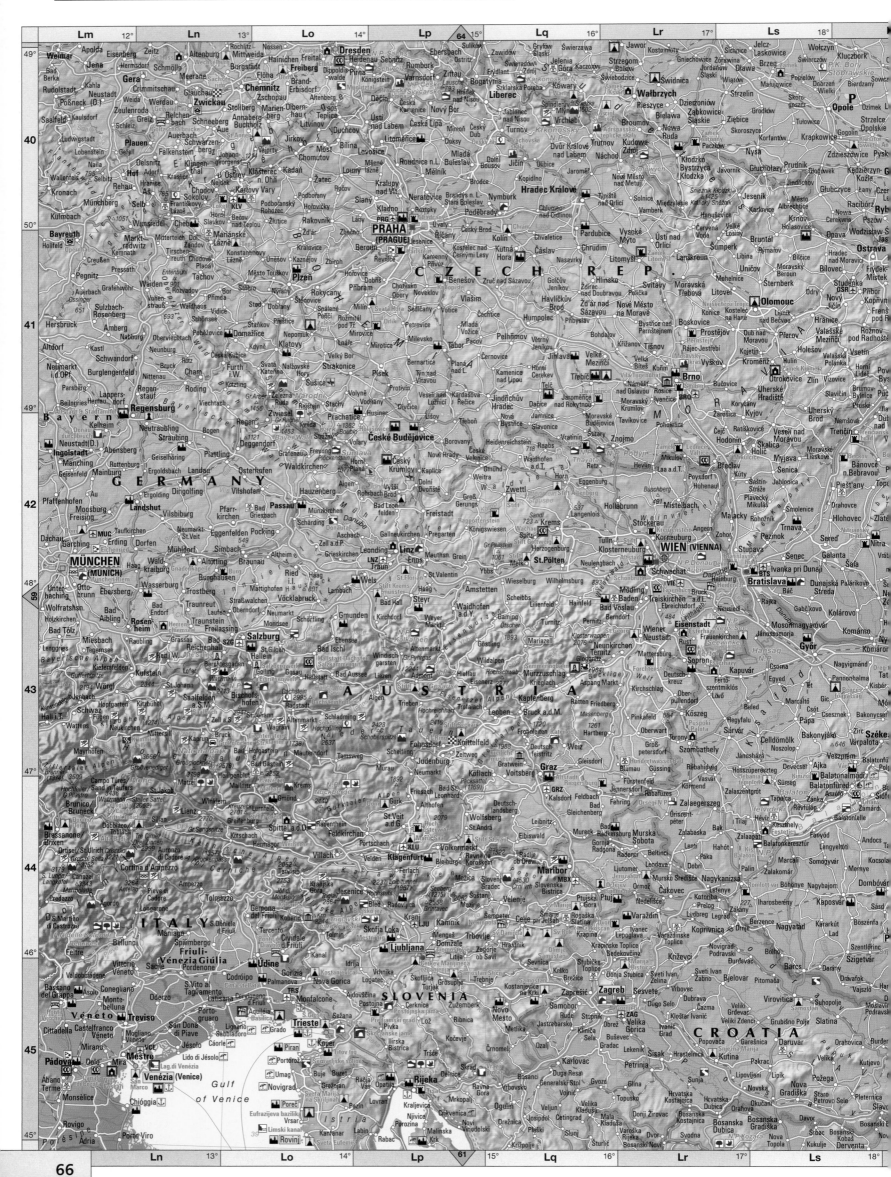

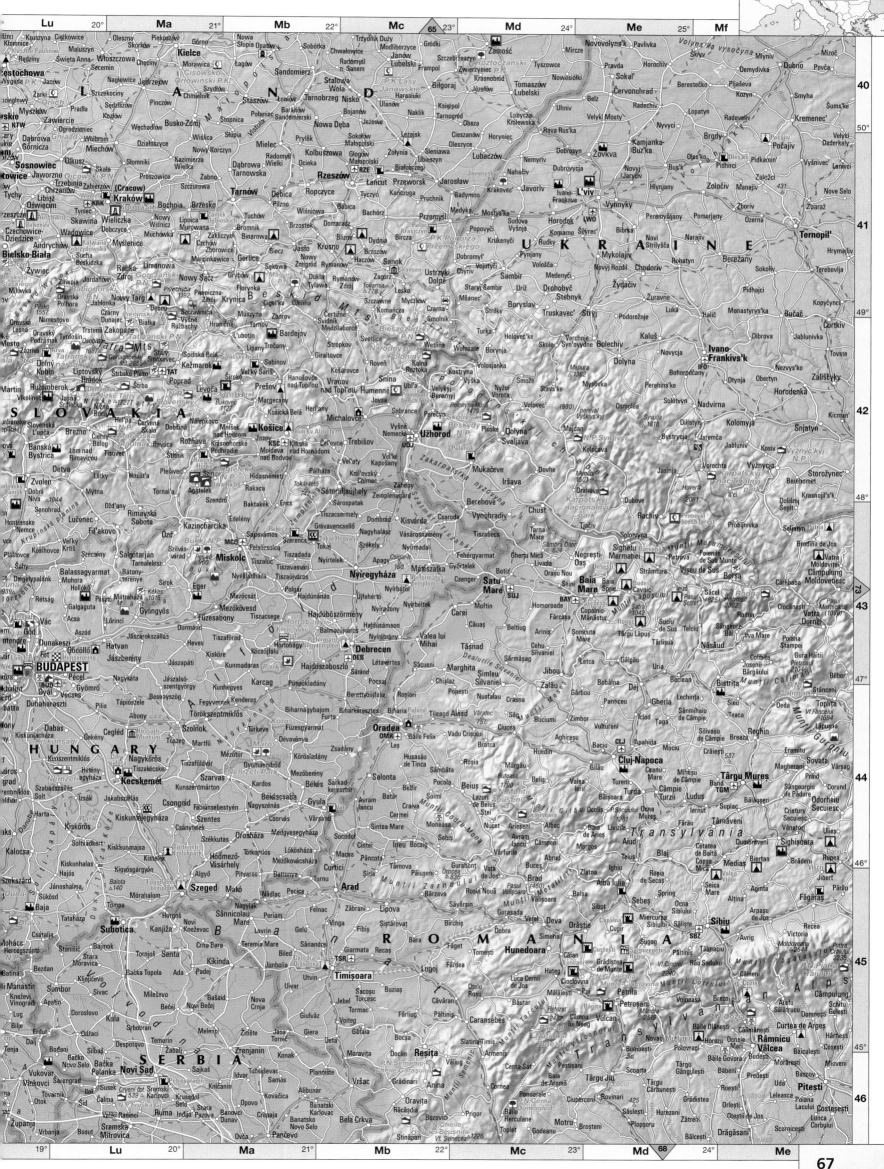

25° Mf 26° Mg 27° Mh 28° 73 Mj 29° Mk 30° Ml

45
45°

ROMANIA

Brașov
Sfântu Gheorghe
Focșani
Galați
Brăila
Buzău
Târgoviște
Ploiești
Pitești
BUCUREȘTI (BUCHAREST)
Călărași
Silistra
Ruse
Giurgiu
Alexandria
Turnu Măgurele
Zimnicea
Svištov
Pleven
Lovech
Veliko Tărnovo
Gabrovo
Dobrich
Novi Pazar
Razgrad
Šumen
Târgovište
Veliki Preslav
Provadija
Varna
Balčik
Kavarna

B L A C K   S E A

Constanța
Mamaia
Ovidiu
Medgidia
Cernavodă
Năvodari
Eforie
Mangalia
Durankulak

Delta of the Danube
Tulcea
Sulina
Sfântu Gheorghe

BULGARIA

Sofia region towns:
Trojan
Sliven
Karnobat
Burgas
Sozopol
Primorsko
Ahtopol
Nesebăr
Pomorie
Slănčev Briag

Karlovo
Kazanlăk
Stara Zagora
Nova Zagora
Jambol
Plovdiv
Asenovgrad
Pazardžik
Dimitrovgrad
Haskovo
Kărdžali
Smoljan

Edirne
Kırklareli
Lüleburgaz
Çorlu
Tekirdağ
İSTANBUL
Gebze
BURSA

T U R K E Y

Çanakkale
Biga
Bandırma
Balıkesir
Gönen
Edremit

Sea of Marmara

G R E E C E

Kavala
Xánthi
Komotiní
Alexandroúpoli
Drama
Thássos
Límnos
Samothráki
Áthos

Gelibolu
Bozcaada
Troy (Troja)

69

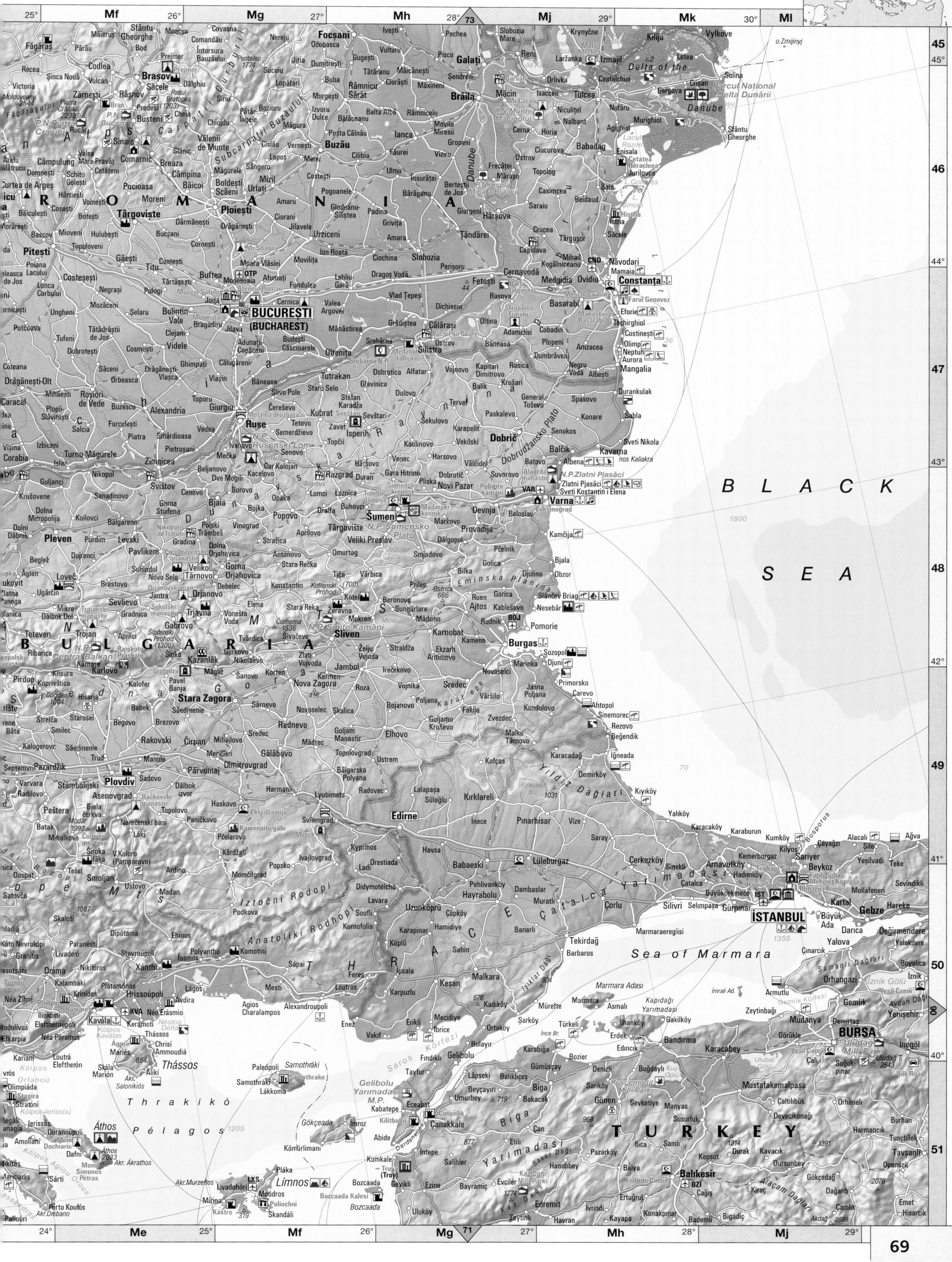

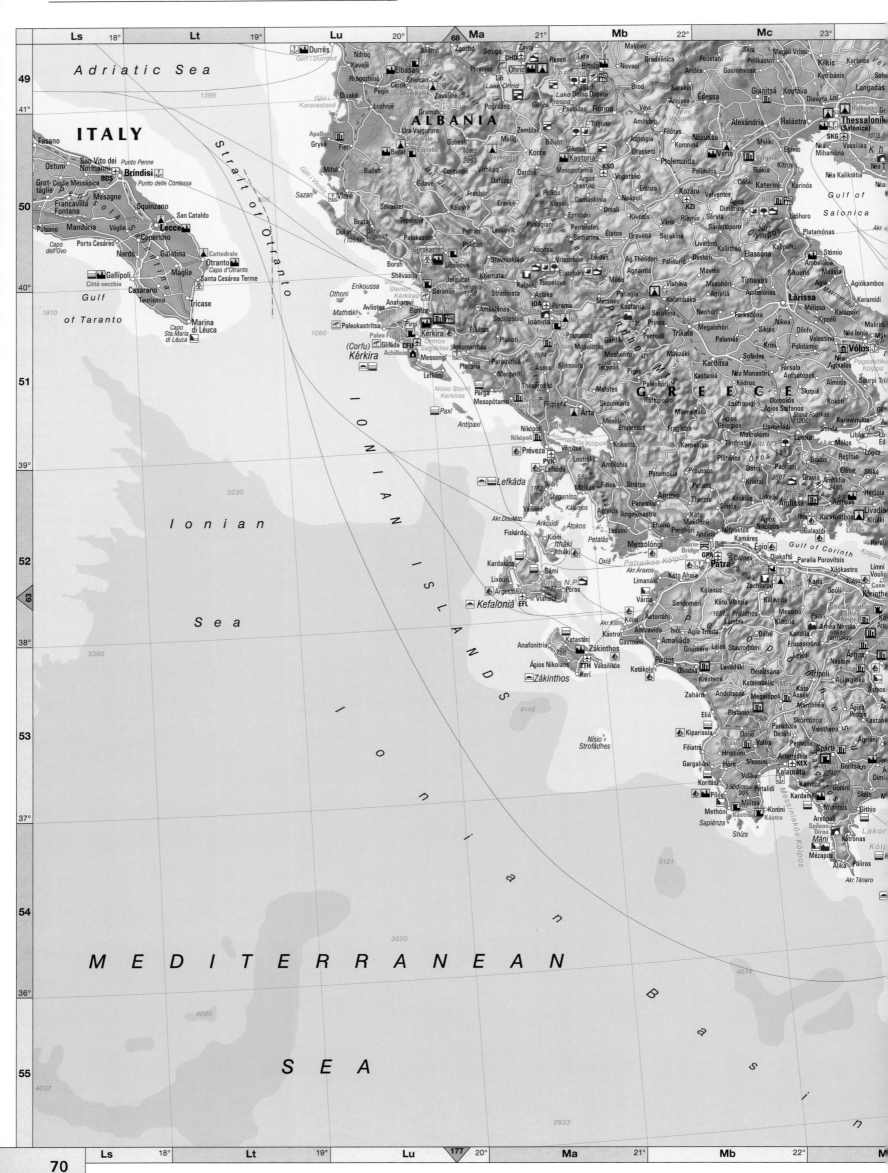

Me 24° 25° Mf 26° Mg 27° Mh 28° Mj

BURSA

T U R K E Y

İZMİR

Manisa

Ödemiş

Aydın

Denizli

Pamukkale

Bandırma

Çanakkale

Gelibolu Yarımadası M.P.

Biga Yarımadası

Balıkesir

Edremit

Bergama

Akhisar

Salihli

Kuşadası

Söke

Milas

Bodrum

Muğla

Marmaris

Dalaman

Gökova Körfezi

Thássos

Samothráki

Límnos

Lésvos

Mytilíni

Áthos

T h r a k i k ó   P é l a g o s

A e g e a n   S e a

N o r t h e r n   S p o r a d e s

Skíros

Psará

Híos

Sámos

Ikaría

Pátmos

Évia

ATHENS

ATHINA

Pireás (Piraeus)

Ándros

Tínos

Míkonos

Náxos

Páros

Síros

Kéa

Kíthnos

Sérifos

Sífnos

Mílos

Íos

Amorgós

Thíra

Anáfi

Astipálea

Kós

Kálimnos

Léros

Níssiros

Tílos

Sími

Rhodes

Ródos (Rhodes)

Lindos

C y c l a d e s

S o u t h e r n   S p o r a d e s

D o d e c a n e s e

Mirtóon Sea

Kárpathos

Kássos

S e a   o f   C r e t e

Crete

Iráklio

Haniá (Khaniá)

Réthimno

Ágios Nikólaos

Ierápetra

L i v i k ó   P é l a g o s

L e v a n t i n e   B a s i n

Md 24° Me 25° Mf 178 26° Mg 27° Mh

71

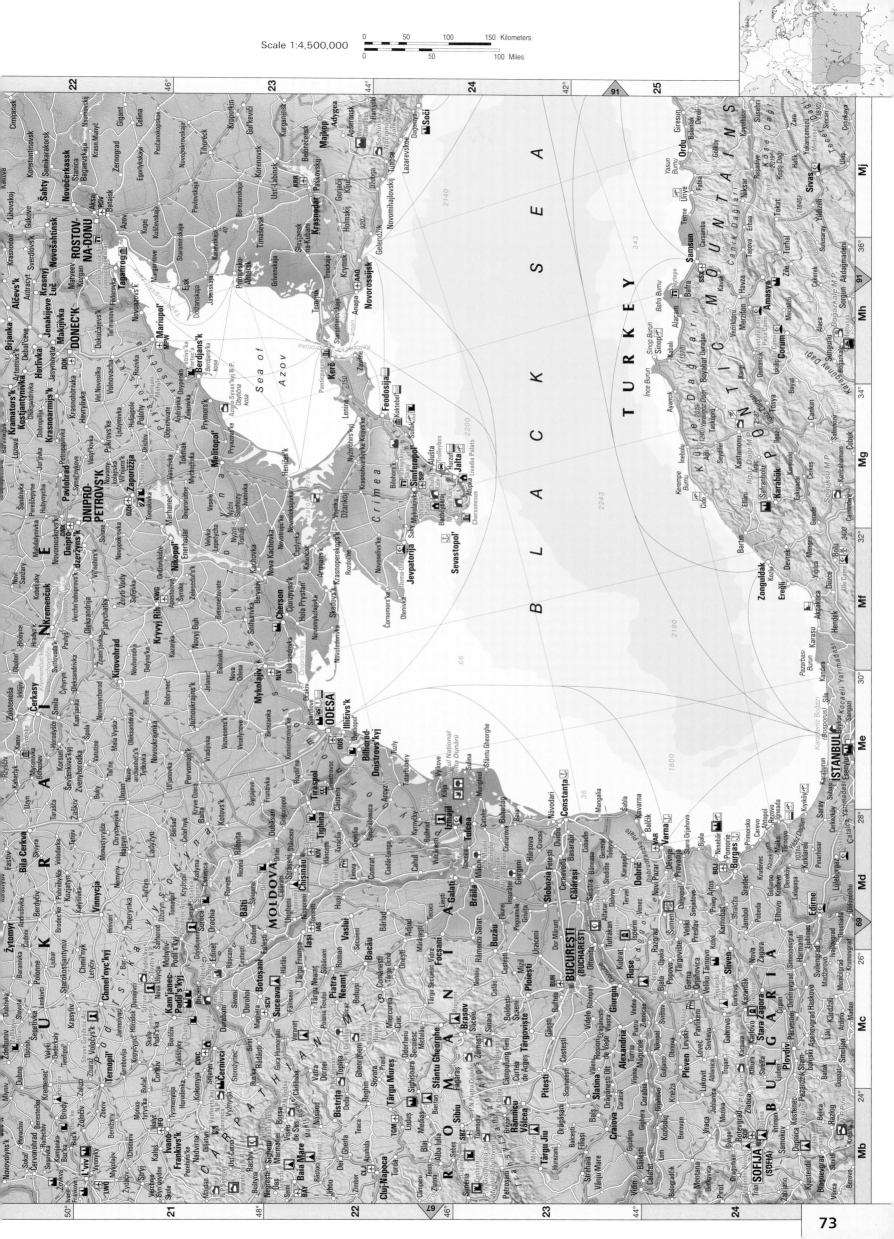

Asia

Asia is the largest continent on Earth. Its huge variety of impressive landscapes range from the Arabian Peninsula to the Siberian lowlands, and from the 8,000-m-high mountains of the Himalayas to the tropical karst topography and rainforests of south-east Asia. On this vast continent, mountains, plateaus, basins and lowlands are all intermingled in no apparent order. Many of the most impressive landscapes of Asia have been formed by plate tectonics – for example, the magnificent Himalayas were created by the folding of the Earth's crust 25 million years ago when the Indian subcontinent collided with

the great continent of Eurasia. The mountains and islands along the Pacific coast are also characterised by tectonic activity. It is here that the Pacific and Philippine plates are pushing beneath the Eurasian plate in a process known as subduction, which also causes volcanic activity.

Wuyi Mountain: a pilgrim's path winds its way up Wuyi Mountain. The valley often remains in cloud while the peak basks in sunlight.

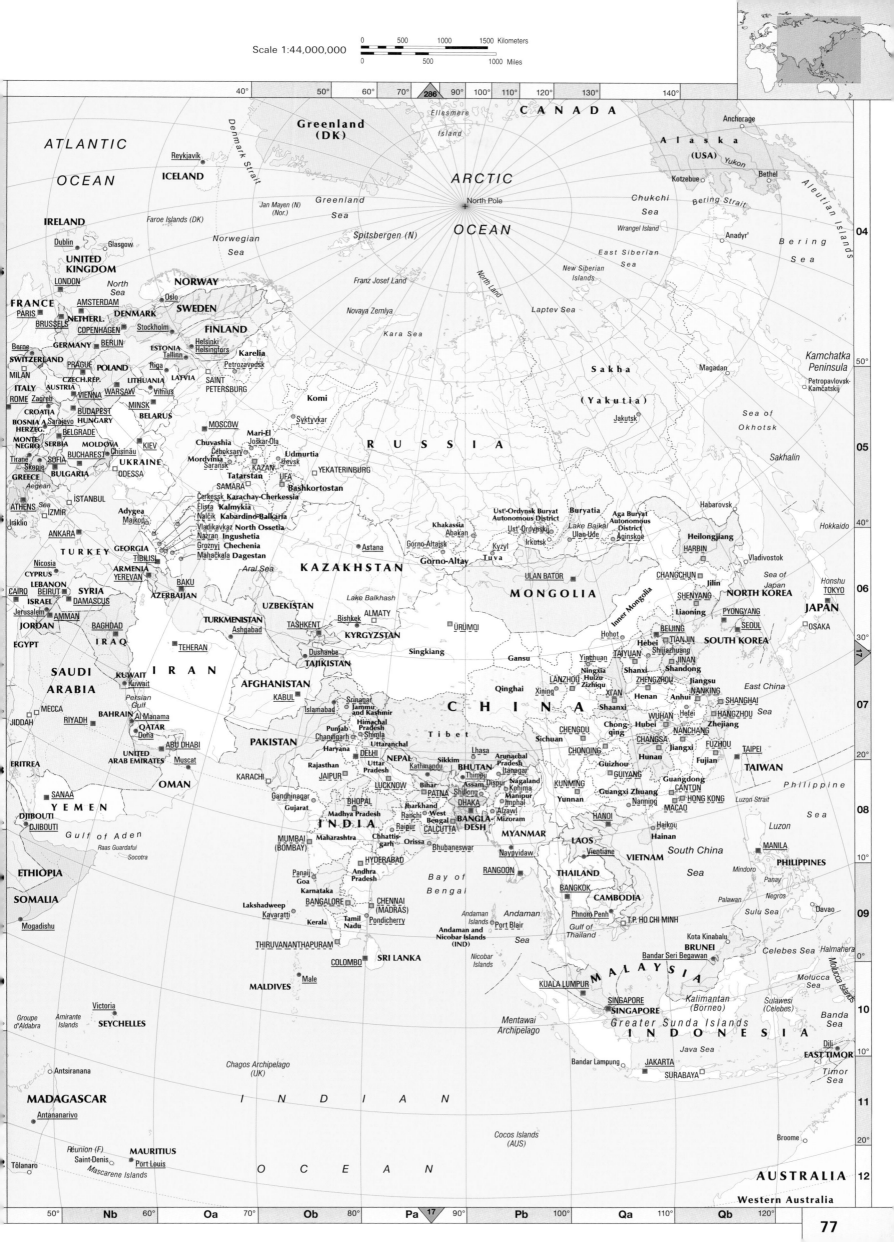

The **Aral Sea** between Kazakhstan and Uzbekistan, which is slightly brackish, once contained many fish. This inland sea was once the fourth largest lake in the world, but the water level has been steadily dropping in recent years.

The effects of low precipitation and high evaporation have contributed to this, but the main problem is that both the rivers that feed the lake, the Amu Darya and Syr Darya, have been dammed for irrigation purposes.

West Siberian Plain and North Siberian Lowland

The fertile **West Siberian Plain** between the Ural Mountains and the Yenisei River is one of the largest areas of lowland on Earth, covering some 2.6 million sq. km. The plain continues north of the Central Siberian Plateau as the North Siberian Lowland, which consists largely of moorland.
The great Ob, Irtysh, Yenisei, Lena, Aldan and Kolyma rivers flow through both regions.
The **West Siberian Plain** has several particularly distinct zones of vegetation. The far north is covered in tundra and permafrost, replaced further south by the taiga. Next comes an area of forest steppe, followed by grassland steppe landscape to the south.

Central Siberian Plateau

A flat, undulating plateau rises between the **Yenisei** and **Lena** rivers and is bordered to the north by the North Siberian Lowland, and to the south by the **Eastern Sayan Mountains**. It covers an area of some 3.5 million sq. km. The plateau has an average altitude of 700 m and

Tigris and Euphrates

The **Tigris River** covers a length of 1,950 km, rising in the East Taurus Mountains and flowing south-east through Iraq. Several large tributaries join the river from the east. At Kut, the Shatt al-Hai branch of the river begins to flow south. At Amara, the Tigris becomes a huge salt marsh, which is not only the traditional home of the Marsh Arabs but also supports a unique flora and fauna.
The **Euphrates River**, including the headwaters – the Murat – flows over a total distance of 3,380 km. It rises in the East Anatolian Plateau as the Kara and Murat Rivers, which merge at the Keban Reservoir. The river then passes through the uplands of Syria and Iraq down through southern Iraq, before merging into the Tigris to form the Shatt al-Arab, which drains into the Persian Gulf.

contains numerous lakes. To the north-west, the region rises to the **Putorana Plateau** at a height of up to 1,701 m.

Lake Baikal

Lake Baikal has a surface area of 32,500 sq. km, making it the largest mountain lake in Asia and one of the biggest freshwater lakes, by volume, on Earth. It also has one of the largest fish populations for its size.
The lake is 636 km long and 79 km wide and is surrounded by densely forested mountains – the **Baikal Mountains** in the west, the **Chamar-Daban** in the south and the **Barguzin Mountains** in the east. The lake is 455 m above sea level, and its greatest depth is 1620 m, making it the deepest lake on Earth. It is fed by 336 tributaries, but the only outlet is the river **Angara**. The only large island is **Olkhon**, with an area of 730 sq. km. Lake Baikal was

formed 60 million years ago in the Palaeogene Period and has some unique endemic wildlife.

Mountains of Eastern Siberia

The **mountains of Eastern Siberia** form a broad arc east of the middle and lower courses of the Lena River. The vast curve of the Verkhoyansk Range enclose the basins of the Kolyma, Yana and Indigirka rivers, an area of marshes and lakes.
The interior of this semi-circle of mountains contains high peaks such as the **Chersky Range** and low mountain ranges such as the Oymyakon Plateau. On the Pacific coast, the **Koryak Mountains** (rising to 2,562 m) merge almost seamlessly into the mountain chains of the Kamchatka Peninsula. The **Sikhote-Alin mountain system** follows the coastline south to the Sea of Japan.

Verkhoyansk Range

The **Verkhoyansk Range** in the inhospitable Sakha region in the far north-east of Russia extends in a wide arc over 1,100 km, parallel to the Lena River in the west. The mountains extend as far as the Laptev Sea. This fold mountain range has an average height of 1,000 m and a maximum height of 2,389 m. The terrain is covered in tundra vegetation, mainly mosses and lichens and is virtually uninhabited.

Chersky Range

These mountains in north-eastern Siberia stretch for 1,500 km from the lower reaches of the Yana River to the upper reaches of the **Kolyma**. The highest point is **Pobeda Peak** at 3,147 m.
The chains of this highly structured fold mountain range are mainly composed of metamorphic rocks and sandstone, in which

numerous rivers have carved out deep gorges and valleys. Parts of the range are covered in imposing glaciers. Forests of larches cover the slopes at medium to high altitudes.

Kolyma Mountains

This mountain chain in north-eastern Siberia has a total length of approximately 1,300 km, consisting of several isolated massifs and ridges. The **Kolyma Mountains** are the watershed between the **Arctic Ocean** and the **Pacific**. Larch forests grow on the lower slopes; the higher altitudes (up to heights of 1,962 m) are covered in mountain tundra.

Kamchatka Peninsula

This peninsula is 1,200 km long and stretches between the Bering Sea and the Sea of Okhotsk. It is one of the most significant volcanic regions on Earth.

Lake Baikal has a depth of 1,620 m, making it the world's deepest lake. It also has one of the largest quantities of water and fish stocks.

Lena, Ob, Irtysh, Yenisei

The **Lena** rises in the Baikal Mountains at a height of 930 m and flows through a narrow valley that slowly broadens out. After 1,450 km, the river is joined by the Vitim. The Lena flows into the Central Yakut Plain, where it is joined by the Aldan.
After some 4,400 km, the river opens into the Laptev Sea in a large delta that covers approximately 30,000 sq. km. The **Ob** is the main

river of the West Siberian Plains and is formed by the confluence of the Katun and Bija Rivers, both flowing down from the Altai Mountains. In the lower reaches of the river, it divides to form two branches, the Greater and Lesser Ob, which reunite after approximately 460 km. After 3,650 km (if the largest tributary, the Irtysh, is included, the total length is 5,410 km) the Ob opens into the Kara Sea in the Gulf of Ob,

which is 900 km long and 30-90 km wide. It is only free of ice for short periods of the year. The fertile Ob Basin covers 85 per cent of the West Siberian Plain. Including its tributaries and branches, the Ob has a drainage basin covering 2.975 million sq. km.
The **Irtysh** rises in the glaciers on the south-west slopes of the Altai and flows west through Lake Saissan, joining the Ob near

Khanty-Mansijsk after 4,248 km.
The **Yenisei** is formed by the confluence of the Greater and Lesser Yenisei Rivers which rise near the Mongolian border and flow north. After 4,130 km, the Yenisei opens into the Kara Sea in the 435 km-long Gulf of Yenisei.
All of the rivers are frozen for between five and eight months of the year, and 80 per cent of the outflow is produced in summer.

*The **Dead Sea**, a terminal or sink sea between Israel and Jordan, has a salt concentration of 28 per cent, one of the highest in the world. Only certain species of algae and micro-organisms can live in it. The sea was formed by a trench and* *has a maximum depth of 400 m, making it the deepest basin on Earth. Irrigation in the surrounding areas, reducing the amount of water fed into it by the river Jordan, has led to a reduction in the water level of the sea.*

A structured chain of mountains extend from north to south down the whole of the western side of **Kamchatka**. The highest point is the **Itchinskaya Sopka** volcano (3,607 m). The central part of the peninsula is up to 450 km wide. Another mountain chain on the eastern side of the peninsula runs parallel to the western chain. These mountains contain 160 volcanoes. The highest of the 29 active volcanoes is the **Klyuchevskaya Sopka** (4,750 m).

The steep cliffs of the **Kamchatka Valley**, irrigated by the Kamchatka River, lie between the two partially glaciated chains. The valley is dominated by taiga vegetation. In the east, the mountains drop down to a marshy coastal plain.

Sikhote-Alin

This mountain system is 1,200 km long and 250 km wide. It runs parallel to the coast from the **mouth of the Amur River** in the north to the southern tip of the **Murvyov-Amursky Peninsula** in the south.

The mountains have an average height of 800 m and comprise several low mountain chains, divided from each other by deep valleys. The chain sits on a bedrock of sandstone, schist and basalt, and the highest point is Anik Mountain (1,933 m). The mountains drop steeply down to the Sea of Japan.

Anatolia

The Anatolian region extends between the Black Sea and the Mediterranean and is divided from the European mainland by the **Sea of Marmara** and the narrow **Bosphorus**.

Extensions of the **Taurus** and **Pontic Mountains** surround the **Anatolian Plateau**, which becomes the **Armenian Highland**. This is bordered by the **Lesser Caucasus** in the north, and by the **Taurus Mountains** in the south. To the south, the Euphrates and the Tigris supply water to a fertile basin, bordered to the east by the **Zagros Mountains**, which in turn descend into the desert terrain of the **Iranian Uplands**.

Anatolian Plateau

The plateau runs along the Black Sea coast from the **Pontic Mountains** and continues parallel to the Mediterranean coast, surrounded by the **Taurus Mountains**, which rise in the east. The plateau descends towards the coast to form fertile plains. The highest peak is **Mount Ararat** at a height of 5,165 m.

The Anatolian Plateau is traversed by numerous rivers (the most important are the Euphrates and the Tigris). The area close to the Taurus Mountains contains numerous terminal lakes, including **Lake Van** at an altitude of 1,646 m.

Taurus Mountains

The **Taurus Mountain system** belongs to the Anatolian fold mountain belt and is composed mainly of limestone and metamorphic rocks, which in places are covered by a young volcanic stratum. The highest mountain in the range is **Buzul Dagı** (4,168 m). The volcanic mass of **Mount Erciyes** (3,917 m) developed to form the tufa walls and peaks of the **Goreme**.

Mesopotamia

Mesopotamia literally means the land 'between two rivers'. The region extends between the middle and lower courses of the **Euphrates** and **Tigris** rivers. It is a fertile basin, provided with ample water by the numerous tributaries and branches of the two rivers. The marshy and silt-covered mouth is dotted with lakes.

Arabian Peninsula

The Arabian Peninsula is the largest peninsula in Asia, covering an area of 3.5 million sq. km. It is a desert plateau which rises to a height of up to 3,000 m and is interspersed with wadis. The **Red Sea** separates the Arabian Peninsula from the continent of Africa. In the west, the long depression, formed by **Mesopotamia** and the Persian Gulf, forms the border with the fold mountains of northern Iran (the **Zagros Mountains**), which extend down to the far southeastern tip of the peninsula at Jabal ash-Sham (3,018 m).

The highest point on the peninsula is in the south-west (Jabal an-Nabi Shu'ayb, 3,760 m), but the mountains then drop steeply to the Red Sea. To the north, the mountains slope down more gradually in several stages. The large depression in the interior of the peninsula is covered by sandy desert and dunes.

Najd

This plateau in the north-east of the Arabian peninsula is mainly covered by stony and sandy desert and is enclosed by **Jabal**

1 Anatolia: Cappadocia's impressive landscape of strange columns and towers has been created by the erosion of soft tufa stone, interspersed with harder rocks.

2 Taurus: hot springs flow over the limestone terraces at Pamukkale. The deposits formed by the high mineral content of the water have created a staggered basin.

3 The tiny settlement of Shaharah in the north of Yemen sits at an altitude of 2,450 m. Foothills of the mountains along the Arabian Peninsula reach a height of 3,000 m.

Himalayas

Seen from the south, the Himalayas form a huge arc stretching across the top of the Indian sub-continent. The steep, thrusting mountain system contains several of the world's highest mountains and is the subject of countless myths and legends among the local peoples living in its shadow. The name 'Himalaya' derives from Sanskrit, meaning 'the snow abode'.

The Himalayas consists of four mountain chains running parallel to each other. These are the Sub-Himalayan Range, also known as the Siwalik Hills, the Lower Himalayan Range and the Great Himalayas. The fourth and most northerly mountain chain, the Gangdise Shan, is separated from the Great Himalayas by an immense valley formed by the Brahmaputra River and has peaks reaching a height of more than 7,000 m. Vast snowfields and glaciers cover some 17 per cent of the mountains and extend as far as the lower valleys, where they feed the sources of Asia's largest rivers, the Brahmaputra, the Ganges and the Indus. The Himalayas system contains a total of 19 rivers, some of which flow south and leave the mountain system in deep gorges with sheer cliff walls that can tower up to 5 km into the sky. The immense size of the Himalayas mean that they also form a significant climate and vegetation divide. The mountains act like a wall, blocking the cold air from the north of the continent, which would otherwise provide cooler temperatures all the way to the south of the Indian sub-continent. At the same time, the mountain barrier prevents the significant precipitation of the summer monsoon from moving northwards. Instead, the rain only affects the southern mountain slopes, and the Tibetan Plateau to the north is one of the driest regions on Earth. The southern slopes of the Himalayas are covered in lush rainforest and cloud forest, but the northern slopes are dominated by dry, alpine steppes. In the upper regions, the alpine climate gives way to a polar climate, and hurricane force winds howl over the glaciers.

It is hard to imagine that the highest mountains on Earth were once a layer of sediment on the ocean floor, but proof comes in the form of fossilised mussel shells and other sea creatures that can be found at an altitude of several kilometres. The Himalayas are a relatively young range of alpidic fold mountains. The story of their creation began 60 million years ago when the Indian continental plate, drifting at a speed of several centimetres a year, began to slide under the Eurasian Plate. Between 55 and 40 million years ago, a fracture formed at the site of this collision in the crust of the Indian Plate. The crust pushed further north below the sinking fracture paths and began to subduct, while the fractured layer of crust was pushed south on to the Indian sub-continent. Approximately 30 million years ago, a new fracture formed much deeper in the crust and this layer was also pushed on to the Indian

sub-continent. The Himalayas began to form at the subduction zone and are still growing today at a rate of a couple of millimetres a year. This folding process is far from complete, and the region is regularly affected by landslides and powerful earthquakes. It is possible to imagine that Mount Everest may one day be higher than 9,000 m, but only if it grows faster than the eroding forces of wind, rain, frost and ice wear it down. It is these substantial erosive powers that have formed the jagged and pointed mountain silhouettes to create the astounding raw beauty of the region.

The people living here believe that the eternally snow-covered peaks are the home of the gods. In the early twentieth century, climbers began to attempt to conquer the mountains in these remote regions, although the area had hardly been mapped. It was not until the 1950s that the peaks were climbed successfully for the first time. Thanks to improved equipment, a French expedition in 1950 was the first to reach the summit of Annapurna I at an altitude of over 8,000 m. After that, new peaks were conquered every year. Even the slopes of the notoriously challenging Kanchenjunga were climbed in 1955. The last of the major peaks to be reached was Sishapangma, conquered by a Chinese expedition in 1964.

Thin air, icy cold and sudden changes in weather conditions remain a danger to mountaineers, despite huge advances in equipment and clothing in recent decades. Since Sir Edmund Hillary and Sherpa Tensing Norgay first reached the top of Mount Everest in 1953, about 700 climbers have mastered the peak. More than 150 people have lost their lives in the attempt, either on the ascent or during the descent. At least 20 have died on the mountainside in the last few years alone.

All of the world's mountains over 8,000 m are located in the Himalayas and the connecting mountain chains. These are Mount Everest (8,863 m), K2 (8,611 m), Kanchenjunga (8,586 m), Lhotse (8,511 m), Makalu (8,481 m), Dhaulagiri (8,167 m), Manaslu (8,156 m), Cho Oyu (8,153 m), Nanga Parbat (8,126 m), Annapurna I (8,091 m), Gasherbrum I (8,068 m), Gasherbrum II (8,035 m), Broad Peak I (8,047 m) and Sisha Pangma (8046 m).

Above: a satellite image showing part of the Himalayas, the highest mountain range in the world. A horseshoe-shaped chain of mountains rising to 8,000 m surrounds almost snow-free valleys in Nepal's Sagarmatha National Park.

Inset: Mount Everest, at 8,863 m the highest mountain on Earth.

The Mongolian **Altai** is the highest mountain chain in Mongolia and one of the country's greatest natural wonders. The chain is approximately 1,000 km long and up to 4,374 m high. The impressive Altai mountain system also extends through Russia and the Gobi Desert, where the slopes can reach a height of up to 4,000 m.

Tuwaik and **Jabal Shammar**, after which the land in the east descends to a sandy desert. The Al-Aramah Plateau is in the centre of this barely inhabited region. The **Najd** lies at an altitude of between 600 m and 1,000 m and is the most populated part of the peninsula, thanks to its numerous oases and wadis.

Rub al Khali

The **Great Arabian Desert** whose name in Arabic means 'Empty Quarter', covers 780,000 sq. km, making it the largest continuous stretch of sand on Earth. The desert is 1,500 km across and contains sand dunes up to 300 m high. The climate is extremely dry and there are almost no oases.

Elburz Mountains

This range of fold mountains lies south of the **Caspian Sea** in northern Iran and forms the climate and vegetation divide between the desert landscape of the **Iranian Highlands** and the coastal landscape around the Caspian. The highest peak is **Damavand** at a height of 5,670 m. On the south side of the mountains is a dry area of mountain steppe. The northern face of the mountains is wetter and is covered in mountain forests and areas of grassland.

Iranian Highland

The highlands and the surrounding mountains are part of the Alpidic mountain chain that runs through Europe and Asia and divides here to form a northern branch, the **Elburz Mountains,** and a southern branch, the **Zagros Mountains**. The interior of the highlands is a basin with no outlets, dissected by mountain ranges. There are large inland deserts, the **Lut Desert** and the **Great Salt Desert**. The mountains in the north and west are volcanic and the area is subject to powerful earthquakes, a sign of the region's continuing tectonic activity.

Zagros Mountains

This young Alpidic fold mountain range divides the Iranian Highland from the southern basin of the Euphrates and Tigris lowlands. The mountain range is about 1,200 km long and extends from the mountains of Armenia to the **Gulf of Oman**. The peaks can rise to altitudes of over 4,500 m, and are interspersed with wide, shallow high-altitude valleys.

'The Roof of the World'

The massive arc of the highest and most impressive mountain system in the world extends for more than 2,500 km and forms a climate and vegetation divide between the **Indian Sub-continent** and the **Tibetan Plateau**. The range contains most of the highest mountains on Earth.
The **Himalayas** are young alpidic fold mountains. They formed at the northern edge of the Indian Continental Plate, which collided with the Eurasian Plate approximately 60 million years ago, pushing this plate upwards from beneath at a speed of a couple of centimetres a year. The folding process began about 20 million years ago, and the Himalayas are continuing to grow. The **Hindu Kush, Karakorams** and **Pamirs** in the north-west all belong to this mountain system.

Pamirs, Hindu Kush, Karakorams

The highest mountain of the **Pamirs** is **Ismail Samani Peak** (7,495 m), formerly known as Communism Peak. The steep mountain folds are covered in a desert landscape and there are broad high valleys in the interior. The **Hindu Kush** is about 700 km long and heavily glaciated. The range has 20 peaks of over 7,000 m, the highest of which is the 7,707-m-high **Tirich Mir**.

The **Karakorams** have four peaks of over 8,000 m, including **K2** (8,611 m), the second highest mountain on Earth.
More than a third of these mountains are covered in glaciers. The **Siachen** and **Baltoro Glaciers** contain some of the largest floes of ice outside the Arctic regions.

Himalayas

The main mountain system of the **Himalayas** is divided into four chains with steep mountain folds. The highest of these is the **Great Himalayas**, which have a maximum distance from north to south of 250 km. Nine of the world's 14 peaks rising over 8,000 m are found in this chain. To the south lies the **Lower Himalayan Range** with altitudes of about 4000 m and broad valleys. This range joins the **Sub-Himalayan Range**, also known as the Siwalik Hills, which descend to the plains of the Indus River. To the north, the **Brahmaputra River** divides the Great Himalayas from the Gangdise Shan.

Gangdise Shan

This range, over 1,000 km long, has a maximum altitude of 7,114 m (**Nyainqentanglha Feng**). The **Gangdise Shan** only joins the **Great Himalayas** in the west. The region has particularly low precipitation and is largely covered in steppe terrain. Only the southern slopes of the mountains are glaciated, the gentle northern slopes have a desert landscape.

Tibetan Plateau

The Tibetan Plateau is both the largest and the highest plateau in the world, covering an area of 2 million sq. km with an average altitude of 4,500 m. It is surrounded by a barrier of mountains 7,000 m to 8,000 m high.
The dry and inhospitable plateau is intersected by a small number of mountain chains, and the areas in between are covered in gravel deposits or salt lakes. The north and west of the plateau is mainly gravel and scree desert, while high steppes and tree steppes are found in the east. The area to the south of the Gangdise Shan forms a trench at an altitude of just 3,600 m, and this is where most of the Tibetan people live.

Tarim Basin

This endorheic drainage basin is surrounded by the **Tian Shan, Kunlun Shan, Altun Shan** and **Pamir** mountains. It stretches

Tibetan Plateau: the ruined Phuntsoling monastery in Central Tibet.

from west to east over a distance of 1,500 km, and is up to 650 km wide. The altitude drops from 1,400 m in the west, to approximately 800 m in the east. The lowest point (780 m) is dominated by **Lop Nur**, a dried-up salt lake which covers an area of about 25,000 sq. km.
The region has a harsh and arid continental climate. A large expanse of the **Tarim Basin** (272,000 sq. km) is covered by the **Taklamakan Desert**, with its immense sand dunes. Tributaries entering the basin from the surrounding mountains disappear or end in salt flats at the edges of this desert. The **Tarim River** only provides enough water to supply a small number of oases in the north of the desert.

Kunlun Shan, Tian Shan, Nan Shan

The **Kunlun Shan** is a late Triassic fold mountain system that stretches for more than 3,000 km and forms the northern border of the Tibetan Plateau. The Western Kunlun Shan joins the Pamirs and reaches a height of 7,546 m (**Muztagh Ata**), before dividing into two chains in the east. The Central Kunlun contains the heavily glaciated **Ulug Muztagh** (6,973 m) and the **Burhan Budai Mountains** (7,720 m). The mountain valleys contain numerous sink salt lakes. Tectonic valleys divide the chain from the Eastern Kunlun, which gradually rise to the **Qin Ling** in the east.
The **Tian Shan** stretch over 2,500 km and are bordered on all sides by deserts and semi-deserts (**Gobi Desert, Dzungaria Desert**). The mountain chain is interspersed with numerous streams and mountain valleys (**Turpan Basin,** 154 m below sea level at its lowest point) and is composed of Precambrian and Palaeozoic rock. The highest point is **the Pobeda Peak** at 7,439 m.
The **Nan Shan** is a series of high alpidic chains, with deep valleys and numerous endorheic basins, salt lakes and marshes.

Gobi Desert

This immense basin in the heart of Asia extends for some 2,000 km and has an area of approximately 1.3 million sq. km. It is surrounded by mountains on all sides. The low foothills of the **Mongolian Altai Mountains** extend far into the **Gobi Desert**, which lies at an altitude of approximately 1,000 m. Only the south-west consists of pure sandy desert (**Badain Jaran Desert**, 47,000 sq. km, **Tengger Desert**, 36,000 sq. km); the rest is steppe terrain.
Water drains from the north-east, via the **Kerulen**, to the **Amur** river. The most important river is the **Etsin Gol**, which provides water for the oases in the valley.

Mongolia

This area of Central Asia is dominated in the west by the **Altai Mountains,** with altitudes of up to 4,374 m, and the **Khangai Mountains** (over 3,500 m).

Pacific Ring of Fire

The Central Oceanic Ridge is one of the main forces driving continental plate movement. Deep sea magma flows out of the side of this ridge, pushing the surrounding plates away from each other as it hardens at a speed of approximately 2 cm per year in the Atlantic and up to 18 cm per year in the South Pacific.

Magma rising from the centre of the Earth to the ocean floor forms approximately 2.5–3 cu. km of new oceanic crust each year. Simultaneously, the same amount of oceanic crust is forced deep underground and re-melted in the deep sea trenches at the edges of the continental plates.

Molten lava can often break through the Earth's crust at the site of these subduction zones, forming volcanoes. The arrangement of volcanoes on the Earth is by no means random. The area around the Pacific Plate alone contains some two-thirds of the

600 active volcanoes on Earth. A ring of fire covering 32,500 km and consisting of volcanic island chains and belts of volcanoes encircles the Pacific Ocean. It stretches from the Antarctic Peninsula, over Tierra del Fuego to the huge volcanic mountain chains of the Southern and Central American Cordillera.

The arc of islands that extends from the volcanoes of Alaska and across the Aleutian Islands marks the northern edge of the Pacific Plate. This string of islands continues on to the Kamchatka Peninsula in Siberia and the Kuril Islands.

It is here that the Pacific Plate pushes below the Eurasian Plate. The series of volcanoes continues with further island chains, stretching from Japan to Taiwan and south to the Mariana Islands. This marks the border between the Pacific Plate and the relatively

small Philippine Plate, which is itself surrounded by three further plates. The edges of the Philippine Plate form the particularly active chains of volcanoes in Indonesia and the Philippines.

The volcanic ring ends along the edge of the Indo-Australian Plate

with the volcanoes of Melanesia and Fiji in the South Pacific, New Zealand and some sub-Antarctic islands. This massive Pacific Ring of Fire does not merely create volcanoes, which can suddenly spring back to life after centuries of lying dormant, but 95 per cent of the world's earthquakes also originate here. Undersea activity off the coast of Indonesia caused the tsunami of December, 2004.

Big picture: a dramatic eruption on the Kamchatka Peninsula in Eastern Siberia.

Inset: Mount Fuji: Japan's highest volcano is currently dormant.

Left: the volcanic White Island in New Zealand is one of a chain of active volcanoes that extends to Mount Ruapehu.

*The **Yangtze Jiang**, the 'long river', rises in the Tibetan Plateau and flows into the sea at Shanghai after 6,300 km. Much of the river is navigable and is of great economic importance for China.*

The fascinating landscape of this river includes the Three Gorges in the provinces of Sichuan and Hubei. Tiger Leaping Gorge is situated on the border between Tibet and Yunnan.

Plateaus at a height of 1,000 m to 1,500 m cover the east of Mongolia. The north-east is covered in taiga vegetation. The rest of the region is dominated by mountain deserts and steppe vegetation, bounded in the south by the **Gobi Desert**. Four-fifths of the region consists of steppe and pastureland. The most important river is the **Selenga**.

Dzungaria

This tectonic trough between the **Mongolian Altai** and the **Eastern Tian Shan** is bordered by the **Gobi Desert** in the east, while the border in the west consists of several mountain chains (**Djungarian Alatau**). The interior of the region is mainly covered by sandy deserts, with salt steppes and lakes around the edges (**Ulungur, Ebinur, Sayram**). The only outlet is the **Irtysh River**.

Altai Mountains

The mountain system splits to form the Russian, Mongolian and Gobi Altai. The Palaeozoic mountains of the **Russian Altai** rise in the centre and east to glaciated peaks with a height

The **Yangtze** is the third-longest river on Earth. It rises at the confluence of several rivers at an altitude of 5,600 m on the Qinghai Plateau. It then flows south-east through high mountain chains. The river crosses the eastern section of the Red Basin, at which point it is 500 m wide, before cutting across the Yunnan-Guizhou Plateau for a distance of 648 km between Chongqing and Yichang. The Yangtze then meanders eastwards across a great plain. At Nanjing, the 'long river' forms a massive delta, and drains into the East China Sea at Shanghai in two branches after covering a total distance of 6,400 km.
Rising in the Qinghai Plateau, the **Huang He** then winds along the southern edge of the Gobi Desert and around the Ordos Plateau into wide plains. It flows into the Yellow Sea north-west of the Shandong Peninsula after covering a total distance of 4,845 km.

of some 4,506 m. The rest of the system consists of plateaus, low mountain chains and steppe-covered valleys. The **Mongolian Altai** begins at the **Tabyn Bogdo Ola** and extends for 1,000 km. The **Gobi Altai** extends for some 500 km, rising to a height of some 3,957 m. They mark the south-eastern boundary of the mountain system.

Khangai Mountains

This range is 700 km long and has an average altitude of 2,500 m. The highest point is the 4,031-m-high Mount **Otgontenger**. The mountains consist of strata of granite, schist and sandstone. The higher altitudes have only a sparse covering of vegetation. The southern slopes consist of steppes and the north faces are covered in dense forest.

North-east China Plain

This region is densely populated and intensively farmed. It extends along the Pacific coast from the fertile plains traversed by the **Huang He River** to the lowlands in the middle and lower reaches of the **Yangtze River**. In the plains of the lower Yangtze, the river's waters and those of its tributaries have formed a series of natural lakes.

Shandong Peninsula

The **Shandong Peninsula** divides **Bo Hai Bay** in the north from the Yellow Sea in the south. The peninsula has numerous small bays, and the western section is part of the flood plain of the **Huang He River**. The interior is covered in hills and mountains.

Dongting Lake, Poyang Lake, Tai Lake

Dongting Lake is one of China's largest freshwater lakes and forms a natural dam, preventing the waters of the **Yangtze** from escaping and regulating the flow of the river. The volume of the lake is decreasing due to the large amount of sediment deposited by the river. The lake covers an area of between 3,600 and 4,700 sq. km. The relatively shallow **Poyang Lake** is fed by the **Gan River**. The lake also serves as a retention basin, and its surface area varies greatly,

depending on the flow of water that enters it (between 3,700 and 5,070 sq. km). **Tai Lake** is fed by a labyrinth of water courses, which are connected to the **Yangtze** by the **Huangpu River** and by canals.

Yangtze Delta

At Nanjing, the **Yangtze** begins to form a wide **delta**, 350 km long and up to 80 km wide, covering an area of more than

80,000 sq. km. It is here that the Yangtze dumps approximately 300 million tons of silt and mud into the sea each year. The area surrounding the fertile delta is one of the most heavily populated regions of China.

Central Chinese Mountains

The **Central Chinese Mountains** separate the North-east China Plain from sub-tropical South China. It consists mainly of ancient, highly eroded mountains, composed of granite.

Qin Ling Mountains

This mountain system stretches 1,550 km and forms the climate divide between the temperate north and the sub-tropical south of China. It is also the watershed between the river systems of the **Huang He** and **Yangtze Rivers**. The Variscan fold mountain chain, composed of granite, limestone

and sandstone, reaches its highest point at the 3,767-m-high **Mount Taibaishan**.

Khingan Range

Both mountain chains stretch from the **Amur River** to the region north of Beijing and form the northern edge of the central lowlands of Manchuria. The **Greater Khingan** separates this lowland from the Mongolian Plateau in the west and is mainly

composed of granite and basalt. The average height is 1,200 m. The mountains are covered in dense forests to an altitude of more than 2,000 m. The **Lesser Khingan** is a low mountain chain to the north-east that rises to a height of some 1,200 m. The **Amur River** flows through a deep gorge to the north-east.

Sichuan

Eastern **Sichuan** is dominated by the large Sichuan Basin (220,000 sq. km) along the middle section of the **Yangtze** River. The abundance of red sandstone in this area has given it the name of the **Red Basin**.
The fertile hills at an altitude of 400 to 800 m are interspersed with shallow valleys and are surrounded on all sides by mountains up to 3,000 m in height and by the Yunnan-Guizhou Plateau. This plateau, at a height of 1,800 to 2,000 m, is mainly composed of limestone and dominates western Sichuan and central Hunan. It is

bordered by the **Sino-Tibetan Mountains** and the **Qinghai Plateau**. The Sino-Tibetan Mountains reach a maximum height of 7,556 m in the **Daxue Shan**.

Mountains of South-east China

The mountains of South-east China are very segmented and can be divided into two systems,

The Gobi Desert covers the whole southern section of Mongolia. Nomads live in this inhospitable place.

the **Nan Ling** and the **Wuyi Shan**. They separate the **South China Lowlands** from the **Yangtze Plain** further north.
The mountains rise to a height of 200 m to 1,100 m, with narrow valleys and wide basins, and they provide some of China's most attractive landscapes.
The whole region once lay beneath the sea. It has only been dry land since the Tertiary Era. The area has huge limestone strata, with an average thickness of 1,100 m, on a granite bedrock. Earth movements have misaligned and uplifted these layers, and erosion has created a magnificent karst topography. The strange karstified limestone towers of the **Guilin** region on the **Lijiang River** are among the strangest and most beautiful natural landscapes on Earth.

Nan Ling

The **Nan Ling mountain system** is an eastern extension of the **Altun Shan**, consisting of a

The Indus River is over 3,000 km long and rises in the Gangdise Shan Mountains around the Tibetan Plateau at a height of 5,000 m. The river winds through the Himalayas cutting spectacular gorges up to 3,000 m deep before flowing out on to the shallow plains in the south-west. The Indus continues southwards across the dry landscape of Pakistan, providing much-needed water for the surrounding regions.

series of staggered mountain chains, which form the watershed between the **Yangtze** and the **Zhujiang** to the south. The main peaks are over 1,500 m high. The highest elevation is 1,902 m. To the south, the mountains descend to form rolling hills.

Wuyi Shan

The mountain system consists of a series of chains which form the border between Fujian and Jiangxi provinces. It has peaks of up to 1,800 m. The southern end of the mountain range includes the **Shanling** with its densely forested slopes, honeycombed with limestone caves. In the north-east, the mountain terrain gives way to the dense bamboo forest of the **Xianxia Mountains**.

The **Wuyi Shan** has a very attractive landscape of cliffs with several peaks and green gorges.

Taiwan

The island of Taiwan (Formosa) is separated from China by the 160-km-wide **Straits of Taiwan**. It has an area of 36,000 sq. km and is dominated by a central, young **fold mountain chain**, which runs through the island from north to south and covers approximately two-thirds of the land area. The craggy, rainforest-covered mountains have more than 60 peaks, which can reach heights of over 3,000 m. The highest point is the 3,997-m-high **Mount Yu Shan**. To the east, the mountains fall steeply, but in the west the peaks drop in terrace-like stages to form a fertile flat coastal strip between 8 and 40 km wide.

In the north of the island, above the **Taipei Basin,** there is a group of extinct volcanoes which are part of the volcanic arc of the **Ryukyu Islands.** Taiwan's position on the join between the Pacific Plate and the Philippine Plate means that the island is often affected by volcanoes as the Earth's crust constantly shifts.

Japan consists of a 2,600-km long arc of about 4,100 islands, which are actually the peaks of an underwater volcanic mountain range. The main islands of **Kyushu** (36,554 sq. km), **Shikoku** (18,260 sq. km), **Honshu** (227,414 sq. km)

and **Hokkaido** (83,511 sq. km) are joined in the north by the **Sakhalin Island** and the **Kuril Islands.** The **Ryukyu Islands,** including **Okinawa,** form the southern extensions of this island chain. The main islands contain numerous bays and peninsulas. Three-quarters are afforested low mountains with deep valleys and steep cliffs, interspersed with interior valleys, terraces and plateaus. Even the two largest basins and eight plains, which are traversed by rivers and open to the sea, are divided into vertical levels. These islands are the main population centres of Japan.

The island chain has experienced a great deal of tectonic activity since

the Neogene period and contains hundreds of volcanoes, of which 40 are still active, including **Mount Aso** (1,592 m).

Honshu

Honshu is by far the largest of the main Japanese islands and contains both volcanic and granite mountain chains, with narrow coastal seams and large peninsulas (including the **Kii, Izu and Noto peninsulas**), some of which are extensions of the mountain chains.

The main mountains are the **Japanese Alps**, which consist of the Akaishi, Kiso and Hida Mountains, and which reach an altitude of 3,192 m in central Japan. **Mount Fuji** rises to a height of 3,776 m and is the highest mountain in the country, and is part of a volcanic chain that extends over the **Izu Peninsula** and into the Sea of Japan.

The largest plain on Honshu, after the 32,000 sq. km **Kanto Plain** around Tokyo, is the region of Kansai, west of the Alps. This

area contains **Lake Biwa** (675 sq. km), which formed in a tectonic hollow; it is Japan's largest lake. **Kansai** is not a flat plain, but is intersected by numerous plateaus, mountains and basins. To the south-west, the mountains rise to form a narrow peninsula, which runs along the **Inland Sea** – a depression filled

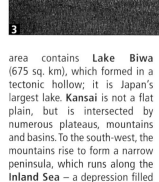

1 The vegetation on the high plains of Mongolia is only suitable for grazing livestock. The yurts (tents) of the native nomads dot the landscape.

2 Green pasture as far as the eye can see: the landscape of the Chinese autonomous region of Xinjiang Uygur,

also known as East Turkestan, is an important habitat for the nomadic peoples of the steppes.

3 Mountains near Lijiang: the karst cliffs in the South China region around Guilin rise almost vertically out of completely flat plains.

*The coast of **Halong Bay**, some 150 km east of the Vietnamese capital Hanoi, provides a stunning landscape. The strange array of weird columns was formed after sea levels rose at the end of the Ice Age. Amazing rock formations of towers and needles are the result of harsh erosion over the course of many hundreds of thousands of years.*

with sea water that separates Honshu from Sjikoku – and which ends at the Kammon Strait.

Sakhalin

This island, with a total area of 76,400 sq. km is located between the Gulf of Tartary and the **Sea of Okhotsk**. It has a length of 948 km and is some 160 km wide. Only the north is mountainous; the highest point is **Mt. Lopatin** (1,609 m). The island is covered in tundra, with mixed woodland to the south.

Indian Sub-continent

The Indian Sub-continent is bordered by the **Arabian Sea** in the west and the **Bay of Bengal** in the east, and terminates in the south in a triangular peninsula, which extends into the Indian Ocean. The north of the sub-continent is covered by part of the **Himalayan mountain system**. South-east of the Himalayas lie the **plains of the Ganges Brahmaputra**, and south-west of the Himalayas there is the **Indus Plain** (the Punjab), that gives way to the dry landscape of the **Thar Desert** in the south.
The **Indian Peninsula** is covered by the **Deccan Plateau**, which contains mountain chains with

heights of up to 1,722 m, formed during the folding that produced the Himalayas. These mountain chains include the **Aravalli Range, Vindhya Range and Satpura Range**. The Deccan is surrounded by the mountains of the **Western Ghats** and the **Eastern Ghats**, which run parallel to the coast. The coastal seam in the west is very narrow, but in the east, north and south, the mountains are bordered by a broad lowland area. Both the **Ganges** and **Indus Rivers** form huge deltas.

Thar Desert

The Thar Desert is a dry landscape covering 250,000 sq. km between the **Aravalli Range** and the **Indus Plain**. It is mostly covered in steppe vegetation, with long stretches of dunes. The region has a very small population and is irrigated by a few canals. The area includes a 15,000 sq.-km-region of desert, which has been created by human activity.

Ganges Plain

At Haridwar, the **Ganges** enters a wide plain covering an area of over 1 million sq. km, providing water to one quarter of the sub-continent. The Ganges meanders east across this extensive plain,

Ganges, Indus

The **Ganges River** rises in the Himalayas at a height of 4,600 m at the confluence of the Bhagirathi and the Alaknanda. The river flows through the Ganges Plain before forming a fertile delta over an area of 56,000 sq. km. After a distance of 2,700 km, the Ganges opens out into the Bay of Bengal.
The **Indus** rises at a height of 5,182 m in the Gangdise Shan and flows between the Karakorams and the Himalayas in a north-westerly direction, before turning south and leaving the mountains behind. The Kabul River joins the Indus as it enters the Indus Plain. In this arid plain, the Indus feeds water to an oasis approximately 150 km wide. After 3,200 km, the river flows into the Arabian Sea, forming a delta of over 7,800 sq. km.

Mekong

The **Mekong** rises at an altitude of approximately 3,000 m on the Tibetan Plateau and flows southeast through deep gorges in the mountains of eastern Tibet. North of Luang Prabang, the river bends sharply to the south and then follows the northern and eastern edges of the Khorat Plateau, where it is joined by the Mun River. Despite the river's shallow gradient it creates several cataracts over this stretch, the most famous being the Khone Falls in Laos near the border with Cambodia. The Mekong forms a flood plain with several other rivers 550 km before its mouth. It then turns south and forms a wide delta before draining into the South China Sea, having covered a distance of more than 4,500 km.

Indonesia: Mount Agung (3,014 m) is the highest volcano on Bali.

at a very slight gradient. Several tributaries join the river, including the **Ghaghara**, the **Gandak**, the **Yamuna** and the **Son**, forming a convoluted river system and a very fertile region which is densely populated as a result.

The Ghats

The **Western Ghats** follow the west coast of India for a distance of 1,500 km and form a fault scarp which drops steeply to the coast of the Arabian Sea.
In the south, the mountains rise to form the **Nilgiri Mountains**, with a height of more than 2,000 m, then dividing into the individual massifs of the **Southern Ghats**, whose highest peak is **Anaimudi** (2,695 m).
The **Eastern Ghats** are a series of hill and mountain chains stretching from north to south, where they reach their highest elevation of 1,628 m, before joining the Western Ghats at the Nilgiri Mountains.

Sri Lanka

The island is separated from the Indian Sub-continent by the shallow Palk Strait and the Gulf of Mannar. Sri Lanka, which until 1972 was known as Ceylon, has an area of 65,610 sq. km, much of which is dominated by lowland and coastal plains, lined with lagoons.
The only mountains are at the southern end of the interior of the island; the highest point is **Pidurutalagala** which rises to an altitude of 2,524 m. The island also has a number of isolated

peaks, such as **Sigiriya** and Sri Pada, also called Adam's Peak (2,243 m). Sri Lanka is composed of Pre-Cambrian stone primarily land. Only the far north-west of the country has partially karstified limestone strata of the Tertiary Period.

South-east Asia

South-east Asia is bordered to the south and east by the South China Sea and extends into the foothills of the **mountains of East Tibet**, which run along the east coast as the **Annamitic Cordillera** (Ngoc Linh, 2,598 m). On the west coast, the **Bilauktaung Mountains** (2,075 m) extend into the **Malay Peninsula**. The steep mountains to the north of south-east Asia are followed by the broad **Khorat Plateau** in the centre of the region, which is surrounded by further mountain ranges, the **Dangrek Mountains** (1,328 m) and the **Cardamom Mountains**. To the south, a broad plain traversed by many rivers ends in the Mekong Delta.

Mekong Delta

The **Mekong River** widens into a delta at Phnom Penh, covering an area of 70,000 sq. km. The growth of this delta to the southwest is affected by ocean currents. The water courses in the delta vary depending on the monsoon rains. To mitigate the effect of the floods, the delta has been dammed to form the **Tonle Sap Lake**.

Hoang Lien Mountain Range

The north of South-east Asia is dominated by this mountain range with deep valleys and an average height of 2,000 m. The range is an extension of the mountains of East Tibet and has numerous plateaus. The highest point is **Fansipan** (3,143 m) in the north-east.

Malay Peninsula

This peninsula, located between the Andaman Sea and the Gulf of Thailand, is 1,500 km long from north to south. The narrowest point is the **Kra Isthmus** (40 km). The peninsula has numerous bays and is traversed by a mountain system which forms one coherent mass in the north but which separates in the south to form staggered mountain chains (**Tahan**, 2,187 m).
To the south, a series of hills lead to a marshy coastal plain. This is dominated by scattered karstified pillars (**Halong Bay** and **Phang Nga Bay**). Tropical rainforest covers most of the peninsula, which gives way to mangrove swamps on the west coast.

Indonesian Islands

The **Malay Archipelago** is a chain of islands covering a distance of 5,000 km which sits on the 200-m-deep continental shelf of the Sunda Plate at the boundary between the Indo-Australian Plate and the Philippine Plate. Several mountain chains have

New Guinea: the mountains of the second-largest island on Earth are covered in rainforest. New Guinea lies on an extension of the Indonesian island chain and also marks the start of Oceania. It is on the border between the two continents. Like many other islands between the Indian and Pacific Oceans, New Guinea is also surrounded by numerous coral reefs and offshore coral islands.

folded here as a result of volcanic activity since the Mesozoic Era. The islands have a bedrock of sandstone and limestone – with the exception of Borneo – but high levels of volcanic and tectonic activity gives them largely volcanic characteristics. The area beween the Pacific and Indian Oceans form the longest uninterrupted volcanic chain on Earth. Seventy of them are young volcanoes that have erupted since the year 1600.

The islands are mountainous and only the larger ones – **Luzon, Mindanao, Java, Sumatra** and **Borneo** – have large flood plains. Some of the islands have offshore coral reefs.

Sumatra

Sumatra, the sixth largest island in the world, covers an area of some 425,000 sq. km and is the most westerly of the Indonesian islands. It is separated from Java by the narrow Sunda Straits.

The landscape in the west of the island is dominated by the densely forested **Barisan Mountains**. This mountain range has several active volcanoes (including **Kerinci**, 3,800 m, and **Merapi**, 2,914 m), and drops steeply on the west coast, but is bounded in the east by a foothill region, followed by undulating lowlands and finally a marshy coastal plain and mangroves. In the interior of the Barisan Mountains, tufa deposits have formed plateaus.

Java

This island, the most populated in Indonesia, covers an area of 126,650 sq. km. It has a volcanic mountain chain running its entire length, with peaks rising to heights of 3,676 m. The mountains descend to the coast of the Java Sea.

Borneo

With an area of 746,950 sq. km, mountainous Borneo is the third largest island on Earth and is composed of schist and Mesozoic rock. The highest point is **Mount Kinabalu** at 4,095 m. The foothills of the central mountains surround a basin containing numerous lakes and marshes.

The coasts have few bays. The interior was once completely covered in dense rainforest but much of it has been cleared to produce grassland.

The Philippines Archipelago

This island group forms the northeastern section of the **Malay Archipelago** and comprises more than 7,100 islands. **Luzon** (108,772 sq. km) and **Mindanao** (94,594 sq. km) alone make up some two- thirds of the total land mass. The islands are covered in densely forested mountain chains and hills, dominated by both extinct and active volcanoes.

New Guinea

New Guinea covers approximately 771,900 sq. km and is

covered by several parallel and densely forested mountain chains along its whole length. In the south, these mountains are bordered by a flood plain about 450 km wide, which has formed alongside the **Digul** and **Fly Rivers**. The coast has numerous bays and peninsulas and is dominated by mangrove swamps.

Mountains of New Guinea

The young fold mountain chains that run the length of the island join in the south-east to form the **Owen Stanley Range** on a peninsula, which continues in the island groups to the east. In the west, the **Maoke Mountains** are covered in dense rainforest. The **Central Range**, whose highest point is **Puncak Jaya** (5,030 m), is glaciated. Tectonic activity is mainly restricted to the northern coastal mountains and the only volcanic region is in the east (**Mount Lamington**, 1,680 m).

1 Mayon on the island of Luzon in the Philippines reaches a height of 2,463 m and is an active volcano.

2 The karstified pillars in Phang Nga Bay north of the Thai city of Phuket are the result of thousands of years of erosion.

3 The active volcano of Bromo is 2,614 m high. It is in the Bromo-Tengger-Semeru National Park on Java and is part of the Tengger Caldera.

4 Rice terraces: mountain slopes in the Philippines transformed by the Ifugao into a unique agricultural landscape.

Alaska
(USA)

Ud

Uc

Ub

Ua

Td

Tc

Tb

Ta

Sd

Sc

Sb

160°

165°

170°

175°

180°

175°

170°

165°

160°

155°

150°

Chukchi Sea
Wevok
Cape Lisburne   *Kotzebue*
Sound   *Seward*
Peninsula   Bethel
Wales   Nome   Alakanuk
Bering Strait
Uelen   Northeast
Lavrentija   Cape
Arctic Circle   St.Matthew
Egvekinot   Island
(USA)
m. Navarin

Wrangel
Island
Ušakovskoe
Mys Šmidta
Prolix Longa
Koljučinskaja guba
Chukotskiy
Poluostrov
Providenija
Gambell
Saint Lawrence Island
(USA)

Bering
Sea

Anadyrskoye Ploskogor'ye   1887
Pevek   Ugol'nye
hrebet Pekulnej   Kopi
ostrov Ajon   *Paljavaam*   Anadyr'   Nagornyj
Čaunskaja guba   *Anadyr*
Čerskij   **Chukchi**
1775 Bilibino   1651
Anjujskij hrebet   **Autonomous District**   3795

O C E A N

New Siberian
Islands

East Siberian
Sea

Laptev Sea

1125
ičkogo
o.Bol.Begičev
o.Arga-
Sagastyr   *Olenëkskij*
zaliv   Muora-Sise
o.Kotel'nyj   o.Novaja
Sibir'
pr.Sannikova
o.Bol.
Ljahovskova
pr.Dmitrija Lapteva
Jano-Indigirskaja
nizmennost'
Kolymskaja
nizmennost'
1797
Olojskij hrebet
Omolon   1503   Kamenskoe

Koryak
Korf
Autonomous District
Karaginskij
Ossora   o.Karaginskij
m. Ozernoj

nsula
land
a
o.Bol.Begičev
kraž Čekanovskogo   Lena Delta
guba
Buor-Haja
Hajyr   Ust'-Kujga
Deputatskij
Saskylah   *Janskij*   Čekurdah
zaliv
Indigirka
Alazejskoe
ploskogor'e
Jukagirskoe
ploskogor'e
1613   1814   1483
1411   m. Oljutorskij
Apuka   2562
g. Ledjanaja   Tc

Sejmčan   1962   *Sirsova Ridge*
Oljutorskij
zaliv
m. Tajgonos

Verhojanskiy
Olenëk   Menkerja
Sakha
Žigansk
Udačnyj   **(Yakutia)**
Viljujskoe
plato
Njurba   Viljujsk
Morkoka   *Vilyuj*
Mimyj
Nakanno
Lensk
Olëkminsk
Range
2243
Bataga   2533
Honuu   *Momskij hrebet*
Lazo   2690
Janskoe
ploskogor'e
2081
Mountains
2120
Sangar   Ust'-Nera
hrebet Suntar-Hajata
2959   Susuman   Jagodnoe
Ojmjakon
Tomtor   Ust'-Omčug
Handyga
2184
Jakutsk   *hrebet Ulahan-Bom*
Central'nojakutskaja
Kerdem   Amga
ravnina   Ust'-Maja
prilenskoe plato
Ulu
Aldan
Aldanskoe
Aldan
nagor'e
Čul'man   2243   1890   1906
Olëkma
Nerjungri   2067
g.Skalistyj Golec
Mogoča   2384

Omolon
Susuman
Magadan
m. Tolstoj
m. Južnyj
Okhotsk
m. Alevina

Ust'-Kamčatsk
Koman dorskie o-va
m. Kamčatskij
4750
vlk. Ključevskaja Sopka
Sredinnyj hrebet
3607
m.Kronockij
vlk. Korjakskaja
Sopka
3456
Petropavlovsk-
Kamčatskij
2460

Kamchatka
Peninsula

Sea of
Okhotsk

m. Lopatka
o. Paramušir
o. Onekotan
o. Šiaškotan
o. Rasšua
o. Simušir

Kuril Islands

ER IA

kut
E   I   A
Lake
Baikal   1702
Patomskoe nagor'e
2193   1702
2630
Buryatia
Stanovoy
3067
Nagor'ye
2467
Stanovoy Khrebet
hr. Tukuringra
Verhnezejskaja
ravnina
Zejskoe vdhr.
Zejsko-
Bureinskaja
ravnina
Shantarskiye
Ostrova
Čumikan
Nikolaevsk-
na-Amure
1609
Sakhalin
Poronajsk
m.Terpenija
Komsomol'sk-
na-Amure
Uglegorsk
Habarovsk
Vanino
Južno-Sahalinsk
Holmsk
La Perouse Strait

Tatarskij Proliv

Wakkanai   Abashiri
o. Urup
o. Simušir
o. Iturup
Kuril Trench

ynsk Buryat
ous District
dzskij
tsk
va
Ulan-Ude
Petrovsk
Zabajkal'skij
Sühbaatar
Baruun-
kharaa
MONGOLIA
ULAN BATOR
Öndörhaan
Baruun Urt
Čita
Karymskoe
Aginskoe
Borzja
Chojbalsan
Yablonovyy Range
Olëkminskij
Stanovik
Mogoča
Mohe
Yimuhe
Mangui
Amur
Šimanovsk
Skovorodino
Zeja
Blagoveščensk
Birobidžan
Jewish
Autonomous Region
Bureinskij hrebet
Bikin
Sihote-Alin
Dal'nerečensk
Ussurijsk
o. Kunašir

Baruun Urt
Aga Buryat
Autonomous District
Ergun Zuoqi
Ergun Youqi
Yakeshi
Manzhouli
Hailar
Hulun Nur
Greater Hingan Range
Lesser Hingan Range
Zhalantun
Bei'an
Yichun   Hegang
Jagdaqi
CHINA
Qiqihar   Mingshui   Jiamusi   Jixi
Tailai   Suihua   Tonghe
Anda   **Heilongjiang**   Lake
Khanka
Chojbalsan   Ulanhot
Baicheng   **HARBIN**   Shangzhi
Qiqihar   Zhalantun   Mudanjiang
Sanchahe
Kherlen Gol
Spassk-
Dal'nij
Rudnaja
Pristan'
Dal'negorsk
2290
Asahi dake
Asahikawa
SAPPORO   Kushiro
Obihiro
Tomakomai
Hakodate

La Perouse Strait
HOKKAIDO
JAPAN

17

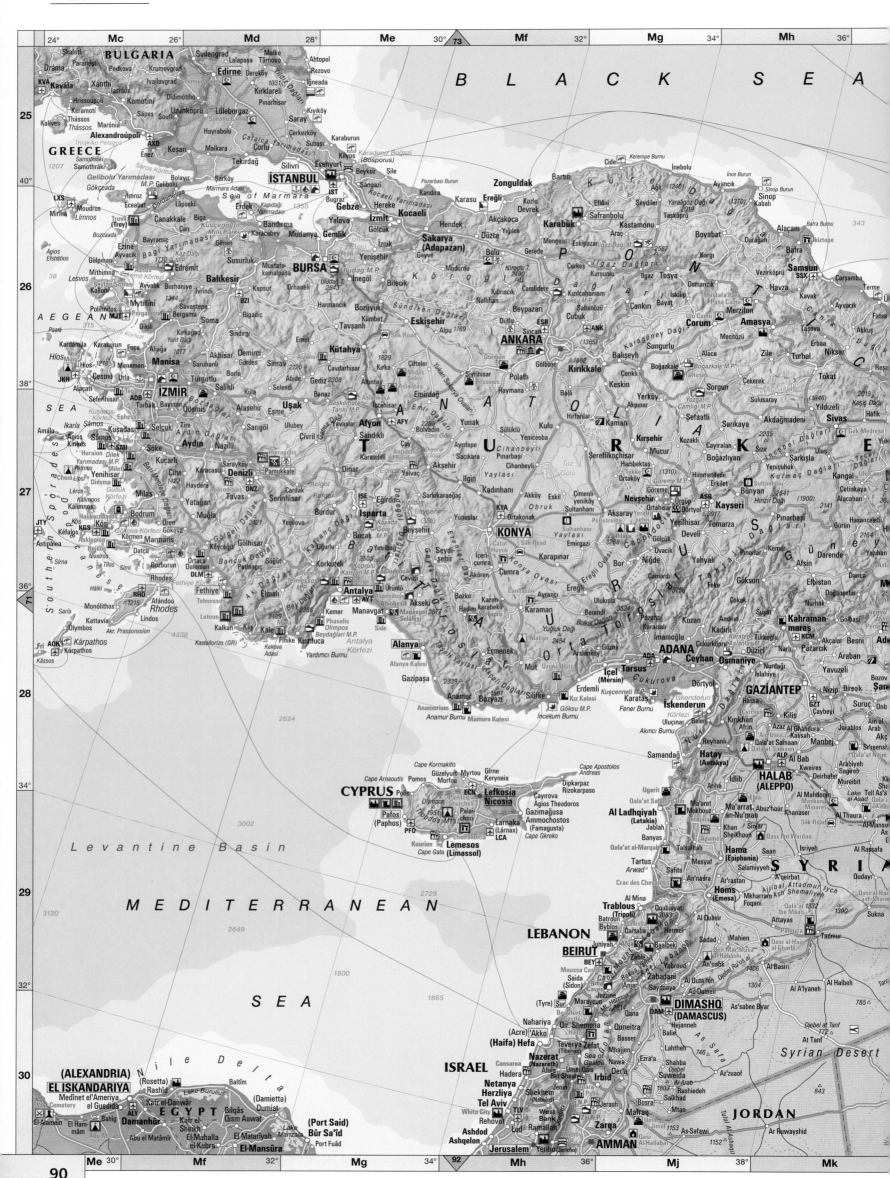

Scale 1:4,500,000

0   50   100   150 Kilometers
0   50   100 Miles

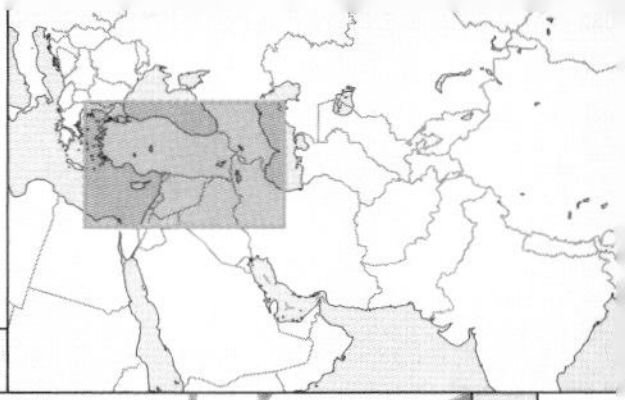

RUSSIA

KAZAKHSTAN

CAUCASUS

GEORGIA

ARMENIA

AZERBAIJAN

IRAN

IRAQ

Abkhazia
North Ossetia
South Ossetia
Chechenia
Ingushetia
Dagestan
Kabardino-Balkaria
Karachay-Cherkessia

Soči
Adler
Gagra
Sokhumi
Očamčire
Zugdidi
Poti
Batumi
Kutaisi
Senaki
Ozurgeti
Kobuleti

Pjatigorsk
Kislovodsk
Nal'čik
Čerkessk
Georgievsk
Mineral'nye Vody
Groznyj
Vladikavkaz
Nazran'
Mahačkala
Kaspijsk
Derbent
Bujnaksk

TBILISI (TIBILISI)
Rustavi
Gori
Mtskheta
Telavi
Kaspi
Khašuri

Gyumri
Vanadzor
YEREVAN
Echmiadzin
Ashtarak
Hrazdan
Sevan (Lake Sevan)
Masis
Artašat
Ararat
Iğdır
Ağrı

Gänžä
Mingeçevir
Šamkir
Yevlax
Šamaxi
Sumqayit
BAKI (BAKU)
Xırdalan
Salyan
Ali Bayramlı
Sabirabad
Imišli
Nagornyy-Karabakh
Xankendi (Stepanakert)
Naxçıvan
Sisian
Göris
Kapan

Trabzon
Gümüşhane
Erzincan
Erzurum
Kars
Ardahan
Artvin
Rize
Hopa
Bayburt
Kelkit
Elazığ
Diyarbakır
Batman
Bitlis
Van
Muş
Bingöl
Tunceli
Ağrı
Tatvan
Silvan
Mardin
Siirt
Hakkâri
Nusaybin
Cizre

Al-Hasaka
Al-Mawsil (AL MAWSIL)
Arbil
Kirkuk
As Sulaymaniyah
Samarra
Tikrit
Ar Ramadi
Al Fallujah
Al Kadhimiya
BAGHDAD
Ba'quba
Deir Al Zor

Tabriz (**TABRIZ**)
Orumiyeh
Khoy
Marand
Maragheh
Mahabad
Miyandoab
Saqqez
Sanandaj
Bukan
Zanjan
Marivan
Kermanshah
Hamadan
Malayer
Borujerd
Arak
Qom
Khorramabad
Ardabil
Bandar-e-Anzali
Rasht
Lahijan
Qazvin
Karaj
TEHRAN (TEHERAN)
Kašan

CASPIAN SEA

Lake Urmia
Van Gölü
Mt. Ararat (5165)

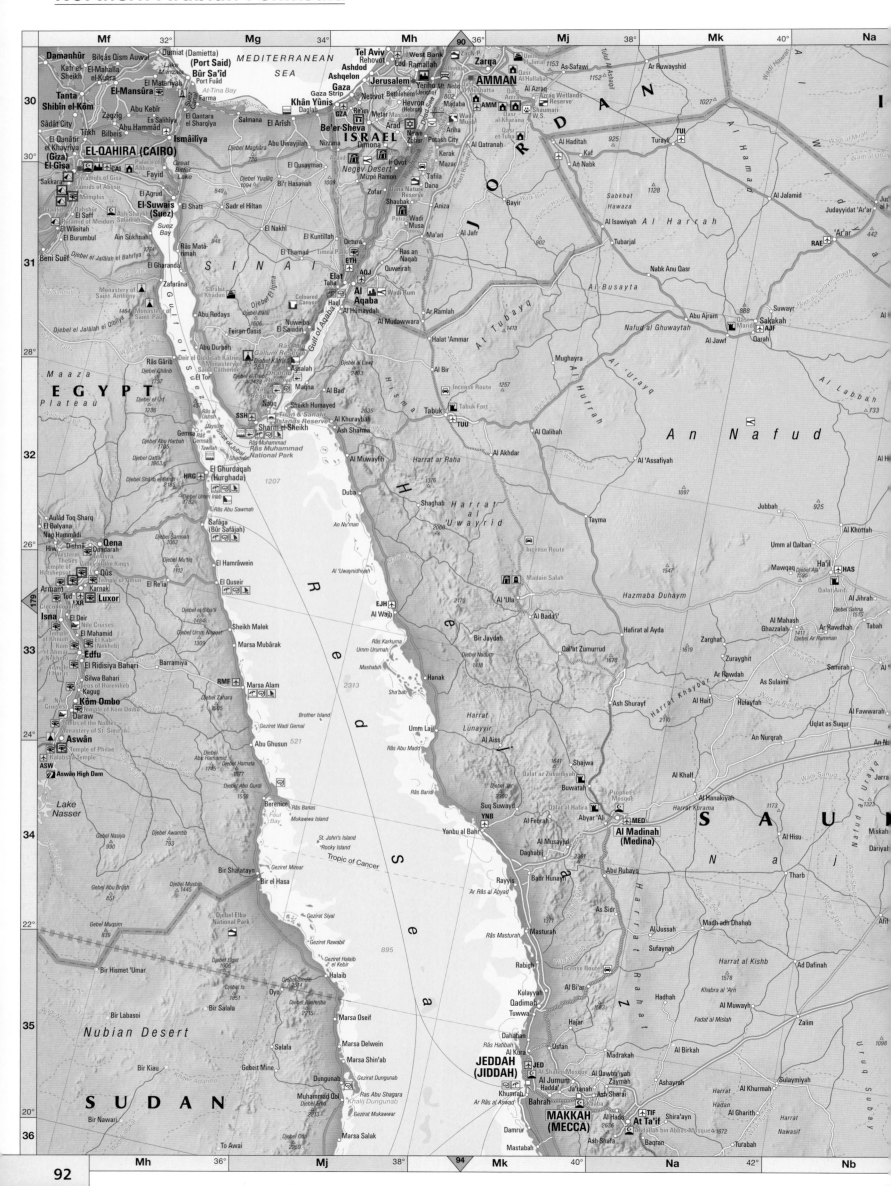

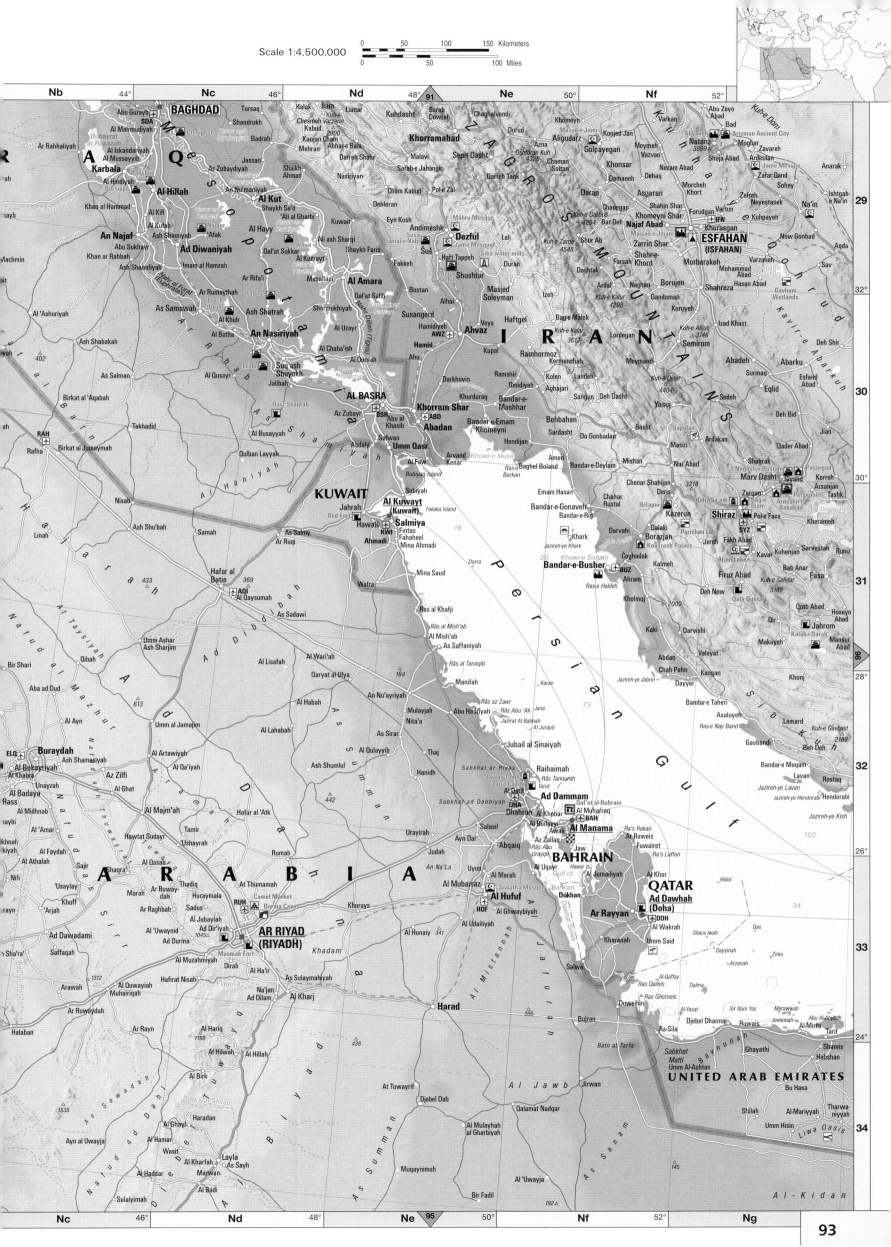

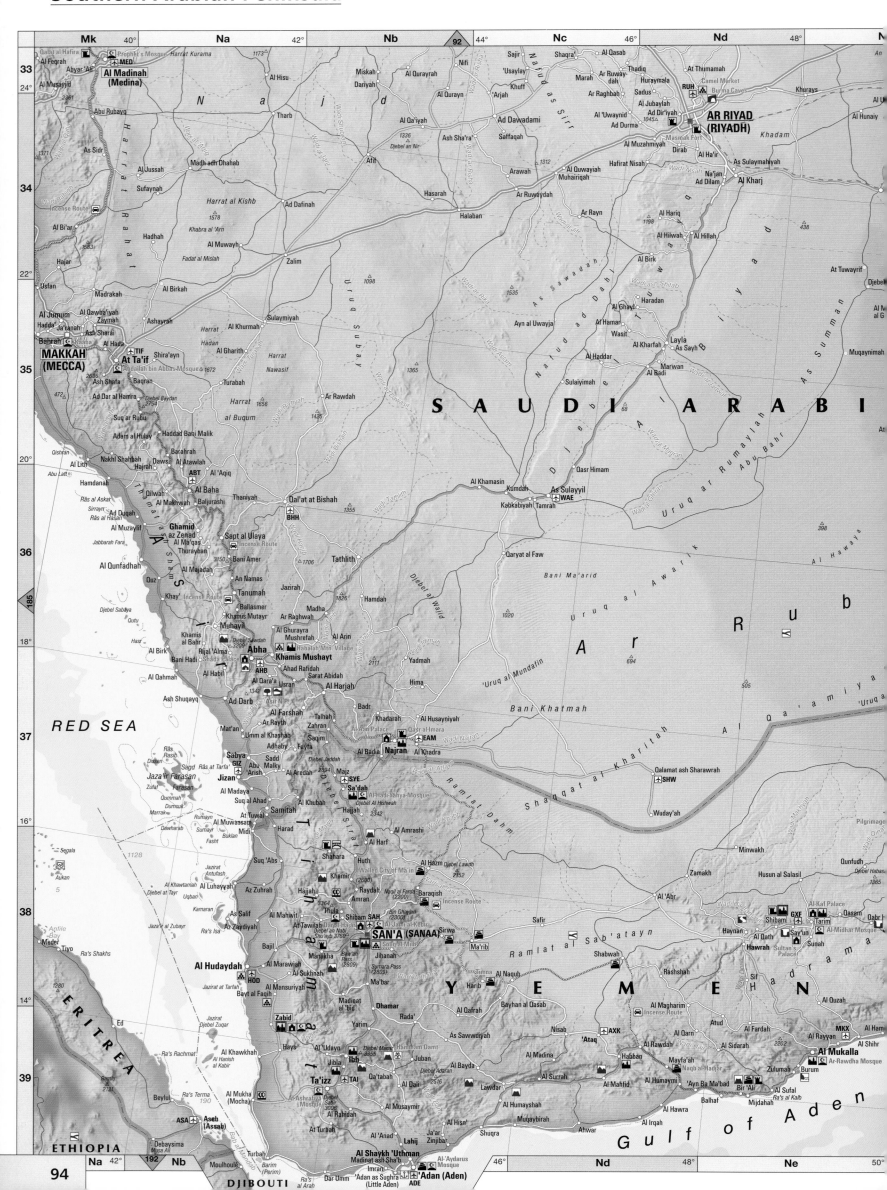

Southern Arabian Peninsula

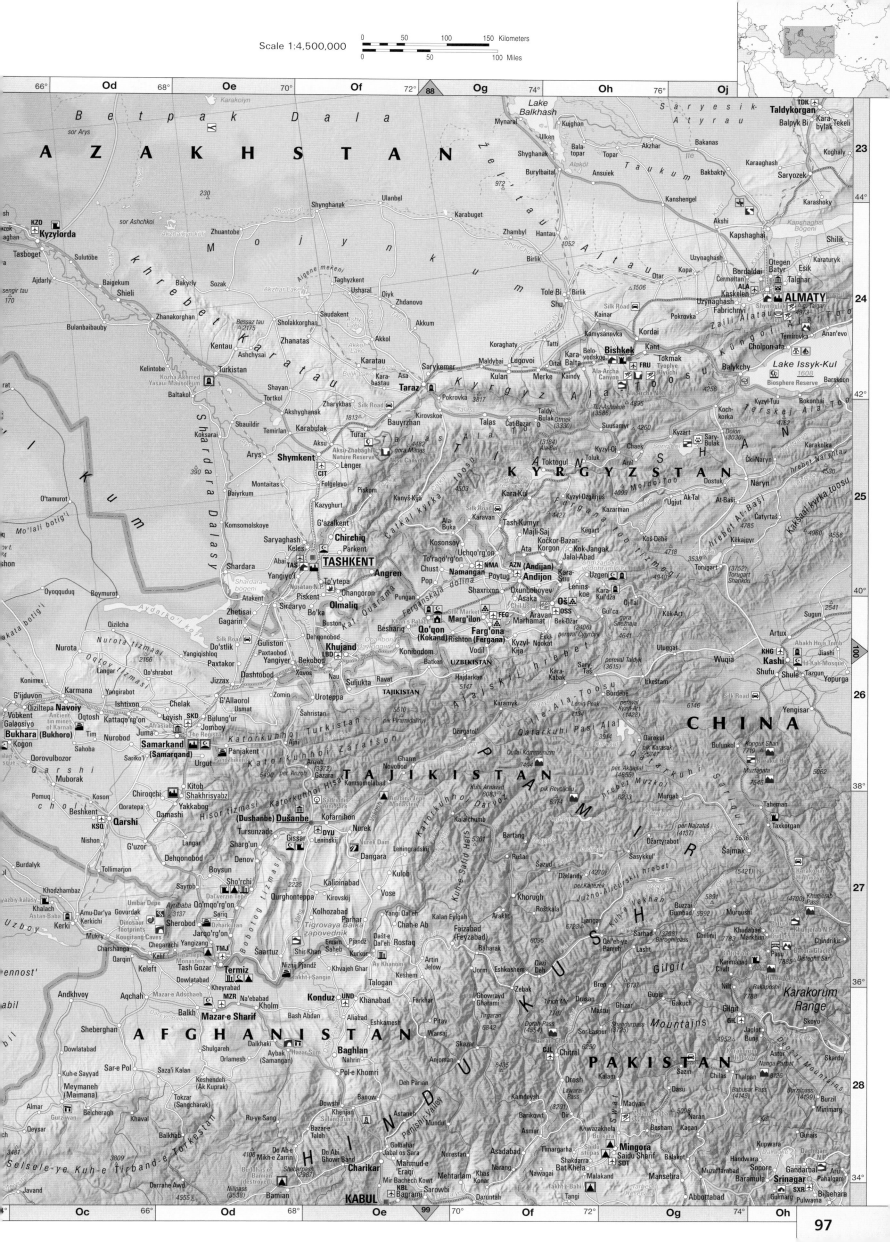

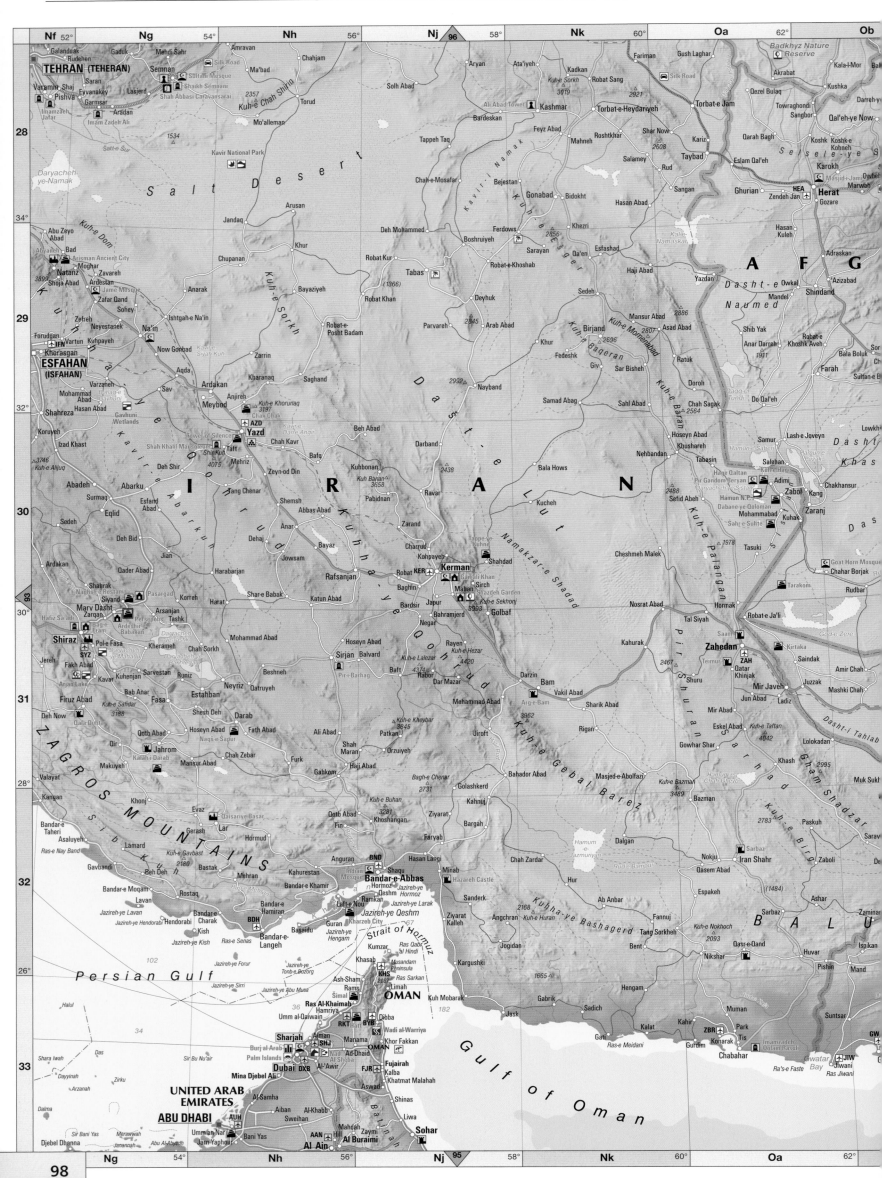

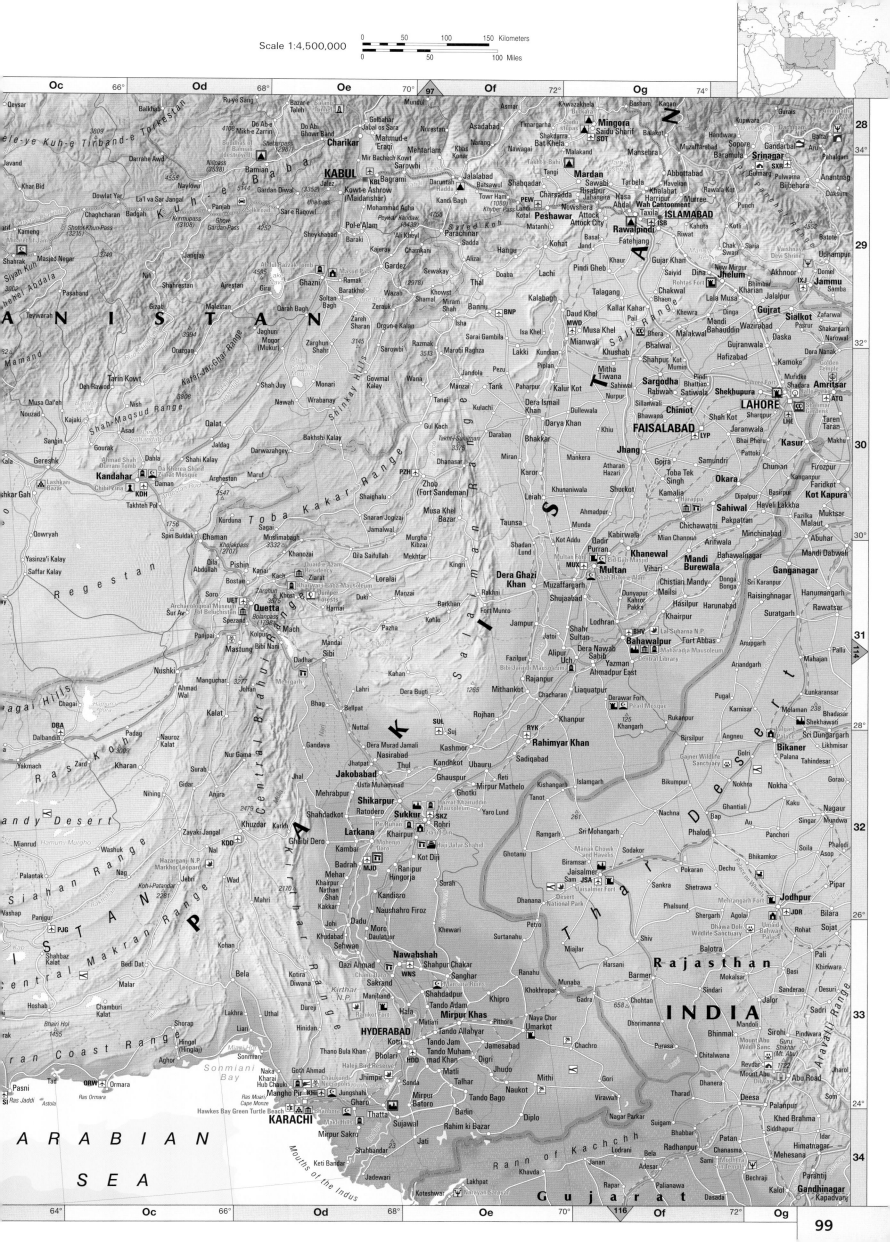

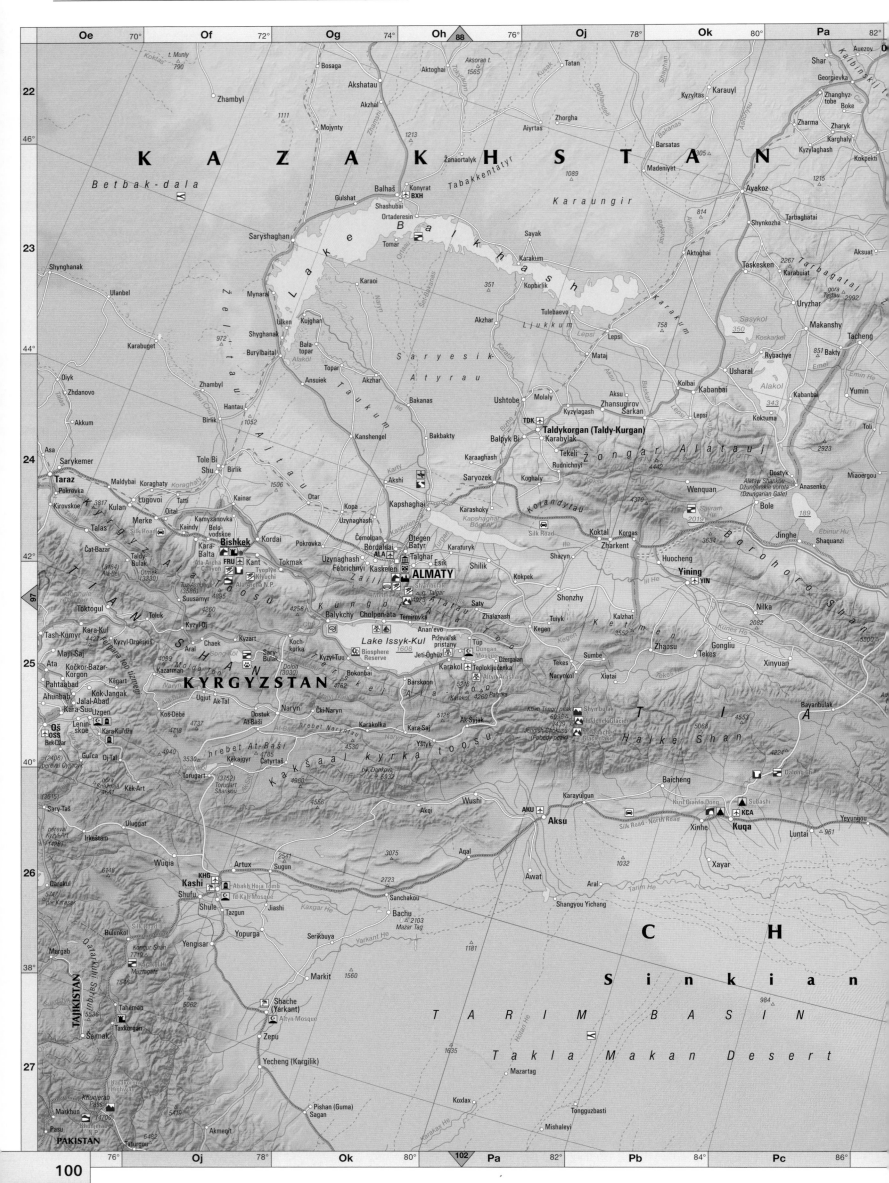

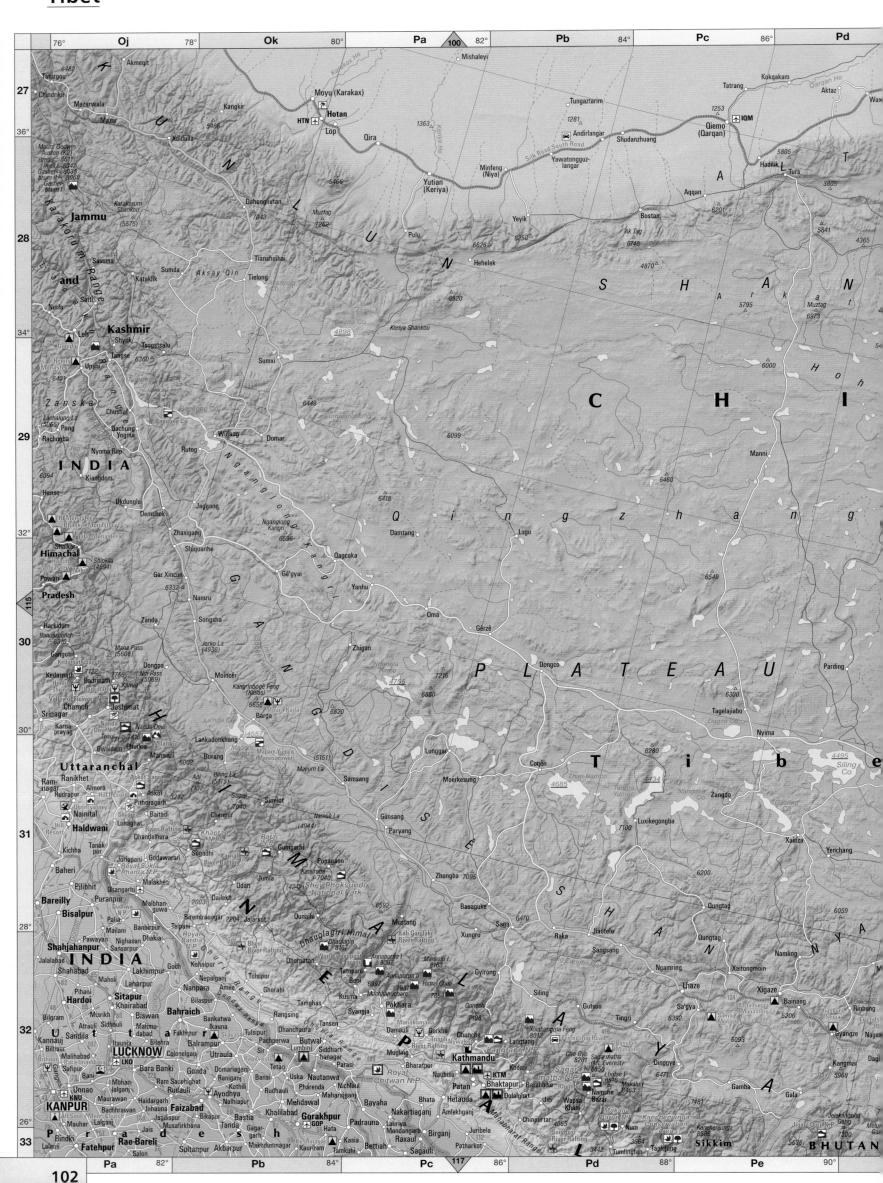

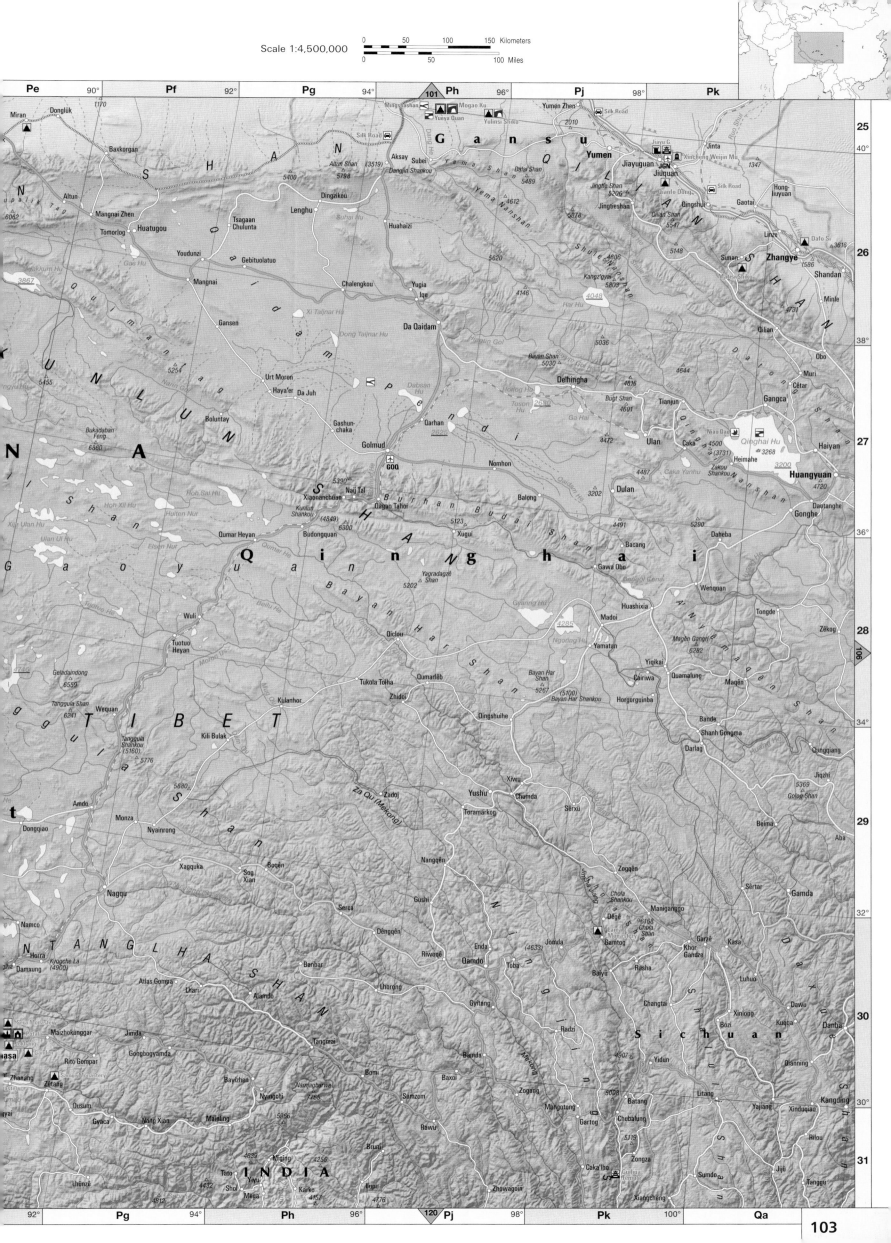

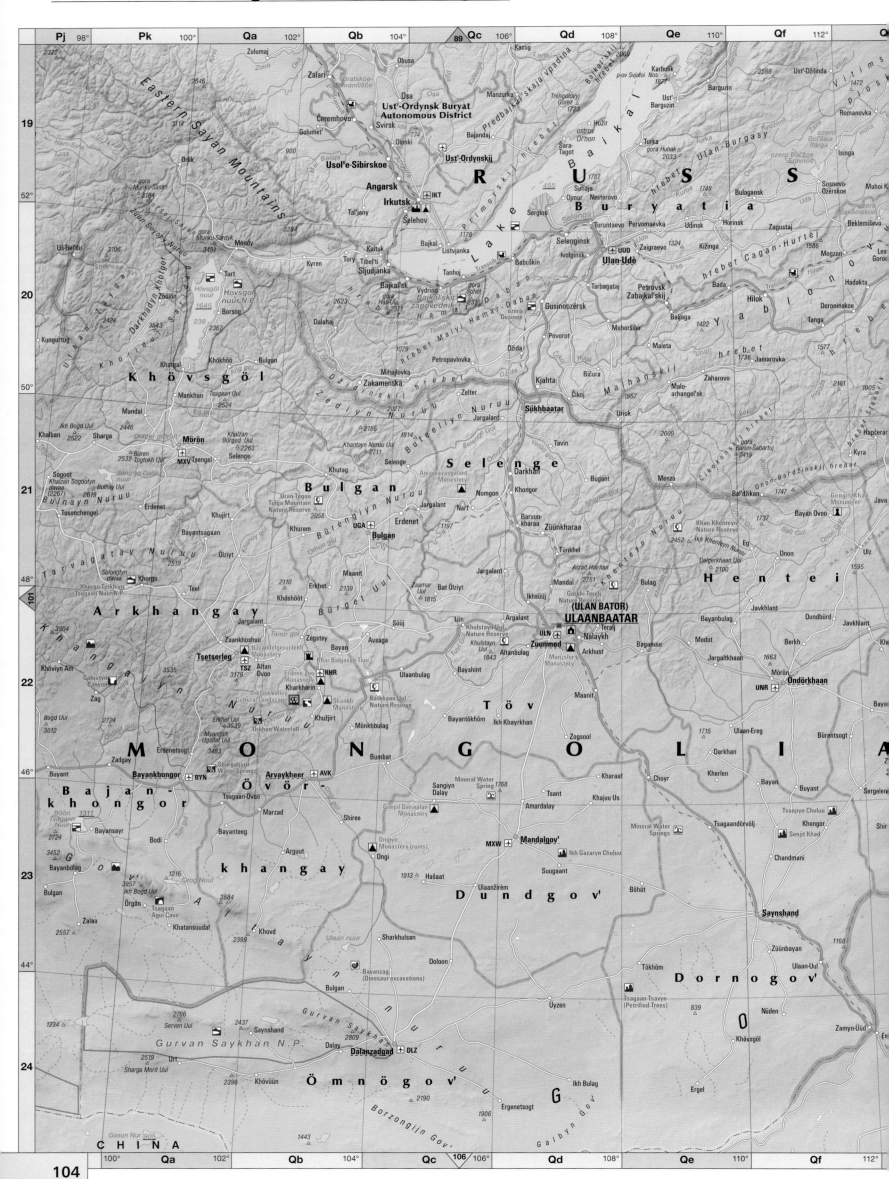

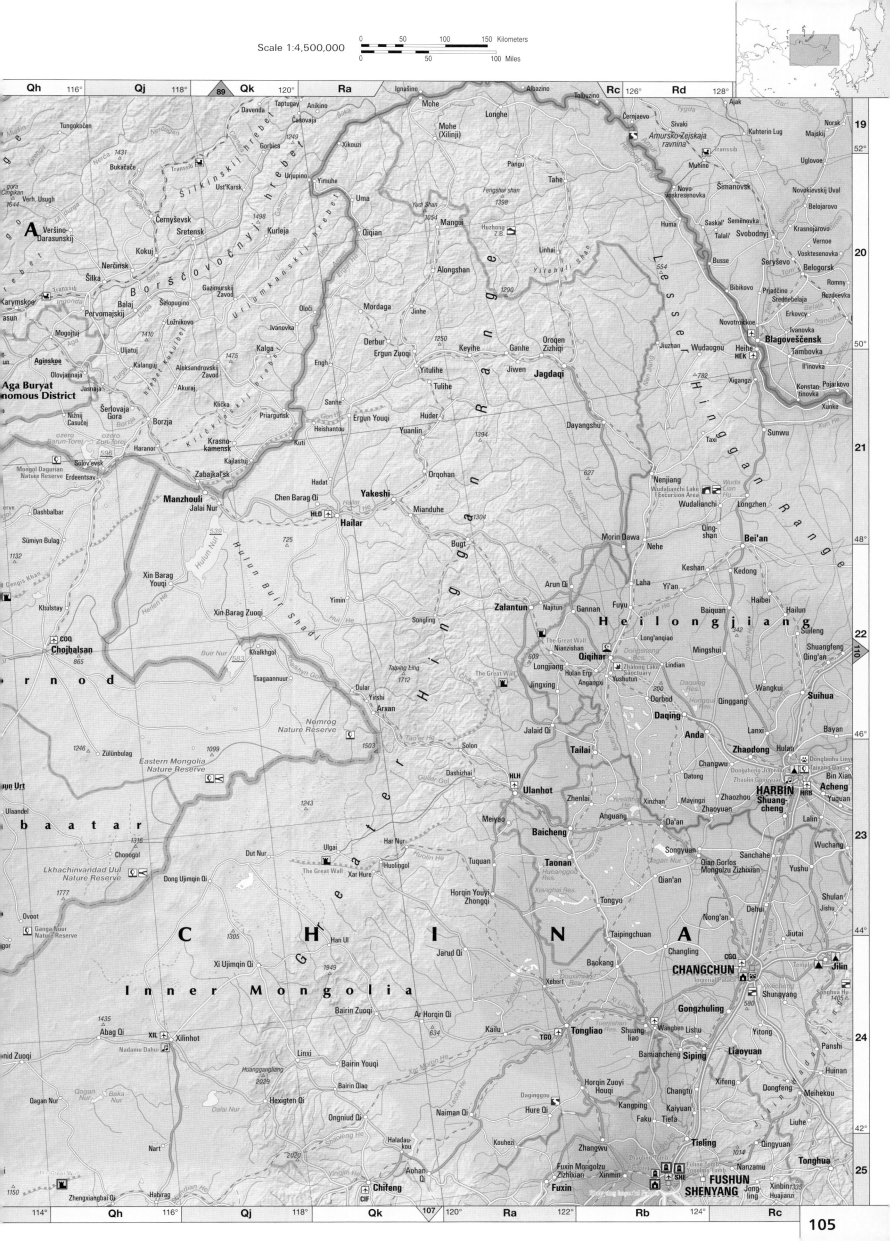

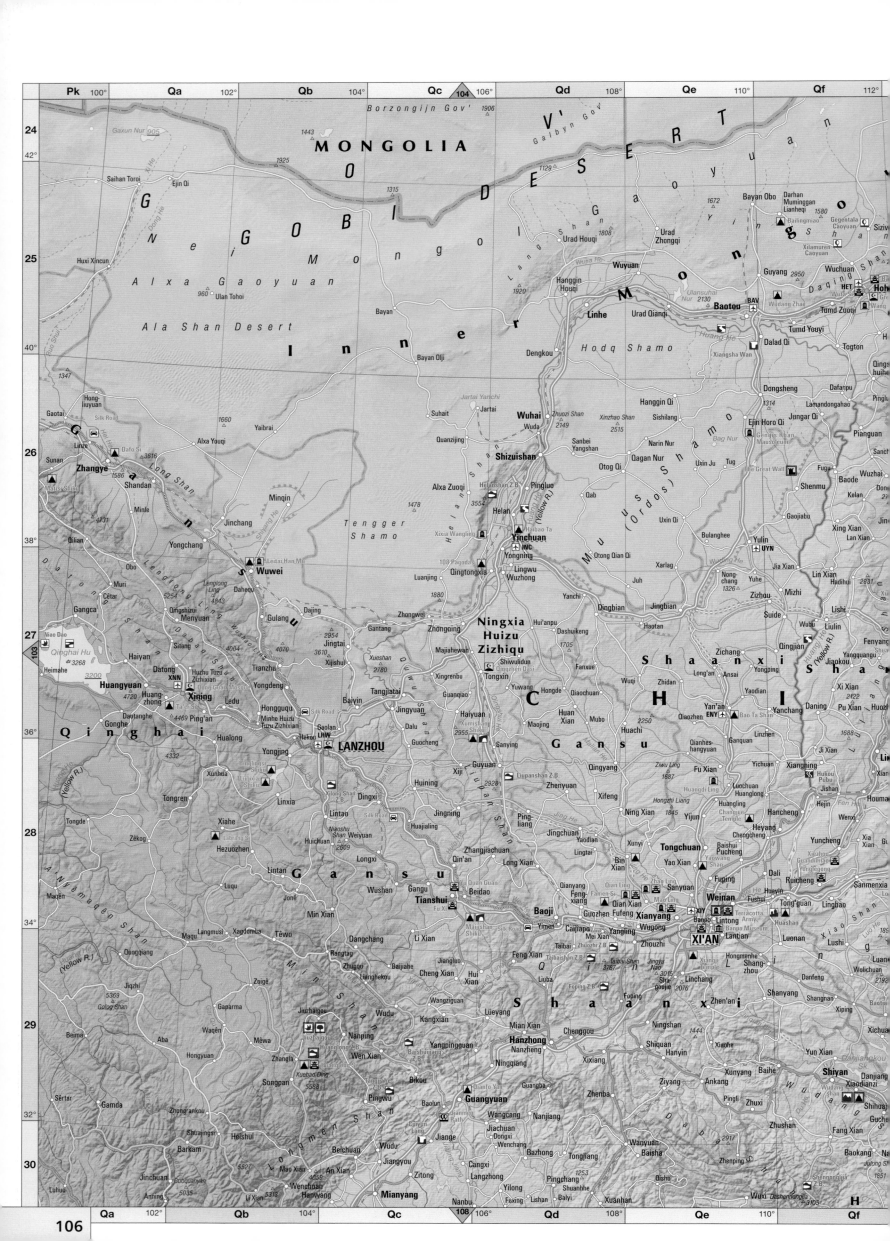

Scale 1:4,500,000

0 50 100 150 Kilometers
0 50 100 Miles

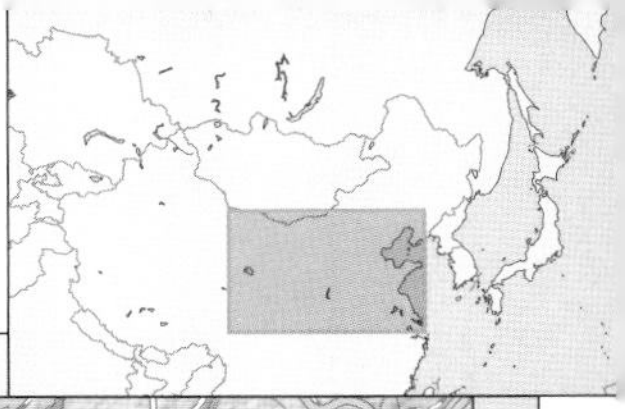

The Great Wall

BEIJING · Beijing Shi · PEK

TIANJIN · Tianjin Shi · TSN

Hebei

Shanxi (A)

Datong · Zhangjiakou · Xuanhua · Chengde · Baoding · Shijiazhuang · Xingtai · Handan · Anyang · Hebi

Liaoning

SHENYANG · **FUSHUN** · **ANSHAN** · Liaoyang · Benxi · Fengcheng · Dandong · Sinuiju · DDG

Fuxin · Beipiao · Chaoyang · Jinzhou · Jinxi · Panjin · Yingkou · Haicheng · Wafangdian · Lüshun (Port Arthur)

DALIAN (LÜDA) · DLC

Gulf of Liaotung · Bo Hai · Bohai Wan · Bohai Haixia

NORTH KOREA · Nampo · Korea Bay

Yellow Sea

Shandong

JINAN · **ZIBO** · **QINGDAO (TSINGTAU)** · TAO · Weifang · WEF · Yantai · YNT · Weihai · Dongying · Tai'an · Laiwu · Zaozhuang · Linyi

Shandong Peninsula · Laizhou Wan · Penglai · Longkou

North China Plain · Yellow River (Huanghe Kou)

Henan

ZHENGZHOU · CGO · Kaifeng · Luohe · Xuchang · Pingdingshan · Xinxiang · Jiaozuo · Nanyang · Zhumadian · Xinyang · Shangqiu · Zhoukou

Jiangsu

NANJING · NKG · Xuzhou · XUZ · Huaiyin · Huai'an · Yancheng · Yangzhou · Zhenjiang · Nantong · Lianyungang · Suqian · Taizhou · Rugao

SHANGHAI · Shanghai Shi · SHA · PVG · Suzhou · SZV · Wuxi · WUX · Changzhou · Taicang · Baoshan · Jiaxing · Huzhou

Anhui

HEFEI · HFE · **HUAINAN** · Bengbu · Wuhu · WHU · Ma'anshan · Chaohu · Lu'an · Bozhou · Fuyang · FUG · Chuzhou

Tai Hu · Hongze Hu · Chao Hu

Yangtze (Changjiang Kou) · Dong Hai Bridge · Shanghai Deepwater Port

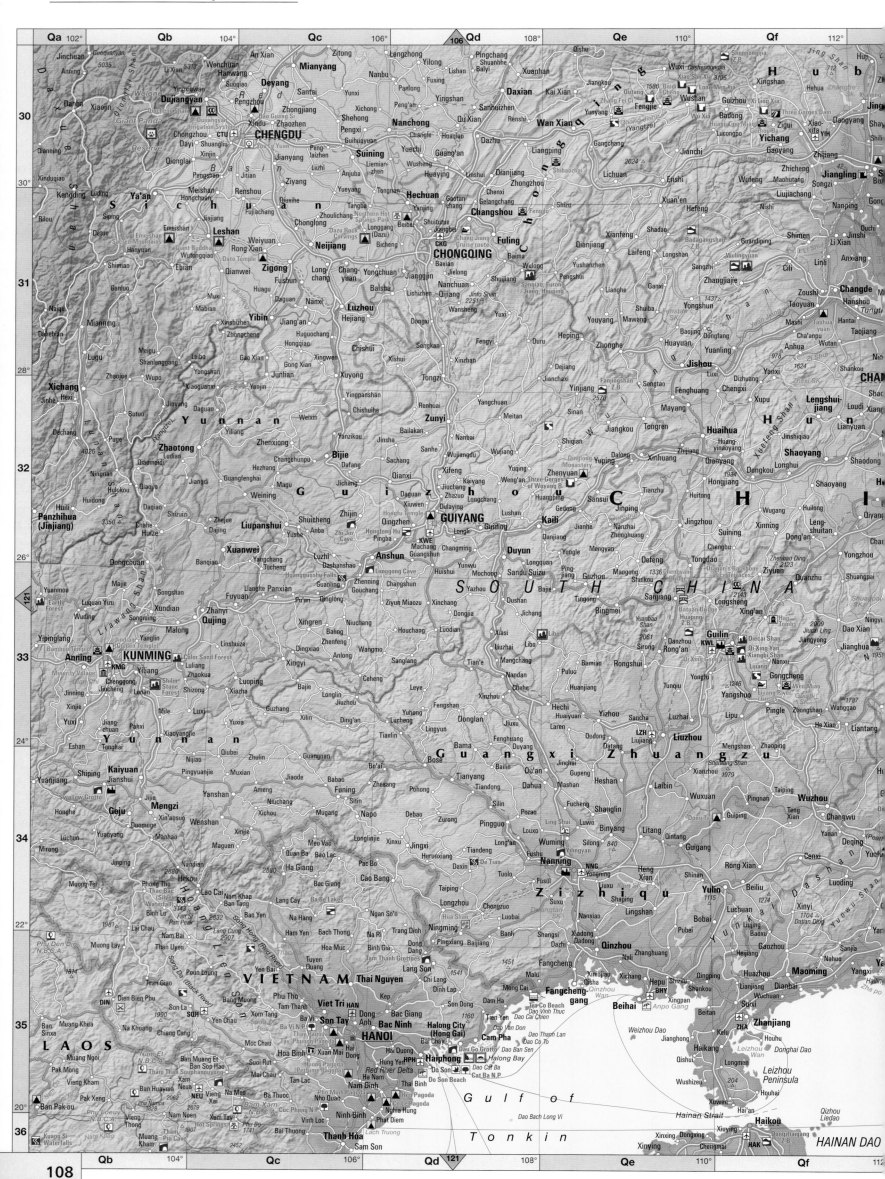

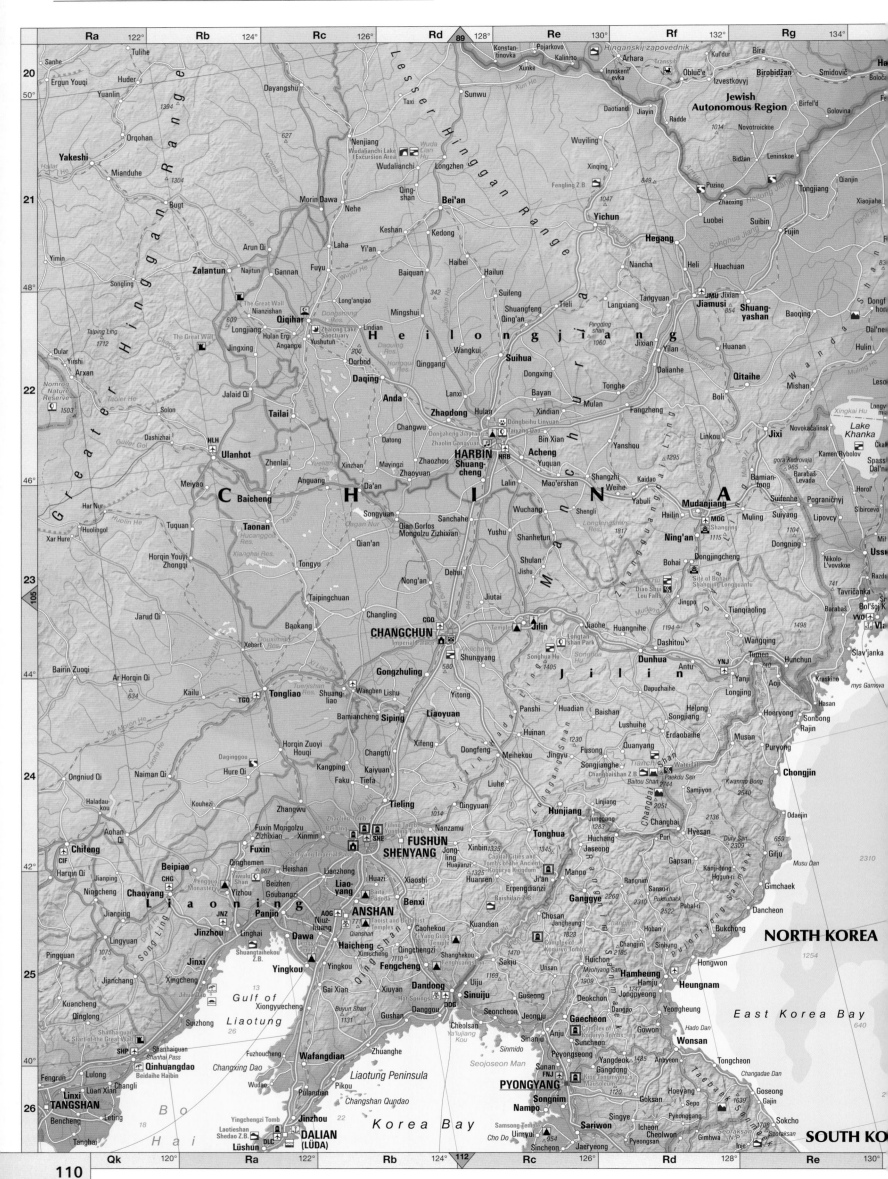

Scale bar: 0 50 100 150 Kilometers
0 50 100 Miles

| Rj 138° | Rk 140° | Sa 142° | Sb 144° | Sc 146° | Sd |

RUSSIA

Sichote Alin'

-Volkonskoe
Nel'ma
Gvasjugi
Samarga
gora Ko 2004
a
Sjain
Svetlaja
Svetlovodnaja
Ust'-Sobolevka
Vostok 1505
Amgu
Velikaja Kema
1745
Ternej 1595
tnoe
vopokrovka
2028
Dal'negorsk
1483
Rudnaja Pristan'
Plastun
Kavalerovo
amensk
Ubovka
1855 gora Oblačnaja
Gornovodnoe
Ol'ga
1380 gora Cernaja
Lazo
Valentin
ansk
povednyj
dka

Sakhalin

Južno-Sahalinsk
UUS
Ožidaevo 1047
Holmsk
Dal'nee Čaplanovo
Anviva
Ozerskij
Ohotskoe
zaliv Mordvinova
Jasnomorskij
Gornozavodsk
Nevel'sk
Šebunino
588
Korsakow
Brjanskoe
Novikovo
zaliv Aniva
670
Kirillovo
Hvostovo
mys Aniva
o. Moneron 439
Kuznecovo 452
Atlasovo
mys Kril'on

Kuril Islands

gora Kamuj 1322
Slavnoe zaliv Prostor
Kuril'sk
Rejdovo
Pioner
o. Iturup
Burevestnik
gora Stokan 1634
Lesozavodskij
mys Lovcova
mys Rikorda
proliv Ekaterinay
vlk. Tjatja 1819
Tjatino
Nemuro-kaikyo Kunaširskij proliv
Kunašir
Južno-Kuril'sk
Serno-vodsk
Golovnino
ozero Šikotan 412
Malokuril'skoe
ozero Zelenyj 880
Malaja Kuril'skaja grjada
proliv Spanberga

La Perouse Strait
Soya-misaki 87
Wakkanai
113
Rebun-to
Funadomari
RBJ
Rishirifuji
Reburi
Rishiri
Rishiri-to 1729
RIS N.P.
Rishiri-Rebun-Sarobetsu N.P.
505
Sarufutsu
Hama-Tombetsu
WKJ 427
Naku-Tombetsu
Esashi
Omu
Mombetsu 93
Okoppe
Nishi Okoppe
Takinoue
MBE
Saroma
Tokoro
Saroma-ko
Abashiri
Shari
Shiretoko-misaki
Shiretoko-hanto
Rausu 1661
Shiretoko N.P.
Noseppu-misaki
Nemuro-hanto
Nemuro
Kiritappu
Akkeshi
Attoko
Naka-Shibetsu
SHB
Shibetsu
Shibecha
Teshikaga
Kawayu
Bihoro
Kitami
Rubeshibe
Akankoshan
Akan N.P.
Meakan-dake 1499
Tsurui
Kushiro-Shitsugen N.P.
Kushiro
KUH
Kushiro-cho
Shiranuka

Otoineppu
Nakagawa
Toyotomi
390
Teuri-to
Jagishiri-to
Haboro
Embetsu 99
Bifuka
Nayoro
Shibetsu
Kamikawa
Aibetsu
Asahi-dake 2290
Asahikawa
Numata
AKJ
Bei 2077
Daisetsuzan N.P.
Tokachi-dake
Kami Shihoro
Ashoro
Rikubetsu
1009
Wassamu
316
Rumoi
Mashike
Fukagawa
Takikawa
802
Hamamasu
Ashibetsu
Furano
Hombetsu
Ikeda
Obihiro
OBO
Urahoro

HOKKAIDO

1293
123
Kitami-Yamato-tai

Atsuta
Ishikari
Bibai
Mikasa
Iwamizawa
Yubari
Shimizu
Hidaka
Biratori
160
Hidaka-sammyaku

Niseko Shakotan Otaru-kaigan Q.N.P.
Furubira
Otaru
Ishikari-santi
Shimizu
Hiro
Hiroo
Erimo-misaki

Yoichi 1298
1021
SPK/CTS
Hiroshima
Yubetsu-dake 1893
Eniwa
SAPPORO
Chitose
Syakotan-hanto
Iwanai
Rakonshi
Shikotsu Toya N.P.
Yotei-zan 1893
Tomakomai
Suttsu
Kuromatsunai
Date
Shiraoi
Shizunai
Urakawa
Noboribetsu
Karumae-zan
Oshamambe
Mombetsu
Kuromatsunai
Kariba-y. 1520
Mitsuishi
Imakane
Yakumo
Hitahiyamam
Mori
Onuma Q.N.P.
Shikabe
Minamikayabe
Kunni
Muroran
85

Okushiri
Kumashi
Nanae
Kamiiso
Esan
Okushiri-to 585
OIR
HKD
Kaminokuni
Hakodate
Esashi
Kikonai 1072
Oma-saki
Shirya-saki
Kaminokuni
Oma
Mutsu
Shimokita
Shimokita Q.N.P. hanto
Daisengendake
Fukushima
Sai
Kawauchi
Matsumae 714
Minmaya
Yokohama
Seikan Tunnel
Wakino-sawa
Mutsu-wan
Rokkasho
Tsugaru Q.N.P.
Kanita
Hiranai
Noheji
Misawa
Tsugaru Strait
Shiura
Nakasato
Sichinoe
MSJ
Aomori
AOJ
Towada
Hachinohe
Goshogawara
Namioka
Genohe
Ajigasawa
Sannohe
Kuji
Hirosaki
Noda
Shirakami Sanchi
Towada-Hachimantai N.P.
Ninohe
Henasi-saki
Shirakami-dake 1235
Odate
Ashiro
Iwaizumi
Kyuroku-jima
Kazuno
Kuzumaki
Noshiro
Kazuno
Miyako
Toda-saki
Towada-Hachimantai N.P.
2041
Iwate-san
Nyudo-saki
Oga-hanto
Kakunodate
Morioka
Yamada
Rikuchu-Kaigan N.P.
Oga Q.N.P.
1914
Fukuroji-ji
Kamaishi
Akita
AXT
Hanamaki
Tono
Samurai Houses
Omagari
Kitakami
Ofunato
Honjo
Yokote
Mizusawa
Kesennuma
Yuzawa
Ichinoseki
Chokai Q.N.P.
Chokai-san 2230
Kurikoma Q.N.P.
1628
Tojima
Hasama
Sakata
Shinjo
Furukawa
Ishinomaki
Tsuruoka
Obanazawa
Izumi
Kinkasan-jima
Shiogama
Bandai-Asahi N.P.
Tendo
Sendai
SDJ
Sendai-wan
JAPAN
Yamagata
Iwanuma
Sanpoku
Zao Q.N.P.
1841 Zao-san
Shiroishi
Awa-jima
Murakami
Nan-yo
Soma
Yone-zawa
Bandai-asahi N.P.
Fukushima
Haramachi
Arakawa
Azuma-san
KIJ
Shibata
2024
Namie
Iide-san 2105
Koriyama
Niigata
SDO
Ryotsu
Nitsu
Aizu-Wakamatsu
Iwaki
Aikawa
Sukagawa
Akadomari
Ogi
1173
Sado-jima
Sado Yahiko Q.N.P.
Teradomari
Sanjo
Tajima
Shirakawa
Yamatsuri
Nagaoka
Echigo-Sanzan-Tadami Q.N.P.
1917
Kitaibaraki
Hegura-jima
Ojiya
Nikko N.P.
Hitachi
Kashiwazaki
Tokamachi
2578
Imaichi
Kuroiso
Suzu-misaki
Joetsu
Nikko
Utsunomiya
Noto-hanto
Sozu
Kubiki Tunnel
Moka
Katsuta
Wajima 567
Arai
2578 Shirane-san
Oya Kannon
Shimodate
Mito
Noto-jima
Toyama
Itoigawa
Joshin Etsu Kogen N.P.
Ashikaga
Togi
Nanao Asahi
Tateyama
Numata
Kiryu
Oyama
Himi
Noto-kongo Coast
Uozu
Maebashi
Kumagaya
Tsuchiura
Hakui
Toyama
Suzuka
Takasaki
Kawagoe
Kashima
Takaoka
TOY
2-2 yama
Omachi
Ueda
Saku
Chichibu
Kasumigaura
Kanazawa
Tonami
Nagano
Chichibu Tama N.P.
Kashiwa
Matto
MMJ
Matsumoto
Chubu Sangaku N.P.
Komoro
TYO/NRT
Tsubata
Hotaka-dake 3015
Tomioka
Tokyo Disneyland
Tsuruoka
Hakusan N.P.
TOKYO
Chiba
Narita
Inubo-saki
Kujukuri-nada
Sawara
Choshi

PACIFIC OCEAN

Sea of Japan

Yamato Rise

Western Sea

HONSHU

Erimo Seamount 3735
Erimo-misaki

Depth/elevation numbers: 1035, 1260, 1740, 2028, 2152, 3669, 3484, 3400, 1600, 3699, 1788, 842, 485, 3039, 1521, 1298, 238, 120, 3063, 366, 259, 1084, 3127, 802, 1021, 3282, 1865, 3022, 7292, 2565, 1230, 2185, 7520, 2179, 7916, 8410, 3600, 8540

| 132° | Rg | 134° | Rh | 136° | Rj | 138° | Rk | 140° | Sa |

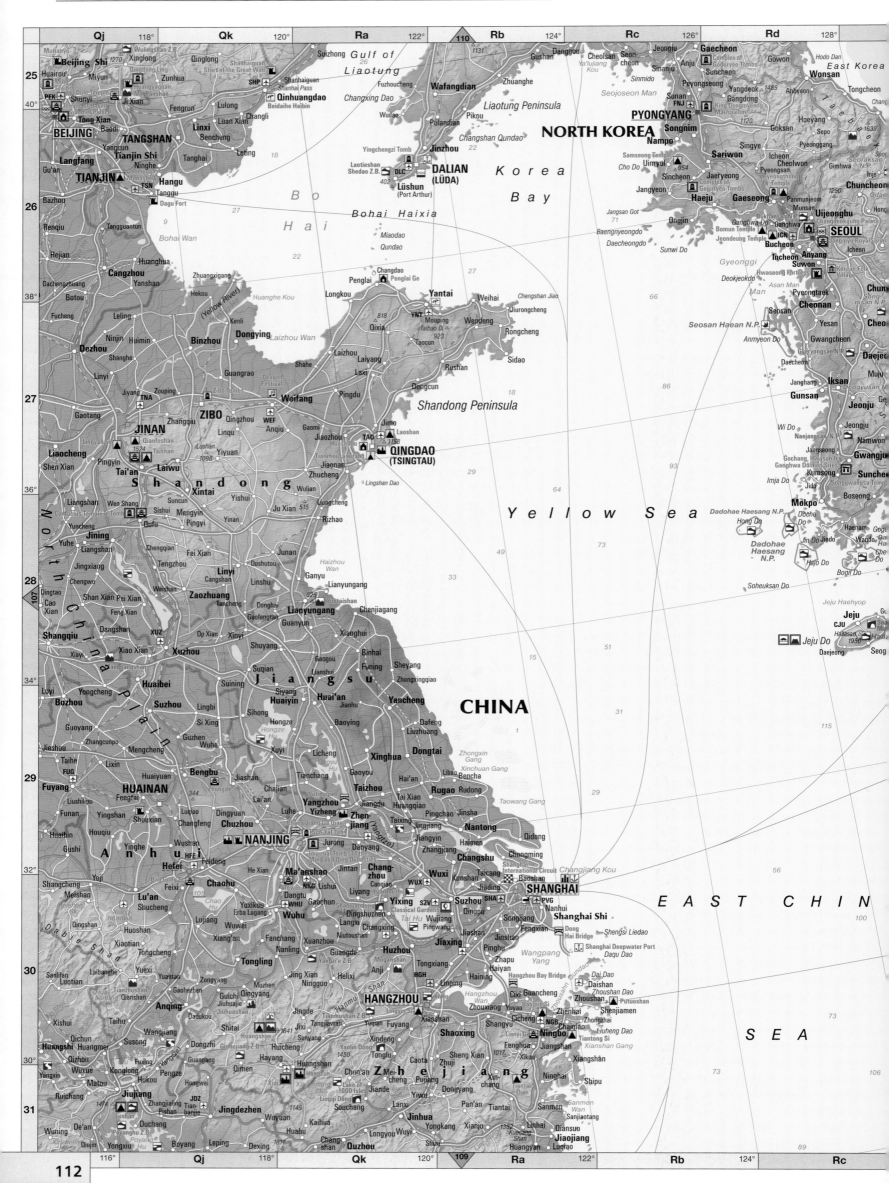

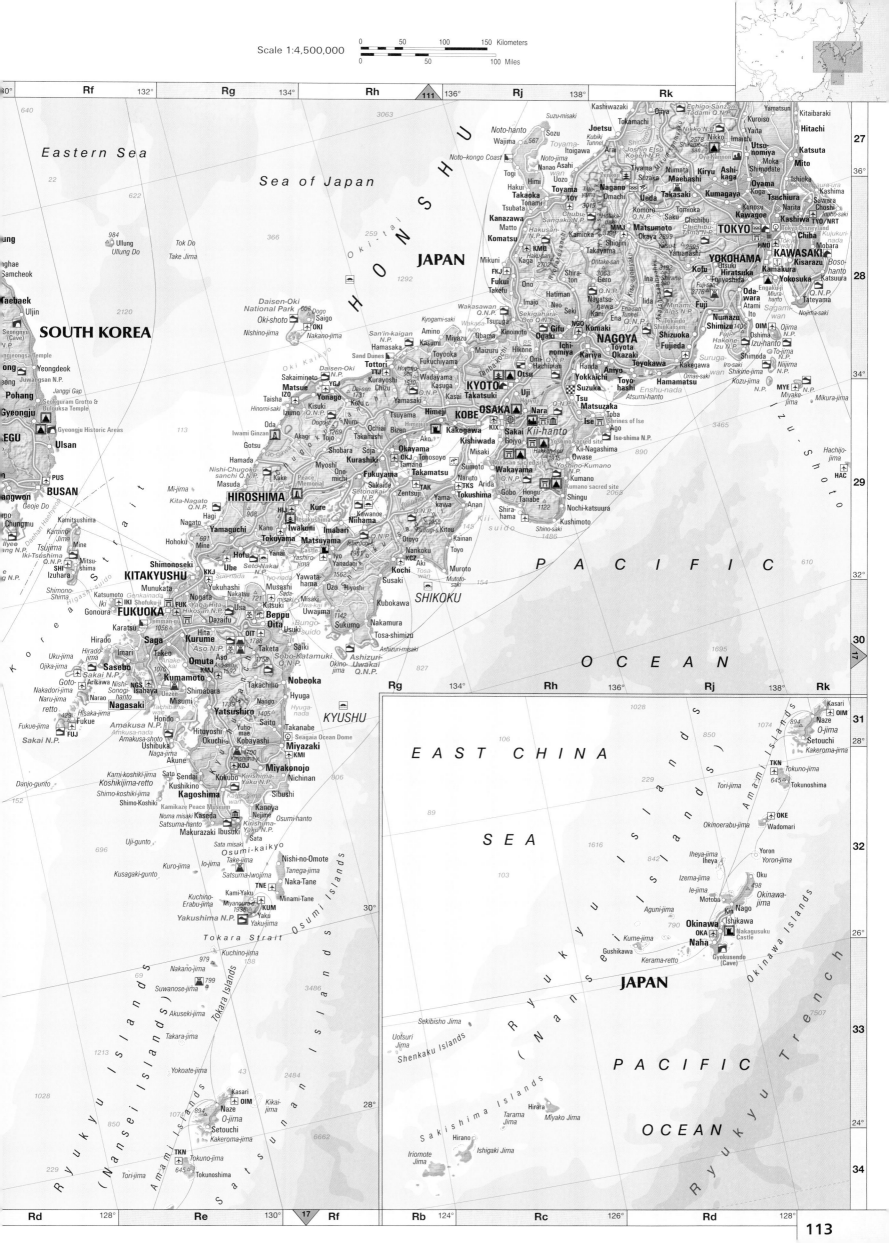

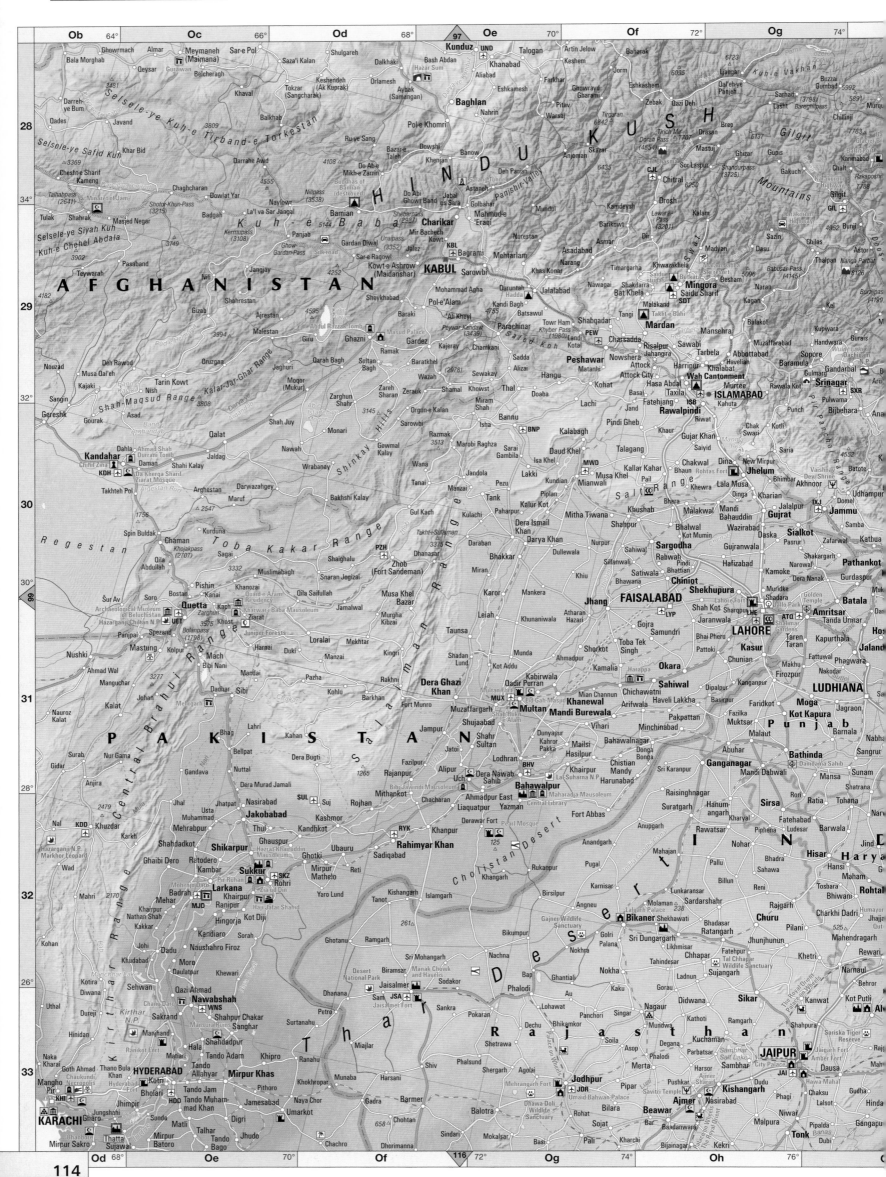

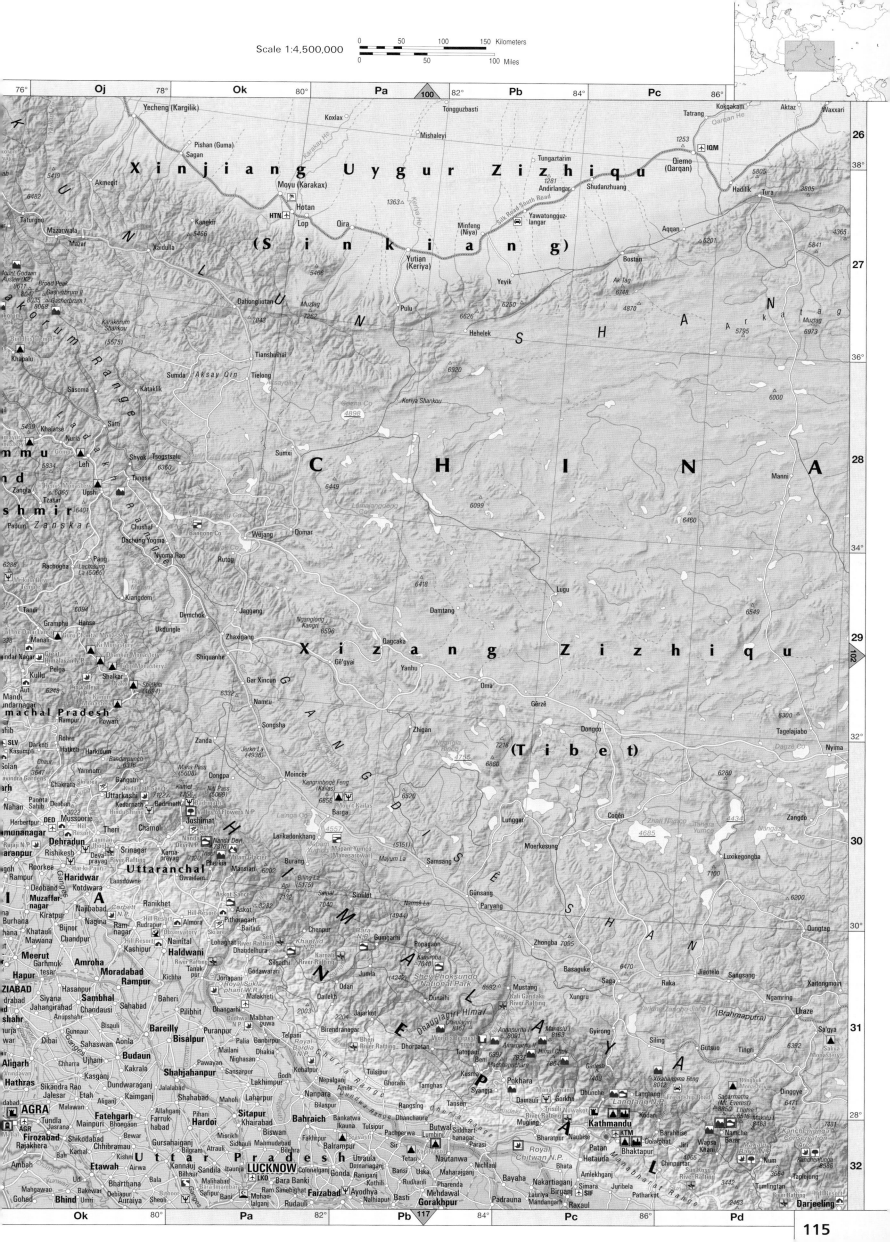

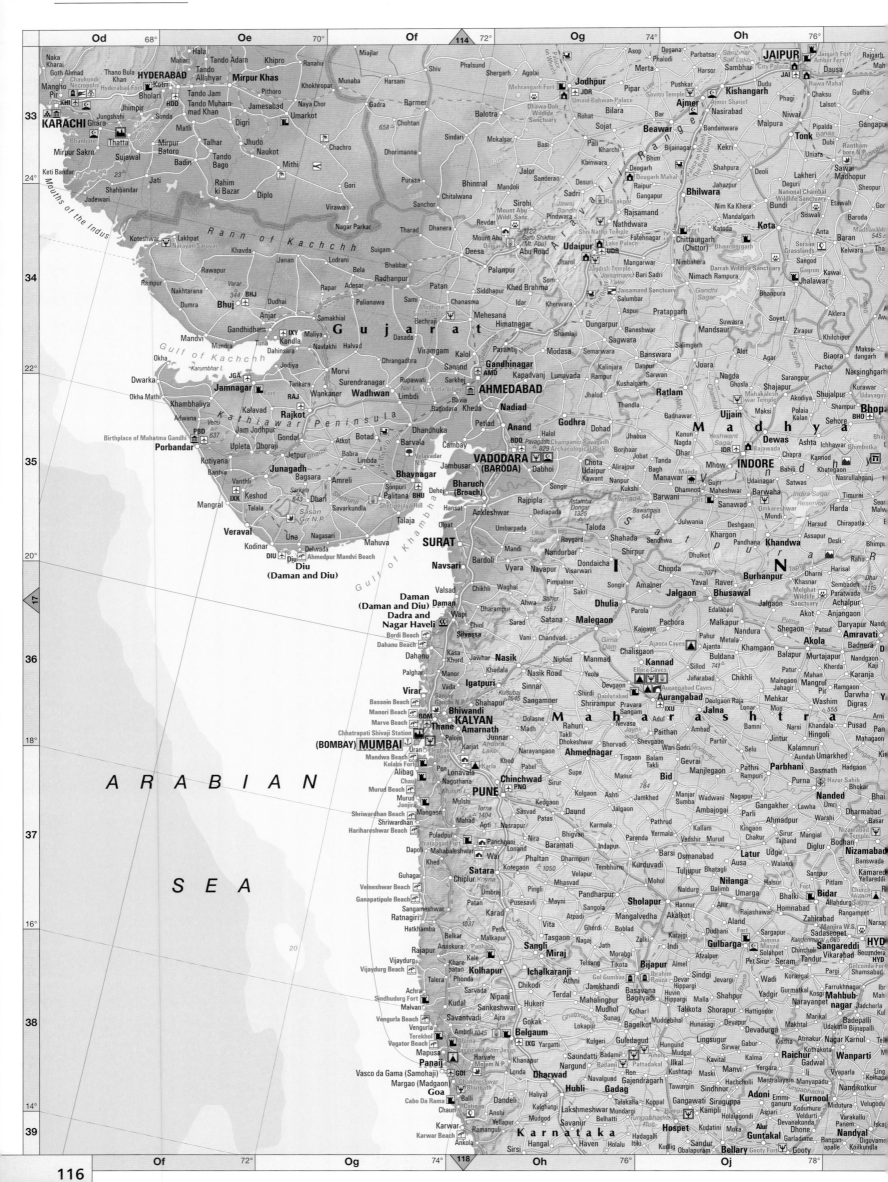

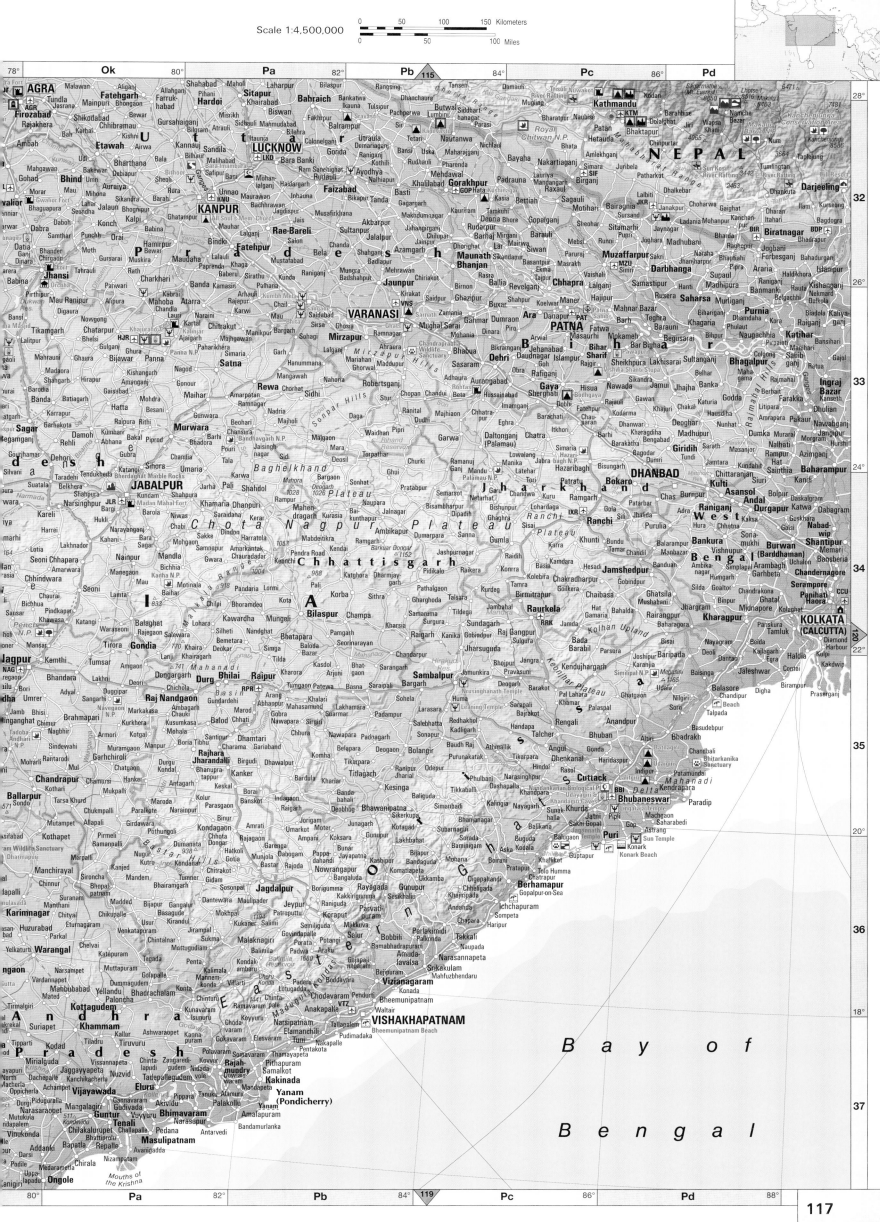

Southern India, Maldives, Sri Lanka

ARABIAN

SEA

Laccadive Islands

Bitra I.

Chetlat I.

Amindivi Islands   Kiltan I.

Perulmar
Par I.   Kadmath I.

Bangaram I.   Amini I.

AGX   Agatti I.

Kavaratti   Andrott I.

Kavaratti I.

Suheli I.

Cannanore Islands   Kalpeni I.

Lakshadweep

Nine Degree Channel

Minicoy I.

Eight Degree Channel   **Lakshadweep**

Sea

Haa-Alifu Atoll
(North Thiladhunmathee Atoll)

Gallandhoo Channel   Dhidhdhoo
Haa-Dhaalu Atoll
(South Thiladhunmathee Atoll)
Makunudu Atoll   Nolhivaranfaru

Shaviyani Atoll
(North Miladhunmadulu Atoll)
Raa Atoll   Farukolhu
(Maalhosmadulu North)
Ugoofaaru   Noonu Atoll
(South Miladhunmadulu Atoll)
Pearl Island   Manadhoo

Neifaru
Moresby Channel   Lhaviyani Atoll
Baa Atoll
(Maalhosmadulu   **MALDIVES**
South)
Eydhafushi   Kaashidhoo
Kardiva Channel
Gaafaru Channel

Tohddoo Atoll   North Male Atoll
Rasdhoo Atoll
Arie Atoll
(Alifu Atoll)   **Male**   MLE

Mahibadhoo   South Male Atoll

Beaches   Scuba diving
Ariadhoo Channel   Felidhoo Channel
Faafu Atoll   Felidhoo Atoll
(North Nilandhoo Atoll)   (Vaavu Atoll)
Magoodhoo   Vaavu Channel
Dhaalu Atoll   Muli
(South Nilandhoo Atoll)   Meemu Atoll
(Mulaku Atoll)
Kudahuvadhoo
Kudahuvadhoo Channel
Thaa Atoll
(Kolhumadulu Atoll)

Veymandhoo

Veymandhoo Channel   Laamu Atoll
(Hadhdhunmathee Atoll)
Hithadhoo

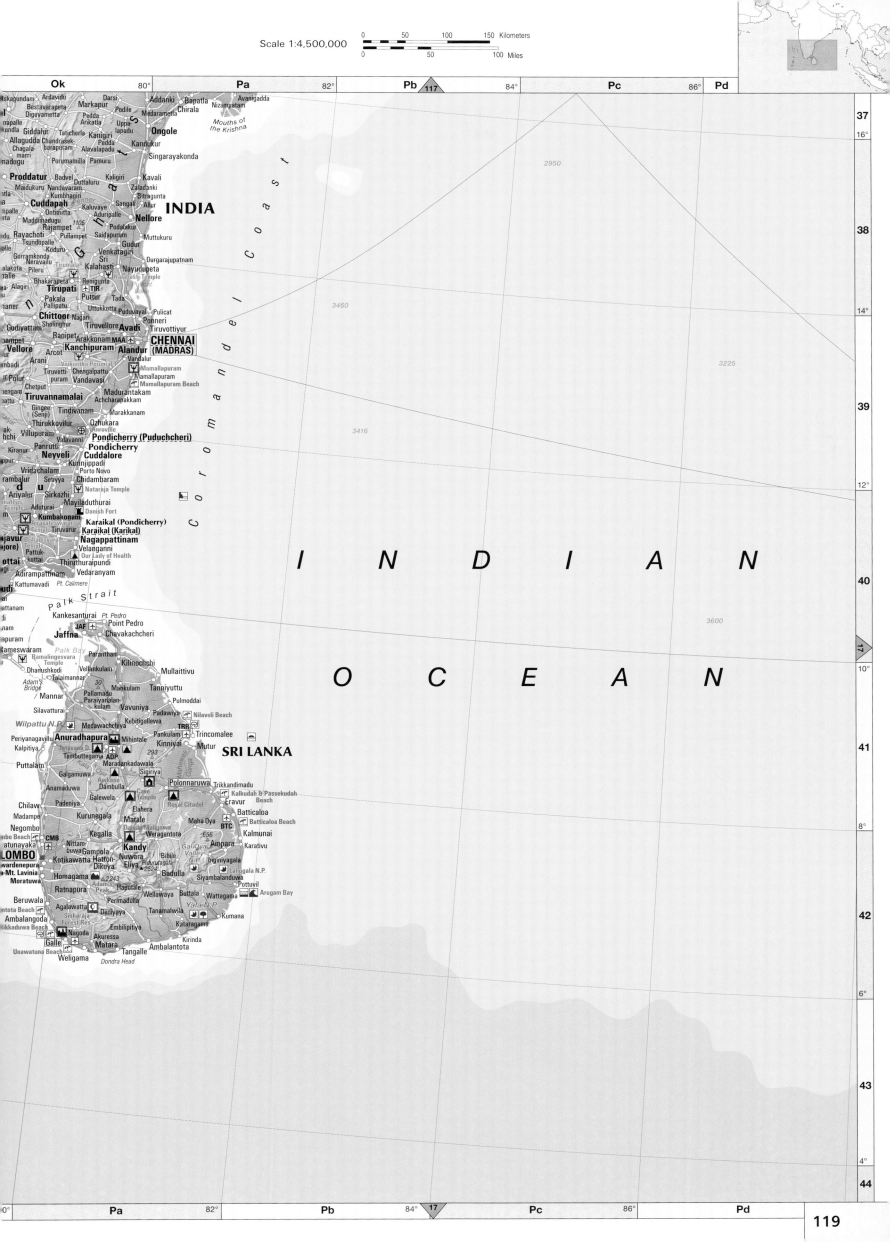

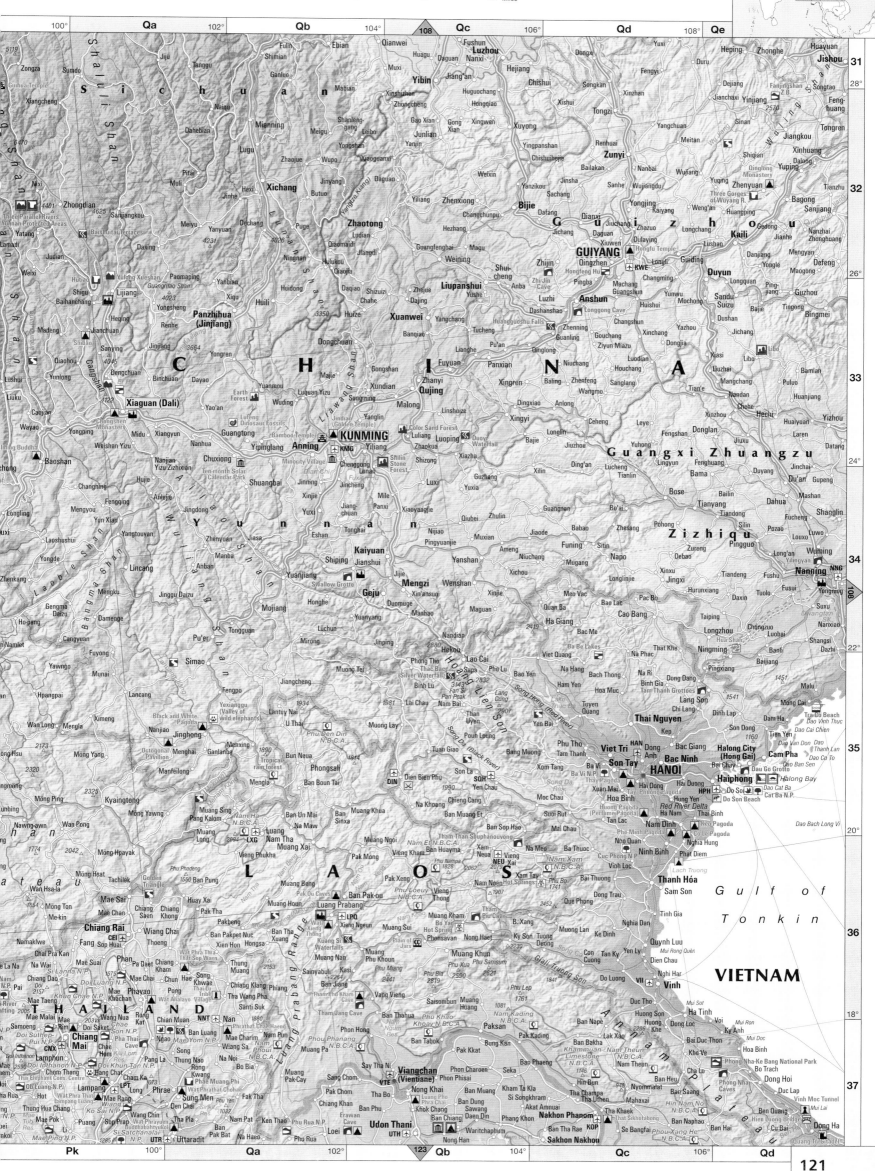

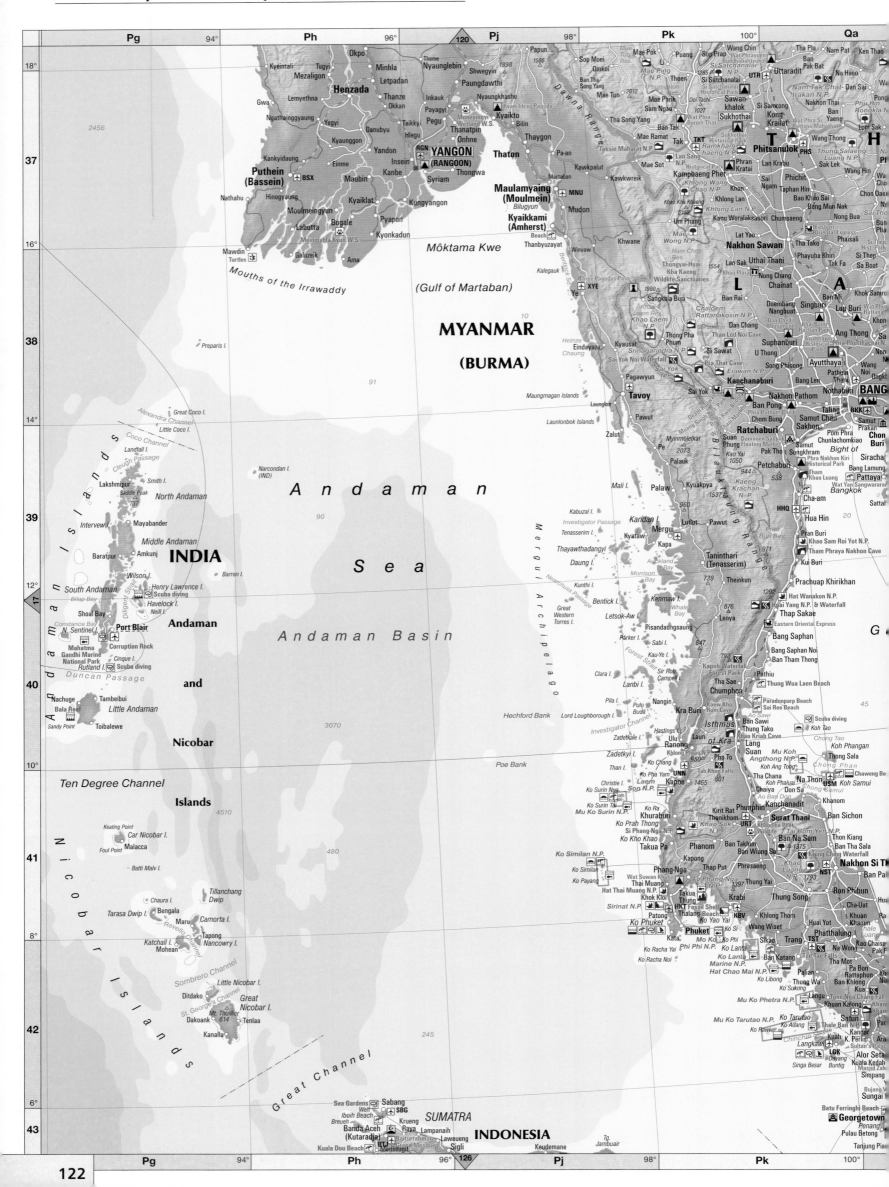

Philippines

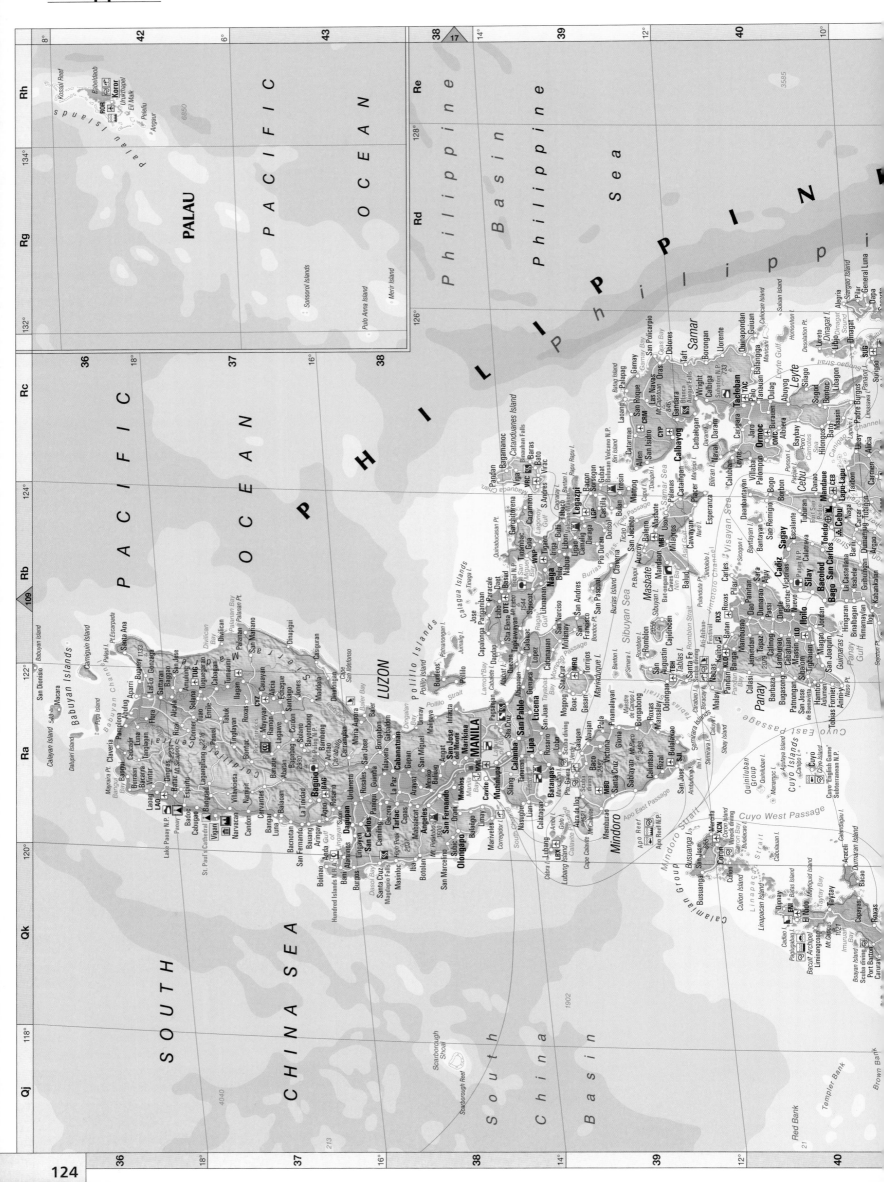

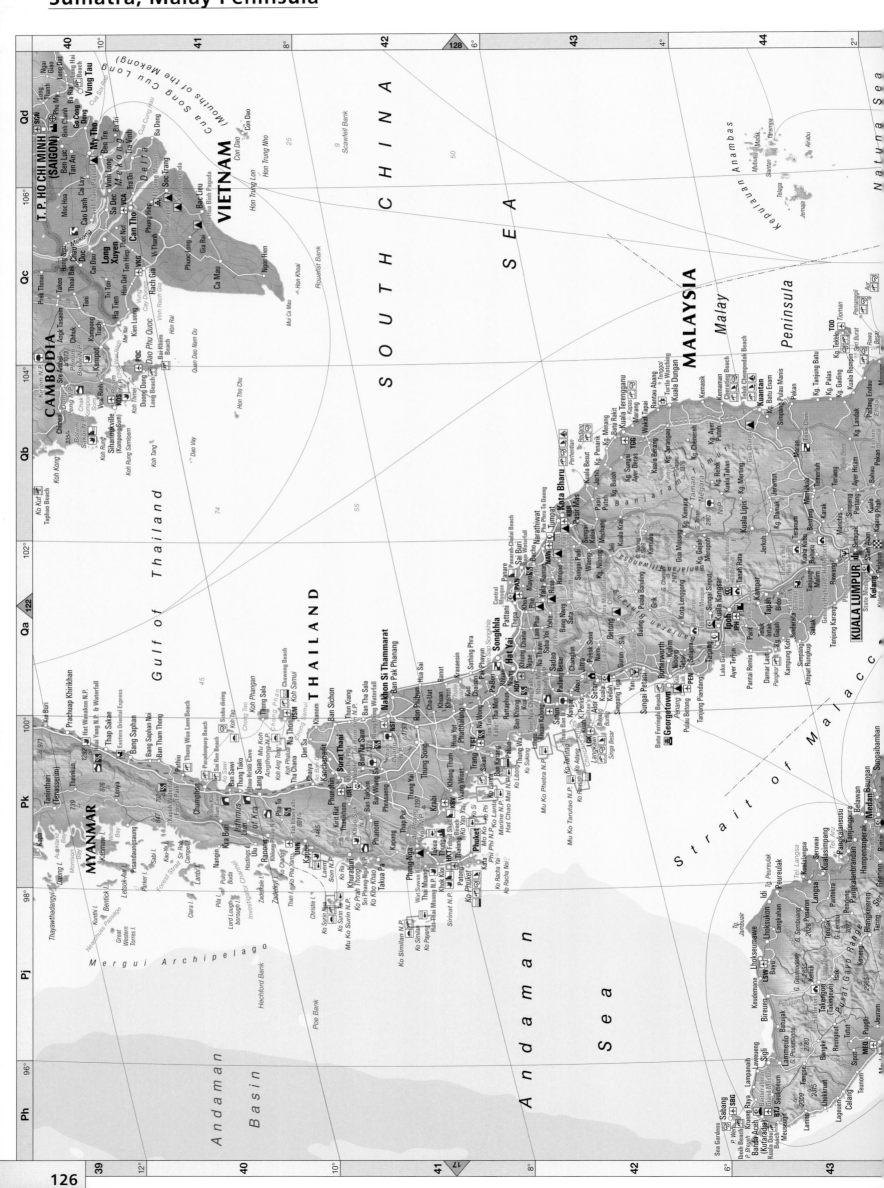

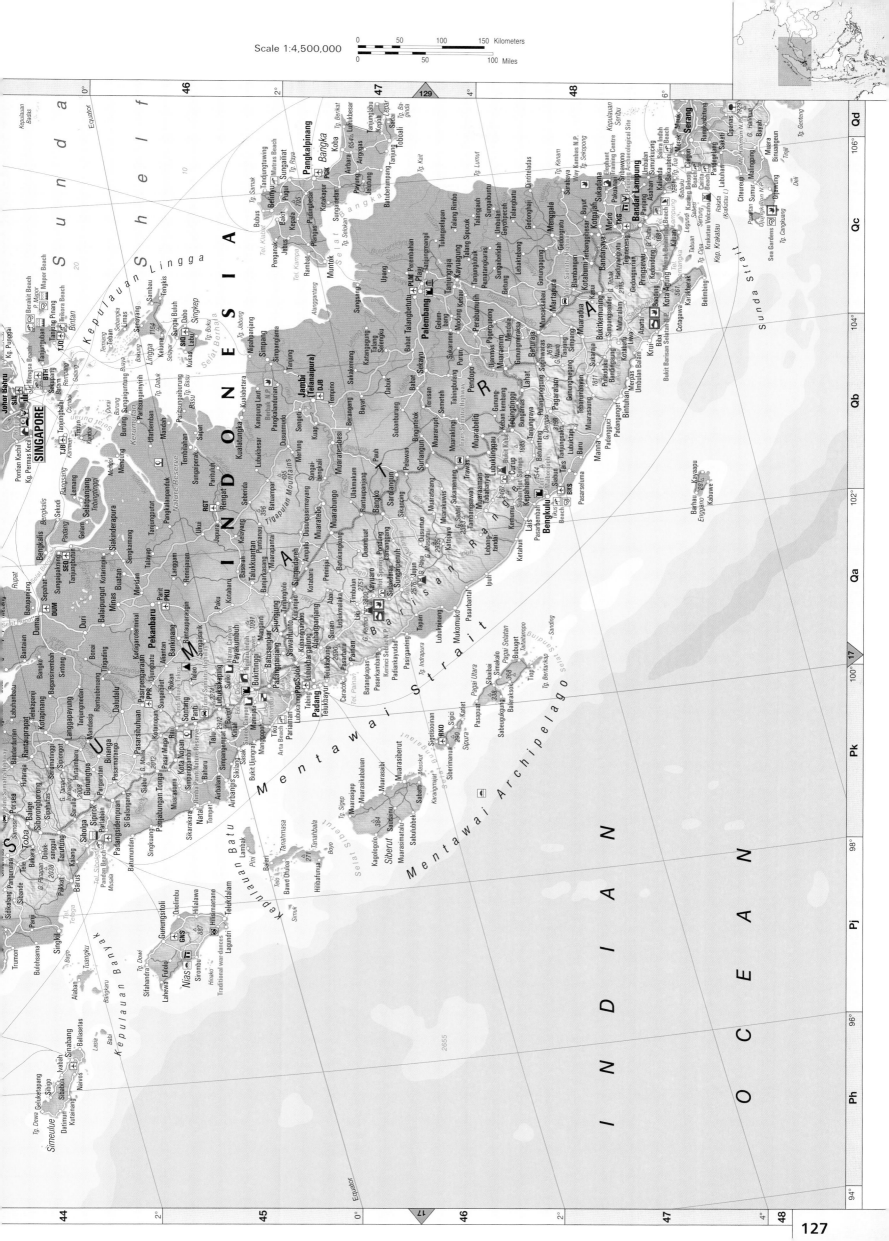

Scale 1:4,500,000

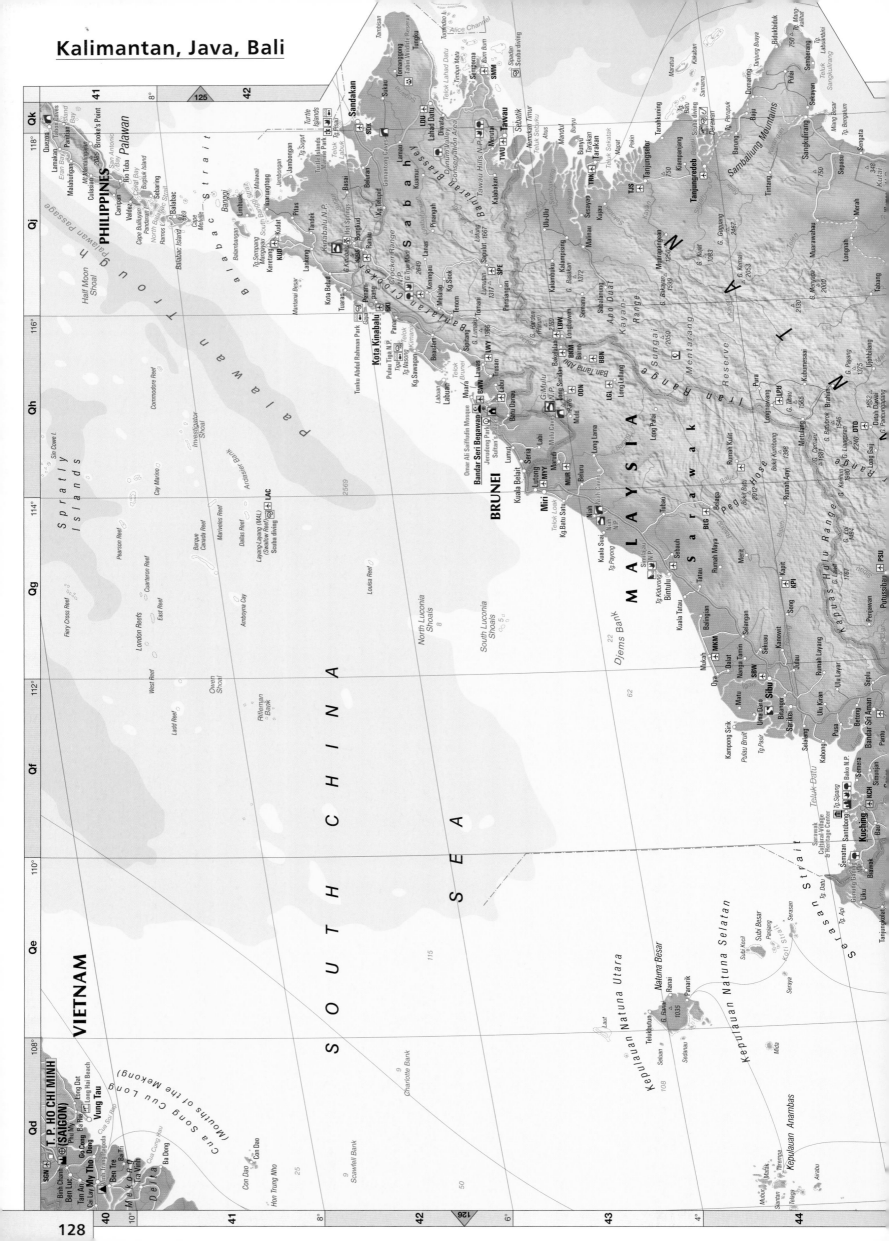

Kalimantan, Java, Bali

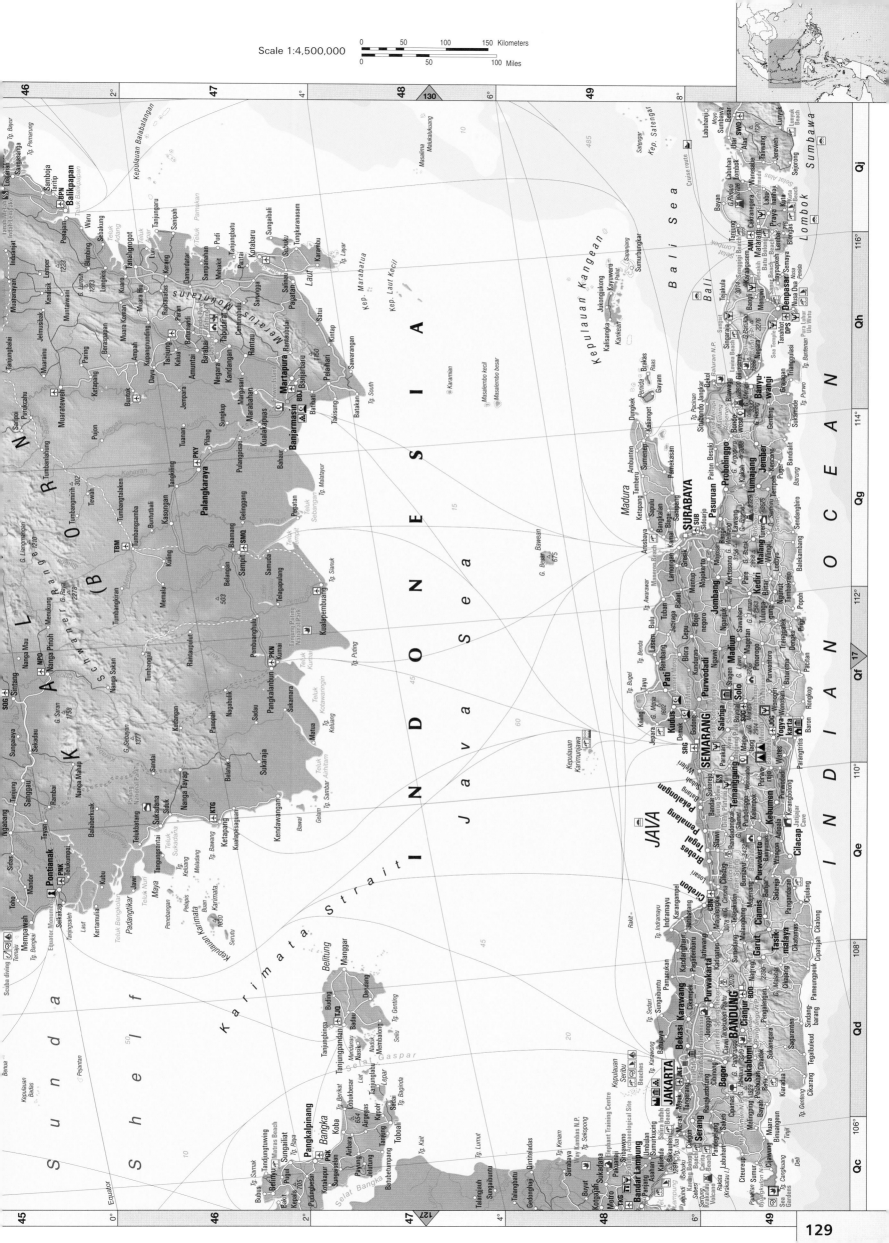

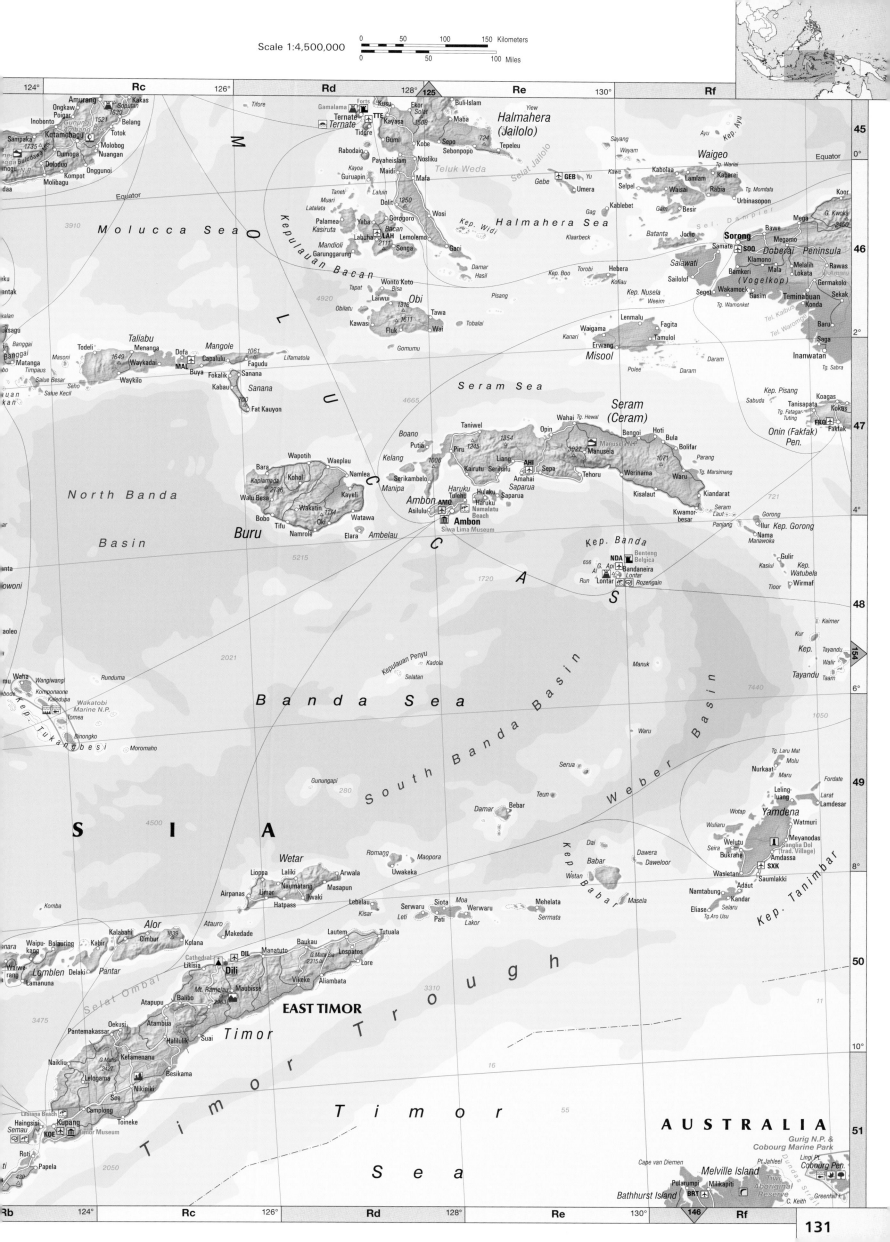

Australia / Oceania

The smallest continent, known as Oceania or Australasia, is the 'island continent' consisting of Australia, a few large islands (such as eastern New Guinea and the two islands of New Zealand) and approximately 7,000 smaller islands scattered over the Pacific. Australia can be sub-divided into three major areas – the West Australian tableland, which occupies about half the country, the adjoining central Australian lowland and the Great Dividing Range, which adjoins it in the east. The mountainous island of Tasmania off the south-east coast and the Great Barrier Reef off the north-east coast are other important physical features. New Zea-

land is predominantly mountainous and covered in sub-tropical and temperate forests. The Pacific islands are divided into three groups: Melanesia, Polynesia and Micronesia. The larger islands are of volcanic origin, the smaller ones are mostly coral atolls.

The Caroline Islands are the largest group of islands in Micronesia. They comprise 963 islands, which are mostly atolls of volcanic origin. Archeological finds have revealed the presence of early settlements.

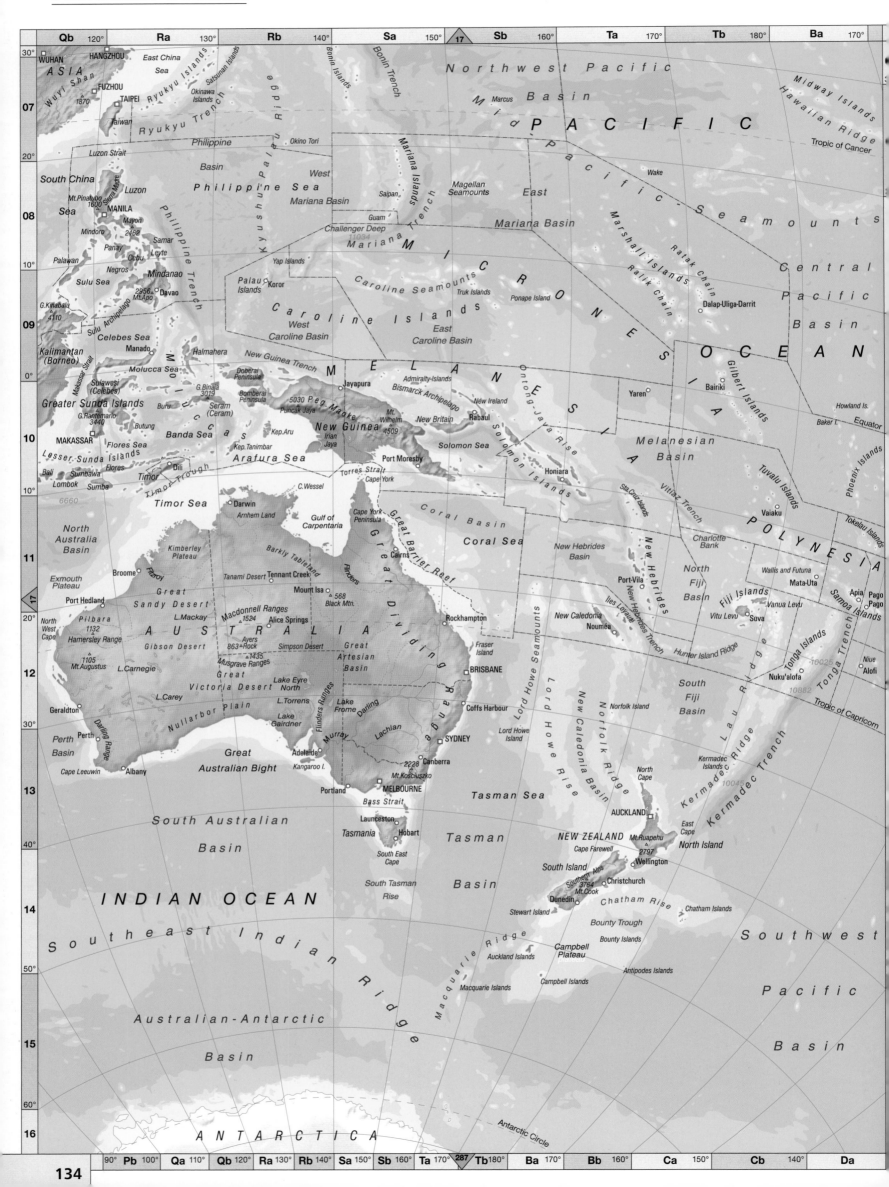

ASIA
WUHAN
HANGZHOU
East China Sea
Wuyi Shan
FUZHOU
1870
TAIPEI
Ryukyu Islands
Satsunan Islands
Taiwan
Ryukyu Trench
Okinawa Islands
Okinawa Trench

Northwest Pacific
Marcus
Basin
PACIFIC

Midway Islands
Hawaiian Ridge
Tropic of Cancer

Philippine
Basin
South China Sea
Mt.Pinatubo 1600
MANILA
Mayon
Mindoro 2462
Luzon
Sierra Madre
Luzon Strait
Okino Tori

Philippine Sea
West
Mariana Basin
Saipan
Guam
Challenger Deep 11034
Mariana Trench

East
Mariana Basin
Wake
Magellan Seamounts

Pacific-Seamounts

Central Pacific Basin

Palawan
Negros
Cebu
Panay
Samar
Leyte
Sulu Sea
Mindanao
G.Kinabalu 4110
2956 Mt.Apo
Davao
Sulu Archipelago
Yap Islands
Palau Islands
Koror

Caroline Seamounts
Truk Islands
Ponape Island

M I C R O N E S I A

Ratak Chain
Ralik Chain
Marshall Islands
Dalap-Uliga-Darrit

O C E A N

Celebes Sea
Manado
Halmahera
Kalimantan (Borneo)
Molucca Sea
Sulawesi (Celebes)
G.Binaja 3019
Greater Sunda Islands
Buru
G.Rantemario 3440
Seram (Ceram)
Butung
Banda Sea
Kep.Aru
MAKASSAR
Flores Sea
Kep.Tanimbar
Makassar Strait
Moluccas

Caroline Islands
West Caroline Basin
East Caroline Basin

New Guinea Trench
M E L A N E S I A

Ontong-Java Rise
Yaren
Bairiki
Gilbert Islands
Howland Is.
Baker I.
Equator

Jayapura
Doberai Peninsula
Bomberai Peninsula
Admiralty Islands
Bismarck Archipelago
New Ireland
New Britain
Rabaul

Lesser Sunda Islands
Bali
Lombok
Sumbawa
Sumba
Flores
Timor
Dili
Timor Trough
6660
Arafura Sea

5030 Peg. Maoke
Puncak Jaya
Irian Jaya
New Guinea
Mt.Wilhelm 4509
Port Moresby
Solomon Sea
Solomon Islands
Honiara
Sta.Cruz Islands
Vitiaz Trench

Melanesian Basin
Vaiaku
Tuvalu Islands
Phoenix Islands
Tokelau Islands

P O L Y N E S I A

Timor Sea
Darwin
Arnhem Land
Gulf of Carpentaria
C. Wessel
Torres Strait
Cape York
Cape York Peninsula

Coral Basin
Coral Sea

New Hebrides Basin

North Fiji Basin
Port-Vila
New Hebrides
Iles Loyaute
Charlotte Bank
Fiji Islands
Vitu Levu
Vanua Levu
Suva
Wallis and Futuna
Mata-Uta
Apia
Pago Pago
Samoa Islands

North Australia Basin
Exmouth Plateau
Broome
Fitzroy
Kimberley Plateau
Barkly Tableland
Cairns
Great Barrier Reef

Port Hedland
North West Cape
Pilbara 1132
Hamersley Range
1105 Mt.Augustus
Geraldton
Great Sandy Desert
Tanami Desert
Tennant Creek
Mount Isa
568 Black Mtn.
Flinders
Rockhampton
Fraser Island

AUSTRALIA
Gibson Desert
L.Mackay
Macdonnell Ranges 1524
Alice Springs
Ayers Rock 863 1435
Simpson Desert
Musgrave Ranges
Great Artesian Basin
Great Dividing Range
BRISBANE

Lord Howe Seamounts
Lord Howe Rise
New Caledonia
Noumea
New Caledonia Basin
Norfolk Island
Norfolk Ridge

South Fiji Basin
Nuku'alofa
Tonga Islands
Niue
Alofi
Tropic of Capricorn

L.Carnegie
L.Carey
Great Victoria Desert
Lake Eyre North
L.Torrens
Lake Frome
Lake Gairdner
Flinders Ranges
Darling
Lachlan
Coffs Harbour
Lord Howe Island

Perth Basin
Perth
Darling Range
Nullarbor Plain
Murray
SYDNEY
Canberra 2228
Hunter Island Ridge
Lau Ridge
Kermadec Islands
North Cape

Cape Leeuwin
Albany
Great Australian Bight
Adelaide
Kangaroo I.
MELBOURNE
Mt.Kosciuszko
Portland
Bass Strait

Tasman Sea
AUCKLAND
East Cape
Kermadec Trench

South Australian Basin
Launceston
Hobart
Tasmania
South East Cape

Tasman Basin
South Tasman Rise

NEW ZEALAND
Mt.Ruapehu 2797
North Island
Cape Farewell
Wellington
South Island
Southern Alps 3764 Mt.Cook
Christchurch
Dunedin
Chatham Rise
Chatham Islands

INDIAN OCEAN
Southeast Indian Ridge

Stewart Island
Macquarie Ridge
Bounty Trough
Bounty Islands
Auckland Islands
Campbell Plateau
Antipodes Islands

Southwest Pacific Basin

Australian-Antarctic Basin
Macquarie Islands
Campbell Islands

ANTARCTICA
Antarctic Circle

134

| 90° | Pb | 100° | Qa | 110° | Qb | 120° | Ra | 130° | Rb | 140° | Sa | 150° | Sb | 160° | Ta | 170° | 287 | Tb | 180° | Ba | 170° | Bb | 160° | Ca | 150° | Cb | 140° | Da |

*'The **Twelve Apostles'** on the coast of Victoria, Australia: these huge needles, up to 40 m high, are an excellent illustration of the erosive power of wind and water. They are part of the Port Campbell National Park.*

Northern Australian mountain ranges

The **Western Australian table-land** which rises west of the **Mac-Donnell Chain** and continues to the west coast encircles the central Australian lowland. The tableland which has an average altitude of 250 m to 800 m has its highest elevations in several mountain ranges that stretch from the West coast to the **Gulf of Carpentaria**. It is traversed by numerous rivers but only those near the coast contain more than a trickle of water all year round. **Darling Scarp** (**Bluff Knoll,** 1,109 m) contains the continent's oldest rocks. Inland, the plateau becomes a vast, desert-like dry landscape, the Simpson Desert, with numerous salt lakes before dropping down to form the central Australian lowland.

Hamersley Basin which adjoins the Darling Scarp in the north reaches altitudes of up to 1,235 m (**Mount Bruce**). **Mount Augustus** which has an altitude of 1,106 m is in this mountainous region and is rocks coloured red due to its iron content.

The **King Leopold Range** forms the southern border of the **Kimberley Plateau**. This mountainous country drops away in the North to form **Arnhem Land**. In the south, it adjoins the limestone **Barkley Tableland**.

Kimberley Highlands

The mountain range bordering the **Kimberley Plateau** stretches from the **Joseph Bonaparte Gulf** in the north where it drops down

Darling

The 2740 km Darling is the longest river in Australia. The headwaters originate in the Darling Downs in the Great Dividing Range. The main headwater is the MacIntyre River. The Darling carries between 340 and 550 million cu. m of water per year on average but when there is no rain it can dry out altogether. After absorbing many tributaries originating in the Great Dividing Range, the Darling flows into the Murray near Wentworth, which in turn eventually drains into the Indian Ocean.

in sheer cliffs to the **Great Sandy Desert** in the south.

The rugged landscape occupies an area of approximately 360,000 sq. km, gradually rising to a height of 937 m (**Mount Ord**). At average temperatures of 38°C, the vegetation is typical of a savannah and is suitable for rearing cattle and sheep.

Rivers have sculpted impressive caverns and remarkable gorges in the sandstone which predominates here.

Millennia of erosion and weathering have produced extraordinary rock formations such as the weird limestone formation in **Purnululu** which was only discovered in 1982.

The foothills of the Kimberleys form richly structured, high cliffs close to the Indian Ocean where

Kimberley: eroded limestone rocks in Purnululu National Park.

extensive breaker platforms made of sandstone can be found upstream. The coastal area is remarkable for its significant iron ore deposits.

Arnhem Land

The peninsula between the **Timor Sea** and the **Gulf of Carpentaria** in the north of the **Northern Territory** occupies an area of approximately 80,000 sq. km.

At the scalloped edges of the coast in the lowlands of the Gulf of Carpentaria, tropical rainforests, mangrove swamps and **wetlands** are typical of the landscape. Vast silt and mud flats and salt marshes cover the estuary.

In the extremely rugged mountainous country inland on the peninsula, water channels have sculpted deep channels and gullies. Savannah and grassland can be found to the south.

Central Australian Desert

Approximately 70 per cent of the total land mass of Australia consists of desert and semi-desert formed by an inland sea that dried up 120 million years ago. The scree deposits and sandy regions stretch over massive distances from the West Australian tableland through the Central Australian Basin to the cordilleras. The **Great Sandy Desert**, the **Tanami Desert**, the **Gibson Desert**, the **Great Victoria Desert** and the **Simpson Desert** are surrounded in the north, west and east by mountain ranges and plateaus. Inland, scattered monadnocks and several mountain ranges predominate. They include the **Musgrave Ranges** and the **MacDonnell Ranges**. Uluru (Ayers **Rock**), the **Olgas** and the 760-m-high **Mount Connor** are among the monadnocks that emerge from the sandstone plains.

The region has few waterways, and those that exist are only full after heavy rainfall, mostly evaporating into great salt-pans. Thus **Lake Eyre**, **Lake Torrens** and **Lake Gardiner** are misleading names as the 'lakes' seldom contain water. In the vast desert of 'the Centre', massive underground reservoirs lie at great depths, including the **Great Artesian Basin** whose Mesozoic sediments store large quantities of water from the last Ice Age.

Gibson Desert

This stony desert in central Western Australia between the Great Sandy Desert and the Great Victoria Desert occupies an area of

approximately 330,000 sq. km. Vast sections of this treeless plain are covered in recent deposits of scree, over which larger sand dunes covered in scrub vegetation have formed.

Individual monadnocks and isolated mountains, reaching altitudes of up to 600 m, tower over the seemingly endless plain.

Numerous salt-pans and salt lakes have formed, including **Lake Disappointment** which, due to the infrequent precipitation, continues to evaporate, ensuring that its salt concentration is constantly increasing.

Victoria Desert

The **Great Victoria Desert** is bordered by the Musgrave Ranges in the North, the Darling Plateau in the West and the Stuart Ranges in the East. Sandy and scree deserts, relieved in places by bushy vegetation, cover the vast, treeless, dry region.

In the eastern and western border regions, the desert turns into salt marshes. In the south, the limestone tableland of the **Nullarbor Plain**, which contains caves carved out by underground currents, leads to the coast where it forms a spectacular, 200 m high, rugged line of cliffs.

Great Sandy Desert

The largest of the continent's four deserts is situated in the northern part of the western Australian desert and occupies an area of approximately 520,000 sq. km. It extends to the south of the Kimberley Plateau, becomes the Gibson Desert in the south and is bordered in the east by the

MacDonnell Ranges. At **Eighty Mile Beach,** the western foothills of the Great Sandy Desert reach the Indian Ocean coast, where it forms vast stretches of dunes. The Great Sandy Desert consists primarily of extensive plains with parallel sand dunes covered in dry grasses. Only sporadically do monadnocks such as **Mount Cornish** (363 m) rise over the vast plains. In the north-west, the desert contains the artesian wells of the **Desert Basin**. Vast salt-pans lie in the south and east.

Simpson Desert

The **Simpson Desert** covers the south-east of the Northern Territory as well as parts of the states of South Australia and Queensland and has a total area of over 250,000 sq. km.

The MacDonnell Ranges form the northern border. In the east, the scree and sandy desert containing massive dunes between 30 and 60 m high becomes the **Great Artesian Basin**.

Central Australian Mountains

The **MacDonnell Ranges** are part of the mountainous regions which divide the vast plains and steppes of central Australia. They were formed approximately 600 to 900 million years ago and are one of the oldest mountain ranges in the world.

The chain of hills runs from east to west and consists of quartz and sandstone. They stretch over the sub-soil of the West Australian tableland which has an average altitude of 600 m and a length of 380 km and reach their peak at **Mount Zeil** which has an altitude of 1,510 m. The arc of the **Musgrave Ranges** to the south is approximately 210 km long and consists of granite formations.

The highest peak is **Mount Woodroffe** (1,435m). The southeastern foothills of the Musgrave Ranges form the **Petermann Ranges,** which are approximately 320 km long.

The numerous monadnocks which sporadically tower over the vast desert plains and steppes are one of the most impressive wonders of nature in Australia. The most famous is the 350 m-high, massive **Uluru (Ayers Rock)** the largest monolith in the world with a breadth of approximately 9 km, and the more than 30 sandstone **Olgas** which cover an area of approximately 28 sq. km.

Monoliths of Australia

On the world's driest continent, erosion, the most powerful force of nature, has created impressive geological formations. These also include the greatest monoliths on Earth.

Australia is the driest inhabited continent. It is also the flattest and has the oldest and least fertile soils, due to the fact that the centre of the country, the deserts, are a vast, dried-up sea bed. As a result, it has always been a playground for the elements of wind and water, which have created spectacular and imposing monoliths over the millennia.
Uluru (Ayers Rock) enchants those who visit it when its sandstone faces, which are interspersed with mica and feldspar, turn a blood-red colour at sunset. Uluru is 3.6 km long and 2 km wide and it rises 350 m above the plateau. As the rocks which consist of harder sandstone weather more slowly than the surrounding area, this monadnock now towers over the

dry plain. Its lower slopes are severely eroded and wind and water have created basins and canyons on its plateau-like top. The precipitation from violent thunderstorms pours down these channels in massive cataracts during the rainy season.
This mountain is the home of the mythical rainbow snake Uluru, which is why the Aborigines have given it this name.
The Olga Mountains lie not far away. These near-circular worn-down rock formations, which number over 36 and which tower over the surrounding plain at altitudes of up to 500 m, have been exposed by millennia of erosion. The 'Kata Tjuta', as the Aborigines call the Olgas, have a mythological significance too. They are con-

sidered to be the fossilised heads of man-eating giants.
The third in the league of great monoliths is Mount Connor, to the east of Ayers Rock, also sacred to the aborigines. This flat-topped limestone and sandstone boulder

is 3 km long and 1.2 km wide. Its lower slopes are extremely rugged and covered in scree, whilst the upper slopes consist of rocky crags. For the aborigines this is where their mythical ice man comes from.

Big picture: the Olga Mountains, called 'Kata Tjuta' by the Aborigines, form a group of approximately 30 small individual mountains in the centre of Australia.

Inset: Ayers Rock, called 'Uluru' by the Aborigines, looks like a red giant at sunset and sunrise. This phenomenon is caused by ferric oxides in the rock surface.

Left: the 'Devil's Marbles', located between Alice Springs and Darwin, are approximately 1.5 million years old. The granite lumps, created by erosion, soar like monolithic peaks straight out of the flat central Australian desert.

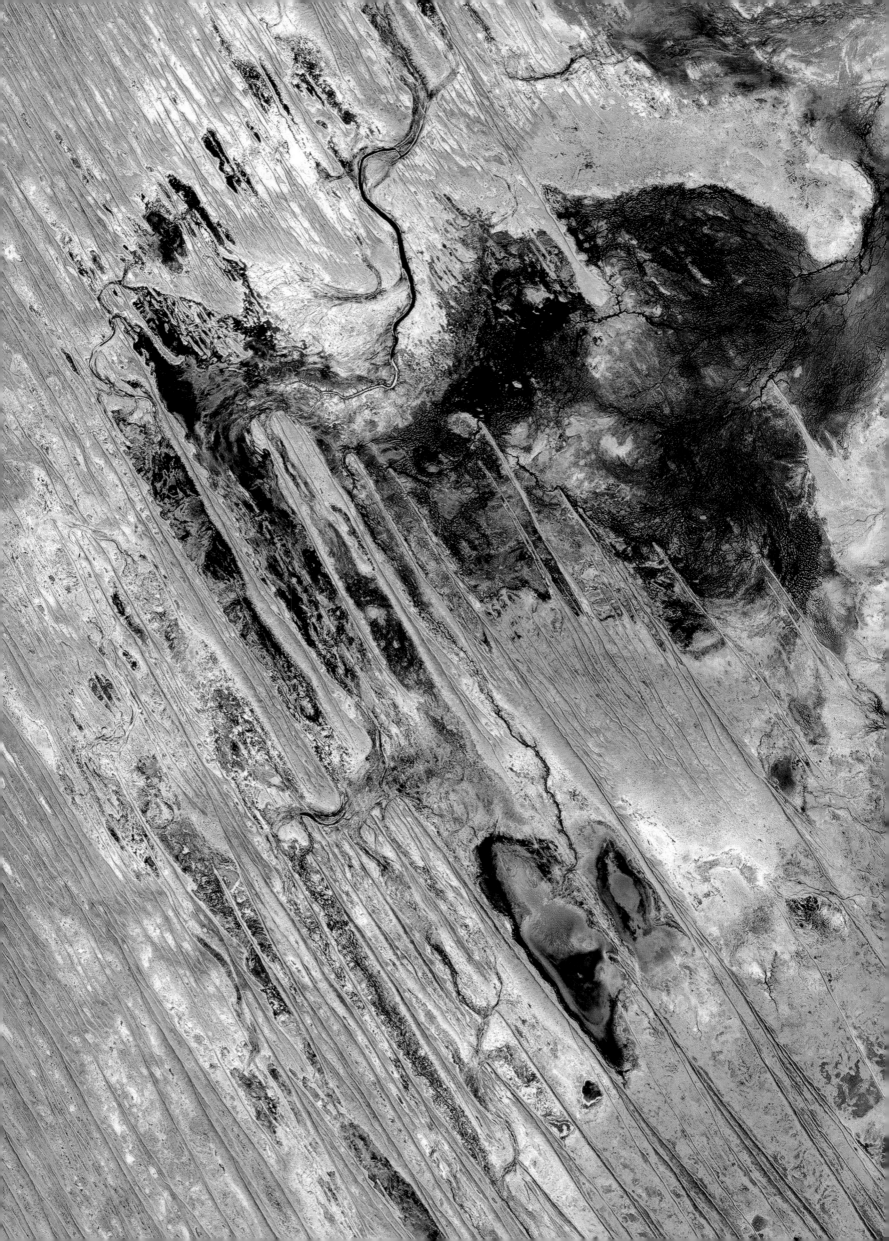

Vast rusty red-sand dunes stretching for 300 kilometres to the north-west that glow in the light of the rising and setting sun are the hallmark of Simpson Desert National Park, one of the last true wilder-nesses on earth. It would not be aerially mapped until 1929. Forty-five years later, in 1973, it was first crossed without the aid of vehicles. Four more years would pass until the woman writer Robin Davidson, riding from South Australia on a camel, succeeded in tracing the Oodnadatta Track, a traditional Aboriginal trading route stretching for more than 615 kilometres, now named after the tiny settlement of Oodnadatta on the south-western fringe of the Simpson Desert.

Mount Cook, called 'Aorangi' by the indigenous Maori, is located in the New Zealand Alps on the South Island. It is New Zealand's highest mountain at 3764 m. The National Park that surrounds it was founded in 1953.

The many glaciers and lakes of this mountain landscape are stunning. The longest glacier on the southern hemisphere is the Tasman Glacier, stretching from Mount Cook almost 30 km into the valley.

Great Dividing Range

The **Australian Cordillera** runs parallel to the Pacific coast around the entire southern and south-eastern coast for approximately 3,000 km, starting in the north at **Cape York Peninsula**, and running north-south to the south coast at Melbourne. It then continues on to the island of **Tasmania**, which is located off the south-eastern tip of the continent. The cordillera consists of a series of ranges: the Great Dividing Range (Australia's most substantial mountain range, also known as the Eastern Highlands,), the New England Range, the Blue Mountains and the Australian Alps.

The mountain chain consists primarily of low mountains and is divided by several plateaus. It reaches its maximum altitude in the north with **Mount Bartle Frere** (1,611 m).

Mount Kosciuszko, near the capital city of Canberra, stands in the southern foothills of the **Australian Alps**. At an altitude of 2,228 m, it is the highest mountain both within the **Great Dividing Range** and in Australia as a whole.

The Australian cordillera forms the continent's main water divide. It was folded upwards through subduction as a result of seismic events in the Tertiary Era. It descends in a steep platform formation in the east and slopes downwards to form vast plains further inland.

Murray

The Murray is Australia's largest river and has water all year round. It originates in the Snowy Mountains and crosses them in its upper reaches through a series of deep gorges 320 km in length. It then crosses the Murray Darling Basin in the central Australian lowland, where, with its tributary the Murrumbidgee, it irrigates the extensive farmland through dams and artificial water courses from the Snowy River. After 2570 km, the Murray flows into Lake Alexandrina and through Encounter Bay, eventually draining into the Indian Ocean.

New South Wales

The state of **New South Wales** lies in the south-east of the continent and occupies a total area of approximately 800,000 sq. km. It can be divided geographically into four sections.

First there is the coastal strip, with climates ranging from temperate on the far south coast to sub-tropical near the Queensland border. Then there are the Australian cordilleras adjoining a narrow coastal strip containing tropical rainforest, vast sandy beaches and expanses of dunes. They reach their highest point in the south at Mount Kosciuszko (altitude: 2,228 m) in the Australian Alps. In the north, the cordilleras run towards the **New England Range** (highest peak: **Round Mountain**, 1,685 m) and the **Blue Mountains** (highest peak: 945 m).

The Australian cordillera gradually slopes down to the west and turns into the western plains which cover approximately two-thirds of the territory and are surrounded by the **Grey Range**. The **Murray River** (length: 2,570 km) which flows through the country, and its tributary the **Darling** which rises in the cordilleras, form the only large inland water systems of the Australian continent that contain water all year round. The plains that are suitable for farming are in the Riverina area around Wagga Wagga. The far north-west consists of arid plains.

Tasmania

The island of **Tasmania**, of the south coast of Australia, was originally part of the Australian mainland. It was first formed 12,000 years ago, at the end of the last Ice Age, when the sea level rose and large parts of the country were flooded. This is when the **Bass Straits** were formed which separate Tasmania from the mainland. The island occupies an area of 67,800 sq. km. It has a central mountainous plateau which is a continuation of the Australian Cordillera and reaches its highest point at **Mount Ossa** (1,617 m) which slopes in a south-easterly direction. The rest of the island is mountainous, with a narrow strip of flat coastal plain along its northern coast.

The island exhibits numerous Ice Age formations. It is covered with rainforest fed by rivers on which there are spectacular cascades and rapids such as the **Russell Falls**. Tasmania promotes itself as the 'Natural State' owing to its large, and relatively unspoilt, natural environment. Forty per cent of the island consists of reserves, National Parks and World Heritage Sites.

New Zealand – North Island

The island occupies an area of 114,500 sq. km and is separated from the South Island by the **Cook**

New Zealand: the volcanic cone of Mount Taranaki (2,518 m).

Straits. It is 38 km wide and displays unusual scenic diversity. The **Northland** and the volcanic **Coromandel Peninsula** in the north are characterised by long, level coastlines with wide sandy beaches and expanses of dunes as well as rocky cliffs. The volcanic region stretches from **White Island** in the **Bay of Plenty**, a volcano that is still active, to Mount Egmont in the Eastern region of **Taranaki**.

A plateau has formed around the three volcanoes in the region of **Tongariro** in the island's centre. Lake Taupo is about 600 sq. km in area. It is a crater lake, formed following a gigantic volcanic explosion. To the north of Lake Taupo lies the famous central geothermal region around **Lake Rotorua**. Here, the entire panoply of volcanic and post-volcanic phenomena can be found: small crater lakes, geysers such as the **Pohutu** and boiling water lakes rich with colourful, shiny mineral deposits, sinter terraces and sulphurous mud flats. **Mount Tarawera** (1,111 m) has been cut in half by a 19-km-long chasm since it last erupted in 1886. Along the east coast, the folds of the cordillera (the **Huiarau, Ruahine, Puketoi** and **Tararua Ranges**) stretch from the East Cape to the southern peak. The northern foothills of the **Southern Alps** reach altitudes of up to 1,700 m. The southern North Island consists of low mountains and hills traversed by numerous rivers such as the **Manawatu** and the **Wanganui**. High cliffs overlook the Cook Straits at this point.

Mount Egmont, Ruapehu

Mount Egmont (2,518 m) rises in the east of New Zealand's North Island, known as **Taranaki** in Maori. It is a dormant volcano which last erupted in 1775. The snow-covered, isolated volcanic peak is located in the centre of an almost circular peninsula with a diameter of approximately 60 km formed by lava deposits.

Three further volcanic craters dominate the centre of the North Island and form the **Tongariro Highland**. **Mount Ruapehu is** the only volcano that is still active and is also the highest mountain on the North Island at 2,797 m. The other two are **Mount Ngauruhoe** (2,287 m), which last erupted in 1975, and the supposedly extinct **Mount Tongariro** (1,968 m).

This mountainous region is glaciated to a large degree and is bisected by deep gorges. The landscape is characterised by strange rock formations.

New Zealand South Island

The north of the **South Island**, which occupies a total area of 150,700 sq. km, is characterised by low mountain ranges such as the **Tasman Mountains** (**Mount Kendall**, 1,762 m, **Mount Anglem**, 979 m) and the picturesque ria coast of the **Marlborough Sound**. The **Freshwater River** flows through a swampy valley, rising close to the north-west coast and flowing south-east into the narrow bay of the **Paterson Inlet**. The **Rakeahua river** also flows into the Paterson Inlet.

The **Southern Alps** are a defining factor of the South Island with their numerous peaks rising above 3,000 m, massive glaciers and beautiful high mountain landscapes. The Alps fall steeply to the west, whilst sloping downwards in the east where they become the vast lowland **Canterbury Plains**. In the south-east, there is the mountainous landscape of **Otago**, reaching altitudes of up to 1,200 m and traversed by the broad river valleys of the **Clutha** and the **Mataura**. On the Otago peninsula this mountain range drops steeply down to the Pacific. In the far south, vast plains stretch all the way to the coast.

The imposing **fjords** in the south-west of the South Island were created during the Ice Age as powerful ice currents flowing towards

*The **Palau-Islands** are situated at the western edge of Micronesia.*
They are atoll islands (the remains of coral reefs). Altogether there are 300 islands surrounded by extensive coral reefs.

the ocean, sculpting granite and shale mountains and forming deep fjords, bays, inlets and numerous islands in the Tasman Sea.
The mountainous region, which contains deep ravines, reaches its highest points at **Mount Irene** (1,879 m) and **Mitre Peak** (1,692 m). The numerous lakes in the east such as **Te Anau** and **Manapouri** were also formed at the end of the Ice Age. As the sheets of ice thawed, the depressions caused by the weight of the ice pressing down on them filled with water.

Southern Alps

The **Southern Alps** are the youngest mountain range in New Zealand, originating approximately 10 million years ago.
The mountains run parallel to the west coast for a distance of around 450 km from the northern foothills of the **Marlboroughs** to the southern foothills of the **Dunstan and Garvie Mountains**.
Mount Cook, New Zealand's highest mountain at 3,764 m, **Mount Tasman** (3,497 m) and **Mount Sefton** (3,157 m) are among the 16 peaks in the centre of the island that are higher than 3,000 m. Over 360 glaciers traverse the mountainous landscape, which rises again to 3,027 m in the southwest with **Mount Aspiring**.
The largest of the glaciers is the **Tasman Glacier** on Mount Cook which is 29 km long and 9 km wide. The **Hooker Glacier** and the **Mueller Glacier** are additional examples of these moving rivers of ice. Towards the west, the Southern Alps descend to the narrow coastal plain which is only 50 km wide, where further imposing ice masses, including the **Franz Josef Glacier** and the **Fox Glacier**, descend from the highest mountainous regions to 300 m above sea level.
The Southern Alps gradually slope downwards in an easterly direction. The Alpine glaciers feed numerous mountain lakes on these gently descending plateaus, including the **Wakatipu**, the **Tekapo**, the **Pukaki** and the **Hawea**.

Canterbury Plains

Like the wide plains of the southern area, the alluvial **Canterbury Plains** in the east of the South Island are also covered in Ice Age sediment. They are bounded by the foothills of the Southern Alps

and the east coast of the South Island. They are situated south of Christchurch, the biggest city on the South Island. They are bounded in the north by Hundalee Hills in the Hurunui District, and in the south they merge into the plains of North Otago beyond the Waitaki River. The Canterbury Plains are formed from the alluvial shingle produced by several large rivers, notably the Waimakariri, the Rakaia, the Selwyn, and the Rangitata Rivers. The land is used for sheep-rearing but is prone to drought, especially when the prevailing wind is from the northwest. At these times, the weather phenomenon known as the

Nor'west Arch, an arch of clouds accompanied by a hot north-westerly wind, can be seen across much of the plain.
The rivers of the Canterbury Plains have a distinctive braided appearance. Beyond the Waitaki, they run in narrow channels, rather than spreading across wide shingle depressions, as is the case in Canterbury, eventually draining into the Pacific Ocean.
The rivers of the Canterbury Plains carry away debris from the South-

ern Alps. These Alps extend to the **Banks Peninsula**, formed in the Tertiary Era, over six million years ago, following violent eruptions of

1 Milford Sound in the Fjordland National Park. Mitre Peak overlooks one of the most beautiful fjords in the world.

2 The steep and mountainous island of Moorea in French Polynesia is a remnant of a once active volcano. The coral reef

two volcanoes. The Banks Peninsula once contained primaeval forest full of New Zealand's native flora and bird species, but most of it was

surrounding the island is clearly seen in the limpid waters of the deep blue sea.

3 Moorea: the island has several rugged mountains up to 1000 m in altitude. The bays north of Moorea include the Baie de Cook and Baie

felled or burned during the first 50 years of European occupation. What remains still provides a refuge for unique birdlife.

d'Opunohu. The coastline is covered in lush, tropical vegetation.

4 Lake Rotorua in the volcanic area of the New Zealand's North Island. Its original sinter terraces were destroyed in a volcano explosion.

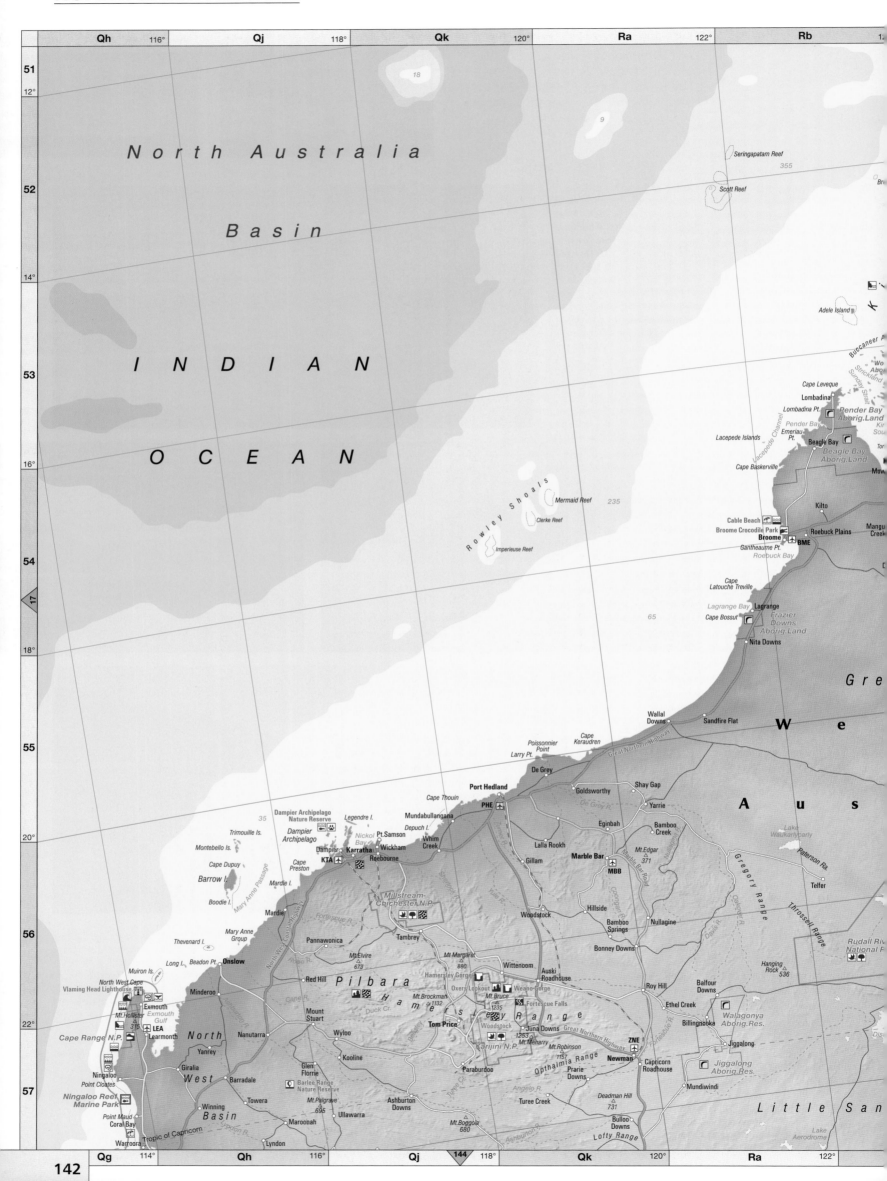

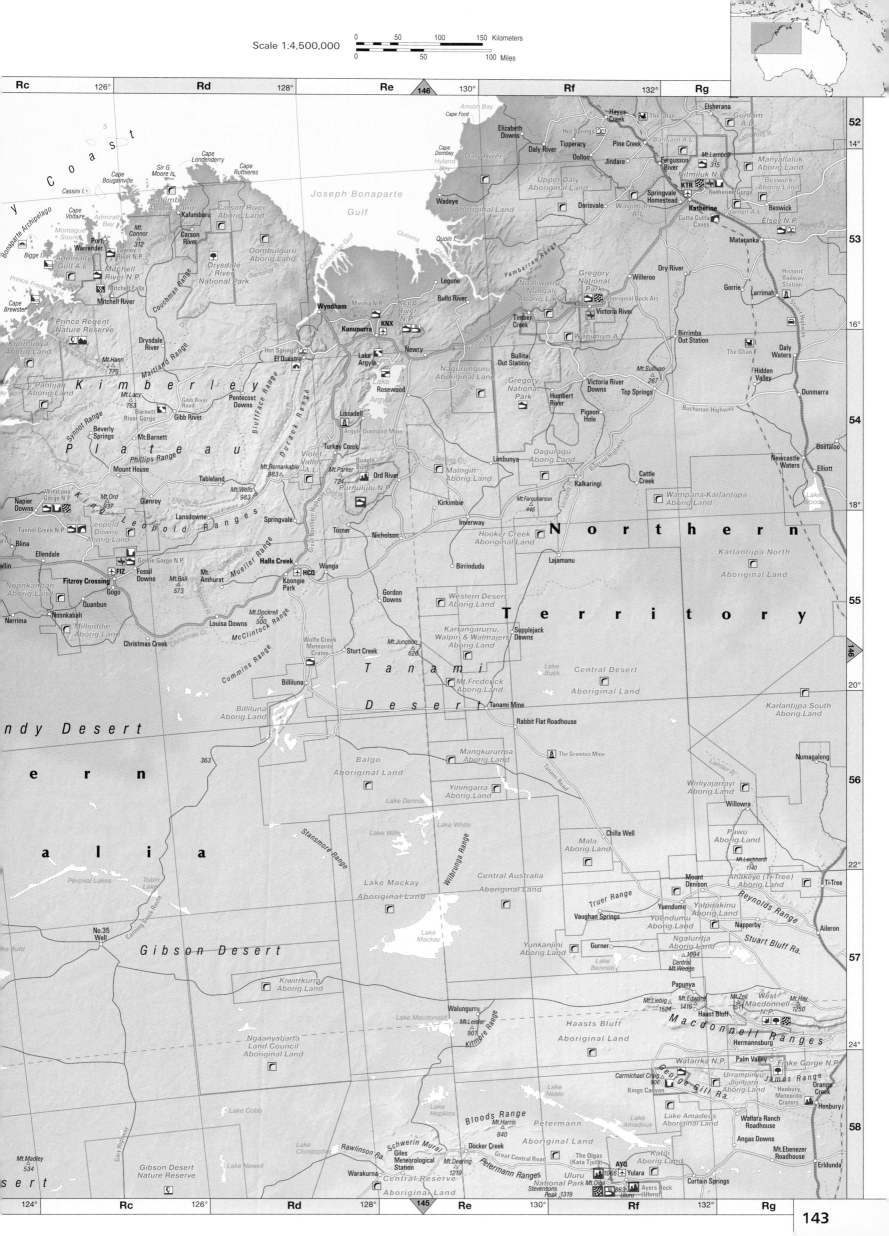

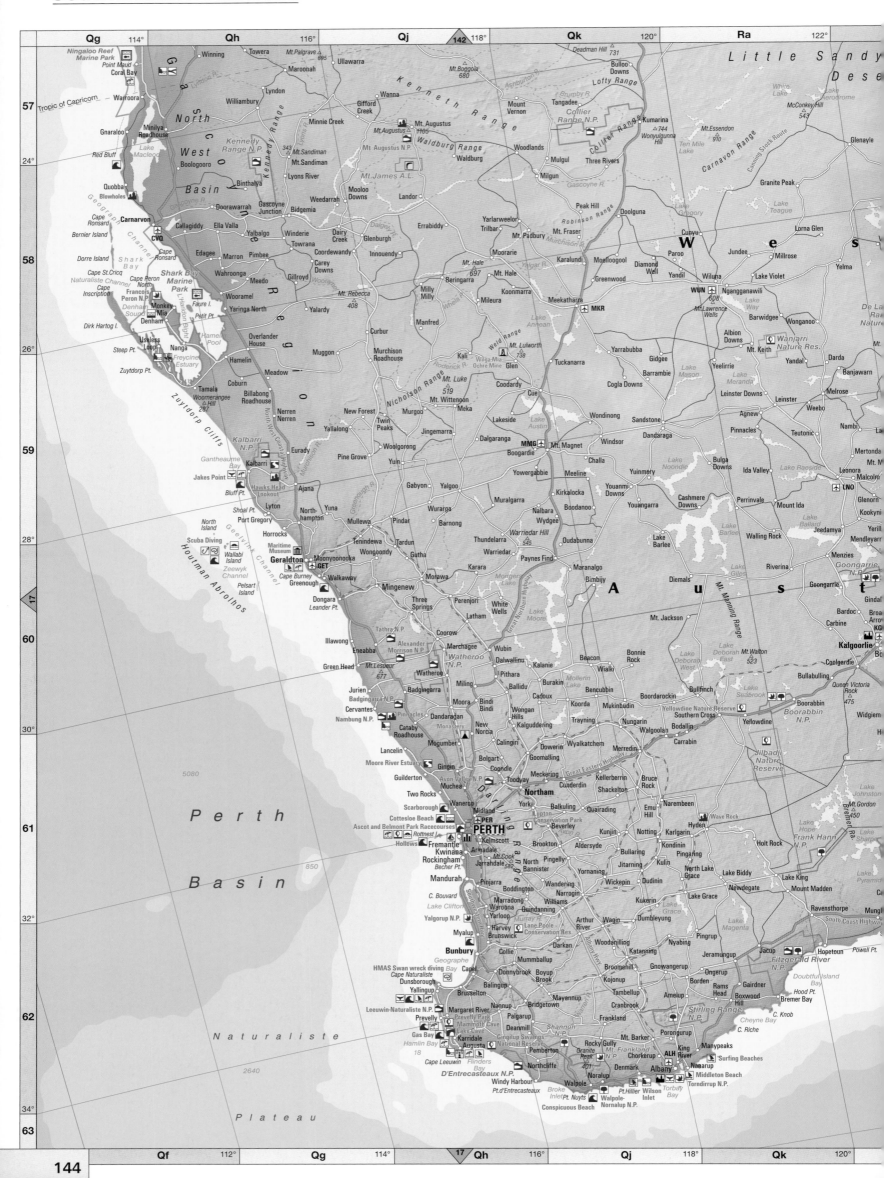

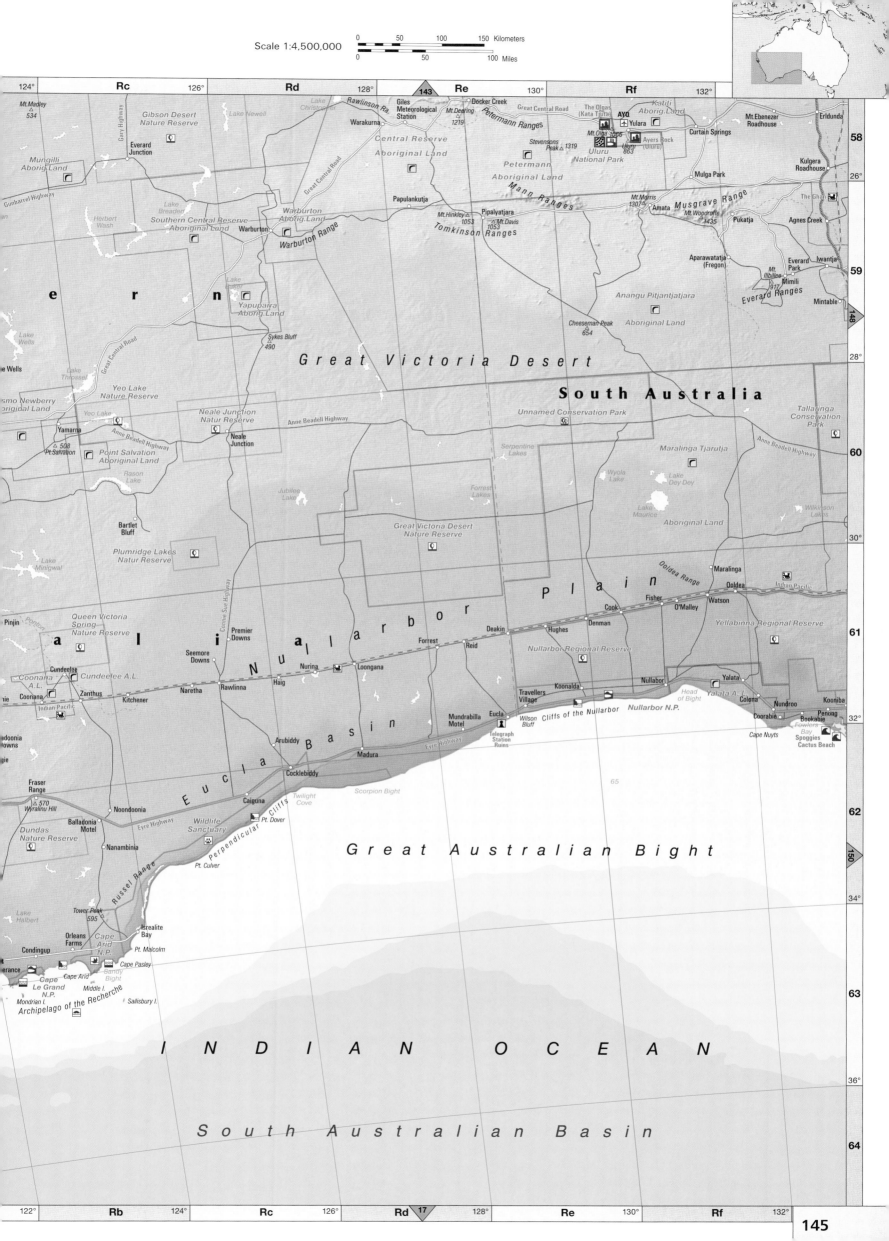

Scale 1:4,500,000

0 50 100 150 Kilometers
0 50 100 Miles

Mt.Madley
534
Gary Highway
Gibson Desert Nature Reserve
Lake Newell
Lake Christopher
Rawlinson Ra.
Giles Meteorological Station
Docker Creek
Great Central Road
The Olgas (Kata Tjuta)
AYO
Katiti Aborig.Land
Mt.Ebenezer Roadhouse
Erlduna

Mungilli Aborig.Land
Everard Junction
Warakurna
Central Reserve Aboriginal Land
Mt.Deering
1219
Petermann Ranges
Mt.Olga 1066
Yulara
Ayers Rock (Uluru)
Uluru
National Park
Curtain Springs
58

Stevensons Peak 1319
Petermann
Kulgera Roadhouse
26°

Gunbarrel Highway
Herbert Wash
Lake Breaden
Southern Central Reserve Aboriginal Land
Warburton Aborig.Land
Warburton
Warburton Range
Papulankutja
Mann Ranges
Aboriginal Land
Mulga Park

The Ghan

Mt.Morris 1307
Amata
Musgrave Range
Mt.Woodroffe 1435
The Ghan

e r n
Lake Wells
Lake Throssel
Lake Luker
Yapuparra Aborig.Land
Mt.Hinkley 1053
Pipalyatjara
Mt.Davis 1053
Tomkinson Ranges
Aparawatatja (Fregon)
Mt.Illbillee 917
Everard Park
Iwantja
59

Anangu Pitjantjatjara
Everard Ranges
Mimili
Mintable

Lake Wells
Sykes Bluff 490
Great Central Road
Great Victoria Desert
Cheeseman Peak 654
Aboriginal Land
28°

Wells
Lake Throssel
Yeo Lake Nature Reserve
South Australia

smo Newberry riginal Land
Yeo Lake
Neale Junction Natur Reserve
Anne Beadell Highway
Unnamed Conservation Park
Tallaringa Conservation Park

Yamarna
508 Pt.Salvation
Point Salvation Aboriginal Land
Neale Junction
Anne Beadell Highway
Serpentine Lakes
Maralinga Tjarutja
Anne Beadell Highway
60

Rason Lake
Forrest Lakes
Wyola Lake
Lake Dey Dey
Wilkinson Lakes

Bartlet Bluff
Jubilee Lake
Great Victoria Desert Nature Reserve
Lake Maurice
Aboriginal Land

Lake Minigwal
Plumridge Lakes Natur Reserve
30°

Ooldea Range
Maralinga

Pinjin
Ponton
Queen Victoria Spring Nature Reserve
Cronie Sue Highway
Premier Downs
Nullarbor Plain
Ooldea
Fisher
Indian Pacific
Watson
Indian Pacific
61

a l i
Seemore Downs
Cook
O'Malley
Yellabinna Regional Reserve

Cundeelee
Coonana A.L.
Cundeelee A.L.
Rawlinna
Haig
Nurina
Loongana
Forrest
Reid
Deakin
Hughes
Denman
Nullarbor Regional Reserve
Nullabor
Yalata

Coonana
Zanthus
Kitchener
Naretha
Koonalda
Travellers Village
Koonalda
Nullabor
Yalata A.L.
Colona
Nundroo
Kooniba

Indian Pacific
Arubiddy
Eucla Basin
Madura
Eyre Highway
Eucla
Wilson Bluff
Cliffs of the Nullarbor
Nullarbor N.P.
Cape Nuyts
Fowlers Bay
Spoggies
Bookabie
Penong
Coorabie
32°

doonia owns
Mundrabilla Motel
Telegraph Station Ruins
Cactus Beach

Fraser Range
Cocklebiddy
Scorpion Bight
65
62

570 Wyralinu Hill
Caiguna
Twilight Cove
Great Australian Bight

Balladonia Motel
Noondoonia
Wildlife Sanctuary
Pt.Dover

Dundas Nature Reserve
Nanambinia
Eyre Highway
Perpendicular Cliffs
Pt.Culver

Russel Range
34°

Lake Halbert
Tower Peak 595
Isrealite Bay

Orleans Farms
Cape Arid N.P.
Pt.Malcolm

Condingup
erance
Cape Arid
Cape Pasley

Cape Le Grand N.P.
Sandy Bight
Middle I.
63

Mondrian I.
Salisbury I.
Archipelago of the Recherche

I N D I A N   O C E A N

S o u t h   A u s t r a l i a n   B a s i n
64

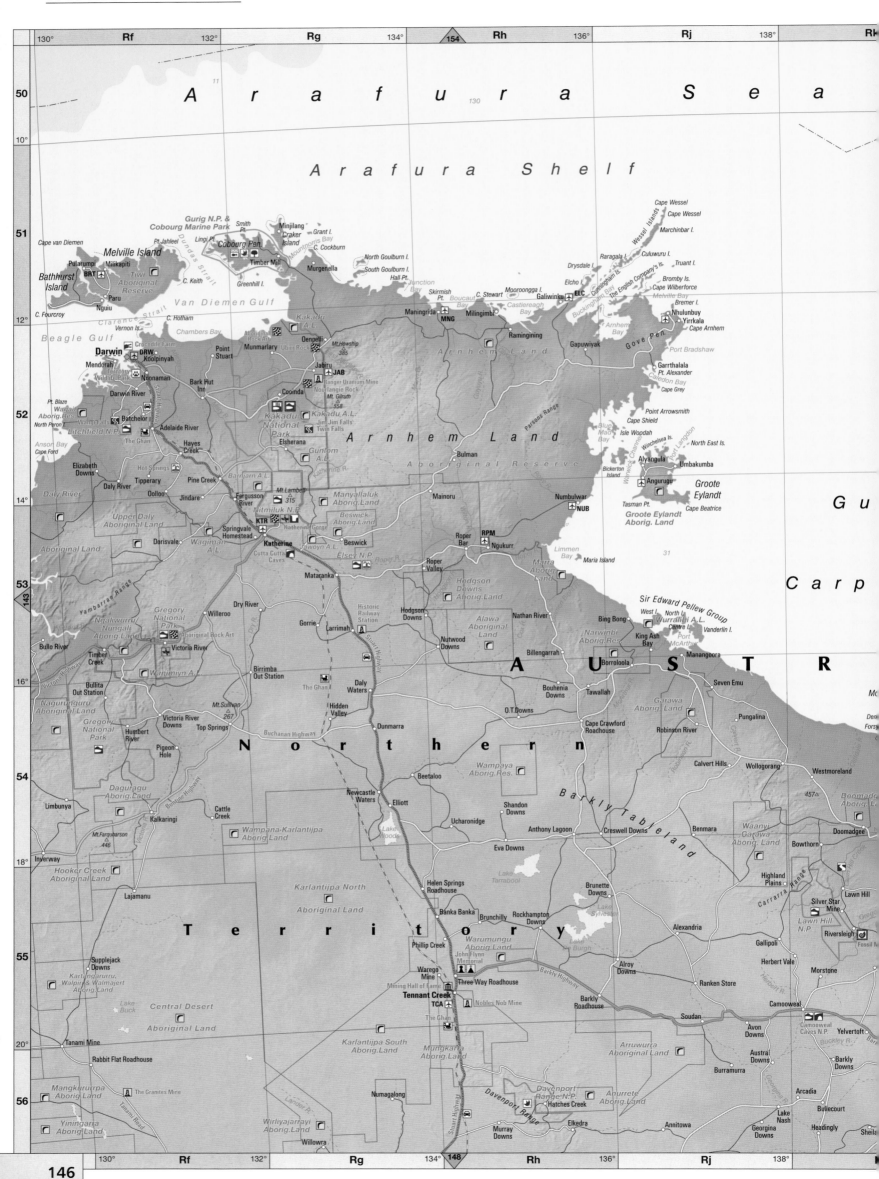

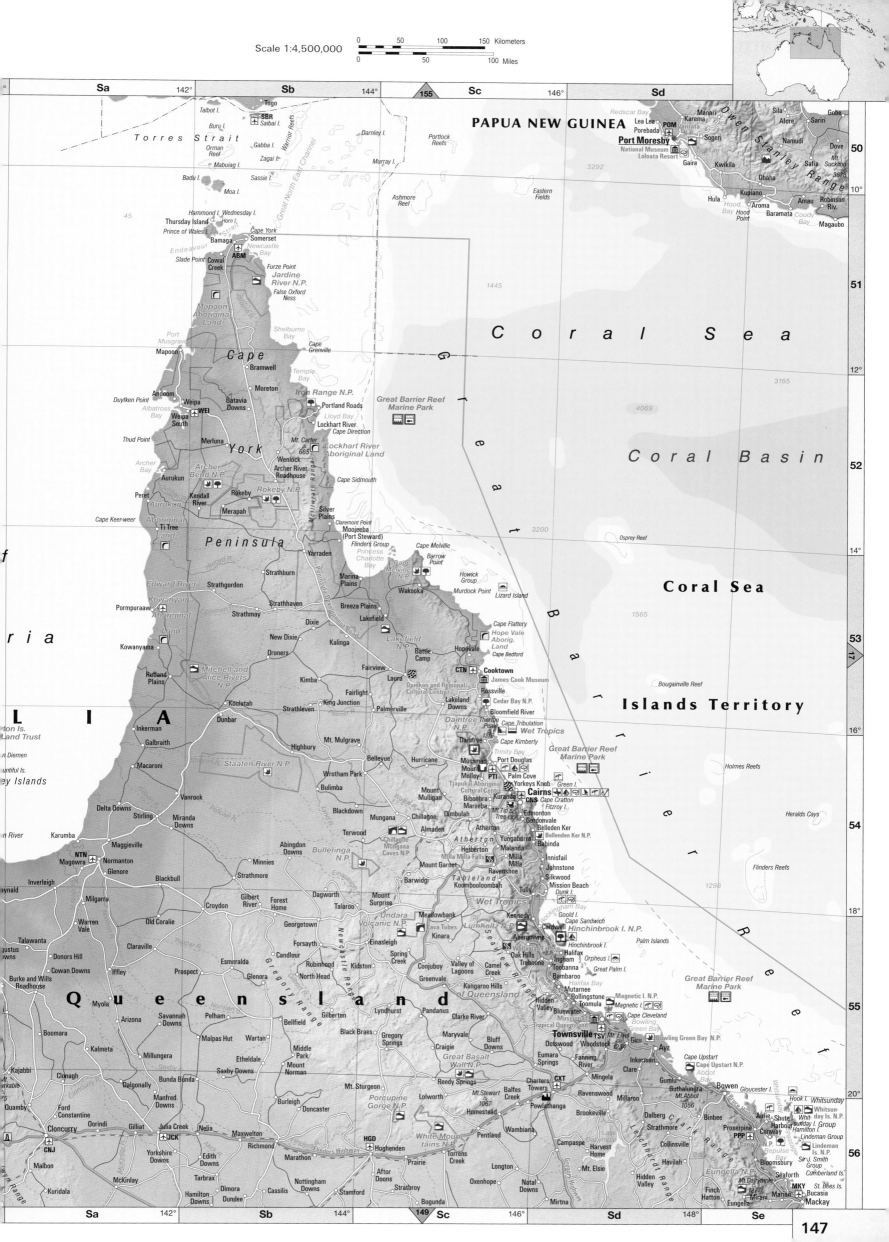

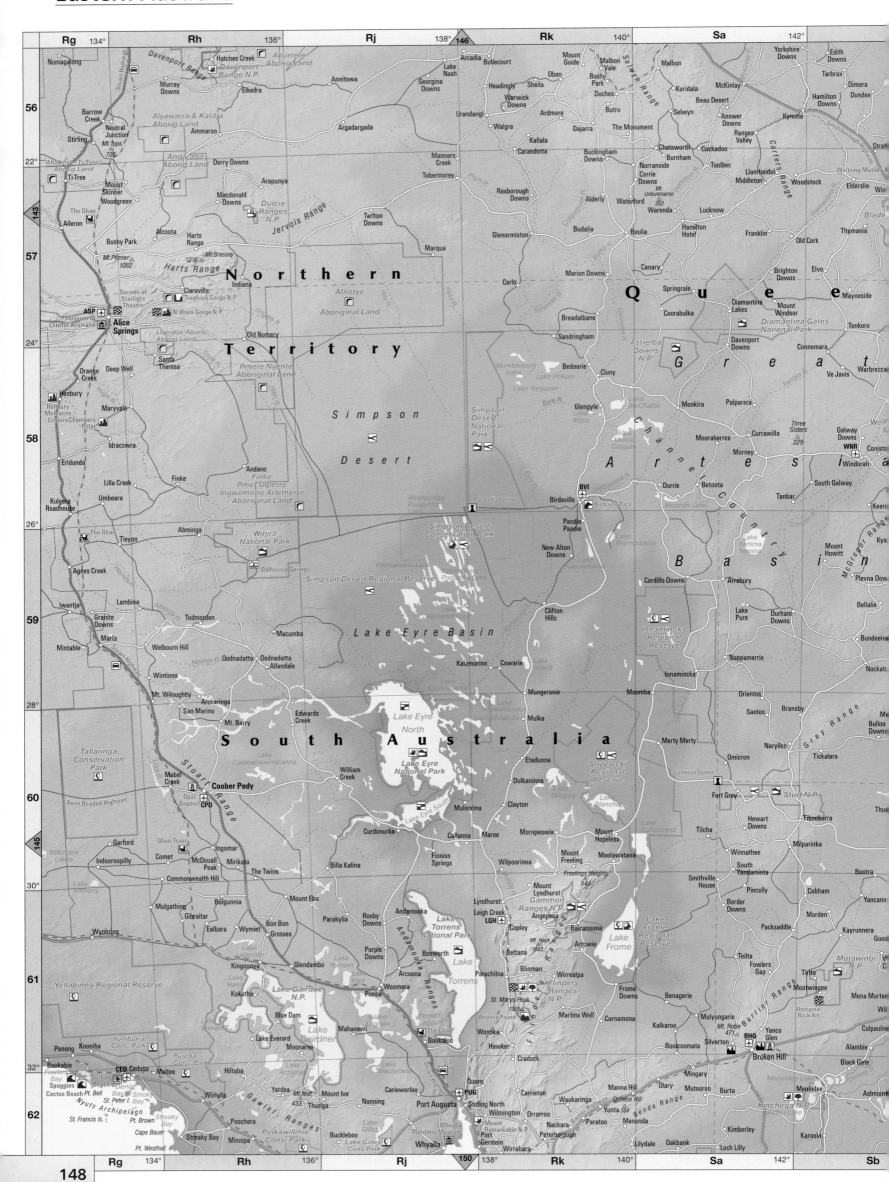

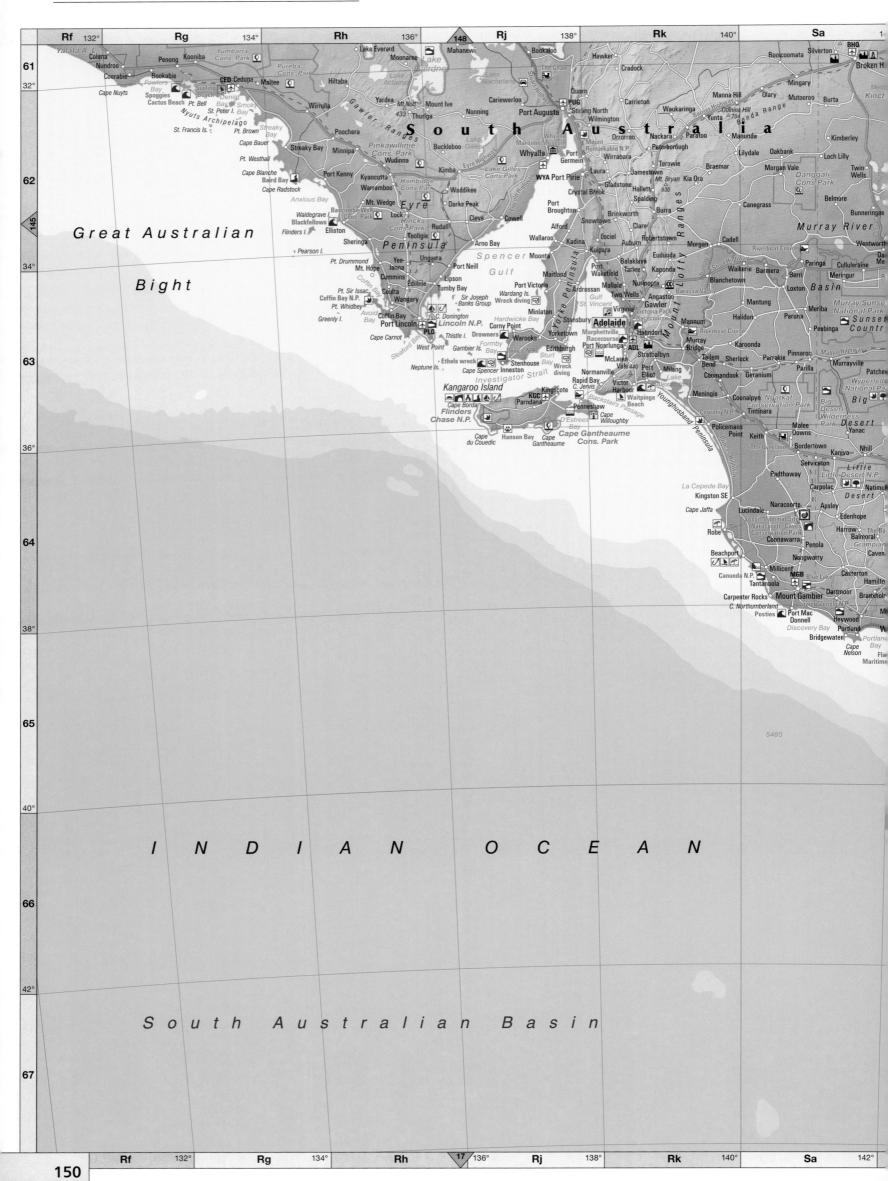

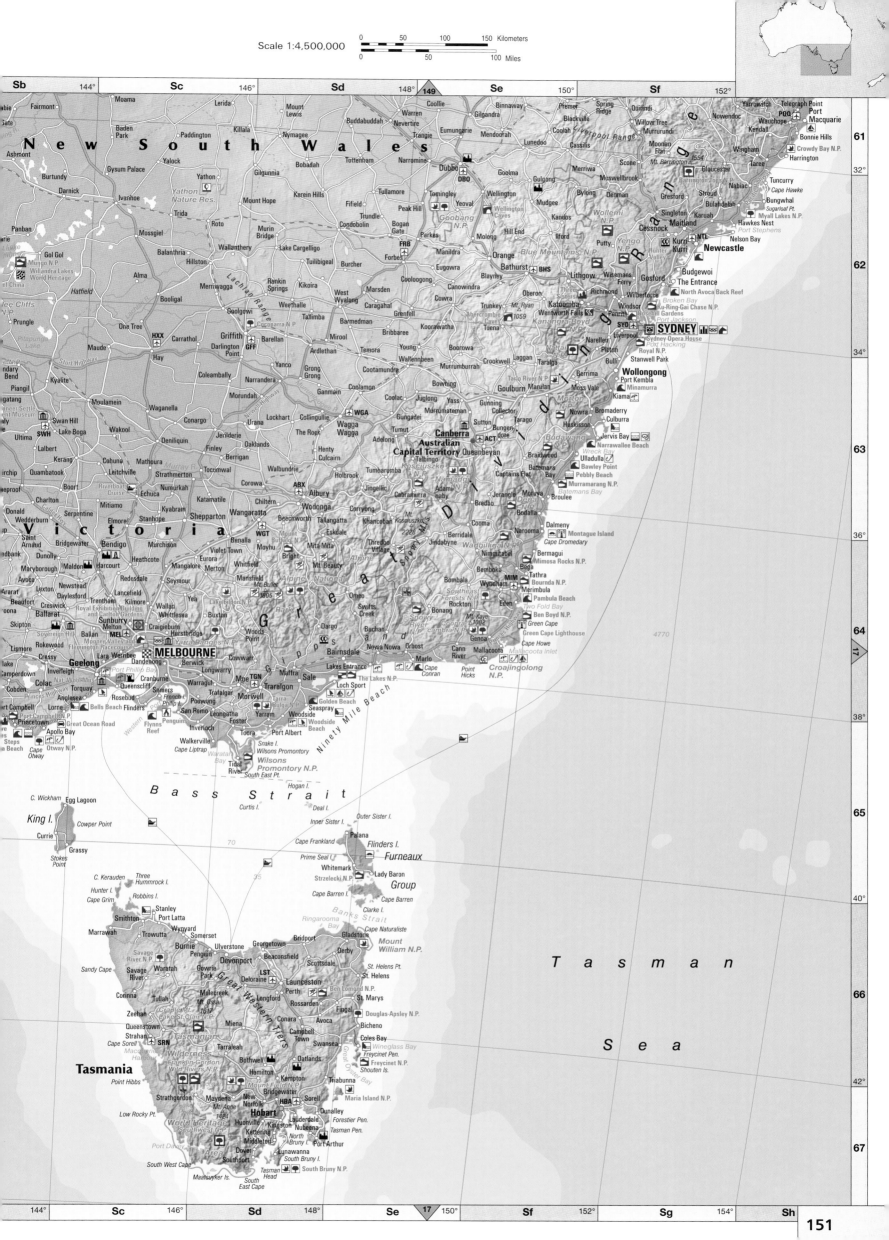

Scale 1:4,500,000

| 0 | 50 | 100 | 150 Kilometers |

| 0 | 50 | 100 Miles |

New South Wales

Fairmont
Moama
Lerida
Mount Lewis
Coollie
Binnaway
Premer
Spring Ridge
Blackville
Willow Tree
Quirindi
Nowendoc
Yarrowitch
Telegraph Point
Port Macquarie

Ashmont
Baden Park
Paddington
Killala
Nymagee
Warren
Nevertire
Buddabuddah
Gilgandra
Coolah
Cassilis
Murrurundi
Moonan Flat
Wingham
Wauchope
Kendall
Bonnie Hills

Burtundy
Gysum Palace
Yalock
Mount Hope
Trangie
Dubbo
DBO
Gulgong
Mudgee
Scone
Mt. Barrington
1554
Gloucester
Nabiac
Crowdy Bay N.P.
Taree

V i c t o r i a

Tasmania

Bass Strait

King I.

Currie
Grassy
Stokes Point

Flinders I.
Furneaux
Group

Hobart

T a s m a n

S e a

New Zealand

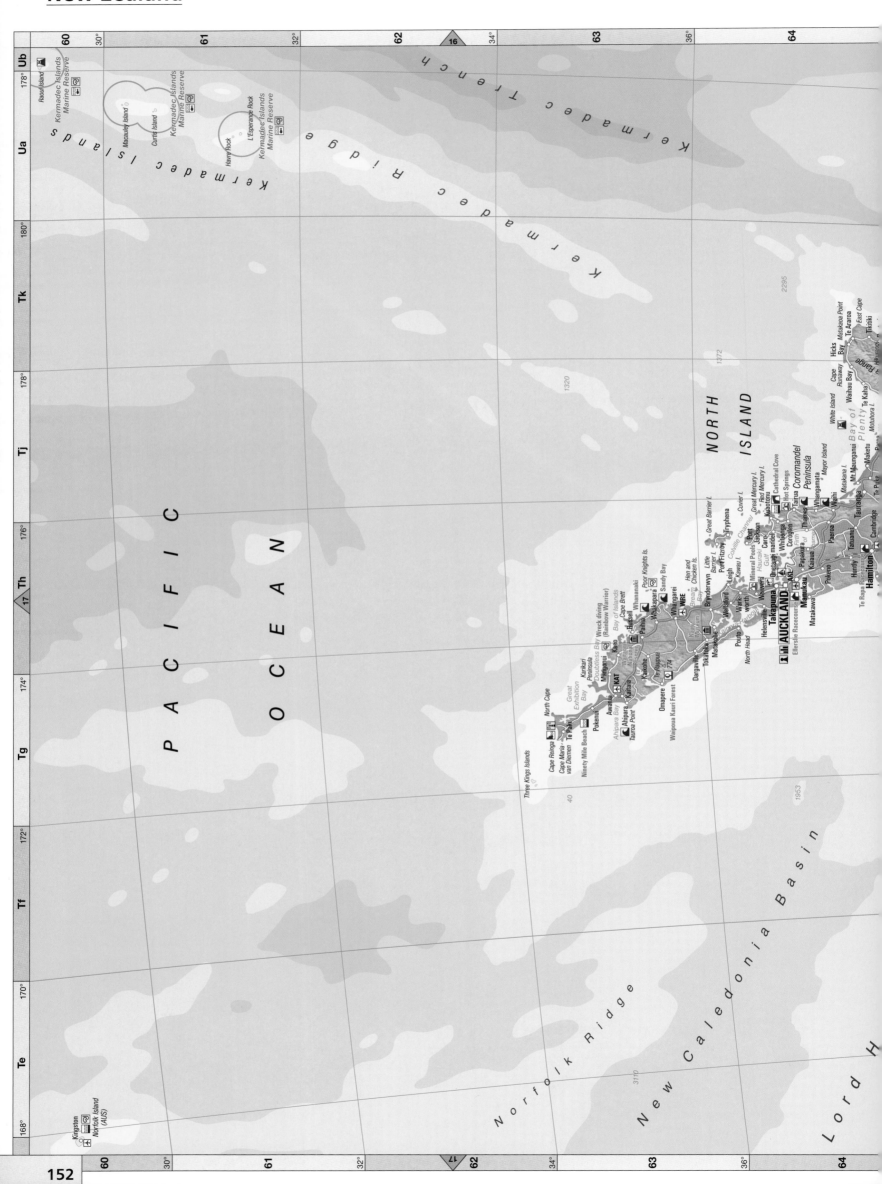

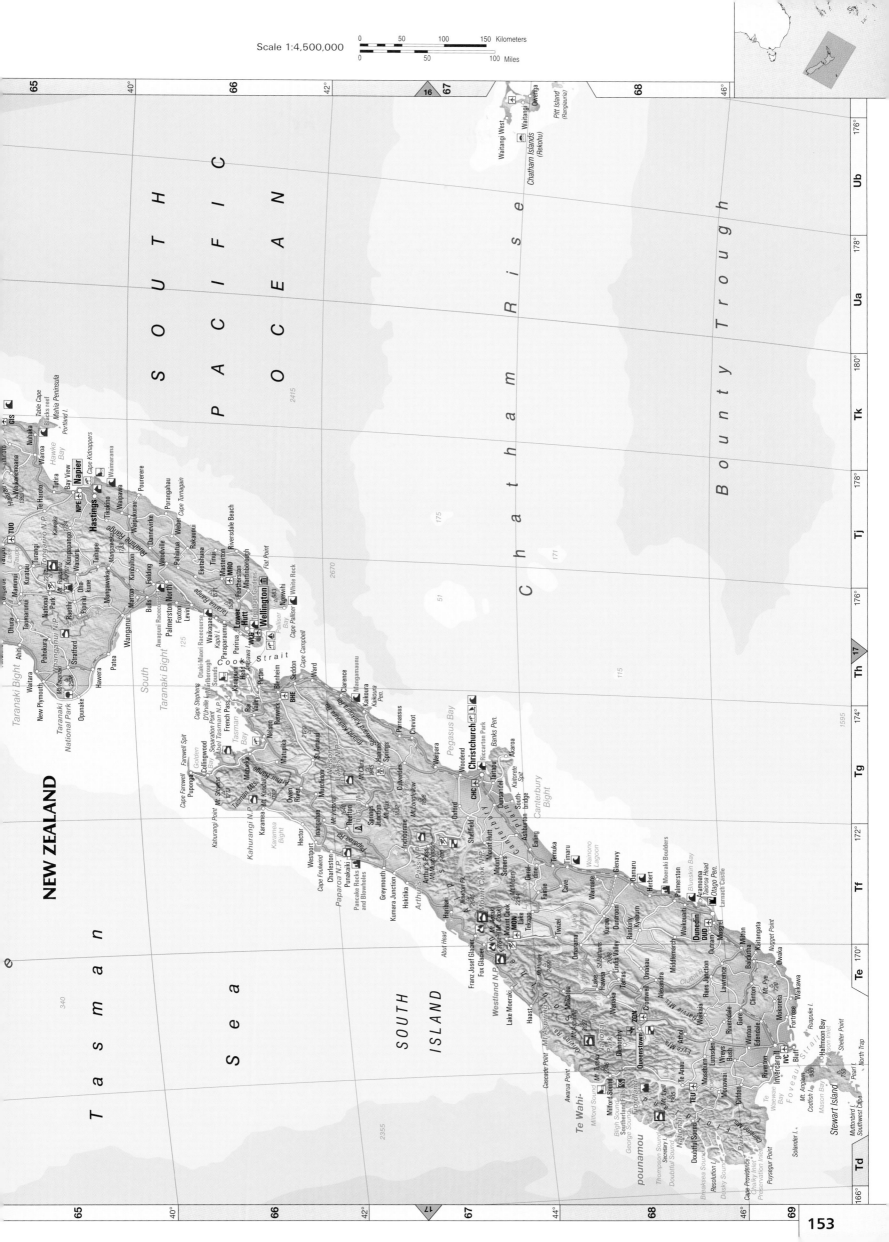

Scale 1:4,500,000

| 0 | 50 | 100 | 150 Kilometers |

| 0 | 50 | 100 Miles |

NEW ZEALAND

T a s m a n

S e a

S O U T H

P A C I F I C

O C E A N

SOUTH ISLAND

Napier

Hastings

Palmerston North

Wellington

Lower Hutt

Cook Strait

Taranaki Bight

New Plymouth

Taranaki National Park

Nelson

Blenheim

Christchurch

Timaru

Oamaru

Dunedin

Invercargill

Queenstown

Chatham Islands
(Rekohu)

Waitangi

Pitt Island
(Rangiauria)

C h a t h a m   R i s e

B o u n t y   T r o u g h

pounamou

Te Wahi-

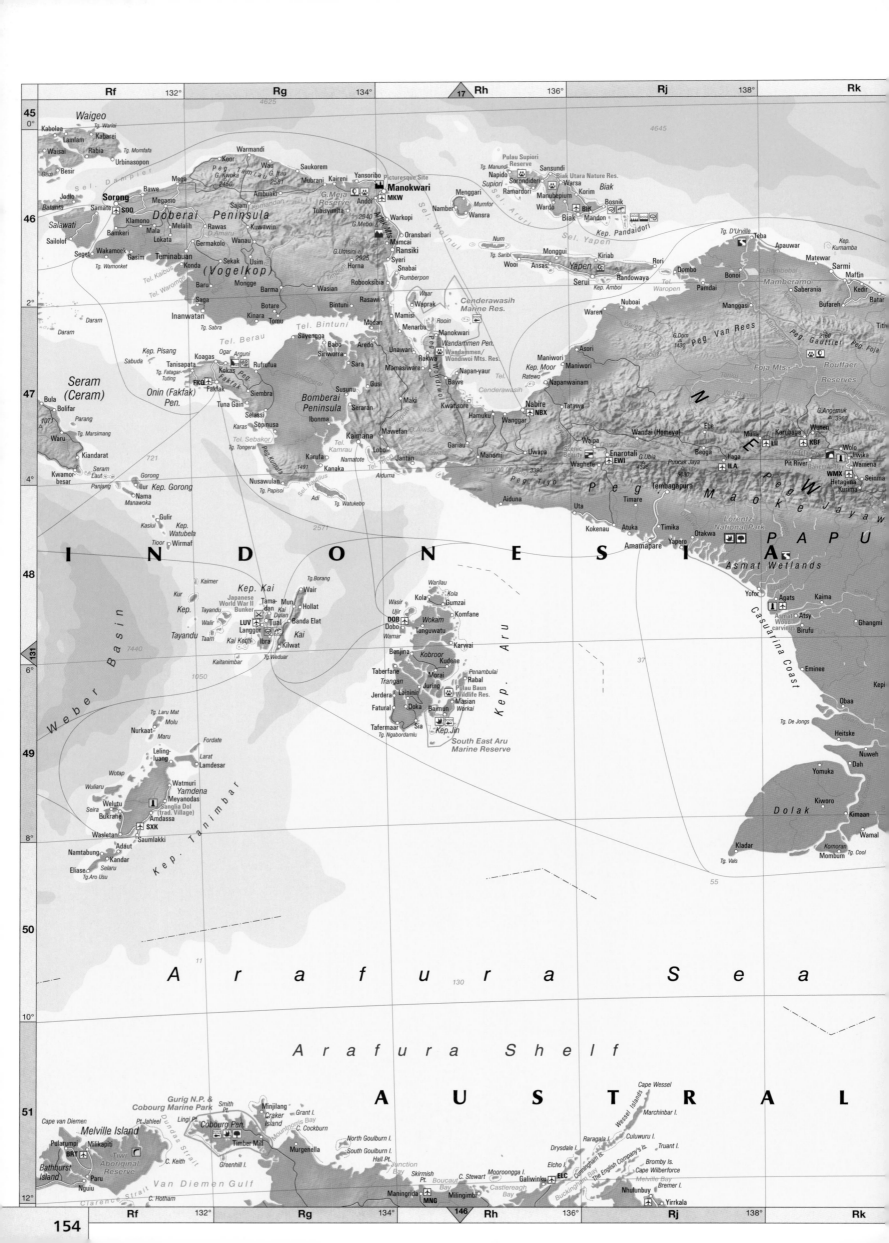

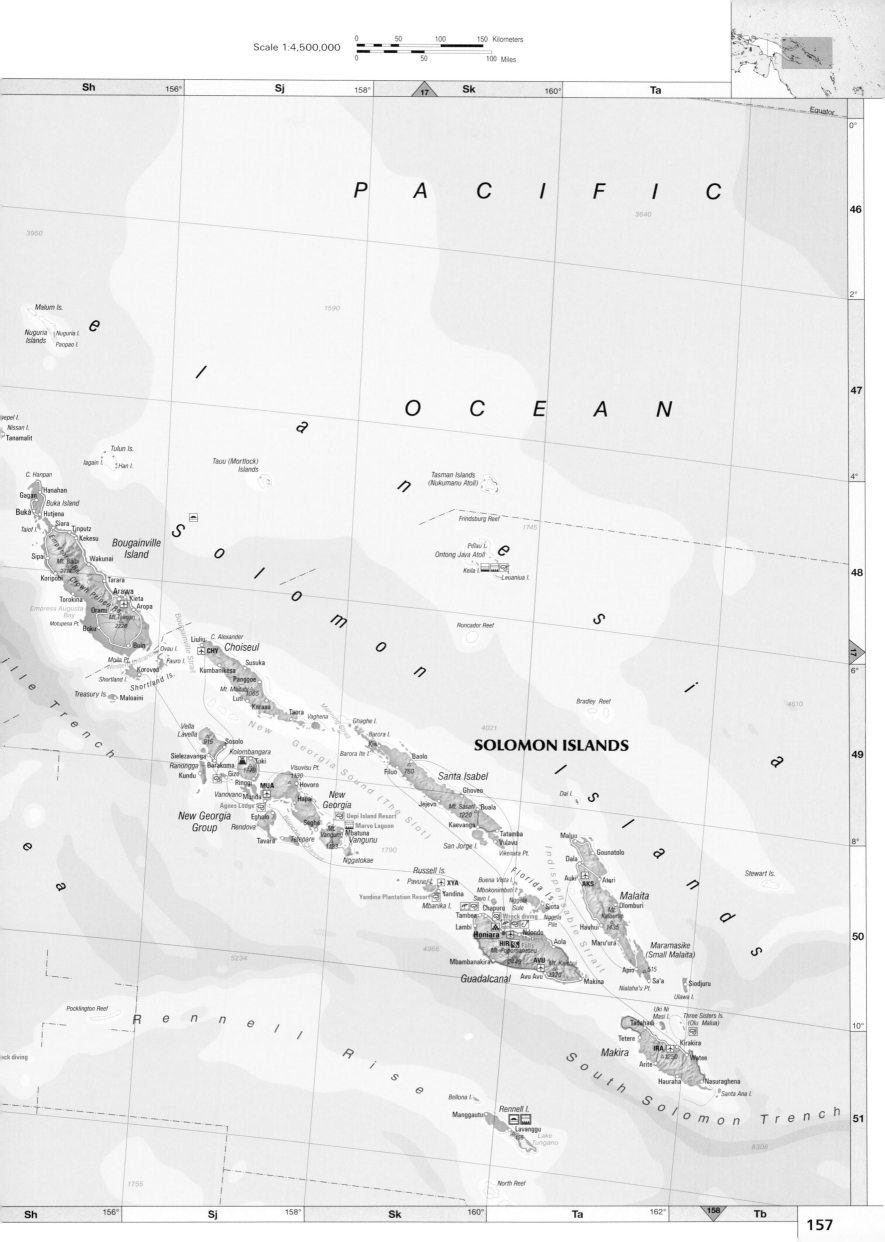

Scale 1:4,500,000

0 50 100 150 Kilometers

0 50 100 Miles

Equator

0°

P A C I F I C

46

3950

3640

2°

1590

e

l

a

O C E A N

47

n

Malum Is.

Nuguria
Islands

Nuguria I.

Paopao I.

eepel I.

Nissan I.

Tanamalit

Tulun Is.

Iagain I.

Han I.

Tauu (Mortlock)
Islands

Tasman Islands
(Nukumanu Atoll)

4°

d

C. Hanpan

Hanahan

Gagan

Buka Island

Buka

Hutjena

Siara

Tinputz

Kekesu

Taiof I.

Sipai

Mt. Balbi
2714

Wakunai

Bougainville
Island

Koripobi

Tarara

Torokina

Arawa

Kieta

Orami

Aropa

Empress Augusta
Bay

Mt. Takuan
2220

Motupena Pt.

Boku

Buin

S

o

l

o

m

o

n

Frindsburg Reef

1745

Pelau I.

Ontong Java Atoll

Keila I.

e

Leuaniua I.

48

Roncador Reef

s

Liuliu

C. Alexander

Choiseul

CHY

Ovau I.

Fauro I.

Moila Pt.

Koroveu

Western

Shortland Is.

Kumbanikesa

Susuka

Panggoe

Mt. Maitabi
1065

Luti

Knrasa

Taora

Vaghena

Ghaghe I.

Barora I.

Barora Ite I.

Kia

i

Bradley Reef

17

6°

ille Trench

Treasury Is.

Maloaini

New

Manning Strait

Baolo

Filuo

760

Santa Isabel

4021

4610

Vella
Lavella

915

Sosolo

Kolombangara

Sielezavanga

Barakoma

Tuki

Ranongga

Gizo

1770

Visuvisu Pt.
1130

Ghoveo

Jejevo

Mt. Sasari
1220

Buala

Dai I.

a

49

e

Kundu

Ringgi

New
Georgia

Hovoro

Hapai

Kaevanga

Vanovano

Munda

Agnes Lodge

MUA

New Georgia
Group

Egholo

Seghe

Uepi Island Resort

Marvo Lagoon

Tatamba

Vulavu

Vikenara Pt.

San Jorge I.

Maluu

Gounatolo

a

s

Rendova

Tavara

Tetepare

Mt.
Vangunu
1123

Mbatuna

Vangunu

1790

Dala

Aukl

Ateri

Stewart Is.

Malaita

i

Nggatokae

Russell Is.

Buena Vista I.

AKS

Pavuvu I.

XYA

Mbokonimbeti I.

Mbanika I.

Yandina Plantation Resort

Yandina

Savo I.

Nggela
Sule

Olomburi

Mt.
Kalourat

Olu Malua

l

e

a

Tambea

Lambi

Chapuru

Nggela
Pile

Siota

Wreck diving

Ndondo

Siota

Hauhui

1435

Apio

515

a

n

Honiara

HIR

Mataniko
Falls

Aola

Maru'ura

Maramasike
(Small Malaita)

Sa'a

Siodjuru

50

4966

Mbambanakira

Mt. Popomaneseu

AVU

Mt. Kaichui
2449

Avu Avu

1920

Makina

Nialaha'u Pt.

Ulawa I.

d

Guadalcanal

Florida Is.

Indispensable Strait

Uki Ni
Masi I.

Three Sisters Is.
(Olu Malua)

s

Pocklington Reef

R

e

n

n

e

l

l

R

i

s

e

Tadahadi

Tetere

Makira

IRA

1250

Kirakira

Watee

10°

eck diving

Arite

Hauraha

Nasuraghena

Bellona I.

Rennell I.

South Solomon Trench

Manggautu

Lavanggu

155

Lake
Tungano

51

5234

8308

1755

North Reef

SOLOMON ISLANDS

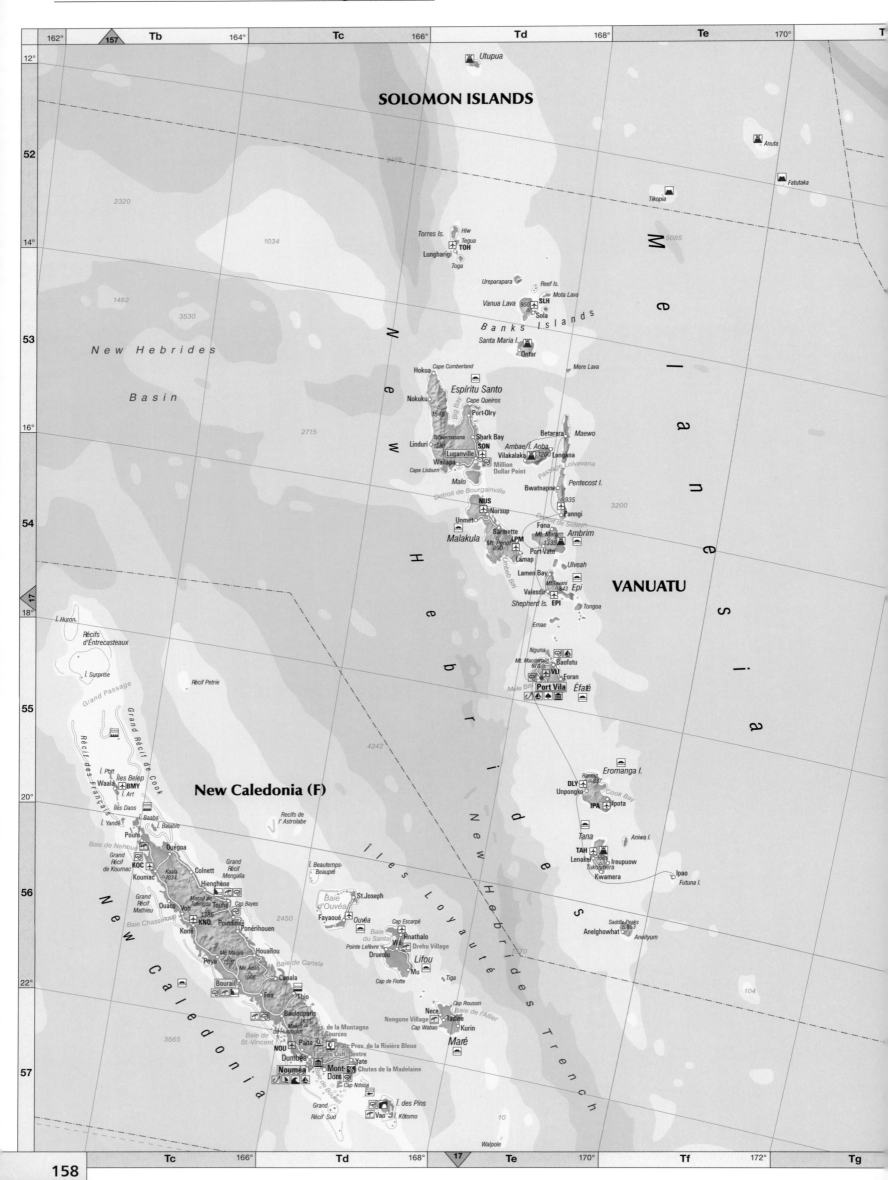

SOLOMON ISLANDS

Utupua

Anuta

Fatutaka

Tikopia

Torres Is.
Hiw
Tegua
TOH
Lungharigi
Toga

Ureparapara
Reef Is.
Mota Lava
Vanua Lava
950
SLH
Sola
Santa Maria I.
Onfar
Mere Lava

Banks Islands

Melanesia

New Hebrides Basin

Hokua
Cape Cumberland
Espíritu Santo
Nokuku
Cape Queiros
1546
Port-Olry
Betarara
Maewo
Tabwemasana
Shark Bay
Linduri
Isao
SON
Ambae/I. Aoba
Longana
Luganville
Vilakalaka
1200
Wailapa
Million Dollar Point
Cape Lisburn
Malo
Bwatnapne
Pentecost I.
NUS
935
Norsup
Panngi
Unmet
Fona
Detroit de Segond
Sarmette
Mt. Marum
LPM
1335
Ambrim
Malakula
Mt. Penot
890
Port-Vato
Lamap
Lamen Bay
Ulveah
Mt. Tavani
843
Valesdir
Epi
Shepherd Is.
EPI
Tongoa
Emae

VANUATU

Nguna
Mt. Macdonald
674
Baofatu
VLI
Foran
Mele Bay
Port Vila
Éfaté

I. Huron.
Récifs d'Entrecasteaux
I. Surprise
Récif Petrie
Eromanga I.
Ranto
837
DLY
Unpongko
Ipota
IPA

New Hebrides Basin

4242

Grand Passage
Récif des Français
Grand Récif de Cook
I. Pott
Waala
BMY
Îles Belep
I. Art
Tana
Aniwa I.
TAH
Lenakel
1084
Ireupuow
Kwamera
Tukosmera
Ipao
Futuna I.

New Caledonia (F)

Îles Daos
Baaba
I. Balabio
Poum
Baie de Nehoue
Grand Récif de Koumac
KOC
Koumac
Kaala
1034
Colnett
Grand Récif Mengalia
Ouégoa
Hienghène
Recifs de l'Astrolabe
St.Joseph
Baie d'Ouvéa
Quaco
Voh
Massif de Tchingou
Touho
Cap Bayes
I. Beautemps-Beaupré
Grand Récif Mathieu
1386
KNQ
Poindimié
Fayaoué
Ouvéa
Kone
Ponérihouen
Cap Escarpé
Baie du Santal
Baie Chasseloup
2450
Pointe Lefèvre
Hnathalo
We
Drehu Village
Houaïlou
Mu Maoya
1507
Druéulu
Lifou
Poya
Mu
Tiga
Mt. Aoùpinié
1006
Baie de Canala
Bourail
Canala
Cap de Fiotte
Foa
Thio
Cap Roussin
Baie de l'Allier
Bouloparis
Nece
Nengone Village
Tadine
Kurin
Cap Wabao
Rés. de la Montagne des Sources
Maré
Mt. Humboldt
1635
Baie de St-Vincent
Païta
NOU
Dumbea
Tjibaou Cult. Centre
Yate
Nouméa
Mont-Dore
Chutes de la Madeleine
Parc Prov. de la Rivière Bleue
Cap Ndoua
Grand Récif Sud
Vao
I. des Pins
I. Kotomo

New Caledonia

Walpole

New Hebrides Trench

Îles Loyauté

Saddle Peaks
863
Anelghowhat
Aneityum

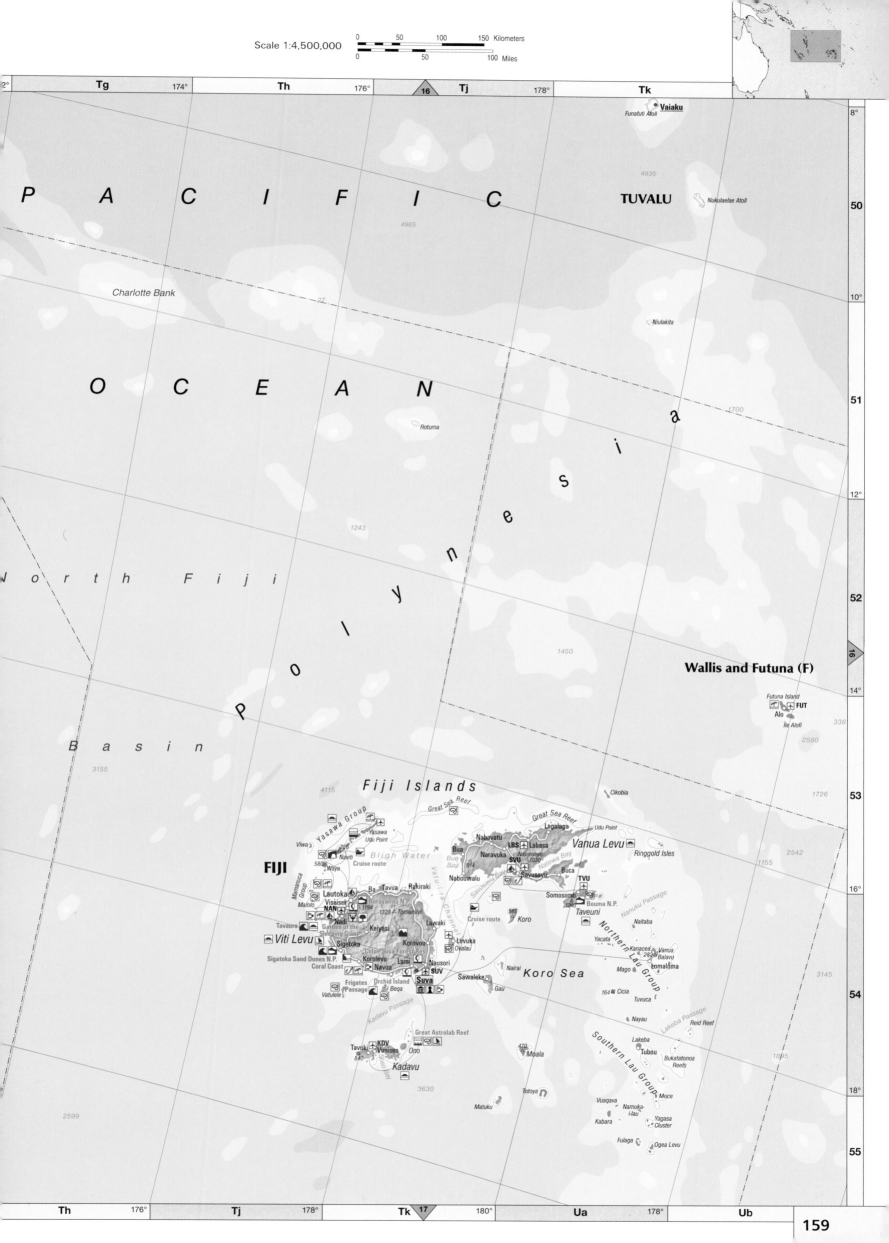

Vaiaku
Funafuti Atoll

P A C I F I C   TUVALU   Nukulaelae Atoll

4935

O C E A N

Charlotte Bank

Niulakita

27

Rotuma

1700

N o r t h   F i j i

1243

B a s i n

3155

4115

Fiji Islands

Cikobia

1726

Great Sea Reef
Yasawa Group
Yasawa
Udu Point   Great Sea Reef   Udu Point
Viwa   Naviti   *Bligh Water*   Lagalaga   Vanua Levu
FIJI   Waya   Ba Tavua Rakiraki   Nabavatu LBS Labasa   Ringgold Isles
Mamanuca Group   Lautoka   SVU   Nasorolevu   Naitaba
Malolo   Viseisei   Korovanitu N.P.   Nabouwalu Savusavu   TVU
NAN   Nadi   Tomanivi   Koro   Bouma N.P.
Tavarua   Garden of the   Keiyasi   Somosomo   *Taveuni*
Viti Levu   Sleeping Giant   Korovou   Levuka   Yacata Vanua Balavu
Sigatoka   Colo-i-Suva Forest Res.   Ovalau   Kanacea Lomaloma
Sigatoka Sand Dunes N.P.   Korolevu   Lami Nausori   Mago
Coral Coast   Navua SUV   Nairai   *Koro Sea*   Cicia
Frigates   Orchid Island   Suva   Sawaieke Gau   Tuvuca
Passage   Beqa   Nayau
Vatulele   Nayau   Reid Reef

Southern Lau Group
Great Astrolab Reef   Lakeba
Tavuki KDV   Ono   Moala   Tubou   Bukatatonoa Reefs
Vunisea   Moce
Kadavu   Vuaqava   Namuka-i-Lau Yagasa Cluster
Kabara
Matuku   Totoya   Fulaga Ogea Levu

TUVALU

a

s

e

n

y

l

o

P

i

s

e

n

Wallis and Futuna (F)

Futuna Island
FUT
Alo
Île Alofi   338

2580

2542

1155

Nanuku Passage

Northern Lau Group

Lakeba Passage

3145

1895

	8°
	50
	10°
	51
	12°
	52
	16
	14°
	53
	16°
	54
	18°
	55

| Th | 176° | Tj | 178° | Tk | 17 | 180° | Ua | 178° | Ub |

Africa

The third largest continent on Earth is a compact land mass between the Atlantic and Indian Oceans, rising to an average height of 650 m. The Mediterranean and Red Seas separate Africa from the neighbouring continents of Europe and Asia. North Africa is primarily shaped by basin landscapes, with the vast Saharan desert covering about a third of the African land mass. Central Africa is very similar in terms of topography, but is covered in rainforest, whereas highlands mostly define the face of southern Africa. The Great Rift Valley fault system is situated on the eastern side of the continent, where there are volcanoes over

5,000 m high. This is the most variable part of the continent in terms of natural geography. Few islands line the coasts, apart from the large island of Madagascar. Africa is neatly segmented in half by the equator, so apart from the uplands, there are only two climates – tropical and sub-tropical.

Quiver trees in Namibia: this South African species of aloe grows up to 10 m high and the circumference of the trunk can be as much as 1 m.

Africa

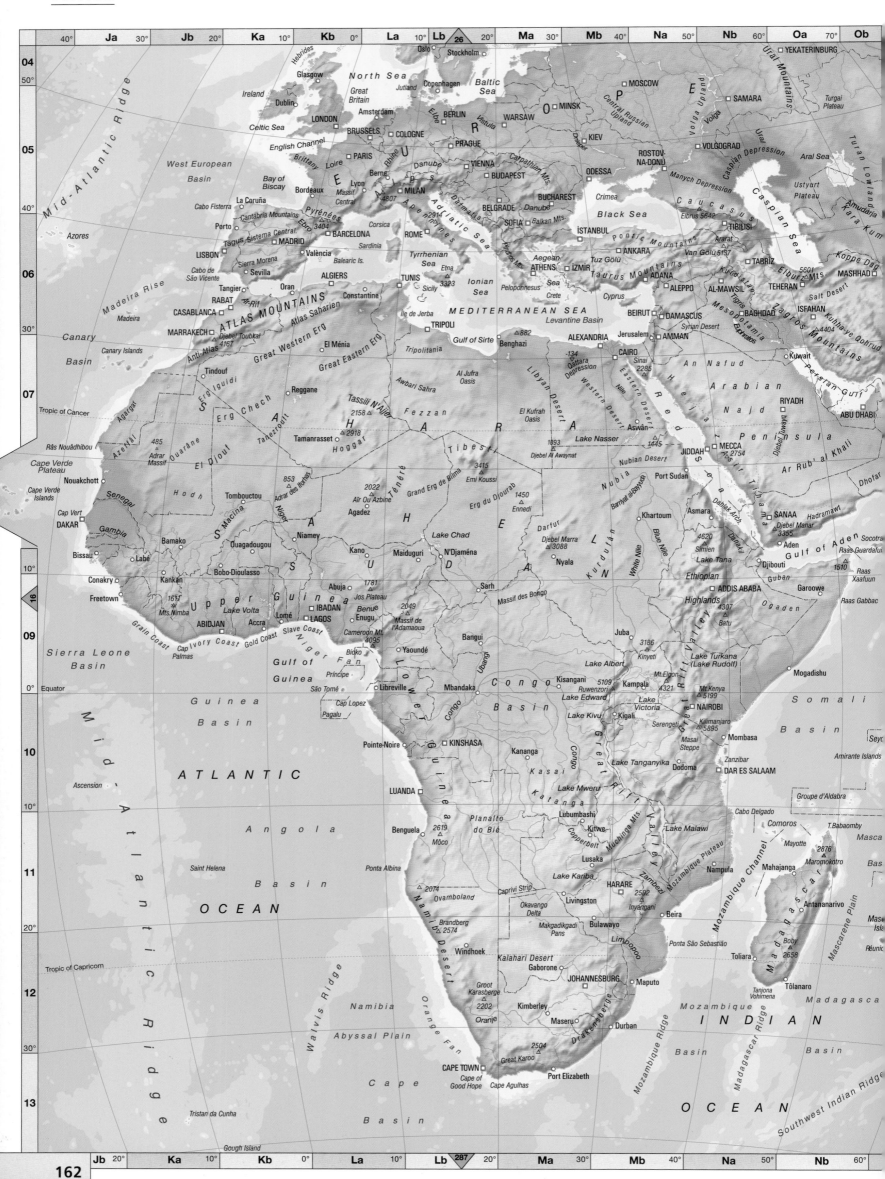

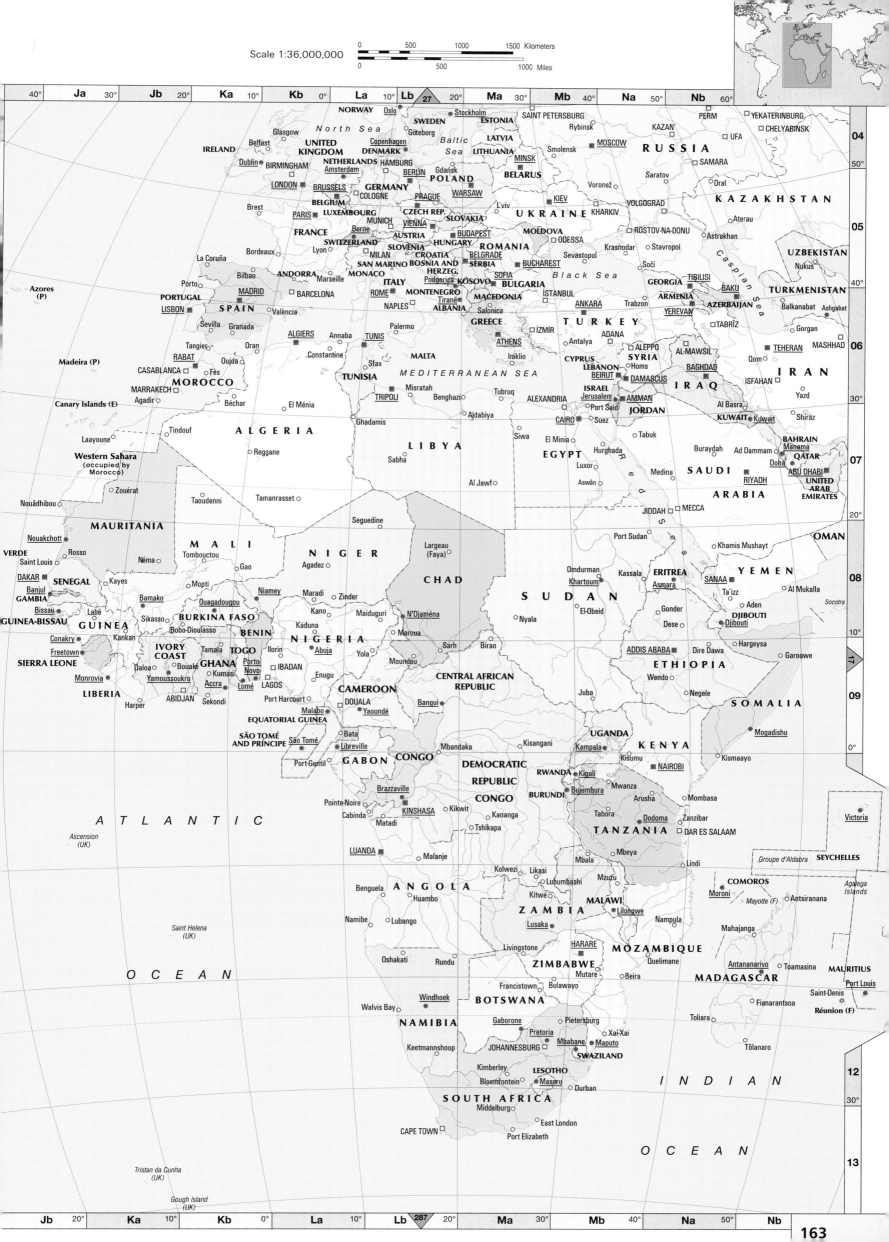

Scale 1:36,000,000

0   500   1000   1500 Kilometers

0   500   1000 Miles

NORWAY   Oslo   SWEDEN   Stockholm   ESTONIA   SAINT PETERSBURG   PERM   YEKATERINBURG
Glasgow   Göteborg   LATVIA   Rybinsk   KAZAN   UFA   CHELYABINSK   04
IRELAND   Belfast   UNITED   Copenhagen   LITHUANIA   Smolensk   MOSCOW   SAMARA   50°
Dublin   BIRMINGHAM   KINGDOM   DENMARK   HAMBURG   Gdańsk   MINSK   Saratov   Oral   KAZAKHSTAN
LONDON   NETHERLANDS   BERLIN   POLAND   BELARUS   Voronež   VOLGOGRAD   Aterau
Brussels   GERMANY   WARSAW   L'viv   KHARKIV   ROSTOV-NA-DONU   UZBEKISTAN
PARIS   LUXEMBOURG   COLOGNE   PRAGUE   UKRAINE   Astrakhan   05
BELGIUM   CZECH REP.   SLOVAKIA   MOLDOVA   Krasnodar   Stavropol   Nukus
FRANCE   MUNICH   VIENNA   BUDAPEST   ODESSA   Sevastopol   Soči   TURKMENISTAN
Brest   SWITZERLAND   AUSTRIA   HUNGARY   ROMANIA   Black Sea   GEORGIA   TBILISI   BAKU   40°
Lyon   Berne   SLOVENIA   CROATIA   BELGRADE   BUCHAREST   ISTANBUL   ARMENIA   AZERBAIJAN   Balkanabat   Ashgabat
Bordeaux   MILAN   SAN MARINO   BOSNIA AND   SERBIA   BULGARIA   ANKARA   YEREVAN   TABRĪZ   Gorgan

*The wide valleys of the **Sahara** desert are known as wadis. In these valleys, when rain falls heavily, the dry river bed fills up rapidly but dries out again as soon as there is another long dry spell. The water table is near the surface, so oases are often found alongside wadis.*

The Atlas region

The **Atlas** and **Rif** mountain chains run parallel to the Mediterranean and Atlantic coasts in the northwest of the African continent, enclosing a partly fertile, partly steppe central plateau.

This plateau consists of the fertile **Sebou Basin**, the **coastal Meseta** next to the Atlantic Ocean and the barren highlands of the east Moroccan Meseta. In the north, the plateau is edged by the foothills of the **Atlas** Mountains and in the south by the **Saharan Atlas range**.

The fold mountains of the Atlas-Rif system are the result of the collision of the European continental plate with the more stable African plate. This event took place in the Palaeozoic period, approximately 600 million years ago, and lasted until the Tertiary period.

Rif Mountains

The **Rif Mountains** stretch over 300 km from the **Straits of Gibraltar** to the **Cape Tres Forcas** and are composed of palaeozoic rock, which appears

Niger

The Niger, which at 4,160 km long and with a catchment area of about 2.1 million sq. km counts as one of the longest rivers on the continent, rises in the Loma Mountains in Guinea, near the border with Sierra Leone. The river then flows in a north-easterly direction to the western Sahara and, with its tributary, the Bani, forms a large inland delta in Mali, where about 40,000 sq. km is inundated for three to six months of the year. Here the Niger loses about half of its water. It then meanders to the southeast in the Niger bend at the Upper Guinea watershed of Tosaye. At Yelwa, the Niger is stemmed by the Kainji dam. The Benue, which flows into the Niger at Lokoja, doubles the amount of water in the river, which reaches a width of between 700 m and 2,000 m at Onitsha. It finally flows in numerous branches into a delta of approximately 25,000 sq. km in the Gulf of Guinea.

on the surface on the Mediterranean coast. Younger sedimentary strata cover the mountains inland. The wild and rugged peaks reach elevations of 2,448 m (**Tidighin**) and are adjacent to the **Middle Atlas** in the south.

The Atlas Mountains

The **Middle Atlas** stretches over a distance of more than 350 km and reaches an average height of 1,300 m. The eastern part, where the Middle Atlas drops in a steep escarpment, has the characteristics of a high mountain region (**Bou Naceur**, 3,340 m), whereas the western part changes into extensive high plateaus that have shifted in a stepped fashion, with protruding mountain peaks of only around 400 m.

The **High Atlas** extends over 800 km from **Cape Ghir** to the east Moroccan **Meseta**, where it branches and becomes the **Saharan Atlas**. The highest peak is the

Toubkal summit (4,167 m). The range slopes away in the west and south into steep rocky cliffs up to 1,000 m high. In the north, it flattens out gently to the Meseta. In the south-east, it lies adjacent to the mountain chains of the Saharan Atlas, reaching heights of more than 2,300 m.

Sahara region

The Sahara, the largest area of desert on Earth, extends over about 12 million sq. km. The vast tableland, which is covered with sand and boulders interspersed with small oases, stretches over approximately 6,000 km along an east-west axis from the **Atlantic** to the **Red Sea** and over 2,000 km in a north-south direction as far as the Sudan.

Whereas the steppe landscape of the **Mediterranean coast** in the north forms a narrow strip

extending to only around 100 km before merging completely with the desert, the shape of the landscape only alters very gradually in the south. The semi-desert and thornbush savannah of the **Sahel** gradually change into desert in a corridor approximately 300 km in width.

Only about 20 per cent of the **Sahara** is covered with sandy desert; the remaining areas are boulder and stone basins, which are covered with a layer of fine gravel (**Serirs**) on the plains and by coarse rock (**Hammadas**) on the plateaus. The stepped rims of the basins slope down to **wadis** or riverbeds, which are only filled with water after rainfall. Interior depressions, covered with huge **ergs** and closed salt lake areas (chotts), characterise other parts of the north as far as the Mediterranean coast. These interior basins extend southwards and form the **Tenere desert** and the **Libyan** and **Arabian deserts**.

These areas, intersected by the **Nile Basin**, extend as far as the **Red Sea**.

The **Central Sahara** contains mountain islands and highlands, such as the **Tademait**, **Tassili** and **Djado**, ringed by high mountain ranges such as the **Ahaggar**, **Tibesti**, **Aïr**, **Iforas** and **Ennedi**. The only permanent stretch of water in the Sahara is the **Nile**.

Excluding the Nile valley region, about 2 million people live in the Sahara desert. They are mostly nomads and oasis farmers.

The Sahara has an extreme desert climate: temperatures can rise to more than 50°C during the day and yet sink to below freezing point at night, even during the summer months.

Ergs

The massive dunes in the interior depressions of **West and Central Sahara**, which contain occasional high, ochre to reddish-yellow sand dunes, only occupy about one fifth of the Sahara. They have created a very definitive image of the desert, however.

The largest of these sand seas are the **Grand Erg Occidental**, which stretches over 500 km between Mauretania and the Saharan Atlas, the **Grand Erg Oriental** and the **Grand Erg du Bilma**. In addition, there are small ergs everywhere, whose drifting dunes change shape and size according to the prevailing wind, so they are continually transforming.

Ahaggar (Tassili N' Ajjer)

The **Ahaggar** is the largest mountainous area in the **Central Sahara**, extending over an area of almost 300,000 sq. km.

The heart of this spectacular mountain region, which was formed about 600 million years ago and reshaped through continuous volcanic activity, is the bizarre basalt landscape of the **Atakor**, with the **Tahat** summit reaching 2,918 m.

To the north and east of the Ahaggar are the **Tassili steppes**, which were formed about 250 million years ago. The sandstone strata on this high plateau have been washed away over millions of years by earlier river courses and eroded by wind and sand into unique shapes, including rock arches. The vast **Tassili N'Ajjer** in Algeria, containing the **Adrar** at a height of 2,158 m, looks like a fantasy moonscape.

Nile: this picture illustrates how much life in the surrounding desert depends on the river.

Nile

At 6,671 km, the Nile is the longest river on Earth and the most important river in Africa. It has a catchment area of approximately 3.35 million sq. km and flows from ten sources in the mountains of Burundi. It then quickly forms the Kagera, which flows into Lake Victoria after a journey of 850 km, in order to leave Uganda at Jinja as the Victoria Nile. This flows through

Lake Kyoga, crosses the ridge at the eastern rim of the Central African rift via the Kabalega Falls and pours into Lake Albert. The Albert Nile, which is known as the Mountain Nile from the Sudanese border, finally reaches the marshy area of the Sudd. From here, as the White Nile it picks up the Gazelle Nile and the Sobat and joins the sediment-rich Blue Nile at Khartoum,

which flows down from the Ethiopian highlands. After the confluence with the Atbara, the Nile covers the final 2,700 km as it flows through the Nubian and Libyan deserts. The first of the six famous Nile cataracts is at Aswan in Egypt. After forming a huge delta, the numerous branches of the Nile finally drain into the Mediterranean Sea near Alexandria.

In one of the most inhospitable regions of the Sahara Desert, in south-east Algeria, near the borders with Libya and Niger, the Tassili N'Ajjer mountain range covers an area roughly the size of England. The highest point is Adrar Afao, at 2,158 m. Concealing a large plateau, it is also known as the Tassili Plateau. Erosion has transformed parts of the rock, sculpting the sandstone into bizarre and spectacular formations, including around 300 rock arches.

The Tibesti Mountains, Djado Plateau

The steep gorges and bizarre weathering of the **Tibesti Mountains** in the central Sahara, which cover an area of approximately 100,000 sq. km, are one of the most impressive landscapes on the continent.

The deeply fissured high mountains jut out like a wedge with a sheer drop of about 450 m to the surrounding low plateau. The substrate of the Tibesti mountain range consists of granite and slate strata, which folded upwards in the Quaternary and Tertiary periods. In the course of these tectonic activities, several volcanoes were formed, whose cooled lava masses now sit on this substrate as mountain peaks.

The massive **Emi Koussi**, which is the Sahara's highest point at 3,415 m, is one of these volcanoes. It has a diameter of 70 km at the base. Volcanic phenomena, such as fumaroles and hot springs, can also be found here.

The surrounding highlands form the transition to the plateaus, including the **Djado Plateau**, which is traversed by huge wadis.

Libyan Desert

The Libyan desert in the north-eastern Sahara covers an area of approximately 1.5 million sq. km. It consists of extensive tablelands with distinct tiers of strata that were separated during the Ice Age by waterways. Where the north is characterised by chalk from the Tertiary period, the south is composed primarily of sandstone. The tablelands rise in the south to several massifs and reach their highest elevation in the **Jabal al-Uwaynat** at 1,898 m. The extremely dry and inhospitable **Libyan Desert** is a gravel desert in most parts, interspersed with vast sand dunes in the basins. From the southern slope of the **Marmarica**, the **Qattara Depression** stretches from the Siwa Oasis to the deepest point, the Qattara Basin (-133 m).

Nubian Desert

The rocky and sandy desert extending east of the **Nile** to the **Red Sea** covers about 400,000 sq. km and is uninhabited as a result of its exceptionally dry climate. The mountainous region rises in an easterly direction, reaching its highest elevation in the **coastal range** at Jabal Oda

(2,259 m) before sloping steeply to the coast. Groundwater is only available inone dry valley in the **Nubian Desert**.

Nile Basin, Nile Delta

On its journey through the **Libyan** and **Nubian Deserts**, the **Nile** has eroded a box canyon approximately 20 km wide and up to 300 m in depth, and forms six cataracts. Before the first of these **cataracts**, at Aswan, a 500-km stretch of river has been dammed to form the Aswan High Dam and Lake Nasser, known as Lake Nubia in the small section in the Sudan.

The extensive sedimentary deposits from the annual Nile floods are caused by the tropical monsoon rains falling on the Ethiopian Highlands which in turn feed water to the **Blue Nile**. This phenomenon has led to the formation of an extremely fertile coastal strip which widens as it flows through Egypt into the vast **Nile Delta**, an area measuring approximately 24,000 sq. km. From the delta, the branches of the Nile, the **Rosetta** and the **Damietta** drain into the Mediterranean. This fertile area has been intensively cultivated for thousands of years and can truly be said to be the cradle of civilisation.

1 This delightful scenic route leads over the 2,260-m-high Tizi-n-Tichka Pass in Morocco's High Atlas Mountains.

2 Tafraoute, Morocco: the Anti-Atlas, lying to the south of the Atlas mountains, was formed considerably earlier than the other Atlas ranges.

3 The Wadi Dadès in Morocco's Atlas Mountains. Wadis are dry river valleys and most have steep valley walls.

4 Sahara: the Ennedi Mountains in north-eastern Chad soar to a height of 1,450 m. The plateau consists of sandstone.

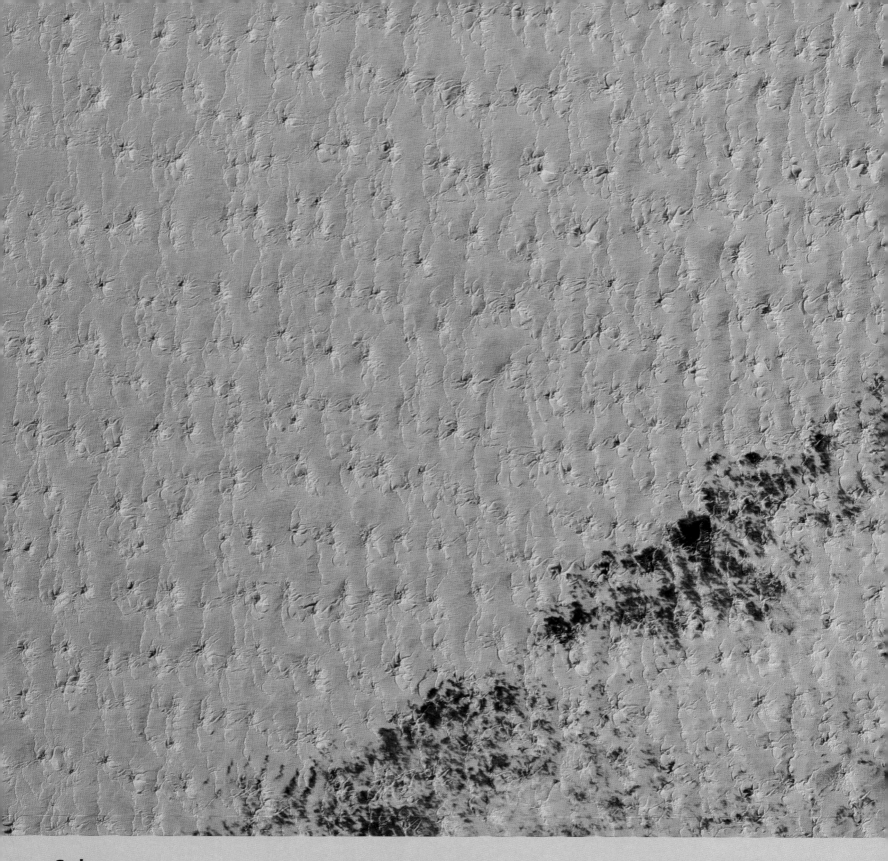

Sahara

The Arabs call the large dunes of the Sahara the 'Bahr bela ma' or the 'Sea without water', as the soft rise and fall of the dune crests are reminiscent of the swell of the ocean. Alexander von Humboldt, the well-travelled natural scientist, believed in the nineteenth century that the Sahara was part of a huge desert belt, extending from the Atlantic to India.

The Sahara is the world's largest hot desert, covering more than 9,000,000 sq. km. Only about 20 per cent of the surface of this large desert is covered with sand and a mere ten per cent of the Sahara can be described as genuine sand dunes. The aeolian shapes carved by the wind make up only a small part of this desert; most of the wealth of geological forms was and is shaped by what surface water there is.

That may sound surprising, as the Sahara is still one of the driest regions on Earth. Yet the comparatively low precipitation, which falls intermittently at the edges of the Sahara and only rarely in the centre, has huge erosive power. The sudden torrents of rain cause flash floods, heavily eroding the stepped slopes and edges of the wadis (dry river beds) and carving deep gorges in the mountains; sand and rubble are washed into the wide dry valleys or the inner Saharan areas.

A large part of the Sahara's very varied geological formations date from a time when the climate was wetter. Over millions of years, the region has been inundated several times and vast layers of sediment have been deposited in the basins, which are 7 km thick in places. These basins, covered by stone and boulder deserts, are lined with folds where the crystalline sub-soil

of the Saharan substrate has become visible. These uplifted folds were formed mainly in the centre of the Sahara and developed further through volcanic activity. The high mountains of the Ahaggar fall into this category. The transition from the basins to the high stepped strata of the mountain regions and plateaus, such as the Tassili n Ajjer, is momentous.

When Europe lay under a thick sheet of ice 1.8 million years ago, the Sahara was a fertile landscape as a result of a wet phase, the pluvial period. At this time, many rivers crisscrossed the steppe landscape and formed deep gorges, today's wadis. In summer, large lakes filled depressions in the landscape.

The Sahara has been a desert for approximately 40,000 years, even though shorter pluvial phases, most recently in 4,000 BC, again caused the completely arid areas to recede. The climate soon became warmer and drier again, and the desert began to grow. Since then, there have been wetter and drier periods, but there is no doubt about the expanse of perpetual desert. For about 200 years, a particularly dry period has prevailed, which has intensified in the last 100 years and manifested itself as severe droughts in the southern zone, at the edge of the Sahel and in the Sahel itself. Additionally, the effect of livestock grazing has led to very evident desertification.

The north-east trade winds are a further significant force of nature that has affected the shape of the Sahara. They not only create the shifting dunes but, working in conjunction with water, they have the power to move boulders and debris. The effect of sand corrosion is particularly great in the southern Sahara, where the trade winds have an extreme effect, and this has led to the formation of strangely shaped rocky outcrops. The hot and often sand-laden winds such as the Sirocco (known as the Ghibli in Libya), the Khamsin, the Simoom or the southerly Harmattan are also feared, as they can suddenly turn into sandstorms lasting only a few minutes

or for days on end. The Saharan winds carry the sand-dust even as far as the European Alps.

Today, only a few areas in the Sahara are habitable, although the area is one of the most ancient of human habitats. Archaeologists have identified signs of human activity dating back 500,000 years, when the rainfall pattern allowed settlement.

Today, those who live in settled communities in the Sahara primarily inhabit the oases, which have

been established in places where favourable conditions have enabled access to the groundwater trapped in the sedimentary strata. These desert gardens, where date palms grow in abundance and limpid pools are stocked with goldfish, are to be found primarily at the northern end of the Sahara where they create a belt of vegetation. The nomadic tribes who roam the area mostly live in the dry valleys, the highlands, plateaus with more favourable climates at the foot of

the high mountains and in some of the dune landscapes that periodically contain water.

Most of the inhabitants of the Sahara live around its edge, in areas such as the Sahel. It is worth noting that the different ethnic groups that live in the Sahara did not previously have a name by which to designate the whole region. They still only rarely use the Arabic word 'sahrâ' today, which means 'yellowish' as well as 'barren'. The regional expressions

for the individual landscapes that the Sahara's inhabitants employ to illustrate the variety of landscapes are symbolic. In this way, the Sahel becomes the rescuing 'shore', which is reached by travellers from the north.

Above: the satellite picture shows a section of the Grand Erg Oriental (Great Eastern 'Erg', or dune field) in the Algerian Sahara Desert. Some of the most impressive features of the Sahara are the star dunes, which grow upwards with three to five arms rising to a central point. The dunes of the central Sahara can rise to 200 m.

Africa

*Although not far from the Equator, the summit of **Kilimanjaro** is covered in snow. Due to its immense height, the mountain massif has a variety of climates and vegetation zones. Up to a height of 3,000 m, land that was previously wooded savannah has been cleared for agricultural use. There is also mountain forest and mountain grassland, which gives way to the icy wastes of the summit.*

Sahel

The landscape of the **Sahel**, Arabic for 'shore', stretches in a 300-km-wide belt from the Atlantic coast to the **Horn of Africa**, across the whole African continent, creating a gradual transition area from the extremely dry **Sahara** and the wetland **savannah** in the south. The Sahel consists mainly of thornbush savannah with isolated grassland that is suitable only for use as grazing land for nomadic herds of livestock. However, further south, in the region of the **Niger** and **Senegal** rivers and in the area around **Lake Chad**, irrigation is possible. As a result of intensive farming and cattle-rearing, large parts of the original tree and bush vegetation have been destroyed. Overgrazing and serious drought have led to large-scale soil erosion, so that every year, several million tonnes of dust from this region is blown away – some of it ends up as far away as Europe.

Sudan region

The area between the **Sahara** in the north and the rainforest regions in the south extends to

Congo

The second largest river in Africa at 4,734 km, the Congo rises in the Mitumba Mountains and flows as the Lualaba across the Lunda and Central African basins, where it forms numerous rapids and lakes. The river loses only 60 m in height at the seven individual waterfalls that make up the 100 km stretch of the Stanley Falls. It flows as a lowland river 14 m wide for more than 1,700 km to Kinshasa. On its long route through the Congo basin, it absorbs many tributaries including the Lomami and the Ubangi. The Lower Guinea Basin is crossed by the Congo at Livingstone Falls (Inga Falls). Below, the valley opens up into a wide basin to the river mouth which is covered in mangrove swamp and continues as a 1,700 m deep gorge to the ocean floor in the Atlantic.

around 4.5 million sq. km. The zone, which spreads from **Fouta Djallon** to **the Ethopian highlands** in the east, is 900 km wide on average.
The difference in height is only small at 250–500 m, although in **Ouaddaï** and **Ennedi**, the plateaus that divide Niger, Chad and the White Nile basins, the elevation is greater.
The Sudan has climate and vegetation zones that are almost parallel in width. The north is covered by dry savannah, which gives way to thornbush savannah at the Sahel. At its southern extremity, the Sudan extends into the wet savannah region.

Guinea highlands

The central **highlands of Guinea** form the western edge of the **Upper Guinea basin** and consist of mountainous regions that overlap the **Fouta Djallon**, which

The 3000-m-high Mulanje-Massif in the South of the Malawi lake.

rises to an altitude of approximately 1,500 m.
It reaches its greatest elevation at the northern end of the **Massif du Tamqué** (1,538 m). In the east, it turns partly into forest, partly into uplands covered in high pasture up to an altitude of around 400 m. The **Senegal** and **Niger** rivers both have their sources in the Guinea highlands.

Niger Basin

With its tributary, the river **Bani**, the **Niger** forms a massive inland delta of around 40,000 sq. km

between Ségou and Timbuktu. The delta is flooded for three to six months of the year, and leaves broad swamps that add their waters to the many smaller and larger lakes.

Chad basin

This extensive depression covers part of the **Sahara** in the north, and the **Sudan** in the south. It is surrounded by the **Tibesti** and **Ennedi** plateaus and the western edges of the **Darfur mountains** as well as the **Azande basin**, and the **Ouaddaï** highlands. The lowest point is the **Bodélé Depression** in the central south (160 m). **Lake Chad** which occupies a large proportion of the depression is a tideless lake, only 3–7 m deep, believed to be the remains of an inland sea. The circumference of the lake is constantly changing due to intense evaporation, but it is thought to be 22,000 sq. km in

size today. The northern part of the lake has almost completely dried out since 1972. The only river flowing into Lake Chad is the **Chari River**, which discharges into a constantly expanding delta at the south of the lake.
The shores are swamps in which reeds and papyrus flourish. On the eastern side there are many islands created by dunes. Lake Chad was once the largest lake in Africa, but that is no longer the case, and there is a danger that it may eventualy disappear altogether due to global warming and demands on its waters.

Darfur region

This mountainous region comprises a broad, sparsely vegetated plateau, which spreads south from the **Libyan desert**, and is dominated by the volcanic highlands of the **Marrah mountains** in the central region. The **Darfur mountains** cover 480,000 sq. km. They consist mainly of a 600 to 1,100-m-high plateau, dominated by the Marrah mountains, which are on average 2,200 m high. This area of basalt rock rises to a peak in the Marrah at 3,088 m. The north of this sparsely-inhabited region is covered with dry savannah, while the south, in contrast, is often flooded during the rainy season.

Sudd

The swamp of the **Sudd** (Arabic for 'barrier') is an extensive floodplain of the **Nile**. It is created by the discharge of the Mountain Nile from the uplands of the **Azande basin** in a broad alluvial plain, where the river, becoming increasingly sluggish, meanders and accommodates the **Sobat River** and the **Bahr el-Ghazal** ('River of the Gazelles').
With its swamps, lagoons and side-channels, the Sudd covers an estimated area of between 100,000 and 130,000 sq. km, and is thickly overgrown with beds of reeds, papyrus and grasses. The Nile loses about 60 per cent of its water through evaporation in the Sudd, before it flows northwards as the White Nile.

Ethiopian highland

The deep **Ethiopian rift**, the continuation of the **East African rift**, divides the **Ethiopian highlands** into a western region, which stretches to the southern basin of **Lake Turkana** and falls steeply into the **Sudan**, and an eastern region, which gently slopes into the **Somali Peninsula**. The Ethiopian rift, which is interspersed with lakes and volcanoes that are still young, opens out to the north-east into the **Afar Depression**. Broad plateaus dominate the landscape, ringed by volcanic massifs.
To the north, the Amhara highlands are riven with deep valleys. The adjacent Simien mountains reach heights of 4,620 m (Ras Dashan), while the lower Kaffa highlands stretch to the southwest. The eastern highlands are

dominated by the 4,377-m-high Mount Batu. Throughout the region, the highland escarpments and the deep river gorges (Omo, Blue Nile, Takaze) are very steep.

Somali Peninsula

This wedge-shaped peninsula, better known as the **Horn of Africa** because of its shape, is bordered to the north by the **Gulf of Aden** and to the south by the open **Indian Ocean**. The Somali Peninsula is a steep massif, dropping to the south, while to the north it slopes gradually to the sea, structured by step faults.
The highest elevation is the 2,416 m **Mount Shimbiris** in the north. Here, the coast is very steep and rocky and descends to a coastal plain up to 100 km wide. The Somali Peninsula is mainly semi-desert.

Central Africa

Central Africa consists mainly of broad plateaus, which gain height towards the east. The central **Congo basin**, which has a narrow channel to the Atlantic coast, is surrounded on all sides by deep valleys of pre-Cambrian rocks. In the west, there is the **Lower Guinea basin**, in the north the **Azande basin**, in the south the Lunda basin and in the east the margins of the **central African rift**. These scoop out the surface of the land and plunge steeply, by up to 3,000 m, at the margins. They are surrounded by huge rocky outcrops such as the Mitumba **mountains**.
The **Virunga volcanoes**, North of **Lake Kivu**, are a mountain range running east to west, with a peak at 4,507 m (**Mount Karisimbi**). The **Rwenzo Mountain range** contains the highest mountain in central Africa, the 5,109-m-high **Mount Stanley**, which is heavily glaciated around the summit. The lower slopes are grassy.

Congo basin

The landscape stretching across both sides of the Equator is drained by the **Congo River** and its tributaries, which form extensive swamps. The river basin contains an almost circular depression with a circumference of more than 1,000 km containing a lake, the

*On the edge of **Lake Chad**, which forms a type of natural border between Chad, Cameroon, Niger and Nigeria, much reed and papyrus grows. Numerous floating papyrus islands* *characterise further parts of the lake surface. The largest tributary to this alluvial lake is the Chari. Lake Chad is also particularly significant for its abundance of fish.*

Malebo Pool, at a height of 400 m. The area is covered in young, tertiary and quaternary sedimentary rocks.

The equatorial tropical climate of the Congo basin is covered in the largest stretch of African evergreen rainforest. The higher borderlands consist of tabular, mesozoic sandstone strata that look like a series of steps in the south, traversed by rivers and rapids.

Upper and Lower Guinea basins

The **Upper Guinea basin** runs parallel to the Atlantic coast in an east-west direction from the **Pepper Coast** to the **Niger delta**. Numerous rivers, such as the Volta river system, which cross the valley, have formed fertile alluvial plains and deltas, often reaching deep into the interior. In the **Nimba mountains**, the Upper Guinea Basin is on a plateau which reaches 1,611 m at its highest point. The **Lower Guinea Basin** runs parallel to the Atlantic coast between **Cape Lopez** and the mouth of the **Cunene River** – a stretch of around 1,800 km. The basins rise steeply from a coastline almost 250 km long and reach heights of between 975 m (**Chaillu Massif**) and 2,619 m (**Moco**). Within the country, the Lower Guinea Basin slopes towards the **Congo Basin**, while they both merge into a plateau in the centre, traversed by numerous streams and rivers.

Bié Plateau

The **Bié Plateau** in the southern region of the **Lower Guinea Basin** is an almost square upland at an altitude of 1,500 m and with Mount **Moco**, rises to 2,619 m. The fertile grasslands, watered by numerous rivers, which cover a large proportion of Angola, slope southwards to the edge of the Namibian desert. Not far from the border with Namibia, the **Cunene**, which has its source in Central Angola, cuts through the rocky outcrops and plunges 120 m at the site of the **Ruacana Waterfall**.

Muchinga Mountains, Mitumba Mountains

The **Mitumba Mountains** form the western edge of the Central African rift over 1,200 km between **Lake Tanganika** (33,000 sq. km) on the eastern border of

Tanzania and the **Rwenzori Mountains**. South of **Lake Kivu** they reach a height of over 2,400 m, then slope steeply down to the rift. The Muchinga Mountains overlook the Lunda basin highlands, at an average altitude of 1,000–1,300 m, west of the Mitumba Mountains, and rise to 1,502 m in the **Chifukunya Hills**.

East African rift system

The tectonic fault line of the East African rift system still contains active volcanos and experiences earthquakes. It stretches from the Jordan River valley in the Near East

right down to the **Zambezi**, a total length of 6,000 km. It is the longest rift valley on Earth, running as far south as Mozambique in southern Africa.

The rift is some 6,400 km long and averages 48–64 km wide. It has been forming for some 30 million years, as Africa and the Arabian Peninsula separate, and has pro-

duced such massifs as Kilimanjaro and Mount Kenya. The system's main branch, the Eastern Rift Valley continues south along the Red Sea to several lakes in Kenya. It is less obvious in Tanzania, where the eastern rim has been eroded. It continues south to the Indian Ocean near Beira. The western branch terminates in Malawi. The

1 In the centre of the Ngorogoro Nature Reserve there is the Ngorogoro volcano, whose crater is one of the largest on the earth with a diameter of 22 km.

2 The rocky needles at the summit of Mount Kenya are the remains of a volcanic crater.

3 Thick vegetation covers the slopes of the Rwenzori massif, which is over 5,000 m high – the highest point is covered in mist for most of the year.

4 At an altitude of almost 6,000 m, the huge Kilimanjaro massif appears to float in the distance.

At 5,895 m, the snow-capped peak of Kilimanjaro rises out of the East African Savannah, which ripples in rich brown tones. The circular caldera of the highest volcano in Africa is clearly visible. The slopes beneath the caldera are covered with a layer of ash, on which a thin covering of vegetation has developed.

A thick green belt of rainforest and cloud forest cloak the volcano. Settlements lie below the wooded zone, farmers are venturing ever further into the north-east and west of the wooded areas. The thorn and dry savannah are crossed by rivers, creating green strips of forest.

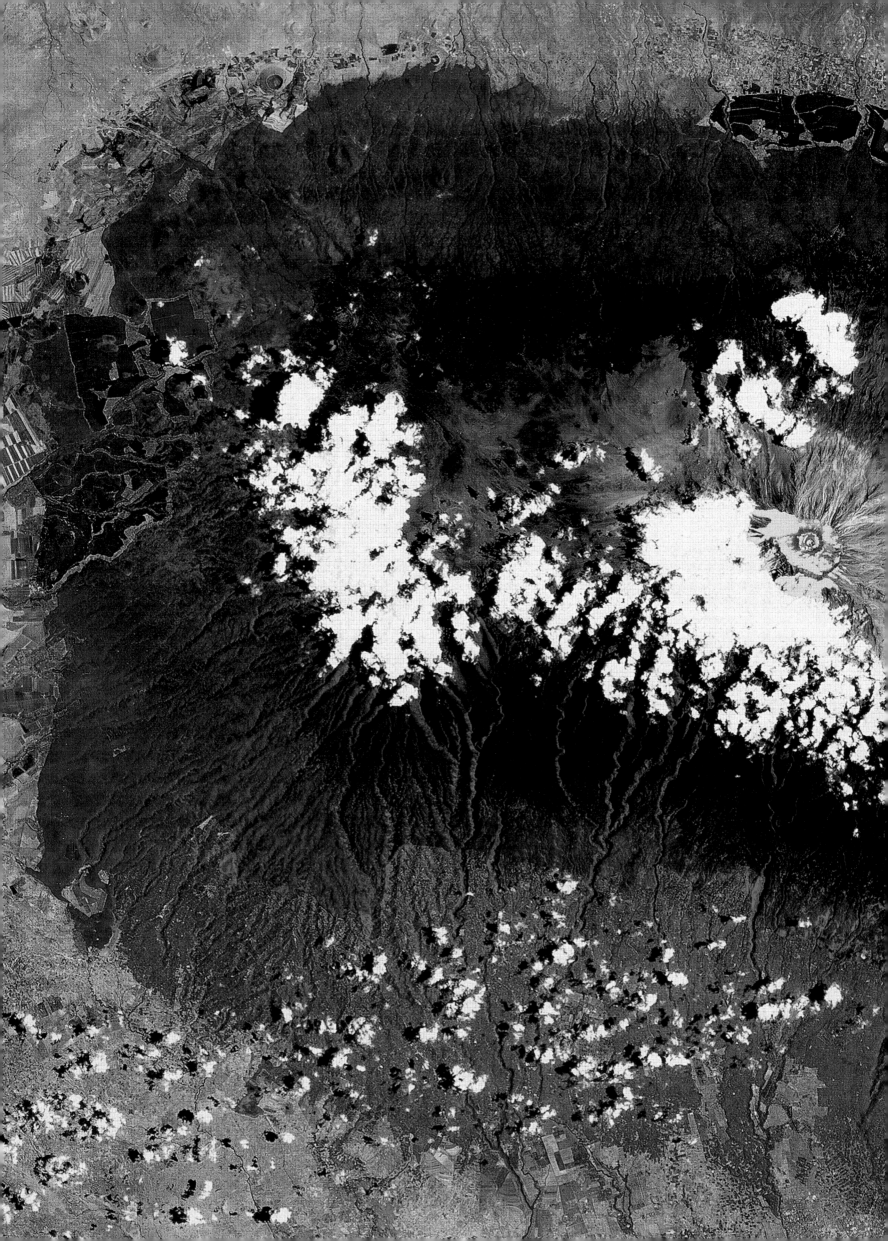

*The **Etosha Plain** in the **Kalahari Desert** is dry almost throughout the year. However, the smaller pools and wells that surround it provide a constant water supply to the area. They are filled from a freshwater reservoir beneath the salt plain and attract large herds of animals. During the rainy periods, the apparent desert suddenly transforms itself for a fleeting period into a green landscape. Wild animals in search of food follow the rainfall.*

East African Rift System was formed as a result of strong movements of the earth's crust at the end of the Tertiary Era.

The **East African Rift System**, also known as the **Rift Valley**, forms the eastern part of the rift valley system. North of **Lake Turkana**, formerly known as **Lake Rudolf**, the Rift Valley continues into the **Ethiopian Rift Valley** and extends to the **Afar Depression**. It determines the shape of the landscape of large parts of Tanzania, Kenya and Ethiopia.

The western edge of the **Central African Rift Valley** is bordered by parallel faults and is 40 to 50 km wide. The valleys contain finger-lakes, such as **Lake Tanganyika**, which is around 650 km long and at one point reaches 655 m below sea level; the lowest point in the valley. Towards the south, the Central African Rift Valley continues into the **Niassa Rift**, containing **Lake** Niassa or **Malawi**.

The East African Rift Valley System marks the point where the African continent splits and the African (Nubian) plate separates from the East African (Somalian) plate. This is most clearly illustrated in the Afar Depression (-116 m) and in a fissure in the Red Sea from which magma erupts.

Highland Lakes

In the **Ethiopian Rift Valley**, **Lake Turkana**, with an area of 8,600 sq. km, forms the closed Lake **Omo** and the **East African Rift Valley** contains a series of lakes, up to a height of 1,500 m. The **Semliki River** connects **Lake Albert** (5,300 sq. km) with **Lake Rutanzige** and **Lake Edward** (2,150 sq. km). **Lake Kivu** (2,650 sq. km), on the other hand, empties into the **Ruzizi River** which flows into Lake **Tanganyika**. **Lake Malawi** is 550 km long and covers an area of 30,800 sq. km. With a depth of 706 m, it is one of the deepest lakes on earth. It drains in the south through the Shire River into the **Zambezi**.

Between the **East African** and the **Central African Rift Valleys**, lies the vast, shallow **Lake Victoria**, which, at 69,484 sq. km, is the largest lake in Africa, the largest tropical lake in the world, and the second-largest freshwater lake in the world in terms of surface area. Being relatively shallow for its size, with a maximum depth of 84 m and a mean depth of 40 m, Lake Victoria ranks as the seventh largest freshwater lake by volume.

Kilimanjaro

The volcanic massif of **Kilimanjaro** (Swahili for 'Shining Mountain') is Africa's highest mountain. There are three volcanoes, Shira (4,300 m), **Mawenzi** (5,355 m) and **Kibo**. The highest point is the **Uhuru Peak** on the Kibo volcano (5,895 m), the only volcano whose crater has a diameter of 2 km. The volcano is still active. Hanging glaciers about 4,300 m long flow from its snowy peaks.

Beneath the glacial zone of the summit there is scree and moraine. Between 3,000 and 4,300 m, there is a belt of trees and tall grass. Between 1,800 and 3,000 m, cloud forests with unique varieties of flora and fauna cover the slopes; dry savannah is found below this point. Kilimanjaro was declared a National Park in 1971.

Victoria falls: the Zambezi plunges 110 m here.

Mount Kenya

This volcano, just south of the equator, has been extinct for a long time. It is the highest mountain in Kenya and the second-highest in Africa. It has a base circumference of 153 km. The highest of the heavily eroded peaks are the **Batian** (5,200 m), **Nelion** (5,188 m) and **Lenana** (4,985 m).

Grasslands extend up to a height of around 3,200 m, above which there is dense rainforest, with alpine vegetation at a height of 4,600 m. Above this, there is a lava field, covered by glaciers at the summit.

Serengeti

The Serengeti is a wide savannah dotted with clumps of trees. It is at an altitude of between 1,500 and 1,800 m in the highlands, south-east of Lake Victoria, the largest of all the African lakes with an area of 68,800 sq. km, which occupies almost half the total area of the Serengeti.

The south-east of the vast grassland, whose name in the Masai language means 'endless plains', has some afforestation along the river banks in the west. Umbrella acacias, typical of the African tree steppes, are found here. The 30,00 sq. km region of the Serengeti, which supports one of the highest populations of wild game on earth, is the heartland of the Serengeti National Park in Tanzania.

The Serengeti became legendary as a result of the annual migration of the massive herds of animals. In May and June, when the rainfall dwindles and the grassy plains of the Serengeti have been grazed, thousands upon thousands of gnus, zebras and gazelles, followed by lions, hyenas and cheetahs as well as numerous species of birds, move north-westwards to the Masai-Mara National Reserve in south Kenya in search of water.

In the autumn, the big herds return once more to the short grass steppes of the Serengeti.

South Africa

The **South African interior** is dominated by a series of undulating plateaus, extending from the Cape Province to central Angola. The **South African Plateau** is part of this area, as are the neighbouring **highlands of Zambia** and **Zimbabwe**, the **Niassa Plateau** and the **Manica Plateau** in the north-east.

The coastlines are characterised by mountain ranges and coastal plains. Such coastal mountains and escarpments are found in the **Mulanje Mountains** (Mulanje Peak: 3,000 m, the highest point in Malawi), the **Lebombo Mountains** and in the **Dragon Mountains** as well as in **Namibia**. Coastal plains are only found in **Mozambique** and **Namibia**.

The **Kalahari Basin**, with an area of approximately 900,000 sq. km, forms the central depression of the South African plateau. It rises to the edge of the plateau up to the **Great Escarpment**, which accompanies the **Zambezi** plateau to Angola. Here it separates the interior from the arid coastal regions.

The Great Escarpment arose as a result of an uplift and now forms the **Dragon Mountains**, the **Stormberg**, the Sneeuberg and the **Nuweveld Mountains**. Some of the mountain ranges in this escarpment were formed by Mesozoic lava deposits.

Namib

This cold desert, whose very name means 'the empty desert', extends for a length of around 1,800 km between Port Nolloth and Namibe along the Atlantic coast. The desert's east-to-west width varies from 80 km to 130 km, until it meets the foot of the **Great Escarpment**. It has a total area of around 50,000 sq. km. The **Kunene Region** in the north consists of a series of isolated mountains; southwards arises the highest peak **Brandberg Mountain** at a height of 2,579 m.

The extreme dryness of the region is caused by the Benguela Current, which frequently produces a sea-mist. Other areas of the north are covered by pebbles and gravel and become the **Kalahari Desert**. This area is almost devoid of vegetation, while the central desert is characterised by wide stretch of dunes, which can reach a height of 300 m.

Kalahari

The dry basin landscape covers an area of around 800,000 sq. km and consists of broad highland areas, covered by the largest continuous stretches of sand on earth. The large dunes typical of the western end have mostly existed since the Ice Age.

The only peaks in the otherwise endlessly flat dry savannah, which is 900 m high, are isolated rocky outcrops. The **Kalahari** contains numerous salt pans and the remains of glacial lakes, among them the **Makgadikgadi Pan** and the **Etosha Pan**, two of the largest on Earth.

In the north, the swampy **Okavango Basin** periodically feeds the Boteti river system when conditions permit.

Okavango-Basin

The **Okavango River** springs from the **Bié Highland**, and after around 1,800 km seeps into a basin in the northern **Kalahari**. Here it forms a 250-km-wide inland delta with several branches and lagoons.

This vast marshy region, which is almost completely flooded during the rainy season extends over an area of around 20,000 sq. km. The marshland is covered in dense beds of reeds and papyrus; at the higher altitudes, there is forest and savannah.

The inland delta is the habitat of many different types of animals. During the dry season elephants, gnus, zebras, antelopes and buffaloes migrate into the savannahs. Various species of birds, such as ospreys, cormorants and cranes live in the swamps.

Zambezi-Basin
(Victoria falls)

The **Zambezi River** emerges from **Luanda** and flows through Angola and western Zambia, forming the border between Zimbabwe and Zambia.

At Maramba the river, now 1,700 m wide, leaves the highland and thunders down into a ravine 110 m deep and 50 m wide, at right angles to the direction of flow. This is the **Victoria Falls**.

In the **Tete Basin**, the Zambezi reaches the **Mozambique Lowlands** and finally, after a total of 2,736 km, forms a delta with its tributary the **Shire**, which is around 5 km widle, before it flows into the Indian Ocean.

*The **Okavango** flows – unusually – not into another river or into open water, but sinks into the sand sea of the Kalahari. The Okavango delta is one of the most impressive landscapes in the world. The delta stretches over 17,000 sq. km and is a swamp area containing a rich variety of flora and fauna.*

South African Highland

The **South African Highland**, the centre of which has wide plains and undulating plateaus, is subdivided into three different regions. These are the **High Veld** (1,200 to 1,800 m), which covers the southern Cape Plateau (up to 1,855 m) and includes the **Basotho Highland**; the transition zone of the **Middle Veld**, which is over 600 m high and covers large parts of the South African highland; and the hilly area of the **Low Veld**, which adjoins the flat coastal plain in the eastern **Transvaal**.

The most important waterway is the **Orange River**, whose tributaries are the **Caledon** and Vaal in the highlands. It finally drains into the **Atlantic**.

Karoo

The desert and semi-desert known as the **Karoo** form a series of basins, which extend between the **great escarpment** and the **Cape Mountains** at a height of 300–900 m. The region is split into the **Great Karoo** in the south and the **Little Karoo** in the west. This area of 395,000 sq. km covers almost a third of the Republic of South Africa, and consists of dry savannahs.

Dragon Mountain

In the **Dragon Mountains** in the **Natal**, the eastern part of the **Great Escarpment** forms a spectacular vertical rock face, rising to up to 1,000 m high. The hilly area known as **Little Berg**, which is between 1,800 and 2,000 m high, is situated close to this steep drop. The Natal-Dragon Mountains consists of massive sandstone strata, which are overlapped by layers of basalt and diabase.

Geologically much older rocks, such as dolomite and quartzite, form the Great Escarpment in the **Transvaal's Dragon mountains**, which rise to 2,286 m. The highest peaks are the **Thabana-Ntlenyana** (3,482 m) and the **Champagne Castle** (3,355 m).

Madagascar

The fourth largest island on the planet is separated from the east coast of Africa by the 400-km-wide **Mozambique Channel**. It is 587,041 sq. km in area.

Over the central mountainous region, which is approximately 800–1,600 m high, increasing in height in an easterly direction, there are individual island mountains and mountain massifs of volcanic origin. **Maromokotro** is the highest peak, at an altitude of 2,876 m.

Due to the tropical climate, the **Andringitra Mountains** (**Pic Boby**, 2,658 m) in the south of the island have been attractively weathered.

Towards the east, the highlands drop steeply towards the coast, while in the west, at a lower altitude, it becomes a relatively wide coastal plain divided by bays. There are off-shore coral reefs.

This asymmetry matches the watershed, which is near the eastern edge of the island, with the larger rivers, such as the **Betsiboka**, to the west.

Madagascar is famous for its extensive rainforests, which are inhabited by several species of fauna such as the lemurs that are unique to the island.

The south-western part of the island, which is drier, is covered by thornbush savannah.

The Manambolo river has created deep canyons and gorges and has some spectacular waterfalls as it meanders through the jungle that surrounds it. The west coast has many protected harbours and broad plains.

1 The giant dunes of the Namibian desert can reach an altitude of 300 m.

2 The Ugab Terraces at the border of the South African interior Highlands: several table mountains and canyons were formed through erosion east of the southern Namib.

3 The Blyde River, a tributary of the Olifants River, cuts through the dolomite limestone of the South African Draken mountains.

4 The symbol of Cape Town is the 1,092-m-high Table Mountain, rising at the Cape of Good Hope.

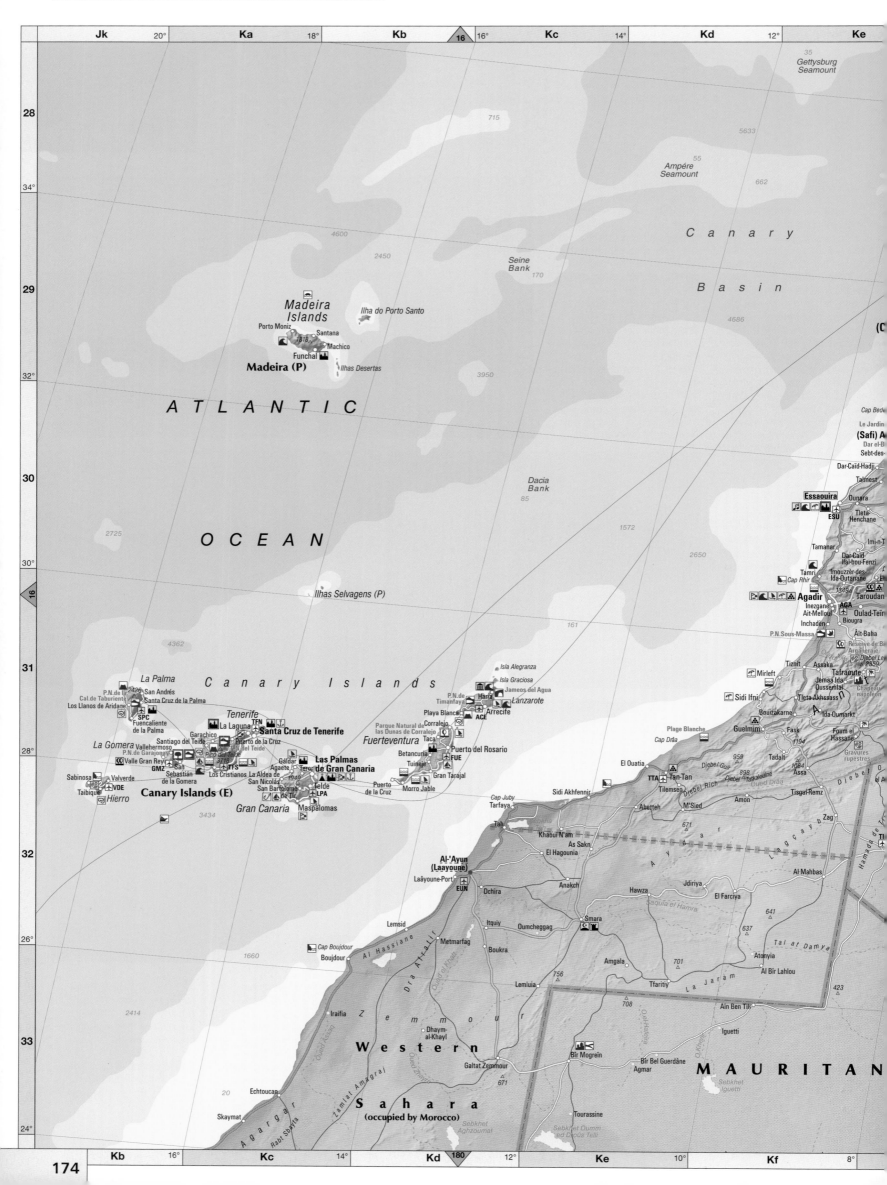

28

34°

Gettysburg Seamount 35

715

5633

Ampére Seamount 55

662

29

C a n a r y

B a s i n

4686

Madeira Islands

Ilha do Porto Santo

32°

Porto Moniz 1818 Santana
Machico
Funchal

Madeira (P) *Ilhas Desertas*

4600

2450

Seine Bank 170

3950

Cap Bede
Le Jardin
(Safi) A
Sebt-des-
Dar-Caïd-Hadji
Talmest

A T L A N T I C

Dacia Bank 85

Essaouira
ESU
Ounara
Tleta-Henchane

30

O C E A N

2725

1572

2650

Tamanar
Imi-n-T
Dar-Caïd-
Ifal-bou-Fenzi
Imouzzèr-des-
Tamri *Cap Rhir* Ida-Outanane
1349

30°

Ilhas Selvagens (P)

161

Agadir
AGA
Inezgane
Aït-Mellou
Inchaden
Biougra
Oulad-Teïr
Aït-Baha
P.N.Sous-Massa

31

C a n a r y   I s l a n d s

4362

Isla Alegranza
Isla Graciosa

Jameos del Agua
P.N.de
Timanfaya Harra
Lanzarote

Reserve de B
Argananeraie
2359
Djebel Le

31°

Tiznit
Mirleft
Tafraoute
Jemâa Ida
Oussenlal
Assaka

Sidi Ifni
Tleta-Akhsass
Ida-Oumarkt

La Palma 2426
San Andrés
Santa Cruz de la Palma
P.N.de
Cal.de Taburiente
Los Llanos de Aridane
SPC
Fuencaliente
de la Palma

Tenerife
TFN
La Laguna
Santa Cruz de Tenerife
Garachico Puerto de la Cruz
Santiago del Teide
Pico del Teide
La Gomera 3715
P.N.de Garajonay TFS
Valle Gran Rey
GMZ San
Sebastián
de la Gomera

Playa Blanca
Corralejo
Parque Natural de
las Dunas de Corralejo
Fuerteventura
Taca
Betancuria
Tuineje

Arrecife
ACE

Puerto del Rosario
FUE

Bouizakarne
Fask Foum el
1194 Hassane
Tadalt
Guelmim

Plage Blanche
Cap Drâa

El Ouatia
TTA Tan-Tan
Tilemsen
Abetteh
Tah

Djebel Guir
Djebel Rich
959
898
Amon

Assa
1064 Tisgui-Remz
Zag

28°

Sabinosa Valverde
Taibique VDE
Hierro

3434

Gáldar
Agaete
Teror
San Bartolomé
de Tir
Gran Canaria
1949
Maspalomas

San
Sebastián
de la Gomera
La Aldea de
San Nicolás
de Tir

**Las Palmas
de Gran Canaria**
LPA
Telde

Gran Tarajal

Puerto de la Cruz

Morro Jable

Cap Juby
Tarfaya

Sidi Akhfennir

Oued Drâa

M'Sied

Taskaloula

32

Canary Islands (E)

Khaoui N'am
As Sakn

671

641

Al-Mahbas

26°

Cap Boujdour
Boujdour

1660

Al Hassiane

Metmarfag
Boukra

El Hagounia

Itquiy
Oumcheggag

**Al-'Ayun
(Laayoune)**
EUN
Laâyoune-Port
Dchira
Anakch
Hawza

Smara

Jdiriya
El Farciya

637

Atonyia
Al Bir Lahlou

33

2414

Lemsid

Echtoucan

Skaymat

Iraifia
Echtoucan

Agargar

Dra Attallit

Z e m m o u r

Dhaym-
al-Khayl

W e s t e r n

S a h a r a
(occupied by Morocco)

20

Lemiuia

Galtat Zemmour

Amgala

756

Tfaritiy
La Jaram

Bir Mogrein

Bir Bel Guerdâne
Agmar

Iguetti

701

708

671

423

Aïn Ben Tili

Tal at Damya

M A U R I T A N

Sebkhet Iguetti

Tourassine

*Sebkhet Oumm
ed Drols Telli*

Scale 1:4,500,000

0 50 100 150 Kilometers
0 50 100 Miles

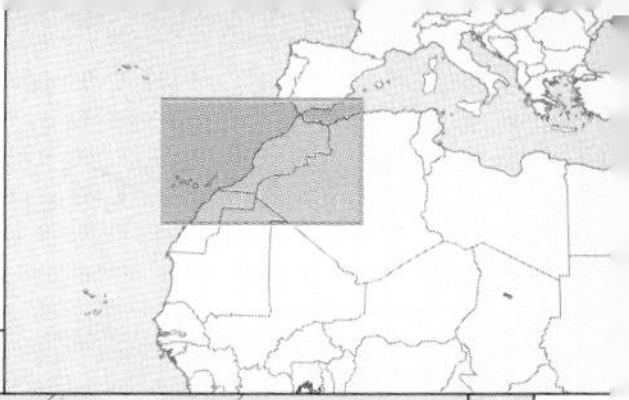

MEDITERRANEAN SEA

SPAIN

MOROCCO

ALGERIA

Golfo de Cádiz
Costa de la Luz
El Puerto de Santa María
Cádiz
San Fernando
Chipiona
Jerez d.l Frontera
Lebrija
Villamartin
Arcos
Olvera
Antequera
Ronda
Coín
Estepona
Marbella
Fuengirola
Torremolinos
Málaga
Vélez-Málaga
Nerja
Almuñécar
Motril
Adra
Berja
Almería
Roquetes de Mar
Sierra Nevada
Tabernas
Sorbas
Carboneras
Geról
Vera
Cuevas
Cabo de Gata
Costa de Almería
Isla del Alborán (E)
Costa del Sol
Marbella
San Roque
La Línea de la Concepción
Algeciras
Tarifa
Punta de Tarifa
Strait of Gibraltar
Gibraltar (UK)
Punta Almina
Ceuta (E) (Sebta)
(Tangier) Tanjah
Asilah
Larache El-Araïche
El-Kebir
Ksar
Moulay-Bousselham
Arbaoua
Souk-el-Arba-des-Beni-Hassan
Titwan (Tétouan)
Martil
Chefchaouen
Bou-Ahmed
El-Tleta-de-Oued-Laou
Cap des Trois Fourches
Al Hoceïma
Ajdir
Torres-de-Alcalá
Bab-Besen
Ketama
Targuist
Melilla (E) Nador
Ras Kebdana
Saïdia
Segangane
Zalo
Drioüch
Midar
Berkane
Marsa-Ben-Mehdi
Ghazaouet
Wahran (Oran)
Les Andalouses
Aïn-el-Türck
Arzew
Mostaganem
Cap Carbon
Sidi Ali
Achaacha
Bouzghaïa
El Marsa
Ténès
Oued Rhiou
Relizane
Mascara
Chlef
Bou Kadir
Rahouia
Tiaret
Souguer
Sidi Bel Abbès
Hennaya
Maghnia
Tlemcen
Sebdou
Ujdah (Oujda)
Taourirt
Guercif
Ahfir
El-Aïoun
Jerada
Debdou
Aïn Benimathar
Tendrara
Figuig
Beni-Ounif
Béchar
Kenadsa
Abadla
Taghit
Beni-Abbès
El Ouata
Ougarta
Kerzaz
Timoudi
Charouïne
Timimoun
Adrar
Reggane
In Salah
Aoulef
Akabli
Sali
Foggâret ez Zoûa

(RABAT) AR-RIBAT
Salé
Mohammedia
DAR-AL-BAYDA
Khemisset
(Meknès) Miknas
Faz (Fès)
Sefrou
Ifrane
Azrou
Taza
Guercif
Beni-Mellal
Azilal
Khouribga
Oued-Zem
Kasba Tadla
Khénifra
Midelt
Er-Rachidia
Goulmima
Tinerhir
Boumalne Dadès
Ouarzazate
Agdz
Zagora
Tagounite
Mhamid
(Kénitra) Al-Q'nitra

Atlas Mountains
Moyen Atlas
Haut Atlas
Anti Atlas
Hauts Plateaux
Monts des Ksour
Atlas Saharien
Plateau du Rekkam
Plateau du Tademaït
Great Western Erg
Erg Chech
Hamada du Guir
Hamada de la Daoura
Hamada Tounassine
Iguidi
Erg Iabès
El Mzereb
Chegga

175

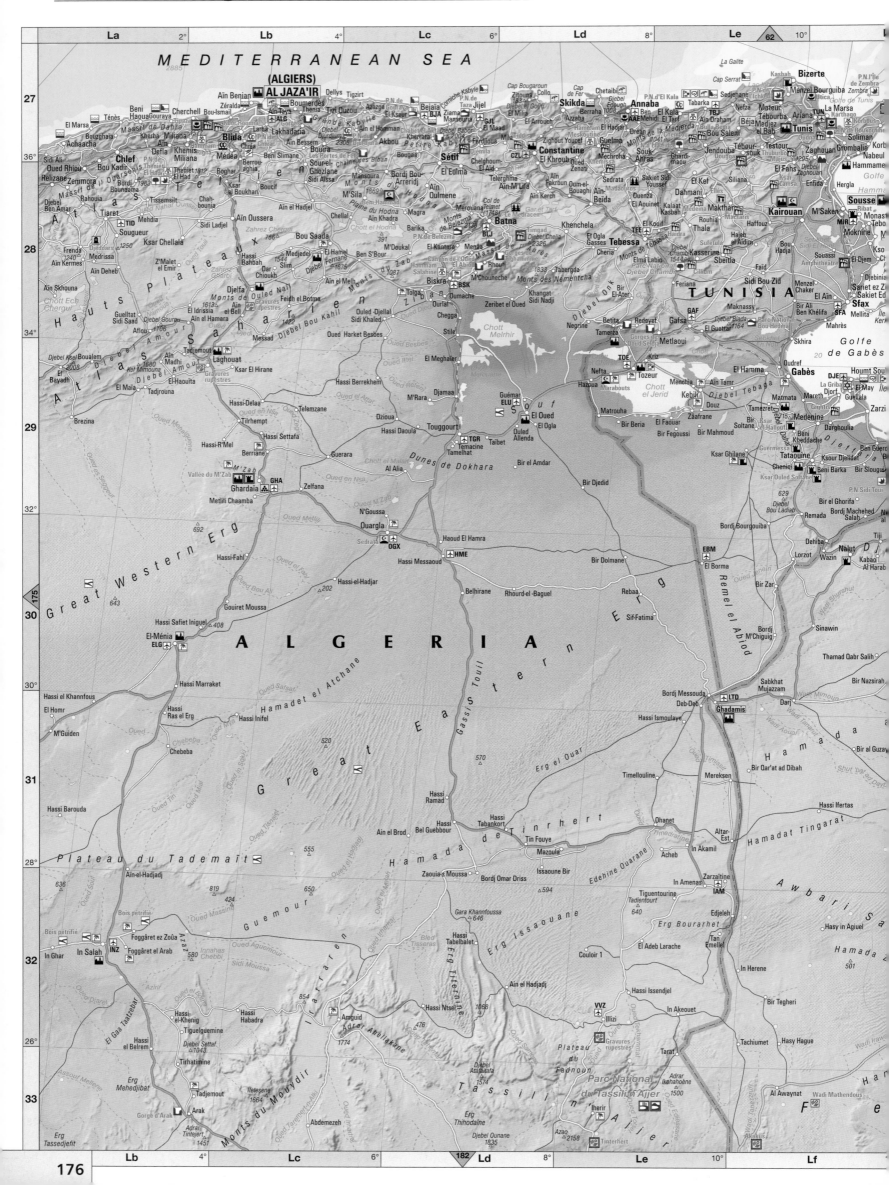

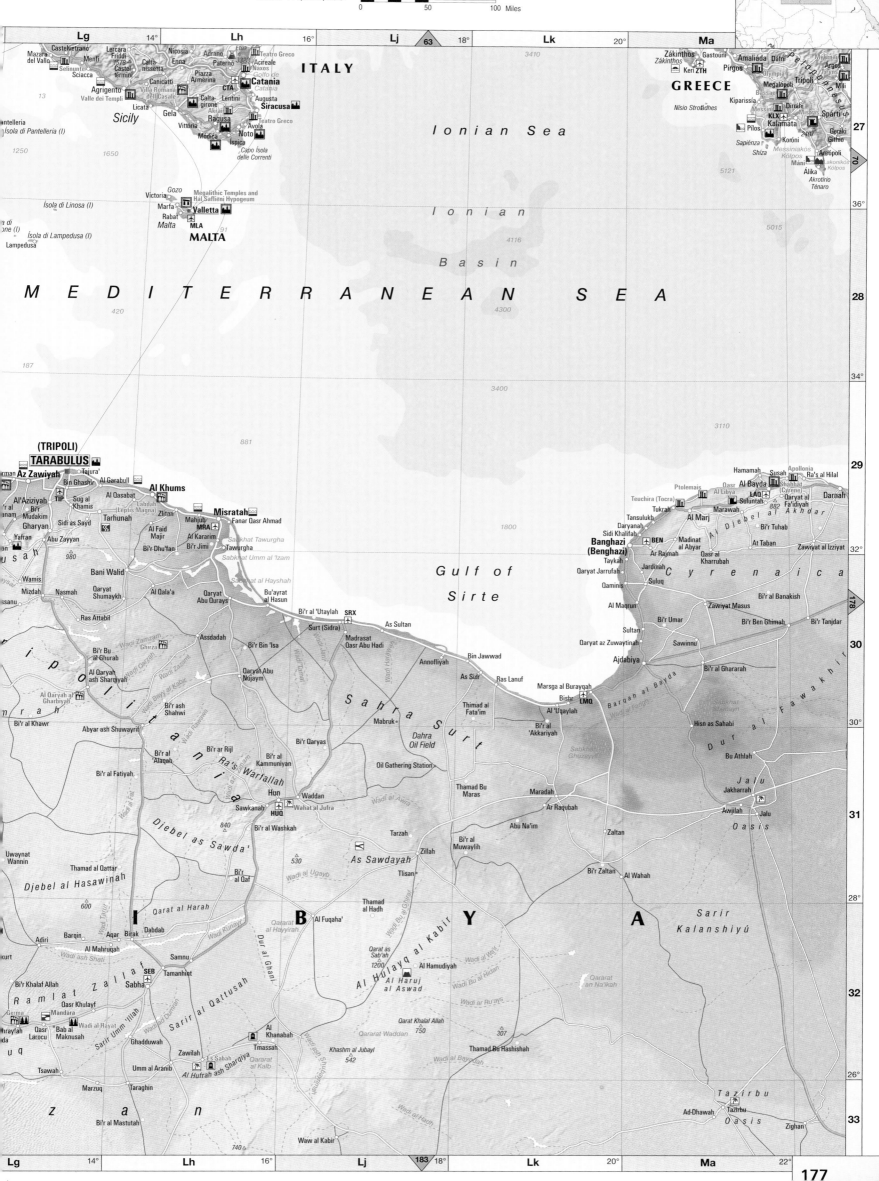

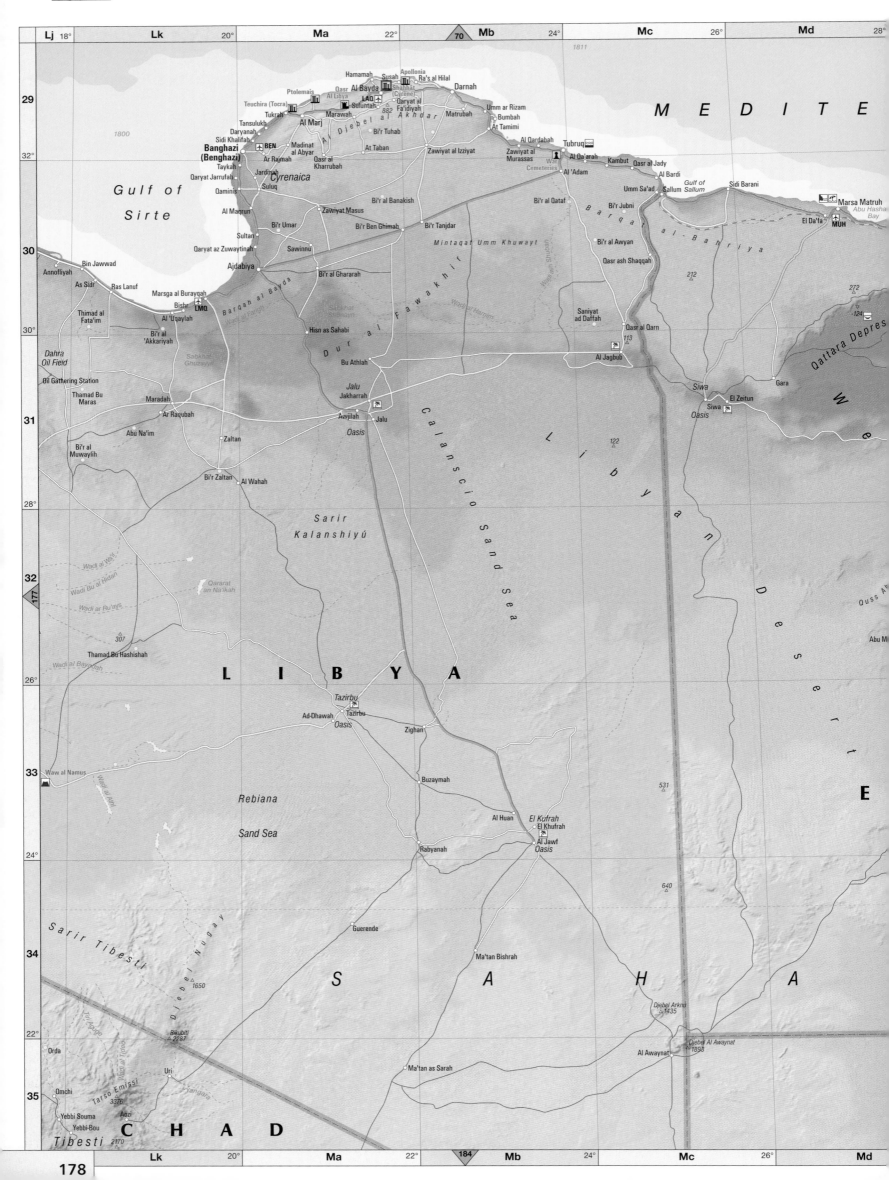

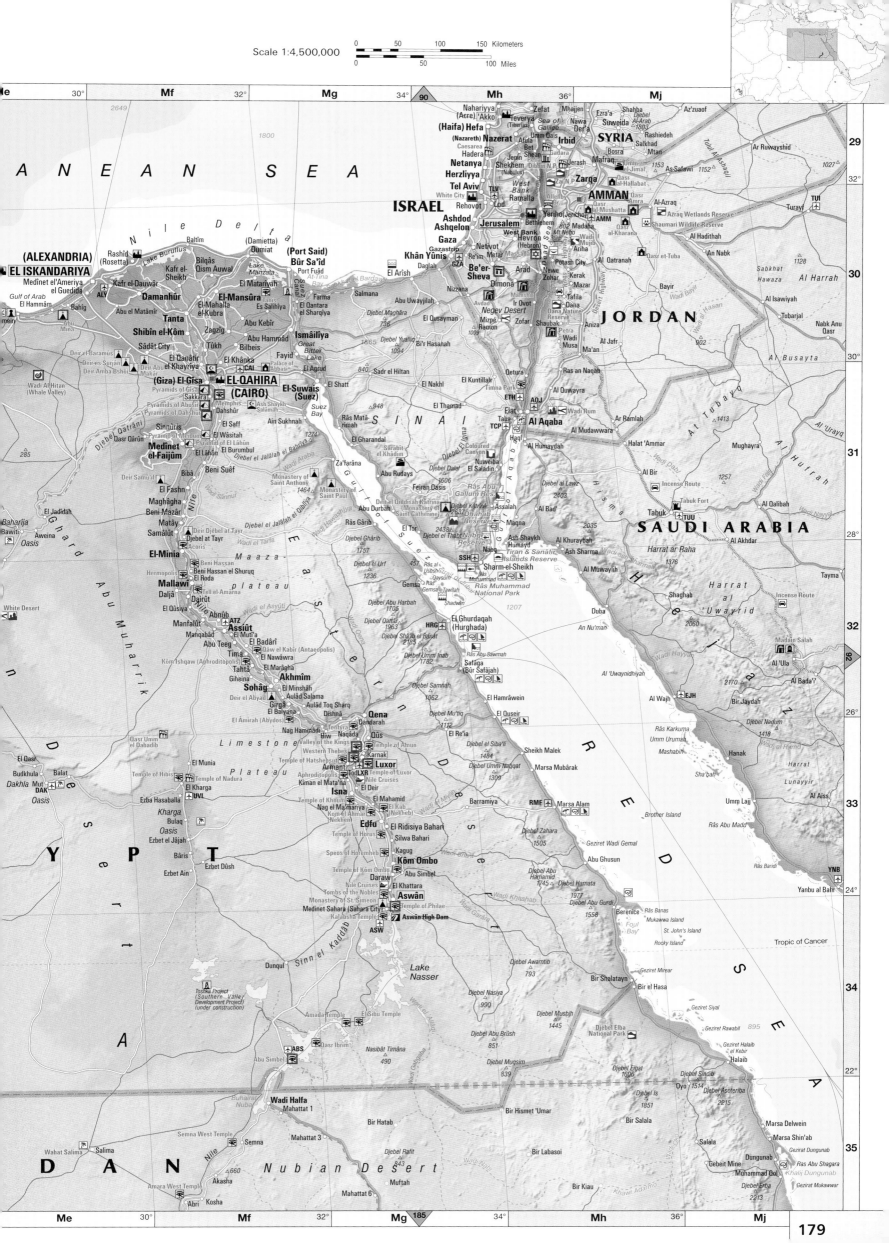

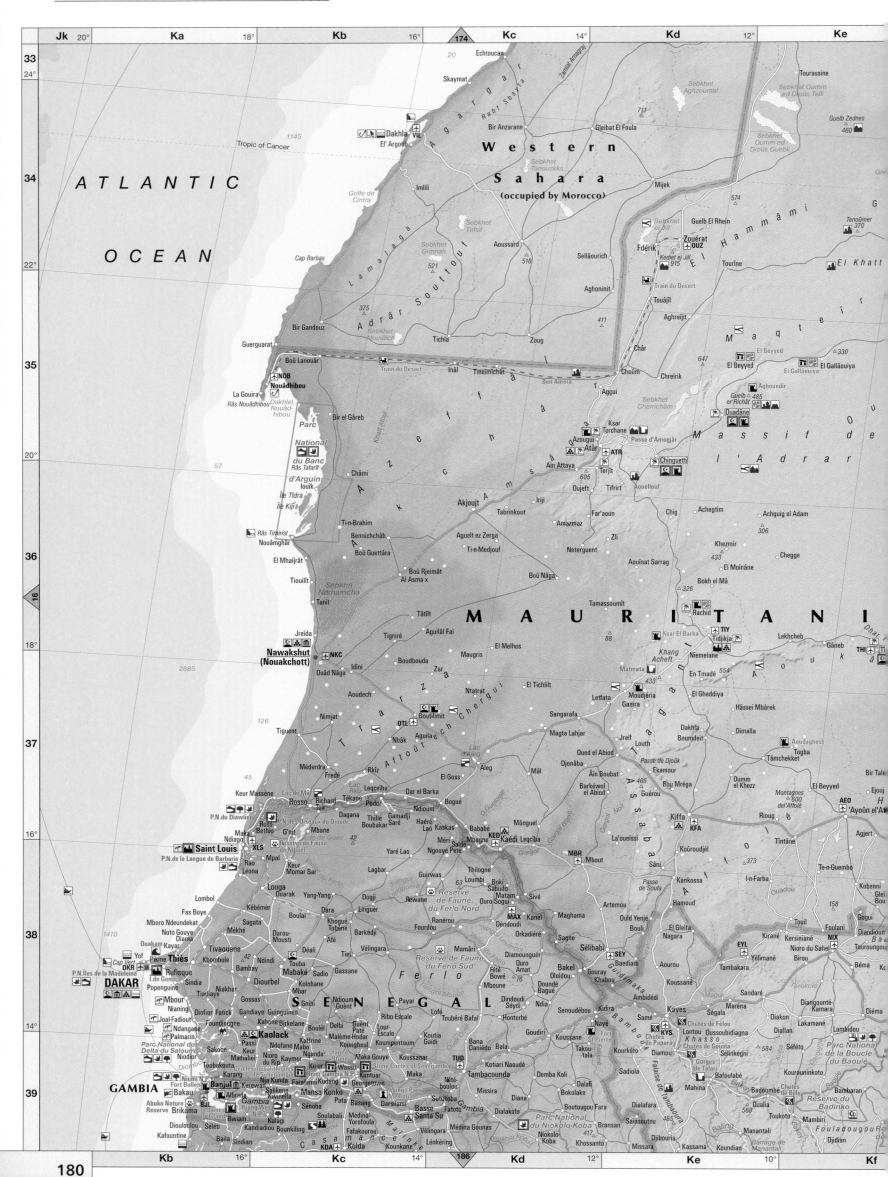

33

A L G E R I A

24°

Grizm

725

El Mzereb

370
333

Oued el Ma
Oued Khârroûb

Bîr 'Amrâne
250

El Mreiti
Ti-n-Bessaïs

Agâraktem

Aoukâr

34

Hamada el Harich

Taoudenni

270

Erg Azennezal

Oued Tamanghasset

Ijoubban

El Guettara

22°

Oglat el Khnâchîch   El Khnâchîch

El Khnâchîch

Bir Ounâne

343   Erg Aït el Khâoua

Erg in Techerène

35

Erg Atouila

Foum el 'Alba
282

324

Douaouir   Erg I-n-Sâkâne

I-n-Techerène

Tessounfat el Bass

Kreb Bekati el Bass

20°

Erîgât

Oued el Hajâr

Boû Nâga

El Mraïti

273

367

I-n-Échai

Tamandouririt

I-n-Akli

Ancien

Tessalit

Abanko

182

I-n-Akhmed

Timétrine
(Ti-n-Kâr)

Tichet

Aguelhok

36

Araouane

Guîr

El Mamouel

El Mâmoûn

Mabroûk

Djebel

Sidi el Mokhtâr   Boû Djébéha

Abelbod

T i m é t r i n e

Adrar
Tachdaït

Tadânet Keyna

El Ma'mour-
Ighichârene

Aghezzaf

Ammouk

18°

A w a n a

Dahr Oualâta

Touérât   271

I-n-Milach

Anéfis

Édjérit

M A L I

Tagoûrâret

Douaya

I-n-Aleï

Tabankort

Hâssi Fouîni
Oualâta

Irîgui

Tigoumatene

I-n-Abaléha

Oudeïka

Almoustarat

Latik   Oureï   Zoûgh
Agoueïnît

Nkhaïlé

El Basriyé

I-n-Amazzagh

Ti-n-Tehoun

I-n-Ouchef

Agamor

Karkabane

Kerchouél

37

Nbeïket Dlim

Ti-n-Tijot

Agounni Jefal

Ti-n-Aguelhaj
(Tangoutranat)

265 Bamba

Téméra Bisane

Hâssi

Bourem

Youani
Tondibi

Karkarichinkat

Taouârdei

Néma

Houeiriye

Outeïd Arkâs

Tombouctou
TOM

Bourem-
Inali

Ber

Gourma-Rharous

Défilé de Tosaye

Niger

Teiskot

EMN
El Bouz

El Arhlaf

Râs el Mâ

Lerneb
(Tilemsi)

Bintagoûngou
Farache

Kahara

499

Korioume

Mandiakoy

440

Oinardene

Karouassa

Tombeau
des Askia

Amakouladji

GAQ
Tacharane

Iménas

Djébok

Houeïriye   Gargango

Danga

Bambou

Gao

Biliali Koyra

Amourj   Nioût   Hâssi Touil

Tonka

Diré

Haïbongo

Haribomo

Fintrou

Adiora

Doro

Haoussa-Foulane
Gargouna

16°

Boû Gâdoûm
Koumbi Saleh

Bassikounou

Tondidarnou

Banikane

Saréyâmou

Lac Garou

Réserve
de Gourma

Gourma

Gossi

Tagarane Gabout

Mobdoua
Adel Bagrou

Fassala Néré

Niafounké

Saraféré

Kanioume

Bambara-
Maoundé

I-n-Adiattafene

Dorey

Lac Do

Balal

Koronga

Medd Allah

Méma

Léré

Ambin

Ngorkou

Lac Aou-
goundou

Ngouma

I-n-Tillit

Léléhoy   Ansongo

Dali   Dilli

Nara   NRM

Fatiba

Farimaké

Gati-Loumo
Youvarou

Lac
Niangay

Tanal

Réserve de
Douentza

Ndaki

Tessit

Tassiga

Bentia
(Koukia)

Goumbou

267

Boundjiguiré

Boulel

Oura-Ndia
Dogo

Korienzé

Nyiminiama

Monts du Hombori
Garmi Tondo
1080 (Main de Fatima)

Hombori
1155
Hombori Tondo

777

Ouatagouna
Labbezanga

38

Falou

Ouagadou

Mourdiah

Dogofri
Diabali

Dioura

Diondiori

Diallombé   Konza

Boré

Dala

Boni

Boumboum

Forage
Christine

Ti-n-Akof

Ouanzerbé

Firgoun

14°

Danfa

Sokolo

Kerké
Ténenkou

Pays
Nirigari

268

Dankabou

Diounlouna

Mondoro

Douna

Kobou

Dunes de Sable

Déou

Oursi

Markoy

Dolbel

Toumkou
Famalé

Warté
Séguéla

Molodo

Ndébougou
Niono

Sossébé
Ouro-Modi
MZI
Mopti
Soma-

Kani-Gogouna
Madougou

Dioungani

Yoro

Barabule

Salmossi

Gorom-Gorom

Bankilaré

Méhana

Sébété
Boron

Monimpé-
bougou

Dia
Diafarabé

Sévaré
Bandiagara

Dogon

Sofara

Yanga

Koumbri

Tibo

Solé

Djibo

Tongo-
mayel

Aribinda

Sikire

Gaïgou

Falagountou

Yatako

Sara Koyra

NIGER

Ségou

Doura

Massina

Koua-kourou

Bankass

Koro

Koporokenité Na

Ban

Pobé Mengao

Gravures
rupestres

Gorgadji   Dori

Foneko   Tillabéri

Dioro

Say

Mougna

Taga

Bandiagara

Sofara

Titao

Bourzanga

Namissiguima

Rollo

Kélbo

Necropoles

Katchirga

Sampelga

Dargol

Markala
SZU
Togou

Kolongotomo

Pogo

Sansanding

Konio
Fangasso

Séguri

Diallassagou

Tou

Bélehédé

Ouahigouya

Dalbo

Pensa

Bouroum

Yalgo

Bangaré

Gotheye

39

Banamba

Séguéla

Niamina

Konodimini
Zinzana

San
Tominian

Koula

Sites d'extraction
de fer de Kindiba

Tori

Sokoura

Louta

Titao

Zogore

Ségénéga

Koala

Lac de Bam
Barsalogo

Bani

Sebba

Bossey
Bangou

B U R K I N A   F A S O

Solna

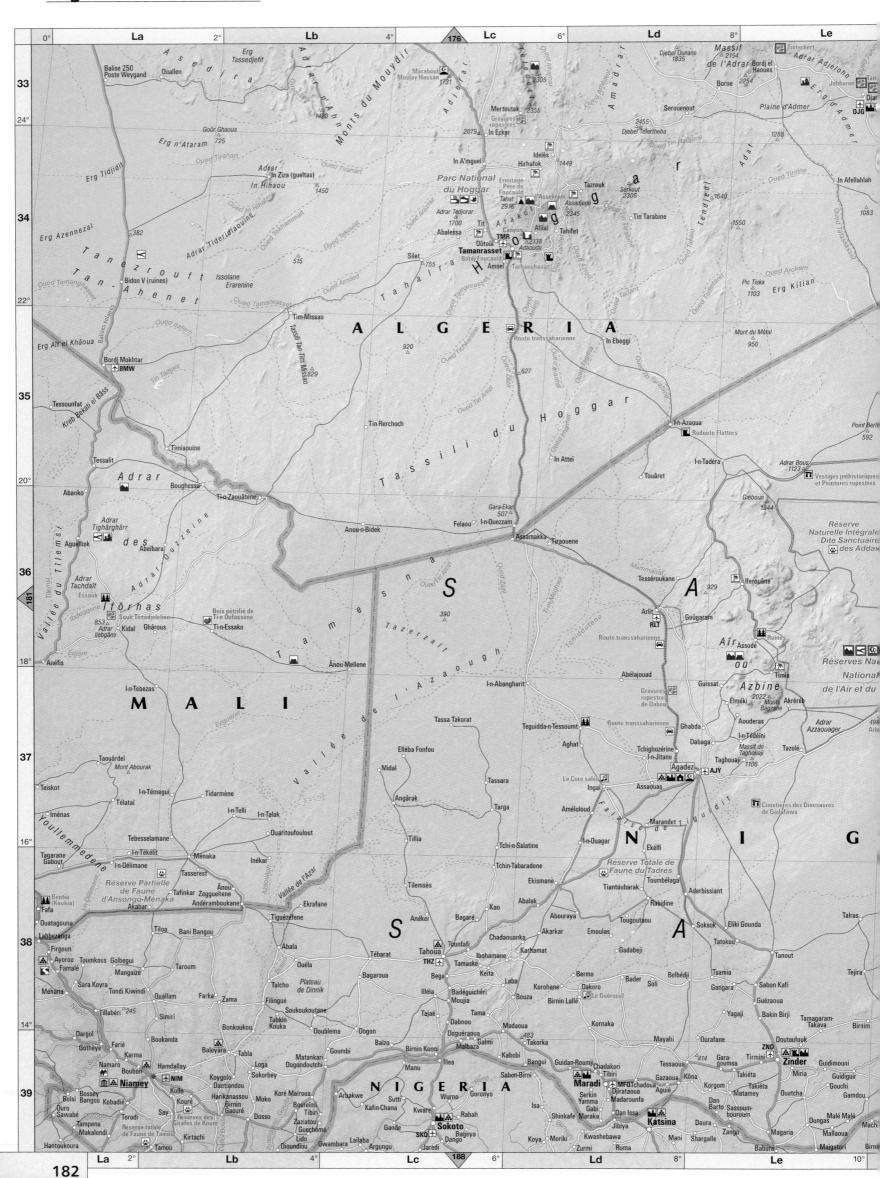

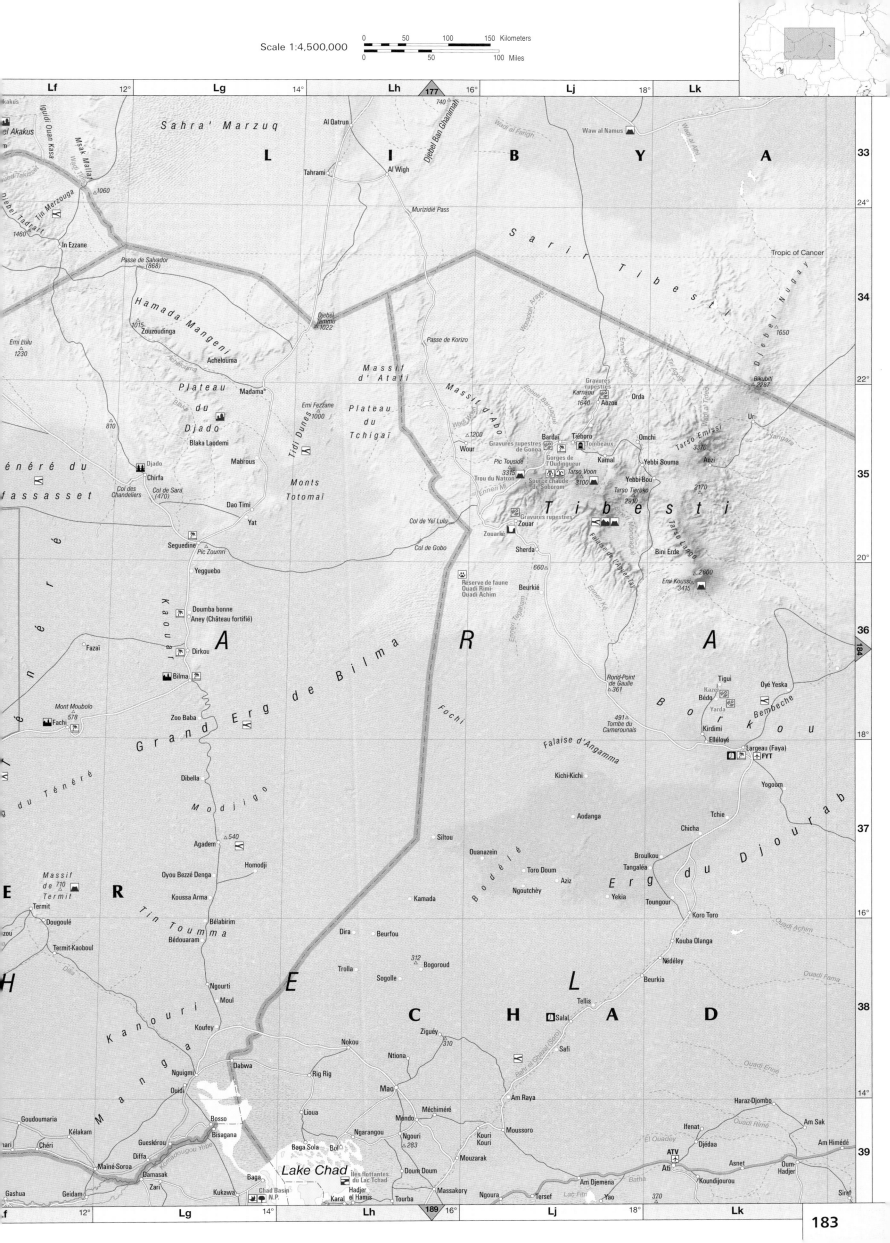

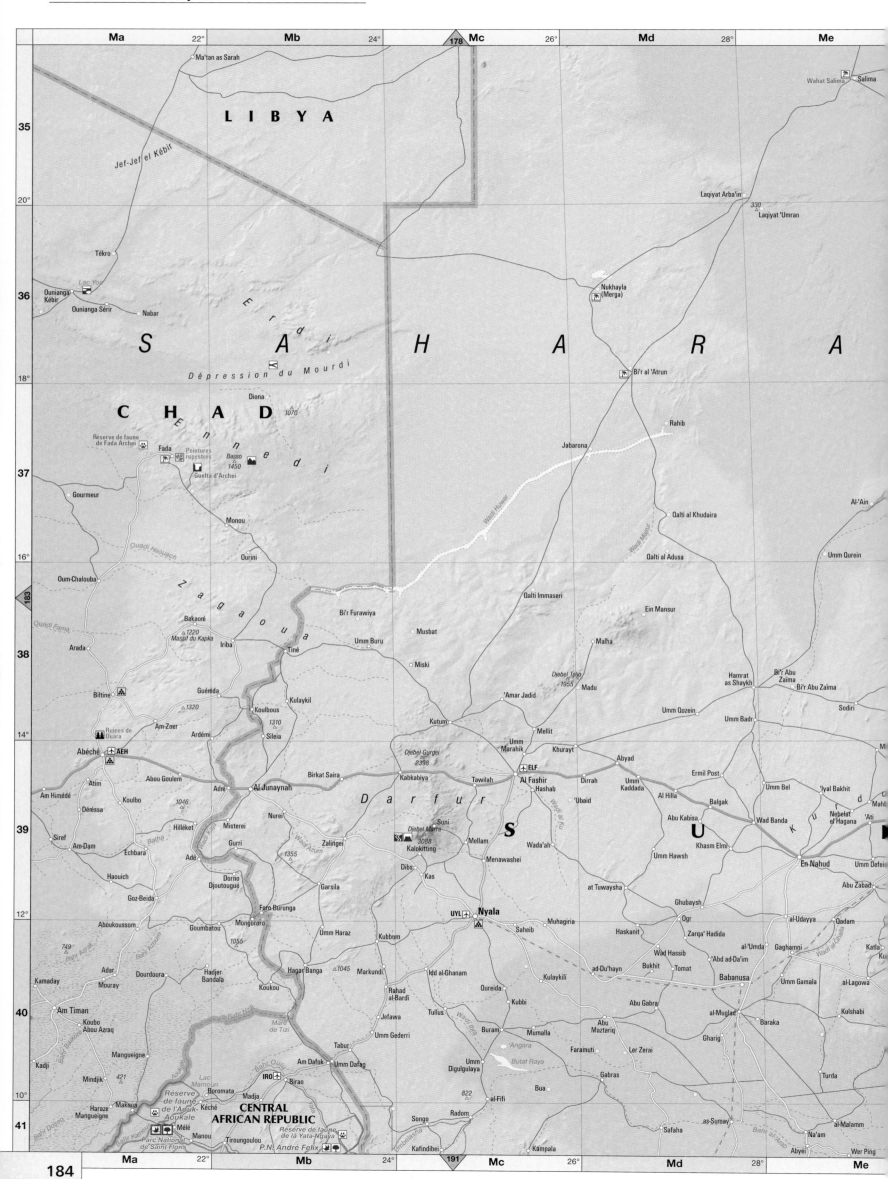

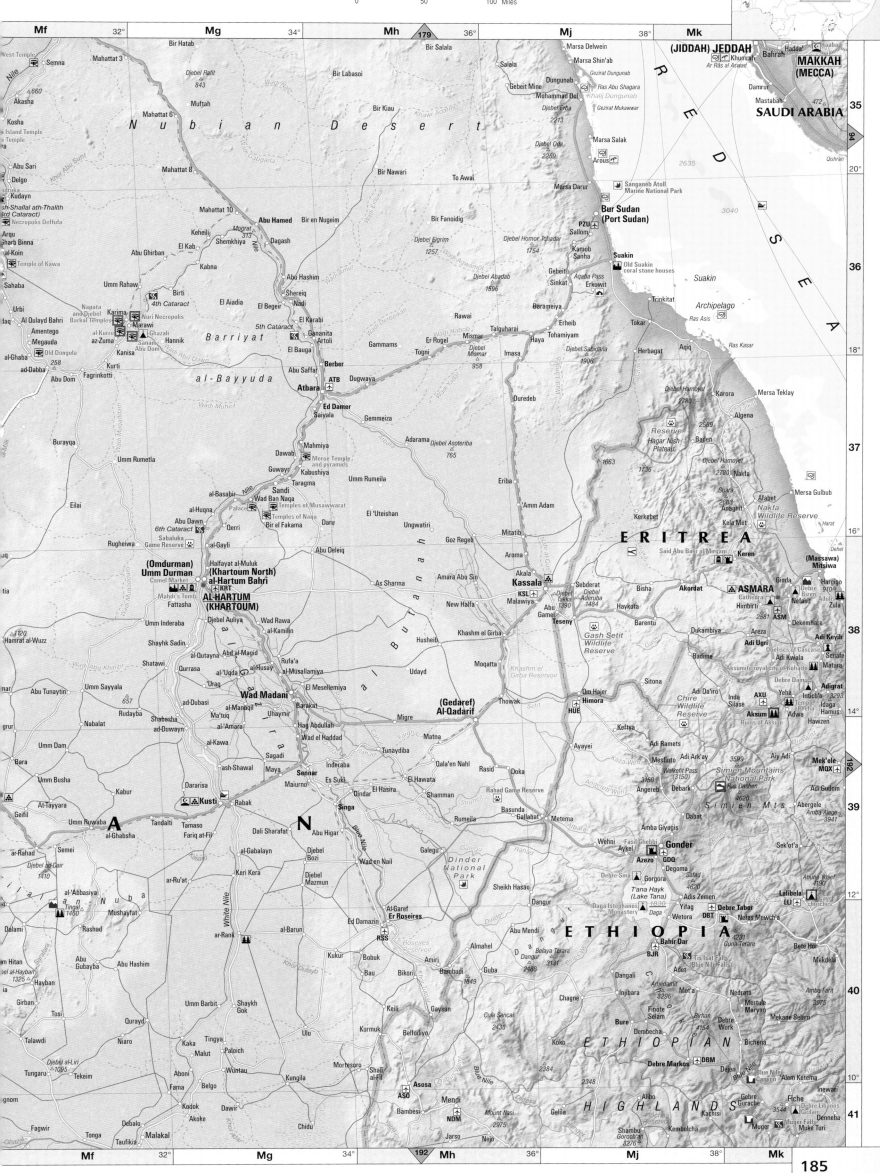

Scale 1:4,500,000

| 0 | 50 | 100 | 150 Kilometers |
| 0 | 50 | | 100 Miles |

RED SEA

Nubian Desert

al-Bayyuda

Barriyat

SAUDI ARABIA

(JIDDAH) JEDDAH

MAKKAH (MECCA)

Bur Sudan (Port Sudan)

Suakin

ERITREA

ASMARA

Kassala

(Massawa) Mitsiwa

Keren

(Omdurman) Umm Durman

(Khartoum North) al-Hartum Bahri

AL-HARTUM (KHARTOUM)

Wad Madani

(Gedaref) Al-Qadarif

S U D A N

Sennar

Kusti

Singa

Ed Damazin Er Roseires

Dinder National Park

ETHIOPIA

Gonder

T'ana Hayk (Lake Tana)

Bahir Dar

Lalibela

Debre Tabor

Mek'ele

Simien Mountains National Park

ETHIOPIAN HIGHLANDS

Debre Markos

185

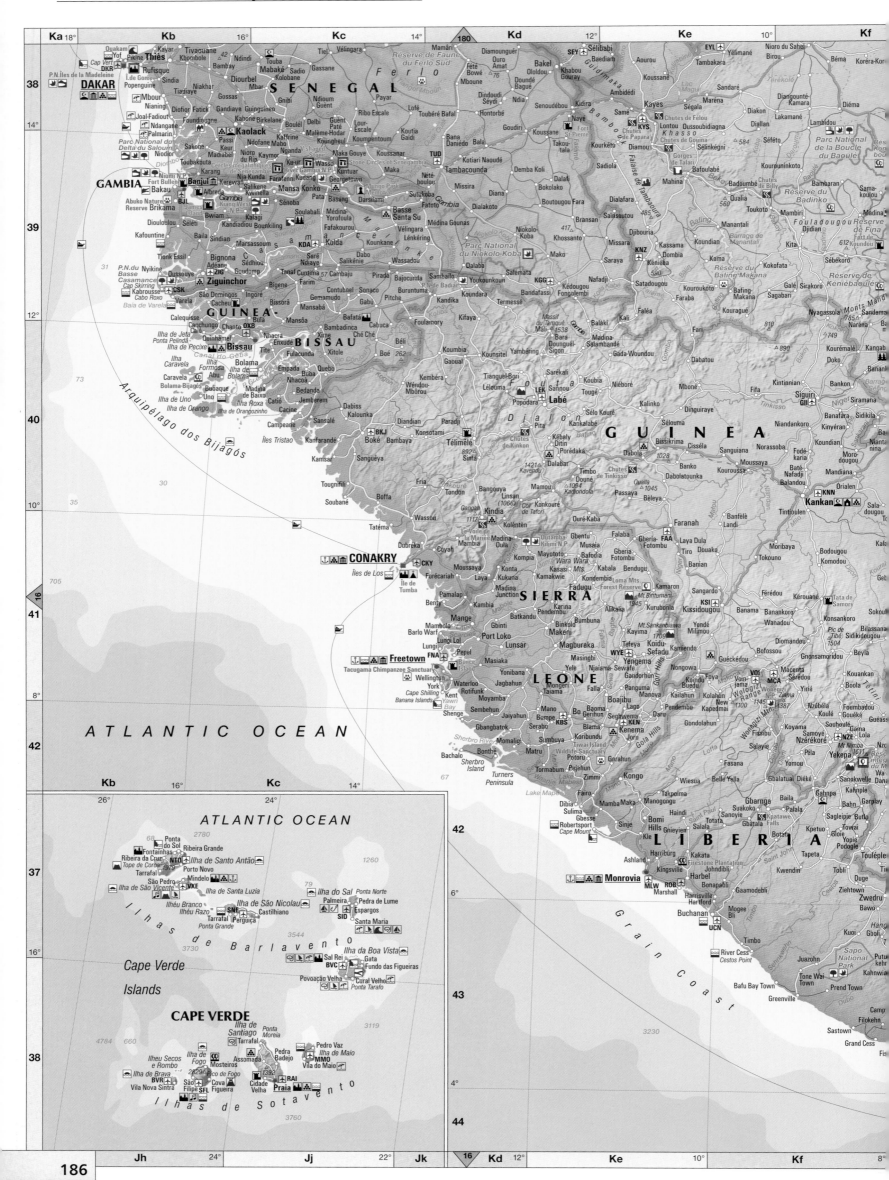

Scale 1:4,500,000

| 0 | 50 | 100 | 150 | Kilometers |

| 0 | 50 | 100 | Miles |

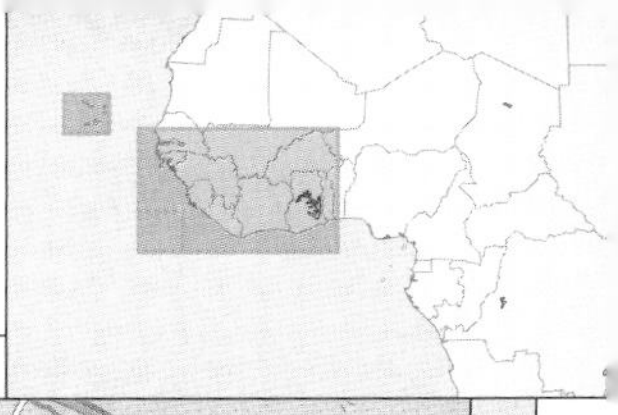

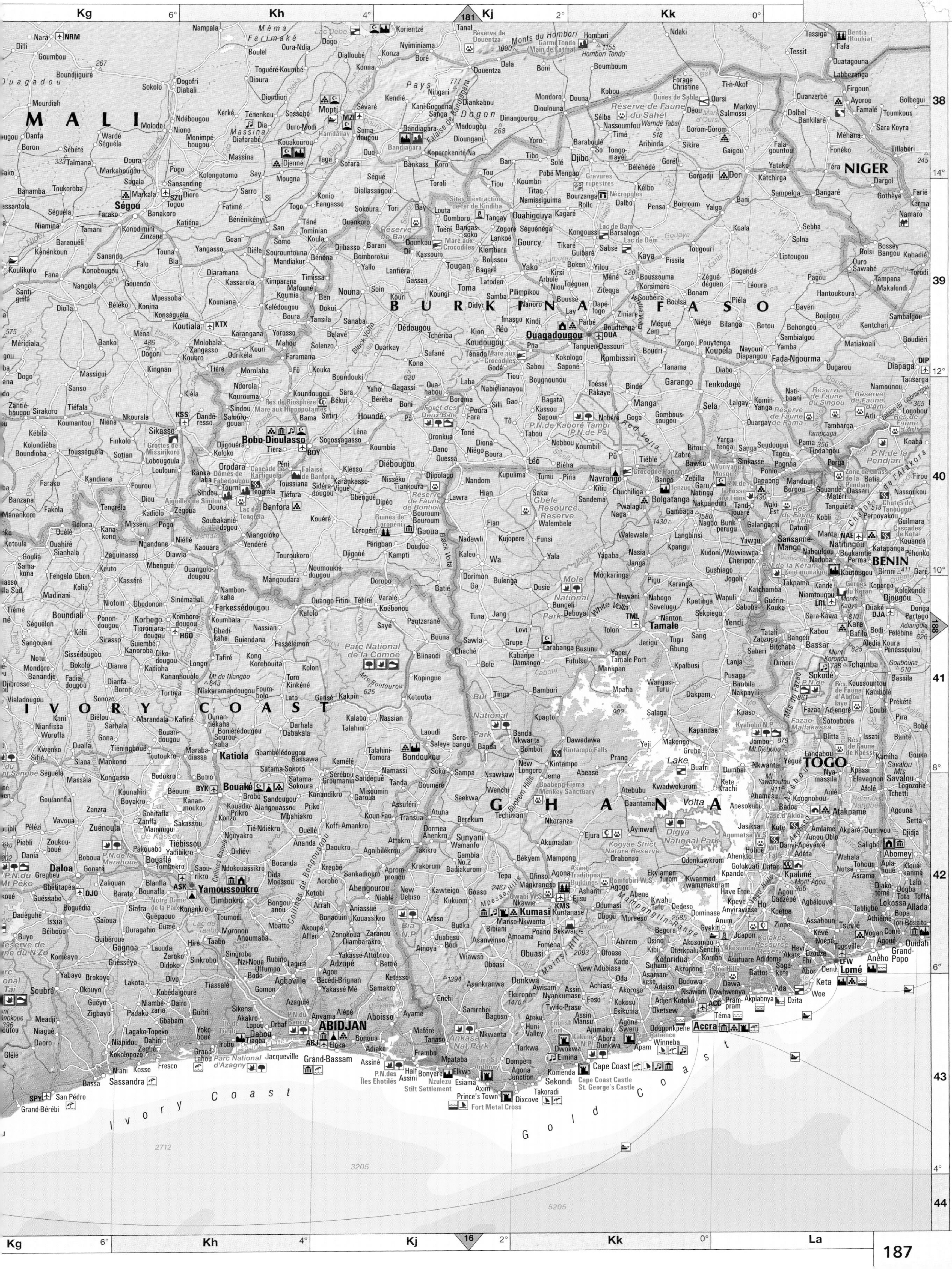

MALI

NIGER

BURKINA FASO

IVORY COAST

GHANA

TOGO

BENIN

Ivory Coast

Gold Coast

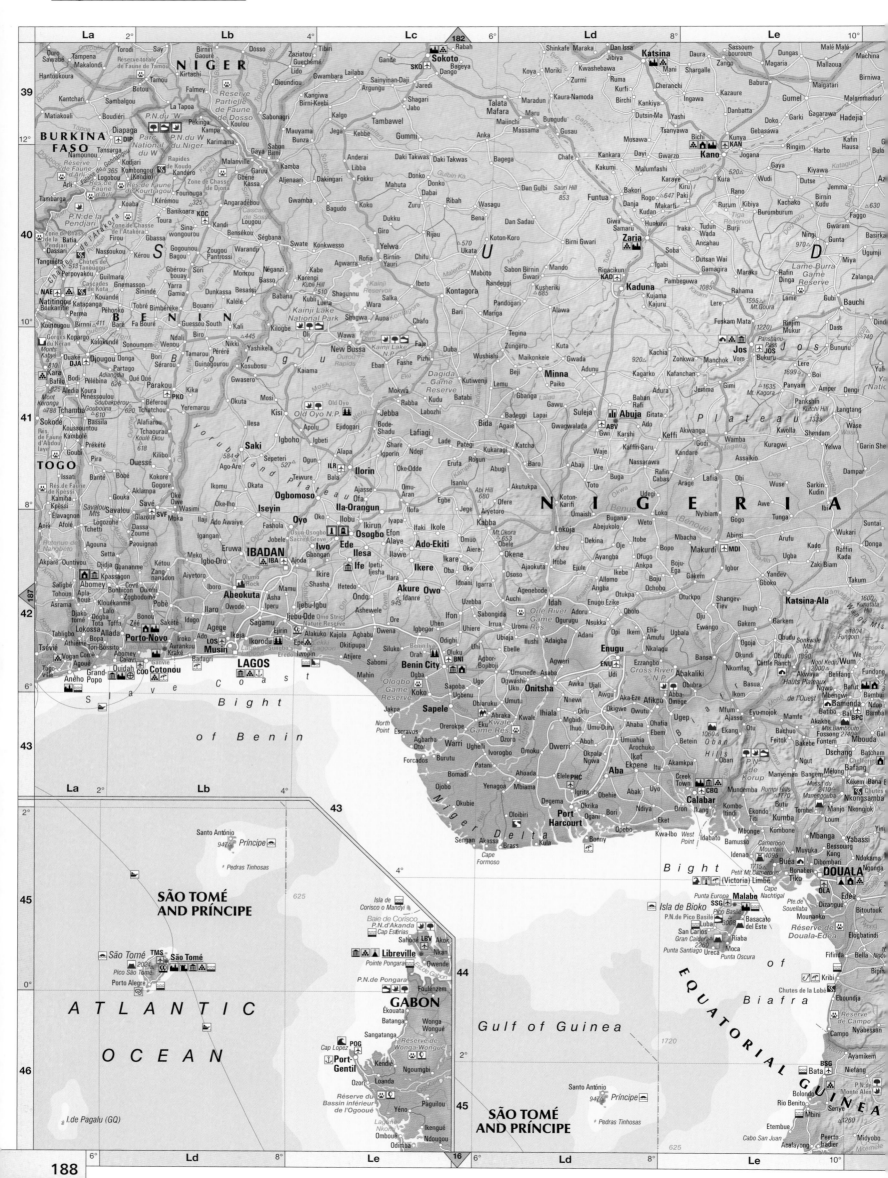

Scale 1:4,500,000

| 0 | 50 | 100 | 150 | Kilometers |

| 0 | 50 | 100 | Miles |

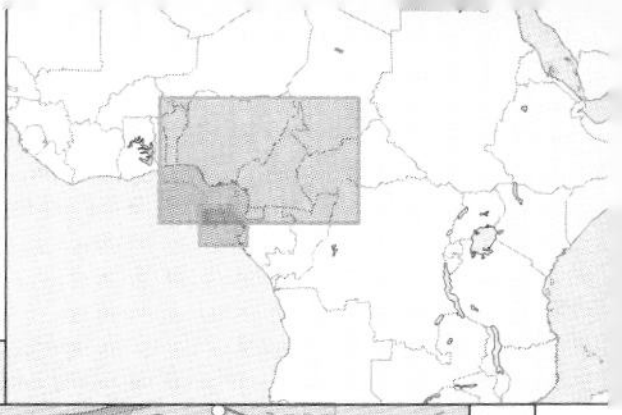

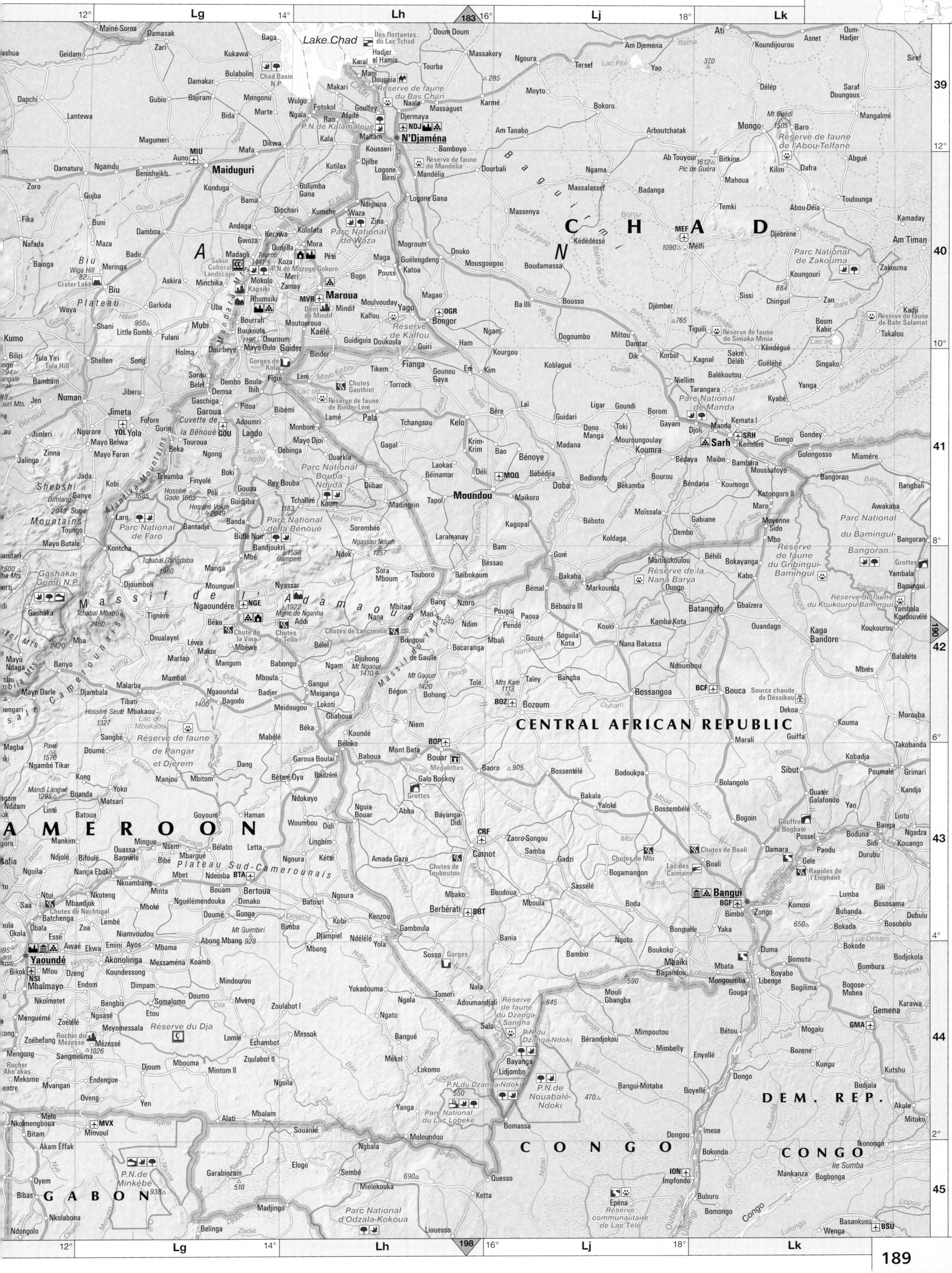

Lake Chad
Îles flottantes du Lac Tchad

CHAD

N'Djaména
NDJ

C H A D

Reserve de faune de l'Abou-Telfane

Parc National de Zakouma
Zakouma

Parc National de Waza

Maiduguri
MIU

Maroua
MVR

Bongor
OGR

Garoua
GOU

Moundou
MQQ

Sarh
SRH

Parc National de Manda

Parc National de Bamingui-Bangoran

Yola
YOL

Parc National de la Bénoué

Parc National Bouba Ndjida

Parc National de Faro

Gashaka-Gumti N.P.

Massif de l'Adamaoua

Ngaoundéré
NGE

CENTRAL AFRICAN REPUBLIC

Bouar
BOP

Bozoum
BOZ

Bossangoa
BCF Bouca

Réserve de faune du Gribingui-Bamingui

Réserve de la Nana Barya

Carnot
CRF

Bouar
Galo Boukoy

Réserve de faune de Pangar et Djèrem

Plateau Sud-Camerounais

CAMEROON

Bertoua
BTA

Berbérati
BBT

Bangui
BGF

Yaoundé
NSI
Mbalmayo

Réserve du Dja

Réserve de faune du Dzanga-Sangha

P.N.du Dzanga-Ndoki

P.N.de Nouabalé-Ndoki

Parc National du Lac Lobeke

MVX

GABON

P.N.de Minkébé

CONGO

Parc National d'Odzala-Kokoua

Réserve communautaire de Lac Télé

ION
Impfondo

DEM. REP.

CONGO

GMA

BSU

39
12°
40
10°
41
8°
190
42
6°
43
4°
44
2°
45

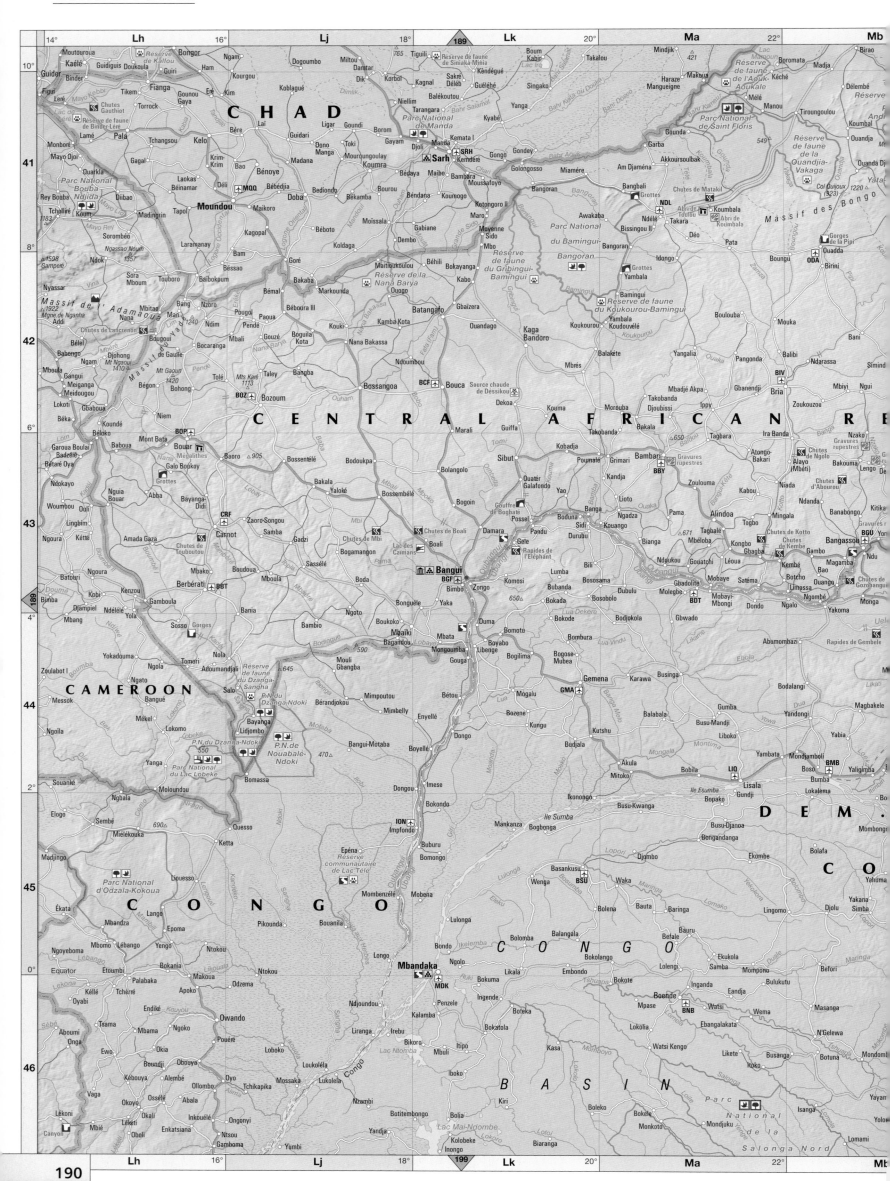

Scale 1:4,500,000

0   50   100   150 Kilometers
0   50   100 Miles

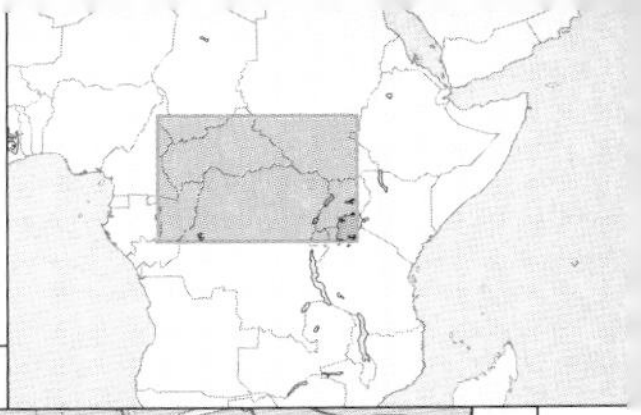

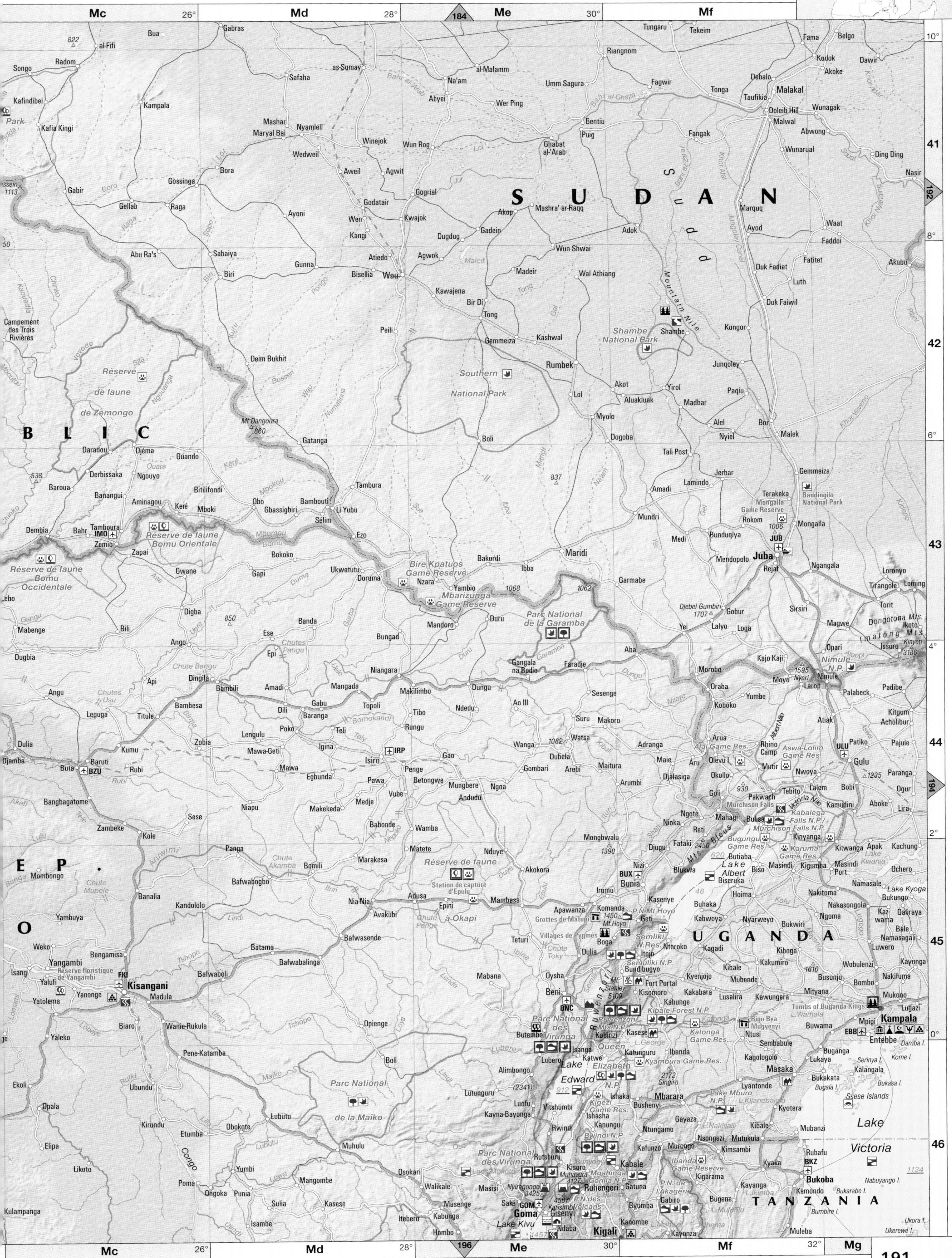

SUDAN

Suud

Mountain Nile

Tungaru Tekeim
Riangnom
Fama Belgo
al-Malamm
Na'am
Umm Sagura Fagwir
Abyei Wer Ping
Kodok Dawir
Akoke
Debalo
Tonga
Malakal
Doleib Hill
Taufikia
Malwal
Wunagak
Abwong
Bentiu
Puig
Ghabat al-'Arab
Fangak
Wunarual
Ding Ding

822
al-Fifi
Bua
Gabras
Songo
Radom
Kampala
Safaha
as-Sumay
Mashar'
Maryal Bai
Nyamlell
Wedweil
Winejok
Wun Rog
Lol
Abu Ra's
Sabaiya
Bora
Aweil
Agwit
Gogrial
Akop
Mashra' ar-Raqq
Adok
Marquq
Waat
Nasir
Gabir
Gellab
Gossinga
Raga
Wen
Kwajok
Godatair
Ayoni
Kangi
Atiedo
Dugdug
Gadein
Gunna
Biri
Bisellia
Wau
Agwok
Wun Shwai
Madeir
Wal Athiang
Ayod
Faddoi
Fatitet
Akubu
Duk Fadiat
Luth
Duk Faiwil
Kongor
Junqoley

Kafia Kingi
Kafindibei
Park
1113
Mashar
Kawajena
Bir Di
Tong
Gemmeiza
Kashwal
Rumbek
Shambe National Park
Shambe

Campement des Trois Rivières
Réserve de faune de Zemongo
Mt Dangoura 860
Gatanga
Boli
Southern National Park
Akot
Lol
Myolo
Dogoba
Aluakluak
Yirol
Madbar
Alel
Nyiel
Malek
Bor

837
Daradou
Djéma
Ouando
Derbissaka
Ngouyo
Bitilifondi
Tambura
Amadi
Lamindo
Jerbar
Gemmeiza
538
Baroua
Banangui
Aminagou
Keré
Mboki
Obo
Gbassigbiri
Bambouti
Li Yubu
Sélim
Ezo
Bokoko
Maridi
Mundri
Medi
Bunduqiya
Terakeka
Mongalla Game Reserve
Bandingilo National Park
Rokom
1006
Mongalla

Dembia
Bahr
Tamboura IMO
Zemio
Zapai
Gwane
Gapi
Duma
Ukwatutu
Doruma
Nzara
Yambio
Bire Kpatuos Game Reserve
Mbarizunga Game Reserve
Mandoro
Duru
Garmabe
Mendopolo
JUB
Juba
Rejat
JUB

Réserve de faune Bomu Orientale
Réserve de faune Bomu Occidentale
Bokoko
Bakordi
Ibba
1068
1062
Djebel Gumbiri 1707
Gobur
Ngangala
Loronyo
Tirangole
Loming

Digba
Bili
Banda
Bungad
Parc National de la Garamba
Yei
Lalyo
Loga
Magwe
Torit
Dongotona Mts.
Ikoto
Matong Mts.
Issoro
Kinyeti 3186

850
Dugbia
Ese
Epi
Chutes Pangu
Niangara
Gangala na Bodio
Garamba
Faradje
Aba
Morobo
Oraba
Kajo Kaji
1595 Nyeri
Nimule N.P.
Nimule
Larop
Palabek
Padibe

Chutes Usu
Api
Dingila
Bambili
Amadi
Mangada
Makilimbo
Dungu
Sesenge
Dungu
Nzoro
Koboko
Yumbe
Kitgum
Achólibur

Angu
Titule
Bambesa
Dili
Gabu
Baranga
Topoli
Tibo
Ndedu
Ao III
Suru
Makoro
Watsa
Adranga
Maie
Arua
Aru
Rhino Camp
Ajai Game Res.
Atiak
Paranga
Ogur

Leguga
Kumu
Zobia
Poko
Teli
Igina
Mawa-Geti
Bomokandi
Tely
Rungu
Gao
Wanga
1082
Dubela
Gombari
Arebi
Maitura
Djalasiga
Okollo
Mutir
Goli
Aswa-Lolim Game Res.
ULU
Gulu
Patiko
Pajule
1235
Lalem
Bobi
Aboke
Lira

Dulia
Djamba
Baruti BZU
Rubi
Rubi
Isiro IRP
Penge
Betongwe
Mungbere
Ngoa
930
Pakwach
Tebito
Kamutini
Apak
Kachung

Buta
Niapu
Medje
Pawa
Vube
Andudu
Mongbwalu
Nioka
Reti
Murchison Falls
Victoria Nile
Kabalega Falls N.P./
Murchison Falls N.P.
Kinyanga
Kitwanga
Ochero

Bangbagatome
Zambeke
Sese
Kole
Panga
Babonde
Wamba
Matete
Nduye
Akokora
Djugu
Fataki 2450
Bunia
1390
Karuma 620
Butiaba
Bugungu Game Res.
Biso
Masindi
Masindi Port
Lake Kwania
Namasale
Lake Kyoga

Mombongo
Bunga
Chute Akamba
Bomili
Marakesa
Réserve de faune
Station de capture d'Epulu
Adusa
Epini
Mambasa
Irumu
BUX
Bunia
Blukwa
Lake Albert
Biseruka
Hoima
Nakitoma
Kafu
Nakasongola
Bale
Namasagali

Weko
Yambuya
Bengamisa
FKI
Kandololo
Nia-Nia
Avakubi
à Okapi
Chute Penge
Komanda
Apawanza
1450 Mt. Hoyo
Grottes de Matupi
P.N. Mt Hoyo
Geti
Buhaka
Kabwoya
Nyarweyo
Bukwiri
Ngoma
Kaz-wami
Galiraya
Luwero
Kayunga

Isang
Yalufi
Yangambi
Réserve floristique de Yangambi
Madula
Kisangani
Batama
Bafwasende
Teturi
Villages de Pygmees
Boga
Dulia
Chute Toky
Semliki W.Res.
Ntoroko
Kagadi
Kibiga
Kakumiro
Mubende
Wobulenzi
Nakifuma
Bombo
Mukono

Yatolema
Yaleko
Biaro
Wanie-Rukula
Madula
Bafwabeli
Mabana
Oysha
Ituri
Bundibugyo
Beni
BNC
1610
Fort Portal
Kisomoro
Kibale Forest N.P.
Kyenjojo
Kibale
Mityana
Busunju
EBB
Kampala
Entebbe
Lugazi

Ekoli
Opala
Ubundu
Obokote
Lubutu
Boli
Parc National de la Maiko
Lenda
Butembo
Kanya-Bayonga
Parc National des Virunga
Stanley 5109 Mt.
Ruwenzori Mts.
Katiri N.P.
Kasese
Queen
L. George
Katonga Game Res.
Bigo Bya Mugyenyi
Tombs of Buganda Kings
Kakabara
Lusalira
Kawungera
Ntusi
Sembabule

Elipa
Likoto
Opienge
Pene-Katamba
Maiko
Ruiki
Lutunguru
Alimbongo
Lubero
Lake Edward
Katwe
Luberu
Kyambura Game Res.
2172 Singiro
Mbarara
Lake Mburo N.P.
Lyantonde
Masaka
Bukakata
Ssese Islands

Kulampanga
Kirundu
Etumba
Obokote
Muhulu
Vitshumbi
Kayna-Bayonga
Luofu
2341
912
Ishaka
Bushenyi
Ntungamo
Gayaza
Nakivali
Kabale
Mubanzi
Lake Victoria
Kalangala
Bugala I.
Serinya I.
Kome I.
Damba I.
Mpigi

Poma
Yumbi
Mangombe
Osokari
Parc National des Virunga
Rutshuru
Kisoro
Muhavura 4127
Mgahinga Gorilla N.P.
Ruhengeri
Gatuna
Kabale
Ibanda Game Reserve
P.N. de l'Akagéra
Kigarama
Kayonza
Bukoba
1134
Nabuyongo I.
Rubafu
BKZ

Ongoka
Punia
Sulia
Isambe
Walikale
Masisi
Nyiragongo 3470
Karisimbi 4507
P.N. des Volcans
Byumba
Gabiro
L. Mugesera
Bugene
L. Mihindi

Kabunga
Musenge
Itebero
Hombo
Sake GOM
Goma
Gisenyi
Ndaba
Lake Kivu
4457
Kigali
Kanombe
Kayonza
Bukoba
Kemondo
Bukarabe I.
Muleba
Ukora I.
Ukerewe I.
Bumbire I.

UGANDA

TANZANIA

EP. O

BLIC

Lake Victoria

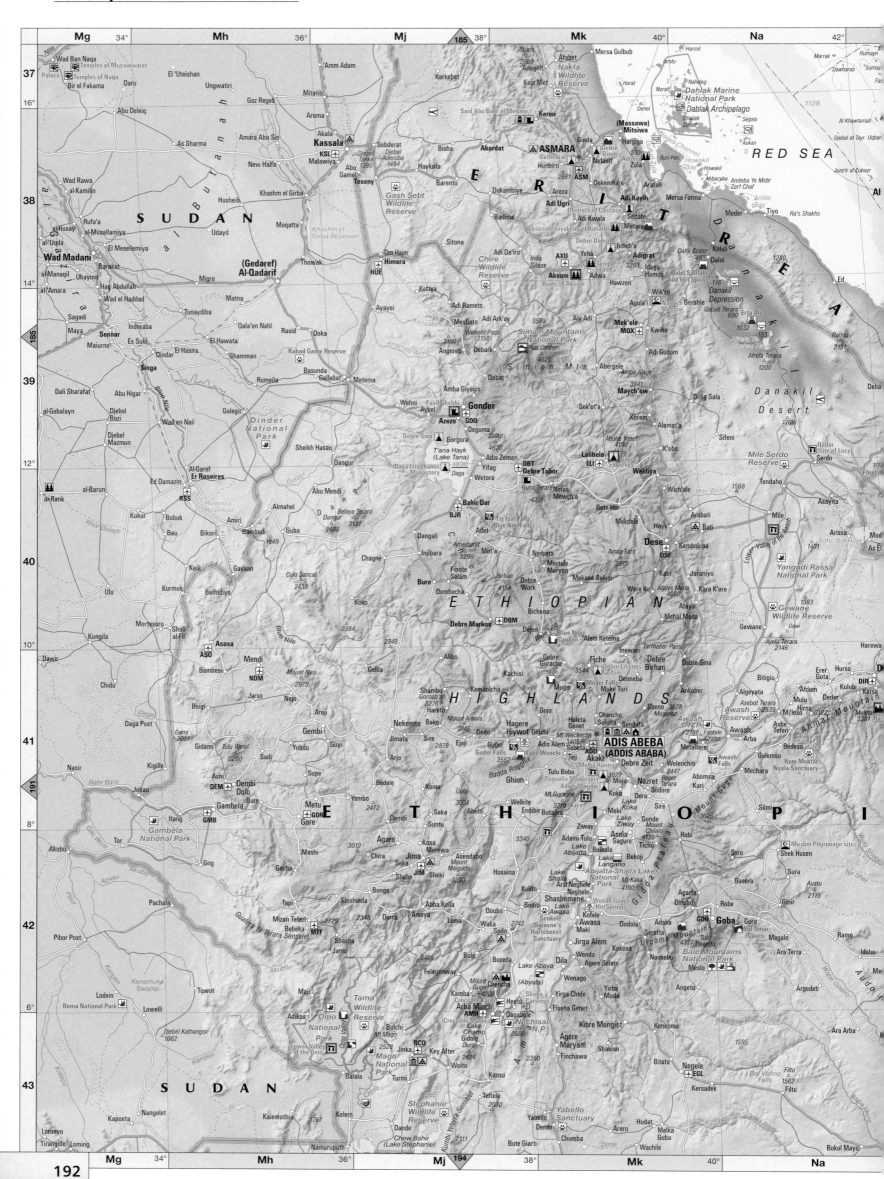

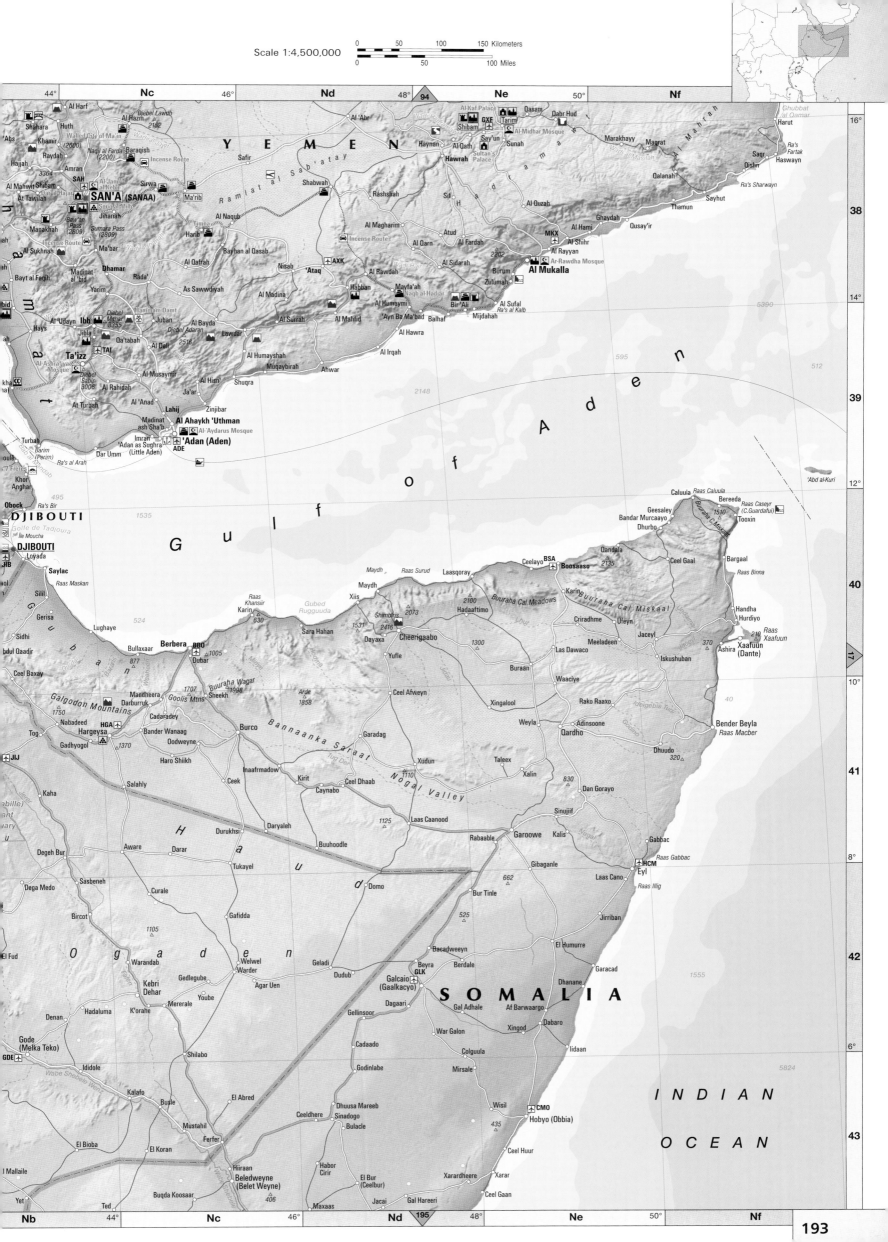

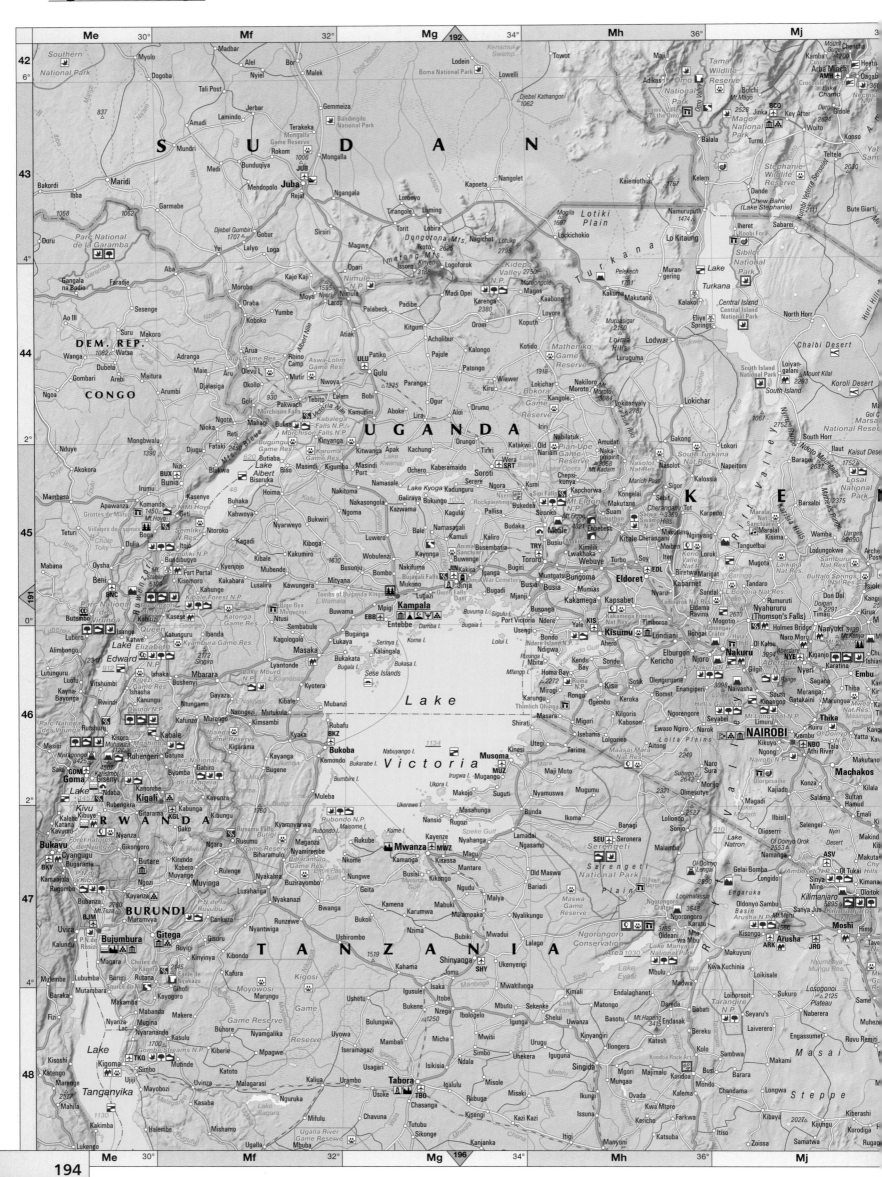

Mk   40°   Na   42°   Nb   193   44°   Nc   46°   Nd

ETHIOPIA

Angetu
Gaba
Gode (Melka Teko)
GDE
Ididole
Shilabo
Cadaado
Colguula
Argedeb
Ara Arba
El Kere
6°
Godinlabe
Mirsale
engist
Konkoma
El Medo
Kalafo
Bitata
El Mallaile
El Abred
Dhuusa Mareeb
1385
Wabe Shebele Wenz
Negele
EGL
Kersadek
Hargele
Bare
Yet
Mustahil
Ferfer
Ceeldhere
Sinadogo
Bulacle
43
1595
Andia Range
Lema Shilindi
Rabdure
Ted
Buqda Koosaar
Hiiraan
Beledweyne (Belet Weyne)
Habor Cirir
El Bur (Ceelbur)
Xarardheere
Ceel Gaan
Melka Guba
Wachile
El Gof
Chelago
Melka Mari
Malka Mari
Dollo Odo
Doolow
Malca Rie
Luuq
Xuddur (Oddur)
Totiyas
Ceel Garas
Jiigley
Cel Duubo
Maxaas
Derri
Jacai
Bud Bud
Nooleeye

SOMALIA

MUQDISHO (MOGADISHU)

Marka (Merca)

Kismaayo
KMU

INDIAN OCEAN

Equator   0°

Nb   44°   Nc   46°   Nd

SEYCHELLES

Amirante Islands

Victoria
SEZ
Mahé

Praslin
La Digue

Amirante Basin

INDIAN OCEAN

Alphonse Group

Mk   40°   Na   42°   Nb   197   Nb   52°   Ng   54°   Nh   56°   Nj

195

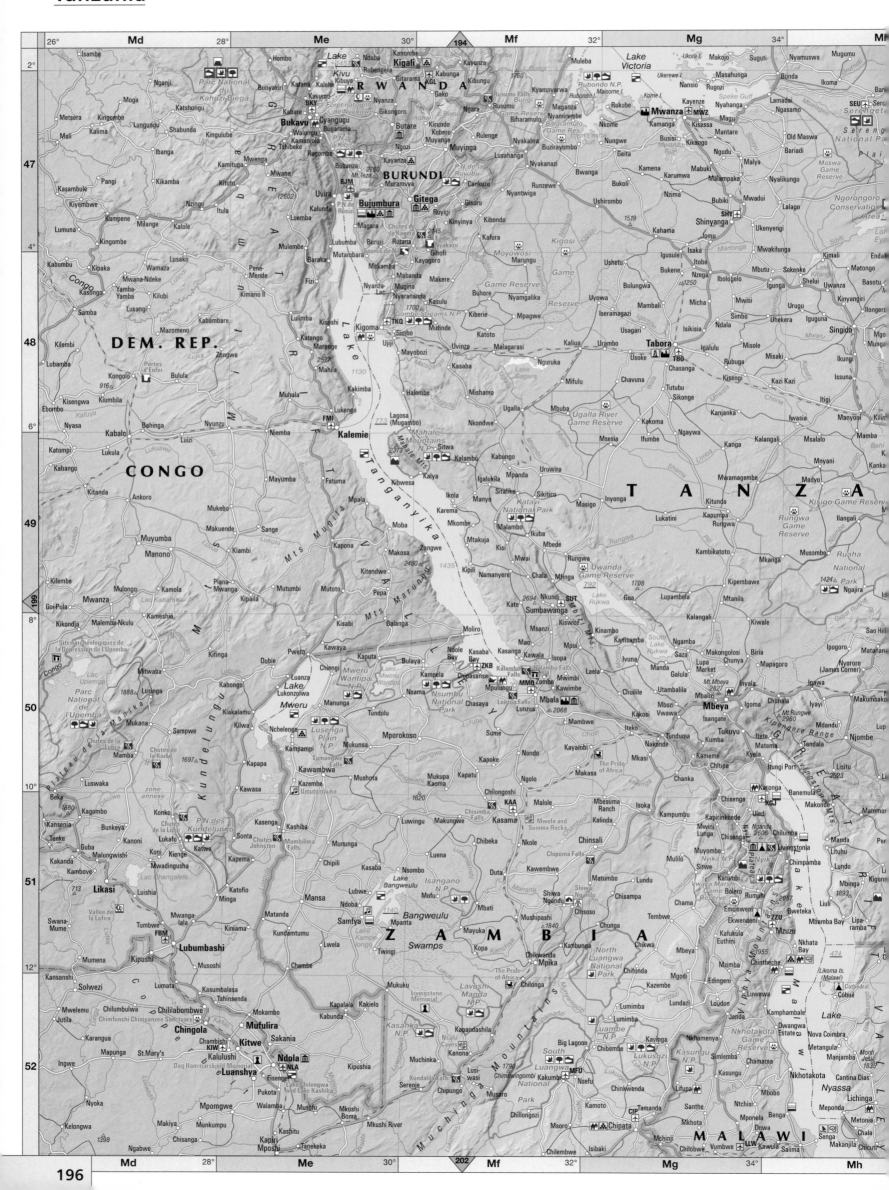

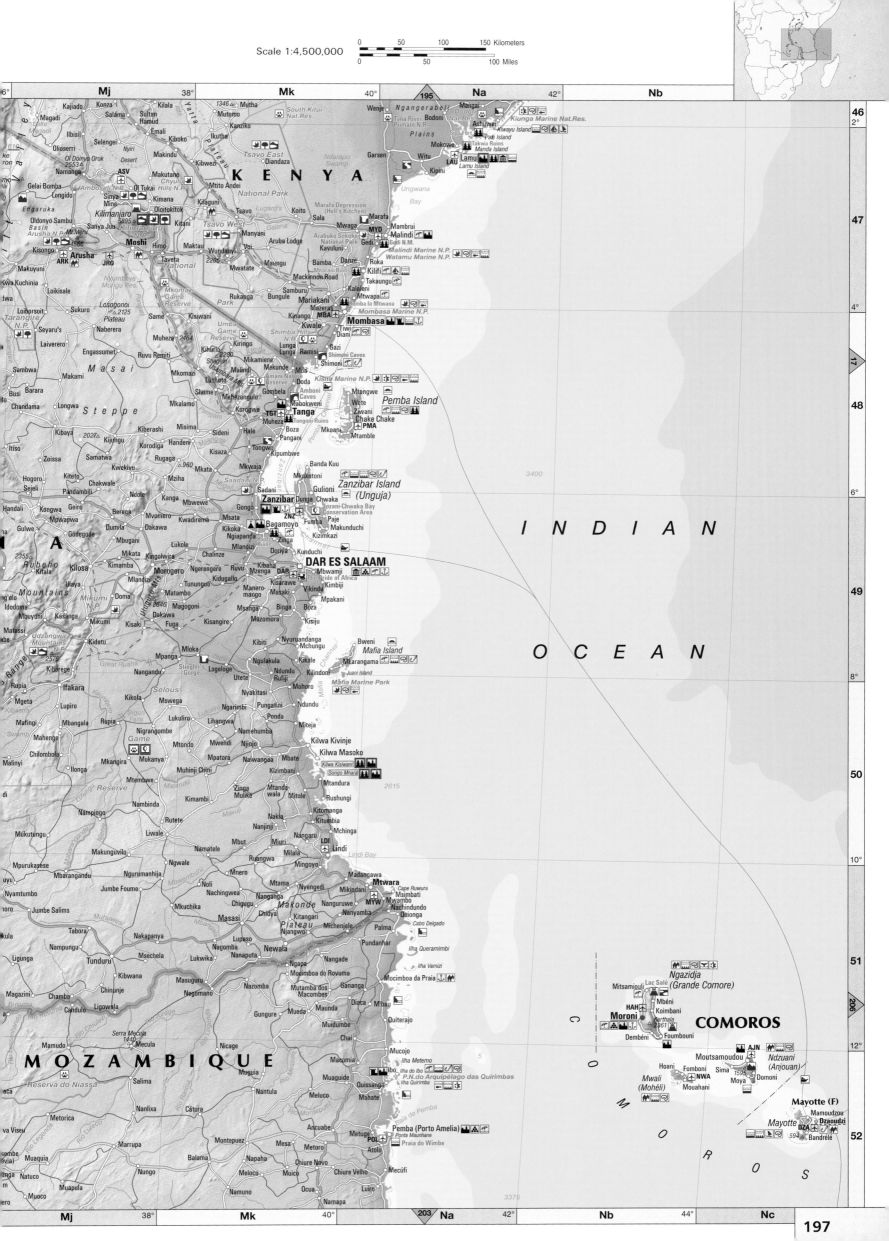

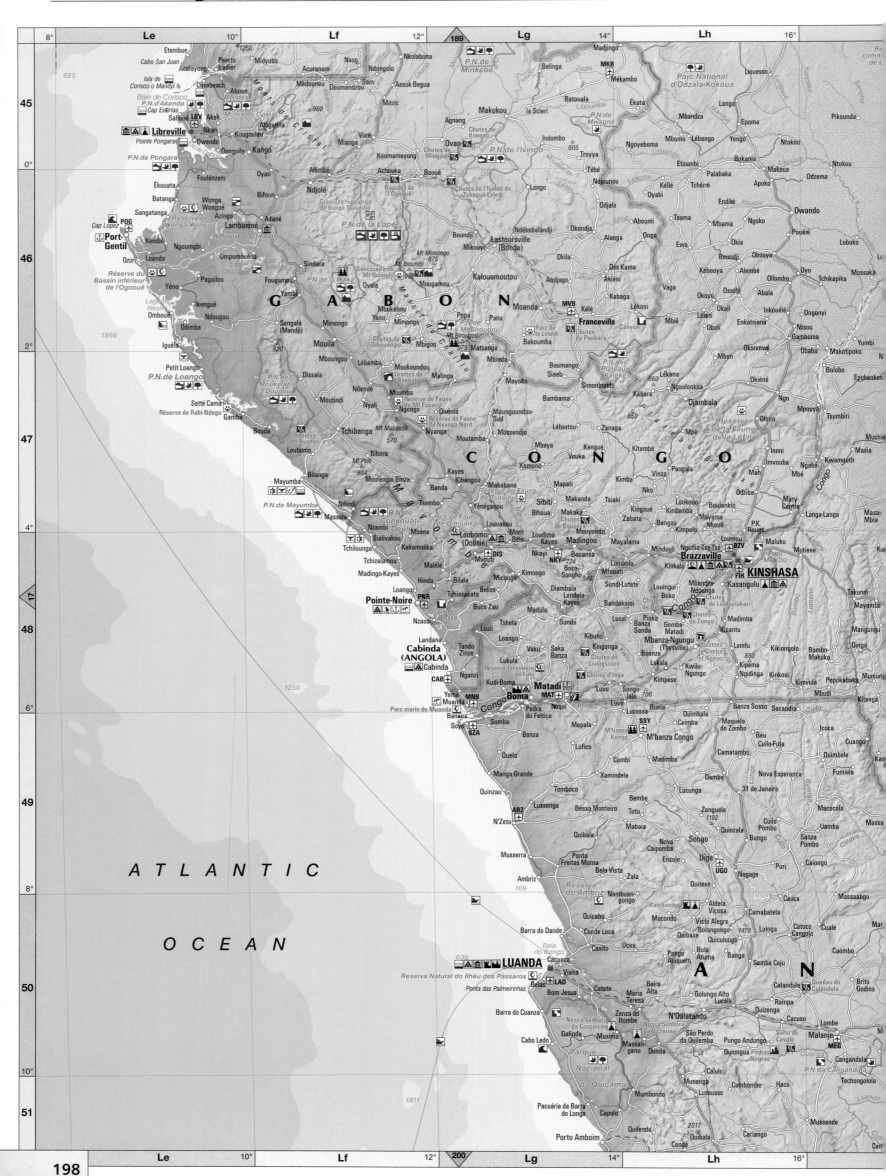

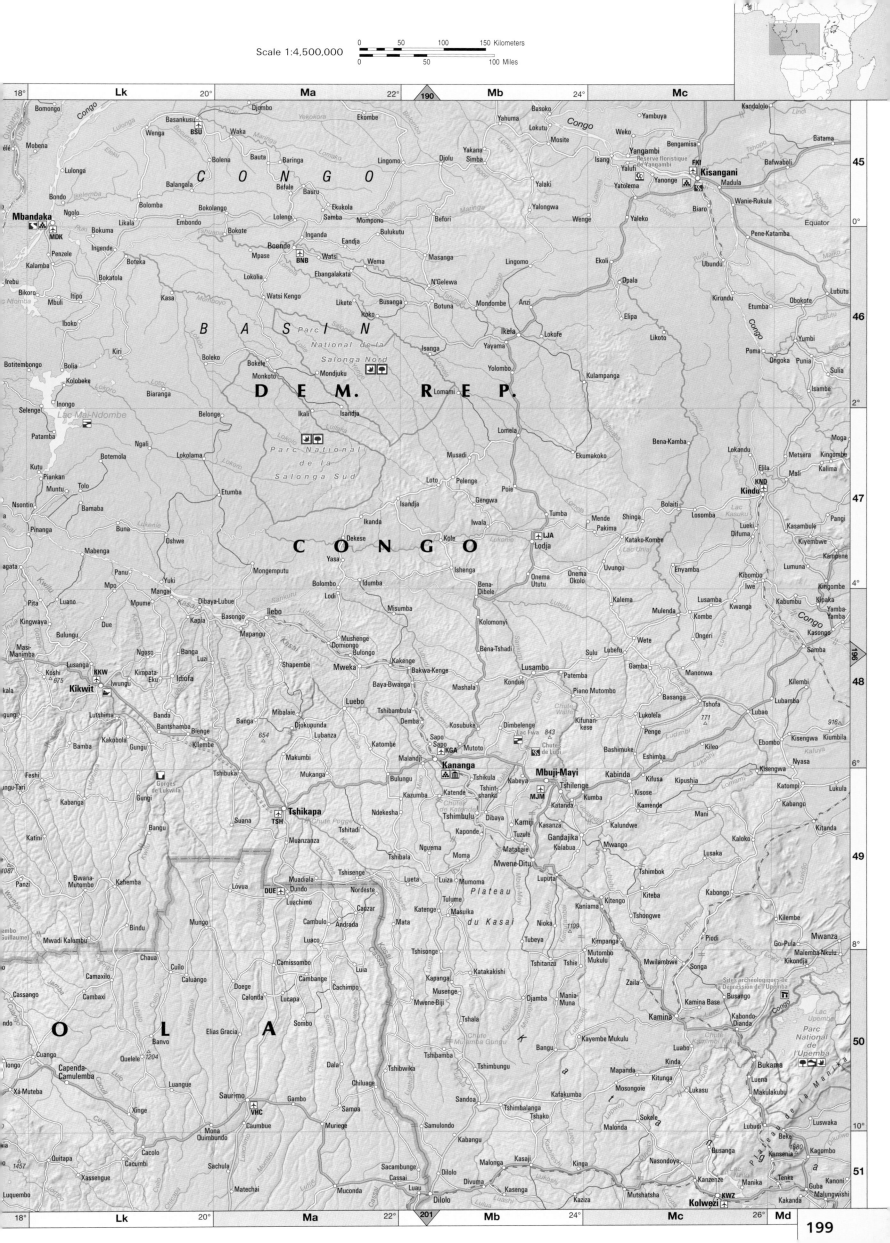

Scale 1:4,500,000

0 50 100 150 Kilometers
0 50 100 Miles

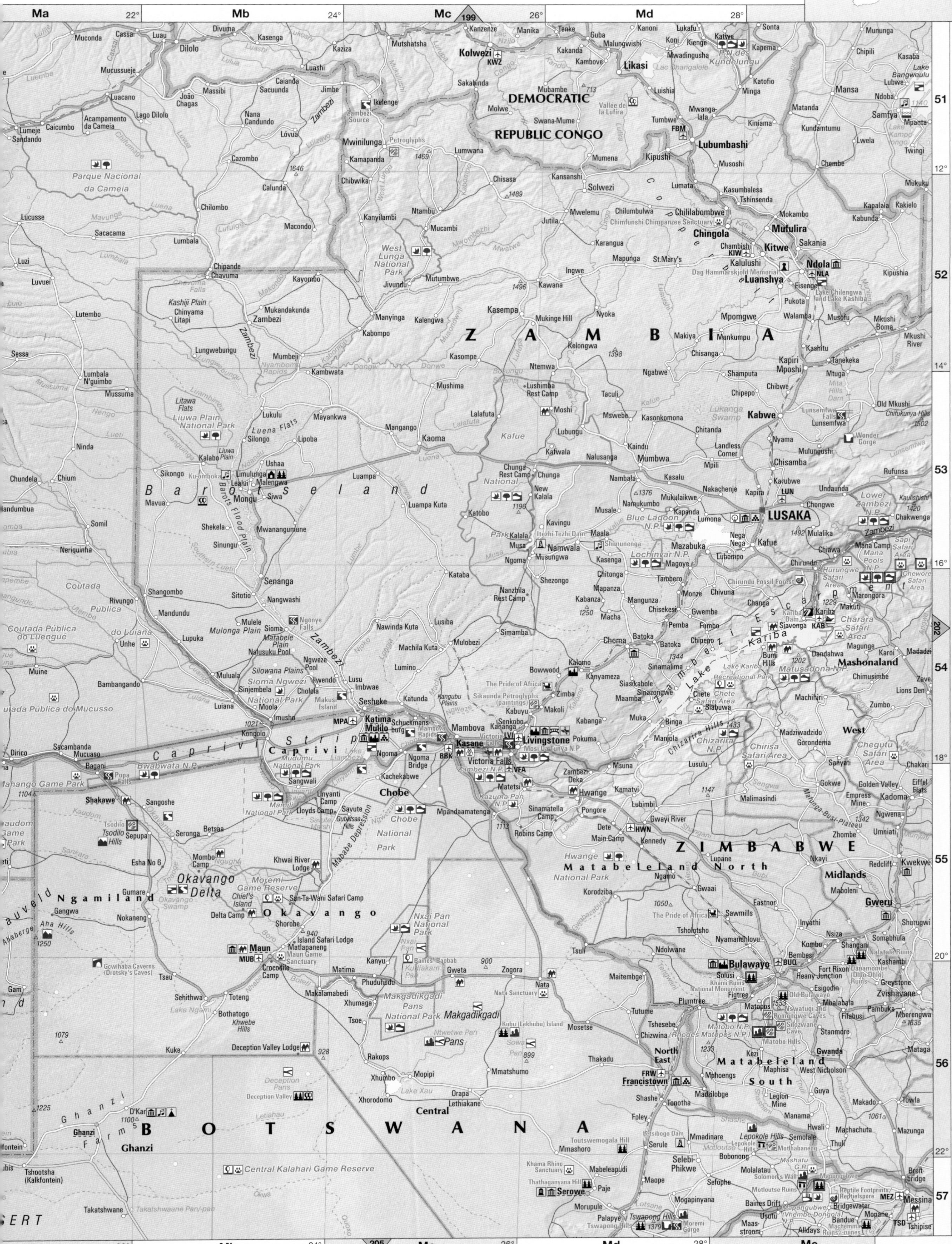

DEMOCRATIC

REPUBLIC CONGO

Kolwezi
KWZ
Likasi
Lubumbashi

ZAMBIA

Chingola
Kitwe
KIW
Ndola
NLA
Luanshya
Mufulira

Solwezi

Kabwe

Mongu
Barotseland

Kaoma

LUSAKA

Mazabuka
Kafue

Namwala

Senanga

Mana Camp
Mana Pools

Livingstone
LVI
Victoria Falls
VFA
Kasane
BBK
Katima Mulilo
MPA

Caprivi Strip

Chobe

Okavango Delta
Ngamiland

Maun
MUB

ZIMBABWE

Matabeleland North

Hwange
HWN

Midlands

Gweru

Bulawayo
BUQ

Francistown
FRW

North East

Matabeleland South

BOTSWANA

Ghanzi
Ghanzi Farms

Central

Central Kalahari Game Reserve

Serowe

Selebi-Phikwe

Makgadikgadi
Makgadikgadi Pans National Park

Okavango
National Park

Nxai Pan National Park

Tsodilo Hills

Shakawe

Kaudom Game Park

Messina
TSD

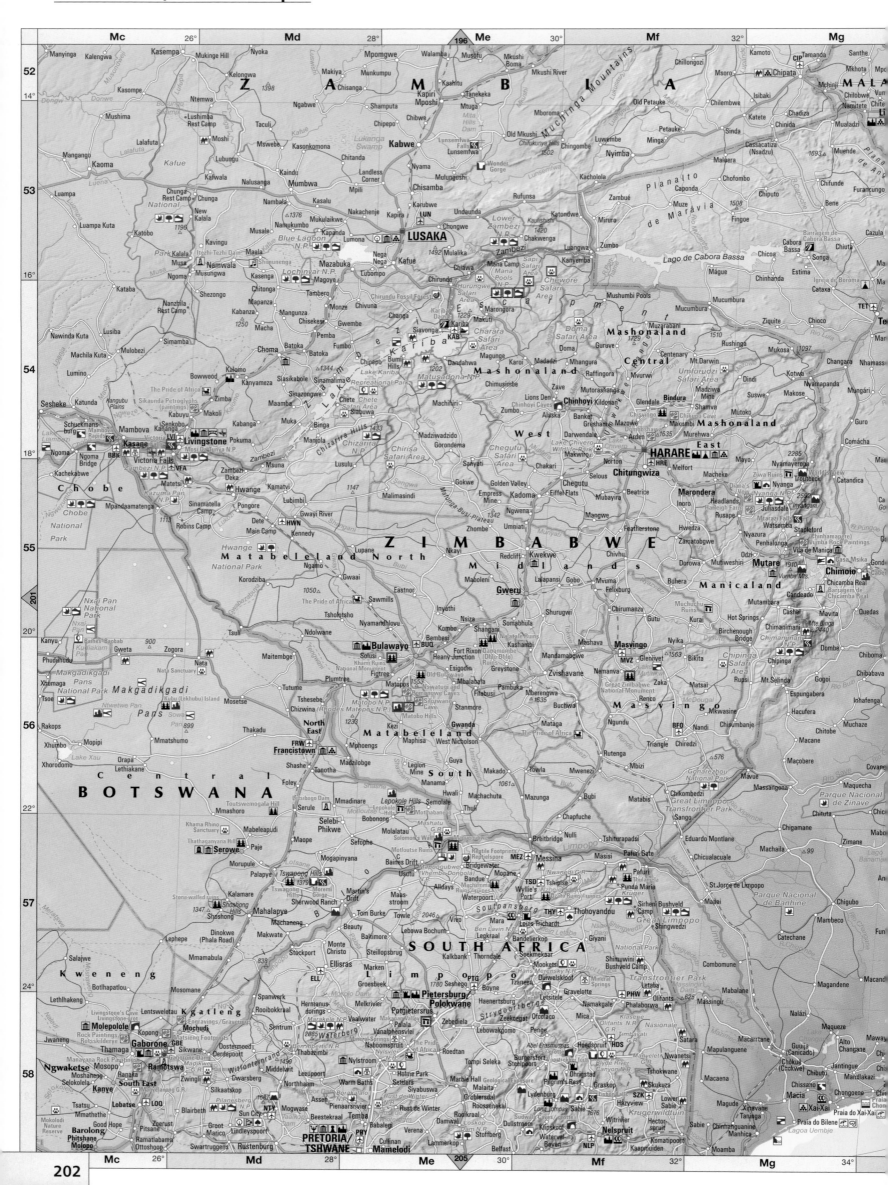

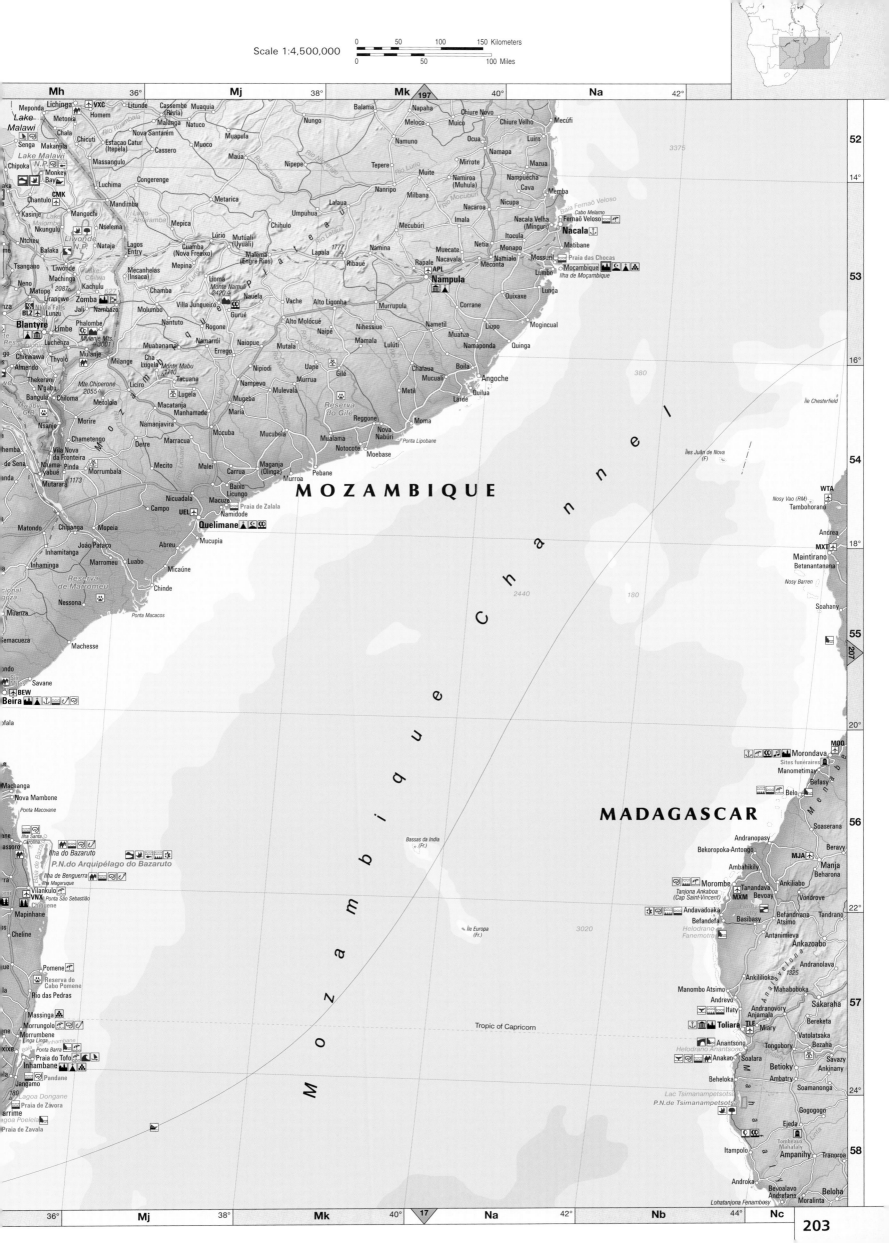

52
14°
53
16°
54
18°
55
207
20°
56
22°
57
24°
58

Lake Malawi

Meponda   Lichinga   VXC   Litunde   Cassembe   Muaquia   Napaha
Metonia   Homem   Malanga   Muapula   Balama   Napaha   Chiure Novo
Chala   Chicuti   Nova Santarém   Natuco   Nungo   Meloco   Muico   Chiure Velho   Mecúfi
Senga   Makanjila   Estação Catur   Cassero   Namuno   Namapa
Chipoka   Massangulo   Maúa   Nipepe   Muite   Mirrote   Mazua
Monkey Bay   Congerenge   Metarica   Lalaua   Nanripo   Milbana   Nampuécha   Memba

Lake Malawi N.P.

CMK
Chantulo   Luchima   Umpuhua   Chihulo   Namiroa (Muhula)   Nacala Velha (Minguri)   Balaô Fernaô Veloso
Kasinje   Mangochi   Mandimba   Mepica   Lúrio   Mutúali (Uyuali)   Imala   Monapo   Fernaô Veloso
Nkungulu   Nselema   Cuamba (Nova Freixo)   Mecanhelas (Insaca)   Malema (Entre Rios)   Ribaué   Netia   Nacala   Nacala   Matibane
Nataja   Lagos Entry   Chamba   Mepinha   Nauela   Vache   Alto Ligonha   Muecate   Namialo   Meconta   Mossuril   Praia das Chocas

APL
Nampula   Moçambique   Ilha de Moçambique

Blantyre   Zomba   Molumbo   Villa Junqueiro   Gurué   Alto Molócué   Naipé   Nihessiue   Nametil   Lúrio   Mogincual
Limbe   Nambazo   Nantuto   Namarrói   Errego   Naiope   Mutala   Mamala   Namaponda   Quinga
Phalombe   Muabanama   Nipiodi   Nampevo   Uape   Gilé   Chalaua   Boila   Angoche

MOZAMBIQUE

Quelimane

Mozambique Channel

MADAGASCAR

Beira

Morondava
Manometimay
Befasy
Belo
Soaserana
Beravy

MJA
Manja
Beharona

Morombe
Tanandava
Bevoay
Ankiliabo
Vondrove

MXM

Andavadoaka
Befandefa
Befandriana Atsimo
Tandrano

Basibasy
Antanimieva
Ankazoabo
Andranolava

Tropic of Capricorn

Toliara
Ifaty
Andranovory Anjamala
Sakaraha
Bereketa

Anantsono
Anakao
Soalara
Tongobory
Bezaha
Savazy
Ankinany

Betioky
Ambatry
Soamanonga

Beheloka

Ejeda
Gogogogo

Itampolo
Ampanihy
Tranoroa
Androka
Bevoalavo
Andrefana
Beloha
Lohatanjona Fenambosy
Moralinta

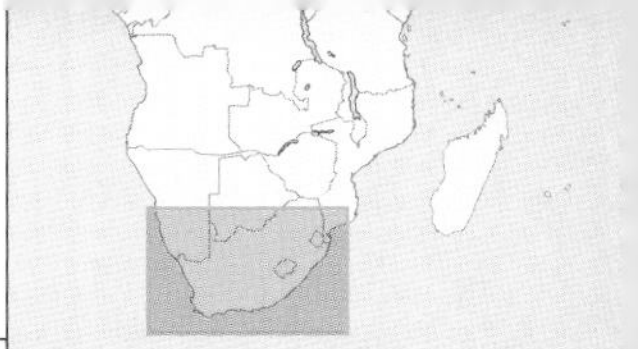

MOZAMBIQUE

BOTSWANA

Morupule Palapye Tswapong Hills Baines Drift Bridgewater
Mahalapye Shoshong Martin's Drift Maas-stroom Mopane Pafuri Gate Chicualacuale
Sherwood Ranch Tom Burke Towle Vivo Masisi Pafuri St.Jorge de Limpopo Chigubo
Makwate Monte Christo Ellisras Marken Kalkbank Thorndale Thohoyandou Combomune Magadene
Mmamabula Stockport Steilloopbrug Seshego Giyani Catechane
Lethlhakeng Groesbeek Pietersburg/Polokwane Tropic of Capricorn
Kgatleng Marakele N.R. Vaalwater Potgietersrus Lebowakgomo Massingir Macarrtane
Molepolole Mochudi Gaborone Ramotswa Nylstroom Zebediela Ocolaco Chókwé Guijá Alto Changane
Kanye South East Northam Warm Baths Settlers Groblersdal Satara Macaena Chibuto Mandlakazi
Lobatse LOO Sun City NTY Mogwase Assen Rust de Winter Lydenburg Skukuza Magude Xai-Xai
Mmathethe Rustenburg Brits Ga-Rankuwa Cullinan Roossenekal Hazyview Chinhacanine Macia Chongoene
Zeerust Mabopane PRETORIA/TSHWANE Mamelodi Middelburg Nelspruit Komatipoort Maputo
Mafikeng Koster Krugersdorp Roodepoort Benoni Witbank Barberton MAPUTO
Lichtenburg Randfontein SOWETO JOHANNESBURG Springs Delmas Mbabane SWAZILAND Manzini Bela Vista
Klerksdorp Vanderbijlpark Heidelberg Bethal Amsterdam Big Bend Ponta do Ouro
Orkney Vereeniging Sasolburg Mpumalanga Ermelo Ndumo
Bothaville Parys Frankfort Volksrust Piet Retief Pongola Kosi Bay N.R.
Welkom Kroonstad Reitz Newcastle Vryheid Jozini Mbaswana
Virginia Lindley Warden Dundee Nongoma Hluhluwe
Kimberley Bethlehem Harrismith Ladysmith Ulundi Richards Bay/Richardsbaai
Bloemfontein Maseru LESOTHO Estcourt Eshowe Empangeni
Free State Thaba Nchu Giant's Castle Pietermaritzburg Stanger Durban
Colesberg Springfontein KwaZulu Natal Kwa-Mashu Umlazi Durban
Aliwal-Noord Kokstad Port Shepstone Margate
Graaff-Reinet Queenstown Umtata Port St.Johns
Cradock King William's Town Bisho Mdantsane Coffee Bay
Somerset-East East London Kei Mouth
Uitenhage Grahamstown/Grahamstad The Haven
Port Elizabeth Port Alfred Kenton on Sea

Eastern Cape

Cape St.Francis Jeffrey's Bay Algoa Bay

INDIAN

OCEAN

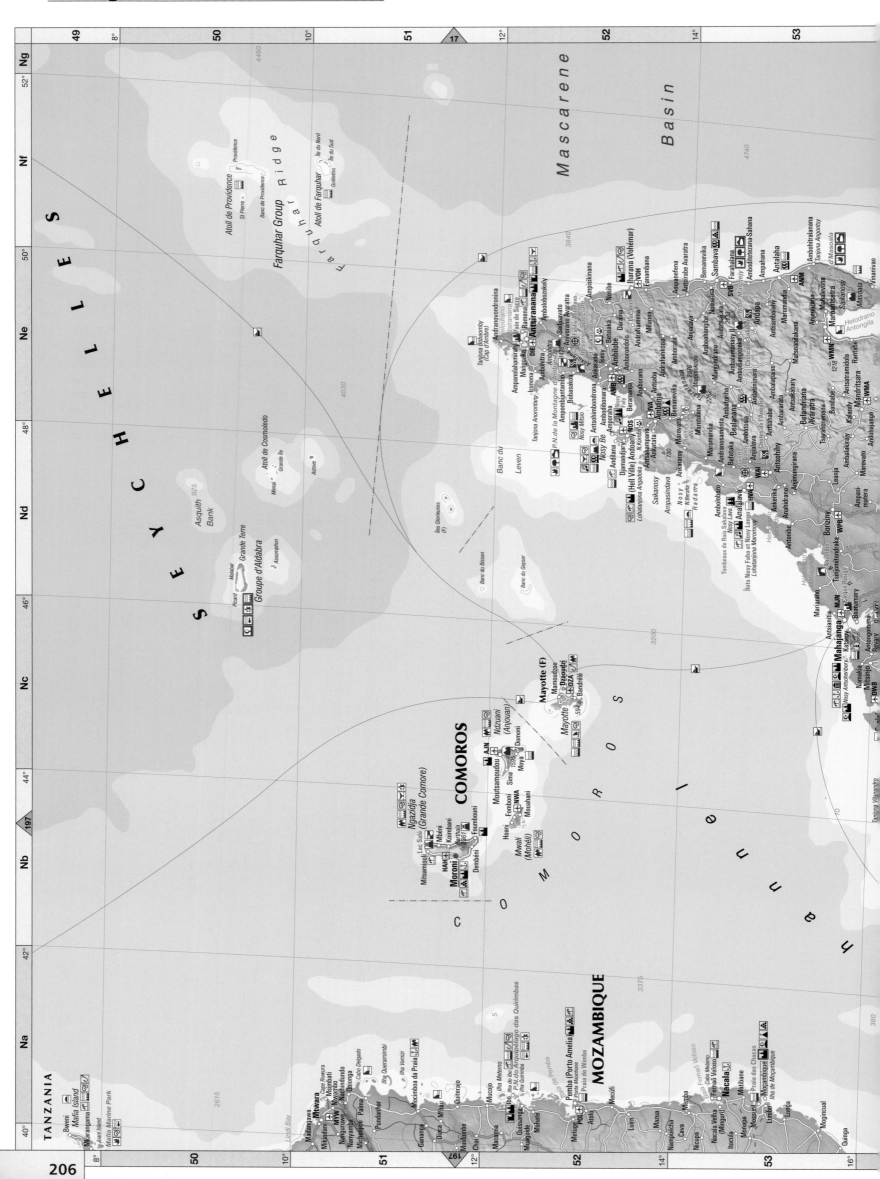

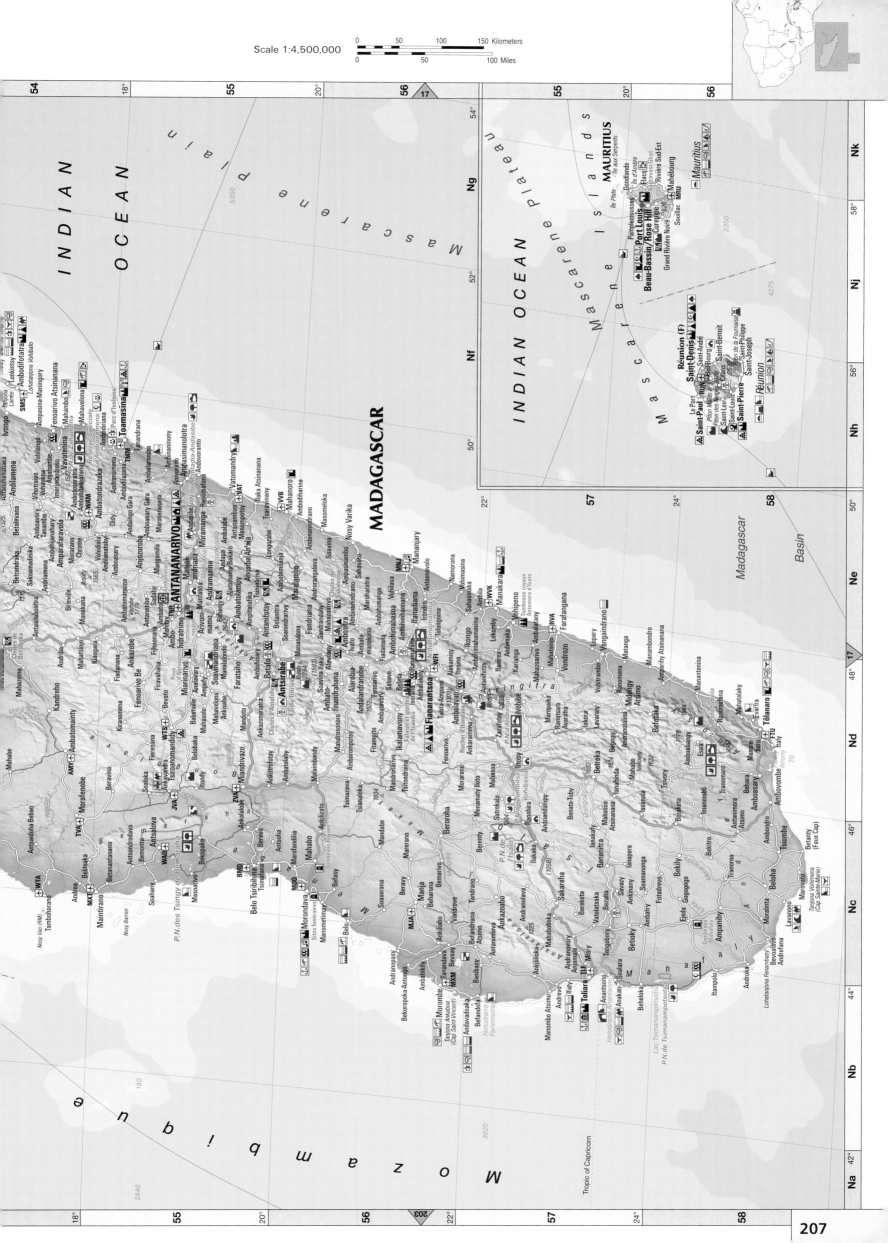

North and Central America

This continent in the northern hemisphere also includes Mexico and Greenland and covers an area of 25 million sq. km. More than two-thirds of the land mass consists of North America. Central America forms a land bridge between this continent and the continent of South America. The great landscapes of the continent stretch between the Pacific and Atlantic Oceans and range from the glaciers of Alaska to the tropical Caribbean islands. In the north-east, the islands and hills of the Canadian Shield surround the expanse of Hudson Bay. Further to the south lies the Great Lakes region, followed by the US Deep South, which is

bordered to the west by the three parallel mountain chains of the Cordilleras, and to the east by the Appalachians. The Cordilleras also extend through Central America, where the Mexican Yucatán Peninsula and the islands of the Greater and Lesser Antilles surround the Caribbean Sea.

A hundred years ago Glacier Bay was still completely covered in ice, but as the glaciers retreat beautiful wildflower meadows emerge along the banks of the meandering meltwater rivers.

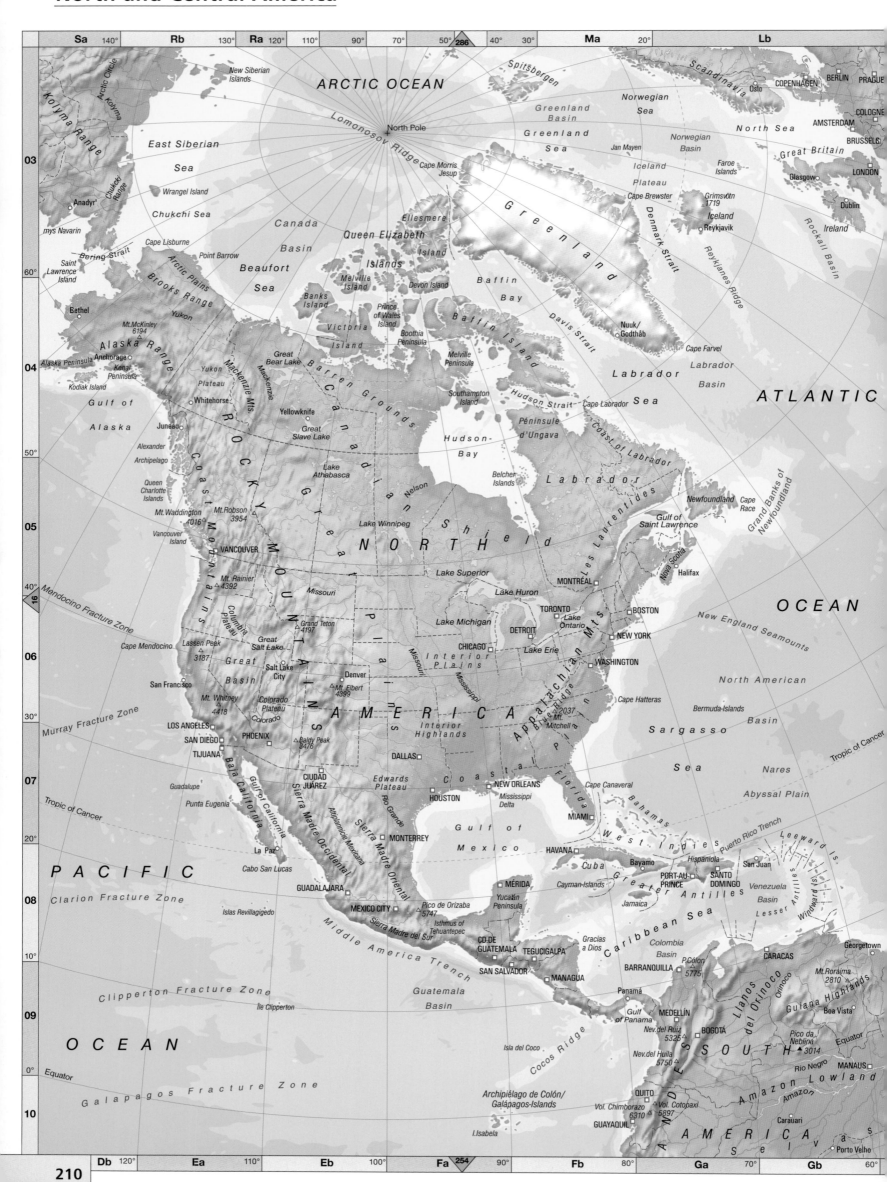

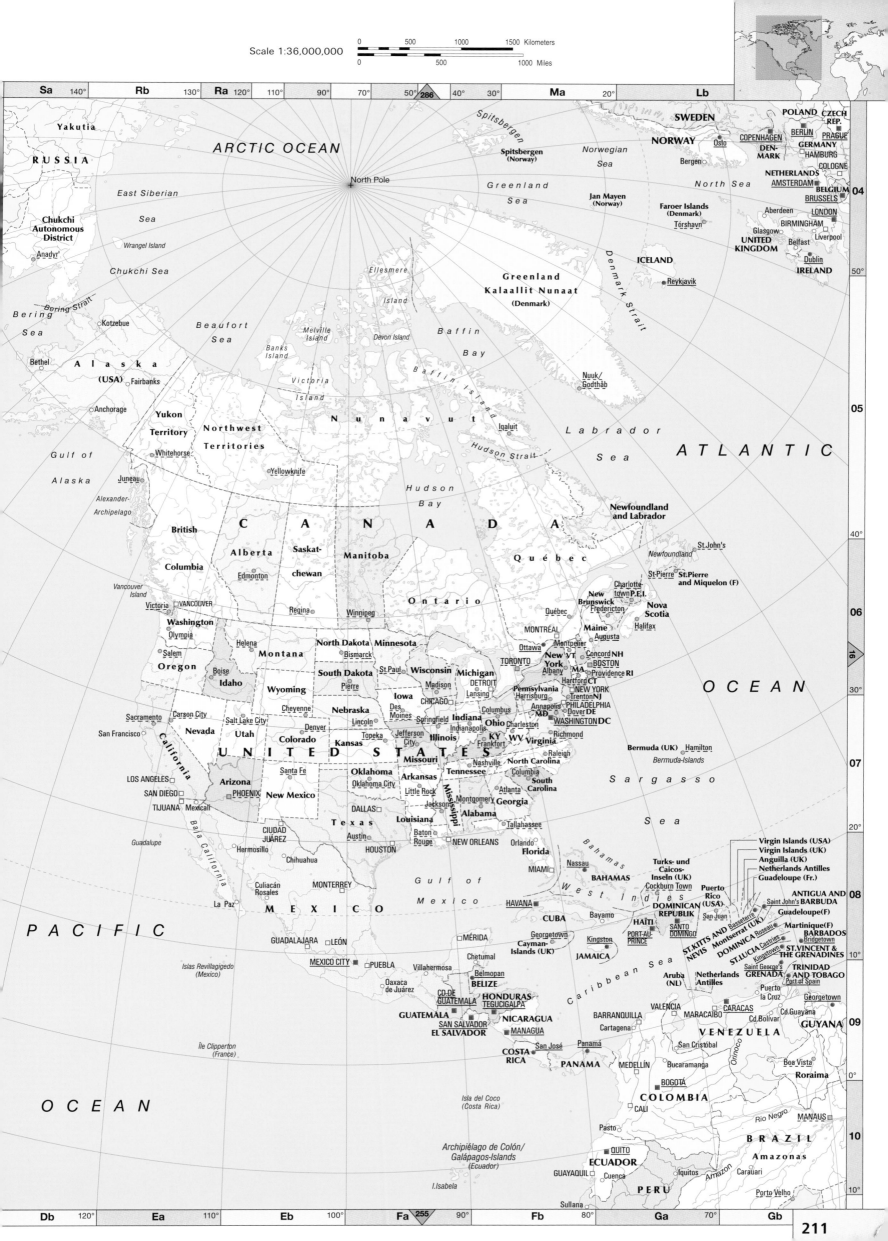

***Greenland**: more than four-fifths of the island is covered with an inland ice sheet. Icebergs are created when the huge valley glaciers move seawards and calve (give birth to icebergs). In summer, above the Arctic Circle, the sun stays above the horizon even at night.*

Greenland

The largest island on Earth at 2,175,600 sq. km is separated from the North American mainland by the **Kane Basin**, **Baffin**

height of 1,800 m and reaching elevations of 3,733 m on the east face. Further inland, the land sinks to some 250 m below sea level, giving it a shape that resembles a huge bowl filled with a vast sheet of ice.

The inland pack-ice rises to 3,300 m in height and has a volume of 2.5 million cu. km. Only the mountain peaks soaring above the ice break up the monotonous white scenery. There are depressions, crevasses and clefts especially

near the coast, but these are mostly covered in snow and are not visible.

Massive glaciers move slowly down through the mountain ranges to the sea, where they often break off abruptly and pro-

duce icebergs. The **Humboldt Glacier**, which is approximately 100 km wide, and the 300 km-wide steep cliff at **Melville Bay** are particularly impressive.

Mount McKinley is reflected in Wonder Lake in Denali National Park.

Hudson

This river in the eastern USA, is named after the English sea captain, Henry Hudson. It rises in the Adirondacks from several small lakes. The Hudson is 507 km long and flows into New York Bay. It is linked to the lower reaches of the St. Lawrence river and to the Great Lakes by several canals. Its most important tributary is the Mohawk, which joins it from the east.

Alaska: in Glacier Bay 16 glaciers flow into the sea.

Yukon

This is Alaska's main river. It is 2,554 km long but if its headwater, the Nisutlin, is taken into account it is even longer, at 3,185 km, making it one of the longest rivers in North America. It has a drainage area of some 830,000 sq. km. The Yukon rises in the Coast Mountains and flows into the Bering Sea. The estuary covers an area of 30,000 sq. km of swamps and lakes.

Alaska

This peninsula in the north-west of the American continent is bordered by the Arctic Sea to the north, the **Bering Sea** to the west and the Pacific to the south. The whole of **Alaska** is mountainous and based on a substrate of crystalline schist, limestone and sandstone, overlaid with subsequent strata from the Jurassic, Cretaceous and Tertiary periods. The shape of the landscape can be traced back to folding and tectonic movements in the Tertiary period. The Earth here is still moving today as is evidenced by the active volcanoes on the **Aleutian Islands** and the numerous earthquakes.

The **Brooks Range** in the north, with elevations of up to 2,816 m, is adjacent to a coastal plain of varying widths, containing many lakes and marshes. In spite of these elevations, the mountain range, with its plateau landscape, has more of the characteristics of a low mountain range.

The mountain ranges of the **Chugach Mountains** and the **Alaska Range** run parallel to the Brooks Range. The southern regions of these ranges are heavily glaciated. In the north-west, the mountains drop steeply to the **Yukon Basin**. The water meadows cover a large area in the direction of the Bering Sea and meet at a coastal plain, which is mostly covered by the **Yukon** and **Kuskokwim** rivers as they flow into the delta.

Almost three-quarters of the area is covered in permafrost, which reaches depths of up to 400 m. Inland, tundra vegetation prevails and in the south there are pine and sitka spruce forests.

The Alaska Range

The **Alaska Range** is a continuation of the **North American Cordillera** and is the highest region in this high mountain range. **Mount McKinley**, at 6,194 m, is the highest mountain in North America. The volcanic **Aleutian Range** is a continuation of the Alaska Range on the Alaskan Peninsula, finally ending in the **Aleutian Islands**.

Bay, the **Kennedy Channel**, the **Davis Straits** and **Smith Sound** in the west and from Svalbard by the Greenland Sea.

Geologically, Greenland is a continuation of the Canadian Shield. It consists of Pre-Cambrian crystalline and intrusive rocks. In the north and east, younger sedimentary and volcanic rocks overlie these ancient formations. Approximately five-sixths of the area is covered by a permanent ice cap. Only a very narrow strip of coast and the seaward **skerries**, small rocky hillocks rounded by the action of glaciation, are free of ice.

Deep **fjords** cut into the coastline. These are lined with mountain ranges rising in the west to a

Mount Wrangell (4317m) in south-east Alaska is an extinct volcano.

Big picture: this view from space shows a section of the east coast of Greenland. On the far side of the picture, the Scoresby Sund, ice-free and around 200 km long, is one of the world's longest fjords. Its individual branches reach another 150 km into the hinterland. Also notable is the narrow Hurryfjord, which projects into the Jameson Land peninsula.

Above: a unique spectacle in the Arctic summer – massive icebergs make their way in stately progress along the coast of Greenland.

North and Central America

Mount Saint Helen's in Washington State was considered to be dormant, until it suddenly erupted violently in 1980, blowing off its cone and killing 60 people. Lava and ash rained down for many miles around. Mount Saint Helen's is one of the volcanos formed during the Tertiary Era in the *Cascades Range*.

The Yukon Basin

The most northerly of North America's intra-mountain basins, the Yukon Basin is situated between the **Coast Mountains** and the **Brooks Range** and slopes gradually from a height of some 1,200 m in the east as it heads towards the west. The landscape is composed of low mountain ranges, hills, basins and the deep gorges of the river valleys, which are very impressive. Both the **Yukon** and the **Kuskokwim** rivers drain into the Yukon Basin.

The Mackenzie Mountains

The **Mackenzie Mountains** are a range in north-western Canada on the Alaskan border. They are the northern continuation of the **Rocky Mountains** and extend over a distance of 800 km. The range, which has had only little exploration, reaches a height of 2,900 m.

Colorado River

The Colorado River rises in the Rocky Mountains and flows for 2,334 km before draining into the Gulf of California in Mexico. It is of great economic importance because of its dams and artificial irrigation systems. The river is renowed for the deep chasms it has cut through the Colorado plateau. The Grand Canyon is on average 1,600 m deep and between 6 km and 29 km wide. The steep sides are stepped with ledges and platforms, and broken up by many intersecting gorges.

The Canadian Shield

The **Laurentian Massif** curves around from the mouth of the **Mackenzie River** in the north via the **Great Bear Lake**, the **Great Slave Lake**, **Lake Athabasca**, the **Reindeer Lake** and **Lake Winnipeg** to the **Labrador** coast. It covers an area of around 5 million sq. km. In the west, the massif is bordered by the **Hudson Bay Basin**, while in the north it ends in the islands of the Canadian-Arctic archipelago. The southern part of the islands generally consists of flat plains,

which are mostly devoid of vegetation, or of gently undulating plateau landscapes that are rarely above 400 m, whereas the northern regions are generally mountainous.

The high **Innuitian Mountains** contain numerous glaciers. **Mount Challenger** on **Ellesmere Island** rises to an altitude of 3,048 m and the range reaches a height of 2,600 m on **Baffin Island**.

The Canadian Shield has an average altitude of between 400 and 500 m and gently curves in the shape of a key around the edges. In the west, the boundaries consist of tiers of strata of the **Interior Plains**, while in the east they are bounded by the Labrador coastal region. The **Torngat Mountains** rise to an altitude of approximately 1,700 m.

The ancient land mass of the Canadian Shield consists of archaic and proterozoic rocks, mostly gneiss, granite, limestone and sandstone. The land mass is covered with rivers and dotted

with lakes, the result of Ice Age glaciation. There are endless expanses of wooded hills, shallow basins and bare flat rocky outcrops, also formed by glaciation.

Baffin Bay

The area of sea that was named after the British seafarer, William Baffin, is a branch of the North Atlantic and extends over an area of 689,000 sq. km between Greenland in the west and Baffin Island in the east. **Baffin Bay** is 1,450 km in length, the width varies between 110 km and 650 km. The **Davis**

Straits connect the Labrador Sea and Baffin Bay; the narrow **Nares Strait** leads to the Arctic Sea. Depths of 2,100 m have been measured in the middle of the Bay in the **Baffin Hollow**; elsewhere, the Bay is between 240 m and 700 m deep. The undersea shelves of Greenland and Canada line the seabed of Baffin Bay. The sediment on the sea bed consists of deposits of debris from the Ice Age.

The prevailing climate in the Bay is extremely cold and even in the height of summer the icebergs barely melt. The tidal range is between 4 m and 9 m.

Baffin Island is Canada's largest Arctic island at 688,808 sq. km. The heavily glaciated mountains reach heights of up to 2,600 m.

Newfoundland

This island in the Atlantic Ocean, measuring 108,860 sq. km, faces the wide estuary of the **St. Lawrence River** of the east coast of Canada. The island's interior

consists of a trunk mountain block, which rises to 814 m as the **Appalachian** foothills in the **Long Range Mountains**. The glaciers from the last Ice Age have created a low hilly relief which and contains many forests, moors, lakes, rivers and waterfalls. The rocky cliff coast is laced with numerous fjords.

Labrador

This peninsula in the north-east of North America forms the eastern part of the Canadian Shield with an area of approximately 1.6 mil-

lion sq. km. Labrador was virtually uninhabited until recent times; it consists of a plateau that reaches 1,700 m in the **Torngat Mountains** in the north-east. Dense pine forests characterise this landscape with its wealth of lakes. In the north, the vegetation gradually changes into Arctic tundra. The Labrador trough, which tretches from **Ungava Bay** to **Lake Mistassini**, contains rich iron ore deposits.

Rocky Mountains

The Rockies stretch for more than 4,300 km down the west coast of North America from the Brooks Range in Alaska via Canada to New Mexico. They are part of the **North American Cordillera**, which continues down the west coast into Central and South America. The mountains were folded upward about 150 million years ago at the transition from the Cretaceous period to the Ter-

tiary and partly uplifted. Around 50 million years ago, the high mountain ranges were uplifted again through volcanic activity. Molten magma welled up in the Earth's crust, solidified into granite or other igneous rocks and penetrated through to the surface as magma again after renewed amalgamation.

The **Rocky Mountains** gained their definitive appearance approximately two million years ago, when immense ice sheets cleared a path during the Ice Age and cut deep gorges into the rock, polishing mountain slopes and carving deep

basins which are now mountain lakes. Ice Age glaciers are also responsible for the trough valleys, corries, moraines and fjords typical of this mountain chain. Some parts of the Rocky Mountains are still heavily glaciated. In total, 74 peaks have elevations of over 3,500 m and 600 mountains exceed the 2,000 m mark. **Mount Elbert** in Colorado at 4,401 m is the highest peak.

In the north, the Rocky Mountains are more densely wooded than in the south and are divided into longitudinal valleys as a result of numerous river resurgences. In the south, the mountains are separated into parallel chains, which include several high basins, such as the Colorado Plateau and the Great Basin.

The Coast Mountains

The **Coast Mountains** are part of the Pacific Mountain System and stretch over 1,600 km from the Alaskan border through British Columbia to the **Fraser River** in

Mount Columbia (3,747 m) at Lake Maligne in the Rocky Mountains.

the south. Many summits are higher than 3,400 m in the **Munday**, **Tiedemann** and **Monarch Mountains**. The highest peak is **Mount Waddington** at 4,016 m. Numerous glaciers have cut deep gorges or canyons in the rock and also created the fjord landscape on the Pacific Coast.

The Cascade Mountains

The **Cascades** stretch for about 1,100 km from British Columbia in the north via the states of Washington and Oregon to California in the south.

*The **Niagara Falls** were formed during the Ice Age. The Niagara River, which marks the border between Canada and the USA, flows from **Lake Erie** into **Lake Ontario**. In the middle of its course, the river drops over a 60-m sheer cliff to form the Niagara Falls which are split in two. The semi-circular Horseshoe Falls are on the Canadian side and on the American side, the American Falls.*

After the mountain range had been levelled down to a trunk area in the Early Tertiary period, it was later raised again by volcanic activity. The numerous peaks of over 3,000 m are extinct volcanoes, which are partly glaciated. There is still some volcanic activity.

The highest elevations in the range are **Mount Rainier** at 4,392 m, **Mount Adams** at 3,751 m and **Mount Hood** (3,427 m).

The densely wooded mountains show a clear climate delineation. Whereas clouds from the Pacific precipitate on the western slopes, there is very little rainfall in the regions situated in the eastern lee of the range. Rainfall only increases in the higher mountain ranges of the Rocky Mountains further to the east. They are called the Cascades due to their numerous rapids and waterfalls.

The Coast Ranges

To the west of the **longitudinal valleys** of the **Willamette** River and the **Puget Sound**, the relatively short chains of the **Coast Ranges** run parallel to the Pacific coast. In the centre, they are approximately only 1,000 m high, but climb to 2,692 m in the **Diabolo Range**.

Several geological faults traverse the high ranges, the most famous being the **San Andreas Fault**. At this point, the Pacific and American continental plates are moving past each other. The tension arising from this, which can be released without warning, means that the region is permanently at risk from earthquakes. The city of San Francisco is built at one of the most vulnerable points, meaning that its inhabitants must always be prepared for earth tremors of varying intensity.

To be convinced of the volcanic activity in the Cascade Range area, one merely has to visit **Lassen Volcanic National Park**, where bubbling fumaroles and hot springs are evidence of how thin the Earth's crust is here.

Sierra Nevada

The Great Basin is a 500,000 sq. km wide desert highland, which stretches between the Columbia Plateau in the north, the Mojave Desert in the south, the Sierra Nevada in the west and the Wasatch Range in the east.

Short, sheer mountain ranges intersect the Great Basin along a north-south axis. In Mount Bonpland and the East Humboldt Range, the mountains reach elevations of 3,450 m.

The basins are situated at an altitude of between 1,000 and 1,500 m in the north; in the south they sink to below sea level in the arid Sonora Desert at the **Salton Sink**, now known as the Salton Sea. The Salton Sink is located in south-eastern California near the Arizona border. In 1905, a levee broke on the Colorado River. The river found the easiest course for the overflow which was a nearby deep natural depression known as the Salton Sink. A huge lake was created, which has no outlet and is brackish as a result. It is now known as the Salton Sea. The Salton Sink is the eighth deepest place on earth.

Death Valley, so named for its hostile climate is a National Park. It reaches the deepest point on the land surface of the United States (-86 m) at the brackish Badwater Basin. This is also one of the hottest places on earth, a temperature of 56.7°C having been recorded there in 1913. Death Valley National Park was established in 1933, covers almost 4,800 sq. km.

Viewed from the top of the 3,368 m Telescope Peak in the Panamint Range Mountains, the floor of Death Valley spreads out almost 3.5 km below. All the great divisions of geological time, the eras and most of their sub-divisions, are represented in the rocks of the mountains that ring Death Valley. The short rivers seep away into the ground,

Great salt crusts and enormous salt lakes, such as the **Salduro Flats** in western Utah make the whole region into a highly inhospitable landscape. The **Great Salt Lake**, on average only 5 m deep, is the remainder of a once considerably larger freshwater lake from the ice age, whose surface area varied between 3,900 and 5,300 sq. km. The playas of the **Mojave** and **Gila Deserts** are extremely arid.

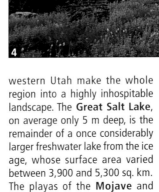

1 Alaska chain: the Kluane National Park, at the border of Canada with Alaska, contains around 4,000 glaciers, some of which are over 10 km in width and up to 100 km long.

2 + **3** Northern Rocky Mountains: lakes formed during the ice age, partly glaciated high mountains and deep, lonely valleys are typical of the Canadian Rockies, as here in the Banff National Park.

4 The Cascade chain: Mount Rainier is 4,392 m high and covered in snow and glacial ice.

Rocky Mountains

The 'Rockies' form the eastern section of the North American Cordillera and run along the west coast of the continent of North America. In total, 74 peaks in the Rocky Mountains reach a height of more than 3,500 m, and 600 mountains are higher than 2,000 m. The mountain range is home to many endangered animals.

The Northern Cordillera extends for 4,500 km from Alaska through Canada and along the West Coast to New Mexico. The mountains form the backbone of the North American Continent. The highest points in the region are the 4,401-m-high Mount Elbert in Colorado and Mount Robson in Canada, (3,954 m).

In geological terms, the Rocky Mountains are a relatively young chain of fold mountains. Their creation began approximately 120 million years ago, when tectonic movements of the Earth's crust caused large areas of land to fold. Powerful subterranean volcanic activity accompanied these forceful movements. Magma welled up from beneath the crust and solidified on the surface as granite and other plutonic rocks, or reached the Earth's surface in the form of lava.

The modern landscape of the Rocky Mountains was shaped by powerful glaciers which formed in the Ice Age that began just two million years ago. Sheets of ice, some several thousand metres thick, thrust over the mountain sides and into the valleys. They cut razor-sharp ridges into the stone, wore down prominent cliff formations, smoothed the mountain slopes and carved out deep bowls, that later filled with meltwater to form mountain lakes.

The natural landscapes of the Rocky Mountains are extremely varied and have been a favourite subject of landscape paintings since the early nineteenth century. The Grand Canyon of northwest Arizona is also part of the Rockies. This amazing sight, the most famous gorge in the world, is the result of slow erosion by the Colorado River over millions of years, eating into the stone strata of the plateau to form a canyon 400 km long, between 6 and 30 km wide and up to 1,800 m deep. The Colorado River has numerous cataracts and rapids, making it a paradise for whitewater rafting enthusiasts. The Rocky Mountains are also North America's main watershed.

The rivers rising in the mountains, often dammed to form lakes, are an important source of water, particularly for the inhabitants of the south-western States which have low rainfall.

In 1807, a fur hunter in the north-western state of Wyoming stumbled across a particularly impres-

At 3,618 m, Mount Assiniboine in Alberta is one of Canada's most beautiful mountains.

sive landscape with dramatic vertical cliffs, rumbling waterfalls, boiling hot springs and geysers. Back in his home town of St. Louis, nobody believed his fanciful descriptions of a weird landscape. Over the following decades, other trappers also described this wondrous area in Yellowstone, in the middle of the Rocky Mountains, until eventually two official expeditions were sent to the region. Their impressive report resulted in the creation in 1872 of the world's first National Park – Yellowstone.

Since then, a series of further nature reserves have been established in the northern Rockies. They are Glacier National Park in Montana, Denali National Park in Alaska, the Grand Tetons in Wyoming and the Rocky Mountains National Park in Colorado – whose large number of mountains over 3,000–4,000 m have given it the nickname 'The Roof of the Continent'. The Guadalupe Mountains National Park in Texas and New Mexico has been created in the southern Rockies.

The Rocky Mountains offer ideal habitats for many rare and endangered mountain animals. The Bald Eagle, the national bird of the United States, rules the skies and the rare Whooping Crane finds refuge here. The dense woodland of the national parks consist mainly of spruce, fir and pine, and the forests are inhabited by elk, wapiti, bighorn sheep, mountain hares and beavers. Nocturnal animals, including foxes, pumas, lynxes and wolves, hunt their prey at night.

The symbol of the North American wilderness is the giant grizzly bear, a sub-species of the brown bear, although the grizzly is now threatened with extinction. Only some 1,000 specimens remain in North America. Before the continent was discovered by European settlers, it was inhabited by 100,000 of these 2.5-m-high bears. Their territory extended from Alaska to Mexico and from the Pacific coast to the endless expanse of the Great Plains.

The mountain goat lives above the tree line of the Rocky Mountains, almost undisturbed by any other creature. This relative of the chamois is incredibly agile on the steep mountain rocks and dangerous cliffs. Another inhabitant of the high mountains is the marmot, which can hibernate for up to eight months of the year and which, in the short time in between, will normally only leave its burrow to collect food. The shy and nimble coyote – a relative of the fox and wolf – has only been reintroduced to the Rocky Mountains in the last few decades. This animal has adapted well to the tough living conditions of its mountain habitat, and it will eat anything. The same cannot be said of the enormous masters of the plains: the bison. These massive wild cattle can be three metres long and have a shoulder height of 2 m, but only eat grass – though in huge quantities of up to 12 kg a day – in order to prepare for the tough, long and strength-sapping winters of the cordillera, during which snow can block the passes as early in the year as November.

During the coldest part of the year, temperatures in the valleys can sink to as low as -20°C. Like so many other natural environments, the wilderness of the Rockies is now threatened with oil exploration.

Big picture: the impressive Grand Tetons in Wyoming rise steeply out of the plains to a height of 2,000 m.

Inset pictures: catching a glimpse grizzly bear is an unforgettable experience.

*Sierra Nevada: the 4,418-m-high **Mount Whitney** in the Californian Central Sierra Nevada, is the highest peak in the USA outside Alaska. The upper slopes of the Sierra Nevada are mainly covered with forests.*

Colorado Plateau

With a total area of around 112,000 sq. km, the tableland of the **Colorado Plateau** spreads across northern Arizona, southern Utah, south-western Colorado and north-western New Mexico. The altitudes can reach between 1,500 m and 3,300 m.

The numerous plateaus are made from different strengths of rock strata that are in various stages of erosion. Mountain streams and rivers have cut deep clefts in the rock. The most famous of these is the massive Grand Canyon.

Grand Canyon

One of the greatest natural wonders on earth is the deep gorge, around 400 km long (greater than the distance from London to Paris!) that the Colorado River has cut through the Colorado Plateau in north-west Arizona.

The gorge is 1,600 m deep in the centre and ranges in width from 6 to 29 km. For a long time it was thought the canyon was created by the collapse of a rift, as it did not seem possible that the Colorado river, which is not that impressive in such a dry landscape, could have cut such a deep and wide gorge through the rock strata. In 1869, John Welsey Powell was able to prove that the rock strata on both sides of the valley belonged to the same faces, so a rift collapse could be ruled out.

The Colorado needed about six million years to mould this massive depression in the rock. Geologists have found the area to be an excellent field of research, as more than 350 m years of natural history has been exposed on the sides of the gorge.

The various rock strata in the Grand Canyon stretch from the Kaibab limestone of the Permian era on the surface, through to archaic formations at the bottom of the gorge. The individual strata are only slightly sloping, and are made up of step-like escarpments. The 100 m-thick **Kaibab limestone** is the youngest and deepest stratum, and was deposited in the Permian era. The numerous marine fossils that are contained in it make it easy to recognise that this white formation was once a sea bed.

The next stratum is composed of yellow Coconino sandstone. It is associated with Supai formation with red and green sandstones,

chalk and slate. The next layer consists of Redwell limestone from the Lower Carboniferous era. The gorge cuts deep into the **Archaean bedrock** that is formed from granite, gneiss and mica schist – rocks that have partly been overlaid with red sandstone, schist and chalk from the Algonkian age.

After the Colorado Plateau was uplifted in the Miocene age, erosion wore away strata from the Eocene, Cretaceous, Jurassic and Triassic eras, and the river was able to carve a course for itself deep in the base of the bedrock. The bizarre rock formations – towers, ledges and crevices, some reminiscent of a Buddhist stupa – are the result of a combination of various factors – the alternating hard and soft rock strata, vertical and horizontal erosion, extreme temperature fluctuations, wind and aridity.

There are three distinct **vegetation zones**. In the dry heat of the valley, only desert plants are able

to prosper. Above this is a temperate zone, where the land is dominated by live-oaks and junipers. At over 2,000 m there are mixed forests containing Douglas firs and aspen. In winter, the high plateau is covered in deep snow. Both the northern rim and the southern rim of the Grand Canyon are open to the public, although visitors are not given access to the northern rim during the winter months. There are also helicopter rides over the canyon, as well as to nearby Lake Havasu. The 72-km-long Lake Havasu on the Colorado River was named by

the Chemehuevi Indians and translates into 'Land of the Blue Green Water'.

Bryce Canyon

Another impressive natural wonder of the Colorado Plateau is **Bryce Canyon** in south-western Utah. The canyon, around 146 sq. km in size, was not formed by a river like the Grand Canyon, but is the result of erosion of the steep edges of the Pansaugunt Plateau.

Bryce Canyon was formed shortly after the Grand Canyon and **Zion Canyon**, which belong together, geomorphologically speaking. The course of natural history can also be read from these slopes.

The rock strata in the west come from the Pre-Cambrian era, and get gradually younger to the east. In the Triassic there was a plateau landscape here that was made from limnic chalk, to which pillars, columns and strangely shaped blocks still bear witness. Around 60 million years ago,

southern Utah was covered by a lake. Chalk, sand and alluvium were deposited on the lake bed and this was compressed into a 600 m-thick rock stratum. When several massive tectonic movements occurred 13 million years ago and squeezed the land into a slope, the lake drained away. The formations that were piled up to 3,000 m high broke apart and were fragmented into massive blocks by the tension. This is where the work of the erosion agents began, carving the shapes that are visible today from the Pansaugunt Plateau.

The massive temperature fluctuations and the composition of the eroded materials, which are hostile to plant life, mean that there is little vegetation in the vicinity of Bryce Canyon.

A certain attraction comes not only from the breath-taking rock formations, but also from the fascinating interplay of colours. The metal oxides in the rocks create widely different impressions of colour, depending on the weather and the position of the sun. Bryce Canyon has been opened up to the public. A well signposted network of paths indicate the places of interest in this fascinating area full of natural history.

Monument Valley

Monument Valley is in the central region of the Colorado Plateau, on the border of Arizona and Utah. This 70-km by 80-km-wide valley within the Navajo Indian reservation reaches elevations of 1,600 m to 2,300 m.

The isolated rock towers and tablelands are made of De Chelley sandstone and stand 600 m above the landscape. Depending on the position of the sun, visitors to this picturesque giant can experience a fascinating show of light, shadow and every shade of red and purple.

The red sandstone dates from the late Permian era. When almost all of North America was covered with a primeval lake in the early Triassic period, a large amount of sand was deposited in Monument Valley. After the sea drained away, the uplift phase of the Colorado

Plateau began, which caused the mountains to break into giant slabs in the process.

Over several million years, wind and water eroded the upper stratum, which was then covered by later formations. The different strata were subjected to various weathering processes in the period following the Quaternary. The formation of the curious red rock giants is mainly the work of the wind, which eroded the soft strata over millions of years. Only the most resilient rocks could resist the force of the wind.

The typically shaped rocks are reminiscent of sculptures, causing people to imagine all kinds of representations. They have been given names such as 'the Totem Pole', 'Big Indian', 'King's Throne' and 'Castle'. The vegetation is rather sparse, consisting of a few isolated barrel cacti, stunted bushes, succulents and some grasses. The lack of ground cover exposes the fascinating mechanism of this unique landscape. The Navajo Indians live dotted around the site in their traditional huts.

Arches National Park

More than 300 m years ago, the foundations of this 300 sq. km National Park were laid in the US state of Utah. On the bed of a primaeval sea, thick layers of salt accumulated. These later expanded into underground domes under the pressure of subsequent deposits. The surrounding rock material advanced and fragmented under the tension into immense parallel rock strata. Precipitation and wind eroded the softer layers of rock from these blocks and created the famous **Arches** – bizarre, free-standing rock arches. The most famous of the rock arches of which there are around 200 – is the so-called Delicate Arch, which stands in isolation 50 m high on a rocky plateau.

Great Plains

With a length of over 5,000 km and a breadth of between 500 km and 1,200 km, the **Great Plains** stretch from the west of the Inner rim from the Arctic coast at the mouth of the Mackenzie River, to the Rio Grande in central Texas, where they meet the Gulf Coast. This plateau was originally covered in grassland. The phenotype changed only after the first white

Great Basin: rocks in the Death Valley.

*The **Joshua Tree National Monument** in the **Great Basin** consists of two different types of desert, the **Colorado desert** and the **Mojave desert**. Joshua Trees – members of the Yucca family of succulents – are found in the High Desert.*

settlers took over the land and allowed their cattle and horses to graze on it. Large fields, on which grain is largely grown as a monoculture, determine the look of the landscape today. While the altitudes in the east are only around 400 to 500 m, the plateaus, traversed by a large number of rivers, rise westwards to heights of up to 1,600 m in the foothills of the Rocky Mountains.

Great Lakes

The five **Great Lakes** are linked together by the St Lawrence Seaway, which drains into the Atlantic. The largest group of freshwater lakes on Earth, said to contain 20 per cent of all the freshwater on the surface of the planet, were created during the last Ice Age – the lakes are the remains of massive glacial basins. On the northern shore of the Great Lakes there is the flat valley of the St Lawrence Seaway, which was shaped by Pleistocene glaciation inland, and still exhibits many glacial forms. The 100 m natural barrier around the river, rises at the lake shores into a rump landscape of a height of 300–400 m.

The banks of the Great Lakes are shaped by a steep fjord-like coast, which gives way to **Georgian Bay,** containing numerous islands and skerries formed during the last Ice Age. The Great Lakes cover a total area of approximately 245,000 sq. km.

Lake Superior is the largest at 82,103 sq. km. It has a maximum depth of 405 m, and is drained by **St Mary's River** into **Lake Huron**. Lake Superior is free of ice for eight months of the year.

Lake Huron is at an altitude of 177 m and has an area of 61,797 sq. km; it is up to 228 m deep. **Lake Michigan**, which lies to the south-west, is 57,757 sq. km. It is linked to Lake Huron by the **Straits of Mackinaw**, and is 282 m deep. The most southerly of the Great Lakes is **Lake Erie** – 25,725 sq. km and up to 64 m deep. This lake is linked to **Lake Ontario** by the **Niagara River**. The difference between the water levels is the reason for the formation of the **Niagara Falls**. Lake Ontario, the smallest and most easterly of the Great Lakes, is 19,011 sq. km, lies 75 m above sea level; it is 244 m deep in places. The canals that connect the lakes make them navigable for ships.

Appalachians

The Appalachian central massif, formed from crystalline rocks, stretches a distance of 2,600 km from Newfoundland to northern Alabama. The 200 to 300-km-wide mountains were created around 300 m years ago during the Appalachian mountain-building phase in the Palaeozoic era, and are therefore considerably older than the Cordillera in the west. After a period of erosion, the Appalachians were lifted again in the Triassic period, and than eroded again, so the highest elevations of the **White Mountains** and the **Green Mountains**

1 The Yosemite national park demonstrates the variety and the beauty of the Sierra Nevada. The fruitful valley is overshadowed by the granite cupola of El Capitán.

2 Aspen, Colorado: snow- and ice-covered mountains, deep ravines and forests are typical

of the Rocky Mountains in this part of Colorado.

3 Big Sur on the southern coast mountains between San Simeon and Carmel in central California. The Pacific breakers hurl themselves against the rugged coastline, making this a surfer's paradise.

Great Plains: the area in the Western Plains of the USA is poor in vegetation and often described as **'The Badlands'.** The Badlands National Park in South Dakota comprises almost 100,000 ha. It contains a fascinating stone landscape, formed through wind and water erosion of the less resistant rocks, resulting in ravines, chines, towers and pyramids.

barely reach 2,000 m. The highest peak is **Mount Mitchell** at 2,037 m. The Appalachians are divided into north and south sections by the **Hudson-Mohawk gorge.** The Northern Appalachians comprise a 750m-high plateau, which was heavily glaciated during the Ice Age but is still easily recognisable due to the glacial deposits and landfill features.

The Southern Appalachians are divided into several thinner ridges. The **Piedmont** is limited by the coastal plain fault lineson. The 100 to 400-m-high undulating plateau is dominated by the **Blue Ridge** to the west.

Until the nineteenth century, the Blue Ridge was only passable through a few mountain passes such as the **Cumberland Gap.** The spine of the Southern Appalachians is the 1,500-km-long and 150-km-wide **Great Appalachian Valley**, that comprises several parallel strata up to 600 m high.

This landscape is traversed by a river system that features numerous rapids, particularly on the **Tennessee River** and its tributaries. A steep escarpment marks the transition from the Great Appalachian Valley to the

Mississippi, Missouri

The 'Great River' river or 'Missi Sepe' as the Indians called it rises in the Itasca lake 445 m above sea level, west of a Upper Lake. It flows through almost the whole length of the Great Plains and has the drainage area of 3,221 sq. km. With the Missouri, it has a combined length of 6,020 km, making it one of the longest rivers in the world. The lower reaches begin after the absorption of its tributraries, the Missouri and Illinois rivers, near St. Louis. Because it flows so slowly, the Mississippi is very meandering and creates ox-bow lakes. It is protected in many places by high embankments called 'levees'. Strong sedimentation means that the Mississippi has a shallow bed, so that it often flows above that of its surroundings. Flooding is therefore not unusual. The Mississippi eventually drains into the Gulf of Mexico at the wide Mississippi Delta.

Appalachian Plateau, the largest area of the Appalachians. The **Allegheny** and **Cumberland**-plateaux are shaped by deep valleys that have been eroded into the rock by numerous rivers. The terrain slopes from around 1,000 m in the east to 300 m in the west, before gradually being replaced by the grassy plains of the central lowland.

Gulf Coast

The northern and central parts of the Gulf Coast were given their current appearance during the Cretaceous period. Low mounds, rarely higher than 200 m and made from ancient rock, shape the landscape. Long sandy beaches, sand banks, swamps and lagoons line the Gulf. There are almost no natural harbours in this northern region of Mexico.

The coastal plain is traversed by the **Rio Grande** (Rio Bravo del Norte) and **Tamesí-Pánuco** rivers. In the central part of the Mexican state of Veracruz, the extremities of the **Sierra Madre Occidental** narrow the plains to a breadth of only 15 km, and at San Andrés Tuxtla, the flat landscape is interrupted by a rocky

coastline and undulating landscape. The rivers **Usumacinta**, **Grijalva**, **Coatzacoalcos** and **Papaloapan** turn into swampland at their estuaries, covered with typical swampland vegetation of mangroves, bulrushes and reeds. Naturally, the area is prone to serious flooding and this causes serious damage to shipping and the oil installations in the region.

Mississippi basin

The immense watershed of the **Mississippi River** is around 3,208,000 sq. km, of which 1,365,000 sq. km are in **Missouri**, and 528,000 sq. km in **Ohio**. In the north, there are glacial plateaus

The Mississippi stores a lot of sediment in its delta.

along the Canadian border, with numerous lakes and marshes. In the central region, a basin covered with recent sediment has determined the landscape, while towards the coast there are flat lagoon-rich alluvial areas. To the east, the Appalachians form the catchment area with the Rocky Mountains to the west.

Florida

The peninsula of **Florida** stretches almost 700 km into the sea, and divides the Gulf of Mexico from the Atlantic.

In the central area, Florida has a breadth of 110–150 km, in the north is the 550-km-wide 'panhandle'. In the south, there is a 600-km-long chain of offshore islands, the so-called **Florida Keys** (from the Spanish 'cay' an island). The last island in the chain, Key West, is the most southerly and westerly point of the continental United States and only 150 km from Cuba.

To the east, Florida is part of the continental shelf, and is made of strong limestone strata, which uplifted from the sea during the Triassic Era. The strong sea level fluctuations determined by cold and warm fronts have led to the formation of rolling uplands stretching towards the centre of the State.

South of **Lake Okeechobee**, the largest of the almost 8,000 lakes, there is a limestone plain containing numerous springs. In the **coastal area** to the west the land is sinking, and the terrain consists of swampland with numerous backwaters and bays, while to the Atlantic side, the coast contains spits – flat tongues of land that form a barrier against the open sea – as well as long flat sandy beaches.

The Florida **Everglades** in the south consist of a huge swamp surrounded by thick mangrove forests, in which manatees have found their most northerly retreat. The Everglades are now a National Park and are full of interesting wildlife, including alligators and crocodiles.

Atlantic Coastal Plain

The fault line marks the transition to the **Atlantic Coastal Plain.** The coast has many bays and fjords and skerries are witness to the glacial formation of this northerly stretch of coastline. Further south, the coast is full of fjords and inlets, along the course of which the coast widens. In the north, the coastal rivers have formed many natural harbours, while the south has more alluvium, lagoons and swamps.

Baja California

Baja California (**Lower California**) is a thin narrow peninsula, separated from the Mexican mainland by the Gulf of California. The peninsula is 1,200 km long and 40 to 240 km wide. Its upper surface is made of rock formations from the Cretaceous and Triassic periods.

In the south, sea sedimentation and volcanic remains from the Pleistocene and Holocene periods characterise the landscape.

Several chains of mountains cross the peninsula, continuing the **Californian coastal mountain range**. In the east, the mountains fall to a steep rim, while they slope more gently in the west.

These crystalline mountains are over 1,500 m high, but occasionally reach heights of 3,000 m.

On both sides of the **Sierra Santa Clara** there are plateaus, broad, flat strips of desert and cactus savannah. At the narrowest corner of the Gulf of California, the Colorado River reaches the sea in a massive delta. During the dry summer months, however, the river may dry up before it reaches its destination.

Mexico

Almost 80 per cent of the surface of Mexico geologically belongs to the mainland, which narrows to barely 200 km at the Isthmus of **Theuantepec**. In the north-west, the thin peninsula of **Lower**

*The red sky of Shenandoah National Park in the State of Virginia: the National Park stretches alongside the **Blue Ridge Mountains**, the main chine of the **Appalaches**, and is mostly afforested.*

It is famous for its rich flora and fauna. The park offers magnificent views, especially in the late summer and autumn when the leaves of the deciduous trees, change to yellow, red and brown.

California is attached to the mainland. South of the Isthmus of Theuantepec, the **Yucatán Peninsula** and the Mexican state of Chiapas make up the **Central American landmass**. The Mexican highland forms the continuation of the North American cordillera system and rises from 1,000 m in the north to 2,000 m further south. Towards the coast, the highlands drop away in steep slopes. To the west of the Mexican highland plateau, the **Sierra Madre Oriental** rises to 3,500 m.

The Meseta Central lies at a height of between 1,500 m and 3,000 m and is divided up into basins by isolated mountain ridges. The largest of these is the **Bolson de Mapimi**. In the east, the highland is bordered by the **Sierra Madre Occidental**, which rises to a height of 4,000 km, and by **Cordillera Volcánica** in the south.

These volcanic regions include the highest mountains in Mexico, like the snow-covered 5,700-m-high **Citlaltépetl** and the only slightly lower **Ixtaccicuatl** and **Popocatépetl**.

Numerous earthquakes and active volcanoes are proof of the continuing tectonic movement in this mountain region. The most impressive proof of volcanic activity is **Paricutin**, a volcano created in 1943.

The highland of **Chiapas**, which can be up to 3,000 m high, is abutted by the Sierra **Madre del Sur** at the coast, with several volcanic cones up to 4,000 m high. To the north east, the highland flattens gradually, and ends at the Yucatán Peninsula. Mangrove forests crossing the coastal lowland of **Tabasco** are interlaced with rivers and lagoons, which continue from the **Gulf of Campeche** to the coastal lowland of Veracruz.

While the **Rio Grande** carries extremely low levels of water during the arid winter, it becomes a raging torrent in the rainy season. The biggest river within the country is the **Rio Grande de Santiago**.

Sierra Madre

The highland of Mexico is abutted by two mountain ridges – the **Sierra Madre Occidental** in the west and the **Sierra Madre Oriental** to the east. The Sierra Madre Occidental runs from north-west to south-east and

is around 1,100 km long and around 160 km wide. The elevation is over 1,800 m in the middle, with the highest elevation even exceeding the 3,000 m mark. The direction of the strata in the massive mountain chain and valleys are the result of the folding in the Mesozoic era. The so-called Barrancas – ravines up to 1,500 m deep – are a tourist attraction. The Sierra Madre Oriental also originated in the Mesozoic period.

South-east of the Rio Grande there is a range of relatively low mountains which rise to a massive chain south of Monterrey with peaks of over 3,000 m.

The Sierra Madre del Sur is a craggy labyrinth of mountain ridges and deep valleys of chalk sediment. The mountains, which rise to a height of 3,000 m, are bordered to the north by the lowlands of the **Balsa-Mezcala** river systems, to the east by the **Sierra Mixteca**, and in the south-west by an intermittent coastal plain.

Mexican highlands

The **highlands of Mexico** reach a height of around 2,500 m in the south, but in the north they are only 1,100 m high. The landscape of the region is formed by seven large basins that are interlaced with a variety of isolated mountain chains and deep fissures in the earth.

The rather monotonous landscape of the northern highlands is shaped by deserts with dunes and desert-like steppes, which gradually give way to grasslands. The mountain ridges stretch from north to south and from north-

west to south-east and rise to an altitude 800 m to 900 m higher than the basins.

During the rainy season, flat lakes develop in the basins, which evaporate again in the dry season. As the lakes have no tidal movement and no outlet, salt remains in the basins, which transform into salt marshes and salt-clay plains.

 **1** Portland: the east coast of the New England states dives relatively smoothly into the Atlantic behind the northern highlands of the Appalaches.

2 Allegheny plateau: Pocahonta's river flow in the plains between the northern Appalaches and the Great Lakes.

3 High Mountains, wide valleys: in the Great Smokey Mountains in Tennessee lie the highest peaks of the Appalachen.

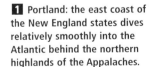 **4** Whitewater Bay: the Everglades are an extended swamp and reed area surrounded by Mangrove forests, at the southern end of Florida.

Big picture: the Mississippi Delta on the Gulf of Mexico. Through the depositing of sediment, the river is gradually building up its delta, pushing out into the sea at a rate of 100 m a year.

Above: the Mississippi near Memphis, Tennessee, with many meanders and partly dried-up tributaries along its course. The hilly landscape, which is farmed intensively, protects the city from rising water.

*The West Indian Island of **Saint Lucia** is one of the Lesser Antilles. It is of volcanic origin, mountainous with rugged slopes rising to a height of 1,000 m partly forested. However only the higher layers display the pristine tropical rain forest vegetation, as most of the island is covered in secondary forest. The signature mark of the island is the steep volcanic cones of Gros Piton and Petit Piton, soaring from the plain near the Soufrières Volcano.*

The southern highlands are shaped by precipitation and have mountains and rolling hills formed by volcanic landfill. Gentle knolls alternate here with craggy volcanic peaks and basins, and high valleys with numerous lakes in between. The region, which is generally mountainous, also has isolated swamps and hot springs.

Sonora

The parallel mountain ranges with their broad valleys and the north Pacific coastal plain in the state of Sonora were created in the mid to late Triassic period. The detrital stone formations, which surround the basins of Sonora, give way to several mountain ranges to the north east. The coast itself is flat and sandy, with rocky areas and lagoons only in certain bays. The arid landscape of the **Sonora desert** begins in the north, and stretches to California and the south east of Arizona.

Yucatán, Central America

Central America forms the mainland bridge between the North limestone plateau of the **Yucatán** peninsula. It is only in the extreme south that the foothills reach the Caribbean coast. Elsewhere, there is a marshy stretch of up to 75 km between the land and sea.

On the coast, there are more than 100 small untouched coral islands, the so-called Cays. In south Belize, the outer reaches of the Central American bedrock rise to **Victoria Peak** at 1,122 m. The **Maya Mountains** are composed of gneiss, schist, shale and granite. The Petén plateau in northern Guatemala is also part of the Yucatán peninsula. It consists of karst formations and swamps. The almost unexploited region is covered by thick rainforest, which gives way to pinewood and eventually savannah.

To the south of the Yucatán peninsula, the landscape changes to become the mountainous region of Central America. The area around Honduras is also part of the highlands encircled by the **Cordilleras.**

The eastern lowlands of Honduras are a humid, thickly-forested alluvial region, also described as **Misquite**. On the edge of the coast there is a marshy alluvial plain with lagoons. It provides an ideal habitat for mosquitoes and with **Lake Nicaragua** and **Lake Managua** divides the broader north from the smaller southern part of the bridging land.

The area is tectonically weak and prone to both earthquakes and volcanic activity. In **Costa Rica**, three consecutive mountain ranges divide the north and the Caribbean lowland, from the low landscape of Guanacaste and the rolling country of the south west. In the canal zone in Panama, the central American strip of land is at its narrowest, at 55 km.

Yucatán Peninsula

The 450-km-wide and 600-km-long **Yucatán** Peninsula lies between the Gulf of Mexico in the north and west, and the **Caribbean** to the east. The large chalk plateau with karst formations gradually rose from the sea after the end of the Triassic period, and the lifting process continues today.

Apart from the **Sierrita** (150-m), the peninsula is completely flat. Although there no watercourses, there are extensive dry forests in the north, and rainforests in the south. This is due to the chalk substrate, which provides sufficient lagoons, and in the south there are coral reefs and smaller islands such as **Cozumel**, which is popular with scuba-divers.

Central American Cordilleras

In southern Guatemala, the cordillera system has two main strands – the north western **Sierra de los Cuchumatanes** and the southern **Sierra Madre**.

The Sierra Madre is made up of craggy cordilleras and extensive plateaux. Here, there are several volcanic cones, of which some are still active. The **Tajumulco volcano** is the highest peak in Central America at 4,220 m.

Although volcanism has formed numerous small mountain ridges in the Honduras region, the volcanic cones, so typical elsewhere, are missing here.

In Nicaragua, the Central American cordillera continues into the Central Cordillera, and divides into several 100 to 200-km-long ridges. Although the **Pico Mogotón** reaches a height of 2,107 m, the mountains in this range are rarely higher than 1,500 m. In the north west of Costa Rica a chain of volcanic cones forms the **Cordillera de Guanacaste**, which reaches 1,971 m with **Orosî**. Further on are the much higher and partly active volcanos of the **Cordillera Central**. **Irazu** is the highest peak of this mountain range at 3,432 m.

The mountains in the **Cordillera de Talamanca**, which are divided by the Valle Central, are higher, peaking with **Chirripó Grande** at 3,820 m. In Panama, the **Cordillera de Talamanca** continues into the volcanic **Serrania de Tabasará** mountain range. The highest point is **Volcán Barú** at 3,478 m. At only 1,000 m high, the mountains on the Caribbean coast of Panama, like the **Cordillera de San Blas**, are considerably lower.

Caribbean Islands

The **Caribbean islands** stretch in a broad arc over 4,000km from the south coast of Florida to the north eastern coast of Venezuela. The overall area of the islands is around 234,000 sq. km.

Around 95 per cent of the islands belong to the Antilles, with the **Greater Antilles** making up 90 per cent of the land surface. The **Lesser Antilles** is made up of innumerable small islands and are divided into the Windward and Leeward islands. The **Bahamas**, as well as the **Turks and Caicos Islands** and the more **remote Cayman Islands** are also part of the Caribbean Islands.

The island arc separates the Caribbean Sea from the Atlantic. Around the islands, large parts of the sea are also part of the continental shelf. The **Bahamas**, **Cuba** and **Trinidad** are dominated by shallow seas, which have formed since the last Ice Age. The remaining regions of the Caribbean are deep sea, with an average depth of 4,000 to 5,000 m. In the Cayman rift, depths of 7,240 m have been measured, in the Puerto Rico rift 8,300 m, and the Milwaukee Deep 9,220 m.

In these rifts, the earth's crust is particularly thin. It is here that the epicentre of earthquakes are often located and the islands themselves are tectonically unstable. Given the abrasion terraces formed in the coral chalk, it is possible to determine to what extent the islands are being pushed out of the water. Often it is in these coastal regions, which are rising step by step, that it is possible to recognise the channels chiselled in the chalk by the surf. Particularly impressive terrace systems are to be seen in the north west part of Hispaniola and on Cape Maisi in Cuba.

The Bolsas and Bocas peculiar to the Netherlands Antilles, Cuba and Curacao are, in contrast, the result of marine flooding.

A particular attraction of the landscape lies in the many coral reefs that stretch from the north to the Bermudas. The reefs on the island coasts are clearly divided into inner reef, reef crest, reef platform and ruckriff. The bank reefs further out to the sea, which are barely under the water surface, are less clearly differentiated.

The Caribbean islands have wonderful sandy beaches, which often cover the coastal rock.

Greater Antilles

The islands of **Cuba**, **Jamaica**, **Hispaniola**, **Puerto Rico** and other small islands make up the Greater Antilles. The North American **Cordillera** continues into this island arc, turning towards the east in Central America.

Several parallel mountain chains make up the island of Hispaniola. In the central cordillera, the **Pico Duarte** rises to 3,175 m. Sierra

Lesser Antilles: the Virgin Islands in the Caribbean island arc.

and Latin American continents. The thin strip of land with mountain ridges can be up to 500 km wide in places.

The flat rolling country in the north west of Belize is part of the has been jokingly called the 'Mosquito coast'.

The western coastal lowlands of the Pacific are also geologically a relatively young alluvial plain. The **Nicaragua basin** water supply through the formation of natural cisterns.

The Yucatan Peninsula is famous for its unspoiled landscapes and tropical wildlife. The west coast consists of sand banks and

Baja California (lower California) is separated by the Gulf from the continent. The desert peninsula is 1,200 km long and its mountain chain over 3,000 m high. Typical of the stark coastal landscape of the peninsula in the North West of Mexico are the numerous cacti, capable of surviving long drought periods. In Baja California alone, 120 different cacti have been counted and almost half of them can only be found there.

Maestra, with **Pico Turquino** at 1,974 m on Cuba, **Blue Mountain Peak** at 2,256 m on **Jamaica** and **El Yunque** at 1,065 m on Puerto Rico are branches of the cordillera system.

Even if the mountains reach high levels, they are different from the Rocky Mountains in that the relief was not formed by ice-age glaciation, but by erosion from rivers and precipitation. larger plains can be only found in the Bahamas and on Cuba. Here there are low chalk plateaux with uniform formations.

Lesser Antilles

A large number of tiny islands make up the Lesse Antilles archipelago, which are divided into two island chains.

The **Leeward Islands** form an arc from the **Virgin Islands** in the north to Trinidad in the south. **Montserrat, Antigua, Guadeloupe** and **Dominica** make up the northern Leeward Islands. **Martinique, Saint Lucia, Saint Vincent** and **Grenada** are part of the Windward Islands.

The Windward Islands lie off the coast of Venezuela, and stretch from east to west from **Aruba** to the **Isla de Margarita**. The South American cordillera continues here, from Aruba to Trinidad, with the only notable heights being 920 m at **Pico San Juan** on Margarita and 941 m at Cerro del Aripo on Trinidad.

The Leeward Islands are of volcanic origin. There are still active volcanoes on Monserrat, Martinique, Guadeloupe and Saint Vincent. These pose a constant and serious threat to the population. In August 1955, the capital of the island of Monserrat was evacuated as there was a threat of an eruption. The extinct volcanoes are now mostly volcanic ruins, but like the **Quill** on Saint Eustacius, some are still complete volcanic cones.

Another obvious sign of the continuing volcanism are the solfatara and fumeroles on **Saint Lucia**. Flat chalkstone regions are a distinguishing feature of the islands located in the island arc of **Anguilla, Antigua** and **Barbuda**. Although many of the Caribbean islands have been spoiled by the over-cultivation of cash crops such as sugar-cane, bananas, coffee and rice, others – such as St. Bath's and Mustique – are completely unspoiled and are playgrounds for wealthy jet-setting tourists from all over the world.

Geologically speaking, the Caribbean islands are only of two origins; volcanic and coral atoll. The most interesting volcano in the Caribbean is Mont Pelée, one of several active volcanoes on the island of Martinique in the French Antilles. Martinique is an island of volcanic nature, as with all of the islands on the Lesser Antilles chain. Like the archipelagos in the 'Pacific Ring of Fire', the islands of the Lesser Antilles consist of volcanoes built up by subduction trenches; something rarely found in the Atlantic Ocean, as most of the Atlantic volcanoes are 'hot spot' volcanoes like those found in Iceland and Hawaii.

Martinique's sole volcano, Mount Pelée last erupted in 1902, destroying the island's capital city of St. Pierre in a pyroclastic flow, and killing approximately 25,000 to 35,000 people.

The type of volcanic explosion that occurred is known as a 'Peléean Eruption'. It is caused by a solidified volcanic dome known as a 'dike' which smashes due to the force of the magma and hot gasses that well up inside it from the magma chamber. The lava flows down the mountain by means of gravity. The force of the Mount Pelée eruption was made worse due to the fact that there was a vee-shaped notch in the cone that directed the explosion and the ensuing lava straight on to the built up area directly below the volcano.

A recent example of the Mount Pelée-type explosion can be found on another of the Lesser Antilles, the British colony of Montserrat. Montserrat has a strato volcano, Mount Souffiière, which was thought to be dormant. Monser-

rat has suffered from minor earthquakes but the volcano suddenly erupted in 1992. Like the Mount Pelée earthquake, the eruption was caused by magma squeezing through the solidified cone of the volcano at very high pressure. The build-up started through the movement of magma through cracks deep in the rocks.

1 The summetrical giant: the 5,465-m-tall Popocatépetl is the highest active volcano in North and Central America.

2 The impressive 'Barranca del Cobre' (Copper Canyon) in the Sierra Madre. It is even bigger than the Grand Canyon in North America.

3 Crater lakes of the volcano Poás (2,700 m) in Costa Rica. The central American Cordilleras are full of volcanoes.

4 Costa Rica: the Central American Cordilleras are mostly covered by tropical mountain and rain forests.

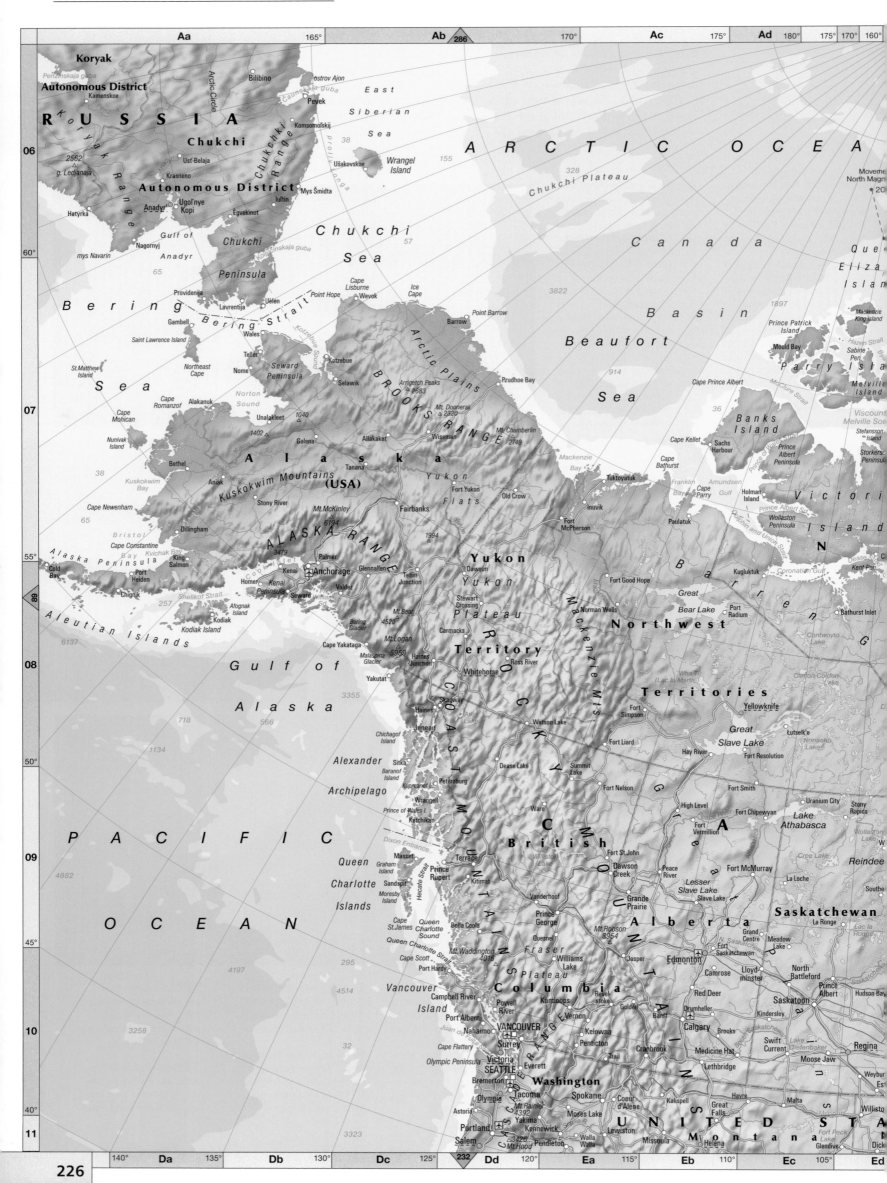

B e r i n g

S e a

Bering St

RUSSIA

Sireniki 1158
Providenija Novoe Jandrakinot Raupeljan Lorino
Urelik Čaplino Lavrentija
PVX
mys Čukotskij Čečen ostrov Močigmenskij
Čaplino Arakamčečen mys Nygligan zaliv

ostrov
Rathmanova
(Big Diomede I.) Little Diomed
Inalik

Northwest Cape Gambell
Ningeehak Wales
Niyrakpak Cape Prince
Lagoon of Wales Lost River Brooks M.
883
Powooiliak Camp Savoonga
Saint Lawrence I. 673 Atuk Mtn. King I. Point Spencer Port
Clarence
Iveetok Camp Sinuk Telle

Lietnik
Southeast Cape 555 Northeast Cape Nome **OME**
Kinipaghulghat Cape Nome
Mts.

Bluff
White Mountain

Rocky Point

16

58°

Hall I.
450
Alaska Maritime
Wildlife Refuge Saint Matthew I.

Cape Upright

67

17

56°

89

95

20

N o r t o n   S o u n d

Yukon Delta
C. Romanzof Waklarok Alakanuk Kwikpak
Askinuk Mts. Kotlik Emmonak Pastol
714 New Akulurak Hamilton Bay Stuart I.
Hooper Bay Knockhock Scammon New Stebbins
Bay Hamilton St. Michael
Chevak Yukon Delta St. Michael Unalakleet
Cape Mohican Mountain **MOU** 701
Village Pitkas Pt. Andreafsky R.
Nash Harbor Chakaktolik 396
Yukon Delta Mekoryuk Cape Etolin Pilot Station
Wildlife Refuge 283 Keyaluvik Marshall
Nunivak I. C. Vancouver Tununak 451 Cahkwaktolik
Nightmate Nelson I. Chiftak National Anvik
Cape Mendenhall Kasigluk Ohogamuit Stuyahok Shageluk
Cape Corwin Chefornak Wildlife Refuge Holy Cross
Kikegtek I. **BET** Kalskag
Pingurbek I. Kipnuk Tuntutuliak Bethel Flat
Napakiak Akiachak Tuluksak **ANI**
Kwigillingok Eek Whitefish Horn Mts. Crooked
Lake 1097 Creek
Kuskokwim Mt. Plummer Cairn Mts.
Bay 1463 1158
Quinhagak Kilbuck Mountains

St. Paul I.
Otter I. **SNP** Northeast Point
St.Paul Walrus I.

St. George I.

Pribilof Islands

18

54°

Carter Spit
Explorer Mtn. Mt. Oratia
Platinum 811 1645 Togiak Chingmiluk
Goodnews Bay National Lake Nogamut
Cape Newenham Goodnews Wildlife Refuge Taylor Mts.
Mining Camp 1091
Calm Point Togiak
544 Togiak A h k l u n   M o u n t a i n s
Hagemeister I. Bay
High I. Holitna R.
Hagemeister Strait Walrus Is. Crooked I.
Aleknagik Aleganik
Lake Koliganek Ketok Mtn. Old Village
Nushagak 517 Telaqua
Peninsula **DLG** Lake
Dillingham New Stuyahok
Clarks Point Lake Clark
B r i s t o l National Park
B a y Cape Nondalton and Preserve
Constantine Hallersville
Etolin
Point Kvichak Bay Igiugig Chigmit
Cape Sarichef Cape Naknek Sugarloaf Mtn. Newhalen Mountains
Mordvinof Anvak I. **AKN** 745 Iliamna
Unimak Shishaldin Otter Pt. King Salmon Lake Pile Bay
Volcano Kudiakof Is. Village
2862 Moffet Pt. Williamsport
Izembek Katmai Chenik
False Pass **CDB** Cold Bay Wildlife Refuge Caribou R. National Burr Pt. Chinitna Pt.
King Cove Mt. Dana Park 1196 Augustine I.
Deer I. 1310 Pavlof Vol. and Preserve Mt. Douglas
Sanak I. Sanak 2504 Ilnik Seal Is. Strogonof Port Heiden 2153 Mt. English Bay
Dolgoi I. Point Pilot Point Katmai **HOM**
Caton I. Port Moller Becharof 2047 Pt. Adam
Sanak Islands Unga I. Mt. Peulik Becharof Portlock
Pavlof Is. 1500 N.W.R. Chugach Is.
Sand Korovin I. Aniakchak Black I.
Point Perryville Veniaminof Mon. Chenik
Chignik Volcano C. Nukshak
Shumagin Islands 2507 Aniakchak Mt. Katmai C. Douglas
Nagai I. Volcano Kanatak *A l e u t i a n* 2144 Wide Bay
Big Koniuji I. Kupreanof *R a n g e* Gulf
Chernabura I. Little Koniuji I. Pt. Chiach I. Castle C. of
Simeonof I. Mitrofania I. Seal C. Nakchamik Foggy Alaska
Cape Cape **19**
Semidi Is. Aghiyuk I. Low Cape Larsen Bay Kodiak
Chowiet I. *Kodiak Island* Fort Abercrombie
Cape Ikolik S.H.S. **ADO**
Sitkinak Strait Old Harbor
Tugidak I.

Alaska Marine Hwy. Alaska Peninsula

Shelikof Strait

Bk 160° **Ca** 158° **Cb** 156° ◆ 16 **Cc** 154° **Cd** 152° **Ce** 150°

Chukchi

Sea

Arctic Circle

Point Hope
Point Hope
Cape Lisburne
Wevok
Mt. Hamlet
620

Lisburne
Peninsula
38

Naokak

Point Lay
Kasegaluk Lagoon
Icy Cape

Wainwright
Point Franklin
Paerd Bay

75

Beaufort

Nulavik
Point Barrow
Barrow
BRW
Elson Lagoon

Titikut

Sea

Kivalina
Mt. Kelly
960
Timmerkpuk Mt.
1154

Thunder Mt.
1462

Atqasak
Ikiak

Cape Simpson
Alaktak
Anakruak

Arctic Plains

115

Cape Krusenstern
Nat.Mon.
Noatak
Cape Krusenstern

Mulgrave Hills

Iglichuk Hills

Kokruagarok

Cape Halkett

Espenberg
Sheshalik

Baird Mountains

National
1516

Lookout Ridge

Valley of Willow

Harrison

C.Espenberg
Kotzebue
OTZ

Brooks Range

Atigaru Point

Kotzebue Sound
Baldwin Peninsula

Noorvik
Kiana

Kobuk Valley
National Park
Schwatka Mts

Endicott Mts

Nuiqsut

Oliktok Point

1640

Deering
Candle
Elephant Point

Buckland

Selawik

Ambler

Gates of the Arctic

1860
Anaktuvuk Pass

Umiat

Beechey Point

Deadhorse
SCC
Prudhoe Bay

70°
72°

Shungnak

National Park
and Preserve

Bullen

Flaxman I.
Brownlow Point

Kobuk
Arrigetch Peaks
2693

Camden Bay

10

Kokrines Hills

Ray Mountains

2440
2152
Mt.Chamberlin
2749

Kaktovik
Griffin Point

Nulato
Koyukuk

Huslia

Zane Hills

Lookout Mt.
713

Horace Mt.
1736

2453
2255

Davidson

Demarcation Point
Gordon

Galena
GAL

Hughes

Allakaket
Bettles
Coldfoot
Wiseman

Arctic Village

National

Ivvavik
National Park

1905

Ruby
Birches

Chandalar

Mountains

Mt.Greenough
1601

226

11

(USA)

Tanana
TAL

Stevens Village

Venetie

Wildlife Refuge

Vuntut
National Park

Old Crow
Flats

Rampart
Beaver

Sheenjek R.

Bear Mt.
1601

Old Crow
YOC

Yukon Flats
National

Fort Yukon
FYU
Birch Creek

Old Rampart

68°
70°

Manley Hot Springs

Livengood

Wildlife Refuge

Chalkyitsik

856

Sharp Mt.
1035

Old Minto

White Mountains

576
Wickersham Dome

Nenana
FAI
Ester Fox
Fairbanks

Eagle Summit
(1104)
Steese Highway

Circle

Chena Hot Springs
Moore Creek

Salmon Fork

Porcupine
Plain

Richardson

The Butt
1390

Twin Mt.
1765

Yukon-Charley

Coal Creek

Nation

Indian Grave Mt.
1292

1905

Ogilvie Mountains

Eagle Plains

1574

12

Alaska Range

Delta Junction

Fort Greely

Mt. Harper
1995

Rivers
Nat. Preserve

Eagle

Glacier Mt.
1905

Mt.Klotz
1799

1343

66°

Mt. Hayes
4171

Rapids
Isabel Pass
(1009)

Chicken

CANADA

Ogilvie

Mt. Kimball
2950

Jack Wade

Mt. Hart
1620

Dawson City
Rock Creek

Tok Junction
Tetlin Junction

Mentasta Pass
(694)
Slana

Klondike

YDA
Glenboyle

Selwyn Mts

2210

13

64°

Yukon

Yukon

Plateau

Mt. Stewart
1240

2515

Stewart

Keno City

Mt. Patterson
2087

Coffee Creek

Coldspring Mtn.
1390

Stewart Crossing

Grey Hunter Peak
2215

Plateau

Ethel Lake

Big Katzas

Mayo
Mayo Lake
670

Wellesley
Basin

Territory

Minto

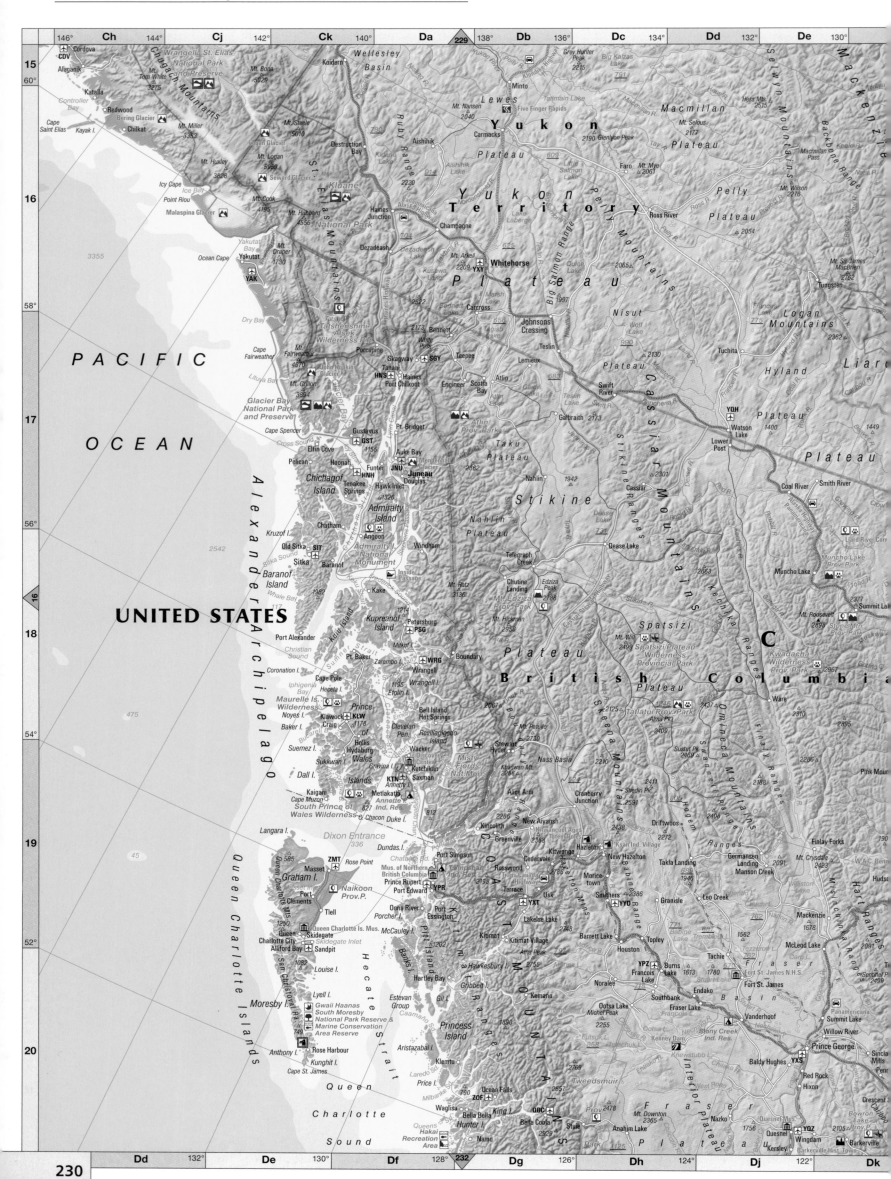

PACIFIC

OCEAN

UNITED STATES

Alexander Archipelago

Chichagof Island

Admiralty Island

Baranof Island

Kupreanof Island

Queen Charlotte Islands

Graham I.

Moresby I.

Yukon

Territory

Plateau

Yukon

Plateau

Whitehorse

Macmillan Plateau

Pelly Plateau

Selwyn Mountains

Logan Mountains

Hyland Plateau

Liard Plateau

Cassiar Mountains

Stikine Ranges

Stikine Plateau

Taku Plateau

Nahlin Plateau

Stikine

Spatsizi Plateau

British Columbia

Plateau

Skeena Mountains

Omineca Mountains

Finlay Ranges

C O A S T   M O U N T A I N S

Prince Rupert

Prince George

Queen Charlotte Sound

Glacier Bay National Park and Preserve

Wrangell St. Elias National Park and Preserve

Chugach Mountains

St. Elias Mountains

Kluane National Park

Cordova

Yakutat

Juneau

Sitka

Ketchikan

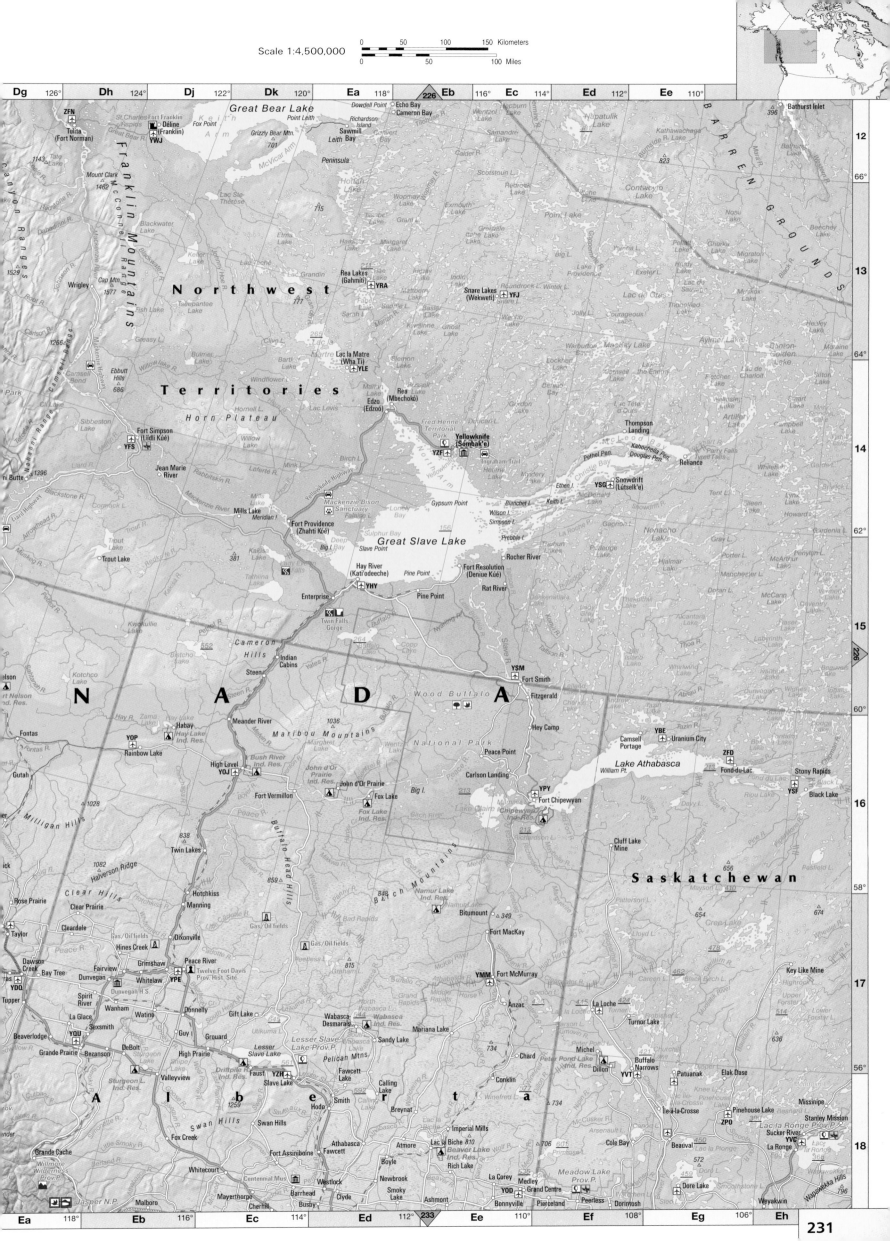

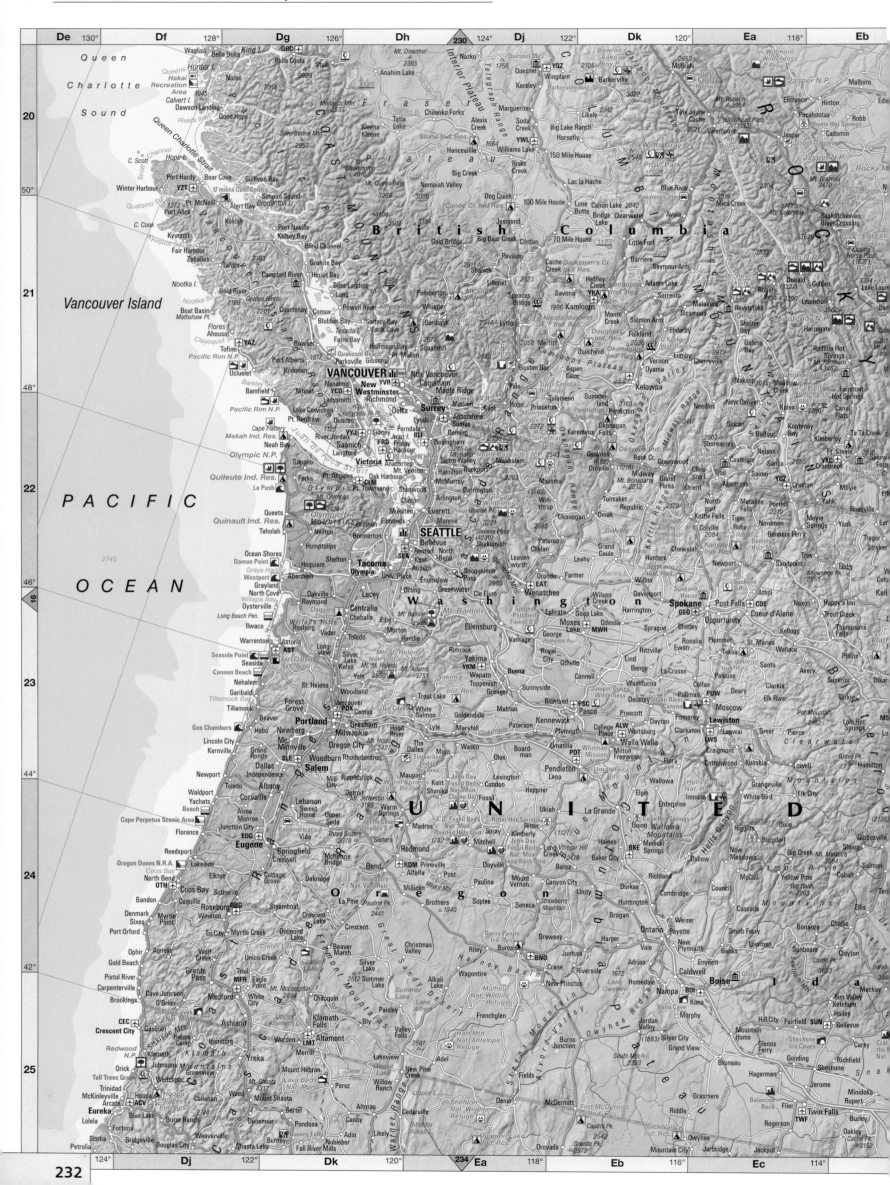

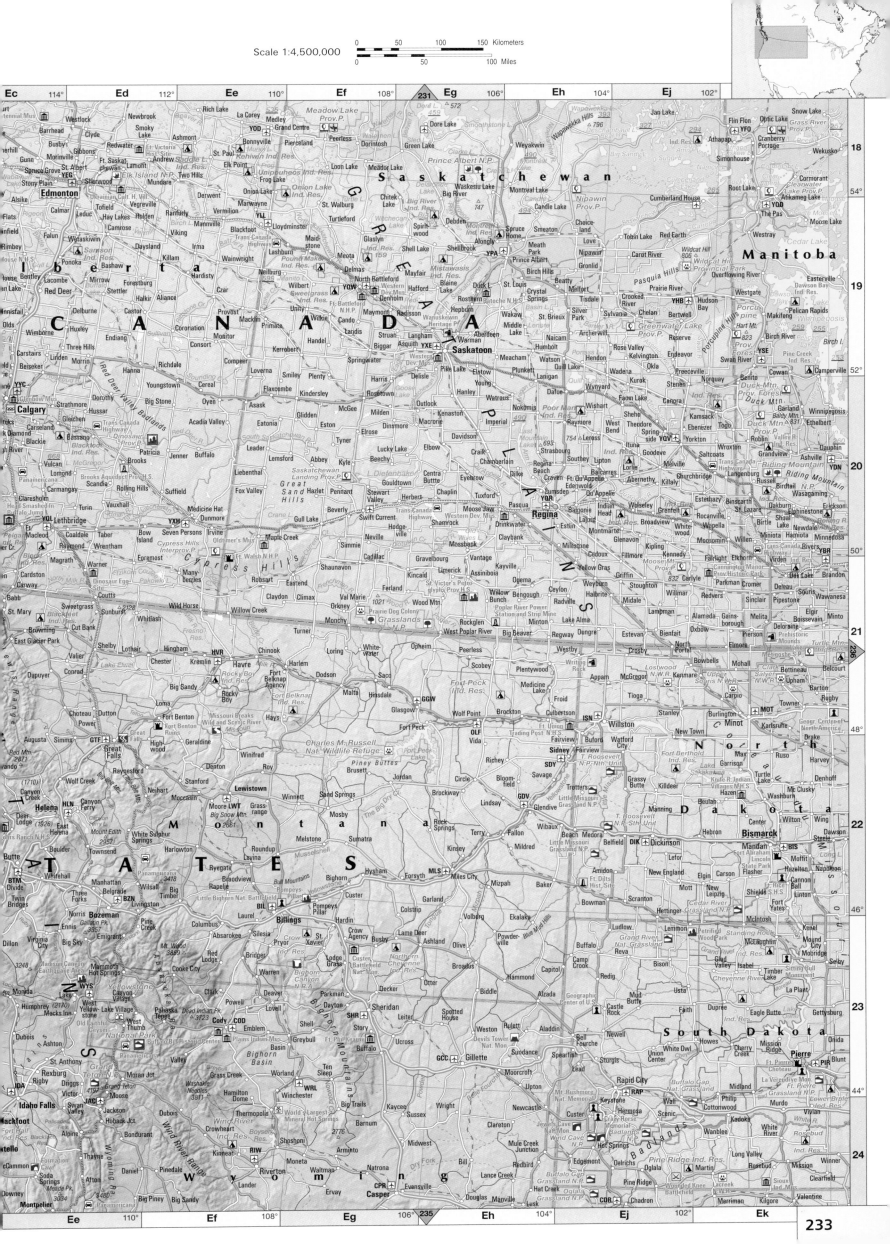

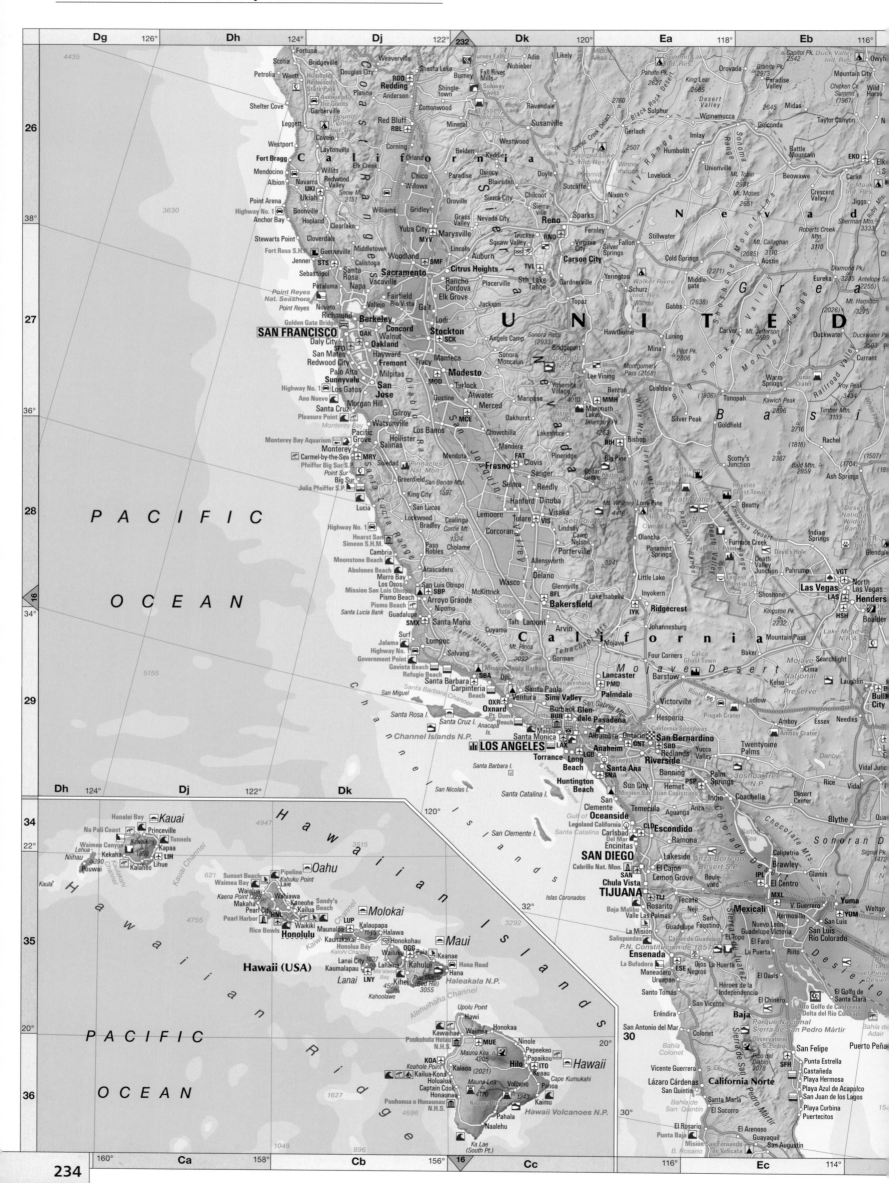

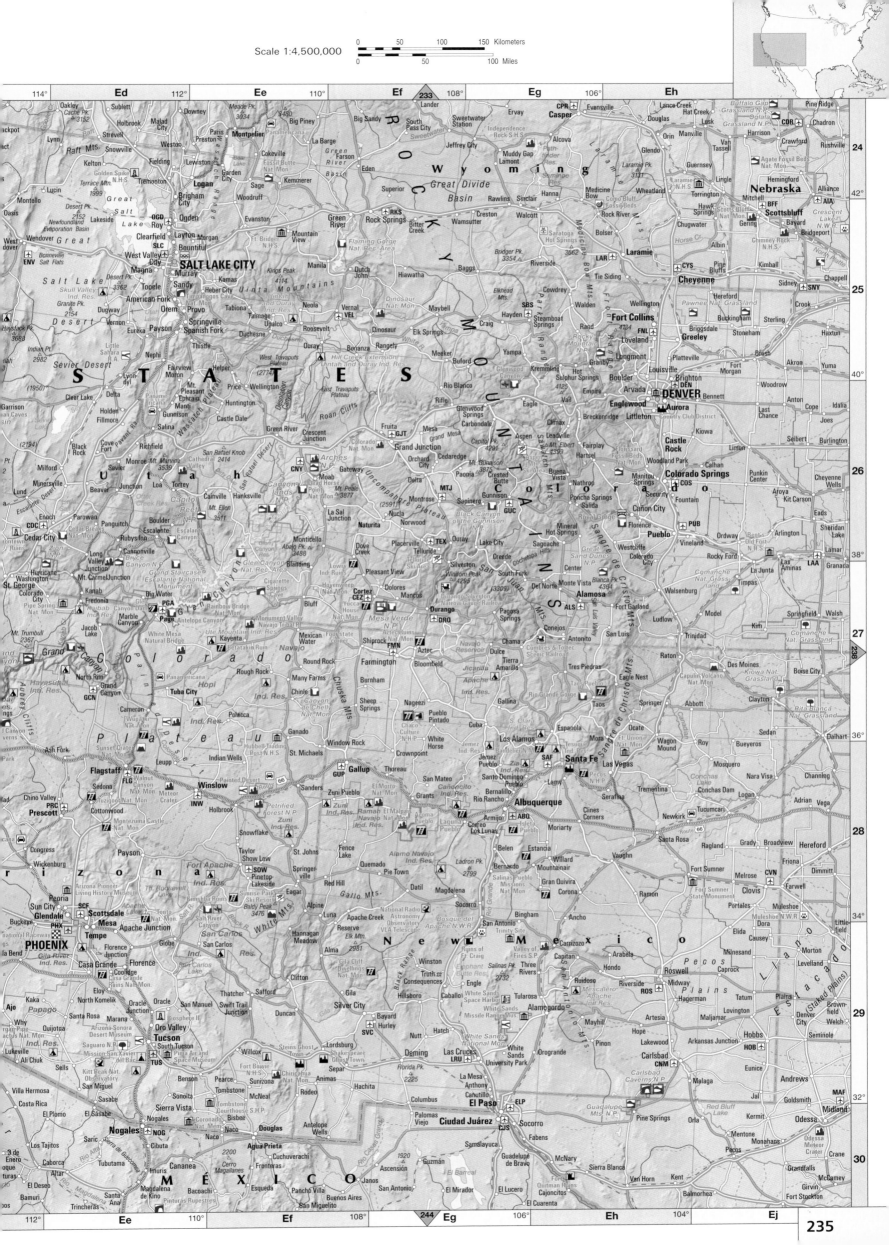

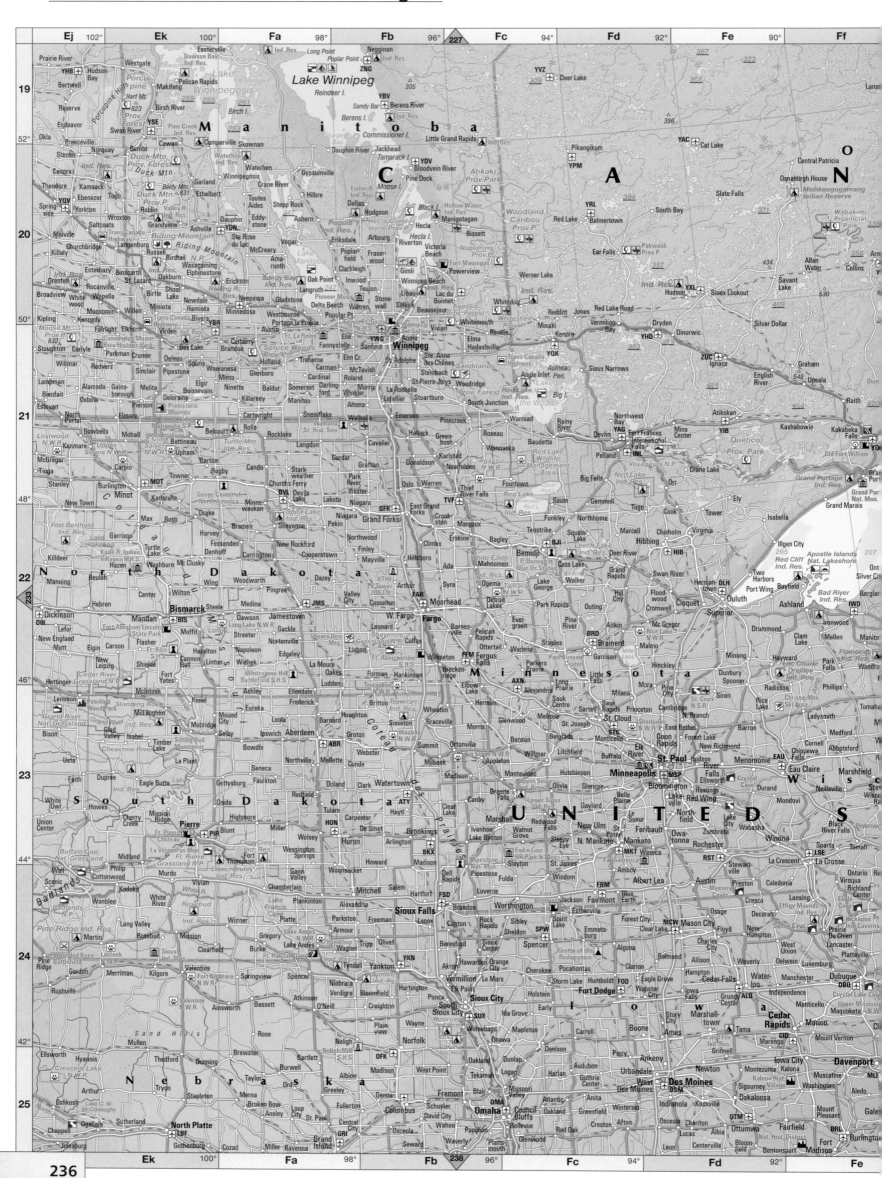

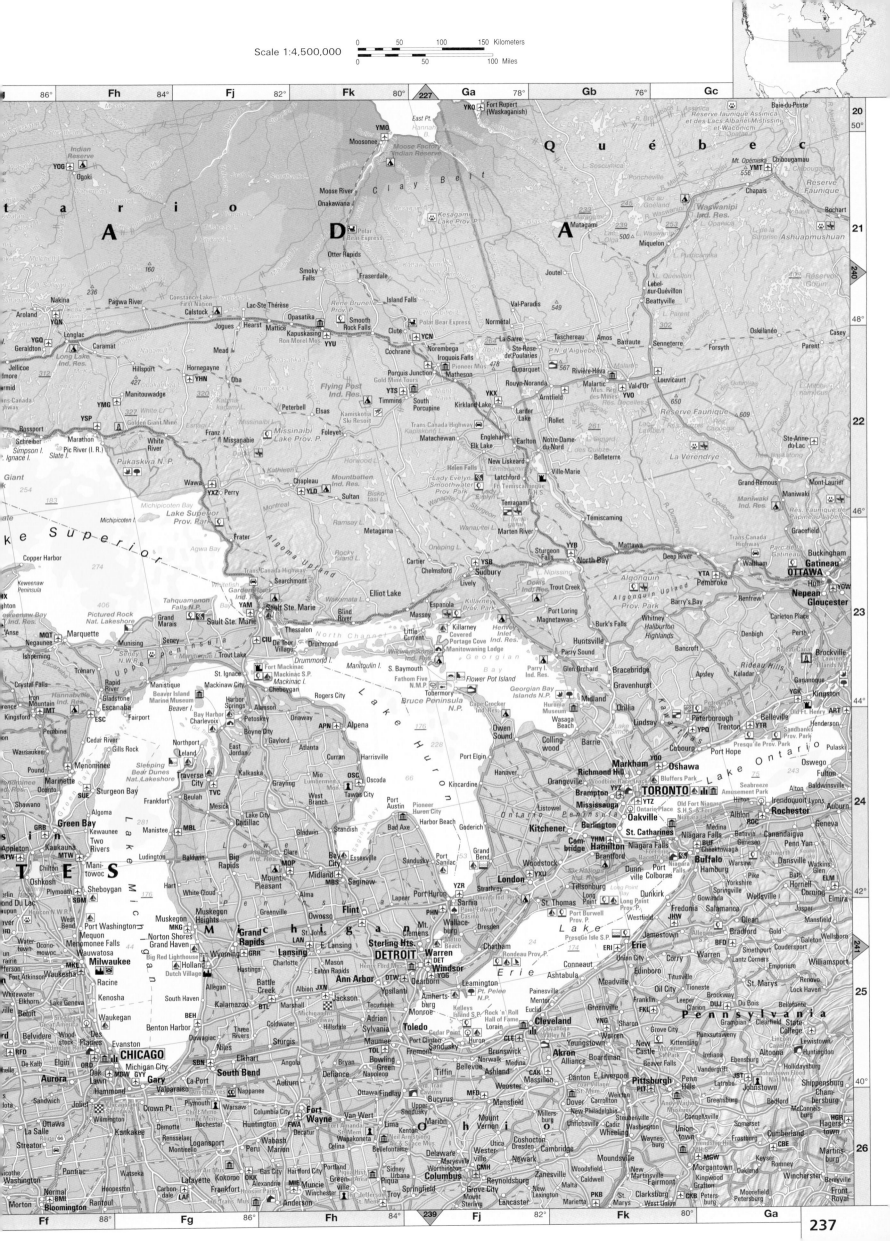

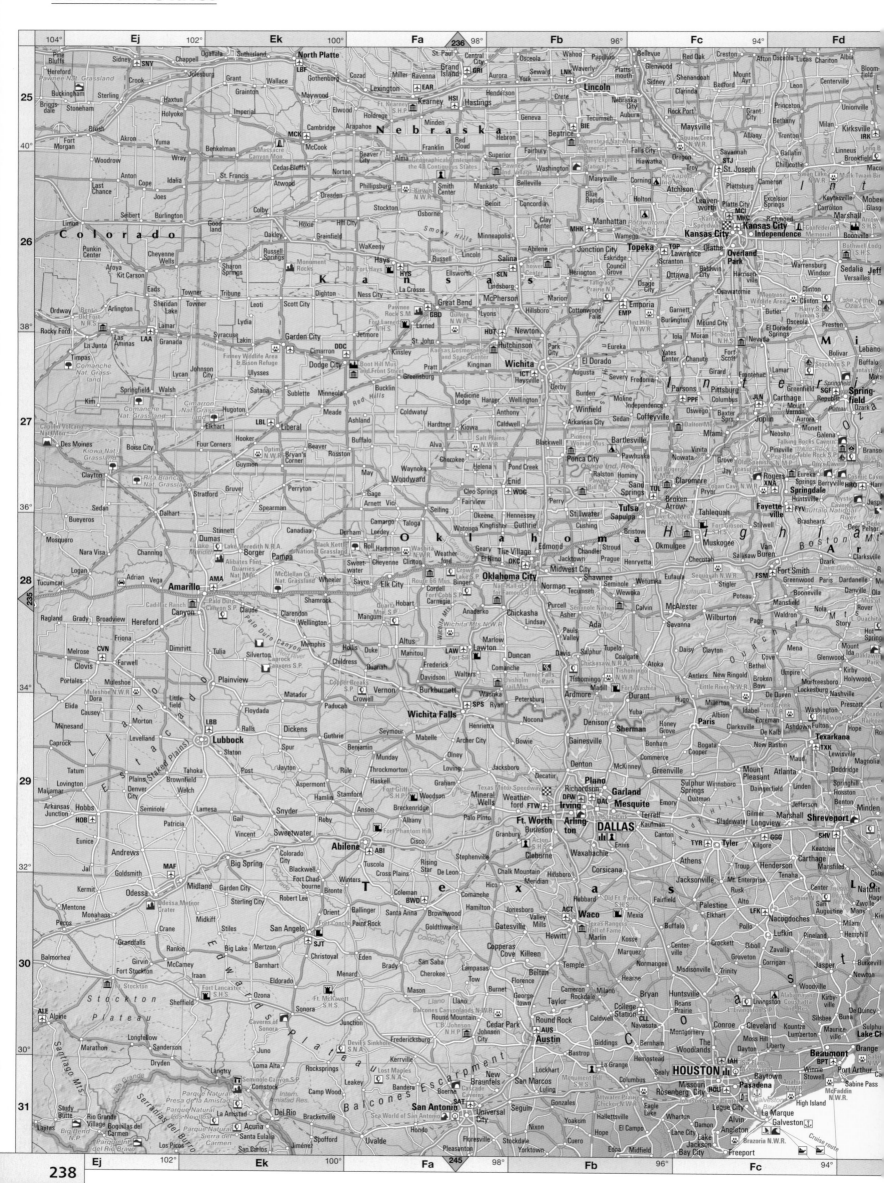

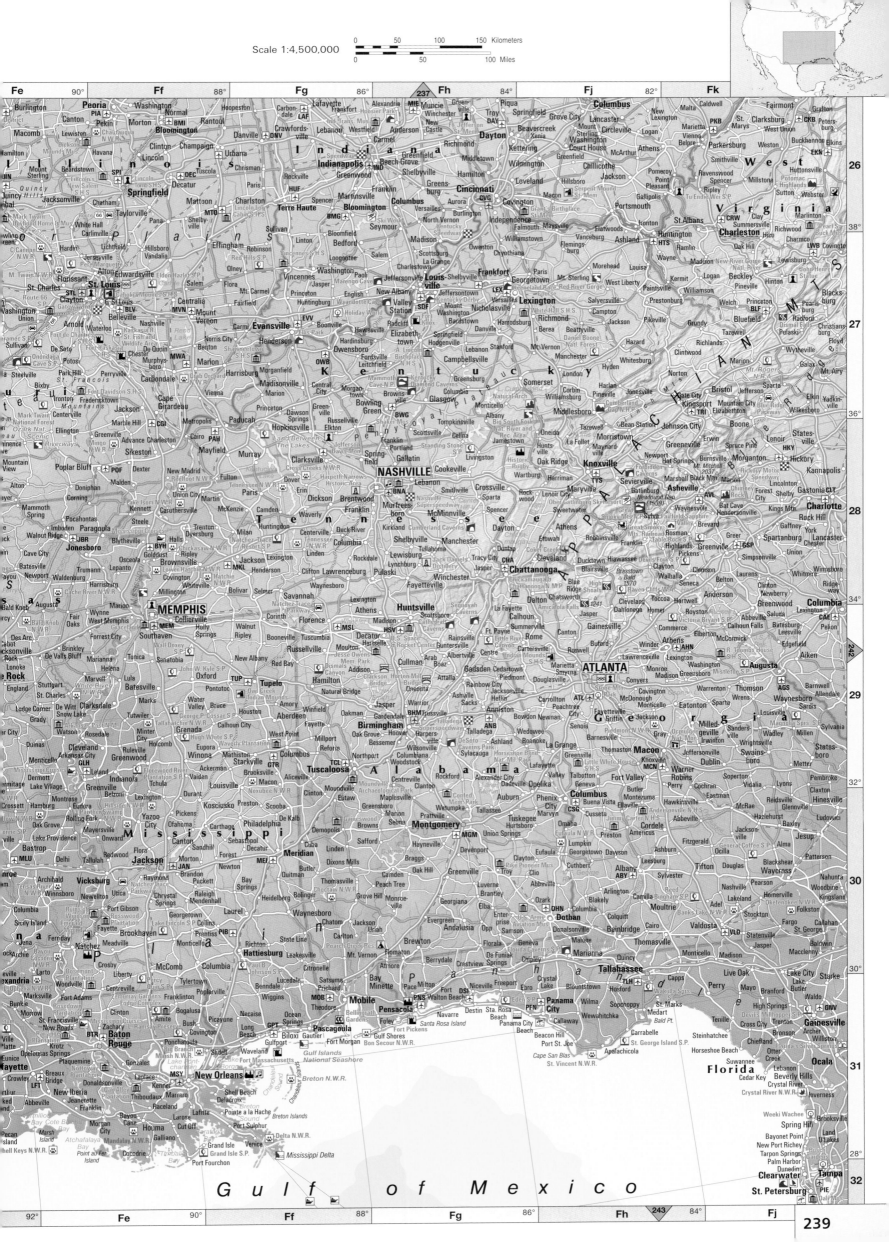

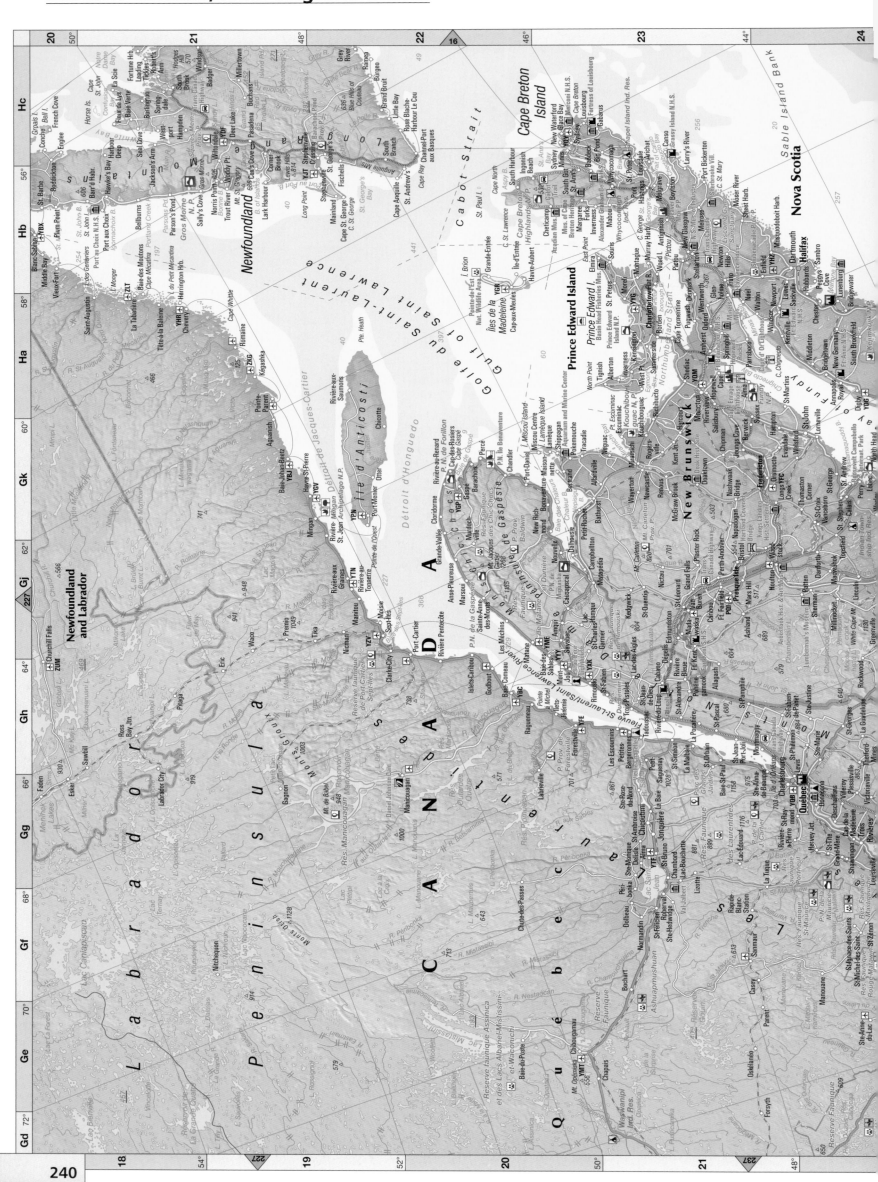

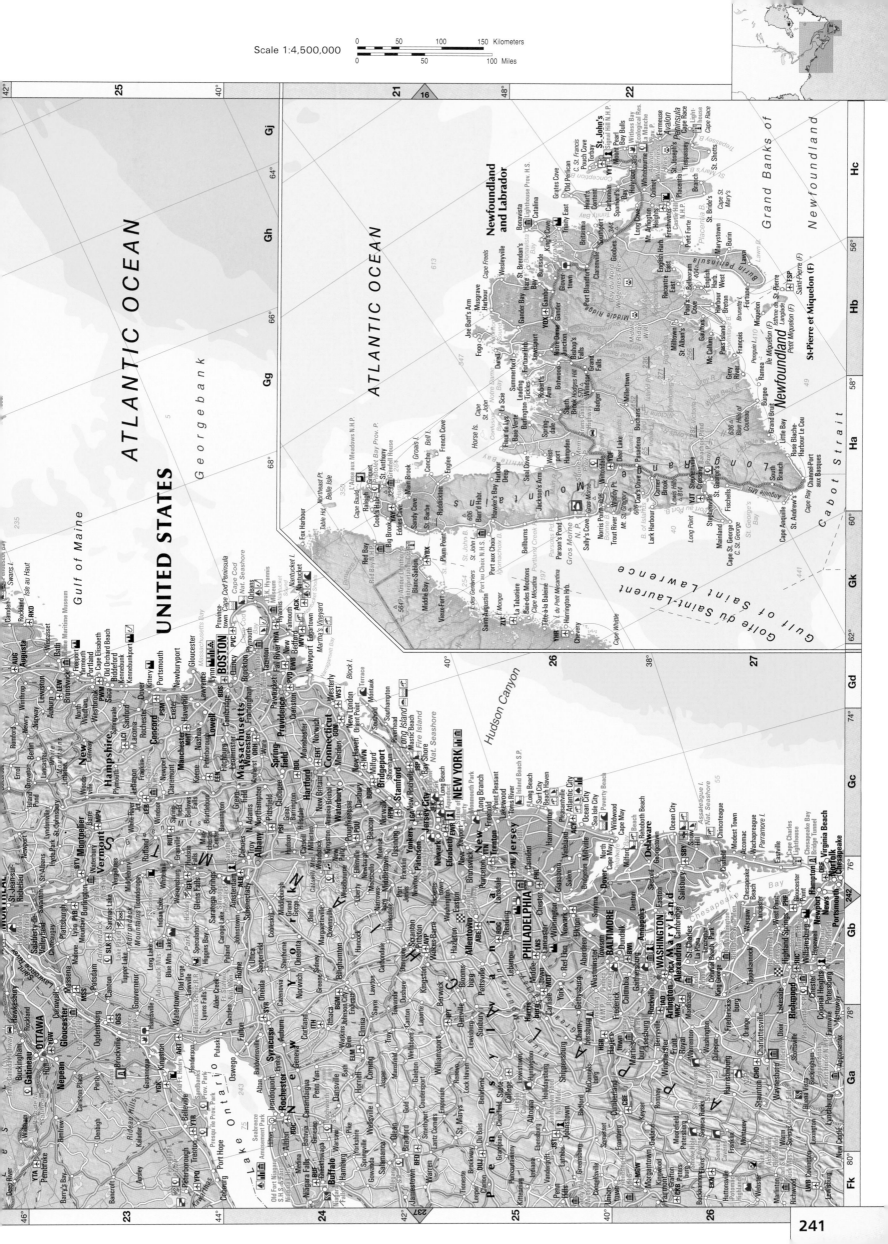

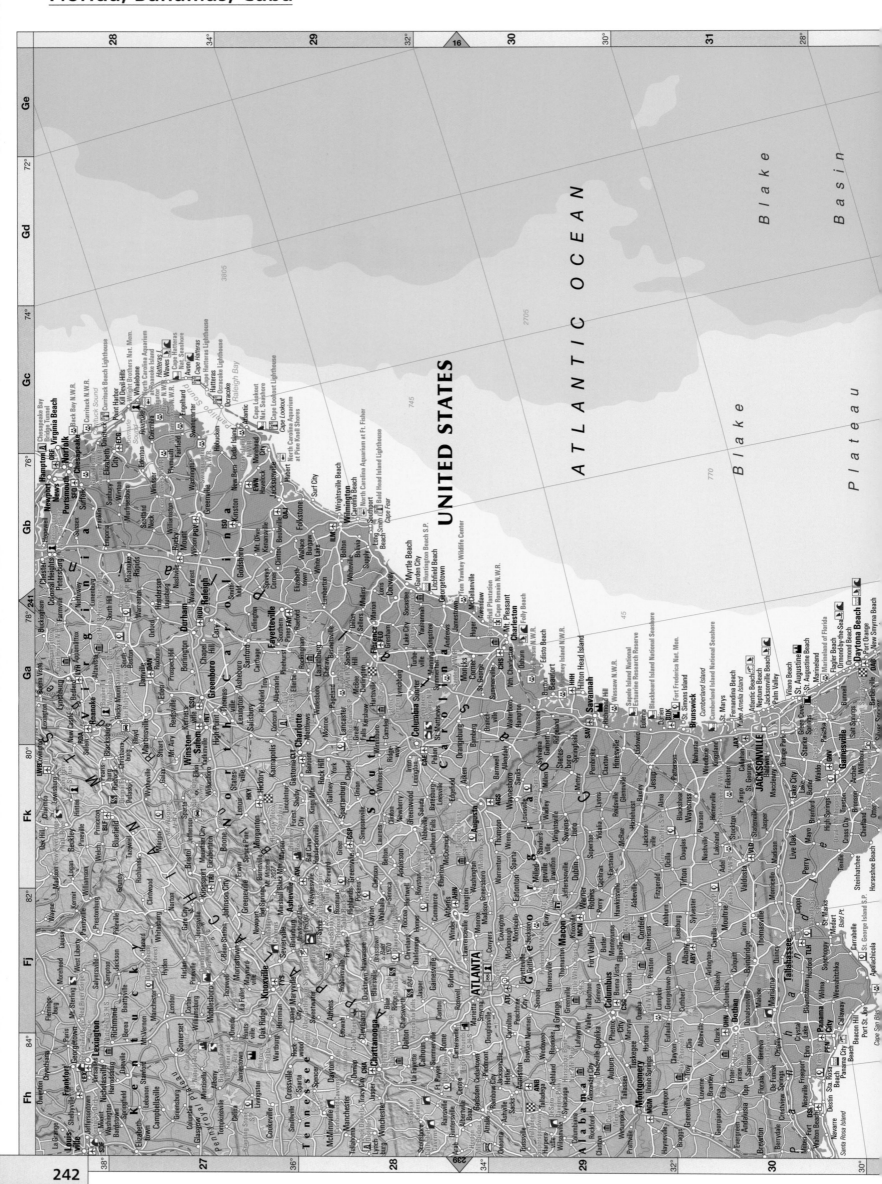

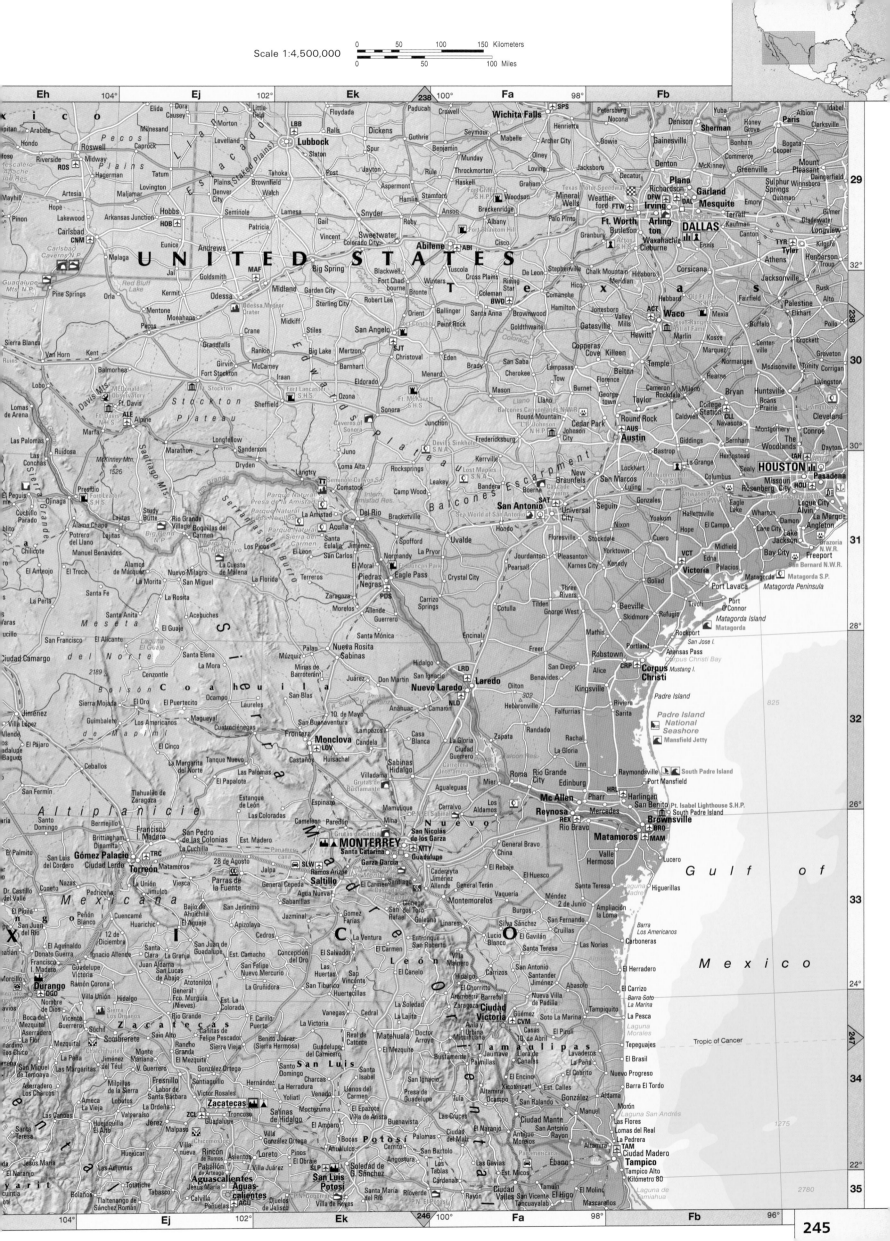

Scale 1:4,500,000

0 50 100 150 Kilometers
0 50 100 Miles

33
24°
34
243
22°
35
20°
36
18°
37
16°
38
14°
39

Mexican

Basin

Cruise route

Sigsbee
4012
Deep

Gulf of Mexico

Tropic of Cancer

3765
3780

2780
3265

55

Cayo Arenas

Cayo Nuevo

Arrecifes
Triángulos

Arrecife
Alacrán

Campeche Bank

Cruise route

MÉXICO

Gulf of
Campeche

Parque Natural
Río Lagartos

Cabo Catoche
Ecab
Isla Holbox
Isla Contoy
Isla Blanca

Cabo Catoche

Parque Natural
San Felipe

El Cuyo
Boca Iglesia
Isla Mujeres

Punta Yalkubul
Río Lagartos
Loché
Yalsihón
Puerto Juárez
Isla Mujeres

CUN Cancún

Dzilam de Bravo
Telchac Puerto
TZM
Yucatán
Leona
Vicario
Puerto Morelos

Progreso
Cansahcab
Motúl
Temax
Tizimín
Calotmul
Espita
Chemax
Playa del Carmen
Xcaret

Sisal
Hunucmá
Kinchil
Izamal
Tunkas
Dzitas
Piste
Valladolid
Cobá
CZM Cozumel
Molas

MÉRIDA MID
CZA
Isla Cozumel

Parque Natural
Río Celestún

Celestún
Chunchucmil
Muna
Tekit
Sotuta
Kantunil
Yaxcabá
Chikindzonot
Akumal
Xel-Ha
Celarain
Punta Celarain

Isla Arena
Moxcané
Tekax
Tihosuco
Tepich
P.N. Tulum
Tulum

La Costa
Holachó
Hecelchakán
Ticul
Oxkutzcab
Peto
San Ramón
Vigia
Chico
Tulum
Parque Marino Nacional
Arrecifes de Cozumel

Jaina
Bolonchén de Rejón
Tzucacab
Santa
Rosa
Punta Allen

Yucatán

Campeche
Lerma

Baluarte de Santiago
CPE
Tiquimul
Hopelchén
Iturbide
Valle Hermoso
Nohbec

Pomuch
Edzná
Pich
Xochob
Dzibalchén
Sabana
San Francisco
Polyuc

Villa Madero
Champotón
Villa de Guadalupe
Hool
Ayala
Arellano
Xmabén
Río Verde

Quintana

Roo

Reforma
Cafetal

Cabeza
de Coral
Reserva de
la Biosfera
Banco Chinchorro

Carillo Puerto
Santa
María
Pixoyal
Yohaltún
Bacalar
CTM

Sabancuy
Dzibalché
Morocoy
Chetumal

Puerto Real
Isla de
Aguada
Chicbul
Constitución
Xpujil
Corozal
Banco
Chinchorro
Cayo
Centro
Cayo Lobos

CME
Laguna
de Términos
18 de Marzo
Francisco
Escárcega
Balamkú
Tomás
Garrido
Sarteneja
Parque Nacional
Arrecifes de Xcalak

Ciudad del Carmen
Kilometro 69
Becan
Chicanná
La Unión
Xcalak

Frontera
El Vapor
Hormiguero
Mariscos
Orange Walk
Ambergris Cay
San Pedro

Nuevo
Campechito
Atasta
Candelaria
Xpujil
Villahermosa
Sand
Hill
BZE
Cay Caulker
Hick's Cay

Paraíso
Palizada
Nuevo Coahuila
Dos Lagunas
Belize City
Turneffe
Northern Cay
Douglas Cay

Tupilco
El Triunfo
San Marcos
Carmelita
P.N. Tikal
Dos
Pilas
Blue Hole
Islands
Long Cay

Tabasco

Villahermosa VSA
Tila
Tenosique
El Naranjo
Tikal
Cd. Melchor de Mencos
Caracol
Dangriga
Cruise route

Cárdenas
Macuspana
Catazajá
Emiliano
Zapata
Mactún
Sayaxché
Poptún
Riverdale
Tobacco
Range
Glovers Reef

Coatzacoalcos
Huimanguillo
Jalapa
Palenque PQM
El Pedregal
Uaxactún
Flores
El Cruce
DGA
Mango Creek
Placencia

Minatitlán
Las Choapas
Chontalpa
Pichucalco
Salto
de Agua
Yajalón
Temó
Ocosingo
La Selva
San Javier
Co-op Bethel
Ixcun
Naj Tunich
FRS
Ranguana Cay
Golfo de

Acayucan
Vasconcelos
Cerro
Nanchital
Raudales
Rayón
El Cañón
El Sumidero
Bonampak
Frontera
Corozal
Dolores
Punta Negra
PND
Honduras

Isthmus of
Tehuantepec
Chicoasén
Coyula
TGZ
San Cristóbal de las Casas
Benemérito de
las Américas
Dos Pilas
Agustina
San Antonio
Punta Gorda
Sapodilla Cays
Isla de Utila
Utila

Chiapas

Tuxtla
Gutiérrez
Flores
Magón
Amatenango
del Valle
Comitán de
Domínguez
R. de la Biosfera
Montes Azules
Modesto
Méndez
C. de Tres Puntas
Puerto Cortés
Turtle Harbour

Sierra Madre de Chiapas

Villaflores
El Parral
El Tenam Puente
Chinkultic
P.N. Lagunas
de Montebello
Chisec
Sebol
Semox
Livingston
PBR
B. de
Omoa
Tela
La Masica 2435
LCE

Revolución
Mexicana
La Trinitaria
Tziscao
Cuevas
Sebol
Castillo de San Felipe
Puerto
Barrios
San Pedro SAP
La Lima
Jílamo

Arriaga
Paso
Hondo
San Mateo Ixtatán
Barillas
P.N. Lachúa
El Estor
La Ruidosa
Canoa
El Progreso ORO

Puerto Arista
El Manguito
La Democracia
Soloma
Santa Cruz
Verapaz
Cobán
Quiriguá
Río Lindo
Yorito
Yoro
Montañas 2378

GUATEMALA
Doña María
La Entrada
Santa
Bárbara

Embarcadero
Trejo
Pajapan
Chicomuselo
Colotenango
Huehuetenango
Aguacatán
Sacapulas
Salamá
Río Hondo
Copán
Santa Rosa
de Copán
HONDURAS

Mapastepec
Motozintla
de Mendoza
Santa Cruz
del Quiché
Joyabaj
Sanarate
Zacapa
Chiquimula
Agua
Azul
SDH
Santa
La Libertad

Escuintla
Huixtla
Unión
Juárez
Totonicapán
Chichicastenango
El Progreso
Esquipulas
Nueva
Ocotepeque
San Miguel
Marale

Quezaltenango
Panajachel
Chimaltenango
Jalapa
Jocotán
Metapán
Agua
Blanca
La Esperanza
Marcala

Tapachula TAP
Retalhuleu
Santiago
Antigua
CD. DE
GUATEMALA
El Progreso
Nueva
Concepción
Chalatenango
La Paz
Comayagüela
TEGUCIGALPA TGU

Puerto Madero
Cd. Hidalgo
Mazatenango
Vol. de
Fuego 3763
Amatitlán
Cuilapa
Santa Ana
Aguilares
San Vicente
Ojojona
Caridad

Ocós
Escuintla
Los Hoyos
Taxisco
Chiquimulilla
Ahuachapán
Ilobasco
San Francisco
Gotera
Yauyupe

Tecojate
Chulamar
Masagua
SAN SALVADOR SAL
Zacatecoluca
San Miguel
Usulután
Choluteca

Sipacate
Pto.
Quetzal
San José
La Barra
Sonsonate
La Libertad
Playa Costa del Sol
Isla Montecristo
El Cuco
Coyolito

EL SALVADOR

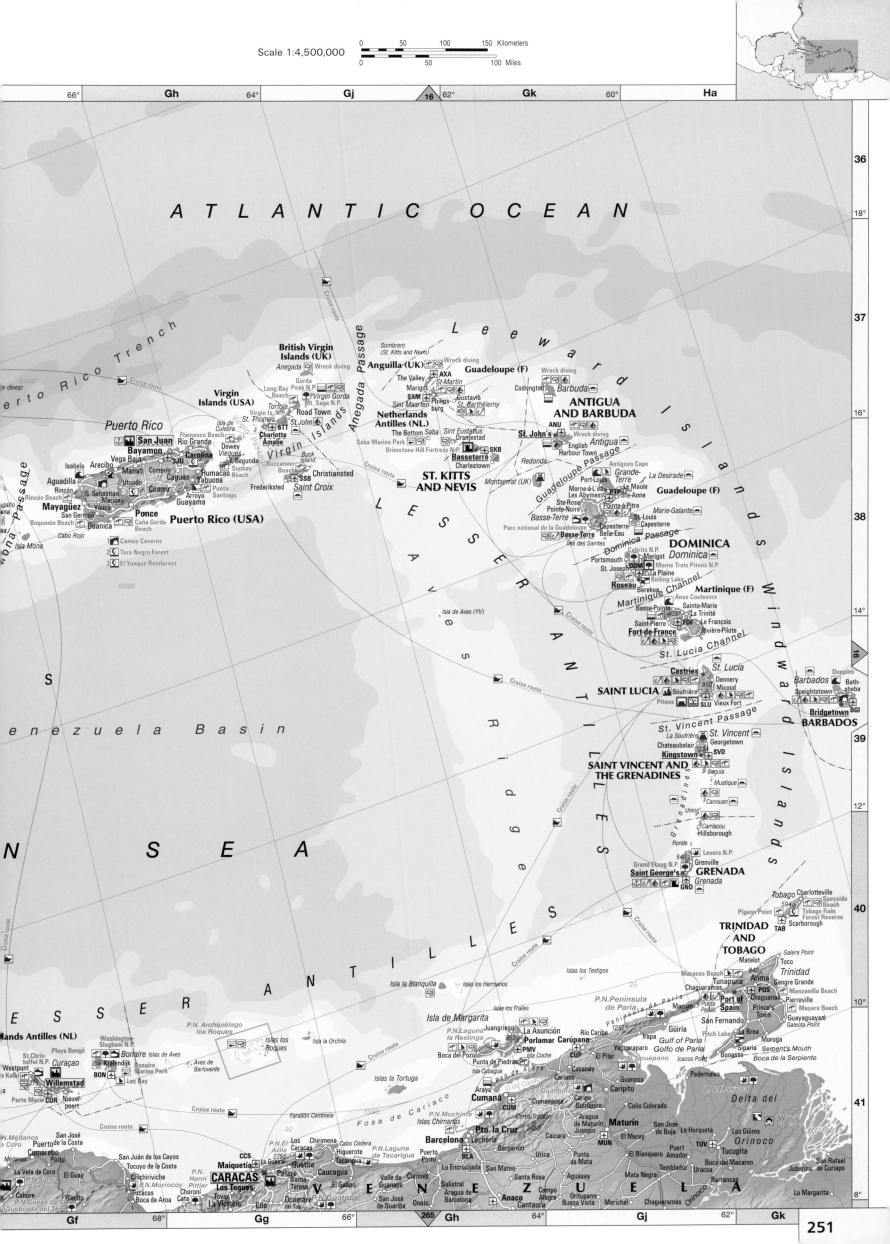

South America

The steeply imposing chain of the Cordillera continues down the Pacific coast right through the southern part of the American double continent. With the Andes it attains its greatest width, measuring some 700 km west to east at the Tropic of Capricorn. Numerous high plains link the upper slopes of the Cordilleras. Lowlands adjoin it in the east, including both the gigantic Amazon basin and the fertile plains of the Pampas. The mountain areas in the north and east are overgrown with tropical vegetation. The north-south axis of South America, some 7,500 km in length, results in extreme climatic differences. In the northern

region, which is closer to the equator, it is hot, humid and wet. The central region has a relatively mild climate, while the cool to temperate region of Patagonia merges into the southern latitudes of Tierra del Fuego, which is affected by the cold climate of the Antarctic.

The Torres del Paine National Park. The highest point in the park is the 3,050-m-high Cerro Torre. Nearby are the Cerro Paine Chico and the three spectacular summits of the Torres (towers) del Paine.

South America

254

Db 120° | Ea 110° | Eb 100° | Fa 90° | Fb 80° | Ga 70° | Gb 60° | 287 | Hb 40° | Ja 30° | Jb 20° | Ka 10° | Kb 0° | La 10° | Lb

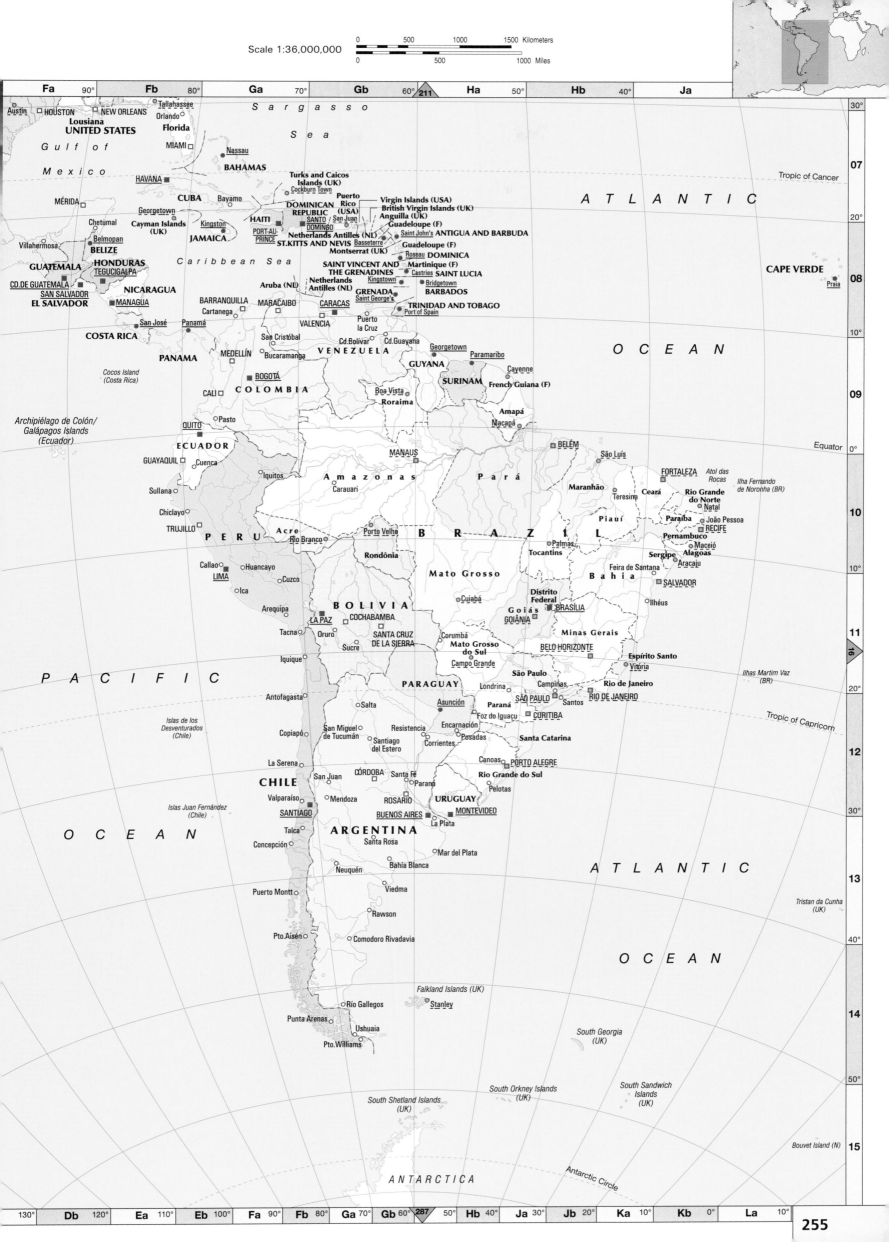

Sargasso Sea

UNITED STATES

Austin ☐ HOUSTON ☐ NEW ORLEANS
Lousiana
Florida
Orlando
Tallahassee
MIAMI ☐

Gulf of Mexico

ATLANTIC

30°
07
Tropic of Cancer

Nassau
BAHAMAS

MÉRIDA ☐

Chetumal

CUBA
Bayamo
HAVANA

Georgetown
Cayman Islands (UK)

Turks and Caicos Islands (UK)
Cockburn Town

DOMINICAN REPUBLIC
HAITI
PORT-AU-PRINCE
SANTO DOMINGO

Puerto Rico (USA)
San Juan

Virgin Islands (USA)
British Virgin Islands (UK)
Anguilla (UK)
Guadeloupe (F)
Saint John's ANTIGUA AND BARBUDA

20°
08
CAPE VERDE
Praia

Villahermosa

Belmopan
BELIZE
GUATEMALA
CD.DE GUATEMALA
SAN SALVADOR
EL SALVADOR

HONDURAS
TEGUCIGALPA

JAMAICA
Kingston

ST.KITTS AND NEVIS
Montserrat (UK)
SAINT VINCENT AND THE GRENADINES
Netherlands Antilles (NL)
Basseterre

Guadeloupe (F)
Martinique (F)
Roseau DOMINICA
Castries SAINT LUCIA
Kingstown
Bridgetown
GRENADA
BARBADOS

NICARAGUA
MANAGUA

Caribbean Sea

Aruba (NL)
Netherlands Antilles (NL)

Saint George's
TRINIDAD AND TOBAGO
Port of Spain

San José
COSTA RICA

Panamá
PANAMA

BARRANQUILLA
Cartanega
MARACAIBO
CARACAS
VALENCIA
Puerto la Cruz

Cd.Bolívar
Cd.Guayana

San Cristóbal
MEDELLÍN
Bucaramanga
CALI
BOGOTÁ

VENEZUELA
GUYANA
Georgetown
Paramaribo
SURINAM

Cayenne
French Guiana (F)

10°

OCEAN

09

Cocos Island (Costa Rica)

COLOMBIA
Pasto

Boa Vista
Roraima

Amapá
Macapá

Archipiélago de Colón/
Galápagos Islands (Ecuador)

QUITO
ECUADOR
GUAYAQUIL
Cuenca

Iquitos

MANAUS

BELÉM
São Luís

FORTALEZA
Atol das Rocas

Equator
0°

Sullana

Amazonas
Carauari

Pará

Maranhão
Teresina

Ceará
Natal

Ilha Fernando de Noronha (BR)

Rio Grande do Norte

10

Chiclayo

TRUJILLO

PERU

Acre
Rio Branco

BRAZIL

Piauí
Paraíba
João Pessoa
RECIFE

Callao
LIMA
Huancayo
Cuzco
Ica

Rondônia

Palmas
Tocantins

Pernambuco
Maceió
Alagoas
Aracaju
Sergipe

10°

Arequipa

BOLIVIA

Mato Grosso

Cuiabá

Distrito Federal
Goiás
GOIÂNIA
BRASÍLIA

Feira de Santana
Bahia
Ilhéus

SALVADOR

11

Tacna

LA PAZ
COCHABAMBA
SANTA CRUZ DE LA SIERRA

Oruro
Sucre

Corumbá
Mato Grosso do Sul

Minas Gerais
BELO HORIZONTE

PACIFIC

Iquique

Campo Grande

Espírito Santo
Vitória

Ilhas Martim Vaz (BR)

16

20°

Antofagasta

Islas de los Desventurados (Chile)

PARAGUAY

São Paulo
Londrina
Campinas
SÃO PAULO
Santos

Rio de Janeiro
RIO DE JANEIRO

Tropic of Capricorn

Copiapó
San Miguel de Tucumán

Salta

Asunción

Paraná
Foz do Iguaçu
CURITIBA
Santa Catarina

La Serena

Resistencia
Santiago del Estero
Corrientes

Encarnación
Posadas

12

CHILE

San Juan
CÓRDOBA
Santa Fé
Paraná

Canoas
PORTO ALEGRE
Rio Grande do Sul
Pelotas

Valparaíso
SANTIAGO

Mendoza

ROSARIO
BUENOS AIRES
La Plata

URUGUAY
MONTEVIDEO

Islas Juan Fernández (Chile)

OCEAN

Talca

ARGENTINA
Santa Rosa

30°

Concepción

Mar del Plata

ATLANTIC

Neuquén

Bahía Blanca

13

Puerto Montt

Viedma

Rawson

Tristan da Cunha (UK)

Pto.Aisén

Comodoro Rivadavia

40°

OCEAN

Falkland Islands (UK)
Stanley

South Georgia (UK)

14

Río Gallegos
Punta Arenas
Ushuaia
Pto.Williams

50°

South Orkney Islands (UK)

South Sandwich Islands (UK)

South Shetland Islands (UK)

Bouvet Island (N)

15

ANTARCTICA

Antarctic Circle

| 130° | Db | 120° | Ea | 110° | Eb | 100° | Fa | 90° | Fb | 80° | Ga | 70° | Gb | 60° | 287 | 50° | Hb | 40° | Ja | 30° | Jb | 20° | Ka | 10° | Kb | 0° | La | 10° |

255

South America

*The Chapada dos Guimaraes in the highlands of **Mato Grosso** adjoins the **Brazilian Highlands**. Chapadas are the extended plateaus occupying most of the Brazilian Highlands. They are mostly covered by tropical rain forests.*

Colombian Cordilleras

In Colombia, the Andes divide into three mountain chains at Nudo de Pasto: the **West**, **Central** and **East Cordilleras**. Deep, long valleys, the **Rio Cauca** and **Rio Magdalena**, which flow to the Caribbean, separate the mountain ranges from each other. In contrast to other high mountain areas, the Andes in Colombia do not present a steep alpine appearance. The landscape is marked by wide plateaus and ridges. The only exception are the highly glaciated, more recent volcanoes in the Central Cordilleras.

The **Cordillera Occidental** has an average height of 3,000 m and consists of crystalline rock. The highest elevation of the barely saperated Cordillera Occidental is the 4,764-m-high **Cumbal**.

The **Cordillera Central** is also composed of crystalline rock, but only its southern part forms a continuous chain. Elsewhere the Cordillera Central forms ridges with an average height of 4,000 m and includes numerous young, semiactive volcanoes. These volcanic cones reach considerable heights and their glaciated peaks are well above the snowline. The tallest of these volcanoes are the 5,750-m-high **Nevado del Huila** and the 5,325 m **Nevado del Ruiz**.

Further north lies the **mountainous country of Ruiz**, 2,000 to 3,000 m high. To the extreme north, the Central Cordillera ends with the isolated mountain block of the **Sierra Nevada de Santa Marta**, which slopes steeply down to the

Amazon

The Amazon is the longest river in South America, with a drainage area of 7 million sq. km and an approximate length of 6,500 km. It originates in the two main headwaters of Marañón and Ucayali, springing up in the Andes. In its middle reaches it is called Solimões. It crosses the Brazilian lowlands and flows with its three main branches into the Atlantic.

By the time it reaches Iquitos, the Amazon is 1.8 km wide, near Manaus it is 5 km wide and the estuary mouth is up to 250 km. The tidal flow and the Pororoca tidal wave can be felt 800 km upstream.

Caribbean. It contains Colombia's highest mountain, **the Pico Cristóbal Colón** (5,775 m).

The **Eastern Cordillera** is on average over 5,000 m high and splits into two branches. The **Cordillera de Mérida** continues beyond Venezuela, while the **Sierra de Perijá** ends on the Guajira peninsula.

These two mountain ranges on Venezuelan soil surround Lake

The Angel Falls: the total drop measures 948 m.

Maracaibo, which is 180 km long and up to 120 km wide. Lake Maracaibo is the largest lake in South America and is also believed to be the second-oldest on earth. Beneath its waters lie the largest petroleum deposits on the South American continent, so the beauty of the lake is marred by more than 5,000 oil derricks. It has an outlet to the Gulf of Venezuela.

The Cordillera Oriental is composed of gneiss and granite, with overlying sediment from the Mesolithic and Quaternary periods. Characteristic features are the basins at an altitude of 2,800 m, which resulted from primaeval lakes and were later filled with ablation rubble.

The **Rio Magdalena** flows for about 1,000 km through a rift valley between the Central and East Cordilleras into the Caribbean. Its most important tributary, the **Rio Cauca**, also flows through a rift valley between the Central and West Cordilleras. The Cauca rises in the western Central Cordillera. It has cut a deep gorge in the rock as it flows northwards. The river banks are lined with thick rainforest. The river is navigable and is an important transport route for the local people.

Guayana Highlands

The **Guyana Highlands** extend over about 1.5 million sq. km between the Orinoco, the Amazon lowlands and the Atlantic Ocean. The granite bedrock consists of high, flat plateaus split by extremely steep canyons.

The rivers carve their paths through shallow valleys, repeatedly broken up by rapids, cascades and waterfalls. The most impressive of these is undoubtedly the **Angel Falls**, at 948 m the highest waterfall on Earth. The falls are named after an American pilot called Jimmy Angel, so the name has no religious connotation as one might expect.

The nearby 226-m-high **Kaieteur Falls** is the world's largest single drop waterfalls, measuring 222 m. For comparison, The drop at Kaieteur is about five times greater than Niagara Falls.

To the west, the wooded highlands rise steeply towards ragged granite plateaus. The **Serranía de Mapichí** rises up to 2,262 m and the **Sierra Marahuaca** reaches a height of 2,579 m. The northern ascent, which consists of a 400 to 600-m-high bedrock and is surmounted by a series of individual, isolated mountains, is the easiest ascent for climbers.

At a height of 1,000 to 1,400 m, there are high plateaus divided into steep steps, consisting of several layers of sandstone. These are composed of deposits from primaeval rivers and seas, which have developed into their present form through erosion over the

Orinoco

The 2,575-km-long Orinoco River rises in the southern mountains of Guyana and at first flows westwards. It then forks into two branches.

The southern Casiquiare joins the Amazon system and the northern branch continues north as the Orinoco, running along the base of Guyana's mountains.

After the absorption of numerous tributaries springing up in the Cordilleras, such as the Meta and Guaviare, the Orinoco turns east and eventually creates a 30,000 sq. km delta from which it drains into the Atlantic Ocean.

course of time. They are punctured with fissures and crevasses.

Gran Sabana

The **Gran Sabana** is a treeless grassy expanse consisting of flat sandstone table mountains on average more than 1,000 m high and rising to 1,400 m in places. It is overshadowed by steeply rising table mountains, including the 2,810-m-high **Mount Roraima**, the highest on earth, which has given its name to the sandstone rock that is found here.

At 2,994 m, the **Pico da Neblina**, whose northern slopes are shared by Brazil and Venezuela and whose southern slopes are in Brazil, are part of the Neblina National Park. Together with the neighbouring Parima-Tapirapeco National Park in Venezuela and the **Canaima** National Park, they form a protected area of about 80,000 sq. km, probably the largest protected tropical rainforest in the world. The sandstone plateaus of the interior are typical savannah landscapes.

Amazon Basin

About 600 million years ago, the **Amazon Basin** was a bay open to the west towards the primaeval Pacific Ocean. After the Andes folded in the Tertiary era, the route to the sea was blocked and the region gradually transformed itself into an enormous inland lake. It was not until the Quaternary Period that the waters were able to break through, this time to the Atlantic Ocean.

At 4 million sq. km, the Amazon lowland is the largest tropical forest on earth (the Brazilians call it **Selvas** 'the woods'). But the highly sensitive ecological system is under threat. The massive deforestation of the jungle to clear land for agricultural use and the associated destruction of countless plant and animal species has become a problem of global importance, transcending all national boundaries.

Brazilian Highlands

North-eastern Brazil is typified by very varied forms of landscape. The coastal plain is between 40 and 60 km wide and was created in the Tertiary Era. Then the land rises inland to a plateau up to

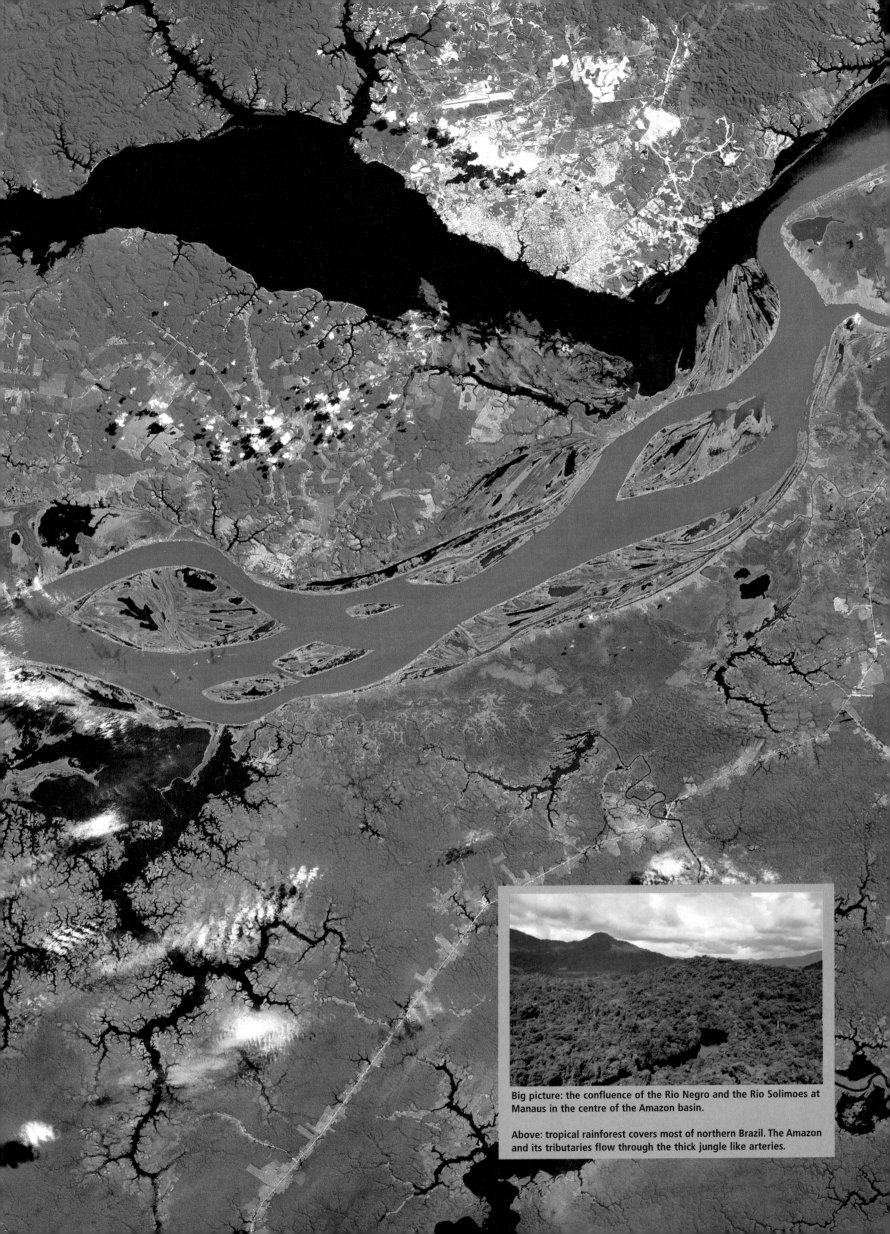

Big picture: the confluence of the Rio Negro and the Rio Solimoes at Manaus in the centre of the Amazon basin.

Above: tropical rainforest covers most of northern Brazil. The Amazon and its tributaries flow through the thick jungle like arteries.

*The volcanic **Galapagos Islands** lie out in the Pacific Ocean 1,000 km from the South American mainland to which they have never been connected. The resulting unique development of the islands' flora and fauna have made them world-famous. The landscape is typical of a volcanic island with lava formations, tufa and cinder cones dominating the bizarre crater landscape with its sparse ground cover. Tourism is heavily restricted to preserve the environment.*

300 m in height, consisting of uniformly ancient sedimentary rock, which in the west has become exposed again after the ablation of more recent rock.

In the interior and in the east these more recent sedimentary deposits have still largely been preserved. Further inland there is a table land up to 800 m high, in which sandstone plateaus have survived from the formerly underground Palaeozoic and Mesozoic sedimentary rock cover.

In the west, the land is only about 150 m above sea level. There are many isolated mountains consisting of gneiss and granite. Particularly fascinating landscape features are the weathered granite rocks and quartzite reefs of the **São Francisco valley**.

In north-western Brazil, the upper strata have not been able to withstand erosion. Remnants are found only in the low sandstone plateaus of the **Serra do Cachimbo** and the **Serra dos Caiabis**.

To the south and east, the area is bordered by the **Chapada dos**

Paraná

The Paraná river emerges through the confluence of the Rio Paranaíba and the Rio Grande in the Brazilian Highlands. In its upper reaches, the river has many waterfalls. After the absorption of the Paraguay River, the Paraná flows southwards as a wide lowland river. Near Rosario it branches into several arms and expands into a wide, swampy delta. North of Buenos Aires it absorbs the Uruguay river to become the Río de la Plata, a mighty, 50 km to 200-km-wide estuary that drains into the Atlantic. The Paraná and its tributaries carry vast amounts of sediment. It is so silted up that it is only navigable if a path is first dredged for the boat.

Parecis, the **Mato Grosso** and the **Serra do Roncador**.

Brazilian Uplands

The largest enclosed area of natural landscape in South America, of which there is about 6 million sq. km, is the Brazilian Uplands, the **Planalto**, which gradually rises out of the Amazon basin. The **Brazilian Uplands** is

on average about 500–1,000 m high, but to the south and east it rises to almost 3,000 m. The highest elevation is the 2,890-m-high **Pico da Bandeira**. This is followed by the 2,787 m **Pico das Agulhas Negras** and the **Pico de Itambé**, which, with its 2,033 m, only just exceeds the 2,000 m boundary.

In the west, the mountainous land of Brazil is bordered by the lowlands of the **Pampas** and the **Gran Chaco**, in the east it drops steeply, often by up to 100 m, in the **Serra do Mar** to the Atlantic, leaving room for only a narrow strip of flat coastline.

This is the site of one of the world's most famous beaches, the **Copacabana** in Rio de Janeiro with its beautiful backdrop, Sugar Loaf mountain.

The **Planalto** consists of a crystalline base, which is largely composed of gneiss, mica shale and quartzite. This massif is very old in terms of earth history and is part of the primaeval South American continent. Ablation and weathering on the Atlantic coast as well as erosion by tributaries of the Amazon have once again exposed this bedrock.

In other areas of the mountainous country, the Palaeozoic and Mesozoic strata have resisted erosion. The varying degrees of weathering in these younger layers, consisting of sandstone, limestone and basalt, are responsible for the variety of the landscapes.

A fascinating natural spectacle can be seen in the south-east of the mountainous country. Only a few kilometres from its estuary in the **Paraná**, the **Iguaçu** tumbles over a broad horseshoe-shaped fracture some 2,700 m wide, into a gorge approximately 80 m deep. This awesome sight is accompanied by the clouds of spray, shimmering in all the colours of the rainbow that are thrown up by the rushing waters.

Mato Grosso

The **Mato Grosso** is a very old, severely eroded mountain range, which covers most of the Brazilian state after which it is named. To the west, it borders the **Serra dos Parecis** and to the south it merges with the flooded savannahs of the **Pantanal**.

The Mato Grosso plateau, which attains an average height of about 600 m, forms the border between the Amazon basin in the north and the Paraguay basin in the south.

While the very sparsely populated highland in the north of the Mato Grosso contains primaeval forests from which rubber is harvested, in the south and east the vegetation consists mainly of grass and tree savannahs. This region is rich agricultural land, where cereals, cotton, tobacco and coffee are cultivated, and there is also cattle-ranching.

The Andes

The **Andes Cordillera** extends some 7,500 km from the Caribbean coast as far as the southernmost tip of the South American continent. This mountain range is between 200 km and 800 km wide. This mountain range piled up when the South American continental plate moved over the Pacific plate. The seismic activity continues as the massif continues to uplift. Earthquakes and volcanic eruptions are evidence of today's continuing plate movements.

Planalto: the Iguaçu Falls, on a tributary of the Paraná.

The **southern Andes** is a narrow high mountain range, which in the **Tierra del Fuego** reaches a height of about 1,500 m, soon rising to 3,500 m. In central Chile and western Argentina, it towers to more than 5,000 m.

This area contains **Aconcagua**. This extinct volcano, at a height of 6,963 m) is not only the highest mountain in the Andes but also the highest in both South and North America.

The Central Andes begins at the **Atacama desert** in Chile. Between the West and East Cordilleras lies the **Altiplano**, containing both the famous mountain lakes, **Titicaca** and **Poopó**. Several mountains over 6,000 m in altitude are part of the Central Cordilleras, including the **Sajama** (6,520 m), **Ausangate** (6,384 m) and, rising east of Lake Titicaca, **Illampu** (6,362 m).

The whole area is highly important in terms of cultural history. The ruins of the 'forgotten city' of Machu Picchu contain significant vestiges of the Inca culture. This city, which is difficult to access even today, escaped destruction by the Spanish conquistadors because of its remoteness. In 1911, the area was rediscovered and made accessible to the public.

In northern Peru, the Andes become noticeably lower and the **North Andes** begin, whose two main chains again reach 6,310 m in Ecuador. Ecuador also includes the rumbling **Cotopaxi**, the

most active volcano on earth, which reaches a height (currently) of 5,897 m. Its apparently perfectly formed cone is actually composed of an older and a younger volcano. Cotopaxi, beneath which hot magma presses close to the earth's surface, is snowcovered all year round. The last eruption of the volcano took place in 1928. Fortunately, the inhabitants of the region did not suffer much from its eruption, but if Mount St. Helen's,

in North America, is anything to go by, that may not be the case in the future. Near the state border between Ecuador and Colombia, at the **Nudo de Pasto**, the Andes divide into three main parallel chains, of which the Central Cordillera again rises to 5,750 m (**Nevado del Huila**), but then gradually declines, as do the West and East Cordilleras.

With the **Cordillera of Mérida**, an area of foothills of the East Cordillera, the Andes continue as far as Venezuela, where they reach their most northerly point.

Atacama Desert

A large desert has formed on the western edge of northern Chile, due to the absence of rainfall. The land is buried under ablation rubble of the **Puna** or Altiplano. The surface of the **Atacama** is covered in salt crusts, the so-called 'salares', gravel and stony detritus. The Atacama is the driest and most inhospitable desert on earth, having no oases or any

Paraguay

The Rio Paraguay rises in the Mato Grosso mountains and flows in its upper reaches through the 100,000 sq. km wide alluvial soil of Pantanal. On its way south, it constitutes the borders of the country of Paraguay – which was named after it – with Brazil and Argentina. The river crosses the Gran Chaco and flows into the Paraná river as its main tributary, near the city of Corrientes. The total length of the Paraguay River is 2,550 km. The most important tributaries are the São Lourenço, entering from the east and the Pilcomayo and Bermejo tributaries entering from the west.

underground source of water. The extremely low rainfall and the dramatic difference between day and night temperatures mean that the desert is virtually devoid of vegetation.

Lake Titicaca

The 8,300-sq. km-wide **Lake Titicaca** is the largest highland lake on earth, 3,812 m above sea level in the heart of the Andes between Peru and Bolivia. Since navigation

Some 60 km away from the Ecuadorian capital Quito, Cotopaxi, at 5,897 m the highest active volcano in the world, is surrounded by the Cotopaxi Nature Reserve. The distinctive cone-shape of the summit is covered with snow and ice above 4,000 m. The volcanic activity on Cotopaxi, which last erupted in 1928, is caused by the collision between the Oceanic and Continental Plates.

is possible on the lake, it is also considered to be the highest navigable waterway in the world. Lake Titicaca is 190 km long, an average of 50 km wide, and up to 281 m deep. On its eastern shore it is overshadowed by the peak of the 6,362-m-high **Illampu**. More than twenty rivers flow into this glacial lake. Depending on precipitation and glacier melt, these convey variable amounts of water at different seasons. The lake is drained by the **Rio Desaguatheo** which itself drains into **Lake Poopó**, which has no outlet.

Lake Titicaca has a very irregular shape and contains 33 islands and several peninsulas. In the mythology of the local Uru Native Americans, the **Isla del Sol** in the middle of the lake plays a significant role. They believe that 'Sun Island' is the birthplace of the Sun and traditional festivals are held here.

Lago Chucuito in the north is linked to **Lago Huinaymarca** in the south by the 80-m-deep Straits of Tiquina, thus making both lakes navigable. Although Huinaymarca has a distinctly brackish taste, it is considered to be a freshwater lake, but the waters are said to have health-giving properties.

Altiplano

The **Altiplano** is a highland at an altitude of 3,600 m to 4,200 m between the West and East Cordilleras and forms the western part of the **Puna block**.

This high plain, with no outlet, is some 700 km long and up to 200 km wide, and is covered only with sparse vegetation. The indigenous Aymarás provide themselves with all they need by the cultivation of potatoes, maize and barley. Sheep and chickens supply meat, milk and eggs. They produce wool from the fleece of llamas, so they are completely self-sufficient. Since the Quaternary Era, a number of 100-m-high layers of rubble have overlaid the ancient **boulders**. Mountain ranges running from north to south divide the Altiplano into individual basin landscapes. The dry steppes of the southern part of the region contain large salt-pans such as the **Salar de Uyuni**.

Cordillera Blanca

To the north of Lima, the Santa Valley separates the West Cordillera of the Andes into two parallel mountain ranges, the **Cordillera Negra** and the **Cordillera Blanca**. The Cordillera Blanca acquired its name from its many towering peaks covered in snow. One of these is **Huascarán**, at 6,768 m the highest mountain in the Peruvian Andes.

This folded mountain range came into existence in the Late Tertiary Era, but the process of uplift has still not been completed. The relief of the Cordillera Blanca was drastically reshaped in the Ice Age. Moraines, cirques and trough valleys are evidence of the power of the mighty ice sheets which poured down the west flank especially on the high mountain range.

Terminal moraines dammed up the smaller lakes. Particularly impressive are the deep trough valleys at a height of around 4,000 m, such as the **Quebrada Santa Cruz** and the **Quebrada Honda**. This inhospitable region has not attracted human habitation; only in the fertile **Santa valley** have a few villages and settlements sprung up.

Gran Chaco

The **Gran Chaco** is a high plateau, some 800,000 sq. km wide, which extends over the territory of Paraguay and Argentina between Paraná in the east and the Andes in the west. The Gran Chaco lies at a height of 100 m to 400 m. The **Chaco Boreal** in the north is succeeded by the **Chaco Central** and further south, the **Chaco Austral**. The Chaco Boreal consists of sand and clay sediment, which forms an uneven plain that tilts upwards in the west.

1 The Andes: in the East, the highlands are edged with numerous cordilleras of different heights. The Cordillera Vilcabamba near Cuzco is one of the smaller peaks.

2 Lake Titicaca, highest lake in the world. Like Lake Poopó, it is a glacial lake of a type that can be found throughout the Andean highlands.

3 Isla Pescado, Bolivia: several salt lakes, swamps and deserts were formed in the southern part of the Andean highlands. Due to evaporation these mostly sink lakes with no outlets become clogged with evaporite minerals and eventually dry out.

4 The Salar de Uyuni, almost 3,700 m above sea level, is the largest of the many salt-pans of the Altiplano. Another problem of glacial lakes is that they turn brackish over time.

Big picture: a section of the Western Cordillera in the heart of the Andes, between Chile and Bolivia. Almost all the numerous strato volcanoes are covered with snow and echo the north-south course of the Western Cordillera. The dazzling white areas are salt lakes (salare), an indicator of the aridity of the area. The largest is the Salar de Ascotán. The mountain peaks drop down to the Altiplano (high plain).

Above: Cerro Torre (3,128 m) in Patagonia's Fitzroy Massif.

The Andes

The Andes Cordillera is the longest chain of mountains in the world, extending over the entire western coastal area of the South American continent. In almost every case several 'partial Cordilleras' run parallel to each other. In the border triangle of Peru, Bolivia and Chile, the mountains cover an area extending more than 700 km.

The Andes Cordillera extends in several chains through the entire length of South America, covering over 7,500 km from the Caribbean Sea in the north to Cape Horn at the southern tip of the continent. Here, the mountain range breaks up into countless small islands.

The Southern Andes consists of a narrow, high mountain range, rising in Tierra del Fuego to 1,500 m; further north the peaks reach 3,000 to 5,000 m in central Chile and western Argentina. This part of the range contains Aconcagua (6,960 m), the highest mountain in the Andes and in the whole American continent. From a latitude of 27° S, the mountains expand into the Central Andes.

Between the West and East Cordilleras lies the Altiplano with its salt lakes and huge freshwater lakes such as Poopó and Titicaca. North-west of Lake Titicaca, the two

chains approach each other again. In the north Peruvian gap, at 5° S, the high ranges flatten out and become narrower. Here, the North Andes begins, dividing in Ecuador into two main chains up to 6,310 m high. Of the three main chains in Colombia, the middle one rises to 5,000 m. The Cordillera of Mérida, the foothills of the Eastern Cordillera, extend into Venezuela.

The Andes came into being through a series of geological processes. The basins of the Mesozoic were filled with deposits from primaeval rivers, which resulted in the formation of a huge mass of strata several kilometres thick. The shifting of the South American Continental Plate and the Oceanic Nazca Plate, in the course of several successive folding periods, caused the original rock to melt and transform under pressure. Erosion finally caused a considerable reduction in

height and the formation of further deposits. The severely broken-down relief forms took shape in the early Pliocene. The shape continued to develop during the Quaternary Era through volcanism and, in the south, volcanoes emerged from beneath the Ice Age glaciers.

The Andes offers a wide variety of landscape. The Altiplano, for example, is a basin landscape at an altitude of 4,000 m. Encircled by high mountains, the Puna is a desert highland dating from the Tertiary era. The basins of the Puna, at up to 4,200 m, are often covered by a salt crust and at deeper points filled with a salty swamp. At the western edge of the Puna is a concentration of younger volcanoes such as the Llullaillaco (6,739 m) and the Ojos del Salado (6,887 m).

The extremely inhospitable Atacama desert turns into a semi-desert in the Altiplano, covered with sparse grassland and cactus.

The high peaks of the Central Cordillera are covered with snow. The melted snow and ice irrigates the agricultural land in the valleys. The snowline above Mendoza in

Argentina starts at 4,500 m, but is lower further south. In Patagonia the Ice Age has left clear traces behind. Heights here hardly reach 4,000 m, but glaciation increases. The mountains on the Pacific coast were formed in the Quaternary by huge icebergs. These cut deep fjords into the land and heaped up moraine banks, behind which huge lakes such as Buenos Aires and Argentino filled up. The glaciers in the 6,000-sq.-km Argentinian Los Glaciares National Park form the largest continuous glacial surface north of the Antarctic.

Among the Andes' most impressive landscapes is the Cordillera Blanca with its rugged giant mountains, glaciers, moraines and glacier lakes and the impressive double peak of Huascarán (6,768 m).

The Andes in Ecuador are strongly volcanic. The heavily glaciated Cotopaxi (5,897 m) is the highest active volcano on Earth.

The great heights and extent of the Andes make this mountain range the greatest climatic borderline on Earth. While the trade winds supply the eastern foothills with high

precipitation, large areas of the range's lee side are very arid.

Agricultural land is rare in the Andes, so the small areas of fertile land on the slopes are terraced to enable the cultivation of grain, vegetables, fruit and tobacco. The extreme altitude determines what crops can be grown. In the valleys, tropical fruits, rice and cotton are grown; the middle slopes are used for cultivating sugar cane, coffee and tobacco. At higher altitudes, winter wheat and potatoes are grown. The high pastures are also used for grazing cattle. The local Quechua population keeps herds of native llama and vicuña. The llamas are used as pack animals and vicuña wool is highly prized, both in its natural state and woven into cloth and vicuña blankets.

Big picture: the 6,400-m-high Parinacota volcano lies in the Chilean Lauca National Park.

Inset: The 3,000-m-high, steep granite rocks dominate the Torres del Paine in the south of Chile.

The San Valentin glacier in Chile, surrounding the San Rafael Lake, transports ancient blocks of ice on its way to the sea. The giant San Rafael glacier, stretches from the Patagonian inland to the Chilean coast.

A few isolated elevations occasionally interrupt the monotony of the featureless landscape. The slight variations in the relief can only be recognised in the rainy season, when the hollows fill up with water and the higher ridges stand out like islands above the flooded plain.

The dry forests are succeeded in the west by thornbush and dry steppes. There are isolated grassy areas, whose meandering forms show that they are, in fact, the beds of ancient rivers that once flowed through here.

In the Argentinian section of the Gran Chaco, unlike the Chaco Boreal, the land is much more fertile. About a third of the land is covered with forest, and between the forests there are areas of open meadowland containing a few isolated trees.

The region's sub-tropical climate results in very hot summers, and in the rainy season large areas are flooded. The main rivers that run through the Gran Chaco are the

landscape, but in fact it is only an oval sunken area of the same terrain. In the rainy season, the 20- to 40-km-wide depression is largely submerged. Swamps, lakes and meandering rivers ensure a varied landscape.

The banks of the **Paraguay** river, which flows through the Pantanal, are covered with rainforest which flourishes in the damp, humid climate.

In the dry season, which lasts as a rule from October to April, the plateaus that adjoin the river are used by farmers from the lowlands as rich pasture in which to fatten their livestock.

Bolivian Lowlands

From the eastern slopes of the Andes the extensive **Bolivian lowlands** change from the humid and hot Amazon basin in the north to the hot arid scrub of the Gran Chaco. This hilly and completely

steppes mark the gradual transition to the **Chaco boreal** in the south. The main rivers are the 1,800-km-long **Rio Mamoré** and the 1,700-km-long Rio Beni, which combine to form the **Rio Madeira**.

The Pampas

The **Pampas** consist of a gigantic plain which stretches between the 30th and 37th southern parallels. To the west it begins at some 500 m at the foot of the Andes, and extends as far as the Atlantic in the east. In the north it gradually changes into the **Gran Chaco** and is bordered in the south by the **Patagonian tableland**. To the east, the Pampas are framed by the heights of the **Brazilian** highlands, while in the west they are dominated by the mighty **Andes**.

The Pampas are part of the central Argentinian lowlands, a geologically relatively young deposit area dating from the Quaternary

wide grain fields and extensive cattle pastures.

The cattle grazing on the Pampas, consisting of herds of Aberdeen Angus and Herefords, have become famous for the delicacy of their flesh. Alfalfa or lucerne, which is grown here and used for animal fodder, also contributes to the flavour of the world-famous Argentinian beefsteaks.

The central and south-eastern region also contains grazing land for cattle herds but the grassy meadows are considerably drier and much less cultivated than those of Europe and North America, so that this area preserves its original wild appearance to a much greater extent.

Patagonia

In the south, the Pampas gradually changes into the **Patagonian tableland**. In the barrel-shaped valley of the Río Negro, crops are

then, as now, exposed to masses of humid air that formed over the Pacific Ocean and then fell as rain over the western slopes of the Cordilleras.

As the glaciers melted, sea water penetrated the valleys, producing a maze of islands and fjords, unique in both the northern and the southern hemisphere.

The huge fjords, up to 1,200 m deep, divide the Andes along the Pacific coast into several ranges, which run parallel to the chains of the Cordilleras. In addition, a dense system of sea channels run at a ninety-degree angle, tracing the oblique course of the original fault lines.

Violent storms rage constantly in the **fjord** areas, and it rains daily, the precipitation being very violent and ice-cold. The Cordilleras here are some 4,000 m high and their countless glaciers often extend far out into the sea.

A breathtaking natural spectacle can be observed in the fjords when, with a mighty roar, amplified by

Patagonia: the mighty Perito Moreno glacier in Los Glaciares National Park.

Pilcomayo, Bermejo and Rio Salado, which contribute only a small part of their waters to the Paraguay river.

Pantanal

The **Pantanal**, one of the planet's most spectacular wetland systems. is a flood plain more than 100,000 sq. km wide covering upper Paraguay, Bolivia and Brazil. Geologists include the Pantanal in the **Brazilian uplands**, since in terms of earth history the plain is part of the same region. It differs from the mountainous area in its

featureless expanse is covered with rich vegetation, in stark contrast to the sparse highlands. In the north, there are extensive rainforests, which change towards the south into open woodland.

Adjacent to these are the grassy savannahs of the **Llanos del Mamoré**. This alluvial area also contains gallery woods and forest islands, the so-called 'montes'.

The **mountain country of Chiquitos**, which rises to an altitude of 1,400 m, is succeeded by a large swamp, which covers the flood plain of the low-lying **Paraguay** river. Dry forests and thornbush

Era, to which **Mesopotamia** and the Gran Chaco also belong.

The original landscape of the Pampas was determined by a treeless grass steppe, but in earlier times the plain may have been covered with forests.

The human race has radically altered the face of the Pampas, for the fertile steppe soil, similar to the black earth of the Ukraine, is admirably suitable as an area for agricultural use and immigrants to the region have created an extensive cultivated area. Today the region, particularly the damp eastern Pampas, is characterised by

grown in a fertile 10 to 15-km-wide strip, where the land resembles that of the Pampas. South of the **Río Negro**, however, the landscape changes dramatically. Bitter, whirling winds, huge glaciers and icy torrential downpours such as are hardly to be met elsewhere, have created a landscape unlike any other on earth.

In the Pleistocene, huge ice sheets covered vast areas of the continent. The icy streams that flowed from the high mountains down to the Pacific cut deep trough valleys through the mountains. The **glaciers** on the Pacific side were

echoes, huge masses of ice burst from the glacier tongues and crash into the water.

The eastern side of the **Cordilleras** are much less exposed to the force of the winds. In the lowlying, sheltered areas, forests are able to flourish, but towards the east the winds again gain strength and only a monotonous dry steppe landscape is able to withstand them. In the Pleistocene Era the glaciers, noticeably smaller than those in the western half, carved depressions into the mountainous landscape , which remained as lakes after the ice had melted.

The beach of South Georgia, one of the Falkland islands. These islands, known in Spanish as the Malvinas, lie some 500 km off the South American coast. The main islands, West and East Falklands, are separated by the Falkland Sound. The landscape, whose sparse vegetation is only suitable for sheep-grazing, is mainly hilly. On both islands, the highest mountains rise 700 m above sea level.

These include the **Lago Argentino**, **Lago Nahuel Huapi** and **Lago Buenos Aires**.

An impressive spectacle can be observed at Lago Argentino. The enormous **Moreno glacier** shifts every couple of years to this lake in south-western Patagonia, where it forms a huge ice barrier, which can rise up to 60 m high. When the build-up of water finally bursts through the barrier, the ice smashes apart with a tremendous crash.

The stratified area slopes down in marked gradations to the Atlantic. The crystalline bedrock that was swept over it in the Ice Age is covered by low-lying sedimentary formations, tufa and layers of black basalt.

The surface has been shaped by river water into countless small **mesas** (table formations) and is strewn with the so-called Patagonian detritus, consisting of pebbles about the size of hens' eggs. The highest mountains of the Patagonian Cordilleras are the towering **San Valentín** at 4,058 m and the **San Lorenzo** at 3,706 m.

Tierra del Fuego

The sheltered east side of the Cordilleras was deeply affected by Pleistocene glaciers. The depressions created by these glaciers filled with water after the Pleistocene Era. One such water-filled sink is the **Straits of Magellan**, named after its Portuguese discoverer, Ferdinand Magellan. When Magellan sailed through the Straits in 1520, a stretch of water some 583 km long, between the Pacific and the Atlantic, he saw a number of small fires burning on the port side of the ship. He named the land on which they were burning **Tierra del Fuego** – land of fire. Tierra del Fuego has a total area of 73,746 sq. km. The rugged inhospitable landscape of **Patagonia** continues on the main island and the many smaller islands off shore. Since they experienced the same geological processes, the tableland is structured in the same way and **fjords** and straits offer the same natural spectacles.

In Tierra del Fuego, the Cordilleras are much lower, reaching a maximum height in **Cerro Yogan** of only 2,469 m. The ice sheets break up only gradually. The glaciated peaks, which tower over the fjords like gigantic icebergs, are

a magnificent sight. The climate here ranges from chilly to temperate, with an annual average temperature of only 5.5°C, and storms occur frequently.

Falkland Islands

The **Falkland Islands** lie 770 km north-east of Cape Horn in the South Atlantic. This island group, known in Spanish as the **Islas Malvinas**, because they were originally discovered by sailors from St. Malo in Britanny, consists of two main islands and almost 200 smaller islands. East Falkland has an area of 6,760 sq. km; West Falkland is 5,280 sq. km in area.

The stony landscape consists of treeless grassland without any notable stretches of water, extending over a hilly tableland, interspersed with stratified mountainous ridges.

The intensive sheep-rearing carried out by the settlers during the last 150 years has almost totally destroyed the native vegetation, which originally consisted of tussock grass, heather and peat moorland.

The South Sandwich Islands and South Georgia in Antarctica are included among the Falkland Islands for political purposes. All are British crown colonies. The capital of the Falkland Islands is Port Stanley. The Falkland Islanders are almost exclusively of British descent.

It is likely that valuable deposits of mineral ores and even petroleum may lie beneath the British territorial waters off the Falkland Islands, but there has been no confirmation of any finds. This is one reason that the sovereignty of the Islands is hotly disputed.

1 Smoke issuing from the Caldera of the 2,840-m-high Villarrica Volcano at Lake Villarrica. Like other smaller volcanos at the southern tip of the South American Cordilleras, it is considered to be extinct.

2 The Atacama Desert lies on the coast between Chile and Peru. It is considered to be the driest in the world. The landscape is dominated by sedimentary strata at different stages of erosion.

3 Northern Patagonia is the foothills of the Pampas. It is a steppe-like dry zone, covered in stunted trees, shrubs and grass.

The climate is inhospitable and it is not suitable for farming.

4 Patagonia, Los Glaciares National Park: the mighty glaciers slide slowly down into the valley, gradually revealing the stark outline of Mount Fitzroy (3,375 m) and the other peaks behind them.

Ga · 78° · Gb · 76° · Gc · 250 · 74° · Gd · 72° · Ge

C A R I B B E A N   S E A

Colombia

Basin

Isthmus of Panama

PANAMA

Gulf of Darién

Gulf of Panama

PACIFIC

OCEAN

Punta Gallinas · Taroa
Bahía Honda · Punta Estrella
Cabo de la Vela · Península de la Guajira · P.N.Macuira · Puerto Estrella
Puerto Bolívar · 853 · Península Paraguaná
Carizal · Puerto Lopez · Los Ta
Uribia · Ceira · Punto M
Manaure · Gulf of
Papurí · Venezuela
3718 · 4214
4220
1936

Riohacha · RCH
Los Flamencos · Pelechua · Palomino · Barbacoas
Cabo de la Aguja · P.N.Tayrona · Maicao · Punta M
Santa Marta · SMR · 2950 · Sierra Nevada · de Santa Marta
P.N.Isla de Salamanca · Ciudad Perdida · Fonseca · MAR · MARACAIBO
BARRANQUILLA · BAQ · Ciénaga · Pico Cristóbal Colón · San Juan · Villanueva · Los Pedales · Cabimas
Soledad · Baranoa · 5775 · del César · Rosario · Cabimas
Cangaru · Sta Cruz de Santa Marta · Campo Mara · Cerro Cerón
Sabanalarga · Valledupar · La Concepción · La Paz · 1990
Cartagena · CTG · Santa Catalina · Remolino · Aracataca · Atanquez · VUP · Robles La Paz · San Juan · Palmarejo · Santa Rita · Ciudad Ojeda · Lagunillas
San Felipe · Turbaco · Arjona · Salamina · Fundación · Pueblo Bello · Caracoli · Negrones · Barranquitas · Bachaquero
P.N.Corales del Rosario Isla Barú · Barú · San Estanislao · Plato · Grenada · Boscónia · Augustín · Cerro Teta · Calle Larga
y San Bernardo · Calamar · Zambrano · Codazzi · 3750 · El Batay · Mene Grande
Islas de San Bernardo · San Juan · El Carmen · La Jagua · P.N.Sierra de Perijá · Lago de · Aguachica
Punta de San Bernardo · Nepomuceno · 820 · Ariguani · Chiriguana · Río de Oro · Santa Rosa · Maracaibo · La Ceiba
Golfo de · Tolú · Ovejas · Chimichagua · 2610 · Puerto · 250
San Antero · Morrosquillo · Corozal · Santa Ana · Guamal · Catatumbo · Mene de Mauroa
Isla Fuerte · Sincé · Santa Cruz · El Banco · P.N.Catatumbo · Encontrados · Bobures · Trujillo
San Bernardo · Sincelejo · de Mompoxi · Margarita · Barrancas · Bari · Gallinazo · Guayabones · Valera
del Viento · Chinú · Caimito · de Loba · 2521 · Puerto Chama
Monitos · Lorica · Sahagún · San Benito Abad · Tamalameque · Tibú · Puerto Santander · Mérida · Barin
Puerto Escondido · Cereté · Sucre · Achí · La Mata · Tres Bocas · El Guayabo · El Vigía · MRD 4765 · Barin
Arboletes · MTR 336 · San Marcos · La Gloria · Convención · 3750 · Morotuto · Ejido · Pico Espejo · Pico Bolívar · 5007
San Juan de Urabá · Monteria · Planeta · Ayapel · Gamarra · Cerro Mina · OCV · Ocaña · Rubio · La Fría · Lagunillas · Santa Bárbara · Boca de Anar
Puerto Mulatos · Rica · Nechi · 2400 · Aguachica · Abrego · Sardinata · El Zulia · CUC · Pregonero · Tabay · Santa
Cabana · La Manta · Caucasia · Simiti · Pedregosa · Cúcuta · San Antonio · Capacho
Acandí · Turbo · Tierralta · Montelíbano · El Darién · Cáchira · SVZ · de Táchira · Santa Bárbara
Golfo de · TRB · 2000 · Puerto Triana · San Pablo · Chinacorta · 3865 · Santo Domingo · Mata de
Urabá · La Rica · Zaragoza · Alto de Tamar · Sabaneta · Rionegro · STD · San Antonio · Palma
Necoclé · P.N.Paramillo · 2350 · Puerto Wilches · California · Pamplona · El Piñal · de Caparo · El Cantón
Riosucio · Ituango · Segovia · Barrancabermeja · Girón · P.N.Páramos · El Nula · P.N.Río Viejo · Apur
Mutatá · 3400 · Peque · Yarumal · Chucuri · EJA · BGA · Berlín · La Victoria · El Amparo de A
Murindó · Paramillo · Amalfi · El Tigre · Bucaramanga · Piedecuesta · Cubara · El Troncal · Arauca
Dabeiba · 3960 · Carolina · Puerto · Lebrija · Cerrito · El Socorro
Cupica · P.N.Las · Sabanalarga · Berrío · San Vicente · Bánadia
Golfo de · Orquídeas · Santa Fe · Galán · Barichara · Málaga · Sierra Nevada · Tame · Santa Fe
Cupica · 4080 · Frontino · 3500 · San Gil · 5493 · Puerto Rondón
Punta Marzo · Bellavista · Sopetran · Cisneros · Socorro · Onzaga · Soata · P.N.El Cocuy · Hato Corozal
Urrao · MEDELLIN · Copacabana · Puerto · Muzo · Vélez · Santana · Chita · del Cocuy · Puerto
Puerto Arquia · Itagui · MDE · Granada · Olaya · Fuente · Barbosa · Duitama · Socota · Las Delicias
BSC · El Valle · Bebarama · Caldas · La Ceja · Cocorná · Cimitarra · Nacional · Belén · Paz del Río · Paz de
Playa Larga · Amagá · Santa Barbara · San Luis · Villa de Leyva · Paipa · Corrales · Aripuro · Pore
Parque Nacional Utria · Tribugá · Fredonia · 4050 · Sonson · 3350 · Arcabuco · Sogamoso · Labranza · El Pinal
Golfo de · 3200 · Aguadas · La Dorada · La Palma · Ráquira · Tunja · Boyaca · Grande
Tribugá · Coqui · UIB · Quibdó · Andes · Ríosucio · Salamina · Victoria · San Cayetano · Susa · Tibaná · Villapinzon · Toca · EYP · Yopal
Cabo Corrientes · Virudó · Cértegui · Apia · 3650 · Honda · Muzo · Ubate · Choconta · Miraflores · Trinidad
Memba · Istmina · P.N.Tatamá · Marsella · Libano · Armero · Guaduas · Pacho · Garagoa · Chameza
Punta Manglares · Novita · Cerro · MZL · Manizales · Nevado del Ruiz · Gachetá · Tauramena · Aguazul
Manglares · Nóvita · San José · Balboa · 4200 · 5225 · Cambao · Tocancipá · Sta María · Chizca · Orocue
Togoroma · Sipi · del Palmar · Chinchina · Mariquita · Albán · Zipaquirá · Sabanalarga · Mani
Buenaventura · Noanama · Pereira · Quimbaya · Nevado Tolima · Fontibon · BOG · Barranca de Upia
PEI · Cartago · La Mesa · Museo del Oro · Guateque · Patio Chiquito
Boca · Versalles · AXM · Armenia · Guatapé · La Poyata · Nuevo Mundo · Guacamayas
Caraugal · La Unión · Calarcá · Alvarado · BOGOTA · P.N. · La Rosita
Punta Magdalena · Zarzal · Sevilla · Buenos Aires · Ibagué · Tocaima · Suacha · Chingaza · Betania · Pto Gaitan
Dagua · Tuluá · Candelaria · 3930 · Girardot · Cáqueza · Cumaral · Paratebueno · Bengala
Buga · Chicoral · Espinal · Fúsagasugá · Fosca · Puerto López · Planas
C O L O M B I A · El Cerrito · Ortega · Saldaña · 1561 · Cabrera · Nazareth · VVC · Pto Porfia
Palmira · Riobланка · La Palmita · Coyaima · Guamo · Cunday · Villavicencio · Cumaribo
CLO · Florida · 4200 · Planadas · Purificación · Pandi · S. Martín · Casazinc · Caño las Viejitas
Verenal · Jamundí · Corinto · Dolores · Colombia · Granada · Carrozas · 220
CALI · Pto. Tejada · Caloto · Toribio · Baraya · La Uribe · S. Carlos · Mapiripán · Siare
Boca Candelaria · Isla Aji · Verenal · Timba · Mondomo · P.N.Nevado del Huila · 3520 · de Guaroa · Guaviare
Lopez · Toez · 5750 · NVA · Cerro · S. Juan · Candilejas · El Olvido · Siare Guajibos
P.N.Isla Gorgona · Isla Gorgona · Puerto Coco · Silvia · Palermo · Neiva · de Aráma · Guaní · Guayabero
Punta Reyes · Isla Soledad · P.N. · Teruel · Campo · P.N. · Pto. Arturo
GPI · Guapi · Parque Nacional · Piendamó · alegre · Serranía · S. José
Munchique · PPN · Río Blanco · Ricaute · Hobo · de la Macarena · del Guaviare
Punta Guascama · Mosquera · Popayán · El Tambo · Tesalia · 2615 · Inírida
Parque Nacional · 4800 · Vol Puracé · Pital · Laberinto · Gigante · Garzón · P.N. · Reserva
Sanquianga · Argelia · Resas · 4580 · La Argentina · Altamira · Guacamayas · Tinigua · Nacional
El Carmen · La Alianza · Vol Sotará · Pitalito · San Vicente · Natural
San Augustín · El Bordo (Patía) · La Vega · Lusitania · de Caguan · Nukak
Ensenada · Sanabria · El Estrecho · Puerto · Apaporis
de Tumaco · Pisanda · Santa Rosa · El Doncello · La Tunia · 870 · Pacuativa
Tumaco · TCO · Mercaderes · Bolívar · Florencia · Cartagena · Rdl. Chiribiquete · Tucunia
Terán · San Antonio · San Pablo · FLA · del Chaira · Dos Ríos · Pto. Silvania · Sta. Rosa
Cabo Manglares · Barbacoas · San José · Morelia · La Chaira
Isla Santa Rosa · Junin · (Albán) · La Florida · Yurayaco · Buenos Aires
La Tolita · Sotomayor · PSO · San Antonio de Getucha · Pto. Nare
San Lorenzo · (Los Andes) · Vol Galeras · Sibundoy · Puerto Limón · Solita · Mecaya
La Tola · Tobar · 4276 · Pasto · Mocoa · Tres Esquinas · Pto. Argentina · Sta. Rita · Cachiporro · Rdl. Yupurari
Limones · Donoso · Guachucal · Vol Cumbal · Túquerres · Ipiales · Valparaiso · Serranía de Chiribiquete · Rdl. Palitó
Bordón · Maldonado · Cumbal · IPI · TUA · Gualmatán · Monopamba · P.N. Chiribiquete
Montañas de Osa · TUQ · Orito · PUU · Puerto Asis
El Angel · San Gabriel

Ga · 78° · Gb · 76° · Gc · 268 · 74° · Gd · 72° · Ge

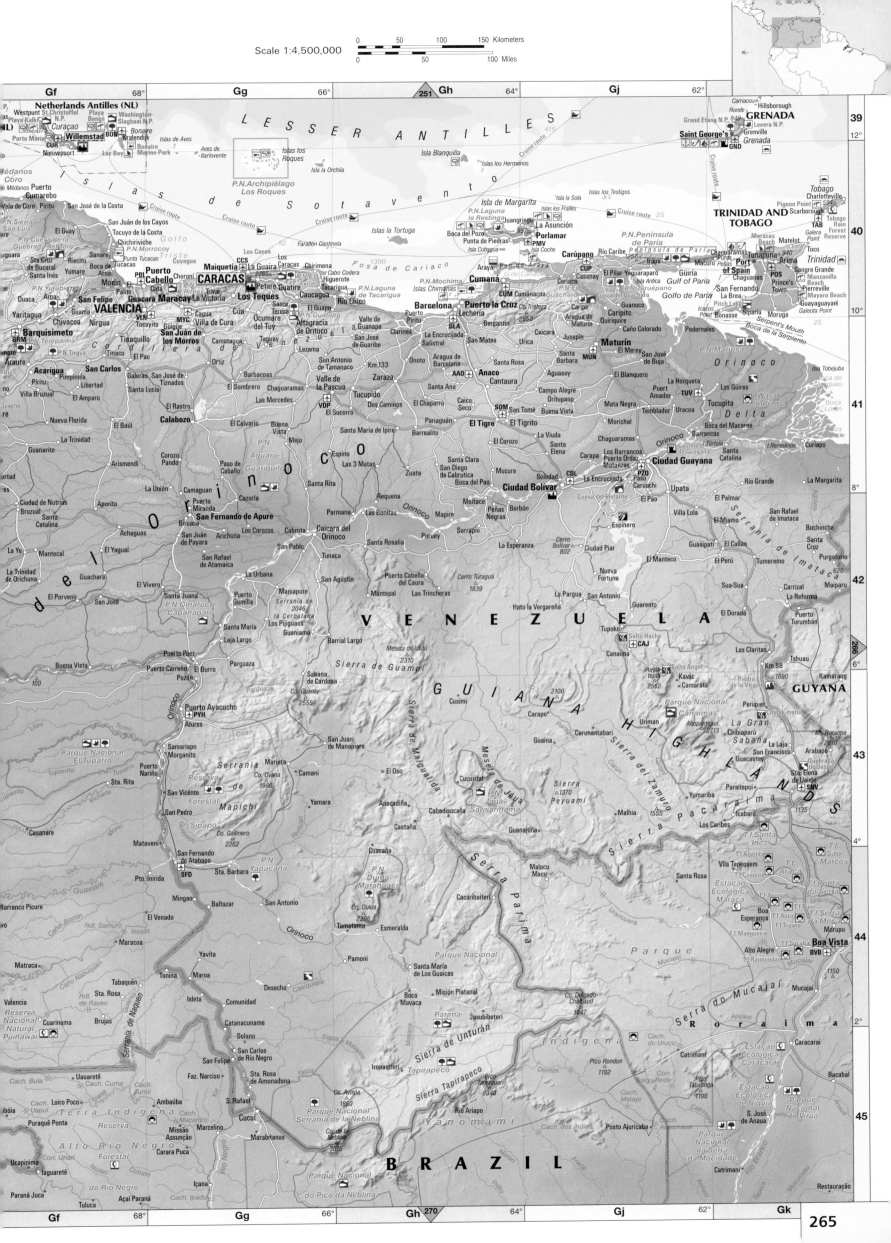

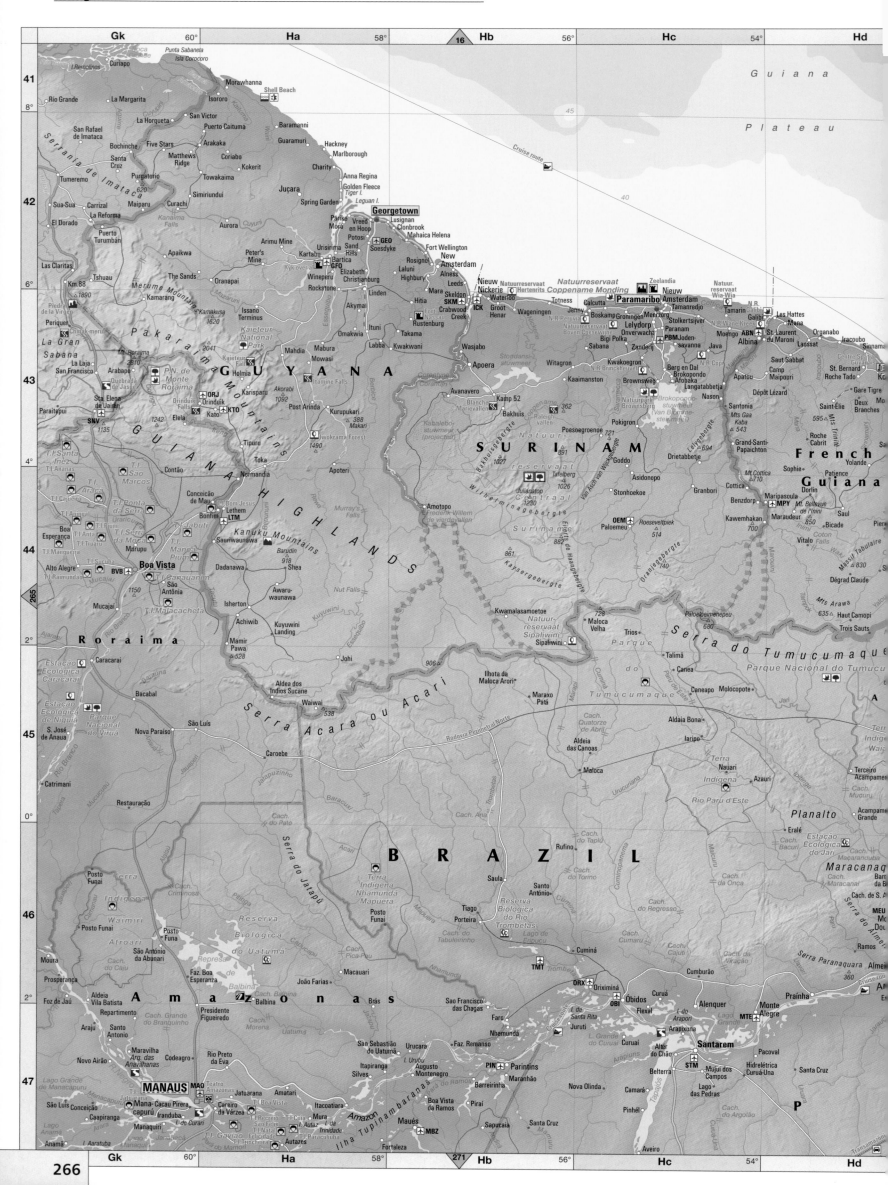

Guyana, Surinam, Mouths of the Amazon

Gk 60° Ha 58° Hb 56° Hc 54° Hd

41 8°

Guiana

Plateau

Cruise route

45

40

42 6°

GUYANA

Georgetown

Paramaribo

SURINAM

French Guiana

43 4°

GUIANA HIGHLANDS

Roraima

44 2°

Boa Vista

265

2°

Serra do Tumucumaque

Parque Nacional do Tumucumaque

45 0°

Serra Acara ou Acari

Planalto

BRAZIL

Maracana

46 2°

AMAZONAS

Amazonas

47

MANAUS

Santarem

Amazon

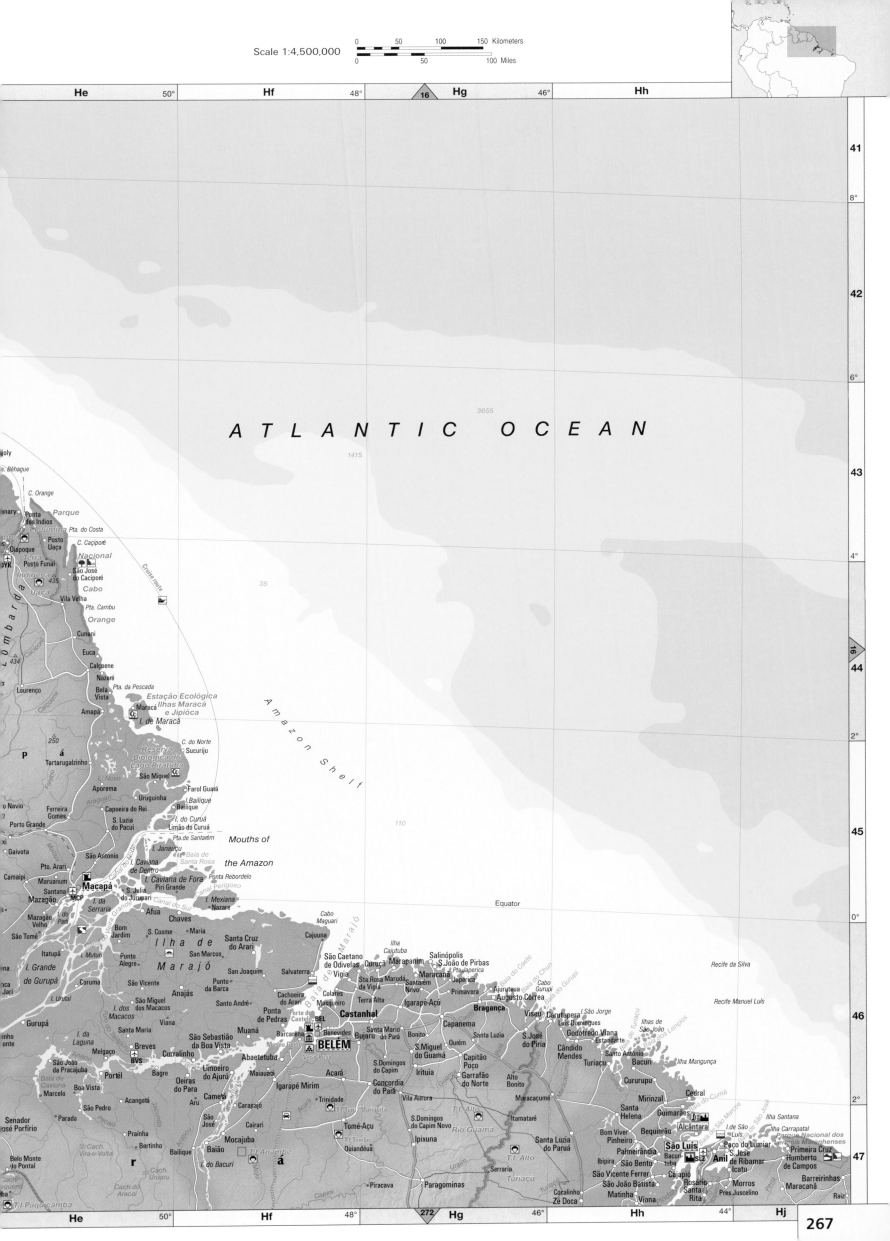

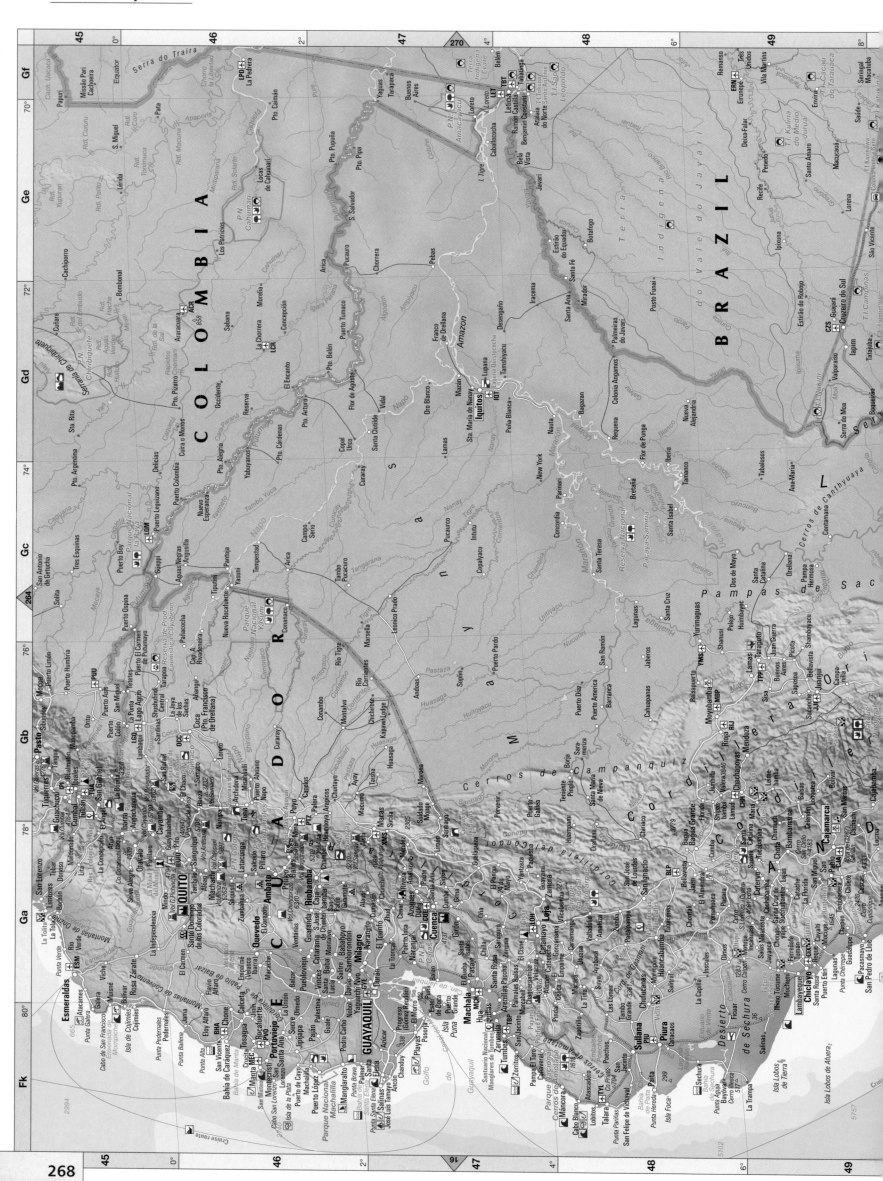

Amazon Lowlands

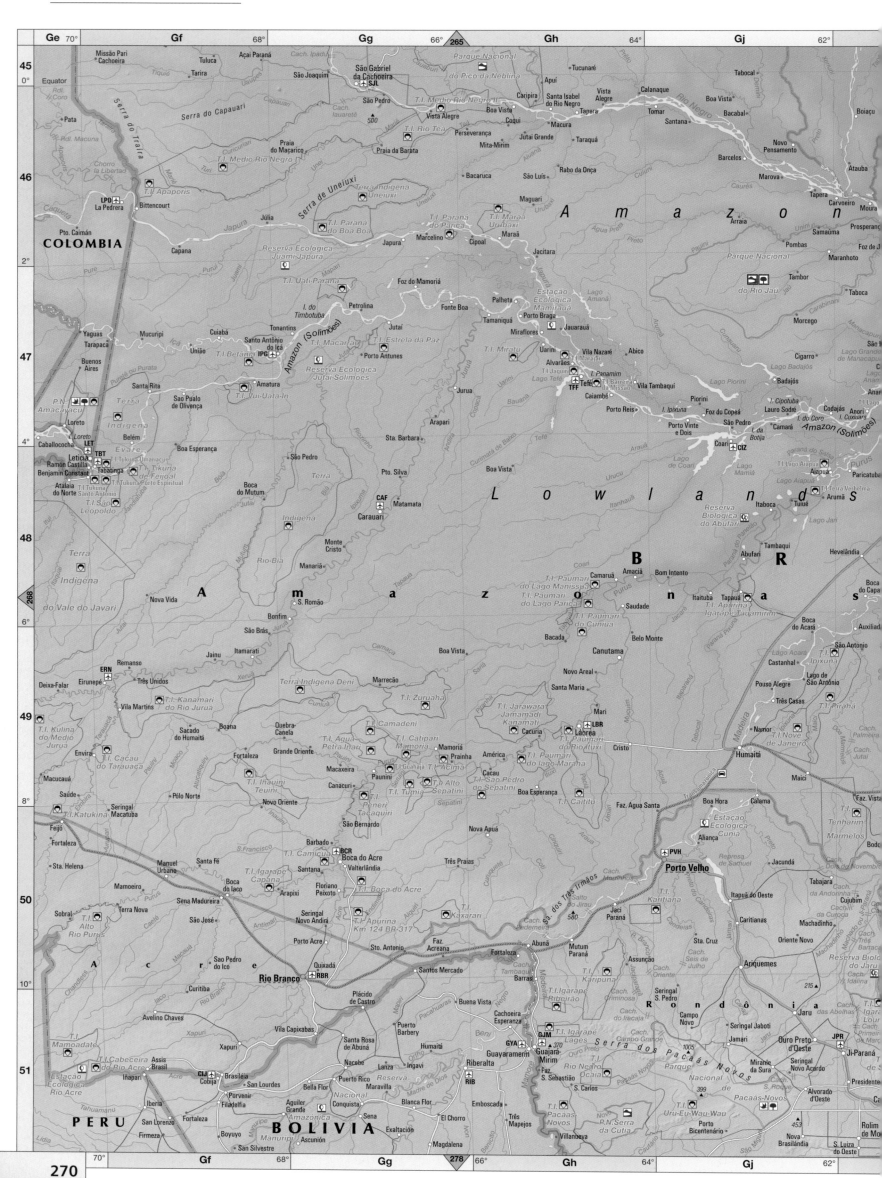

COLOMBIA

PERU

BOLIVIA

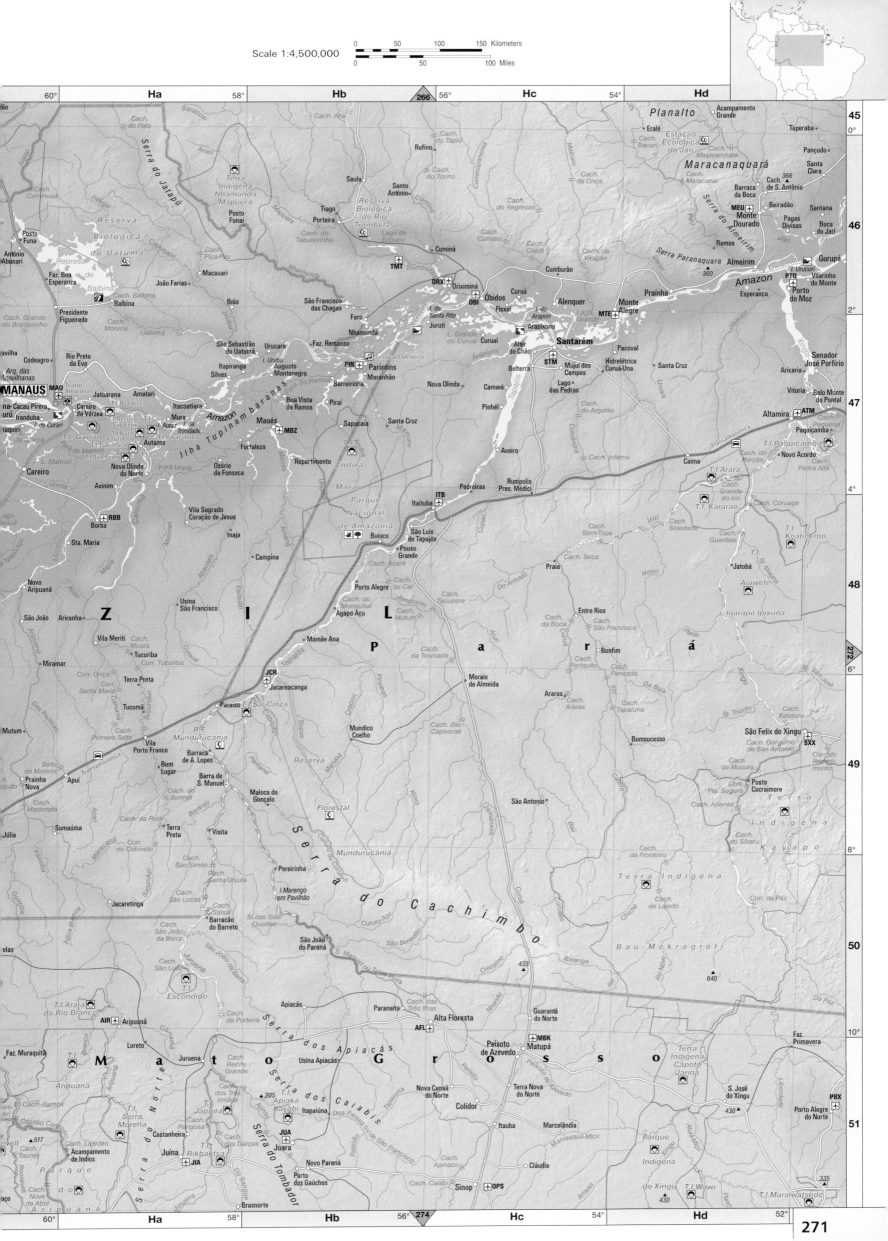

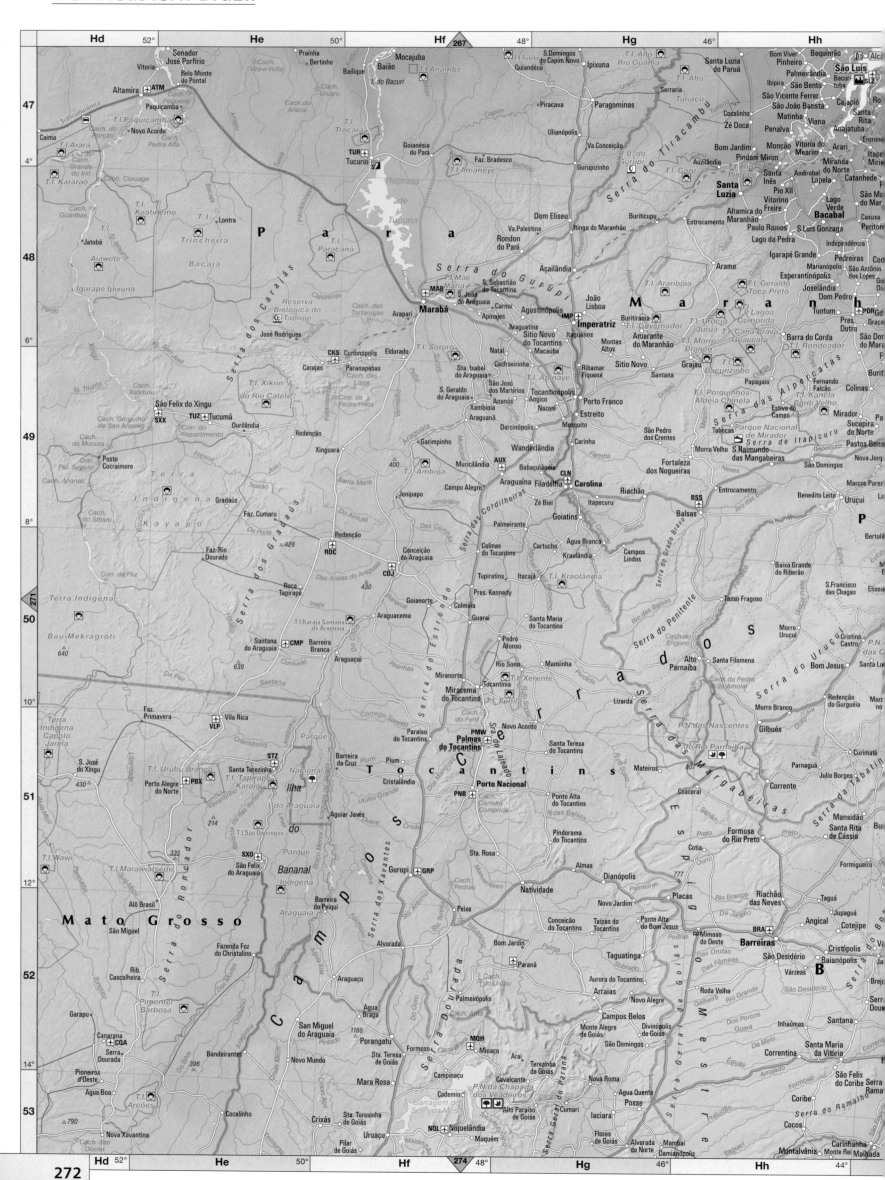

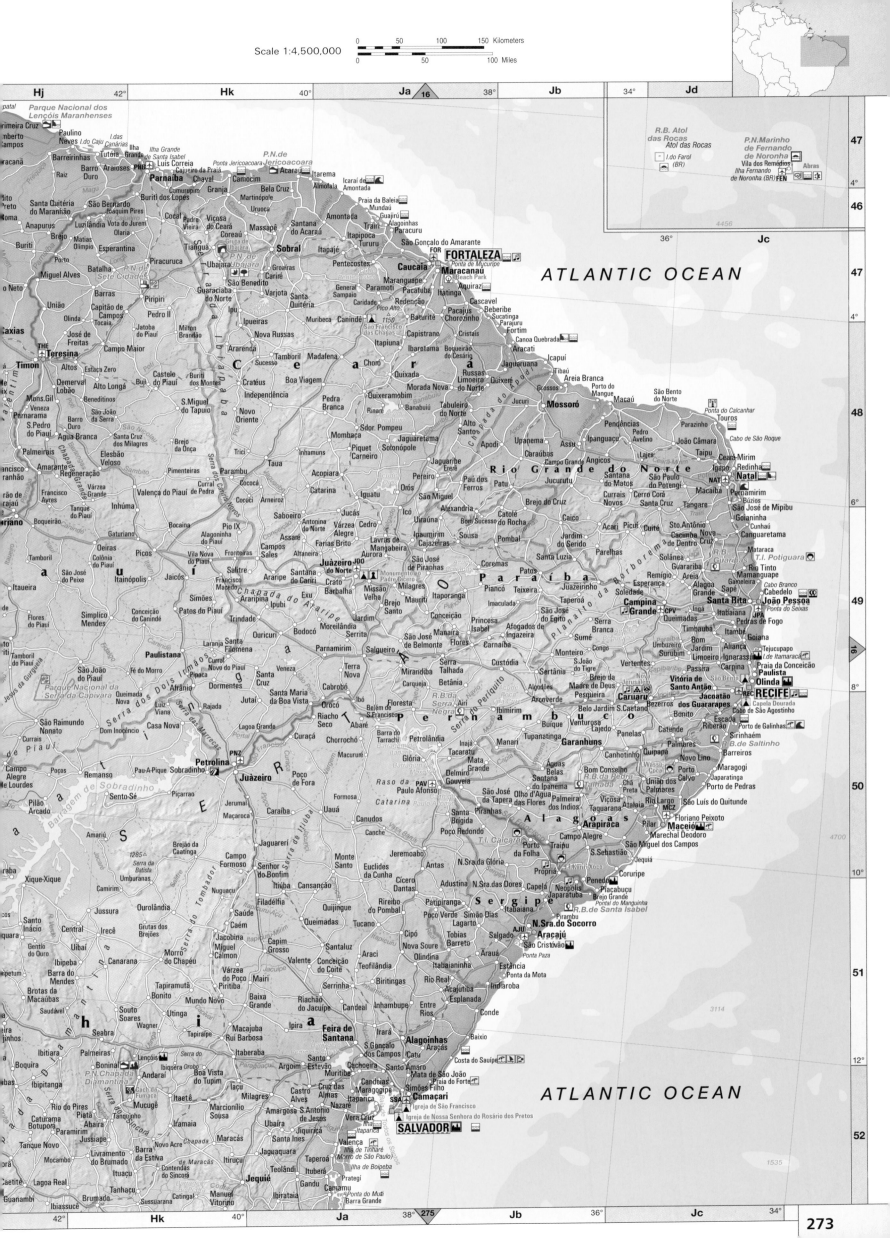

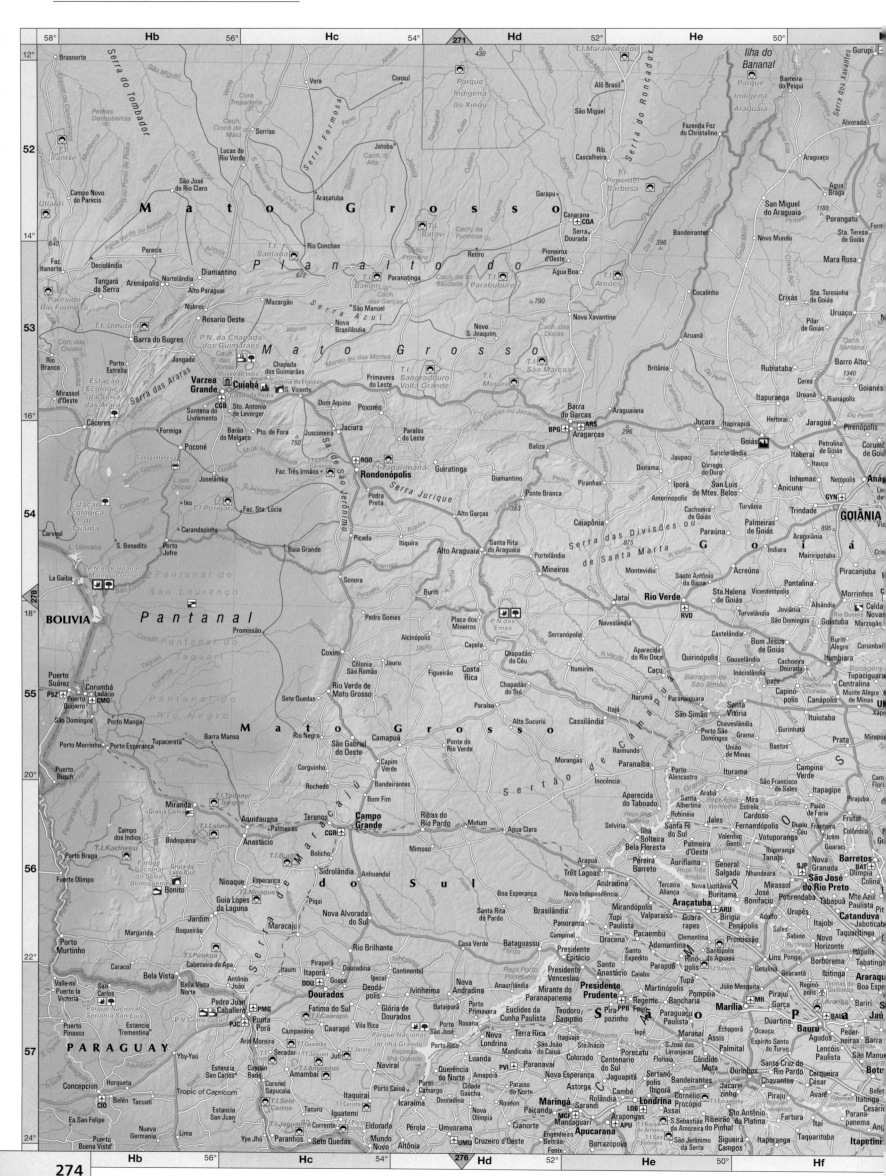

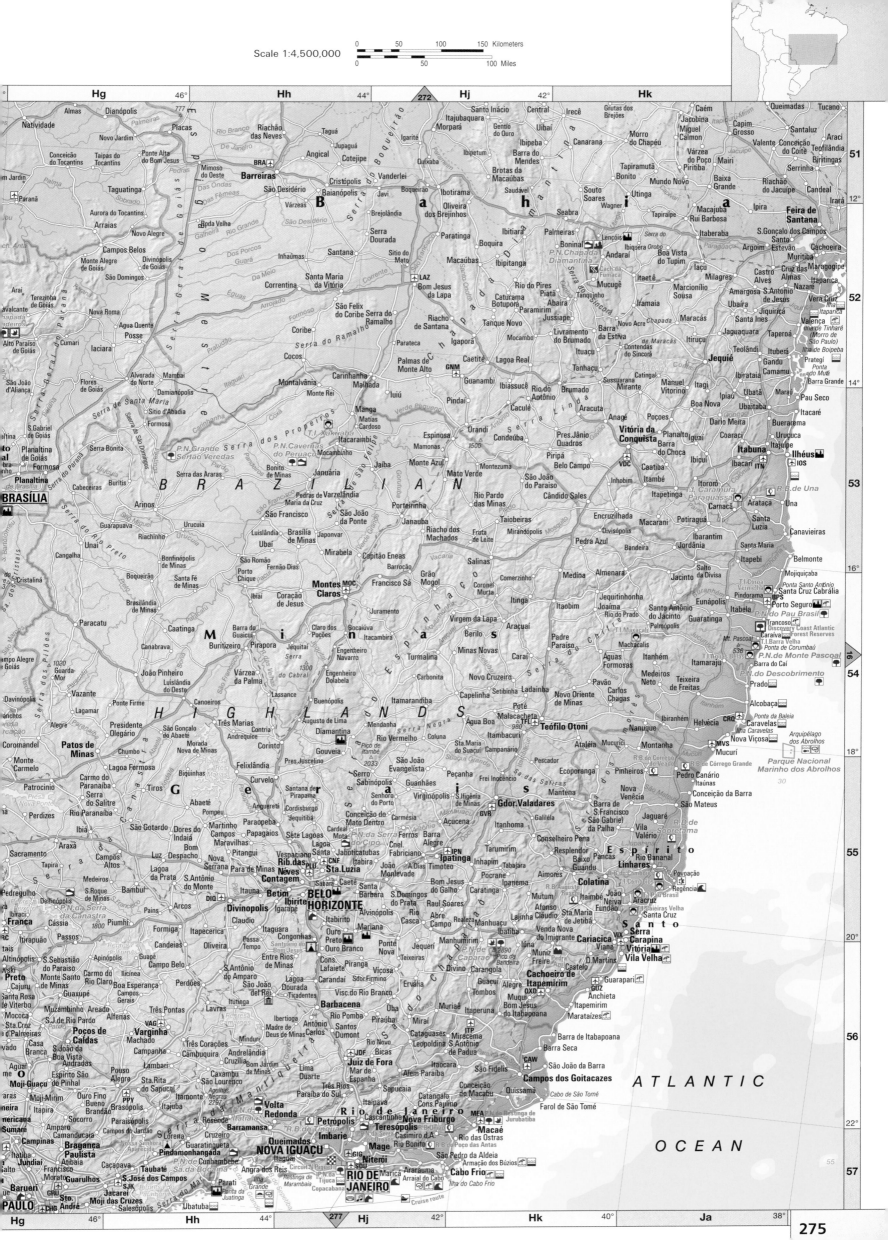

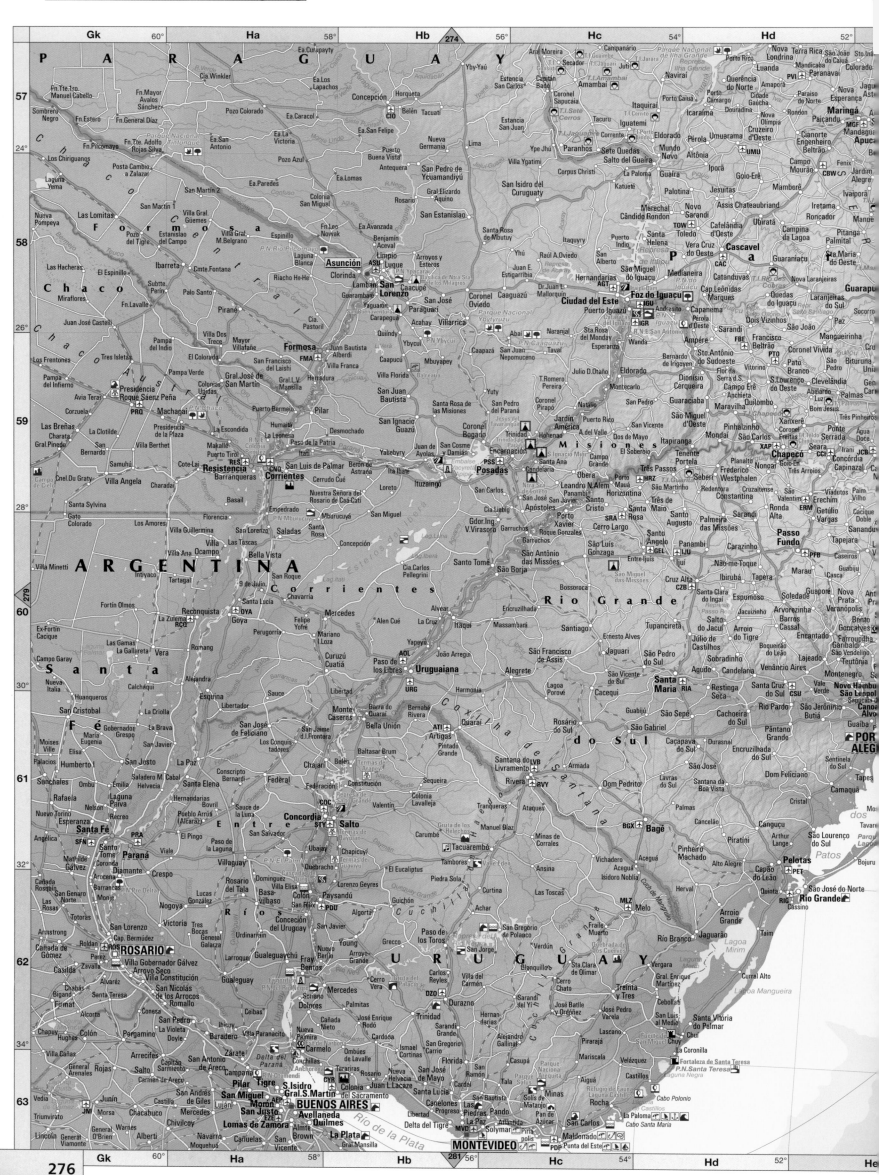

0   50   100   150 Kilometers
0   50   100 Miles

22°

José das
aranjeiras
Cândido   Palmital   Espírito Santo   Barra Bonita
Mota   do Turvo   Lençóis   São Manuel   Moji-Mirim   Itapira   Bueno   Brasópolis   Itajubá   Agulhas Negras   Paraíba do Sul   Conceição   Quissamã
Bandeirantes   Santa Cruz do   Paulista   São Pedro   Limeira   Socorro   Brandão   Itatiaia   P.N.de   Volta   Cascantina   Nova Friburgo   do Macabu
Jacareí   Rio Pardo   Cerqueira   Piracicaba   Americana   Amparo   Paraisópolis   Campos do Jordão   Resende   Barramansa   Redonda   Petrópolis   Teresópolis   Rio das Ostras   Macaé
Cornélio   Chavantes   César   Sta.Bárbara   Sumaré   Camanducaia   Cruzeiro   Queimados   Imbarie   Casimiro d.A.   Poço das Antas
Procópio   Piraju   Capivari   Campinas   Bragança   Guaratinguetá   NOVA IGUAÇU   Mage   Rio Bonito   São Pedro da Aldeia
Sto.Antônio   Fartura   Indaiatuba   Jundiaí   Paulista   Atibaia   Francisco   Pindamonhangada   Itaguai   Niterói   Maricá   Araruama   Cabo Frio
Ribeirão da Platina   Itaí   Salto   Morato   Taubaté   Angra dos Reis   RIO DE   Arraial do Cabo   Ilha do Cabo Frio
Sigueira Campos   Itaporanga   Sorocaba   S.Roque   Guarulhos   S.José dos Campos   JANEIRO   Copacabana
Ibaiti   Wenceslau   Taquarituba   Votorantim   Barueri   Moji das Cruzes   Ubatuba   Cruise route
Braz   Itararé   Salto de Piraporá   SÃO PAULO   Sto.   Jacareí   Caraguatatuba   Tropic of Capricorn
Arapoti   Piedade   André   S.Bernardo do Campo   Ilhabela
Telêmaco   Ventania   Capão   São Miguel   Diadema   Santos   São Sebastião   Ilha de São Sebastião
Borba   Jaguariaíva   Bonito   Arcanjo   São Vicente   Guarujá   Ponta do Boi
Tibagi   Guapiara   Itanhaém   Praia   Pitangueiras   I.de Alcatrazes
Piraí   Apiaí   Juquiá   Grande   Peruíbe
do Sul   Ponta do   I.Queimada

24°

Castro   Carambeí   Adrianópolis   Arpoador   Pequena
Ponta Grossa   Cerro Azul   Registro   Barra
Almirante   R.Branco   Jaguatirica   Eldorado   Iguape   Ilha Comprida
Tamandaré   do Sul   Serra Negra   Jacupiranga   Atlantic Forest
CURITIBA   Palmeira   Guaraqueçaba   Cananéia   Southeast Reserves

Campo Largo   Colombo   Cruise route   80
Pinhais
Araucária   Morretes   P.N.do Superagui
São João   Lapa   São José   Ilha do Mel   Baía de Paranaguá
do Triunfo   Faz.Rio   dos Pinhais   Paranaguá
São Mateus   Grande   P.N.de Saint-Hilaire/Lange   40
do Sul   Quitandinha   Matinhos

58

Mafra   Rio Negro   Pirabeiraba   Guaratuba   BRAZIL
Canoinhas   Garuva
Papanduva   Rio Negrinho   São Bento   São Francisco do Sul
Itaió   do Sul   Ilha de São Francisco
Doutor   Guaramirim   Joinville
Lajeadinho   Pedrinho   Jaraguá   Massa-   Barra Velha

26°

Santa   Santa   Timbó   do Sul   randuba
Cecília   Terezinha   Indaial   Gaspar   Navegantes
S.Cristovão   Pres.   Blumenau   NVT
do Sul   Getúlio   Ibirama   Brusque   Itajaí
Taió   Ibirama   S.João   Tijucas   Balneário Camboriú
Rio do   Batista   Ponta de Porto Belo
Pouso   Sul   Canasvieiras   Reserva Biológica
Redondo   Alfredo   São José   Ponta do Rapa   Marinha do Arvoredo
Otacílio   Wagner   Barreiros   Gdor.Celso Ramos
Costa   Rancho   Palhoça   Ilha de Santa Catarina
LAJ   Bocaina   Queimado   São José   Florianópolis

59

Lages   do Sul   Ituporanga   Pântano do Sul
Painel   Urubici   Ibié   Ponta dos Naufragados
P.N.de   Morro   Três Barras
São Joaquim   da Igreja   Garopaba
São Joaquim   Orleans   Braço   Lagoa do Mirim
Lauro Muller   do Norte   Imbituba

28°

Cambará   Urussanga   Imaruí
do Sul   Rio Maina   Laguna
ainhas   Turvo   Meleiro   Tubarão
Grande   Forquilhinha   Içara   Jaguaruna
cisco   Criciúma
la   CCM   Araranguá
P.N.Serra
Sombrio

Terra de Areia   Torres
Lagoa do Itapera
Lagoa dos Quadros
Osório   Capão da Canoa

60

Tramandaí

Pinhal

61

A T L A N T I C   O C E A N   3775

62

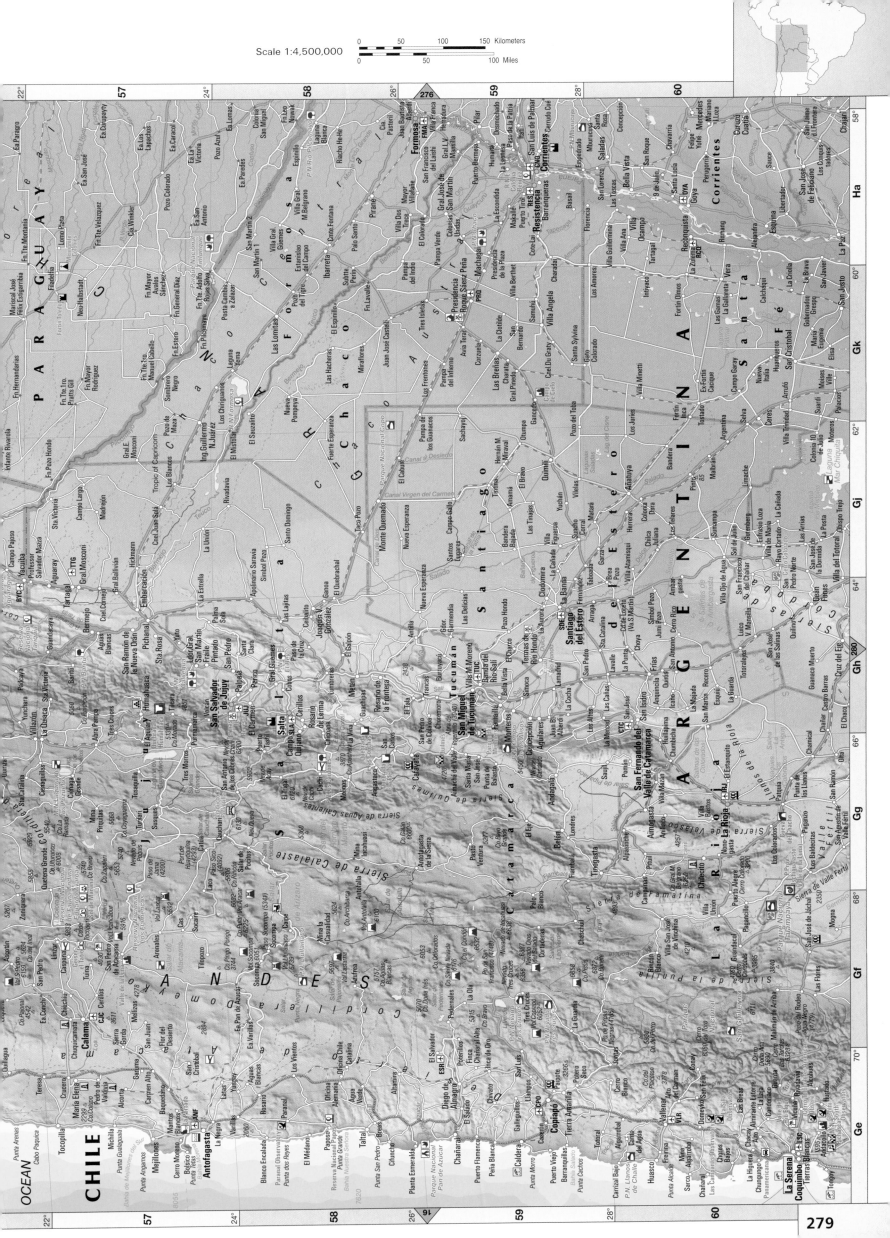

Central Chile, Central Argentina

0	50	100	150 Kilometers
0		50	100 Miles

67

44°

5155

A r g e n t i n e

Cruise route

5850

68

5570

B a s i n

46°

69

A T L A N T I C

48°

O C E A N

150

390

70

16

173

50°

176

71

212

*Falkland Islands
(Islas Malvinas)*

Isla Jason

Pepple Island

Cape Colphin

Cape Bougainville

2035

Westpoint

Port
Howard

Douglas

Cape
Carysfort

Berkeley
Sound

△705

King George Bay

558△
Mount Maria

681
△
East
Falkland

458△

Weddell
Island △289

West
Falkland

Darwin

55△

Stanley

Falkland Sound

PSY ⊕ Fitzroy

△339

△89

Choiseul Sound

Lively Island

52°

Port Stephens

North Arm

Falkland Islands (UK)

Cabo Meredith

Speedwell
Island

Bleaker Island

George Island

Engle Passage

Sea Lion Island

18

322

Beauchêne Isla

72

1339

2170

550

304

29

B u r d w o o d   *B a n k*

S c o t i a   *R i d g e*

54°

1892

S c o t i a

75

5055

73

S c o t i a   S e a

Cruise route

2179

120

4812

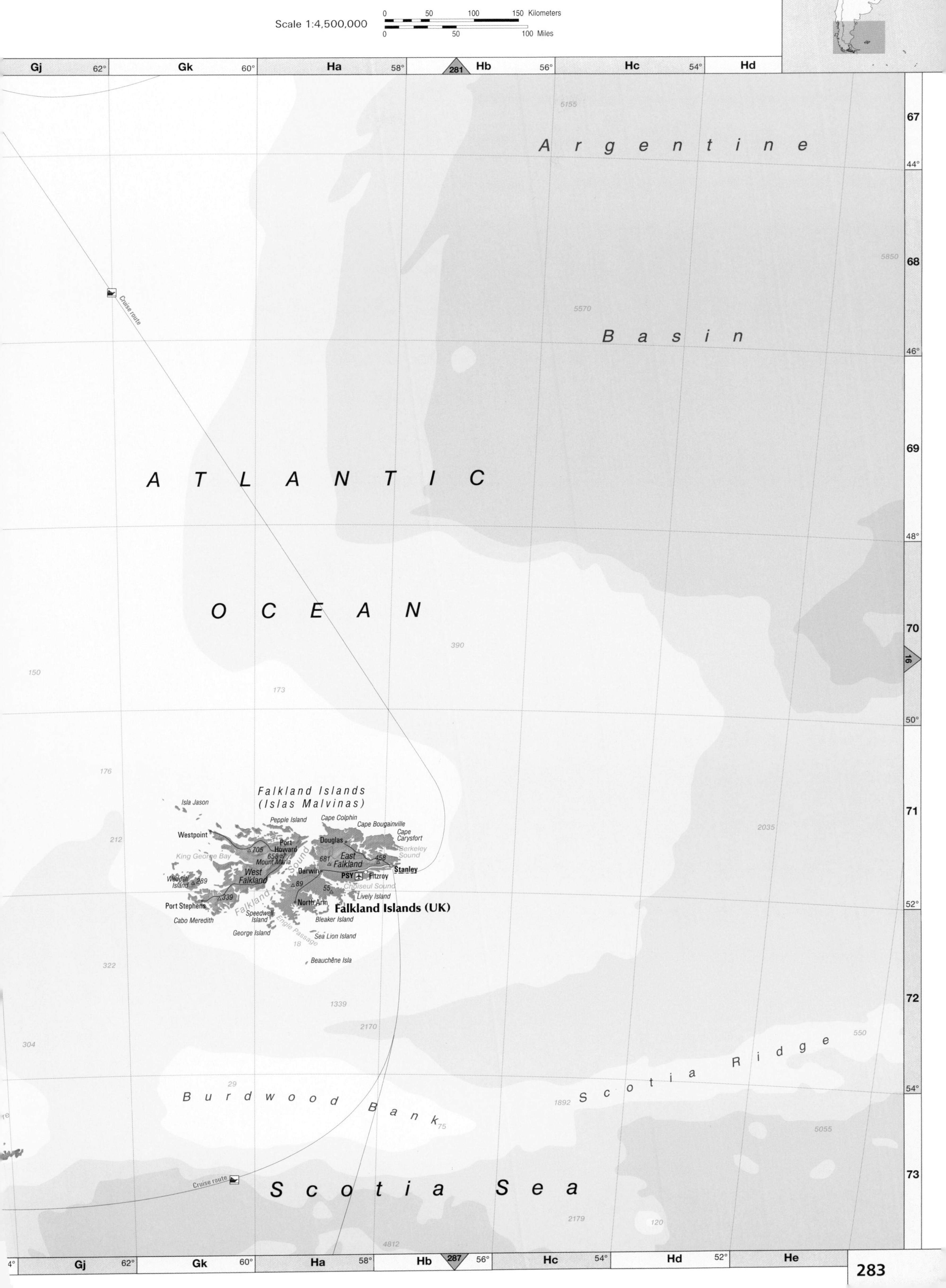

Arctic Region / Antarctica

Antarctica is the coldest of all the continents. More than 90 per cent of the total amount of ice on Earth amasses here around the South Pole. The land mass of the continent, which is about the same size as Europe, is permanently covered by a layer of ice with a thickness of approximately 2 km. At the centre of the continent, this ice sheet may reach a depth of up to 4.5 km. The immense weight of the ice pushes the submerged mountains far below sea level. The surface area of the continent changes, depending on the time of year – it can as much as double in size in winter as a result of the increased ice mass. Only those mountains located on

the Pacific edge are not entirely covered in ice. The Antarctic ice desert is divided into five regions, distinguishable from each other only by the characteristics of the ice sheet. The area of land and sea surrounding the North Pole is described as the Arctic or North Polar region, a large part of which is formed by the Arctic Ocean.

The Antarctic ice desert is uninhabited by mammals. Only penguins occasionally live on parts of the immense sheet of ice.

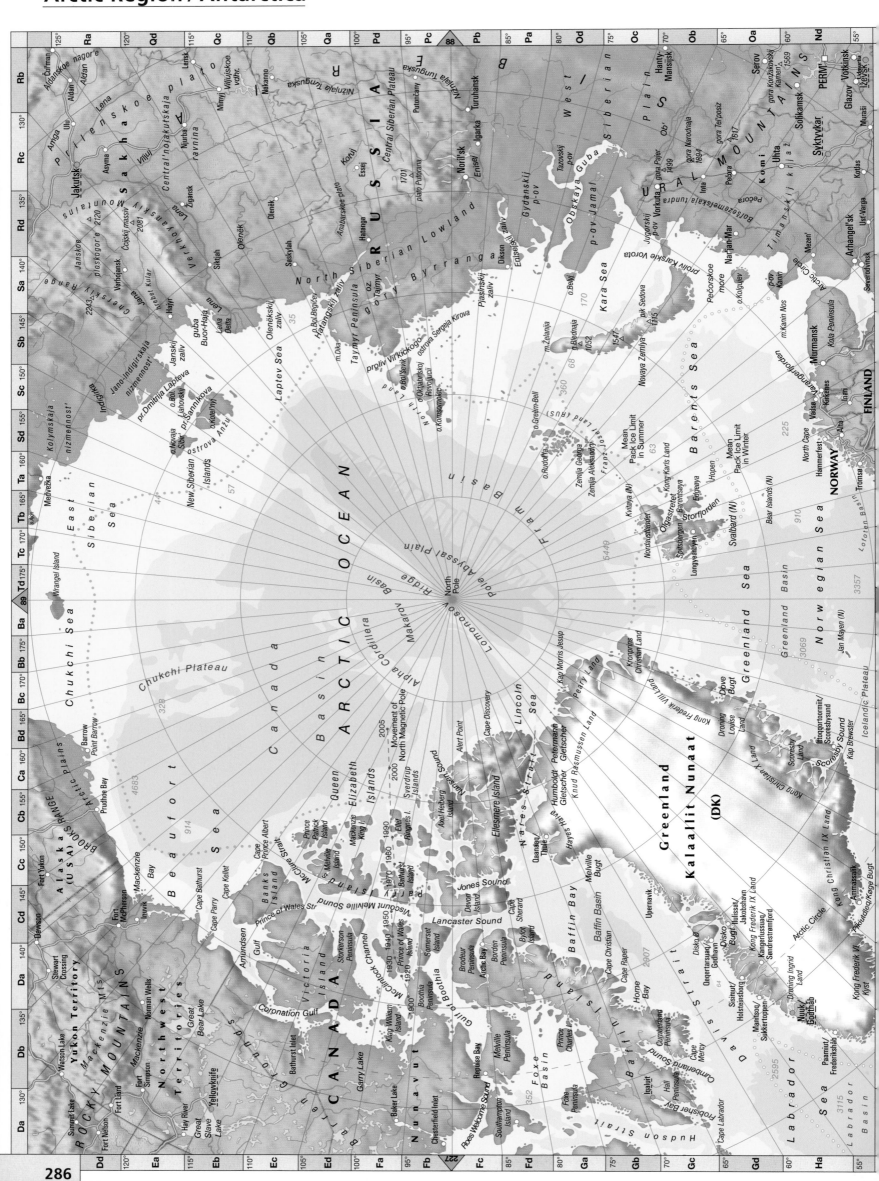

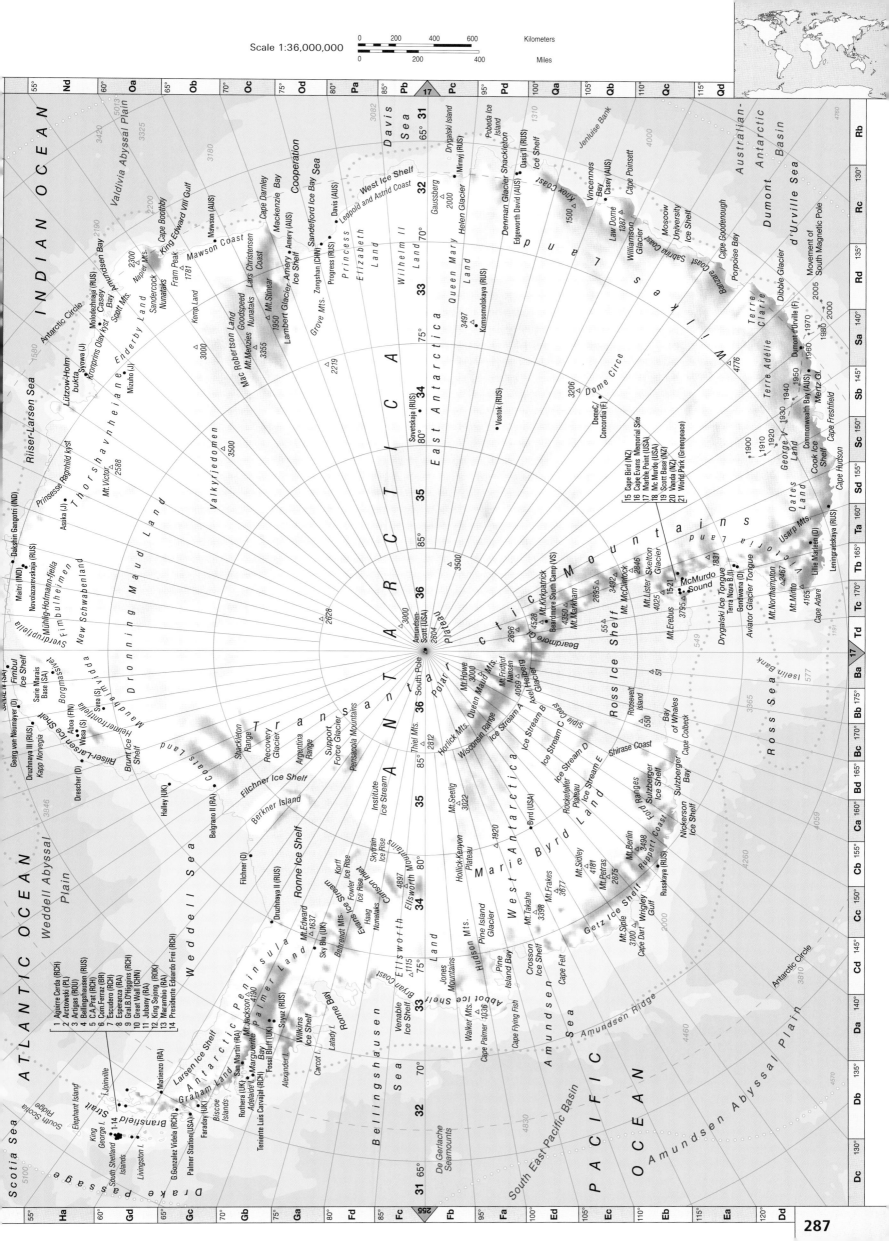

An iceberg is trapped by the frozen sea at Kloa Point on the Mawson Coast: icebergs are formed ('calved') when part of the inland ice mass or a valley glacier breaks off. 'Tabular icebergs' are sheets that have broken off from the Antarctic ice-shelf. These can be several kilometres in length and they can float around the Southern Ocean for several months.

South Orkney Islands
South Shetland Islands

In addition to the main land mass of the Antarctic Continent, the territory of the Antarctic also includes several offshore sub-antarctic island groups. The **South Orkney Islands** lie between the **Scotia Sea** in the north and the **Weddell Sea** in the South Atlantic. The island group consists of the main islands, **Coronation** and **Laurie**, and a number of smaller islands. The whole island group covers an area of 622 sq. km.

The inhospitable islands are mainly mountainous and can reach altitudes of up to 2,100 m. The landscape is heavily glaciated. The scant vegetation consists of mosses, algae and lichen. Apart from two research stations on the islands of **Signy** and **Laurie**, the archipelago is uninhabited.

The **South Shetland Islands** lie in the **Drake Passage**, approximately 90 km north of the **Antarctic Peninsula**. The island chain is 510 km long and has an Alpine, glaciated landscape, composed mainly of volcanic stone. It covers an area of 4,622 sq. km. Seismic and volcanic activity beneath the ice sheet persists to this day. Only lichen and algae grow on the inhospitable island group, which is uninhabited, with the exception of a research station on **Deception Island**.

Filchner-Ronne Ice Shelf

The massive ice shelf in the south **Weddell Sea** is divided by **Berkner Island** into the eastern **Ronne Ice Shelf** and the western **Filchner Ice Shelf**. It is the second largest ice shelf in the Antarctic and covers an area of some 530,000 sq. km. The extensive ice shelves form when the glaciers of the mainland move towards the sea and enter it at such a shallow gradient that they do not break apart. Near the coast, the ice shelf almost sits on the ocean floor. The ice shelf also consists of frozen precipitation and sea water and has a thickness of approximately 250 m in the far north, and up to 1,800 m in the south, where it extends more than 840 km into the mainland. Where the sheet meets the water, the ice is still about 30 m thick.

Icebergs and sheets of ice frequently break away from this huge ice shelf to form tabular icebergs with an area of more than 10,000 sq. km and drift-ice which can float out many kilometres into the Southern Ocean.

Trans-antarctic Mountains

The **Trans-antarctic Mountains** were formed through a process of uplift and denudation beginning 450 million years ago at the edge of the Antarctic Plate. The mountain range has a total length of 4,800 km and it separates the continent into a smaller eastern section and a significantly larger western part.

East Antarctica has a table shape composed of Precambrian igneous and metamorphic rocks from the former great southern continent. West Antarctica is composed of younger rock.

The Trans-antarctic Mountains are completely covered by ice in the central sections and stretch from **Victoria Land** in the south to the **Weddell Sea** to the northeast of the continent. In the north, glaciers extend from the mountains into the sea to form **Edith Ronne Land**. The glacial extensions in the east reach out far into the **Ross Sea**, forming the immense **Ross Ice Shelf** that covers an area of 540,000 sq. km.

The eastern side of the mountains contains volcanoes and areas of seismic activity, stretching from Ellsworth Land all the way to the Scotia Arc. The mountain system reaches its greatest height in the steep mountain chain running along the Ross Sea (**Kirkpatrick**, 4,528 m and **Markham**, 4,350 m). At this point, the mountains drop away very steeply into the sea. The Trans-antarctic Mountains extend into Victoria Land to form an island in the centre of the Ross Ice Shelf. This island, **Mount Erebus**, is the highest active volcano on the continent.

Very few places in the Antarctic are free of ice (just 1.5 per cent of the total area). These include the **Dry Valleys** in Victoria Land near the U.S. McMurdo Station on the edge of the Ross Ice Shelf. This region covers an area of

Drift-ice on the coast of the Antarctic Peninsula.

some 3,000 sq. km, and was formed by strong dry winds, called katabatic winds, that blow through the region at extremely high speeds.

The Dry Valleys are subject to unusual temperature fluctuations and have seen no precipitation for approximately two million years. The area also contains some salt lakes, such as **Lake Vanda**, formed by melting glaciers during warmer periods.

Antarctic Mountains

The Antarctic also contains other mountain chains or individual peaks, known by the Inuit term of **Nunataks**, which protrude above the 2-km-thick layer of ice in the central Antarctic and the coastal regions. These include the **Sentinel Range** whose highest peak, **Mount Vinson**, reaching an altitude of 4,897 m, is also

the highest mountain on the continent, and the mountain chains that extend from the north coast to the Leopold and Astrid Coast, which can reach heights of 3,600 m and which formed 80 million years ago at the fractured edge of the former continent of Gondwanaland. In **MacRobertson Land**, the glaciers on **Mount Menzies** (3,355 m) fall steeply to form the **Amery Ice Shelf**.

Antarctic Peninsula

The **Antarctic Peninsula**, which was formerly called **Graham Land** or the **Palmer Peninsula**, lies between the Weddell Sea and the Bellingshausen Sea in West Antarctica. The peninsula is some 1,300 km long and is the largest in Antarctica.

The Antarctic peninsula forms the northernmost extension of the continent and its highest point, **Mount Jackson** (4,191 m), in the ice-free Antarctic Andes, is actually an extension of the South American Cordillera. In geological terms, it is the youngest mountain on the continent.

The edge of the peninsula contains numerous volcanoes, some of which are still active, and other signs of volcanic activity.

Off the west coast of the peninsula there are some islands, including **Alexander Island**, at 390 km long the largest island in Antarctica, as well as other large ice shelves. This area has relatively mild summer temperatures and is the site of a number of permanently manned scientific research stations.

Queen Maud Land

Queen Maud Land is an extensive upland area covering a large part of the north-east between 20° W and 45° E. In this region, the ice layer can be more than 4.5 km thick. The weight of this immense mass of ice has pushed the underlying mountains below sea-level. The endless ice desert is only interrupted by a small number of scattered, steep cliffs and strange peaks, rising above the frozen white landscape.

New Swabia, a section of land near the coast of Queen Maud Land, is covered by mountains for a length of more than 1,000 km. These include the **Mühlig Hoffmann Mountains**, maximum altitude 3,090 m, and the **Wohlthat Massif**, with a maximum altitude of 2,980 m.

South of these mountains, the land rises to form the **Wegener Plateau** at more than 4,000 m above sea level. New Swabia is also the site of the German Neumayer Research Station.

Wilkes Land

Wilkes Land, along the southeast coast facing the Indian Ocean, between the **Queen Mary Coast** and the **George V Land**, covers the area between 100° E and 142° E, representing most of eastern Antarctica.

This wide, barren region is almost entirely covered by a uniform ice sheet, more than 4,700 m thick. There are outlet glaciers along the coast. **Bunger Oasis** is on in **Knox Land**, and **Adélie Land**, which covers some 390,000 sq. km, is located in the east.

Kerguelen Islands

The archipelago of the **Kerguelen Islands** at the southern end of the Indian Ocean, approximately 2,800 km south-east of Madagascar, comprises the main island, Kerguelen (5,800 sq. km), also called Desolation Island, and a further 300 small islands and protruding mountain peaks, which together cover an area of 7,215 sq. km. The heavily glaciated Kerguelen Island is dominated by mountain peaks, the highest of which is **Mount Ross** rising to 1,960 m. The island is of volcanic origin, and there is still some volcanic activity in the form of hot springs.

The Weddell Sea has a maximum depth of 5,000 m and large parts are covered in floating drift-ice and icebergs. In the south, the sea is dominated by a permanent ice shelf. It was named after the *English explorer J. Weddell and forms a southern part of the Atlantic, cutting deep into the continental mass of the South Polar region and dividing it into West and East Antarctica.*

Research Stations

The Antarctic Treaty was signed by 12 countries in 1959 and enforced in 1961. The treaty states that Antarctica is a continent for conducting research, and can only be used for peaceful purposes. In 1991, 40 nations signed an additional treaty.

Since then, approximately 46 research stations belonging to different countries have been established in this inhospitable region. About 1,200 scientists live on these stations during the winter months, with a further 2,500 in the summer.

The main focus of the research is the circulation systems in the ocean, water and ice in the Antarctic. It is becoming increasingly important to use the ice sheet to detect traces of climate change with the aim of drawing conclusions about the current trends in the world's climate.

The following are the research stations belonging to the different nations:

USA: McMurdo Station, on the southernmost extension of the Ross Sea; **Amundsen Scott South Pole Station**, at the geographic South Pole; **Palmer Station**, Anvers Island

Russia: Vostok Station, on the inland ice of East Antarctica (Station Vostok II), it was here that the lowest temperature on Earth was recorded at -91.5°C; **Bellingshausen**, King George Island on the South Shetland Islands; **Molodezhnaya Station; Novolazarevskaya Station; Progress Station; Mirny Station; Russkaya Station**

Australia: Davis Station, Princess Elizabeth Land; **Casey Station**, Wilkes Land; **Mawson Station**, MacRobertson Land; **Macquarie Base**, Macquarie Island

New Zealand: Scott Base, Ross Island, Victoria Land, on Mount Erebus

Argentina: Esperanza Base; Orcadas Base; San Martín Station

Germany: Georg von Neumayer Station, New Swabia

Great Britain: Halley Research Station; Rothera Research Station, Adelaide Island

Italy: Mario Zucchelli Station, Terra Nova Bay, Ross Sea

India: Dakshin Gangotri Station; Maitri Station, Schirmacher Region

China: Great Wall Station, King George Island, South Shetland Islands; **Zhongshan Station**, Amery Ice Shelf

Chile: Professor Julio Escudero Base, King George Island, South Shetland Islands; **Capitán Arturo Prat Base**, Greenwich Island, South Shetland Islands; **Bernardo O'Higgins Station**, Antarctic Peninsula

France: Dumont d'Urville Station, Adélie Land

South Africa: SANAE IV

Japan: Showa Station

Brazil: Comandante Ferraz Station

South Korea: King Sejong Station, King George Island

Norway: Troll Station, Queen Maud Land

Finland: Aboa Station, Queen Maud Land

Spain: Juan Carlos I, Livingston Island

Ukraine: Akademik Vernadsky Station, Galindez Island

Poland: Henryk Arctowski Station, King George Island

Uruguay: General Artigas Station, King George Island

1 Floating islands: pack-ice, drift-ice and icebergs are characteristic of the Southern Ocean. Strange 'mountains' are created, which disappear within a relatively short space of time. The temperature variations between the seasons ensure that the cycle is kept in motion.

2 Mount Melbourne volcano in Victoria Land, rises to a height of 2,733 m. The peaks of the Trans-antarctic Mountains are among the few places in Antarctica that are not completely covered in ice.

3 Mount Erebus (3,795 m), the world's southernmost active volcano, is situated on an island in the Ross Sea. It last erupted in 2006.

4 The peaks of the Transantarctic Mountains, the highest range in Antarctica. Glacial ice has formed over centuries as the winter snows have gradually compacted.

The Arctic Ocean

The Arctic Ocean includes the Barents Sea, Baffin Bay and Hudson Bay, and is sometimes considered to be an extension or part of the Atlantic Ocean.

The **Arctic Ocean** is located in an area between Eurasia, America and Greenland and is the smallest of the world's five major oceanic divisions. It has an area of 12,173 sq. km and an average depth of 1,000 m. At the deepest point, the depth is 5,626 m.

The Arctic Ocean consists of four main basins (**the North American, Siberian, Eurasian and Fram Basins**), separated from each other by three great ocean ridges. The largest of these, the **Lomonosov Ridge**, stretches from north-west to south-east for a distance of over 1,750 km. The **Mid-Arctic Ridge**, a branch of the **Mid-Atlantic Ridge,** runs parallel to it. The **Alpha Ridge** is situated on the Canadian side of the Lomonosov Ridge.

The continental shelf off the coast of northern Asia is much broader than that of other oceans. In some places it is as wide as 1,600 km and nowhere is it narrower than 480 km. The **Kara, Laptev, Chukchi, Beaufort, Lincoln** and **East Siberian Seas all form** part of this shelf.

The Atlantic Ocean joins the Arctic Ocean in the region around the Greenland Sea. This narrow channel between Greenland and Spitsbergen produces 80 per cent of the water transfer between the two oceans.

During the winter months, the Arctic Ocean is covered by a layer of sea-ice between 2.5 and 3.5 m thick. In summer, the continental fringes are free of ice. The ice is in a state of continuous motion, caused by the rotating currents (**pack-ice drift**).

Most Arctic icebergs originate from glaciers. They can tower up to 80 m above the water and may be more than 1,000 m long. Another form of iceberg is found off the shores of **Ellesmere Island** and North Greenland. These 'islands of ice' consist of very old ice masses. They are only about 5 m in height and appear to be relatively small, but they may be up to 200 m wide.

The **Barents Sea**, between the coast of northern Europe, Spitsbergen and Novaya Zemlya, has a surface area of 1.4 million sq. km and is mainly ice-free in the south. **Baffin Bay** covers an area of 500,000 sq. km north of the pack-ice border and is up to 2,377 m deep. Hudson's Bay (1.4 million sq. km) is a shallow sea in the north-east of North America that extends far inland and is connected to the Arctic Ocean via the **Foxe Channel** and to the **North Atlantic** via the **Hudson Straits**. Hudson Bay is covered in ice from November to May.

The Arctic Ocean and the seas bordering it have large oil and gas reserves, but the difficult conditions that prevail here – the extreme cold, the strong winds and the constantly shifting sea-ice – prevent the extraction of these resources.

Big picture: the Geographic North Pole ('True North') has a fixed position, unlike the Magnetic North Pole. The North Pole lies in the Arctic Ocean and is occasionally free of ice, despite the cold temperatures in the area.

Inset: the Arctic is home to several large mammal species including Polar Bears.

All of the places named on the maps in the atlas are listed in the atlas index. The place names are listed alphabetically. Special symbols and letters including accents and umlauts are ignored in the order of the index. For example, the letters Á, Ä, Â are all categorized under A, and è, °, Î are all treated as the standard Latin letter Z. Written characters consisting of two letters joined together (ligatures) are treated as two separate characters in the index: for example, words beginning with the character Æ would be indexed under AE.

The most commonly used abbreviations in the atlas – including N.P. for national park or N.W.R. for national wildlife refuge – are also used in the index. These abbreviations are listed and explained on this page (below). Generic geographic terms (sea, bay, etc.) and word articles (the, le, el, etc.)

were used in the order of the index: for example, the Gulf of Mexico is listed under G and Le Havre, France is listed under L.

A special aspect of the atlas is the detailed and specially developed system of pictograms it features. These pictograms highlight famous travel routes, scenic landscapes, natural attractions, man-made attractions, cultural sites, as well as sporting, vacation, and recreation facilities. These pictograms also appear in the index (up to three per place name). The pictograms provide a basic overview of the attractions featured in a particular area. The meanings of all of the pictograms featured in the atlas are explained on the following page. In addition to these pictograms, the index also features special symbols to provide information about the political status of certain

places including states, provinces, and capital cities. Virtually all of the places listed in the atlas have a country reference; these nations are identified by their international license (registration) plate codes. The various international license codes are identified on page 292. In the case of communities and areas that are located on or between the borders of two nations, the license

plate codes of both nations are listed and separated by a slash.

The names of areas and geographic features that cannot be assigned to specific states, such as the Atlantic Ocean, are followed by the page number of a map featuring the area and the number of the map grid box in which the area is depicted on the map.

Antigua	⌂ ⌂ ⌂	**AG**	187	Gk37
Place name	Pictograms	Nation	Page	Map grid

Abbreviations

Abb.	Abbey, abbaye (French), abbadia (Span.), abbazia (Ital.)	Ind.	Indian/ Native Americans, First Nation	N.R.	Nature Reserve, Natuurreservaat (Dutch)	Sr.	Sredn -e, -ij, -jaja (Russian) = central, middle
Abor.	Aboriginal (indigenous inhabitants of Australia)	Ind.Res.	Indian Reservation = Native American land reserves in North America	N.R.A.	National Recreation Area	Sra.	Sierra (Span.), serra (Port./Ital.) = mountain range
Aborig.	Aboriginal (indigenous inhabitants of Australia)	Is.	Islands	N.S.	National Seashore	St./St	Saint (English and French), sankt (German, Dutch)
Ad.	Adas (Turkish) = Island	Îs.	Îles (French) = islands	N.Sra.	Nossa Senhora (Port.) = our lady (Mary, the mother of Jesus)	Sta.	Santa (Span./Port./Ital.) = saint
Ág.	Ági -os, -a, -i (Greek) = Saint	Jaz.	Jazovir (Bulg.) = reservoir	Nva.	Nueva (Span.) = new-	Star.	Star -o, -yj, -aja, -oe (Russian) = old-
A.L.	Aboriginal Land = Aboriginal land reserve in Australia	Jct.	Junction	Nvo.	Nuevo (Span.) = new-	Ste	Sainte (French) = saint
Ban.	Banjaran (Malaysian) = mountain range	Jez.	Jezioro (Pol.), jezero (Czech/Slovak./Serb./Croat./Slov.) = lake	N.W.R.	National Wildlife Refuge	Sth.	South, southern
Bol'.	Bol'-šoj, -šaja, -šoe (Russian) = large-	Kan.	Kanal (Turk./Rus.), kanaal (Dutch), kana (Pol.) = canal	o.	Ostrov (Rus.) = island	St.Mem.	State Memorial
C.	Cape, cap (French), cabo (Span./Port.), capo (Ital.)	Kep.	Kepulauan (Malaysian) = archipelago	P.	Port (English and French), puerto (Span./Port.), porto (Ital.) = harbor	Sto.	Santo (Span./Port.) = Saint
Can.	Canal	Kg.	Kampong (Malaysian), kampung (Khmer) = village	Peg.	Pegunungan (Indonesian) = mountain	Str.	Street, Strait, stretto (Italian), stræde (Danish), stret (Norwegian)
Cast.	Castle, castel (French), castillo (Span.), castelo (Port.), castello (Ital.)	Kör.	Körfezi (Turk.) = gulf, bay	Pen.	Peninsula, péninsule (franz.), península (Span.), penisola (Ital.)	t.	tau (Kaz.) = mountain
Cd.	Ciudad (Span.), cidade (Port.) = city	L.	Lake, lac (French), lago (Ital./Span./Port.), loch, lough (Gaelic)	Pk.	Peak	T.	Take (Jap.) = peak, summit
Co.	Cerro (Span.) = mountain, hill	M.	Mys (Rus./Ukr.) = cape	P.N.	Parc National (French), parque nacional (Span./Port.), parco nazionale (Ital.) = national park	T.	Temple
Conv.	Convento (Span.) = monastery	Mal.	Malo, -yj, -aja, -oe (Rus.) = small			Tel.	Teluk (Indonesian) = bay
Cord.	Cordillera (Span.) = mountain range	Mem.	Memorial	p-ov.	Poluostrov (Rus.) = peninsula	Tg.	Tanjung (Indonesian) = cape
Corr.	Corrente (Port.), corriente (Ital./Span.) = river	Mon.	Monastery, monastère (French), monasterio (Span.), monastero (Ital.)	Pres.	Presidente (Span./Port.) = president	T.I.	Terra Indígena (Port.), territorio indigena (Span.) = indigenous land reservation in Latin America
Cr.	Creek	M.P.	Milli Parki (Turk.) = national park	Prov.	Provincial, Province		
D.	Dake (Jap.) = mountain	Mt.	Mount, mont (French)	Pse.	Passe (French) = Pass	Vdhr.	Vodohranilišče (Russian) = reservoir
D.	Danau (Indonesian) = lake	Mta.	Montagna (Ital.), montaña (Span.) = mountain range	Pso.	Paso (Span.), passo (Ital.) = Pass	Vel.	Velik -o, -ij, -yki, -oe (Rus.) = large-
Dağ.	Dağlar, dağlari (Turkish) = mountain range	Mte.	Monte (Ital./Span./Port.), montagne (French) = mountain	Pt.	Point	Verh.	Verhn -ee, -ie, -ij, -jaja (Rus.) = mountain
Ea.	Estancia (Span.) = estate	Mtes.	Montes (Span./Port.), montagnes (French) = mountains	Pta.	Punta (Span./Port.) = point	Vill.	Village
Emb.	Embalse (Span.), embassament (catalonian) = reservoir	Mţii	Munţii (Romanian) = mountain range	Pte.	Pointe (French) = point	vlk.	Vulkan (Rus.) = volcano
Ens.	Ensenada (Span./Port.) = small bay	Mti.	Monti (Ital.) = mountain range	Pto.	Punto (Ital.) = point	Vol.	Volcano, volcan (French), volcán (Span.)
Erm.	Ermita (Span.) = hermitage	Mtn.	Mountain	Q.N.P.	Quasi National Park (Jap.) = national park	Vul.	Vulkan (German), Vulcano (Ital./Romanian) = volcano
Est.	Estación (Span.) = train station	Mtns.	Mountains	R.	River, rivière (French), río (Span.), ribeiro, rio (Port.), rîu (Romanian), reka (Bulgarian)	W.A.	Wilderness Area
Faz.	Fazenda (Port.) = estate	Mts.	Mountains, Monts (French)			Wildl.	Wildlife
Fl.	Fleuve (French) = river	Mus.	Musée (French), museo (Span.), museu (Port.) = museum	Ra.	Range	W.S.	Wildlife Sanctuary
Fs.	waterfalls	N.	North, Northern, Norte (Ital./Span./Port.), Norra (Swedish), Nørdre (Norwegian), Nørre (Danish), Nord (German)	Rep.	Republic, république (French), república (Span./Port.), republicca (Ital.)	Y.	Yama (Jap.) = mountain, mountain range
g.	gawa (Jap.) = river			Repr.	Represa (Port.) = dam	Zal.	Zaliv (Russian), zalew (Polish) = bay
G.	Gora (Russian), góra (Polish), gunung (Indonesian) = mountain			Res.	Reserva (Span.), réserve (French) = nature reserve	Zap.	Zapovednik (Russian) = nature reserve
Gde.	Grande (Span./French) = large	Nac.	Nacional (Span.), Nacional'-nyj, -aja, -oe (Russian) = national	Res.	Reservoir, réservoir (French)	Z.B.	Nature reserve in the People's Republic of China
Geb.	Gebirge (German), gebergte (Dutch) = mountain range	Naz.	Nazionale (Ital.) = national	Resp.	Respublika (Russian) = Republik		
Grd.	Grand (French) = large	N.B.C.A.	National Biodiversity and Conservation Area = protected natural area	s.	San (Jap.) = mountain	Zp.	Zapadn -e, -ji, -aja, -noe (Russian) = west, western
Gt.	Great-	Nev.	Nevado (Span.) = snow-covered mountain peaks	S.	San (Span./Ital.), são (Port.) = saint		
Hist.	Historic, historical	N.H.P.	National Historic Park	Sanc./Sanct.	Sanctuary		
Hr.	Hrebet (Russian) = high	N.H.S.	National Historic Site	Sd.	Sound (German, Danish, Norwegian, Swedish)		
Ht.	Haut (French) = high-	Niž.	Niž-e, -nij, -naja, -neje (Russian) = lower-	Sel.	Selat (Indonesian) = strait		
Hte.	Haute (French) = high-	Nižm.	Nižmennost' (Rus.) = plain	Sg.	Song (Vietnamese) = river		
Hts.	Haut -s, -es (French) = high-	N.M.P.	National Military Park	S.H.P.	State Historic Park		
Hwy.	Highway	N.P.	National Park, Nationalpark (Swedish), nasjonal park (Norwegian), Nemzeti Park (Hungarian)	S.H.S.	State Historic Site		
I.	Isla (Span.), ilha (Port.) = island			Sk.	Shuiku (Chinese) = reservoir		
Î.	Île (French) = island			S.M.	State Monument		
				S.P.	State Park		

The index explained

International license (registration) plate code

A	Austria	CR	Costa Rica	GR	Greece	MC	Monaco	RCA	Central Africa Republic	TCH	Chad
AFG	Afghanistan	CV	Cape Verde	GUY	Guyana	MD	Moldova	RCB	Republic of the Congo	TG	Togo
AG	Antigua and Barbuda	CY	Cyprus	H	Hungary	MEX	Mexico	RCH	Chile	THA	Thailand
AL	Albania	CZ	Czech Republic	HN	Honduras	MH	Marshall Islands	RDC	Dem. Republic of the Congo	TJ	Tajikistan
AND	Andorra	D	Germany	HR	Croatia	MK	Macedonia	RG	Guinea	TLS*	East Timor
ANG	Angola	DARS	Western Sahara	I	Italy	MNE	Montenegro	RH	Haiti	TM	Turkmenistan
ARM	Armenia	DJI	Djibouti	IL	Israel	MNG	Mongolia	RI	Indonesia	TN	Tunisia
AUS	Australia	DK	Denmark	IND	India	MOC	Mozambique	RIM	Mauritania	TO	Tonga
AZ	Azerbaijan	DOM	Dominican Republic	IR	Iran	MS	Mauritius	RL	Lebanon	TR	Turkey
B	Belgium	DY	Benin	IRL	Ireland	MV	Maldives	RM	Madagascar	TT	Trinidad and Tobago
BD	Bangladesh	DZ	Algeria	IRQ	Iraq	MW	Malawi	RMM	Mali	TUV	Tuvalu
BDS	Barbados	E	Spain	IS	Iceland	MYA	Myanmar (Burma)	RN	Niger	UA	Ukraine
BF	Burkina Faso	EAK	Kenya	J	Japan	N	Norway	RO	Romania	UAE	United Arab Emirates
BG	Bulgaria	EAT	Tanzania	JA	Jamaica	NAM	Namibia	ROK	Korea, South	USA	United States of
BH	Belize	EAU	Uganda	JOR	Jordan	NAU	Nauru	ROU	Uruguay		America
BHT	Bhutan	EC	Ecuador	K	Cambodia	NEP	Nepal	RP	Philippines	UZ	Uzbekistan
BIH	Bosnia and Herzegovina	ER	Eritrea	KIR	Kiribati	NIC	Nicaragua	RSM	San Marino	V	Vatican City
BOL	Bolivia	ES	El Salvador	KNA*	Saint Kitts and Nevis	NL	Netherlands	RUS	Russia	VN	Vietnam
BR	Brazil	EST	Estonia	KS	Kyrgyzstan	NZ	New Zealand	RWA	Rwanda	VU	Vanuatu
BRN	Bahrain	ET	Egypt	KSA	Saudi Arabia	OM	Oman	S	Sweden	WAG	Gambia
BRU	Brunei	ETH	Ethiopia	KSV	Kosovo	P	Portugal	SD	Swaziland	WAL	Sierra Leone
BS	Bahamas	F	France	KWT	Kuwait	PA	Panama	SGP	Singapore	WAN	Nigeria
BU	Burundi	FIN	Finland	KZ	Kazakhstan	PAL	Palau	SK	Slovakia	WD	Dominica
BY	Belarus	FJI	Fiji	L	Luxembourg	PE	Peru	SLO	Slovenia	WG	Grenada
C	Cuba	FL	Liechtenstein	LAO	Laos	PK	Pakistan	SME	Suriname	WL	Saint Lucia
CAM	Cameroon	FSM	Micronesia	LAR	Libya	PL	Poland	SN	Senegal	WS	Samoa
CDN	Canada	G	Gabon	LB	Liberia	PNG	Papua New Guinea	SOL	Solomon Islands	WV	Saint Vincent and
CH	Switzerland	GB	Great Britain	LS	Lesotho	PRK*	Korea, North	SP	Somalia		the Grenadines
CHN*	China	GCA	Guatemala	LT	Lithuania	PY	Paraguay	SRB	Serbia	YE	Yemen
CI	Cote d'Ivoire	GE	Georgia	LV	Latvia	Q	Qatar	STP	São Tomé and Príncipe	YV	Venezuela
CL	Sri Lanka	GH	Ghana	M	Malta	RA	Argentina	SUD	Sudan	Z	Zambia
CO	Colombia	GNB	Guinea-Bissau	MA	Morocco	RB	Botswana	SY	Seychelles	ZA	South Africa
COM	Comoros	GQ	Equatorial Guinea	MAL	Malaysia	RC	Taiwan	SYR	Syria	ZW	Zimbabwe

* Some countries do not have official vehicle registration codes. In these cases, the international three-letter code (ISO 3166) is shown.

Symbols used in the index

City
State
Capital
Province
Provincial Capital

Principal travel routes

Auto route
Rail road
Highspeed train
Shipping route

Remarkable landscapes and natural monuments

UNESCO World Natural Heritage
Mountain landscape
Rock landscape
Ravine/canyon
Extinct volcano
Active volcano
Geyser
Cave
Glacier
River landscape
Waterfall/rapids
Lake country
Desert
Oasis
Fossil site
Depression
Nature park
National park (landscape)
National park (flora)
National park (fauna)
National park (culture)
Biosphere reserve
Wildlife reserve
Whale watching

Turtle conservation area
Protected area for sea-lions/seals
Protected area for penguins
Zoo/safari park
Crocodile farm
Coastal landscape
Beach
Coral reef
Island
Underwater reserve

Remarkable Cities and cultural monuments

UNESCO World Cultural Heritage
Pre- and early history
Prehistoric rockscape
The Ancient Orient
Ancient Egypt
Ancient Egyptian pyramids
Minoan culture
Phoenecian culture
Early African culture
Etruscan culture
Greek antiquity
Roman antiquity
Nabatean culture
Vikings
Ancient India
Ancient China
Ancient Japan
Mayan culture
Inca culture
Aztec culture
Other ancient American cultures
Places of Jewish cultural interest
Places of Christian cultural interest
Places of Islamic cultural interest
Places of Buddhist cultural interest
Places of Hindu cultural interest

Places of Jainist cultural interest
Places of Sikh cultural interest
Places of Shinto cultural interest
Places of cultural interest to other religions
Places of cultural interest to indigenous peoples (native peoples)
Aborigine reservation
Places of Aboriginal cultural interest
Indian reservation
Indian Pueblo culture
Places of Indian cultural interest
Amazonian Indians/protected area
Cultural landscape
Historical city scape
Impressive skyline
Castle/fortress/fort
Caravanserai
Palace
Technical/industrial monument
Dam
Remarkable lighthouse
Remarkable bridge
Tomb/grave
Theater of war/battlefield
Monument
Memorial
Space mission launch site
Space telescope
Market
Festivals
Museum
Theater
World exhibition
Olympics

Sport and leisure destinations

Arena/stadium
Race track

Golf
Horse racing
Skiing
Sailing
Diving
Windsurfing
Surfing
Canoeing/rafting
Seaport
Deep-sea fishing
Waterskiing
Beach resort
Mineral/thermal spa
Amusement/theme park
Casino
Hill resort
Lodge

Special index pictograms

Bodies of Water
Canal
Other physical names
Pass
Underwater topography

2 de Junio – Al 'Adam

2 de Junio MEX 245 Fa33
3 Castelli CH 60 Lk44
3 de Enero MEX 244 Ed30
9 de Julio RA 276 Ha60
9 de Julio RA 281 Gk63
10. de Abril MEX 246 Fa34
10. de Mayo MEX 245 Ek32
12 de Diciembre MEX 245 Ej33
16 de Julio RA 281 Gk64
18 de Marzo MEX 247 Fe36
24 de Mayo EC 268 Ga47
25 de Mayo RA 280 Gf63
25 de Mayo RA 280 Gg64
25 de Mayo RA 281 Gk63
27 de Abril CR 248 Fh40
27 de Enero MEX 244 Eb30
28 de Agosto MEX 245 Ej33
31 de Janeiro ANG 198 Lh49
70 Mile House CDN 232 Dk20
100 Mile House CDN 232 Dk20
108 Pagodas CHN 106 Qd26
150 Mile House CDN 232 Dk19

A

Å N 40 Ll27
A1-Ring A 61 Lp43
Aabenraa DK 42 Lk35
Aabybro DK 42 Lk33
Aachen D 58 Lg40
Aadan Yabaal SP 195 Nd44
Aakirkeby DK 43 Lp35
Aalborg DK 42 Lk33
Aalen D 59 Ll42
Aalestrup DK 42 Lk34
Aalst B 51 Le40
Aalten NL 51 Lg39
Aalter B 51 Ld39
Aamuda SYR 91 Na27
Äänekoski FIN 44 Mf28
Aansluit ZA 204 Mb59
Aapravasi Ghat (Port Louis) MS 207 Nj56
Aarau CH 60 Lj43
Aareschlucht CH 60 Lj44
Aars DK 42 Lk34
Aarschot B 51 Le40
Aarup DK 42 Ll35
Aba CHN 106 Qa29
Aba RDC 194 Mf44
Aba WAN 188 Ld43
Aba ad Dud KSA 93 Nc32
Abaco Island BS 243 Gb32
Abadan IR 93 Ne30
Abadla DZ 175 Kj30
Abaeté BR 275 Hh55
Abaetetuba BR 267 Hf46
Abag Qi CHN 105 Qh23
Abai KZ 97 Oe25
Abaí PY 276 Hc58
Abai RI 127 Qa46
Abaíra BR 273 Hk52
Abaji WAN 188 Ld41
Abajo Peak USA 235 Ef27
Abaj Takalik GCA 248 Fe38
Abak WAN 188 Ld43
Abakaliki WAN 188 Le42
Abakan RUS 88 Pc08
Abakh Hoja Tomb CHN 100 Oj26
Abala RCB 198 Lh46
Abala RN 182 Lb38
Abalak RN 182 Ld38
Abalessa DZ 182 Lc34
Ab Anbar IR 98 Nk32
Abancay PE 269 Gd52
Abanilla E 57 Kt52
Abanko RMM 181 La36
Ábano Terme I 60 Lm45
Abapó BOL 278 Gj55
Abarán E 57 Kt52
Abaré BR 273 Ja50
Abashiri J 111 Sc23
Abasolo MEX 245 Fa33
Abasolo MEX 246 Ek35
Abastumani GE 91 Nb25
Abatan RP 124 Ra37
Abay Wenz ETH 192 Mj40
Abba RCA 190 Lh43
Abbadia San Salvatore I 60 Lm48
Abba Kella ETH 192 Mj42
Abba-Omege WAN 188 Le42
Abbas Abad IR 91 Nf27
Abbas Abad IR 96 Nj27
Abbas Abad IR 98 Nh30
Abbasanta I 62 Lj50
Abbaye aux Dames de Saintes F 52 Ku45
Abbaye aux Hommes de Caen F 50 Ku41
Abbaye de Fontenay F 53 Le43
Abbaye de Fontfroide F 53 Lc47
Abbaye de Jumièges F 50 La41
Abbaye de la Chaise-Dieu F 53 Ld45
Abbaye de Saint-Benoît-sur-Loire F 53 Lc43
Abbaye de Saint-Guilhem-le-Désert F 53 Ld47
Abbaye de Sénanque F 53 Lf47
Abbaye d'Orval B 51 Lf41
Abbaye Sainte-Foy F 53 Lc46
Abbaye Saint-Pierre F 52 Ku44
Abbazia della Trinità di Venosa I 63 Lq50
Abbazia di Casamari I 62 Lo49
Abbazia di Montecassino I 62 Lo49
Abbeville F 51 Lb40
Abbeville USA 239 Fh30
Abbeville USA 239 Fd31
Abbeville USA 242 Fj28
Abbeville USA 242 Fj30
Abbey CDN 233 Ef20
Abbeyfeale IRL 47 Kl38
Abbeyleix IRL 47 Kn38
Abbiategrasso I 60 Lj45
Abbieglassie AUS 149 Sd59
Abbot, Mount AUS 147 Sd56
Abbotsbury GB 49 Ks40
Abbotsford CDN 232 Dj21
Abbotsford USA 236 Fe23
Abbott USA 235 Eh27
Abbottabad PK 99 Og28
'Abd ad-Da'im SUD 184 Md40
'Abd al Kuri YE 95 Ng39
Abdallah bin Abbas Mosque KSA 94 Na35
Abd al-Magid SUD 185 Mg38
Abdaly KWT 93 Nd30
Abdan IR 93 Nf31
Abdemezeh DZ 176 Lc33
'Abdin SUD 184 Me39
Abdul Razzak Tomb AFG 99 Oe29
Abease GH 187 Kk41
Abéché TCH 184 Ma39
Abeïbara RMM 182 La36
Abejar E 56 Ks49
Abejukolo WAN 188 Ld42
Abélajouad RN 182 Ld37
Abelardo Luz BR 276 Hd59
Abelbod RMM 181 Kk36
Abel Erasmuspas ZA 205 Mf58
Abel Tasman N.P. NZ 153 Tg66
Abelti ETH 192 Mj41
Abemarre RI 155 Sa49
Abene GH 187 Kk42
Abengourou CI 187 Kj42
Abenójar E 55 Kq52
Abensberg D 59 Lm42
Abeokuta WAN 188 Lb42
Aberaeron GB 49 Kq38
Abercrombie Caves AUS 151 Se62
Aberdare N.P. EAK 194 Mj46
Aberdare Range EAK 194 Mj46
Aberdeen CDN 233 Eg19
Aberdeen GB 48 Ks33
Aberdeen USA 232 Dj22
Aberdeen USA 236 Fa23
Aberdeen USA 239 Ff29
Aberdeen USA 241 Gb26
Aberdeen ZA 205 Mc62
Aberdeen Road ZA 205 Mc62
Aberfeldy GB 48 Kr34
Aberfoyle AUS 149 Sc56
Abergavenny GB 49 Ks39
Abergele ETH 192 Mk39
Abergele GB 49 Kr37
Abergowrie AUS 147 Sc55
Abernethy CDN 233 Ej20
Abersoch GB 49 Kq38
Aberystwyth GB 49 Kq38
Abetone I 60 Ll46
Abetteh MA 174 Ke31
Ab Garm IR 91 Ne28
Abgué TCH 189 Lk40
Abha KSA 94 Nb36
Abhana IND 117 Ok34
Abhanpur IND 117 Pa35
Abhar IR 91 Ne27
Abhar-e Bala IR 93 Nd29
Abico BR 270 Gh47
Abide TR 69 Mg50
Abide TR 71 Mk52
Abidjan CI 187 Kj43
Abi Hill WAN 188 Ld42
Abijatta-Shalla Lakes N.P. ETH 192 Mk42
Abilene USA 238 Fa29
Abilene USA 238 Fb26
Abingdon = Isla Pinta EC 269 Fe45
Abingdon GB 49 Kt39
Abingdon Downs AUS 147 Sb54
Abington GB 48 Kr35
Abinsi WAN 188 Le42
Abirem GH 187 Kk42
Abisko S 38 Lt22
Abisko fjällstation S 38 Lt22
Abisko n.p. S 38 Lt22
Abjarovščyna BY 65 Md38
Abkhazia GE 91 Na24
Abminga AUS 148 Rh59
Abnûb ET 179 Mf32
Åbo = Turku FIN 44 Mc30
Aboa ANT 286 Kb33
Aboh WAN 188 Ld43
Aboisso CI 187 Kj43
Aboke EAU 194 Mg44
Abolones Beach USA 234 Dk28
Abomey DY 188 La42
Abomey Calavi DY 188 Lb42
Abomsa ETH 192 Na41
Abong WAN 189 Lf42
Abong Mbang CAM 189 Lg44
Aboni SUD 185 Mg40
Abony H 67 Lu43
Abor GH 187 La42
Abora Dunkwa GH 187 Kk43
Aboriginal Rock Art AUS 148 Sb61
Aboriginal Rock Art AUS 149 Se58
Aborlan RP 125 Qk41
Aborlan, Mount RP 125 Qk41
Abou-Déïa TCH 189 Lk40
Abou Goulem TCH 184 Ma39
Aboukoussom TCH 184 Ma40
Aboumi G 198 Lh46
Aboun G 198 Le45
Abouraya RN 182 Ld38
Abovian ARM 91 Nc25
Aboyne GB 48 Ks33
Abqaiq KSA 93 Ne33
Abra Anticona PE 269 Gb51
Abra de Gavilán PE 268 Ga49
Abra de Ilog RP 124 Ra39
Abra del Ingernillo RA 279 Gh59
Abraham's Bay BS 250 Gc34
Abra Huashuaccasa PE 269 Gd53
Abraka WAN 188 Ld43
Abrantes P 55 Km51
Abra Pampa RA 279 Gh57
Abras BR 273 Jd47
Abra Tapuna PE 269 Gd52
Abre Campo BR 275 Hj56
Abrego CO 264 Gd41
Abrene = Pytalovo RUS 45 Mh33
Abrene Pytalovo RUS 45 Mh33
Abreu MOC 203 Mj55
Abri SUD 185 Mf35
Abri de Koumbala RCA 190 Ma41
Abri de Toulou RCA 190 Ma41
Abritus BG 69 Mg47
Abrud RO 67 Md44
Abruka saar EST 45 Mc32
Abruzzo I 62 Lo48
Abruzzo, P.N. d' I 62 Lo49
Absaroka Range USA 233 Ee23
Absarokee USA 233 Ef23
Abtei Einsiedeln CH 60 Lj43
Abtei Stams A 60 Lm43
Ab Torsh IR 91 Ne27
Ab Touyour TCH 189 Lk40
Abu GNB 186 Kc40
Abu Ajram KSA 92 Mk31
Abu Al-Abyadh UAE 95 Ng33
Abu al Khasib IRQ 93 Nd30
Abu 'Arish KSA 94 Nb37
Abu at Tabul OM 95 Nh35
Abu Bahr KSA 94 Nd35
Abu Dawn SUD 185 Mg37
Abu Deleiq SUD 185 Mg38
Abu Dhabi UAE 95 Nh33
Abu Dhabi Icerink UAE 95 Nh33
Abu Dom SUD 185 Mf37
Abu Durbah ET 179 Mg31
Abu el Matâmir ET 179 Mf30
Abufari BR 270 Gj48
Abu Gabra SUD 184 Md40
Abu Gamel SUD 185 Mj38
Abu Ghirban SUD 185 Mg36
Abu Ghusun ET 179 Mh33
Abugi WAN 188 Ld41
Abu Gubayba SUD 185 Mf40
Abu Gurayb IRQ 91 Nc29
Abu Hadriyah KSA 93 Ne32
Abu Hamed SUD 185 Mg36
Abu Hammâd ET 179 Mf30
Abuhar IND 114 Oh30
Abu Hashim SUD 185 Mf40
Abu Hashim SUD 185 Mg36
Abu Higar SUD 185 Mg39
Abuja WAN 188 Ld41
Abu Kabisa SUD 184 Md39
Abu Kamal SYR 91 Na28
Abu Kebîr ET 179 Mf30
Abuki Mountains RI 130 Ra47
Abuko Nature Reserve WAG 186 Kb39
Abukuma-koti J 111 Sa27
Abu Latt KSA 94 Na36
Abulug RP 124 Ra36
Abu Maztariq SUD 184 Md40
Abu Mendi ETH 192 Mh40
Abu Mina ET 179 Me30
Abu Minqar ET 178 Md32
Abumombazi RDC 190 Mb44
Abu, Mount = Guru Shikhar IND 116 Og33
Abunã BR 270 Gh50
Abu Na'im LAR 177 Lk31
Abu Ra's SUD 191 Mc42
Abu Road IND 116 Og33
Abu Rubayq KSA 92 Mk34
Abu Rudays ET 179 Mg31
Abu Saffar SUD 185 Mg37
Abu Sari SUD 185 Mf35
Abu Simbel ET 179 Mf34
Abu Simbel ET 179 Mg33
Abu Sukhayr IRQ 93 Nc30
Abuta J 111 Sa24
Abu Teeg ET 179 Mf32
Abut Head NZ 153 Tf67
Abu Tunaytin SUD 185 Mf38
Abu 'Uruq SUD 185 Mf38
Abu Uwayjilah ET 179 Mh30
Abuyog RP 124 Rc40
Abu Zabad SUD 184 Me39
Abu Zayyan LAR 177 Lg29
Abu Zeyo Abad IR 91 Nf29
Abuz'hour SYR 90 Mj28
Abwong SUD 191 Mg41
Åby S 43 Lp32
Åby S 43 Lr32
Abyad SUD 184 Md39
Abyaneh IR 93 Nf29
Abyar 'Ali KSA 92 Mk33
Abyar ash Shuwayrif LAR 177 Lh31
Abydos = El Âmirah ET 179 Mf32
Abyei SUD 191 Me41
Abyek IR 91 Nf27
Åbyggeby S 43 Ls30
Åbytorp S 43 Lq31
Acadian Museum CDN 240 Gk22
Acadia N.P. USA 241 Gf23
Acadia Valley CDN 233 Ee20
Acahay PY 276 Hb58
Açailândia BR 272 Hg48
Açai Paraná BR 270 Gf45
Acajutiba BR 273 Ja51
Acajutla ES 248 Ff39
Acalayong GQ 188 Le45
Acambaro MEX 246 Ek35
Acampamento da Cameia ANG 201 Ma51
Acampamento de Indios BR 271 Ha51
Acampamento Grande BR 266 Hd45
Acandi CO 264 Gb41
Acangatá BR 267 He47
A Cañiza E 54 Km48
Acaponeta MEX 245 Eh34
Acapulco MEX 246 Fa37
Acará BR 267 Hf46
Acaraú BR 273 Hk47
Acari BR 273 Jb49
Acari PE 269 Gc53
Acarigua YV 265 Gf41
Acasio BOL 278 Gg55
Acatlán de Juárez MEX 246 Ej35
Acatlán de Osorio MEX 246 Fa36
Acat zingo MEX 246 Fb36
Acay, Nevado de RA 279 Gg58
Acayucan MEX 247 Fc37
Accéglio I 60 Lh46
Accomac USA 241 Gc27
Accra GH 187 Kk43
ACE Basin N.W.R. USA 242 Fk29
Acebuches MEX 245 Ej31
Aceguá BR 276 Hc61
Aceguá ROU 276 Hc61
Acerenza I 63 Lq50
Achaacha DZ 175 La27
Achacachi BOL 278 Gf54
Achaguas YV 265 Gf42
Achalpur IND 116 Oj35
Achampet IND 117 Pa37
Achao RCH 280 Gd67
Achar ROU 276 Hb62
Achcharapakkam IND 119 Ok39
Acheb DZ 176 Le31
Achegtim RIM 180 Ke36
Achelouma RN 183 Lg34
Acheng CHN 110 Rd23
Achensee A 60 Lm43
Achguig el Adam RIM 180 Ke36
Achí CO 264 Gc41
Achiasi GH 187 Kk43
Achilleio GR 70 Lu51
Achill Head IRL 47 Kk37
Achill Island IRL 47 Kk37
Achim D 58 Lk38
Achiras RA 280 Gh62
Achiri BOL 278 Gf54
Achiwib GUY 266 Ha44
Achnasheen GB 48 Kp33
Acholibur EAU 194 Mg44
Achouka G 198 Lf46
Achra IND 116 Og37
Aci Castello I 63 Lq53
Aci Catena I 63 Lq53
Acima, T.I. BR 270 Gg49
Ačinsk RUS 88 Pc07
Acireale I 63 Lq53
Ackerman USA 239 Ff29
Acklins Island BS 250 Gc34
Acle GB 49 Lb38
Acobamba PE 269 Gc52
Acoma Pueblo USA 235 Eg28
Acomayo PE 269 Ge52
Aconcagua, Cerro RA 280 Ge62
Aconchi MEX 244 Ee31
Acopantepui YV 265 Gj43
Acopiara BR 273 Ja49
Acoris ET 179 Mf31
A Coruña E 54 Km47
Acos PE 269 Gb51
Acostambo PE 269 Gc52
Acoyapa NIC 249 Fh40
Acqua Doria F 62 Lj49
Acquapendente I 60 Lm48
Acquasanta Terme I 61 Lo48
Acquasparta I 60 Ln48
Acquaviva delle Fonti I 63 Lr50
Ácqui Terme I 60 Lj46
Acre BOL/BR 270 Gf51
Acre BR 255 Ga10
Acre IL 90 Mh29
Acreúna BR 274 He54
Acri I 63 Lr51
Acsa H 67 Lu43
Acton S.H.S. USA 238 Fb29
Actopan MEX 246 Fa35
Açucena BR 275 Hj55
Acueducto romano de Segovia E 54 Kq50
Acuña MEX 245 Ek31
Acurenam GQ 188 Lf45
Ada GH 187 La43
Ada SRB 68 Ma45
Ada USA 236 Fb22
Ada USA 238 Fb28
Adaba ETH 192 Mk42
Adadi Mariam ETH 192 Mk41
Adaigba WAN 188 Ld42
Adaiso GH 187 Kk43
Adam OM 95 Nj34
Adam al Hulay KSA 94 Na35
Adamantina BR 274 He56
Adámas GR 71 Me54
Adamclisi RO 69 Mh46
Adamello I 60 Ll44
Adaminaby AUS 151 Se63
Adami Tulu ETH 192 Mk42
Adamova BY 45 Mj35
Adam's Bridge IND/CL 119 Ok41
Adams Lake CDN 232 Ea20
Adams, Mount USA 232 Dk22
Adam's Peak CL 119 Pa42
Adamuz E 55 Kq52
Adana TR 90 Mh27
Adan as Sughra YE 94 Nc39
Adané G 198 Lf46
Adani WAN 188 Ld42
Adaouda DZ 182 Lc34
Adapazarı = Sakarya TR 90 Mf25
Adar TCH 184 Ma40
Adarama SUD 185 Mh37
Adare IRL 47 Km38
Adaut RI 131 Rf50
Adavale AUS 149 Sc58
ad-Dabba SUD 185 Mf36
Ad Dafinah KSA 94 Nb34
Ad Dahna KSA 93 Nc32
Ad Dali YE 95 Nf36
Ad Dammam KSA 93 Nf32
Addanki IND 117 Ok38
Ad-Dar-al-Bayda MA 175 Kg29
Ad Dar al Hamra KSA 94 Na35
Ad Darb KSA 94 Nb37
Ad-Dariz OM 95 Nj34
Ad Dawadami KSA 93 Nc33
Ad Dawhah Q 93 Nf33
Ad Dawr IRQ 91 Nb28
Ad-Dhaid UAE 95 Nh33
Ad-Dhawah LAR 178 Ma33
Addi CAM 189 Lh42
Ad Dibdibah KSA 93 Nc32
Ad Dikakah KSA 95 Nf36
Ad Dilam KSA 93 Nd33
Ad Dir'iyah KSA 93 Nd33
Addis Ababa ETH 192 Mk41
Addison USA 239 Fg28
Ad Diwaniyah IRQ 93 Nc30
Addo ZA 205 Mc62
Addo Elephant N.P. ZA 205 Mc62
ad-Dubasi SUD 185 Mg38
ad-Du'hayn SUD 184 Md40
Ad Dulaymiyah KSA 93 Nb32
Ad Dulu'iyah IRQ 91 Nc28
Ad-Dumeir SYR 90 Mj29
Ad Duqah KSA 94 Na36
Ad Durma KSA 93 Nd33
Ad Duwayd KSA 93 Nb30
ad-Duwayn SUD 185 Mg39
Adé TCH 184 Ma39
Adéane SN 186 Kb39
Adel USA 232 Ea24
Adel USA 242 Fj30
Adelaide AUS 150 Rk63
Adelaide ZA 205 Md62
Adelaide Island 286 Gc32
Adelaide River AUS 146 Rf52
Adelaide River AUS 146 Rf52
Adel Bagrou RIM 181 Kg38
Adelbert Range PNG 155 Sc48
Adelboden CH 60 Lh44
Adele Island AUS 142 Rb53
Adelia Maria RA 280 Gh62
Adelong AUS 149 Sc57
Adelong AUS 151 Se63
Ademuz E 57 Kt50
Aden YE 94 Nc39
Adenau D 59 Lg40
Adendorp ZA 205 Mc62
Aderbissiant RN 182 Ld38
Adesar IND 116 Of34
Adet ETH 192 Mj40
Adéta TG 187 La42
Adhaby KSA 94 Nb37
Adhaura IND 117 Pb33
Adi RI 154 Rg48
Adiake CI 187 Kj43
Adiangdia DY 188 La41
Adi Ark'ay ETH 192 Mj39
Adicora YV 265 Gf40
Adi Da'iro ETH 192 Mk38
Adidome GH 187 La42
Adigala ETH 192 Nb40
Ádige = Etsch I 60 Ln45
Adigrat ETH 192 Mk38
Adi Gudom ETH 192 Mk39
Adikas ETH 194 Mh43
Adi Keyih ER 192 Mk38
Adi Kwala ER 192 Mk38
Adilabad IND 117 Ok36
Adilcevaz TR 91 Nb26
Adimi IR 98 Oa30
Adin USA 234 Dk25
Adinsoone SP 193 Ne41
Adiora RMM 181 Kk37
Adipala RI 129 Qe49
Adi Ramets ETH 192 Mj39
Adirampattinam IND 119 Ok40
Adiri LAR 177 Lg32
Adirondack Mountains USA 241 Gc24
Adirondack Museum USA 241 Gc24
Adirondack Park USA 241 Gc24
Adirondack Scenic R.R. USA 241 Gc24
Adis Alem ETH 192 Mk41
Adis Zemen ETH 192 Mj39
Adi Ugri ER 192 Mk38
Adıyaman TR 90 Mk27
Adjengré TG 187 La41
Adjen Kotoku GH 187 Kk43
Adjerar DZ 182 Lc33
Adjud RO 73 Md22
Adler RUS 91 Mk24
Adliswil CH 60 Lj43
Admiralty Inlet CDN 227 Fc04
Admiralty Bay AUS 143 Rc53
Admiralty Gulf A.L. AUS 143 Rc53
Admiralty I. National Monument USA 230 Dc17
Admiralty Islands PNG 156 Sd47
Admiralty Island USA 230 Dc17
Admjany BY 45 Mf36
Admont A 61 Lp43
Ado WAN 188 Lb42
Ado WAN 188 Ld41
Ado Awaiye WAN 188 Lb42
Ado-Ekiti WAN 188 Lc42
Adok SUD 191 Mf41
Adolfo BR 274 Hf56
Adolfo González Chaves RA 281 Gk65
Adolfo López Mateos MEX 244 Ed33
Adolfo López Mateos (La Junta) MEX 244 Eg31
Adonara RI 131 Rb50
Adoni IND 116 Oj38
Adony H 67 Lt43
Adorf D 59 Ln40
Adoru WAN 188 Ld42
Adoumandjali RCA 190 Lh44
Adoumri CAM 189 Lg41
Adra E 55 Kr54
Adra IND 117 Pd34
Adrall E 56 Lb48
Adranga RDC 194 Mf44
Adrano I 63 Lp53
Adrar DZ 175 Kk32
Adrar Ahellakane DZ 176 Lc32
Adrar Azzaouager RN 182 Le37
Adrar des Ifôrhas RMM 182 La36
Adrar Ikohahoène DZ 176 Le32
Adrar-n-Aklim MA 175 Kg30
Adrar-n-Deren MA 175 Kg30
Adrar-n-Imchech MA 175 Kg30
Adrâr Souttouf DARS 180 Kc34
Adrar Tedjorar DZ 182 Lc34
Adrar Tighârghârr RMM 182 La36
Adrar Tintejert DZ 176 Lb33
Adraskan AFG 98 Ob29
Adré TCH 184 Mb39
Ádria I 60 Ln45
Adrian USA 232 Eb24
Adrian USA 237 Fh25
Adrian USA 238 Ej28
Adrianópolis BR 277 Hf58
Adriatic Sea 26 Lb05
Adršpašsko-teplické skály CZ 66 Lq40
Adul IND 116 Oh36
Adulis ER 192 Mk38
Adunații-Copăceni RO 69 Mg46
Adunkur Daban CHN 100 Pc24
Adunu WAN 188 Ld41
Adur IND 118 Oj41
Adura WAN 188 Lc43
Aduripalle IND 119 Ok38
Adusa RDC 191 Me45
Adustina BR 273 Ja51
Adutiškis LT 45 Mg35
Aduturai IND 119 Ok40
Advance USA 239 Ff27
Adwa ETH 192 Mk38
Adwana IND 116 Oe35
Adyal IND 117 Ok35
Adygea RUS 77 Mb05
Adzharia GE 91 Na25
Adzhina Tepe Monastery TJ 97 Oe26
Adzopé CI 187 Kj42
Aegean Sea 71 Me51
Aegviidu EST 44 Mf31
Aekanopan RI 127 Pk44
Ærø DK 42 Ll36
A Estrada E 54 Km48
Aetorráhi GR 70 Mb53
Äetsä FIN 44 Mc29
Afabet ER 185 Mk37
Afadé CAM 189 Lh39
'Afak IRQ 93 Nc29
Afándou GR 71 Mj54
Af Barwaargo SP 193 Ne42
Afdem ETH 192 Na41
Afé SN 180 Kc38
Afétes GR 68 Md51
Afféri CI 187 Kj42
Afghanistan AFG 77 Oa06
Afgooye SP 195 Nc44
Afhir MA 175 Kj28
Afif KSA 94 Nb34
Afikpo WAN 188 Ld43
Afilal DZ 182 Lc34
Aflaj Irrigation Systems OM 95 Nj34
Aflou DZ 176 Lb28
Afmadow SP 195 Nb45
Afobaka SME 266 Hc43
Afogados de Ingazeira BR 273 Jb49
Afognak Island USA 228 Ce16
Afognak Mtn. USA 228 Cd16
Afolé TG 187 La42
Afonso Cláudio BR 275 Hk56
Afore PNG 156 Se50
Afqa RL 90 Mh28
Afrânio BR 273 Hk50
Afrasiab UZ 97 Od26
Afrera Terara ETH 192 Na39
Afrin SYR 90 Mj27
Afşin TR 90 Mj26
Afsluitdijk NL 51 Lf37
Afton USA 233 Ee24
Afton USA 236 Fc25
Aftor Doons AUS 147 Sc56
Aftoût ech Chergui RIM 180 Kc37
Afua BR 267 He46
Afula IL 90 Mh29
Afumați RO 69 Mg46
Afyon TR 90 Mf26
Afzalpur IND 116 Oj37
Aga-Batyr RUS 91 Nc24
Aga Buryat Autonomous District RUS 89 Qd08
Agadem RN 183 Lg37
Agadez RN 182 Ld37
Agadir MA 174 Kf30
Agadir-Tissint MA 175 Kg31
Agaete E 174 Kc31
Agaie WAN 188 Ld41
Agalawatta CL 119 Pa42
Agalega Islands MS 162 Nb11
Agamor RMM 181 La37
Agana USA 135 Sa08
Agápi GR 71 Mf53
Agapo Açu BR 271 Hb48
Agar IND 116 Oh34
Agâraktem RMM 181 Kg34
Agarfa ETH 192 Mk42
Agaro ETH 192 Mj42
Agartala IND 120 Pf34
Agar Uen ETH 193 Nc42
Agassiz Prov. Forest CDN 236 Fc20
Agastya Malai IND 118 Oj41
Agate Fossil Beds Nat. Mon. USA 235 Ej24
Agathonisi GR 71 Mg53
Agats RI 154 Rk48
Agatti Island IND 118 Og40
Agave Landscape MEX 246 Ej35
Agbabu WAN 188 Lc42
Agbarha-Otor WAN 188 Lc43
Agbélouvé TG 187 La42
Agbor-Bojiboji WAN 188 Ld42
Agboville CI 187 Kh43
Agdam AZ 91 Nd25
Agdas AZ 91 Nd25
Agde F 53 Ld47
Agdz MA 175 Kg30
Agdžabedi AZ 91 Nd25
Agege WAN 188 Lb42
Agen F 52 La46
Agenebode WAN 188 Ld42
Agerbæk DK 42 Lj35
Agere Maryam ETH 194 Mk43
Agere Selam ETH 192 Mk42
Aggeneys ZA 204 Lk60
Agger DK 42 Lj34
Aggtelek H 67 Ma42
Aggteleki N.P. H 67 Ma42
Aggui RIM 180 Kd35
Aghajari IR 93 Ne30
Agha Mosque IR 91 Nf28
Aghat RN 182 Ld37
Agh Bolagh IR 91 Nc27
Aghdas Cave IR 91 Ne28
Aghezzaf RMM 181 Kk36
Aghireșu RO 67 Md44
Aghoninit DARS 180 Kd34
Aghor PK 99 Oc33
Aghouedir RIM 180 Ke35
Aghreïjit RIM 180 Kd35
Aghrijit RIM 180 Kf36
Agiá GR 70 Mc51
Agiabampo MEX 244 Ef32
Agía Galíni GR 71 Me55
Agía Marína GR 69 Md53
Agía Marína GR 71 Me52
Agía Pelagía GR 71 Mc54
Agía Triáda GR 70 Mb53
Agía Varvára GR 71 Mf55
Agighiol RO 69 Mj45
Ágii Apóstoli GR 69 Md54
Ágii Theódori GR 69 Md53
Ágii Theódori GR 70 Mb51
Aginskoe RUS 105 Qh20
Aginta RO 67 Me45
Agiokambos GR 68 Md52
Agiókambos GR 70 Mc51
Agiorgítika GR 70 Mc53
Ágios Andréas GR 70 Mc53
Ágios Charalampos GR 69 Mf50
Ágios Christós GR 70 Mc50
Ágios Dimítrios GR 70 Mc50
Ágios Dimítrios GR 70 Mc50
Ágios Dimítrios GR 70 Mc54
Ágios Efstrátios GR 71 Me51
Ágios Efstrátios GR 71 Mf51
Ágios Geórgios GR 70 Mb52
Ágios Kírikos GR 71 Mg53
Ágios Mámas GR 71 Me55
Ágios Nikolaos GR 70 Ma53
Ágios Nikólaos GR 70 Mc52
Ágios Nikólaos GR 71 Mf55
Ágios Pétros GR 70 Mc53
Ágios Stéfanos GR 70 Mc51
Ágios Stéfanos GR 71 Mh54
Ágios Theodoros = Çayırova CY 90 Mh28
Ágira I 63 Lp53
Agjert RIM 180 Kf37
Aglal RMM 181 Kj37
Åglen BG 69 Me47
Ağlı TR 90 Mg25
Aglona LV 45 Mg34
Agmar RIM 174 Ke33
Agnang G 198 Lg45
Agnantiá GR 70 Mb51
Agnes Creek AUS 148 Rg59
Agnes Lodge SOL 157 Sj50
Agness USA 232 Dh24
Agnes Waters AUS 149 Sf58
Agnew AUS 144 Ra60
Agnibilékrou CI 187 Kj42
Agnone I 63 Lp49
Ago J 113 Rj28
Ago-Are WAN 188 Lb41
Agogo GH 187 Kk42
Agohay Beach RP 125 Rc41
Agolai IND 114 Og32
Agona GH 187 Kk42
Agona Junction GH 187 Kk43
Agona-Sweru GH 187 Kk43
Agoo RP 124 Ra37
Agora GR 69 Me50
Agordo I 60 Ln44
Agostadero de Aguirre MEX 244 Eg32
Agotu PNG 155 Sc49
Agou CI 187 Kj43
Agoudal MA 175 Kh30
Agoué TG 187 La42
Agoueïnît RIM 181 Kg37
Agou Gadzépé TG 187 La42
Agouna DY 188 La42
Agounni Jefal RMM 181 Kj37
Agouti MA 175 Kg30
Agra IND 115 Ok32
Agra Fort IND 115 Oj32
Agrahanskij poluostrov RUS 91 Nd24
Agramunt E 57 Lb49
Ágreda E 56 Kt49
Agreliá GR 70 Mb51
Ağrı TR 91 Nb26
Agriáni GR 70 Mc53
Ağri Dağı TR 91 Nc26
Agrigento I 62 Lo53
Agrínio GR 70 Mb52
Agriovótano GR 69 Md51
Agrópoli I 63 Lp50
Agua Azul HN 248 Fg38
Agua Blanca GCA 248 Ff38
Agua Blanca de Iturbide MEX 246 Fa35
Agua Boa BR 274 Hd53
Água Boa BR 275 Hj54
Agua Braga BR 272 Hf52
Agua Branca BR 272 Hg49
Agua Branca BR 273 Hj48
Agua Caliente PE 269 Gc50
Aguacatán GCA 248 Fe38
Aguachica CO 264 Gd41
Agua Clara BR 274 Hd56
Agua Comprida BR 274 Hf56
Aguada Cecilio RA 280 Gh66
Aguada de Pasajeros C 243 Fk34
Aguadas CO 264 Gc43
Aguadilla USA 251 Gg36
Água Doce BR 276 He59
Agua Dulce MEX 247 Fc36
Aguadulce PA 249 Fk41
Agua Escondida RA 280 Gf64
Agua Grande MEX 244 Ee31
Agua Hedionda, Cerro RA 280 Gg62
Aguaí BR 275 Hg57
Agualeguas MEX 245 Fa32
Aguanga USA 234 Eb29
Aguanish CDN 240 Gj20
Agua Nueva MEX 245 Ek33
Água Petra Inari, T.I. BR 270 Gg49
Agua Prieta MEX 244 Ef30
Agua Quente BR 272 Hg52
Aguaragüe, P.N. BOL 279 Gj56
Aguaray RA 279 Gj57
A Guarda E 54 Km49
Aguaro-Guariquito, P.N. YV 265 Gg41
Aguasay YV 265 Gj41
Águas Belas BR 273 Jb50
Águas Belas, T.I. BR 275 Ja54
Aguas Blancas PE 279 Gf58
Aguas Blancas RA 279 Gh57
Aguas Blancas, Cerro RA/RCH 279 Gf58
Aguascalientes MEX 246 Ej35
Aguascalientes MEX 246 Ej34
Águas Formosas BR 275 Hk54
Aguas Negras PE 268 Gc46
Aguas Turbias, P.N. BH 248 Ff37
Aguateca GCA 247 Fe37
Agua Verde PE 279 Gf58
Agua Viva YV 264 Ge41
Aguaytia PE 269 Gc50
Aguazul CO 264 Gd43
A Gudiña E 54 Kn48
Agudo BR 276 Hd60
Agudo E 55 Kq52
Agudos BR 274 Hf57
Águeda P 54 Km50
Aguelhok RMM 181 La36
Aguelt ez Zerga RIM 180 Kc36
Aguiar Javés BR 272 Hf51
Aguié RN 182 Ld39
Aguila RIM 180 Kc37
Aguila USA 235 Ed29
Aguilâl Faï RIM 180 Kc36
Aguilar E 55 Kq53
Aguilar de Campóo E 54 Kq48
Aguilares ES 248 Ff39
Aguilares RA 279 Gh59
Águilas E 57 Kt53
Aguiler Grande BOL 270 Gf51
Aguililla MEX 246 Ej36
Aguirre Cerda ANT 286 Gd31
Aguja, Cerro RA/RCH 282 Ge67
Aguja, Cerro RCH 282 Gf73
Agula'i ETH 192 Mk39
Agulhas Negras BR 277 Hh57
Agulhas N.P. ZA 204 Lk63
Agumatsa W.S. GH 187 La42
Agumbe IND 118 Oh39
Aguni-jima J 113 Rd32
Agustinópolis BR 272 Hf48
Agutaya Island RP 124 Ra40
Ağva TR 69 Mk49
Agwarra WAN 188 Lc40
Agweri WAN 188 Ld42
Agwit SUD 191 Md41
Agwok SUD 191 Me42
Ahaba WAN 188 Ld43
Ahaberge NAM 201 Ma55
Ahad Rafidah KSA 94 Nb36
Aha Hills RB 201 Ma55
Ahakeye (Ti-Tree) A.L. AUS 143 Rg57
Ahamasu GH 187 La42
Ahar IR 91 Nd26
Ahaus D 58 Lh38
Åheim N 40 Lf28
Ahenkto GH 187 La42
Ahero EAK 194 Mh46
Ahipara NZ 152 Tg63
Ahipara Bay NZ 152 Tg63
Ahiti NZ 153 Th65
Ahklun Mountains USA 228 Cc15
Ahladiá GR 69 Me49
Ahladohóri GR 68 Md49
Ahlainen FIN 44 Mb29
Ahlainen FIN 44 Mb29
Ahlat TR 91 Nb26
Ahlbeck D 58 Lp37
Ahlen D 58 Lh39
Ahmadi KWT 93 Ne31
Ahmadpur IND 116 Oj36
Ahmadpur PK 99 Of30
Ahmadpur East PK 99 Of31
Ahmad Shah Durrani Tomb AFG 99 Oc30
Ahmad Wal PK 99 Oc31
Ahmar Mountains ETH 192 Na41
Ahmedabad IND 116 Og34
Ahmednagar IND 116 Oh36
Ahmedpur Mandvi Beach IND 116 Of35
Ahmetli TR 71 Mh52
Ahoada WAN 188 Ld43
Ahome MEX 244 Ef33
Ahousat CDN 232 Dg21
Ahram IR 93 Nf31
Ahraura IND 117 Pb33
Ahrensbök D 58 Ll36
Ahrensburg D 58 Ll37
Ahsu AZ 91 Ne25
Ahtamar TR 91 Nb26
Ähtäri FIN 44 Me28
Ahtme EST 44 Mh31
Ahtopol BG 69 Mh48
Ahty RUS 91 Nd25
Ahu IR 93 Ne30
Ahuachapan ES 248 Ff39
Ahualulco MEX 246 Ek34
Ahualulco de Mercado MEX 246 Ej35
Ahuano EC 268 Gb46
Ahuas HN 249 Fh38
Ahuasbila HN 249 Fh38
Ahun F 53 Lc44
Ahus RI 128 Qj44
Åhus S 43 Lp35
Ahvaz IR 93 Ne30
Ahvenanmaa = Åland FIN 44 Lu30
Ahwa IND 116 Og35
Ahwar YE 94 Nd39
Ai-Ais NAM 204 Lj59
Ai-Ais Hot Springs NAM 204 Lj59
Ai-Ais Warmwaterbronne NAM 204 Lj59
Aiaktalik Island USA 228 Cd17
Aialik Cape USA 228 Cf16
Aiapuá BR 270 Gj48
Aiaweté Igarapé Ipixuna , T.I. BR 271 Hd48
Aiban UAE 95 Nh33
Aibar E 56 Kt48
Aibetsu J 111 Sb24
Aichach D 59 Lm42
Aiduma RI 154 Rh48
Aiduna RI 154 Rh48
Aiere WAN 188 Ld42
Aigamas Caves NAM 200 Lj55
Aigen A 61 Lp43
Aigen A 66 Lo42
Aigene mekeni KZ 97 Oe23
Aigiali GR 71 Mf54
Aigle CH 60 Lg44
Aignay-le-Duc F 53 Le43
Aigre F 52 La45
Aigrefeuille-d'Aunis F 52 Ku44
Aiguá ROU 281 Hc63
Aiguebelle F 53 Lg45
Aiguebelle, P.N. d' CDN 237 Ga21
Aigues-Mortes F 53 Le47
Aigüestortes i Estany de Sant Maurici, P.N. de E 56 La48
Aiguilete, Cerro RCH 282 Gd71
Aiguille du Midi F 53 Lg45
Aiguilles F 53 Lg46
Aiguilles de Sindou BF 187 Kh40
Aiguillon F 52 La46
Aigurande F 52 Lb44
Aihole IND 116 Oh38
Aija PE 269 Gb50
Aikawa J 111 Rk26
Aiken USA 242 Fk29
Ailao Shan CHN 121 Qa33
Ailefroide F 53 Lg46
Aileron AUS 148 Rg57
Ailigandi PA 249 Ga41
Ailly-sur-Noye F 51 Lc41
Aimachá del Valle RA 279 Gh59
Aimogasta RA 279 Gg60
Aimorés BR 275 Hk55
Ain al Arab SYR 90 Mk27
Ain Attaya RIM 180 Kd35
Ainaži LV 45 Me33
Aïn-Beïda DZ 176 Ld28
Aïn Benian DZ 176 Lb27
Aïn Benimathar MA 175 Kj28
Aïn Ben Tili RIM 174 Kf33
Aïn Bessem DZ 176 Lb27
Âïn Boubat RIM 180 Kd37
Aïn Dara SYR 90 Mj27
Aïn Defla DZ 176 La27
Aïn Deheb DZ 176 La28
Aïn Draham TN 176 Le27
Aïn-Ech-Chair MA 175 Kj29
Aïn el Bell DZ 176 Lb28
Aïn el Brod DZ 176 Lc31
Aïn el Hadja DZ 175 La28
Aïn el Hadjadj DZ 176 Ld32
Aïn-el-Hadjadj DZ 176 Lb31
Aïn el Hadjel DZ 176 Lb28
Aïn el Hamara DZ 176 Lb28
Aïn el Hamman DZ 176 Lc27
Aïn el Melh DZ 176 Lc28
Aïn-el-Orak DZ 175 La29
Aïn-el-Türck DZ 175 Kk28
Aïn Fakroun DZ 176 Ld28
Aïn Fekan DZ 175 La28
Ainggyi MYA 120 Ph35
Ainhoa F 52 Kt47
Aïn Kerch DZ 176 Ld28
Aïn Kermes DZ 175 La28
Aïn Khadra DZ 176 Lc28
Âïn-Leuh MA 175 Kh29
Aïn Madhi DZ 176 Lb29
Aïn-M'Lila DZ 176 Ld27
Ainos N.P. GR 70 Ma52
Aïn Oulmene DZ 176 Lc28
Aïn Oussera DZ 176 Lb28
Ainsa E 56 La48
Aïn Sefra DZ 175 Kk29
Aïn Skhouna DZ 175 La28
Ain Sukhnah ET 179 Mg31
Ainsworth USA 236 Fa24
Aïn Tamr TN 176 Le29
Aïn Taya DZ 176 Lb27
Aïn Tédelès DZ 175 La28
Aïn Témouchent DZ 175 Kk28
Aintree GB 49 Ks37
Aiome PNG 155 Sc48
Aiome, Mount PNG 155 Sc48
Aiquile BOL 278 Gh55
Airabu RI 126 Qd44
Airaines F 51 Lb41
Airasca I 60 Lh46
Airavateswarar Temple IND 119 Ok40
Airbalam RI 127 Pk45
Airbangis RI 127 Pk45
Airbara RI 129 Qd47
Airdrie CDN 233 Ec20
Aire-sur-l'Adour F 52 Ku47
Aire-sur-la-Lys F 51 Lc40
Airgegas RI 129 Qd47
Airi BR 273 Ja50
Airlie AUS 147 Se56
Airolo CH 60 Lj44
Aïr ou Azbine RN 182 Le36
Airpanas RI 131 Rc49
Airvault F 52 Ku44
Airwa IND 117 Ok32
Aisch D 59 Ll41
Aishihik CDN 230 Db15
Aitana E 57 Ku52
Aitape PNG 155 Sb47
Âït-Baha MA 174 Kf30
Âït Ben Haddou MA 175 Kg30
Aiteke Bi KZ 96 Ob23
Âït-Hamane MA 175 Kg30
Aitkin USA 236 Fd22
Ait-Melloul MA 174 Kf30
Âït Morrhad MA 175 Kh30
Aitong EAK 194 Mh46
Âït-Ourir MA 175 Kg30
Âït Saadane MA 175 Kh30
Aiud RO 67 Md44
Aix-en-Othe F 51 Ld42
Aix-en-Provence F 53 Lf47
Aixe-sur-Vienne F 52 Lb45
Aix-les-Bains F 53 Lf45
Aiy Adi ETH 192 Mk39
Aiyetoro WAN 188 Lb42
Aiyetoro WAN 188 Lc42
Aiyrtas KZ 100 Oj21
Aizawl IND 120 Pg34
Aizenay F 52 Kt44
Aizkrāukle LV 45 Mf34
Aizpute LV 45 Mb34
Aizu-Wakamatsu J 111 Rk27
Ajabshir IR 91 Nc27
Ajaccio F 62 Lj49
Ajai Game Reserve EAU 194 Mf44
Ajaigarh IND 117 Pa33
Ajak RUS 105 Rd19
Ajana AUS 144 Qh59
Ajanta IND 116 Oh35
Ajanta Caves IND 116 Oh35
Ajaokuta WAN 188 Ld42
Ajasse WAN 188 Lc41
Ajasso WAN 188 Le43
Ajax, Mount NZ 153 Tg67
Aj Bogd Uul MNG 101 Ph23
Ajdabiya LAR 177 Ma30
Ajdarly KZ 97 Oc23
Ajdir MA 175 Kj28
Ajdovščina SLO 66 Lo45
Ajigasawa J 111 Sa25
Aj'jawdiyeh SYR 91 Na27
Ajjibal Attadmur lych SYR 90 Mj28
Ajka H 66 Ls43
Ajman UAE 95 Nh33
Ajmer IND 114 Oh32
Ajmer Sharief IND 114 Oh32
Ajni TJ 97 Oe26
Ajo USA 235 Ed29
Ajoda WAN 188 Lc42
Ajoya MEX 244 Eg33
Ajra IND 116 Oh37
Ajrestan AFG 99 Od29
Ajtos BG 69 Mh48
Ájtte S 38 Lu24
Ajumaku GH 187 Kk43
Ajuruteua BR 267 Hg46
Ajuy RP 124 Rb40
Akabar RMM 182 La38
Akabli DZ 175 La32
Akadomari J 111 Rk27
Aka-Eze WAN 188 Ld43
Akagera, P.N. de l' RWA 194 Mf46
Akagi J 113 Rg28
Akaishi-sanmyahku J 113 Rk28
Akakbe CAM 188 Le43
Akaki ETH 192 Mk41
Akakro CI 187 Kh43
Akakus LAR 183 Lf33
Akala SUD 185 Mj38
Akalkot IND 116 Oj37
Akam Éffak G 189 Lf45
Akamkpa WAN 188 Le43
Akanda, P.N. d' G 198 Le45
Akankoshan J 111 Sc24
Akan N.P. J 111 Sc24
Akarkar RN 182 Ld38
Akarnaniká GR 70 Mb52
Akaroa NZ 153 Tg67
Akasame PNG 155 Sb49
Akasha SUD 185 Mf35
Akashat IRQ 90 Mk29
Akassa WAN 188 Ld43
Akat Amnuai THA 121 Qb37
Akats GH 187 La42
Akbarpur IND 117 Pb32
Akbou DZ 176 Lc27
Akçaabat TR 91 Mk25
Akçakale TR 90 Mk27
Akçakoca TR 90 Mf25
Akçalar TR 90 Mj27
Akçalı Dağları TR 90 Mg27
Akçaova TR 71 Mj53
Akçay TR 91 Nb25
Akcjabrski BY 72 Me19
Akdağ TR 71 Mj51
Akdağ TR 71 Mj53
Ak Dağlar TR 90 Me27
Akdağmadeni TR 90 Mh26
Akdepe TM 96 Nk24
Akébou TG 187 La42
Akelamo RI 125 Rd45
Akelamo RI 125 Re45
Aken D 58 Ln39
Åkernes N 42 Lh32
Åkersberga S 43 Lt31
Åkers styckebruk S 43 Ls31
Aketi RDC 191 Mb44
Akhalkalaki GE 91 Nb25
Akhaltsikhe GE 91 Nb25
Akhiok USA 228 Cc17
Akhisar TR 71 Mh52
Akhmeta GE 91 Nc25
Akhmim ET 179 Mf32
Akhnoor 114 Oh29
Akhpat and Sanain Monasteries ARM 91 Nc25
Aki J 113 Rg29
Akiachak USA 228 Bk15
Akiéni G 198 Lg46
Akıncı Burnu TR 90 Mh27
Akinum PNG 156 Se49
Akita J 111 Sa26
Akividu IND 117 Pa37
Akjoujt RIM 180 Kc36
Akka MA 174 Kf31
Akkeshi J 111 Sc24
'Akko IL 90 Mh29
Akkol KZ 97 Of24
Akkoursoulbak RCA 190 Ma41
Akköy TR 71 Mh53
Akköy TR 90 Mg26
Akkum KZ 97 Of24
Ak Kuprak = Keshendeh AFG 97 Od27
Akkuş TR 90 Mj25
Aklampa DY 188 Lb41
Aklera IND 116 Oj33
Akmektep KZ 100 Pb22
Akmenrags LV 45 Mb34
Akmeqit CHN 100 Oj27
Akniste LV 45 Mf34
Aknoul MA 175 Kj28
Ako J 113 Rh28
Akodiya IND 116 Oj34
Akok G 198 Le45
Akoke SUD 191 Mg41
Akokora RDC 191 Me45
Akola IND 116 Oj35
Akolica BY 45 Mh36
Akoma PNG 155 Sc49
Akom II CAM 188 Lf44
Akono CAM 189 Lf44
Akonolinga CAM 189 Lg44
Akop SUD 191 Me41
Akorabi GUY 266 Ha43
Akordat ER 192 Mj38
Akören TR 90 Mg27
Akoroso GH 187 Kk43
Akosombo GH 187 La42
Akosombo Dam GH 187 La42
Akot IND 116 Oj35
Akot SUD 191 Mf42
Akoupé CI 187 Kj42
Akparé TG 187 La42
Akpınar TR 90 Mg26
Akplabnya GH 187 La43
Akposso TG 187 La42
Akqi CHN 100 Ok25
Akrabat TM 96 Oa28
Akraberg DK 46 Ko29
Åkrahamn N 42 Lf31
Akrai I 63 Lp53
Akranes IS 46 Js26
Akrar IS 46 Js26
Akre IRQ 91 Nb27
Akréréb RN 182 Le37
Åkrestrømmen N 40 Lm29
Akron USA 236 Fb24
Akron USA 237 Fk25
Akron USA 238 Ej25
Akrópolis GR 69 Md53
Akrópolis GR 71 Mj54
Akropong GH 187 Kk42
Akrotiri GR 71 Mf54
Akrotiri Ágios Ioánnis GR 71 Mf55
Akrotiri Ákrathos GR 69 Me50
Akrotiri Áraxos GR 70 Mb52
Akrotiri Doukáto GR 70 Ma52
Akrotiri Drébano GR 69 Md51
Akrotiri Kassándra GR 68 Md51
Akrotiri Kilíni GR 70 Mb53
Akrotiri Kímis GR 71 Me52
Akrotiri Kriós GR 69 Md55
Akrotiri Lithári GR 71 Me52
Akrotiri Líthino GR 71 Me56
Akrotiri Maléas GR 69 Md54
Akrotiri Murzeflos GR 71 Mf51
Akrotiri Palioúri GR 69 Md51
Akrotiri Salonikiós GR 69 Me50
Akrotiri Soúnio GR 71 Me53
Akrotiri Ténaro GR 70 Mc54
Akša RUS 104 Qg20
Aksaj RUS 73 Mk22
Akşar TR 91 Nb25
Aksaray TR 90 Mh26
Aksay CHN 103 Ph26
Aksay Qin 102 Ok28
Aksdal N 42 Lf31
Akşehir TR 90 Mf26
Aksekı TR 90 Mf27
Akshatau KZ 100 Og22
Akshyghanak KZ 97 Oe24
Aksoran tau KZ 100 Oh21
Aksu CHN 100 Pa25
Aksu KZ 97 Oe24
Aksu KZ 100 Ok23
Aksuat KZ 100 Pb22
Aksuat KZ 101 Pb21
Aksu Canyon KZ 97 Of24
Aksum ETH 192 Mk38
Aksumite royal city of Kohaito ER 192 Mk38
Aksu-Zhabaghly Nature Reserve KZ 97 Of24
Ak-Šyjak KS 100 Ok25
Ak Tag CHN 102 Pc27
Ak-Tal KS 100 Oh25
Aktaš RUS 101 Pd20
Aktau KZ 96 Nf24
Aktaz CHN 102 Pd26
Aktoghai KZ 100 Oh21
Aktoghai KZ 100 Ok22
Aktuzla TR 91 Nb26
Akubu SUD 192 Mg42
Akula RDC 190 Ma44
Akulurak USA 228 Bh14
Akumadan GH 187 Kk42
Akumal MEX 247 Fg35
Akune J 113 Rf29
Akuraj RUS 105 Qj20
Akure WAN 188 Lc42
Akuressa CL 119 Pa42
Akureyri IS 46 Kb25
Akuseki-jima J 113 Re31
Akutukpa WAN 188 Ld41
Akwanga WAN 188 Le41
Akwaya CAM 188 Le42
Akyab = Sittwe MYA 120 Pg35
Akyma GUY 266 Ha43
Akzhal KZ 100 Oh22
Akzhar KZ 100 Oh23
Akzhar KZ 100 Oj23
Akzhar KZ 100 Pb22
Ål N 40 Lj30
Al RI 131 Re48
Al A'amiyah IRQ 91 Nc29
Al-Aan Palace KSA 94 Nc37
Ala-Archa Canyon KS 100 Oh24
Ala-Archa N.P. KS 100 Oh24
Alabama USA 239 Fg29
Alabama and Coushatta Ind. Res. USA 238 Fc30
Alaban RI 127 Pj44
Alabat Island RP 124 Rb38
Al-'Abbasiya SUD 185 Mf39
Ala-Bel KS 100 Og24
Alabel RP 125 Rc42
Al 'Abr YE 94 Nd37
Ala-Buka KS 97 Of25
Alaca TR 90 Mh25
Alacahan TR 90 Mj26
Alacalı TR 69 Mk49
Alaçam TR 90 Mh25
Alaçam Dağları TR 71 Mj51
Alacant E 57 Ku52
Alaçatı TR 71 Mg52
Ala Dağlar TR 91 Nb26
Al 'Adam LAR 178 Mb30

Aladdin – Ambulong Island

Aladdin USA 233 Eh23
Aladdin Tomb Tower IR 91 Nf28
Aladža džamija MK 68 Ma48
Aladžda manastir BG 69 Mh47
Aladzha TM 96 Ng26
Alaejos E 54 Kp49
Alafiarou DY 188 Lb41
Alaganik USA 229 Ch15
Alagir RUS 91 Nc24
Alagiri IND 119 Ok39
Alag Khayrkhan Uul MNG 101 Ph23
Alagna Valésia I 60 Lh45
Alagoa Grande BR 273 Jc49
Alagoas BR 255 Ja11
Alagoinhas BR 273 Ja47
Alagoinhas BR 273 Ja52
Alagón E 56 Kt49
Alagoninha do Piauí BR 273 Hk49
Alahan TR 90 Mg27
Alahanpanjang RI 127 Qa46
Alaharma FIN 41 Mc27
Al-'Ain SUD 184 Me37
Al Ain UAE 95 Nh33
Al Aiss KSA 92 Mk33
Al-Ajaiz OM 95 Nj36
Alajärvi FIN 44 Md28
Alajskij hrebet KS 97 Of26
Alajuela CR 249 Fh40
Alakamisy Itenina RM 207 Nd56
Alakanuk USA 228 Bh14
Al Akhdar KSA 92 Mj31
Alakol KZ 100 Pa22
Alaktak USA 229 Cc10
Alakuko WAN 188 Lc42
Alakurtti RUS 39 Ml24
Al Alia DZ 176 Lc29
Al A'lyaneh SYR 90 Mk28
Al Amadiyah IRQ 91 Nb27
Al 'Amar KSA 93 Nc33
Al Amara IRQ 93 Nd30
Al-'Amara SUD 185 Mg38
Alamat'a ETH 192 Mk39
Alambie AUS 148 Sb61
Alamdo CHN 103 Ph30
Alameda CDN 233 Ej21
Alamikamba NIC 249 Fh39
Alaminos RP 124 Qk37
Alamo MEX 246 Fb35
Álamo Chapo MEX 245 Eh31
Alamogordo USA 235 Eh29
Alamo Navajo Ind. Res. USA 235 Eg28
Alamor EC 268 Fk47
Álamos MEX 244 Ef32
Alamosa USA 235 Eh27
Alamos de Márquez MEX 245 Ej31
Al Amrashi YE 94 Nc37
Alamuru IND 117 Pa37
Al 'Anad YE 94 Nc39
Åland = Ahvenanmaa FIN 44 Lu30
Aland IND 116 Oj37
Al Andalus Expreso E 55 Kr53
Ålandsbro S 41 Ls28
Alandur IND 119 Pa39
Alanga G 198 Lg46
Alang Besar RI 127 Qa44
Alange E 55 Ko52
Alanggantang RI 127 Qc46
Alangouassou CI 187 Kh42
Alanis E 55 Kp52
Alanjeq IR 91 Nd26
Alanson USA 237 Fh23
Alanta LT 45 Mf35
Alantika Mountains WAN 189 Lg41
Alanya TR 90 Mf27
Alanya Kalesi TR 90 Mf27
Alapa WAN 188 Lc41
Alappuzha IND 118 Oj40
Al 'Aqiq KSA 94 Na35
Alaraz E 54 Kp50
Alarcón E 57 Ks51
Al Aredah KSA 94 Nb37
Al Arin KSA 94 Nb36
Alarobia-Andalandranobe RM 207 Nd56
Al Artawiyah KSA 93 Nc32
Alas RI 130 Qj50
Alaşehir TR 71 Mj52
Ala Shan Desert CHN 106 Qa25
Al-Ashkhara OM 95 Nk35
Al-Ashrafiya Mosque YE 94 Nb39
Al 'Ashuriyah IRQ 93 Nb30
Alaska USA 226 Ca06
Alaska ZW 202 Mf54
Alaska Highway USA 229 Ch14
Alaska Marine Highway USA 228 Cb17
Alaska Peninsula USA 226 Bd07
Alaska Peninsula Wildlife Refuge USA 228 Ca17
Alaska Range USA 229 Ce14
Al Asma x RIM 180 Kc36
Al 'Assafiyah KSA 92 Mk31
Al 'Assah LAR 176 Lf29
Alássio I 60 Lj47
Alasso RMM 181 Kf38
Alastaro FIN 44 Mc30
Alat AZ 91 Ne26
Al Atawlah KSA 94 Na35
Alataw Shankou KZ/CHN 100 Pb23
Al Athalah KSA 93 Nb33
Alati CAM 189 Lg44
Alatri I 62 Lo49
Alatsinainy Bakaro RM 207 Nd55
Alatskivi EST 44 Mh32
Alatyr' RUS 72 Nd18
Alausí EC 268 Ga47
Alaverdi ARM 91 Nc25
Alavus FIN 44 Md28
Alawa WAN 188 Ld40
Alawa A.L. AUS 146 Rh53
Al-'Awabi OM 95 Nj34
Al Awaynat LAR 176 Lf33
Al Awaynat LAR 178 Mc35
Al-'Awir UAE 95 Nh33
Al-'Aydarus Mosque YE 94 Nc39
Al Ayn KSA 93 Nc32
Al-Ayn OM 95 Nj34
Alayo RCA 190 Mb43
Al-'Ayun MA/DARS 174 Kd32
Alazejskoe ploskogor'e RUS 89 Sb05
Al 'Aziziyah LAR 177 Lg29
Al Azraq JOR 92 Mj30
Alba I 60 Lj46
Al Ba'aj IRQ 91 Na27
Al Bab SYR 90 Mj27
Albac RO 67 Mc44
Albacete E 57 Kt52
Al Bad' KSA 92 Mh31
Al Bada'i' KSA 92 Mk32
Al Badaya KSA 93 Nb33
Alba de Tormes E 54 Kp50
Al Badi IRQ 91 Na28
Al Badi KSA 94 Nd35
Al Badia KSA 94 Nc37
Ålbæk DK 42 Ll33
Ålbæk Bugt DK 42 Ll33
Al Baha KSA 94 Na36
Albaida E 57 Ku52
Alba Iulia RO 67 Md44
Albalate del Arzobispo E 57 Ku49
Albalate de Zorita E 57 Ks50
Al Baleed OM 95 Nh37
Alban CO 264 Gc43
Alban = San José CO 264 Gb45
Alban F 52 Lc47
Albania AL 70 Lu50
Albano Laziale I 60 Ln49
Albany AUS 144 Qj63
Albany USA 232 Dj23
Albany USA 238 Fa29
Albany USA 238 Fc25
Albany USA 239 Fh27
Albany USA 239 Fh30
Albany USA 241 Gd24
Albanyà E 52 Lc48
Albany Downs AUS 149 Se59
Al Bardi LAR 178 Mc30
Albardón RA 280 Gf61
Al Barit IRQ 93 Nb30
Albarracín E 57 Kt50
al-Barun SUD 185 Mg40
al-Basabir SUD 185 Mg37
Al Basira SYR 91 Na28
Al Basiri SYR 90 Mj28
Al Basra IRQ 93 Nd30
Al Basra IRQ 93 Nd30
Al Batha IRQ 93 Nc30
Albatross Bay AUS 147 Sa52
Albatross-eiland NAM 204 Lh59
Albatross Island NAM 204 Lh59
Al Bayda LAR 177 Ma29
Al Bayda YE 94 Nc38
Albazino RUS 105 Rc19
Albemarle USA 242 Fk28
Albena BG 69 Mj47
Albenga I 60 Lj46
Albentosa E 57 Ku50
Albergaria-a-Velha P 54 Km50
Albermarle = Isla Isabela EC 269 Fe46
Albernoa P 55 Kn53
Alberobello I 63 Ls50
Albersdorf D 58 Lk36
Albert F 51 Lc40
Alberta CDN 226 Ea08
Albert Edward, Mount PNG 155 Sd50
Albert Falls ZA 205 Mf60
Alberti RA 281 Gk63
Albert I Land N 38 Lf06
Albertinia ZA 204 Ma63
Albert Lea USA 236 Fd24
Albert Nile EAU 191 Mf44
Alberto de Agostini, P.N. RCH 282 Ge73
Alberton CDN 240 Gh22
Albert Town BS 250 Gc34
Albertville F 53 Lg45
Albertville USA 239 Fg28
Albeşti RO 69 Mj47
Albi F 52 Lc47
Albia USA 236 Fd25
Al Bi'ar KSA 92 Mk34
Albilbah AUS 149 Sc58
Albin USA 235 Eh25
Albina SME 266 Hc43
Albion USA 234 Dj26
Albion USA 237 Fh24
Albion USA 237 Ga24
Albion USA 238 Fc29
Albion Downs AUS 144 Ra59
Al Bir KSA 92 Mj31
Al Birk KSA 94 Na36
Al Birk KSA 94 Nd34
Al Birkah KSA 94 Na34
Al Bīr Lahlou DARS 174 Kf32
Al Biyad KSA 94 Nd35
Albocàsser E 57 La50
Alborea E 57 Kt51
Ålborg DK 42 Lm36
Ålborg Bugt DK 42 Ll34
Albox E 55 Ks53
Albreda WAG 186 Kb39
Albro AUS 149 Sd57
Albstadt D 59 Lk42
Al Budayyi BRN 93 Nf32
Albuera RP 124 Rc40
Albufeira P 55 Km53
Al Bukayriyah KSA 93 Nb32
Albuñol E 55 Kr54
Albuquerque E 55 Kn51
Albuquerque USA 235 Eg28
Al Buraimi OM 95 Nh33
Albury AUS 151 Sd64
Al Busayta KSA 92 Mk30
Al Busayyah IRQ 93 Nd30
al Butanah SUD 185 Mh38
Alcácer do Sal P 55 Km52
Alcáçovas P 55 Km52
Alcala RP 124 Ra37
Alcalá de Guadaira E 55 Kp53
Alcalá de Henares E 55 Kr50
Alcalá del Júcar E 57 Kt51
Alcalá de los Gazules E 55 Kp54
Alcalá del Río E 55 Kp53
Alcalà de Xivert E 57 La50
Alcalá la Real E 55 Kr53
Álcamo I 62 Ln53
Alcanar E 57 La50
Alcanede P 55 Km51
Alcañices E 54 Ko49
Alcañiz E 57 Ku49
Alcântara BR 267 Hh47
Alcántara E 55 Ko51
Alcántara I 63 Lq53
Alcantarilla E 57 Kt53
Alcaracejos E 55 Kq52
Alcaraz = Pueblo Arrúa RA 276 Ha61
Alcarràs E 57 La49
Alcaudete E 55 Kq53
Alcaudete de la Jara E 55 Kq51
Alcazaba de Almería E 55 Ks54
Alcázar de San Juan E 55 Kr51
Alcedo, Volcán EC 269 Fe46
Alcester GB 49 Kt38
Alcester Island PNG 156 Sg50
Alčevs'k UA 73 Mk21
Al Chaba'ish IRQ 93 Nd30
Alcinópolis BR 274 Hd55
Alcira RA 280 Gh62
Alcobaça BR 275 Ja54
Alcoba de los Montes E 55 Kq51
Alcoentre P 55 Km51
Alcohuas RCH 279 Ge61
Alcoi E 57 Ku52
Alcolea del Pinar E 57 Ks49
Alconchel E 55 Kn52
Alcoota AUS 148 Rh57
Alcorisa E 57 Ku50
Alcorta RA 281 Gk62
Alcorta RCH 279 Gf57
Alcoutim P 55 Kn53
Alcova USA 235 Eg24
Alcoy = Alcoi E 57 Ku52
Alcublas E 57 Ku51
Alcúdia E 57 Ld51
Aldaia Bona BR 266 Hc45
Al Dali YE 94 Nc39
Aldama MEX 244 Eh31
Aldama MEX 246 Fa34
Aldan RUS 89 Rb07
Aldan RUS 89 Rc07
Aldanskoe nagor'e RUS 89 Ra07
Aldar MNG 101 Pj22
Aldeadávila de la Ribera E 54 Ko49
Aldea del Rey E 55 Kr52
Aldea dos Indios Sucane GUY 266 Ha45
Aldeburgh GB 49 Lb38
Aldeia das Canoas BR 266 Hc45
Aldeia Viçosa ANG 198 Lh50
Aldeia Vila Batista BR 270 Gk46
Aldenueva del Codonal E 54 Kq49
Alder Creek USA 241 Gc24
Alder Flats CDN 233 Ec19
Alderly AUS 148 Rk57
Alderney GB 50 Ks41
Aldershot GB 49 Ku39
Aldersyde AUS 144 Qj62
Aldeyjarfoss IS 46 Kc25
Al Dibin YE 95 Nf37
Al Djebel al Akhdar LAR 177 Ma29
Al Eatrah KSA 92 Nb33
Åled S 42 Ln34
Aledia Koura DY 188 La41
Aledo USA 236 Fe25
Aleg RIM 180 Kd37
Alegre BR 275 Hg55
Alegre BR 275 Hk56
Alegrete BR 276 Hc60
Alegria RP 124 Rb41
Alegria RP 124 Rd40
Alejandra RA 276 Ha60
Alejandria BOL 278 Gh52
Alejandro Gallinal ROU 276 Hc62
Alejandro Humboldt, P.N. C 250 Gc35
Aleknagik USA 228 Ca16
Aleksandrov RUS 72 Mk17
Aleksandrovac SRB 68 Mb46
Aleksandrovac SRB 68 Mb47
Aleksandrów Kujawski PL 64 Lt38
Aleksandrów Łódzki PL 65 Lu39
Alekseevka RUS 72 Mk20
Alekseevka RUS 72 Nb20
Alekseevskaja RUS 72 Nb20
Aleksin RUS 72 Mj18
Aleksinac SRB 68 Mb47
Alekšycy BY 65 Md37
Alel SUD 191 Mf42
Ålem S 43 Lr34
Alémbé G 198 Lf46
Alembé RCB 198 Lh46
'Alem Ketema ETH 192 Mk40
Alem Maya ETH 192 Na41
Alem Paraíba BR 275 Hj56
Alençon F 50 La42
Alen Cué RA 276 Hb60
Alenquer BR 266 Hc46
Alenquer P 55 Km52
Alentejo P 55 Kn52
Alépé CI 187 Kj43
Aleppo SYR 90 Mj28
Alerce Andino, P.N. RCH 280 Gd66
Alert CDN 227 Gd02
Alerta PE 269 Ge51
Alert Bay CDN 232 Dg20
Alert Point CDN 227 Fb02
Alès F 53 Le46
Aleşd RO 67 Mc43
Alessándria I 60 Lj46
Ales stenar S 43 Lp35
Ålesund N 40 Lg28
Aletschgletscher CH 60 Lh44
Aleutian Basin USA 76 Tb04
Aleutian Islands USA 226 Bd08
Aleutian Range USA 228 Cb17
Alexander USA 229 Ce15
Alexander Archipelago USA 226 Da07
Alexanderbaai ZA 204 Lj60
Alexander Bay ZA 204 Lj60
Alexander City USA 239 Fh29
Alexander Graham Bell N.H.S. CDN 240 Gk22
Alexander Island 286 Ga32
Alexander Morrison N.P. AUS 144 Qh60
Alexander-Nevski BG 68 Md48
Alexandra NZ 153 Te68
Alexandria AUS 146 Rj55
Alexandria BR 273 Ja49
Alexandria ET 179 Me30
Alexándria GR 70 Mc50
Alexandria RO 69 Mf47
Alexandria USA 236 Fa24
Alexandria USA 236 Fc23
Alexandria USA 237 Fh25
Alexandria USA 239 Fd30
Alexandria USA 241 Gb26
Alexandria ZA 205 Md62
Alexandroupoli GR 69 Mf50
Aleksandrovskij Zavod RUS 105 Qj20
Alexis Creek CDN 232 Dj19
Alexishafen PNG 155 Sc48
Al Faid Majir LAR 177 Lh29
Alfalfa USA 232 Dk23
Al Fallujah IRQ 91 Nb29
Al Fardah YE 94 Ne38
Alfaro E 56 Kt48
Alfarràs E 57 La49
Al Farshah KSA 94 Nb37
Al Fashir SUD 184 Mc39
Al-Fatah OM 95 Nj34
Alfatar BG 69 Mh47
Al Fathah IRQ 91 Nb28
Al Fatk YE 95 Ng37
Al Faw IRQ 93 Ne31
Al Fawwarah KSA 92 Nb32
Al Faydah KSA 93 Nc33
Al Faydami YE 95 Ng37
Alfeld D 58 Lk39
Alfenas BR 275 Hh56
Al Feqrah KSA 92 Mk33
al-Fifi SUD 184 Mc40
Alföld H 67 Ma43
Alfonsina MEX 244 Ec31
Alfonsine I 60 Ln46
Alford AUS 150 Rj62
Alford GB 48 Ks33
Alford GB 49 La37
Alfredo Wagner BR 277 Hf59
Al Fuqaha' LAR 177 Lj32
al-Gabalayn SUD 185 Mg39
Al-Gabir SUD 185 Me39
Al Garabull LAR 177 Lg29
Ålgård N 42 Lf32
Al-Garef SUD 185 Mh40
Algarroba RA 281 Gj65
Algarrobal RCH 279 Ge60
Algarrobo CO 264 Gc40
Algarrobo RCH 280 Ge62
Algarrobo del Aguila RA 280 Gg64
Algarve P 55 Km53
al-Gayli SUD 185 Mg37
Algeciras E 55 Kp54
Algena ER 185 Mk37
Algeria DZ 163 Kb07
Algeyata ETH 192 Na41
al-Ghaba SUD 185 Mf36
al-Ghabsha SUD 185 Mf39
Al Ghandura SYR 90 Mj27
Al Gharith KSA 94 Na35
Al Ghat KSA 93 Nc32
Al Ghaydah YE 95 Ng37
Al Ghayl KSA 94 Nd34
Alghero I 62 Lj50
Al Ghrayfah LAR 177 Lg32
Al Ghurayra KSA 94 Nb36
Al Ghwaybiyah KSA 93 Ne33
Algiers DZ 176 Lb27
Algodões BR 273 Jb50
Algodonales E 55 Kp54
Algoma USA 237 Fg23
Algoma Upland CDN 237 Fj22
Algona USA 236 Fc24
Algonquin Prov. Park CDN 237 Ga23
Algonquin Upland CDN 237 Ga23
Algorta ROU 276 Hb62
Algyő H 67 Ma44
Al Habah KSA 93 Nd32
Al Habariyah IRQ 93 Nb29
Al Habbaniyah IRQ 91 Nb29
Al Habil KSA 94 Nb36
Al Hada KSA 94 Na35
Al Haddar KSA 94 Nc34
Al Haditah KSA 92 Mj30
Al Hadithah IRQ 91 Nb28
Al-Hadi-Yahya-Mosque YE 94 Nb37
Al Hadr IRQ 91 Nb28
Alhai IR 93 Ne30
Al Ha'ir KSA 93 Nd33
Al Hait KSA 92 Na33
Al-Hajar OM 95 Nk34
Al Hajarah KSA 93 Nb31
Al Halbeh SYR 90 Mk28
Al Hallaniyah OM 95 Nh37
Al Hallaniyat Bay OM 95 Nh37
Al Hamad KSA 92 Mk30
Alhama de Aragón E 57 Kt49
Alhama de Granada E 55 Kr54
Alhama de Murcia E 57 Kt53
Al Hamar KSA 94 Nd34
Alhambra E 55 Kr52
Alhambra E 55 Kr53
Alhambra USA 234 Ea28
Al Hami YE 94 Ne38
Al-Hamra OM 95 Nj34
Al Hamudiyah LAR 177 Lj32
Al Hanakiyah KSA 92 Na33
Al Hanish al Kabir YE 94 Nb39
Al Haniyah KSA 93 Nc31
Al Haqlaniyah IRQ 91 Nb28
Al Harabah LAR 176 Lf30
Al Harf YE 94 Nc37
Al Hariq KSA 94 Nd34
Al Harjah KSA 94 Nb36
Al Harrah KSA 92 Mk30
Al Haruj al Aswad LAR 177 Lj32
Al-Hasaka SYR 91 Na27
Alhaurín el Grande E 55 Kq54
Al Hawaya KSA 94 Ne35
Al Hawra YE 94 Nd39
Al Hayy IRQ 93 Nc29
Al Hayyaniyah KSA 92 Nb31
Al-Hazm OM 95 Nj34
Al Hazm YE 94 Nc37
Alheit ZA 204 Ma60
Al-Hibak KSA 95 Ng35
Al Hilla SUD 184 Md39
Al-Hillah IRQ 93 Nc29
Al Hillah KSA 94 Nd34
Al Hilwah KSA 94 Nd34
Al Hindiyah IRQ 93 Nc29
Al Hisn' YE 94 Nc39
Al Hisu KSA 92 Na33
Al Hoceima MA 175 Kj28
Al Hol SYR 91 Na27
Al Huan LAR 178 Mb33
Al Hudaydah YE 94 Nb38
Al Hufrah KSA 92 Mk31
Al-Hufrah al-Janubiyah OM 95 Nh36
Al Hufrah ash Sharqiya LAR 177 Lh32
Al Hufuf KSA 93 Ne33
Al Hulayq al Kabir LAR 177 Lj32
Al Humaydah KSA 92 Mh31
Al Humaymi YE 94 Nd38
Al Humayshah YE 94 Nc39
Al-Humrah UAE 95 Nh34
Al Hunaiy KSA 93 Ne33
al-Huqna SUD 185 Mg37
Al Hurriyeh SYR 91 Na28
al-Husay SUD 185 Mg38
Al Husayniyah KSA 94 Nc37
Al-Huwaysah OM 95 Nj35
Ália I 62 Lo53
Aliabad AFG 97 Oe27
Ali Abad IR 96 Nh27
Ali Abad IR 98 Nh31
Ali Abad Tower IR 98 Nk28
Aliaga E 57 Ku50
Aliağa TR 71 Mg52
'Ali al Gharbi IRQ 93 Nd29
Aliambata TLS 131 Rd50
Aliança BR 270 Gj50
Aliança BR 273 Jc49
Aliance CDN 233 Ee19
Aliantan RI 127 Qa45
Alíartos GR 69 Md52
Ali ash Sharqi IRQ 93 Nd29
Alibag IND 116 Og36
Alibates Flint Quarries Nat. Mon. USA 238 Ek28
Ali Bayramli AZ 91 Ne26
Alibo ETH 192 Mj41
Alibunar SRB 68 Ma45
Alicante = Alacant E 57 Ku52
Alice AUS 149 Sg60
Alice USA 245 Fa32
Alice ZA 205 Md62
Alice Arm CDN 230 Df18
Alice Channel MAL/RP 125 Qk43
Alice Springs AUS 148 Rg57
Alice Town BS 243 Ga33
Alice Town BS 243 Gb33
Aliceville USA 239 Ff29
Ali Chuk USA 235 Ed30
Alicia RP 124 Ra37
Alicia RP 124 Rc41
Alifu Atoll = Arie Atoll MV 118 Og44
Alifuuto Nature Reserve SP 195 Nc44
Aliganj IND 115 Ok32
Aligarh IND 115 Ok32
Alignements de Pagliaju F 62 Lj49
Aligudarz IR 93 Ne29
Álika GR 70 Mc54
Alikalia WAL 186 Ke41
'Ali Kheyl AFG 99 Oe29
Al Ikhwan YE 95 Ng39
Alikí GR 69 Me50
Alíko GR 71 Mf54
Alima RCB 198 Lj46
Alimbongo RDC 191 Me46
Alimiá GR 71 Mh54
Alinda TR 71 Mh53
Alindau RI 130 Qk46
Alindoa RCA 190 Ma43
Alingsås S 42 Ln33
Alipur IND 120 Pe34
Alipur PK 99 Of31
Alipura IND 115 Ok33
Alipur Duar IND 120 Pe32
Alirajpur IND 116 Oh34
Al Irqah YE 94 Nd39
Ali Sabieh DJI 193 Nb40
Al Isawiyah KSA 92 Mk30
Aliseda E 55 Ko51
Alishan RC 109 Ra34
Alishan RC 109 Ra34
Al Iskandariyah IRQ 93 Nc29
Alista MEX 246 Ej36
Alivéri GR 71 Me52
Aliwal-Noord ZA 205 Md61
Aliwal North ZA 205 Md61
Alizai PK 99 Of29
Al Jafr JOR 92 Mj30
Al Jafurah KSA 93 Nf33
Al Jagbub LAR 178 Mc31
Al Jalamid KSA 92 Na30
Al-Jami'al-Kebir YE 94 Nc38
Al Jawb KSA 95 Nf34
Al Jawf KSA 92 Mk31
Al Jawf LAR 178 Mb33
Al Jaza'ir DZ 163 Kb07
Aljenaari WAN 188 Lb40
Aljezur P 55 Km53
Al Jihrah KSA 92 Nb32
Al Jubaylah KSA 93 Nd33
Al Jufra Oasis 162 Lb07
Al Jumailiyah Q 93 Nf33
Al Jumum KSA 92 Mk35
Al Junaynah SUD 184 Mb39
Al Jurayd KSA 93 Ne32
Al Jussah KSA 94 Na34
Aljustrel P 55 Km53
Al Kabar SYR 91 Mk28
Al Kadhimiya IRQ 91 Nc29
Al-Kaf Palace YE 94 Ne37
Alkali Lake USA 232 Ea24
Alkamari RN 183 Lf39
Al- Kamil OM 95 Nk34
al-Kamilin SUD 185 Mg38
Al Karabilah IRQ 91 Na28
Al Karameh SYR 91 Mk28
Al Kararim LAR 177 Lh29
al-Kawa SUD 185 Mg39
Al-Khabb UAE 95 Nh33
Al-Khabbah OM 95 Nk34
Al Khabra KSA 93 Nb32
Al-Khabura OM 95 Nj34
Al Khadra KSA 94 Nc37
Al Khafah KSA 93 Nb32
Al Khalf KSA 92 Na33
Al Khalis IRQ 91 Nc29
Al Khamasin KSA 94 Nc35
Al Khanabah LAR 177 Lh32
Al Khandaq SUD 185 Mf36
Al Kharfah KSA 94 Nd34
Al Kharj KSA 93 Nd33
Al Khawkhah YE 94 Nb39
Al-Khawrah UAE 95 Nh33
Al Khawtamah YE 94 Nb38
Al Khidr IRQ 93 Nc30
Al Khobar KSA 93 Nf32
Al Khor Q 93 Nf33
Al Khottah KSA 92 Na32
Al Khubah KSA 94 Nb37
Al Khums LAR 177 Lh29
Al Khuraybah KSA 92 Mh31
Al Khurmah KSA 94 Nb35
Al Khushaybi KSA 93 Nb33
Al-Kidan KSA 95 Ng34
Al Kifl IRQ 93 Nc29
Al Kisrah SYR 91 Mk28
Alkmaar NL 51 Le38
al-Koin SUD 185 Mf36
Al Kufah IRQ 93 Nc29
Al Kumayt IRQ 93 Nd29
Al Kura KSA 92 Mk35
al-Kurru SUD 185 Mf36
Al Kut IRQ 93 Nc29
Al Kuwayt KWT 93 Nd31
Al Labbah KSA 92 Na31
Allada DY 188 Lb42
Allagash USA 240 Gf22
al-Lagowa SUD 184 Me40
Allagudda IND 119 Ok38
Allahabad = Tirth Raj Prayag IND 117 Pa33
Al Lahabah KSA 93 Nd32
Allahdurg IND 116 Oj37
Allahganj IND 115 Ok32
Allakaket USA 229 Cd12
Allanche F 53 Lc45
Allandale AUS 148 Rh59
Allanmyo MYA 120 Ph36
Allanridge ZA 205 Md59
Allansford AUS 151 Sb65
Allan Water CDN 236 Fe20
Allapali IND 117 Pa36
Allardville CDN 240 Gh22
Allariz E 54 Kn48
Allauch F 53 Lf47
Alldays ZA 202 Me57
Alleen N 42 Lh32
Allegan USA 237 Fh24
Allegany S.P. USA 237 Ga24
Allen RA 280 Gg65
Allen RP 124 Rc39
Allendale USA 242 Fk29
Allende MEX 245 Ek31
Allende MEX 245 Ek33
Allen Island AUS 146 Rk54
Allensworth USA 234 Ea28
Allentown USA 241 Gc25
Alleppey = Alappuzha IND 118 Oj40
Alleppey Beach IND 118 Oj41
Aller D 58 Ll38
Aller = Cabañaquinta E 54 Kp47
Allersberg D 59 Lm41
Allevard F 53 Lg45
Allgäu D 59 Ll43
Allgäuer Alpen D/A 59 Ll43
Alliance USA 235 Ej24
Alliance USA 237 Fk25
Alliford Bay CDN 230 De19
Alligator Pond JA 250 Gb37
Alligator River N.W.R. USA 242 Gc28
Allinge DK 43 Lp35
Al Lisafah KSA 93 Nd32
Allison USA 236 Fd24
Allison Island PNG 155 Sb46
Al Lith KSA 94 Na35
Allo E 56 Ks48
Allomo WAN 188 Ld42
Allones F 50 La43
Allora AUS 149 Sf60
Allos F 53 Lg46
All Soul's Memorial Church (Kanpur) IND 117 Pa32
Allu RI 130 Ra48
Al Luhayyah YE 94 Nb38
Allur IND 119 Pa38
Alma AUS 151 Sc62
Alma CDN 240 Ge21
Alma CDN 240 Gh23
Alma USA 235 Ef29
Alma USA 237 Fh24
Alma USA 238 Fa25
Alma USA 242 Fj30
Al Ma'aniyah IRQ 93 Nb30
Almacelles E 57 La49
Al Machmin IRQ 93 Nb30
Almada P 55 Kl52
Al Madaya KSA 94 Nb37
Almaden AUS 147 Sc54
Almadén E 55 Kq52
Al Madina YE 94 Nd38
Almafuerte RA 280 Gh62
Al Magharim YE 94 Nd38
Almagro E 55 Kr52
Al Mahash KSA 92 Na32
Al Mahatta Ath'thania SYR 91 Na28
Al Mahbas DARS 174 Kf32
Al Mahdoom SYR 90 Mj27
Almahel ETH 192 Mh40
Al Mahfid YE 94 Nd38
Al Mahmudiyah IRQ 93 Nc29
Al Mahrah YE 95 Nf38
Al Mahruqah LAR 177 Lh32
Al Mahwit YE 94 Nb38
Al Majadah KSA 94 Na36
Al Majm'ah KSA 93 Nc33
Al Makhwah KSA 94 Na36
al-Malamm SUD 191 Me41
Al-Malkyer SYR 91 Nb27
Alma, Mount AUS 149 Sf58
Al Manajier SYR 91 Na27
Al Manama BRN 93 Nf32
Al Manama UAE 95 Nh33
al-Manaqil SUD 185 Mg38
Almandar IR 91 Nc26
Almansa E 57 Kt52
Al-Mansura SYR 90 Mk28
Al Mansuriyah YE 94 Nb38
Almanza E 54 Kp48
Alma Peak CDN 230 Dg17
Al Ma'qas KSA 94 Na36
Al Maqrun LAR 177 Ma30
Almar AFG 97 Oc28
Al Marah KSA 93 Ne33
Al Marawiah YE 94 Nb38
Almaraz E 55 Kp51
Al-Mariyyah UAE 95 Ng34
Al Marj LAR 177 Ma29
Almarza E 56 Ks49
Almas BR 272 Hg51
Almaty KZ 100 Oj24
Al Mawsil IRQ 91 Nb27
Al-Mawsil IRQ 91 Nb27
Al Mayadin SYR 91 Na28
al-Maysar OM 95 Nk34
Al Mayyah KSA 92 Nb32
Almazán E 56 Ks49
Almeida P 54 Ko50
Almeirim BR 271 Hd46
Almeirim P 55 Km51
Almel IND 116 Oj37
Almelo NL 51 Lg38
Almenara BR 275 Hk54
Almenara E 57 Ku51
Almenar de Soria E 56 Ks49
Almendo MW 203 Mh54
Almendral E 55 Ko52
Almendralejo E 55 Ko52
Almere NL 51 Lf38
Almería E 55 Ks54
Almerimar E 55 Ks54
Älmhult S 43 Lp34
Al-Midhar Mosque YE 94 Ne38
Al Midhnab KSA 93 Nc33
Al-Mihrad KSA 95 Ng35
Al Mina RL 90 Mh28
Al-Mintirib OM 95 Nk34
Almirante PA 249 Fj41
Almirante Brown RA 281 Ha63
Almirante Latorre RCH 279 Ge60
Almirante Tamandaré BR 277 Hf58
Al-Mirfa UAE 95 Ng33
Almiropótamos GR 71 Me52
Almirós GR 70 Mc51
Al Mish'ab KSA 93 Ne31
Al Mistannah KSA 93 Ne33
Almodôvar P 55 Km53
Almodóvar del Campo E 55 Kq52
Almodóvar del Río E 55 Kp53
Almofala BR 273 Ja47
Almoharín E 55 Ko51
Almonte E 55 Ko53
Almora AUS 146 Rk55
Almora IND 115 Ok31
Almoustarat RMM 181 La37
Älmsta S 43 Lt31
Al Mubarraz KSA 93 Ne33
Al-Mudaiba OM 95 Nk34
Al Mudawwara JOR 92 Mh31
Almudévar E 56 Ku48
al-Muglad SUD 184 Md40
Al Muharraq BRN 93 Nf32
Al Mukalla YE 94 Ne38
Al Mukha YE 94 Nb39
Al Mulayhah al Gharbiyah KSA 94 Ne34
Almuñécar E 55 Kr54
Almunge S 43 Lt31
Al Muqdadiyah IRQ 91 Nc29
Al-Musalla OM 95 Nk34
al-Musallamiya SUD 185 Mg38
Al-Musana'a OM 95 Nj34
Al Musayjid KSA 92 Mk33
Al Musaymir YE 94 Nc39
Al Mussayyib IRQ 93 Nc29
Al Muwassam KSA 94 Nb37
Al Muwayh KSA 94 Na34
Al Muwaylih KSA 92 Mh32
Al Muzahmiyah KSA 93 Nd33
Al Muzaylif KSA 94 Na36
Al Naqub YE 94 Nc38
Alness GB 48 Kq33
Alness GUY 266 Hb42
Alnif MA 175 Kh30
Alnwick GB 48 Kt35
Alo F 159 Ua53
Ålö FIN 44 Mc30
Alóag EC 268 Ga46
Aloândia BR 274 Hf54
Alô Brasil BR 272 He52
Alofi NZ 135 Bb11
Alogatina G 198 Lf45
Aloi EAU 194 Mg44
Aloja LV 45 Me33
Aloja LV 45 Me33
Along IND 120 Ph31
Alongly CDN 233 Eh19
Alongshan CHN 105 Rb20
Alónissos GR 69 Md51
Alonso de Rojas C 243 Fj34
Alor E 55 Kn52
Alor RI 131 Rc50
Álora E 55 Kq54
Alorna IND 116 Og38
Alor Setar MAL 126 Qa42
Alot IND 116 Oh34
Alota BOL 279 Gg56
Alotau PNG 156 Sf51
Alpachiri RA 281 Gj64
Alpalhão P 55 Kn51
Alpamayo PE 269 Gb50
Alpasinche RA 279 Gg60
Alpena USA 237 Fj23
Alpera E 57 Kt52
Alpes du Valais CH 60 Lh44
Alpha AUS 149 Sd57
Alpha Cordillera 286 Ea01
Alphen a/d Rijn NL 51 Le38
Alphonse Group SY 195 Ng49
Alpiarça P 55 Km51
Alpi Carniche I 61 Lo44
Alpi Lepontine I/CH 60 Lj44
Alpi Maríttime I 60 Lh46
Alpine USA 233 Ee24
Alpine USA 235 Ef29
Alpine USA 245 Ej30
Alpine Lake Wilderness USA 232 Dk22
Alpine N.P. AUS 151 Sd64
Alpi Oróbie I 60 Lk44
Alpi Venoste I 60 Ll44
Alps 26 La05
Alpu TR 90 Mf26
Alpujarras E 55 Kr54
Al Qa'amiyat KSA 94 Ne36
Al Qa'arah LAR 178 Mc30
Al-Qabil OM 95 Nh34
Al-Qaffay UAE 95 Nf33
Al Qafrah YE 94 Nc38
Al Qahmah KSA 94 Na37
Al Qa'iyah KSA 93 Nb33
Al Qa'iyah KSA 93 Nc32
Al Qala'a LAR 177 Lh30
Al Qalibah KSA 92 Mj31
Al Qara'a KSA 94 Nb36
Al Qardabah LAR 178 Mb29
Al Qarn YE 94 Nd38
Al Qaryah ash Sharqiyah LAR 177 Lg30
Al Qaryah al Gharbiyah LAR 177 Lg30
Al Qasab KSA 93 Nc33
Al Qasabat LAR 177 Lh29
Al Qath YE 94 Ne38
Al Qatif KSA 93 Nf32
Al Qatranah JOR 92 Mj30
Al Qatrun LAR 183 Lh33
Al Qawba'iyah KSA 92 Mk35
Al Qaysumah KSA 93 Nd31
Al-Qua'a UAE 95 Nh34
Al Quasir SYR 90 Mj28
Alquézar E 56 La48
Al Qulayd Bahri SUD 185 Mf36
Al Qulayyib KSA 93 Ne32
Al Qunfadhah KSA 94 Na36
Al Qurayn KSA 93 Nb33
Al Qurayrah KSA 93 Nb33
Al Qurnah IRQ 93 Nd30
Al Qusayr IRQ 93 Nc30
Al Qutaifeh SYR 90 Mj29
al-Qutayna SUD 185 Mg38
Al Quwarah KSA 93 Nb32
Al Quwayiah KSA 93 Nc33
Al Quzah YE 94 Ne38
Al Rahibat LAR 176 Lf30
Al Rahidah YE 94 Nc39
Al Rassafa SYR 90 Mk28
Al Rawdah YE 94 Nd38
Al Rayyan YE 94 Ne38
Alroy Downs AUS 146 Rj55
Als DK 42 Lk35
Als DK 42 Ll34
Alsace F 51 Lh42
Alsace F 51 Lh43
Alsa Craig GB 48 Kp35
Al-Samha UAE 95 Nh33
Alsasua E 56 Ks48
Alsea USA 232 Dj23
Alsfeld D 58 Lk40
Al-Shafee Mosque KSA 92 Mk35
Al Shaykh 'Uthman YE 94 Nc39
Alshi EC 268 Ga47
Al Shihr YE 94 Ne38
Al Sidarah YE 94 Ne38
Alsike CDN 233 Ec19
Alsike S 43 Ls31
Alsterbro S 43 Lq34
Alstermo S 43 Lq34
Al Sufal YE 94 Ne38
Al Sukhnah YE 94 Nb38
Al Surrah YE 94 Nd39
Alta N 39 Md21
Alta Badia I 60 Lm44
Alta Floresta BR 271 Hc50
Altagracia NIC 248 Fh40
Alta Gracia RA 280 Gh61
Altagracia YV 264 Ge40
Altagracia de Orituco YV 265 Gg41
Alta Italia RA 280 Gh63
Altamira BR 271 Hd47
Altamira CO 264 Gc44
Altamira MEX 246 Fa34
Altamira MEX 246 Fb34
Altamira PE 279 Gf58
Altamira do Maranhão BR 272 Hh48
Altamont USA 232 Dk24
Altamura I 63 Lr50
Alta Murgia, P.N. dell' I 63 Lr50
Altan MNG 101 Ph21
Altanbulag MNG 101 Pj21
Altanbulag MNG 104 Qd22
Altaneira BR 273 Ja49
Altan ovoo CHN/MNG 101 Pf23
Altan Ovoo MNG 104 Qa22
Altar MEX 244 Ee30
Altar-Est DZ 176 Le31
Altar, Volcán EC 268 Ga46
Altata MEX 244 Eg33
Altavista USA 242 Ga27
Altay CHN 101 Pe22
Altay MNG 101 Pj21
Altay MNG 101 Pj22
Altay RUS 88 Pb08
Altay Mountains MNG 76 Pa05
Altayn Caadah Gov' MNG 101 Pj24
Altay Shan CHN 101 Pd21
Altdorf CH 60 Lj44
Altdorf D 59 Lm41
Altea E 57 Ku52
Altenberg D 58 Lo40
Altenburg D 58 Ln40
Altenkirchen D 58 Lh40
Altenmarkt A 61 Lo43
Altenmarkt A 61 Lp43
Altensteig D 59 Lj42
Altentreptow D 58 Lo37
Altér do Chão BR 271 Hc47
Alter do Chão P 55 Kn51
Alte Saline Bad Reichenhall D 59 Ln43
Al Thaura SYR 90 Mk28
Altheim A 66 Lo42
Althofen A 61 Lp44
Alțina RO 67 Me45
Altinbesik TR 90 Mf27
Altındere Vadisi Milli Parkı TR 91 Mk25
Altin Köprü IRQ 91 Nc28
Altinópolis BR 275 Hg56
Altınova TR 71 Mg51
Altıntaş TR 90 Mf26
Altıntepe TR 91 Mk26
Altiplanicie del Payún RA 280 Gf64
Altiplano BOL 278 Gf54
Altiri IND 117 Pd35
Altja EST 44 Mg31
Altkirch F 53 Lh43
Altmark D 58 Lm38
Altmühl D 59 Lm42
Altnaharra GB 48 Kq32
Alto USA 238 Fc30
Alto Alegre BR 265 Gk44
Alto Alegre BR 276 Hd61
Alto Araguaia BR 274 Hd54
Alto Bonito BR 267 Hg46
Alto Bonito BR 269 Ge50
Alto Cedro C 243 Gb35
Alto Changane MOC 205 Mg58
Alto Chicapa ANG 200 Lk51
Alto del Carmen RCH 279 Ge60
Alto de Tamar CO 264 Gc42
Alto Garças BR 274 Hd54
Alto Golfo de California y Delta del Río Colorado MEX 244 Ec30
Alto Hama ANG 200 Lh52
Alto Ligonha MOC 203 Mk53
Alto Longá BR 273 Hj48
Alto Molócuè MOC 203 Mj53
Alton GB 49 Ku39
Alton USA 239 Fe26
Alton USA 239 Fe27
Alton USA 241 Gb24
Altona CDN 236 Fb21
Alto Nevado, Cerro RCH 282 Gd68
Altônia BR 274 Hd57
Altoona USA 237 Ga25
Alto Paraguai BR 274 Hb53
Alto Paraíso de Goiás BR 275 Hg53
Alto Parnaíba BR 272 Hh50
Alto Pelado RA 280 Gg62
Alto Pencoso RA 280 Gg62
Alto Purus PE 269 Ge51
Alto Rio Guamá, T.I. BR 267 Hg47
Alto Rio Mayo RA 282 Ge68
Alto Rio Negro, T.I. BR 265 Gf45
Alto Rio Purus, T.I. BR 269 Ge50
Alto Rio Senguer RA 282 Ge68
Altos BR 273 Hj48
Alto Santo BR 273 Ja48
Alto Sepatini, T.I. BR 270 Gg49
Alto Sucuriú BR 274 Hd55
Altotonga MEX 246 Fb36
Altötting D 59 Ln42
Alto Turiaçu, T.I. BR 272 Hg47
Altun CHN 103 Pe26
Altun-alem džamija SRB 68 Ma47
Altun Ha BH 248 Ff37
Altun Shan CHN 103 Pg26
Altun Shan CHN 102 Pc27
Altura E 57 Ku51
Alturas USA 232 Dk25
Alturitas YV 264 Gd41
Altus USA 238 Fa28
Altyn Arashan KS 100 Ok24
Altyn-Mosque CHN 100 Oj26
Aluakluak SUD 191 Mf42
Al Ubaydi IRQ 91 Na28
Al Ubaylah KSA 95 Nf34
Al Udailiyah KSA 93 Ne33
Al 'Udayn YE 94 Nb39
al-Udayya SUD 184 Me39
Alu Grottos CHN 121 Pk33
Alūksne LV 45 Mh33
Al 'Ula KSA 92 Mj32
al-'Umda SUD 184 Md40
Aluminé RA 280 Ge65
Alunda S 43 Lt30
Alungdaw Kathapa National Park MYA 120 Ph34
Aluoi VN 123 Qd37
Alupka UA 73 Mh23
Al 'Uqaylah LAR 177 Lk30
Al Uqayr KSA 93 Nf33
al-'Uqda SUD 185 Mg38
Alur IND 116 Oj37
Alur IND 116 Oj38
Al 'Urayq KSA 92 Mk31
Al-Uruq al-Muraridah KSA 95 Ng36
Alušta UA 73 Mh23
Al Uwaylah KSA 92 Nb30
Al 'Uwayja KSA 95 Nf34
Al 'Uwaynid KSA 93 Nc33
Al 'Uwaynidhiyah KSA 92 Mh32
Al Uzaym KSA 92 Nb32
Al Uzayr IRQ 93 Nd30
Alva USA 238 Fa27
Alvalade P 55 Km53
Älvängen S 42 Ln33
AlvarAalto-museo FIN 44 Mf28
Alvarado CO 264 Gc43
Alvarado MEX 247 Fc36
Alvarães BR 270 Gh47
Alvaréz RA 281 Gk62
Álvaro Obregón MEX 244 Eg31
Alvdal N 40 Ll28
Älvdalen S 41 Lp29
Älvdalen S 43 Lo30
Alvear RA 276 Hb60
Alvesta S 43 Lp34
Ålvik N 42 Lg30
Alvin USA 238 Fc31
Alvinópolis BR 275 Hj56
Alvito P 55 Kn52
Älvkarleby S 43 Ls30
Alvorada BR 272 Hf52
Alvorada BR 276 He61
Alvorada do Gurguéia BR 272 Hj50
Alvorado do Norte BR 275 Hg53
Alvorado d'Oeste BR 270 Gj51
Alvord Valley USA 232 Ea24
Älvros S 41 Lp28
Älvsbyn S 41 Ma25
Älvsered S 42 Ln33
Al Wahah LAR 177 Lk31
Al Wajh KSA 92 Mj32
Al Wakrah Q 93 Nf33
Alwar IND 114 Oj32
Al Wari'ah KSA 93 Nd32
Al Widyan IRQ/KSA 91 Na29
Al Wigh LAR 183 Lh33
Al Wittyah LAR 176 Lf29
Alxa Gaoyuan CHN 106 Qa25
Alxa Youqi CHN 106 Qa26
Alxa Zuoqi CHN 106 Qc26
Alyangula AUS 146 Rj52
Al Yaroubiyeh SYR 91 Nb27
Al-Yasat UAE 95 Ng33
Alyawarra & Katitja A.L. AUS 148 Rh56
Alytus LT 45 Me36
Alzada USA 233 Eh23
Alzey D 59 Lj41
Alzira E 57 Ku51
Ama MYA 122 Ph38
Ama PNG 155 Sa48
Amacayacu, P.N. CO 270 Gf47
Amaciã BR 270 Gh48
Amaculi MEX 244 Eg33
Amada Gaza RCA 190 Lh43
Amada Temple ET 179 Mg34
Amadi BD 120 Pe34
Amadi RDC 191 Md44
Amadi RDC 191 Me44
Amadi SUD 194 Mf43
Amadjuak Lake CDN 227 Gb05
Amadora P 55 Kl52
Amadrar DZ 182 Ld33
Amaga CO 264 Gc42
Amager DK 42 Ln35
Amahai RI 131 Re47
Amakouladji RMM 181 Kk37
Amakusa N.P. J 113 Re29
Amakusa-shoto J 113 Re29
Amal OM 95 Nh36
Åmål S 42 Ln31
Amalapuram IND 117 Pb37
Amalfi CO 264 Gc42
Amalfi I 63 Lp50
Amalia ZA 205 Mc59
Amaliáda GR 70 Mb53
Amalner IND 116 Oh35
Amaluza EC 268 Ga47
Amaluza EC 268 Ga48
Amamá RA 279 Gj59
Amamapare RI 154 Rj48
Amambaí BR 274 Hc57
Amambai, T.I. BR 274 Hc57
Amami Islands J 113 Re32
Amanab PNG 155 Sa47
Aman Abad IR 96 Nk27
Amancio Rodríguez C 243 Gb35
Amandit River Rafting RI 129 Qh47
Amándola I 61 Lo48
Amaneyé, T.I. BR 272 Hf47
Amanganj IND 117 Pa33
Amani Nature Reserve EAT 197 Mk48
Amantea I 63 Lr51
Amanzimtoti ZA 205 Mf61
Amapá BR 267 He44
Amapá BR 255 Ha09
Amaporã BR 274 Hd57
Amar ETH 194 Mj43
Amara RO 69 Mh46
Amara Abu Sin SUD 185 Mh38
Amarante BR 273 Hj49
Amarante P 54 Km49
Amarante do Maranhão BR 272 Hg48
Amaranth CDN 236 Fa20
Amărăştii de Jos RO 69 Me47
Amara West Temple SUD 185 Mf35
Amarbayasgalant Monastery MNG 104 Qc21
Amardalay MNG 104 Qd22
Amareleja P 55 Kn52
Amargosa BR 273 Ja52
Amargosa Desert USA 234 Eb27
Amargosa Range USA 234 Eb27
Amarillas C 243 Fk34
Amarillo USA 238 Ek28
Amárinthos GR 69 Md52
Amariú BR 273 Hk51
'Amar Jadid SUD 184 Mc38
Amarkantak IND 117 Pa34
Amarnath IND 116 Og36
Amarnath Cave PK 114 Oh28
Amarpatan IND 117 Pa33
Amarpur IND 120 Pf34
Amaru RO 69 Mg46
Amarwara IND 117 Ok34
Amasya TR 90 Mh25
Amata AUS 148 Rf59
Amatari BR 271 Ha47
Amatenango del Valle MEX 247 Fd37
Amatitlán GCA 248 Fe38
Amatrice I 61 Lo48
Amatura BR 270 Gf47
Amau PNG 156 Se51
Amaya E 54 Kq48
Amazmaz RIM 180 Kd36
Amazon 271 Ha47
Amazonas BR 255 Gb10
Amazônia, P.N. de BR 271 Hb48
Amazon Lowlands BR 270 Gh46
Amazon Shelf 267 Hf44
Ambad IND 116 Oh36
Ambae VU 158 Td53
Ambagarh Chauki IND 117 Pa35
Amba Giyogis ETH 192 Mj39
Ambah IND 117 Ok32
Ambahikily RM 207 Nb56
Ambajogai IND 116 Oj36
Ambala IND 115 Oj30
Ambalabe RM 207 Ne55
Ambalabongo RM 207 Nd54
Ambalajanakomby RM 207 Nd54
Ambalakely RM 207 Nd56
Ambalakirajy RM 206 Ne53
Ambalamanakana RM 207 Nd56
Ambalamanasy II RM 206 Ne53
Ambalangoda CL 119 Pa42
Ambalantota CL 119 Pa42
Ambalapaiso RM 206 Ne53
Ambalarondra RM 207 Ne55
Ambala Sadar IND 115 Oj30
Ambalatany RM 207 Nd57
Ambalavao RM 207 Nd56
Ambam CAM 189 Lf44
Ambanja RM 206 Ne52
Ambar PE 269 Gb51
Ambararata RM 206 Ne53
Ambargasta RA 279 Gj60
Ambasa IND 120 Pf34
Ambathala AUS 149 Sc58
Ambato EC 268 Ga46
Ambato RM 207 Nd55
Ambato Boeny RM 206 Nd54
Ambatofinandrahana RM 207 Nd56
Ambatolahy RM 207 Nc56
Ambatolampy RM 207 Nd55
Ambatomainty RM 207 Nc54
Ambatomanoina RM 207 Nd55
Ambatondrazaka RM 207 Ne54
Ambatoriha RM 206 Ne53
Ambatosia RM 206 Ne53
Ambatovory RM 207 Nd56
Ambatry RM 207 Nc57
Ambaúba BR 265 Gg45
Ambazac F 52 Lb45
Ambelákia GR 70 Mc51
Ambelau RI 131 Rd47
Ambelónas GR 70 Ma51
Ambelónas GR 70 Mc51
Ambered ARM 91 Nc25
Amber Fort IND 114 Oh32
Amberg D 59 Lm41
Ambergris Cay BH 247 Fg36
Ambérieu-en-Bugey F 53 Lf45
Ambert F 53 Ld45
Ambidédi RMM 180 Ke38
Ambikanagar IND 117 Pd34
Ambikapur IND 117 Pb34
Ambila RM 207 Nd56
Ambil Island RP 124 Ra39
Ambilobe RM 206 Ne52
Ambin RMM 181 Kh38
Ambinanindrano RM 207 Nd56
Ambinanindrano RM 207 Ne56
Ambinaninony RM 207 Ne55
Ambioa, T.I. BR 272 Hf49
Ambitle Island PNG 156 Sg48
Ambjörby S 43 Lo30
Amble GB 48 Kt35
Ambler USA 229 Cb12
Ambleside GB 49 Ks36
Ambo PE 269 Gb51
Amboahangibe RM 206 Ne53
Amboahangy RM 207 Nd58
Amboasary RM 207 Nd55
Amboasary RM 207 Nd58
Amboasary Gara RM 207 Ne55
Amboavory RM 207 Ne54
Ambodiangezoka RM 206 Ne53
Ambodiatafana RM 207 Ne54
Ambodibonara RM 206 Ne52
Ambodifotatra RM 207 Ne54
Ambodiharina RM 207 Ne55
Ambodilazana RM 207 Ne55
Ambodiriana RM 207 Ne54
Ambodıtetezana-Sahana RM 206 Nf53
Ambohidratrimo RM 207 Nd55
Ambohijanahary RM 207 Ne54
Ambohimahamasina RM 207 Nd56
Ambohimahasoa RM 207 Nd56
Ambohimanga RM 207 Nd55
Ambohimanga RM 207 Nd56
Ambohimilanja RM 207 Nd55
Ambohinihaonana RM 207 Nd56
Ambohipaky RM 206 Nc54
Ambohisary RM 207 Nd55
Ambohitra RM 206 Ne52
Ambohitra RM 206 Ne52
Ambohitralanana RM 206 Nf53
Ambohitsilaozana RM 207 Ne54
Amboise F 52 Lb43
Amboiva ANG 200 Lh51
Amboli IND 116 Og38
Ambolobozo RM 206 Nd53
Ambolobozokely RM 206 Ne52
Ambolomoty RM 206 Nd54
Ambon RI 131 Rd47
Ambon RI 131 Re47
Ambondro RM 207 Nc58
Ambondromamy RM 206 Nd54
Ambongo RM 207 Nc54
Amboni Caves EAT 197 Mk48
Amboriala RM 206 Ne52
Amborompotsy RM 207 Nd56
Amborondolo RM 206 Ne52
Amboró, P.N. BOL 278 Gj54
Amboseli N.P. EAK 194 Mj47
Ambositra RM 207 Nd56
Ambotosoratra RM 207 Ne54
Ambovombe RM 207 Nd58
Amboy USA 234 Ec28
Amboy USA 236 Fc24
Amboy Crater USA 234 Ec28
Amboyna Cay 128 Qg42
Ambrim VU 158 Te54
Ambriz ANG 198 Lg49
Ambrolauri GE 91 Nb24
Ambuaki RI 154 Rg46
Ambulong Island RP 124 Ra39

Ambunten – Argostóli

Ambunten RI 129 Qg49
Ambunti PNG 155 Sb48
Ambur IND 119 Ok39
Am Dafok RCA 184 Mb40
Am-Dam TCH 184 Ma39
Amdassa RI 131 Rf49
Amderma RUS 88 Oa05
Am Djaména RCA 190 Ma41
Am Djemena TCH 183 Lj39
Amdo CHN 103 Pf29
Amealco MEX 246 Ek35
Ameca MEX 245 Eh35
Ameca La Vieja MEX 245 Eh34
Ameghino RA 281 Gj63
Ameib NAM 200 Lh56
Ameixial P 55 Kn53
Ameland NL 51 Lf37
Amélia I 60 Ln48
Amelia Island USA 242 Fk30
Amélie-les-Bains F 52 Lc48
Amelinghausen D 58 Ll37
Améloloud RN 182 Ld37
Amelup AUS 144 Qk63
Amendolara I 63 Lr51
Ameng CHN 121 Qc34
Amenia USA 241 Gd25
Amentego SUD 185 Mf36
Ameri IR 93 Nf30
América BR 270 Gh49
Americana BR 275 Hg57
American Falls USA 232 Ed24
American Fork USA 235 Ee25
American Samoa USA 135 Bb11
Americus USA 239 Fh29
Amersfoort NL 51 Lf38
Amersfoort ZA 205 Me59
Amery ANT 286 Oc32
Ames USA 236 Fd24
Amesbury GB 49 Kt39
Ameya ETH 192 Mj42
Amfíklia GR 70 Mc52
Amfilohía GR 70 Mb52
Ámfissa GR 70 Mc52
Amfiteatri AL 68 Lu49
Amga RUS 89 Rc06
Amga RUS 89 Rc06
Amgala DARS 174 Ke32
Amgaon IND 117 Pa35
Amgu RUS 111 Rj23
Amguid DZ 176 Lc32
Amguri IND 120 Ph32
Amherst CDN 240 Gh23
Amherst = Kyaikkami MYA 122 Pj37
Amherst USA 241 Gd24
Amhertsburg CDN 237 Fj24
Am Himédé TCH 184 Ma39
Amhuinnsuidhe Castle GB 48 Ko33
Amicalola Falls USA 239 Fh28
Amidon USA 233 Ej22
Amiens F 51 Lc41
Amile NEP 115 Pb32
Amili IND 120 Ph31
Amilly F 53 Lc43
Aminagou RCA 191 Mc43
Amíndeo GR 70 Mb50
Amindivi Islands IND 118 Og40
Amini Island IND 118 Og40
Åminne S 43 Lt33
Amino J 113 Rh28
Aminuis NAM 204 Lk57
Amir Abad IR 96 Oa27
Amirante Basin 195 Nh49
Amirante Islands SY 195 Ng48
Amir Chah PK 98 Ob31
Amiri SUD 185 Mh40
Amirkala IR 96 Ng27
Amish Acres USA 237 Fg25
Amite USA 239 Fe30
Amity Point AUS 149 Sg59
Amizmiz MA 175 Kf30
Amkunj IND 122 Pg39
Amla IND 117 Ok35
Amlakhi IND 120 Pg33
Amlamé TG 187 La42
Amlekhganj NEP 117 Pc32
Åmli N 42 Lj32
Amlwch GB 49 Kq37
Amm Adam SUD 185 Mj37
Amman JOR 92 Mh30
Ammarnäs S 41 Lr25
Ammaroo AUS 148 Rh56
Ammassalik DK 227 Ja05
Ammersee D 59 Lm43
Ammouk RMM 181 Kk36
Amnat Charoen THA 123 Qc38
Amoama GH 187 Kj42
Amol IR 96 Ng27
Amolianí GR 69 Md50
Amon MA 174 Ke31
Amontada BR 273 Ja47
Amorgós GR 71 Mf54
Amorgós GR 71 Mf54
Amorinopolis BR 274 He54
Amory USA 239 Ff29
Amos CDN 237 Ga21
Åmot N 42 Lj31
Åmot N 42 Lk31
Amotape, Cerros de PE 268 Fk48
Åmotfors S 42 Ln31
Amotopo SME 266 Hb44
Amou F 52 Ku47
Amouguèr MA 175 Kh29
Amou Oblo TG 187 La42
Amourj RIM 181 Kg37
Amoy = Xiamen CHN 109 Qk33
Amoya GH 187 Kj42
Ampah RI 129 Qh46
Ampahana RM 206 Nf53
Ampalu RI 127 Qa46
Ampana RI 130 Ra46
Ampanefena RM 206 Ne52
Ampang RI 130 Qj50
Ampani IND 117 Pb36
Ampanihy RM 207 Nc58
Ampanolahamiraty RM 206 Ne52
Ampara CL 119 Pa42
Amparafaravola RM 207 Ne54
Amparihy Atsinanana RM 207 Nd57
Amparo BR 275 Hg57
Ampasimanolotra RM 207 Ne55
Ampasimatera RM 206 Nd53
Ampasina-Maningory RM 207 Ne54
Ampasinambo RM 207 Ne56
Ampefy RM 207 Nd55
Amper WAN 188 Le41
Ampére BR 276 Hd58
Ampère Seamount 174 Kd28
Ampezzo I 61 Ln44
Amphitheâtre d'El Djem TN 176 Lf28
Ampisikinana RM 206 Ne52
Ampitatafika RM 207 Nd55
Amplepuis F 53 Le45
Ampliación la Loma MEX 245 Fa33
Ampombiantambo RM 206 Ne52
Amporaha RM 206 Ne52
Amposta E 57 La50
Amqui CDN 240 Gg21
Amrabad IND 116 Ok37
Amran YE 94 Nb38
Amrapara IND 117 Pd33
Amrati IND 117 Pa36
Amravan IR 96 Nh28
Amravati IND 116 Oj35
Am Raya TCH 183 Lj38
Amreli IND 116 Of35
Amritsar IND 114 Oh30
Amroha IND 115 Ok31
Amrum D 58 Lj36
Am Sak TCH 183 Lk39
Amsel DZ 182 Lc34
Amsterdam NL 51 Le38
Amsterdam USA 241 Gc24
Amsterdam ZA 205 Mf59
Amsterdamøya N 38 Lf06
Amstetten A 66 Lp42
Amtali BD 120 Pf34
Am Tanabo TCH 189 Lj39
Am Timan TCH 184 Ma40
Amudalavalsa IND 117 Pb36
Amudarja TM 96 Ob26
Amu-Dar'ya TM 97 Oc27
Amudat EAU 194 Mh45
Amulung RP 124 Ra37
Amund Ringnes Island CDN 227 Fa03
Amundsen Bay 286 Nc32
Amundsen Gulf CDN 226 Dd04
Amundsen Ridge ANT 287 Eb32
Amundsen Sea ANT 287 Ec32
Amungwiwa, Mount PNG 155 Sd49
Amuntai RI 129 Qh47
Amur RUS/CHN 76 Ra04
Amurang RI 125 Rc45
Amursko-Zejskaja ravnina RUS 105 Rd19
Amusquillo E 54 Kq49
Amzacea RO 69 Mj47
Am-Zoer TCH 184 Ma38
Anabanua RI 130 Ra47
Anabar RUS 89 Qc04
Anabarskoe plato RUS 89 Qb04
Anaborano RM 206 Ne52
Anacadiña YV 265 Gh43
Anacapa Is. USA 234 Ea29
Anaco YV 265 Gh41
Anaconda USA 233 Ed22
Anacortes USA 232 Dj21
Anadarko USA 238 Fb28
Anadyr RUS 89 Tc05
Anadyr' RUS 89 Td06
Anadyrskoye Ploskogor'ye RUS 89 Tc05
Anáfi GR 71 Mf54
Anáfi GR 71 Mf54
Anafonitria GR 70 Ma53
Anagé BR 275 Hk53
Anaghit ER 185 Mk37
Anagni I 62 Lo49
Anagodu IND 118 Oj38
Anah IRQ 91 Na28
Anaharavi GR 70 Lu51
Anaheim USA 234 Eb29
Anahidrano RM 206 Nd53
Anahim Lake CDN 230 Dh19
Anahita IR 91 Ne28
Anáhuac MEX 245 Ek32
Anahuac N.W.R. USA 238 Fc31
Anai Mudi IND 118 Oj40
Anajás BR 267 Hf46
Anajatuba BR 272 Hh47
Anakalang RI 130 Qk50
Anakao RM 207 Nb57
Anakapalle IND 117 Pb37
Anakch DARS 174 Kd32
Anakie AUS 149 Sd57
Anakopia Caves GE 91 Na24
Anakruak USA 229 Cd10
Anaktuvuk Pass USA 229 Ce11
Analalava RM 206 Nd53
Analavory RM 207 Nd55
Anamã BR 270 Gk47
Anamaduwa CL 119 Pa42
Ana-Maria PE 268 Gc49
Anambe, T.I. BR 267 Hf47
Anamorium TR 90 Mg27
Anamur TR 90 Mg27
Anamur Burnu TR 90 Mg27
Anan J 113 Rh29
Ananás BR 272 Hf49
Ananas, T.I. BR 265 Gk44
Anand IND 116 Og34
Ananda CI 187 Kh42
Anandgarh IND 114 Og31
Anandpur IND 117 Pd35
Anandpur Sahib IND 115 Oj30
Anan'evo KS 100 Oj24
Añangu EC 268 Gb46
Angangu Pitjantjatjara A.L. AUS 145 Rf59
Ananthapur IND 118 Oj38
Anantnag 114 Oh29
Anantsono RM 207 Nb57
Anapa RUS 73 Mj23
Anápolis BR 274 Hf54
Anapurus BR 273 Hj47
Anar IR 98 Nh30
Anarak IR 98 Ng29
Anar Darreh AFG 98 Oa29
Anasazi MEX 244 Ef31
Anascaul IRL 47 Kk38
Anasenko CHN 100 Pb23
Anaskura IND 116 Og37
Anastácio BR 274 Hc56
Anatai RI 127 Qc48
Anatolia TR 90 Mf26
Anatoliki Rodhopi GR 69 Mf49
Añatuya RA 279 Gj60
Anau TM 96 Nk27
Anaurilândia BR 274 Hd57
Anba CHN 121 Qc32
Anban CHN 121 Qa34
Anbyon PRK 112 Rd26
Ancahau WAN 188 Le40
Ance LV 45 Mc33
Ancenis F 52 Kt43
Ancerville F 51 Lf42
Anchetti IND 118 Oj39
Anchieta BR 275 Hk56
Anchieta BR 276 Hd59
Ancho USA 235 Eh29
Anchorage USA 229 Cf15
Anchorage Reef PNG 156 Sf51
Anchor Bay USA 234 Dj26
Anchorena RA 280 Gh63
Anchorena, P.N. ROU 281 Hb63
Ancien RMM 181 Kk35
Ancient tin mines of Karnab UZ 97 Oc26
Ancohuma, Nevado BOL 278 Gf53
Ancón EC 268 Fk47
Ancón PE 269 Gb51
Ancona I 61 Lo47
Ancuabe MOC 197 Mk52
Ancud RCH 280 Gd66
Ancy-le-Franc F 53 Le43
Anda CHN 110 Rc22
Anda RP 124 Qk37
Andacollo RCH 279 Ge61
Andaga WAN 189 Lg40
Andagalá RA 279 Gg59
Andagua PE 269 Gd53
Andahuaylas PE 269 Gd52
Andaingo Gara RM 207 Ne55
Andal IND 117 Pd34
Åndalsnes N 40 Lh28
Andalucía E 55 Ko53
Andalusia USA 239 Fg30
Andaman and Nicobar Islands IND 122 Pg40
Andaman and Nicobar Islands IND 122 Pg40
Andaman Basin 122 Ph40
Andaman Islands IND 122 Pg40
Andaman Sea IND 122 Ph39
Andamarca PE 269 Gc53
Andamooka AUS 148 Rj61
Andamooka Ranges AUS 148 Rj61
Andanda IND 117 Pc36
Andano AUS 148 Rh58
Andapa RM 206 Ne53
Andapa RM 207 Nd55
Andaraí BR 273 Hk52
Andasibe RM 207 Ne55
Andasinimaro RM 206 Ne53
Andatsakala RM 206 Ne53
Andavadoaka RM 207 Nb57
Andebu N 42 Ll31
Andelot F 51 Lf42
Andemaka RM 207 Nd57
Andenes N 38 Lr21
Anderai WAN 188 Lc40
Andéramboukane RMM 182 Lb38
Ånderdalen n.p. N 38 Ls21
Anderlecht B 51 Le40
Andermatt CH 60 Lj44
Andernach D 59 Lh40
Andernos-les-Bains F 52 Kt46
Anderson USA 234 Dj25
Anderson USA 237 Fh25
Anderson USA 242 Fj28
Anderson Gate NAM 200 Lh55
Andersonville N.H.S. USA 239 Fh29
Anderstorp S 43 Lo33
Andes CO 264 Gc43
Andes 254 Ga10
Andhra Pradesh IND 117 Ok37
Andijan UZ 97 Og25
Andilamena RM 207 Ne54
Andilana RM 206 Ne52
Andilanatoby RM 207 Ne54
Andimeshk IR 93 Ne29
Anding CHN 109 Qg31
Andirá Marau, T.I. BR 271 Hb47
Andırın TR 90 Mj27
Andírio GR 70 Mb52
Andirlangar CHN 102 Pb27
Andirobal BR 272 Hh47
Andjogo G 198 Lg46
Andkhvoy AFG 97 Oc27
Andoain E 56 Ks47
Andoany RM 206 Ne52
Andoas PE 268 Gb47
Andocollo RA 280 Ge64
Andocs H 66 Ls44
Andohahela, P.N. d' RM 207 Nd58
Andohajango RM 206 Ne53
Andoi RI 154 Rg46
Andong ROK 113 Re27
Andoni Gate NAM 200 Lj55
Andoom AUS 147 Sa52
Andorra AND 56 Lb48
Andorra E 57 Ku50
Andorra la Vella AND 56 Lb48
Andover GB 49 Kt39
Andovoranto RM 207 Ne55
Andøya N 38 Lq21
Andrada ANG 199 Ma49
Andradas BR 275 Hg57
Andradina BR 274 He56
Andrafainkona RM 206 Ne52
Andramasina RM 207 Nd55
Andranofasika RM 206 Nd54
Andranolalina RM 207 Nd57
Andranolava RM 207 Nc57
Andranomavo RM 207 Nc54
Andranomena RM 207 Ne55
Andranopasy RM 207 Nb56
Andranosamonta RM 206 Ne53
Andranovondronina RM 206 Ne52
Andranovory RM 207 Nc57
Andratx E 57 Lc51
Andravída GR 70 Mb53
Andrea RM 207 Nc54
Andreapol' RUS 72 Mg17
Andrée-Land N 38 Lh06
André Felix, P.N. RCA 190 Mb41
Andrelândia BR 275 Hh56
Andrequice BR 275 Hh55
Andresito RA 276 Hc58
Andrevo RM 207 Nb57
Andrew CDN 233 Ed19
Andrews USA 238 Ej29
Andrews USA 242 Ga29
Ándria I 63 Lr49
Andriamena RM 207 Nd54
Andriandampy RM 207 Nc57
Andriba RM 207 Nd54
Andriesvale ZA 204 Ma59
Andrijevica MNE 68 Lu48
Andrijivka UA 73 Mj22
Andringitra RM 207 Nd57
Andringitra, P.N. d' RM 207 Nd57
Andrítsena GR 70 Mb53
Androfiamena RM 206 Ne52
Androka RM 207 Nc58
Androrangalova RM 207 Nd56
Ándros GR 71 Me53
Ándros GR 71 Me53
Andros Island BS 243 Ga33
Andros Town BS 243 Gb33
Andrott Island IND 118 Og40
Andrušivka UA 73 Me20
Andrychów PL 65 Lu41
Andselv N 38 Lt21
Andújar E 55 Kq52
Andulo ANG 200 Lj51
Anduze F 53 Ld46
Andy Warhol Museum USA 237 Ga25
Aneby S 43 Lp33
Anecón Chico, Cerro RA 280 Gf66
Anecón Grande, Cerro RA 280 Ge66
Anéfis RMM 181 La36
Anegada GB 251 Gh36
Anegada Passage 251 Gj36
Aného TG 187 La42
Aneityum VU 158 Te56
Anekal IND 118 Oj39
Anéker RN 182 Lc38
Anelghowhat VU 158 Te56
Añelo RA 280 Gf65
Anepahan RP 125 Qk41
Aney RN 183 Lg36
Anfu CHN 109 Qh32
Angahuán MEX 246 Ej36
Angalimp PNG 155 Sc48
Angamali IND 118 Oj40
Angamarut PNG 155 Sa49
Angangxi CHN 105 Rb22
Angara RUS 89 Qa08
Angaradébou DY 188 Lb40
Angârak RN 182 Lc37
Angarapa A.L. AUS 148 Rh57
Angarsk RUS 104 Qb19
Angarskij krjaž RUS 89 Qa07
Angas Downs AUS 143 Rg58
Angastaco RA 279 Gg58
Angaston AUS 150 Rk63
Angat RP 124 Ra38
Angatuba BR 277 Hf57
Angaur PAL 124 Rh42
Angba WAN 188 Ld42
Angchran IR 98 Nj32
Ånge S 41 Lq28
Angeles RP 124 Ra38
Ängelholm S 42 Ln34
Angélica RA 281 Gk61
Angelókastro GR 68 Md53
Angelókastro GR 70 Mb52
Ängelsberg S 43 Lq31
Angels Camp USA 234 Dk26
Angemuk, Gunung RI 154 Rk47
Angepena AUS 148 Rk61
Angereb ETH 192 Mj39
Ångermanland S 41 Lr27
Angermünde D 58 Lo37
Angern A 66 Lr42
Angers F 52 Ku43
Angerville F 51 Lb42
Ängesön S 41 Ma27
Angetu ETH 192 Mk42
Anggoro RI 130 Ra47
Angical BR 272 Hh51
Angico BR 272 Hg49
Angicos BR 273 Hj51
Angicos BR 273 Jb48
Angkor Wat K 123 Qb39
Angk Tasaom K 123 Qc40
Angle Inlet USA 236 Fc21
Anglem, Mount NZ 153 Td69
Anglès E 57 Lc49
Angles F 52 Kt44
Anglesea AUS 151 Sc65
Anglesey GB 49 Kq37
Angleton USA 238 Fc31
Anglure F 51 Ld42
Angneu IND 114 Og31
Ango RDC 191 Mc43
Angochangua EC 268 Ga45
Angoche MOC 203 Mk54
Angol RCH 280 Gd64
Angola ANG 163 Lb11
Angola USA 237 Fh25
Angola Basin 162 La11
Angoon USA 230 Dc17
Angoram PNG 155 Sc48
Angostura MEX 244 Ef33
Angostura MEX 246 Ek34
Angostura Inglesa RCH 282 Gc70
Angoulême F 52 La45
Angourie AUS 149 Sg60
Angpawing Bum MYA 120 Ph32
Angra dos Reis BR 277 Hh57
Angren KS 97 Of25
Ängsö n.p. S 43 Lt31
Ang Thong THA 122 Qa38
Ang Tra Peang Thmor W.S. K 123 Qb39
Angu RDC 191 Mc44
Anguang CHN 105 Rb23
Angueretá BR 275 Hh55
Angüés E 56 Ku48
Anguilla GB 251 Gj36
Anguilla GB 251 Gj36
Anguilla Cays BS 243 Ga34
Anguille Mts. CDN 241 Ha21
Angul IND 117 Pc35
Anguo CHN 107 Qh26
Anguran IR 98 Nh32
Angurugu AUS 146 Rj53
Anguse EST 44 Mg31
Angusilla PE 268 Gc46
Anhai CHN 109 Qk33
Anholt DK 42 Lm34
Anhua CHN 108 Qf31
Anhuanduí BR 274 Hc56
Anhui CHN 112 Qj29
Ani TR 91 Nb25
Aniak USA 228 Ca15
Aniakchak Nat.Mon. and Preserve USA 228 Ca17
Aniassué CI 187 Kj42
Anicuns BR 274 Hf54
Anié TG 187 La42
Anikino RUS 105 Ra19
Anil BR 267 Hh47
Anillaco RA 279 Gg60
Animas USA 235 Ef30
Añimbo BOL 278 Gh56
Anina RO 68 Mb45
Aningal, T.I. BR 265 Gk44
Anini-y RP 124 Ra40
Anísio de Abreu BR 273 Hj50
Anita USA 236 Fc25
Aniva RUS 111 Sb22
Anivorano RM 207 Ne55
Anivorano Avaratra RM 206 Ne52
Aniwa Island VU 158 Te55
Aniyo J 113 Rj28
Aniza JOR 92 Mh30
Anjahambe RM 207 Ne54
Anjalankoski FIN 44 Mg30
Anjamala RM 207 Nb57
Anjanazana RM 206 Ne53
Anjangaon IND 116 Oj35
Anjar IND 116 Of34
Anjar RL 90 Mh29
Anji CHN 112 Qk30
Anjialava RM 206 Ne53
Anjialava RM 206 Ne53
Anjimangirana RM 206 Nd53
Anjira PK 99 Od31
Anjireh IR 98 Nh29
Anjohibe RM 206 Nd53
Anjoman AFG 97 Of28
Anjou F 50 Ku42
Anjouan = Ndzuani COM 206 Nc52
Anjozorobe RM 207 Nd55
Anju PRK 110 Rc26
Anjuba CHN 108 Qc30
Anjujskij hrebet RUS 89 Ta05
Anka WAN 188 Lc39
Ankalalobe RM 207 Nc55
Ankang CHN 106 Qe29
Ankara TR 90 Mg26
Ankarafantsika, P.N. d' RM 206 Nd54
Ankaramena RM 207 Nd56
Ankaramy RM 206 Ne52
Ankarana RM 206 Ne52
Ankarana RM 206 Ne52
Ankaratra RM 207 Nd55
Ankarsrum S 43 Lr33
Ankasakasa RM 206 Nc54
Ankasa Nature Park GH 187 Kj43
Ankatata RM 206 Ne52
Ankavandra RM 207 Nc55
Ankazoabo RM 207 Nc57
Ankazobe RM 207 Nd55
Ankazomborona RM 206 Nd54
Ankazomiriotra RM 207 Nd55
Ankeny USA 236 Fd25
Ankerika RM 206 Nd53
An Khe VN 123 Qe39
Ankiliabo RM 207 Nb56
Ankililioka RM 207 Nb57
Ankilizato RM 207 Nc56
Ankinany RM 207 Nc57
Ankirihitra RM 207 Nd54
Ankisabe RM 207 Nd55
Anklam D 58 Lo37
Ankleshwar IND 116 Og35
Ankober ETH 192 Mk41
Ankofa RM 206 Ne54
Ankola IND 118 Oh38
Ankoro RDC 196 Md49
Ankotrofotsy RM 207 Nc55
Ankpa WAN 188 Ld42
Anlejie CHN 121 Qa33
Anliu CHN 109 Qh34
An Loc VN 123 Qd40
Anlong CHN 121 Qc33
Anlong Veng K 123 Qc38
Anlu CHN 109 Qg30
Anmyon Do ROK 112 Rd27
Anna RUS 72 Na20
Annaba DZ 176 Ld27
Annaberg PNG 155 Sc48
Annaberg-Buchholz D 59 Ln40
An Nabhaniyah KSA 92 Nb33
An Nabk KSA 92 Mj30
An'nabk SYR 90 Mj28
An Nafud KSA 92 Mk31
An Najaf IRQ 93 Nc29
An Na'La KSA 93 Ne33
An Namas KSA 94 Nb36
Annam Plateau LAO/VN 121 Qc36
Annan GB 48 Kr36
Anna Paulowna NL 51 Le38
Annapolis USA 241 Gb26
Annapolis Royal CDN 240 Gh23
Annapurna I NEP 115 Pb31
Annapurna II NEP 115 Pc31
An-Naqdah OM 95 Nk35
Ann Arbor USA 237 Fj24
Anna Regina GUY 266 Ha42
An Nashash UAE 95 Nh34
An Nasiriyah IRQ 93 Nd30
An'nasra SYR 90 Mj28
Annecy F 53 Lg45
Annemasse F 53 Lg44
Anne, Mount AUS 151 Sd67
Annette Island USA 230 De18
Annette Island Ind. Res. USA 230 De18
Anning CHN 108 Qa30
Anning CHN 121 Qb33
Anniston USA 239 Fh29
Annitowa AUS 146 Rj56
Annofliyah LAR 177 Lj30
Annonay F 53 Le45
Annopol PL 65 Mb40
Annot F 53 Lg47
Annotto Bay JA 250 Gb36
Annoual MA 175 Kj28
An Nu'ayriyah KSA 93 Ne32
An Nukhayb IRQ 93 Nb29
An Nu'man KSA 92 Mh32
An Nu'maniyah IRQ 93 Nc29
An Nurqrah KSA 92 Na33
Anola CDN 236 Fb21
Áno Merá GR 71 Mf53
Ano Nuevo USA 234 Dj27
Áno Poróia GR 68 Md49
Anori BR 270 Gk47
Anosibe An'ala RM 207 Ne55
Anosy RM 207 Nd58
Anoual MA 175 Kj29
Anoumaba CI 187 Kh42
Ânou Mellene RMM 182 Lc36
Anou-n-Bidek DZ 182 Lc36
Ânou Zegguehene RMM 182 Lb38
Áno Vrondoú GR 69 Md49
An Ping Qiao CHN 109 Qk33
Anqing CHN 112 Qj30
Anqiu CHN 107 Qk27
Anquincila RA 279 Gh60
Anröchte D 58 Lj39
Anroville IND 119 Ok40
Ans B 51 Lf40
Ansai CHN 106 Qe27
Ansas RI 154 Rh46
Ansbach D 59 Ll41
Anse-á-Galets RH 250 Gd36
Anse-áVeau RH 250 Gd36
Anse Couleuvre F 251 Gk38
Anse-Pleureuse CDN 240 Gh21
Anserma CO 264 Gc43
Anshan CHN 110 Rb25
Anshi IND 116 Oh38
Anshun CHN 121 Qc32
Ansilta, Cerro de RA 280 Gf61
Ansina ROU 276 Hc61
Ansley USA 236 Fa25
Anson USA 238 Fa29
Ansongo RMM 181 La38
Ansuiek KZ 100 Oh23
Answer Downs AUS 148 Sa56
Anta IND 116 Oj33
Anta PE 269 Gd52
Antabamba PE 269 Gd53
Antaeopolis = Qâw el Kabir ET 179 Mf32
Antagarh IND 117 Pa35
Antakya TR 90 Mj27
Antalaha RM 206 Nf53
Antalya TR 90 Mf27
Antalya Körfezi TR 90 Mf27
Antanambao Manampotsy RM 207 Ne55
Antanambe RM 207 Ne54
Antananarivo RM 207 Nd55
Antanetibe RM 207 Nd55
Antanifotsy RM 207 Nd55
Antanifotsy RM 207 Nd57
Antanimenabaka RM 207 Ne54
Antanimieva RM 207 Nb57
Antanimora Atsimo RM 207 Nc58
Antarctica ANT 287 Ga35
Antarctic Peninsula ANT 287 Gd32
Antares, Gunung RI 155 Sa48
Antarvedi IND 117 Pa37
Antas BR 273 Ja51
Anta, T.I. BR 265 Gk44
Antauta PE 269 Ge53
Antelao I 60 Ln44
Antelope Canyon USA 235 Ee27
Antelope Summit USA 234 Ec26
Antelope Wells USA 235 Ef30
Antequera E 55 Kq54
Antequera PY 276 Hb58
Antetezampandrana RM 207 Ne54
Anthony USA 235 Eg29
Anthony USA 238 Fb27
Anthony Island CDN 230 De19
Anthony Lagoon AUS 146 Rh54
Anthótopos GR 70 Mc51
Anti-Atlas MA 174 Kf31
Antibes F 53 Lh47
Antigo USA 237 Ff23
Antigonish CDN 240 Gj23
Antigua AG 251 Gk37
Antigua GCA 248 Fe38
Antigua and Barbuda 251 Gk37
Antigues Cape F 251 Gk37
Antiguo Morelos MEX 246 Fa34
Antikíthira GR 69 Md55
Anti Lebanon RL 90 Mj29
Antilla C 250 Gc35
Antilla RA 279 Gh59
Antímilos GR 71 Me54
Antiochia ad Pisidiam TR 90 Mf26
Antipajuta RUS 88 Od05
Antíparos GR 71 Mf53
Antíparos GR 71 Mf54
Antípaxi GR 70 Ma51
Antipodes Islands 134 Ba14
Antisana, Volcán EC 268 Ga46
Antissa GR 71 Mg51
Anti-Taurus Mountains TR 90 Mj26
Antlers USA 238 Fc28
Antnäs S 41 Mb25
Antofagasta RCH 279 Ge57
Antofagasta de la Sierra RA 279 Gg59
Antofalla RA 279 Gg58
Antofalla, Volcán RA 279 Gg58
Anton USA 238 Ej26
Antongomena-Bevary RM 206 Nc53
Antonibe RM 206 Nd53
Antonin PL 64 Ls39
Antonina BR 277 Hf58
Antonina do Norte BR 273 Ja49
António MOC 202 Mh57
Antônio Carlos BR 275 Hj56
Antonio de Biedma RA 282 Gg69
Antônio Dias BR 275 Hj55
Antônio João BR 274 Hc57
Antônio Prado BR 276 He60
Antonito USA 235 Eg27
Antonovo BG 69 Mg47
Antopal' BY 65 Me38
Antracyt UA 73 Mk21
Antranoambo RM 207 Ne54
Antrim GB 47 Ko36
Antrim Mountains GB 47 Ko35
Antrodoco I 61 Lo48
Antsaba RM 206 Ne52
Antsahabe RM 206 Ne53
Antsahampano RM 206 Ne52
Antsaidoha Bebao RM 207 Nc54
Antsakabary RM 206 Ne53
Antsalova RM 207 Nc55
Antsambalahy RM 206 Ne53
Antsatramidola RM 206 Ne53
Antsenavolo RM 207 Ne56
Antsiafabositra RM 207 Nd54
Antsianitia RM 206 Nd53
Antsirabe RM 207 Nd55
Antsirabe Afovoany RM 206 Ne53
Antsirabe Avaratra RM 206 Ne52
Antsiranana RM 206 Ne52
Antsla EST 45 Mg33
Antsoha RM 207 Nc55
Antsohihy RM 206 Nd53
Antsohimbondrona RM 206 Ne52
Antsondrodava RM 207 Nc55
Anttola FIN 44 Mh29
Antu CHN 110 Re24
Antuco, Volcán RCH 280 Ge64
Antwerp B 51 Le39
Anučino RUS 110 Rg24
Anum GH 187 La42
Anupgarh IND 114 Og31
Anupshahr IND 115 Ok31
Anuradhapura CL 119 Pa41
Anurrete A.L. AUS 146 Rh56
Anuta SOL 158 Te51
Anvak Island USA 228 Bj18
Anvik USA 228 Bk14
Anxi CHN 101 Pk25
An Xian CHN 106 Qc30
Anxiang CHN 109 Qg31
Anxious Bay AUS 150 Rh62
Anyama CI 187 Kh43
Anyang CHN 107 Qh27
Anyang ROK 112 Rd27
A'Nyêmaqên Shan CHN 103 Pk28
Anyi CHN 109 Qh31
Anyirawase GH 187 La42
Anykščiai LT 45 Mf35
Anyuan CHN 109 Qh33
Anza USA 234 Eb29
Anza-Borrego Desert S.P. USA 234 Eb29
Anzac CDN 231 Ee17
Anze CHN 107 Qg27
Anzi RDC 199 Mb46
Anzin F 51 Ld40
Ánzio I 62 Ln49
Anzob TJ 97 Oe26
Aoba Lodge NAM 200 Lj55
Aodanga TCH 183 Lj37
Aohan Qi CHN 105 Qk24
Aoiz E 56 Kt48
Aoji PRK 110 Rf24
Aojiang CHN 109 Ra32
Aola SOL 157 Ta50
Aomen = Macao CHN 109 Qg34
Aomori J 111 Sa25
Aonla IND 115 Ok31
Ao Phang-Nga N.P. THA 122 Pk41
Aorobo CI 187 Kj42
Aosta I 60 Lh45
Aoudaghost RIM 180 Ke37
Aoudech RIM 180 Kc37
Aouderas RN 182 Le37
Aouelloul RIM 180 Kd35
Aoufouss MA 175 Kh30
Aouhinet bel Egra DZ 175 Kg32
Aouînât ez Zbil RIM 180 Kf37
Aouïnat Sarrag RIM 180 Kd36
Aoukâr RIM 180 Ke36
Aoulef DZ 175 La32
Aoulouz MA 175 Kf30
Aourir-n'-Ouassel MA 175 Kg30
Aourou RMM 180 Ke38
Aoussard DARS 180 Kc34
Aozi TCH 183 Lk35
Aozou TCH 183 Lj35
Apache Creek USA 235 Ef29
Apache Junction USA 235 Ee29
Apache Lake USA 235 Ee29
Apacheta, Cerro RA 279 Gg58
Apagy H 67 Mb43
Apahida RO 67 Md44
Apaikwa GUY 266 Gk42
Apak EAU 194 Mg45
Apalachicola USA 239 Fh31
Apam GH 187 Kk43
Apamea SYR 90 Mj28
Apan MEX 246 Fa36
Apaporis, T.I. BR 270 Gf46
Aparados da Serra, P.N. BR 277 He60
Aparawatatja AUS 148 Rh59
Aparecida, Nossa Senhora BR 277 Hh57
Aparecida do Rio Doce BR 274 He55
Aparecida do Taboado BR 274 He56
Aparri RP 124 Ra36
Apatin SRB 68 Lt45
Apatity RUS 88 Mc05
Apatou F 266 Hc43
Apatzingán de la Constitución MEX 246 Ej36
Apauwar RI 154 Rk46
Apawanza RDC 191 Me45
Ape LV 45 Mg33
Apečki BY 65 Mg37
Apeldoorn NL 51 Lg38
Apen D 58 Lh37
Apennines I 26 Lb05
Apesokubi GH 187 La42
Aphéas GR 69 Md53
Aphrodisias TR 71 Mj53
Aphroditopolis ET 179 Mg33
Aphroditopolis = Kôm Ishqaw ET 179 Mf32
Api NEP 115 Pa30
Api RDC 191 Mc44
Apia CO 264 Gc43
Apia WS 135 Ba11
Apiacás BR 271 Hb50
Apiaí BR 277 Hf58
Apiaka Kayabi, T.I. BR 271 Hb51
Apidiá GR 70 Mc54
Api, Gunung RI 131 Re48
Apinajes BR 272 Hf48
Apinayé, T.I. BR 272 Hg49
Apinópolis BR 275 Hg56
Apio SOL 157 Ta50
Apizolaya MEX 245 Ej33
Aplahoué DY 188 La42
Aplao PE 269 Gd54
Apodi BR 273 Jb48
Apo Duat Range RI 128 Qh44
Apo East Passage RP 124 Ra39
Apoera SME 266 Hb43
Apoko RCB 198 Lh46
Apolda D 58 Lm39
Apolinario Saravia RA 279 Gj58
Apollo Bay AUS 151 Sb65
Apollonia AL 70 Lu50
Apollonia LAR 178 Mb29
Apolo BOL 278 Gf53
Apólonas GR 71 Mf53
Apolu WAN 188 Lc41
Apo, Mount RP 125 Rc42
Apo N.P. RP 125 Rc42
Apopka USA 242 Fk31
Aporé BR 274 Hd55
Apo Reef RP 124 Ra39
Apo Reef N.P. RP 124 Ra39
Aporema BR 267 He45
Apostle Islands Nat. Lakeshore USA 236 Fe22
Apóstoles RA 276 Hc59
Apostolove UA 73 Mg22
Apoteri GUY 266 Ha43
Appalachian Mountains USA 210 Fb06
Appam USA 233 Ej21
Äppelbo S 43 Lo30
Appenino Lucano I 63 Lq50
Appennino Abruzzese I 62 Lo48
Appennino Calabro I 63 Lr52
Appennino Campano I 63 Lp49
Appennino Ligure I 60 Lj46
Appennino Tosco-Emiliano I 60 Ll46
Appennino Umbro-Marchegiano I 60 Ln47
Appenzell CH 60 Lk43
Appingedam NL 51 Lg37
Appleby-in-Westmorland GB 49 Ks36
Appleton USA 236 Fc23
Appleton USA 237 Ff23
Appomattox USA 242 Ga27
Appomattox Court House N.H.P. USA 242 Ga27
Apricena I 63 Lq49
Apriki LV 45 Mb34
Aprilci BG 69 Me48
Aprília I 62 Ln49
Aprilovo BG 69 Mg47
Aprompronou CI 187 Kj42
Apšeronsk RUS 73 Mk23
Apšeronskij poluostrov AZ 91 Ne25
Apsley AUS 150 Sa64
Apsley CDN 237 Ga23
Apšupe LV 45 Md34
Apt F 53 Lf47
Apti IND 116 Og36
Apucarana BR 274 He57
Apuí BR 270 Gh46
Apuí BR 271 Ha49
Apuka RUS 89 Tb06
Apure YV 265 Gg41
Apurímac PE 269 Gd52
Apurinã Igarapé Tauamirim, T.I. BR 270 Gj48
Apurina Km 124 BR-317, T.I. BR 270 Gg50
Apurito YV 265 Gf41
Aqabah IRQ 91 Nb29
Aqaba Pass SUD 185 Mj36
Aqal CHN 100 Ok25
Aqar LAR 177 Lh32
Aqchah AFG 97 Od27
Aqda IR 98 Ng29
A'qeirbat SYR 90 Mj28
Aqiq SUD 185 Mk36
Aqitag CHN 101 Pf25
Aq Qaleh IR 96 Nh27
Aqqan CHN 102 Pc27
Aqua Downs AUS 149 Sd59
Aquarium and Marine Center (Shippagan) CDN 240 Gh22
Aqueduct USA 241 Gd25
Aquidauana BR 274 Hc56
Aquila MEX 246 Ej36
Aquiléia I 61 Lo45
Aquiles Serdán MEX 244 Eh31
Aquin RH 250 Gd36
Aquiraz BR 273 Ja47
Aquismón MEX 246 Fa35
Aquitaine F 52 Ku46
Ara IND 117 Pc33
Ara Arba ETH 195 Na43
Arab USA 239 Fg28
Arabá BR 274 He55
Arab Abad IR 98 Nj29
Araban TR 90 Mj27
Arabapo YV 265 Gk43
Arabati ETH 192 Mk40
Arabela USA 235 Eh29
Arabian Oryx Sanctuary OM 95 Nj35
Arabian Peninsula 76 Na07
Arabian Sea 76 Oa08
Arabiyeh Sagireh SYR 90 Mk27
Arabuko Sokoke N.P. EAK 195 Mk47
Araç TR 90 Mg25
Aracá BR 265 Gj45
Aracajú BR 273 Jb51
Aracar, Volcán RA 279 Gg58
Araçás BR 273 Ja52
Aracataca CO 264 Gc40
Aracá, T.I. BR 265 Gk44
Aracati BR 273 Jb48
Araçatuba BR 274 Hc52
Araçatuba BR 274 He56
Araceli RP 124 Ra40
Aracena E 55 Ko53
Araci BR 273 Ja51
Aracruz BR 275 Hk55
Aracu BOL 278 Gg54
Araçuaí BR 275 Hj54
Aracuta BR 275 Hk53
Arad IL 92 Mh30
Arad RO 67 Mb44
Arada TCH 184 Ma38
Aradan IR 98 Ng28
Arafali ER 192 Mk38
Arafura Sea AUS/RI 154 Rf50
Arafura Shelf 154 Rg51
Aragarças BR 274 Hd53
Arage WAN 188 Le41
Aragoiânia BR 274 Hf54
Aragón E 56 Kt49
Aragona I 62 Lo53
Araguacema BR 272 Hf50
Araguaçu BR 272 Hf52
Araguaçui BR 272 Hf50
Aragua de Barcelona YV 265 Gh41
Aragua de Maturín YV 265 Gj41
Araguaia BR 272 He51
Araguaiana BR 274 He53
Araguaína BR 272 Hf49
Araguanã BR 272 Hf49
Araguari BR 274 Hf55
Araguatins BR 272 Hf48
Aráhova GR 70 Mc52
Arai BR 272 Hg52
Arai J 111 Rk27
Araioses BR 273 Hj47
Araju BR 270 Gk47
Arak DZ 176 Lb33
Arak IR 91 Ne28
Arakaka GUY 266 Ha42
Arakawa J 111 Rk26
Arakht AFG 97 Of27
Arakkonam IND 119 Ok39
Araku IND 117 Pb36
Aral CHN 100 Pa25
Aral KS 100 Oh25
Aralık TR 91 Nc26
Aralkı TR 91 Na25
Aralkum KZ 96 Ob22
Aral Moreira BR 274 Hc57
Aral Sea KZ/UZ 96 Nk23
Aralsk KZ 88 Oa09
Aramah KSA 93 Nc32
Arambagh IND 117 Pd34
Aramberri MEX 245 Fa33
Arame BR 272 Hh48
Aramits F 52 Ku47
Aramoana NZ 153 Tf68
Aran IR 91 Nf28
Arancay PE 269 Gb50
Aranda de Duero E 54 Kr49
Aranda de Moncayo E 56 Kt49
Arandis NAM 200 Lh57
Arandjelovac SRB 68 Ma46
Arang IND 117 Pa35
Arani IND 119 Ok39
Aran Island IRL 47 Km36
Aran Islands IRL 47 Kl37
Aranjuez E 55 Kr50
Aranos NAM 204 Lk58
Aransas Pass USA 245 Fb32
Arantangi IND 119 Ok40
Arantzazu E 56 Ks48
Araouane RMM 181 Kj36
Arapahoe USA 238 Fa25
Arapari BR 270 Gg47
Arapari BR 272 Hf48
Arapawa Island NZ 153 Th66
Arapicos EC 268 Gb46
Arapiraca BR 273 Jb50
Arapixi BR 270 Gf50
Arapixuna BR 271 Hc47
Arapkir TR 90 Mk26
Arapongas BR 274 He57
Arapoti BR 277 Hf58
Arapuá BR 274 He56
Arapunya AUS 148 Rh57
Araputanga BR 278 Ha53
'Ar'ar KSA 92 Na30
Araracuara CO 268 Gd46
Arara do Rio Branco, T.I. BR 271 Ha50
Araranguá BR 277 Hf60
Araraquara BR 274 Hf56
Araras BR 271 Hc49
Araras BR 275 Hg57
Ararat ARM 91 Nc26
Ararat AUS 151 Sb64
Ararat = Ağri Daği TR 91 Nc26
Arara, T.I. BR 271 Hd47
Ararauma BR 277 Hj57
Ararendá BR 273 Hk48
Arari BR 272 Hh47
Araria IND 117 Pd32
Arariba, T.I. BR 274 Hf57
Araribóia, T.I. BR 272 Hg48
Araripe BR 273 Hk49
Araripina BR 273 Hk49
Aras IR 91 Nd27
Aras de Alpuente E 57 Kt51
Arataca BR 275 Ja53
Aratâne RIM 181 Kf36
Ara Terra ETH 192 Na42
Arau MAL 126 Qa42
Arauá BR 273 Jb51
Arauca CO 264 Ge42
Araucária BR 277 Hf58
Arauco RCH 280 Gd64
Araure YV 265 Gf41
Aravakkurichchi IND 118 Oj40
Aravalli Range IND 116 Og33
Aravan KS 97 Og25
Aravete EST 44 Mf31
Arawa PNG 157 Sh49
Arawah KSA 94 Nc34
Arawale National Reserve EAK 195 Na46
Arawe Islands PNG 156 Se49
Araxá BR 275 Hg55
Araya YV 265 Gh40
Arayat RP 124 Ra38
Arba ETH 192 Na41
Arbadin SP 195 Nb45
Arbakwe WAN 182 Lc39
Arba Minch ETH 194 Mj43
Arba Minch Crocodile Market ETH 194 Mj43
Arbaoua MA 175 Kh28
Arbat IRQ 91 Nc28
Árbatax I 62 Lk51
Arbil IRQ 91 Nc27
Arboga S 43 Lq31
Arbois F 53 Lf44
Arbolé BF 187 Kj39
Arboledas RA 281 Gk64
Arboletes CO 264 Gb41
Arboréa I 62 Lj51
Arbourg CDN 236 Fb20
Arboutchatak TCH 189 Lj39
Arbre du Ténéré RN 182 Le37
Arbroath GB 48 Ks34
Árbus I 62 Lj51
Arcabuco CO 264 Gd43
Arcachon F 52 Kt46
Arcadia AUS 146 Rk56
Arcadia AUS 149 Se58
Arcadia USA 243 Fk32
Arčadinskaja RUS 72 Nb21
Arcahaie RH 250 Gd36
Arcata USA 232 Dh25
Arc de Triomphe d'Orange F 53 Le46
Arcelia MEX 246 Ek36
Arc-en-Barrois F 53 Lf43
Arc-et-Senans F 53 Lf43
Archaeological Museum of Beluchistan PK 99 Od30
Archangelskij sobor RUS 72 Nb17
Archäologischer Park Xanten D 58 Lg39
Archena E 57 Kt52
Archer USA 242 Fj31
Archer Bay AUS 147 Sa52
Archer Bend N.P. AUS 147 Sb52
Archer City USA 238 Fa29
Archer River Roadhouse AUS 147 Sb52
Archers Post EAK 194 Mj45
Archerwill CDN 233 Eh19
Arches N.P. USA 235 Ef26
Archibald USA 239 Fe29
Archibarca, Cerro RA 279 Gg58
Archidona E 55 Kq53
Archidona EC 268 Gb46
Archie USA 239 Fe30
Archipelago of the Recherche AUS 145 Rb63
Archipel des 7 Frères DJI 193 Nb39
Archipiélago de Bocas del Toro PA 249 Fj41
Archipiélago de Camagüey C 243 Ga34
Archipiélago de Juan Fernández, P.N. RCH 269 Ga62
Archipiélago de las Perlas PA 249 Ga41
Archipiélago de los Canarreos C 243 Fj35
Archipiélago de los Colorados C 243 Fh34
Archipiélago de los Jardines de la Reina C 243 Ga35
Archipiélago de Sabana C 243 Fk34
Archipiélago de San Blás PA 249 Ga41
Archipiélago de Solentiname NIC 249 Fh40
Archipiélago Guayaneco RCH 282 Gc69
Archipiélago Los Roques, P.N. YV 265 Gg40
Archipiélago Reina Adelaide RCH 282 Gc72
Arcidosso I 60 Lm48
Arcipélago de la Maddalena, P.N. dell' I 62 Lk49
Arcipélago Toscano, P.N. dell' I 60 Lk47
Arcis-sur-Aube F 51 Le42
Arckaringa AUS 148 Rh59
Arco I 60 Ll45
Arco USA 232 Ed24
Arco de Baúlhe P 54 Kn49
Arcoona AUS 148 Rj61
Arcos BR 275 Hh56
Arcos de Jalón E 57 Ks49
Arcos de la Frontera E 55 Kp54
Arcot IND 119 Ok39
Arcoverde BR 273 Jb50
Arctic Bay CDN 227 Fd04
Arctic Circle Hot Springs USA 229 Ch13
Arctic National Wildlife Refuge USA 229 Ch11
Arctic Ocean 286 Dd02
Arctic Plains USA 229 Cb11
Arctic Village USA 229 Ch11
Arctowski ANT 286 Ha31
Arcyz UA 73 Me23
Ardabil IR 91 Ne26
Ardahan TR 91 Nb25
Ardakan IR 93 Nf30
Ardakan IR 98 Nh29
Ardal IR 93 Nf30
Ardara IRL 47 Km36
Ardasier Bank 128 Qh42
Ardatov RUS 72 Nb18
Ardavidu IND 116 Ok38
Ardboe GB 47 Ko36
Arde SP 193 Nd41
Ardèche F 53 Le46
Ardee IRL 47 Ko37
Ardémi TCH 184 Mb38
Arden DK 42 Lk34
Arden ZW 202 Mf54
Ardennes B/F 51 Le41
Ardentes F 53 Lb44
Ardes F 53 Ld45
Ardeşen TR 91 Na25
Ardeshir-e-Babakan IR 98 Ng31
Ardestan IR 98 Ng29
Ardgartan GB 48 Kq34
Ardino BG 69 Mf49
Ardisa E 56 Ku48
Ardlethan AUS 151 Sd63
Ardmore AUS 148 Rk56
Ardmore USA 238 Fb28
Ardon RUS 91 Nc24
Ardres F 51 Lb40
Ardrossan AUS 150 Rj63
Ardrossan GB 48 Kq35
Ards Peninsula GB 47 Kp36
Ardvasar GB 48 Kp33
Åre S 40 Lo27
Areado BR 273 Hj51
Areado BR 275 Hg56
Área Natural Apolobamba BOL 278 Gf53
Área Natural de Manejo Integrado Kaa-Iya del Gran Chaco, P.N. y BOL 278 Gk55
Área Natural de Manejo Integrado Otuquis, P.N. y BOL 278 Ha55
Área Natural de Manejo Integrado San Matías BOL 278 Ha54
Área Natural El Palmar BOL 278 Gh55
Arecibo USA 251 Gg36
Aredo RI 154 Rg47
Åre-Duved S 40 Ln27
Arefu RO 67 Me45
Aregaon IND 117 Ok35
Aregue YV 264 Ge40
Areia BR 273 Jc49
Areia Branca BR 273 Jb48
Arellano MEX 247 Fe36
Arena Island RP 125 Ra41
Arenal CR 249 Fh40
Arenales RCH 279 Gg57
Arenales, Cerro RCH 282 Gd69
Arenal, P.N., Volcán CR 249 Fh40
Arenápolis BR 274 Hb53
Arenas PA 249 Fk42
Arenas de San Pedro E 55 Kp50
Arendal N 42 Lj32
Arendsee D 58 Lm38
Arenillas EC 268 Fk47
Arenys de Mar E 57 Lc49
Arenzano I 60 Lj46
Areões, T.I. BR 274 He53
Areópoli GR 70 Mc54
Arequipa PE 269 Ge54
Arequita, P.N. ROU 281 Hc63
Arero ETH 195 Mk43
Arévalo E 54 Kq49
Areza ER 192 Mk38
Arezzo I 60 Lm47
Arfak Mountains RI 154 Rh46
Argadargada AUS 148 Rj56
Argalant MNG 104 Qd22
Argalastí GR 68 Md51
Argamasilla de Alba E 55 Kr51
Argamasilla de Calatrava E 55 Kq52
Argan CHN 101 Pe25
Arganda E 55 Kr50
Arganil P 54 Km50
Argao RP 124 Rb41
Argaybulak Daban CHN 101 Pe24
Arg-e-Bam IR 98 Nk31
Argedeb ETH 192 Na42
Argelès-Gazost F 52 Ku48
Argelès- sur-Mer F 53 Ld48
Argelia CO 264 Gb44
Argenta I 60 Lm46
Argentan F 50 La42
Argentat F 52 Lb45
Argenteuil F 51 Lc42
Argentina RA 279 Gj60
Argentina RA 255 Gb13
Argentina Range 286 Ja35
Argentine Basin 254 Hb14
Argenton-Château F 52 Ku44
Argenton-sur-Creuse F 52 Lb44
Argent-sur-Sauldre F 53 Lc43
Arghestan AFG 99 Od30
Argoim BR 273 Ja52
Argolikós Kólpos GR 70 Mc53
Argonne F 51 Le41
Argopuro, Gunung RI 129 Qg49
Árgos GR 70 Mc53
Árgos GR 70 Mc53
Árgos Orestikó GR 70 Mb50
Argostóli GR 70 Ma52

Arguedas ⬚ E 56 Kt48
Argun ⬚ RUS 91 Nc24
Argungu ⬚ WAN 188 Lc39
Arguni ⬚ RI 154 Rg47
Argyle ⬚ MNG 104 Qb23
Argyle Diamond Mine ⬚ AUS 143 Re54
Arhangel'sk ⬚ RUS 88 Na06
Arhara ⬚ RUS 110 Rf21
Arhauli ⬚ IND 117 Pa33
Arhavi ⬚ TR 91 Na25
Arhéa Kórinthos ⬚ GR 70 Mc53
Arhéa Neméa ⬚ GR 70 Mc53
Arhéa Neméa ⬚ GR 70 Mc53
arheologičeskij zapovednik Tanais ⬚ RUS 73 Mk22
Arheologikó Mousío ⬚ GR 71 Mf55
Ar Horqin ⬚ CHN 110 Ra24
Århus ⬚ DK 42 Ll34
Århus Bugt ⬚ DK 42 Ll34
Ariadnoe ⬚ RUS 111 Rh23
Ariana ⬚ TN 176 Lf27
Ariano Irpino ⬚ I 63 Lq49
Arias ⬚ RA 281 Gj62
Aribinda ⬚ BF 181 Kk38
Arica ⬚ CO 268 Ge47
Arica ⬚ PE 268 Gc46
Aricagua ⬚ YV 264 Ge41
Aricaria ⬚ BR 271 Ha51
Arichuna ⬚ CDN 240 Ga23
Arichuna ⬚ YV 265 Gg42
Arida ⬚ J 113 Rd34
Aridéa ⬚ GR 70 Mc50
Aride Atoll ⬚ MV 118 Oq44
Ariel ⬚ RA 281 Ha64
Arieşeni ⬚ RO 72 Md19
Arifwala ⬚ PK 99 Og30
Ariguani ⬚ CO 264 Gc41
Ariha ⬚ JOR 92 Mh35
Ariha ⬚ SYR 90 Mj28
Arikawa ⬚ J 113 Re29
Arikok N.P. ⬚ NL 265 Gf39
Arilje ⬚ SRB 68 Ma47
Arima ⬚ TT 251 Ge44
Arimu Mine ⬚ GUY 266 Ha42
Arinagour ⬚ GB 48 Ko34
Aringay ⬚ RP 124 Ra37
Arinis ⬚ RO 67 Md43
Arinos ⬚ BR 271 Hb51
Arinos ⬚ BR 275 Hg53
Arinthod ⬚ F 53 Lf44
Ariogala ⬚ LT 45 Md35
Aripuanã ⬚ BR 271 Hb48
Aripuanã ⬚ BR 271 Ha50
Aripuaná, T.I. ⬚ BR 271 Ha50
Ariquemes ⬚ BR 270 Gj50
Ariquida ⬚ RCH 278 Gf55
Ariranha ⬚ BR 271 Ha45
Aris ⬚ NAM 200 Lj57
Arisaig ⬚ GB 48 Kp34
Arisba ⬚ GR 71 Mg51
Arisman Ancient City ⬚ IR 98 Ng29
Arisménd ⬚ YV 265 Gf41
Arisba ⬚ GR 71 Mg51
Aristazabal Island ⬚ CDN 230 Df19
Aristóbulo del Valle ⬚ RA 276 Hc59
Aritao ⬚ RP 124 Ra37
Arite ⬚ SOL 157 Ta61
Aritzo ⬚ I 62 Lk51
Arivonimamo ⬚ RM 207 Nd55
Ariyalur ⬚ IND 119 Ok40
Ariza ⬚ E 57 Ks49
Arizona ⬚ AUS 147 Sa55
Arizona ⬚ RA 280 Gh63
Arizona ⬚ USA 204 Bb60
Arizona Pioneer Living History Museum ⬚ USA 235 Ee29
Arizona Sonora Desert Museum ⬚ USA 235 Ee29
Arizpe ⬚ MEX 244 Ee30
'Arjah ⬚ KSA 93 Nc33
Ārjāng ⬚ S 42 Ln31
Arjeplog ⬚ S 38 Ma24
Arjo ⬚ ETH 192 Mj41
Arjona ⬚ CO 264 Gc40
Arjona ⬚ E 56 Kr53
Arjuni ⬚ IND 117 Pb35
Arkadak ⬚ RUS 72 Nb19
Arkadelphia ⬚ USA 238 Fd28
Arkadia ⬚ PL 65 Ma38
Arkalgud ⬚ IND 118 Oj39
Arkalyk ⬚ KZ 88 Ob08
Arkansas ⬚ USA 238 Ez27
Arkansas City ⬚ USA 238 Fb27
Arkansas City ⬚ USA 239 Fa29
Arkansas Junction ⬚ USA 238 Fc29
Arkansas Post N.M. ⬚ USA 239 Fe29
Arkassa ⬚ GR 71 Mh55
Arkatag ⬚ CHN 102 Pa27
Arkell, Mount ⬚ CDN 230 Dc15
Arkesini ⬚ GR 71 Mf54
Arkhangay ⬚ MNG 104 Pk22
Arkhust ⬚ MNG 104 Qb24
Arki ⬚ GR 71 Mg53
Arkitsa ⬚ GR 68 Md52
Arklow ⬚ IRL 47 Ki38
Arkö ⬚ S 43 Lr32
Arkösund ⬚ S 43 Lr32
Arkoúdi ⬚ GR 70 Mc53
Arktikum ⬚ FIN 39 Mf24
Arla ⬚ S 43 Lr31
Arlanc ⬚ F 53 Ld45
Arles ⬚ F 53 Le47
Arli ⬚ BF 187 La40
Arlington ⬚ USA 232 Dj21
Arlington ⬚ USA 236 Fb23
Arlington ⬚ USA 238 Ej26
Arlington ⬚ USA 238 Fz29
Arlington ⬚ USA 239 Fh30
Arlington ⬚ USA 241 Gd26
Arlington ⬚ USA 205 Md60
Arlington Park ⬚ USA 237 Ff24
Arlit ⬚ RN 188 Lf41
Arlon ⬚ B 51 Lf41
Arma ⬚ GR 69 Md52
Arma ⬚ PE 269 Gc52
Armada ⬚ BR 276 Hc61
Armadale ⬚ AUS 144 Qj62
Armagh ⬚ GB 47 Ko36
Armand Bermúdez, P.N. ⬚ DOM 250 Ge36
Armant ⬚ ET 179 Mg33
Armenia ⬚ ARM 91 Nc25
Armenia ⬚ CO 264 Gc43
Armenia ⬚ RO 68 Mc45
Armentières ⬚ F 51 Lc40
Armidale ⬚ AUS 149 Sf61
Armijo ⬚ USA 235 Eg28
Armjans'k ⬚ UA 73 Mg22
Armona ⬚ IND 117 Ok35
Armour ⬚ USA 236 Fa24
Armraynald ⬚ AUS 147 Rk55
Armstrong ⬚ CDN 236 Fl20
Armstrong ⬚ RA 281 Gk62
Armutlu ⬚ TR 69 Mg50
Armutova ⬚ TR 71 Mg51
Arnac-Pompadour ⬚ F 52 Lb45
Arnäsvall ⬚ S 39 Lp27
Arnavutköy ⬚ TR 69 Mj49
Arnes ⬚ IS 46 Jr25
Árnes ⬚ N 42 Lm30
Arnett ⬚ USA 238 Fa27
Arnhem ⬚ NL 51 Lf39
Arnhem Bay ⬚ AUS 146 Rj52
Arnhem Cave ⬚ NAM 201 Lk57
Arnhem Land ⬚ AUS 146 Rh52
Arnhem Land Aboriginal Reserve ⬚ AUS 146 Rh52
Arnö ⬚ IND 116 Oj35
Arno ⬚ AUS 149 Sb58
Arno ⬚ S 43 Ls32
Arno Bay ⬚ AUS 150 Rj62
Arnö ⬚ AUS 149 Sb58
Arnsberg ⬚ D 58 Lj39
Arntfield ⬚ CDN 238 Ga21

Aroa ⬚ YV 265 Gf40
Aroab ⬚ NAM 201 Lj59
Arocena ⬚ RA 281 Gk62
Arochuku ⬚ WAN 188 Ld43
Aroji ⬚ ETH 192 Mh41
Aroland ⬚ CDN 237 Fg20
Aroma ⬚ PNG 155 Sa50
Aroma ⬚ SUD 185 Mj38
Aron ⬚ CL 119 Pa42
Arona ⬚ I 60 Lj45
Aroostook Hist. & Art Mus. ⬚ USA 240 Gf22
Aropa ⬚ PNG 157 Sh49
Aroroy ⬚ RP 124 Rb39
Arosa ⬚ CH 60 Lk44
Arosbaya ⬚ RI 129 Qg49
Arous ⬚ SUD 185 Mj35
Arovi ⬚ USA 238 Ej26
Åröysund ⬚ N 42 Ll31
Arpajon la Norville ⬚ F 51 Lc42
Arpaşu de Jos ⬚ RO 67 Me45
Árpino ⬚ I 62 Lo49
Arqu ⬚ BD 117 Pf33
Arquata del Tronto ⬚ I 61 Lo48
Arriola ⬚ USA 234 Ea28
Arvorezinha ⬚ BR 276 Hd60
Arwad ⬚ SYR 90 Mj28
Arwal ⬚ IND 117 Pc33
Arwala ⬚ RI 131 Rd47
Arxan ⬚ CHN 105 Qk22
Aryan ⬚ IR 96 Nj28
Arys ⬚ KZ 97 Oe24
Arzachena ⬚ I 62 Lk49
Aramas ⬚ RUS 72 Nb18
Arzanah ⬚ UAE 95 Ng32
Arzew ⬚ DZ 175 Kk28
Arzignano ⬚ I 60 Lm45
Arzúa ⬚ E 54 Kn48
Aš ⬚ CZ 66 Ln40
Aš ⬚ S 42 Ll31
Ås ⬚ S 41 Lp27
Åsa ⬚ KZ 97 Of24
Asab ⬚ NAM 200 Lj58
Asab ⬚ UAE 95 Nh34
Asaba ⬚ WAN 188 Ld43
Asadabad ⬚ AFG 97 Of29
Asadabad ⬚ IR 98 Ne29
Asad ⬚ IR 98 Da29
Aşağiçonak ⬚ TR 90 Mm27
Asahan ⬚ RI 127 Qc48
Asahi ⬚ J 111 Rj27
Asahi-dake ⬚ J 111 Sb24
Asahikawa ⬚ J 111 Sb24
Asaka ⬚ UZ 97 Og25
Asalem ⬚ IR 91 Ne27
Asaluyeh ⬚ IR 98 Ng32
Asamankese ⬚ GH 187 Kk43
Asan Abad ⬚ IR 98 Ng29
Asandh ⬚ IND 114 Oj31
Asandi ⬚ IND 118 Oj39
Asankranwa ⬚ GH 187 Kj42
Asansol ⬚ IND 117 Pd34
Asanwinso ⬚ GH 187 Kj42
Asarna ⬚ S 41 Lp28
Asaro ⬚ PNG 155 Sc49
Åsarp ⬚ S 43 Lp32
Asarum ⬚ S 43 Lq34
Asasp ⬚ F 52 La48
Asau ⬚ CDN 233 Ef20
Åsbäck ⬚ S 43 Lr31
Ascochinga ⬚ RA 280 Gh61
Ascoli Piceno ⬚ I 61 Lo48
Ascoli Satriano ⬚ I 63 Lq49
Ascona ⬚ CH 60 Lj44
Ascope ⬚ PE 268 Gb50
Ascot ⬚ GB 49 Ku39
Ascotán ⬚ RCH 279 Gf56
Ascunción ⬚ BOL 270 Gg51
Aseb ⬚ ETH 193 Na39
Asedabad ⬚ DZ 182 La33
Aseki ⬚ PNG 155 Sd49
Ås Éla ⬚ J 92 Mj28
Asela ⬚ ETH 192 Mk42
Åsele ⬚ S 39 Lp26
Åseli ⬚ S 40 Lo29
Asendabo ⬚ ETH 192 Mj42
Asenovgrad ⬚ BG 69 Me48
Åseral ⬚ N 42 La32
Asermanuevo ⬚ CO 264 Gd43
Aserradero la Flor ⬚ MEX 245 Eh34
Aserradero Los Charcos ⬚ MEX 245 Eh34
Aserradero Yerbitas ⬚ MEX 244 Eg32
Asfaka ⬚ GR 70 Ma51
Asfi ⬚ MA 174 Kf29
Asgapour ⬚ MA 175 Kg30
Asgaran ⬚ IR 91 Nf29
Ash ⬚ WAN 188 Lc42
Ashabha ⬚ EAK 195 Na34
Ashanti ⬚ GH 187 Kk42
Ashara ⬚ SYR 91 Na28
Ashayrah ⬚ KSA 94 Na35
Ashbourne ⬚ GB 49 Kt37
Ashburton ⬚ USA 242 Fj37
Ashburton ⬚ NZ 153 T67
Ashburton Downs ⬚ AUS 142 Qj57
Ashburton River ⬚ AUS 142 Qh57
As Sawdah ⬚ KSA 94 Nc34
As Sawwah ⬚ LAR 177 Lj31
As Sawwdiyah ⬚ YE 94 Na36
Ashchysai ⬚ KZ 97 Oe24
Ashdown ⬚ USA 242 Fa30
Asheboro ⬚ USA 242 Ga26
Asher ⬚ USA 238 Fb28
Ashern ⬚ CDN 236 Fa20
Asherton ⬚ USA 244 Fa32
Ashewele ⬚ WAN 188 Lc42
Ashford ⬚ AUS 149 Sf60
Ashford ⬚ GB 49 La39
Ash Fork ⬚ USA 235 Ed28
Ashgabad ⬚ TM 96 Nj27
Ashibetsu ⬚ J 111 Sb24
Ashikaga ⬚ J 111 Rk27
Ashington ⬚ GB 48 Kt35
Ashizuri-misaki ⬚ J 113 Rg29
Ashizuri-Uwakai Q.N.P. ⬚ J 113 Rg29
Ashland ⬚ LB 186 Ka42
Ashland ⬚ USA 233 Eg22
Ashland ⬚ USA 236 Fb22
Ashland ⬚ USA 237 Fj25
Ashland ⬚ USA 238 Fd27
Ashland ⬚ USA 239 Fg28
Ashland ⬚ USA 239 Fj29
Ashley ⬚ AUS 149 Se60
Ashley ⬚ USA 236 Fa22
Ashmont ⬚ CDN 233 Ee18
Ashmore Islands ⬚ AUS 142 Rb52
Ashmore Reef ⬚ PNG 155 Sc51
Ashoknagar ⬚ IND 116 Oj38
Ashoro ⬚ J 111 Sb24
Ashqelon ⬚ IL 92 Mg30
Ash Shabkah ⬚ IRQ 93 Nb30
Ash Shafa ⬚ KSA 94 Na34
Ash Shakk ⬚ IRQ 93 Nd31
Ash Sham ⬚ UAE 98 Nj32
Ash Shamaliyah ⬚ SYR 90 Mj28
Ash Shamasiyah ⬚ KSA 93 Nc30
Ash Shamiyah ⬚ IRQ 93 Nc30
Ash Shamiyah ⬚ IRQ 93 Nc30
Ash Sha'ra' ⬚ KSA 93 Nc30
Ash Sharqat ⬚ IRQ 91 Nb28

Aruanã ⬚ BR 274 He53
Aruba ⬚ NL 265 Gf40
Aruba ⬚ NL 250 Ge39
Aruba ⬚ CRO 264 Ge39
Aruba Lodge ⬚ EAK 195 Mk47
Arididy ⬚ AUS 145 Rd61
Arufi ⬚ PNG 155 Sa50
Arufu ⬚ WAN 188 Le42
Arumã ⬚ BR 270 Gj48
Arumi ⬚ RDC 194 Mf44
Arumuganeri ⬚ IND 118 Ok41
Arunachal Pradesh ⬚ IND 120 Pg32
Arundel ⬚ GB 49 Ku40
Aruppukkottai ⬚ IND 118 Ok41
Arusan ⬚ IR 98 Nh28
Arusha ⬚ EAT 194 Mj47
Arusha N.P. ⬚ EAT 194 Mj47
Aruwimi ⬚ RDC 191 Mc45
Arva ⬚ SK 67 Lu41
Arvada ⬚ USA 235 Eh26
Arvand Kenar ⬚ IR 93 Ne30
Arvaykheer ⬚ MNG 104 Qb22
Arvi ⬚ IND 116 Ok35
Arviat ⬚ CDN 227 Fb06
Arvidsjaur ⬚ S 41 Lu25
Arwad ⬚ SYR 90 Mj28
Asa ⬚ WAN 188 Lc42
Asaita ⬚ ETH 193 Na39
As'Shaykh Salamah ⬚ ET 179 Mf31
Ash Shatrah ⬚ IRQ 93 Nd30
ash-Shawal ⬚ SUD 185 Mg39
Ash Shihr ⬚ YE 94 Nc38
Ash Shubaykiyah ⬚ KSA 93 Nb33
Ash Shumlul ⬚ KSA 93 Nd32
Ash Shuqayq ⬚ KSA 94 Na35
Ash Shurayf ⬚ KSA 92 Mk33
Ash Springs ⬚ USA 235 Ec27
Ashta ⬚ IND 116 Oj34
Ashtabula ⬚ USA 237 Fk25
Ashtarak ⬚ ARM 91 Nc25
Ashti ⬚ IND 116 Oj36
Ashtiyan ⬚ IR 91 Ne28
Ashton ⬚ RA 204 Mab9
Ashton ⬚ ZA 204 Ma60
Ashton ⬚ EAK 195 Na46
Ashville ⬚ CDN 236 Ek20
Ashville ⬚ USA 239 Fg29
Ashwaraopet ⬚ IND 117 Pa37
Asia ⬚ PE 269 Gb52
Asia 76 Pa04
Asiago ⬚ I 60 Lm45
Asidonopo ⬚ SME 266 Hc44
Asientos ⬚ MEX 246 Ej34
Asifabad ⬚ IND 116 Ok36
Asikkala ⬚ FIN 44 Mf29
Asilah ⬚ MA 175 Kg28
Asilo ⬚ PE 269 Ge53
Asilulu ⬚ RI 131 Rd47
Asinara, P.N. dell' ⬚ I 62 Lj49
Asir ⬚ KSA 94 Na36
Asir N.P. ⬚ KSA 94 Nb37
Asir N.P. ⬚ KSA 94 Nb37
Asir N.P. ⬚ IND 117 Pc36
Askale ⬚ TR 91 Na26
Askeaton ⬚ IRL 47 Km38
Asker ⬚ N 42 Ll31
Askersund ⬚ S 43 Lq32
Askhanehi ⬚ IR 96 Nj27
Askim ⬚ N 42 Ln31
Askinuk Mts. ⬚ USA 228 Bg15
Askira ⬚ WAN 189 Lg40
Askja ⬚ IS 46 Kd25
Asklepieion ⬚ GR 71 Mh54
Askö ⬚ S 43 Lr31
Askola ⬚ FIN 44 Mf30
Åskopping ⬚ S 43 Lq32
Askot ⬚ IND 115 Pa31
Askvoll ⬚ N 40 Lj29
Aslanduz ⬚ IR 91 Nd26
Aslankaya ⬚ TR 90 Mh50
Aslanlu ⬚ IR 91 Nd26
Aslantepe ⬚ TR 90 Mk52
Asluman ⬚ RP 124 Ra60
Asmali ⬚ TR 69 Mh50
Asmar ⬚ AFG 97 Of28
Asmara ⬚ ER 192 Mk38
Asmat Wetlands ⬚ RI 154 Rk49
Asmat Woodcarvings ⬚ RI 154 Rk49
Asmunti ⬚ FIN 39 Mg25
Asnes ⬚ DZ 182 Lc33
Asnæs ⬚ DK 42 Lm35
Asni ⬚ MA 174 Kf29
Asò ⬚ J 111 Rk28
Asola ⬚ IND 114 Og32
Asòrno ⬚ RI 117 Pa37
Aspe ⬚ E 57 Ku52
Aspen ⬚ USA 235 Eg27
Aspen Cove ⬚ CDN 232 Dk21
Aspendos ⬚ TR 90 Mf27
Aspermont ⬚ USA 238 Ej29
Aspet ⬚ F 52 Lb47
Aspiring, Mount ⬚ NZ 153 T68
Aspres-sur-Buëch ⬚ F 53 Lf46
Asprógia ⬚ RO 70 Mb50
Aspromonte, P.N. dell ⬚ I 63 Lr52
Asprópirgos ⬚ GR 69 Md52
Aspur ⬚ IND 116 Og34
Asquith ⬚ CDN 233 Eg19
Asquith Band ⬚ PE 269 Nd50
Asralt Hairhan ⬚ MNG 104 Qb22
Asrama ⬚ TG 187 La42
Assa ⬚ MA 174 Kf31
Assab = Aseb ⬚ ER 193 Nb39
As'sabeewa'arbaien ⬚ SYR 90 Mj28
As'sabkha ⬚ SYR 90 Mk28
As Sadawi ⬚ KSA 93 Nd31
Assadjem ⬚ DZ 182 Ld34
As'safkha ⬚ SYR 90 Mj28
As Safwani ⬚ JOR 92 Mh29
Assahoun ⬚ TG 187 La42
Assai ⬚ BR 274 He57
Assaikio ⬚ WAN 188 Le41
As Sakn ⬚ DARS 174 Ke32
Assaka ⬚ MA 174 Kf31
As Salif ⬚ YE 94 Na36
As Salman ⬚ IRQ 93 Nc30
As Salmy ⬚ KSA 93 Nd31
Assamaka ⬚ RN 182 Lc36
As Samawah ⬚ IRQ 93 Nc30
As Sanam ⬚ KSA 95 Nf34
Assaouas ⬚ RN 182 Ld37
Assaré ⬚ BR 273 Ja49
As Sawadah ⬚ IND 116 Oj38
As Sharma ⬚ SUD 185 Mh38
As Sidr ⬚ LAR 177 Lh30
As Sila ⬚ UAE 95 Nh34
As-Sila ⬚ IRQ 93 Nc30
Assikuri ⬚ CI 187 Kj43
Assiniboia ⬚ CDN 232 Eh21
Assiniboine, Mount ⬚ CDN 232 Ec20
Assin Mansu ⬚ GH 187 Kk43
As Sirar ⬚ KSA 94 Ne33
Assis ⬚ BR 274 He57
Assis Brasil ⬚ BR 270 Gf51
Assis Chateaubriand ⬚ BR 276 Hd58
Aššûr ⬚ IRQ 91 Nb28
Ašlār ⬚ D 58 Lj40
As Sulaimi ⬚ KSA 93 Nb33
As Sulayyil ⬚ KSA 94 Nc35
As Sulaymaniyah ⬚ IRQ 91 Nc28
As Summan ⬚ KSA 93 Nd32
As Summan ⬚ KSA 94 Ne34
As-Suwayq ⬚ OM 95 Nj34
Astacós ⬚ GR 70 Mb52
Astana ⬚ KZ 88 Oc08
Astana-Baba ⬚ TM 96 Nk31
Astaneh ⬚ IR 91 Ne27
Astaneh ⬚ IR 91 Ne28
Astaffort ⬚ F 52 Lb46
Astara ⬚ AZ 91 Ne26
Asten ⬚ NL 51 Lf39
Asti ⬚ I 60 Lj46
Astipálaia ⬚ GR 71 Mg54
Astipálea ⬚ GR 71 Mg54
Astola ⬚ PK 99 Ob33
Astor ⬚ 114 Oh28
Astorga ⬚ BR 274 He57
Astorga ⬚ E 54 Ko48
Astoria ⬚ USA 232 Dj22
Astorga ⬚ USA 239 Dj22
Astove ⬚ SY 206 Nd51
Astra ⬚ RA 282 Gg68
Astravec ⬚ BY 45 Mf36
Astrasevca ⬚ GR 69 Nd51
Astrolabe Bay ⬚ PNG 155 Sc48
Ástros ⬚ GR 70 Mc53
Astryna ⬚ BY 65 Me37
Astudillo ⬚ E 54 Ko47
Asturias ⬚ E 54 Ko47
Astuvansalmi ⬚ FIN 44 Mh29
Asuka ⬚ ANT 286 Ma33
Asuka ⬚ J 113 Rd29
Asunción Nochixtlán ⬚ MEX 246 Ek37
Asūne ⬚ LV 45 Mh34
Asutuare ⬚ GH 187 La42
Asveja ⬚ BY 45 Mj34
Aswad ⬚ OM 95 Nj33
Aswa-Lolim Game Reserve ⬚ EAU 194 Mh44
Aswan ⬚ ET 179 Mg33
Aswan High Dam ⬚ ET 179 Mg34
Aszód ⬚ H 67 Lu43
Aszófö ⬚ H 66 Ls44
Ata ⬚ KS 97 Og25
Ata Bupu D. ⬚ RI 130 Ra50
Atacames ⬚ EC 268 Ga45
Ata'iyeh ⬚ IR 96 Nk28
Atajaña, Cerro ⬚ RCH 278 Ge55
Atakent ⬚ KZ 97 Oe26
Ata Koo Fai-Nuwa Puri D. ⬚ RI 130 Ra50
Atakor ⬚ DZ 182 Lc34
Atalaia ⬚ BR 273 Jb50
Atalaia do Norte ⬚ BR 268 Ge48
Atalaia ⬚ PE 269 Gd51
Atalaya, Cerro ⬚ PE 269 Gc52
Atalén ⬚ BR 275 Hk55
Atamí ⬚ J 113 Rk28
Atanquez ⬚ CO 264 Gd40
Ata Polo D. ⬚ RI 130 Ra50
Atapuerca ⬚ E 56 Kr48
Atapupu ⬚ RI 131 Rc50
Atâr ⬚ RIM 180 Kd35
Atarfe ⬚ E 55 Kr53
Ataturk Baraji ⬚ TR 90 Mk27
Atauro ⬚ RI 131 Rc50
Ataúro ⬚ RI 131 Rc50
Ataya ⬚ ETH 192 Mk39
Atbara ⬚ SUD 185 Mj37
Atbara ⬚ SUD 185 Mj37
At-Baši ⬚ KS 100 Oh25
Atebubu ⬚ GH 187 Kk42
Ateca ⬚ E 57 Kt49
Atebubu ⬚ GH 187 Kk42
Ath ⬚ B 51 Ld40
Athabasca ⬚ CDN 231 Ed18
Athabasca Falls ⬚ CDN 232 Ea19
Athabasca River ⬚ CDN 233 Ee16
Athapapu ⬚ CDN 233 Ek18
Atharan Hazari ⬚ PK 99 Og30
Atherton ⬚ AUS 147 Sd54
Athens ⬚ USA 238 Fc29
Athens ⬚ USA 239 Fe28
Athens ⬚ USA 239 Fg28
Athens ⬚ USA 239 Fg28
Athens ⬚ USA 239 Fj26
Atherstone ⬚ GB 49 Kt38
Atherton ⬚ AUS 147 Sd54
Atherton Tableland ⬚ AUS 147 Sc54
Athiéme ⬚ DY 187 La42
Athi River ⬚ EAK 194 Mj46
Athlone ⬚ IRL 47 Kn37
Athmallik ⬚ IND 117 Pc35
Athni ⬚ IND 118 Oj38
Áthos ⬚ NZ 153 Te68
Áthos ⬚ GR 69 Me50
Athy ⬚ IRL 47 Ko38
'Ati ⬚ SUD 185 Mf38
Ati ⬚ TCH 183 Lk39
Atiak ⬚ EAU 194 Mg44
Ati-Atihau-Festival (Kalibo) ⬚ RP 124 Rb40
Ático ⬚ PE 269 Gd54
Atiedo ⬚ SUD 191 Md42
Atienza ⬚ E 57 Ks49
Atigaru Point ⬚ USA 229 Ce10
Atijere ⬚ WAN 188 Lc42
Atikaki Prov. Park ⬚ CDN 236 Fb20
Atikameg Lake ⬚ CDN 233 Ek18
Atikokan ⬚ CDN 236 Fd21
Atim ⬚ TCH 184 Ma39
Atimonan ⬚ RP 124 Ra39
Atitlan, Volcán ⬚ GCA 248 Fe38
Atizapán de Zaragoza ⬚ MEX 246 Fa36
Atjaševo ⬚ RUS 72 Nd18
Atkamba Mission ⬚ PNG 155 Sa48
Atkinson ⬚ USA 236 Fa24
Atkot ⬚ IND 116 Of35
Atlacomulco ⬚ MEX 246 Fa36
Atlanta ⬚ USA 239 Fd29
Atlanta ⬚ USA 239 Fh29
Atlanta ⬚ USA 242 Gb28
Atlantic ⬚ USA 239 Fb25
Atlantic Beach ⬚ USA 242 Ga26
Atlantic City ⬚ USA 241 Gc24
Atlantic Forest Southeast Reserves ⬚ BR 277 Hg58
Atlántida ⬚ ROU 281 Hc63
Atla pexco ⬚ MEX 246 Fa35
Atlas Gompa ⬚ CHN 103 Pg30
Atlas Mountains ⬚ MA 162 Kb06
Atlasovo ⬚ RUS 111 Sh20
Atlaxco ⬚ MEX 246 Fb36
Atlin ⬚ CDN 230 Dd16
Atlin Prov. Park ⬚ CDN 230 Dd16
Atlixco ⬚ MEX 246 Fb36
Atmakur ⬚ IND 116 Oj37
Atmakur ⬚ IND 118 Ok38
Atmore ⬚ USA 239 Fg30
Atna Peak ⬚ CDN 230 Df19
Atnetye A.L. ⬚ AUS 146 Rg57
Atocha ⬚ BOL 278 Gg56
Atoka ⬚ USA 238 Fb28
Atoll de Bora-Bora ⬚ ⬚ Nd50
Atoll de Cosmoledo ⬚ SY 206 Nd50
Atoll de Providence ⬚ SY 206 Nf50
Atolo ⬚ MOC 197 Na52

Atome ⬚ ANG 200 Lh51
Atongo-Bakari ⬚ RCA 190 Ma43
Atonyia ⬚ DARS 174 Ke32
Atotonilco ⬚ MEX 245 Ej33
Atotonilco El Alto ⬚ MEX 246 Ej35
Atouat, Mount ⬚ VN 123 Qd38
Atoyac de Alvarez ⬚ MEX 246 Ek37
Atpadi ⬚ IND 118 Oj38
Atqan ⬚ CHN 98 Qb10
Atqasuk ⬚ USA 229 Cb10
Atrai ⬚ IND 117 Pe33
Atrauli ⬚ IND 115 Pa32
Atri ⬚ I 61 Lp48
Atsabe ⬚ RI 131 Rc50
Atsapangthong ⬚ LAO 123 Qc37
Atsumi-hanto ⬚ J 113 Rj28
Atsy ⬚ RI 154 Rk48
Atta ⬚ CAM 189 Lg42
At Taban ⬚ LAR 177 Ma29
At-Taff ⬚ UAE 95 Nh34
At Taif ⬚ KSA 94 Na35
At Taji ⬚ IRQ 91 Nc29
Attakoro ⬚ CI 187 Kj42
Attalea ⬚ TR 90 Mf27
Attapeu ⬚ LAO 123 Qd38
At Tamimi ⬚ LAR 178 Mb29
At Tanf ⬚ SYR 90 Mk29
Attawapiskat ⬚ CDN 227 Fd08
At Tawilah ⬚ YE 94 Na36
Attayas ⬚ SYR 90 Mj28
At Taysiyah ⬚ KSA 93 Nc32
At-Tayyara ⬚ SUD 185 Mf39
Atteridgeville ⬚ ZA 205 Me58
Attersee ⬚ A 61 Lo43
At Thumamah ⬚ KSA 93 Nd33
Attingal ⬚ IND 118 Oj41
Attleborough ⬚ GB 49 La38
Attock ⬚ PK 99 Og29
Attock City ⬚ PK 99 Og29
Attoko ⬚ J 111 Sc24
Attu ⬚ IND 119 Ok40
Attungga ⬚ AUS 149 Sf61
At Turabah ⬚ KSA 94 Na35
At Turbah ⬚ YE 94 Nc39
At Tuwal ⬚ KSA 94 Na35
At Tuwayfih ⬚ KSA 94 Ne35
At Tuwaysha ⬚ SUD 184 Md39
Atud ⬚ YE 94 Ne38
Atuka ⬚ RI 154 Rj48
Atuk Mountain ⬚ USA 228 Be14
Atuntaqui ⬚ EC 268 Ga45
Atura ⬚ BD 120 Pe33
Atures ⬚ YV 265 Gg43
Åtvidaberg ⬚ S 43 Lq32
Atwater ⬚ USA 234 Dz27
Atwood ⬚ USA 238 Ek26
Au ⬚ D 59 Lm42
Au ⬚ AUS 229 Cb10
Aua Island ⬚ PNG 155 Sb46
Auasberge ⬚ NAM 200 Lj57
Aubagne ⬚ F 53 Lf47
Aube ⬚ B 51 Li41
Aubenas ⬚ F 53 Le46
Aubergenville ⬚ F 51 Lb42
Auberive ⬚ F 53 Lf43
Aubiet ⬚ F 52 Lb47
Aubigny-sur-Nère ⬚ F 53 Lc43
Aubin ⬚ F 52 Lc46
Aubrey Cliffs ⬚ USA 235 Ed28
Auburn ⬚ AUS 150 Rk63
Auburn ⬚ USA 232 Dz26
Auburn ⬚ USA 234 Dz26
Auburn ⬚ USA 237 Fh29
Auburn ⬚ USA 239 Fg29
Auburn ⬚ USA 241 Gd24
Auburn Range ⬚ AUS 149 Sf58
Auca Mahuida ⬚ RA 280 Gf64
Aucanquilcha, Cerro ⬚ RCH 278 Gf56
Aucayacu ⬚ PE 269 Gb50
Auch ⬚ F 52 Lb47
Auche ⬚ MYA 120 Pj33
Auchinleck ⬚ GB 48 Kr34
Auchterarder ⬚ GB 48 Kr33
Auckland ⬚ NZ 152 Th64
Auckland Islands ⬚ NZ 134 Ta15
Auden ⬚ CDN 237 Fg20
Audierne ⬚ F 50 Kq42
Audincourt ⬚ F 53 Lg43
Audru ⬚ EST 45 Me31
Audubon ⬚ USA 236 Fc25
Aue ⬚ D 59 Ln40
Auerbach ⬚ D 59 Lm41
Auerbach ⬚ D 59 Lm41
Auezov ⬚ KZ 100 Pa21
Augathella ⬚ AUS 149 Sd58
Aughnacloy ⬚ GB 47 Ko36
Augrabies ⬚ ZA 204 Ma60
Augrabies Falls ⬚ ZA 204 Ma60
Augrabies Falls N.P. ⬚ ZA 204 Ma60
Augrabiesvalle ⬚ ZA 204 Ma60
Augsburg ⬚ D 59 Ll42
Augusta ⬚ AUS 144 Qh63
Augusta ⬚ I 63 Lq53
Augusta ⬚ USA 238 Fb27
Augusta ⬚ USA 239 Fe28
Augusta ⬚ USA 241 Ge24
Augustin Codazzi ⬚ CO 264 Gd40
Augustine Island ⬚ USA 228 Cd16
Augusto Correa ⬚ BR 267 Hh47
Augusto Montenegro ⬚ BR 271 Hb47
Augusto, Island ⬚ AUS 143 Rc53
Augustów ⬚ PL 65 Mc37
Augustus, Mount ⬚ AUS 142 Qj58
Aukan ⬚ ER 192 Na38
Auke Bay ⬚ USA 230 Dc16
Aukrug ⬚ SOL 157 Ta50
Auki ⬚ SOL 157 Ta50
Aukstaitijos n.p. ⬚ LT 45 Mg35
Auld Ski area ⬚ IND 116 Oh30
Aulla ⬚ I 60 Lk46
Aulnay ⬚ F 52 Ka44
Aulneau Pen. ⬚ CDN 236 Fc21
Ault ⬚ F 51 Lb41
Aulum ⬚ DK 42 Ll34
Aumale ⬚ F 51 Lb41
Aumont-Aubrac ⬚ F 53 Ld46
Auna Dheegle ⬚ SP 195 Nc45
Aunay-sur-Odon ⬚ F 50 Ku42
Aundah ⬚ IND 116 Oj36
Auneau ⬚ F 51 Lb42
Auning ⬚ DK 42 Lm34
Auno ⬚ WAN 189 Lg40
Aup ⬚ RI 131 Rd47
Aur ⬚ MAL 126 Qc44
Aura ⬚ FIN 44 Md30
Auraiya ⬚ IND 117 Pa33
Auki ⬚ SOL 157 Ta50
Aurangabad ⬚ IND 117 Pc33
Aurangabad ⬚ IND 116 Oj36
Aurangabad Caves ⬚ IND 116 Oh36
Aur ⬚ J 50 Ks43
Aurdal ⬚ N 40 Ll30
Aure ⬚ N 40 Lk28
Aurich ⬚ D 58 Lh37
Auriflama ⬚ BR 274 He56
Aurillac ⬚ F 53 Ld46
Aurland ⬚ N 40 Lj30
Aurlandsvangen ⬚ N 40 Lj30
Aurora ⬚ GUY 266 Ha42
Aurora ⬚ RO 69 Mh47
Aurora ⬚ RP 125 Rb42
Aurora ⬚ USA 229 Bh13
Aurora ⬚ USA 235 Eg27
Aurora ⬚ USA 237 Fz25
Aurora ⬚ USA 238 Fd27
Aurora ⬚ USA 239 Fh26
Aurora ⬚ ZA 204 Lk60
Aurora de Tocantins ⬚ BR 272 Hg52
Aurukun ⬚ AUS 147 Sa53
Aurukun A.L. ⬚ AUS 147 Sa53
Ausa ⬚ IND 116 Oj36
Ausai Roadhouse ⬚ AUS 142 Qk57
Auski Madulì ⬚ EAK 195 Na44
Austad ⬚ N 42 La32
Austevoll ⬚ N 42 Lf30
Austin ⬚ CDN 236 Ek20
Austin ⬚ USA 234 Eb26
Austin ⬚ USA 235 Eb26
Austin ⬚ USA 238 Fb30
Austmarka ⬚ N 42 Ln30
Austral Downs ⬚ AUS 146 Rj56
Australia ⬚ AUS 135 Ra12
Australian-Antarctic Basin ⬚ 287 Ra30
Australian Capital Territory ⬚ AUS 151 Se63
Austria ⬚ A 61 Lo43
Austvågøya ⬚ N 38 Lp22
Autan ⬚ IND 115 Oj30
Autazes ⬚ BR 271 Ha47
Auterive ⬚ F 52 Lb47
Authon-du-Perche ⬚ F 50 La42
Autlán de Navarro ⬚ MEX 246 Eh36
Autodromo Interlagos ⬚ BR 277 Hg57
Autostadt Wolfsburg ⬚ D 58 Ll38
Auttoinen ⬚ FIN 44 Mf29
Autun ⬚ F 53 Le44
Auvergne ⬚ F 53 Lc45
Auvergne ⬚ F 53 Lc45
Auvillar ⬚ F 52 Lb46
Auxerre ⬚ F 53 Ld43
Auxi-le-Château ⬚ F 51 Lc40
Auxonne ⬚ F 53 Lf43
Auyan-tepui ⬚ YV 265 Gj43
Auzances ⬚ F 53 Lc44
Auziladila ⬚ BR 267 Hh47
Ava ⬚ USA 238 Fd27
Avadi ⬚ IND 119 Pa40
Avadkhara ⬚ GE 91 Na24
Availles-Limousine ⬚ F 52 La44
Avaj ⬚ IR 91 Nd28
Avaldsnes ⬚ N 42 Lf31
Avallon ⬚ F 53 Ld43
Avanahti ⬚ IND 118 Oj39
Avanavero ⬚ SME 266 Hb43
Avangapda ⬚ IND 117 Pa38
Avaré ⬚ BR 274 Hf57
Avdira ⬚ GR 69 Me50
Avdira ⬚ TM 92 Mg20
Avdijivka ⬚ UA 72 Mg20
Avdan Dagı ⬚ TR 69 Mk50
Avdira ⬚ GR 69 Me50
Aveiro ⬚ BR 271 Hc47
Aveiro ⬚ P 54 Km50
Avelimona ⬚ BR 272 Hj51
Avelino Chaves ⬚ BR 270 Gf51
Avelino Lopes ⬚ BR 272 Hj51
Avellaneda ⬚ RA 281 Ha63
Avellino ⬚ I 63 Lp50
Avén d'Orgnac ⬚ F 53 Le46
Avenue of the Giants ⬚ USA 234 Dj25
Aversa ⬚ I 63 Lp50
Avesta ⬚ S 43 Lq30
Avezzano ⬚ I 61 Lo48
Aviemore ⬚ GB 48 Kr33
Avigliana ⬚ I 60 Lh46
Avigliano ⬚ I 63 Lq50
Avignon ⬚ F 53 Le47
Ávila ⬚ E 54 Kp50
Avila y Urbina ⬚ MEX 246 Fa34
Avilés ⬚ E 54 Ko47
Avinurme ⬚ EST 44 Mg32
Avize ⬚ F 51 Le42
Avispa, Cerro ⬚ BR/YV 265 Gh45
Avize ⬚ F 51 Le42
Avlémonas ⬚ GR 69 Md54
Avliotes ⬚ GR 70 Lu51
Avliona ⬚ GR 69 Md52
Avlona ⬚ USA 151 Sb64
Avoca ⬚ AUS 151 Sd66
Avola ⬚ I 63 Lq53
Avola ⬚ CDN 232 Ec20
Avon ⬚ USA 242 Gc28
Avon Downs ⬚ AUS 146 Rj56
Avon Park ⬚ USA 243 Fk32
Avontuur ⬚ ZA 204 Mb62
Avon Valley National Park ⬚ AUS 144 Qj62
Avram Iancu ⬚ RO 67 Md44
Avram Iancu ⬚ RO 67 Md44
Avranches ⬚ F 50 Kt42
Avrankou ⬚ DY 188 Lb42
Avrig ⬚ RO 67 Me45
Avrille ⬚ F 52 Ku43
Awasaga ⬚ MNG 104 Qb22
Avu Avu ⬚ SOL 157 Ta50
Awaê ⬚ CAM 189 Lf44
Awa-jima ⬚ J 111 Rk26
Awakino ⬚ NZ 153 Th65
Awan ⬚ IND 116 Oj33
Awang ⬚ BRN 130 Qj44
Awanui ⬚ NZ 152 Tg63
Awara ⬚ PNG 156 Sf48
Awara Plain ⬚ EAK 195 Na44
Awarua Point ⬚ NZ 153 Te68
Awaruawanwa ⬚ GUY 266 Ha44
Awasa ⬚ ETH 192 Mj41
Awash ⬚ ETH 192 Na40
Awash Falls eth ⬚ ETH 192 Na41
Awash Reserve ⬚ ETH 192 Na41
Awat ⬚ CHN 100 Pa25
Awbari ⬚ LAR 177 Lg32
Awdal ⬚ SP 195 Nb44
Awe ⬚ WAN 188 Le41
Aweil ⬚ SUD 191 Md41
Aweina ⬚ ET 179 Mg32
Awgu ⬚ WAN 188 Ld43
Awio ⬚ PNG 156 Sf49
Awisam ⬚ GH 187 Kk43
Awjilah ⬚ LAR 178 Mb31
Awka ⬚ WAN 188 Ld43
Awo ⬚ RI 154 Rj48
Awu ⬚ RI 131 Rc46
Ax-les-Thermes ⬚ F 52 Lb48
Axamarby ⬚ S 43 Lq30
Axchiapan ⬚ MEX 246 Fa36
Axvall ⬚ S 43 Lp32
Ayabaca ⬚ PE 268 Ga49
Ayacara ⬚ RCH 279 Gd68
Ayacucho ⬚ PE 269 Gc52
Ayacucho ⬚ RA 281 Ha64
Ayakoz ⬚ KZ 100 Pa22
Ayamé ⬚ CI 187 Kj43

Ayamiken ⬚ GQ 188 Lf44
Ayamonte ⬚ E 54 Kn53
Ayancik ⬚ TR 90 Mk25
Ayangba ⬚ WAN 188 Ld43
Ayanur ⬚ IND 118 Oh39
Ayapata ⬚ PE 269 Ge52
Ayapel ⬚ CO 264 Gc41
Ayaviri ⬚ PE 269 Ge53
Aybak ⬚ AFG 97 Oe27
Aydar ⬚ ETH 192 Mj39
Aydat ⬚ MAL 126 Qd45
Aydin ⬚ E 56 Ku48
Ayer Hitam ⬚ MAL 126 Qc44
Ayer Tawar ⬚ MAL 126 Qb43
Ayer Terjun ⬚ MAL 125 Rd58
Ayinwafi ⬚ GH 187 Kk42
Aykel ⬚ ETH 192 Mj39
Ay Khanom ⬚ AFG 97 Oe27
Aylesbury ⬚ GB 49 Ku39
Ayllón ⬚ E 56 Kr49
Aylsham ⬚ GB 49 La38
Ayn al Uwayja ⬚ KSA 94 Nc34
'Ayn Ba Ma'bad ⬚ YE 94 Nc38
Ayn Dar ⬚ KSA 93 Ne32
Ayod ⬚ SUD 191 Mf41
Ayodhya ⬚ IND 117 Pb32
Ayo El Grande ⬚ MEX 246 Ek35
Ayora ⬚ E 57 Kt51
Ayoûn el Atroûs ⬚ RIM 180 Kf37
Ayr ⬚ AUS 147 Sd55
Ayr ⬚ GB 48 Kq35
Ayranci ⬚ TR 90 Mg27
Ayritepe ⬚ TR 90 Mf26
Aysha ⬚ ETH 193 Nb40
Ayton ⬚ GB 48 Ks35
Aytre ⬚ F 52 Ka44
Ayu ⬚ RI 131 Rf47
Ayun ⬚ OM 95 Ng37
Ayutla de los Libres ⬚ MEX 246 Fa37
Ayutthaya ⬚ THA 122 Qa38
Ayutthaya Historical Park ⬚ THA 122 Qa38
Ayvacik ⬚ TR 71 Mg51
Ayvacik ⬚ TR 91 Ma25
Ayvalik ⬚ TR 71 Mg51
Azad Shar ⬚ IR 96 Ng27
Azagny ⬚ CI 187 Kj43
Azaguié ⬚ CI 187 Kj43
Azaila ⬚ E 57 Ku49
Azamgarh ⬚ IND 117 Pb32
Azamagues, Cerro ⬚ BOL 278 Gg55
Azaouagh ⬚ RMM 182 Lb38
Azare ⬚ WAN 188 Lf40
Azar Shahr ⬚ IR 91 Nc27
Azarichy ⬚ BY 72 Me19
Azay-le-Rideau ⬚ F 52 La43
Azaz ⬚ SYR 90 Mj27
Azazga ⬚ DZ 176 Lc27
Azemmour ⬚ MA 174 Kf29
Azerbaijan ⬚ AZ 91 Nd25
Azezo ⬚ ETH 192 Mj39
Azilal ⬚ MA 175 Kg29
Azimganj ⬚ IND 117 Pd34
Azinga ⬚ G 198 Lh46
Aziory ⬚ BY 65 Me37
Aziz ⬚ TCH 183 Lj37
Aziz-abad ⬚ IR 98 Nj30
Azizabad ⬚ AFG 98 Ok29
Azizie ⬚ USA 147 Rk55
Azmer ⬚ IR 91 Nd28
Azogues ⬚ EC 268 Ga47
Azopardo ⬚ RA 282 Jb06
Azores ⬚ P 163 Jk06
Azougui ⬚ RIM 180 Kd35
Azov ⬚ RUS 73 Mk22
Azovo-Syvas'kyj N.P. ⬚ UA 73 Mj22
Azrou ⬚ MA 175 Kg29
Aztec ⬚ USA 235 Eg27
Aztec ⬚ USA 234 Ed29
Aztec Ruins Nat. Mon. ⬚ USA 235 Eg27
Azua ⬚ DOM 250 Ge36
Azuaga ⬚ E 55 Kp52
Azúcar ⬚ EC 268 Fk47
Azufrera ⬚ PE 279 Gf58
Azul ⬚ RA 281 Ha64
Azuman-san ⬚ J 111 Sa27
Azumbilla ⬚ MEX 246 Fb36
Azurduy ⬚ BOL 278 Gh55
Az Zabadani ⬚ SYR 90 Mj29
Az Zabbaq ⬚ IRQ 93 Nd32
Az Zallaq ⬚ BRN 93 Nf32
Az Zawiyah ⬚ LAR 177 Lg29
Az Zaydiyah ⬚ YE 94 Na36
Az Zilfi ⬚ KSA 93 Nc32
Az Zintan ⬚ LAR 177 Lg30
Az Zubayr ⬚ IRQ 93 Nd30
Az Zubaydiyah ⬚ IRQ 93 Nc29
Az Zubayr ⬚ IRQ 93 Nd30
Az Zuhrah ⬚ YE 94 Nb38
az-Zuma ⬚ SUD 185 Mf36

B

Ba ⬚ FJI 159 Tj54
Ba ⬚ RI 131 Rb51
Baa Atoll ⬚ MV 118 Og43
Baadheere ⬚ SP 195 Nb44
Baal ⬚ SP 195 Nb45
Baamang ⬚ RI 129 Qg47
Baan Baa ⬚ AUS 149 Se61
Baan Chuem Beach ⬚ THA 123 Qb40
Baanta ⬚ SP 195 Nb45
Baantama ⬚ GH 187 Kk42
Baar ⬚ IND 117 Pb32
Baba ⬚ BG 69 Md48
Baba ⬚ RIM 180 Kd37
Babadag ⬚ RO 69 Mh46
Babacuiándia ⬚ BR 272 Hg49
Babadaykhan ⬚ TM 96 Ng27
Babaera ⬚ ANG 200 Lh52
Babaeski ⬚ TR 69 Mh49
Babahoyo ⬚ EC 268 Ga46
Babahoyo ⬚ EC 268 Ga46
Bab al Maknusah ⬚ LAR 177 Lg32
Bab Anar ⬚ IR 98 Ng31
Baban Rafi ⬚ WAN 188 Ld41
Babanusa ⬚ SUD 184 Md40
Babar ⬚ RI 131 Re49
Babase Island ⬚ PNG 156 Sg48
Babati ⬚ EAT 194 Mj47
Babatngon ⬚ RP 125 Rc40
Babbage ⬚ CDN 229 Ck12
Babbitt ⬚ USA 236 Fc22
Babelsberg ⬚ D 59 Ln38
Babelthuap ⬚ PAL 124 Rh42
Babel, Mount de ⬚ CDN 240 Gf22
Babek ⬚ BY 91 Ma26
Babengo ⬚ RCA 190 Ma43
Baberu ⬚ IND 117 Pb33
Babetville ⬚ CDN 240 Ge22
Babi ⬚ RI 127 Pj44
Babi-Babi ⬚ NAM 200 Lk57
Babica ⬚ PL 65 Mb41
Babile ⬚ ETH 193 Na41
Babine ⬚ CDN 230 Df18
Babo ⬚ RI 154 Rf48
Babo-Rani ⬚ ETH 192 Mj39
Baboua ⬚ RCA 189 Lh43
Babra ⬚ IND 116 Of35
Babusar Pass ⬚ 114 Og28
Babushkin ⬚ RUS 108 Qc20
Babuyan ⬚ RP 124 Ra36
Babuyan Channel ⬚ RP 124 Ra36
Babuyan Islands ⬚ RP 124 Ra36
Babylon ⬚ IRQ 93 Nc29
Babina ⬚ IND 117 Ok33

Babinda AUS 147 Sc54
Babine Range CDN 230 Dg18
Babiogórski P.N. PL 65 Lu41
Babo RI 154 Rg47
Babol IR 96 Ng27
Babol Sar IR 96 Ng27
Babonde RDC 191 Md44
Babonde RDC 191 Me44
Babonga CAM 189 Lh42
Babongo MEX 244 Eg32
Baboua RCA 190 Lh43
Babra IND 116 Oj35
Babriškés LT 45 Mo36
Babrongan Tower AUS 142 Rb55
Babrujsk BY 72 Me19
Babtai LT 45 Md35
Bab-Taza MA 175 Kh28
Babura WAN 188 Le39
Babusar Pass 114 Oh28
Babuškin RUS 104 Qd20
Babuyan RP 124 Qk41
Babuyan Channel RP 109 Ra36
Babuyan Island RP 109 Ra36
Babuyan Islands RP 124 Ra36
Babylon IRQ 93 Nc29
Bacabal BR 266 Gk45
Bacabal BR 270 Gj46
Bacabal BR 272 Hh48
Bacabalzinho BR 278 Gj52
Bacada BR 270 Gh49
Bacadweeyn SP 193 Nd42
Bacalar MEX 247 Ff36
Bacan RI 151 Rf44
Bacang CHN 103 Pk28
Bacanora CAM 244 Ef31
Bacao RP 124 Qk40
Bacarra RP 124 Ra36
Bacaruca BR 270 Gh46
Bacău RO 73 Md22
Bacău RI 131 Qe40
Baccarat F 51 Lg42
Baceracac MEX 244 Ef30
Bac Giang VN 121 Qc34
Bac Giang VN 121 Qd35
Bachalo WAL 186 Ka42
Bachaquero YV 264 Ge41
Bacharach D 59 Lh40
Bachčysaraj UA 73 Mg23
Bächhrawan IND 117 Pa32
Bachiniva RI 101 Qh36
Bachmač UA 72 Mg20
Bacho THA 123 Qa42
Bachórz PL 65 Mc41
Bac Thong VN 121 Qc34
Bachu CHN 100 Og26
Bachuo CAM 188 Le43
Baciu SRB 68 Mj47
Baciu RO 67 Md44
Bacicuity PL 65 Mc37
Bačka Palanka SRB 68 Lu45
Bačka Topola SRB 68 Lu45
Bačkebo S 43 Lr34
Bäckefors S 42 Lo32
Bäckhammar S 43 Lq31
Backnang D 59 Lk42
Bačko Novo Selo SRB 68 Lu45
Bäckovski manastir BG 69 Mf47
Backstairs Passage AUS 150 Rk63
Backwaters IND 118 Oj41
Bac Lieu VN 123 Qd41
Bac Ninh VN 121 Qd35
Bacnotan RP 124 Ra37
Baco RP 124 Ra39
Bacoachi MEX 244 Ef30
Bacobampo MEX 244 Ef32
Bacolod RP 124 Rb40
Baco, Mount RP 124 Ra39
Bacon RP 124 Rc39
Baconao, P.N. C 250 Gc36
Bacopari BR 277 He61
Bacot RP 277 Hh48
Bacouri RP 124 Qk40
Bacungan RP 124 Qk41
Bacuri BR 267 Hh46
Bacurituba BR 267 Hh47
Bacurizinho, T.I. BR 272 Hh48
Bad D 93 Nf29
Bada RUS 104 Qe20
Bada Barabil IND 117 Pc34
Badaganshan Z.B. CHN 108 Qe31
Badagara WAN 189 Lg39
Bad Aibling D 59 Ln43
Badai-Tugai Nature Reserve UZ 96 Oa25
Badajós BR 270 Gj47
Badajoz E 56 Ko52
Badaling CHN 109 Qj38
Badalona E 57 Lc49
Badami IND 116 Oh38
Badanga TCH 190 Lj40
Bad Arolsen D 58 Lk39
Badarpur IND 120 Pg33
Badau RI 129 Qd47
Bad Aussee A 61 Lo43
Bad Axe USA 237 Fj24
Bad Bederkesa D 58 Lj37
Bad Bentheim D 58 Lh38
Bad Bergzabern D 59 Lh41
Bad Berka D 58 Lm40
Bad Berleburg D 58 Lj39
Bad Bevensen D 58 Ll37
Bad Bibra D 58 Lm39
Bad Bramstedt D 58 Lk37
Bad Brückenau D 59 Lk40
Bad Camberg D 59 Lj40
Baddeck CDN 240 Gk22
Bad Doberan D 58 Lm36
Bad Driburg D 58 Lk39
Bad Düben D 58 Ln39
Bad Dürkheim D 59 Lj41
Bad Dürrenberg D 58 Ln39
Bade RI 154 Rk49
Badeggi WAN 188 Ld41
Badéguichéri RN 182 Lc38
Bademli TR 71 Mj51
Baden D 58 Lk39
Baden CH 60 Lj43
Baden ER 185 Mk37
Baden-Baden D 59 Lj42
Bad Endorf D 59 Ln43
Baden Park AUS 151 Sc62
Baden-Württemberg D 59 Lk41
Baden IND 116 Ok37
Bader RN 182 Ld38
Bad Freienwalde D 58 Lp38
Bad Friedrichshall D 59 Lk41
Badgah AFG 99 Od28
Bad Gandersheim D 58 Lk39
Badgaon BD 120 Pg33
Bad Gastein A 61 Lo43
Badger CDN 241 Hd21
Badgingarra AUS 144 Qh61
Badgingarra N.P. AUS 144 Qh61
Bad Gleichenberg A 61 Lq44
Bad Griesbach D 59 Ln42
Bad Hall A 66 Lp42
Bad Harzburg D 58 Ll39
Bad Herrsfeld D 58 Lk40
Bad Hofgastein A 61 Lo43
Bad Homburg D 59 Lj40
Bad Honnef D 58 Lh40
Badia Gran E 57 Lc51
Badiakurom GH 187 Kj42
Badine ETH 192 Md39
Badin PK 99 Oe33
Bad Iburg D 58 Lj38
Bad Ischl A 61 Lo43
Badiraguato MEX 244 Ef33
Badjer CAM 189 Lg42
Bad Karlshafen D 58 Lk39
Bad Kissingen D 59 Ll40
Bad Kleinen D 58 Lm37
Bad Königshofen D 59 Ll40
Bad Kreuznach D 59 Lh41
Bad Krozingen D 59 Lh43
Bad Laasphe D 58 Lj40
Badlands USA 233 Ej24
Badlands N.P. USA 233 Ej24
Bad Langensalza D 58 Ll40
Bad Lauchstädt D 58 Ln39
Bad Lausick D 58 Ln39

Bad Lauterberg D 58 Ll39
Bad Leonfelden A 66 Lp42
Bad Liebenwerda D 58 Lo39
Bad Mergentheim D 59 Lk41
Bad Münstereifel D 58 Lg40
Bad Muskau D 58 Lp39
Bad Nauheim D 59 Lj40
Badnawar IND 116 Oh34
Bad Neuenahr-Ahrweiler D 58 Lh40
Bad Neustadt D 59 Ll40
Badoc RP 124 Ra37
Bad Oeynhausen D 58 Lj38
Badogo RMM 186 Kh40
Bad Oldesloe D 58 Ll37
Badong CHN 108 Qf30
Ba Dong VN 123 Qd41
Badonviller F 51 Lg42
Badou TG 187 La42
Badoumbe RMM 186 Ke39
Badou MEX 244 Ec31
Bad Pyrmont D 58 Lk39
Bad Radkersburg A 61 Lq44
Badrah IRQ 93 Nc29
Badrah PK 99 Oj32
Badranlu IR 96 Nj27
Bad Reichenhall D 59 Ln43
Badr Hunayn KSA 92 Mk34
Badrinath IND 115 Ok30
Badrinath IND 116 Oj36
Badu AUS 143 Sd51
Badu CHN 109 Qh32
Badulla CL 119 Pa42
Badvel IND 119 Ok38
Bad Vöslau A 61 Lr43
Bad Waldsee D 59 Lk43
Bad Wildungen D 58 Lk39
Bad Windsheim D 59 Ll41
Bad Wörishofen D 59 Ll43
Bad Wurzach D 59 Lk43
Baedaem RIM 180 Ke38
Baena E 55 Kq53
Baeza E 55 Kr53
Bafang CAM 189 Lf43
Bafatá GNB 186 Kd39
Baffin Basin 227 Gc04
Baffin Island CDN 227 Ga04
Bafia CAM 189 Lf43
Bafilo TG 187 La41
Bafing RMM 186 Ke40
Bafing-Makana RMM 186 Ke39
Bafodia WAL 186 Ke41
Bafoulabé RMM 186 Ke39
Bafoussam CAM 188 Lf43
Bafq IR 98 Nh30
Bafra TR 90 Mh25
Bafra Burnu TR 90 Mh25
Baft IR 98 Nh31
Bafwaboli RDC 191 Md45
Bafwabalinga RDC 191 Md45
Bafwabogbo RDC 191 Md45
Bafwaboli RDC 191 Md45
Bafwasende RDC 191 Md45
Baga TCH 189 Lh40
Baga IND 122 Pj33
Baga WAN 189 Lg39
Bagabag RP 124 Ra37
Bagabag Island PNG 155 Sd48
Bagaces CR 249 Fh40
Bagala SUD 185 Mf40
Bagalkot IND 116 Oh37
Bagamanoc RP 124 Rc39
Bagamoyo EAT 197 Mk49
Bagan MYA 120 Ph35
Bagandou RCA 190 Lk44
Baganga RP 125 Rd42
Bagani NAM 201 Ma55
Bagansiapiapi RI 127 Qa44
Bagansinembah RI 127 Qa45
Baganuur MNG 104 Qe22
Bagaraas TM 71 Mh53
Bagaré RP 187 Kj39
Bagaroua RN 182 Lc38
Baga Sola TCH 183 Lh39
Bagassi BF 187 Kj40
Bagata RDC 190 Lj46
Bagazan PE 268 Gd48
Bagdogra IND 120 Pe32
Bage BR 276 Hc61
Bag-e-Eram IR 98 Ng31
Bagega WAN 188 Lc40
Bage-Malek IR 98 Nf30
Bagenalstown IRL 47 Ko38
Bageo DK 42 Ll36
Bagepalli IND 118 Oj39
Bageriel BD 120 Pe34
Bageya WAN 182 Lc39
Baggao RP 124 Ra37
Baggs USA 235 Eg25
Baghadan TM 96 Nj26
Baghag IR 98 Ng31
Bagh-e Chenar IR 98 Nj31
Baghel Boland IR 93 Ne30
Bagheikhand Plateau IND 117 Pb34
Bagheria I 62 Lo52
Bagherta GB 98 Nj30
Baghlan AFG 99 Od27
Bagienice PL 65 Mc37
Bagjan GH 102 Pg32
Bagley USA 236 Fc22
Bago RP 40 Lk30
Bagnacavallo I 60 Lm46
Bagnara Cálabra I 63 Lq52
Bagnères-de-Bigorre F 52 La47
Bagnères-de-Luchon F 52 La48
Bagni Contursi I 63 Lq50
Bagno di Romagna I 60 Lm47
Bagnoles-de-l'Orne F 50 Ku42
Bagnoli del Trigno I 63 Lp49
Bagnols-sur-Cèze F 53 Le46
Bago RP 127 Pj44
Bagodara IND 116 Og34
Bagoé RMM 187 Kg40
Bagoline I 60 Ll45
Bagou DY 188 La40
Bago Yoma MYA 120 Ph36
Bagpat IND 115 Oj31
Bagratlonovsk = Eylau RUS 45 Ma36
Bagua PE 268 Gb48
Bagua Grande PE 268 Gb48
Bagudo RP 124 Ra37
Baguinéda RMM 186 Kh40
Bagurato BR 267 Hj47
Bagyurdu TR 71 Mh52
Bah IND 115 Ok32
Bahadur Abad IND 117 Pd33
Bahadurganj IND 117 Pd32
Bahalda IND 117 Pd34

Bahama Islands 243 Gb32
Baia do Bengo ANG 198 Lg50
Baia do Caeté BR 267 Hg46
Baia do Chun BR 267 Hh47
Baia do Cumã BR 267 Hh47
Baharampur IND 120 Pe33
Baharîya Oasis ET 179 Me31
Baharu RI 127 Pk45
Bahau MAL 126 Qb44
Baher IR 91 Ne28
Baheri IND 115 Ok31
Bahi EAT 196 Mh48
Bahia RA 255 Hb11
Bahía Adventure RCH 282 Gc68
Bahia Aguirre RA/RCH 282 Gd71
Bahía Algodones MEX 245 Fb33
Bahía Blanca MEX 244 Ec31
Bahía Blanca RA 281 Gj65
Bahía Bufadero MEX 246 Ej36
Bahía Bustamante RA 282 Gg68
Bahía Chanco RCH 280 Gd63
Bahía Chiquinata RCH 278 Ge56
Bahía Colonet MEX 244 Ec30
Bahía Conchalí RCH 280 Ge61
Bahía Cook RCH 282 Ge73
Bahía Creek RA 281 Gj66
Bahía Culebra CR 248 Fh40
Bahía Ilha Grande BR 277 Hh57
Bahía Darwin RCH 282 Gc68
Bahía de Adair MEX 244 Ed30
Bahía de Amatique CA 248 Ff38
Bahía de Banderas MEX 246 Eh35
Bahía de Bluefields NIC 249 Fj40
Bahía de Buenaventura CO 264 Gb44
Bahía de Caballos PE 269 Gc53
Bahía de Caráquez EC 268 Fk46
Bahía de Chetumal MEX 247 Fg36
Bahía de Coronado CR 249 Fj41
Bahía de Corrientes C 243 Fh35
Bahía de Guadiana C 243 Fh34
Bahia de Independencia PE 269 Gb53
Bahía de la Ascensión MEX 247 Fg36
Bahía del Espíritu Santo MEX 247 Fg36
Bahia de Lobos MEX 244 Ee32
Bahía de Loreto, P.N. MEX 244 Eb29
Bahía de los Ángeles MEX 244 Ed31
Bahía de Manta EC 268 Fk46
Bahía de Mejillones del Sur RCH 279 Ge57
Bahía de Ocoa DOM 250 Ge36
Bahía de Omoa GCA 248 Ff38
Bahía de Paita PE 268 Fk48
Bahía de Palmas MEX 244 Ec33
Bahía de Panamá PA 249 Ga41
Bahía de Paracas PE 269 Gb53
Bahía de Portete CO 264 Ge39
Bahía de Salinas PE 269 Gb51
Bahía de Samaná DOM 250 Gf36
Bahía de San Esteban MEX 244 Ef33
Bahía de San Quintín MEX 244 Eb30
Bahía de Santa Elena CR 248 Fh40
Bahía de Santa Inés MEX 244 Ee32
Bahía de Santa María MEX 244 Ef33
Bahía de Sechura PE 268 Fk48
Bahía de Sepetiba BR 277 Hh57
Bahía de Tablazo YV 264 Gb40
Bahía de Tela HN 248 Fg38
Bahía de Tepoca MEX 244 Ed30
Bahía de Tortugas MEX 244 Ec32
Bahía Elizabeth EC 269 Fe46
Bahía Engaño RA 282 Gh67
Bahía Escocesa DOM 250 Gf36
Bahía Grande RA 282 Gf71
Bahia Honda C 243 Fj34
Bahía Inútil RCH 282 Gf72
Bahía Kino RA 244 Ee31
Bahía las Cañas RCH 280 Gd63
Bahía Laura RA 282 Gg69
Bahía Lomas RCH 282 Gf72
Bahia Magdalena MEX 244 Ec33
Bahia Mansa RCH 280 Gd66
Bahía Morena RCH 279 Ge57
Bahía Nassau RCH 282 Gg73
Bahía Negra PY 278 Ha56
Bahía Nuestra Señora RCH 279 Ge58
Bahía Otway RCH 282 Gc72
Bahía Posesión RCH 282 Gf72
Bahía Puerto de Lobos MEX 244 Ed30
Bahía Punta Gorda NIC 249 Fj40
Bahía Rosario MEX 244 Ec31
Bahía Salado RCH 279 Ge59
Bahía Salvación RCH 282 Gc71
Bahía Samborombón RA 281 Hb63
Bahían San Blas RA 281 Gj66
Bahían San Carlos MEX 244 Ec31
Bahían San Carlos MEX 244 Ed32
Bahían San Felipe MEX 244 Ed30
Bahían San Jorge MEX 244 Ed30
Bahía San Luis Gonzaga MEX 244 Ec31
Bahía San Nicolás PE 269 Gc53
Bahía San Sebastián RA 282 Gf72
Bahía San Vicente RCH 280 Gd64
Bahía Sargento MEX 244 Ed31
Bahías de Huatulco MEX 244 Ec31
Bahía Sebastián Vizcaíno MEX 244 Ec31
Bahía Solano CO 264 Gb42
Bahía Solano RA 282 Gg68
Bahía Stokes RCH 282 Gj65
Bahía Vera RA 282 Gh67
Bahili ET 179 Me30
Bahili IND 116 Oj34
Bahinga RDC 196 Md48
Bahir Dar ETH 192 Mj40
Bahla OM 95 Nj34
Bahla Fort OM 95 Nj34
Bahn IR 186 Kt42
Bahr IR 91 Ne28
Bahr KSA 92 Mh33
Bahrah BR 100 Lh49
Bahraich IND 115 Pa31
Bahr Al-Arab SUD 191 Me41
Bahr al-Ghazal SUD 191 Me41
Bahram Abad IR 91 Nf27
Bahramjerd IR 98 Nh31
Bahramteppe AZ 91 Nd26
Bahr Baru ETH/SUD 192 Mg41
Bahr el Ghazal TCH 183 Lj38
Bahuaja-Sonene, P.N. PE 269 Gf52
Bubuilu RI 130 Rd47
Bahuichivo MEX 244 Ef32
Bahuluang RI 130 Ra49
Bahusai RI 130 Ra47
Baia RO 69 Mj46
Baia de Aramã RO 67 Md44
Baia Farta ANG 200 Lg53
Baia de Aries RO 67 Md44
Baia de Bazaruto MOC 203 Mh56
Baia de Caxiuna BR 267 Hd47
Baia de Inhambane MOC 203 Mh57
Baia de Maputo MOC 205 Mg58
Baia de Marajó BR 267 Hf47
Baia de Paranaguá BR 277 He58
Baia de Pemba MOC 203 Mk54
Baia de Santa Rosa BR 267 Hh47
Baia de São Marcos BR 267 Hh47
Baia de Todos os Santos BR 273 Ja52
Baia de Turiaçu BR 267 Hh46
Baia de Varela GNB 186 Kb39

Bak H 66 Lr44
Baká NIC 249 Fh39
Bakala RCH 190 Lj42
Bakalak TR 69 Mh50
Bakakeng RI 124 Ra40
Bakala RCA 190 Lj43
Bakala RCA 190 Ma42
Bakalak KZ 100 Oj23
Bakaore TCH 184 Ma38
Bakara RI 127 Pk44
Bakau WAG 186 Kb39
Bakauheni RI 127 Qc48
Bakay, Gunung RI 128 Qd47
Bakbakty KZ 100 Oj23
Bakdak RI 130 Ra48
Bakebe SN 180 Kd38
Bakel SN 180 Kd38
Bakelalan MAL 128 Qh44
Baker USA 233 Eb28
Baie-Comeau CDN 240 Gf21
Baker City USA 232 Dk21
Baie de Concarneau F 50 Kq43
Baker Island USA 134 Ba10
Baie de Gaspé CDN 240 Gh22
Baker Island USA 149 Se56
Baie-des-Sables CDN 240 Ga21
Bakersfield USA 234 Ea28
Baie du Mont-Saint-Michel F 50 Kt42
Bakerville D 225 Md58
Baie-Johan-Beetz CDN 240 Gj22
Bakewar IND 117 Ok32
Baiersbronn D 59 Lj42
Bakewell GB 49 Kt37
Baie Verte CDN 241 Hb33
Bakhardok TM 96 Nk26
Bigekum KZ 97 Od23
Bakhmut UA 73 Mh21
Baigneux-les-Juifs F 53 Le43
Bakhshi Kalay AFG 99 Oe30
Baihanchang CHN 121 Qa32
Bakhuis SME 266 Hb43
Baihar IND 117 Pa33
Baie CHN 106 Qf29
Baiheng CHN 108 Qd34
Baihe CI 187 Kg41
Baijiang CHN 108 Qd34
Bakel SN 180 Kd38
Baijnath IND 115 Ok30
Bakesiir CHN 108 Qc32
Baikonyr KZ 96 Oa27
Bakeng RI 151 Rf44
Bakel CHN 109 Qg32
Baikunthapur IND 117 Pb34
Bakonycsernye H 66 Lr43
Baihar IND 131 Qe40
Bakori WAN 188 Ld40
Baila SN 186 Kb39
Baikal CHN 108 Qd32
Bakor CI 187 Kg41
Bakan CHN 108 Qe31
Baile Átha Cliath = Dublin IRL 47 Ko37
Bakouma RCA 190 Ma43
Bäile Felix RO 67 Mb43
Baile Govora RO 67 Me45
Bäile Herculane RO 68 Mc46
Bakubung RI 128 Qd47
Bakta KZ 100 Oj23
Bakty KZ 100 Pb22
Baku AZ 91 Ne25
Bakung RI 127 Qc45
Baleesti RO 68 Me45
Baleia CHN 108 Qd31
Baliquabo CHN 106 Qf25
Baliguê CHN 108 Qd33
Bakum D 58 Lj38
Bakuma RCH 190 Ma43
Bakuriani GE 91 Nb25
Baliri CHN 109 Qg32
Baliliu CHN 106 Qk24
Baililu TCH 189 Lh40
Bailleul CI 187 Kg41
Bailleul F 51 Lc40
Ba'lii TCH 189 Lh40
Bailubo ANG 200 Lh52
Baima CHN 108 Qd31
Baimajing CHN 109 Qe34
Ba Ma Si CHN 107 Qa28
Bakwa-Kenge RDC 199 Mb48
Bainang CHN 102 Pe31
Bainbridge USA 239 Fh30
Bakyrly KZ 97 Od23
Bala, Cerros de BOL 278 Gg53
Bala GB 49 Kr38
Baing RI 154 Rh49
Bainville USA 235 Eg24
Baino CHN 109 Qg32
Baird Inlet USA 228 Bj15
Bains-les-Bains F 53 Lg42
Baalbek F 51 Lf41
Baia CHN 103 Pi30
Baiquan CHN 110 Rd22
Baiaginila IND 117 Pc32
Baligê IND 127 Qa45
Baira USA 229 Bk12
Balakan AZ 91 Nd25
Bala CHN 108 Qc33
Bairiki KIR 135 Tb09
Balikalal MEX 247 Ff37
Bairin Qiao CHN 105 Qk24
Balaken AZ 91 Nd25
Bairin Youqi CHN 105 Qj24
Balakété RCA 190 Lk42
Bairinsdale AUS 151 Sd64
Balaklava AUS 150 Rk63
Bais RP 124 Rb41
Balaklija UA 72 Mj21
Baishan CHN 110 Rd25
Balakot PK 99 Og30
Baishanzu CHN 109 Qk32
Balal RMM 181 Kg38
Baishizi Z.B. CHN 110 Rc25
Balabo D'Alsace F 53 Lg43
Baisinata Terraces CHN 121 Pk32
Balaghat IND 117 Pa33
Baisinga IND 117 Pd35
Balaghat RDC 190 Lk45
Bäisoara RO 67 Md44
Balaguier F 53 Lf47
Baisogala LT 45 Md35
Balama MOC 197 Mk51
Bai Ta CHN 109 Qe32
Balambangan Island RP 125 Ra43
Baitadi NEP 115 Pa31
Balamku CAM 247 Ff36
Baita Pagoda CHN 110 Rb25
Balan CHN 109 Qg32
Bait Na'amm OM 95 Nj34
Balangir IND 117 Pb35
Baitou Shan CHN/PRK 110 Rd25
Balakudê CHN 105 Qk24
Baiturrahman Grand Mosque RI 126 Ph43
Balam Takli IND 116 Oj36
Baixa Grande BR 273 Hk51
Balamorghab AFG 99 Ob28
Baixa Grande do Ribeirão BR 272 Hh50
Balam Takli IND 116 Oj36
Bai Xang VN 121 Qc36
Balanced Rock USA 232 Ec24
Baixio BR 273 Jb52
Balandou RG 186 Kf40
Baixo Guandu BR 273 Hk55
Balanga RDC 196 Me50
Baixo Longa ANG 200 Lk53
Balangiga RP 124 Rc40
Baiyer River PNG 155 Sc48
Balango RP 124 Ra37
Baiyin CHN 106 Qf27
Balanguingui Island RP 125 Ra43
Bairyrkum KZ 97 Oe24
Balantak RI 151 Rb46
Baiyü CHN 103 Pk30
Balánti USA 151 Sc62
Baja H 67 Lt44
Balanthira AUS 151 Sc62
Baja California MEX 244 Eb31
Balao EC 268 Gb46
Baja California Norte MEX 244 Ec30
Balaoan RP 124 Ra37
Baja California Sur MEX 244 Ed32
Balapur IND 116 Oj35
Baja del Agrio RA 280 Gf65
Balatonfüred H 66 Lr44
Baja Malibu MEX 244 Ec19
Balashi ND 182 Lc39
Bajadarú RUS 104 Pk29
Balasinor IND 116 Og34
Bajau RI 126 Qa44
Balatina MD 67 Mh43
Bajalan RI 127 Pk44
Balatonboglár H 66 Lr44
Bajalta RUS 106 Qc23
Balanka WAN 189 Lf41
Bajil YE 94 Na38
Balashov RUS 72 Na19
Bajima, Mount AUS 149 Sg60
Balassagyarmat H 67 Lu42
Bajina Bašta SRB 68 Lu47
Balat ET 179 Me33
Bajío de Ahuichila MEX 245 Ej33
Balta Alba RO 69 Mh45
Bajk'al RUS 104 Qc20
Balat RO 69 Mh46
Bajkal'skij zapovednik RUS 104 Qc20
Balau RO 67 Mc44
Bajmok SRB 68 Lu45
Balcad SP 195 Nc44
Bajo C RA 130 Rd50
Balcanoona AUS 148 Rk61
Bajo Caracoles RA 282 Gg69
Balcarce RA 281 Ha64
Bajocunde GNB 186 Kc39
Bald Head Island Lighthouse USA 242 Gb30
Balce CAM 188 Lf42
Bajo de la Tierra Colorada RA 280 Gg67
Bald Knob USA 238 Fe28
Bajo del Gualicho RA 280 Gh67
Bald Knob N.W.R. USA 236 Fe28
Bajo de los Menidos RA 280 Gg67
Balçová TR 71 Mh52
Bajo de Santa Rosa RA 280 Gg66
Baldone LV 45 Me34
Bajo Hondo RA 280 Gh61
Bald Pt. USA 239 Fh31
Bajo Izozog BOL 278 Gj55
Baldwin USA 237 Fh24
Bajo Nuevo C 250 Gd39
Baldwin USA 237 Fh24
Bajonpaqui PE 269 Gc51
Baldwin City USA 237 Fh24
Bajoví Polje MNE 68 Lt47
Baldwin Peninsula USA 229 Bj12
Bajpakli zālītājs MJ 68 Mc44
Baldwinsville USA 237 Gb24
Bajram Curri AL 68 Ma48
Baldy Mtn. USA 235 Ef29
Bajy KS 100 Qk25
Baldy Peak USA 234 Ee29
Bale EAU 194 Mg45
Baldzarkačan RUS 104 Qf21

Baleares E 57 Lc51
Balearic Islands E 57 Lb51
Balearic, Gunung RI 130 Ra47
Balehoomur IND 118 Oh39
Balekamba RI 151 Rb46
Bale Mountains N.P. ETH 192 Mk42
Balessang RI 151 Qk46
Balfate HN 248 Fg38
Baler RP 124 Ra38
Balerakok RI 127 Qc48
Baler Bay RP 124 Ra38
Balesberg ZA 205 Mf59
Bales Creek AUS 147 Sc56
Balfour CDN 232 Eb21
Balfour ZA 205 Me59
Balfour Downs AUS 142 Ra57
Balgak SUD 184 Md39
Balgazyn RUS 101 Ph20
Balgo AUS 143 Rd57
Balguntay CHN 101 Pd24
Balhaf YE 94 Ne38
Balho DJI 192 Nb39
Bali DJI 192 Nb39
Bali Barat N.P. RI 129 Qh50
Bali RCA 190 Ma42
Balibo TLS 131 Rc50
Balie SYR 90 Mj29
Baliem Valley RI 154 Rk48
Balifondo RCA 190 Ma43
Balige RI 127 Pj44
Baliguda IND 117 Pb35
Balik BG 69 Mh47
Balik BG 69 Mh47
Balikana IND 117 Pc36
Balikeşir TR 71 Mh51
Balikiçes TR 69 Mh50
Balikpapan RI 129 Qj46
Balimila IND 117 Pb36
Balimo PNG 155 Sb50
Baling MAL 126 Qa43
Balingasag RP 125 Rc41
Balinge S 43 Ls31
Balingen D 59 Lj42
Balingup AUS 144 Qh62
Balise 250 Poste Weygand DZ 182 La33
Bali Sea 130 Qk49
Baliseyh TR 90 Mg26
Baliuag RP 124 Ra38
Baliza BR 272 Hd54
Baliuag CAM 188 Lf42
Balk NL 58 Lf38
Balkanabat TM 96 Nh26
Balkan Mountains BG 68 Mc47
Balkh AFG 97 Od27
Balkhab AFG 99 Od28
Balkhash KZ 100 Oh22
Balkhulish GB 48 Kp34
Balladonia Motel AUS 145 Rb62
Balladiata AUS 150 Sa60
Ballaghaderreen IRL 47 Km36
Ballan AUS 151 Sc64
Ballangen N 38 Lr22
Ballantrae GB 48 Kq35
Ballarat AUS 151 Sb64
Ballaroo AUS 149 Se59
Ballarpur IND 117 Ok36
Ballasetas PE 269 Gc51
Ballater GB 48 Kr34
Ballenas Whale watching MEX 244 Ec32
Ballenrieff Castle GB 48 Ks33
Balleza MEX 244 Ej32
Balli IND 116 Oh37
Ballia IND 117 Pc33
Ballidu AUS 144 Qj61
Ballina AUS 151 Sg60
Ballina IRL 47 Km37
Ballinasloe IRL 47 Km37
Balling DK 42 Lj34
Ballinger USA 236 Fa30
Ballon d'Alsace F 53 Lg43
Ballston Spa USA 237 Gd24
Ballum DK 42 Lj34
Balluta GB 49 Ks40
Ballstad N 38 Lp21
Ballybofey IRL 47 Kn36
Ballycastle IRL 47 Kf38
Ballycastle IRL 47 Kn35
Ballyconneely IRL 47 Kl37
Ballyhaunis IRL 47 Km37
Ballymena GB 47 Ko35
Ballymoney GB 47 Ko35
Ballynahinch GB 47 Kp36
Ballyshannon IRL 47 Km36
Balmaceda, Cerro RCH 282 Gc71
Balmaceda RCH 282 Gf71
Balmazújváros H 67 Ma43
Balmertown CDN 236 Fd20
Balmoral AUS 151 Sb64
Balmoral Castle GB 48 Kr34
Balmorhea USA 235 Ek30
Balneário MEX 245 Ej30
Balneário Camboriú BR 277 Hf59
Balneario del Sol C 250 Gc36
Balneário Gaivotas BR 277 Hf58
Balneario las Grutas RA 280 Gh66
Balnearío Massini RA 281 Gj66
Balneario Oriente RA 281 Gk65
Balo IR 131 Rb46
Baloa RO 130 Rb46
Baloarí IR 130 Rd47
Balodabazang RI 130 Rd47
Balod IND 116 Ok35
Baloda Bazar IND 117 Pb35
Balombe ANG 200 Lh52
Balotra IND 116 Og32
Baluti IR 98 Ng31
Balpyk Bi KZ 100 Ok23
Balrampur IND 115 Pb31
Balš AL 70 Lu49
Balsa RO 67 Md44
Balsa IND 117 Pb32
Balsam RMM 181 Kh38
Balsas BR 272 Hg50
Balsas MEX 246 Ek37
Balsas PE 268 Gb49
Balta ZA 205 Me61
Baltanás E 56 Kq49
Baltar E 54 Ko49
Baltasi RUS 73 Ng17
Baltasound GB 48 Ku30
Balti MD 67 Mh43
Baltic Sea 26 Lb04
Baltíjsk LV 45 Ma36
Baltim ET 178 Me30
Baltimore IRL 47 Kk40
Baltimore USA 241 Gb26
Baltimore ZA 202 Me57
Baltinava LV 45 Mg34
Baltit Fort PK 114 Oh27

Bandar-e-Gonaveh IR 93 Nf31
Bandar-e Hamiran IR 98 Nh32
Bandar-e Kharmi IR 98 Nh32
Bandar-e-Kiya Shahr IR 91 Ne27
Bandar-e-Langeh IR 98 Nh32
Bandar-e-Mashhar IR 93 Ne30
Bandar-e Moqam IR 98 Nh32
Bandar-e-Rig IR 93 Nf31
Banderas, Bahía de MEX 246 Nh27
Bandarjaya RI 127 Qc48
Bandar Lampung RI 127 Qc48
Bandar Murcaayo SP 193 Nf40
Bandarpunch IND 115 Ok30
Bandar Seri Begawan BRU 128 Qh44
Bandar Siri Aman MAL 128 Qf45
Banda Sea RI 131 Rc48
Bande CHN 103 Pk29
Bande E 54 Kn48
Bandeira BR 275 Hk53
Bandeira BR 272 Ke52
Banderantes RI 129 Qg50
Bandeirantes BR 272 Hd51
Bandelierkop ZA 202 Me57
Bandelier M.N. USA 235 Eg28
Bandera USA 245 Fa31
Bandera RA 279 Gj59
Bander Wanaag SP 193 Nc41
Bandhavgarh N.P. IND 117 Pa34
Bandiagara RMM 181 Kj38
Bandiagara RMM 181 Kj38
Bandialit RI 129 Qg50
Banding RI 127 Qa45
Bandingung RI 127 Qb48
Bandipur N.P. IND 118 Oj40
Bandipur N.P. IND 119 Oj40
Bandirma TR 69 Mh50
Bandjoukri CAM 189 Lg41
Bandjoun CAM 189 Lf43
Bandol F 53 Lf47
Bandon IRL 47 Km39
Bandon USA 232 Dh24
Bandua MOC 203 Mh56
Bandula RO 69 Mh46
Bandundu RDC 199 Lj47
Bandung RI 129 Qd49
Bandung RI 129 Qd49
Bane RUS 104 Rb59
Bane EAK 195 Mk45
Banémo RO 69 Mj46
Baneh IR 91 Nc28
Banemfala RG 186 Ke40
Baneshwar IR 98 Nh30
Baneswar IND 116 Oh34
Banfélé RG 186 Ke40
Banff CDN 232 Ec20
Banff GB 48 Ks33
Banff N.P. CDN 232 Ec20
Banfora BF 187 Kh40
Banga RCA 190 Lh42
Banga ANG 198 Lh50
Banga RDC 199 La48
Banga RDC 199 Ma48
Banga RDC 199 Me48
Bangalore IND 118 Oj39
Bangaluda IND 117 Pb36
Bangana RCA 190 Ma44
Bangana IND 116 Oj36
Bangaon IND 117 Pc33
Bangar RP 124 Ra37
Bangaram Island IND 118 Og40
Bangared IND 118 Ok39
Bangare RN 187 La39
Bangassoko BF 187 Kj39
Bangassou RCA 190 Mb43
Bangba RCA 190 Lk43
Bangbagatome RDC 191 Mc44
Bangbong RI 129 Qg50
Bangeta, Mount PNG 155 Sd49
Banggai RI 131 Rb46
Banggi MAL 128 Qj43
Banggong Co IND 114 Oj30
Bangi RI 129 Qd49
Bangka RI 125 Rc45
Bangka RI 127 Qc46
Bangka, Selat RI 127 Qc46
Bangkalan RI 129 Qf49
Bangkaru RI 127 Pj45
Bangkinang RI 127 Qa45
Bangko RI 127 Qb46
Bangkog Co CHN 102 Pd29
Bangkok THA 122 Qa40
Bangla Sahib IND 115 Oj31
Bangladesh BD 120 Pf33
Bangolo CI 187 Kg42
Bangor USA 241 Gf23
Bangor GB 49 Kq37
Bangor GB 47 Kp35
Bangor RCA 190 Lk41
Bangoran RCA 190 Ma41
Bangoran RCA 198 Lk47
Bangpuan CAM 189 Lg41
Bangsa Putih RI 128 Qd47
Bangued RP 124 Ra37
Bangui RCA 190 Lk43
Banguru RDC 191 Mc44
Bangweulu Swamps Z 196 Mf51
Banha ET 178 Me30
Bangui CHN 109 Qe36
Ban Hai LAO 121 Qd35
Ban Houayxay LAO 121 Qc35
Ban Het LAO 121 Qd36
Ban Heum LAO 121 Qc35
Banhine, P.N. de MOC 202 Mg57
Ban Hin Kiong Temple RI 125 Rc45
Ban Huayma CAM 121 Qb35
Bani BF 187 Kj40
Bani RP 124 Qk37
Bani DOM 250 Ge36
Bani IND 117 Pd34
Bani, Jebel MA 175 Kf30
Bania RCA 190 Lj44
Banié CI 187 Kf42
Banie PL 64 Lq38
Banifing RMM 187 Kh40
Banikoara DY 188 La39
Banima RCA 191 Mc44
Banister Fork USA 234 Ee28
Bani Nkasim LAO 121 Qd36
Banja RI 129 Qd47
Banja SRB 68 Lu46
Banja Koviljača SRB 68 Lt46
Banjar RI 129 Qe49
Banjaran RI 129 Qd49
Banjaran Bintang MAL 126 Qa43
Banjaran Brassey MAL 128 Qj44
Banjaran Tama Abu MAL 128 Qh44

Banjaran Titiwangsa – Bélédougou

Banjaran Titiwangsa ▲ MAL 126 Qa43
Banjarbaru RI 129 Qh46
Banjarkasang RI 127 Qa46
Banjarmasin RI 129 Qh47
Banjawarn AUS 144 Ra59
Ban Jiang LAO 121 Qb36
Banjul ● WAG 186 Kb39
Banka AZ 91 Nd26
Banka IND 117 Pd33
Banka Banka AUS 146 Rh55
Bankass RMM 181 Kj38
Ban Katang THA 122 Pk42
Bankatwa IND 117 Pb32
Bankaulang LAO 121 Qd35
Bankberg ▲ ZA 205 Mc62
Bankeryd S 43 Lg33
Banket ZW 202 Mf54
Ban Khlong Kua THA 122 Qa42
Ban Khlong Son THA 123 Qb39
Bankilaré RN 181 La38
Bankinang RI 127 Pd33
Banks BG 68 Md48
Ban Klan LAO 123 Qd38
Banko RG 186 Ke40
Bankon RI 186 Kf40
Bankou mana RMM 186 Kf39
Banks Island CDN 230 De19
Banks Island CDN 226 Dd04
Banks Island VU 158 Td53
Banks Lake N.W.R. USA 242 Fj30
Banks Peninsula NZ 153 Tg67
Banks Providence SY 206 Nf50
Banks Strait AUS 151 Sd64
Bankura IND 117 Pd34
Ban Lampoy LAO 123 Qc37
Banli CHN 106 Qd34
Ban Luang THA 121 Qa36
Ban Lung K 123 Qd39
Ban Mai LAO 123 Qd38
Banmanki IND 117 Pd33
Ban Mi THA 122 Qa38
Ban Muang THA 121 Qb36
Ban Muang Et LAO 121 Qc35
Ban Nabo LAO 123 Qd37
Bannalec F 50 Kr43
Ban Napa LAO 121 Qc36
Ban Naphao LAO 121 Qc36
Ban Na Sam THA 122 Pk41
Bannerghatta N.P. IND 118 Oj39
Bannerman Town BS 243 Gb33
Banning USA 234 Eb29
Bannu IND 117 Pd32
Baños EC 268 Ga46
Baños PE 269 Gb51
Baños de Benasque E 56 Ld48
Báňovce nad Bebravou SK 66 Lf42
Banovci Dunav SRB 68 Ma46
Banovići BiH 68 Lf46
Banów AFG 97 Oe28
Ban Pak Bat THA 121 Qa37
Ban Pak-ou LAO 121 Qb35
Ban Pakpet Nuc LAO 121 Qa36
Ban Pak Phanang THA 122 Qa41
Ban Phaeng THA 121 Qc37
Ban Phai THA 123 Qd37
Ban Phe THA 123 Qa38
Ban Phon LAO 123 Qd38
Banpo CHN 106 Qe28
Banpo Museum CHN 106 Qe28
Ban Pua THA 122 Pk39
Ban Pung LAO 121 Qa37
Banqiao CHN 107 Qg30
Banqiao CHN 121 Qc32
Ban Rai THA 122 Pk38
Bansa WAN 188 Le42
Ban Saang LAO 121 Qc37
Ban Salak Phet THA 123 Qd40
Ban San Chao Po THA 123 Qd40
Ban San Keo K 123 Qd38
Ban Sawi THA 122 Pk40
Bansberia IND 117 Qk38
Bansi IND 117 Ok33
Bansi IND 117 Pb32
Ban Sichon THA 122 Pk41
Bansihari IND 120 Pd33
Bansin D 58 Ld37
Ban Sinxa LAO 121 Qd35
Banská Bystrica SK 67 Lf42
Banská Štiavnica SK 67 Lf42
Banskol IND 117 Pc36
Ban Sop Hao LAO 121 Qc35
Banstead GB 49 Kj39
Banswada IND 116 Oj36
Banswara RI 116 Oh34
Ban Tabok LAO 121 Qc36
Bantadjé CAM 189 Lg41
Bantaji IND 130 Ra48
Bantaian IND 127 Qa45
Ban Tak THA 122 Pk37
Ban Takhun THA 122 Pk41
Bantan Island RP 124 Rc39
Bantayan Island RP 124 Rb40
Bantè DY 188 La41
Banteay Chhmar K 123 Qb39
Banteay Chhmar K 123 Qb39
Ban Thahua LAO 121 Qb36
Ban Tham Thong THA 122 Pk40
Ban Tha Rae THA 121 Qc37
Ban Tha Sala THA 122 Pk41
Ban Tha Song Yang THA 122 Pj37
Ban Tha Tum THA 123 Qb38
Ban Thu Xuang LAO 121 Qc36
Bantimurung RI 130 Ra48
Ban Tomo Nawk LAO 123 Qd35
Banton Island RP 124 Rb39
Bantry IRL 47 Kl39
Bantshamba RDC 199 Lk49
Bantva IND 116 Of35
Bantval IND 118 Oh39
Ban Un Mai LAO 121 Qa35
Banvo ANG 199 Lk50
Ban Wiang Sa THA 122 Pk41
Ban Yaeng THA 122 Qa37
Banyalbufar E 57 Lc51
Banyo SYR 90 Mh28
Banyoles E 57 Lc48
Banyumas RI 129 Qe49
Banyuwangi RI 129 Qh50
Banzana RMM 187 Kg40
Banzare Coast AN 286 Rb52
Banza Sanda RDC 198 Lh48
Banza Sosso ANG 198 Lh48
Bao RCA 190 Md43
Bao CHN 190 Lg41
Baode CHN 106 Qd26
Baodi CHN 107 Qh26
Baoding CHN 107 Qh26
Baoding Shan CHN 108 Qd31
Baofeng CHN 107 Qg28
Bao Gong Ci CHN 108 Qa30
Baoguo CHN 112 Ra30
Baojing CHN 108 Qe31
Baokang CHN 105 Rb23
Baokang CHN 107 Qf28
Bao Khao Sai THA 123 Qa37
Bao Lac VN 121 Qd34
Baolo SOL 157 Sk49
Baolun CHN 106 Qe29
Baonu WAL 186 Kd41
Baoro RCA 190 Lh42
Baoro CHN 112 Ra29
Baorong CHN 110 Rg22
Baoshan CHN 112 Ra30
Baoshan CHN 111 Pk33
Bao Ta Shan CHN 106 Qe27
Baotianmam Z.B.D. CHN 106 Qf29
Baotou CHN 106 Qe25
Baoulé RMM 186 Kf39
Baoxu CHN 108 Qf34
Bao Yen VN 121 Qd34
Bap IND 114 Og32
Bapaume F 51 Lc40
Baqer Abad IR 91 Nf28

Baqran KSA 94 Na35
Baquba IRQ 91 Nc29
Baguedano RCH 279 Gf57
Bar IND 114 Oh37
Bar MNE 68 Lu48
Bar UA 73 Md21
Bara RG 186 Kd39
Bara RI 131 Rd47
Bara RO 68 Mb45
Bara SUD 185 Mf39
Bara WAN 188 Lf40
Baraawe SP 195 Nc45
Bara Sagar IND 117 Pa34
Bara Banki IND 117 Pa32
Barabaš-Levada RUS 110 Rf23
Barabinskaja nizmennost' ▲ RUS 88 Oc07
Baracoa C 250 Gc35
Baraderes RH 250 Gd36
Baradero RA 276 Ha62
Baradla-barlang H 67 Ma42
Baraga USA 237 Ft22
Bărăganu RO 69 Mh46
Barago SAK 194 Mj45
Barah T.I. IND 117 Pa32
Barahona DOM 250 Ge36
Barahtsa SK 66 Na35
Bara Imambara IND 117 Pa32
Barajas de Melo E 57 Ks50
Baraka EAT 192 Mj38
Baraka RDC 196 Ma48
Barakak SUD 184 Ma40
Barakaldo E 56 Ks47
Barakat SUD 185 Mg38
Barakatha IND 117 Pc33
Baraki AFG 99 Oe29
Barakoma SOL 157 Sj49
Barakot IND 117 Pd34
Barale AUS 149 Se58
Baramanni GUY 266 Ha44
Baramata PNG 156 Se51
Baramati IND 116 Oh36
Baran IND 116 Oj33
Baranavičy BY 65 Mg37
Baranga RDC 191 Md44
Barangbarang RI 130 Ra48
Baranet GB 49 Kg39
Baranivka UA 73 Md20
Baranoa CO 264 Gc40
Baranof USA 230 Dc17
Baranof Island USA 230 Dc17
Baranów PL 65 Mc39
Baranowo Sandomierski PL 65 Mb40
Barão de Antonia, T.I. BR 274 He57
Barão de Grajaú BR 273 Hj49
Barão de Melgaço BR 271 Gk51
Barão de Melgaço BR 274 Hc54
Baraouelli RMM 187 Kg39
Baraqish F 94 Nb38
Baraqueville F 52 Lc46
Barara EAT 197 Mj48
Baras RP 124 Rb39
Bara Sagar IND 117 Pa34
Barate CI 187 Kh42
Baratkhel AFG 99 Oe29
Baratpur IND 117 Pc32
Barauli IND 117 Pc32
Barauni IND 117 Pd33
Baravaky BY 65 Mg37
Baraya CO 264 Gc44
Barbacena BR 275 Hj56
Barbacoas CO 264 Ga45
Barbacoas CO 264 Gb44
Barbacoas YV 265 Gg41
Barbado BR 270 Gg50
Barbados BDS 251 Ha39
Barbados 251 Ha39
Barbalha BR 273 Ja49
Barbastro E 56 Ld48
Barbastro E 56 Kp54
Barbate E 55 Kp54
Barbazum CAM 95 Nh37
Barbèle LV 45 Me34
Bar Bigha IND 117 Pc33
Barberino CO 264 Gc42
Barberville USA 242 Fk31
Barbuda 46 251 Gk47
Barbude RO 68 Md47
Barca de Alva E 54 Kp49
Barcaldine AUS 149 Sc57
Barcarena BR 267 Hf46
Barcatat USA 142 Qf7
Barcelona E 57 Lc49
Barcelona YV 265 Gg41
Barcelonette F 53 Lg44
Barcelos BR 270 Gk46
Barcelos P 54 Kn49
Bárcena de Pie de Concha E 54 Kq47
Barcin PL 64 Ls38
Barcoo AZ 91 Nd25
Barczewo PL 65 Ma37
Barô IS 46 La45
Barda BR 275 Hj61
Barda del Medio RA 280 Gf65
Bardaï TCH 183 Lj35
Bardaskan IR 97 Nh30
Bardbārbunga IS 46 Kc26
Bardas Blancas RA 280 Gf63
Bardawell IND 117 Ph34
Bar Dabh IR 93 Nf29
Bardejov SK 67 Mb41
Bardeskan IR 98 Nj28
Bardi I 60 Lf46
Bardoc AUS 144 Ra61
Bardoli IND 116 Og35
Bardonecchia I 60 Lg42
Bardsey Island GB 49 Kg38
Bardsir IR 98 Nj30
Bardula IND 117 Pd35
Baré ETH 195 Na43
Barekuma IND 115 Ok31
Bareli IND 117 Ok34
Barellan AUS 151 Sd63
Barentin F 51 La41
Barentsburg N 38 Lh06
Barentu ER 192 Mj38
Bareo MAL 128 Qj44
Barfleur F 50 Kt41
Barfloievka RUS 111 Rg23
Barga CHN 102 Pa30
Bargaal SP 193 Nf40
Barga IND 117 Oh34
Bargatheide D 58 Lf37
Barguzin RUS 104 Qe19
Barguzinski Hrebet ▲ RUS 89 Qb08
Barh IND 117 Pc33
Bar Harbor USA 241 Gf23
Barhaj IND 117 Pa33
Barharwa IND 117 Pd33
Bari I 63 Lh51
Bari IND 116 Oj33
Bari WAN 188 Lc40
Baria RO 69 Mf45
Bariadi EAT 194 Mg47

Barichara CO 264 Gd42
Barika DZ 176 Lc28
Barikowt AFG 97 Of28
Barili RP 124 Rb40
Barillas GCA 248 Fe38
Barim YE 94 Nb38
Baringa RDC 190 Ma45
Barinitas YV 264 Ge41
Baripada IND 117 Pd35
Báris ET 179 Mf33
Bari Sadri IND 117 Ok33
Barisal BD 119 Pf34
Barisan Range RI 127 Qa46
Barisan Range RI 127 Qa46
Baritú RA 279 Gh57
Barjac PE 268 Fk48
Barjols F 52 Lf44
Barka OM 95 Nj34
Barkam CHN 106 Qb30
Barkava LV 45 Mg34
Barkédji SN 180 Kc38
Barkerville Hist. Town CDN Dk19
Barkhan PK 99 Oe31
Bark Hut Inn AUS 146 Rf52
Barkly Downs AUS 146 Rk56
Barkly East ZA 205 Md61
Barkly Highway AUS 146 Rh55
Barkly Highway AUS 146 Rh55
Barkly Pass ZA 205 Md61
Barkly Roadhouse AUS 146 Rh55
Barkly Tableland AUS 146 Rh54
Barkly West ZA 205 Mc60
Barkol CHN 101 Pg24
Barkuar Dongar IND 117 Ph34
Bar-le-Duc F 51 Lf42
Barlee Range Nature Reserve AUS 142 Qh57
Barletta I 63 Lr49
Barlinek PL 64 Lq37
Barlo Warf WAL 186 Kd41
Barma RI 154 Rg46
Barmedman AUS 151 Sd63
Barmer IND 116 Of34
Barmera AUS 150 Sa63
Barmouth GB 49 Kg38
Barnala IND 114 Oh30
Barnard USA 236 Fa23
Barnaul RUS 104 Qc19
Barnaul RUS 88 Pa08
Barnesville USA 236 Fb22
Barnesville USA 239 Fh29
Barnet GB 49 Kj39
Barnett River Gorge AUS 143 Rd54
Barnsley GB 49 Kj37
Barnstaple GB 49 Kg39
Barnstorf D 58 Le38
Barnum USA 233 Jj24
Barnwell USA 242 Fk29
Baro TCH 189 Lk39
Baro WAN 188 Ld41
Barobo RP 125 Rd41
Baroda IND 116 Og33
Barodia = Vadodara IND 116 Og34
Barodia IND 117 Ok33
Baroe DZ 205 Md62
Baroghilpass AFG/PK 97 Og27
Barola IND 117 Pa34
Barolong RB 205 Mc58
Barona Island SOL 157 Sk49
Barona Ite Island AUS 150 Rk63
Barossa Valley AUS 150 Rk63
Barotac Nuevo RP 124 Rb40
Barotseland BR 201 Mb53
Baroua RCA 191 Md43
Barovo MK 68 Mc49
Barpeta IND 120 Pf32
Barqah al Bayda LAR 177 Ma30
Barqah al-Bahriya ET/RN 178 Mc31
Barqin LAR 177 Lg32
Barque Canada Reef 122 Qj41
Barra BR 275 Hj54
Barra BR 270 Gg48
Barra Alegre BR 275 Hj55
Baraba AUS 149 Sf61
Barra Bonita BR 274 Hf57
Barraca da Boca BR 271 Hd46
Barraca de A.Lopes BR 271 Hd46
Barraca de A.Lopes BR 276 Ho55
Barração do Barreto BR 271 Ha50
Barracas F 57 Ku50
Barra da Estiva BR 273 Hk52
Barradale AUS 142 Qf57
Barra de Cazones MEX 246 Fb35
Barra de Itabapoana BR 275 Hk56
Barra de Navidad MEX 246 Ed37
Barra de São Francisco BR 275 Hk55
Barra de São Manuel BR 271 Ha49
Barra de Tuxpan MEX 246 Fb35
Barra do Bugres BR 274 Hb53
Barra do Cai BR 275 Hj54
Barra do Choça BR 275 Hk53
Barra do Dande ANG 198 Lg52
Barra do Guaicuí BR 275 Hh54
Barra do Mendes BR 273 Hj51
Barra do Tarrachi BR 273 Ja50
Barra El Tordo MEX 246 Fb34
Barrafranca I 63 Lp53
Barragem de Manantiali RMM 186 Ke39
Barragem de Matadi RDC 198 Lg48
Barragem de Sélingué RMM 186 Kf40
Barragem do Alqueva P 55 Kn51
Barragem de Moxoto BR 273 Ja50
Barragem de Pedra BR 273 Hk52
Barragem de Pracana BR 55 Kn53
Barragem de São Simão I BR 274 Hf55
Barragem de Serra da Mesa BR 274 Hf53
Barragem de Sobradinho BR 273 Ho50
Barragem do Alqueva P 55 Kn52
Barragem do Caia P 55 Kn51
Barragem do Maranhão P 55 Kn51
Barragem Itumbiara BR 274 Hf55
Barragem Mohamed V MA 175 Kj28
Barragem Pedro do Cavalo BR 273 Ja52
Barragem S.M. Ben Abdellah MA 175 Kg29
Barragem de Cabora Bassa MOC 202 Mg53
Barragem de Castelo de Bode P 55 Kn51
Barragem de Chicamba Real MOC 202 Mg55
Barragem de Itaparica BR 273 Ja50

Barramiya ET 179 Mg33
Barranca PE 268 Gb48
Barranca RP 269 Gb51
Barrancabermeja CO 264 Gd42
Barranca del Cobre MEX 244 Eg32
Barranca del Cobre, P.N. MEX 244 Eg32
Barranca de Upia CO 264 Gd43
Barrancas CO 264 Ge41
Barrancas TV 265 Gj41
Barranc d'Algendar E 57 Ld51
Barranco de Loba CO 264 Gc41
Barranco Picure CO 265 Gd44
Barrancos P 55 Ko52
Barranda E 57 Kt52
Barranqueras RA 276 Ha59
Barranquilla CO 264 Gc40
Barranquitas RCH 279 Ge59
Barras YV 264 Gd40
Barras BR 273 Hj48
Barra Seca BR 275 Hk56
Barra Soto La Marina MEX 246 Fb34
Barraute CDN 237 Gb21
Barre USA 241 Gd23
Barra Velha BR 277 Hf59
Barra Velha, T.I. BR 275 Ja54
Barrax E 57 Ks51
Bar'd Harbour CDN 241 Hb20
Barreal RA 280 Gf62
Barreales VV 265 Gh41
Barreira Branca BR 272 He50
Barreira da Cruz BR 272 Hf51
Barreira do Peiquí BR 272 Hf52
Barreiras BR 271 Hb47
Barreirinhas BR 267 Hj47
Barreiro P 55 Ki52
Barreiros BR 273 Jc50
Barreiros BR 277 Hf59
Barrême F 53 Lg47
Barren Grounds CDN 227 Gb07
Barren Grounds CDN 226 Dd05
Barren Is. USA 228 Cd16
Barren Island MA 122 Pg39
Barretal MEX 245 Fa33
Barretos BR 274 Hf56
Barrett Lake CDN 230 Dg18
Barrhead CDN 237 Eb20
Barrial Largo YV 265 Gg42
Barrie CDN 237 Fk23
Barrière CDN 230 Dk20
Barrington AUS 148 Sa61
Barrington = Isla Santa Fé EC 269 Fe46
Barrington, Mount AUS 151 Sf62
Barrington Tops N.P. AUS 151 Sf62
Barrington USA 149 Sc60
Barriyat al-Bayyuda SUD 185 Mg36
Barro Alto BR 274 Hf53
Barroção BR 275 Hj54
Barro Duro BR 273 Hj47
Barro Duro BR 273 Hj47
Barron USA 236 Fd23
Barros Arana, Cerro RCH 282 Gd67
Barros Cassal BR 276 Hd60
Barrow USA 229 Cb10
Barrow Creek AUS 148 Rg56
Barrow-in-Furness GB 49 Kh36
Barrow Island AUS 142 Qf56
Barrow Point AUS 147 Sc53
Barruelo de Santuillán E 54 Kq48
Barry GB 49 Kh39
Barry Church AZ 204 Ma63
Barrydale ZA 204 Ma62
Barry's Bay CDN 241 Gb23
Barsalogo BF 187 Kk39
Barsanii EAK 194 Mj45
Bârsana RO 67 Mc45
Barsatas KZ 100 Ok21
Barsi IND 116 Oj36
Barskoon KS 100 Oj24
Barsoi IND 117 Pd33
Barssatas BR 271 Ha45
Barstow USA 234 Eb29
Bartang TJ 97 Of26
Bartel USA 232 Ej25
Bartica GUY 266 Ha42
Bartin TR 90 Mg25
Bartlesville USA 238 Fb27
Bartlett Bluff AUS 145 Rc60
Barton USA 236 Fa25
Barton-upon-Humber GB 49 Kj37
Bartoszyce PL 65 Ma36
Baru CO 264 Gc41
Baru BR 277 Hg57
Baruku IND 130 Ra47
Baruni IND 117 Pd33
Barung RI 128 Qj45
Barung RI 129 Qf49
Baruth D 58 Lo38
Baruti RDC 191 Mc44
Baruunharaa MNG 104 Qd21
Baruunturuun MNG 105 Qg22
Barvala IND 116 Of35
Barvas GB 48 Kf33
Barvinkove UA 73 Mj21
Barwala IND 114 Oh31
Barwani IND 116 Oh34
Barwice PL 64 Lr37
Barwidgee AUS 144 Ra59
Barwidgi AUS 147 Sd58
Bary KZ 72 Ne16
Baryulgil AUS 149 Sg60
Bârzava RO 67 Mb45
Basacato del Este GQ 188 Le44
Basadude IND 117 Pa36
Basaidu IR 98 Nh32
Basail RA 276 Ha60
Basail MAL 128 Qj43
Basaid SRB 68 Ma45
Basaidu IR 98 Nh32
Basail IND 128 Qj44
Basanga PK 99 Og29
Basang WAG 186 Kc39
Basankusu RDC 190 Lk45
Basapa WAG 188 Le42
Basara RDC 191 Mb45
Basarabeasca MD 73 Me22
Basarabi RO 69 Mj46
Basaseachic MEX 244 Ef31
Basavana Bagevadi IND 116 Oh37
Basavilbaso RA 276 Ha62
Bascom RO 69 Me46
Baseer SYR 90 Mj29
Basel Naval Azopardo RA 281 Ha64
Baseráh ET 179 Mf33
Bashaw CDN 237 Eb21
Bashee Bridge ZA 205 Me61
Bashkimak RDC 199 Mc48
Bashkortostan RUS 72 Nb04
Basht IR 91 Nf31
Basi IND 116 Oj33
Basiano RI 130 Rb47
Basi IND 117 Pc34
Basian RI 130 Ra47
Basilaki Island PNG 156 Sf51
Basilan Strait RP 125 Rb42

Basildon GB 49 La39
Basilan CAM 189 Lh43
Basilica d'Aquila E 61 Lo48
Basilica d'Aquileia I 62 Lo47
Basilica de Nuestra Señora de los Milagros PY 276 Hb58
Basílica di Lecce I 63 Lt50
Basílica di San Francesco d'Assisi I 62 Ln49
Basílica di San Pietro □ I 62 Ln49
Basílica di Bom Jesus □ IND 116 Og38
Basílica San Gavino □ I 62 Lj51
Basilicata I 63 Lr50
Basílique de Saint-Nicolas-de-Port F 51 Lg42
Basilique Notre-Dame de Paray-le-Monial F 53 Le44
Basilique Notre Dame de Port de Clermont-Ferrand F 53 Ld45
Basin USA 233 Ej23
Basin Head Fisheries Mus. CDN 240 Gj22
Basirka WAN 188 Ld40
Basirpur PK 99 Og30
Baska HR 61 Lp45
Başkale TR 91 Nb26
Başkomutan Tarihi Milli Parkı TR 90 Me26
Basle CH 60 Lh43
Basmath IND 116 Oj36
Basoda IND 117 Oj34
Basoko RDC 191 Mb45
Basongo RDC 199 Ma48
Basongo RDC 199 Ma48
Basotu EAT 196 Mh48
Basra IR 91 Nd30
Basra IR 187 Kg43
Bassano I 60 To Mb53
Bassano CDN 233 Ed20
Bassano del Grappa □ I 60 Lm45
Bassas da India I 62 Mk56
Basse à Puthein MYA 122 Ph39
Bassein Beach IND 116 Og36
Bassein E 56 Lb48
Basse-Pointe F 251 Gk38
Basse Santa Su WAG 186 Kc39
Basse Terre F 251 Gk37
Basse-Terre F 251 Gk37
Basseterre KN 251 Gk37
Bassikounou RIM 181 Kh38
Bassila DY 188 La41
Basso DY 188 La41
Basso TCH 184 Mb37
Basso Strait USA 151 Sc65
Bassum D 58 Lj38
Bast IR 98 Nh31
Bastak IR 98 Nh31
Bastakaravan-Dames F 53 Lg43
Basti IND 117 Pa34
Bastia Umbria I 60 Lk47
Bastogne B 51 Lf41
Bastos BR 274 Hf55
Bastrop USA 238 Fd29
Basu IR 98 Nh31
Basudebpur IND 117 Pd35
Basuna BY 65 Mg38
BasHills IND 117 Pa34
Basu IR 98 Nh31
Basua RI 129 Qe49
Baswa IND 114 Oj32
Bat OM 95 Nj34
Báta H 66 Lu42
Batagarusa RUS 89 Rc05
Batan YE 94 Nb38
Batak RI 129 Qh48
Batakan RI 129 Qh48
Batala IND 114 Oh30
Batam RI 127 Qb45
Batama RDC 191 Mc44
Batan RP 124 Rb40
Batang CHN 109 Pk31
Batangafo RCA 190 Lk42
Batangas RP 124 Ra39
Batan Island RP 109 Rb35
Batan Islands RP 109 Ra35
Batanovci BG 68 Mc48
Batanta RI 154 Rf46
Batar RO 67 Mb44
Batas Island RP 124 Ra39
Bataszék H 67 Lt42
Batatais BR 275 Hg56
Batavia USA 241 Fk24
Batavia Downs AUS 147 Sb52
Bat Cave USA 242 Fj28
Batchelor AUS 146 Rf52
Batchelor CAM 189 Lf43
Batchenga CAM 189 Lf43
Batea E 57 La49
Bate-Nafadji RG 186 Kf40
Batemans Bay AUS 151 Sf63
Batesburg-Leesville USA 242 Fk29
Batesville USA 239 Ff28
Bath GB 49 Kh39
Bath GB 205 Md61
Batha TCH 183 Lj39
Batha-S TCH 184 Li37
Bathgate USA 236 Fa22
Bathinda IND 114 Oh30
Bathsheba BDS 251 Ha39
Ba Thuoc VN 121 Qc35
Bathurst AUS 151 Se62
Bathurst CDN 240 Gh22
Bathurst ZA 205 Md62
Bathurst Island AUS 146 Rf51
Bathurst Island CDN 227 Fa03
Bathurst Inlet CDN 226 Ec05
Batié BF 187 Kk41
Batié Mentese Dagları TR 71 Mh53
Batina IR 61 Lt45
Batinah OM 95 Nj33
Batken KS 100 Oh24
Batkhaan Uul Nature Reserve MNG 104 Qb23
Batoka Z 202 Mf54
Baton Rouge USA 239 Ff30
Batna DZ 176 Lc28
Batoche N.H.S. CDN 233 Eg19
Batman TR 91 Na27
Batnorov MNG 105 Qj22
Bato RP 124 Rc39
Bato RP 125 Qk43
Bat'ozek CZ 66 Lr42
Batoche N.H.S. CDN 233 Eg19
Batomga RUS 89 Rc07
Bat Öl MNG 104 Qa22
Bat-öngan Caves RP 124 Rc39

Batouala G 198 Lg45
Batouri CAM 189 Lh43
Batovi, T.I. BR 274 Hd52
Batovi G 198 Lg45
Batrahalli IND 118 Ok39
Batroun RL 90 Mh28
Battambang K 123 Qc40
Battchang CAM 189 Lf42
Batt Doeng K 123 Qc40
Battenberg D 58 Lj39
Batti Malv Island IND 122 Pg39
Batticaloa CL 119 Pa42
Batticaloa Beach CL 119 Pa42
Battipaglia I 63 Lr50
Battistero di Firenze □ I 60 Lm47
Battistero di Parma □ I 60 Lm46
Battle Camp AUS 147 Sc53
Battle Creek USA 237 Fh24
Battle of Colenso ZA 234 Eb25
Battle of Talana ZA 205 Mf60
Battonya □ H 67 Mb44
Batu RI WAN 188 Ld40
Batu Bolong Beach RI 130 Qh50
Batu Caves MAL 126 Qa44
Batudaka RI 130 Ra46
Batudaka RI 130 Ra46
Batu Danau MAL 128 Qh43
Batu Ferringhi Beach MAL 126 Pk43
Batum GE 91 Na25
Batum IR 91 Na25
Batumundan RI 127 Pd45
Batu Pahat MAL 127 Qb45
Batupanjang RI 127 Qa45
Baturetno RI 129 Qf50
Baturité BR 273 Ja49
Baturaja RI 127 Qc48
Batu Rakit MAL 126 Qb43
Batu Tambang RI 130 Ra48
Batyrevo RUS 72 Nd18
Bau MAL 128 Qf45
Bauang RP 124 Ra37
Bauchi WAN 188 Le40
Baud F 50 Kr43
Baude RG IND 117 Pc35
Baudh Raj IND 117 Pc35
Bauchan AUS 147 Sc36
Bauhaus E 52 Ku43
Bauhaus □ D 58 Ln40
Bauhausbauten und klassisches Weimar □ D 58 Lm40
Bauhinia Downs AUS 149 Se58
Bauk-Mekraproti, T.I. BR 271 Hd50
Baume-les-Dames F 53 Lg43
Bauna □ D 58 Lo39
Bauna I 62 Lk50
Baungan RP 126 Pk44
Baures BOL 270 Gj52
Bauru BR 274 Hf57
Bausendorf D 58 Lh41
Bauska LV 45 Me34
Bauta RDC 191 Mb45
Bautzen □ D 58 Lp39
Bauyrzhan KZ 97 Of24
Bavaria D 59 Lm42
Bavanište SRB 68 Ma45
Bavaro MEX 204 Ee31
Bavelloons □ MEX 204 Ee31
Baveno I 60 Lj44
Bavi VN 121 Qd35
Bavilla F 62 Lk49
Ba VI N.P. VN 121 Qd35
Bawal JI AUS 142 Qh56
Bawean RI 129 Qf48
Bawinkel D 58 Lh38
Bawku GH 187 Kk40
Bawlake MYA 120 Pj36
Bawley Point AUS 151 Sf63
Bawo Ofuloa RI 127 Pd46
Baxoi CHN 108 Q43
Baxter USA 236 Fc22
Baxter Springs USA 238 Fc27
Bay MNG 187 Kj39
Bay Bulls CDN 241 Hd22
Bay City USA 237 Fj24
Bay de Nord Wilderness Res. CDN 241 Hc21
Bayamo C 243 Gb35
Bayamón USA 251 Gg37
Bayan C 243 Gb35
Bayan CHN 106 Qc25
Bayan CHN 110 Rc22
Bayan MNG 101 Pk22
Bayan MNG 104 Qa22
Bayan MNG 104 Qa22
Bayan CHN 106 Qc25
Bayan MNG 104 Qd22
Bayan RI 130 Qj50
Bayan MNG 104 Qd22
Bayanaul MNG 100 Ok19
Bayanbaraat MNG 104 Qa22
Bayanbulag MNG 101 Pk22
Bayanda-Didi RCA 190 Lh43
Bayangol RCA 101 Qj44
Bayan Har Shan CHN 103 Pj28
Bayan Har Shankou CHN 103 Pj28
Bayankhongor MNG 104 Qa22
Bayankhoshuu MNG 101 Qj44
Bayan Obo CHN 106 Qc26
Bayan Olji CHN 106 Qc25
Bayan-Ovoo MNG 101 Pk23
Bayan-Ovoo MNG 105 Qj22
Bayansayr MNG 104 Pk23
Bayan Shan CHN 106 Qb26
Bayard USA 235 Eg28
Baydhabo SP 195 Nb44
Bayef USA 235 Ej25
Bayerischer Wald □ D 59 Ln41
Bayeux F 50 Ku41
Bayfield CDN 237 Fj24
Bayburt TR 91 Na26
Bayonet Point USA 242 Fj31
Bayombong RP 124 Ra37

Bayhan al Qasab YE 94 Nc38
Bayindir TR 71 Mh32
Bayir JOR 92 Mj30
Bayizhen CHN 103 Ph31
Bayji IRQ 91 Nb28
Bayju KZ 96 Ob23
Bayh Dat PK 99 Oc32
Bediondo IND 117 Lj41
Baykonur Cosmodrome KZ 96 Ob23
Bay Minette USA 239 Fg30
Baynes Mountains NAM 200 Lg54
Baynunah UAE 95 Nh34
Bayo, Cerro RCH 282 Gd68
Bayo, Cerro MEX 247 Fd36
Bay of Biscay F/E 52 Ks46
Bay of Campeche MEX 247 Fd36
Bay of Fundy CDN 240 Gg23
Bay of Islands CDN 241 Ha21
Bay of Islands NZ 152 Tj64
Bay of Plenty NZ 152 Tj64
Bay Grande, Cerro RA 282 Gg59
Bayombong RP 124 Ra37
Bayonne USA 233 Ej22
Bayón E 51 Lg42
Bayonet Point USA 243 Fj31
Bayonne F 52 Ks44
Bayou Cocodrie N.W.R. USA 239 Fe30
Bayóvar PE 268 Fk48
Bayramaly TM 96 Ob27
Bayramiç TR 71 Mg51
Bayreuth D 59 Lm41
Bayshint MNG 104 Qf22
Bay Shore USA 241 Ga24
Bay Springs USA 239 Ff30
Bayt al Faqih YE 94 Nb38
Baytik Shan CHN/MNG 101 Pf23
Baytown USA 238 Fc31
Bay Tree CDN 231 Ea18
Bayu RI 126 Pj43
Bayu-Undur MNG 104 Qc22
Bay View NZ 153 Tj65
Baza E 55 Kt53
Bazar-e Taleh AFG 97 Oe28
Bazas F 52 Ku44
Bazhong CHN 106 Qd28
Bazman IR 98 Nk31
Bazar Abad IR 91 Nf28
Behara RM 207 Nc56
Beharona RM 207 Nc56
Behbahan IR 91 Nf30
Beh Deh IR 98 Nj32
Behm Canal USA 230 De18
Behramkale TR 71 Mg51
Behrendt Mountains AN 286 Gb34
Behring Point BS 243 Gb33
Behror IND 114 Oj32
Bei'an CHN 105 Rd21
Beibei CHN 112 Rb30
Béibouco CI 187 Kg42
Beichuan CHN 106 Qc30
Beidaihe Haibin CHN 107 Qk28
Beidao CHN 106 Qd28
Beidaud RO 69 Mj46
Beigi ETH 192 Mh41
Beijing ● CHN 107 Qh26
Beijing Shi CHN 107 Qj25
Beilen NL 51 Lg38
Bei Ling CHN 110 Rb25
Beilngries D 59 Lm42
Beinamar TCH 190 Lh41
Beira MOC 203 Mh55
Beira Alta ANG 183 Lh50
Beira Alta I 54 Kn50
Beiring I 54 Kn50
Beirut ● RL 90 Mh29
Beisaren A 59 Mf36
Beiseker CDN 233 Ec20
Bei Shan CHN 101 Ph25
Beitun CHN 101 Pd22
Beirus RO 67 Mc44
Beizhangdian CHN 107 Qg27
Béja TN 176 Le27
Bejaïa DZ 176 Lc27
Béjar E 55 Kq50
Bejestan IR 98 Nj28
Bejucal C 250 Ga34
Bejpuram IND 117 Pb36
Bejnou KZ 96 Ob23
Beka CAM 189 Lg41
Beka CAM 189 Lh42
Bekaa Valley RL 90 Mh28
Bekal Beach IND 118 Oh39
Bekal Fort IND 118 Oh39
Bekaman TCH 190 Lj41
Bekandze IR 98 Nj32
Bekasi RI 129 Qd49
Békés □ H 67 Mb44
Békéscsaba □ H 67 Mb43
Bekily RM 207 Nc56
Bekipay RM 206 Nb54
Bekkal RM 207 Nc55
Bekobod UZ 97 Oe25
Bekobokar CDN 233 Ep20
Bekoboka RM 206 Nb54
Bekodoka RM 206 Nb53
Bekol RI 129 Qh49
Bekol RM 207 Nc55
Bekoropoka-Antongo RM 207 Nb56
Bekwai GH 187 Kk42
Bekwai GH 187 Kk42
Bela IND 116 Of34
Bela IND 116 Of34
Béla PNG 155 Sd49
Bela-Bela ZA 205 Md58
Belabo CAM 189 Lg43
Bel Air ● MS 207 Nj56
Bela Palanka SRB 68 Mc47
Belaer CZ 66 Ls41
Bela Vista BR 275 Hj54
Bela Vista ANG 200 Lg28
Bela Vista BR 268 Hd44
Bela Vista MOC 205 Mf59
Belau CHN 190 Lh41
Belaya RM 207 Nc55
Belchatów PL 65 Lu39
Belcheragh AFG 97 Oe28
Belcher Islands CDN 227 Ff07
Belchite E 57 Kt49
Beled H 66 Ls43
Belée CZ 66 Ls41
Belediweyne SP 195 Nc44
Bélédougou RMM 186 Kf39

Bedele ETH 192 Mj41
Bederkesa D 58 Li37
Bedford GB 49 Kj38
Bedford USA 238 Fe25
Bedford USA 239 Fg26
Bedford USA 241 Fk25
Bedford USA 239 Fk29
Bedi Dat PK 99 Oc32
Bediondo IND 117 Lj41
Bédouaram RN 183 Lg38
Bedourie AUS 148 Rk58
Beechwood USA 151 Sd64
Beechy Point USA 229 Cc10
Beech Grove USA 239 C710
Beechworth AUS 151 Sd64
Beelitz D 58 Ln38
Beer Arqo ETH 192 Mk41
Beer-Sheva IL 92 Mh30
Beerwah AUS 149 Sg59
Beeskow D 58 Lp38
Beethoven Peninsula AN 286 Gb33
Beeville USA 245 Fb31
Befale RDC 207 Nb57
Befandefa RM 207 Nb56
Befasy RM 207 Nc56
Beforta DY 188 La41
Befori RDC 190 Mb45
Befotaka RM 206 Nb53
Befotaka RM 207 Nc57
Bega AUS 151 Se64
Begamganj BD 120 Pf34
Begamganj IND 117 Ok34
Bégard F 50 Kr42
Bégendik TR 69 Mj49
Begogo RM 207 Nd57
Begogo RCA 190 Lh42
Begovo GH 187 Kk42
Begunicy RUS 44 Mk31
Beg Abad IR 98 Nh30
Behara RM 207 Nc56
Beharona RM 207 Nc56
Behbahan IR 91 Nf30
Beh Deh IR 98 Nj32
Behm Canal USA 230 De18
Behramkale TR 71 Mg51
Behrendt Mountains AN 286 Gb34
Behring Point BS 243 Gb33
Behror IND 114 Oj32
Bei'an CHN 105 Rd21
Beibei CHN 112 Rb30
Béibouco CI 187 Kg42
Beichuan CHN 106 Qc30
Beidaihe Haibin CHN 107 Qk28
Beidao CHN 106 Qd28
Beidaud RO 69 Mj46
Beigi ETH 192 Mh41
Beijing ● CHN 107 Qh26
Beijing Shi CHN 107 Qj25
Beilen NL 51 Lg38
Bei Ling CHN 110 Rb25
Beilngries D 59 Lm42
Beinamar TCH 190 Lh41
Beira MOC 203 Mh55
Beira Alta ANG 183 Lh50
Beira Litoral P 54 Kn50
Beirut ● RL 90 Mh29
Beisaren A 59 Mf36
Beiseker CDN 233 Ec20
Bei Shan CHN 101 Ph25
Beitun CHN 101 Pd22
Beius RO 67 Mc44
Beizhangdian CHN 107 Qg27
Béja TN 176 Le27
Bejaïa DZ 176 Lc27
Béjar E 55 Kq50
Bejestan IR 98 Nj28
Bejucal C 250 Ga34
Bejpuram IND 117 Pb36
Bejnou KZ 96 Ob23
Beka CAM 189 Lg41
Beka CAM 189 Lh42
Bekaa Valley RL 90 Mh28
Bekal Beach IND 118 Oh39
Bekal Fort IND 118 Oh39
Bekaman TCH 190 Lj41
Bekandze IR 98 Nj32
Bekasi RI 129 Qd49
Békés H 67 Mb44
Békéscsaba H 67 Mb43
Bekily RM 207 Nc56
Bekipay RM 206 Nb54
Bekkal RM 207 Nc55
Bekobod UZ 97 Oe25
Bekoboka RM 206 Nb54
Bekodoka RM 206 Nb53
Bekol RI 129 Qh49
Bekoropoka-Antongo RM 207 Nb56
Bekwai GH 187 Kk42
Bela IND 116 Of34
Bela PNG 155 Sd49
Bela-Bela ZA 205 Md58
Belabo CAM 189 Lg43
Bel Air ● MS 207 Nj56
Bela Palanka SRB 68 Mc47
Bela Vista BR 275 Hj54
Bela Vista ANG 200 Lg28
Bela Vista BR 268 Hd44
Bela Vista MOC 205 Mf59
Belaya RM 207 Nc55
Belchatów PL 65 Lu39
Belcheragh AFG 97 Oe28
Belcher Islands CDN 227 Ff07
Belchite E 57 Kt49
Beled H 66 Ls43
Belediweyne SP 195 Nc44
Bélédougou RMM 186 Kf39

Béléhédé – Bi'r Tanjdar

Béléhédé BF 181 Kk38
Béléko RMM 187 Kg39
Bélel CAM 189 Lh42
Belel WAN 189 Lg41
Belém BR 267 Hf46
Belém BR 270 Gf47
Belém de São Francisco BR 273 Ja50
Belen CO 264 Gd42
Belén CR 248 Fh40
Belén PA 249 Fk41
Belén PY 274 Hb57
Belén RA 279 Gg59
Belén RCH 278 Gf55
Belén ROU 276 Hb61
Belen TR 90 Mj27
Belen USA 235 Eg28
elet Weyne SP 193 Nc43
elev RUS 72 Mj19
èleya RG 186 Ke40
elezma, P.N. de DZ 176 Lc28
elfast GB 47 Kp36
elfast USA 241 Gf23
elfast ZA 205 Mf58
elfield USA 233 Ej22
elfir RO 67 Mb44
elfodiyo ETH 192 Mh40
elford GB 48 Kt35
elfort F 53 Lg43
elgachhi IND 117 Pd33
elgaum IND 116 Oh38
elgaum Fort IND 116 Oh38
elgern D 58 Lo39
elgium B 51 Le40
elgo SUD 185 Mg40
elgodère F 60 Lk48
elgorod RUS 72 Mj20
elgrade SR 68 Ma46
elgrade USA 233 Ee23
elgrade USA 236 Fc23
elgrano, Cerro RA 282 Ge69
elgrano II ANT 286 Jb34
elhar IND 117 Pd33
elhatti IND 116 Oh38
elhirane DZ 176 Ld30
éli GNB 186 Kd40
eli WAN 189 Lf42
elic C 243 Gb36
elica MK 68 Ma49
elidzi RUS 91 Ne25
elifang CAM 188 Lf42
eli Izvor BG 68 Md47
eli Manastir HR 61 Lt45
elimbing RI 127 Qc48
elin-Béliet F 52 Ku46
elinga G 189 Lg45
elinyu RI 127 Qc46
eliş RO 67 Md44
elišće HR 61 Lt45
elitsaka RM 207 Nc54
elitung RI 129 Qd47
elize ANG 198 Lg48
elize 248 Ff37
elize Barrier Reef System BH 248 Fg37
elize City BH 248 Ff37
eljanovo BG 69 Mf47
elkar IND 116 Og37
elkhera IND 117 Ok34
el'ki BY 45 Mh35
l'kovo RUS 72 Mg19
ll AUS 149 Sf59
ll ZA 205 Md62
lla CAM 188 Lf44
lla Bella CDN 230 Df19
llac F 52 Lb44
lla Coola CDN 230 Dg19
lladère DOM 250 Ge36
lla Flor BOL 270 Gg51
llágio I 60 Lk45
llalie AUS 148 Sb59
llária-Igea Marina I 60 Ln46
llary IND 118 Oj38
llata AUS 149 Se60
lla Unión ROU 276 Hb61
llavista CO 264 Gb42
llavista PE 268 Ga48
llavista PE 268 Gb49
lla Vista RA 276 Ha60
lla Vista RA 279 Gh59
lla Vista Norte PY 274 Hb57
l Brook AUS 149 Sg61
lburns CDN 241 Hb20
lle Anse RH 250 Gd36
lleden Ker AUS 147 Sc54
llefontaine USA 237 Fj25
llefonte USA 241 Gb25
llegarde F 53 Lc43
llegarde-sur-Valserine F 53 Lf44
le Glade USA 243 Fk32
le-Île F 50 Kr43
le Isle CDN 241 Hc20
lême F 50 La42
lenden Ker N.P. AUS 147 Sd54
leoram CDN 241 Hc22
le Plaine USA 236 Fd23
leterre CDN 237 Ga22
leville CDN 241 Gb23
leville F 53 Le44
leville USA 238 Fb26
leville USA 239 Fe26
leville ZA 204 Lk62
leville-sur-Vie F 52 Kt44
levue AUS 147 Sc54
levue USA 232 Dj22
levue USA 232 Ec24
levue USA 236 Fc25
levue USA 237 Fj25
ley F 53 Lf45
le Yella LB 186 Kf42
lfield AUS 147 Sb55
l Fourche USA 233 Ej23
lingham USA 232 Dj21
lingrath Gardens USA 239 Ff30
lingshausen ANT 286 Ha30
lingshausen Sea ANT 287 Fd32
linzona CH 60 Lk44
l Island CDN 241 Hc20
l Island Hot Springs USA 230 De18
lo CO 264 Gc42
locq RA 281 Gk63
lows Falls USA 241 Gd24
lpat PK 99 Od31
l Peninsula CDN 227 Fd06
lpuig E 57 Lb49
l River CDN 229 Db12
l Rock 48 Ks34
rose AUS 149 Sd59
's Beach AUS 151 Sc65
uno I 60 Ln44
Ville RA 281 Gj62
mez E 55 Kp52
mond USA 236 Fd24
mont GB 48 Ku30
mont USA 242 Fk28
mont ZA 205 Mc60
monte BR 275 Ja53
monte E 57 Ks51
monte P 54 Kn50
monte de Miranda E 54 Ko47
mont Park USA 241 Gd25
mont Park Racecourse AUS 144 Qh61
mopan BH 248 Ff37
mopan BH 248 Ff37
more AUS 150 Sa62
mullet IRL 47 Kl36
o RM 207 Nc56
obaka RM 207 Nc55
o Campo BR 275 Hk53
œil B 51 Ld40
ogorsk RUS 105 Re20
ogradčik BG 68 Mc47
ogradčiški Skali BG 68 Mc47
oha RM 207 Nc58
o Horizonte BR 275 Hj55
oit USA 237 Ff24
oit USA 238 Fa26
o Jardim BR 273 Jb50
ojarovo RUS 105 Re20
ojarskij RUS 88 Ob06
oko RCA 190 Lh43
o Monte BR 270 Gh49
o Monte do Pontal BR 267 He47
onge RDC 199 Ma47
orado E 56 Kr48
orečensk RUS 73 Mk23
Beloslav BG 69 Mh47
Belotinci BG 68 Mc47
Belo Tsiribihina RM 207 Nc55
Belovodskoe KS 100 Oh24
Belpasso I 63 Lp53
Belper GB 49 Kt37
Belpre USA 239 Fk26
Belsay GB 48 Kt35
Bel'skaja vozvyšennost' RUS 72 Mg18
Beltana AUS 148 Rk61
Belterra BR 271 Hc47
Beltinci SLO 66 Lr44
Beltiug RO 67 Mc43
Belton USA 238 Fb30
Belton USA 242 Fj28
Beltov Qirlari UZ 96 Oa24
Belturbet IRL 47 Kn36
Beluguppa IND 118 Oj38
Belur IND 118 Oh39
Beluran MAL 128 Qj43
Beluru MAL 128 Qh44
Belvedere Maríttimo I 63 Lq51
Belvès F 52 La46
Belvidere USA 237 Ff24
Belvidere Kerk ZA 204 Mb63
Belyj RUS 72 Mg18
Belz UA 65 Me40
Belzig D 58 Ln38
Belzoni USA 239 Fe29
Bełżyce PL 65 Mc39
Béma RMM 180 Kf38
Bémal RCA 190 Lj42
Bemanevika RM 206 Ne52
Bemanevika RM 206 Nf53
Bemarivo RM 207 Nc56
Bembe ANG 198 Lh49
Bembeche TCH 183 Lk36
Bembesi ZW 202 Me56
Bemboka AUS 151 Se64
Bemetara IND 117 Pa35
Bemidji USA 236 Fc22
Bemonto RM 207 Nc55
Ben BF 187 Kh39
Bena WAN 188 Lc40
Benabarre E 56 La48
Bena-Dibele RDC 199 Mb48
Benagerie AUS 148 Sa61
Ben-Ahmed MA 175 Kg29
Bena-Kamba RDC 199 Mc47
Ben Alberts Nature Reserve ZA 205 Md58
Benalla AUS 151 Sc64
Benalup de Sidonia E 55 Kp54
Benamaurel E 55 Ks53
Ben Amera RIM 180 Kd35
Benato-Toby RM 207 Nc57
Bena-Tshadi RDC 199 Mb48
Benavente E 54 Kp49
Benavides E 54 Kp48
Benavides USA 245 Fa32
Ben Badis DZ 175 Kk28
Ben Boyd N.P. AUS 151 Se64
Bencés főapátság H 66 Ls43
Bencha CHN 112 Ra29
Bencheng CHN 107 Qk26
Bencubbin AUS 144 Qj61
Bend USA 232 Dk23
Béndana TCH 190 Lk41
Benda Range AUS 150 Sa62
Bendela RDC 199 Lj47
Bendeleben Mts. USA 229 Bj13
Bendemeer AUS 149 Sf61
Bender Beyla SP 193 Nf41
Bendigo AUS 151 Sc64
Bend of the Boyne IRL 47 Ko37
Bendorf D 58 Lh40
Bendugu WAL 186 Ke41
Bene MOC 202 Mg53
Beneditinos BR 273 Hj48
Benedito Leite BR 272 Hh49
Benejama E 57 Ku52
Benemérito de las Américas MEX 247 Fe37
Bénéna RMM 187 Kh39
Bénénikényi RMM 187 Kh39
Benenitra RM 207 Nc57
Benešov CZ 66 Lp41
Benevento I 63 Lp49
Benevides BR 267 Hf46
Benga MOC 202 Mg54
Benga MW 196 Mh52
Bengabad IND 117 Pd33
Bengala CO 264 Gd43
Bengala IND 122 Pg41
Bengamisa RDC 191 Mc45
Bengbis CAM 189 Lg44
Bengbu CHN 112 Qj29
Benge USA 232 Ea22
Benghazi LAR 177 Ma29
Bengkalis RI 127 Qb45
Bengkalis RI 127 Qb45
Bengkulu RI 127 Qb47
Bengoi RI 131 Rf47
Bengough CDN 233 Eh21
Beng Per W.S. K 123 Qc39
Bengtsfors S 42 Ln31
Benguela ANG 200 Lg52
Ben Guerdane TN 176 Lf29
Ben Guerir MA 175 Kg29
Beni BOL 270 Gh51
Beni NEP 115 Pb31
Beni RDC 191 Me45
Beni-Abbès DZ 175 Kj30
Beni Barka TN 176 Lf29
Benicarló E 57 La50
Benicasim = Benicàssim E 57 La50
Benicàssim E 57 La50
Benidorm E 57 Ku52
Benifaió E 57 Ku51
Beni Hammad DZ 176 Lc28
Beni Haoua DZ 176 La27
Beni Hassan ET 179 Mf32
Beni Hassan el Shuruq ET 179 Mf32
Beni Kheddache TN 176 Lf29
Beni Mazâr ET 179 Mf31
Beni-Mellal MA 175 Kg29
Benin WAN 188 Lc43
Benin 163 La08
Benin City WAN 188 Lc42
Benin Iya WAN 188 Lc42
Beni-Ounif DZ 175 Kk29
Beni Saf DZ 175 Kk28
Benisheikh WAN 189 Lg40
Beni Slimane DZ 176 Lb27
Beni-Smir DZ/MA 175 Kk29
Beni Suêf ET 179 Mf31
Beni-Tajjite MA 175 Kj29
Benito CDN 236 Ek20
Benito Juárez MEX 244 Eg30
Benito Juárez MEX 244 Eg31
Benito Juárez MEX 246 Ej35
Benito Juárez MEX 247 Fd37
Benito Juárez RA 281 Ha64
Benito Juárez, P.N. MEX 246 Fb37
Benito Juárez (Sierra Hermosa) MEX 246 Ek34
Beni-Yal MA 175 Kj29
Benjamin USA 238 Fa29
Benjamín Aceval PY 276 Hb58
Benjamin Constant BR 268 Ge48
Benjamin Hill MEX 244 Ee30
Benjina RI 154 Rh49
Benkayang RI 129 Qe45
Benkelman USA 238 Ek25
Benkovac HR 61 Lq46
Ben Lavin Nature Reserve ZA 202 Me57
Ben Lawers GB 48 Kq34
Ben Lomond N.P. AUS 151 Sd66
Ben Luc VN 123 Qd40
Ben Macdui GB 48 Kr33
Benmara AUS 146 Rj54
Ben Mehidi DZ 176 Ld27
Ben More GB 48 Ko34
Ben More GB 48 Kq34
Ben More Assynt GB 48 Kq32
Ben Moussa MA 175 Kg29
Benndale USA 239 Ff30
Bennetsville USA 242 Ga28
Bennett CDN 230 Dc16
Bennett USA 235 Eh26
Bennett Dam, W.A.C. CDN 230 Dj17
Ben Nevis GB 48 Kq34
Bennichchâb RIM 180 Kc36
Bennington USA 241 Gd24
Bénodet F 50 Kq43
Benoni ZA 205 Me59
Benoud DZ 175 La29
Bénoué = Benue WAN 188 Le42
Bénoué, P.N. de la CAM 189 Lg41
Bénoye TCH 190 Lj41
Ben Quang VN 121 Qd37
Ben S'Bour DZ 176 Lc28
Bensékou DY 188 Lb40
Bensheim D 59 Lj41
Ben-Slimane MA 175 Kg29
Benson USA 235 Ee30
Benson USA 236 Fc23
Ben Starav GB 48 Kp34
Bent IR 98 Nk32
Benteng RI 130 Ra49
Benteng Belgica RI 131 Rf48
Bentia RMM 181 La38
Bentick Island MYA 122 Pj40
Bentinck Island AUS 147 Rk54
Bentinck Sound MYA 122 Pj38
Bentiu SUD 191 Me41
Bentley CDN 233 Ec19
Bento Gonçalves BR 276 He60
Benton USA 234 Ea27
Benton USA 238 Fd28
Benton USA 238 Fd29
Benton USA 239 Ff27
Bentong MAL 126 Qa44
Benton Harbor USA 237 Fg24
Bentonsport USA 236 Fe25
Bentonsport Nat. Hist. District USA 236 Fe25
Bentota Beach CL 119 Ok42
Bentuang Karimun Nature Reserve RI 128 Qg45
Benty RG 186 Kd41
Benua RI 129 Qd45
Benue WAN 188 Ld41
Benwee Head IRL 47 Kl36
Benxi CHN 110 Rb25
Benza ANG 198 Lg49
Benzdorp SME 266 Hc44
Ben-Ziareg DZ 175 Kk30
Beo RI 125 Rd43
Beoga RI 154 Rj47
Beograd-Surcin SRB 68 Ma46
Beohari IND 117 Pa33
Béoumi CI 187 Kh42
Beowawe USA 234 Eb25
Beppu J 113 Rf29
Beqa FJI 159 Tk55
Bequia WV 251 Gk39
Bequimão BR 267 Hh47
Ber RMM 181 Kj37
Berabevu RA 281 Gk62
Berahle ETH 192 Mk39
Beraketa RM 207 Nc58
Berakit Beach RI 127 Qc45
Beramanja RM 206 Ne52
Bérandjokou RCB 190 Lj44
Berangang RI 127 Qb46
Berasia IND 116 Oj34
Beraspapan RI 129 Qh46
Berastagi RI 126 Pk44
Berat AL 70 Lu50
Berat Fortesë AL 70 Lu50
Beravina RM 207 Nc55
Beravy RM 207 Nc56
Berazino BY 45 Mj36
Berazino BY 72 Me19
Berbak National Park RI 127 Qb46
Berber SUD 185 Mg36
Berbera SP 193 Nc40
Berbérati RCA 190 Lh43
Berbinzana E 56 Kt48
Berceto I 60 Lk46
Berchtesgaden D 59 Ln43
Berchtesgaden, N.P. D 59 Ln43
Berck-Plage F 51 Lb40
Berdaale SP 195 Nb44
Berdale SP 193 Nd42
Berdía E 54 Km48
Berdjans'k UA 73 Mj22
Berdjans'ka kosa UA 73 Mj22
Berdsk RUS 88 Pa08
Berdyčiv UA 73 Me21
Bére TCH 190 Lj41
Berea USA 239 Fh27
Béréba BF 187 Kj40
Berebere RI 125 Re44
Bereeda SP 193 Nf40
Berega EAT 197 Mj49
Berehomet UA 67 Mf42
Berehove UA 67 Mc42
Bereina PNG 155 Sd50
Bereketa RM 207 Nc57
Bereku EAT 197 Mh48
Berekua WD 251 Gk38
Berekum GH 187 Kj42
Berendi TR 90 Mh27
Berenice ET 179 Mh34
Berens Island CDN 236 Fb19
Berens River CDN 236 Fb19
Berenty RM 207 Nc57
Bere Regis GB 49 Ks40
Beresford USA 236 Fb24
Berestečko UA 65 Mf40
Berestjane UA 65 Mf40
Berettyóújfalu H 67 Mb43
Berevo RM 207 Nc55
Berezanka UA 73 Mf22
Berezanskaja RUS 73 Mk23
Berežany UA 67 Me41
Berezinsky Biosphere Nature Reserve BY 45 Mj36
Berezna UA 72 Mf20
Berezne UA 72 Md20
Bereznehuvate UA 73 Mg22
Berezniki RUS 88 Nd07
Berežnycja UA 65 Mg39
Berga E 56 Lb48
Bergama TR 71 Mh51
Bergamo I 60 Lk45
Bergantin YV 265 Gh41
Bergantiños E 54 Km47
Bergara E 56 Ks47
Bergen D 43 Lo36
Bergen D 58 Lk38
Bergen N 42 Lf30
Berg en Dal SME 266 Hc43
Bergen op Zoom NL 51 Le39
Bergensbanen N 40 Lg30
Berger N 42 Ll31
Bergerac F 52 La46
Bergheim D 58 Lg40
Bergland CDN 236 Fc21
Bergland NAM 204 Lj57
Bergland USA 236 Ff22
Bergo FIN 41 Mb28
Bergo FIN 41 Mb28
Bergshamra S 43 Lt31
Bergsig NAM 200 Lh56
Bergsjö S 41 Ls29
Bergues F 51 Lc40
Bergville ZA 205 Me60
Berhait IND 117 Pd33
Berhamapur IND 117 Pc36
Berilo BR 275 Hj54
Beringarra AUS 144 Qj59
Beringen B 51 Lf39
Bering Glacier USA 230 Cj15
Bering Land Bridge National Preserve USA 229 Bh13
Bering Sea USA/RUS 226 Ba06
Bering Strait USA/RUS 210 Ba03
Berisu IR 91 Nc27
Berja E 55 Ks54
Berkane MA 175 Kj28
Berkeley USA 234 Dj27
Berkh MNG 104 Qf22
Berkner Island 286 Hc34
Berkovica BG 68 Md47
Berkovici BIH 68 Lt47
Berlanga E 55 Kp52
Berlanga de Duero E 56 Ks49
Berlenga P 55 Kl51
Berlevåg N 39 Mj20
Berlin CO 264 Gd42
Berlin D 58 Lo38
Berlin USA 237 Ff24
Berlin USA 241 Ge23
Berlin, Mount 286 Da34
Bermagui AUS 151 Sf64
Bermejillo MEX 245 Ej33
Bermejo BOL 279 Gh57
Bermejo BOL/RA 279 Gh57
Bermejo PE 269 Gb51
Bermejo RA 279 Gf61
Bermeo E 56 Ks47
Bermillo de Sayago E 54 Ko49
Bermo RN 182 Ld38
Bermuda GB 211 Gb06
Bermuda Islands GB 210 Gb06
Bernabé Rivera ROU 276 Hb61
Bernalda I 63 Lr50
Bernalillo USA 235 Eg28
Bernardo C 250 Gc35
Bernardo USA 235 Eg28
Bernardo de Irigoyen RA 276 Hd59
Bernardo O'Higgins, P.N. RCH 282 Gc70
Bernartice CZ 66 Lp41
Bernāti LV 45 Ma34
Bernau D 58 Lo38
Bernaville F 51 Lc40
Bernay F 50 La41
Bernburg D 58 Lm39
Berndorf A 61 Lr43
Berne CH 60 Lh44
Berner Alpen CH 60 Lh44
Berneray GB 48 Kn33
Berner Oberland CH 60 Lg44
Bernham USA 238 Fb30
Bernice USA 239 Fd29
Bernier Island AUS 144 Qg58
Bernkastel-Kues D 59 Lh41
Bernsdorf D 58 Lp39
Berón de Astrada RA 276 Hb59
Beronovo BG 69 Mg48
Beroroha RM 207 Nc56
Beroun CZ 66 Lp41
Berounka CZ 66 Lo41
Berovo MK 68 Mc49
Berraha DZ 176 Ld27
Berraondo RA 281 Gj65
Berrechid MA 175 Kg29
Berre-l'Étang F 53 Lf47
Berri AUS 150 Sa63
Berriane DZ 176 Lb29
Berridale AUS 151 Se64
Berrigan AUS 151 Sc63
Berrima AUS 151 Sf63
Berrouaghia DZ 176 Lb27
Berrydale USA 239 Fg30
Berry Islands BS 243 Gb33
Berryville USA 238 Fd27
Berryville USA 241 Gb26
Beršad' UA 73 Me21
Berseba NAM 204 Lj59
Bersenbrück D 58 Lh38
Berteştii de Jos RO 69 Mh46
Bertincourt F 51 Ld40
Bertinho BR 267 He47
Bertolínia BR 273 Hj49
Bertoua CAM 189 Lg43
Bertrand CDN 240 Gh22
Bertrix B 51 Lf41
Bertwell CDN 233 Ej19
Beruniy UZ 96 Oa25
Beruri BR 270 Gk47
Beruwala CL 119 Ok42
Berwick AUS 151 Sc64
Berwick CDN 240 Gh23
Berwick USA 241 Gb25
Berwick-upon-Tweed GB 48 Ks35
Beryslav UA 73 Mg22
Berzence H 66 Ls44
Bērzpils LV 45 Mh34
Besakih RI 129 Qh50
Besalampy RM 207 Nc54
Besalú E 56 Lc48
Besançon F 53 Lg43
Besani IND 117 Pa33
Bešankovičy BY 72 Me18
Besar MAL 126 Qb44
Besar MAL 126 Qc44
Besar RI 130 Rb50
Besar, Gunung RI 129 Qg48
Besassi DY 188 Lb40
Beschoky tau KZ 96 Ng23
Besedino RUS 72 Mj20
Besenyszög H 67 Ma43
Beshahr IR 96 Ng27
Besham PK 97 Og28
Beshariq UZ 97 Of25
Beshkent UZ 97 Oc26
Beshneh IR 98 Nh31
Beshtom UZ 96 Oa24
Besikama RI 131 Rc50
Besir RI 131 Rf46
Beskid Mountains PL/SK 67 Mb41
Beskid Wysoki PL 65 Lu41
Beslan RUS 91 Nc24
Besni TR 90 Mj27
Bessa Monteiro ANG 198 Lg49
Béssao TCH 190 Lh42
Bessarabia MD 73 Me22
Bessaz tau KZ 97 Oe24
Bessèges F 53 Le46
Bessemer USA 239 Fg29
Bessoung Kang CAM 188 Le43
Best NL 51 Lf39
Bestavarapeta IND 119 Ok38
Bestwig D 58 Lj39
Besuki RI 129 Qg49
Beswick AUS 146 Rg53
Beswick A.L. AUS 146 Rg53
Beta IND 117 Pb33
Betafo RM 207 Nd55
Betalevana RM 207 Ne54
Betanantanana RM 207 Nc55
Betancuria E 174 Kc31
Betânia BR 273 Ja50
Betânia BR 278 Gk53
Betania CO 264 Gd43
Betânia, T.I. BR 270 Gf47
Betanty RM 207 Nc58
Betanzos BOL 278 Gh55
Betanzos E 54 Km47
Betarara VU 158 Te53
Bétaré Oya CAM 189 Lh43
Betatakin Ruin USA 235 Ee27
Bete Hor ETH 192 Mk40
Betein WAN 188 Le43
Bétera E 57 Ku51
Beteta E 57 Ks50
Bethal ZA 205 Me59
Bethanie NAM 204 Lj59
Bethany USA 238 Fc25
Bethel USA 228 Bk15
Bethel USA 238 Fc28
Bethlehem IL 92 Mh30
Bethlehem ZA 205 Me60
Bethulie ZA 205 Mc61
Béthune F 51 Lc40
Betim BR 275 Hh55
Betioky RM 207 Nc57
Betita DZ 176 Ld28
Betong MAL 128 Qf45
Betong THA 123 Qa43
Betoota AUS 148 Sa58
Bétou RCB 190 Lk44
Betpak Dala KZ 88 Ob09
Betrandraka RM 207 Nd54
Betroka RM 207 Nd57
Betsaa RB 201 Mb55
Bet Shean IL 90 Mh29
Betsiaka RM 206 Ne52
Betsy Bay BS 250 Gd34
Bettiah IND 117 Pc32
Bettié CI 187 Kj42
Bettiesdam ZA 205 Me59
Bettles USA 229 Ce12
Bettloua DZ 175 Kk28
Bettna S 43 Lr32
Béttola I 60 Lk46
Betton F 50 Kt42
Bettyhill GB 48 Kq32
Betul IND 116 Oj35
Betulia CO 264 Gb42
Betung RI 127 Qc47
Betws-y-Coed GB 49 Kr37
Betzdorf D 58 Lh40
Béu ANG 198 Lh49
Beulah AUS 150 Sb63
Beulah USA 236 Ek22
Beulah USA 237 Fg23
Beulaville USA 242 Gb28
Beurfou TCH 183 Lh38
Beurkia TCH 183 Lj38
Beurkié TCH 183 Lj36
Bevato RM 207 Nd55
Beveren B 51 Le39
Beverley AUS 144 Qj62
Beverley GB 49 Ku37
Beverly CDN 233 Ef20
Beverly Hills USA 242 Fj31
Beverly Springs AUS 143 Rc54
Beverstedt D 58 Lj37
Beverungen D 58 Lk39
Bevoalavo Andrefana RM 207 Nc58
Bevoay RM 207 Nb56
Bewani PNG 155 Sa47
Bewar IND 115 Ok32
Bewar IND 117 Ok33
Beyağaç TR 71 Mj53
Beyazçeşme Şelâlesi TR 91 Nb26
Beyçayırı TR 69 Mg50
Beydağ TR 71 Mj52
Bey Dağları TR 90 Mf27
Beykoz TR 69 Mk49
Beyla RG 186 Kf41
Beylaqan AZ 91 Nd26
Beylul ER 192 Nb39
Beypazarı TR 90 Mf25
Beypore IND 118 Oh40
Beyra SP 193 Nd42
Beyşehir TR 90 Mf27
Beyşehir Gölü TR 90 Mf27
Beytüşşebap TR 91 Nb27
Bezaha RM 207 Nc57
Bežanickaja vozvyšennost' RUS 72 Me17
Bežanicy RUS 72 Me17
Bezanson CDN 231 Ea18
Bezas E 57 Kt50
Bezdan SRB 68 Lt45
Bežeck RUS 72 Mj17
Bežeckij verhnij RUS 72 Mj17
Bezeklik Qianfo Dong CHN 101 Pe24
Bezerros BR 273 Jc50
Béziers F 53 Ld47
Bez'va RUS 44 Mj32
Bhabbar IND 116 Of33
Bhabua IND 117 Pb33
Bhadasar IND 114 Oh31
Bhadora IND 117 Pa34
Bhadra IND 114 Oh31
Bhadrachalam IND 117 Pa37
Bhadrakh IND 117 Pd35
Bhadrapur NEP 120 Pe32
Bhadravati IND 118 Oh39
Bhadra W.S. IND 118 Oh39
Bhadreswar IND 120 Pe34
Bhag PK 99 Od31
Bhagalpur IND 117 Pd33
Bhagamandala IND 118 Oh39
Bhaguapura IND 117 Ok32
Bhainsrorgarh IND 116 Oh33
Bhai Pheru PK 99 Og30
Bhairab Bazar BD 120 Pf33
Bhairamgarh IND 117 Pa36
Bhairi Hol PK 99 Oc33
Bhaisa IND 116 Oj36
Bhakarapeta IND 119 Ok39
Bhakkar PK 99 Of30
Bhaktapur NEP 115 Pc32
Bhalki IND 116 Oj37
Bhaluka BD 120 Pf33
Bhalwal PK 99 Og29
Bhamo MYA 120 Pj33
Bhanbore PK 99 Od33
Bhandara IND 117 Ok35
Bhandari IND 120 Ph32
Bhandarwah 114 Oh29
Bhander IND 117 Ok33
Bhanga BD 120 Pf34
Bhanjanagar IND 117 Pc36
Bhanpura IND 116 Oj33
Bhanupratappur IND 117 Pa35
Bhaptiahi IND 117 Pd32
Bharatpur IND 115 Oj32
Bharatpur NEP 115 Pc32
Bharatpur National Park = Keoladeo National Park IND 114 Oj32
Bharda NEP 117 Pd32
Bharthana IND 117 Ok32
Bharuch IND 116 Og35
Bhata NEP 117 Pc32
Bhatagli IND 116 Oj36
Bhatapara IND 117 Pa35
Bhatgaon IND 117 Pb35
Bhatiapara BD 120 Pe34
Bhatkal IND 118 Oh39
Bhattiprolu IND 117 Pa37
Bhaun PK 99 Og29
Bhavani IND 118 Oj40
Bhavnagar IND 116 Og35
Bhawal N.P. BD 120 Pf33
Bhawana PK 99 Og30
Bhawanipatna IND 117 Pb36
Bhawra IND 116 Oj34
Bheemunipatnam IND 117 Pb37
Bheemunipatnam Beach IND 117 Pb37
Bhelsi IND 117 Ok33
Bhera PK 99 Og29
Bherdaghat Marble Rocks IND 117 Ok34
Bheri River Rafting NEP 115 Pb31
Bhigvan IND 116 Oh36
Bhikamkor IND 114 Og32
Bhilai IND 117 Pa35
Bhilwara IND 116 Oh33
Bhim IND 116 Oh33
Bhimavaram IND 117 Pa37
Bhimbar PK 99 Oh29
Bhimbetka IND 116 Oj34
Bhimpur IND 116 Oj35
Bhind IND 117 Ok32
Bhinmal IND 116 Og33
Bhisi IND 117 Ok35
Bhita IND 117 Pa33
Bhitarkanika Sanctuary IND 117 Pd35
Bhitarwar IND 117 Ok33
Bhiwandi IND 116 Og36
Bhiwani IND 114 Oj31
Bhognipur IND 117 Ok32
Bhojpur IND 116 Oj34
Bhojpur IND 117 Pc35
Bhokar IND 116 Oj36
Bhola BD 120 Pf34
Bholari PK 99 Oe33
Bhongaon IND 115 Ok32
Bhongir IND 117 Ok37
Bhopal IND 116 Oj34
Bhopalpatnam IND 117 Pa36
Bhoramdeo IND 117 Pa34
Bhore IND 117 Pc32
Bhorvadi IND 116 Oh36
Bhuban IND 117 Pc35
Bhubaneswar IND 117 Pc35
Bhuj IND 116 Oe34
Bhusawal IND 116 Oh35
Bhutan BHT 120 Pe32
Biadola IND 120 Pe33
Biafra WAN 188 Le43
Biak RI 130 Rb46
Biak RI 154 Rj46
Biak RI 154 Rj46
Biak Utara Nature Reserve RI 154 Rh46
Biała Piska PL 65 Mc37
Biała Podlaska PL 65 Md38
Białka PL 65 Ma41
Białobrzegi PL 65 Ma39
Białobrzegi PL 65 Mc40
Białogard PL 64 Lq36
Białopole PL 65 Md40
Białowieski P.N. PL 65 Md37
Białowieża PL 65 Md38
Biały Bór PL 64 Lr37
Białystok PL 65 Md37
Bianco I 63 Lr52
Bianga RCA 190 Ma43
Biankouma CI 187 Kg42
Bia N.P. GH 187 Kj42
Biaora IND 116 Oj34
Biaranga RDC 199 Lk46
Biaro RDC 191 Mc45
Biaro RI 125 Rc44
Biarritz F 52 Kt47
Biasca CH 60 Lj44
Biawak MAL 128 Qe45
Bibâ ET 179 Mf31
Biba RI 127 Qc48
Bibai J 111 Sa24
Bibala ANG 200 Lg53
Bibas G 189 Lf45
Bibbiena I 60 Lm47
Bibé CAM 189 Lg43
Bibémi CAM 189 Lg41
Biberach D 59 Lk42
Bibiani GH 187 Kj42
Bibi-Jawindi Mausoleum PK 99 Of31
Bibikovo RUS 105 Rd20
Bibile CL 119 Pa42
Bibi Nani PK 99 Od31
Biboohra AUS 147 Sc54
Bibora G 198 Lf47
Bibrka UA 67 Me41
Bicade F 266 Hd44
Bicaj AL 68 Ma49
Bicanak asr. ARM/AZ 91 Nc26
Bicas BR 275 Hj56
Bicaz RO 73 Md22
Bicester GB 49 Kt39
Bičevaja RUS 111 Rh22
Bichena ETH 192 Mk40
Bicheng CHN 108 Qd31
Bicheno AUS 151 Se66
Bichhia IND 117 Pa34
Bichhua IND 117 Ok35
Bichi WAN 188 Le39
Bickerton Island AUS 146 Rj52
Bicol N.P. RP 124 Rb39
Bicske H 67 Lt43
Bicuar, P.N. do ANG 200 Lh53
Bičura RUS 104 Qd20
Bid IND 116 Oh36
Bida WAN 188 Ld41
Bida WAN 189 Lg39
Bidar IND 116 Oj37
Bidar Fort IND 116 Oj37
Bidbid OM 95 Nk34
Bidde SP 195 Nb45
Biddeford USA 241 Ge24
Biddle USA 233 Eh23
Bideford GB 49 Kq39
Bidgemia AUS 144 Qh58
Bidokht IR 98 Nk28
Bidon V DZ 182 La34
Bidor MAL 126 Qa43
Bidukbiduk RI 125 Qk45
Bidžan RUS 110 Rf22
Bie S 43 Lr31
Biebrzański Park Narodowy PL 65 Mc37
Biecz PL 65 Mb41
Biedenkopf D 58 Lj40
Biéha BF 187 Kk40
Biei J 111 Sb24
Biel = Bienne CH 60 Lh43
Biel E 56 Ku48
Bielawa PL 64 Lr40
Bielefeld D 58 Lj38
Bieler See CH 60 Lh43
Bielice PL 65 Lu37
Biella I 60 Lj45
Biélou CI 187 Kg41
Bielsa E 56 La48
Bielsk PL 65 Lu38
Bielsko-Biała PL 65 Lu41
Bielsk Podlaski PL 65 Md38
Bienenbüttel D 58 Ll37
Bienfait CDN 233 Ej21
Bienge RDC 199 Lk48
Bien Hoa VN 123 Qd40
Bieniów PL 64 Lq39
Bienne = Biel CH 60 Lh43
Bierbank AUS 149 Sc59
Bierdzany PL 64 Lt40
Biertan RO 67 Me44
Bierutów PL 64 Ls39
Biescas E 56 Ku48
Biesiekierz PL 64 Lr36
Biesiesvlei ZA 205 Mc59
Bieszczady PL 67 Mc41
Bieszczadzki P.N. PL 67 Mc41
Bièvre B 51 Lf41
Bieżuń PL 65 Lu38
Bifoulé CAM 189 Lg43
Bifoun G 198 Lf46
Bifuka J 111 Sb23
Biga TR 69 Mh50
Bigadiç TR 71 Mj51
Big Ambergris Cay GB 250 Ge35
Bigand RA 281 Gk62
Biga Yarımadası TR 69 Mg50
Big Baldy USA 232 Ec23
Big Bear Creek CDN 232 Dj20
Big Beaver CDN 233 Eh21
Big Belt Mts. USA 233 Ee22
Big Bend SD 205 Mf59
Big Bend N.P. USA 245 Ej31
Big Branch Marsh N.W.R. USA 239 Fe30
Big Brook CDN 241 Hb20
Big Creek CDN 232 Dj20
Big Creek USA 232 Ec23
Big Cypress Seminole Ind. Res. USA 243 Fk32
Big Desert AUS 150 Sa63
Big Desert Wilderness Park AUS 150 Sa63
Bigene GNB 186 Kc39
Big Falls USA 236 Fd21
Bigfork USA 232 Ec21
Biggar CDN 233 Eg19
Biggar GB 48 Kr35
Bigge Island AUS 143 Rc53
Biggenden AUS 149 Sg58
Biggleswade GB 49 Ku38
Big Hole ZA 205 Mc60
Big Hole Nat. Battlefield USA 232 Ed23
Bighorn USA 233 Eg22
Bighorn Basin USA 233 Ef23
Bighorn Canyon N.R.A. USA 233 Ef23
Bighorn Mountains USA 233 Eg23
Bight of Bangkok T 122 Qa39
Bight of Benin 188 Lb43
Bight of Biafra 188 Ld43
Bigi Polka SME 266 Hc43
Big Island CDN 231 Eb15
Big Island CDN 231 Ed16
Big Island CDN 236 Fc21
Big Koniuji Island USA 228 Ca18
Big Lagoon Z 196 Mg52
Big Lake USA 238 Ek30
Big Lake Ranch CDN 232 Dk19
Bignona SN 186 Kb39
Bigo Bya Mugyenyi EAU 194 Mf45
Big Pine USA 234 Ea27
Big Pine USA 243 Fk33
Big Piney USA 235 Ee24
Big Pond CDN 240 Gk23
Big Rapids USA 237 Fh24
Big Red Lighthouse USA 237 Fg24
Big River CDN 233 Eg19
Big River Ind. Res. CDN 233 Eg19
Big River Roadhouse USA 229 Cc14
Big Rock USA 234 Eb29
Big Salmon Range CDN 230 Dd15
Big Salmon River CDN 230 Dc15
Big Sandy USA 233 Ee21
Big Sandy USA 235 Ef24
Big Sky USA 233 Ee23
Big Smokey Valley USA 234 Eb26
Big Snow Mtn. USA 233 Ef22
Big South Fork Nat. River and Rec. Area USA 239 Fh27
Big Spring USA 238 Ek29
Big Stone CDN 233 Ee20
Big Stone N.W.R. USA 236 Fb23
Big Sur USA 234 Dk27
Big Timber USA 233 Ef23
Big Trails USA 233 Eg24
Biguaçu BR 277 Hf59
Big Water USA 235 Ee27
Big Wood Cay BS 243 Gb33
Bihać BIH 61 Lq46
Bihar IND 117 Pc33
Biharamulo EAT 194 Mf47
Biharamulo Game Reserve EAT 194 Mf47
Biharia RO 67 Mb43
Bihariganj IND 117 Pd33
Biharkeresztes H 67 Mb43
Biharnagybajom H 67 Mb43
Bihar Sharif IND 117 Pc33
Bihé Plateau ANG 200 Lj52
Bihoro J 111 Sc24
Bihoua RCB 198 Lg47
Bihpur IND 117 Pd33
Bijainagar IND 116 Oh33
Bijaipur IND 116 Oj32
Bijapur IND 116 Oh37
Bijapur IND 117 Pa36
Bijapur IND 117 Pb36
Bijar IR 91 Nd28
Bijawar IND 117 Ok33
Bijbehara 114 Oh29
Bijeljina BIH 68 Lu46
Bijelo Polje MNE 68 Lu47
Bijie CHN 121 Qc32
Bijnapalli IND 116 Ok37
Bijnor IND 115 Ok31
Bijsk RUS 88 Pb08
Bikaner IND 114 Og31
Bikapur IND 117 Pb32
Bikin RUS 111 Rh22
Bikita ZW 202 Mf56
Bikok CAM 189 Lf44
Bikori SUD 185 Mh40
Bikoro RDC 199 Lk46
Bikou CHN 106 Qc29
Bikramganj IND 117 Pc33
Bikumpur IND 114 Og32
Bila Cerkva UA 73 Mf21
Bilad Bani Bu Ali OM 95 Nk34
Bilad Bani Bu Hasan OM 95 Nk34
Bilala RCB 198 Lg48
Bilanga BF 187 Kk39
Bilanga G 198 Lf47
Bilara IND 114 Og32
Bilaspur IND 115 Oj30
Bilaspur IND 115 Pa32
Bilaspur IND 117 Pb34
Bilassana RG 186 Kf41
Bilauktaung Range MYA/THA 122 Pk39
Bilbao = Bilbo E 56 Ks47
Bilbeis ET 179 Mf30
Bilbo = Bilbao E 56 Ks47
Bilbor RO 67 Mf43
Bílčice CZ 66 Ls41
Bíldudalur IS 46 Jr25
Bileća BIH 68 Lt48
Bilecik TR 90 Me25
Biled RO 68 Ma45
Bilehra IND 115 Pa32
Bilesha Plain EAK 195 Na45
Bilesuvar AZ 91 Ne26
Biłgoraj PL 65 Mc40
Bilgorod-Dnistrovs'kij UA 73 Mf22
Bilgram IND 115 Pa32
Bilhaur IND 117 Pa32
Bili RDC 190 Lk43
Bili RDC 191 Mc43
Biliali Koyra RMM 181 Kk37
Bilibino RUS 89 Tb05
Bilin MYA 122 Pj37
Bílina CZ 66 Lo40
Biling La CHN/NEP 102 Pa30
Biliran Island RP 124 Rc40
Biliri WAN 189 Lf41
Bilisht AL 70 Ma50
Bilis Qoogaaoi SP 195 Na45
Bilje HR 61 Lt45
Bilka BG 69 Mh48
Bill USA 233 Eh24
Billabong Roadhouse AUS 144 Qh59
Billa Kalina AUS 148 Rj60
Billdal S 42 Lm33
Billengarrah AUS 146 Rh53
Billiluna AUS 143 Rd55
Billiluna A.L. AUS 143 Rd55
Billingen S 43 Lo32
Billingnooka AUS 142 Ra57
Billings USA 233 Ef23
Billingsfors S 42 Ln32
Bill of Portland GB 49 Ks40
Billom F 53 Ld45
Billun IND 114 Oh31
Billy Island BS 243 Ga33
Bilma RN 183 Lg36
Biloela AUS 149 Sf58
Bilohors'k UA 73 Mh23
Bilokurakyne UA 72 Mk21
Biloo SP 195 Nb45
Bilopillja UA 72 Mh20
Bílovec CZ 66 Ls41
Bilovods'k UA 72 Mk21
Biloxi USA 239 Ff30
Bilqâs Qism Auwal ET 179 Mf30
Biltine TCH 184 Ma38
Bilto N 38 Mb21
Bilugyun MYA 122 Pj37
Bilungala RI 125 Rb45
Bilverdi IR 91 Nd26
Bilwi = Puerto Cabezas NIC 249 Fj38
Bima RI 130 Qk50
Bimba CAM 189 Lh43
Bimbe ANG 200 Lh51
Bimbéréke DY 188 Lb40
Bimbijy AUS 144 Qk60
Bimbila GH 187 La41
Bimbo RCA 190 Lk43
Bimini Islands BS 243 Ga33
Bina Etawa IND 117 Ok33
Binalbagan RP 124 Rb40
Binanga RI 127 Pk45
Binarowa PL 65 Mb41
Binauhan Falls RP 124 Rc39
Binbee AUS 147 Sd56
Binche B 51 Le40
Binchuan CHN 121 Qa33
Bindé BF 187 Kk40
Binder TCH 190 Lh41
Bindi Bindi AUS 144 Qj61
Bindki IND 117 Pa32
Bindloe = Isla Marchena EC 269 Fe45
Bindoy RP 124 Rb41
Bindu RDC 199 Lk49
Bindura ZW 202 Mf54
Binéfar E 56 La49
Bin-el-Ouidane MA 175 Kg29
Binga EAT 197 Mk49
Binga ZW 202 Md54
Bingara AUS 149 Sf60
Bing Bong AUS 146 Rj53
Bingen D 59 Lh41
Binger USA 238 Fa28
Bingham GB 49 Ku38
Bingham USA 235 Eg29
Bingham USA 240 Gf23
Binghamton USA 241 Gc24
Bin Ghashir LAR 177 Lg29
Bin Ghaylan YE 94 Nc38
Bingintelok RI 127 Qb47
Binglingsi Shiku CHN 106 Qb28
Bingmei CHN 108 Qe33
Bingöl TR 91 Na26
Bingöl Dağları TR 91 Na26
Bingsjö S 41 Lq29
Binhai CHN 112 Qk28
Binh Chanh VN 123 Qd40
Binh Chau Hot Springs VN 123 Qd40
Binh Dinh VN 123 Qe39
Binh Gia VN 121 Qd35
Binh Lu VN 121 Qb34
Binh Son VN 123 Qe38
Binibihali PNG 156 Sf51
Bini Erde TCH 183 Lk35
Binjai RI 126 Pk44
Bin Jawwad LAR 177 Lk30
Binkolo WAL 186 Ke41
Bin Lam VN 123 Qe38
Binnaway AUS 149 Se61
Binneringie AUS 145 Rb61
Binongko RI 131 Rc48
Binpur IND 117 Pd34
Binscarth CDN 236 Ek20
Bintagoungou RMM 181 Kj37
Bintan RI 127 Qc45
Binthalya AUS 144 Qh58
Bintuhan RI 127 Qb48
Bintulu MAL 128 Qg44
Bintumani, Mount WAL 186 Ke41
Bintuni RI 154 Rg47
Binur IND 117 Pa36
Bin Xian CHN 106 Qe28
Bin Xian CHN 110 Rd23
Binyang CHN 108 Qe34
Binz D 58 Lo36
Binzhou CHN 107 Qk27
Bio Addo SP 195 Nc44
Bioča MNE 68 Lu48
Biograd na moru HR 61 Lq47
Biogradska Gora, N.P. MNE 68 Lu48
Biokovo HR 61 Ls47
Biosphere II USA 235 Ee29
Biotopo del Quetzal GCA 248 Fe38
Biotopo Monterrico-Hawaii GCA 248 Fe39
Biougra MA 174 Kf30
Bipindi CAM 188 Lf44
Bipok CAM 188 Lf43
Biquinhas BR 275 Hh55
Bira RUS 110 Rg21
Bira Beach Resort RI 130 Ra48
Bi'r Abu Zaïma SUD 184 Me38
Birak LAR 177 Lh32
Bi'r Al 'Akkariyah LAR 177 Lk30
Bi'r Al 'Alaqah LAR 177 Lh31
Bi'r Al 'Atrun SUD 184 Md36
Bi'r al Awyan LAR 178 Mc30
Bi'r al Banakish LAR 177 Ma30
Bi'r al Fatiyah LAR 177 Lh31
Bi'r al Ghanam LAR 177 Lg29
Bi'r al Ghararah LAR 177 Ma30
Bir al Guzayyil LAR 176 Lf31
Bir 'Ali YE 94 Ne38
Bir Ali Ben Khélifa TN 176 Lf28
Bi'r al Jadid LAR 177 Lg32
Bi'r al Kammuniyan LAR 177 Lj31
Bi'r al Khawr LAR 177 Lg30
Bi'r Allaq LAR 176 Lf30
Bi'r al Mastutah LAR 177 Lh33
Bi'r al Muwaylih LAR 177 Lk31
Bi'r al Qaf LAR 177 Lh31
Bi'r al Qataf LAR 178 Mb30
Bi'r al 'Utaylah LAR 177 Lj30
Bi'r al Washkah LAR 177 Lh31
Birampur IND 117 Pd35
Bîr 'Amrâne RIM 181 Kf34
Biramsar IND 114 Of32
Bir Anzarane DARS 180 Kc34
Birao RCA 184 Mb40
Bi'r ar Rijl LAR 177 Lh31
Bi'r ash Shahwi LAR 177 Lh30
Biratnagar NEP 117 Pd32
Biratori J 111 Sb24
Bi'r A'yad LAR 177 Lg29
Bîr Bel Guerdâne RIM 174 Ke33
Bi'r Ben Ghimah LAR 177 Ma30
Bir Beria TN 176 Le29
Bi'r Bin ,Isa LAR 177 Lh30
Bi'r Bu al Ghurab LAR 177 Lg30
Birch Creek USA 229 Ch12
Birchenough Bridge ZW 202 Mg55
Birches USA 229 Cd13
Birch Hills CDN 233 Eh19
Birchi WAN 188 Ld39
Birchip AUS 151 Sb63
Birchiş RO 68 Mc45
Birch Island CDN 236 Fa19
Birch Mountains CDN 231 Ed17
Birch River CDN 233 Ek19
Bircot ETH 193 Nb42
Bircza PL 65 Mc41
Bi'r Dhu'fan LAR 177 Lh30
Bir Di SUD 191 Me42
Bird Island = Île aux Vaches SY 195 Nh47
Bird Island ZA 204 Lk62
Bir Djedid DZ 176 Ld29
Bir Dolmane DZ 176 Le30
Bird Rock Lighthouse BS 250 Gc34
Birdsville AUS 148 Rk58
Birdsville Race AUS 148 Rk58
Birdtail CDN 236 Ek20
Birecik TR 90 Mk27
Bire Kpatuos Game Reserve SUD 191 Me43
Bir el Amdar DZ 176 Ld29
Bir El-Ater DZ 176 Le28
Bir el Fakama SUD 185 Mg37
Bir el Gâreb RIM 180 Kb35
Bir el Ghorifa TN 176 Lf29
Bir el Hasa SUD 179 Mh34
Birendranagar NEP 115 Pa31
Bir en Nugeim SUD 185 Mh36
Biretwa EAK 194 Mh45
Bireuen RI 126 Pj43
Bir Fadil KSA 95 Ne34
Bir Fanoidig SUD 185 Mh36
Bir Faysan KSA 94 Ne35
Bir Fegoussi TN 176 Le29
Birfel'd RUS 110 Rg21
Bi'r Furawiya SUD 184 Mb38
Bir Gandouz DARS 180 Kb35
Birganj NEP 117 Pc32
Birgi TR 71 Mj52
Birgudi IND 117 Pa35
Bir Hadi KSA 95 Nf36
Birhan ETH 192 Mj40
Bi'r Hasanah ET 179 Mg30
Bir Hatab SUD 179 Mg35
Bir Hismet 'Umar SUD 179 Mh35
Biri N 40 Ll30
Biri SUD 191 Md42
Biria EAT 196 Mg50
Birigüi BR 274 He56
Biri Island RP 124 Rc39
Birini RCA 190 Mb42
Biritingas BR 273 Ja51
Birjand IR 98 Nk29
Bir Jaydah KSA 92 Mj32
Bir-Jdid MA 175 Kg29
Bi'r Jimi LAR 177 Lh29
Bi'r Jubni LAR 178 Mc30
Birka S 43 Ls31
Birkat Al 'Aqabah IRQ 93 Nb30
Birkat al Jumaymah KSA 93 Nb31
Birkat Saira SUD 184 Mb39
Birkeland N 42 Lh32
Birkeland N 42 Lj32
Birkelane SN 180 Kc38
Birkenau PL 65 Lu41
Birkenfeld D 59 Lh41
Birkenhead AUS 149 Sd58
Birkenhead GB 49 Kr37
Birkerød DK 42 Ln35
Bi'r Khalaf Allah LAR 177 Lg32
Bir Kiau SUD 185 Mh35
Bir Labasoi SUD 179 Mh35
Birlik KZ 100 Og23
Birlik KZ 100 Og24
Bir Mahmoud TN 176 Le29
Birmingham GB 49 Ks38
Birmingham USA 239 Fg29
Birmitrapur IND 117 Pc34
Bîr Mogreïn RIM 174 Ke33
Bi'r Mudakim LAR 177 Lg29
Bir Nawari SUD 185 Mh35
Bir Nazsirah LAR 176 Lf30
Birni Gwari WAN 188 Ld40
Birni-Keebi WAN 188 Lc39
Birnim RN 182 Le38
Birnin Gaouré RN 182 Lb39
Birnin Konni RN 182 Lc39
Birnin Kudu WAN 188 Le40
Birnin Lallé RN 182 Ld38
Birnin-Yauri WAN 188 Lc40
Birniwa WAN 188 Lf39
Birnni DY 188 La41
Birnon IND 117 Pb33
Biro DY 188 Lb41
Birobidžan RUS 110 Rg21
Birou RMM 180 Kf38
Bir Ounâne RMM 181 Kj35
Birpara IND 120 Pe32
Bir Qar'at ad Dibah LAR 176 Le31
Bi'r Qaryas LAR 177 Lj31
Birr IRL 47 Kn37
Birricannia AUS 149 Sc57
Birrimba Out Station AUS 146 Rg53
Birrindudu AUS 143 Re55
Bir Salala SUD 179 Mh35
Birsay GB 48 Kr31
Bir Senia DZ 175 Kk29
Bir Shalatayn ET 179 Mh34
Bir Shari KSA 93 Nb32
Birsilpur IND 114 Og31
Bir Slougui TN 176 Lf29
Bir Soltane TN 176 Le29
Birštonas LT 45 Me36
Bi'r Tabankurt LAR 177 Lg32
Bir Taleb RIM 180 Kf37
Bir-Tam-Tam MA 175 Kh29
Bi'r Tanjdar LAR 178 Mb30

Bi'r Taziet ☐ LAR 177 Lg33
Bir Tegheri ☐ LAR 176 Lf32
Birthplace of Mahatma Gandhi ☐ IND 116 Oe35
Birthplace of Sun Yat-sen ☐ CHN 109 Qg34
Birti ☐ SUD 185 Mg36
Bi'r Tin Abunda ☐ LAR 177 Lg32
Bi'r Tlakshin ☐ LAR 177 Lg30
Birtle ☐ CDN 236 Ek20
Bir Tuhab ☐ LAR 177 Ma29
Biruaca ☐ YV 265 Gg42
Birufu ☐ RI 154 Rk48
Bi'r Umar ☐ LAR 177 Ma30
Birżai ☐ LT 45 Me34
Bir Zaltan ☐ LAR 177 Lk31
Birżi ☐ LV 45 Mf34
Birżi pilis ☐ LT 45 Me34
Bisa ☐ RI 131 Rd46
Bisaccia ☐ I 63 Lq49
Bisagno ☐ WAN 183 Lg39
Bisal ☐ IND 117 Pd34
Bisalpur ☐ IND 115 Ok31
Bisamberg ☐ IND 117 Pb34
Bisanadi National Reserve ☐ EAK 195 Mk45
Bisane ☐ RMM 181 Kk37
Bišåpur ☐ IR 93 Nf31
Bisauli ☐ IND 115 Ok31
Bisbalha ☐ S 56 Ku48
Bisbee ☐ USA 235 Eh30
Biscarrosse ☐ F 52 Ke44
Biscéglie ☐ I 63 Le49
Bischofsheim ☐ D 58 Lp39
Bischofswerda ☐ D 58 Ma41
Bischwiller ☐ F 51 Ln42
Biscoe Islands ☐ 286 Gc32
Biscucuy ☐ YV 265 Gf41
Bisellia ☐ SUD 191 Md42
Biseruka ☐ EAU 194 Mf45
Biševo ☐ HR 61 Lq48
Bisha ☐ ER 192 Mj38
Bishkek ☐ ⬤ ★ KS 100 Oh24
Bisho ☐ ZA 205 Md62
Bishop ☐ USA 234 Ea27
Bishop Auckland ☐ GB 49 Kt36
Bishop Hill S.H.S. ☐ USA 236 Fe25
Bishop's Falls ☐ CDN 241 Hc21
Bishop's Stortford ☐ GB 49 La39
Bishri ☐ LAR 177 Lk30
Bishunpur ☐ IND 117 Pc34
Bishu Shanzhuang ☐ CHN 107 Qj25
Biskra ☐ DZ 176 Lc28
Biskupiec ☐ PL 65 Ma36
Bislig ☐ RP 125 Rd41
Bismarck ☐ USA 233 Ej23
Bisonó ☐ DOM 250 Ge36
Bismarck Archipelago ☐ PNG 156 Se47
Bismarck Sea ☐ PNG 156 Sd48
Bismark ☐ D 58 Lm38
Bismil ☐ TR 91 Na27
Bismo ☐ N 40 Lj29
Bison ☐ EAU 194 Mf45
Bison ☐ USA 233 Ej23
Bisonó ☐ DOM 250 Ge36
Bisotun ☐ ⬛ IR 91 Nd28
Bisotun ☐ IR 91 Nd28
Bispgården ☐ S 41 Lr28
Bissau ☐ ⬤ ★ GNB 186 Kc40
Bisset ☐ CDN 236 Fc20
Bissikrima ☐ RG 186 Ke40
Bissingou II ☐ RCA 190 Ma41
Bistcho Lake ☐ CDN 236 Ea18
Bistra ☐ BIH 61 Ls46
Bistrica ☐ MNE 68 Lu47
Bistrica ☐ SRB 68 Lu47
Bistrița ☐ RO 67 Md48
Bisungarh ☐ IND 117 Pc33
Biswan ☐ IND 115 Pb32
Bisztynek ☐ PL 65 Ma36
Bitam ☐ G 189 Lf44
Bitangor ☐ MAL 128 Qf44
Bitata ☐ ETH 195 Mk43
Bitburg ☐ D 59 Lj41
Bitchabé ☐ TG 187 La41
Bitche ☐ F 51 Ln41
Bitévinta ☐ GE 91 Na24
Bithoor ☐ IND 117 Pb34
Bitili ☐ ETH 192 Na41
Bitilifondi ☐ RCA 191 Md43
Bitkine ☐ TCH 189 Lk40
Bitlis ☐ TR 91 Nb27
Bitola ☐ ⬛ MK 68 Mb49
Bitonto ☐ I 63 Le49
Bitra ☐ BF 187 Kh40
Bitoutouk ☐ CAM 188 Lf44
Bitragunta ☐ IND 119 Ok38
Bitra Island ☐ IND 118 Og40
Bittencourt ☐ BR 264 Gf47
Bitter Creek ☐ USA 235 Ef25
Bitterfeld ☐ D 58 Ln39
Bitterfontein ☐ ZA 204 Lk61
Bitterroot Range ☐ USA 232 Ec22
Bitti ☐ I 62 Lk50
Bittuang ☐ RI 130 Qe47
Bitung ☐ RI 125 Rb45
Bituruna ☐ BR 276 He59
Biu ☐ WAN 189 Lg40
Bivona ☐ I 62 Lo53
Biwinapada ☐ RI 130 Rb48
Bixby ☐ USA 239 Fe27
Biyang ☐ CHN 107 Qg29
Biye K'obe ☐ ETH 193 Nb40
Biyoley ☐ SP 195 Nc44
Bizana ☐ ZA 205 Me61
Bizen ☐ J 113 Rh28
Bizerte ☐ TN 176 Le27
Bjahoml' ☐ BY 45 Mj36
Bjala ☐ BG 69 Mf47
Bjala ☐ BG 69 Mh48
Bjala čerkva ☐ BG 69 Me49
Bjala Slatina ☐ BG 69 Md47
Bjalynicy ☐ BY 72 Me19
Bjarézina ☐ BY 45 Mg36
Bjargtangar ☐ IS 46 Jq25
Bjarnarey ☐ IS 46 Ju25
Bjärnum ☐ S 43 Lo34
Bjaroza ☐ BY 65 Me38
Bjarozavka ☐ BY 65 Mf37
Bjärred ☐ S 42 Ln35
Bjästa ☐ S 41 Lt27
Bjelašnica ☐ ⬛ BIH 68 Ls47
Bjelovar ☐ HR 61 Lr45
Bjerkvik ☐ N 38 Lk22
Bjerringbro ☐ DK 42 Lk34
Björbo ☐ S 43 Lp30
Bjørkelangen ☐ N 42 Lm31
Björkö ☐ S 43 Lt31
Bjorkoby ☐ FIN 41 Mb27
Bjorkon ☐ FIN 41 Mb27
Björksele ☐ S 41 Lt26
Björna ☐ S 41 Lt26
Bjørneborg ☐ S 43 Lp32
Björne Peninsula ☐ CDN 227 Fc03
Björnlandets n.p. ☐ S 41 Lt27
Bjurholm ☐ S 41 Lu27
Bjursås ☐ S 43 Lq30
Bjuv ☐ S 42 Ln34
Bla ☐ RMM 187 Kh39
Blaa londi ☐ IS 46 Ju26
Blace ☐ SRB 68 Mb47
Blackall ☐ AUS 149 Sc58
Black and White Pagoda ☐ CHN 121 Qa54
Blackbeard Island National Seashore ☐ USA 242 Fk54
Blackbird Cay ☐ BH 248 Fg37
Blackbull ☐ AUS 147 Sa54
Blackbutt ☐ AUS 149 Se59
Black C. ☐ USA 228 Cd16
Black Canyon of the Gunnison N.P. ☐ USA 235 Eg26
Black Diamond ☐ USA 235 Ec20
Blackduck ☐ USA 237 Fb22
Blackdown Tableland N.P. ☐ AUS 149 Se57
Blackfeet Ind. Res. ☐ USA 233 Ed21
Blackfoot ☐ CDN 233 Ee19

Blackfoot ☐ USA 233 Ed22
Blackfoot ☐ USA 233 Ed24
Blackfoot Ind. Res. ☐ CDN 233 Ed20
Blackfoot Res. ☐ USA 233 Ee24
Black Forest ☐ D 59 Lh43
Black Gate ☐ AUS 151 Sb62
Black Head ☐ IRL 47 Kf37
Blackie ☐ CDN 233 Ed21
Black Island ☐ CDN 236 Fb20
Black Kettle National Grassland ☐ USA 238 Fa28
Black Lake ☐ CDN 231 Eh16
Black Mountain ☐ IND 120 Pf32
Black Mountain ☐ USA 234 Ea27
Black Mountain N.P. ☐ BHT 120 Pf32
Black Mountains ☐ USA 241 Gb25
Black Mountains N.P. ☐ ☐ AUS 151 Sf62
Blackpool ☐ GB 49 Kr36
Black River ☐ VN 121 Qb35
Black River ☐ JA 250 Ga36
Black River Falls ☐ USA 236 Fe23
Black Rock ☐ NAM 204 Lh59
Black Rock ☐ USA 234 Ea27
Black Rock Desert ☐ USA 234 Ea25
Black Sea ☐ 26 Mb05
Blackshear ☐ USA 242 Fj30
Black's reef ☐ NZ 153 Tj65
Blackville ☐ AUS 149 Se59
Black Volta ☐ GH/BF 187 Kj40
Blackwater ☐ AUS 149 Se57
Blackwell ☐ USA 238 Ek29
Blackwell ☐ USA 148 Sb57
Bladgrond ☐ ZA 204 Lk60
Blaenavon ☐ GB 49 Kr39
Blagaj ☐ BIH 61 Ls47
Blagoevgrad ☐ BG 68 Md48
Blagojščenka ☐ RUS 88 Pa08
Blagojščenka ☐ RUS 105 Rd20
Blahovēščensky svobor ☐ UA 72 Mj20
Blain ☐ F 50 Kt43
Blaine Lake ☐ CDN 233 Eg17
Blair ☐ USA 236 Fb25
Blair Athol ☐ AUS 149 Sd57
Blairbeth ☐ ZA 205 Md60
Blair Castle ☐ GB 48 Kr34
Blairgowrie ☐ GB 48 Ks34
Blairmore ☐ CDN 233 Ec21
Blairquhan Castle ☐ ☐ GB 48 Kq33
Blaisden ☐ USA 234 Dk26
Blairsville ☐ USA 242 Fj29
Blaj ☐ RO 67 Md44
Blà Jungfrun ☐ S 43 Lr33
Blà Jungfrun n.p. ☐ S 43 Lr33
Blaka Laodemi ☐ RN 183 Lg35
Blakely ☐ PL 65 Mc36
Blake Basin ☐ 242 Gc31
Blakely ☐ USA 239 Fh30
Blake Plateau ☐ 242 Ga30
Blama ☐ WAL 186 Ke42
Blamangan ☐ RI 127 Qc48
Blamont ☐ F 51 Lg42
Blanca Aurora Falls ☐ RP 124 Rc40
Blancagrande ☐ RA 281 Gk64
Blanca Peak ☐ USA 235 Eh27
Blanchard Springs Caverns ☐ USA 239 Fd28
Blanche Channel ☐ SOL 157 Sj50
Blanche Marievallen ☐ SME 266 Hb43
Blanchet Island ☐ CDN 231 Ed15
Blanchetown ☐ AUS 151 Rk62
Blanco Encalada ☐ PE 279 Ge58
Blanco, P.N. Juan Castro ☐ CR 249 Fh40
Blanc-Sablon ☐ CDN 241 Hb20
Blandford Forum ☐ GB 49 Ks40
Blanding ☐ USA 235 Ef27
Blanes ☐ E 57 Lc49
Blanfla ☐ CI 187 Kh42
Blangkejeren ☐ RI 126 Pj43
Blangpidie ☐ RI 126 Pj44
Blangy-sur-Bresle ☐ F 51 Lb41
Blankenholm ☐ S 43 Lr33
Blanzac ☐ F 52 La45
Blarney ☐ IRL 47 Kf38
Blarney Castle ☐ IRL 47 Kf38
Blasket Islands ☐ IRL 47 Kd38
Blaszki ☐ PL 64 Lt39
Blatnica ☐ BIH 61 Ls46
Blato ☐ HR 61 Lr48
Blaubeuren ☐ D 59 Lk42
Blaufelden ☐ D 59 Lk41
Blåvands Huk ☐ DK 42 Lj35
Blåvands Huk ☐ DK 42 Lj35
Blawagg ☐ RI 129 Qh50
Blaye ☐ F 52 Ku45
Blayney ☐ AUS 151 Se62
Blazevo ☐ SRB 68 Ma47
Blâzma ☐ LV 45 Md33
Bleaker Island ☐ GB 283 Ha72
Blebo ☐ LB 186 Kg43
Bleckede ☐ D 58 Ll37
Bled ☐ SLO 66 Lp44
Bleialf ☐ D 59 Lh41
Bleiburg ☐ A 61 Lq44
Bleikvassli ☐ N 38 Lo25
Blejsko jezero ☐ SLO 66 Lp44
Blekinge ☐ S 43 Lq34
Blenheim ☐ CDN 241 Gd21
Blenheim ☐ AUS 149 Se59
Blenheim ☐ NZ 153 Tg66
Blenheim Palace ☐ ☐ GB 49 Kt39
Bleré ☐ F 52 La43
Blerick ☐ NL 51 Lg39
Blesmanspos ☐ ZA 205 Mc59
Blettarans ☐ F 53 Lf44
Blida ☐ DZ 176 Lb27
Blieskastel ☐ D 59 Lh41
Blimbing ☐ RI 127 Qc47
Blina ☐ AUS 143 Rc54
Blinadi ☐ CI 187 Kj41
Blind Channel ☐ CDN 232 Dh20
Blind River ☐ CDN 237 Fj22
Blinisht ☐ AL 68 Lu49
Blinman ☐ AUS 148 Rk61
Blinnenhorn ☐ CH 60 Lj44
Bliss Landing ☐ CDN 232 Dh20
Blitar ☐ RI 127 Qc48
Blitta ☐ TG 187 La41
Blizne ☐ CI ☐ PL 65 Mb41
Block Island ☐ USA 246 Ga25
Bloemfontein ☐ ⬤ ★ ZA 205 Md60
Bloemhoek ☐ ZA 204 Lk60
Bloemhof ☐ ZA 205 Mb59
Bloemhof Dam Nature Reserve ☐ ZA 205 Md59
Blois ☐ F 52 La43
Blokhus ☐ DK 42 Lk33
Blombacka ☐ S 43 Lo31
Blomdalss ☐ N 38 Lo25
Blongas ☐ RI 130 Qj50
Btonie ☐ PL 65 Ma38
Blood Ind. Res. ☐ CDN 233 Ed21
Bloods Range ☐ AUS 143 Re58
Bloodvein River ☐ CDN 236 Fb20
Bloody Foreland ☐ IRL 47 Kh35
Bloomfield ☐ USA 233 Eh22
Bloomfield ☐ USA 235 Eg27
Bloomfield ☐ USA 236 Fb24
Bloomfield ☐ USA 239 Fg26
Bloomfield River ☐ AUS 147 Sc53
Bloomington ☐ USA 236 Fc23
Bloomington ☐ USA 239 Fg25
Bloomington ☐ USA 239 Ff26
Bloomsbury ☐ AUS 147 Se56
Blora ☐ RI 127 Qb48
Blossom Village ☐ 243 Fk36
Blötno ☐ PL 64 Lg37
Bloukrans Bridge ☐ ZA 204 Mb63
Blountstown ☐ USA 239 Fh30
Blowhole ☐ IND 117 Pd34
Blowholes (Quobba) ☐ AUS 144 Qg58
Blubber Bay ☐ CDN 232 Dh21

Bludenz ☐ A 60 Lk43
Bluefield ☐ USA 241 Ga27
Bluefields ☐ NIC 249 Fj39
Blue Grotto ☐ M 63 Lp55
Blue Hills of Couteau ☐ CDN 241 Hb22
Blue Hole ☐ BH 248 Fg37
Blue Lagoon N.P. ☐ ☐ Z 202 Md53
Blue Lake ☐ AUS 150 Sa64
Blue Lake ☐ USA 232 Dj25
Blue Lake ☐ S 43 Lt33
Bodalangi ☐ RDC 190 Ma44
Blue Mountains ☐ AUS 241 Gc24
Blue Mountains ☐ JA 250 Gb36
Blue Mountains ☐ USA 232 Eb23
Blue Mountains N.P. ☐ ☐ JA 250 Gb36
Blue Mountains N.P. ☐ ☐ AUS 151 Sf62
Blue Mud Hills ☐ USA 233 Ef22
Blue Nile ☐ ETH 185 Mh40
Blue Nile ☐ SUD 162 Mb50
Blue Nile Canyon ☐ ETH 192 Mh40
Blue Nile Falls = Tis Isat Falls ☐ ETH 192 Mj40
Blue Rapids ☐ USA 238 Fb26
Blue Ridge ☐ USA 239 Fh25
Blue Ridge ☐ USA 242 Fk27
Blue Ridge Parkway ☐ USA 242 Fk27
Blue River ☐ CDN 232 Ea19
Blue Stack Mountains ☐ IRL 47 Km36
Blue Train H.B. ☐ J 142 Qe61
Blue Train (Garden Route) ☐ ZA 205 Mc62
Bluewater ☐ AUS 147 Sd55
Bluff ☐ NZ 153 Te69
Bluff ☐ USA 235 Ef27
Bluff ☐ PA 247 Fg41
Bluff ☐ USA 235 Ef27
Bluff Downs ☐ AUS 147 Sc55
Bluffers Park H. ☐ CDN 237 Ga24
BluffFace Range ☐ AUS 143 Rd54
Bluff Point ☐ AUS 144 Qh59
Blukwa ☐ RDC 194 Mf45
Blumau ☐ A 61 Lr43
Blumberg ☐ D 59 Lj43
Blumenau ☐ BR 277 Hf59
Blunt ☐ USA 236 Fa24
Blup Blup Island ☐ PNG 155 Sc47
Bly ☐ USA 232 Dk24
Blyde River Canyon Nature Reserve ☐ ZA 205 Mf58
Blydeverwaghterplato ☐ ZA 204 Mb61
Blyth ☐ GB 49 Kt35
Blythe ☐ USA 234 Ec29
Blytheville ☐ USA 239 Ft28
Bni-Boufrah ☐ MA 175 Kh28
Bo ☐ N 42 Lk31
Bo ☐ WAL 186 Ke42
Boabeng-Fiema Monkey Sanctuary ☐ GH 187 Kk42
Boac ☐ RP 124 Ra39
Boaco ☐ NIC 249 Fh39
Boa Esperança ☐ BR 265 Gk44
Boa Esperança ☐ BR 270 Gj48
Boa Esperança ☐ BR 274 Hd56
Boa Esperança do Sul ☐ BR 274 Hf55
Boagis ☐ PNG 156 Sg50
Boa Hora ☐ BR 270 Gj48
Bo'ai ☐ CHN 107 Qd30
Boali ☐ RCA 190 Lk43
Boana ☐ PNG 155 Sd49
Boanda ☐ CAM 188 Lf44
Boane ☐ MOC 205 Mg59
Boang Island ☐ PNG 156 Sg47
Boano ☐ RI 131 Rd47
Boa Nova ☐ BR 275 Hk53
Boardman ☐ USA 232 Ea23
Boardman ☐ RP 124 Rc41
Boat Basin ☐ CDN 232 Dg21
Boat of Garten ☐ GB 48 Kr33
Boa Viagem ☐ BR 273 Ja48
Boa Vista ☐ ⬤ BR 265 Gg45
Boa Vista ☐ BR 267 He47
Boa Vista ☐ BR 270 Gh48
Boa Vista ☐ BR 270 Gj46
Boa Vista da Ramos ☐ BR 271 Hb47
Boa Vista do Tupim ☐ BR 273 Hk52
Boa Vista, T.I. ☐ BR 271 Ha47
Boayan Island ☐ RP 124 Qk40
Boaz ☐ USA 239 Fg28
Bobadah ☐ AUS 151 Sd62
Bobadilla ☐ RDC 190 Ma44
Bobingen ☐ D 59 Ll42
Böblingen ☐ D 59 Lj42
Bobo ☐ RI 131 Rd47
Bobo-Dioulasso ☐ BF 187 Kh40
Bobolice ☐ PL 64 Lr37
Bobonong ☐ BW 200 Md56
Bobowo ☐ RN 68 Md48
Bobotop tizmasi ☐ UZ 97 Od27
Bobr ☐ CI 187 Kg42
Bobrov ☐ RUS 72 Na20
Bobrovycja ☐ UA 72 Mf20
Bobrowice ☐ UA 73 Mg21
Boburés ☐ YV 264 Ge41
Böbs ☐ BF 187 Kj40
Boby ☐ 206 Mk54
Boca Apiza ☐ MEX 246 Ea36
Boca Barranca ☐ CR 249 Fh41
Boca de Aroa ☐ YV 265 Gf40
Boca de la Serpiente ☐ YV 265 Gk41
Boca de la Vinorama ☐ MEX 244 Ef34
Boca del Macareo ☐ YV 265 Gk41
Boca del Pao ☐ YV 265 Gh41
Boca del Rio ☐ MEX 247 Fb36
Boca de Pascuales ☐ MEX 246 Eb36
Boca de Pijijiapan ☐ MEX 247 Fd38
Boca de Rio Indio ☐ PA 249 Fk41
Boca de Tomatlán ☐ MEX 246 Ea35
Boca de Yuma ☐ DOM 251 Gf36
Boca Grande ☐ YV 265 Gk41
Boca Iglesia ☐ MEX 247 Fh35
Bocaina do Sul ☐ BR 277 Hf59
Bocaiúva ☐ BR 275 Hj54
Boca Mavaca ☐ YV 265 Gh43
Bocanda ☐ CI 187 Kj41
Bocanó ☐ YV 264 Ge41
Boca Raton ☐ USA 243 Fk34
Boca do Acre ☐ BR 270 Gg49
Boca do Acre, T.I. ☐ BR 270 Gg49
Boca do Iaco ☐ BR 270 Gf50
Boca do Jari ☐ BR 267 He46
Bocas ☐ MEX 246 Ek34
Bocaranga ☐ RCA 190 Lj42
Bocas del Toro ☐ PA 249 Fj41
Bocхолma ☐ CHN 103 Ph31
Bochnia ☐ PL 65 Ma41
Bocholt ☐ D 58 Lh39
Bochum ☐ D 58 Lh39
Bockenem ☐ D 58 Ll38
Bockheo ☐ K 123 Qd39

Bolesławiec ☐ PL 64 Lq39
Bolgart ☐ AUS 144 Qj61
Bolhò ☐ H 66 Ls44
Bolhov ☐ RUS 72 Mj19
Bolhrad ☐ UA 73 Mf45
Bolia ☐ RDC 190 Ma46
Boli ☐ CHN 110 Rf23
Boli ☐ RDC 191 Md48
Boli ☐ SUD 191 Md42
Bolintin-Vale ☐ RO 69 Mf46
Bolivar ☐ CO 264 Gb45
Bolivar ☐ PE 268 Gb49
Bolívar ☐ CO 264 Gd45
Bolivar 802, Cerro ☐ YV 265 Gj42
Bolivia ☐ ☐ 243 Ga34
Bolivia ☐ ☐ 242 Ga28
Bolkar Dağları ☐ TR 90 Mf27
Bolków ☐ PL 64 Lq40
Bollène ☐ F 53 Le46
Bollnäs ☐ S 41 Lr29
Bollon ☐ AUS 149 Sd60
Bollullos del Condado ☐ E 55 Ko53
Bolmen ☐ S 43 Lo34
Bolnisi ☐ GE 91 Nb25
Bologma ☐ RDC 190 Ma44
Bologna ☐ ⬛ I 61 Ll46
Bologoes ☐ RUS 72 Mg17
Bologoe ☐ RUS 72 Mg17
Bolomba ☐ RDC 190 Ma44
Bolon ☐ RP 124 Rc41
Bolotnoe ☐ RUS 96 Ph08
Bolo

Bom Jesus de Goiás ☐ BR 274 Hf55
Bom Jesus do Galho ☐ BR 275 Hj55
Bom Jesus do Itabapoana ☐ BR 275 Hk56
Bom Jesus do Monte ☐ P 54 Kn39
Bom Jesus, T.I. ☐ BR 266 Ha44
Bømlafjorden ☐ N 42 Lf31
Bømlo ☐ N 42 Lf31
Bom Lugar ☐ BR 271 Ha49
Bom Retiro ☐ BR 270 Lk45
Bomotu ☐ RDC 190 Lk44
Bomsucesso ☐ BR 271 Hd49
Bom Sucesso ☐ BR 273 Jb49
Bom Viver ☐ BR 267 Hh47
Bonab ☐ IR 91 Nd27
Bonaberi ☐ CAM 188 Le43
Bonai ☐ RN 265 Gf39
Bonamga ☐ AUS 151 Se64
Bonanza ☐ NIC 249 Ck15
Bonanza ☐ USA 232 Ec25
Bonao ☐ DOM 250 Ge36
Bonaparte Archipelago ☐ AUS 143 Rc53
Bonaparte, Mount ☐ USA 232 Ea21
Boñar ☐ E 54 Kq48
Bonar Bridge ☐ GB 48 Kq33
Bonasse ☐ TT 251 Gk40
Bonaventure ☐ CDN 241 Hd21
Bonavista ☐ CDN 241 Hd21
Bonavista Bay ☐ CDN 241 Hd21
Bon Bon ☐ AUS 148 Rh60
Boncuk Dağları ☐ TR 90 Me27
Bonda ☐ EAK 194 Mh46
Bondo ☐ CI 187 Kj41
Bondo ☐ RDC 191 Md44
Bondoc Point ☐ RP 124 Rb39
Bondokodi ☐ RI 130 Qk50
Bondolav ☐ BR 267 Hd45
Bondoukou ☐ CI 187 Kj41
Bondowoso ☐ RI 129 Qg48
Bonds Cay ☐ BS 243 Gb33
Bondurant ☐ USA 233 Ee24
Bone ☐ RI 130 Rb48
Bonelipu ☐ RI 130 Rb48
Bone-Dumoga N.P. ☐ RI 125 Rb45
Bonekraal ☐ ZA 204 Lk60
Bonerate ☐ RI 130 Ra49
Bohov ☐ RUS 72 Mj19
Boa, Cerro ☐ PE 279 Gf59
Bonifim ☐ BR 264 Haeq

Bosanska Dubica ☐ BIH 61 Lr45
Bosanska Gradiška ☐ BIH 61 Ls45
Bosanska Kostajnica ☐ BIH 61 Lr45
Bosanski Kozac ☐ BIH 61 Lr46
Bosanski Brod ☐ BIH 61 Ls45
Bosanski Kobaš ☐ BIH 61 Ls45
Bosanski Novi ☐ BIH 61 Lr45
Bosanski Petrovac ☐ BIH 61 Lr46
Bosanski Šamac ☐ BIH 68 Lt45
Bosanski Stari Most ☐ BIH 61 Lr45
Bosanska Gahovo ☐ BIH 61 Lr45
Bosavi, Mount ☐ PNG 155 Sb49
Bos Chek Prey ☐ K 123 Qc39
Boscia ☐ CO 264 Gd40
Bose ☐ CHN 108 Qc34
Boshof ☐ ZA 205 Mc60
Boshruyeh ☐ IR 98 Nj29
Bosilegrad ☐ SRB 68 Mc48
Bösjökloster ☐ S 43 Lo35
Boskamp ☐ SME 266 Hc43
Boskovice ☐ CZ 66 Lr41
Bosnia and Herzegovina ☐ ■ BIH 27 Lb05
Bosnik ☐ RI 154 Rj46
Boso ☐ RDC 190 Ma44
Bosobolo ☐ RDC 190 Lk43
Boso-hanto ☐ J 113 Sa28
Bososama ☐ RDC 190 Ma44
Bosporus ☐ TR 69 Mk49
Bosque de Fray Jorge, P.N. ☐ RCH 280 Ge61
Bosque El Apache N.W.R. ☐ USA 235 Eg29
Bosque Petrificado J.Ormachea ☐ RA 282 Gf68
Bosque Petrificado Victor Szlapelisi ☐ RA 282 Gf68
Bossangoa ☐ RCA 190 Lj42
Bossbeen ☐ N 42 Lj31
Bossembélé ☐ RCA 190 Lj43
Bossentélé ☐ RCA 190 Lj43
Bossey Bangou ☐ RN 187 La39
Bosso ☐ RN 182 Lg38
Bosso ☐ RN 183 Lg39
Bossoroca ☐ BR 276 Hc60
Bostan ☐ CHN 102 Pc27
Bostan ☐ PAK 99 Od30
Bostan Abad ☐ IR 91 Nd27
Bostankum ☐ KZ 96 Ng24
Boston ☐ GB 49 Ku38
Boston ☐ ⬛ USA 246 Ga25
Bo'ston ☐ UZ 96 Nk24
Boston Bar ☐ CDN 232 Dk21
Boston Mts. ☐ USA 238 Fd28
Bosut ☐ SRB 68 Lu46
Bosworth ☐ AUS 148 Rj61
Bószénfa ☐ H 66 Ls44
Botafogo ☐ BR 268 Ge48
Botana ☐ RCA 190 Lj43
Botata ☐ LB 186 Kf42
Botcho ☐ RCA 190 Lj43
Boteti ☐ RDC 190 Mf45
Botevgrad ☐ BG 68 Md47
Bothaville ☐ ZA 205 Md60
Bothwell ☐ AUS 151 Sd67
Bothwell Lodge S.H.S. ☐ USA 239 Fc27
Boticas ☐ P 54 Kn39
Bottineau ☐ USA 236 Fa21
Botna ☐ IS 46 Jt26
Botro ☐ CI 187 Kj41
Botshabelo ☐ ZA 205 Md60
Botswana ☐ ■ 163 Ma12
Bottenvika ☐ S 236 Ek21
Bottle Creek ☐ 239 Ga25
Bottrop ☐ D 58 Lg39
Botucatu ☐ BR 274 Hf57
Botumirim ☐ BR 275 Hj54
Boturoaçu ☐ BR 273 Ja48
Botwood ☐ CDN 241 Hc21
Bouaflé ☐ CI 187 Kh42
Bouafle N.A. ☐ CI 187 Kh42
Bou-Ahmed ☐ MA 175 Kh28
Bou Akba ☐ DZ 175 Kj31
Bou Alba ☐ RIM 181 Kf32
Bou Ali ☐ DZ 175 Kk32
Bouam ☐ CAM 189 Lg43
Bouânane ☐ MA 175 Kk29
Bouandougou ☐ CI 187 Kh41
Bouanga ☐ RCA 190 Lh43
Bouanri ☐ BF 188 Lb40
Bouansa ☐ RCB 190 Lg47
Bouar ☐ RCA 190 Lh43
Bou Ngjida, P.N. de ☐ ● CAM
Boubin ☐ CZ 66 Lg41
Boubon ☐ RN 187 La39
Bouca ☐ RCA 190 Lj42
Bouches du Bonifacio ☐ F/I 62 Lk
Boucle du Baoulé, P.N. de la ☐ ● RMM 180 Kf38
Boú Ctaila ☐ RIM 181 Kf38
Bouda ☐ DZ 175 Kj31
Boudamasa ☐ TCH 189 Lh41
Boudenib ☐ MA 175 Kk29
Boudo ☐ RMM 181 Kg38
Boudoukou ☐ RCA 191 Md43
Bouenza ☐ RCB 190 Lg47
Boufarik ☐ DZ 176 Lb27
Bougaa ☐ DZ 176 Lc28
Bou Gâdoúm ☐ RIM 181 Kh36
Bouga Guettara ☐ RMM 182 Kk36
Bou-Hajla ☐ TN 176 Le29
Bou-Hanifia ☐ DZ 175 Lq28
Bou Hedma, P.N. ☐ TN 176 Le28
Bouila ☐ RMM 181 Kg40
Bougainville Island ☐ PNG 157 Sh50
Bougainville Reef ☐ AUS 147 Sd55
Bougainville Strait ☐ SOL 157 Sh50
Bougen ☐ RMM 181 Kg38
Bougetrao ☐ BR 268 Ge48
Bougoi ☐ RCA 190 Lj42
Bougouni ☐ RMM 186 Kg41
Bougtob ☐ DZ 175 La29
Boui Lapraire ☐ CDN 236 Fb19
Bou Kadir ☐ DZ 176 Lb27
Bouka N.A. ☐ RMM 181 Kg40
Boukombé ☐ BF 187 Kk40
Boukornine, P.N. de ☐ TN 176 Lf27
Boukra ☐ DARS 174 Kd31
Boula ☐ RCA 190 Lj43
Boulal ☐ RMM 181 Kf38
Boulaïd ☐ RCB 190 Lh47
Boulandour ☐ SN 186 Kd39
Bou Lanjar ☐ CHN 101 Pe26
Boulder ☐ USA 233 Ef24
Boulder City ☐ USA 234 Ec28

Bushman Drawings – Cape Chignecto

Cape Chiniak – Čehov

Cape Chiniak USA 228 Cd17
Cape Christian CDN 227 Gc04
Cape Clear IRL 47 Kl39
Cape Cleare USA 229 Cf16
Cape Cleveland AUS 147 Sd55
Cape Clinton AUS 149 Sf57
Cape Coast GH 187 Kk43
Cape Coast Castle GH 187 Kk43
Cape Cockburn AUS 146 Rg51
Cape Cod Bay USA 241 Ge25
Cape Cod Nat. Seashore USA 241 Gf25
Cape Cod Peninsula USA 241 Gf25
Cape Colphin GB 283 Ha71
Cape Comorin IND 118 Oj41
Cape Conran AUS 151 Se64
Cape Conran AUS 151 Se64
Cape Constantine USA 228 Ca16
Cape Cook CDN 232 Df20
Cape Coral USA 243 Fk32
Cape Corwin AUS 148 Bh16
Cape Cratton AUS 147 Sd54
Cape Crauford CDN 227 Fd04
Cape Crawford Roadhouse AUS 146 Rh54
Cape Crocker Ind. Res. CDN 237 Fk23
Cape Cross NAM 200 Lg56
Cape Cross Seal Reserve NAM 200 Lg56
Cape Cumberland VU 158 Td53
Cape Darby USA 228 Bj13
Cape Darnley 286 Oc32
Cape Dart 286 Dc33
Cape Denbigh USA 228 Bk13
Cape Dernburg NAM 204 Lh59
Cape Direction AUS 147 Sb52
Cape Discovery CDN 227 Fd02
Cape Dombey AUS 143 Re52
Cape Donington AUS 150 Rj63
Cape Dorchester CDN 227 Ga05
Cape d' Or Lighthouse CDN 240 Gh23
Cape Dorset CDN 227 Ga06
Cape Douglas USA 228 Cd16
Cape Dromedary AUS 151 Sf64
Cape du Couedic AUS 150 Rj64
Cape Dupuy AUS 142 Qh56
Cape Dyer CDN 227 Gd05
Cape Elisabeth USA 241 Ge24
Cape Enrage Lighthouse CDN 240 Gh23
Cape Espenberg USA 229 Bj12
Cape Etolin USA 228 Bg15
Cape Evans Memorial Site ANT 287 Tb34
Cape Fairweather CDN 230 Da16
Cape Farewell NZ 153 Tg66
Cape Fear USA 242 Gb29
Cape Felt 286 Eb33
Cape Flattery AUS 147 Sc53
Cape Flattery CDN 232 Dh21
Cape Floral Region Protected Areas ZA 204 Lj63
Cape Florida USA 243 Fk33
Cape Flying Fish 286 Ed33
Cape Ford AUS 143 Re52
Cape Formoso WAN 188 Ld43
Cape Foulwind NZ 153 Tf66
Cape Fourcroy AUS 146 Rf51
Cape Frankland AUS 151 Sd65
Cape Freels CDN 241 Hd21
Cape Freshfield 286 Sc32
Cape Fria NAM 200 Lf55
Cape Gantheaume AUS 150 Rj64
Cape Gantheaume Conservation Park AUS 150 Rj64
Cape Gaspé CDN 240 Gj21
Cape Gata CY 90 Mg28
Cape George CDN 240 Gk23
Cape Girardeau USA 239 Ff27
Cape Girgir PNG 155 Sc47
Cape Gkreko CY 90 Mh28
Cape Goodenough 286 Rb32
Cape Graham Moore CDN 227 Gb04
Cape Green AUS 151 Sf64
Cape Grenville AUS 147 Sb51
Cape Grey AUS 146 Rj52
Cape Grim AUS 151 Sc66
Cape Guardafui = Raas Caseyr SP 193 Nf40
Cape Halkett USA 229 Cd10
Cape Hanpan PNG 157 Sh48
Cape Harrison CDN 227 Ha07
Cape Hatteras USA 242 Gc28
Cape Hatteras Lighthouse USA 242 Gc28
Cape Hatteras Nat. Seashore USA 242 Gc28
Cape Horn 254 Gb15
Cape Hotham AUS 146 Rf52
Cape Howe AUS 151 Sf64
Cape Hudson 286 Sc32
Cape Ikolik USA 228 Cc17
Cape Iktugitak USA 228 Cc16
Cape Inscription AUS 144 Qg58
Cape Jaffa AUS 150 Rk64
Cape Jervis AUS 150 Rk63
Cape Keer-weer AUS 147 Sa52
Cape Keith AUS 146 Rf51
Cape Kekurnoi USA 228 Cc17
Cape Kellet CDN 226 Dc04
Cape Kerauden AUS 151 Sc66
Cape Keraudren AUS 142 Qk55
Cape Kidnappers NZ 153 Tj65
Cape Kimberly AUS 147 Sc54
Cape Knob AUS 144 Qk63
Cape Kormakitis CY 90 Mg28
Cape Krusenstern USA 229 Bj12
Cape Krusenstern Nat.Mon. USA 229 Bh12
Cape Kumukahi USA 234 Cc36
Cape Kunmik USA 228 Cb17
Capel AUS 144 Qh62
Capela BR 273 Jb51
Capela BR 274 Hd55
Cape Labrador CDN 227 Gd06
Capela Dourada BR 273 Jc50
Cape Latouche Treville AUS 142 Ra55
Cape Leeuwin AUS 144 Qh63
Cape Le Grand N.P. AUS 145 Rb62
Cape Leveque AUS 142 Rb54
Capelinha BR 275 Hj54
Cape Liptrap AUS 151 Sc65
Cape Lisburn VU 158 Td53
Cape Lisburne USA 229 Bg11
Capel'ka RUS 45 Mj32
Capella AUS 149 Se57
Cape Londonderry AUS 143 Rd52
Cape Lookout USA 242 Gb28
Cape Lookout Lighthouse USA 242 Gb28
Cape Lookout Nat. Seashore USA 242 Gb28
Cape Low CDN 227 Fc06
Cape Manifold AUS 149 Sf57
Cape Maria van Diemen NZ 152 Tg63
Cape May USA 241 Gc26
Cape Mécatina CDN 240 Ha20
Cape Melville AUS 147 Sc53
Cape Melville RP 128 Qj42
Cape Melville N.P. AUS 147 Sc53
Cape Mendenhall USA 228 Bg16
Cape Mercy CDN 227 Gd06
Cape Mohican USA 228 Bg15
Cape Monze PK 99 Od33
Cape Mordvinof USA 228 Bh18
Cape Moreton AUS 149 Sg59
Cape Mount LB 186 Ke42
Cape Muzon USA 230 Dd18
Cape Nachtigal CAM 188 Le44
Cape Naturaliste AUS 144 Qh62
Cape Naturaliste AUS 151 Se66
Capenda-Camulemba ANG 199 Lk50
Cape Nelson AUS 150 Sa65
Cape Nelson PNG 156 Se50
Cape Newenham USA 228 Bj16
Cape Nome USA 228 Bh13
Cape North CDN 240 Gk22
Cape Northumberland AUS 150 Sa65
Cape Nuyts AUS 150 Rg62
Cape of Good Hope ZA 204 Lk63
Cape Otway AUS 151 Sb65
Cape Palliser NZ 153 Th66
Cape Palmer 286 Fa33
Cape Palmerston AUS 149 Se56
Cape Pankof USA 228 Bj18
Cape Parry CDN 226 Dd04
Cape Pasley AUS 145 Rb62
Cape Peron North AUS 144 Qg58
Cape Perpetua Scenic Area USA 232 Dh23
Cape Poinsett 286 Qc32
Cape Pole USA 230 Dd17
Cape Preston AUS 142 Qj56
Cape Prince Albert CDN 226 Dc04
Cape Prince of Wales USA 228 Bf13
Cape Providence NZ 153 Td68
Cape Providence USA 228 Cb17
Cape Queen CDN 227 Ga06
Cape Queiros VU 158 Td53
Cape Race CDN 241 Hd22
Cape Race Lighthouse CDN 241 Hd22
Cape Radstock AUS 150 Rh62
Cape Range N.P. AUS 142 Qg57
Cape Raper CDN 227 Gc05
Cape Ray CDN 241 Ha22
Cape Recife ZA 205 Mc63
Cape Reinga NZ 152 Tg63
Cape Rhir MA 174 Kf30
Cape Riche AUS 144 Qk63
Cape Romain N.W.R. USA 242 Ga29
Cape Romanzof USA 228 Bg15
Cape Ronsard AUS 144 Qg58
Cape Ronsard AUS 144 Qg58
Cape Runaway NZ 152 Tj64
Cape Ruthieres AUS 143 Rd52
Cape Ruwura EAT 197 Na51
Cape Sable USA 243 Fk33
Cape Sable Island CDN 241 Gh24
Cape Saint Cricq AUS 144 Qg58
Cape Saint Elias USA 230 Ch16
Cape Saint Francis CDN 241 Hd22
Cape Saint Francis ZA 205 Mc63
Cape Saint Francis ZA 205 Mc63
Cape Saint George CDN 241 Ha21
Cape Saint George CDN 241 Ha21
Cape Saint James CDN 230 De19
Cape Saint John CDN 241 Hc20
Cape Saint Lawrence CDN 240 Gk22
Cape Saint Mary CDN 240 Gk23
Cape Saint Mary's CDN 241 Hc22
Cape San Agustin RP 125 Rd42
Cape San Blas USA 239 Fh31
Cape Sandwich AUS 147 Sd55
Cape San Ildefonso RP 124 Rb37
Cape Santa Maria BS 250 Gc34
Cape Sarichef USA 228 Bh18
Cape Scott CDN 232 Df20
Cape Sherard CDN 227 Ga04
Cape Shield AUS 146 Rj52
Cape Shilling WAL 186 Kd41
Cape Sibbald 286 Tb33
Cape Sidmouth AUS 147 Sb52
Cape Simpson USA 229 Cc10
Cape Smith CDN 227 Ga06
Cape Sorell AUS 151 Sc67
Cape Spencer AUS 150 Rj63
Cape Spencer CDN 230 Db16
Cape Stephens NZ 153 Tg66
Cape Sterling 286 Fb32
Cape Stewart AUS 146 Rh51
Cape Thouin AUS 142 Qk56
Cape Tormentine CDN 240 Gj22
Cape Town ZA 204 Lk62
Cape Tribulation AUS 147 Sc54
Cape Turnagain NZ 153 Tj66
Cape Upright USA 228 Bd15
Cape Upstart AUS 147 Sd55
Cape Upstart N.P. AUS 147 Sd55
Cape Vancouver USA 228 Bh15
Cape van Diemen AUS 146 Rf51
Cape Verde 11 Jb08
Cape Verde Islands CV 186 Jh38
Cape Verde Plateau 162 Jb08
Cape Vogel PNG 156 Sf50
Cape Voltaire AUS 143 Rc53
Cape von Diemen AUS 147 Rk54
Cape Wessel AUS 146 Rj51
Cape Whittle CDN 240 Ha20
Cape Wickham AUS 151 Sb65
Cape Wilberforce AUS 146 Rj51
Cape Willoughby AUS 150 Rk63
Cape Wrath GB 48 Kp32
Cape York AUS 147 Sb51
Cape York Peninsula AUS 147 Sb52
Cap Ferret F 52 Kt46
Cap Fréhel F 50 Ks42
Cap Gris-Nez F 51 Lb40
Cap-Haïtien RH 250 Gd36
Capidava RO 69 Mj46
Capilla del Monte RA 280 Gh61
Capim Grosso BR 273 Hk51
Capim Verde BR 274 Hc55
Capinazal BR 276 He59
Capinha P 55 Kn50
Capinópolis BR 274 Hf55
Capinota BOL 278 Gg54
Capira PA 249 Ga41
Capiro-Calentura, P.N. HN 248 Fh38
Cap Island RP 125 Ra43
Capistrano BR 273 Ja48
Capitan USA 235 Eh29
Capitán Augusto Rivadeneira EC 268 Gc46
Capitán Bado PY 274 Hc57
Capitán Bermúdez RA 281 Gk62
Capitán Leónidas Marques BR 276 Hd58
Capitán Pablo Lagerenza PY 278 Gk55
Capitán Sarmiento RA 281 Ha63
Capitão de Campos BR 273 Hk48
Capitão Eneas BR 275 Hj54
Capitão Poço BR 267 Hg46
Capitol Reef N.P. USA 235 Ee26
Capitol Peak USA 233 Eh23
Capitol Peak USA 232 Eb25
Capitol Reef N.P. USA 235 Ee26
Capivari BR 275 Hg57
Capivari do Sul BR 277 He61
Cap Juby MA 174 Kd31
Čaplanovo RUS 111 Sb22
Čapljina BIH 61 Ls47
Cap Lopez G 198 Le46
Čaplygin RUS 72 Mk19
Čaplynka UA 73 Mg22
Cap Mountain CDN 231 Dj14
Cap Ndoua F 158 Td57
Capoas, Mount RP 124 Qk40
Capo Bellavista I 62 Lk51
Capo Boeo I 62 Ln53
Capo Bonifati I 63 Lq51
Capo Càccia I 62 Lj50
Capo Calavà I 63 Lp52
Capo Carbonara I 62 Lk51
Capo Coda Cavallo I 62 Lk50
Capo Colonna I 63 Ls52
Capo Comino I 62 Lk50
Capo del Falcone I 62 Lj50
Capo dell'Argentiera I 62 Lj50
Capo dell'Orso I 63 Lr51
Capo di Ferro I 62 Lk49
Capo di Fasca I 62 Lj51
Capo di Milazzo I 63 Lq52
Capo di Monte Santu I 62 Lk50
Capo di Pula I 62 Lk52
Capo d'Orlando I 63 Lp52
Capo d'Orlando I 63 Lp52
Capo d'Otranto I 63 Lt50
Capoeira do Rei BR 267 He45
Capo Ferrato I 62 Lk51
Capo Gallo I 62 Lo52
Capo Granitola I 62 Ln53
Capo Ísola delle Correnti I 63 Lq54
Capo Linaro I 62 Lm48
Capolo ANG 198 Lg51
Capo Mannu I 62 Lj50
Capo Marárgiu I 62 Lj50
Capo Mele I 60 Lj47
Capo Murro di Porco I 63 Lq54
Caponda MOC 202 Mf53
Capo Palinuro I 63 Lq50
Capo Pàssero I 63 Lq54
Capo Pecora I 62 Lj51
Capo Rizzuto I 63 Ls52
Capo San Marco I 62 Lj51
Capo San Marco I 62 Lo53
Capo Santa Croce I 63 Lq53
Capo Santa Maria di Léuca I 63 Lt51
Capo San Vito I 62 Ln52
Capo San Vito I 63 Ls50
Capo Scarámia I 63 Lp54
Capo Senino F 60 Lj48
Capo Sferracavallo I 62 Lk51
Capo Spartivento I 62 Lj52
Capo Spartivento I 63 Lr53
Capo Sperone I 62 Lj52
Capo Spulico I 63 Lr51
Capo Testa I 62 Lk49
Capo Teulada I 62 Lj52
Capotoan, Mount RP 124 Rc39
Capoto Jarina, T.I. BR 271 Hd51
Capo Trionto I 63 Lr51
Capo Vaticano I 63 Lq52
Cappadocia TR 90 Mh26
Cap Palmas CI 187 Kg43
Cappella Palatina I 62 Lo52
Capps USA 242 Fj30
Cap Rhir MA 174 Kf30
Capri I 63 Lp50
Capriana MD 73 Me22
Capricorn Highway AUS 149 Sd57
Capricorn Roadhouse AUS 142 Qk57
Caprivi NAM 201 Mb54
Caprivi Strip NAM 201 Mb54
Caprock USA 238 Ej29
Caprock Canyons S.P. USA 238 Ek28
Cap Roussin F 158 Td56
Cap Saint-André = Tanjona Vilanandro RM 206 Nc54
Cap Sainte-Marie = Tanjona Vohimena RM 207 Nc58
Cap Saint-Vincent = Tanjona Ankaboa RM 207 Nb56
Cap Serrat TN 176 Le27
Cap Skirring SN 186 Kb39
Cap Spartel MA 55 Kp45
Captain Cook USA 234 Cc36
Captains Flat AUS 151 Se63
Captieux F 52 Ku46
Capua ANG 200 Lk53
Cápua I 63 Lp49
Capu di Muru F 62 Lj49
Capulin Volcano Nat. Mon. USA 235 Eh27
Capul Island RP 124 Rc39
Capunda ANG 200 Lj51
Capu Rossu F 60 Lj48
Cap Vert SN 180 Kb38
Cap Wabao F 158 Td56
Caquetá CO 268 Ge46
Caqueza CO 264 Gd43
Caraballo RP 124 Ra37
Carabao Island RP 124 Ra39
Caracal RO 69 Me46
Caracaraí BR 265 Gk45
Caracas YV 265 Gg40
Caracol BOL 278 Gf56
Caracol BR 273 Hj50
Carácol BR 274 Hb56
Carácol BR 274 Hb56
Caracol CO 264 Gd40
Caracolli BOL 278 Gg54
Carácuaro MEX 246 Ek36
Caraculo ANG 200 Lg53
Caraga RP 125 Rd42
Caragahal AUS 151 Sd62
Caraguatatuba BR 277 Hh57
Carahue RCH 280 Gd65
Caraí BR 275 Hk54
Caraíba BR 273 Ja50
Caraíva BR 275 Ja54
Carajas BR 272 He49
Caraman F 52 Lb47
Caramoan RP 124 Rb39
Caramoan RP 124 Rb39
Caramat CDN 237 Fg21
Caramura Paraguassa, T.I. BR 275 Ja53
Caramut AUS 151 Sb64
Caranavi BOL 278 Gg53
Carancho RA 280 Gh64
Carandai BR 275 Hj56
Carandazinho BR 274 Hb54
Carandotta AUS 148 Rk56
Caranga de Abajo E 54 Ko47
Carangola BR 275 Hj56
Caransebeș RO 68 Mc45
Carantec F 50 Kr42
Carapa PE 269 Ge53
Carapa YV 265 Gj41
Carapajó BR 267 Hf47
Carapeguá PY 276 Hb58
Carapinha BR 275 Hk56
Carapo YV 265 Gj43
Carara Puca BR 265 Gg45
Carare CO 264 Gd42
Carari BR 271 Gk46
Caratinga BR 275 Hj55
Carauari BR 270 Gg48
Caraúbas BR 273 Jb48
Caravaca de la Cruz E 57 Kt52
Caravela GNB 186 Kb40
Caravelí PE 269 Gd53
Caravelas BR 275 Ja54
Caraz PE 269 Gb50
Carazinho BR 276 Hd60
Carazinho BR 276 Hd60
Carballiño E 54 Km48
Carballo E 54 Km47
Carberry CDN 236 Fa21
Carbinie AUS 144 Ra61
Carbo MEX 244 Ee31
Carbonara I 62 Lk52
Carbondale USA 235 Eg26
Carbondale USA 239 Ff27
Carbondale USA 239 Fg25
Carbondale USA 241 Gc25
Carbonear CDN 241 Hd22
Carboneras E 57 Kt54
Carboneras MEX 245 Fb33
Carboneras de Guadazaón E 57 Kt51
Carbónia I 62 Lj51
Carbonita BR 275 Hj54
Carbonne F 52 Lb47
Carcans F 52 Kt45
Carcans-Plage F 52 Kt45
Carcar RP 124 Rb40
Carcassonne F 52 Lc47
Carcastillo E 56 Kt48
Carcelén E 57 Kt51
Carcot Island 286 Ga32
Carcross CDN 230 Dc15
Carcuma AUS 150 Sa63
Cardal ROU 281 Hb63
Cardamom Mountains K 123 Qb39
Cardeal Mota BR 275 Hj55
Cardeña E 55 Kq52
Cárdenas C 243 Fk34
Cárdenas MEX 246 Fa34
Cárdenas MEX 247 Fd37
Cardiff GB 49 Kr39
Cardigan GB 49 Kq38
Cardigan Bay GB 49 Kq38
Cardinal CDN 236 Fa21
Cardona E 57 Lb49
Cardona ROU 276 Hb62
Cardoso BR 274 Hf56
Cardwell AUS 147 Sd55
Careí RO 67 Mc43
Careiro BR 271 Gk47
Careiro da Várzea BR 271 Ha47
Carembei BR 277 He58
Carén RCH 280 Ge61
Carentan F 50 Kt41
Carevo BG 69 Mh48
Carev Vrh MK 68 Mc48
Carey USA 232 Ed24
Carey Downs AUS 144 Qh58
Carfield AUS 149 Sc57
Cargèse F 60 Lj48
Carhaix-Plouguer F 50 Kr42
Carhuamayo PE 269 Gb51
Carhuanca PE 269 Gd52
Carhuas PE 269 Gb50
Carhué RA 281 Gj64
Cariacica BR 275 Hk56
Cariaco YV 265 Gj40
Cariamanga EC 268 Ga48
Cariango ANG 200 Lh51
Cariati I 63 Lr51
Caribbean Sea 210 Fb08
Cariboo Mountains CDN 232 Dk19
Caribou CDN 227 Fa07
Caribou USA 240 Gf22
Caribou Lake CDN 236 Ff20
Caribou Mountain USA 229 Ce12
Carichic MEX 244 Eg32
Caridad HN 248 Fg39
Caridade BR 273 Ja48
Cariewerloo AUS 150 Rj62
Carigara RP 124 Rc40
Carignan F 51 Lf41
Carillo Puerto MEX 247 Fe36
Carinda AUS 149 Sd61
Cariñena E 57 Kt49
Carinha BR 272 Hg49
Carinhanha BR 275 Hj53
Carini I 62 Lo52
Carinish GB 48 Kn33
Carinola I 63 Lo49
Caripe YV 265 Gj40
Caripira BR 270 Gh46
Caripito YV 265 Gj40
Cariré BR 273 Hk47
Carita Beach RI 127 Qc49
Caritianas BR 270 Gj50
Carizal CO 264 Gd39
Car Kalojan BG 69 Mg47
Carles RP 124 Rb40
Carleton, Mount CDN 240 Gg22
Carleton Place CDN 241 Gb23
Cârlibaba RO 67 Mf43
Carlin USA 234 Eb25
Carlisle GB 49 Ks36
Carlisle USA 241 Gb25
Carlo AUS 148 Rk57
Carloforte I 62 Lj51
Carlos A. Carrillo MEX 247 Fc36
Carlos Chagas BR 275 Hk54
Carlos Pellegrini RA 281 Gk62
Carlos Reyles ROU 276 Hb62
Carlos Sasares RA 281 Gk63
Carlos Tejedor RA 281 Gj63
Carlow IRL 47 Ko38
Carloway GB 48 Ko32
Carlsbad USA 234 Eb29
Carlsbad USA 235 Eh29
Carlsbad Caverns N.P. USA 235 Eh29
Carlson Landing CDN 231 Ee16
Carlton AUS 149 Sd61
Carlton USA 239 Fg30
Carlyle CDN 233 Ej21
Carmacks CDN 230 Db14
Carmagnola I 60 Lh46
Carman CDN 236 Fb21
Carmangay CDN 233 Ed20
Carmarthen GB 49 Kq39
Carmaux F 52 Lc46
Carmel USA 239 Fg26
Carmel Beach USA 234 Dk27
Carmel Head GB 49 Kq37
Carmelita GCA 247 Fe37
Carmelo ROU 276 Ha62
Carmen RP 124 Rc41
Carmen Alto RCH 279 Gf57
Carmen de Areco RA 281 Ha63
Carmen de Patagones RA 281 Gj66
Cármenes E 54 Kp48
Carmésia BR 275 Hj55
Carmichael AUS 149 Sd56
Carmichael Craig AUS 143 Rf58
Carmila AUS 149 Se56
Carmo BR 272 Hf48
Carmo do Paranaíba BR 275 Hg55
Carmo do Rio Claro BR 275 Hg56
Carmona CR 249 Fh40
Carmona E 55 Kp53
Carnac F 50 Kr43
Carnaíba BR 273 Jb49
Carnarvon AUS 144 Qg58
Carnarvon AUS 149 Sd58
Carnarvon ZA 204 Mb61
Carnarvon N.P. AUS 149 Sd58
Carnarvon Range AUS 144 Ra58
Carnatic Shoal 124 Qj40
Carnavon Range AUS 149 Se58
Carndonagh IRL 47 Kn35
Carnegie AUS 145 Rb58
Carnegie USA 238 Fa28
Carn Eige GB 48 Kp33
Carnew IRL 47 Ko38
Carnforth GB 49 Ks36
Car Nicobar Island IND 122 Pg41
Carnikava LV 45 Me33
Čarnjany BY 65 Me39
Carnot RCA 190 Lh43
Carnoustie GB 48 Ks34
Carnsore Point IRL 47 Ko38
Caroebe BR 266 Ha45
Caroga Lake USA 241 Gc24
Carolina BR 272 Hg49
Carolina CO 264 Gc42
Carolina RA 280 Gg62
Carolina USA 251 Gh36
Carolina ZA 205 Mf59
Carolina Beach USA 242 Gb29
Carolina Sandhills N.W.R. USA 242 Fk28
Caroline CDN 233 Ec19
Caroline Islands 134 Rb09
Carolinensiel D 58 Lh37
Caroline Seamounts 134 Sa09
Caroni YV 265 Gj43
Carora YV 264 Ge40
Carot River CDN 233 Ej19
Carpathian Mountains RO 26 Ma05
Carpathian Mountains UA 67 Md42
Carpathian Mountains 73 Mb21
Carpaţii Curburii RO 69 Mf45
Carpen RO 68 Md46
Carpenter USA 236 Fb23
Carpenter Rocks AUS 150 Sa64
Carpenterville USA 232 Dh24
Carpentras F 53 Lf46
Carpi I 60 Ll46
Carpina BR 273 Jc49
Carpinteria USA 234 Ea28
Carpio E 55 Kp51
Carpolac AUS 150 Sa64
Carquefou F 52 Kt43
Carqueja BR 273 Ja50
Carrabelle USA 239 Fh31
Carrabin AUS 144 Qk61
Carrapia CO 264 Gd40
Carranglan RP 124 Ra37
Carrara I 60 Ll46
Carrarra Range AUS 146 Rj55
Carrasco, P.N. BOL 278 Gh54
Carrascosa del Campo E 57 Ks50
Carrasquero YV 264 Gd40
Carrathol AUS 151 Sc63
Carrauntoohil IRL 47 Kl38
Carrbridge GB 48 Kr33
Carre Four RH 250 Gd36
Carrenleufú RCH 282 Ge67
Carrere, Cerro RA 280 Gf64
Carretera Austral RCH 282 Gd67
Carriacou WV 251 Gk39
Carrickfergus GB 47 Kp36
Carrickmacross IRL 47 Ko37
Carrick-on-Shannon IRL 47 Km37
Carrick-on-Suir IRL 47 Kn38
Carrieton AUS 150 Rk62
Carrington USA 236 Fa22
Carrington CDN 240 Gd20
Carrion de los Condes E 54 Kq48
Carrizal YV 265 Gk42
Carrizal Bajo RCH 279 Ge60
Carrizos MEX 245 Fa33
Carrizo Springs USA 245 Fa31
Carrizozo USA 235 Eh29
Carroll USA 236 Fc24
Carrollton USA 237 Fk25
Carrollton USA 239 Fh29
Carrollton USA 238 Fd26
Carrouges F 50 Ku42
Carruamayo PE 264 Gd44
Carrua MOC 203 Mj54
Carryduff GB 47 Kp36
Çarşamba TR 90 Mj25
Carseland CDN 233 Ed20
Carson USA 236 Ek22
Carson City USA 234 Ea26
Carson River AUS 143 Rd53
Carson River A.L. AUS 143 Rd53
Carstairs CDN 233 Ec20
Cartagena CO 264 Gc40
Cartagena E 57 Ku53
Cartagena del Chaira CO 264 Gc45
Cartago CO 264 Gc43
Cartago CR 249 Fj41
Cartaxo P 55 Km51
Cartaya E 55 Kn53
Carter Bar Pass GB 48 Ks35
Carter, Mount AUS 147 Sb52
Carter Spit USA 228 Bj16
Carters Range AUS 148 Sa57
Cartersville USA 239 Fh28
Carthage TN 176 Lf27
Carthage USA 238 Fc27
Carthage USA 239 Ff29
Carthage USA 242 Ga28
Cartier CDN 237 Fk22
Cartier Island AUS 142 Rb52
Carti Suitupo PA 249 Ga41
Cartucho BR 272 Hg50
Cartwright CDN 227 Ha08
Cartwright CDN 236 Fa21
Caruaru BR 273 Jc50
Carumbé ROU 276 Hb61
Carunantabari YV 265 Gj43
Carúpano YV 265 Gj40
Caruray RP 124 Qk40
Carutapera BR 267 Hh46
Caruthersville USA 239 Ff27
Caru, T.I. BR 272 Hg47
Čárvarica BG 68 Mc48
Caravelas BR 275 Ja54
Carver USA 234 Eb26
Carvin F 51 Lc40
Carvoal BR 274 Hb54
Carvoeiro BR 270 Gk46
Carwarna Downs AUS 145 Rb61
Carway CDN 233 Ed21
Carwell AUS 149 Sd58
Cary USA 242 Ga28
Cas RCH 279 Gg57
Casablanca MA 175 Kg29
Casa Blanca MEX 245 Ek32
Casablanca RCH 280 Ge62
Casa Branca BR 275 Hg56
Casacalenda I 63 Lp49
Casa de Juan Núñez E 57 Kt51
Casadepaga USA 228 Bh13
Casa de Piedra RA 280 Gg65
Casa Grande USA 235 Ee29
Casa Grande Ruins Nat. Mon. USA 235 Ee29
Casalbordino I 63 Lp48
Casale Monferrato I 60 Lj45
Casalins RA 281 Ha64
Casalmaggiore I 60 Ll46
Casalpusterlengo I 60 Lk45
Casamance SN 186 Kc39
Casamassima I 63 Lr50
Casamozza F 60 Lk48
Casa Msika MOC 202 Mg55
Casanare CO 265 Gf43
Casanay YV 265 Gj40
Casa Nova BR 273 Hk50
Casarabi BOL 278 Gh53
Casarano I 63 Lt50
Casares NIC 248 Fg40
Casas MEX 246 Fa34
Casas Colgadas de Cuenca E 57 Ks50
Casas del Puerto E 57 Kt52
Casas de Lázaro E 55 Ks52
Casas Grandes MEX 244 Ee31
Casas Grandes MEX 244 Eg30
Casas-Ibáñez E 57 Kt51
Casas Viejas MEX 244 Eh34
Casa Verde BR 274 Hd56
Casa Verde MEX 246 Fa37
Casavieja E 55 Kq50
Casazinc CO 264 Gd44
Casbas RA 281 Gj64
Casca BR 276 He60
Cascada Coda de Caballo MEX 245 Ek33
Cascadas Agua Azul MEX 247 Fd37
Cascadas de Agoyán EC 268 Ga46
Cascadas de Basaseachic MEX 244 Ef31
Cascadas de Basaseachic, P.N. MEX 244 Ef32
Cascadas del Queguay ROU 276 Ha62
Cascadas de San Rafael EC 268 Gb46
Cascadas de Tzaráracua MEX 246 Ej36
Cascadas Misol-Há MEX 247 Fd37
Cascade AUS 144 Ra62
Cascade USA 232 Eb23
Cascade Caverns USA 245 Fa31
Cascade d'Akloa TG 187 La42
Cascade de Daravangy RM 206 Ne54
Cascade de Karfiguela BF 187 Kh40
Cascade de Vierges MA 175 Kh29
Cascade Mtn. Ski Area USA 236 Ff24
Cascade Point NZ 153 Te68
Cascade Range CDN 232 Dk21
Cascade Range USA 232 Dj24
Cascades de Kota DY 187 La40
Cascades d'Ouzoud MA 175 Kg29
Cascais P 55 Kl52
Cascajal C 243 Fk34
Cascante E 56 Kt49
Cascantinha BR 277 Hj57
Cascas PE 268 Ga49
Cascavel BR 273 Ja48
Cascavel BR 276 Hd58
Cáscia I 61 Lo48
Casciana Terme I 60 Ll47
Cáscina I 60 Ll47
Cásciorele RO 69 Mg46
Cascorro C 243 Gb35
Caseiros BR 276 He60
Caselle Torinese I 60 Lh45
Casentinesi-Monte Falterona-Campigna, P.N. I 60 Lm47
Caserón RCH 279 Ge59
Caserta I 63 Lp49
Casey CDN 240 Gc22
Casey ANT 286 Qc32
Cashel IRL 47 Kn38
Cashel ZW 202 Mg55
Cashmere Downs AUS 144 Qk60
Casigua YV 264 Gd41
Casiguran RP 124 Rb37
Casilda RA 281 Gk62
Casimcea RO 69 Mj46
Casimiro Castillo MEX 246 Eh36
Casimiro de Abreu BR 277 Hj57
Casinos E 57 Ku51
Casiquiare YV 265 Gg44
Casiquiare YV 265 Gg45
Čáslav CZ 66 Lq41
Casma PE 269 Ga50
Cašniki BY 72 Me18
Casoli I 63 Lp48
Casória I 63 Lp50
Caspana RCH 279 Gf57
Caspe E 57 Ku49
Casper USA 233 Eg24
Caspian Depression 76 Na05
Caspian Sea 76 Nb06
Cassacatiza MOC 202 Mg53
Cassai ANG 201 Ma51
Cassai ANG/RDC 199 Ma50
Cassamba ANG 201 Ma52
Cassango ANG 199 Lj50
Cassano allo Iónio I 63 Lr51
Cassapa MOC 203 Mk54
Cassasala ANG 200 Lk51
Cassel F 51 Lc40
Casselton USA 236 Fb22
Cassembe MOC 197 Mj52
Cassero MOC 203 Mj52
Cássia BR 275 Hg56
Cassiar CDN 230 Df16
Cassiar Mountains CDN 230 Df16
Cassiar-Stewart Highway CDN 230 Df17
Cassilândia BR 274 He55
Cassilis AUS 148 Sb56
Cassinga ANG 200 Lj53
Cassini Island AUS 143 Rc52
Cassino BR 276 Hd62
Cassino I 62 Lo49
Cassis F 53 Lf47
Cass Lake USA 236 Fc22
Cassongue ANG 200 Lh51
Castagneto Carducci I 60 Ll47
Castaña YV 265 Gh43
Castañar de Ibor E 55 Kp51
Castañeda MEX 244 Ec30
Castanhal BR 267 Hg46
Castanhal BR 270 Gj49
Castanheira BR 271 Ha51
Castanheira de Pira P 55 Km51
Castaños MEX 245 Ek32
Castaño Viejo RA 280 Gf61
Castejón de Valdejasa E 56 Ku49
Castelândia BR 274 He55
Castelbuono I 63 Lp53
Castel del Monte I 63 Lr49
Castel di Sangro I 63 Lp49
Castelfidardo I 61 Lo47
Castelfranco Emilia I 60 Lm46
Castelfranco Véneto I 60 Lm45
Castelgar CDN 232 Eb21
Casteljaloux F 52 La46
Castellabate I 63 Lp50
Castellammare del Golfo I 62 Ln52
Castellammare di Stábia I 63 Lp50
Castellane F 53 Lg47
Castellaneta I 63 Lr50
Castellanea Marina I 63 Lr50
Castellar de Santiago E 55 Kr52
Castell'Arquato I 60 Lk46
Castelldans E 57 La49
Castelldefels E 57 Lb49
Castell de Ferro E 55 Kr54
Castelli RA 281 Hb64
Castello Aragonese d'Ischia I 62 Lo50
Castello dei Ruffo I 63 Lq52
Castelló de la Plana E 57 Ku51
Castello di Castelsardo I 62 Lj50
Castello di Manfredonia I 63 Lq49
Castello di Manta I 60 Lh46
Castelnaudary F 52 Lb47
Castelnau-de-Médoc F 52 Ku45
Castelnau-Magnoac F 52 La47
Castelnovo ne'Monti I 60 Ll46
Castelnuovo di Garfagnana I 60 Ll46
Castelo BR 275 Hk56
Castelo Branco P 55 Kn51
Castelo de Vide P 55 Kn51
Castelo do Piauí BR 273 Hk48
Castel San Giovanni I 60 Lk45
Castel San Pietro Terme I 60 Lm46
Castelsardo I 62 Lj50
Castelsarrasin F 52 Lb46
Castelterrmini I 62 Lo53
Castelvetrano I 62 Ln53
Casterton AUS 150 Sa64
Castets F 52 Kt47
Castiglioncello I 60 Ll47
Castiglione della Pescáia I 60 Ll48
Castiglione delle Stiviere I 60 Ll45
Castiglione sul Lago I 60 Ln47
Castiglion Fiorentino I 60 Lm47
Castilblanco E 55 Kp51
Castilhiano CV 186 Jh37
Castilla RA 281 Ha63
Castilla RP 124 Rb39
Castilla - La Mancha E 55 Kr51
Castilla la Vieja E 54 Kp50
Castilla Nueva E 57 Kr51
Castilla y León E 54 Kp49
Castillejo de Martín Viejo E 54 Ko50
Castillo-Convento de Calatrava la Nueva E 55 Kr52
Castillo de Ampudia E 54 Kq49
Castillo de Biar E 57 Ku52
Castillo de Fonseca E 54 Kq49
Castillo de Frías E 56 Kr48
Castillo de Granadilla E 55 Ko50
Castillo de Jagua C 243 Fk34
Castillo de Javier E 56 Kt48
Castillo de la Mota E 54 Kq49
Castillo de Loarre E 56 Ku48
Castillo de los Reyes de Navarra E 56 Kt48
Castillo del Puente del Congosto E 55 Kp50
Castillo de Manzanares el Real E 55 Kr50
Castillo de Medellín E 55 Kp52
Castillo de Mombeltrán E 55 Kp50
Castillo de Montearagón E 56 Ku48
Castillo de Peñafiel E 54 Kq49
Castillo de San Felipe GCA 248 Ff38
Castillo de San Marcos USA 242 Fk31
Castillo de Villalonso E 54 Kp49
Castillon-en-Couserans F 52 Lb48
Castillonnès F 52 La46
Castillos ROU 281 Hd63
Castillos de Guayana YV 265 Gj41
Castlebar IRL 47 Kl37
Castlebay GB 48 Kn34
Castleblayney IRL 47 Ko36
Castle Cove USA 228 Ca17
Castlecombe GB 47 Kn36
Castle Dale USA 235 Ee26
Castle Douglas GB 48 Kr36
Castle Hill N.H.P. CDN 241 Hd22
Castle Island BS 250 Gc34
Castleisland IRL 47 Kl38
Castle Mount USA 234 Dk28
Castle Peak USA 232 Ec23
Castlepollard IRL 47 Kn37
Castlerea IRL 47 Km37
Castlereagh Bay AUS 146 Rh52
Castle Rock USA 233 Ej23
Castle Rock USA 235 Eh26
Castles of the Assassins IR 91 Nf27
Castletown GB 48 Kr32
Castletown GB 49 Kq36
Castletownbere IRL 47 Kl39
Castlevale AUS 149 Sd58
Castle Venlaw GB 48 Kr35
Castor CDN 233 Ee19
Castres F 52 Lc47
Castricum NL 51 Le38
Castries WL 251 Gk38
Castril E 55 Ks53
Castro BR 277 He58
Castro RCH 280 Gd67
Castro Alves BR 273 Ja52
Castro Barras RA 279 Gh61
Castrocaro Terme I 60 Lm46
Castro Daire P 54 Kn50
Castro del Río E 55 Kq53
Castrojeriz E 54 Kq48
Castropol E 54 Kn47
Castroreale I 63 Lq52
Castro-Urdiales E 56 Kr47
Castro Verde P 55 Km53
Castro Viejo RA 280 Gf61
Castrovillari I 63 Lr51
Castrovirreyna PE 269 Gc52
Castuera E 55 Kp52
Casuarina Coast RI 154 Rk49
Casuarina Coast RI 154 Rj48
Casuli NIC 248 Fh39
Casupá ROU 281 Hc63
Caswell USA 229 Ce15
Çat TR 91 Na26
Čata YV 265 Gg40
Catabola ANG 200 Lh52
Catabola ANG 200 Lj52
Cataby Roadhouse AUS 144 Qh61
Catacamas HN 248 Fh38
Catacaos PE 268 Fk48
Catache PE 268 Ga49
Catacocha EC 268 Ga48
Cataguases BR 275 Hj56
Catahoula Lake USA 238 Fe30
Catahuasi PE 269 Gc52
Cataingan RP 124 Rb39
Çatak TR 71 Mj52
Çatak TR 91 Nb26
Catalão BR 275 Hg55
Çatalca TR 69 Mj49
Çatalca Yarımadası TR 69 Mh49
Çatal Hüyük TR 90 Mg27
Catalina CDN 241 Hd21
Catalina PE 279 Gf58
Catalonia E 57 La49
Catama SP 195 Na44
Catamarca RA 279 Gg59
Catamayo EC 268 Ga47
Catambué ANG 200 Lk54
Catanacuname YV 265 Gg44
Catanauan RP 124 Rb39
Catandica MOC 202 Mg55
Catanduanes Island RP 124 Rc39
Catanduva BR 274 Hf56
Catanduvas BR 276 Hd58
Catangalo BR 275 Hj57
Catanhede BR 272 Hh47
Catania I 63 Lq53
Catán Lil RA 280 Ge65
Catanzaro I 63 Lr52
Catanzaro Marina I 63 Lr52
Catarama EC 268 Ga46
Cataratas del Iguazú BR/RA 276 Hc58
Catarina BR 273 Ja49
Catarman RP 124 Rc39
Catata-a-Nova ANG 200 Lh52
Catatumbo-Bari, P.N. CO 264 Gd41
Catavi BOL 278 Gf55
Cataxa MOC 202 Mg53
Catazajá MEX 247 Fd37
Catbalogan RP 124 Rc40
Cat Ba N.P. VN 121 Qd35
Ćat-Bazar KS 100 Og24
Cat Cays BS 243 Ga33
Catechane MOC 202 Mg57
Catedral de Ávila E 55 Kq50
Catedral de Barbastro E 56 La48
Catedral de Burgos E 56 Kr48
Catedral de Ciudad Rodrigo E 54 Ko50
Catedral de Cuenca E 57 Ks50
Catedral de León E 54 Kp48
Catedral de Sal CO 264 Gd43
Catedral de Sigüenza E 57 Ks49
Catedral de Toledo E 55 Kq51
Catedral de Tortosa E 57 La50
Catedral de València E 57 Ku51
Catedral de Viseu P 54 Kn50
Catedral de Zamora E 54 Kp49
Catedral La Seo de Zaragoza E 56 Ku49
Cateel Bay RP 125 Rd42
Catemaco MEX 247 Fc36
Catembe MOC 205 Mg59
Catende BR 273 Jc50
Catengue ANG 200 Lg52
Cateraggio F 62 Lk48
Catete ANG 198 Lg50
Cathcart ZA 205 Md62
Cathedral Cave AUS 149 Sd58
Cathedral Caverns USA 239 Fg28
Cathedral Cove NZ 152 Th64
Cathédrale de Clermont-Ferrand F 53 Ld45
Cathédrale de Lausanne CH 60 Lg44
Cathédrale de Narbonne F 53 Lc47
Cathédrale de Reims F 51 Le41
Cathédrale de Saint-Bertrand-de-Commingen F 52 La47
Cathédrale de Strasbourg F 51 Lh42
Cathédrale de Vienne F 53 Le45
Cathédrale d'Orléans F 51 Lb43
Cathédrale du Puy-en-Velay F 53 Ld45
Cathedral Gorge S.P. USA 234 Ec27
Cathedral Peak ZA 205 Me60
Cathedral Prov. Park CDN 232 Dk21
Cathedral Rock N.P. AUS 149 Sg61
Cathedral Valley USA 235 Ee26
Catingal BR 275 Hk53
Catió GNB 186 Kc40
Catipari Mamoria, T.I. BR 270 Gg49
Cat Island BS 250 Gc33
Ćatkal kyrka toosu KS 97 Of25
Cat Lake CDN 236 Fe20
Catoco Cangola ANG 198 Lh50
Catolé do Rocha BR 273 Jb49
Catolo ANG 199 Lj50
Caton Island USA 228 Bj18
Catoute E 54 Ko48
Catriel RA 280 Gg64
Catriló RA 281 Gj64
Catrimani BR 265 Gj45
Catrimani BR 266 Gk45
Catskill USA 241 Gd24
Catskill Mts. USA 241 Gc24
Catskill Park USA 241 Gc25
Cattedrale di Bari I 63 Lr49
Cattedrale d'Otranto I 63 Lt50
Cát Tien N.P. VN 123 Qd40
Cattle Creek AUS 146 Rf54
Cattólica I 61 Ln47
Cattolica di Stilo I 63 Lr52
Catu BR 273 Ja52
Catúa RA 279 Gg57
Catuane MOC 205 Mg59
Catulene MOC 203 Mh54
Catura MOC 197 Mk52
Caturama BR 273 Hj52
Ćatyrtaš KS 100 Oj25
Cáuas RO 67 Mc43
Cauayan RP 124 Ra37
Cauayan RP 124 Rb41
Cauca CO 264 Gb44
Cauca ANG 198 Lh50
Caucaia BR 273 Ja47
Caucaia CO 264 Gc42
Caucasia CO 264 Gc42
Caucasus RUS/GE 91 Na24
Caucete RA 280 Gf61
Cauchari RA 279 Gg58
Caudry F 51 Ld40
Cauit Point RP 124 Rd41
Caumbue ANG 199 Ma50
Caumont-l'Éventé F 50 Ku41
Caunes-Minervois F 52 Lc47
Čaunskaja guba RUS 89 Tb04
Caupolicán BOL 278 Gf52
Cauquenes RCH 280 Gd63
Caura YV 265 Gh42
Cauro F 62 Lj49
Causapscal CDN 240 Gg21
Căușeni MD 73 Me22
Causey USA 238 Ej29
Caussade F 52 Lb46
Cauterets F 52 Ku48
Cauto Embarcadero C 243 Gb35
Cava MOC 203 Na53
Cava de' Tirreni I 63 Lp50
Cavaillon F 53 Lf47
Cavalaire-sur-Mer F 53 Lg47
Cavalcante BR 272 Hg52
Cavalese I 60 Lm44
Cavalier USA 236 Fb21
Cavalla LB 187 Kg43
Cavalo MOC 202 Mh55
Cavan IRL 47 Kn37
Cávaran RO 68 Mc45
Čavdarhisar TR 90 Me26
Cave NZ 153 Tf68
Cave City USA 239 Fh27
Cave Junction USA 232 Dj24
Cavendish AUS 150 Sb64
Cave paintings (Alem Maya) ETH 192 Nd41
Caverna de Santana BR 277 Hf58
Caverna do Diabo BR 277 Hf58
Cavernas de Francés C 243 Fk34
Cavernas de Jumandi EC 268 Gb46
Cavernas do Peruaçu, P.N. BR 275 Hh53
Caverns of Sonora USA 238 Ek30
Cave Rock ZA 205 Mf61
Cave Temple (Dambulla) CL 119 Pa42
Cavili Island RP 125 Ra41
Cavite RP 124 Ra38
Cavnic RO 67 Md43
Cavour I 60 Lh46
Čavusy BY 72 Mf19
Cavustepe TR 91 Nb26
Cavusy BY 72 Mf19
Cawayan RP 124 Rb40
Cawdor Castle GB 48 Kr33
Caxambu BR 275 Hh56
Caxias BR 273 Hj48
Caxias do Sul BR 276 He60
Caxito ANG 198 Lg50
Caxiuxa BR 272 Hh48
Çay TR 90 Mf26
Çayagzı TR 69 Mk49
Cayaltí PE 268 Ga49
Cayambe EC 268 Ga45
Cayambe, Volcán EC 268 Ga45
Çaybeyi TR 90 Mj27
Cay Caulker BH 248 Fg37
Çayeli TR 91 Na25
Cayenne F 267 Hd43
Cayeux-sur-Mer F 51 Lb40
Çaygören Baraj TR 71 Mj51
Çayiralan TR 90 Mh26
Çayırova = Agios Theodoros CY 90 Mh28
Çaylar TR 91 Na26
Çayli AZ 91 Nd25
Cay Lobos C 243 Gb34
Caylus F 52 Lb46
Cayman Brac GB 243 Ga36
Cayman Islands GB 243 Fk36
Cayman Ridge 243 Fj36
Cayman Trench 243 Fk36
Cay Marino 128 Qh41
Caynabo SP 193 Nd41
Cayo Arenas MEX 247 Fe34
Cayo Becerro HN 249 Fj38
Cayo Becerro HN 249 Fj38
Cayo Caballones C 243 Ga35
Cayo Cabeza del Este C 243 Ga35
Cayo Cantiles C 243 Fj35
Cayo Caratasca HN 249 Fj37
Cayo Caratasca HN 249 Fj38
Cayo Centro MEX 247 Fg36
Cayo Coco C 243 Ga34
Cayo del Rosario C 243 Fj35
Cayo de Santa María C 243 Ga34
Cayo Fragoso C 243 Ga34
Cayo Gorda HN 249 Fj38
Cayo Gorda HN 249 Fj38
Cayo Grande C 243 Ga35
Cayo Guajaba C 243 Gb35
Cayo Guillermo C 243 Ga34
Cayo Largo C 243 Fj35
Cayo Largo C 243 Fk35
Cayo Lobos MEX 247 Fg36
Cayo Mambí C 250 Gc35
Cayo Nuevo MEX 247 Fd35
Cayo Ramona C 243 Fk34
Cayo Romano C 243 Gb34
Cayo Sabinal C 243 Gb35
Cayos Anctitas C 243 Ga35
Cayos Blancos del Sur C 243 Fk34
Cayos Cajones HN 249 Fj37
Cayos Cajones HN 249 Fj37
Cayos Cinco Balas C 243 Ga35
Cayos Cocorocuma HN 249 Fj38
Cayos Cocorocuma HN 249 Fj38
Cayos de Albuquerque CO 249 Fk39
Cayos de E.S.E. CO 249 Fk39
Cayos de Perlas NIC 249 Fj39
Cayos de Roncador CO 249 Fk39
Cayos de San Felipe C 243 Fj35
Cayos Guerrero NIC 249 Fj39
Cayos King NIC 249 Fj39
Cayos los Indios C 243 Fj35
Cayos Mayores del Cabo Falso HN 249 Fj38
Cayos Mayores del Cabo Falso HN 249 Fj38
Cayos Miskitos NIC 249 Fj38
Cayos Morrison Dennis NIC 249 Fj38
Cayo Vivorillo HN 249 Fj38
Cayo Tyara NIC 249 Fj39
Cayo Vivorillo HN 249 Fj38
Cayo Vivorillo HN 249 Fj38
Cay Sal BS 243 Fk34
Cay Santo Domingo BS 250 Gc35
Cay Verde BS 250 Gc35
Cazage ANG 201 Ma51
Cazalla de la Sierra E 55 Kp53
Čažaši GE 91 Nb24
Cazaubon F 52 Ku47
Cazenovia USA 241 Gc24
Čazin BIH 61 Lq46
Čazma HR 61 Lr45
Cazombo ANG 201 Mb51
Cazones MEX 246 Fb35
Cazorla E 55 Ks53
Cazorla YV 265 Gg41
Cazula MOC 202 Mg53
Cazuza Ferreira BR 277 He60
Ccatca PE 269 Ge52
Cea E 54 Kp48
Ceahlău, P.N. RO 73 Mc22
Ceanu Mare RO 67 Md44
Ceará BR 255 Hb10
Ceara Abyssal Plain 254 Hb09
Ceará-Mirim BR 273 Jc48
Ceará-Mirim BR 273 Jc48
Ceatalchioi MOC 69 Mj45
Ceballos MEX 245 Eh32
Čeboksary RUS 72 Nd17
Cebollati ROU 276 Hd62
Cebreros E 55 Kq50
Cebu RP 124 Rb40
Cebu RP 124 Rc40
Čečava BIH 61 Ls46
Ceccano I 62 Lo49
Cece H 67 Lt44
Čečel'nyk UA 73 Me21
Čechtice CZ 66 Lq41
Cecil Plains AUS 149 Sf59
Cécina I 60 Ll47
Cedar Bay N.P. AUS 147 Sc53
Cedar Bluffs USA 238 Ek26
Cedar Breaks Nat. Mon. USA 235 Ed27
Cedar City USA 235 Ed27
Cedaredge USA 235 Eg26
Cedar Falls USA 236 Fd24
Cedar Grove USA 234 Ea27
Cedar Harbour BS 243 Gb32
Cedar Island USA 242 Gb28
Cedar Island N.W.R. USA 242 Gb28
Cedar Key USA 243 Fj31
Cedar Lake CDN 233 Ek19
Cedar Park USA 238 Fb30
Cedar Point USA 237 Fj25
Cedar Rapids USA 236 Fe24
Cedar River USA 237 Fg23
Cedar River Grassland N.P. USA 236 Ek22
Cedartown USA 239 Fh29
Cedarvale CDN 230 Df18
Cedarville USA 232 Dk25
Cedarville ZA 205 Me61
Ceddin E 54 Km47
Cedeño HN 248 Fg39
Cederberg ZA 204 Lk62
Cederberg Wilderness Area ZA 204 Lk62
Cedillo E 55 Kn51
Cedoux CDN 233 Ej21
Cedral BR 267 Hh46
Cedral MEX 246 Ek34
Cedrillas E 57 Ku50
Cedro BR 273 Ja49
Cedros MEX 245 Ek33
Cedros Trench 244 Eb32
Ceduna AUS 150 Rg62
Cée E 54 Kl48
Ceek SP 193 Nc41
Ceel Afweyn SP 193 Nd41
Ceelayo SP 193 Ne40
Ceel Baxay ETH 193 Nb40
Ceelbur = El Bur SP 195 Nd43
Ceel Dhaab SP 193 Nd41
Ceeldheer SP 195 Nd44
Ceeldhere SP 195 Nd44
Ceel Duubo SP 195 Nc44
Ceel Gaal SP 193 Nf40
Ceel Gaan SP 195 Nd43
Ceel Garas SP 195 Nc43
Ceel Huur SP 193 Ne43
Cefalù I 63 Lp52
Cegléd H 67 Lu43
Céglie Messàpica I 63 Ls50
Cehegín E 57 Kt52
Ceheng CHN 121 Qc33
Čehov RUS 72 Mj18

Curral Alto ☐ BR 276 Hd62
Curral de Pedra ☐ BR 273 Hk49
Curralinho ☐ BR 267 Hf46
Curral Novo do Piauí ☐ BR 273 Hk50
Curran ☐ USA 234 Ec26
Curranyalpa ☐ AUS 149 Sc61
Currawilla ☐ AUS 148 Sa58
Currawinya ☐ AUS 149 Sc60
Currawinya N.P. ☐ AUS 149 Sc60
Current ☐ BS 243 Gb33
Current Island ▲ BS 243 Gb33
Currie ☐ AUS 151 Sb65
Currie ☐ USA 235 Ec25
Currituck ☐ USA 242 Gb27
Currituck Beach Lighthouse ☐ USA 242 Gc27
Currituck N.W.R. ▤ USA 242 Gc27
Curtain Springs ☐ AUS 145 Rf58
Curtea de Arges ☐ RO 67 Me45
Curtici ☐ RO 67 Mb44
Curtina ☐ ROU 276 Hd47
Curtis Island ▲ AUS 149 Sf57
Curtis Island ▲ AUS 151 Sd65
Curtis Island ▲ NZ 152 Ua61
Curuá ☐ BR 266 Hc46
Curtina ☐ BR 271 Hc47
Curucá ☐ BR 267 Hg46
Curug Sewu ☐ RI 129 Qe49
Curup ☐ RI 127 Qb47
Cururupu ☐ BR 267 Hh46
Curuzú Cuatiá ☐ RA 276 Ha60
Curvelo ☐ BR 275 Hh55
Cushamen ☐ RA 280 Ge67
Cushing ☐ USA 238 Fb28
Cusimi ☐ YV 265 Gh43
Cusipata ☐ PE 269 Ge52
Cusset ☐ F 53 Ld44
Cusseta ☐ USA 239 Fh29
Custer ☐ USA 233 Eg22
Custer ☐ USA 233 Ej24
Custer Battlefield Nat. Mon. ☐ USA 233 Eg23
Custódia ☐ BR 273 Jb50
Cusuco, P.N. ☐ HN 248 Ff38
Cutalo ☐ ANG 200 Lj52
Cutato ☐ ANG 200 Lj53
Cut Bank ☐ USA 233 Ed21
Cuteevo ☐ RUS 72 Nd18
Cutenda ☐ ANG 200 Lh53
Cutervo ☐ PE 268 Ga49
Cutervo, P.N. de ☐ ▤ PE 268 Ga49
Cutiburi ☐ USA 239 Fh30
Cut Off ☐ USA 239 Fe31
Cutove ☐ UA 73 Mh21
Cutral-Co ☐ RA 280 Gf65
Cutro ☐ I 63 Lr51
Cuttack ☐ IND 117 Pc35
Cutta Cutta Caves ☐ AUS 146 Rg53
Cutzamala de Pinzon ☐ MEX 246 Ek36
Cuvelar ☐ ANG 200 Lh53
Cuvette de Doany ☐ RM 206 Nd53
Cuvier Island ▲ NZ 152 Tb64
Cuxhaven ☐ D 58 La37
Cuya ☐ RCH 278 Ge55
Cuyagua ▲ YV 265 Gg40
Cuyagua ▲ YV 265 Gg40
Cuyahoga Valley N.P. ☐ USA 237 Fk25
Cuyama ☐ USA 234 Ea28
Cuyamel ☐ HN 248 Ff38
Cuyo ☐ RP 124 Ra40
Cuyoaco ☐ MEX 246 Fb36
Cuyo East Passage ☐ RP 124 Ra40
Cuyo 'English Game Subterranean N.P. ☐ RP 124 Ra40
Cuyo Islands ▲ RP 124 Ra40
Cuyo Islands ▲ RP 124 Ra40
Cuyo West Passage ☐ RP 124 Ra40
Cuyuni ☐ GUY 266 Ha42
Cuyutlán ☐ MEX 246 Eh36
Cuzco ☐ ☐ ▤ PE 269 Ge52
Cwmcarn ☐ GB 49 Kr39
Cyangugu ☐ RWA 196 Me47
Cybinka ☐ PL 64 Lg38
Cyclades ☐ GR 71 Mf53
Cyclops Mountains ▲ RI 155 Sa47
Cyhoyn ☐ UA 73 Mg21
Cylinder ▲ AUS 149 Sf58
Cynthia ☐ AUS 149 Sf58
Cypress Gardens ☐ USA 243 Fk31
Cypress Hills ▲ CDN 233 Ef21
Cypress Hills Interprov. Park ☐ CDN 233 Ee21
Cyprus ☐ CY 90 Mg28
Cyran ☐ BY 65 Mg37
Cyrenaica ☐ LAR 177 Ma31
Cyrene = Shahhat ☐ ☐ LAR 177 Ma29
Cyrrhus ☐ SYR 90 Mj27
Czchetherea ☐ AUS 149 Sd59
Czaplinek ☐ PL 64 Lf37
Czar ☐ CDN 233 Ed19
Czarna ☐ PL 65 Mc41
Czarna Białostocka ☐ PL 65 Md37
Czarna Dąbrówka ☐ PL 64 Lf36
Czarnków ☐ PL 64 Lf38
Czarny Dunajec ☐ PL 65 Lu41
Czchów ☐ PL 65 Ma41
Czechowice-Dziedzice ☐ PL 65 Lu41
Czech Republic ☐ CZ 66 Lp41
Czekarzewice ☐ PL 65 Mb39
Czermno ☐ PL 65 Ma39
Czersk ☐ PL 64 Lg37
Czerwieńsk ☐ PL 64 Le38
Czerwionka-Leszczyny ☐ PL 64 Lt40
Czerwony Dwór ☐ PL 65 Mc36
Częstochowa ☐ PL 65 Lu40
Człopa ☐ PL 64 Lf37
Człuchów ☐ PL 64 Lg37
Czyżew-Osada ☐ PL 65 Mc38

D

Da'an ☐ CHN 110 Rc23
Daanbantayan ☐ RP 124 Rc40
Daan Viljoen Game Park ☐ ☐ NAM 200 Lj57
Dabaga ☐ EAT 197 Mh50
Dabaga ☐ RN 182 Lc37
Dabagram ☐ IND 120 Pe34
Dabai ☐ WAN 188 Lc40
Dabajuro ☐ YV 264 Ge40
Dabaka ☐ IND 120 Pg32
Dabakala ☐ CI 187 Kh41
Dabancheng ☐ CHN 101 Pe24
Dabane-ye-Qoloman ▲ IR 98 Oa30
Daban Shan ▲ CHN 106 Qa27
Dabaro ☐ SP 193 Ne42
Daba Shan ▲ CHN 106 Qe29
Dabas ☐ H 67 Lu43
Dabat ☐ ETH 192 Mj39
Dabbagh, Jabal ▲ KSA 188 Mf33
Dabdab ☐ LAR 177 Lh32
Dabeiba ☐ CO 264 Gd42
Dabeiyuan Monastery ▲ CHN 107 Qg26
Dabenoris ☐ ZA 204 Lk60
Dabhoi ☐ IND 116 Og34
Dabie ☐ PL 64 Lg38
Dabie Shan ▲ CHN 107 Qh30
Dabo ☐ RI 127 Qc46
Dabo ☐ SN 186 Kc39
Dabola ☐ RG 186 Ke40
Dabola ☐ IND 117 Ok33
Dabolatounka ☐ RG 186 Ke40
Dabou ☐ CI 187 Kh43
Daboya ☐ GH 187 Kk41
Dabou ☐ IND 117 Ok33
Dabrabraslavka ☐ BY 65 Mg38
Dabrowa ☐ PL 65 Me38
Dąbrowa Białostocka ☐ PL 65 Md37
Dąbrowa Górnicza ☐ PL 65 Lu41
Dąbrowa Tarnowska ☐ PL 65 Ma40
Dabryn' ☐ BY 72 Me20
Dabrynyeva ☐ BY 45 Mh37
Dabugami ☐ IND 117 Pb36
Dabuleni ☐ RO 69 Me47
Dabwa ☐ TCH 183 Lg38

Dac Glei ☐ VN 123 Qd38
Dachau ☐ D 59 Lm42
Dacheng ☐ CHN 109 Qh31
Dachengzhuang ☐ CHN 107 Qj26
Dachepalle ☐ IND 117 Ok37
Dachstein ☐ A 61 Lo43
Dachsteinhöhlen ▲ A 61 Lo43
Dachung Yogma ☐ 115 Ok29
Dacia Seamount ☐ 174 Kd30
Dačice ☐ CZ 66 Lq41
Dac Song ☐ VN 123 Qd39
Dac To ☐ VN 123 Qd38
Dadadi ☐ EAK 195 Na45
Dadanawa ☐ GUY 266 Ha44
Daddato ☐ DJI 193 Nb39
Dade City ☐ USA 243 Fj31
Dadeville ☐ USA 239 Fh29
Dadgo ☐ CHN 108 Qe34
Dadong ☐ CHN 108 Qe34
Dadra and Nagar Haveli ☐ IND 116 Og35
Dadra and Nagar Haveli ☐ IND 116 Og35
Dadu ☐ PK 99 Od32
Daduan ☐ CHN 109 Qh31
Dadukou ☐ CHN 112 Qj30
Daet ☐ RP 124 Rb38
Dafang ☐ CHN 121 Qc32
Dafanpu ☐ CHN 106 Qf26
Dafar ☐ GH 187 La42
Dafeng ☐ CHN 112 Ra29
Dáfnes ☐ GR 70 Mb52
Dafni ☐ GR 69 Me50
Dafni ☐ GR 69 Md53
Dafni ☐ GR 70 Mc52
Dafni ☐ GR 70 Mc53
Dafoe ☐ CDN 233 Eh20
Dafo Si ▲ CHN 106 Qa26
Daga ☐ IND 117 Pb33
Dagaari ☐ SP 193 Nd42
Dagabule ☐ RM 194 Mj43
Daga Istephanos Monastery ▲ ETH 192 Mj40
Dagana ☐ SN 180 Kc37
Daga Post ☐ SUD 192 Mg41
Dagárdi ☐ TR 71 Mj51
Dagasuli ▲ RI 125 Rd44
Dagdari ☐ LV 45 Mh34
Dagdere ☐ TR 71 Mj54
Dagestan ☐ RUS 91 Nd24
Dagestanskij zapovednik ☐ RUS 91 Nd23
Daghabij ☐ KSA 92 Mk34
Dag Hammarskjöld Memorial ☐ Z 196 Me51
Daghmar ☐ OM 95 Nk34
Dagida Game Reserve ▤ WAN 188 Lc41
Daginggou ▲ CHN 110 Ra24
Dagingshan ☐ 187 Mh30
Daglung ☐ CHN 102 Pf31
Dago ☐ RI 125 Rb42
Dagomys ☐ RUS 73 Mk24
Dagua ☐ CO 264 Gb44
Daguan ☐ CHN 108 Qc31
Daguan ☐ CHN 108 Qd32
Daguan ☐ CHN 121 Qd32
Daguán ☐ CHN 107 Qj26
Dagu Fort ▲ CHN 107 Qj26
Dagupan ☐ RP 124 Ra37
Daguragua A.L. ☐ AUS 146 Rf54
Dagworth ☐ AUS 147 Sb54
Dah ☐ RI 154 Rk49
Dahaban ☐ KSA 92 Mk35
Dahanu ☐ IND 116 Og36
Dahana Beach ☐ IND 116 Og35
Daheba ☐ CHN 103 Pk28
Dahegun ☐ CHN 121 Qa31
Dahenu ☐ CHN 108 Qb27
Dahinsara ☐ IND 116 Of34
Dahiri ☐ CI 187 Kh43
Dahla ☐ AFG 99 Oc30
Dahlak Archipelago ☐ ER 192 Na38
Dahlak Marine N.P. ☐ ER 192 Na38
Dahlonega ☐ USA 242 Fj28
Dahmani ☐ TN 176 Le28
Dahme ☐ D 59 Lh41
Dahoma ☐ CHN 107 Qg30
Dahra Oil Field ☐ LAR 177 Lj31
Dahshûr ☐ ET 179 Mf31
Dahuk ☐ IRQ 91 Nb28
Dahuk ☐ IRQ 91 Nb28
Da Huoai ☐ VN 123 Qd40
Dai ▲ RI 131 Re49
Dai Dao ☐ CHN 113 Ra29
Dai Island ▲ SOL 157 Ta49
Dai Lanh Beach ☐ VN 123 Qe39
Daik ☐ RI 127 Qc46
Daimiel ☐ E 55 Kr51
Daingerfield ☐ USA 238 Fc29
Daintree ☐ AUS 147 Sc54
Daintree N.P. ☐ AUS 147 Sc54
Daireaux ☐ RA 281 Gk64
Dairo ☐ CI 187 Kh43
Dairût ☐ ET 179 Mf32
Dairy Creek ☐ AUS 144 Qh58
Daisen ▲ J 113 Rg28
Daisengendake ▲ J 111 Sa25
Daisen-Oki N.P. ☐ J 113 Rg28
Daisen-Oki N.P. ☐ J 113 Rg28
Daisetsuzan N.P. ☐ J 111 Sb24
Daishan ☐ CHN 112 Rb30
Daitari ☐ IND 117 Pc34
Dai Xian ☐ CHN 107 Qg28
Daiyun Shan ▲ CHN 109 Qk33
Dajabón ☐ DOM 250 Ge36
Dajarra ☐ AUS 148 Rk56
Dajing ☐ CHN 106 Qd27
Dajing ☐ CHN 121 Qb32
Dajin ☐ CHN 103 Pg27
Dakawa ☐ EAT 197 Mh50
Dakawa ☐ EAT 197 Mh49
Da Kherga Sherif Ziarat Mosque ☐ AFG 99 Oc31
Dakhla ☐ ▲ DARS 180 Kc34
Dakhla ☐ RIM 180 Ke37
Dakhla Oasis ☐ ET 179 Me33
Dakhlet Nouâdhibou ☐ RIM 180 Kb35
Dakingari ☐ WAN 188 Lc40
Dak Takwas ☐ WAN 188 Lc40
Dak Mil ☐ VN 123 Qd39
Dak Nong ☐ VN 123 Qd40
Dakoank ☐ IND 122 Pg42
Dakoro ☐ RN 182 Ld38
Đakovica ☐ KSV 68 Ma48
Đakovo ☐ HR 61 Lt45
Katerdala u Dakovu ▲ HR 61 Lt45
Dakpam ☐ GH 187 Kk41
Dakshin Gangotri ☐ ANT 286 Lc55
Daksum ☐ 114 Oh29
Daku, Gunung ▲ RI 125 Rd45
Dala ☐ ANG 199 Ma50
Dala ☐ ANG 200 Ma51
Dala ☐ RMM 181 Kj38
Dalaba ☐ SOL 157 Ta50
Dalaba ☐ RG 186 Kd40
Dalabar ☐ RG 186 Kd40
Dalada Maligawa (Kandy) ☐ ☐ CL 119 Pa42
Dalad Qi ☐ CHN 106 Qf25
Dalahaji ☐ RUS 104 Qb20
Dalai Nur ☐ CHN 107 Qj24
Dalai Shan ▲ CHN 103 Pj26
Dalâlî ☐ IR 93 Nf31
Dalâliven ☐ S 43 Lq32
Dalaman ☐ TR 71 Mj54
Dalandzadgad ☐ MNG 104 Qb24
Dalanganem Islands ▲ RP 124 Rb40
Dalangyun ☐ MYA 120 Ph36
Danau Tigi ▲ RI 154 Rh48
Dalarö ☐ S 43 Lt35
Dalarö ☐ S 43 Lt35
Dalälven ☐ S 43 Lq33
Dalay ☐ MNG 104 Qb24
Dalbandin ☐ PK 99 Oc31
Dalbeattie ☐ GB 48 Kr36

Dalberg ☐ AUS 147 Sd56
Dalbosjön ☐ S 42 Lo35
Dálbok Dol ☐ BG 69 Me46
Dálbok izvor ☐ BG 69 Mf48
Dalby ☐ AUS 149 Sf59
Dalby Söderskog n.p. ☐ ☐ S 43 Lo35
Dalcahue ☐ ☐ RCH 280 Gd67
Dale ☐ N 40 Lf29
Dale ☐ ☐ N 42 Lj31
Dalfoss ☐ IS 46 Ju25
Dalfsen ☐ NL 51 Lg38
Dalgan ☐ IR 98 Nk32
Dalgaranga ☐ AUS 144 Qj59
Dálghiu ☐ RO 69 Mf45
Dálgi Del ☐ BG 68 Mc47
Dalgonally ☐ AUS 147 Sa56
Dalgopol ☐ BG 69 Mh47
Dalhalla ☐ S 41 Lq30
Dalhousie ☐ IND 114 Oj29
Dalhousie ☐ CDN 240 Gg21
Dalhousie Springs ☐ AUS 148 Rh59
Dali ☐ CHN 106 Qe28
Dali = Xiaguan ☐ ☐ CHN 121 Qa33
Dali ☐ RMM 181 Kj38
Dalianhe ☐ CHN 110 Re22
Dalias ☐ E 55 Ks54
Dalimb ☐ IND 116 Oj37
Dali Museum (Saint Petersburg) ☐ ☐ USA 243 Fj32
Dali Sharafat ☐ SUD 185 Mg39
Dalj ☐ HR 61 Lt45
Dalja ☐ ET 179 Mf32
Dalkeith ☐ GB 48 Kr35
Dalkhaki ☐ AFG 97 Od27
Dalkola ☐ IND 117 Pd33
Dallas ☐ CHN 108 Qa31
Dallas ☐ USA 232 Dj23
Dallas ☐ USA 238 Fb29
Dallas Reef ▲ 128 Qg42
Dall Island ▲ USA 230 Dd18
Dalma ▲ UAE 95 Ng33
Dalmacija ▲ HR 61 Lq46
Dalmally ☐ GB 48 Kq34
Dalmeny ☐ AUS 151 Se64
Dal'nee ☐ USA 42 Lm35
Dal'nee ☐ RUS 111 Sb22
Dal'negorsk ☐ RUS 111 Rh23
Daľnerečensk ☐ RUS 110 Rg23
Daloa ☐ CI 187 Kg42
Dalol ☐ CI 187 Kg42
Dalol Crater ☐ ER 192 Na38
Dalol Saltlake and Hot Springs ☐ ETH 192 Na38
Dalong ☐ CHN 108 Qc32
Dalong Chi ☐ CHN 100 Pb24
Dalrymple, Mount ▲ AUS 149 Se56
Dalsbruk = Taalintehdas ☐ FIN 44 Mc30
Dalsjöfors ☐ S 42 Lo33
Dals Långed ☐ S 42 Ln32
Dalton ☐ USA 239 Fh28
Dalton ☐ IND 117 Pc33
Dalton Mus. ☐ USA 238 Fc27
Dalu ☐ IND 120 Pf34
Dalu ☐ IND 120 Pt33
Daludalu ☐ RI 127 Qa45
Dalupiri Island ▲ RP 124 Ra36
Dalupiri Island ▲ RP 124 Rb38
Dal'verzin Tepe ☐ ☐ UZ 97 Od27
Dalvik ☐ IS 46 Kb25
Dalwallinu ☐ AUS 144 Qj61
Dalwhinnie ☐ GB 48 Kq34
Daly City ☐ USA 234 Dj27
Daly River ☐ AUS 146 Rf52
Daly River A.L. ☐ AUS 146 Rf53
Dalyup ☐ AUS 145 Ra62
Daly Waters ☐ AUS 146 Rg54
Damaguete ☐ RP 125 Rb41
Da Mai ☐ VN 123 Qd39
Damakar ☐ WAN 189 Lg39
Daman ☐ AFG 99 Oc30
Daman ☐ IND 116 Og35
Daman ☐ IND 116 Og35
Damaneh ☐ IR 93 Nf29
Damango ☐ GH 187 Kk41
Damanhûr ☐ ET 179 Mf31
Damar ▲ RI 131 Re49
Damar ▲ RI 131 Rd49
Damara ☐ RCA 190 Lk43
Damaraland ☐ NAM 200 Lj56
Damardaʻtar ☐ RI 129 Qd47
Damar Laut ☐ MAL 126 Qa43
Damasak ☐ WAN 183 Lg39
Damas Cays ▲ BS 243 Fk34
Damascus ☐ ☐ SYR 90 Mj29
Damaskinia ☐ GR 70 Mb50
Damaturu ☐ WAN 189 Lg40
Damau ☐ RI 125 Rd44
Dame Marie ☐ RH 250 Gc36
Damenge ☐ CHN 121 Qc34
Damghan ☐ IR 98 Nh27
Damghan Caravansarai ☐ IR 96 Nh27
Dam Ha ☐ VN 121 Qd35
Damianópolis ☐ BR 275 Hg53
Damietta ☐ ET 179 Mf30
Damji ☐ BHT 120 Pe32
Damlacık ☐ TR 90 Mj27
Dammartin-en-Goële ☐ F 51 Lc41
Damme ☐ D 58 Lj38
Damnica ☐ PL 64 Lg36
Damnoen Saduak Floating Market ☐ THA 122 Pk39
Damoh ☐ IND 117 Ok34
Damon ☐ USA 238 Fc31
Damon Point ☐ USA 232 Dh22
Dampar ☐ WAN 188 Le41
Dampier ☐ AUS 142 Qj56
Dampier Archipelago ▲ AUS 142 Qj56
Dampier Archipelago Nature Reserve ☐ AUS 142 Qj56
Dampier Downs ☐ AUS 142 Rb55
Dampierre-sur-Salon ☐ F 53 Lf43
Dampier Strait ☐ PNG 156 Sd48
Dampu ☐ 193 Nc41
Damqawt ☐ YE 95 Ng37
Damroh ☐ IND 120 Pg32
Damuk ☐ IND 120 Ph31
Damulla ☐ CL 119 Pa42
Damdama Sahib ☐ ☐ IND 114 Oh31
Damxung ☐ CHN 103 Pf30
Dana ☐ USA 238 Ej27
Dana ▲ RI 130 Ra51
Danakil Depression ☐ ETH 192 Na39
Danakil Desert ☐ ETH 192 Na39
Danamombe (Dhlo Dhlo) Ruins ☐ ZW 202 Me55
Danané ☐ CI 186 Kf42
Da Nang ☐ VN 123 Qd38
Danao ☐ RP 124 Rc40
Danapur ☐ IND 117 Pc33
Danau Aiwsa ▲ RI 154 Rh47
Danau Gigi ▲ RI 154 Rg46
Danau Gita ▲ RI 154 Rg46
Danau Kamakawalar ▲ RI 154 Rh47
Danau Paniai ▲ RI 154 Rj47
Danau Rombebai ▲ RI 154 Rj46
Danau Sentani ▲ RI 155 Sa47
Danau Tigi ▲ RI 154 Rh48
Danau Yamur ▲ RI 154 Rh47
Dana ☐ CHN 103 Qa30
Dan Barto ▲ RI 154 Rh47
Danbury ▲ USA 234 Eb27
Dancheng ☐ CHN 107 Qh29
Dandahura ☐ ZW 202 Me54
Dandaraga ☐ AUS 144 Qh61

Dariv ☐ MNG 101 Ph22
Dariyin Nuruu ▲ MNG 101 Ph22
Dariyah ☐ KSA 92 Nb33
Darjeeling ☐ IND 120 Pe32
Darjeeling Himalayan Railway ☐ ☐ IND 120 Pe32
Därjiu ☐ RO 67 Mf44
Darkan ☐ AUS 144 Qj62
Darke Peak ☐ AUS 150 Rj62
Darkhadyn Khotgor ☐ MNG 104 Pk20
Darkhan ☐ MNG 104 Qd21
Darkhovin ☐ IR 93 Ne30
Darkoti ☐ IND 115 Oj30
Darlag ☐ CHN 103 Pk29
Darling ☐ ZA 204 Lk62
Darling Downs ▲ AUS 149 Se59
Darling Mts. ▲ AUS 144 Qj61
Darling Range ▲ AUS 144 Qj61
Darling River ☐ AUS 151 Sc62
Darlington ☐ GB 49 Kt36
Darlington Point ☐ AUS 151 Sd63
Darlington Raceway ☐ USA 242 Ga28
Darłowo ☐ PL 64 Lf36
Dărmăneşti ☐ RO 69 Mf46
Darnah ☐ LAR 178 Mb29
Darnah ☐ ZA 205 Mf60
Darney ☐ F 53 Lg42
Darnick ☐ AUS 151 Sb62
Darnley Island ▲ AUS 147 Sb50
Daroca ☐ ▲ E 57 Kt49
Darou-Mousti ☐ SN 180 Kb38
Darrahe Awd ☐ AFG 99 Od28
Darrah Wildlife Sanctuary ☐ IND 116 Oh33
Darrington ☐ USA 232 Dk21
Dʻ Arros ▲ SY 195 Nq48
Darsa ▲ YE 95 Nj33
Darsi ☐ IND 117 Ok38
Darsiami ☐ WAG 186 Kc39
Darß ▲ D 58 Lm37
Dannevirke ☐ NZ 153 Tj66
Dannhauser ☐ ZA 205 Mf60
Dano ☐ BF 187 Kj41
Danpu ☐ IND 116 Oh34
Dan Sadau ☐ WAN 188 Lc40
Dan Sai ☐ THA 122 Qa38
Danskøya ▲ N 38 Lf06
Dansville ☐ USA 241 Gb24
Dantan ☐ IND 117 Pd35
Dante = Xaafuun ☐ SP 193 Nf40
Dantewara ☐ IND 117 Pa36
Danube ☐ RN 182 Lb39
Danube ☐ 26 Ma05
Danubyu ☐ MYA 122 Ph37
Danum Valley Conservation Area ☐ MAL 128 Qj43
Danville ☐ IND 116 Oj35
Danville ☐ USA 239 Fh27
Danville ☐ USA 241 Gb24
Danville ☐ USA 242 Ga27
Dan Xian ☐ CHN 109 Qe36
Danxiashan ▲ CHN 109 Qg33
Danyang ☐ CHN 112 Qk29
Danyi-Apéyémé ☐ TG 187 La42
Danzhou ☐ CHN 108 Qe33
Dao ▲ RP 124 Rd41
Dao Bach Long Vi ▲ VN 121 Qd35
Dao Ban Sen ▲ VN 121 Qd35
Dao Cai Chien ▲ VN 121 Qd35
Dao Cat Ba ▲ VN 121 Qd35
Dao Co To ▲ VN 121 Qd35
Dao Hon Lon ▲ VN 123 Qe39
Dao Phu Quoc ▲ VN 123 Qc40
Daoro ☐ CI 187 Kg43
Daotanghe ☐ CHN 106 Qa27
Dao Thanh Lan ▲ VN 121 Qd35
Daotiandi ☐ CHN 110 Rf21
Dao Timi ☐ RN 183 Lg35
Daouda ☐ RP 249 Gf42
Dao Van Don ▲ VN 121 Qd35
Dao Vay ▲ VN 123 Qb41
Dao Vinh Thuc ▲ VN 121 Qd35
Dao Xian ☐ CHN 108 Qf33
Dapa ☐ RP 124 Rd41
Dapaong ☐ TG 187 La40
Dapchi ☐ WAN 189 Lf39
Dapdap ☐ RP 125 Rb41
Dapelogo ☐ BF 187 Kk39
Dapitan ☐ RP 125 Rb41
Dapoli ☐ IND 116 Og37
Dapuchaihe ☐ CHN 110 Re24
Dar Qaidam ☐ CHN 103 Pk27
Daqing ☐ CHN 110 Rc22
Daqing ☐ CHN 110 Rc22
Daqing Shan ▲ CHN 106 Qf25
Daqu Dao ▲ CHN 112 Rb30
Dar'a ☐ SYR 90 Mj29
Darab ☐ IR 98 Nh31
Darab ☐ SP 195 Na45
Daraban ☐ PK 99 Of30
Darabani ☐ RO 73 Md21
Daradou ☐ RCA 191 Mc43
Dara el-Bahri ☐ ET 179 Mf32
Darain ☐ RM 206 Ne52
Dar al-Hajar ▲ YE 94 Nc38
Daram ▲ RI 131 Rf47
Daram ☐ RP 124 Rc40
Darán ☐ RI 93 Nf29
Darany ☐ H 66 Ls45
Darar ☐ ETH 193 Nc41
Dararisa ☐ SUD 185 Mg39
Darasun ☐ RUS 105 Qd20
Darazo ☐ WAN 188 Lf40
Darband ☐ IR 98 Nj30
Darband-i Khan ☐ IRQ 91 Nc28
Darbénai ☐ LT 45 Mb34
Darbhanga ☐ IND 117 Pc32
Darburrah ☐ SP 193 Nc41
Dar-Caïd-Hadji ☐ MA 174 Kf30
Dar-Caïd-llai-bou-Fenzi ☐ MA 174 Kf30
Dar Chioukh ☐ DZ 176 Lb28
Darçinskoye ☐ BR 272 Hg49
Darda ☐ HR 61 Lt45
Darda ☐ AUS 144 Ra59
Dardanelle ☐ USA 238 Fd28
Dardanelles ☐ TR 69 Mg50
Dardesheim ☐ D 58 Ll39
Dareau ☐ EAT 197 Mk49
Dareen ☐ AUS 149 Sf58
Dar el-Bahr ☐ MA 174 Kf29
Dar el Barka ☐ RIM 180 Kc37
Darende ☐ TR 90 Mk26
Dares Salaam ☐ ☐ EAT 197 Mk49
Dareton ☐ AUS 150 Sb63
Darfo-Boário Terme ☐ I 60 Ll45
Darfur ☐ SUD 184 Mc39
Darganata ☐ TM 96 Ob25
Dargaz ☐ IR 96 Nk27
Dargeçit ☐ TR 91 Na28
Dargholia ☐ TN 176 Lf29
Dargol ☐ RN 182 La39
Darhala ☐ CI 187 Kh41
Darhan Muminggan Lianhegi ☐ CHN 106 Qf25
Darica ☐ TR 69 Mk50
Darien ☐ CO 264 Gd44
Darién ▲ PA 264 Ga42
Darién, P.N. del ☐ ☐ PA 249 Gb42
Daring ☐ AUS 151 Sc62
Dario Meira ☐ BR 275 Ja53

Davis, Mount ▲ USA 145 Re59
Davis Mts. ▲ USA 245 Eh31
Davis Strait ☐ 227 Ha05
Davor ☐ LR 61 La45
Davos ☐ CH 60 La44
Davud-Haradok ☐ BY 72 Md19
Dawa ☐ CHN 107 Qj24
Dawab ☐ SUD 185 Mg37
Dawadawa ☐ GH 187 Kk41
Dawa Dawa ☐ RP 125 Rb42
Daweloor ▲ RI 131 Rf49
Dawera ▲ RI 131 Rf49
Dawes Range ▲ AUS 149 Sf58
Dawharah ▲ YE 94 Na37
Dawhwenya ☐ GH 187 La43
Dawir ☐ SUD 191 Mg41
Dawna Range ☐ MYA 122 Pj37
Dawson ☐ KSA 94 Na35
Dawson Bay Ind. Res. ▲ CDN 233 Ek19
Dawson City ☐ CDN 229 Da13
Dawson Creek ☐ CDN 231 Dk18
Dawson Landing ☐ CDN 232 Dg20
Dawson Range ▲ CDN 229 Da14
Dawson River ☐ AUS 149 Sf58
Dawson Springs ☐ USA 239 Fg27
Dawu ☐ CHN 103 Qa30
Dawu ☐ CHN 107 Qh30
Dawwah ☐ OM 95 Nk35
Dax ☐ F 52 Kt47
Daxian ☐ CHN 108 Qd30
Daxin ☐ CHN 108 Qd34
Daxing ☐ CHN 107 Qj26
Daxing ☐ CHN 121 Qa32
Daxue Shan ▲ CHN 103 Qa30
Dayao ☐ CHN 121 Qa33
Dayaxa ☐ SP 193 Nd41
Dayay ☐ CHN 109 Qh30
Dayi ☐ CHN 108 Qb30
Dayi ☐ WAN 188 Ld40
Dayipur ☐ IND 116 Oh35
Daylesford ☐ AUS 151 Sc64
Daysland ☐ CDN 233 Ed19
Dayton ☐ USA 232 Ec22
Dayton ☐ USA 232 Ec22
Dayton ☐ USA 233 Ed30
Dayton ☐ USA 233 Ec30
Dayton ☐ USA 239 Fh26
Daytona Beach ☐ USA 243 Fk31
Daytona Intl. Speedway ☐ USA 242 Fk31
Dayu ☐ CHN 109 Qh33
Dayu ☐ RJ 129 Qh46
Dayville ☐ USA 232 Ea23
Dayyer ☐ IR 93 Nf32
Dayyinah ▲ UAE 95 Ng33
Dazaifu ☐ J 113 Rf29
Dazey ☐ USA 236 Fa22
Dazu ☐ CHN 108 Qc34
Dazu = Longgang ☐ ☐ CHN 108 Qc31
Dazu Rock Carvings ☐ ☐ CHN 108 Qc31
Dchira ☐ DARS 174 Kd32
Dead Indian Peak ▲ USA 233 Ef23
Deadman Hill ▲ AUS 142 Qj56
Deadman's Cay ☐ BS 250 Gc34
Deadman's Cr. Ind. Res. ▲ CDN 232 Dk20
Dead Sea ☐ IL 92 Mh30
Deakin ☐ AUS 145 Re61
Deal ☐ GB 49 La39
Dealba ☐ USA 180 Kc38
Deal Island ▲ AUS 151 Sd65
Dealsville ☐ ZA 205 Mc60
Dealul Silvaniei ☐ RO 67 Mc43
De'an ☐ CHN 109 Qh31
Dean Funes ☐ RA 279 Gh61
Deanmill ☐ AUS 144 Qj62
Dearborn ☐ USA 237 Fj24
Deary ☐ USA 232 Ec22
Dease Lake ☐ CDN 230 Df16
Dease Strait ☐ CDN 226 Ec05
Death Railway ☐ THA 122 Pk38
Death Valley ☐ USA 234 Eb27
Death Valley Junction ☐ USA 234 Eb27
Death Valley N.P. ☐ ☐ USA 234 Ec27
Deauville ☐ ☐ F 50 La41
Deaver ☐ USA 233 Ef23
Debal Ceeve ☐ UA 73 Mk21
Debalo ☐ SUD 191 Mf41
Debao ☐ CHN 108 Qe32
Debark ☐ ETH 192 Mj39
Debauch Mts. ▲ USA 229 Ca13
Debaysima ☐ ETH 192 Na39
Debben ☐ CDN 233 Ed19
Debdou ☐ MA 175 Kj29
Debel ☐ ▲ BG 69 Mf47
Debel bordo ☐ IND 108 Qe33
Debenham ☐ GB 49 La38
Debiapur ☐ IND 117 Ok32
De Brug ☐ ZA 205 Mc60
Debrznica ☐ PL 64 Le38
Deçani ☐ KSV 68 Ma48
Decatur ☐ USA 237 Fh25
Decatur ☐ USA 238 Fb29
Decatur ☐ USA 239 Fg29
Decatur ☐ USA 239 Fg25
Decatur ☐ USA 239 Fh26
Decazeville ☐ F 52 Lb46
Deccan ☐ IND 76 Ob08
Deception Pans ☐ RB 201 Mb56
Deception Valley ☐ RB 201 Mb56
Deception Valley Lodge ☐ RB 201 Mb56
Dechang ☐ CHN 121 Qb32
Dechu ☐ IND 114 Og32
Děčín ☐ CZ 66 Lp40
Decize ☐ F 53 Ld43
Decono ☐ RP 125 Rc41
Decorah ☐ USA 236 Fe24
Deda ☐ RO 67 Me44
Dédougli Daglari ▲ TR 90 Mf27
Dedemsvaart ☐ NL 51 Lg38
Deder ☐ ETH 193 Nb40
Dédi ☐ BF 187 Kk42
Dedo ☐ CDN 233 Eg23
Dedoplis Tskaro ☐ GE 91 Nc25
Dedougou ☐ BF 187 Kj40
Dédováci ☐ RUS 72 Mh18
Dedza ☐ MW 203 Mh53
Deenethorpe ☐ GB 49 Kt38
Deep Bay ☐ ☐ BS 243 Fk33
Deep River ☐ CDN 237 Gb22
Deep Well ☐ AUS 146 Rg57
Deep Well ☐ AUS 146 Rg57
Deepwater ☐ AUS 149 Sf60
Deer Lake ☐ CDN 236 Fc19

Deer Lake ☐ CDN 241 Hb21
Deer Lodge ☐ USA 233 Ed22
Deer River ☐ USA 236 Fd22
Deesa ☐ IND 116 Og33
Defeng ☐ CHN 108 Qe32
Defensores del Chaco, P.N. ☐ ☐ PY 278 Gk56
Defferrari ☐ RA 281 Ha65
Defiance ☐ USA 237 Fj24
De Funiak Springs ☐ USA 239 Fg30
Dega Medo ☐ ETH 193 Nb42
Degana ☐ IND 114 Oh32
De Gaulle ☐ RCA 190 Lh42
Degeh ☐ CHN 103 Pk30
Degeberga ☐ S 43 Lp35
Degeh Bur ☐ ETH 193 Nb41
Dégelis ☐ CDN 240 Gf22
Degema ☐ WAN 188 Ld43
Degel Mas ☐ ETH 192 Mj39
Degoma ☐ ETH 192 Mj39
Degrad Claude ☐ F 266 Hd44
De Grey ☐ AUS 142 Qk56
De Grey River ☐ AUS 142 Qk56
De Groote Peel, N.P. ☐ NL 51 Lf39
Deguçiai ☐ LT 45 Mb35
Deguri ☐ IND 116 Oh33
Dehaj ☐ IR 98 Nh30
Dehak ☐ IR 98 Ob32
Dehak ☐ IR 98 Ob32
Dehej ☐ IND 116 Og35
Dehgaon ☐ IND 117 Ok34
Dehgolan ☐ IR 91 Nd28
Dehibat ☐ TN 176 Lf30
Dehiwala-Mount Lavinia ☐ CL 119 Ok42
Dehloran ☐ IR 93 Nd29
Deh Mohammed ☐ IR 98 Nj28
Dehna ☐ IR 98 Nj31
De Hoop ☐ ZA 204 Mb62
De Hoop Nature Reserve ☐ ☐ ZA 204 Ma63
Dehori ☐ IND 117 Ok34
Deh Parian ☐ AFG 97 Oe28
Deh Shir ☐ IR 98 Nj30
Deh Bid ☐ IR 98 Ng30
Deh Dasht ☐ IR 93 Nf30
Dehej ☐ IND 116 Og35
Dehgaon ☐ IND 117 Ok34
Dehna ☐ IR 98 Nj31
De Hoop ☐ ZA 204 Mb62
Dehra Dun ☐ IND 115 Ok30
Deh Rawod ☐ AFG 99 Oc29
Dehri ☐ IND 117 Pc33
Deh Shir ☐ IR 98 Nj30
Deh Bid ☐ IR 98 Ng30
Deh Shu ☐ AFG 99 Ob30
Dehua ☐ CHN 109 Qk33
Dehui ☐ CHN 110 Rc23
Deim most ☐ RUS 45 Mb36
Deim Bukhit ☐ SUD 191 Md42
Deine ☐ D 58 Ll39
Deir Abu Makar ▲ ET 179 Mf31
Deir Al Zor ☐ SYR 91 Na28
Deir Amba Bishoi ▲ ET 179 Mf30
Deir Djebel at Tayr ▲ ET 179 Mf32
Deir el-Abyad ▲ ET 179 Mf32
Deir el-Baramus ▲ ET 179 Mf30
Deir el Qiddisah Kâtrînâ ▲ ☐ ET 179 Mj31
Deir es-Surján ▲ ET 179 Mf30
Deirhafer ☐ SYR 90 Mj27
Deir Mar Musa al-Habashi ▲ SYR 90 Mj28
Deir Samu'il ▲ ET 179 Mf31
Déise-Falar ☐ BR 268 Ge49
Dej ☐ RO 67 Md43
Déje ☐ S 43 Lp33
Déjé ☐ USA 192 Mk40
Dejiang ☐ CHN 108 Qe31
De Kalb ☐ USA 237 Ff25
De Kalb ☐ USA 239 Ff25
De Kalb ☐ USA 239 Fc29
Dekemhare ☐ ER 192 Na39
Dekese ☐ RDC 199 Ma47
Dekeman ☐ DK 42 Lj35
De Koekenhof ☐ NL 51 Le38
Dekhistan ☐ TM 96 Nh26
Dekoa ☐ RCA 190 Lk42
De Koog ☐ NL 51 Le37
Delacroix ☐ USA 239 Ff31
De la Garma ☐ RA 281 Gk64
Delaki ☐ RI 131 Rd50
Delano ☐ USA 234 Eb28
Delano Peak ▲ USA 235 Ed26
Delareyville ☐ ZA 205 Mc59
Delaware ☐ USA 237 Fj25
Delaware ☐ USA 241 Gc26
Delaware Bay ☐ USA 241 Gc26
Delaware City ☐ USA 241 Gc26
Delbrück ☐ D 58 Lj39
Delčevo ☐ MK 68 Mc49
Delдеleu ☐ CDN 268 Ga46
Delegate ☐ AUS 151 Se64
De Leon ☐ USA 238 Fa29
Deléplis ☐ ☐ BR 275 Hg56
Delfinópolis ☐ BR 275 Hg55
Delft ☐ NL 51 Lg37
Delgado, Cabo ☐ MOC 197 Na53
Delgany ☐ IRL 47 Kp38
Delgo ☐ SUD 185 Mg37
Delhi ☐ IND 115 Oj31
Delhi ☐ ☐ IND 114 Oj31
Delhi ☐ USA 239 Fe29
Delhi ☐ USA 241 Gc24
Delhi ☐ USA 241 Gc24
Delhinga ☐ CHN 103 Pj27
Deli ☐ RI 127 Qc49
Deli ☐ TCH 190 Lh41
Delia ☐ CDN 233 Ed20
Delicias ☐ MEX 245 Eh31
Delingha ☐ CHN 103 Pk27
Delijan ☐ IR 93 Nf29
Déline ☐ CDN 231 Dj13
Delingha ☐ CHN 103 Pk27
Delia ☐ RO 68 Mb46
Delitzsch ☐ D 59 Ln39
Dell ☐ USA 233 Ed23
Dell Rapids ☐ USA 236 Fb24
Dellys ☐ DZ 176 Lb27
Delmas ☐ ZA 205 Me59
Delmenhorst ☐ D 58 Lj37
Del Norte ☐ USA 235 Eg27
Deloraine ☐ AUS 151 Sd66
Delphi ☐ ☐ GR 70 Mc52
Delray Beach ☐ USA 243 Fk32
Del Rio ☐ USA 245 Ek31
Del Rio ☐ USA 245 Ek31
Delsbo ☐ S 41 Lr29
Delta ☐ CDN 232 Dk21
Delta ☐ USA 235 Ed26
Delta ☐ USA 235 Ef25
Delta dei Po ☐ I 60 Lm46
Delta del Río Colorado, Alto Golfo de California y ☐ MEX 244 Ec30
Delta del Tigre ☐ ROU 281 Hb62
Delta Downs ☐ AUS 147 Sa54
Delta Dunării, P.N. ☐ ☐ RO 69 Mk45
Delta du Saloum, P.N. du ☐ ☐ SN 186 Kb39
Delta Junction ☐ USA 229 Ch13
Delvádia ☐ IND 116 Og34
Delta of the Danube ☐ RO 69 Mk45
Delungra ☐ AUS 149 Sf60

Delvin ☐ IRL 47 Kn37
Delwada ☐ IND 116 Of35
Demak ☐ RI 129 Qf49
Demänová ☐ SK 67 Lu41
Démarcation Point ☐ USA 229 Ck11
Demba ☐ RDC 199 Mb48
Demba Koli ☐ SN 186 Kd39
Dembeni ☐ ETH 192 Mj40
Dembeni ☐ COM 206 Nb51
Dembi ☐ ETH 192 Mk41
Dembia ☐ RCA 191 Mc43
Dembi Dolo ☐ ETH 192 Mh41
Dembo ☐ CAM 189 Lg41
Demchok ☐ 115 Ok30
Demerariplateau ☐ 254 Hb09
Demerval Lobão ☐ BR 273 Hj48
Demidov ☐ RUS 72 Mf18
Deming ☐ USA 235 Ef29
Demini ☐ BR 71 Mj51
Demirci ☐ TR 71 Mj52
Demirköprü Baraji ☐ TR 71 Mj52
Demirtaş ☐ TR 69 Mh49
Demitsana ☐ GR 70 Mb53
Demjansk ☐ RUS 72 Mg17
Demmin ☐ D 58 Ln37
Demnate ☐ MA 175 Kg30
Democratic Republic Congo ☐ 163 Ma10
Demonia ☐ GR 70 Mc54
de Monte Roraima, P.N. ☐ ☐ BR 266 Gk43
Demopolis ☐ USA 239 Fg29
Demotte ☐ USA 237 Fg25
Dempo, Gunung ▲ RI 127 Qb47
Dempster Highway ☐ CDN 229 Da13
Demsa ☐ CAM 189 Lg41
Demta ☐ RI 155 Sa47
Demydivka ☐ UA 65 Mf40
Denain ☐ F 51 Ld40
Denali Highway ☐ USA 229 Cg14
Denali National Park ☐ ☐ USA 229 Ce14
Denali National Park ☐ USA 229 Cf14
Denan ☐ ETH 193 Nb42
Denbigh ☐ CDN 241 Gb23
Denbigh ☐ GB 49 Kr37
Den Burg ☐ NL 51 Le37
Den Chai ☐ THA 121 Qa38
Dendang ☐ RI 127 Qc47
Dendâra ☐ RIM 181 Kg37
Dendermonde ☐ ▲ B 51 Le39
Denghuan ☐ CHN 121 Qa33
Dengfeng ☐ CHN 107 Qg28
Dengi ☐ WAN 188 Le41
Dengkou ☐ CHN 106 Qe26
Dêngqên ☐ CHN 103 Ph30
Denguiro ☐ RCA 190 Mb43
Dengzhou ☐ CHN 107 Qg29
Denham ☐ AUS 144 Qg58
Denham Sound ☐ AUS 144 Qg58
Den Helder ☐ NL 51 Le38
Denhoff ☐ USA 236 Fa22
Denia ☐ ☐ E 57 Kt52
Denial Bay ☐ AUS 150 Rg62
Deniliquin ☐ AUS 151 Sc63
Denio ☐ USA 232 Ea25
Denison ☐ USA 236 Fc24
Deníz ☐ USA 238 Fb29
Deniže Kué = Fort Resolution ☐ CDN 231 Ed15
Deniyaya ☐ CL 119 Pa42
Deniz Kampi Yeri ☐ TR 71 Mg52
Denizli ☐ TR 69 Mh53
Denizli ☐ TR 71 Mk53
Denkanikota ☐ IND 118 Oj39
Denman ☐ AUS 151 Sf62
Denmark ☐ AUS 145 Qj63
Denmark ☐ USA 151 St62
Denmark ☐ DK 42 Lj35
Denmark Strait ☐ 286 Jb04
Dennebrog ☐ USA 236 Fb25
Denneg ☐ ETH 192 Mk41
Denness ☐ WL 251 Gk39
Den Oever ☐ NL 51 Lf38
Denow ☐ UZ 97 Oc26
Denpasar ☐ RI 129 Qh50
Dent de Mindif ☐ CAM 189 Lh40
Denton ☐ USA 233 Ef22
Denton ☐ USA 238 Fb29
Denton ☐ USA 241 Gc26
d'Entrecasteaux Islands ▲ PNG 156 Sf50
D'Entrecasteaux Is. ▲ AUS 144 Qh63
Dents du Midi ▲ CH 60 Lg44
Denver ☐ GH 187 La42
Denver ☐ USA 235 Eh26
Denver City ☐ USA 238 Ej29
Déo ☐ RCA 190 Ma41
Deoband ☐ IND 115 Oj30
Deoghar ☐ IND 117 Pc33
Deodápolis ☐ BR 274 Hc57
Deogarh ☐ IND 117 Pb35
Deogarh ☐ IND 116 Oh33
Deogarh ☐ IND 116 Oh33
Deogarh ☐ IND 117 Pb34
Deogarh Mahal ▲ IND 116 Oh33
Deoghar ☐ IND 117 Pc33
Deoli ☐ IND 116 Oh33
Deoli ☐ IND 116 Oh33
Deoli ☐ IND 117 Pa36
Deori ☐ IND 117 Ok34
Deoria ☐ IND 117 Pb32
Depalpur ☐ IND 116 Oh34
Déou ☐ BF 181 Kk38
Depapre ☐ RI 155 Sa47
Dépôt Lézard ☐ F 266 Hd43
Dépression du Mourdi ☐ TCH 184 Mb36
Depuch Island ▲ AUS 142 Qj56
Deputatskij ☐ RUS 89 Ra05
Déqên ☐ CHN 121 Pk31
Deqing ☐ CHN 108 Qf34
De Queen ☐ USA 238 Fc28
De Quincy ☐ USA 238 Fd30
Dera ☐ ETH 192 Mk41
Dera Bugti ☐ PK 99 Oe32
Dera Ghazi Khan ☐ PK 99 Oe31
Dera Ismail Khan ☐ PK 99 Oe30
Dera Murad Jamali ☐ PK 99 Oe31
Derajie ☐ CHN 103 Pk30
Deräne ☐ UA 65 Mg40
Derawar Fort ☐ ▲ PK 99 Of31
Derazhnya ☐ UA 73 Me20
Derbent ☐ RUS 91 Ne25
Derbent ☐ UZ 97 Ob26
Derby ☐ AUS 142 Rb54
Derby ☐ AUS 151 Sd66
Derby ☐ ☐ GB 49 Kt38
Derby ☐ USA 238 Fb27
Derdepoort ☐ ZA 205 Md58
Dereköy ☐ TR 69 Mh49
Dereli ☐ TR 91 Mk25
Derik ☐ ☐ TR 91 Na28
Dérksen Island ☐ ☐ CAM 189 Lh40
Derdáci ☐ RM 206 Ne52
De Ridder ☐ USA 238 Fd30
Deris ☐ ETH 192 Mk41
Derm ☐ NAM 204 Lk58
Dermeköy ☐ TR 69 Mh49
Dermott ☐ USA 238 Fe29
Derná ☐ MOC 203 Mj54
Derre ☐ MOC 203 Mj54
Derri ☐ SP 195 Nd43
Derry = Londonderry ☐ ☐ GB 47 Kn36
Derry Downs ☐ AUS 148 Rh57
De Rust ☐ ZA 204 Mb62

Derval ☑ F 50 Kt43
Derventa ☑ BIH 61 Ls46
Derwent ☑ CDN 233 Ee19
Derwent Valley Mills ☑ GB 49 Kt37
Des Arc ☑ USA 239 Fe28
Desaru MAL 127 Qc45
Desaru Beach ☑ MAL 127 Qc45
Descartes ☑ F 52 La44
Deschaillons ☑ CDN 240 Gd22
Deschambault Lake ☑ CDN 233 Ej18
Descobrimento, P.N. do ☑ BR 275 Ja54
Desdunes ☑ RH 250 Gd36
Dese ☑ ETH 192 Mk40
Desecho ☑ YV 265 Gg44
Desembarco del Granma, P.N. ☑ C 243 Gb36
Desengaño ☑ PE 268 Gd47
Desenzano del Garda ☑ I 60 Lj45
Desert Center ☑ USA 234 Ec27
Desert Express ☑ NAM 200 Lh57
Desert Highway ☑ JOR 180 Mf32
Desert Lake, Mount ☑ USA 241 Gf23
Desert National Wildlife Range ☑ USA 234 Ec27
Desert N.P. ☑ IND 114 Oh32
Desert Peak ☑ USA 235 Ed25
Desert Valley ☑ USA 234 Ea25
Desesti ☑ RO 67 Md43
Deshgaon ☑ IND 116 Oj35
Desierto de Altar ☑ MEX 234 Ed30
Desierto de Sechura ☑ PE 268 Fk48
Desierto de Vizcaino ☑ MEX 244 Ed32
Deskáti ☑ GR 70 Mb51
Desli ☑ IND 116 Oj35
De Smet ☑ USA 236 Fb23
Desmochado ☑ PY 276 Ha59
Desmoncos ☑ USA 256 Fd25
Desmar ☑ YE 94 Nc38
Desnyano-Staroguts'kyj N.P. ☑ UA 72 Mg19
Desolation Canyon ☑ USA 235 Ee26
Desolation Point ☑ RP 124 Rc40
De Soto ☑ USA 239 Fe26
DeSoto Caverns Park ☑ USA 239 Fg29
Despatch ☑ ZA 205 Mc62
Despeñaderos ☑ RA 280 Gh61
Des Plaines ☑ USA 237 Ff24
Despotovac ☑ SRB 68 Mb46
Despotovo ☑ SRB 68 Lu45
Dessau ☑ D 58 Ln39
Destacamento São Simão ☑ BR 278 Gk53
Destin ☑ USA 239 Fg30
Destruction Bay ☑ CDN 230 Da15
Desuri ☑ IND 116 Og33
Desvres ☑ F 51 Lb40
Dete ☑ RO 68 Mb45
Dete ☑ ZW 202 Md55
De Tian ☑ CHN 108 Od34
Detkovo ☑ RUS 44 Mj32
Detmold ☑ D 58 Lk39
De Tour Village ☑ USA 237 Fj23
Detroit ☑ USA 237 Fj24
Detroit de Bougainville ☑ VU 158 Td53
Détroit de Jacques-Cartier ☑ CDN 240 Gj21
Détroit d'Honguedo ☑ CDN 240 Gh21
Detroit Lakes ☑ USA 236 Fc22
Dettifoss ☑ IS 46 Kd25
Det Udom ☑ THA 123 Qc38
Detuo ☑ CHN 108 Qd31
Deua N.P. ☑ AUS 151 Se63
de Ubajara, P.N. ☑ BR 273 Hk47
Deukeskenkala ☑ IM 96 Nk24
Deulgaon Raja ☑ IND 116 Oj35
Deurne ☑ NL 51 Lf38
Deustua ☑ PE 269 Ge53
Deutschfeistritz ☑ A 61 Lq43
Deutschheim S.H.S. ☑ USA 239 Fe26
Deutschkreuz ☑ A 61 Lr43
Deutschlandsberg ☑ A 61 Lq44
Deva Branches ☑ F 266 Hd43
Deva ☑ RO 68 Mc45
Devadurga ☑ IND 116 Oj37
Devakottai ☑ IND 119 Ok37
De Valls Bluff ☑ USA 239 Fe29
Devanakonda ☑ IND 116 Oj38
Devaprayag ☑ IND 115 Ok30
Devapur ☑ IND 116 Oj37
Devar Hipparig ☑ IND 116 Oj37
Devarshola ☑ IND 118 Oj40
Dévaványa ☑ H 67 Ma43
Devaz ☑ AZ 91 Ne25
Devecicchiogü ☑ TR 71 Mj51
Deveci ☑ TR 66 Ls43
Develi ☑ TR 90 Mh26
Deventer ☑ NL 51 Lf38
Deveril ☑ AUS 149 Se57
Devetak ☑ BIH 68 Lt46
Devgadh Bariya ☑ IND 116 Oh34
Deviation Peak ☑ USA 229 Bk12
Devikolhi ☑ IND 115 Oj29
Devil Mount ☑ USA 229 Bb12
Devils Fork S.P. ☑ USA 242 Fj28
Devil's Hole ☑ USA 234 Ec27
Devil's Hole ☑ IM 48 La34
Devils Lake ☑ USA 236 Fa21
Devils Marbles S.P. ☑ AUS 146 Rh56
Devil's Millhopper S.P. ☑ USA 242 Fj31
Devils Point ☑ BS 250 Gc33
Devils Point ☑ BS 250 Gd34
Devils Postpile Nat. Mon. ☑ USA 234 Ea27
Devil's Sinkhole S.N.A. ☑ USA
Devils Tower Nat. Mon. ☑ USA 233 Eh23
Devin ☑ SK 66 Lr42
Devipattinam ☑ IND 119 Ok41
Devizes ☑ GB 49 Kt39
Devli ☑ CDN 236 Fd21
Devnja ☑ BG 69 Mh47
Devon ☑ ZA 205 Me59
Devon Island ☑ CDN 227 Fc03
Devonport ☑ AUS 151 Sd66
Devonshire ☑ AUS 149 Sc57
Devoto ☑ RA 281 Gj61
Devrek ☑ TR 90 Mf25
Dewakangbesar ☑ RI 130 Qd48
Dewas ☑ IND 116 Oj34
Dewanassar ☑ PK 99 Oc30
De Weerribben, N.P. ☑ NL 51 Lf38
Dewele ☑ ETH 193 Nd41
Dewelsdorp ☑ ZA 205 Md60
Dewey ☑ USA 235 Gh36
De Witt ☑ USA 239 Fe28
Dexing ☑ CHN 109 Qj31
Dexter ☑ USA 239 Ff27
Deyang ☑ CHN 108 Qe31
Deyhuk ☑ IR 98 Nj29
Deza ☑ E 56 Ks49
Dezadeash ☑ CDN 230 Db15
Dezfül ☑ IR 93 Ne29
Dezhou ☑ CHN 107 Qj27
Dhaalu Atoll ☑ MV 118 Og44
Dhahran ☑ KSA 93 Nf32
Dhaje ☑ BHT 120 Pf32
Dhaka ☑ BD 120 Pf33
Dhaka ● BD 120 Pf33
Dhakala ☑ IND 115 Pa31
Dhakala Desert ☑ NEP 117 Pb30
Dhalai ☑ NEP 117 Pb32
Dhalkut ☑ OM 95 Ng37
Dhamangaon ☑ IND 116 Ok35
Dhamar ☑ YE 94 Nc38
Dhamdaha ☑ IND 117 Pd33
Dhamnod ☑ IND 116 Oh34
Dhamtari ☑ IND 117 Pa35
Dhana ☑ IND 116 Oj34
Dhanana ☑ SP 193 Nd42
Dhanasar ☑ PK 99 Oc30
Dhanaura ☑ IND 115 Ok31
Dhanbad ☑ IND 117 Pc34
Dhanchaura ☑ NEP 115 Pb32
Dhandhuka ☑ IND 116 Of34
Dhangarhi ☑ NEP 115 Pa31

Dhankar Monastery ☑ IND 115 Ok29
Dhankuta ☑ NEP 117 Pd32
Dhanpuri ☑ IND 117 Pd33
Dhanushkodi ☑ IND 119 Ok41
Dhanwar ☑ IND 117 Pd33
Dhar ☑ IND 114 Oh29
Dhar ☑ IND 116 Oh34
Dhar ☑ IND 116 Oj35
Dharan ☑ NEP 117 Pd32
Dharapuram ☑ IND 115 Oj29
Dharan ☑ IND 116 Of35
Dharmabad ☑ IND 116 Oj36
Dharmanagar ☑ IND 120 Pg33
Dharmapura ☑ IND 118 Oj38
Dharmapuri ☑ IND 118 Ok39
Dharmapuri ☑ IND 118 Ok39
Dharmasthala ☑ IND 118 Oh39
Dharmavaram ☑ IND 118 Oj38
Dharmjamgarh ☑ IND 117 Pb34
Dharmpuri ☑ IND 116 Oh37
Dhar Tichit ☑ IND 114 Oj31
Dhar ☑ IND 116 Ok35
Dhaulagiri Himal ☑ NEP 115 Pb31
Dhaulagiri ☑ NEP 115 Pb31
Dhawa Doli Wildlife Sanctuary ☑ IND 114 Og32
Dhawa Doli W.S. ☑ IND 114 Og32
Dhawalpur ☑ IND 117 Pb35
Dhaya ☑ DZ 175 Kk28
Dhaym-al-Khayl ☑ IND 119 Ok38
Dhekiajuli ☑ IND 120 Pg32
Dhenkanal ☑ IND 117 Pc34
Dhidhdhoo ☑ MV 118 Og42
Dhing ☑ IND 120 Pg32
Dholpur ☑ IND 115 Oj31
Dhone ☑ IND 118 Oj38
Dhoraji ☑ IND 116 Of35
Dhorighat ☑ IND 117 Pb32
Dhorimanna ☑ IND 116 Of33
Dhorpatan ☑ NEP 115 Pb31
Dhrangadhra ☑ IND 116 Of34
Dhuburi ☑ IND 120 Pf32
Dhulia ☑ IND 116 Oh35
Dhulian ☑ IND 117 Pd33
Dhunche ☑ NEP 115 Pc31
Dhupaigari ☑ IND 120 Pe32
Dhuudo ☑ SP 193 Nf41
Dhuusa Mareeb ☑ SP 195 Nd43
Dia ☑ RMM 181 Kf38
Diabali ☑ RMM 181 Kf38
Diablo Range ☑ USA 234 Dk27
Diabo ☑ BF 187 Kj40
Diaca ☑ MOC 197 Na51
Diafarabé ☑ RMM 181 Kh38
Diakofto ☑ GR 70 Mc52
Diaou ☑ RMM 180 Ke38
Dialafara ☑ RMM 186 Ke39
Dialakoto ☑ SN 186 Kd39
Dialian ☑ RMM 188 Kd39
Diallassagou ☑ RMM 187 Kj39
Dialloubé ☑ RMM 181 Kh38
Diamante ☑ I 63 Lq51
Diamante ☑ RA 281 Gk62
Diamantina Gates N.P. ☑ AUS 148 Sa57
Diamantina River ☑ AUS 148 Sa57
Diamantino ☑ BR 274 Ha52
Diamantino ☑ BR 274 Hd51
Diambala ☑ RCB 198 Lg48
Diambarasco ☑ CI 187 Kj42
Diamond Harbour ☑ IND 120 Pe34
Diamond Lake ☑ USA 232 Ea23
Diamond Mine ☑ NAM 204 Lg60
Diamond Peak ☑ USA 234 Ea25
Diamond Well ☑ AUS 144 Qj56
Diamouguene ☑ SN 180 Kd38
Diana ☑ SN 186 Kd39
Dianalund ☑ DK 42 Lm35
Diana's Vow ☑ ZW 202 Mg55
Dianbai ☑ CHN 108 Qf35
Dianbabou ☑ RMM 181 Kj38
Diano Marina ☑ I 60 Lj47
Diandopolis ☑ BR 272 Hg51
Dianra ☑ CI 187 Kg41
Diao Shui Lou Falls ☑ CHN 110 Re23
Diapaga ☑ BF 187 Kj39
Diapangou ☑ BF 187 La39
Diaramana ☑ RMM 187 Kh39
Diassa = Madina ☑ RMM 187 Kg40
Diavata ☑ GR 70 Mc50
Diawling, P.N. du ☑ RIM 180 Kb37
Diaz Cross ☑ ZA 205 Md62
Diaz Point ☑ NAM 204 Lh59
Dibaga ☑ IND 115 Ok31
Dibaya ☑ RDC 199 Mb49
Dibaya-Lubue ☑ RDC 199 Lk48
Dibba ☑ UAE 95 Nj33
Dibbin N.P. ☑ JOR 180 Mf29
Dibble Glacier ☑ 286 Tc33
Dibella ☑ RN 182 Lg37
Dibeng ☑ ZA 204 Mb59
Dibla ☑ WAL 186 Ke42
Dibis ☑ IRQ 91 Nc28
Diboll ☑ USA 238 Fc30
Dibombari ☑ CAM 188 Le43
Dibrova ☑ UA 67 Md42
Dibrugarh ☑ IND 120 Ph32
Dichato ☑ RCH 280 Gd64
Dichiseni ☑ RO 69 Mh46
Dickinson ☑ USA 233 Ej22
Dickson ☑ USA 239 Fg27
Dickson Mounds Mus. ☑ USA 239 Fe25
Dida Galgalu Desert ☑ EAK 195 Mk44
Didan ☑ NL 51 Lg39
Dida Moessou ☑ CI 187 Kh42
Didcot ☑ GB 49 Kt39
Didiéni ☑ RMM 187 Kf38
Didié ☑ CI 187 Kh42
Didwana ☑ IND 114 Oh32
Didy ☑ RM 207 Ne55
Didyma ☑ GR 69 Md53
Didyma ☑ TR 71 Mh53
Didymoteícho ☑ GR 69 Mg49
Didyr ☑ BF 187 Kj39
Die ☑ F 53 Lf45
Die Bos ☑ ZA 204 Lk61
Diébougou ☑ BF 187 Kh40
Dieburg ☑ D 59 Lk41
Diecai Shan ☑ CHN 108 Qf33
Diego Cão's Cross ☑ NAM 200 Lg56
Diego de Almagro ☑ RCH 279 Gf59
Diego de Alvear ☑ RA 281 Gj63
Diéké ☑ RMM 186 Kf42
Diekirch ☑ L 51 Lg42
Diéma ☑ RMM 180 Ke38
Diemansputs ☑ ZA 204 Ma60
Diemen ☑ NL 51 Le38
Dien Bien Phu ☑ VN 121 Qc34
Dien Chau ☑ VN 121 Qc36
Diendiori ☑ RMM 181 Kh38
Dinisáes ☑ GR 71 Mg55
Dien Khanh ☑ VN 123 Qd39
Dien Mon ☑ VN 123 Qd37

Dioro ☑ RMM 187 Kh39
Dioşti ☑ RO 69 Me46
Diou ☑ RMM 187 Kh40
Diouatebdougou ☑ CI 187 Kg41
Diouloulou ☑ SN 186 Kb39
Dioulouna ☑ RMM 181 Kk38
Dioumara ☑ RMM 181 Kg38
Dioundiou ☑ RN 188 Kf38
Dioura ☑ RMM 181 Kh38
Diourbel ☑ SN 180 Kb38
Dipadih ☑ IND 117 Pb34
Dipalpur ☑ PK 99 Og30
Dipkarpaz = Rizokarpaso ☑ CY 90 Mh28
Diplo ☑ PK 99 Oe33
Dipolog ☑ RP 124 Qk40
Dipótama ☑ RP 125 Rb41
Dipoldis walde ☑ D 58 Ln40
Dir ☑ PK 97 Of28
Dira ☑ TCH 183 Lh38
Dirā ☑ KSA 93 Nd33
Dire Dawa ☑ ETH 192 Na41
Dirfis ☑ GR 69 Me52
Dirico ☑ ANG 201 Ma54
Dirk Hartog Island ☑ AUS 144 Qg58
Dirkou ☑ RN 183 Lg38
Dirranbandi ☑ AUS 149 Se60
Dişaj ☑ IR 91 Nc27
Discovery Bay ☑ AUS 150 Sa65
Discovery Center (Ketchikan) ☑ USA 230 De18
Dishkakat ☑ USA 229 Cb14
Dishná ☑ ET 179 Mg32
Disko Bugt ☑ DK 227 Hb05
Disko Ø ☑ DK 227 Hb05
Dismal Falls ☑ USA 242 Fk27
Disneyland ☑ USA 239 Fg28
Disney ☑ AUS 149 Sc66
Disneyland ☑ USA 234 Dk28
Dispur ☑ IND 120 Pf32
Diss ☑ GB 49 Lb38
Dissala ☑ G 198 Lh47
Dissen ☑ D 58 Lk38
Disteghil Sar ☑ IND 115 Oj28
Distrito Federal ☑ BR 255 Hb11
Ditdako ☑ IND 117 Pg42
Diu ☑ IND 116 Of35
Diuta Point ☑ RP 125 Rc41
Divakê ☑ AL 70 Lu50
Divandarreh ☑ IR 91 Nc28
Divčibare ☑ SRB 68 Ma46
Divčice ☑ CZ 66 Lp41
Dilwara ☑ IND 116 Og33
Dimalla ☑ IND 189 Lg43
Dimalla ☑ IND 180 Ke37
Dimapur ☑ IND 120 Pg33
Dimaro ☑ C 243 Fh44
Dimashq ● SYR 90 Mg29
Dimbelenge ☑ RDC 199 Mb48
Dimbokro ☑ CI 187 Kh42
Dimbulah ☑ AUS 147 Sc54
Dimiao ☑ RP 124 Rc41
Dimisis ☑ PNG 155 Sb50
Dimitrovgrad ☑ BG 69 Mf48
Dimitrovgrad ☑ SRB 201 Mb51
Dimitrovgrad ☑ RUS 44 Nh19
Dimitang-Wadi ☑ IND 119 Ok39
Dimmifjallgarður ☑ IS 46 Ke25
Dimmitt ☑ USA 238 Ej28
Dimona ☑ IL 92 Mh30
Dimori ☑ TG 187 La41
Dimovo ☑ BG 68 Mc47
Dimpam ☑ CAM 189 Lg44
Dimpolis ☑ BR 269 Ge50
Dina ☑ PK 99 Og29
Dinagat ☑ RP 124 Rc41
Dinagat Island ☑ RP 124 Rc40
Dinagat Sound ☑ RP 124 Rc40
Dinaig ☑ RP 125 Rc42
Dinajpur ☑ BD 120 Pe33
Dinalongan ☑ RP 124 Ra37
Dinan ☑ F 52 Kt42
Dinangourou ☑ RMM 181 Kj38
Dinapigui ☑ RP 124 Rb37
Dinara ☑ HR 61 Lr46
Dinard ☑ F 52 Kt42
Dinaric Alps ☑ 26 Lb05
Dindar N.P. ☑ SUD 185 Mh39
Dinder N.P. ☑ SUD 202 Mg54
Dindigul ☑ IND 118 Oj40
Dindima ☑ WAN 188 Lf40
Dindon ☑ IND 117 Pa34
Dindouli Seydi ☑ SN 180 Kd38
Ding'an ☑ CHN 109 Qf36
Ding'an ☑ CHN 121 Qc33
Dingbian ☑ CHN 106 Qd27
Ding Ding ☑ SUD 191 Mg41
Dingé ☑ RDC 199 Mb48
Dinggye ☑ CHN 102 Pd31
Dinghushan Z.B. ☑ CHN 108 Qg34
Dingia ☑ RDC 190 Mf44
Dingjia ☑ RDC 199 Mb49
Dingle ☑ IRL 47 Kh38
Dingle ☑ RP 124 Rb40
Dingle Bay ☑ IRL 47 Kh38
Dingolfing ☑ D 59 Lo42
Dingolshausen ☑ IND 117 Pa34
Dingras ☑ RP 124 Ra36
Dingshuzhenn ☑ CHN 112 Qk30
Dingtao ☑ CHN 107 Qg28
Dinguraye ☑ RG 186 Ke40
Dingwall ☑ GB 48 Kq33
Dingxi ☑ CHN 106 Qc28
Dingxiang ☑ CHN 107 Qg26
Dingxiang ☑ CHN 107 Qg26
Dingzhou ☑ CHN 103 Pg26
Dinh Lap ☑ VN 121 Qd34
Dinira, P.N. ☑ YV 264 Ge41
Dinklage ☑ D 58 Lj38
Dinokwe ☑ RB 202 Md57
Dinorwic ☑ CDN 236 Fd21
Dinosaur ☑ USA 235 Eg25
Dinosaur Egg Site ☑ CDN 233 Ed21
Dinosaur Footprints (Moyeni) ☑ LS 205 Md61
Dinosaur Nat. Mon. ☑ USA 235 Eg25
Dinosaur Prov. Park ☑ CDN 233 Ee22
Dinosaur's Footprints ☑ NAM 200 Lj56
Dinslaken ☑ D 58 Lh39
Dinsmore ☑ CDN 233 Ed20
Dintiteladss ☑ RI 127 Qc48
Diö ☑ S 43 Lp44
Dioila ☑ RMM 187 Kg39
Diola ☑ RMM 180 Ke38
Dioklecjanova palača ☑ HR 61 Lr47
Diomandou ☑ RG 186 Kf41
Diona ☑ TCH 184 Mb38
Diondiori ☑ RMM 181 Kh38
Dionisádes ☑ GR 71 Mg55
Dionisio Cerqueira ☑ BR 276 Hd59
Diorama ☑ BR 274 He54

Djebel el Jalālah el Qiblīya ☑ ET 179 Mf31
Djebel el Kahla ☑ DZ 176 Lc28
Djebel Fernane ☑ DZ 176 Lc28
Djebel Gourou ☑ DZ 176 Lb28
Djebel Grouz ☑ DZ/MA 175 Kk29
Djebel Gumbiri ☑ SUD 194 Mf43
Djebel Habashiyah ☑ YE 94 Ne37
Djebel Hafit ☑ OM/UAE 95 Nh34
Djebel Hamrin ☑ IRQ 91 Nc28
Djebel In Azzene ☑ DZ 175 La32
Djebel Is ☑ SUD 179 Mh34
Djebel Jaddah ☑ YE 94 Nb37
Djebel Jar al ☑ KSA 92 Mh33
Djebel Kathangor ☑ SUD 194 Mh43
Djebel Khadar ☑ OM 95 Nk34
Djebel Ksel ☑ DZ 175 La29
Djebel Lawdh ☑ YE 94 Nc39
Djebel Lekst ☑ MA 174 Kf31
Djebel Mahrat ☑ YE 94 Nf38
Djebel Manar ☑ YE 94 Nc38
Djebel Marra ☑ KSA 94 Nb35
Djebel Mazmun ☑ SUD 185 Mg39
Djebel Meschkakur ☑ MA 175 Kj29
Djebel Mouchchene ☑ MA 175 Kj29
Djebel Mourik ☑ MA 175 Kh29
Djebel Nafusah ☑ LAR 177 Lg30
Djebel Nasiya ☑ ET 179 Mg32
Djebel Onk ☑ DZ 176 Lc28
Djebel Ouarkziz ☑ DZ/MA 174 Kf31
Djebel Qatrani ☑ ET 179 Mf31
Djebel Qattâr ☑ ET 179 Mg32
Djebel Ru'us al Tiwal ☑ SYR 90 Mg19
Djebel Sabir ☑ YE 94 Nc38
Djebel Salma ☑ KSA 92 Nb32
Djebel Samhah ☑ ET 179 Mg32
Djebel Sarhro ☑ MA 175 Kh29
Djebel Sawdah ☑ KSA 94 Nb36
Djebel Settat ☑ DZ 176 Lb32
Djebel Shaïb el Banat ☑ ET 179 Mg32
Djebel Sindib ☑ SUD 179 Mg34
Djebel Sirat ☑ YE 94 Nb37
Djebel Tammu ☑ LAR/RN 183 Lh34
Djebel Tasakalouine ☑ MA 174 Ke31
Djebel Tazzeka ☑ MA 175 Kh28
Djebel Tazzeka, P.N. ☑ MA 175 Kh28
Djebel Tebaga ☑ TN 176 Le29
Djebel Tenouchfi ☑ DZ 175 Kk28
Djebel Tidirhine ☑ MA 175 Kh28
Djebel Touaris ☑ DZ 175 Kj31
Djebel Toubkal ☑ MA 175 Kg29
Djebel Toucha ☑ DZ 175 La29
Djebel Tuwayq ☑ KSA 94 Nc35
Djebel Umm Inab ☑ ET 179 Mg32
Djebel Zaghouan ☑ TN 176 Le29
Djebobo, Mount ☑ GH/TG 187 La41
Djébok ☑ RMM 181 Kk38
Djébrène ☑ TCH 189 Lk40
Djedada ☑ TCH 183 Lk39
Djedars ☑ DZ 175 La29
Djeffara ☑ TN 176 Le30
Djelfa ☑ DZ 176 Lb29
Djéma ☑ RCA 191 Mc42
Djèmber ☑ TCH 189 Lj40
Djémila ☑ DZ 176 Lc28
Djema Bank ☑ MAL 128 Qg44
Dien-Bou Rezg ☑ DZ 175 Kk30
Djenné ☑ RMM 187 Kh39
Djérem ☑ CAM 189 Lg42
Djermaya ☑ TCH 189 Lh39
Djibasso ☑ BF 187 Kh40
Djibo ☑ BF 187 Kj39
Djibouria ☑ RMM 166 Kf42
Djibouti ☑ DJI 193 Nd40
Djibouti ● DJI 193 Nd40
Djibouti ☑ 163 Na08
Djibrosso ☑ CI 187 Kg41
Djidja ☑ DY 188 La42
Djigoue ☑ BF 187 Kh40
Djiguéni ☑ RIM 181 Kf38
Djilbe ☑ CAM 189 Lh41
Djiljet ☑ BF 187 Kh40
Djiratoutou ☑ CI 187 Kg41
Djohong ☑ CAM 189 Lh42
Djokpunuto ☑ RDC 199 Ma48
Djoli ☑ TCH 190 Lk41
Djoli ☑ RDC 190 Mb40
Djombo ☑ RDC 190 Mf44
Djonaba ☑ RIM 180 Kd37
Djort ☑ RN 182 La38
Djort Torba ☑ DZ 175 Kj30
Djoubissi ☑ RCA 190 Ma42
Djougou ☑ DY 188 La42
Djoum ☑ CAM 189 Lg44
Djoumboli ☑ CAM 189 Lg42
Djugu ☑ RDC 194 Mf45
Djulino ☑ BG 69 Mh48
Djupivogur ☑ IS 46 Kf26
Djurås ☑ S 43 Lq32
Djurdjura, P.N. du ☑ DZ 176 Lc27
Djuro n.p. ☑ S 43 Lo32
Djursland ☑ DK 42 Lm34
Djurs Sommerland ☑ DK 42 Lj34
D'Kar ☑ RB 201 Ma57
Dlolwana ☑ ZA 205 Mf60
Dmitriyev-L'govskij ☑ RUS 72 Mh19
Dmitrov ☑ RUS 72 Mj17
Dmytrivka ☑ UA 67 Mc41
Dolak ☑ RI 154 Rk49
Dolalghat ☑ NEP 115 Pc32
Dolanes ☑ IND 116 Oh36
Dolavon ☑ RA 282 Gg67
Dolbeau ☑ CDN 240 Gd21
Dolbel ☑ RN 181 La38
Doleib Hill ☑ SUD 191 Mf41
Đelemo ☑ N 42 Lj32
Dolfinarium ☑ NL 51 Lf38
Dolgellau ☑ GB 49 Kr38
Dolgoi Island ☑ USA 228 Bk18
Dolgorukovo ☑ RUS 45 Mk19
Dolianova ☑ I 62 Lk51
Dolisié = Loubomo ☑ RCB 198 Lg48
Dolití Septi ☑ G 67 Mf42
Doljani ☑ BIH 61 Ls47
Dollard ☑ NL 51 Lh37
Dollo Odo ☑ ETH 195 Na43
Dolna Banja ☑ BG 69 Me48
Dolna Mitropolija ☑ BG 69 Me47
Dolna Orjahovica ☑ BG 69 Mf47
Dolni Bousov ☑ CZ 66 Lp40
Dolni Čam ☑ CHN 108 Qd31
Dolni Kubin ☑ BG 68 Md47
Dolni Zandov ☑ CZ 66 Lo40
Dolno Dupeni ☑ MK 70 Mb50
Dolný Kubin ☑ SK 67 Lu41
Dolo ☑ I 60 Ln45
Dolo ☑ RI 130 Qk46
Dolokmarawan ☑ RI 126 Pk44
Dolokmarawan ☑ RI 126 Pk44
Doloksanggul ☑ RI 127 Pk44
Dolomite ☑ NAM 200 Lh56
Dolomiti ☑ I 60 Ln44
Dolomiti Bellunesi, P.N. delle ☑ I 60 Ln44
Dolon ☑ KS 100 Oh25
Dolong ☑ RI 130 Rb46
Dolonnur ☑ MNG 104 Qc23
Dolores ☑ CO 264 Gc44
Dolores ☑ E 57 Ku52
Dolores ☑ GCA 247 Ff37
Dolores ☑ RA 281 Ha64
Dolores ☑ ROU 276 Ha62
Dolores ☑ RP 124 Rc39
Dolores ☑ USA 235 Eg27
Dolores Hidalgo ☑ MEX 246 Ek35
Dolores Hidalgo ☑ MEX 247 Fc37
Dolphin and Union Strait ☑ CDN 226 Ea05
Do Luong ☑ VN 121 Qc36
Dolyna ☑ UA 67 Md42
Dolyna ☑ UA 67 Md42
Dolyns'ka ☑ UA 73 Mh20
Dolżanskaja ☑ RUS 73 Mj21
Dolzičy ☑ RUS 44 Mh32
Doma Safari Area ☑ ZW 202 Mf54
Domázlice ☑ CZ 66 Lo41
Dombai ☑ RUS 91 Na24
Dombás ☑ N 42 Lk30
Dombe ☑ MOC 202 Mg55
Dombe Grande ☑ ANG 200 Lg52
Dombóvár ☑ H 68 Lu44
Dombrau ☑ BG 69 Mh47
Dombresson ☑ CH 53 Lh43
Dobrina ☑ RI 154 Rh48
Dobrinka ☑ RUS 45 Mk19
Dombrovica ☑ UA 72 Me18
Domda ☑ RG 186 Ke41
Domashingila ☑ ET 192 Mk40
Dombóvár ☑ H 68 Lu44

Docker Creek ☑ AUS 143 Re58
Dockrell, Mount ☑ AUS 143 Rd55
Doclea ☑ MNE 68 Lu48
Doc Let Beach ☑ VN 123 Qe39
Doc. Juan L.Mallorquín ☑ PY 276 Hc58
Doda ☑ EAT 197 Mk48
Doda ☑ RI 130 Ra46
Dodaga ☑ RI 125 Re45
Dodaballapur ☑ IND 118 Oj39
Doddridge ☑ USA 238 Fd29
Dodecanese ☑ GR 71 Mg54
Dodge City ☑ USA 236 Fa26
Dodol ☑ SN 180 Kc38
Dodoma ● EAT 197 Mh49
Dodoni ☑ GR 70 Ma51
Dodori National Reserve ☑ EAK 195 Na46
Dodoyo ☑ GH 187 Kk43
Doembang Nangbuat ☑ THA 122 Qa38
Doetinchem ☑ NL 51 Lg39
Doğanbey ☑ TR 71 Mg50
Doğankent ☑ TR 91 Mk25
Doğanşehir ☑ TR 90 Mj26
Doğanyol ☑ TR 91 Mk26
Dog Creek ☑ CDN 232 Dj20
Dogji ☑ SN 180 Kc38
Dogliani ☑ I 60 Lh46
Dogo ☑ J 113 Rg27
Dogo ☑ RMM 187 Kk40
Dogoba ☑ SUD 190 Mf41
Dogofri ☑ RMM 181 Kh38
Dogon, P.N. de ☑ RN 182 Lc38
Dogondoutchi ☑ RN 182 Lc38
Dogonti ☑ RMM 187 Kh39
Dogoumbo ☑ TCH 189 Lj40
Dogri ☑ SN 186 Ke39
Dogon-yama ☑ J 113 Rg28
Doğubeyazıt ☑ TR 91 Nc26
Doğuéraoua ☑ RN 182 Lc38
Doğu Karadeniz Dağları ☑ TR 91 Mk25
Doğu Menteşe Dağları ☑ TR 71 Mj53
Dogwood Trail ☑ USA 239 Fd30
Dohad ☑ IND 116 Oh34
Dohazari ☑ BD 120 Pg34
Doi ☑ THA 121 Pk36
Doigan ☑ EAK 194 Mj45
Doi Inthanon ☑ THA 121 Pk36
Doi Khun Tan N.P. ☑ THA 121 Pk36
Doi Luang N.P. ☑ THA 121 Pk36
Doimara ☑ IND 120 Pg32
Doi Pagoda ☑ VN 123 Qd37
Doi Saket ☑ THA 121 Pk36
Do Suthep-Pui N.P. ☑ THA 121 Pk36
Dos Vizinhos ☑ BR 276 Hd58
Doi Tachi ☑ THA 122 Pk37
Dojevice ☑ SRB 68 Ma47
Doka ☑ ETH 192 Mk40
Doka ☑ SUD 185 Mh39
Dokan ☑ IRQ 91 Nc28
Dokis Ind. Res. ☑ CDN 237 Fj22
Doko ☑ G 40 Lc30
Dokkum ☑ NL 51 Lg37
Doko ☑ RG 186 Kf40
Doko ☑ WAN 188 Le39
Doksy ☑ CZ 66 Lp40
Dokukajewk S.J. ☑ UA 73 Mj22
Dolak ☑ RI 154 Rk49
Dolalghat ☑ NEP 115 Pc32
Dolan Springs ☑ USA 234 Ec28
Dolant ☑ ZA 205 Mf56
Dom Eliseu ☑ BR 272 Hg48
Dom Eliseu ☑ BR 276 Hd61
Domart ☑ F 53 Lc44
Dômes de Fabedougou ☑ BF 187 Kh40
Domeyko ☑ RCH 279 Ge60
Don, Gunung ☑ RI 154 Rj47
Domica ☑ SK 67 Ma42
Dominase ☑ GH 187 Kk42
Domingos Martins ☑ BR 275 Hk56
Domínguez ☑ RA 276 Ha62
Dominica ☑ WD 251 Gk38
Dominica ☑ WD 251 Gk38
Dominical ☑ CR 249 Fj41
Dominican Republic ☑ DOM 250 Ge37
Dominica Passage ☑ 251 Gk38
Dom Inocencio ☑ BR 273 Hj50
Domiongo ☑ RDC 199 Ma48
Dömitz ☑ D 58 Lm37
Domme ☑ F 52 Lb44
Domnești ☑ RO 68 Me45
Domnovo ☑ RUS 42 Mb19
Domo ☑ ETH 193 Nd42
Domokós ☑ GR 70 Mc51
Domoni ☑ COM 206 Nc52
Dompaire ☑ F 53 Lg43
Dom Pedro ☑ BR 276 Hc61
Dom Pedro ☑ BR 272 Hh48
Dompem ☑ GH 187 Kj43
Dompierre-sur-Besbre ☑ F 53 Ld44
Dompu ☑ RI 130 Qk50
Domuel ☑ MOC 202 Mg53
Dom und Sankt Michael in Hildesheim ☑ D 58 Lk38
Domusnovás ☑ I 62 Lj51
Domuyo, Volcán ☑ RA 280 Ge64
Domżale ☑ SLO 66 Lq44
Dom zu Aachen ☑ D 58 Lg40
Dom zu Braunschweig ☑ D 58 Ll39
Dom zu Eichstätt ☑ D 59 Lm42
Dom zu Erfurt ☑ D 58 Lm40
Dom zu Freiberg ☑ D 58 Ln40
Dom zu Freising ☑ D 59 Lm42
Dom zu Fulda ☑ D 59 Lk40
Dom zu Greifswald ☑ D 58 Lo36
Dom zu Gurk ☑ A 61 Lp44
Dom zu Halberstadt ☑ D 58 Lm39
Dom zu Köln ☑ D 58 Lg40
Dom zu Limburg ☑ D 59 Lj40
Dom zu Mainz ☑ D 59 Lj41
Dom zu Merseburg ☑ D 58 Lm39
Dom zu Minden ☑ D 58 Lk38
Dom zu Münster ☑ D 58 Lj39
Dom zu Naumburg ☑ D 58 Lm39
Dom zu Paderborn ☑ D 58 Lj39
Dom zu Speyer ☑ D 59 Lj41
Dom zu Stendal ☑ D 58 Lm38
Dom zu Worms ☑ D 59 Lj41
Don ☑ GB 48 Kr33
Doña Ana, Cerro ☑ RCH 279 Ge60
Donacona ☑ CDN 240 Ge22
Doña Inés, Cerro ☑ RCH 279 Gf59
Doña Juana, Volcán ☑ CO 264 Gb45
Donald ☑ AUS 151 Sb64
Donald ☑ CDN 232 Eb20
Donalda ☑ CDN 233 Ec19
Donaldsonville ☑ USA 239 Fe30
Donalsonville ☑ USA 242 Fh30
Dos Córregas ☑ BR 274 He57
Dos Irmãos ☑ BR 274 Hf53
Doña María ☑ GCA 248 Ff38
Doñana, P.N. de ☑ E 55 Kq53
Donauwörth ☑ D 59 Lm42
Donaueschingen ☑ D 59 Lj43
Donautal ☑ A 66 Lo42
Donauwörth ☑ D 59 Lm42
Dome Anemkro ☑ CI 187 Kj42
Doncaster ☑ GB 49 Kt37
Doncaster Ind. Res. ☑ CDN 240 Gc22
Donduri ☑ A 60 Ld43
Dornes ☑ F 53 Ld44
Dornoch ☑ GB 48 Kq33
Dorno Djouatogbe ☑ TCH 184 Mb39
Dornogov' ☑ MNG 104 Qe23
Doro ☑ RMM 181 Kk37
Doroh ☑ IR 98 Nj30
Dorohoi ☑ RO 73 Md42
Dorohusk ☑ PL 65 Md39
Dorondovy Island ☑ RP 125 Ra42
Dorong ☑ IN 123 Qd40
Dondusani ☑ MD 73 Md21
Dorosiovo ☑ SRB 68 Lu45
Dorosyny ☑ UA 65 Mf40
Dorota ☑ S 41 Lr26
Dorre Island ☑ AUS 144 Qg58
Dorowa ☑ ZW 202 Mf55
Đorpen ☑ D 58 Lj38
Dorra ☑ KWT 93 Ne31
Dorre Island ☑ AUS 149 Sg61
Dorrigo N.P. ☑ AUS 149 Sg61
Dorsale Camerounaise ☑ CAM 189 Lf42
Dorset Coast ☑ GB 49 Ks40
Dorsland Trekkers Monument ☑ NAM 200 Lh55
Dorsten ☑ D 58 Lg39
Dortmund ☑ D 58 Lj39
Dörtyol ☑ TR 90 Mj27
Dörud ☑ IR 93 Ne29
Doruma ☑ RDC 191 Md43
Dörzbach ☑ D 59 Lk41
Dos Caminos ☑ YV 265 Gh41
Dos de Mayo ☑ PE 268 Gd49
Dos de Mayo ☑ RA 276 Hd60
Dos Hermanas ☑ E 55 Kp53
Dos Lagunas ☑ GCA 247 Ff37
Do Son ☑ VN 121 Qd35
Dos Palos ☑ USA 234 Dk27
Dos Ríos ☑ CR 249 Fg40
Dosso ☑ RN 182 Lc38
Do'stlik ☑ UZ 97 Oe26
Dostuk ☑ KS 100 Oh25
Dothan ☑ USA 239 Fg30
Dotswood ☑ AUS 147 Sd55
Douai ☑ F 51 Ld41
Douako ☑ RG 186 Ke41
Doualayel ☑ CAM 189 Lg42
Douala ● CAM 188 Le43
Douar ☑ RMM 181 Kj37
Doubabougou ☑ RMM 181 Kg38
Double Island Point ☑ AUS 149 Sg58
Doublemi ☑ RN 182 La38
Double Mountain ☑ AUS 149 Sf57
Doubtful Bay ☑ AUS 143 Rc54
Doubtful Island Bay ☑ AUS 149 Qk62
Doubtful Island Bay ☑ NZ 153 Td68
Doubtful Sound ☑ NZ 153 Td68
Douchy-les-Mines ☑ F 51 Ld41
Doucier ☑ F 53 Lf44
Doudou ☑ BF 187 Kj40
Doué-la-Fontaine ☑ F 52 Ku43
Douentza ☑ RMM 181 Kj38
Douglas ☑ GB 283 Ha71
Douglas ☑ USA 230 Dc16
Douglas ☑ USA 235 Eh24
Douglas ☑ USA 233 Eh23
Douglas ☑ USA 205 Mb60
Douglas ☑ ZA 204 Mb60
Douglas-Apsley National Park ☑ AUS 151 Se66
Douglas Cay ☑ BH 248 Fg37
Douglas City ☑ USA 234 Dj25
Douglas, s. Ind. Res. ☑ CDN 232 Dj20
Douglas, Mount ☑ USA 228 Cd18
Douglas Range ☑ 286 Ge32
Douglasville ☑ USA 239 Fh29
Doukhobor Hist. Village ☑ CDN 232 Eb21
Doukoula ☑ CAM 189 Lh40

Elesbão Veloso – Etolikó

Etolin Island – Fort Greely

Etolin Island USA 230 Dd17
Etolin Point USA 228 Ca16
Etorohaberge NAM 200 Lg54
Etosha N.P. NAM 200 Lh55
Etosha Pan NAM 200 Lj55
Etou CAM 189 Lg44
Etoumbi RCB 190 Lh45
Etowah USA 239 Fh28
Etrépagny F 51 Lb41
Etretat F 50 La41
Etropole BG 68 Md48
Etropolski manastir BG 69 Me48
Etsch = Ádige I 60 Ll44
Ettelbruck L 51 Lg41
Ettenheim D 59 Lh42
Etten-Leur NL 51 Le39
Et-Tleta-de-Oued-Laou MA 175 Kh28
Ettlingen D 59 Lj42
Et-Tnine MA 174 Kf30
ttumanur IND 118 Oj41
tumba RDC 199 Ma47
tumba RDC 199 Mc46
turnagaram IND 117 Pa36
u F 51 Lb40
uca BR 267 He44
ucaliptus BOL 278 Gg54
ucla AUS 145 Re61
ucla Basin AUS 145 Rc62
uclid USA 237 Fk25
uclides da Cunha BR 273 Ja51
uclides da Cunha Paulista BR 274 Hd57
udora USA 239 Fe29
udunda AUS 150 Rk63
ufaula USA 238 Fc28
ufaula USA 239 Fh30
ufaula N.W.R. USA 239 Fh29
ufrasio Loza RA 279 Gj60
ufrazijeva bazilika HR 61 Lo45
ugene USA 232 Dj23
ugowra AUS 151 Se62
ulo AUS 149 Sc60
ulonia USA 242 Fk30
umara Springs AUS 147 Sd55
umungarie AUS 149 Se61
unápolis BR 275 Ja54
ungella AUS 149 Se56
ungella N.P. AUS 149 Se56
unice USA 238 Ej29
unice USA 239 Fd30
upen B 51 Lg40
uphrates IRQ 91 Na28
upora USA 239 Ff29
ura FIN 44 Mc29
urady AUS 144 Qh59
urajoki FIN 44 Mb29
ureka USA 232 Dh25
ureka USA 232 Ec21
ureka USA 234 Ec26
ureka USA 235 Ed26
ureka USA 236 Fa23
ureka USA 238 Fb27
ureka Springs USA 238 Fd27
urimbula N.P. AUS 149 Sf58
uromba AUS 149 Se58
uropa Park D 59 Lh42
urope 26 La05
uropoort NL 51 Ld39
uropos parkas LT 45 Mf36
urora AUS 151 Sc64
uro Speedway D 58 Lo39
uskirchen D 58 Lg40
uston AUS 151 Sb63
utaw USA 239 Fg29
uthini MW 196 Mg51
utin D 58 Ll36
va Downs AUS 146 Rh55
vale ANG 200 Lh54
vandale CDN 240 Gg23
vangelístria GR 71 Mf53
vans Strait CDN 227 Fd06
vanston USA 235 Ee25
vanston USA 237 Fg24
vansville USA 239 Fg27
vare, T.I. BR 270 Gf47
vartra RM 207 Nd58
vaton ZA 205 Md59
vaux-les-Bains F 53 Lc44
vaz IR 98 Ng32
vciler TR 71 Mg51
vdilos GR 71 Mg53
venki Autonomous District RUS 88 Pc05
vensville USA 233 Eg24
verard Junction AUS 145 Rc58
verard Park AUS 145 Rg59
verard Ranges AUS 145 Rg59
verest, Mount NEP/CHN 115 Pd31
verett USA 232 Dj22
vergem B 51 Ld39
verglades City USA 243 Fk33
verglades National Park USA 243 Fk33
vergreen USA 232 Ec21
vergreen USA 236 Fc22
vergreen USA 239 Fg30
vertsberg S 40 Lo29
vesham AUS 149 Sb57
vesham GB 49 Kt38
via GR 69 Md52
via GR 71 Me52
vian-les-Bains F 53 Lg44
vijärvi FIN 44 Md27
vinayong GQ 188 Lf45
visa F 60 Lj48
vje N 42 Lh32
ksinograd BG 69 Mh47
vlanovo RUS 72 Mj19
vodoula CAM 189 Lf43
Oghli IR 91 Nc26
voikós Kólpos GR 69 Md52
volène CH 60 Lh44
vora P 55 Kn52
voramonte P 55 Kn52
vora Romana P 55 Kn52
vreux F 51 Lb41
vron F 50 Ku42
vros GR 69 Mg49
vry F 51 Lc42
van USA 232 Eb22
vango WAN 188 Le42
vaso Ngiro EAK 194 Mh46
vaso Ngiro EAK 195 Mk45
vasse PNG 156 Sf48
vo RCB 198 Lh46
altación BOL 270 Gg51
altación BOL 278 Gh52
arhos GR 70 Mc52
celsior ZA 205 Md60
celsior Springs USA 238 Fc26
e GB 49 Kr39
eter GB 49 Kr40
eter USA 241 Ge24
-Fortín Cacique RA 279 Gk60
il-Home of the Dalai Lama IND 115 Oj29
moor N.P. GB 49 Kr39
mouth AUS 142 Qh56
mouth Gulf AUS 142 Qh57
mouth Plateau AUS 134 Qb11
pedition N.P. AUS 149 Se58
pedition Range AUS 149 Se58
plorerbank 249 Fk37
plorer Mtn. USA 228 Bk16
tremadura E 55 Ko51
tremo P 54 Km49
u BR 273 Ja49
uma Cays BS 243 Gb33
uma Cays Land and Sea Park BS 243 Gb33
uma Sound BS 243 Gb33
dehavn N 42 Lj32
dhafushi MV 118 Og43
ebrow CDN 233 Eg20
emouth GB 48 Ks35
e of Kuruman ZA 204 Mb59
e Peninsula GB 48 Ko32
gurande F 53 Lc45
l SP 193 Ne42
lau = Bagrationovsk PL 65 Ma36
moutiers F 52 Lb45
n Kush IR 93 Nd29
rarbakki IS 46 Jt27
re Highway AUS 145 Rc62
re Mountains NZ 153 Te68
re Peninsula AUS 150 Rh62
Eysturoy DK 46 Ko28
Eyu-mojok CAM 188 Le43
Eyvan IR 91 Nd29
Eyvanakey IR 98 Ng28
Ezba Hasaballa ET 179 Mf33
Ezbet Ain ET 179 Mf33
Ezbet Dûsh ET 179 Mf33
Ezbet el Jâjah ET 179 Mf33
Ezcaray E 56 Ks48
Ezere LV 45 Mc34
Ežerėlis LT 45 Md36
Ezernieki LV 45 Mh34
Ezhou CHN 109 Qh30
Ezibeleni ZA 205 Md61
Ezine TR 71 Mg51
Ezo SUD 191 Md43
Ezra'a SYR 90 Mj29
Ezulwini Valley SD 205 Mf59
Ezzangbo WAN 188 Ld42
Ez-Ziliga MA 175 Kg29

F

Faaborg DK 42 Ll35
Faadippolhu Atoll = Lhaviyani Atoll MV 118 Og43
Faafu Atoll MV 118 Og44
Fabens USA 235 Eg30
Fåberg N 40 Ll29
Fábiánsebestyén H 67 Ma44
Fäboda FIN 41 Mc27
Fa Bouré DY 188 Lb40
Fabriano I 61 Ln47
Fábricas de Riópar E 55 Ks52
Fabrichnyi KZ 100 Oj24
Facatativa CO 264 Gc43
Fachi RN 183 Lf36
Facundo RA 282 Gf68
Fada TCH 184 Ma37
Fada-Ngourma BF 187 La39
Fadat al Mislah KSA 94 Na34
Faddoi SUD 191 Mg41
Faden CDN 240 Gg18
Fadhi OM 95 Nh37
Fadiadougou CI 187 Kg41
Fadugu WAL 186 Ke41
Faenza I 60 Lm46
Fafa RMM 181 La38
Fafadun SP 195 Na44
Fafakourou SN 186 Kc39
Fafe P 54 Km49
Făgăraș RO 67 Me45
Fagerås S 42 Lo31
Fagerhult S 42 Lm32
Fagerhult S 43 Lq33
Fagernes N 40 Lk30
Fagersta S 43 Lq30
Făget RO 68 Mc45
Faggo WAN 188 Le40
Fagita RI 131 Rf46
Fagne B 51 Le40
Fagrinkotti SUD 185 Mf37
Fagudu RI 131 Rd46
Fagurhólsmýri IS 46 Kd27
Fagwir SUD 191 Mf41
Fahaheel KWT 93 Ne31
Faïd TN 176 Le28
Failaka Island KWT 93 Ne31
Faille de Nyakazu BU 196 Mf47
Fairbairn Reservoir AUS 149 Sd57
Fairbanks USA 229 Cg13
Fairbury USA 238 Fb25
Fairfield USA 232 Ec24
Fairfield USA 234 Dj26
Fairfield USA 236 Fe25
Fairfield USA 238 Fb30
Fairfield USA 241 Gf23
Fairfield USA 242 Gb28
Fairfield Sapphire Valley USA 242 Fj28
Fair Harbour CDN 232 Dg20
Fair Head GB 47 Ko35
Fairhill AUS 149 Se57
Fair Isle GB 48 Kt31
Fairlie NZ 153 Tf68
Fairlight AUS 147 Sc53
Fairlight CDN 236 Ek21
Fairmont AUS 148 Sb61
Fairmont USA 236 Fc24
Fairmont USA 237 Fk26
Fairmont Hot Springs CDN 232 Ec20
Fairo WAL 186 Ke42
Fair Oaks USA 239 Fe28
Fairplay USA 235 Eh26
Fairport USA 237 Fg23
Fairview AUS 147 Sc53
Fairview AUS 149 Sd61
Fairview CDN 231 Ea17
Fairview USA 233 Eh22
Fairview USA 235 Ee26
Fairview USA 238 Fa27
Fairweather, Mount CDN 230 Db16
Fairyhouse Racetrack IRL 47 Ko37
Fairyland AUS 149 Sf59
Faisalabad PK 99 Og30
Faith USA 233 Ej23
Faiyiba SUD 185 Mf38
Faizabad AFG 97 Of27
Faizabad IND 117 Pb32
Faje WAN 188 Lc41
Fakenham GB 49 La38
Fakfak = Onin Peninsula RI 131 Rf47
Fakfak RI 154 Rg47
Fakh Abad IR 98 Ng31
Fakhrpur IND 115 Pa32
Fakija BG 69 Mh48
Fakkeh IR 93 Nd29
Fakola RMM 187 Kg40
Fakse DK 42 Ln35
Fakse Bugt DK 42 Ln35
Fak Tha THA 121 Qa37
Faku CHN 110 Rb24
Falaba WAL 186 Ke41
Faladié RMM 186 Kf39
Falagountou BF 181 La38
Falaise F 50 Ku42
Falaise d'Amont F 50 La41
Falaise d'Aval F 50 La41
Falaise de Bandiagara RMM 181 Kj38
Falaise de Banfora BF 187 Kh40
Falaise de l'Aguer-Tay TCH 183 Lj35
Falaise de Tambaoura RMM 186 Ke39
Falaise de Tiguidit RN 182 Ld37
Falaise du Gobnangou BF 188 La40
Falaise et grottes de l'Isandra RM 207 Nd56
Falakata IND 120 Pe32
Falam MYA 120 Pg34
Falconara Maríttima I 61 Lo47
Faléa RMM 186 Ke39
Falémé SN 180 Kd38
Falerum S 43 Lr32
Fălești MD 73 Md22
Falfurrias USA 245 Fa32
Fali Mountains WAN 188 Lf42
Falkenberg D 58 Lo39
Falkenberg S 42 Ln34
Falkensee D 58 Lo38
Falkenstein D 59 Ln40
Falkirk GB 48 Kr34
Falkland CDN 232 Ea20
Falkland Islands GB 255 Ha15
Falkland Islands GB 283 Ha71
Falkland Plateau 254 Ha15
Falkland Sound GB 283 Ha71
Falköping S 43 Lo32
Falla WAL 186 Ke41
Fallingbostel D 58 Lk38
Fallon USA 233 Eh22
Fallon USA 234 Ea26
Fall River USA 241 Ge25
Fall River Mills USA 234 Dk25
Falls City USA 238 Fc25
Falls of Measach GB 48 Kp33
Falmey RN 188 Lb39
Falmouth GB 49 Kp40
Falmouth JA 250 Gb36
Falmouth USA 239 Fh26
Falmouth USA 241 Ge25
Falo RMM 187 Kg39
Falou RMM 181 Kg38
False Bay CDN 232 Dh21
False Oxford Ness AUS 147 Sb51
False Pass USA 228 Bj18
Falset E 57 La49
Falso Cabo de Hornos RCH 282 Gf73
Falster DK 42 Ln36
Falsterbo S 42 Ln35
Fălticeni RO 73 Md22
Falu gruva S 43 Lq30
Falun CDN 233 Ed19
Falun S 43 Lq30
Fama SUD 185 Mf40
Famagusta CY 90 Mg28
Famaillá RA 279 Gh59
Famalé RN 181 La38
Fameck F 51 Lg41
Famenin IR 91 Ne28
Famen Si CHN 106 Qd28
Fana N 42 Lf30
Fana RMM 187 Kg39
Fanambana RM 206 Ne52
Fanandrana RM 207 Ne55
Fanar Qasr Ahmad LAR 177 Lh29
Fanchang CHN 112 Qk30
Fandriana RM 207 Nd56
Fang THA 121 Pk36
Fangak SUD 191 Mf41
Fangasso RMM 187 Kh39
Fangcheng CHN 107 Qg29
Fangcheng CHN 108 Qe35
Fangchenggang CHN 108 Qe35
Fangliao RC 109 Ra34
Fångö S 43 Lr32
Fang Xian CHN 106 Qf29
Fangzheng CHN 110 Re23
Fanipal' BY 45 Mh37
Fanjingshan Z.B. CHN 108 Qe31
Fanning River AUS 147 Sd55
Fannuj IR 98 Nk32
Fannystelle CDN 236 Fb21
Fanø DK 42 Lj35
Fano I 61 Lo47
Fanø Bugt DK 42 Lj35
Fanshan CHN 109 Ra32
Fanshi CHN 107 Qg26
Fansipan VN 121 Qb34
Fantale Crater ETH 192 Mk41
Fantastic Caverns USA 238 Fd27
Fan Xian CHN 107 Qh28
Fanxue CHN 106 Qd27
Faom Lake CDN 233 Ej20
Faqih Soleyman IR 91 Nd28
Fara BF 187 Kj40
Faraba RMM 186 Ke39
Farache RMM 181 Kj37
Faraday ANT 286 Gd32
Farafangana RM 207 Nd57
Farafenni WAG 186 Kc39
Farafra Oasis ET 179 Me32
Farági Samariás GR 69 Md55
Farági Vouriakoú GR 70 Mc52
Faragouran RMM 187 Kg40
Farah AFG 98 Ob29
Farahalana RM 206 Nf53
Farakka IND 117 Pd33
Farako RMM 187 Kg39
Farako RMM 187 Kg40
Farallón Centinela YV 265 Gg40
Farallones de Cali, P.N. CO 264 Gb44
Faramana BF 187 Kh39
Faramuti SUD 184 Md40
Faranah RG 186 Ke40
Far'aoun RIM 180 Kd36
Farasan KSA 94 Na37
Faratsiho RM 207 Nd55
Fărău RO 67 Me44
Fărcașa RO 67 Md43
Fârdea RO 68 Mc45
Fareham GB 49 Kt40
Farestad N 42 Lh33
Farewell USA 229 Cd14
Farewell Spit NZ 153 Tg66
Färgelanda S 42 Lm32
Fargo USA 236 Fb22
Fargo USA 242 Fj30
Fari RMM 186 Ke39
Farias Brito BR 273 Ja49
Faribault USA 236 Fd23
Faridabad IND 115 Oj31
Faridkot IND 114 Oh30
Faridpur BD 120 Pe34
Farié RN 182 La39
Farihy Alaotra RM 207 Ne54
Farihy Antanavo RM 206 Ne52
Farihy Ihotry RM 207 Nb57
Farihy Itasy RM 207 Nd55
Farihy Kinkony RM 206 Nc54
Farihy Tritriva RM 207 Nd56
Färila S 41 Lq29
Farilhões P 55 Kl51
Farim GNB 186 Kc39
Fariman IR 96 Nk28
Faringdon GB 49 Kt39
Farini I 60 Lk46
Fariq at-Fil SUD 185 Mg39
Färjestaden S 43 Lr34
Farka RN 182 Lb38
Farkadóna GR 70 Mc51
Farkhar AFG 97 Oe27
Farkwa EAT 197 Mh48
Fârliug RO 68 Mb45
Farma ET 179 Mg30
Farmakas GR 70 Mc53
Farmakonisi GR 71 Mh53
Farmamerica USA 236 Fd24
Farmer USA 232 Ea22
Farmerville USA 239 Fd29
Farmington USA 235 Ef27
Farmington USA 241 Ge23
Farmville USA 242 Ga27
Färnebofjärdens n.p. S 43 Lr30
Farne Deep GB 48 Ku35
Farne Islands GB 48 Kt35
Farnham GB 49 Ku39
Farnham, Mount CDN 232 Eb20
Faro BR 271 Hb47
Faro CDN 230 Dd14
Faro P 55 Kn53
Faro RA 281 Gk65
Fårö S 43 Lu33
Faroe Islands DK 26 Kb03
Faroe Islands DK 27 Kb03
Farol de São Tomé BR 275 Hk57
Farol Guará BR 267 Hf45
Faro, P.N. de CAM 189 Lg41
Fårösund S 43 Lu33
Fårösund S 43 Lu33
Farquhar Group SY 206 Nf50
Farquhar Ridge SY 206 Nf50
Farquharson, Mount AUS 146 Rf54
Farranfore IRL 47 Kl38
Farroupilha BR 276 He60
Farrukhabad IND 115 Ok32
Farrukhnagar IND 116 Ok37
Farsah IR 93 Nf29
Fársala GR 70 Mc51
Farsø DK 42 Lk34
Farson USA 235 Ef24
Farsund N 42 Lg32
Fartura BR 277 Hf57
Faruj IR 96 Nk27
Farukolhu MV 118 Og42
Farul Genovez RO 69 Mj46
Farum DK 42 Ln35
Fårup Sommerland DK 42 Lk33
Farwell USA 238 Ej28
Faryab IR 98 Nj32
Fasa IR 98 Ng31
Fasad OM 95 Ng36
Fasana LB 186 Kf42
Fasano I 63 Ls50
Fas Boye SN 180 Kb38
Fashe WAN 188 Lc41
Fashola WAN 188 Lb42
Fasht YE 94 Nb37
Fasil Ghebbi ETH 192 Mj39
Fask MA 174 Kf31
Fáskrúðsfjörður IS 46 Kf26
Fassala Néré RIM 181 Kh38
Fassanu LAR 177 Lg30
Fastiv UA 73 Me20
Fataki RDC 194 Mf44
Fatehabad IND 114 Oh31
Fatehgarh IND 115 Ok32
Fatehjang PK 99 Og29
Fatehnagar IND 116 Oh33
Fatehpur IND 114 Oh32
Fatehpur IND 117 Pa33
Fatehpur IND 117 Pc33
Fatehpur Sikri IND 115 Oj32
Fatež RUS 72 Mh19
Fath Abad IR 98 Nh31
Fathom Five N.M.P. CDN 237 Fk23
Fatiba RMM 181 Kg38
Fatick SN 180 Kb38
Fatih Sultan Mehmet Köprüsü TR 69 Mk49
Fátima P 55 Km51
Fatima do Sul BR 274 Hc57
Fatima Masume IR 91 Nf28
Fatimé RMM 187 Kh39
Fatitet SUD 191 Mf42
Fat Kauyon RI 131 Rd47
Fatoto WAG 186 Kd39
Fatsa TR 90 Mj25
Fattasha SUD 185 Mg38
Fattuwal IND 114 Oh30
Fatuma RDC 196 Me49
Fatunda RDC 198 Lj48
Fatural RI 154 Rh49
Fatutaka SOL 158 Tf51
Fatwa IND 117 Pc33
Faulkton USA 236 Fa23
Faulquemont F 51 Lg41
Faura E 57 Ku51
Făurei RO 69 Mh45
Faure Island AUS 144 Qg58
Fauresmith ZA 205 Mc60
Fauro Island SOL 157 Sj49
Fauske N 38 Lq23
Faust CDN 231 Ec18
Fauville-en-Caux F 50 La41
Faux Cap = Betanty RM 207 Nc58
Fåvang N 40 Ll29
Favara I 62 Lo53
Faverges F 53 Lg45
Faversham GB 49 La39
Favignana I 62 Ln53
Favone F 62 Lk49
Fawcett CDN 231 Ec18
Fawcett Lake CDN 231 Ed18
Fawnleas ZA 205 Mf60
Fawn Pt. USA 228 Bj18
Fawn Trough 287 Oc30
Faxaflói IS 46 Js26
Faxinal BR 276 He58
Faxinal, T.I. BR 276 He58
Faya = Largeau TCH 183 Lk37
Fayala RDC 198 Lj47
Fayaoué F 158 Td56
Fayd KSA 92 Nb32
Fayence F 53 Lg47
Fayette USA 239 Fe30
Fayette USA 239 Fg29
Fayetteville USA 238 Fc27
Fayetteville USA 239 Fg28
Fayetteville USA 239 Fh29
Fayetteville USA 242 Ga28
Fayfa KSA 94 Nb37
Fayid ET 179 Mg30
Fayl-Billot F 53 Lf43
Fayón E 57 La49
Fay-sur-Lignon F 53 Le46
Fazaï RN 183 Lf36
Fazao TG 187 La41
Fazao-Malfakassa, P.N. de TG 187 La41
Fazenda Acreana BR 270 Gg50
Fazenda Agua Santa BR 270 Gj50
Fazenda Boa Esperanza BR 271 Gk46
Fazenda Bradesco BR 272 Hf47
Fazenda Cumaru BR 272 He49
Fazenda Foz do Christalino BR 272 He52
Fazenda Itanorte BR 274 Hb53
Fazenda Muraquitã BR 271 Gk51
Fazenda Narciso BR 265 Gg45
Fazenda Primavera BR 271 Hd51
Fazenda Remanso BR 271 Hb47
Fazenda Rio Dourado BR 272 He50
Fazenda Rio Grande BR 277 Hf58
Fazenda Santa Lúcia BR 274 Hc54
Fazenda São Sebastião BR 270 Gh51
Fazenda Três Irmãos BR 274 Hc54
Fazenda Vista Alegre BR 270 Gk50
Fazilka IND 114 Oh30
Fazilpur PK 99 Of31
F. Carillo Puerto MEX 246 Ej34
Fdérik RIM 180 Kd34
Featherston NZ 153 Th66
Featherstone ZW 202 Mf55
Fécamp F 50 La41
Feda N 42 Lg32
Federación RA 276 Hb61
Federal RA 276 Ha61
Fedeshk IR 98 Nk29
Fé do Morro BR 273 Hk50
Fëdorovka RUS 73 Mk22
Fegyvernek H 67 Ma43
Fehérgyarmat H 67 Mc43
Fehmarn D 58 Lm36
Fehmarnbelt D 58 Lm36
Fehmarnsund D 58 Ll36
Fehring A 61 Lr44
Feidh el Botma DZ 176 Lb28
Feidong CHN 112 Qj30
Feijó BR 268 Ge50
Feilding NZ 153 Th66
Feira de Santana BR 273 Ja52
Feiran Oasis ET 179 Mg31
Feitok CAM 188 Le43
Feixi CHN 112 Qj30
Fei Xian CHN 112 Qj28
Feke TR 90 Mh27
Felanitx E 57 Ld51
Felaou DZ 182 Lc36
Feldbach A 61 Lq44
Feldberg D 58 Lo37
Feldberg D 59 Lj43
Feldkirch A 60 Lk43
Feldkirchen A 61 Lp44
Felegenway ETH 192 Mj42
Felidhoo Atoll MV 118 Og44
Felidhoo Channel MV 118 Og44
Felipe Carrillo Puerto MEX 247 Ff36
Felipe Yofré RA 276 Ha60
Felixburg ZW 202 Mf55
Felixlândia BR 275 Hh55
Felixstowe GB 49 Lb39
Fellabær IS 46 Kf25
Fellegvár H 67 Lt43
Felletin F 53 Lc45
Fellingsbro S 43 Lq31
Felnac RO 67 Mb44
Felsberg D 58 Lk39
Felsenthal N.W.R. USA 239 Fd29
Felsőzsolca H 67 Ma42
Feltre I 60 Lm44
Femern Bælt DK 42 Lm36
Femundsmarka n.p. N 40 Ln28
Fence ZA 205 Mc63
Fence Lake USA 235 Ef28
Fener Burnu TR 90 Mh27
Fener Burnu TR 91 Mk25
Feng'an CHN 109 Qh34
Fengcheng CHN 109 Qh31
Fengcheng CHN 110 Rc25
Fengdu CHN 108 Qd31
Fengelo CI 187 Kg41
Fengguo Monastery CHN 110 Ra25
Fenghua CHN 109 Ra31
Fenghuang CHN 108 Qd33
Fenghuang CHN 108 Qe32
Fenghuang CHN 109 Qj34
Fenghuangshan CHN 110 Rc25
Fengjie CHN 108 Qe30
Fengjiu CHN 107 Qh28
Fengkou CHN 109 Qg30
Fengliang CHN 109 Qj34
Fengling Guan CHN 109 Qk31
Fengling Z.B. CHN 110 Re21
Fengning CHN 107 Qj25
Fengpin RC 109 Ra34
Fengpo CHN 121 Qa34
Fengqing CHN 121 Pk33
Fengrun CHN 107 Qk26
Fengshan CHN 108 Qd33
Fengshan RC 109 Ra34
Fengshui shan CHN 105 Rb19
Fengshun CHN 109 Qj34
Fengtai CHN 112 Qj29
Feng Xian CHN 106 Qd29
Feng Xian CHN 112 Qj28
Fengxian CHN 112 Ra30
Fengxiang CHN 106 Qd28
Fengxin CHN 109 Qh31
Fengxue Si CHN 107 Qg28
Fengyi CHN 108 Qd31
Fengyuan RC 109 Ra33
Fengzhen CHN 107 Qg25
Feni BD 120 Pf34
Feni Islands PNG 156 Sg48
Fenix BR 274 He57
Fenoarivo RM 207 Nd56
Fenoarivo RM 207 Nd56
Fenoarivo Atsinanana RM 207 Ne54
Fenoarivo Be RM 207 Nd55
Fensmark DK 42 Lm35
Fenyang CHN 106 Qf27
Fenyi CHN 109 Qh32
Feodosija UA 73 Mh23
Ferdjioua DZ 176 Lc27
Ferdows IR 98 Nk29
Ferdowsi Tomb IR 96 Nk27
Fère-Champenoise F 51 Ld42
Férédou RG 186 Kf41
Fère-en-Tardenois F 51 Ld41
Ferentillo I 61 Ln48
Ferentino I 62 Lo49
Feres GR 69 Mg50
Ferfer ETH 195 Nc43
Fergana UZ 97 Of25
Fergana too tizmegi KS 97 Og25
Ferganskaja dolina UZ 97 Of25
Fergus Falls USA 236 Fb22
Fergusson Island PNG 156 Sf50
Fergusson River AUS 146 Rf53
Ferhadiju džamija BIH 61 Ls46
Feriana TN 176 Le28
Ferkessédougou CI 187 Kh41
Ferlach A 61 Lp44
Ferland CDN 233 Eg21
Ferland CDN 236 Ff20
Fermo I 61 Lo47
Fermoselle E 54 Ko49
Fermoy IRL 47 Km38
Fernández RA 279 Gj59
Fernandez Bay BS 250 Gc33
Fernandina Beach USA 242 Fk30
Fernandina, Volcán EC 269 Fe46
Fernando Falcão BR 272 Hh48
Fernandópolis BR 274 He56
Fernão Dias BR 275 Hh54
Fernaõ Veloso MOC 203 Na53
Ferndale USA 232 Dj21
Fernie CDN 232 Ec21
Fernley USA 234 Ea26
Ferokh IND 118 Oh40
Ferrandina I 63 Lr50
Ferrara I 60 Lm46
Ferraz, Com. ANT 286 Ha31
Ferreira ZA 205 Md60
Ferreira do Alentejo P 55 Km52
Ferreira Gomes BR 267 He45
Ferreñafe PE 268 Ga49
Ferrette F 53 Lh43
Ferriday USA 239 Fe30
Ferriere I 60 Lk46
Ferrocarril Chihuahua al Pacífico MEX 244 Ef32
Ferrol E 54 Km47
Ferros BR 275 Hj55
Fertő-Hanság N.P. H 66 Lr43
Fertőszentmiklós H 66 Lr43
Fès MA 175 Kh28
Fès-el-Bali MA 175 Kh28
Feshi RDC 199 Lk49
Fessélémon CI 187 Kh41
Fessenden USA 236 Fa22
Festetics H 66 Ls44
Festival Folclórico (Parintins) BR 271 Hb47
Fété Bowé SN 180 Kd38
Fetești RO 69 Mh46
Fethard IRL 47 Kn38
Fethiye TR 90 Me27
Fetisovo KZ 96 Ng24
Fetlar GB 48 Ku30
Fetsund N 42 Lm31
Feuchtwangen D 59 Ll41
Feurs F 53 Le45
Fevik N 42 Lj32
Feyzabad = Faizabad AFG 97 Of27
Feyz Abad IR 98 Nk28
Fezna MA 175 Kh30
Fezzan LAR 177 Lg33
Ffestiniog GB 49 Kr38
Fiadanana RM 207 Nd55
Fiadanana RM 207 Nd56
Fiambalá RA 279 Gg59
Fian GH 187 Kj40
Fianarantsoa RM 207 Nd56
Fianga TCH 190 Lh41
Fibiș RO 68 Mb45
Fiche ETH 192 Mk41
Fichtelgebirge D 59 Lm40
Ficksburg ZA 205 Md60
Ficuar PE 268 Fk48
Fidenza I 60 Ll46
Fielding USA 235 Ed25
Fields USA 232 Ea24
Fier AL 70 Lu50
Fierenana RM 207 Nc55
Fiery Cross Reef 128 Qg41
Fierzë AL 68 Ma48
Fiésole I 60 Lm47
Fifa RG 186 Kf40
Fife Ness GB 48 Ks34
Fifield AUS 151 Sd62
Fifinda CAM 188 Lf44
Fifth Cataract SUD 185 Mg36
Figari F 62 Lk49
Figeac F 52 Lc46
Figeholm S 43 Lr33
Figiás GR 71 Me52
Figtree ZW 202 Me56
Figueira da Foz P 54 Km50
Figueira de Castelo Rodrigo P 54 Ko50
Figueirão BR 274 Hd55
Figueiras, T.I. BR 278 Ha53
Figueiró dos Vinhos P 55 Km51
Figueres E 56 Lc48
Figui CAM 189 Lg41
Figuig MA 175 Kk29
Fijhaonana RM 207 Nd55
Fiji 135 Tb11
Fiji Islands 134 Tb11
Fik ETH 192 Nb41
Fika WAN 189 Lf40
Filabusi ZW 202 Me56
Filadelfia BOL 270 Gf51
Filadélfia BR 272 Hg49
Filadélfia BR 273 Hk51
Filadélfia I 63 Lr52
Filadelfia PY 279 Gk57
Fil'akovo SK 67 Lu42
Filamana RMM 186 Kg40
Filchner ANT 286 Hb34
Filchner Ice Shelf 286 Hd35
Filer USA 232 Ec24
Filey GB 49 Ku36
Filiași RO 68 Md46
Filiátes GR 70 Ma51
Filiatrá GR 70 Mb53
Filingué RN 182 Lb38
Filinskoe RUS 72 Nb18
Filipiáda GR 70 Ma51
Filipstad S 43 Lp31
Filitosa F 62 Lj49
Filiya WAN 189 Lf41
Fillmore CDN 233 Ej21
Fillmore USA 235 Ed26
Filokehn LB 186 Kf43
Filótas GR 70 Mb50
Filóti GR 71 Mf53
Filtu ETH 195 Na43
Filtu ETH 195 Na43
Filuo SOL 157 Sk49
Fimbulheimen 286 Lb33
Fimbul Ice Shelf 286 Kd33
Fin IR 98 Nh32
Finale Emília I 60 Lm46
Finale Lígure I 60 Lj46
Finaly Ranges CDN 230 Dh17
Finaña E 55 Ks53
Finca Chañaral Alta RCH 279 Gf59
Finchawa ETH 194 Mk43
Finch Hatton AUS 149 Se56
Fındıklı TR 69 Mg50
Findlay USA 237 Fj25
Fingal AUS 151 Sd66
Fingoe MOC 202 Mf53
Fínikas GR 71 Me53
Finike TR 90 Mf27
Finisterre Range PNG 155 Sc48
Fink Creek USA 229 Bj13
Finke AUS 148 Rh58
Finke Gorge N.P. AUS 143 Rg58
Finke Pmer Ulperre Ingwemirne Arletherre A.L. AUS 148 Rh58
Finkolo RMM 187 Kg40
Finland FIN 27 Ma03
Finlay Forks CDN 230 Dj17
Finley USA 236 Fb22
Finnerödja S 43 Lp32
Finney Wildlife Area & Bison Refuge USA 238 Ek27
Finniss Springs AUS 148 Rj60
Finnmarksvidda N 39 Mc21
Finnøy N 42 Lf31
Finnsnes N 38 Lt21
Finote Selam ETH 192 Mj40
Fins OM 95 Nk34
Finschhafen PNG 155 Sd49
Finskij zaliv 44 Md31
Finspång S 43 Lq32
Finsteraarhorn CH 60 Lj44
Finsterwalde D 58 Lo39
Fintas KWT 93 Ne31
Fintown IRL 47 Km36
Fintrou RMM 181 Kk37
Finyolé CAM 189 Lg41
Fionnphort GB 48 Ko34
Fiordland NZ 153 Td68
Fiordland N.P. NZ 153 Td68
Fiorenzuola d'Arda I 60 Lk46
Firat Nehri TR 91 Mk26
Firavahana RM 207 Nd55
Fire Island USA 229 Ce15
Fire Island Nat. Seashore USA 241 Gd25
Firenzuola I 60 Lm46
Firestone Plantation LB 186 Ke42
Firgoun RN 181 La38
Firmat RA 281 Gk62
Firmeza PE 270 Gf51
Firminy F 53 Le45
Firou DY 188 La40
Firovo RUS 72 Mg17
Firozabad IND 115 Ok32
Firozpur IND 114 Oh30
Firozpur Jhirka IND 114 Oj32
First Coffee Plantations C 250 Gc36
Firth of Forth GB 48 Ks34
Firth of Thames NZ 152 Th64
Firuz Abad IR 91 Ne28
Firuz Abad IR 98 Ng31
Firuz Bey Camii TR 71 Mh53
Firyuza TM 96 Nk27
Fischells CDN 241 Ha21
Fischersbrunn NAM 204 Lh58
Fiseha Genet ETH 192 Mk42
Fisenge Z 196 Me52
Fish Cays BS 243 Gb32
Fisher AUS 145 Rf61
Fishermen's Cottages ZA 204 Ma63
Fisher R. Ind. Res. CDN 236 Fb20
Fisher Strait CDN 227 Fd06
Fishguard GB 49 Kq39
Fish River NAM 204 Lj58
Fish River ZA 204 Ma61
Fish River Canyon Park NAM 204 Lj59
Fish Town LB 186 Kg43
Fiskárdo GR 70 Ma52
Fiskebäckskil S 42 Lm32
Fismes F 51 Ld41
Fissibu LB 186 Kf42
Fissoa PNG 156 Sf47
Fitampito RM 207 Nd56
Fitchburg USA 241 Ge24
Fities GR 70 Mb52
Fitjar N 42 Lf31
Fitzcarrald PE 269 Gd51
Fitzgerald CDN 231 Ee16
Fitzgerald USA 242 Fj30
Fitzgerald River N.P. AUS 144 Qk62
Fitzroy GB 283 Ha71
Fitz Roy RA 282 Gg69
Fitzroy Crossing AUS 143 Rc55
Fitzroy Island AUS 147 Sd54
Fitzroy River AUS 142 Rb54
Fiuggi I 62 Lo49
Fiumicino I 62 Ln49
Five Cays Settlements GB 250 Gd35
Five Civilized Tribes Mus. USA 238 Fc28
Five Finger Rapids CDN 230 Db14
Five Stars GUY 266 Gk42
Fivizzano I 60 Ll46
Fizi RDC 196 Me48
Fjadory BY 65 Mg39
Fjæra N 42 Lg31
Fjällbacka S 42 Lm32
Fjallfoss = Dynjandifoss IS 46 Jr25
Fjellerup DK 42 Ll34
Fjerritslev DK 42 Lk33
Fjugesta S 43 Lp31
Fkih-Ben-Salah MA 175 Kg29
Flacq MS 207 Nj56
Fladen 42 Lm33
Fladungen D 59 Ll40
Flagler Beach USA 242 Fk31
Flagstaff USA 235 Ee28
Flagstaff ZA 205 Me61
Flagstaff Hill Maritime Museum AUS 150 Sb65
Flambeau Ind. Res. USA 236 Ff23
Flamborough Head GB 49 Ku36
Flamenco Beach USA 251 Gh36
Fläming D 58 Ln38
Flaming Gorge Nat. Rec. Area USA 235 Ef25
Flamingo USA 243 Fk33
Flanders B 51 Lc40
Flannan Isles GB 48 Kn32
Flasher USA 236 Ek22
Flat USA 228 Ca14
Flatey IS 46 Js25
Flatey IS 46 Kc24
Flathead Ind. Res. USA 232 Ec22
Flat Point NZ 153 Th66
Flat River CDN 240 Gj22
Flatwoods USA 239 Fj26
Flavio Alfaro EC 268 Ga46
Flaxcombe CDN 233 Ef20
Flaxman Island USA 229 Ch10
Flecha Point RP 125 Rb42
Fleetwood GB 49 Kr37
Flekkefjord N 42 Lg32
Flekkerøy N 42 Lh32
Flemingsburg USA 239 Fj26
Flemington Racecourse AUS 151 Sc64
Flen S 43 Lr31
Flensburg D 58 Lk36
Flensburger Förde D 58 Ll36
Flers F 50 Ku42
Flesberg N 42 Lk31
Flesjarnar DK 46 Ko29
Fletcher Lake CDN 231 Ef14
Fletcher Promontory 286 Fd34
Fleurance F 52 La47
Fleur de Lys CDN 241 Hb20
Fleury-les-Aubrais F 51 Lb43
Fleuve Saint-Laurent CDN 240 Gf21
Flevoland NL 51 Lf38
Flexal BR 266 Hc46
Flims CH 60 Lk44
Flinders AUS 151 Sc65
Flinders Bay AUS 144 Qh62
Flinders Chase N.P. AUS 150 Rj63
Flinders Group AUS 147 Sc53
Flinders Highway AUS 147 Sb56
Flinders Island AUS 150 Rh62
Flinders Island AUS 151 Se65
Flinders Ranges AUS 148 Rk61
Flinders Ranges N.P. AUS 148 Rk61
Flinders Reefs AUS 147 Se54
Flinders River AUS 147 Sa54
Flin Flon CDN 233 Ek18
Flint USA 237 Fj24
Flint Hills USA 238 Fb27
Flint Hills N.W.R. USA 238 Fc26
Flisa N 42 Lm30
Flix E 57 La49
Flize F 51 Le41
Fljótsdalsheiði IS 46 Ke25
Floating Gardens MYA 120 Pj35
Floating Market (Phung Hiep) VN 123 Qc41
Floby S 43 Lo32
Flogny-la-Chapelle F 53 Ld43
Flöha D 58 Lo40
Flomaton USA 239 Fg30
Floodwood USA 236 Fd22
Flora RP 124 Ra36
Flora USA 232 Eb23
Flora USA 239 Fe29
Florac F 53 Ld46
Florala USA 239 Fg30
Florange F 51 Lg41
Flor da Serra do Sul BR 276 Hd59
Flor de Agosto PE 268 Gd47
Flor del Desierto RCH 279 Gf57
Flor de Punga PE 268 Gc48
Florena o Charles = Isla Santa María EC 269 Fe46
Florence I 60 Lm47
Florence USA 232 Dh24
Florence USA 235 Ee29
Florence USA 235 Eh26
Florence USA 237 Ff23
Florence USA 238 Fb30
Florence USA 239 Fg28
Florence USA 242 Ga28
Florence Junction USA 235 Ee29
Florence Vale AUS 149 Sd57
Florencia CO 264 Gc45
Florencia RA 276 Ha60
Florennes B 51 Le40
Florenville B 51 Lf41
Flores BR 273 Jb49
Flores GCA 247 Ff37
Flores RI 130 Ra50
Flores de Goiás BR 275 Hg53
Flores do Piauí BR 273 Hj49
Flores Island CDN 232 Dg21
Flores Magón MEX 247 Fd37
Flores Sea RI 130 Qk49
Floresta BR 273 Ja50
Florești MD 73 Me22
Floresville USA 245 Fa31
Florewood River Plantation S.P. USA 239 Fe29
Floriano BR 273 Hj49
Floriano Peixoto BR 270 Gg50
Floriano Peixoto BR 273 Jc50
Florianópolis BR 277 Hf59
Florida C 243 Ga35
Florida CO 264 Gb44
Florida PE 268 Gb48
Florida ROU 281 Hb63
Florida USA 243 Fk32
Florida Bay USA 243 Fk33
Florida Caverns S.P. USA 239 Fh30
Florida Islands SOL 157 Ta50
Florida Keys USA 243 Fk33
Florida Peak USA 235 Eg29
Florida's Silver Springs USA 242 Fj31
Florídia I 63 Lq53
Flórina GR 70 Mb50
Florínia BR 274 He57
Florissant USA 239 Fe26
Florissant Fossil Beds Nat. Mon. USA 235 Eh26
Florø N 40 Lf29
Florynka PL 65 Ma41
Flower Island RI 129 Qh47
Flower Pot Island CDN 237 Fk23
Floyd USA 236 Fd24
Floyd USA 242 Fk27
Floydada USA 238 Ek29
Flúðir IS 46 Ju26
Flüelapass CH 60 Lk44
Fluk RI 131 Rd46
Fluminimaggiore I 62 Lj51
Flying Post Ind. Res. CDN 237 Fj21
Flynns Reef AUS 151 Sc65
Fô BF 187 Kh40
Foa F 158 Tc56
Foča BIH 68 Lt47
Foça TR 71 Mg52
Fochabers GB 48 Kr33
Fochi TCH 183 Lh36
Focșani RO 69 Mh45
Fodé RCA 190 Mb43
Fodékaria RG 186 Kf40
Fofore WAN 189 Lg41
Fogadalmi templom H 67 Ma44
Fogang CHN 109 Qg34
Foggâret el Arab DZ 176 Lb32
Foggâret ez Zoûa DZ 176 Lb32
Fóggia I 63 Lq49
Foggy Cape USA 228 Cb17
Föglö FIN 44 Ma31
Fogo CDN 241 Hc21
Foguang Si CHN 107 Qg26
Fohnsdorf A 61 Lp43
Föhr D 58 Lj36
Fóia P 55 Km53
Foix F 52 Lb48
Fojnica BIH 61 Ls47
Fokalik RI 131 Rc47
Fokino RUS 72 Mh19
Fokku WAN 188 Lc40
Folégandros GR 71 Me54
Folégandros GR 71 Me54
Folelli F 60 Lk48
Foley RB 202 Md56
Foley USA 239 Fg30
Foleyet CDN 237 Fj21
Folgares ANG 200 Lh53
Folgefonna N 42 Lg30
Folgelevo KZ 97 Oe24
Foligno I 60 Ln48
Folkestone GB 49 Lb39
Folkston USA 242 Fk30
Folkstone USA 242 Gb28
Folk Village Museum IRL 47 Km35
Folldal N 40 Lk28
Follingbo S 43 Lt33
Föllinge S 41 Lp27
Follónica I 60 Ll48
Folly Beach USA 242 Ga29
Fomboni COM 206 Nb52
Fomena GH 187 Kk42
Fomento C 243 Ga34
Fominki RUS 72 Nb18
Fona VU 158 Te54
Fondation P.Gianadda in Martigny CH 60 Lh44
Fond Du Lac USA 237 Ff24
Fond-du-Lac CDN 231 Eg16
Fondi I 62 Lo49
Fonéko RN 181 La38
Fongolembi SN 186 Ke39
Fonni I 62 Lk50
Fonsagrada E 54 Kn47
Fonseca CO 264 Gd40
Fontainebleau F 51 Lc42
Fontaine-Française F 53 Lf43
Fontaínhas CV 186 Jh37
Fontas CDN 231 Dk16
Fontdepou E 56 La49
Fonte Avellana I 61 Ln47
Fonte Boa BR 270 Gg47
Fontenay-le-Comte F 52 Ku44
Fontenay-Trésigny F 51 Lc42
Fontevraud-l'Abbaye F 52 La43
Fontibón CO 264 Gc43
Fontiveros E 54 Kq50
Font-Romeu F 52 Lc48
Font-Romeu F 52 Lc48
Fontur IS 46 Kf24
Fonyód H 66 Ls44
Foping CHN 106 Qd29
Foping Z.B. CHN 106 Qd29
Fóppolo I 60 Lk44
Forage Christine BF 181 Kk38
Foran VU 158 Te54
Forbach F 51 Lg41
Forbes AUS 151 Sd62
Forbesganj IND 117 Pd32
Forbes Reef SD 205 Mf59
Forbidden Caverns USA 242 Fj28
Forcados WAN 188 Lc43
Forcalquier F 53 Lf47
Forcarei E 54 Km48
Forchheim D 59 Lm41
Forchtenstein A 61 Lr43
Ford, Cerro el RCH 282 Ge72
Fordate RI 131 Rg49
Ford Constantine AUS 147 Sa56
Førde N 42 Lf31
Ford Ranges 286 Cc34
Fords Bridge AUS 149 Sc60
Fordsville USA 239 Fg27
Fordyce USA 239 Fd29
Forécariah RG 186 Kd41
Foreman USA 238 Fc29
Foremost CDN 233 Ee21
Forest USA 239 Ff29
Forestburg CDN 233 Ed19
Forest City USA 236 Fd24
Forest City USA 242 Fk28
Forest Grove USA 232 Dj23
Forest Home AUS 147 Sb55
Forestier Peninsula AUS 151 Se67
Forest Lake USA 236 Fd23
Forest Vale AUS 149 Sd58
Forestville CDN 240 Gf21
Forêt des Deux Balé BF 187 Kj40
Forêt du Day, P.N. de la DJI 192 Nb40
Forêt naturelle de Nyungwe RWA 196 Me47
Forfar GB 48 Ks34
Forges-les-Eaux F 51 Lb41
Forillon, P.N. de CDN 240 Gh21
Forked Island USA 239 Fd31
Forks USA 232 Dh22
Forlandet n.p. N 38 Lf06
Forlì I 60 Ln46
Forlimpópoli I 60 Ln46
Forman USA 236 Fb22
Formation Cave USA 233 Ee24
Formazza I 60 Lj44
Formby GB 49 Kr37
Formentera E 57 Lb52
Fórmia I 62 Lo49
Formiga BR 274 Hb54
Formiga BR 275 Hh56
Formigueiro BR 272 Hh51
Formosa BR 273 Ja50
Formosa BR 275 Hg53
Formosa BR 275 Hg53
Formosa RA 276 Ha59
Formosa RA 279 Gk58
Formosa 76 Ra07
Formosa do Rio Preto BR 272 Hh51
Formoso BR 272 Hf52
Fornæs DK 42 Ll34
Fornells E 57 Le50
Fornos MOC 203 Mh57
Fornovo di Taro I 60 Ll46
Foro Burunga SUD 184 Mb39
Foro Romano I 62 Ln49
Føroya Fornminnissavn DK 46 Ko28
Forquilhinha BR 277 Hf60
Forres GB 48 Kr33
Forrest AUS 145 Re61
Forrestal Range 286 Hb35
Forrest City USA 239 Fe28
Fors S 43 Lr30
Forsayth AUS 147 Sb55
Forserum S 43 Lp33
Forshaga S 43 Lo31
Förslöv S 42 Ln34
Forsmo S 41 Ls27
Forsnes N 40 Lj27
Forssa FIN 44 Md30
Forst D 58 Lp39
Forsvik S 43 Lp32
Forsyth CDN 237 Gb21
Forsyth USA 233 Eg22
Forsyth Island AUS 146 Rk54
Forsyth Range AUS 148 Sb57
Fort (Maheshwar) IND 116 Oh34
Fort Abbas PK 99 Og31
Fort Abercrombie S.H.S. USA 236 Fb22
Fort Abercrombie State Historic Park USA 228 Cd17
Fort Adams USA 239 Fe30
Fort Alexander RH 250 Gd36
Fortaleza BOL 270 Gf51
Fortaleza BOL 270 Gh50
Fortaleza BOL 278 Gg52
Fortaleza BR 268 Ge50
Fortaleza BR 270 Gf49
Fortaleza BR 271 Ha47
Fortaleza BR 273 Ja47
Fortaleza de Santa Teresa ROU 276 Hd62
Fortaleza dos Nogueiras BR 272 Hg49
Fort Amanda St. Mem. USA 237 Fh25
Fort Anne N.H.S. CDN 240 Gh23
Fort Apache Ind. Res. USA 235 Ee29
Fort Assiniboine CDN 231 Ec18
Fort Atkinson USA 237 Ff24
Fort Augustus GB 48 Kq33
Fort Battleford N.H.P. CDN 233 Ef19
Fort Beaufort ZA 205 Md62
Fort Beauséjour N.H.S. CDN 240 Gh23
Fort Belknap Agency USA 233 Ef21
Fort Belknap Ind. Res. USA 233 Ef21
Fort Belmont USA 236 Fc24
Fort Benton USA 233 Ee22
Fort Benton Ruins USA 233 Ee22
Fort Berthold Ind. Res. USA 233 Ej22
Fort Bowie N.H.S. USA 235 Ef29
Fort Bragg USA 234 Dj26
Fort Bridger N.H.S. USA 235 Ee25
Fort Brown ZA 205 Md62
Fort Bullen WAG 186 Kb39
Fort Chadbourne USA 238 Ek29
Fort Charlotte BS 243 Gb33
Fort-Chimo = Kuujjuaq CDN 227 Gc07
Fort Chipewyan CDN 231 Ee16
Fort Clatsop National Memorial USA 232 Dj22
Fort Cobb S.P. USA 238 Fa28
Fort Collins USA 235 Eh25
Fort Concho USA 238 Ek30
Fort Davidson S.H.S. USA 239 Fe27
Fort Davis USA 245 Ej30
Fort Davis N.H.S. USA 245 Eh30
Fort de Chartres S.H.S. USA 239 Fe26
Fort de Chartres S.H.S. USA 239 Fe26
Fort de Cock RI 127 Qa46
Fort-de-France F 251 Gk38
Fort de Koundou RMM 186 Kf39
Fort Dilts Hist. Site USA 233 Ej22
Fort Dodge USA 236 Fc24
Fort Duncan Park USA 245 Ek31
Forte da Principe da Beira BR 278 Gh52
Forte dei Marmi I 60 Ll47
Forte do Castelo (Belém) BR 267 Hf46
Fort Edward N.H.S. CDN 240 Gh23
Fort Erie Race Track CDN 237 Ga24
Fortescue Falls AUS 142 Qk57
Fort Fairfield USA 240 Gg22
Fort Frances CDN 236 Fd21
Fort Franklin CDN 231 Dj13
Fort Frederica Nat. Mon. USA 242 Fk30
Fort Frederick ZA 205 Mc63
Fort Garland USA 235 Eh27
Fort Gibson S.H.S. USA 238 Fc28
Fort Good Hope CDN 226 Dc05
Fort Greely USA 229 Ch14

Fort Grey – Gayaza

Fort Grey ◻ AUS 148 Sa60
Fort Griffin S.H.P. ◻ USA 238 Fa29
Fort Hall Ind. Res. ◻ USA 233 Gd24
Forthassa-Rharbia ◻ DZ 175 Kk29
Fort Hope ◻ CDN 236 Ft20
Fort Hope Ind. Res. ◻ CDN 237 Eg20
Forth Rail Bridge ◻ GB 48 Kt34
Fortín ◻ BR 273 Jb48
Fortín 1° de Mayo ◻ RA 280 Ge65
Fortín Carlos A.López ◻ PY 279 Ha56
Fortín Coronel Bogado ◻ PY 278 Ha56
Fortín Defensores del Chaco ◻ PY 278 Ha56
Fortín Estero ◻ PY 279 Gk57
Fortín Ingall ◻ CDN 240 Gf22
Fortín General Díaz ◻ PY 279 Gk57
Fortín Hernandarias ◻ PY 279 Gk56
Fortín Inca ◻ RA 279 Gk58
Fortín Lavalle ◻ RA 279 Gk58
Fortín Leo Nowak ◻ PY 276 Ha58
Fortín Malal-Hué ◻ RA 280 Gf63
Fortín Mayor Avalos Sánchez ◻ PY 279 Gk57
Fortín Mayor Infante Rivarola ◻ PY 279 Gj56
Fortín Mayor Rodríguez ◻ PY 279 Gk57
Fortín Pilcomayo ◻ PY 279 Gk57
Fortín Pozo Hondo ◻ PY 279 Gk57
Fortín Ravelo ◻ BOL 278 Ge72
Fortín Teniente tro.Manuel Cabello ◻ PY 279 Gk57
Fortín Teniente tro.Pratts Gill ◻ PY 279 Gk57
Fortín Teniente Adolfo Rojas Silva ◻ PY 279 Ha57
Fortín Teniente Montania ◻ PY 279 Ha57
Fortín Teniente Picco ◻ PY 278 Ha55
Fortín Teniente Velazquez ◻ PY 279 Ha57
Fort Toledo ◻ PY 279 Gk57
Fort Jacques ◻ RH 250 Gd36
Fort Jefferson National Park ◻ USA 243 Fj33
Fort Jefferson St. Mem. ◻ USA 237 Fb25
Fort Kaskasia S.H.S. ◻ USA 239 Fd26
Fort Kearney S.H.P. ◻ USA 238 Fa25
Fort Kent ◻ USA 240 Gf22
Fort Kent S.H.S. ◻ USA 240 Gf22
Fort Knox ◻ USA 239 Fj27
Fort Kochi ◻ IND 118 Oj41
Fort Lancaster S.H.S. ◻ USA 238 Ek30
Fort Langley N.H.S. ◻ CDN 232 Dj21
Fort Laramie N.H.S. ◻ USA 235 Eh24
Fort La Reine ◻ CDN 236 Fa21
Fort Lennard N.H.S. ◻ USA 232 Ek22
Fort Lauderdale ◻ USA 243 Fk32
Fort Leaton S.H.S. ◻ USA 238 Ed23
Fort Lemhi Mon. ◻ USA 232 Ed23
Fort Liard ◻ CDN 231 Dj15
Fort Liberté ◻ RH 250 Ge36
Fort MacKay ◻ CDN 231 Ee17
Fort Mackinac ◻ USA 237 Fh23
Fort Macleod ◻ CDN 233 Ed21
Fort Madison ◻ USA 239 Fe26
Fort-Mahon-Plage ◻ F 51 Lb40
Fort Malborough ◻ RI 127 Qd47
Fort Massachusetts ◻ USA 239 Ff30
Fort Maurepas ◻ CDN 236 Fb20
Fort McDermitt Ind. Res. ◻ USA 232 Eb25
Fort McKavett S.H.S. ◻ USA 238 Ek30
Fort McMurray ◻ CDN 231 Ee17
Fort McPherson ◻ CDN 226 Db05
Fort Metal Cross ◻ GH 187 Kj43
Fort Morgan ◻ USA 235 Ee24
Fort Mtobeni ◻ ZA 205 Mf60
Fort Munro ◻ PK 99 Oe31
Fort Murray ◻ ZA 205 Md62
Fort Myers ◻ USA 243 Fj32
Fort Nassau ◻ GUY 266 Hb43
Fort Nelson ◻ CDN 231 Di16
Fort Niobrara N.W.R. ◻ USA 236 Ek24
Fort Norman ◻ CDN 231 Dh13
Fort Ogden ◻ USA 243 Fk32
Fort Patience ◻ GH 187 Kf43
Fort Payne ◻ USA 239 Fh28
Fort Peck ◻ USA 233 Eg22
Fort Peck Ind. Res. ◻ USA 233 Eh21
Fort Phantom Hill ◻ USA 238 Fa29
Fort Phil Kearny ◻ USA 233 Eh24
Fort Pickens ◻ USA 239 Ff30
Fort Pierce ◻ USA 243 Fk32
Fort Pierre Choteau N.P. ◻ USA 236 Ek23
Fort Pierre Grassland N.P. ◻ USA 236 Ek23
Fort Portal ◻ EAU 194 Mf45
Fort Providence ◻ CDN 231 Eb15
Fort Qu'Appelle ◻ CDN 233 Eg20
Fort Quitman Ruins ◻ USA 238 Eh30
Fort Randall Dam ◻ USA 236 Fa24
Fort Resolution ◻ CDN 231 Ed15
Fortress of Louisbourg ◻ CDN 240 Gk23
Fort Rice S.H.S. ◻ USA 236 Ek22
Fort Rixon ◻ ZW 202 Me56
Fortrose ◻ GB 48 Kq33
Fortrose ◻ NZ 153 Td69
Fort Ross S.H.P. ◻ USA 234 Dj26
Fort Rupert (Waskaganish) ◻ CDN 237 Ga20
Fort Saint Anthony ◻ GH 187 Kj43
Fort Saint James ◻ CDN 230 Dh18
Fort Saint James N.H.S. ◻ CDN 230 Dh18
Fort Saint John ◻ CDN 231 Dk17
Fort Saint-Pierre ◻ SN 180 Kd38
Fort Sandeman – Zhob ◻ PK 99 Oe30
Fort San Pedro ◻ RP 124 Rb40
Fort Saskatchewan ◻ CDN 233 Ed19
Fort Scott ◻ USA 238 Fc27
Fort Scott N.H.S. ◻ USA 238 Fc27
Fort Sesfontein ◻ NAM 200 Lg55
Fort Severn ◻ CDN 237 Fc07
Fort-Shevchenko ◻ KZ 91 Nf23
Fort Simpson ◻ CDN 231 Dk15
Fort Smith ◻ CDN 231 Ed15
Fort Smith ◻ USA 238 Fc28
Fort Stanwix Nat. Mon. ◻ USA 241 Gc24
Fort Steele ◻ CDN 232 Ec21
Fort Steele Heritage Town ◻ CDN 232 Ec21
Fort Stockton ◻ USA 245 Ej30
Fort Stockton ◻ USA 245 Ej30
Fort Sumner ◻ USA 235 Eh28
Fort Sumner State Monument ◻ USA 235 Eh28
Fort Témiscamingue N.H.S. ◻ CDN 237 Ga22
Fort Thompson ◻ USA 236 Fa23
Fort Ticonderoga ◻ USA 241 Gd24
Fortuna ◻ RA 272 Hh48
Fortuna ◻ E 57 Kt52
Fortuna ◻ USA 232 Dh25
Fortune ◻ CDN 241 Hc22
Fortune Harbour ◻ CDN 241 Hc21
Fortuneswell ◻ GB 49 Ks40
Fort Union Nat. Mon. ◻ USA 235 Eh28
Fort Union Trading Post N.H.S. ◻ USA 233 Eh21
Fort Valley ◻ USA 242 Fj29
Fort Vermilion ◻ CDN 231 Eb16
Fort Victoria Hist. Site ◻ CDN 231 Ed18
Fort Walsh N.H.P. ◻ CDN 233 Ef21
Fort Walton Beach ◻ USA 239 Ff30
Fort Wayne ◻ USA 237 Fh25
Fort Wellington ◻ GUY 266 Hb42
Fort William ◻ GB 48 Kq33
Fort Worth ◻ USA 238 Fa29
Fort Yates ◻ USA 236 Ek22
Fort Yukon ◻ USA 229 Ch12
Fort Zeelandia ◻ RC 109 Ra34

Fort Zeelandia ◻ SME 266 Hc43
Forudgan ◻ IR 93 Nf29
Forvika ◻ N 40 Ln25
Fosa de Cariaco ◻ YV 265 Gh40
Fosca ◻ CO 264 Gd43
Foshan ◻ CHN 109 Qg34
Fosheim Peninsula ◻ CDN 227 Fd03
Foso ◻ GH 187 Kf43
Fossacésia Marina ◻ I 63 Lp48
Fossano ◻ I 60 Lh44
Fosse aux Lions, P.N. de la ◻ TG 187 La40
Fosses-la-Ville ◻ B 51 Le40
Fossil ◻ USA 232 De23
Fossil Bluff ◻ ANT 286 Gc33
Fossil Butte Nat. Mon. ◻ USA 235 Ee25
Fossil Downs ◻ AUS 143 Rc55
Fossil Mammal Site (Naracoorte) ◻ AUS 150 Sa64
Fossil Mammal Site (Riversleigh) ◻ AUS 146 Rk55
Fossil ◻ N 42 Lh30
Fossombrone ◻ I 61 Ln47
Fossong Fontem ◻ CAM 188 Le43
Fos-sur-Mer ◻ F 53 Le47
Fouénan ◻ CI 187 Kg41
Fougamou ◻ G 198 Lf46
Fougères ◻ F 50 Kt42
Foula ◻ GB 48 Kt31
Foulaba ◻ RMM 187 Kg40
Fouladougou ◻ RMM 186 Kf39
Foulamory ◻ RG 186 Kd39
Foulani ◻ CI 187 Kh41
Foulenzem ◻ G 198 Le46
Foul Point ◻ IND 122 Pg41
Foumbadou ◻ RG 186 Kf41
Fouman ◻ IR 91 Ne26
Foumban ◻ CAM 188 Lf43
Foumbolo ◻ CI 187 Kh41
Foumbot ◻ CAM 189 Lf43
Foumbouni ◻ COM 206 Nb51
Found Lake ◻ CDN 237 Ga22
Foum de Hassane ◻ MA 174 Kf31
Foum-Zguid ◻ MA 175 Kg30
Founougne ◻ SN 180 Kb38
Founounga ◻ DY 188 Ld40
Fountain ◻ USA 235 Eh27
Fountains Abbey ◻ GB 49 Kt36
Fourchambault ◻ F 53 Ld43
Fourdou ◻ SN 180 Kd38
Fouriès ◻ GR 71 Me55
Fouriesburg ◻ ZA 204 Me60
Fourmies ◻ F 51 Le40
Foúrni ◻ GR 71 Mg53
Fourou ◻ RMM 187 Kg40
Fours ◻ F 53 Ld44
Fox Creek ◻ CDN 231 Eb18
Foxe Basin ◻ CDN 227 Ga05
Foxe Channel ◻ CDN 227 Fd06
Foxe Peninsula ◻ CDN 227 Ga06
Foxford ◻ IRL 47 Kl37
Fox Glacier ◻ NZ 153 Tf67
Fox Harbour ◻ CDN 241 Hc19
Fox Lake Ind. Res. ◻ CDN 231 Ec16
Fox Point ◻ CDN 231 Dj13
Foxton ◻ NZ 153 Th66
Fox Valley ◻ CDN 233 Ef20
Foya ◻ LB 186 Ke41
Foyle ◻ GB 47 Kf38
Foyneya ◻ N 38 Md05
Foz ◻ E 54 Kn47
Foz de Jaú ◻ BR 270 Gk46
Foz de Odeleite ◻ P 55 Kn53
Foz do Breu ◻ BR 269 Ge46
Foz do Copeá ◻ BR 270 Gj47
Foz do Cunene ◻ ANG 200 Lf54
Foz do Iguaçu ◻ BR 276 Hc58
Foz do Jordão ◻ BR 269 Gd46
Foz do Mamoriá ◻ BR 270 Gg47
Frackí ◻ PL 65 Md37
Fraga ◻ E 57 La49
Fraga ◻ RA 280 Gh62
Fragistra ◻ GR 70 Mb53
Fraiburgo ◻ BR 277 He59
Fraile Muerto ◻ ROU 276 Hc62
Fraile Pintado ◻ RA 279 Gh57
Fraize ◻ F 53 Lg42
Frakes, Mount ◻ ANT 286 Ea34
Fram Basin ◻ CDN 227 Fc05
Framingham ◻ USA 241 Ge24
Framlev ◻ DK 42 Lk34
Frammersbach ◻ D 59 Lk40
Fram Peak ◻ ANT 286 Nd32
Frampol ◻ PL 65 Mc40
Franca ◻ BR 275 Hg56
Francaville al Mare ◻ I 61 Lp48
Francavilla di Sicilia ◻ I 63 Lp54
Francavilla Fontana ◻ I 63 Lq50
France ◻ F 27 La05
Franche-Comté ◻ F 53 Lg43
Franche-Comté ◻ F 51 Lf43
Franceville ◻ G 198 Lg46
Franche Lake ◻ CDN 230 Df15
Franciscan Missions in the Sierra Gorda of Querétaro = Arroyo Seco, Jalpan de Serra, Landa de Matamoros ◻ MEX 246 Fa35
Francisco Ayres ◻ BR 273 Hh49
Francisco Beltrão ◻ BR 276 Hd59
Francisco Escárcega ◻ MEX 247 Fe36
Francisco I. Madero ◻ MEX 245 Eh33
Francisco I. Madero ◻ MEX 246 Fa35
Francisco I. Madero ◻ MEX 245 Ek34
Francisco Magnano ◻ RA 281 Gj49
Francisco Morato ◻ BR 277 Hg58
Franciscotown ◻ BR 275 Hf54
Franco de Orellana ◻ PE 268 Gd47
Francoforte ◻ I 63 Lp54
François ◻ CDN 241 Hb22
Francois Lake ◻ CDN 230 Dh18
François Peron N.P. ◻ AUS 144 Qg58
Franeker ◻ NL 51 Lf37
Frankenberg ◻ D 58 Lj39
Frankenthal ◻ D 59 Lj40
Frankenwald ◻ D 59 Lm40
Frankfort ◻ USA 149 Sd57
Frankfort ◻ USA 237 Fg27
Frankfort ◻ USA 239 Fg25
Frankfort ◻ ZA 204 Me60
Frankfurt ◻ D 59 Lj39
Frankfurt ◻ USA 239 Fh26
Frankfurt ◻ D 59 Lj40
Frankfurt (Oder) ◻ D 58 Lp38
Frankhann N.P. ◻ AUS 144 Qh62
Frankische market ◻ OM 95 Nh37
Frankische Trail ◻ OM 95 Nh37
Frankische Alb ◻ D 59 Lm41
Franklin ◻ AUS 148 Sa57
Franklin ◻ USA 144 Qc63
Franklin ◻ USA 239 Fe31
Franklin ◻ USA 239 Fd27
Franklin ◻ USA 239 Fe31
Franklin ◻ USA 239 Ff29
Franklin ◻ USA 241 Gd26
Franklin ◻ USA 241 Gd25
Franklin ◻ USA 241 Ge25
Franklin ◻ ZA 205 Me61
Franklin Bay ◻ CDN 226 Dc04
Franklin – Déline ◻ CDN 231 Dj13
Franklin-Gordon Wild Rivers N.P. ◻ AUS 151 Sa57
Franklin Strait ◻ CDN 227 Fa04
Franklinton ◻ USA 239 Fe30
Fransfontein ◻ NAM 200 Lh56
Fransteinberge ◻ NAM 200 Lh56
Frantiskovy Lázné ◻ CZ 66 Ln40
Franz ◻ CDN 237 Fh21
Franz Josef Glacier ◻ NZ 153 Tf67
Franz Josef Land ◻ RUS 88 Nb03
Frascati ◻ I 62 Ln49
Fraser Basin ◻ CDN 230 Di18
Fraserburg ◻ ZA 204 Ma61
Fraserburgh ◻ GB 48 Ks33
Fraserdale ◻ CDN 237 Fh21
Fraser Lake ◻ CDN 230 Dh18
Fraser Lake ◻ AUS 149 Sg58
Fraser Plateau ◻ CDN 231 Dj19
Fraser Plateau ◻ CDN 230 Dh18
Fraser Range ◻ AUS 145 Rb62
Fraserwood ◻ CDN 236 Fb20
Frashër ◻ AL 70 Ma50
Frater ◻ CDN 237 Fh22
Frátsia ◻ GR 71 Mc54
Frauenfeld ◻ CH 60 Lj43
Frauenkirchen ◻ A 67 Ls43
Fray Bentos ◻ ROU 276 Ha62
Fray Jorge ◻ RCH 280 Ge61
Frazier Downs A.L. ◻ AUS 142 Ra55
Frechen ◻ D 58 Lg40
Frede ◻ RIM 180 Kf37
Frederica ◻ DK 42 Lk34
Frederick ◻ USA 238 Fa28
Frederick ◻ USA 238 Fa28
Fredericksburg ◻ USA 238 Fa35
Fredericksburg ◻ USA 241 Gb26
Fredericktown ◻ USA 239 Fe27
Frederico Westphalen ◻ BR 276 Hd60
Fredericton ◻ CDN 240 Gj23
Frederiksborg ◻ DK 42 Ld35
Frederikshåb = Paamiut ◻ DK 227 Hb06
Frederikshavn ◻ DK 42 Ll33
Frederikssund ◻ DK 42 Lc35
Frederiksværk ◻ DK 42 Lc35
Fred Henne Territorial Park ◻ CDN 231 Ec14
Fredonia ◻ CO 264 Gc43
Fredonia ◻ USA 235 Ed27
Fredonia ◻ USA 234 Ga24
Fredonia ◻ USA 238 Fc27
Fredriksberg ◻ S 43 Lp30
Fredrikstad ◻ N 42 Ll31
Freehold ◻ USA 241 Gd25
Freelings Heights ◻ AUS 148 Rk61
Freeman ◻ USA 236 Fb24
Freeport ◻ BS 243 Ga32
Freeport ◻ USA 237 Ff24
Freeport ◻ USA 238 Fc31
Free State ◻ ZA 205 Md60
Freetown ◻ WAL 186 Kd41
Frégate ◻ SY 195 Nj48
Fregenal de la Sierra ◻ E 55 Ko52
Fregon = Aparawatatja ◻ AUS 145 Rh59
Freiberg ◻ D 58 Lo40
Freiburg ◻ D 59 Lh43
Frei Inocêncio ◻ BR 275 Hk55
Freilassing ◻ D 59 Ln43
Freilichtmuseum Ballenberg ◻ CH 60 Lj44
Freilichtmuseum Stübing ◻ A 61 Lq43
Freire ◻ RCH 280 Gd65
Freirina ◻ RCH 279 Ge60
Freising ◻ D 59 Lm42
Freistadt ◻ A 66 Lp42
Freital ◻ D 58 Lo40
Fréjus ◻ F 53 Lg47
Fremantle ◻ AUS 144 Qh62
Fremont ◻ USA 234 Dc27
Fremont ◻ USA 236 Fb25
Fremont ◻ USA 237 Fj25
Fremont Mountains ◻ USA 232 Dk24
French Bay ◻ BS 250 Gc34
French Cove ◻ CDN 241 Hc20
Frenchglen ◻ USA 232 Ea24
French Guiana ◻ F 255 Ha09
French Island ◻ AUS 151 Se67
French Pass ◻ NZ 153 Tg66
Frenda ◻ DZ 175 La28
Frenštát pod Radhoštěm ◻ CZ 66 Lt41
Frere ◻ ZA 205 Me60
Freren ◻ D 58 Lh38
Fresco ◻ CI 187 Kh43
Freshwater ◻ CDN 241 Hc22
Fresia ◻ RCH 280 Gd66
Fresnay-sur-Sarthe ◻ F 50 La42
Fresnillo ◻ MEX 246 Ej34
Fresno ◻ USA 234 Ea27
Fresno-Alhándiga ◻ E 54 Kq50
Fresno de Caracena ◻ E 54 Kr49
Freudenberg ◻ D 58 Lh40
Freudenstadt ◻ D 59 Lj42
Frévent ◻ F 51 Lc40
Freyburg ◻ D 58 Lm39
Freycinet Estuary ◻ AUS 144 Qg59
Freycinet N.P. ◻ AUS 151 Se67
Freycinet Peninsula ◻ AUS 151 Se67
Freyming-Merlebach ◻ F 51 Lg41
Freyre ◻ RA 281 Gj61
Freyung ◻ D 59 Lo42
Fria ◻ RG 186 Kd40
Frias ◻ RA 279 Gh60
Fribourg ◻ CH 60 Lh44
Friday Harbour ◻ USA 232 Dj21
Friðland að Fjallabaki ◻ IS 46 Ka26
Fridtjof Nansen, Mount ◻ ANT 286 Ab33
Friedberg ◻ D 59 Lj40
Friedberg ◻ D 59 Lm42
Friedeburg ◻ D 58 Lh37
Friedewald ◻ D 58 Lk40
Friedland ◻ D 58 Lo37
Friedland ◻ D 58 Lj38
Friedrichshafen ◻ D 59 Lk43
Friedrichstadt ◻ D 58 Lk36
Friendship Hill N.H.S. ◻ USA 241 Ga26
Friendship Road ◻ CHN 102 Pf31
Friesach ◻ A 61 Lp44
Friesack ◻ D 58 Ln38
Friesoythe ◻ D 58 Lh37
Frigatas Passage ◻ FJI 159 Tj55
Friggesund ◻ S 41 Lr29
Frigorífico ◻ ROU 276 Ha62
Frillesås ◻ S 43 Ll32
Frindsbury Reef ◻ SOL 157 Sk48
Friol ◻ E 54 Kn47
Friona ◻ USA 238 Ej28
Fristad ◻ S 43 Ll32
Fritsla ◻ S 42 Lk33
Frittlar ◻ D 58 Lk39
Friuli-Venezia Giulia ◻ I 61 Ln44
Friville-Escarbotin ◻ F 51 Lb40
Frjanovo ◻ RUS 72 Mk17
Frobisher Bay ◻ CDN 227 Ga07
Frohburg ◻ D 58 Ln39
Frog Lake ◻ CDN 233 Ee19
Frohnleiten ◻ A 61 Lq43
Froid ◻ USA 233 Eh22
Frombork ◻ PL 65 Lu36
Frome Downs ◻ AUS 148 Rk61
Frómista ◻ E 54 Kq48
Fronteira ◻ BR 274 Hf56
Fronteiras ◻ BR 273 Hk49
Frontenac ◻ USA 238 Fc27
Frontenac Islands ◻ MEX 245 Fd32
Frontera ◻ MEX 247 Fd36
Frontera Corozal ◻ MEX 247 Fe37
Frontignan ◻ F 53 Ld47
Front Range ◻ USA 235 Eh25
Front Royal ◻ USA 241 Gb26
Frosinone ◻ I 62 Lo49
Frostburg ◻ USA 241 Ga26
Froussiana ◻ GR 70 Mb53
Frövi ◻ S 43 Lq31

Frøya ◻ N 40 Lj27
Frozen Strait ◻ CDN 227 Fd05
Fruges ◻ F 51 Lc40
Fruita ◻ USA 235 Ef26
Frunzivka ◻ UA 73 Me22
Frúrio ◻ GR 70 Ma51
Fruška Gora, N.P. ◻ SRB 68 Lu45
Frutal ◻ BR 275 Hf55
Frutigen ◻ CH 60 Lh44
Frutillar ◻ RCH 280 Gd66
Frýdek-Místek ◻ CZ 66 Lt41
Frýdlant ◻ CZ 66 Lq40
Fu'an ◻ CHN 109 Qk32
Fuchsskauten ◻ D 58 Lj40
Fuding ◻ CHN 109 Ra32
Fuego, Volcán de ◻ GCA 248 Fe38
Fuengirola ◻ E 55 Kq54
Fuensalida ◻ E 55 Kq50
Fuensanta ◻ E 57 Kt53
Fuente-Álamo ◻ E 57 La52
Fuente de Cantos ◻ E 55 Ko52
Fuente del Arco ◻ E 55 Kp52
Fuente el Fresno ◻ E 55 Kp52
Fuente Obejuna ◻ E 55 Kp52
Fuentes de Ebro ◻ E 57 Kt49
Fuerte Bulnes ◻ RCH 282 Ge72
Fuerte Corral ◻ RCH 280 Gd65
Fuerte de San Miguel ◻ ROU 276 Hd62
Fuerte Esperanza ◻ RA 279 Gk58
Fuerte Olimpo ◻ PY 274 Hb56
Fuerte San Lorenzo ◻ PA 249 Fk41
Fuerte San Rafael ◻ RA 280 Gf63
Fufuiluu ◻ CHN 106 Qd28
Fuga ◻ EAT 197 Mj49
Fuga Island ◻ RP 124 Ra36
Fügen ◻ A 60 Lm43
Fuhai ◻ CHN 101 Pd23
Fuhat ◻ CHN 101 Pd22
Fujairah ◻ UAE 95 Nj33
Fuji ◻ J 113 Rk28
Fujian ◻ CHN 109 Qj32
Fujian ◻ CHN 109 Qj32
Fujieda ◻ J 113 Rk28
Fuji-Hakone-Izu N.P. ◻ J 113 Rk28
Fujin ◻ CHN 110 Rg22
Fuji-san ◻ J 113 Rk28
Fujiyoshida ◻ J 113 Rk28
Fukagawa ◻ J 111 Sb24
Fukang ◻ CHN 101 Pd23
Fukuchiyama ◻ J 113 Rg28
Fukue-jima ◻ J 113 Re29
Fukui Chiao A. ◻ RC 109 Ra33
Fukue-jima ◻ J 113 Re29
Fukul ◻ J 113 Rj27
Fukuoka ◻ J 113 Rf29
Fukusen-ji ◻ J 111 Sa26
Fukushima ◻ J 111 Sa25
Fukushima ◻ J 111 Sa27
Fukuyama ◻ J 113 Rg28
Fulacunda ◻ GNB 186 Kc40
Fulaga ◻ FJI 159 Ua55
Fulani ◻ WAN 189 Lg40
Fulda ◻ D 58 Lk40
Fulda ◻ USA 236 Fb24
Full ◻ RC 109 Ra34
Fuling ◻ CHN 108 Qd31
Fuling ◻ CHN 108 Qd31
Fulingu ◻ CHN 109 Qh32
Fulleborn ◻ PNG 156 Sf49
Fullers ◻ USA 237 Fd24
Fulolo ◻ RI 127 Pj45
Fulton ◻ USA 238 Fd29
Fulton ◻ USA 239 Fe26
Fulton ◻ USA 239 Ff27
Fulton ◻ USA 238 Fd27
Fulton ◻ USA 241 Gb24
Fulufjällets n.p. ◻ S 41 Ln29
Fulung Seaside Park ◻ RC 109 Ra33
Fuman ◻ IR 91 Ne27
Fumba ◻ EAT 197 Mk49
Fumbelo ◻ ANG 200 Lk51
Fumbo ◻ Z 202 Md50
Fumel ◻ F 52 La46
Fumiela ◻ USA 188 Lj49
Funadomari ◻ J 111 Sa23
Funan ◻ CHN 107 Qh29
Funäsdalen ◻ S 40 Ln28
Funchal ◻ P 174 Kb29
Funche Cave ◻ CI 243 Fk35
Fundación Eclética ◻ BR 274 Hf53
Fundación ◻ CO 264 Gc41
Fundão ◻ BR 275 Hk55
Fundão ◻ P 55 Kn50
Fundición, Cerro ◻ RA 279 Gk57
Fundo das Figueiras ◻ CV 186 Jc37
Fundulea ◻ RO 69 Mg46
Fundunba ◻ ANG 200 Lk51
Fundy N.P. ◻ CDN 240 Gh23
Funes ◻ RA 282 Gj67
Funhalouro ◻ MOC 205 Mh57
Funil, T.I. ◻ BR 271 Gk49
Funing ◻ CHN 112 Qk29
Funing ◻ CHN 107 Qh28
Funkley ◻ USA 236 Fc21
Funsi ◻ GH 187 Kk40
Funtua ◻ WAN 188 Ld40
Fuping ◻ CHN 106 Qe28
Fuping ◻ CHN 107 Qh26
Fuqing ◻ CHN 109 Qk33
Fur ◻ DK 42 Lk33
Furancungo ◻ MOC 202 Mg53
Furano ◻ J 111 Sb24
Furculeşti ◻ RO 69 Mf47
Furcy ◻ RH 250 Gd36
Furk ◻ IR 98 Nh31
Furmanov ◻ RUS 72 Na17
Furneaux Group ◻ AUS 151 Se66
Furong ◻ CHN 108 Qf31
Furstenwalde ◻ EAK/ETH 194 Mk44
Furqlu ◻ BR 274 Hf53
Furstenberg ◻ D 58 Lh38
Fürstenberg ◻ D 58 Ln38
Fürstenfeld ◻ A 61 Lr43
Fürstenfeldbruck ◻ D 59 Lm42
Fürstenwalde ◻ D 58 Lp38
Furta ◻ H 67 Mb43
Furth ◻ D 59 Ll41
Furth im Wald ◻ D 59 Ln41
Furtwangen ◻ D 59 Lj42
Furudal ◻ S 41 Lq29
Furukawa ◻ J 111 Sa26
Fürur ◻ DK 42 Lk33
Furuya ◻ CO 264 Gc43
Fushë-Muhur ◻ AL 68 Ma49
Fushun ◻ CHN 108 Qd31
Fushun ◻ CHN 110 Qk25
Fushun ◻ CHN 110 Rb25
Fusong ◻ CHN 110 Rd24
Fussen ◻ D 59 Ll43
Fusui ◻ CHN 108 Qf34
Futaleufú ◻ RCH 282 Ge67
Futaleufú ◻ RA 282 Ge67
Futuna Island ◻ VU 158 Tf55
Futuna ◻ CO 264 Gc43
Futuroscope ◻ F 52 La44
Fuwairet ◻ Q 93 Nf32
Fu Xian ◻ CHN 106 Qe28
Fuxian ◻ CHN 108 Qd32
Fuxin ◻ CHN 110 Qk24
Fuxin Mongolzu Zizhixian ◻ CHN 110 Ra24
Fuyang ◻ CHN 107 Qh29
Fuyang ◻ CHN 109 Qk31
Fuyu ◻ CHN 110 Rb22
Fuyuan ◻ CHN 121 Qc33

Fuyuan ◻ CHN 110 Rh22
Füzuli ◻ AZ 91 Nd26
Füzesabony ◻ H 67 Mb43
Füzesgyarmat ◻ H 67 Mb43
Fuzhou ◻ CHN 109 Qk33
Fuzhoucheng ◻ CHN 107 Ra26
Fylingdales ◻ GB 49 Ku35
Fyn ◻ DK 42 Ll35
Fynshav ◻ DK 42 Lk36
Fyns Hoved ◻ DK 42 Ll35
Fyresdal ◻ N 42 Lj31
Fyrkat ◻ DK 42 Lk34
Fyvie Castle ◻ GB 48 Ks33

G

Ga ◻ GH 187 Kj41
Gaa Kaba Montagnes ◻ F 266 Hc43
Gaalkacyo = Galcaio ◻ SP 193 Nd42
Gaamodebli ◻ LB 186 Kf42
Gaba ◻ ETH 193 Nb42
Gabaldon ◻ RP 124 Ra38
Gabare ◻ BG 69 Md47
Gabarus ◻ CDN 240 Gk23
Gabbac Island ◻ AUS 147 Sb50
Gabbs ◻ USA 234 Eb26
Gabcíkovo ◻ SK 66 Lt42
Gabela ◻ ANG 200 Lg50
Gabès ◻ TN 176 Lf29
Gabi ◻ RN 188 Ld39
Gabia ◻ RN 189 Lg39
Gabiano, Monte ◻ TCH 190 La41
Gabindanti ◻ BD 120 Pf33
Gabir ◻ SUD 191 Mb41
Gabiro ◻ RWA 194 Mf46
Gabol ◻ DK 42 Lk35
Gabon ◻ G 163 Lb10
Gabon, Estuaire de ◻ G 198 Le45
Gaborone ◻ RB 205 Mc58
Gaborone Dam ◻ RB 205 Mc58
Gabras ◻ SUD 184 Md40
Gabrik ◻ IR 98 Nh32
Gabrovo ◻ BG 69 Mf48
Gabu ◻ RN 188 Le39
Gabu ◻ RDC 191 Md44
Gabu ◻ RDC 191 Me44
Gabuli Terara ◻ ETH 192 Na39
Gabur ◻ IR 116 Oj37
Gabyon ◻ AUS 144 Qj60
Gacé ◻ F 50 La42
Gacheta ◻ CO 264 Gd43
Gackle ◻ USA 236 Fa22
Gacko ◻ BIH 68 Lt47
Gadabay ◻ PNG 156 Se51
Gadamai ◻ IND 117 Ok34
Gadarwara ◻ IND 117 Ok34
Gadebusch ◻ D 58 Lm37
Gadein ◻ SUD 191 Me41
Gadhyogil ◻ SP 193 Nd42
Gading N.P., Gunung ◻ MAL 128 Qe45
Gádor ◻ E 56 Kt54
Gádor ◻ PK 99 Of33
Gadsden ◻ USA 239 Fh29
Gaduk ◻ IR 96 Nf28
Gadwal ◻ IND 116 Oj37
Gadzi ◻ RCA 190 Lj43
Gadzi ◻ RCA 190 Lj43
Gaesafjöll ◻ IS 46 Kc25
Gäestj ◻ RO 69 Mf46
Gaeta ◻ I 62 Lo49
Gaffney ◻ USA 242 Fk28
Gafida ◻ ETH 193 Nc42
Gafsa ◻ TN 176 Le29
Gag ◻ RI 131 Rf46
Gagachin ◻ IR 91 Ne27
Gagal ◻ PNG 157 Sh48
Gagan ◻ PNG 157 Sh48
Gagarawan ◻ WAN 188 Le39
Gagarin ◻ RUS 72 Mh17
Gagarin ◻ UZ 97 Oc25
Gagau, Gunung ◻ MAL 126 Qb39
Gage ◻ USA 238 Fa27
Gaggenau ◻ D 59 Lj42
Gaghamol ◻ SUD 184 Md40
Gagino ◻ RUS 72 Nc18
Gagnef ◻ S 43 Lq30
Gagnoa ◻ CI 187 Kh42
Gagra ◻ GE 91 Na24
Gag'ya ◻ RI 131 Re46
Gahavisuka Provincial Park ◻ PNG 155 Sc49
Gahkom ◻ IR 98 Nh31
Gahmar ◻ IND 117 Pb33
Gahmiti = Rea Lakes ◻ CDN 231 Eb13
Gahnpa ◻ LB 186 Kf42
Gai ◻ EAK 194 Mh46
Gaibanda ◻ BD 120 Pe33
Gaighat ◻ NEP 117 Pd32
Gaik ◻ CHN 117 Ok38
Gaikii ◻ LV 45 Mc34
Gail ◻ USA 238 Ek29
Gaildorf ◻ D 59 Lk41
Gailey ◻ USA 148 Sb58
Gailjac ◻ F 52 Lc47
Gaimersdorf ◻ D 59 Ln42
Gaiman ◻ RA 282 Gg67
GaimNarmai ◻ PNG 156 Se50
Gaindakes ◻ TM 97 Ob26
Gaines ◻ D 58 Lh40
Gainesville ◻ USA 243 Fj31
Gainesville ◻ USA 238 Fd27
Gainesville ◻ USA 242 Fj28
Gainsborough ◻ GB 49 Ku37
Gainsborough ◻ CDN 236 Ek21
Gairdner ◻ AUS 144 Qk63
Gairloch ◻ GB 48 Kp33
Gaisabad ◻ IND 117 Ok35
Gaithersburg ◻ USA 241 Gb26
Gaivota ◻ BR 267 He45
Gai Xian ◻ CHN 110 Qk25
Gajalinkalrns ◻ LV 45 Mf38
Gajapatinagaram ◻ IND 117 Pb36
Gajendragarh ◻ IND 116 Oh38
Gajiram ◻ WAN 189 Lg39
Gajner Wildlife Sanctuary ◻ IND 114 Og33
Gajner W.S. ◻ IND 114 Og32
Gajol ◻ IND 120 Pe33
Gajutino ◻ RUS 72 Mk16
Gakem ◻ WAN 188 Le42
Gakem ◻ WAN 188 Le42
Gakilköy ◻ TR 69 Mj49
Gakko ◻ RN 189 Lg39
Gakkovo ◻ RUS 45 Me30
Gakuara ◻ EAK 194 Mh44
Gala ◻ CHN 102 Pe31
Galábovo ◻ BG 69 Mf48
Gal Adhale ◻ SP 193 Nd42
Gal ◻ CHN 102 Pe31
Galán, Cerro ◻ RA 279 Gg59
Galanduak ◻ IR 91 Nd38
Galanga ◻ ANG 200 Lj52
Galangue ◻ ANG 200 Lj52
Galanta ◻ SK 66 Lt42
Galanino ◻ RUS 97 Oj23
Galápagos Islands ◻ EC 269 Fe45
Galashiels ◻ GB 48 Ks35
Fu Xian ◻ CHN 106 Qe28
Galatíni ◻ GR 68 Mb50
Galatista ◻ GR 68 Md50
Galatone ◻ I 63 Lq50
Galb ◻ RIM 180 Kc36
Galbet ◻ DT 93 Nc42
Galbraith ◻ AUS 147 Sa54
Galbraith ◻ CDN 230 Df16
Galbyn Gov' ◻ MNG 104 Qd24
Galcaio ◻ SP 193 Nd42
Galdar ◻ E 174 Kc32
Galdhøpiggen ◻ N 40 Lj29
Galé ◻ RMM 186 Kf39

Galegu ◻ SUD 185 Mh39
Galeia ◻ RG R45
Galena ◻ USA 238 Fd27
Galena ◻ USA 229 Cb20
Galena Bay ◻ USA 232 Eb20
Galenbecker See ◻ D 58 Lo37
Galeota Point ◻ TT 251 Gk43
Galera ◻ E 56 Kt53
Galera ◻ RP 124 Ra38
Galera Point ◻ TT 251 Gk43
Galeras ◻ YV 265 Gk41
Galeras, Volcán ◻ CO 264 Gb45
Galéria ◻ F 60 Lj48
Galería degli Uffizi ◻ I 60 Lm47
Galeton ◻ USA 241 Gb25
Galgaguta ◻ H 67 Lu43
Galgalo ◻ SP 195 Nb45
Galgdon Mountains ◻ SP 193 Nb41
Gal Hareeri ◻ SP 195 Nd44
Galíbi ◻ SME 266 Hc43
Galicea ◻ RP 124 Rb38
Galich ◻ RUS 72 Nb16
Galilaeí ◻ F 53 Ld44
Galim ◻ CAM 188 Lf43
Galinda ◻ ANG 198 Lg50
Galiraya ◻ CAM 194 Mg45
Galiwdu ◻ IND 119 Og46
Galiwinku ◻ AUS 146 Rh52
Gallabat ◻ SUD 185 Mj39
Gallan Head ◻ GB 48 Kn32
Galle ◻ CL 119 Pa42
Gallabat ◻ SUD 185 Mj39
Gallipoli ◻ I 63 Lq50
Gallabbat ◻ SUD 185 Mj39
Gallargues ◻ RCH 279 Ge59
Gállego ◻ E 57 Kt48
Galliano ◻ USA 239 Fe31
Gallinazo ◻ YV 265 Gg43
Gallinero, Cerro ◻ YV 265 Gj43
Gallo Mts. ◻ USA 235 Eg28
Galloway ◻ GB 48 Kq35
Gallup ◻ USA 235 Ef28
Gallur ◻ E 57 Kt49
Galma ◻ WAN 188 Le40
Galmudug ◻ SP 195 Nd45
Galoc ◻ CI 187 Kh42
Galong ◻ AUS 149 Se62
Galoya ◻ CL 119 Pa42
Gal Oya Valley N.P. ◻ CL 119 Pa42
Galsi ◻ IND 117 Pd34
Galt ◻ USA 234 Dk26
Gal Tardo ◻ SP 195 Nc44
Galteen ◻ S 43 Lo33
Galtimukti ◻ RUS 97 Oj23
Galtür ◻ A 60 Ll43
Galufitk ◻ RI 127 Qc48
Galula ◻ EAT 196 Mg50
Galway ◻ IRL 47 Kl38
Galway ◻ IRL 47 Kj37
Galway Downs ◻ AUS 148 Sb58
Gam ◻ NAM 201 Ma56
Gam ◻ RI 131 Re46
Gama ◻ RI 131 Rf54
Gama ◻ ETH 192 Nb42
Gamá ◻ PNG 156 Se50
Gamalama ◻ RI 131 Re46
Gamambo ◻ USA 249 Ga41
Gamarra ◻ CO 264 Gd41
Gamawa ◻ WAN 188 Lf39
Gamay ◻ RP 124 Rb39
Gamba ◻ G 198 Le47
Gamba ◻ RDC 199 Me48
Gambaga ◻ GH 187 Kk40
Gambela ◻ ETH 192 Mg42
Gambela N.P. ◻ ETH 192 Mg42
Gambell ◻ USA 210 Bb06
Gambéla ◻ ETH 228 Be14
Gambey ◻ RI 131 Re46
Gambia ◻ WAG 163 Ka08
Gambia ◻ WAG 186 Kb39
Gambiell Islands ◻ AUS 150 Ra63
Gambo ◻ CDN 241 Hc21
Gambo ◻ RCA 190 Lk43
Gamboa ◻ PA 249 Ga41
Gambula ◻ RCA 190 Lh43
Gambula ◻ RCA 190 Lh43
Gambuta, Gunung ◻ RI 125 Rb45
Gameh ◻ IR 91 Nd27
Gameleira ◻ BR 273 Jc49
Gamia ◻ RI 131 Re46
Gamia ◻ D 188 Lj40
Gamkab ◻ NAM 204 Lk59
Gamboma ◻ RCG 198 Lg48
Gamkahe ◻ RI 131 Re46
Gamleby ◻ S 43 Lq32
Gammelstaden ◻ S 41 Md25
Gammertingen ◻ D 59 Lk42
Gammon Ranges N.P. ◻ AUS 148 Rk61
Gamoep ◻ ZA 204 Lk60
Gamperá ◻ ANG 189 Lh42
Gampola ◻ CL 119 Pa42
Gamud ◻ ETH 193 Nb43
Gamzigrad ◻ SRB 68 Mb47
Gan ◻ CHN 107 Qh29
Gan Gan ◻ RA 282 Gf67
Gananoque ◻ CDN 114 Og31
Ganapatipule Beach ◻ IND 116 Og37
Gananoque ◻ CDN 241 Gc24
Ganaz ◻ CHN 102 Pe29
Gandeh ◻ WAN 188 Le42
Gandak ◻ IND 117 Pb33
Ganceviči ◻ RUS 44 Mf37
Gančá Dvorac ◻ RUS 44 Mf37
Gancheng ◻ CHN 109 Qe36
Gandajika ◻ RDC 199 Mb49
Gandajika ◻ RDC 199 Mb49
Gandaki ◻ WAN 189 Lg39
Gandai ◻ RP 124 Rc39
Gandari ◻ IND 114 Oh28
Gandar ◻ RP 124 Rb38
Gander ◻ CDN 241 Hc21
Gander Lake ◻ CDN 241 Hc21
Gandesa ◻ E 57 La49
Gandhidham ◻ IND 116 Of34
Gandhinagar ◻ IND 116 Og35
Gandía ◻ E 57 Ku52
Gandia ◻ SN 180 Kb38
Gandole ◻ WAN 188 Le42
Gandu ◻ RWA 194 Mf45
Gané ◻ RMM 187 Kg40
Gâneb ◻ RIM 180 Kc36
Ganda ◻ WAN 189 Lg40
Gando ◻ ANG 200 Lj52
Gandia ◻ D 59 Lm42
Gandu ◻ CHN 114 Og37
Ganesabad ◻ IR 96 Nh30
Ganga ◻ IND 117 Pd34
Ganganagar ◻ IND 114 Og31
Gangapur ◻ IND 116 Oj33
Gangapur ◻ IND 116 Oj33
Gangaw ◻ MYA 120 Ph34
Gangca ◻ CHN 105 Qb27
Gangdisé Shan ◻ CHN 102 Pa29
Ganges ◻ F 53 Ld47
Ganghwa Dolmen Site ◻ ROK 112 Rd28
Gangi ◻ I 63 Lp53
Gangmo ◻ CHN 115 Oj31
Gangola ◻ BHT 120 Pf32
Gangnampur ◻ IND 115 Ok39
Gangoa ◻ BR 276 Hd59
Gangte Goemba ◻ BHT 120 Pf32
Gangte Goemba ◻ BHT 120 Pf32
Gangtok ◻ IND 120 Pe32
Gangula ◻ ANG 200 Lg51
Ganguan ◻ RB 201 Ma55
Ganhe ◻ CHN 105 Rb20
Gani ◻ RI 131 Re46
Ganjam ◻ IND 117 Ok33
GanjNameh ◻ IR 91 Ne29
Ganjgal Khan ◻ IR 98 Ng28
Gankuoqin ◻ CHN 107 Qh27
Ganmain ◻ AUS 149 Sd63
Gannan ◻ CHN 105 Rb22
Gannat ◻ F 53 Ld44
Gannavaram ◻ IND 117 Pa36
Ganne Valley ◻ AUS 148 Rg60
Gannoa ◻ CI 187 Kh42
Ganqu ◻ CHN 106 Qe27
Gansbaai ◻ ZA 204 Lk63
Gansé ◻ CI 187 Kj41
Gansen ◻ CHN 103 Pg27
Gansu ◻ CHN 77 Pb06
Gantan ◻ I 59 Lm42
Gantheaume Point ◻ AUS 142 Rb55
Ganviè ◻ DY 188 La42
Ganzata ◻ SUD 184 Mb39
Ganxi ◻ CHN 108 Qf31
Ganyesa ◻ ZA 205 Mc59
Ganyu ◻ CHN 107 Qj28
Gänzä ◻ AZ 91 Nd25
Ganzhou ◻ CHN 109 Qh33
Gao ◻ BF 187 Kj40
Gao'an ◻ CHN 108 Qh31
Gaocheng Gucheng ◻ CHN 101 Pe24
Gaofengji ◻ CHN 112 Qk28
Gaogou ◻ CHN 112 Qk28
Gaolan ◻ CHN 106 Qb27
Gaohezhen ◻ CHN 112 Qk28
Gaojiabu ◻ CHN 110 Qd30
Gaonan ◻ NZ 153 Te68
Gaoping ◻ CHN 107 Qg28
Gaoshan ◻ CHN 109 Qk33
Gaotai ◻ CHN 103 Pk26
Gaoyang ◻ CHN 107 Qh26
Gaoyi ◻ CHN 107 Qg27
Gaoyou ◻ CHN 107 Qj29
Gaozhou ◻ CHN 108 Qf35
Gap ◻ F 53 Lg46
Gapan ◻ RP 124 Ra38
Gaparma ◻ CHN 106 Qb29
Gapuwiyak A. ◻ AUS 146 Rh52
Gara ◻ ET 178 Md31
Garabekevyul ◻ TM 97 Oc26
Garacad ◻ SP 193 Ne42
Garachine ◻ PA 249 Ga42
Garachine ◻ PA 249 Ga42
Gara-Ekar ◻ DZ 182 Lc36
Garagoa ◻ CO 264 Gd43
Garagua ◻ RN 182 Le39
Gara Khanrössa ◻ DZ 176 Le32
Gara Lâkemik ◻ RG 68 Md47
Garalo ◻ RMM 187 Kg40
Garamba, P.N. de la ◻ RDC 191 Me43
Garam Chasma ◻ PK 97 Of27
Garamped ◻ IND 120 Pg33
Garango ◻ BF 187 Kj40
Garanhuns ◻ BR 273 Jb49
Garapuava ◻ PNG 156 Se50
Gara-River ◻ CHN 284 Hd52
Garawa ◻ PNG 124 Rd45
Gara A.L. ◻ LB 186 Kf43
Garawe ◻ LB 186 Kf43
Garayalde ◻ RA 282 Gf67
Garba ◻ CV 186 Jj37
Garberville ◻ USA 232 Dj24
Garbarville ◻ USA 232 Dj24
Garbahárrey ◻ SP 195 Nb44
Gárbenville ◻ USA 232 Dj24
Garbe Tula ◻ EAK 195 Mk45
Garberville ◻ PL 65 Mb39
Garbsen ◻ D 58 Lk38
Garça ◻ CHN 103 Pk30
Garçanta ◻ CHN 103 Pk30
García García ◻ MEX 245 Ek33
Garza ◻ RA 279 Gj60
Gardno ◻ CHN 103 Pk30
Gardar ◻ CHN 103 Pk30
Gargan ◻ RP 124 Ra38
Gasan ◻ RP 124 Ra38
Gassan ◻ BF 187 Kj39
Gasdane ◻ SN 180 Kc38
Gassi Touil ◻ DZ 176 Lc30
Gassol ◻ WAN 188 Le41
Gastonia ◻ USA 242 Fk28
Gata ◻ CV 186 Jj37
Gata, Cabo de ◻ E 56 Kt54
Gateway ◻ USA 235 Ef26
Gateway International Raceway ◻ USA 239 Fd26
Gati ◻ IR 98 Nh31
Gati-Loumo ◻ RMM 181 Kh38
Gatineau ◻ CDN 241 Gc23
Gatinburg ◻ USA 242 Fj28
Gatma Oga ◻ TR 90 Me26
Gato Colorado ◻ RA 279 Gk60
Gattaran ◻ RP 124 Ra36
Gatton ◻ AUS 149 Sg59
Gatun ◻ PA 249 Fk41
Gaturiano ◻ BR 273 Hk49
Gau ◻ FJI 159 Tk55
Gaua Island ◻ VU 158 Te54
Gaub Caves ◻ NAM 200 Lj55
Gaudan ◻ TM 96 Nk27
Gaujas n.p. ◻ LV 45 Md34
Gault ◻ F 52 La43
Gaumla ◻ IND 117 Pb35
Gaurbe Riviera ◻ I 60 Lj45
Gauri ◻ CHN 102 Pe29
Gauribidanur ◻ IND 118 Oj39
Gauri ◻ CHN 102 Pe29
Gaussberg ◻ ANT 287 Pb33
Gaustatoppen ◻ N 42 Lj31
Gauting ◻ D 59 Lm42
Gauya ◻ BF 187 Kj39
Gavarr ◻ ARM 91 Nc25
Gávavá ◻ CHN 277 Hf59
Gavião ◻ P 55 Kn51
Gavin ◻ IR 91 Ne27
Gaviet ◻ PNG 155 Se48
Gavdopoúla ◻ GR 71 Me56
Gávë ◻ RUS 45 Mf30
Gävle ◻ S 43 Lr30
Gäveliukbten ◻ S 43 Lr30
Gaviel ◻ USA 239 Fd26
Gaviotas ◻ CO 265 Ge43
Gavorrano ◻ I 60 Ll48
Gávrio ◻ GR 71 Me53
Gavry ◻ RUS 45 Mf34
Gawachab ◻ NAM 204 Lj59
Gawan ◻ IND 117 Pc34
Gawilgarh Fort ◻ IND 116 Oj35
Gawler ◻ AUS 148 Rk63
Gawler Ranges N.P. ◻ AUS 148 Rh62
Gaworzyce ◻ PL 64 Lq39
Gaxun Nur ◻ CHN 104 Qa25
Gay ◻ MAL 128 Qg42
Gaya ◻ IND 117 Pc34
Gaya ◻ RN 188 La40
Gaya ◻ WAN 188 Le39
Gaya ◻ RI 131 Re46
Gayam ◻ RI 129 Qj49
Gayam ◻ TCH 190 Lj41
Gayan ◻ AFG 99 Oc30
Gayaza ◻ EAU 194 Mf45

Gayéri 🏳 BF 187 La39
Gaylord 🏳 USA 236 Fc23
Gaylord 🏳 USA 237 Fh23
Gayndah 🏳 AUS 149 Sf58
Gaza 🏳 SUD 185 Mh40
Gaza 🏳 IL 92 Mh30
Gaz-Achak 🏳 TM 96 Oa25
G'azalkent 🏳 UZ 97 Oe25
Gazanak 🏳 IR 96 Ng28
Gazandzhyk 🏳 TM 96 Nh26
Gazara 🏳 IS 182 Ld39
Gazara 🏳 TJ 97 Oe26
Gaza Strip 🏳 IL 92 Mh30
Gazelle Peninsula 🏳 PNG 156 Sf48
Gazi 🏳 EAK 197 Mk48
Gaziantep 🏳 TR 90 Mj27
Gazi-Husrev-begova džamija 🏳 BIH 68 Lh47
Gazimurskij Zavod 🏳 RUS 105 Qk20
Gazli 🏳 UZ 96 Ob25
Gbabam 🏳 CI 187 La39
Gbabaoua 🏳 CAM 189 Lh42
Gbadikaha 🏳 CI 187 Kh41
Gbadolite 🏳 RDC 190 Ma43
Gbagba 🏳 RCA 190 Ma43
Gbaizera 🏳 RCA 190 La42
Gbalatuai 🏳 LB 186 Kf42
Gbambélédougou 🏳 CI 187 Kh41
Gbanamme 🏳 DY 188 La39
Gbanannah 🏳 RCA 190 Ma42
Gbanga 🏳 WAN 188 Le41
Gbangbatok 🏳 WAL 186 Kd42
Gbarnga 🏳 LB 186 Kf42
Gbasa 🏳 DY 188 Lb40
Gbassigbiri 🏳 RCA 191 Md43
Gbatala 🏳 LB 186 Kf42
Gbéle Resource Reserve 🏳 GH 187 Kj40
Gbéné 🏳 DY 188 Lb40
Gbéssé 🏳 BF 187 Kj40
Gbentu 🏳 WAL 186 Ke41
Gberia-Fotombu 🏳 RG 186 Ke41
Gberia Fotombu 🏳 WAL 186 Ke41
Gbéroubouay 🏳 DY 188 Lb40
Gbesse 🏳 LB 186 Ke42
Gbéttapea 🏳 CI 187 Kg42
Gbinti 🏳 WAL 186 Kd41
Gbodonon 🏳 CI 187 Kh41
Gboko 🏳 WAN 188 Le42
Gboli 🏳 LB 186 Kf43
Gbon 🏳 CI 187 Kg41
Gbwado 🏳 WAN 188 Lc42
Gburug 🏳 GH 187 Kf41
Gbwado 🏳 RDC 190 Ma44
Gciwihaba Caverns 🏳 RB 201 Ma56
Gdańsk 🏳 PL 64 Lf36
Gdov 🏳 RUS 63 Ma34
Gdyel 🏳 DZ 175 Kh28
Gdynia 🏳 PL 64 Lf36
Geary 🏳 USA 238 Fa28
Gebasawa 🏳 WAN 188 Le39
Gebe 🏳 RI 131 Re46
Gebeit 🏳 SUD 185 Mj35
Gebelein 🏳 CI 186 Kf41
Gebituolatuo 🏳 CHN 103 Pg26
Gebre Gurache 🏳 ETH 192 Mk41
Gebze 🏳 TR 69 Me50
Gecha 🏳 ETH 192 Mh42
Gedaref 🏳 SUD 185 Mh38
Gede 🏳 EAK 195 Mk47
Gedi National Monument 🏛 EAK 195 Na47
Gediz 🏳 TR 90 Me26
Gedlegube 🏳 ETH 193 Nc42
Gedik 🏳 ETH 192 Mj43
Gedong 🏳 CHN 108 Qe32
Gedonghaji 🏳 RI 127 Qc48
Gedongratu 🏳 RI 127 Qc48
Gedong Songo Temple 🏳 RI 129 Qf49
Gedser 🏳 DK 42 Lm36
Geel 🏳 B 51 Lf39
Geelong 🏳 AUS 151 Sc65
Geesaley 🏳 SP 193 Nf40
Geeste 🏳 D 58 Lh38
Geesthacht 🏳 D 58 Ll37
Gefell 🏳 D 59 Lm40
Gentala Caoyuan 🏳 CHN 106 Qf25
Ighard 🏳 🇦🇷 ARM 91 Nc25
'gyai 🏳 CHN 102 Pa29
iro 🏳 EAT 197 Mj43
iselhöring 🏳 D 59 Ln42
isenfeld 🏳 D 59 Lm42
iser el Tatio 🏳 RCH 279 Gf57
isingen 🏳 D 59 Lk43
ita 🏳 EAT 194 Mg47
ithus 🏳 N 42 Lk31
iju 🏳 CHN 121 Qb34
kdepe 🏳 TM 96 Nk26
kehn 🏳 LB 186 Kf42
kehn 🏳 SUD 194 Mf43
idz 🏳 I 63 Lp53
ladaindong 🏳 CHN 103 Pf29
iadi 🏳 EAT 193 Nd42
iai 🏳 EAT 194 Mj47
iai Bomba 🏳 EAT 194 Mj47
iam 🏳 RI 129 Qf47
langchang 🏳 CHN 108 Qd30
iati Monastery 🏳 GE 91 Nb24
ideh 🏳 D 58 Lg39
itfeop 🏳 N 42 Lk31
ie 🏳 RDC 190 Lk43
ieen 🏳 NL 51 Lf40
iembe 🏳 TR 71 Mj51
iemso 🏳 ETH 192 Na41
iendzik 🏳 TR 69 Me52
igaudiškis 🏳 LT 45 Mc35
ibolu 🏳 TR 69 Mg50
ibolu Yarımadası Milli Parkı 🏞 TR 69 Mg50
ila 🏳 ETH 192 Mj41
igmgang 🏳 CHN 121 Qg47
iiai 🏳 SUD 191 Mk41
iiinsoor 🏳 SP 193 Nd42
itting 🏳 D 59 Lk40
iluketapang 🏳 RI 127 Pk44
ilumbang 🏳 RI 127 Qc48
imamudo 🏳 GNB 186 Kc39
imbloux sur-Orneau 🏳 🇩🇪 B 51 Le40
imbogl 🏳 PNG 155 Sc48
imbu 🏳 RI 130 Ra44
ila 🏳 ETH 192 Mj41
imena 🏳 RDC 190 La44
imen 🏳 RI 129 Qf47
iminí South Observatory 🔭 RCH 279 Ge61
imilk 🏳 TR 69 Mj50
immeiza 🏳 SUD 185 Mh37
immeiza 🏳 SUD 191 Mh42
immell 🏳 USA 236 Fc22
imontell del Friuli 🏳 I 61 Lc44
imsa 🏳 ET 179 Mf32
imsbok N.P. 🏞 NAM 204 Ma58
imsbokvlakte 🏞 ZA 205 Mc58
imünden 🏳 D 58 Lj40
imünden 🏳 D 59 Lk40
imale Wenz 🏳 ETH 192 Mk42
imeral Acha 🏳 RA 280 Gh64
imeral Alvear 🏳 RA 281 Gk64
imeral Alvear 🏳 RA 281 Gk64
imeral Arenales 🏳 RA 280 Sb33
imeral Ballivián 🏳 RA 279 Gk61
imeral Bravo 🏳 MEX 245 Fa33
imeral Cabrera 🏳 RA 280 Gf62

General Camacho 🏳 BOL 278 Gf54
General Carneiro 🏳 BR 276 He59
General Cepeda 🏳 MEX 245 Ek33
General Coffee S.P. 🏞 USA 242 Fj30
General Conesa 🏳 RA 280 Gh66
General Conesa 🏳 RA 281 Hb64
General Daniel Cerri 🏳 RA 281 Gj65
General Elizardo Aquino 🏳 PY 276 Hb58
General Enrique Martinez 🏳 ROU 276 Hd62
General Enrique Mosconi 🏳 RA 279 Gj57
General Francisco Murguia (Nieves) 🏳 MEX 245 Ej33
General Galarza 🏳 RA 276 Ha62
General Güemes 🏳 RA 279 Gh58
General Guido 🏳 RA 281 Hb64
General José de San Martín 🏳 RA 276 Ha59
General Juan Madariaga 🏳 RA 281 Hb64
General Juan N. Álvarez, P.N. 🏞 MEX 246 Fa37
General La Madrid 🏳 RA 281 Gk64
General Lavalle 🏳 RA 281 Hb64
General Lavalle 🏳 RA 280 Gj62
General Lucio Victorio Mansilla 🏳 RA 276 Ha59
General Luna 🏳 RP 124 Rd41
General Mansilla 🏳 RA 281 Hb63
General M. Belgrano, Cerro 🏔 RA 279 Gg60
General Mosconi 🏳 RA 279 Gj57
General O'Brien 🏳 RA 281 Gk64
General Pico 🏳 RA 281 Gj63
General Pinedo 🏳 RA 279 Gk59
General Pinto 🏳 RA 281 Gk63
General Roca 🏳 RA 280 Gg65
General Salgado 🏳 BR 274 He56
General Sampaio 🏳 BR 273 Ja68
General San Martin 🏳 RA 281 Gd64
General San Martin 🏳 RA 281 Ha63
General Santos 🏳 RP 125 Rc42
General Terán 🏳 MEX 245 Fa33
General Toševo 🏳 BG 69 Mj47
General Viamonte 🏳 RA 281 Gk63
General Villegas 🏳 RA 281 Gj63
Geneseo 🏳 USA 241 Gb24
Geneva 🏳 CH 60 Lg44
Geneva 🏳 USA 238 Fb25
Geneva 🏳 USA 239 Fj39
Geneva 🏳 USA 239 Fh30
Geneva 🏳 USA 241 Gb24
Gengenbach 🏳 D 59 Lj42
Gengis Khan Mausoleum 🏛 CHN 106 Qe26
Gengis Khan Monument 🏛 MNG 104 Qf21
Gengma Daizu 🏳 CHN 121 Pk34
Gengwa 🏳 RDC 199 Mb47
Genk 🏳 B 51 Lf40
Genlis 🏳 F 53 Lf43
Genoa 🏳 NL 51 Lg39
Genoa 🏳 AUS 151 Se64
Genoa 🏳 I 60 Lj46
Genoa 🏳 USA 236 Fb25
Genohe 🏳 J 111 Sa25
Génolhac 🏳 F 53 Ld46
Gent 🏳 B 51 Le40
Genteng 🏳 RI 129 Qh50
Genthin 🏳 D 58 Ln38
Genting 🏳 RI 126 Pk44
Genting Highlands Hill Resort 🏞 MAL 126 Qa44
Gentio do Ouro 🏳 BR 273 Hj51
Genyem 🏳 RI 155 Sa47
Genzano di Lucània 🏳 I 63 Lr50
Geograph Channel 🏳 AUS 144 Qg58
Geographe Bay 🏞 AUS 144 Qh62
Geographic Center of North America 🏳 USA 236 Fa21
Geographic Center of U.S. 🏳 USA 233 Ej23
Geological Exposure 🏳 ZA 205 Mf58
George 🏳 ZA 204 Mb63
George VI Ice Shelf 🏞 286 Gc33
George Gill Range 🏞 AUS 143 Rf58
George Island 🏳 GB 283 Ha72
George P. Cossar S.P. 🏞 USA 239 Ff28
George Reservoir 🏞 USA 239 Fh30
George R. Parks Highway 🛣 USA 229 Ce14
George Sound 🏳 NZ 153 Td68
Georgetown 🏳 AUS 147 Sb55
George Town 🏳 BS 250 Gc34
Georgetown 🏳 GB 243 Fk36
Georgetown 🏳 GUY 266 Ha42
Georgetown 🏳 MAL 126 Qa43
Georgetown 🏳 USA 238 Fb30
Georgetown 🏳 USA 239 Fh30
Georgetown 🏳 USA 239 Fh30
Georgetown 🏳 USA 242 Ga29
George V and 🏞 286 Sb33
George Washington Birthplace Nat. Mon. 🏞 USA 241 Ga26
George West 🏳 USA 245 Fa31
Georgia 🏳 GE 91 Nb24
Georgia 🏳 USA 239 Fh29
Georgian Bay 🏞 CDN 237 Fk23
Georgian Bay Islands N.P. 🏞 CDN 237 Ga23
Georgievka 🏳 KZ 100 Pa21
Georgievsk 🏳 RUS 91 Nb23
Georgina Downs 🏳 AUS 146 Rj56
Georg von Neumayer 🏳 ANT 286 Kc33
Gera 🏳 D 58 Ln40
Geraardsbergen 🏳 B 51 Ld40
Gerace 🏳 I 63 Lr52
Gerakárou 🏳 GR 68 Md50
Geraki 🏳 GR 70 Mc53
Geraldine 🏳 NZ 153 Tf68
Geraldine 🏳 USA 233 Ee22
Geraldo Toco Preto, T.I. 🏞 BR 272 Hh48
Geraldton 🏳 AUS 144 Qh60
Gerânia Óri 🏔 GR 68 Md52
Geranium 🏳 AUS 150 Sa63
Gérardmer 🏳 F 53 Lg42
Gerdau 🏳 ZA 205 Md59
Gerdine, Mount 🏔 USA 229 Cd15
Geroúbarg 🏳 IS 46 Jc26
Gerede 🏳 TR 90 Mf25
Gerena 🏳 E 55 Ko53
Gergal 🏳 E 55 Ks53
Gergi 🏳 AFG 98 Ob29
Gergova 🏳 RO 69 Mk45
Gerickes 🏳 ZA 204 Mb63
Gerihun 🏳 WAL 186 Ke42
Gerisa 🏳 SP 193 Nd40
Gerlach 🏳 USA 232 Ea26
Gerlachovský štit 🏔 SK 67 Ma41
Germa 🏳 LAR 177 Lg32
Germakolo 🏳 RI 154 Rg46
German Bight 🏞 D 58 Lh38
German Creek 🏳 AUS 149 Sd57
Germania 🏳 RA 281 Gj63
Germansen Landing 🏳 CDN 230 Dh18
Germany 🏳 D 58 Lm40
Germencik 🏳 TR 71 Mh53
Germering 🏳 D 59 Lm42
Germiston 🏳 ZA 205 Me59
Gernika 🏳 E 56 Ks47
Gernsheim 🏳 D 59 Lj41
Gero 🏳 J 111 Rj28
Gerolstein 🏳 D 59 Lh40
Gerolzhofen 🏳 D 59 Ll41

Gerona 🏳 RP 124 Ra38
Gerpir 🏞 IS 46 Kg25
Gersfeld 🏳 D 59 Ll40
Gersthofen 🏳 D 59 Ll42
Gërzë 🏳 CHN 102 Pc29
Gesäuse, N.P. 🏞 A 61 Lp43
Gescher 🏳 D 58 Lh39
Gesves 🏳 B 51 Lf40
Geta 🏳 FIN 44 Lu30
Getafe 🏳 E 55 Kr50
Geti 🏳 RDC 194 Mf45
Getinge 🏳 S 42 Ln34
Getúlio Vargas 🏳 BR 276 He59
Getty Center 🏛 USA 234 Ea28
Gettysburg 🏳 USA 236 Fa21
Gettysburg 🏳 USA 241 Gb26
Gettysburg N.M.P. 🏞 USA 241 Gb26
Getúlina 🏳 BR 274 Hf56
Getúlio Vargas 🏳 BR 276 Hd59
Getxo 🏳 E 56 Kr47
Geureudong, Mount 🏔 RI 126 Pj43
Gevaş 🏳 TR 91 Nb26
Gevgelija 🏳 MK 68 Mc49
Gevral 🏳 IND 116 Oh36
Gewandhaus in Zwickau 🏛 D 58 Ln40
Gewane 🏳 ETH 192 Na40
Gewane Wildlife Reserve 🏞 ETH 192 Na40
Geyik Dağları 🏔 TR 90 Mf27
Geyikli 🏳 TR 71 Mg51
Geysir 🏞 IS 46 Ju26
Geyve 🏳 TR 90 Mf25
Gezhou Ba 🏞 CHN 108 Qf30
Ghabat Al-Arab 🏳 SUD 191 Me41
Ghabda 🏳 RN 182 Le37
Ghadamis 🏳 LAR 176 Lg30
Ghadduwah 🏳 LAR 177 Lh32
Ghafargaon 🏳 BD 120 Pf33
Ghaghra, T.I. 🏞 IND 117 Pc34
Ghaibi Dero 🏳 PK 99 Oc32
Ghairatganj 🏳 IND 117 Ok34
Ghamid az Zenad 🏳 KSA 94 Na36
Gham Shadzar 🏳 IR 98 Oa31
Ghana 🏳 🇬🇭 163 Kh09
Ghanem Ali 🏳 SYR 90 Mk28
Ghangmi 🏳 RI 154 Rk48
Ghanim 🏳 KSA 95 Nh36
Ghantiali 🏳 IND 114 Og32
Ghanpur 🏳 RB 201 Ma56
Ghanzi 🏳 RB 201 Ma56
Ghanzi Farms 🏞 RB 201 Ma56
Ghar Ali Sadr Sarab 🏞 IR 91 Ne28
Gharb Binna 🏳 SUD 185 Mf36
Ghard Abu Muharrik 🏞 ET 179 Mf31
Ghardaïa 🏳 DZ 176 Lc29
Ghardimaou 🏳 TN 176 Le27
Gharghoda 🏳 IND 117 Pb34
Gharig 🏳 SUD 184 Md40
Gharm 🏳 TJ 97 Of26
Gharo 🏳 PK 99 Oj33
Gharous 🏳 RMM 182 La36
Gharyan 🏳 LAR 177 Lg29
Ghat 🏳 LAR 183 Lf33
Ghatal 🏳 IND 117 Pd34
Ghatampur 🏳 IND 116 Ok35
Ghatanji 🏳 IND 116 Ok35
Ghatgaon 🏳 IND 117 Pc35
Ghatsila 🏳 IND 117 Pd34
Ghaura 🏳 IND 117 Ok33
Ghauspur 🏳 PK 99 Oe31
Ghayathi 🏳 UAE 95 Ng34
Ghazali 🏳 SUD 185 Mg36
Ghazali Cinema Town 🏳 IR 96 Nf28
Ghaziabad 🏳 IND 115 Oj31
Ghazi Khan 🏳 IR 96 Nf28
Ghazni 🏳 AFG 99 Oe29
Ghazzalah 🏳 KSA 92 Na32
Ghedi 🏳 I 61 Ll45
Gheorgheni 🏳 RO 69 Mf46
Gherdi 🏳 IND 116 Oh37
Gherla 🏳 RO 67 Md43
Gherm 🏳 IR 91 Ne26
Gherta Mică 🏳 RO 67 Md43
Ghilarza 🏳 I 62 Lj50
Ghimpați 🏳 RO 69 Mf46
Ghion 🏳 ETH 192 Mj41
Ghirán 🏳 CO 264 Gd42
Ghisonaccia 🏳 F 62 Lk48
Ghisoni 🏳 F 62 Lk48
Ghizar 🏳 IND 114 Og27
Ghorahi 🏳 NEP 115 Pb31
Ghorwal 🏳 IND 117 Pa32
Ghosia 🏳 IND 117 Pb33
Ghosla 🏳 IND 116 Oh34
Ghotaru 🏳 IND 114 Of32
Ghoveo 🏳 SOL 157 Sk50
Ghow-Gardan-Pass 🏞 AFG 98 Od31
Ghowrayd Gharami 🏳 AFG 97 Od27
Ghowrmach 🏳 AFG 97 Od28
Ghubaysh 🏳 SUD 184 Md39
Ghudaf 🏳 IND 117 Pb34
Ghura 🏳 IND 117 Pa32
Ghurian 🏳 AFG 98 Oa30
Giali Truong Son 🏳 VN/LAO 121 Qc36
Giang Jamaame 🏳 SP 195 Nb45
Giang 🏳 VN 123 Qd38
Giang Trung 🏳 VN 123 Qe39
Gianitsá 🏳 GR 70 Mc50
Giant Buddha 🏛 CHN 108 Qb31
Giant's Causeway 🏞 GB 48 Kd34
Giant's Playground 🏞 NAM 204 Lk59
Gia Rai 🏳 VN 123 Qc41
Giardini-Naxos 🏳 I 63 Lq53
Giarmata 🏳 RO 68 Mb45
Giarre 🏳 I 63 Lq53
Gia Vực 🏳 VN 123 Qe38
Gibapame 🏳 SP 193 Ne41
Gibara 🏳 C 243 Gb35
Gibbons 🏳 CDN 233 Ed19
Gibbonsville 🏳 USA 232 Ed23
Gibb River 🏳 AUS 145 Rf52
Gibb River Road 🛣 AUS 143 Rd54
Gibellina 🏳 I 62 Ln53
Gibeon 🏳 NAM 204 Ma58
Gibeon Station 🏳 NAM 204 Lj58
Gibralaón 🏳 E 55 Ko53
Gibraltar 🏳 AUS 148 Rh61
Gibraltar 🏳 GB 55 Kp54
Gibraltar Ranges N.P. 🏞 AUS 149 Sg60
Gibson 🏳 AUS 145 Ra62
Gibson Desert 🏞 AUS 134 Ra12
Gibson Desert Nature Reserve 🏞 AUS 145 Rc58
Gibsons 🏳 CDN 232 Dj21
Gibson Steps 🏞 AUS 151 Sb65
Gibzde 🏳 LV 45 Mc33
Gic 🏳 H 66 Ls43
Gichigniu Nuruu 🏔 MNG 101 Pj23
Gidam 🏳 IND 117 Pa34
Gidami 🏳 ETH 192 Mh41
Gidar 🏳 PK 99 Oj31
Giddalur 🏳 IND 119 Ok38
Gidda Plateau 🏔 ETH 192 Mk42
Giddings 🏳 USA 238 Fb30
Gien 🏳 F 53 Lc42
Giebelstadt del Coro 🏳 RA 280 Gh61
Giengen 🏳 D 59 Ll42
Giens 🏳 F 53 Lg47
Giera 🏳 RO 68 Ma45
Gierloz 🏳 PL 65 Mb36
Giessen 🏳 D 59 Lj40
Giethoorn 🏞 NL 51 Lg38
Gietrzwald 🏳 PL 65 Ma37
Gifhorn 🏳 D 58 Ll38
Gifu 🏳 J 111 Rj28
Gigant 🏳 RUS 73 Na22
Gigante 🏳 CO 264 Gc43
Gigante de Atacama 🏛 RCH 278 Gd55

Gigha 🏞 GB 48 Kp35
Gighera 🏳 RO 68 Md47
Gighits 🏳 TN 176 Lf29
Gignac 🏳 F 53 Ld47
Gihena 🏳 ET 179 Mf32
Gihofi 🏳 BU 196 Mf47
Gijduvon 🏳 UZ 96 Ob25
Gijón 🏳 E 54 Kq47
Gikongoro 🏳 RWA 196 Me47
Gila 🏳 USA 235 Ee29
Gila 🏳 USA 235 Ee29
Gila Bend 🏳 USA 235 Ed29
Gila Cliff Dwellings Nat. Mon. 🏛 USA 235 Ef29
Gila River Ind. Res. 🏞 USA 235 Ee29
Gilău 🏳 RO 67 Md44
Gilavë 🏳 AL 70 Lu50
Gilberto de San 🏳 USA 147 Sb55
Gilbert Islands 🏞 134 Tb09
Gilbert River 🏳 AUS 147 Sb55
Gilberts Dome 🏞 USA 94 Se57
Gilbués 🏳 BR 272 Hh50
Gilf Kebir 🏞 ET 179 Ma33
Gilgai 🏳 AUS 149 Sf60
Gilgandra 🏳 AUS 149 Se61
Gilgil 🏳 EAK 194 Mk46
Gilgit 🏳 114 Oh28
Gilgit Mountains 🏔 114 Og27
Gilgunnia 🏳 AUS 151 Sd62
Gilimanuk 🏳 RI 129 Qh50
Gil Island 🏞 CDN 230 Dj19
Gilleleje 🏳 DK 42 Ln34
Gillette 🏳 USA 233 Eh24
Gilla Rock 🏞 USA 237 Fg23
Gilmer 🏳 USA 238 Fc29
Gilroy 🏳 USA 234 Dk27
Gilruth, Mount 🏔 AUS 146 Rg52
Gima 🏳 EC 268 Ga47
Gimi 🏳 WAN 188 Le41
Gimli 🏳 CDN 236 Fb20
Gimo 🏳 S 43 Lt32
Gimone 🏳 F 52 La47
Gimpil Darjaalan Monastery 🏛 MNG 104 Qc23
Gimpu 🏳 RI 130 Ra46
Ginchi 🏳 ETH 192 Mk41
Ginda 🏳 ER 192 Mk38
Gindalbie 🏳 AUS 144 Ra61
Gindie 🏳 AUS 149 Se57
Gindulisi 🏳 LT 45 Mb35
Gingee 🏳 IND 119 Ok39
Gingilup Swamps National Reserve 🏞 AUS 144 Qh63
Gingin 🏳 AUS 144 Qh61
Gin Gin 🏳 AUS 149 Sf58
Gingindlovu 🏳 ZA 205 Mf60
Gingko Petrified Forest S.P. 🏞 USA 232 Dk22
Gingong 🏳 RP 125 Rc41
Ginir 🏳 ETH 192 Na42
Ginosa 🏳 I 63 Lr50
Gintu 🏳 RI 130 Ra46
Gióia del Colle 🏳 I 63 Lr50
Gióia Táuro 🏳 I 63 Lq52
Gioiosa Iónica 🏳 I 63 Lr52
Gioùra 🏞 GR 71 Me51
Gippsland 🏞 AUS 151 Sd64
Giraffenberge 🏞 NAM 200 Lg55
Girai 🏳 IND 117 Pd33
Girardota 🏳 CO 264 Gc43
Girardot 🏳 CO 264 Gc43
Girban 🏳 SUD 185 Mf40
Girdawara 🏳 IND 117 Pa36
Girdwood 🏳 USA 229 Cf15
Giresun 🏳 TR 91 Mk25
Giresun Dağları 🏔 TR 91 Mk25
Girgá 🏳 ET 179 Mf32
Giri 🏳 PNG 155 Sd48
Giri 🏳 IND 117 Pd33
Girilambone 🏳 AUS 149 Sd61
Girne Kerynéia 🏳 CY 90 Mg28
Giro 🏳 WAN 188 Lc40
Giromagny 🏳 F 53 Lg43
Girón 🏳 CO 264 Gd42
Girona 🏳 E 57 Lc48
Gironde 🏞 F 52 Ku45
Girraween N.P. 🏞 AUS 149 Sg60
Giru 🏳 AFG 99 Od29
Girvan 🏳 GB 48 Kq35
Girwa 🏳 IND 117 Pd34
Gisborne 🏳 NZ 153 Tk65
Gisburn 🏳 GB 49 Ks36
Gisenyi 🏳 RWA 191 Me46
Gislaved 🏳 S 43 Lp33
Gisors 🏳 F 51 Lb41
Gisuru 🏳 BU 196 Mf47
Gitarama 🏳 RWA 196 Me47
Gitata 🏳 WAN 188 Ld41
Gitega 🏳 BU 196 Mf47
Githio 🏳 GR 70 Mc54
Giulianova 🏳 I 61 Lo48
Giulvăz 🏳 RO 68 Ma45
Giurgeni 🏳 RO 69 Mh46
Giurgiu 🏳 RO 69 Mh47
Giv 🏳 IR 98 Nk29
Givar 🏳 IR 96 Nh27
Give 🏳 DK 42 Lk35
Givet 🏳 F 51 Le40
Givors 🏳 F 53 Le45
Givry 🏳 F 53 Le44
Givry-en-Argonne 🏳 F 51 Le42
Giwa 🏳 WAN 188 Ld40
Giyani 🏳 ZA 202 Mf57
Giza 🏳 ET 179 Mf31
Gizab 🏳 AFG 99 Oc29
Gizatki 🏳 PL 64 Ls38
Gizo 🏳 SOL 157 Sj50
Gizycko 🏳 PL 65 Mb37
Gjakovë 🏳 🇽🇰 68 Ma48
Gjermundshamn 🏳 N 42 Lf30
Gjerstad 🏳 N 42 Lj32
Gjirí i Vlorës 🏞 AL 70 Lu50
Gjirokastër 🏳 🇦🇱 AL 70 Ma50
Gjoa Haven 🏳 CDN 227 Fa05
Gjøgur 🏳 IS 46 Ju25
Gjøjfjorden 🏞 IS 46 Kb24
Gjøvik 🏳 N 42 Ll31
Glace Bay 🏳 CDN 240 Gk22
Glaciated Rocks and Engravings 🏞 ZA 205 Mf58
Glacier Bay National Park and Preserve 🏞 USA 230 Db16
Glacier Express 🏞 CH 60 Lj44
Glacier Mount 🏔 USA 230 Dd17
Glacier N.P. 🏞 USA 233 Ed20
Glacier N.P. (Montana) 🏞 USA 233 Ec20
Glacier Peak 🏔 USA 232 Dk21
Glacier Peak Wilderness Area 🏞 USA 232 Dk21
Gladbach 🏳 D 58 Lj40
Gladewater 🏳 USA 238 Fc29
Gladstad 🏳 N 40 Lm25
Gladstone 🏳 AUS 149 Sf57
Gladstone 🏳 USA 151 Ri66
Gladstone 🏳 USA 238 Fc26
Gladstone 🏳 USA 237 Fg24
Gladwin 🏳 USA 237 Fh24
Glamis 🏳 USA 235 Ed29
Glamis Castle 🏛 GB 48 Ks34
Glamoč 🏳 BIH 61 Lr46
Glamsbjerg 🏳 DK 42 Ll35
Glamoč 🏳 BIH 61 Lr46
Glandorf 🏳 D 58 Lj38
Glanton 🏳 GB 49 Ks35
Glaris 🏳 CH 60 Lk43
Glasgow 🏳 GB 48 Kr35
Glasgow 🏳 USA 233 Eh21
Glasgow 🏳 USA 239 Fg26
Glasnevin 🏳 🇮🇪 IRL 47 Ka36
Glaslyn 🏳 CDN 233 Ef19

Glassboro 🏳 USA 241 Gc26
Glasshouse Mountains 🏔 AUS 149 Sg59
Glass Window Bridge 🏞 BS 243 Gb33
Glastonbury 🏳 GB 49 Ks39
Glauchau 🏳 D 58 Ln40
Glaumbær 🏳 IS 46 Ka25
Glavatícevo 🏳 BIH 68 Lt47
Glávinica 🏳 BG 69 Mg47
Glazoue 🏳 DY 188 La42
Głębokie 🏳 PL 65 Md39
Gleibat Boukenni 🏳 RIM 180 Kf38
Gleibat El Fouula 🏳 DARS 180 Kd34
Gleiberg 🏳 CDN 233 Ed20
Gleinalpe 🏔 A 61 Lq43
Gleisdorf 🏳 A 61 Lq43
Glave 🏳 AL 70 Lu50
Glénans, les 🏞 F 52 Ks43
Glencoe 🏳 USA 239 Sf58
Glen Coe 🏳 GB 48 Kp34
Glencoe 🏳 ZA 205 Mf60
Glencoe 🏳 CDN 237 Fd07
Glencolumbkille 🏳 IRL 47 Kg37
Glendale 🏳 USA 234 Ea28
Glendale 🏳 USA 235 Ed29
Glendale 🏳 ZW 202 Mf54
Glendalough 🏳 IRL 47 Kc37
Glendambo 🏳 AUS 148 Rh61
Glenden 🏳 AUS 149 Se56
Glendive 🏳 USA 233 Eh21
Glendo 🏳 USA 235 Eh24
Glenfiddich Distillery 🏛 GB 48 Kr33
Glenfinnan 🏳 GB 48 Kp34
Glen Florrie 🏳 AUS 142 Qj57
Glengarry Castle 🏛 GB 48 Kq33
Glengorm Castle 🏛 GB 48 Kp34
Glenhope 🏳 AUS 148 Rk58
Glenholme 🏳 CDN 230 Dc14
Glen Innes 🏳 AUS 149 Sf60
Glen Isla 🏳 AUS 148 Rj57
Glenluce 🏳 GB 48 Kq36
Glen Lyon Peak 🏔 CDN 230 Dc14
Glen More 🏞 GB 48 Kq33
Glenmorgan 🏳 AUS 149 Se59
Glenmorgan 🏳 USA 229 Ch14
Glenmorrison 🏳 AUS 148 Rk57
Glennallen 🏳 USA 229 Cg16
Glenn Highway 🛣 USA 229 Cg14
Glenn Ferry 🏳 USA 232 Ec24
Glennville 🏳 USA 234 Ea28
Glennville 🏳 USA 239 Fh29
Glenora 🏳 AUS 147 Sb55
Glen Orchard 🏳 USA 235 Ee26
Glenormiston 🏳 AUS 148 Rk57
Glenreagh 🏳 AUS 149 Sg61
Glenrothes 🏳 GB 48 Kr34
Glenéisia do Pará 🏳 BR 272 Hf47
Glenéisia do Pará 🏳 BR 272 Hf47
Glenties 🏳 IRL 47 Km36
Glenwood 🏳 USA 235 Eg27
Glenwood 🏳 USA 236 Fc23
Glenwood 🏳 USA 236 Fc25
Glenwood Canyon 🏞 USA 235 Eg26
Glenwood Springs 🏳 USA 235 Eg26
Glettinganes 🏞 IS 46 Kg25
Glidden 🏳 CDN 233 Ef19
Glide 🏳 GR 70 Mc52
Glimmenghus 🏳 S 43 Lp35
Glina 🏳 HR 61 Lr45
Glina 🏳 RO 69 Mg46
Gličko 🏳 PL 64 Ls40
Glogov 🏳 J 113 Rh28
Glogów 🏳 PL 64 Lr39
Glogovek 🏳 PL 64 Ls40
Glogovnica 🏳 HR 61 Lr45
Glomel 🏳 F 52 Ks43
Glommerträsk 🏳 S 41 Lu25
Glória 🏳 BR 273 Hk51
Glória 🏳 RP 124 Ra39
Gloria de Dourados 🏳 BR 274 Hc57
Glossa 🏳 GR 69 Me51
Gloucester 🏳 AUS 151 Sf62
Gloucester 🏳 CDN 241 Gc23
Gloucester 🏳 GB 49 Ks39
Gloucester Island 🏞 AUS 147 Sd55
Gloucester Point 🏳 USA 241 Gb27
Glovers Reef 🏞 BH 248 Fg37
Glovertown 🏳 CDN 241 Hc21
Glöbasi 🏳 TR 90 Mj27
Glöbasi 🏳 TR 90 Nj27
Glöbegui 🏳 IR 96 Nj27
Glöbet 🏳 TR 90 Mg27
Glögebyek 🏳 PL 64 Ls40
Glubokij 🏳 RUS 72 Na21
Glubczyce 🏳 PL 64 Ls40
Glubokij 🏳 RUS 72 Na21
Gluchołazy 🏳 PL 64 Ls40
Glučhowo 🏳 PL 65 Lu39
Gluckstadt 🏳 D 58 Lk37
Glukhove 🏳 RUS 73 Mh19
Glymur 🏞 IS 46 Ju26
Gmünd 🏳 A 61 Lo44
Gmünd 🏳 A 61 Lp42
Gmunden 🏳 A 61 Lo43
Gnadenkapelle Altötting 🏛 D 59 Ln42
Gniew 🏳 PL 64 Lf37
Gnarp 🏳 S 41 Ls28
Gnarrenburg 🏳 D 58 Lj38
Gnemasson 🏳 DY 188 La40
Gnesta 🏳 S 43 Ls31
Gniazdowo 🏳 PL 65 Mb38
Gniben 🏞 DK 42 Lm34
Gniew 🏳 PL 64 Lf37
Gniewino 🏳 PL 64 Lf36
Gnieyien 🏳 LB 186 Ke42
Gniezno 🏳 PL 64 Lr38
G'nit 🏳 SN 180 Kc37
Gnjilane 🏳 🇽🇰 KSV 68 Mb48
Gnoien 🏳 D 58 Ln37
Gnosonamidou 🏳 RG 186 Kf41
Gnosjö 🏳 S 43 Lp33
Goa 🏳 IND 116 Og38
Goa 🏳 RP 124 Rb39
Goageb 🏳 NAM 204 Lj59
Goalen Head 🏞 AUS 151 Se64
Goalpara 🏳 IND 120 Pf32
Goaso 🏳 GH 187 Kh42
Goat Fell 🏔 GB 48 Kp35
Goat Horn Mosque (Chahar Borjak) 🏛 AFG 98 Ob32
Goba 🏳 ETH 192 Mk42
Gobabis 🏳 NAM 201 Ma57
Gobabeb 🏳 NAM 204 Lh57
Gobernador Ayala 🏳 RA 280 Gg64
Gobernador Duval 🏳 RA 280 Gg65
Gobernador Gregores 🏳 RA 281 Gd69
Göle 🏳 TR 91 Nb25
Gobernador Mayano 🏳 RA 282 Gf69
Gobesh 🏳 AL 70 Ma50

Gobi Desert 🏞 CHN 106 Qa25
Gobindpur 🏳 IND 117 Pd34
Gobo 🏳 J 113 Rh29
Gobo 🏳 ZW 202 Me54
Goboboseberge 🏞 NAM 200 Lh56
Gobra Nawapara 🏳 IND 117 Pa35
Gobustan 🏳 AZ 91 Nh25
Göbyeyli 🏳 TR 71 Mh51
Gocchar 🏳 IND 117 Pb33
Goce Delčev 🏳 BG 68 Md49
Goce Delčev 🏳 BG 69 Md49
Goch 🏳 D 58 Lg39
Gochang Dolmen Site 🏛 ROK 112 Rd28
Gochas 🏳 NAM 204 Lk58
Go Cong Dong 🏳 VN 123 Qd40
Göd 🏳 H 67 Lu43
Godar-e Alizak 🏳 IR 96 Nj27
Godataïr 🏳 SUD 191 Md41
Godavari 🏳 IND 117 Pb33
Godawarari 🏳 NEP 115 Pa31
Godbout 🏳 CDN 240 Gg21
Godby 🏳 FIN 44 Lu30
Godda 🏳 IND 117 Pd33
Godda 🏳 SME 266 Hc43
Godé 🏳 BF 187 Kj39
Godech 🏳 BG 68 Mc47
Godcollore Viana 🏳 BR 267 Hh46
Godech 🏳 BG 68 Mc47
Godegode 🏳 EAT 197 Mj49
Godeli 🏳 ETH 193 Nb42
Godec 🏳 BG 68 Mc47
Godegode 🏳 EAT 197 Mj49
Godeli 🏳 ETH 193 Nb42
Goden 🏳 IND 115 Pa32
Godhavn = Qeqertarsuaq 🏳 DK 227 Hb05
Godhra 🏳 IND 116 Og34
Godinlabe 🏳 SP 195 Nd43
Godofredo Viana 🏳 BR 267 Hh46
Goderich 🏳 CDN 237 Fk24
Goderville 🏳 F 51 La41
Godo 🏳 IND 115 Pa32
Gödwarari 🏳 NEP 115 Pa31
Godoy Cruz 🏳 RA 280 Gf62
Gods Lake 🏳 CDN 227 Fb08
Gods Lake Narrows 🏳 CDN 227 Fb08
Godthåb = Nuuk 🏳 DK 227 Hb06
Godwin Austen, Mount 🏔 PK 115 Og28
Goe 🏳 PNG 155 Sa50
Goegap Nature Reserve 🏞 ZA 204 Lk60
Goes 🏳 NL 51 Ld39
Göfis 🏳 A 61 Lk43
Gogango 🏳 AUS 149 Se57
Gogo 🏳 AUS 143 Rc55
Gogo 🏳 WAN 188 Le41
Gogol 🏳 MOC 202 Mg55
Gogolin 🏳 PL 64 Ls40
Gogorrón, P.N. 🏞 MEX 246 Ek35
Gogounou 🏳 DY 188 Lb41
Gohad 🏳 IND 117 Ok32
Gohana 🏳 IND 114 Oj31
Gohitafla 🏳 CI 187 Kh42
Goiám 🏳 E 54 Lo39
Goianorte 🏳 BR 272 Hf50
Goiana 🏳 BR 273 Ka51
Goiandira 🏳 BR 275 Hf55
Goiânésia 🏳 BR 274 Hf53
Goianésia do Pará 🏳 BR 272 Hf47
Goiânia 🏳 BR 274 Hf54
Goianinha 🏳 BR 273 Ka51
Goianorte 🏳 BR 272 Hf50
Goiás 🏳 BR 274 He53
Goiás 🏳 BR 255 Ha11
Goiatins 🏳 BR 272 Hg49
Goiatuba 🏳 BR 274 Hf54
Goidhoo Atoll 🏞 MV 118 Og43
Goilkera 🏳 IND 117 Pc34
Goio-En 🏳 BR 276 Hd58
Goio-Erê 🏳 BR 276 Hd58
Goito 🏳 I 61 Ll45
Gojo 🏳 ETH 192 Mk41
Gojra 🏳 PK 99 Oj30
Gojsk 🏳 PL 65 Lu38
Gojyo 🏳 J 113 Rh28
Gokak 🏳 IND 116 Og37
Gokavaram 🏳 IND 117 Pa37
Gökçeada 🏞 TR 71 Mf50
Gökçedag 🏳 TR 91 Na26
Gökçekaya Baraji 🏞 TR 90 Mf25
Göksun 🏳 TR 90 Mj26
Gökova Körfezi 🏞 TR 71 Mh54
Göksu Milli Parkı 🏞 TR 90 Mg26
Göksun 🏳 TR 90 Mj26
Göktepe 🏳 TR 71 Mg53
Göl 🏳 N 42 Lj30
Gola 🏳 IND 117 Pc34
Golaghat 🏳 IND 120 Ph32
Golak-Kagari 🏔 WAN 191 Mc42
Golan 🏳 IL/SYR 90 Mh29
Golashkerd 🏳 IR 96 Nj31
Golbahar 🏳 AFG 97 Oe28
Gölbasi 🏳 TR 90 Nj31
Golbey 🏳 F 53 Lg42
Gölçük 🏳 TR 71 Mh54
Golconda 🏳 USA 234 Eb25
Gölcük 🏳 TR 71 Mh51
Gölcük 🏳 TR 90 Mf25
Golconda Fort 🏛 IND 116 Ok37
Gold Beach 🏳 USA 232 Dh24
Goldap 🏳 PL 65 Mc36
Gold Bridge 🏳 CDN 232 Dj20
Gold Coast 🏳 AUS 149 Sg59
Gold Coast 🏳 GH 187 Kh43
Goldcreek 🏳 USA 233 Fg24
Golddust 🏳 USA 239 Ff28
Golden 🏳 CDN 232 Ea20
Golden Bay 🏞 NZ 153 Tg66
Golden Beach 🏳 USA 232 Dh24
Golden Ears Prov. Park 🏞 CDN 232 Dj21
Golden Fleece 🏳 GUY 266 Ha42
Golden Gate 🏞 USA 243 Fk32
Golden Gate Bridge 🏛 USA 234 Dj27
Golden Gate Highlands N.P. 🏞 ZA 205 Me60
Golden Giant Mine 🏳 CDN 237 Fg22
Golden Hinde 🏔 CDN 232 Dh21
Golden Spike N.H.S. 🏛 USA 235 Ed25
Golden Temple = Jindian 🏛 CHN 121 Qb33
Golden Triangle 🏞 LAO/MYA/THA 121 Qa35
Golden Triangle Express 🏞 MYA 121 Pk33
Golden Valley 🏳 ZW 202 Me55
Gold River 🏳 CDN 232 Dh21
Gold Mine Tours 🏞 CDN 237 Fa21
Goldfield 🏳 USA 234 Ec27
Goldsboro 🏳 USA 239 Ga28
Goldstone 🏳 USA 234 Eb28
Goldsworthy 🏳 AUS 142 Qk56
Goldthwaite 🏳 USA 238 Fa30
Gölcücük 🏳 TR 71 Mg53
Göle 🏳 TR 91 Nb25
Golegã 🏳 P 55 Ko51
Golela 🏳 ZA 205 Mf59
Golen 🏳 IND 114 Og27
Goleniów 🏳 PL 64 Lq37
Golestan 🏳 AFG 99 Ob29
Golfe d'Ajaccio 🏞 F 62 Lj49
Golfe de Gabès 🏞 TN 176 Lf28

Golfe de Gascogne 🏞 F/E 52 Ks46
Golfe de Hammamet 🏞 TN 176 Lf27
Golfe de la Gonâve 🏞 RH 250 Gc36
Golfe de Porto 🏞 F 62 Lj48
Golfe de Sagone 🏞 F 62 Lj48
Golfe de Saint-Florent 🏞 F 60 Lk48
Golfe de Saint-Malo 🏞 F 50 Ks42
Golfe de Saint-Tropez 🏞 F 53 Lg47
Golfe de Tadjoura 🏞 DJI 193 Nb40
Golfe de Tunis 🏞 TN 176 Lf27
Golfe de Valinco 🏞 F 62 Lj49
Golfe du Lion 🏞 F 53 Ld47
Golfe du Morbihan 🏞 F 50 Ks43
Golfe de Coro 🏞 YV 265 Gf40
Golfito 🏳 CR 249 Fj41
Golfo Almirante Montt 🏞 RCH 282 Gd71
Golfo Aranci 🏳 I 62 Lk49
Golfo de Almeria 🏞 E 55 Ks54
Golfo de Ana Maria 🏞 C 243 Gb35
Golfo de Ancud 🏞 RCH 280 Gd66
Golfo de Arauco 🏞 RCH 280 Gc64
Golfo de Batabanó 🏞 C 243 Fj34
Golfo de Cádiz 🏞 E 55 Kn54
Golfo de Cariaco 🏞 YV 265 Gh40
Golfo de Cazones 🏞 C 243 Fk35
Golfo de Chiriquí 🏞 PA 249 Fj41
Golfo de Corcovado 🏞 RCH 280 Gd67
Golfo de Cupica 🏞 CO 264 Gb42
Golfo de Fonseca 🏞 ES/HN/NIC 248 Fg39
Golfo de Guanacaybo 🏞 C 243 Gb35
Golfo de Guayaquil 🏞 EC 268 Fk47
Golfo de Honduras 🏞 HN 248 Fg37
Golfo de Humboldt 🏞 CO 264 Gb42
Golfo de la Masma 🏞 E 54 Kn47
Golfo dell' Asinara 🏞 I 62 Lj49
Golfo de los Mosquitos 🏞 PA 249 Fk41
Golfo de Morrosquillo 🏞 CO 264 Gc41
Golfo de Nicoya 🏞 CR 249 Fh41
Golfo de Papagayo 🏞 CR 248 Fh40
Golfo de Paria 🏞 YV 265 Gh41
Golfo de Paria 🏞 PA 249 Fk41
Golfo de Peñas 🏞 RCH 282 Gc69
Golfo de San Blás 🏞 PA 249 Ga41
Golfo de San Miguel 🏞 PA 249 Ga41
Golfo de Tribugá 🏞 CO 264 Gb42
Golfo de Urabá 🏞 CO 264 Gb41
Golfo di Cagliari 🏞 I 62 Lk51
Golfo di Follónica 🏞 I 60 Ll48
Golfo di Gaeta 🏞 I 62 Lo49
Golfo di Gioia 🏞 I 63 Lq52
Golfo di Manfredónia 🏞 I 63 Lr49
Golfo di Nápoli 🏞 I 62 Lp50
Golfo di Óbia 🏞 I 62 Lk50
Golfo di Oristano 🏞 I 62 Lj50
Golfo di Orosei 🏞 I 62 Lk50
Golfo di Orosei e del Gennargentu, P.N. del 🏞 I 62 Lk50
Golfo di Palmas 🏞 I 62 Lj51
Golfo di Policastro 🏞 I 63 Lq51
Golfo di Squillace 🏞 I 63 Lr52
Golfo Dulce 🏞 CR 249 Fj41
Golfo Nuevo 🏞 RA 281 Gk67
Golfo San Esteban 🏳 RCH 282 Gc69
Golfo San Jorge 🏞 RA 282 Gg68
Golfo San José 🏞 RA 280 Gh67
Golfo San Matías 🏞 RA 280 Gh66
Golfo Trinidad 🏞 RCH 282 Gc70
Golfo Triste 🏞 YV 265 Gf40
Gölgeli Dağları 🏔 TR 90 Mf27
Gol Gol 🏳 AUS 151 Sb62
Gol Gumbaz (Bijapur) 🏛 IND 116 Og37
Gölhisar 🏳 TR 90 Mf27
Goli 🏳 EAU 194 Mf44
Goliad 🏳 USA 245 Fb31
Golica 🏳 BG 69 Mh48
Goličovo 🏳 RUS 72 Mj18
Golija 🏔 BIH 68 Lt47
Golina 🏳 PL 64 Ls38
Golmatongo 🏳 RDC 199 Md48
Golmberg 🏔 D 58 Lo38
Golmud 🏳 CHN 103 Ph27
Gölog Shan 🏔 CHN 106 Qa26
Golokuati 🏳 GH 187 La42
Golotf 🏳 RUS 91 Nd22
Golovin 🏳 USA 228 Bj13
Golovina 🏳 RUS 110 Rg21
Golovnino 🏳 RUS 111 Sc24
Golpayegan 🏳 IR 93 Nf29
Golspie 🏳 GB 48 Kr33
Gol Tappeh 🏳 IR 91 Ne27
Gol Tappeh 🏳 IR 91 Ne27
Golub-Dobrzyn 🏳 PL 65 Lu37
Golungo Alto 🏳 ANG 198 Lh50
Golyam 🏳 BG 69 Mf48
Gölyaka 🏳 TR 90 Mf25
Golynki 🏳 RUS 63 Me36
Gománcheng 🏳 CHN 108 Qf33
Gomba 🏳 WAN 189 Lh42
Gombe 🏳 EAT 197 Mh48
Gombe-Matadi 🏳 RDC 198 Lh48
Gombe Streams N.P. 🏞 EAT 196 Me48
Gomboro 🏳 BF 187 Kj39
Gombouasougou 🏳 BF 187 Kk39
Gómez Carneiro, T.I. 🏞 BR 274 Hc54
Gómez Farias 🏳 MEX 244 Ej31
Gómez Palacio 🏳 MEX 245 Ej33
Gómez Rendón = Progreso 🏳 EC 268 Fk47
Gomishan 🏳 IR 96 Nh26
Gommern 🏳 D 58 Lm38
Gomon 🏳 CI 187 Kh43
Gomui 🏳 PK 115 Oj28
Gommu 🏳 RI 131 Rd46
Gomti 🏳 IND 117 Pb33
Gonáives 🏳 RH 250 Gc36
Gonave 🏳 MV 202 Mf56
Gonbad-e Kavus 🏳 IR 96 Nh26
Gonçalves Dias 🏳 BR 272 Hh49
Goncelin 🏳 F 53 Lf45
Gonda 🏳 IND 117 Pb32
Gondal 🏳 IND 116 Of34
Gondar 🏳 ETH 192 Mj39
Gondia 🏳 IND 117 Pa34
Göreme Milli Parkı 🏞 TR 90 Mh26
Gore 🏳 ETH 192 Mh41
Gore 🏳 TCH 190 Lj41
Gore 🏳 NZ 153 Te69
Gore Highway 🛣 AUS 149 Sf59
Goreli 🏳 BF 187 Kk39
Gorelki 🏳 RUS 72 Mj18
Gorelovo 🏳 RUS 63 Ma34
Gorey 🏳 IRL 47 Kd37
Gorgan 🏳 IR 96 Ng27
Gorge d'Arak 🏞 DZ 176 Lb33
Gorges Li 🏞 DZ 176 Lc30
Gorges d'Aouli 🏞 MA 175 Kh29
Gorges de Kola la CAM 189 Lh42
Gorges de l'Apijk 🏞 F 53 Le46
Gorges de la Piche 🏞 F 53 Le46
Gorges de la Restonica 🏞 F 60 Lk48
Gorges de l'Asco 🏞 F 60 Lk48
Gorges de l'Oued Seldja 🏞 TN 176 Le29
Gorges de l'Oudinguuer 🏞 TCH 184 Lk38
Gorges de Lukwila 🏞 RDC 199 Lk49
Gorges de Spelunca 🏞 F 60 Lj48
Gorges de Talari 🏞 RMM 186 Ke39
Gorges de Tighanimine 🏞 DZ 176 Ld28
Gorges Diasso 🏞 RCB 198 Lg48
Gorges du Dadès 🏞 MA 175 Kg30
Gorges du Kadéï 🏞 RCA 190 Lh44
Gorges du Keran 🏞 TG 187 La41
Gorges du Prunelli 🏞 F 62 Lj49
Gorges du Verdon 🏞 F 53 Lg47
Gorges du Ziz 🏞 MA 175 Kh30
Gorgona 🏳 ETH 192 Mh41
Gorgota 🏳 RO 69 Mg46
Gorham 🏳 USA 241 Gd24
Gori 🏳 GE 91 Nb24
Gorichem 🏳 NL 51 Le39
Gorinchem 🏳 NL 51 Le39
Goris 🏳 ARM 91 Nd25
Goritsa 🏳 BG 69 Mh48
Gorizia 🏳 I 61 Lo45
Gorki 🏳 BY 72 Mf18
Gorki 🏳 RUS 72 Mk17
Görkiz 🏳 NEP 115 Pc31
Gorkha 🏳 NEP 115 Pc31
Gorkhi-Terelj Nature Reserve 🏞 MNG 104 Qd21

Gorki – Gulf of Gdansk

Gorki RUS 44 Mk31
Gørlev DK 42 Lm35
Gorlice PL 65 Mb41
Görlitz D 58 Lp39
Gorman USA 234 Ea28
Gormanstown IRL 47 Ko37
Gorna Bešovica BG 68 Md47
Gorna Orjahovica BG 69 Mf47
Gorna Studena BG 69 Mf47
Gorni Okol BG 68 Md48
Gornjackij RUS 73 Na21
Gornja Radgona SLO 66 Lq44
Gornja Sabanta SRB 68 Ma47
Gornje Peulje BIH 61 Lr46
Gornji Jabolčište MK 68 Mb49
Gornji Milanovac SRB 68 Ma46
Gornji Vakuf = Uskoplje BIH 61 Ls47
Górno PL 65 Ma40
Gorno-Altajsk RUS 88 Pb08
Gorno-Altay RUS 88 Pb08
Gornovodnoe RUS 111 Rh24
Gornozavodsk RUS 111 Sa22
Goro ETH 192 Na42
Gorodec RUS 72 Nb17
Gorodišče RUS 72 Nc19
Gorogoro RI 131 Rd46
Goroka PNG 155 Sc49
Goroka Show PNG 155 Sc49
Gorom-Gorom BF 181 Kk38
Gorondema ZW 202 Me54
Gorong RI 131 Rf47
Gorongosa MOC 202 Mh55
Gorongoza MOC 202 Mh55
Gorongoza, P.N. de MOC 203 Mh55
Gorontalo RI 125 Rb45
Goronyo WAN 182 Lc39
Górowo Iławeckie PL 65 Ma36
Gorrie AUS 146 Rg53
Gorron F 50 Ku42
Goršečnoe RUS 72 Mj20
Gór Stołowych, P.N. PL 64 Lr40
Gort IRL 47 Km37
Górtis GR 71 Me55
Görukle TR 69 Mj50
Gorumna Island IRL 47 Kl37
gory Byrranga RUS 88 Pc04
gory Koymatdag TM 96 Nh25
gory Prževal'skogo RUS 111 Rg24
Gorzkowice PL 65 Lu39
Gorzków-Osada PL 65 Md40
Gorzów Wielkopolski PL 64 Lq38
Gorzyń PL 64 Lq38
Gosau A 61 Lo43
Goschen Strait PNG 156 Sf51
Gościkowo Jordanowo PL 64 Lq38
Gosford AUS 151 Sf62
Gosforth GB 49 Kr36
Goshogawara J 111 Sa25
Goshute Ind. Res. USA 235 Ec26
Goslar D 58 Ll39
Gospić HR 61 Lq46
Gossas SN 180 Kb38
Gossi RMM 181 Kk38
Gossinga SUD 191 Mc41
Gostilja BG 69 Me47
Gostivar MK 68 Ma49
Göstling A 61 Lp43
Gostomia PL 64 Lr37
Gostyń PL 64 Ls39
Gostynin PL 65 Lu38
Göta kanal S 43 Lp32
Göta kanal S 43 Lr32
Göteborg S 42 Lm33
Götene S 43 Lo32
Gotha D 58 Ll40
Goth Ahmad PK 99 Od33
Gothenburg USA 236 Ek25
Gothèye RN 182 La39
Gothiahalvøya N 38 Lk06
Gotia IND 117 Pa36
Gotland S 43 Lt33
Götlunda S 43 Lq31
Goto-retto J 113 Re29
Gotska Sandön S 43 Lu32
Gotska Sandön n.p. S 43 Lu32
Gotsu J 113 Rg28
Göttingen D 58 Lk39
Gottskär S 42 Lm33
Gouandé DY 187 La40
Gouatchi RCA 190 Ma43
Goubangzi CHN 110 Ra25
Goubi TG 187 La41
Goubouna DY 188 La41
Goucester PNG 156 Se48
Gouchang CHN 121 Qc33
Gouchi RN 182 Le39
Gouda NL 51 Le38
Gouda ZA 204 Lk62
Goudiri SN 180 Kd38
Goudomp SN 186 Kc39
Goudoumaria RN 183 Lf39
Gouéké RG 186 Kf41
Gouendo RMM 187 Kg39
Gouffre de Bogbaté RCA 190 Lk43
Gouffre de Friouato MA 175 Kh28
Gouga RCB 190 Lk44
Goûgaram RN 182 Ld36
Gough Island GB 163 Kb13
Gouiné CI 187 Kg42
Gouiret Moussa DZ 176 Lb30
Gouka DY 188 La41
Goulaonfla CI 187 Kg42
Goulburn AUS 151 Se63
Gouldtown CDN 233 Eg20
Goulfey CAM 189 Lh39
Goulia CI 187 Kg40
Goulmina MA 175 Kh30
Goumbatou TCH 184 Mb40
Goumbi RN 182 Lc39
Goumbou RMM 181 Kg38
Gouménissa GR 70 Mc50
Gouméré CI 187 Kj42
Goúmero GR 70 Mb53
Gouna CAM 189 Lg41
Gounatolo SOL 157 Ta50
Gounda RCA 190 Ma41
Goundam RMM 181 Kj37
Goundi TCH 190 Lj41
Gounou Gaya TCH 190 Lh41
Gourak AFG 99 Oc29
Gourara DZ 175 La31
Gouray RIM 180 Kd38
Gouraya DZ 176 La27
Gouraya, P.N. de DZ 176 Lc27
Gourcy BF 187 Kj39
Gourdon F 52 Lb46
Gouré RN 182 Lf38
Goûr Ghaoua DZ 182 La33
Gourie JA 250 Gb36
Gourin F 50 Kr42
Gouritsmond ZA 204 Ma63
Gourjhamar IND 117 Ok34
Gourma-Rharous RMM 181 Kk37
Gourmeur TCH 184 Ma37
Gournay-en-Bray F 51 Lb41
Gourniá GR 71 Mf55
Gourrama MA 175 Kh29
Goush LAR 176 Lf29
Gouveia BR 275 Hj55
Gouveia P 54 Kn50
Gouvelândia BR 274 He55
Gouverneur USA 241 Gc23
Gouzé RCA 190 Lj42
Gouzon F 53 Lc44
Gov'-Altay MNG 101 Ph22
Gov' Altayn Nuruu MNG 76 Pb05
Goveđari HR 61 Ls48
Gove Peninsula AUS 146 Rj52
Goverdor Celso Ramos BR 277 Hf59
Goverdor Garmendia RA 279 Gh59
Goverdor Ingeniero V.Virasoro RA 276 Hb60
Governador Eugênio Barros BR 272 Hh48
Governador, T.I. BR 272 Hg48
Governador Valadares BR 275 Hk55
Government Point USA 234 Dk28
Governor Generoso RP 125 Rd42
Governor's Harbour BS 243 Gb33
Govindapalle IND 117 Pb36
Govurdak TM 97 Od27
Gowanda USA 237 Ga24
Gowhar Shad Mosque IR 96 Nk27
Gowhar Shar IR 98 Oa31
Gowidlino PL 64 Ls36
Gowmal Kalay AFG 99 Oe29
Gowran Park IRL 47 Kn38
Gowrie Park AUS 151 Sd66
Goya RA 276 Ha60
Göyçay AZ 91 Nd25
Goyerkata IND 120 Pe32
Goyllarisquizga PE 269 Gb51
Goyoum CAM 189 Lg43
Gozare AFG 98 Ob28
Goz-Beida TCH 184 Ma39
Gozdnica PL 64 Lq39
Gözne TR 90 Mh27
Gozo M 63 Lp54
Goz Regeb SUD 185 Mh37
Graaff-Reinet ZA 205 Mc62
Graafwater ZA 204 Lk62
Grabarka PL 65 Mc38
Graben-Neudorf D 59 Lj41
Grabo CI 187 Kg43
Grábóc H 67 Lt44
Grabovica SRB 68 Lu46
Grabovica SRB 68 Mc46
Grabow D 58 Lm37
Grabów nad Prosną PL 64 Lt39
Grabowno PL 64 Lr37
Grabowo PL 65 Mc36
Graça Aranha BR 272 Hh48
Gračac HR 61 Lq46
Gračanica BIH 61 Ls47
Gračanica BIH 68 Lt46
Gračanica SRB 68 Mb48
Graçay F 53 Lb43
Gracefield CDN 237 Gb22
Gracemere AUS 149 Sf57
Graceville USA 236 Fb23
Gracias HN 248 Ff38
Gradac HR 61 Lq45
Gradačac BIH 68 Lt46
Gradaús BR 272 He49
Gradec BG 68 Mc46
Gradešnica MK 68 Mb49
Gradgery AUS 149 Sd61
Gradina BG 69 Mf47
Grădinari RO 68 Mb45
Gradište HR 61 Lt45
Grădistea RO 68 Md46
Grădiștea RO 69 Mh46
Grădiștea de Munte RO 68 Md45
Grădiștea de Munte-Cioclovina, P.N. RO 68 Md45
Gradnica BG 69 Me48
Grado E 54 Ko47
Grado I 61 Lo45
Gradojević SRB 68 Lu46
Gradski bedemi MNE 68 Lt48
Grady USA 238 Ej28
Grady USA 239 Fe28
Grafenau D 59 Lo42
Gräfenberg D 59 Lm41
Gräfenhainichen D 58 Ln39
Grafenwöhr D 59 Lm41
Gråfjell N 42 Lk30
Grafton AUS 149 Sg60
Grafton USA 236 Fb21
Grafton USA 241 Ga26
Graham CDN 236 Fe21
Graham USA 238 Fa29
Graham Island USA 230 Dd19
Graham Lake CDN 231 Ec17
Graham Land 286 Gd32
Grahamstad ZA 205 Md62
Grahamstown ZA 205 Md62
Graiguenamanagh IRL 47 Ko38
Grain Coast LB 186 Ke43
Grainfield USA 238 Ek26
Grainton USA 238 Ek25
Grajagan RI 129 Qh50
Grajaú BR 272 Hg48
Grajewo PL 65 Mc37
Grajvoron RUS 72 Mh20
Gram DK 42 Lk35
Grama BR 274 He55
Gramado BR 276 He60
Graman AUS 149 Sf60
Gramat F 52 Lb46
Grambling USA 238 Fd29
Grammichele I 63 Lp53
Gramphu IND 115 Oj29
Grampian USA 237 Ga25
Grampianfjella N 38 Lf06
Grampian Mountains GB 48 Kq34
Grampians N.P. AUS 150 Sb64
Gramsh AL 70 Ma50
Gramzow D 58 Lo37
Gran N 42 Ll30
Granaatboskolk ZA 204 Lk61
Granada CO 264 Gc42
Granada CO 264 Gd44
Granada E 55 Kr53
Granada NIC 248 Fh40
Granada USA 238 Ej26
Gran Altiplanicie Central RA 282 Gf70
Granard IRL 47 Kn37
Gran Bajo del Gualicho RA 280 Gh66
Gran Bajo Oriental RA 282 Gf69
Granbori SME 266 Hc44
Granbury USA 238 Fb29
Granby CDN 241 Gd23
Granby USA 235 Eh25
Gran Caldera GQ 188 Le44
Gran Campo de Hielo Patagónico RA/RCH 282 Gd70
Gran Canaria E 174 Kc32
Gran Chaco RA/PY 279 Gj58
Grandas de Salime E 54 Ko47
Grand Bahama Island BS 243 Ga32
Grand Ballon F 53 Lh43
Grand Banks of Newfoundland CDN 241 Hc22
Grand Barra DJI 193 Nb40
Grand-Bassam CI 187 Kj43
Grand Bend CDN 237 Fk24
Grand Bérard F 53 Lg46
Grand-Bérébi CI 187 Kg43
Grand Bruit CDN 241 Ha22
Grandcamp-Maisy F 50 Kt41
Grand Canal IRL 47 Kn37
Grand Canyon USA 235 Ed27
Grand Canyon USA 235 Ed27
Grand Canyon Caverns USA 235 Ed28
Grand Canyon du Verdon F 53 Lg47
Grand Canyon N.P. USA 235 Ed27
Grand Cayman GB 243 Fk36
Grand Centre CDN 233 Ee18
Grand Cess LB 186 Kf43
Grand Colombier F 53 Lg45
Grand Combin CH 60 Lh45
Grand Coule USA 232 Ea22
Grande Cache CDN 231 Ea19
Grande Cayemite RH 250 Gd36
Grande-Entrée CDN 240 Gk22
Grande Île SY 206 Nd50
Grande Kabylie DZ 176 Lb27
Grande Oriente BR 270 Gg49
Grande Prairie CDN 231 Ea18
Grand Erg de Bilma RN 183 Lg36
GrandesBergonnes CDN 240 Gf21
Grande Sertão Veredas, P.N. BR 275 Hh53
Grand Etang N.P. WG 251 Gk39
Grande Terre F 251 Gk37
Grande Terre SY 206 Nd50
Grande-Vallée CDN 240 Gh21
Grande Village USA 245 Ej31
Grand Falls CDN 240 Gg22
Grand Falls CDN 241 Hc21
Grandfalls USA 245 Ej30
Grand Forks CDN 232 Ea21
Grand Forks USA 236 Fb22
Grand Gorge USA 241 Gc24
Grand Haven USA 237 Fg24
Grand Island USA 238 Fa25
Grand Isle USA 239 Ff31
Grand Isle S.P. USA 239 Ff31
Grand Junction USA 235 Ef26
Grand-Lahou CI 187 Kh43
Grand Lake CDN 240 Gg22
Grand Lake CDN 241 Hb21
Grand Lake USA 239 Fd31
Grand Lake USA 240 Gf23
Grand Marais USA 236 Fe22
Grand Marais USA 237 Fh22
Grand-Mère CDN 240 Gd22
Grand Mesa USA 235 Eg26
Grândola P 55 Km52
Grand-Popo DY 188 La42
Grand Portage USA 236 Ff22
Grand Portage Ind. Res. USA 236 Ff22
Grand Portage Nat. Mon. USA 236 Ff22
Grand Rapids CDN 231 Ed17
Grand Rapids USA 236 Fd22
Grand Rapids USA 237 Fh24
Grand Récif de Cook F 158 Tb55
Grand Récif de Koumac F 158 Tc56
Grand Récif Mathieu F 158 Tc56
Grand Récif Mengalia F 158 Tc56
Grand Récif Sud F 158 Td57
Grand-Remous CDN 240 Gc22
Grandrieu F 53 Ld46
Grand River Nat. Grassland USA 233 Ej23
Grand Rivière Noire MS 207 Nj56
Grand Ronde USA 232 Dj23
Grand-Santi-Papaichton F 266 Hc43
Grand Staircase Escalante National Monument USA 235 Ee27
Grand Teton USA 233 Ee24
Grand Teton N.P. USA 233 Ee24
Grand Traverse Bay USA 237 Fh23
Grand Turk GB 250 Ge35
Grand Turk Island GB 250 Ge35
Grandview CDN 236 Ek20
Grand View USA 232 Eb24
Grandvillars F 53 Lg43
Grandvilliers F 51 Lb41
Grañén E 56 Ku49
Graneros RCH 280 Ge63
Grangärde S 43 Lp30
Grangemouth GB 48 Kr34
Granger USA 232 Dk22
Grängesberg S 43 Lp30
Grangeville USA 232 Eb23
Granisle CDN 230 Dg18
Granite Bay CDN 232 Dh20
Granite Downs AUS 148 Rg59
Granite Falls USA 236 Fc23
Granite Peak AUS 144 Qj63
Granite Peak AUS 144 Ra58
Granite Peak USA 232 Eb25
Granite Peak USA 235 Ed25
Granites Mine, The AUS 143 Rf56
Granítis GR 69 Md49
Granja BR 273 Hk47
Granja Caimã BR 274 Hb56
Grankullavik S 43 Ls33
Gränna S 43 Lp32
Granö S 41 Lu26
Granollers E 57 Lc49
Gran Pajatén PE 268 Gb49
Gran Pajonal PE 269 Gc51
Gran Pampa Salada BOL 278 Gg56
Gran Paradiso I 60 Lh45
Gran Paradiso, P.N. del I 60 Lh45
Gran Piedra, P.N. C 250 Gc35
Gran Pilastro = Hochfeiler A/I 60 Lm44
Gran Quivira USA 235 Eg28
Gran Sasso d'Italia I 61 Lo48
Gran Sasso e Monti della Laga, P.N. del I 61 Lo48
Gransee D 58 Lo37
Gransherad N 42 Lk31
Grant USA 238 Ek25
Gran Tarajal E 174 Kc31
Grant City USA 238 Fc25
Grantham GB 49 Ku38
Grant Island AUS 146 Rg51
Grant-Kohrs Ranch N.H.S. USA 233 Ed22
Grantown-on-Spey GB 48 Kr33
Grants USA 235 Eg28
Grant's Birthplace St. Mem. USA 239 Fh26
Grants Pass USA 232 Dj24
Granville AUS 149 Sc59
Granville F 50 Kt42
Granville USA 241 Gd24
Grão Mogol BR 275 Hj54
Grapska BIH 68 Lt46
Grasa, Cerro la RA 280 Ge65
Gräsgård S 43 Lr34
Graskop ZA 205 Mf58
Grasmere USA 232 Ec24
Gräsö S 43 Lt30
Grassano I 63 Lr50
Grassau D 59 Ln43
Grass Creek USA 233 Ef24
Grasse F 53 Lg47
Grasslands N.P. CDN 233 Eg21
Grass Patch AUS 145 Ra62
Grassrange USA 233 Ef22
Grass River Prov. Park CDN 233 Ek18
Grass Valley USA 234 Dk26
Grassy AUS 151 Sc66
Grassy Butte USA 233 Ej22
Grassy Island N.H.S. CDN 240 Gk23
Gråsten DK 42 Lk36
Grästorp S 42 Ln32
Grates Cove CDN 241 Hd21
Gratwein A 61 Lq43
Graulhet F 52 Lb47
Graus E 56 La48
Gravataí BR 276 He60
Grávavencsellő H 67 Mb42
Gravedona I 60 Lk44
Gravelbourg CDN 233 Eg21
Gravelines F 51 Lc40
Gravelotte ZA 202 Mf57
Gravenhurst CDN 237 Ga23
Grave Peak USA 232 Ec22
Graverings RB 205 Md58
Gravesend GB 49 La39
Graviá GR 70 Mc52
Gravier F 266 Hd43
Gravina in Púglia I 63 Lr50
Gravina Island USA 230 Dd18
Gravures rupestres DZ 176 Lb28
Gravures rupestres (Aozou) TCH 183 Lj35
Gravures rupestres (Bambari) RCA 190 Ma43
Gravures rupestres de Dabous RN 182 Ld37
Gravures rupestres de Gonoa TCH 183 Lj35
Gravures rupestres de Kongo Moumba G 198 Lf46
Gravures rupestres de Laghouat DZ 176 Lb29
Gravures rupestres de Mertoutek DZ 182 Lc33
Gravures rupestres (Lengo) RCA 190 Mb43
Gravures rupestres (Mapé) RCA 190 Mb43
Gravures rupestres (Nzako) RCA 190 Mb43
Gravures rupestres (Oued Ouret) DZ 176 Le32
Gravures rupestres (Pobé Mengao) BF 187 Kk39
Gravures rupestres (Taghit) DZ 175 Kj30
Gravures rupestres (Zouar) TCH 183 Lj35
Gray F 53 Lf43
Gray USA 242 Fj29
Grayland USA 232 Dh22
Grayling USA 237 Fh23
Grayling Fork USA/CDN 229 Ck12
Graz A 61 Lq43
Gražiškiai LT 45 Mc36
Great Artesian Basin AUS 134 Sa12
Great Astrolab Reef FJI 159 Tk55
Great Australian Bight 134 Ra13
Great Ayton GB 49 Kt36
Great Bahama Bank 243 Ga33
Great Barrier Island NZ 152 Th64
Great Barrier Reef AUS 134 Sa11
Great Barrier Reef Marine Park AUS 147 Sc52
Great Barrington USA 241 Gd24
Great Basalt Wall N.P. AUS 147 Sc55
Great Basin USA 234 Eb26
Great Basin N.P. USA 235 Ec26
Great Bear Lake CDN 226 Dd05
Great Belt DK 42 Ll35
Great Bend USA 238 Fa26
Great Bitter Lake ET 179 Mg30
Great Britain GB 26 La04
Great Channel 122 Ph42
Great Coco Island MYA 122 Pg38
Great Dismal Swamp N.W.R USA 242 Gb27
Great Divide Basin USA 235 Ef25
Great Dividing Range AUS 151 Sd64
Great Dividing Range AUS 134 Sa11
Great Eastern Erg DZ 162 La07
Great Eastern Highway AUS 144 Qj61
Greater Antilles 210 Ga08
Greater Hinggan Range CHN 76 Qb05
Greater Sunda Islands RI 76 Qa10
Great Exhibition Bay NZ 152 Tg63
Great Exuma Island BS 243 Gb34
Great Falls USA 233 Ee22
Great Falls USA 242 Fk28
Great Fish River Reserves ZA 205 Md62
Great Guana Cay BS 243 Gb32
Great Guana Cay BS 243 Gb33
Great Harbour Cay BS 243 Ga33
Great Himalayan N.P. IND 115 Oj29
Great Inagua Island BS 250 Gd35
Great Isaac BS 243 Ga32
Great Karoo ZA 204 Ma62
Great Keppel Island AUS 149 Sf57
Great Limpopo Transfrontier Park ZW/ZA/MOC 202 Mf57
Great Malvern GB 49 Ks38
Great Mercury Island NZ 152 Th64
Great Mosque CHN 106 Qf25
Great Nicobar Island IND 122 Pg42
Great North East Channel AUS 147 Sb51
Great Northern Highway AUS 142 Qk57
Great Northern Highway AUS 143 Rd54
Great Ocean Road AUS 151 Sb65
Great Ormes Head GB 49 Kr37
Great Oyster Bay AUS 151 Se67
Great Palm Island AUS 147 Sd55
Great Papuan Plateau PNG 155 Sb49
Great Pedro Bluff JA 250 Gb37
Great Plain of the Koukdjuak CDN 227 Gb05
Great Plains CDN/USA 210 Ea04
Great Rift Valley 162 Mb10
Great Ruaha EAT 197 Mj49
Great Sale Cay BS 243 Ga32
Great Salt Lake USA 235 Ed25
Great Salt Lake Desert USA 235 Ed25
Great Sand Dunes N.P. USA 235 Eh27
Great Sand Hills CDN 233 Ef20
Great Sandy Desert AUS 134 Ra12
Great Sandy Desert USA 232 Dk24
Great Sandy N.P. AUS 149 Sg58
Great Sea Reef FJI 159 Tk54
Great Sea Reef FJI 159 Tk54
Great Slave Lake CDN 226 Eb06
Great Smoky Mts. N.P. USA 242 Fj28
Great Smoky Mts. Railroad USA 242 Fj28
Great Tiras NAM 204 Lj59
Great Valley USA 241 Gb25
Great Victoria Desert AUS 134 Ra12
Great Victoria Desert Nature Reserve AUS 145 Re60
Great Wall ANT 287 Ha30
Great Western Erg DZ 175 Kk30
Great Western Tiers AUS 151 Sd66
Great Western Torres Island MYA 122 Pj40
Great White Heron N.W.R. USA 243 Fk33
Great Yarmouth GB 49 Lb38
Great Zab IRQ 91 Nb28
Great Zimbabwe National Monument ZW 202 Mf56
Grebbestad S 42 Lm32
Grebenhain D 59 Lk40
Grębocin PL 64 Lt37
Grecco ROU 276 Hb62
Greece GR 27 Ma06
Greeley USA 235 Eh25
Greeley USA 236 Fa25
Green Bay USA 237 Fg23
Green Bay USA 237 Fg23
Greenboro USA 242 Ga27
Greenbush USA 236 Fb21
Green Cape AUS 151 Sf64
Green Cay BS 243 Gb33
Green Cove Springs USA 242 Fk31
Greene USA 241 Gc24
Greeneville USA 242 Fj27
Greenfield USA 234 Dk27
Greenfield USA 236 Fc25
Greenfield USA 238 Fd27
Greenfield USA 239 Fh26
Greenfield USA 239 Fj26
Greenfield USA 241 Gd24
Green Head AUS 144 Qh60
Greenhill Island AUS 146 Rg51
Green Island AUS 147 Sd54
Green Island = Lutao RC 109 Ra34
Green Island Bay RP 124 Qk40
Green Islands PNG 157 Sh48
Green Lake CDN 233 Eg18
Greenland DK 227 Hd03
Greenland Basin 26 Kb02
Greenland Sea 26 Kb02
Greenlaw GB 48 Ks35
Greenly Island AUS 150 Rh63
Green Mts. USA 241 Gd24
Greenock GB 48 Kq35
Greenodd GB 49 Kr36
Greenough AUS 144 Qh60
Green Point ZA 205 Mf61
Green River PNG 155 Sa47
Green River USA 235 Ee26
Green River USA 235 Ef25
Green River Basin USA 235 Ef24
Greensboro USA 239 Fg29
Greensboro USA 242 Fj29
Greensburg USA 237 Ga25
Greensburg USA 238 Fa27
Greensburg USA 239 Fh26
Greensburg USA 239 Fh27
Green Turtle Cay BS 243 Gb32
Greenvale AUS 147 Sc55
Greenview USA 232 Dj25
Greenville CDN 230 Df18
Greenville LB 186 Kf43
Greenville USA 237 Fh24
Greenville USA 237 Fh25
Greenville USA 237 Fk25
Greenville USA 238 Fb29
Greenville USA 239 Fe27
Greenville USA 239 Fe29
Greenville USA 239 Fg27
Greenville USA 239 Fg30
Greenville USA 239 Fh29
Greenville USA 240 Gf23
Greenville USA 242 Fj28
Greenville USA 242 Gb28
Greenwater USA 232 Dk22
Greenwater Lake Prov. Park CDN 233 Ej19
Greenwich GB 49 La39
Greenwood AUS 144 Qj59
Greenwood CDN 232 Ea21
Greenwood USA 238 Fc28
Greenwood USA 239 Fe29
Greenwood USA 239 Fg26
Greenwood USA 242 Fj28
Greer USA 232 Eb22
Greer USA 242 Fj28
Greetsiel D 58 Lh37
Gregbeu CI 187 Kg42
Gregory USA 236 Fa24
Gregory Downs AUS 146 Rk55
Gregory N.P. AUS 146 Rf53
Gregory N.P. AUS 146 Rf54
Gregory Range AUS 142 Ra56
Gregory Range AUS 147 Sb55
Gregory Springs AUS 147 Sc55
Greifenburg A 61 Lo44
Greifswald D 58 Lo36
Greifswalder Bodden D 58 Lo36
Grein A 66 Lp42
Greiz D 59 Ln40
Gremiha RUS 88 Md05
Gremjač'e RUS 72 Mk20
Grenaa DK 42 Ll34
Grenada CO 264 Gc41
Grenada USA 239 Ff29
Grenada WG 251 Gk40
Grenada 251 Gk39
Grenade F 52 Lb47
Grenade-sur-l'Adour F 52 Ku47
Grenadines WV 251 Gk39
Grenchen CH 60 Lh43
Grendill IS 46 Ke26
Grenen DK 42 Ll33
Grenfell AUS 151 Se62
Grenfell CDN 233 Ej20
Grenfell House CDN 241 Hc20
Grenivík IS 46 Kb25
Grenoble F 53 Lf45
Grenville WG 251 Gk39
Gresford AUS 151 Sf62
Gresham USA 232 Dj23
Gresham USA 242 Ga29
Gresham ZW 202 Mf54
Gresik RI 129 Qg49
Gressåmoen n.p. N 40 Lo26
Gressoney-la-Trinité I 60 Lh45
Gretna Green GB 48 Kr36
Greve in Chianti I 60 Lm47
Greven D 58 Lh38
Grevená GR 70 Mb50
Grevenbroich D 58 Lg39
Grevenmacher L 51 Lg41
Grevesmühlen D 58 Lm37
Greve Strand DK 42 Ln35
Grevie S 42 Ln34
Greybull USA 233 Ef23
Grey Cairns GB 48 Kr32
Grey Hunter Peak CDN 229 Dc14
Greylingstad ZA 205 Me59
Grey Mare's Tail GB 48 Kr35
Greymouth NZ 153 Tf67
Grey Range AUS 148 Sb60
Grey Range AUS 149 Sc59
Grey River CDN 241 Hb22
Greystone ZW 202 Me56
Greystones IRL 47 Ko37
Greyton ZA 204 Lk63
Greytown ZA 205 Mf60
Grgurnica MK 68 Mb49
Grianan of Aileach IRL 47 Kn35
Gribanovskij RUS 72 Na20
Gribbelt Island CDN 230 Df19
Gridley USA 234 Dk26
Griekwastad ZA 204 Mb60
Grieskirchen A 66 Lo42
Griffin CDN 233 Ej21
Griffin USA 239 Fh29
Griffin Point USA 229 Cj10
Griffith AUS 151 Sd63
Grigor'evskoe RUS 72 Nb17
Grigoriopol MD 73 Me22
Grik MAL 126 Qa43
Grillby S 43 Ls31
Grillon, Mount USA 230 Db16
Grimari RCA 190 Ma43
Grimma D 58 Ln39
Grimmen D 58 Lo36
Grimsby GB 49 Ku37
Grimsey IS 46 Kb24
Grímsey IS 46 Kb24
Grimshaw CDN 231 Eb17
Grímsstaðir IS 46 Kd25
Grimstad N 42 Lj32
Grimsvötn IS 46 Kc26
Grindavík IS 46 Js27
Grindelwald CH 60 Lj44
Grindsted DK 42 Lj35
Grinkiškis LT 45 Md35
Grinnell USA 236 Fd25
Grinnel Peninsula CDN 227 Fb03
Grintavec SLO 66 Lp44
Gripsholm S 43 Ls31
Griquatown ZA 204 Mb60
Griquet CDN 241 Hc20
Grise Fiord CDN 227 Fc03
Griškabūdis LT 45 Md36
Grisolles F 52 Lb47
Grisslehamn S 43 Lt30
Grissom Air Mus. USA 237 Fg25
Grivenskaja RUS 73 Mk23
Grivița RO 69 Mh46
Grizzly Bear Mountain CDN 231 Dk13
Grjady RUS 72 Mf16
Grjazi RUS 72 Mk19
Grmeč BIH 61 Lr46
Groaíras BR 273 Hk47
Groais Island CDN 241 Hc20
Grobiņa LV 45 Mb34
Groblersdal ZA 205 Me58
Groblershoop ZA 204 Mb60
Grobniza BG 69 Mf48
Grocka SRB 68 Ma46
Gródek PL 65 Md37
Gröditz D 58 Lo39
Gródki PL 65 Ma37
Gródki PL 65 Mc40
Grodków PL 64 Ls40
Grodziczno PL 65 Lu37
Grodzisk Mazowiecki PL 65 Ma38
Grodzisk Wielkopolski PL 64 Lr38
Groeninge-Museum B 51 Ld39
Groenriviersmond ZA 204 Lj61
Groesbeek ZA 202 Me57
Groix F 50 Kr43
Groix F 50 Kr43
Grójec PL 65 Ma39
Grombalia TN 176 Lf27
Grömitz D 58 Ll36
Gromnik PL 65 Ma41
Gröna Lund S 43 Ls31
Gronau D 58 Lh38
Grong N 40 Ln26
Grong Grong AUS 151 Sd63
Gröningen D 58 Lm39
Groningen NL 51 Lg37
Groningen SME 266 Hc43
Groninger Museum NL 51 Lg37
Gronlid CDN 233 Eh19
Grønligrotta N 38 Lp24
Grönskåra S 43 Lq33
Grootberg NAM 200 Lh55
Grootdrink ZA 204 Ma60
Groote Eylandt AUS 146 Rj53
Groote Eylandt A.L. AUS 146 Rj53
Grootfontein NAM 200 Lk55
Groot Henar SME 266 Hb43
Groot Jongensfontein ZA 204 Ma63
Groot Karasberge NAM 204 Lk59
Grootkraal ZA 204 Mb62
Groot Marico ZA 205 Md58
Grootrivierhoogte ZA 204 Mb62
Groot Waterberg NAM 200 Lj55
Grootwinterhoekberge ZA 205 Mc62
Groot Winterhoek Wilderness Area ZA 204 Lk62
Gropeni RO 69 Mh45
Gros Morne CDN 241 Hb21
GrosMorne RH 250 Gd36
Gros Morne N. P. CDN 241 Hb21
Gross Barmen NAM 200 Lj57
Gross Barmen Hot Springs NAM 200 Lj57
Großenhain D 58 Lo39
Großenkneten D 58 Lj38
Großer Arber D 59 Lo41
Großer Beerberg D 58 Ll40
Großer Feldberg D 59 Lj40
Großer Garten D 58 Lk38
Großer Inselsberg D 58 Ll40
Großer Peilstein A 66 Lq42
Großer Plöner See D 58 Ll36
Großer Pyhrgas A 61 Lp43
Großer Rachel D 59 Lo42
Grosses AUS 148 Rh61
Große Sandspitze A 61 Ln44
Grosseto I 60 Lm47
Grosseto Prugna F 62 Lj49
Groß-Gerau D 59 Lj41
Groß Gerungs A 66 Lp42
Großglockner A 61 Ln43
Großglockner Straße A 61 Ln43
Grossos BR 273 Jb48
Großpetersdorf A 61 Lr43
Großräschen D 58 Lo39
Gross Ums NAM 204 Lk57
Großvenediger A 60 Ln43
Grosuplje SLO 66 Lp45
Groton USA 236 Fa23
Grotta Azzurra I 63 Lp50
Grotta del Genovese I 62 Ln52
Grotta di Nettuno I 62 Lj50
Grotta di San Michele I 62 Lk50
Grottáglie I 63 Ls50
Grottaminarda I 63 Lq49
Grottammare I 61 Lo47
Grotte de Clamouse F 53 Ld47
Grotte de Grand-Roc F 52 La46
Grotte de Lascaux F 52 Lb45
Grotte de Niaux F 52 Lb48
Grotte de Pech Merle F 52 Lb46
Grotte des Demoiselles F 53 Ld47
Grotte de Villars F 52 La45
Grotte di Castellana I 63 Ls50
Grotte di Catullo I 60 Ll45
Grotte di Frasassi I 61 Ln47
Grotte du Mas-d'Azil F 52 Lb47
Grottes (Bangbali) RCA 190 Ma41
Grottes d'Azé F 53 Le44
Grottes de Beni-Add DZ 175 Kk28
Grottes de Bétharram F 52 Ku47
Grottes de Bongolo G 198 Lf47
Grottes de Dimba et Ngovo RDC 198 Lh48
Grottes de Matupi RDC 191 Me45
Grottes de Missirikoro RMM 187 Kh40
Grottes de Remouchamps B 51 Lf40
Grottes de Yambala RCA 190 Ma42
Grottes du Galo Boukoy RCA 190 Lh43
Grotto of the Redemption USA 236 Fc24
Grouard CDN 231 Eb18
Groumania CI 187 Kj42
Groundbirch CDN 231 Dk18
Groupe d'Aldabra SY 206 Nd50
Grov N 38 Ls22
Grove USA 238 Fc27
Grove City USA 237 Fj26
Grove City USA 237 Fk25
Grove Hill USA 239 Fg30
Grove Mountains 286 Oc32
Groveton USA 238 Fc30
Groveton USA 241 Ge23
Grožnjan HR 61 Lo45
Groznyj RUS 91 Nc24
Grube GH 187 Kk41
Grube Messel D 59 Lj41
Grubišno Polje HR 61 Ls45
Grudusk PL 65 Ma37
Grudziądz PL 64 Lt37
Grumento Nova I 63 Lq50
Grums S 42 Lo31
Grünau NAM 204 Lk59
Grünberg D 58 Lj40
Grundarfjörður IS 46 Jr26
Grundkallen 43 Lt30
Grundy USA 242 Fj27
Grundy Center USA 236 Fd24
Grünstadt D 59 Lj41
Grunwald PL 65 Ma37
Grupe GH 187 Kj41
Gruppo di Sella I 60 Lm44
Gruszka PL 65 Ma39
Gruta de Intihuasi RA 280 Gh62
Gruta de la Paz EC 268 Gb45
Gruta de las Maravillas E 55 Ko53
Gruta de los Helechos ROU 276 Hb61
Gruta del Palacio ROU 276 Hb62
Gruta de Ubajara BR 273 Hk47
Gruta do Lago Azul BR 274 Hb56
Grutas de Bustamante MEX 245 Ek32
Grutas de García MEX 245 Ek33
Grutas de Lanquin GCA 248 Ff38
Grutas de Loltún MEX 247 Ff35
Grutas de Xtacumbilxunán MEX 247 Fe36
Grutas dos Brejões BR 273 Hk51
Grutas Lázaro Cárdenas MEX 247 Fc37
Gruver USA 238 Ek27
Gruža SRB 68 Ma47
Gruzdžiai LT 45 Md34
Grybów PL 65 Ma41
Grycksbro S 43 Lq30
Gryfice PL 64 Lq37
Gryfino PL 64 Lp37
Gryfów Śląski PL 64 Lq39
Grykë AL 70 Lu50
Gryllefjord N 38 Ls21
Gryt S 43 Lr32
Grythyttan S 43 Lp31
Gstaad CH 60 Lh44
Gua EAT 196 Mg49
Guabalá PA 249 Fk41
Guabiju BR 276 He60
Guabijú BR 276 Hc61
Guabún RCH 280 Gd66
Guacamayas CO 264 Gc44
Guacamayas CO 264 Ge43
Guacara YV 265 Gg40
Guacautey YV 265 Gk43
Guachara YV 265 Gf42
Gua Charah MAL 126 Qb43
Guachimetas de Arriba MEX 244 Eg33
Guachipas RA 279 Gh58
Guachochi MEX 244 Eg32
Guachucal CO 264 Gb45
Guaco CO 264 Ge44
Guaçu BR 274 Hc57
Guaçuí BR 275 Hk56
Guadalajara E 55 Kr50
Guadalajara MEX 246 Ej35
Guadalcanal E 55 Kp52
Guadalcanal SOL 157 Sk50
Guadalest E 57 Ku52
Guadalupe BR 273 Hj49
Guadalupe MEX 245 Ek33
Guadalupe MEX 246 Ej34
Guadalupe PE 268 Ga49
Guadalupe USA 234 Dk28
Guadalupe de Bagues MEX 245 Eh32
Guadalupe Mts. N.P. USA 235 Eh30
Guadalupe y Calvo MEX 244 Eg32
Guadeloupe F 251 Gk37
Guadeloupe Passage 251 Gk37
Guadelupe de Bravo MEX 244 Eg30
Guadelupe del Carnicero MEX 246 Ek34
Guadelupe de los Reyes MEX 244 Eg33
Guadelupe Victoria MEX 244 Ec29
Guadelupe Victoria MEX 245 Eh33
Guadix E 55 Kr53
Guaduas CO 264 Gc43
Guahaja, T.I. BR 270 Gg49
Guaíba BR 276 He61
Guaimaca HN 248 Fg38
Guáimaro C 243 Gb35
Guaimbe, T.I. BR 274 Hc57
Guaina YV 265 Gj43
Guaíra BR 274 Hf56
Guaíra BR 276 Hc58
Guajará BR 268 Gd49
Guajará-Mirim BR 270 Gh51
Guajirú BR 273 Ja47
Gualán GCA 248 Ff38
Gualaquiza EC 268 Ga47
Gualdo Tadino I 60 Ln47
Guale EC 268 Fk46
Gualeguay RA 276 Ha62
Gualeguaychú RA 276 Ha62
Gualjaina RA 280 Ge67
Guallatiri RCH 278 Gf55
Guallatiri, Volcán RCH 278 Gf55
Gualmatán CO 264 Gb45
Guam USA 135 Sa08
Guama YV 265 Gf40
Guamal CO 264 Gc41
Guamal San Martin CO 264 Gd44
Gua Mampu RI 130 Ra48
Guamini RA 281 Gj64
Guamo CO 264 Gc43
Guamote EC 268 Ga46
Guamúchil MEX 244 Ef33
Gua Musang MAL 126 Qb43
Gu'an CHN 107 Qj26
Guanabo C 243 Fj34
Guanacaste N.P. BH 248 Ff37
Guanacaste, P.N. CR 248 Fh40
Guanacevi MEX 244 Eh33
Guanaco Muerto RA 279 Gh61
Guanahani Island = San Salvador BS 250 Gc33
Guanaja HN 248 Fh37
Guanajay C 243 Fj34
Guanajuato MEX 246 Ek35
Guanajuato MEX 246 Ek35
Guanajuña YV 265 Gj43
Guanambi BR 275 Hj53
Guanare YV 265 Gf41
Guanarito YV 265 Gf41
Guanay BOL 278 Gg53
Guanay, Cerro YV 265 Gg43
Guancheng CHN 112 Ra30
Guandacaya BOL 279 Gh57
Guandacol RA 279 Gf60
Guandiping CHN 108 Qf31
Guandong CHN 109 Qg34
Guang'an CHN 108 Qd30
Guangang CHN 109 Qj31
Guangba CHN 106 Qd29
Guangchang CHN 109 Qj32
Guangde CHN 112 Qk30
Guangdong CHN 109 Qg34
Guangfenghai CHN 121 Qc32
Guanghai CHN 109 Qg35
Guangmao Shan CHN 121 Qa32
Guangnan CHN 121 Qc33
Guangning CHN 108 Qg34
Guangrao CHN 107 Qk27
Guangshan CHN 107 Qh30
Guangsheng Si CHN 106 Qf27
Guangshui CHN 107 Qh30
Guangshuishi CHN 107 Qg30
Guangshun CHN 108 Qd32
Guangtong CHN 121 Qa33
Guangxi Zhuangzu Zizhiqu CHN 108 Qd33
Guangyuan CHN 106 Qc29
Guangze CHN 109 Qj32
Guangzhou CHN 109 Qg34
Guanhães BR 275 Hj55
Guaní CO 264 Gd44
Guaniamo YV 265 Gg42
Guanica USA 251 Gg37
Guanling CHN 121 Qc33
Guanoco YV 265 Gj40
Guanqiao CHN 106 Qc27
Guanta RCH 279 Ge60
Guantánamo C 250 Gc35
Guantanamo Bay US Naval Base USA 250 Gc36
Guantao CHN 107 Qh27
Guanyun CHN 112 Qk28
Guapé BR 275 Hh56
Guapi CO 264 Gb44
Guapiara BR 277 Hf58
Guápiles CR 249 Fj40
Guaporé BOL 278 Gk52
Guaporé BR 276 Hd60
Guaporé BR 276 He60
Guaporé BR 278 Ha53
Guaqui BOL 278 Gf54
Guará BR 275 Hg56
Guara E 56 Ku48
Guaraci BR 274 Hf56
Guaraciaba BR 276 Hd59
Guaraciaba do Norte BR 273 Hk48
Guaraí BR 272 Hf50
Guaramacal, P.N. YV 264 Ge41
Guarambaré PY 276 Hb58
Guaramirim BR 277 Hf59
Guaramuri GUY 266 Ha42
Guaranda EC 268 Ga46
Guaraní BOL 278 Gj56
Guaraniaçu BR 276 Hd58
Guarantã BR 274 Hf56
Guarantã do Norte BR 271 Hc50
Guarapari BR 275 Hk56
Guarapuava BR 275 Hg54
Guarapuava BR 276 He58
Guaraqueçaba BR 277 Hf58
Guararapes BR 274 He56
Guarariba BR 273 Jc49
Guaratinga BR 275 Ja54
Guaratingueta BR 277 Hh57
Guaratuba BR 277 Hf58
Guarayos BOL 278 Gf52
Guarda P 54 Kn50
Guardalavaca C 250 Gc35
Guardamar del Segura E 57 Ku52
Guarda-Mor BR 275 Hg54
Guardiagrele I 63 Lp48
Guardia Mitre RA 281 Gj66
Guardian Seamounts 248 Fg41
Guardo E 54 Kq48
Guareña E 55 Ko52
Guarento YV 265 Gj42
Guari PNG 155 Sd50
Guariba BR 274 Hf56
Guarita, T.I. BR 276 Hd59
Guarujá BR 277 Hg58
Guarulhos BR 277 Hg57
Guasave MEX 244 Ef33
Guasca CO 264 Gd43
Guasdualito YV 264 Ge42
Guasipati YV 265 Gk42
Guasizaco MEX 244 Ef32
Guasopa PNG 156 Sg50
Guastalla I 60 Ll46
Guasuti, T.I. BR 274 Hc57
Guatacondo RCH 278 Gf56
Guataqui CO 264 Gc43
Guatemala 248 Fe38
Guatemala Basin 210 Fa08
Guatimape MEX 245 Eh33
Guatire YV 265 Gg40
Guatopo, P.N. YV 265 Gg40
Guatraché RA 281 Gj64
Guaviare CO 265 Gf44
Guaxupé BR 275 Hg56
Guayabal C 243 Gb35
Guayabones YV 264 Ge41
Guayaguayaré TT 251 Gk40
Guayama USA 251 Gg37
Guayaquil EC 268 Ga47
Guayaquil MEX 244 Ec31
Guayaramerín BOL 270 Gh51
Guayllabamba EC 268 Ga46
Guaymas MEX 244 Ee32
Guayubin DOM 250 Ge36
Guayzimi EC 268 Ga48
Guba ETH 192 Mh40
Guba RDC 196 Md51
Guban SP 193 Nb40
Gubat RP 124 Rc39
Gubatsaa Hills RB 201 Mc55
Gúbbio I 60 Ln47
Guben D 58 Lp39
Gubi WAN 188 Le40
Gubin PL 64 Lp39
Gubio WAN 189 Lg39
Gubkin RUS 72 Mj20
Gubra IND 117 Ok34
Guča SRB 68 Ma47
Gucheng CHN 106 Qf28
Gucheng CHN 106 Qf29
Guci Hot Water Spring RI 129 Qe49
Gudalur IND 118 Oj40
Gudauta GE 91 Na24
Gudbrandsdalen N 40 Lk29
Guder ETH 192 Mj41
Guder Falls ETH 192 Mj41
Gudermes RUS 91 Nd24
Guderup DK 42 Lk36
Gudgaon IND 116 Oj35
Gudha IND 114 Oj32
Gudhjem DK 43 Lp35
Gudi WAN 188 Le41
Gudivada IND 117 Pa37
Gudiyattam IND 119 Ok39
Gudong CHN 121 Pk33
Gudur IND 119 Ok38
Guéassou RG 186 Kf41
Guebwiller F 53 Lh43
Guechémé RN 182 Lb39
Guéckédou RG 186 Ke41
Guelb El Makhsar RIM 181 Kf36
Guelb El Rhein RIM 180 Kd34
Guelb er Richât RIM 180 Ke35
Guelb Makhrouga RIM 181 Kf36
Guelb Ragoum RIM 181 Kf36
Guelb Zednes RIM 180 Ke33
Guéléhé TCH 190 Lk41
Guélengdeng TCH 189 Lh40
Guellala TN 176 Lf29
Guelltat Sidi Saad DZ 176 La28
Guelma DZ 176 Ld27
Guelmim MA 174 Ke31
Guelta d'Archei TCH 184 Ma37
Guémar DZ 176 Ld29
Guémené-Penfao F 50 Kt43
Guémené-sur-Scorff F 50 Kr42
Güémez MEX 246 Fa34
Guemour DZ 176 Lc32
Guènt Paté SN 180 Kc38
Guépaouo CI 187 Kh42
Güeppí PE 268 Gc46
Guer F 50 Ks43
Güer Aike RA 282 Gf71
Guérande F 50 Ks43
Guerara DZ 176 Lc29
Guercif MA 175 Kj28
Guéréda TCH 184 Mb38
Guerende LAR 178 Ma34
Guéret F 52 Lb44
Guerguarat DARS 180 Kb35
Guérin-Kouka TG 187 La41
Guermessa TN 176 Lf29
Guerneville USA 234 Dj26
Guernsey GB 50 Ks41
Guernsey USA 235 Eh24
Guérou RIM 180 Ke37
Guerrero MEX 244 Eg31
Guerrero MEX 245 Ek31
Guerrero MEX 246 Ek36
Guerrero Negro MEX 244 Ec32
Guerzim DZ 175 Kk31
Gueskérou RN 183 Lg39
Guéssabo CI 187 Kg42
Guésséyo CI 187 Kg42
Guessou South DY 188 Lb40
Gueugnon F 53 Le44
Guéyo CI 187 Kg43
Guézaoua RN 182 Le38
Guffertspitze A 60 Lm43
Gufudalur IS 46 Js25
Gugești RO 69 Mh45
Guglionesi I 63 Lp49
Guguang, Gunung RI 128 Qj44
Gugurtli UZ 96 Ob25
Guhagar IND 116 Og37
Guia Lopes da Laguna BR 274 Hb56
Guiana Basin 254 Ha08
Guiana Highlands 254 Gb09
Guiana Plateau 266 Hc41
Guiarote BOL 278 Gj55
Guibaré BF 187 Kk39
Guibéroua CI 187 Kg42
Guicán CO 264 Gd42
Guichi CHN 112 Qj30
Guichón ROU 276 Hb62
Guidan-Roumji RN 182 Ld39
Guidari TCH 190 Lj41
Guider CAM 189 Lg41
Guidiguir RN 182 Le39
Guidiguis CAM 189 Lh40
Guidimaka RIM/RMM 180 Ke38
Guidimouni RN 182 Le39
Guiding CHN 108 Qd32
Guidjiba CAM 189 Lg41
Guidong CHN 109 Qg32
Guiembé CI 187 Kh41
Guiendana CI 187 Kh41
Guiengola MEX 247 Fc37
Guiffa RCA 190 Lk42
Guigang CHN 108 Qe34
Guiglo CI 187 Kg42
Güigüe YV 265 Gg40
Guihua Temple CHN 103 Pk31
Guihuayuan CHN 108 Qc30
Guihulñgan RP 124 Rb40
Guijuelo E 55 Kp50
Guilderton AUS 144 Qh61
Guildford GB 49 Ku39
Guilin CHN 108 Qf33
Guillaumes F 53 Lg46
Guillestre F 53 Lg46
Guilmara DY 187 La40
Guilvinec F 50 Kq43
Guimarães BR 267 Hh47
Guimarães P 54 Km49
Guimaras Island RP 124 Rb40
Guimba RP 124 Ra38
Guimbalete MEX 245 Ej32
Guimiliau F 50 Kr42
Guinagourou DY 188 Lb41
Guinchos Cay BS 243 Ga34
Guindulman RP 124 Rc41
Guinea 163 Ka08
Guinea Basin 162 Kb10
Guinea-Bissau 163 Ka08
Güines C 243 Fj34
Guînes F 51 Lb40
Guingamp F 50 Kr42
Guinguineo SN 180 Kc38
Guipavas F 50 Kq42
Guiping CHN 108 Qf34
Guîr RMM 181 Kj36
Güira de Melena C 243 Fj34
Guiratinga BR 274 Hd54
Guiri CAM 189 Lh40
Güiria YV 265 Gj40
Guirwas SN 180 Kc38
Guisa C 243 Gb35
Guisborough GB 49 Kt36
Guiscard F 51 Ld41
Guise F 51 Ld41
Guishi Shuiku CHN 108 Qf33
Guissat RN 182 Le37
Guissèr MA 175 Kg29
Guissona E 57 Lb49
Guitiriz E 54 Kn47
Guitri CI 187 Kh43
Guiuan RP 124 Rc40
Guiyang CHN 108 Qd32
Guiyang CHN 109 Qg33
Gui Yuan Si CHN 109 Qh30
Guizhou CHN 108 Qf30
Guizhou CHN 108 Qc32
Gujan-Mestras F 52 Kt46
Gujarat IND 116 Of34
Gujar Khan PK 99 Og29
Gujba WAN 189 Lf40
Gujiao CHN 106 Qg27
Gujranwala PK 99 Oh29
Gujrat PK 99 Oh29
Gujri IND 116 Oh34
Gukovo RUS 73 Mk21
Gulabgarh 115 Oj29
Gulagambone AUS 149 Se61
Gulang CHN 106 Qb27
Gulangyu RC 109 Qk33
Gulbarga IND 116 Oj37
Gulbarga Fort IND 116 Oj37
Gulbene LV 45 Mg33
Gul'ca KS 97 Og25
Guledagud IND 116 Oh38
Gulf Islands National Seashore USA 239 Ff30
Gulf of Aden 76 Na08
Gulf of Alaska USA 226 Cc07
Gulf of Aqaba ET/KSA 92 Mh31
Gulf of Arab ET 179 Me30
Gulf of Bahrain KSA 93 Nf33
Gulf of Bone RI 130 Ra48
Gulf of Boothia CDN 227 Fc05
Gulf of Bothnia S/FIN 41 Lt28
Gulf of California MEX 244 Ed31
Gulf of Carpentaria AUS 146 Rk53
Gulf of Corinth GR 70 Mc52
Gulf of Darién PA/CO 249 Gb41
Gulf of Finland 44 Md31
Gulf of Gdansk PL 65 Ltu6

Gulf of Genoa ■ I 60 Lj46
Gulf of Guinea ■ 162 La09
Gulf of Hikma ■ ET 178 Me30
Gulf of Kachchh ■ IND 116 Oe34
Gulf of Khambhat ■ IND 116 Og35
Gulf of Liaotung ■ CHN 110 Ra25
Gulf of Lingayan ■ RP 124 Ra37
Gulf of Maine ■ 119 Ok41
Gulf of Mannar ■ IND/CY 119 Ok41
Gulf of Martaban ■ MYA 122 Pj38
Gulf of Masirah ■ OM 95 Nk35
Gulf of Mexico ■ 210 Fa07
Gulf of Oman ■ 76 Nb07
Gulf of Panama ■ PA 249 Ga42
Gulf of Papua ■ PNG 155 Sc50
Gulf of Riga ■ EST/LV 45 Md33
Gulf of Saint Lawrence ■ CDN 240 Gj21
Gulf of Sallum ■ ET 178 Mc30
Gulf of Salonica ■ GR 70 Mc50
Gulf of Sirte ■ LAR 177 Lj30
Gulf of Suez ■ ET 179 Mg31
Gulf of Taranto ■ I 63 Ls50
Gulf of Tehuantepec ■ MEX 247 Fc38
Gulf of Thailand ■ T 122 Qa40
Gulf of Tomini ■ RI 130 Rb47
Gulf of Tonkin ■ VN/CHN 121 Qd36
Gulf of Valencia ■ E 57 La51
Gulf of Venice ■ I 61 Ln45
Gurport ■ USA 210 Fa07
Gulf Saint Vincent ■ AUS 150 Rk63
Gulgong ■ AUS 151 Se62
Gulioni ■ EAT 197 Mk49
Gulistan ■ UZ 97 Oe25
Gul'janci ■ BG 69 Me47
Gul Kach ■ PK 99 Oe30
Gul'kevici ■ RUS 73 Na23
Gull Lake ■ CDN 233 Ef20
Gullspång ■ S 43 Lg32
Güllük ■ TR 71 Mk52
Güllü Dağları ■ TR 91 Na25
Güllük ■ TR 71 Mh53
Gulmarg ■ IND 114 Oh28
Gülpınar ■ TR 71 Mg51
Gulshat ■ KZ 100 Oh22
Gulsvik ■ N 42 Lk30
Gulu ■ EAU 194 Mg44
Gulumba Gana ■ WAN 189 Lh40
Gumare ■ EAT 197 Mj49
Guma = Pishan ■ CHN 100 Ok27
Gumaca ■ RP 124 Ra37
Gumare ■ RB 201 Mb55
Gumba ■ ANG 200 Lh51
Gumba ■ RDC 190 Ma44
Gumbardo ■ AUS 149 Sc59
Gumbiro ■ EAT 196 Mh51
Gumdag ■ TM 96 Nh26
Gumel ■ WAN 188 Le39
Gumgarhi ■ NEP 115 Pb31
Gumla ■ IND 117 Pc34
Gumlu ■ AUS 147 Sd55
Gummersbach ■ D 58 Lh39
Gummi ■ WAN 188 Lc39
Gumsi ■ WAN 182 Lf39
Gümüşcay ■ TR 69 Mh50
Gümüşhane ■ TR 91 Mk25
Gumu Uen ■ SP 195 Nd45
Gunan ■ CHN 109 Qj31
Gunib ■ RUS 91 Nd26
Gunbad-e-Haruniyeh ■ IR 96 Nk27
Gundabooka N.P. ■ AUS 149 Sc61
Gundardehi ■ IND 117 Pa35
Gundelfingen ■ D 59 Ll42
Gundji ■ RDC 190 Ma44
Gundulpet ■ IND 118 Oj40
Güney ■ TR 71 Mh52
Güney ■ TR 71 Mk52
Güney Doğu Toroslar ■ TR 90 Mj26
Gungadel ■ ANG 200 Ls53
Gungadel ■ AUS 151 Se63
Gungu ■ RDC 199 Lk49
Gungu ■ ANG 200 Lh51
Gungure ■ MOC 197 Mk51
Gunjunijung ■ RI 128 Qh45
Gunlom A.L. ■ AUS 146 Rg52
Gunn ■ CDN 233 Ec19
Gunna ■ SUD 191 Md42
Gunnaur ■ IND 115 Ok31
Gunnebo ■ S 43 Lr33
Gunnedah ■ AUS 149 Sf61
Gunnerus Ridge ■ 287 Mc32
Gunning ■ AUS 151 Se63
Gunnison ■ USA 235 Ee26
Gunnison ■ USA 235 Eg25
Gunnison, Mount ■ USA 235 Eg26
Gunpowder ■ AUS 146 Rk55
Guns ■ NAM 200 Li57
Günsang ■ CHN 102 Pb30
Gunta ■ WAN 188 Le40
Guntakal ■ IND 118 Oj38
Guntersville ■ USA 239 Fg28
Guntín de Pallares ■ E 54 Kn48
Gunua ■ IND 117 Pa37
Gununa ■ AUS 146 Rk54
Gunung Ambang Reserve ■ RI 125 Rc45
Gunung Angemuk ■ RI 154 Rk47
Gunung Antares ■ RI 155 Sa48
Gunung Api ■ RI 131 Re48
Gunungapi ■ RI 131 Rd49
Gunung Argopuro ■ RI 129 Qg49
Gunung Bakayan ■ RI 128 Qj44
Gunung Balease ■ RI 130 Ra47
Gunung Basakan ■ RI 128 Qh45
Gunung Batukau ■ RI 128 Qh50
Gunung Besar ■ RI 129 Qg48
Gunung Bromo ■ RI 129 Qg49
Gunung Butak ■ RI 129 Qg49
Gunung Cemaru ■ RI 128 Qh45
Gunung Chamah ■ MAL 126 Qa43
Gunung Cirema ■ RI 129 Qe49
Gunung Daku ■ RI 125 Ra45
Gunung Dempo ■ RI 127 Qd46
Gunung Dom ■ RI 154 Rj47
Gunung Gading N.P. ■ MAL 128 Qe45
Gunung Gagau ■ MAL 126 Qb43
Gunung Gambuta ■ RI 125 Rb45
Gunung Gandadiwata ■ RI 130 Qk47
Gunung Guguang ■ RI 129 Qd49
Gunung Halimun ■ RI 129 Qd49
Gunung Harden ■ RI 128 Qh43
Gunung Irau ■ RI 154 Rg46
Gunung Kambuno ■ RI 130 Ra47
Gunung Katoposo ■ RI 130 Ra46
Gunung Kemal ■ RI 128 Qj45
Gunung Kemben ■ RI 127 Qd47
Gunung Kerihun ■ RI 128 Qg45
Gunung Kerinci ■ RI 127 Qc46
Gunung Kinabalu ■ MAL 128 Qj44
Gunung Kujat ■ RI 128 Qj44
Gunung Kwoka ■ RI 154 Rg46
Gunung Lawit ■ RI 128 Qg45
Gunung Lawu ■ RI 129 Qf49
Gunung Leuser N.P. ■ RI 126 Pj44
Gunung Liangmangari ■ RI 129 Qg46
Gunung Liangpran ■ RI 128 Qj45
Gunung Liman ■ RI 129 Qf49
Gunung Loi ■ RI 128 Qj45
Gunung Lompobatang ■ RI 130 Ra48
Gunung Lumaku ■ MAL 128 Qh43
Gunung Lumut ■ RI 129 Qf46
Gunung Malabar ■ RI 129 Qd49
Gunung Malea ■ RI 127 Pk45
Gunung Malino ■ RI 130 Qk46
Gunung Masurai ■ RI 127 Qc46
Gunung Mata Bia ■ TLS 131 Rd50
Gunung Mebo ■ RI 154 Rg46
Gunungmegang ■ RI 127 Qd46
Gunung Meja Reserve ■ RI 154 Rg46
Gunung Mekongga ■ RI 130 Ra47

Gunung Menyapa ■ RI 128 Qj45
Gunungmeraksa ■ RI 127 Qc47
Gunung Merapi ■ RI 129 Qf49
Gunung Merapi ■ RI 129 Qh50
Gunung Mulu N.P. ■ MAL 128 Qh43
Gunung Muria ■ RI 129 Qf49
Gunung Mutis ■ RI 131 Rc50
Gunung Nanti ■ RI 127 Qd48
Gunung Niut ■ RI 128 Qe45
Gunung Noring ■ MAL 126 Qa43
Gunung Pancungapang ■ RI 128 Qh45
Gunung Pangrango ■ RI 129 Qd49
Gunung Payang ■ RI 128 Qh45
Gunung Ranakah ■ RI 130 Ra50
Gunung Rantemario ■ RI 130 Ra47
Gunung Ratai ■ RI 127 Qd46
Gunung Raung ■ RI 129 Qh50
Gunung Raya ■ RI 127 Qa47
Gunung Raya ■ RI 129 Qg46
Gunung Rinjani ■ RI 130 Qj50
Gunung Saran ■ RI 128 Qg45
Gunung Sebayan ■ RI 129 Qf45
Gunungsitoli ■ RI 127 Pj45
Gunung Slamet ■ RI 129 Qe49
Gunung Tahan ■ MAL 126 Qa43
Gunung Takan ■ RI 130 Qj50
Gunung Tamborra ■ RI 130 Qj50
Gunung Tampu Inanajing ■ RI 127 Pk45
Gunung Tata Mailau = Mount Ramelau ■ TLS 131 Rd50
Gunung Tebak ■ RI 127 Qc48
Gunung Tenamatua ■ RI 130 Ra46
Gunung Tentolomatinan ■ RI 125 Rb45
Gunung Tibau ■ RI 128 Qh45
Gunung Trus Madi ■ MAL 128 Qj43
Gunungtua ■ RI 127 Pk45
Gunung Tuham ■ RI 128 Qg45
Gunung Ubia ■ RI 154 Rj48
Gunung Umsini ■ RI 154 Rg46
Gunung Wanggamet ■ RI 130 Ra51
Gunung Welirang ■ RI 129 Qg49
Gunupur ■ IND 117 Pb36
Gunupur ■ IND 117 Pb36
Gunware ■ IND 117 Pa33
Günz ■ D 59 Ll42
Günzburg ■ D 59 Ll42
Gunzenhausen ■ D 59 Ll41
Guocheng ■ CHN 106 Qc27
Guodao ■ CHN 107 Qg27
Guoquanyan ■ CHN 106 Qb30
Guoyang ■ CHN 112 Qj29
Guozhen ■ CHN 106 Qd28
Gupeng ■ CHN 108 Qe34
Gupis ■ 114 Og27
Guptapur ■ IND 117 Pc36
Gura Halitii ■ RO 67 Mf43
Gurahont ■ RO 67 Mc44
Gura Humorului ■ RO 73 Mc22
Gurais ■ 114 Oh28
Gurampod ■ IND 117 Ok37
Guran ■ IR 98 Nh32
Gurasada ■ RO 68 Mc45
Gurbantunggüt Shamo ■ CHN 101 Pd23
Gurdaspur ■ IND 114 Oh29
Gurdim ■ IR 98 Oa33
Gurdim ■ IR 98 Nc25
Güre ■ TR 71 Mk52
Gur'evsk ■ RUS 45 Ma36
Gurgaon ■ IND 114 Oj30
Gurguéia ■ BR 272 Hj49
Gurig N.P. & Cobourg Marine Park ■ AUS 146 Rg51
Guri Hattnur ■ IND 116 Ok36
Gurk ■ A 61 Lp44
Gurinhatã ■ BR 274 Hf55
Gurkovo ■ BG 69 Mf48
Gurktaler Alpen ■ A 61 Lo44
Gurlan ■ UZ 96 Oa25
Gurmatkal ■ IND 116 Oj37
Gurner ■ AUS 143 Rf57
Guro ■ MOC 202 Mg54
Güroymak ■ TR 91 Nb26
Gurramkonda ■ IND 119 Ok39
Gurri ■ SUD 184 Mb39
Gursahaiganj ■ IND 115 Ok32
Gursarai ■ IND 117 Ok34
Guruapin ■ RI 125 Rd45
Gunujiang N.P. ■ CHN 109 Qj31
Gunlom A.L. ■ AUS 146 Rg52
Gurué ■ MOC 203 Mj53
Gurun ■ MAL 126 Qa43
Gürün ■ TR 90 Mj26
Gurupi ■ BR 267 He46
Gurupi ■ BR 267 Hg46
Gurupi ■ BR 272 Hf51
Gurupizinho ■ BR 272 Hg47
Guru Sai Baba ■ IND 118 Oj38
Guru Shikhar ■ IND 116 Og33
Gurvee ■ ZW 202 Mf54
Gurvan Saykhan ■ MNG 104 Qb24
Gurvan Saykhan N.P. ■ MNG 104 Qa24
Gury ■ AUS 149 Se60
Gurziwann ■ AFG 97 Oc28
Gusau ■ WAN 188 Ld39
Gusev ■ RUS 45 Mc36
Gushan ■ CHN 107 Rb26
Gushan ■ CHN 109 Qk32
Gushgy ■ TM 97 Ob28
Gushiago ■ GH 187 Kk41
Gushikawa ■ J 113 Rd32
Gush Laghar ■ IND 116 Oa28
Gusinje ■ MNE 68 Lu48
Gusinoozërsk ■ RUS 104 Qd20
Gushkara ■ IND 117 Pd34
Güspini ■ I 62 Lj51
Gusselby ■ S 43 Lg31
Güssing ■ A 61 Lr43
Gustavel ■ N 38 Li06
Gustavia ■ F 251 Gj37
Gustavsberg ■ S 43 Lt31
Gustavus ■ USA 230 Dc16
Gustav V Land ■ N 38 Lk05
Gustine ■ USA 234 Dk27
Gusum ■ S 43 Lr32
Gus'-Zeleznyj ■ RUS 72 Na18
Gutai ■ CDN 231 Dk17
Gutcher ■ GB 48 Ku30
Gutenberg ■ RA 279 Gj60
Gutenko Mountains ■ 286 Gd33
Gütersloh ■ D 58 Li39
Gutha ■ AUS 144 Qh60
Guthalungra ■ AUS 147 Sd55
Guthrie ■ USA 238 Fb28
Guthrie Center ■ USA 236 Fc25
Gutian ■ CHN 109 Qk32
Guthrie ■ USA 238 Fa28
Gutu ■ ZW 202 Mf55
Gutsuo ■ CHN 102 Pd31
Gützkow ■ D 59 Ln37
Gutulia n.p. ■ N 40 Ll28
Gütkow ■ D 59 Ln37
Gutukia ■ MOC 205 Mg58
Guwahati ■ IND 120 Pf32
Guwari ■ SUD 185 Mg37
Güzar ■ UZ 97 Od28
Guyana ■ 255 Ha09
Guyang ■ CHN 106 Qf25
Guyi ■ ETH 192 Mh41
Guyra ■ AUS 149 Sf61
Guyuan ■ CHN 106 Qe29
Guyuan ■ CHN 106 Qf26
Guyuan ■ CHN 107 Qg25
Güzelbahçe ■ TR 71 Mh53
Güzelçamlı ■ TR 91 Nb26
Güzelsu ■ TR 91 Nb26
Güzelyurt = Morfou ■ CY 90 Mg28
Guzhen ■ CHN 112 Qj29
Guzmán ■ MEX 244 Eg30
Guzmán ■ MEX 244 Eg30
Gvardeysk ■ RUS 45 Mb36
Gvarv ■ N 42 Lk31

Gvasjugi ■ RUS 111 Rj22
Gvozd ■ HR 61 Lq45
Gwa ■ MYA 122 Ph37
Gwaai ■ ZW 202 Md55
Gwabegar ■ AUS 149 Se61
Gwada ■ WAN 188 Ld41
Gwadar ■ PK 98 Ob33
Gwadar East Bay ■ PK 98 Ob33
Gwagwalada ■ WAN 188 Ld41
Gwaidam ■ IND 115 Ok30
Gwaii Haanas South Moresby National Park Reserve & Marine Conservation Area Reserve ■ CDN 230 De19
Gwalior ■ IND 117 Ok33
Gwalior Fort ■ IND 117 Ok32
Gwalishtap ■ PK 98 Ob31
Gwamba ■ WAN 188 Lc40
Gwambara ■ WAN 188 Lc39
Gwanda ■ ZW 202 Me55
Gware ■ RDC 191 Mc43
Gware ■ IND 117 Pa34
Gwaram ■ WAN 188 Le40
Gwarit ■ RI 154 Rk47
Gwarzo ■ WAN 188 Ld40
Gwatar Bay ■ PK 98 Oa33
Gwayi River ■ ZW 202 Md55
Gwembe ■ Z 202 Md54
Gweru ■ ZW 202 Me55
Gweta ■ RB 201 Mc56
Gwi ■ WAN 188 Ld41
Gwoza ■ WAN 189 Lg40
Gy ■ F 53 Lf43
Gyaca ■ CHN 103 Pg31
Gyangze ■ CHN 102 Pe31
Gyaring Hu ■ CHN 103 Pg27
Gydanskaja guba ■ RUS 84 Od04
Gydanskiy Poluostrov ■ RUS 88 Od04
Gyekiti ■ GH 187 La42
Gyeongju ■ ROK 113 Re28
Gyeongju Historic Areas ■ ROK 113 Re28
Gyltang ■ CHN 102 Pc31
Gyldenlovehøj ■ DK 42 Lm35
Gylien ■ S 39 Mc24
Gympie ■ AUS 149 Sg59
Gyobingauk ■ MYA 120 Ph36
Gyokusendo ■ J 113 Rd32
Gyomaendrőd ■ H 67 Ma44
Gyömrő ■ H 67 Lu43
Gyöngyös ■ H 67 Lu43
Győr ■ H 66 Ls43
Gypsum ■ USA 235 Eg26
Gypsum Palace ■ AUS 151 Sc62
Gyttorp ■ S 43 Lg31
Gyula ■ H 67 Mb44
Gyumri ■ ARM 91 Nb25
Gyzylarbat ■ TM 96 Nj26
Gyzylsu ■ TM 96 Nj26
Gżatsk ■ RUS 72 Mh18

H

Haa-Alifu Atoll ■ MV 118 Og42
Häädemeeste ■ EST 45 Me32
Haa-Dhaalu Atoll ■ MV 118 Og42
Haag am Hausruck ■ A 66 Lo42
Haag in Oberbayern ■ D 59 Ln42
Haag, Niederösterreich ■ A 66 Lp42
Haakon VII Land ■ N 38 Lf04
Haaksbergen ■ NL 51 Lg38
Haarlem ■ NAM 204 Li59
Haamstede ■ NL 51 Ld39
Haanja kõrgustik ■ EST 45 Mg33
Haapsalu ■ EST 44 Md32
Haarl ■ NL 51 Le38
Haarlem ■ Z 204 Mb62
Haast ■ NZ 153 Te67
Haastbergat ■ N 38 Ma06
Haast Bluff ■ AUS 143 Rf57
Haasts Bluff A.L. ■ AUS 143 Rf57
Haaway ■ SP 195 Nb45
Habaha ■ CHN 101 Pd21
Habalah Mountain Village ■ KSA 94 Nb36
Ha Baroana Rock Paintings ■ LS 205 Md60
Habarovsk ■ RUS 110 Rh21
Habarut ■ OM 95 Nj37
Habaswein ■ EAK 195 Mk45
Habay ■ CDN 231 Ea16
Habay-la-Neuve ■ B 51 Lf41
Habaj ■ IR 98 Nk29
Habarana ■ CL 119 Ok41
Habirag ■ CHN 107 Qh24
Habo ■ S 43 Lp33
Habor Cirir ■ SP 195 Nd43
Haboro ■ J 112 Sa23
Habshan ■ UAE 95 Ng34
Hachcholli ■ IND 116 Oj38
Hachenburg ■ D 58 Lh40
Hachijo-jima ■ J 113 Rk29
Hachinohe ■ J 111 Sa25
Hachita ■ USA 235 Ek30
Hacibektaş ■ TR 90 Mh26
Haciömer ■ TR 91 Na26
Haci Zeynalabdin ■ AZ 91 Ne25
Hackás ■ S 41 Lg28
Hackettstown ■ USA 241 Gc25
Hack, Mount ■ AUS 148 Rk61
Hackney ■ GUY 266 Ha42
Haco ■ ANG 198 Lh51
Hacufera ■ MOC 202 Mg56
Haczów ■ PL 65 Mb41
Hadaaftimoo ■ SP 193 Ne40
Hadagalli ■ IND 118 Oj38
Hadalhuma ■ ETH 193 Nd42
Hadamar ■ D 59 Li40
Hadar (site of Lucy) ■ ETH 192 Na39
Hadashville ■ CDN 236 Fc21
Hadbin ■ OM 95 Nh37
Hadda ■ AFG 99 Oc28
Hadda ■ KSA 92 Mk35
Hadagan ■ IND 116 Oj36
Hadagaon ■ IND 116 Oj36
Hadhah ■ KSA 94 Na34
Hadh Bani Zaynan ■ KSA 94 Ne35
Hadhdhunmathee Atoll = Laamu Atoll ■ MV 118 Og45
Hadiboh ■ YE 95 Ng39
Hadihui ■ CHN 106 Qd27
Hadilik ■ CHN 102 Ph27
Hadim ■ TR 90 Mg27
Hadithah ■ IRQ 93 Na30
Hadjaç ■ UA 72 Mh20
Hadjer Bandala ■ TCH 184 Ma40
Hadjer el Hamis ■ TCH 189 Lh39
Hado Dan ■ PRK 110 Rd28
Hadranium ■ IRQ 91 Nb28
Hadraniyeh ■ IRQ 91 Nb28
Hadrian's Wall ■ GB 48 Ks36
Hadselaya ■ N 38 Lp22
Hadsten ■ DK 42 Ll34
Hadsund ■ DK 42 Ll34
Haduyangratu ■ IND 117 Pf37
Hadilici ■ BIH 68 Lt47
Hae ■ THA 121 Qa38
Hagedand ■ N 42 Lh32
Haeinsa Temple ■ ROK 112 Re28
Hae-nam ■ ROK 112 Rd28
Haenertsburg ■ ZA 202 Me57
Haërë Lao ■ SN 180 Kc37
Hafar al Batin ■ KSA 93 Nd31
Hafar al Batin ■ KSA 93 Nc31
Hafford ■ CDN 233 Eg19
Haffouz ■ TN 176 Le28
Hafik ■ TR 90 Mj26

Hafirat al Ayda ■ KSA 92 Mk32
Hafirat Nisah ■ KSA 93 Nd33
Hafizabad ■ PK 99 Og29
Hafiz Sa'adi ■ IR 98 Ng31
Hafjell alpincenter ■ N 40 Ll29
Hafnaberg ■ IS 46 Js27
Hafnarfjörður ■ IS 46 Jt26
Hafrir ■ IS 46 Js27
Hafratindur ■ IS 46 Jt25
Haftgel ■ IR 93 Ne30
Haft Tappeh ■ IR 93 Ne29
Hag Abdullah ■ SUD 185 Mg38
Hagadera ■ EAK 195 Na45
Hagar Banga ■ SUD 184 Mb40
Hagar Nish Plateau ■ ER 185 Mj37
Hagelberg ■ D 58 Ln38
Hagemeister Island ■ USA 228 Bk16
Hagen ■ D 58 Lh39
Hagen (Saale) ■ D 58 Lm39
Hagenow ■ D 58 Lm37
Hag Qaltan Pir Gandom Beryan ■ IR 98 Oa30
Hagere Hiywot ■ ETH 192 Mj41
Hagerman ■ USA 232 Ec24
Hagerman ■ USA 235 Eg26
Hagerstown ■ USA 241 Gb26
Hagetmau ■ F 52 Ku47
Hagewood ■ USA 238 Fd30
Hagfors ■ S 43 Lo30
Haggenäs ■ S 41 Lf28
Häggenäs ■ S 41 Lf28
Hagi ■ J 113 Rf28
Ha Giang ■ VN 121 Qc34
Hagia Sophia ■ TR 69 Mj49
Hagia Sophia (Trabzon) ■ TR 91 Mk25
Hagondange ■ F 51 Lg41
Hagony ■ RP 124 Ra38
Hagony ■ RP 125 Rc42
Haguenau ■ F 51 Lh42
Hahndorf ■ AUS 150 Rk63
Hahot ■ H 66 Lr44
Haia ■ PNG 155 Sc48
Hai'an ■ CHN 109 Qf35
Hai'an ■ CHN 112 Ra29
Haibao Ta ■ CHN 106 Qd26
Haibei ■ CHN 110 Rd22
Haibongo ■ RMM 181 Kj37
Haicheng ■ CHN 110 Rb25
Haidargarh ■ IND 117 Pa32
Hai Dong ■ VN 121 Qc35
Haidra ■ TN 176 Le28
Hai Duong ■ VN 121 Qd35
Haifa ■ IL 90 Mh29
Haifeng ■ CHN 109 Qh34
Haig ■ AUS 145 Rd61
Haikang ■ CHN 108 Qf35
Haikou ■ ● CHN 109 Qf35
Ha'il ■ KSA 92 Na32
Hailakandi ■ IND 120 Pg33
Hailar ■ CHN 105 Qk21
Hailey ■ USA 232 Ec24
Hailin ■ CHN 110 Re23
Hailing Dao ■ CHN 108 Qf35
Hailun ■ CHN 110 Rd22
Hailuoto ■ FIN 41 Me25
Hailuoto ■ FIN 41 Me25
Haima ■ OM 95 Nj36
Haimen ■ CHN 112 Ra30
Hainan ■ CHN 109 Qe36
Hainan Dao ■ CHN 109 Qf35
Hainan Strait ■ CHN 108 Qe35
Hainburg ■ A 66 Lr42
Haindi ■ LB 186 Ke42
Haines ■ USA 230 Dc16
Haines City ■ USA 243 Fk31
Haines Highway ■ CDN 230 Db16
Haines Junction ■ CDN 230 Db15
Hainfeld ■ A 66 Lq42
Haingsisi ■ RI 131 Rb51
Hainichen ■ D 58 Ln40
Hainich, N.P. ■ D 58 Ll39
Haiphong ■ VN 121 Qd35
Haiti ■ RH 250 Gd36
Haiton ■ CHN 109 Qe36
Hai Van ■ VN 123 Qe37
Haiyan ■ CHN 106 Qa27
Haiyang ■ CHN 112 Ra30
Haiyuan ■ CHN 106 Qe28
Hajdarkan ■ KS 97 Of26
Hajdúböszörmény ■ H 67 Ma43
Hajeb el Aïoun ■ TN 176 Le28
Hajiganj ■ BD 120 Pf34
Haji Abad ■ IR 98 Nh31
Haji Abad ■ IR 98 Nk29
Haji Jafar Shahid ■ PK 99 Oe32
Hajiki-saki ■ J 111 Rh26
Hajin ■ SYR 91 Na28
Hajipur ■ IND 117 Pc33
Hajjah ■ YE 94 Nb37
Hajjah ■ YE 94 Nb38
Hajo ■ IND 120 Pf32
Hajo Do ■ ROK 112 Rd28
Hajós ■ H 67 Lu44
Hajrah ■ KSA 94 Na35
Hajsyn ■ UA 73 Me21
Hajyr ■ RUS 89 Rc04
Hakai Recreation Area ■ CDN 232 Dd20
Hakha ■ MYA 120 Pg34
Hakkâri ■ TR 91 Nb27
Hakkâri Dağları ■ TR 91 Nb27
Hakken-san ■ J 113 Rh28
Hakodate ■ J 111 Sa25
Hakul ■ J 111 Rj27
Haku-san ■ J 113 Rj27
Hakusan N.P. ■ J 113 Rj27
Halab ■ ● SYR 90 Mj27
Halaban ■ KSA 94 Nc34
Halabiyeh ■ SYR 91 Mk28
Halabja ■ IRQ 91 Nc28
Halacho ■ MEX 247 Fe35
Haladakuvu ■ CHN 105 Qk24
Halaib ■ SUD 179 Mj34
Halali ■ NAM 200 Lj55
Halaludowa ■ PL 64 Lr39
Halaska ■ USA 230 Cc15
Halat 'Ammar ■ KSA 92 Mj31
Halawa ■ USA 228 Ca34
Halberstadt ■ D 58 Lm39
Halbrite ■ CDN 233 Ej21
Halden ■ N 42 Ll31
Haldensleben ■ D 58 Lm38
Haldia ■ IND 120 Pe34
Haldibari ■ IND 120 Pe32
Haldikhora ■ IND 117 Pd34
Haldwani ■ IND 115 Ok31
Hale ■ EAT 197 Mk48
Haleakala N.P. ■ USA 234 Cb35
Halebid ■ IND 118 Oj39
Haleji Bird Reserve ■ PK 99 Od33
Halembe ■ EAT 196 Mf48
Hale, Mount ■ AUS 144 Qj58
Halesworth ■ GB 49 Lb38
Half Assini ■ GH 187 Kj43
Halfayat al-Muluk ■ SUD 185 Mg38
Halfmoon Bay ■ NZ 153 Tc69
Halfmoon Bay ■ USA 234 Dj27
Half Moon Shoal ■ 128 Qj41
Halfweg ■ Z 204 Ma61
Halgan ■ SP 195 Nc43
Halgeri ■ IND 118 Oh38
Halhul ■ WB 90 Mh30
Hali ■ KSA 94 Na36
Haliaeetus N.P. ■ USA 234 Cb35
Halibab ■ RI 130 Qk47

Hálki ■ GR 71 Mh54
Halkía ■ GR 69 Md52
Halkirk ■ CDN 233 Ed19
Halkirk ■ GB 48 Kr32
Halland ■ S 42 Ln33
Hallandale ■ USA 243 Fd34
Hallands Väderö ■ S 42 Ln34
Hallasan N.P. ■ ROK 112 Rd29
Hallbeck ■ USA 228 Cb16
Halle (Saale) ■ D 58 Lm39
Halleck ■ USA 234 Ec25
Halleforsnäs ■ S 43 Lr31
Hallein ■ A 61 Lo43
Hallettsville ■ USA 245 Fb31
Halley ■ ANT 286 Jc34
Halligen ■ D 58 Lj36
Hallingdal ■ N 42 Lk30
Hallingskarvet ■ N 42 Lj30
Hall in Tirol ■ A 60 Lm43
Hall Island ■ USA 228 Bd15
Hällnäs ■ S 41 Lu26
Hallock ■ USA 236 Fb21
Hallormsstaður ■ IS 46 Kf25
Hall Peninsula ■ CDN 227 Gc06
Hall Point ■ AUS 143 Rc53
Hall Point ■ AUS 146 Rg51
Hails ■ S 42 Lm32
Halls ■ S 42 Lm32
Halls Creek ■ AUS 143 Rd54
Halls Gap ■ AUS 150 Sb64
Hällsta ■ S 43 Lr31
Hallstahammar ■ S 43 Lr31
Hallstatt ■ A 61 Lo43
Hallstatt-Dachstein Salzkammergut ■ A 61 Lo43
Hallstätter See ■ A 61 Lo43
Hallsvik ■ S 43 Lt30
Hallyo Haesang N.p. ■ ROK 113 Re28
Halmahera ■ RI 125 Re45
Halmahera Sea ■ RI 131 Re46
Halmstad ■ S 42 Ln34
Halol ■ IND 116 Og34
Halong Bay ■ VN 121 Qd35
Halong City ■ VN 121 Qd35
Hal Safieni Hypogeum ■ M 63 Lp55
Hal'savy ■ BY 45 Mg36
Hälsingland ■ S 41 Lg29
Halsön ■ FIN 41 Mb28
Halsteren ■ NL 51 Le39
Halstuna ■ S 43 Lr31
Haltern ■ D 58 Lh39
Haltwhistle ■ GB 48 Ks36
Haluaghat ■ BD 120 Pf33
Halul ■ Q 95 Ng33
Halvad ■ IND 116 Of34
Halvarsgårdarna ■ S 43 Lq30
Halvmáneoya ■ N 38 Mb07
Ham ■ F 51 Ld41
Ham ■ TCH 189 Lh40
Hamab ■ NAM 204 Lk60
Hamada al Hamrah ■ LAR 176 Lf31
Ham ada de la Dao ura ■ DZ 175 Kj31
Hamada de Tindouf ■ DZ 174 Kf32
Hamada deTinrhert ■ DZ 176 Ld31
Hamada du Drâa ■ DZ 175 Kj31
Hamada du Guir ■ DZ 175 Kj30
Hamada Marzuq ■ LAR 177 Lg32
Hamadan ■ IR 93 Ne28
Hamada Tounassine ■ DZ 175 Kj31
Hamadat Tingarat ■ LAR 176 Lf31
Hamada Zegher ■ LAR 176 Lf32
Hamadet Bet Touadjine ■ DZ 175 Kk30
Hamadet el Atchane ■ DZ 176 Lc30
Hamaguir ■ DZ 175 Kj30
Hamamah ■ LAR 177 Ma29
Hamamasu ■ J 111 Sa24
Hamamatsu ■ J 113 Rj28
Hamar ■ N 40 Ll30
Hamar S ■ N 40 Lm30
Hamardomen ■ N 40 Lm30
Hamarro Hadad ■ ETH 193 Nd42
Hamasaka ■ J 113 Rh28
Hama-Tometsu ■ J 111 Sb26
Hambidge Conservation Park ■ AUS 150 Rh62
Hamburg ■ ● D 58 Ll37
Hamburg ■ D 232 Dj25
Hamburg ■ USA 236 Fb25
Hamburg ■ USA 239 Fe29
Hamdah ■ KSA 94 Nb36
Hamdallay ■ RMM 181 Kk38
Hamdallay ■ RN 182 Lb39
Hamdanah ■ KSA 94 Na36
Hame ■ TR 71 Mh51
Hämeenkyrö ■ FIN 44 Md29
Hämeenlinna ■ FIN 44 Me30
Hämeenselkä ■ FIN 44 Mf29
Hamelin ■ AUS 144 Qh59
Hamelin Island ■ AUS 143 Rd54
Hamersley Gorge ■ AUS 142 Qj57
HamersleyRange ■ AUS 142 Qj57
Hamhung ■ PRK 110 Rd26
Hamhung ■ CHN 110 Qg32
Hamid ■ D 93 Ne30
Hamidiye ■ TR 69 Mj49
Hamidiyeh ■ IR 93 Ne30
Hamilton ■ ● NZ 151 Sd64
Hamilton ■ USA 232 Dj21
Hamilton ■ USA 235 Ee29
Hamilton ■ USA 239 Fg28
Hamilton ■ USA 239 Fg28
Hamilton Dome ■ USA 233 Ef24
Hamilton Downs ■ AUS 146 Rf57
Hamilton Hotel ■ AUS 148 Sa57
Hamilton Island ■ AUS 147 Sd56
Hamilton River ■ AUS 148 Sa57
Hamilton Sound ■ CDN 241 Hc21
Hamim ■ UAE 95 Nh34
Hamina ■ FIN 44 Mg30
Hamirpur ■ IND 117 Ok34
Hamirpur ■ IND 114 Oj29
Hamju ■ PRK 110 Rd26
Hamlin ■ USA 238 Fa29
Hamlin Bay ■ AUS 144 Qh63
Hamm ■ D 58 Lh39
Hammam al Alil ■ IRQ 91 Na28
Hammam at-Turkman ■ SYR 90 Mk28
Hammam Boughrara ■ DZ 175 Kj29
Hammam Meskoutine ■ DZ 176 Lc27
Hammam-Righa ■ DZ 176 La27
Hammam Salahine ■ DZ 176 Lc28
Hammamet ■ TN 176 Le27
Hammar ■ S 43 Lg31
Hammarn ■ DZ 175 La30
Hammarö ■ S 43 Lg31
Hammaslahti ■ FIN 44 Mh28
Hammel ■ DK 42 Lk34
Hammelburg ■ D 59 Lk40
Hammeren ■ DK 43 Lp35
Hammerfest ■ N 39 Mb21
Hammerum ■ DK 42 Lj34
Hammick ■ USA 237 Fh24
Hammon ■ USA 238 Fa28
Hammond ■ USA 237 Fg25
Hammond ■ USA 238 Ff30
Hammonton ■ USA 241 Gc26
Hamna ■ N 38 Lg22
Hamont ■ B 51 Lf39
Hamoud ■ RIM 180 Kf37
Hampden ■ NZ 153 Te68
Hampden ■ CDN 241 Hb21

Hampenanperak ■ RI 126 Pk44
Hampi ■ IND 116 Oj38
Hampton ■ CDN 240 Gh22
Hampton ■ USA 236 Fd24
Hampton ■ USA 239 Fd29
Hampton ■ USA 242 Fk29
Hamra ■ LAR 185 Ma40
Hamra n.p. ■ S 41 Lp29
Hamrat al-Wuzz ■ SUD 185 Mf38
Hamrat as Shaykh ■ SUD 184 Md38
Hamriya ■ UAE 95 Nh33
Ham Tan ■ VN 123 Qe40
Ham Thuam Nam ■ VN 123 Qe40
Hamtic ■ RP 124 Ra40
Hamuku ■ RI 154 Rh47
Ham Yen ■ VN 121 Qc34
Hamyski ■ RUS 73 Na23
Han ■ USA 234 Cc35
Hanagal ■ IND 118 Oj38
Hanahan ■ USA 241 Ga30
Hanak ■ KSA 92 Mj32
Hanalei Bay ■ USA 234 Ca34
Ha Nam ■ VN 121 Qd35
Hanamaki ■ J 111 Sa26
Hanam Plateau ■ NAM 204 Lj58
Hanang, Mount ■ EAT 196 Mh48
Hana Road ■ USA 234 Cc35
Hanasi Itu ■ CHN 103 Rc53
Hanau ■ D 59 Lj40
Hancavičy ■ BY 65 Mg38
Hâncešti ■ MD 73 Me22
Hanceville ■ CDN 232 Dj20
Hancheng ■ CHN 106 Qf28
Hanchuan ■ CHN 109 Qg30
Hancock ■ USA 237 Ff22
Hancock ■ USA 241 Ga30
Handa ■ J 113 Rj28
Handagajty ■ RUS 101 Pd20
Handaki ■ EAT 197 Mh49
Handan ■ CHN 107 Qh27
Handapa ■ IND 117 Pc35
Handel ■ CDN 233 Ef19
Handeni ■ EAT 197 Mk48
Handlová ■ SK 67 Lt42
Handwa ■ IND 116 Oj35
Handsworth ■ AUS 149 Sd58
Handwara ■ 114 Oh28
Handyga ■ RUS 89 Rb06
Hanford ■ USA 234 Dj27
Hangal ■ IND 118 Oh38
Han Garaučica ■ MNE 68 Lu48
Hanga Roa ■ RCH 269 Gc54
Hang Chat ■ THA 121 Pk36
Hanggan Houqi ■ CHN 106 Qd25
Hanggin Qi ■ CHN 106 Qe26
Hangö = Hanko ■ FIN 44 Mc31
Hanging Rock ■ AUS 142 Ra57
Hangu ■ CHN 107 Qj26
Hangu ■ PK 99 Oj29
Hangzhou ■ ● CHN 112 Ra30
Hangzhou Bay Bridge ■ CHN 112 Ra30
Hanh ■ LAR 176 Lf31
Hani ■ TR 91 Na26
Hanidh ■ KSA 93 Ne32
Haniótis ■ GR 69 Md50
Han Island ■ PNG 157 Sh48
Hankasalmi ■ FIN 44 Mf28
Hankensbüttel ■ D 58 Ll38
Hankou ■ CHN 109 Qg30
Hanko = Hangö ■ FIN 44 Mc31
Hanksville ■ USA 235 Ee26
Hanle ■ IND 114 Oj30
Hanmer Springs ■ NZ 153 Tg67
Hanna ■ CDN 233 Ee20
Hanna ■ USA 235 Eg25
Hannaford ■ USA 236 Fa22
Hannagan Meadow ■ USA 235 Ef29
Hannahville Ind. Res. ■ USA 237 Fg23
Hannibal ■ USA 239 Fe26
Hannik ■ SUD 185 Mg36
Hann, Mount ■ AUS 143 Rc53
Hannover ■ D 58 Lk38
Hannoversch Münden ■ D 58 Lk39
Hannuu ■ CHN 106 Qf27
Hannut ■ B 51 Lf40
Hanö ■ S 43 Lp35
Hanöbukten ■ S 43 Lp35
Hanoi ■ ● VN 121 Qd35
Hanover ■ CDN 237 Fk23
Hanover ■ ZA 205 Mc61
Hanover Road ■ ZA 205 Mc61
Han Pijesak ■ BIH 68 Lt46
Hanshangpu ■ D 58 Li36
Hansi ■ IND 114 Oh31
Hanson ■ USA 240 Gh22
Hansweert ■ NL 51 Le39
Hanumangarh ■ IND 114 Oh31
Hanusovce nad Topl'ou ■ SK 67 Mb41
Hanušovice ■ CZ 66 Lr40
Hanwang ■ CHN 108 Qc30
Hanyang ■ CHN 109 Qg30
Hanyuan ■ CHN 108 Qb31
Hanzhong ■ CHN 106 Qe29
Haora ■ IND 120 Pe34
Haotan ■ CHN 106 Qe27
Haoud El Hamra ■ DZ 176 Ld30
Hãpai ■ SOL 157 Sj50
Haparanda ■ S 41 Me25
Haparanda skärgårds n.p. ■ S 41 Md25
Hapčeranga ■ RUS 104 Qg21
Hapo ■ RI 125 Re44
Happy Camp ■ USA 232 Dj25
Happy Corner ■ USA 241 Ge23
Hapsu ■ PRK 110 Re26
Hapur ■ IND 115 Oj31
Haputale ■ CL 119 Pa42
Haql ■ KSA 92 Mh31
Harabarjan ■ IR 98 Nh30
Haradh ■ KSA 93 Ne33
Harads ■ S 39 Ma24
Haradzec ■ BY 65 Mg37
Harakas ■ GR 71 Mf55
Haramosh ■ J 114 Og27
Haranor ■ RUS 105 Qj20
Harappa ■ PK 99 Og30
Harare ■ ● ZW 202 Mf54
Harasseeb ■ ETH 192 Nb41
ER ■ 193 Nc41
Haraze-Djombo ■ TCH 183 Lk39
Haraze Mangueigne ■ TCH 190 Ma41
Harbang ■ BD 120 Pg34
Harbel ■ LB 186 Ke42
Harbin ■ ● CHN 110 Rd22
Harboøre ■ DK 42 Lj34
Harbor Beach ■ USA 237 Fj24
Harbor Springs ■ USA 237 Fh23
Harbour Breton ■ CDN 241 Hb21

Harbour Deep ■ CDN 241 Hb20
Harcourt ■ AUS 151 Sc64
Harcourt ■ CDN 240 Gh22
Harda ■ IND 116 Oj34
Hardangerfjorden ■ N 42 Lf31
Hardangervidda ■ N 42 Lh30
Hardangervidda N.p. ■ N 42 Lh30
Hardap ■ NAM 204 Li58
Hardap Dam ■ NAM 204 Li58
Hardapdam ■ NAM 204 Lj58
Hardap Recreational Resort ■ NAM 204 Lj58
Hard Bargain ■ BS 243 Gb32
Hardegsen ■ D 58 Lk39
Hardelot-Plage ■ F 51 Lb40
Harden, Gunung ■ RI 128 Qh43
Harderwijk ■ NL 51 Lf38
Hardheim ■ D 59 Lk41
Hardin ■ USA 233 Eg20
Hardin ■ USA 239 Fe26
Hardinsburg ■ USA 239 Fg27
Hardisty ■ CDN 233 Ee19
Hardoi ■ IND 115 Pa32
Hardtner ■ USA 238 Fa27
Hare Bay ■ CDN 241 Ha21
Harem(Ems) ■ D 58 Lh38
Hareto ■ ETH 192 Mj41
Harewa ■ ETH 192 Na41
Harewood ■ GB 49 Kt37
Hargeisa ■ ● SP 193 Nc41
Hargigo ■ ER 192 Mk38
Hargshamn ■ S 43 Lt30
Haria ■ E 174 Kd31
Harib ■ YE 94 Nc38
Haribomo ■ RMM 181 Kj37
Haridaspur ■ IND 117 Pc35
Haridwar ■ IND 115 Ok31
Harihar ■ IND 118 Oh38
Harihareshwar Beach ■ IND 116 Og37
Harikari ■ NZ 153 Tf67
Harinakunj ■ IND 182 Lb39
Harippad ■ IND 118 Oj41
Haripur ■ IND 117 Pc36
Harirad ■ IND 116 Oj31
Harjavalta ■ FIN 44 Mc29
Härjedalen ■ S 40 Lo28
Harkany ■ H 66 Lt45
Harkidun ■ IND 115 Ok30
Harlan ■ USA 236 Fc25
Harlan ■ USA 236 Fc25
Harlan ■ USA 242 Fj27
Harleston ■ GB 49 Kq38
Harlech ■ GB 49 Kq38
Harlem ■ USA 233 Ef21
Harleigh Farm ■ ZW 202 Mg55
Harlingen ■ NL 51 Lf37
Harlingen ■ USA 245 Fb33
Harlow ■ GB 49 La39
Harlowton ■ USA 233 Ef22
Harmancik ■ TR 71 Mk51
Harmanli ■ BG 69 Mg48
Harmonia ■ BR 276 Hb60
Harnai ■ PK 99 Od30
Harness ■ F 51 Lc40
Harney Basin ■ USA 232 Ea24
Harnosand ■ S 41 Lt28
Härnösand ■ S 41 Ls28
Haro ■ E 56 Ks48
Haro Shiikh ■ SP 193 Nc41
Harpanahalli ■ IND 118 Oj38
Harper ■ LB 186 Kg43
Harper ■ USA 238 Fa28
Harper, Mount ■ USA 229 Cj13
Harpers Ferry N.H.P. ■ USA 241 Gb26
Harpersville ■ USA 239 Fg29
Harpeth Narrows Historic Area ■ USA 239 Fg27
Harput Kalesi ■ TR 91 Mk26
Harqin Qi ■ CHN 107 Qk25
Harrat al Buqum ■ KSA 94 Na35
Harrat al Kishb ■ KSA 94 Na34
Harrat Hadan ■ KSA 94 Na35
Harrat Khaybar ■ KSA 92 Mk33
Harrat Kurama ■ KSA 92 Mk33
Harrat Lunayyir ■ KSA 92 Mj33
Harrat Nawasif ■ KSA 94 Nb35
Harrat Rahat ■ KSA 92 Mk34
Harrat Rahat ■ KSA 94 Na34
Harricana ■ CDN 240 Ga20
Harrington ■ AUS 149 Sg61
Harrington ■ USA 232 Ea22
Harrington Harbour ■ CDN 240 Ha20
Harriospur ■ PK 99 Oj29
Harris ■ CDN 233 Eg20
Harris ■ GB 48 Ko33
Harrisburg ■ USA 239 Ff27
Harrisburg ■ ● USA 241 Gb25
Harrismith ■ ZA 205 Md60
Harris, Mount ■ AUS 143 Re58
Harrisonburg ■ USA 241 Ga26
Harrisville ■ LB 186 Ke42
Harrisville ■ USA 237 Fj23
Harrisville ■ USA 241 Ga26
Harrodsburg ■ USA 239 Fg27
Harrogate ■ CDN 233 Eb20
Harrogate ■ GB 49 Kt37
Harrow ■ AUS 150 Sa64
Harrström ■ FIN 41 Mb28
Harry S. Truman S.P. ■ USA 239 Fd27
Harsani ■ IND 116 Of33
Harsefeld ■ D 58 Lk38
Harsin ■ IR 91 Nd29
Harsova ■ RO 69 Mh45
Harsprånget ■ S 39 Ma23
Harstad ■ N 38 Lp22
Harsud ■ IND 116 Oj35
Harsvika ■ N 40 Lk26
Hart ■ USA 237 Fg24
Hartbeesfontein ■ ZA 205 Md59
Hartberg ■ A 61 Lq43
Hartford ■ ● USA 241 Ge25
Hartford City ■ USA 237 Fh25
Hartford ■ USA 239 Fg29
Hartha ■ D 58 Ln39
Hartington ■ USA 236 Fb24
Hartland ■ CDN 240 Gh22
Hartland Point ■ GB 49 Kq39
Hartley Bay ■ CDN 232 De19
Hartmannberge ■ NAM 200 Lg54
Hart, Mount ■ CDN 229 Ck14
Hart Ranges ■ CDN 232 Dj18
Hart Ranges ■ CDN 232 Dj18
Hartola ■ FIN 44 Mf29
Harts Range ■ AUS 146 Rg57
Hartsville ■ USA 241 Ga28
Hartswater ■ ZA 205 Mc59
Hartville ■ USA 236 Fa25
Hartwell ■ USA 239 Fh28
Haruj ■ LAR 178 Lj31
Haruku ■ RI 131 Re47
Harunabad ■ PK 99 Og31
Harur ■ IND 118 Oh39

Har us nuur ■ MNG 101 Pg21
Harut ■ YE 95 Ng38
Harvale ■ IND 116 Oh38
Harvest Home ■ AUS 147 Sd56
Harvey ■ AUS 144 Qh62
Harvey ■ USA 236 Fa22
Harwich ■ GB 49 Lb39
Harwood ■ AUS 149 Sg60
Haryana ■ IND 114 Oj31
Harz ■ D 58 Ll39
Harzgerode ■ D 58 Lm39
Harz, N.P. ■ D 58 Ll39
Hasa Abdal ■ PK 99 Og29
Hasaart ■ MNG 104 Qa23
Hasama ■ J 111 Sa26
Hasan ■ RUS 110 Rf24
Hasanabad ■ IND 117 Ok36
Hasan Abad ■ IR 98 Nj28
Hasan Abad ■ IR 98 Ng29
Hasanabad ■ IR 93 Ne29
Hasançelebi ■ TR 90 Mj26
Hasankale ■ TR 91 Na26
Hasankale ■ TR 91 Na27
Hasankeyf ■ TR 91 Na27
Hasan Kuleh ■ AFG 98 Ob29
Hasan Langi ■ IR 98 Nj32
Hasanpur ■ IND 115 Ok31
Hasarah ■ KSA 94 Na34
Hasardag Reserve ■ TM 96 Nj26
Hasavjurt ■ RUS 91 Nd24
Haselünne ■ D 58 Lh38
Hashab ■ SUD 184 Mc39
Hashtrud ■ IR 91 Nd27
Hasik ■ OM 95 Nh37
Hasil ■ RI 131 Rd46
Hasilpur ■ PK 99 Og31
Haskanit ■ SUD 184 Md40
Haskell ■ USA 238 Fa29
Haskovo ■ BG 69 Mg48
Hasnabad ■ IND 120 Pe34
Hasnabad ■ BD 120 Pf33
Hasparren ■ F 52 Kt47
Hassa ■ TR 90 Mj27
Hassel Mbarek ■ RIM 180 Ke37
Hassela ■ S 41 Lr28
Hasselö ■ S 43 Lr33
Hasselt ■ B 51 Lf40
Hasselt ■ NL 51 Lg38
Hadfurt ■ D 59 Ll40
Hassi Bahbah ■ DZ 176 La28
Hassi Barouda ■ DZ 175 La31
Hassi Bel Guebbour ■ DZ 176 Lf31
Hassi Berrekhem ■ DZ 176 Lc29
Hassi-Bou-Allala ■ DZ 175 Kj30
Hassi Daoula ■ DZ 176 Lc29
Hassi Defla ■ MA 175 Kj29
Hassi-Delaa ■ DZ 176 Lb29
Hassi-el-Ahmar ■ MA 175 Kj29
Hassi el Belrem ■ DZ 176 Lb32
Hassi el Ghella ■ DZ 175 Kk28
Hassi-el-Hadjar ■ DZ 176 Lc30
Hassi el Khannfous ■ DZ 176 Lb31
Hassi-el-Khenig ■ DZ 176 Lb32
Hassi el Klebi ■ DZ 175 Kk31
Hassi el Mouar ■ DZ 175 Kg31
Hassi-Fahl ■ DZ 176 Lb31
Hassi Fougani ■ MA 175 Kj29
Hassi Fouini ■ RIM 181 Kg37
Hassi Hadhour ■ DZ 176 Lc32
Hassi Hassana ■ MA 175 Kj30
Hassi Inertas ■ LAR 176 Lf31
Hassi Inifel ■ DZ 176 Lb31
Hassi Issendjel ■ DZ 176 Lc31
Hassi Karkabane ■ RMM 181 Kk37
Hassi Kord Myriem ■ DZ 175 Kj31
Hassi-Mahrez ■ DZ 175 Kk31
Hassi Marraket ■ DZ 176 Lc30
Hassi Messaoud ■ DZ 176 Ld30
Hassi Moussa ■ DZ 175 La31
Hassi Ntsel ■ DZ 176 Lc30
Hassi Ramad ■ DZ 176 Lc30
Hassi Ras el Erg ■ DZ 176 Lb30
Hassi-R'Mel ■ DZ 176 Lc29
Hassi Safiet Iniguel ■ DZ 176 Lb30
Hassi Settafa ■ DZ 176 Lb29
Hassi Tabelbalet ■ DZ 176 Ld32
Hassi Tartrat ■ DZ 174 Kg32
Hassi Touil ■ RIM 181 Kh37
Hässleholm ■ S 43 Lo34
Håssjö ■ S 41 Ls28
Hastière ■ B 51 Le41
Hastings ■ GB 49 La40
Hastings ■ ● NZ 153 Tj65
Hastings ■ USA 236 Fc25
Hastings ■ USA 239 Fh24
Hastings Island ■ MYA 122 Pk49
Hastings Island ■ PNG 156 Sf51
Haštpar ■ IR 91 Ne27
Håstveda ■ S 43 Lo34
Hasvik ■ N 39 Ma21
Hasways ■ YE 95 Nd38
Hasy in Agüei ■ LAR 176 Lg32
Hasy Tissan ■ LAR 177 Lg31
Hatanga ■ RUS 88 Qa04
Hatangskij zaliv ■ RUS 89 Qb04
Hatch ■ USA 235 Ej29
Hat Chao Mai N.P. ■ THA 122 Pk41
Hatches Creek ■ AUS 146 Rh56
Hatchie N.W.R. ■ USA 239 Fe28
Hat Creek Hist. Ranch ■ CDN 232 Dk20
Hateg ■ RO 68 Mc45
Hatfield ■ AUS 151 Sb62
Hat Gamaria ■ IND 117 Pc34
Hathazari ■ BD 120 Pg34
Hat Head N.P. ■ AUS 149 Sg61
Hatherleigh ■ GB 49 Kq40
Hathras ■ IND 115 Ok32
Ha Tien ■ VN 123 Qc40
Hatiman ■ J 113 Rj28
Ha Tinh ■ VN 123 Qd37
Hatkhamba ■ IND 116 Og37
Hatkoti ■ IND 115 Ok30
Hato Corozal ■ CO 264 Ge42
Hato la Vergareña ■ YV 265 Gj42
Hatol ■ YE 94 Nc37
Hatpara ■ IND 117 Pc34
Hatra ■ IRQ 91 Na28
Hatrik ■ N 42 Lf31
Hatsavan, Cerro ■ RA 282 Gd70
Hatta ■ IND 117 Ok34
Hatta ■ UAE 95 Nh33
Hattah ■ AUS 150 Sb63
Hattah Kulkyne N.P. ■ AUS 151 Sb63
Hatteras ■ USA 242 Gc28
Hatteras, Cape ■ USA 242 Gc28
Hatteras Abyssal Plain ■ 212 Gb06
Hatteras Island ■ USA 242 Gc28
Hat Thai Muang N.P. ■ THA 122 Pk41
Hattfjelldal ■ N 40 Ln25
Hattiesburg ■ USA 238 Ff30
Hattigudur ■ IND 117 Ok36
Hatton ■ CL 119 Pa42
Hatton ■ GB 48 Ks33
Hatton-Dikoya ■ CL 119 Pa42
Hattstatt ■ F 53 Lh43
Hattuşaş ■ TR 90 Mh25
Hat Wanakon N.P. ■ THA 122 Pk40
Hat Yai ■ THA 122 Qa42
Hatzfeldhafen ■ PNG 155 Sc48
Haud ■ ETH 193 Nc41
Haugastøl ■ N 42 Lh30
Haugesund ■ N 42 Lf31
Hauho ■ FIN 44 Me29
Hauhui ■ SOL 157 Ta50
Haukeligrend ■ N 42 Lh31
Haukivuori ■ FIN 44 Mf29
Haukiputi ■ FIN 41 Me25
Haukivesi ■ FIN 45 Mg29
Haultain ■ CDN 233 Ef17
Hauraki Gulf ■ NZ 152 Td64
Hausach ■ D 59 Li42
Hausruck ■ A 66 Lo42
Hautajärvi ■ FIN 39 Mh24
Haut Atlas ■ MA 174 Kf30

Hourtin ◻ F 52 Kt45
Hourtin-Plage ≈ ◻ F 52 Kt45
House of Schmelen ⌂ NAM 204 Lj59
Houston ◻ CHN 230 Dg18
Houston ◻ USA 229 Cf15
Houston ◻ USA 238 Fc31
Houston ◻ USA 239 Ff27
Houtbaai ◻ ZA 204 Lk63
Houtman Abrolhos ◻ AUS 144 Qg60
Houton ◻ GB 48 Kr32
Houtskari ◻ FIN 44 Mb30
Houtsklär ◻ FIN 44 Mb30
Houxia ◻ CHN 101 Pd24
Hov ◻ DK 42 Li35
Hova S 43 Lp32
Høvåg ◻ N 42 Lj32
Hovden ◻ N 42 Lh31
Hove ◻ GB 49 Ku40
Hoverla ◻ UA 67 Me42
Hovoro ◻ SOL 157 Sj50
Hövsan ◻ AZ 91 Nf25
Hövsgöl nuur ◻ MNG 104 Qa20
Hövsgöl nuur N.P. ⌂ MNG 104 Qa20
Hovsta ◻ S 43 Lq31
Hova-Aksy ◻ RUS 101 Pg20
Howakil ◻ ER 192 Na38
Howard ◻ AUS 149 Sg58
Howard ◻ USA 236 Fb23
Howden ◻ GB 49 Ku37
Howe ◻ USA 233 Ej23
Howick ◻ ZA 205 Mf60
Howick Group ◻ AUS 147 Sc53
Howland Islands ◻ USA 134 Ba09
Howli ◻ IND 120 Pf32
Howship, Mount ◻ AUS 146 Rg52
Howth ◻ IRL 47 Kc37
Hoxie ◻ USA 238 Ek26
Höxter ◻ D 58 Lk39
Hoxtolgay ◻ CHN 101 Pd22
Hoxud ◻ CHN 101 Pd24
Hoya ◻ D 58 Lk38
Høyanger ◻ N 42 Lg29
Hoyerswerda ◻ D 58 Lp39
Høylandet ◻ N 40 Ln26
Hoyono-sen ◻ J 113 Rh28
Hoyos ◻ E 55 Ko50
Hoža ◻ BY 65 Md37
Hozviótissa ◻ GR 71 Mf54
Hpakant ◻ MYA 120 Pj33
Hpangngal ◻ MYA 120 Pk34
Hpawngtut ◻ MYA 120 Pj33
Hpungan Pass ◻ IND/MYA 120 Pj32
Hradčany ◻ CZ 66 Lp40
Hradec Králové ◻ CZ 66 Lq40
Hradec nad Moravicí ◻ CZ 66 Ls41
Hrádek nad Nisou ◻ CZ 66 Lp40
Hradzy'k ◻ UA 73 Mg21
Hrafnagíl ◻ IS 46 Kb25
Hrafnseyri ◻ IS 46 Jr25
Hranice ◻ CZ 66 Ls40
Hranice ◻ CZ 66 Ls41
Hraničné ◻ SK 67 Ma41
Hrasnica ◻ BIH 68 Lt47
Hrastelnica ◻ HR 61 Lr45
Hrastnik ◻ SLO 66 Lq44
Hraun ◻ IS 46 Kc26
Hraunfossar ◻ IS 46 Ju26
Hraungerdi ◻ IS 46 Kb27
Hrazdan ◻ ARM 91 Nc25
Hrebet At-Baši ◻ KS 100 Oh25
Hrebet Cagan-Hurtej ◻ RUS 104 Qf20
Hrebet Čerskogo ◻ RUS 104 Qg20
Hrebet Črmana ◻ MNG 104 Qg21
Hrebet Hamar-Daban ◻ RUS 104 Qb20
Hrebet Horumnug Tajga ◻ RUS 101 Pj20
Hrebet Kukulbej ◻ RUS 105 Qj20
Hrebet Malyi Hamar-Daban ◻ RUS 104 Qc20
Hrebet Muzkol ◻ TJ 97 Og26
Hrebet Naryntau ◻ KS 100 Oj25
Hrebet Pekulnej ◻ RUS 89 Td05
Hrebet Sajljuge ◻ MNG/RUS 101 Pe21
Hrebet Sengilan ◻ RUS 101 Pj20
Hrebet Sinij ◻ RUS 111 Rg24
Hrebet Stanovik ◻ MNG 104 Qg21
Hrebet Suntar-Hajata ◻ RUS 89 Rd06
Hrebet Tukuringra ◻ RUS 89 Ra08
Hrebet Turana ◻ RUS 89 Rc08
Hrebet Ulahan-Bom ◻ RUS 89 Rd06
Hrebet Ulan-Burgasy ◻ RUS 104 Qe19
Hrebet Vostočnnyj Sinij ◻ RUS 111 Rg24
Hrebinka ◻ UA 73 Mg20
Hrisey ◻ IS 46 Kb25
Hrissoupoli ◻ GR 69 Me50
Hristiáni ◻ GR 70 Mb53
Hrodna ◻ BY 65 Md37
Hronsky Benadik ◻ SK 66 Lt42
Hrubiesów ◻ PL 65 Md40
Hrušovský hrad ◻ SK 66 Lt42
Hrušuvacha ◻ UA 73 Mj21
Hrvatska Dubica ◻ HR 61 Lr45
Hrvatska Kostajnica ◻ HR 61 Lr45
Hsenwi ◻ MYA 121 Pk34
Hsi-hseng ◻ MYA 120 Pj35
Hsinchu ◻ RC 109 Ra34
Hsinying ◻ RC 109 Ra34
Hsuen Shan ◻ RC 109 Ra33
Hti lin ◻ MYA 120 Ph35
Hua'an ◻ CHN 109 Qk31
Huabu ◻ CHN 109 Qj33
Huacachina ◻ PE 269 Gc53
Huacaya ◻ BOL 278 Gj56
Huacaybamba ◻ PE 269 Gb50
Huachón ◻ PE 269 Gc51
Huachuan ◻ CHN 111 Rf22
Huacrachuco ◻ PE 269 Gb50
Huacullani ◻ PE 278 Ge54
Huade ◻ CHN 107 Qg25
Huadian ◻ CHN 110 Rd24
Huagu ◻ CHN 108 Qc31
Huahai ◻ CHN 103 Ph26
Hua Hin ◻ THA 122 Pk39
Huai'an ◻ CHN 112 Qk29
Huaibei ◻ CHN 112 Qj29
Huaibin ◻ CHN 107 Qh29
Huaidian ◻ CHN 107 Qh29
Huai Hom Karen Village ◻ THA 121 Pj36
Huaihua ◻ CHN 108 Qf32
Huai Huat N.P. ◻ THA 123 Qc37
Huaiji ◻ CHN 108 Qg34
Huailaj ◻ CHN 107 Qh25
Huai Nam Dang N.P. ◻ THA 121 Pk36
Huairen ◻ CHN 107 Qg25
Huairou ◻ CHN 107 Qj25
Huaiyang ◻ CHN 107 Qh29
Huai Yang N.P. & Waterfall ◻ THA 122 Pk40
Huaiyin ◻ CHN 108 Qj31
Huai Yot ◻ THA 122 Pk42
Huaiyuan ◻ CHN 108 Qe33
Huaiyuan ◻ CHN 106 Qd27
Huaiyu Shan ◻ CHN 109 Qj31
Huajapan de León ◻ MEX 246 Fb37
Huajialing ◻ CHN 106 Qc28
Huajicori ◻ MEX 246 Eh35
Huajuapan Ind. Res. ◻ CHN 246 Fb37
Huajlapai Mountain Park ◻ USA 235 Ec28
Hualien ◻ RC 109 Ra33
Huallanca ◻ PE 269 Gb50
Huallaga ◻ PE 269 Gc50
Hualqui ◻ RCH 280 Gd64
Huamachuco ◻ PE 269 Gb50
Huamali ◻ PE 269 Gc51
Huambo ◻ ANG 200 Lh52
Huambo ◻ PE 269 Gc53
Huamuxtitlan ◻ MEX 246 Fa37
Huañamarca ◻ PE 269 Gd54

Huanan ◻ CHN 110 Rf22
Huancabamba ◻ PE 268 Ga48
Huancane ◻ PE 269 Gc52
Huancane ◻ PE 278 Gf53
Huancapi ◻ PE 269 Gc52
Huancapallac ◻ PE 269 Gb50
Huanca Sancos ◻ PE 269 Gc52
Huancavelica ◻ PE 269 Gc52
Huancayo ◻ PE 269 Gc52
Huanchaca, Cerro ◻ BOL 278 Gg56
Huancilla ◻ RA 281 Gj62
Huandacareo ◻ MEX 246 Ek36
Huanengchuan ◻ CHN 107 Qh29
Huangdi Ling ◻ CHN 106 Qe28
Huanggang ◻ CHN 109 Qh30
Huanggang ◻ CHN 109 Qh30
Huanggangliang ◻ CHN 105 Qj24
Huanggang Shan ◻ CHN 109 Qj32
Huangguoshu Falls ◻ CHN 121 Qc33
Huang He Lou ◻ CHN 109 Qh30
Huanghua ◻ CHN 107 Qj26
Huanglianggu ◻ CHN 109 Qj33
Huangling ◻ CHN 106 Qe28
Huang Ling Miao ◻ CHN 108 Qf30
Huanglong ◻ CHN 109 Qk31
Huanglong Si ◻ CHN 106 Qb29
Huanglong Z.B. ◻ CHN 106 Qb29
Huangnihe ◻ CHN 111 Rd24
Huangni ◻ CHN 109 Qh30
Huangping ◻ CHN 108 Qd32
Huangqiao ◻ CHN 112 Ra29
Huangsha ◻ CHN 109 Qk32
Huangshan ◻ CHN 109 Qj31
Huangshan ◻ CHN 112 Qj30
Huangshi ◻ CHN 109 Qh30
Huangyaguan ◻ CHN 107 Qj25
Huangyan ◻ CHN 109 Ra31
Huangyinaoyang ◻ CHN 108 Qf32
Huangyuan ◻ CHN 105 Qb21
Huangzhong ◻ CHN 106 Qa27
Huangzhong ◻ CHN 109 Qf36
Huanjiang ◻ CHN 108 Qe33
Huanquelén ◻ RA 281 Gk64
Huanqueros ◻ RA 279 Gk61
Huanren ◻ CHN 110 Rc25
Huanta ◻ PE 269 Gc52
Huánuco ◻ PE 269 Gc50
Huánuco Viejo ◻ PE 269 Gb50
Huanuni ◻ BOL 278 Gg55
Huan Xian ◻ CHN 106 Qd27
Huanza ◻ PE 269 Gb51
Huaping Yü ◻ RC 109 Ra33
Huaping Z.B. ◻ CHN 108 Qd33
Huaqiao ◻ CHN 108 Qd30
Huaquillas ◻ EC 268 Fk47
Huara ◻ RCH 278 Gf56
Huaral ◻ PE 269 Gb51
Huarazo ◻ PE 269 Gc52
Huari ◻ PE 269 Gb50
Huari ◻ PE 269 Gc52
Huari Belén ◻ BOL 278 Gf54
Huarichic ◻ MEX 244 Ef31
Huarina ◻ BOL 278 Gf54
Huarmey ◻ PE 269 Ga51
Huarong ◻ CHN 108 Qg31
Huásabas ◻ MEX 244 Ef31
Huasaga ◻ EC 268 Gb47
Hua Sai ◻ THA 122 Qa42
Huascarán, P.N. ◻ PE 269 Gb50
Huasco ◻ RCH 279 Ge60
Huashan ◻ CHN 106 Qf28
Hua Shan ◻ CHN 108 Qd34
Huashaoying ◻ CHN 107 Qh25
Huashixia ◻ CHN 103 Pk28
Huatabampo ◻ MEX 244 Ee31
Huatugou ◻ CHN 103 Pf26
Huatusco ◻ MEX 246 Fb36
Huauchi nango ◻ MEX 246 Fa35
Huautla ◻ MEX 246 Fb36
Hua Xian ◻ CHN 107 Qh28
Hua Xian ◻ CHN 107 Qn28
Huayacocotla ◻ MEX 246 Fa35
Huayin ◻ CHN 108 Qf28
Huaying ◻ CHN 108 Qd30
Huayllay ◻ PE 269 Gb51
Huayna Potosi, Nevado ◻ BOL 278 Gf54
Huaytará ◻ PE 269 Gc52
Huaytiquina, Port.de ◻ RA/RCH 279 Gg57
Huayuan ◻ CHN 108 Qe31
Huay Xai ◻ LAO 121 Qa35
Huazhou ◻ CHN 108 Qf35
Huazi ◻ CHN 110 Rb25
Hubbard ◻ USA 238 Fb30
Hubbard, Mount ◻ CDN 230 Da15
Hubbards ◻ CDN 240 Gj23
Hubbell Trading Post N.H.S. ◻ USA 235 Ef28
Hub Chauki ◻ PK 99 Od33
Hubei ◻ CHN 108 Qf30
Hubei ◻ CHN 242 Gb28
Hubli ◻ IND 116 Oh38
Hubynycha ◻ UA 73 Mh21
Huchacalla ◻ BOL 278 Gf55
Huchang ◻ PRK 110 Rd25
Hucknall ◻ GB 49 Ku37
Huckesfield ◻ GB 49 Kt37
Huder ◻ D 58 Lj37
Hüder ◻ CHN 105 Ra20
Hudiksvall ◻ S 41 Ls29
Hudson ◻ CDN 236 Fd20
Hudson, Cerro ◻ RCH 282 Gd69
Hudson ◻ USA 241 Gd24
Hudson Bay ◻ CDN 233 Ej19
Hudson Bay ◻ CDN 227 Gb06
Hudson Canyon ◻ USA 227 Gb24
Hudson Falls ◻ USA 241 Gd24
Hudson Mountains ◻ 286 Fa33
Hudson's Hope ◻ CDN 231 Dk17
Hudson Strait ◻ CDN 227 Fc06
Hue ◻ VN 123 Qd37
Huedin ◻ RO 67 Md44
Huehuetenango ◻ GCA 248 Fe38
Huejcolla ◻ RCH 280 Gd66
Huejúcar ◻ MEX 246 Ej34
Huejuquilla El Alto ◻ MEX 246 Ej34
Huejutla de Reyes ◻ MEX 246 Fa35
Huelgoat ◻ F 50 Kr42
Huelma ◻ E 55 Kr53
Huelva ◻ E 55 Ko53
Huepac ◻ MEX 244 Ee31
Huépil ◻ RCH 280 Ge64
Huequi, Volcán ◻ RCH 282 Gd67
Huercal-Overa ◻ E 57 Kr53
Huertecillas ◻ MEX 245 Ek33
Huesca ◻ E 56 Ku48
Huéscar ◻ E 55 Ks53
Huetamo de Nuñez ◻ MEX 246 Ek36
Huete ◻ E 57 Ks50
Huétraray ◻ N 42 Lt30
Hugenden ◻ AUS 147 Sc56
Hughes ◻ AUS 145 Re61
Hughes ◻ USA 229 Cc12
Hugh White S.P. ◻ USA 239 Ff29
Hugo ◻ USA 238 Ek27
Hugoton ◻ USA 238 Ek27
Huguochang ◻ CHN 108 Qd31
Huhehot → Hohhot ◻ CHN 107 Qh25
Huíb-Hochplato ◻ NAM 204 Lj59
Huichang ◻ CHN 109 Qh32
Huichapan ◻ MEX 246 Fa35
Huida ◻ IND 120 Pe33
Huido ◻ CHN 109 Qh34
Huidong ◻ CHN 121 Qb32
Huila ◻ CO 264 Gc44
Huila Plateau ◻ ANG 200 Lh53
Huilai ◻ CHN 121 Qb32
Huillapima ◻ RA 279 Gh61
Huimbayo ◻ MEX 244 Ed37
Huimin ◻ CHN 108 Qj27
Huimilpan ◻ MEX 246 Ek35
Huinin ◻ CHN 107 Qd27
Huinan ◻ CHN 110 Rd24
Huinca Renancó ◻ RA 280 Gh63

Huining ◻ CHN 106 Qc28
Huisachal ◻ MEX 245 Ek32
Huishui ◻ CHN 108 Qd32
Huitong ◻ CHN 108 Qf32
Huitlong ◻ PE 269 Gc52
Huittinen ◻ FIN 44 Md29
Huitzila ◻ MEX 246 Ej35
Hui Wangmu ◻ CHN 101 Pg24
Hui Xian ◻ CHN 106 Qg29
Huixtla ◻ MEX 247 Fd38
Huiyang ◻ CHN 109 Qh34
Huizhou ◻ CHN 109 Qh34
Huji ◻ CHN 107 Qg30
Hujiang ◻ CHN 121 Qa33
Hukeri ◻ IND 116 Oh37
Hukou ◻ CHN 109 Qh31
Hukou ◻ CHN 110 Qk34
Hukou Pubu ◻ CHN 106 Qf28
Hukuntsi ◻ RB 204 Ma57
Hula ◻ PNG 155 Sd51
Hulaku ◻ RI 131 Re47
Hulan ◻ CHN 110 Rd23
Hulan Ergi ◻ CHN 105 Rb22
Hulayfah ◻ KSA 92 Na32
Hulett ◻ USA 233 Eh23
Hulin ◻ CHN 111 Rg23
Hulín ◻ CZ 66 Ls41
Huljaipole ◻ UA 73 Mj22
Hüls ◻ D 58 Lh39
Hulst ◻ NL 51 Ld39
Hultsfred ◻ S 43 Lq33
Hultsfredsfestivalen ◻ S 43 Lq33
Hulubești ◻ RO 69 Mf46
Hulukou ◻ CHN 106 Qd27
Hulun Buir Shadi ◻ CHN 105 Qk21
Hulun Nur ◻ CHN 105 Qj21
Huma ◻ CHN 105 Rd20
Huma ◻ IND 117 Pb35
Humacao ◻ USA 251 Gh36
Humahuaca ◻ RA 279 Gh57
Humaitá ◻ BR 270 Gj49
Humaitá ◻ PY 276 Ha59
Humanes ◻ E 55 Kr51
Humansdorp ◻ ZA 205 Mc63
Humantla ◻ MEX 246 Fb36
Humariza ◻ MEX 244 Eg32
Humay ◻ PE 269 Gc52
Humay'un's Tomb ◻ IND 114 Oj31
Humboe ◻ ANG 200 Lh54
Humberstone ◻ RCH 278 Gf56
Humberstone and Santa Laura Salpeter Works ◻ RCH 278 Gf56
Humboldt ◻ CDN 233 Eh19
Humburn ◻ AUS 149 Sc59
Humenné ◻ SK 67 Mb42
Humennt ◻ IND 117 Pd34
Humfrey ◻ USA 233 Ed23
Humpolec ◻ CZ 66 Lq41
Humppila ◻ FIN 44 Md30
Humptulips ◻ USA 232 Dj22
Hum ◻ LAR 177 Lh31
Húnafloí ◻ IS 46 Ju25
Hunan ◻ CHN 108 Qf32
Hunasagi ◻ IND 116 Oj37
Hunderwasser-Bad ◻ A 61 Lr43
Hundested ◻ DK 42 Lm35
Hundorp ◻ N 40 Lk29
Hundred Islands N.R.A. ◻ RP 124 Qk37
Hunedoara ◻ RO 68 Mc45
Hünfeld ◻ D 58 Lk40
Hungarioring ◻ H 67 Lu43
Hungary ◻ H 66 Lt43
Hungen ◻ D 59 Lj40
Hungerford ◻ AUS 149 Sc60
Hungnam ◻ PRK 110 Rd26
Hungund ◻ IND 116 Oj37
Huni Valley ◻ VN 121 Qd35
Hunjiang ◻ CHN 110 Rd25
Hunkuvi ◻ WAN 188 La40
Hunnebostrand ◻ S 42 Lm32
Hunsberge ◻ NAM 204 Lj59
Hunsrück ◻ D 59 Lh41
Hunstanton ◻ GB 49 La38
Hunstein Range ◻ PNG 155 Sb48
Hunsur ◻ IND 116 Oj39
Hunter Island ◻ AUS 151 Sc66
Hunter Island ◻ CDN 232 Df20
Hunters ◻ USA 232 Ea21
Hunter Valley ◻ AUS 151 Sf62
Huntingburg ◻ USA 239 Fg26
Huntingdon ◻ GB 49 Ku38
Huntingdon ◻ USA 237 Ga25
Huntington ◻ USA 239 Ff28
Huntington ◻ USA 239 Fg25
Huntington ◻ USA 237 Fh25
Huntington ◻ USA 232 Eb24
Huntington ◻ USA 237 Fj26
Huntington Beach ◻ USA 234 Eb29
Huntington Beach S.P. ◻ USA 242 Gg29
Huntly ◻ GB 48 Kt33
Huntly ◻ NZ 152 Th64
Hunto-Chac ◻ MEX 247 Ff36
Huntsville ◻ USA 237 Fd30
Huntsville ◻ USA 238 Fc30
Huntsville ◻ USA 238 Fd27
Huntsville ◻ USA 239 Ff27
Hunucma ◻ MEX 247 Ff35
Hunyuan ◻ CHN 107 Qg26
Hunza ◻ PK 114 Oh27
Hunza Valley ◻ PK 114 Oh27
Huocheng ◻ CHN 100 Oh23
Huolongji ◻ CHN 105 Qk23
Huong Diem ◻ VN 123 Qd37
Huong Khe ◻ VN 121 Qc36
Huong Pagoda ◻ VN 121 Qc35
Huong Son ◻ VN 121 Qc36
Huon Gulf ◻ PNG 155 Sd49
Huon Peninsula ◻ PNG 155 Sd49
Huonville ◻ AUS 151 Sd67
Huoshan ◻ CHN 112 Qj30
Huoyan Shan ◻ CHN 101 Pe24
Huozhou ◻ CHN 106 Qf27
Hurama ◻ IR 98 Na32
Hure J ◻ IND 117 Pd34
Hurayah ◻ KSA 93 Nd33
Hurbanovo ◻ SK 66 Lt43
Hurdal ◻ N 42 Lm30
Hurdiyo ◻ SP 193 Nf40
Hure Qi ◻ CHN 105 Ra25
Hurezani ◻ RO 68 Md46
Hurghada ◻ ET 179 Mg32
Huri Hills ◻ EAK 194 Mj44
Hurley ◻ USA 236 Fa27
Huron ◻ USA 233 Ej23
Huron ◻ USA 236 Fa23
Huronia Museum ◻ CDN 237 Ga23
Hurricane ◻ AUS 147 Sc54
Hurricane ◻ USA 235 Cf14
Hurricane River Cave ◻ USA 238 Fd27
Hurso ◻ ETH 192 Na41
Hurstbridge ◻ AUS 151 Sc64
Hurtado ◻ RCH 279 Gf61
Hurtigruta ◻ N 40 Lt21
Hurtulu ◻ RI 129 Qh44
Hurunga Safari Area ◻ ZW 202 Me54
Hurunxuing ◻ CHN 108 Qd34
Hurzuf ◻ UA 73 Mh23
Husafell ◻ IS 46 Ju26
Húsávik ◻ IS 46 Kb24
Husašáu de Tinca ◻ RO 67 Mb44
Húsavík ◻ IS 46 Kb25
Husheib ◻ SUD 185 Mh38
Husinec ◻ CZ 66 Lp41

Huskisson ◻ AUS 151 Sf63
Huskvarna ◻ S 43 Lp33
Huslia ◻ USA 229 Cb13
Husn ◻ JOR 90 Mh30
Hus Salaam ◻ CDN 232 Eb19
Hussainabad ◻ IND 117 Pc33
Hussar ◻ CDN 233 Ed20
Husum ◻ D 58 Lk36
Husum ◻ S 41 Lu27
Husun al Salasil ◻ YE 94 Nd37
Hutaraja ◻ RI 127 Pk44
Hutchinson ◻ USA 232 Ea19
Hutchinson ◻ USA 238 Fb27
Hutchinson ◻ ZA 204 Mb61
Huth ◻ YE 94 Nb37
Hutiao La ◻ CHN 121 Qa32
Hutjena ◻ PNG 157 Sh48
Hutou ◻ CHN 111 Rg23
Hutovo Blato ◻ BIH 61 Ls47
Hutton, Mount ◻ AUS 149 Se58
Hutubi ◻ CHN 101 Pd23
Huu ◻ RI 130 Qk50
Huu Beach ◻ RI 130 Qk50
Huvar ◻ IR 98 Oa32
Huvin Hipparoj ◻ IND 116 Oj37
Huwan ◻ CHN 107 Qh30
Huxi Xincun ◻ CHN 106 Qa25
Huxley ◻ CDN 233 Ed20
Huxley, Mount ◻ AUS 150 Qj37
Huxley, Mount ◻ USA 230 Ck15
Huy ◻ B 51 Lf40
Huzhong Z.B. ◻ CHN 105 Rb20
Huzhou ◻ CHN 112 Ra30
Huzhu Tuzu Zizhixian ◻ CHN 106 Qa27
Hužir ◻ RUS 104 Qd19
Hvalba ◻ N 42 Lm31
Hvalnes ◻ IS 46 Kf26
Hvalvík ◻ DK 46 Kn28
Hvammstangi ◻ IS 46 Ju25
Hvammstangi ◻ IS 46 Ji26
Hvammur ◻ IS 46 Ji26
Hvannadalshnúkur ◻ IS 46 Kd26
Hvanneyri ◻ IS 46 Ju26
Hvannigiljafoss ◻ IS 46 Ka26
Hvar ◻ HR 61 Lr47
Hvar ◻ HR 61 Lr47
Hvastovići ◻ RUS 72 Mh19
Hveragerdi ◻ IS 46 Jt27
Hveravellir ◻ IS 46 Ka26
Hvide Sande ◻ DK 42 Lj35
Hvittingfoss ◻ N 42 Lk31
Hvolsvöllur ◻ IS 46 Ju27
Hvostovo ◻ RUS 111 Sh22
Hwange ◻ ZW 202 Mc55
Hwange N.P. ◻ ZW 202 Md55
Hwaseong Fortress ◻ ROK 112 Rd27
Hwedza ◻ ZW 202 Mf55
Hweiziyeh ◻ SYR 91 Na27
Hyades, Cerro ◻ RCH 282 Gd69
Hyannis ◻ USA 241 Ge25
Hyannis ◻ USA 236 Ej23
Hyaburg ◻ USA 230 Dd18
Hyden ◻ AUS 144 Qj61
Hyden ◻ USA 242 Fj27
Hyde Park ◻ USA 241 Gd23
Hyderabad ◻ IND 116 Ok37
Hyderabad ◻ PK 99 Oe33
Hyères ◻ F 53 Lg47
Hyesan ◻ PRK 110 Re25
Hyland Plateau ◻ CDN 230 Df15
Hyltebruk ◻ S 42 Ln34
Hyperittlösen ◻ N 42 Lj36
Hyrax Hill ◻ EAK 194 Mj46
Hysham ◻ USA 233 Eg22
Hyuga ◻ J 113 Rf29
Hyvinkää ◻ FIN 44 Me30

I

Ia ◻ GR 71 Mf54
Iaciara ◻ BR 275 Hg53
Iacu ◻ BR 275 Hj54
Iagain Island ◻ PNG 157 Sh48
Iaguareté ◻ BR 265 Gf45
Iakora ◻ RM 207 Nd57
Iamara ◻ PNG 155 Sb50
Ianabinda ◻ RM 207 Nc57
Ianakafy ◻ RM 207 Nc57
Ianapera ◻ RM 207 Nd56
Ianca ◻ RO 69 Mh45
Iapim ◻ BR 268 Gd49
Iaripo ◻ BR 266 Hc45
Iba ◻ RP 124 Qk38
Ibacari ◻ BR 275 Hj56
Ibague ◻ CO 264 Gc43
Iballë ◻ AL 68 Lu47
Iballë ◻ AL 68 Lu47
Ibans ◻ WAN 188 La42
Ibar ◻ SRB 68 Ma47
Ibara ◻ WAN 188 Lb42
Ibaraki ◻ J 113 Rg27
Ibarra ◻ EC 268 Ga45
Ibarra ◻ RA 276 Ha58
Ibatiba ◻ BR 275 Hj56
Ibb ◻ YE 94 Nc39
Ibba ◻ SUD 191 Md43
Ibbenbüren ◻ D 58 Lh38
Ibeas de Juarros ◻ E 56 Kr48
Ibembo ◻ RDC 191 Mb44
Ibeto ◻ WAN 188 La41
Ibeto ◻ WAN 188 Le41
Ibiá ◻ BR 275 Hg55
Ibiai ◻ BR 275 Hh54
Ibiassucé ◻ BR 275 Hj53
Ibibobo ◻ BOL 279 Gj56
Ibicuí ◻ BR 275 Ja53
Ibicuy ◻ RA 276 Ha62
Ibihy ◻ RM 207 Nd56
Ibimirim ◻ BR 273 Jb50
Ibipeba ◻ BR 273 Hj51
Ibipetum ◻ BR 273 Hj51
Ibipira ◻ BR 267 Hh47
Ibipitanga ◻ BR 273 Hj52
Ibiquera ◻ BR 273 Hj53
Ibiraba ◻ BR 273 Hj51
Ibiraci ◻ BR 275 Hg56
Ibirama ◻ BR 277 Hf59
Ibiranhém ◻ BR 275 Hk54
Ibirataia ◻ BR 275 Ja53
Ibirité ◻ BR 275 Hh55
Ibirubá ◻ BR 276 Hd60
Ibitiara ◻ BR 273 Hj53
Ibitinga ◻ BR 274 Hf56
Ibiza = Eivissa ◻ E 57 Lb51
Ibiza = Eivissa ◻ E 57 Lb52
Ibó ◻ BR 273 Ja50
Ibo ◻ MOC 197 Na52
Ibohamane ◻ RN 182 Lc39
Iboih Beach ◻ RI 126 Ph43
Iboko ◻ RDC 199 La46
Ibologo ◻ EAT 196 Mg48
Ibonma ◻ RI 154 Rg47
Iboro ◻ WAN 188 Lb42
Ibotirama ◻ BR 273 Hj53
Ibra ◻ OM 95 Nk34
Ibri ◻ OM 95 Nj34
Ibrahimpatan ◻ IND 116 Ok37
Ibrahim Rauza ◻ IND 116 Oj37
Ibri ◻ IND 125 Rd45
Ibsuki ◻ J 113 Rf30
Ica ◻ PE 269 Gc52
Icabaru ◻ YV 265 Gj43
Icacos Point ◻ YV 265 Gk40

Içana ◻ BR 265 Gg45
Icapuí ◻ BR 273 Jb48
Içara ◻ BR 277 Hf60
Içara ◻ BR 277 Hf60
Icaraíma ◻ BR 274 Hd57
Icatu ◻ BR 267 Hh47
Icatú, T.I. ◻ BR 274 He56
Içel ◻ TR 90 Mh27
Iceland ◻ IS 46 Ju24
Iceland Basin ◻ 226 Jb04
Iceland Faeroe Rise ◻ 227 Kb06
Icelandic Plateau ◻ 210 Ka03
Icem ◻ BR 274 Hf56
Içeriçumra ◻ TR 90 Mg27
Ice Stream A ◻ 286 Cd35
Ice Stream B ◻ 286 Cc35
Ice Stream C ◻ 286 Cb35
Ice Stream D ◻ 286 Cd35
Ice Stream E ◻ 286 Cc35
Ichabo-eiland ◻ NAM 204 Lh59
Ichabo Island ◻ NAM 204 Lh59
Ichalkaranji ◻ IND 116 Oj37
Ichchapuram ◻ IND 117 Pc36
Iche ◻ MA 175 Kk29
Ichenhausen ◻ D 59 Ll42
Icheu ◻ WAN 188 Ld42
Ichhawar ◻ IND 116 Oj34
Ichinomiya ◻ J 113 Rj28
Ichkeul, P.N. de l' ◻ TN 176 Le27
Ich'on ◻ PRK 112 Rd26
Ich'on ◻ ROK 112 Rd27
Ichuña ◻ PE 269 Ge54
Icó ◻ RO 67 Md44
Içmeler ◻ TR 71 Mj54
Içó ◻ BR 273 Ja49
Icoca ◻ ANG 198 Lj49
Icy Cape ◻ USA 229 Bk10
Icy Cape ◻ USA 230 Ck16
Icy Reef ◻ USA 229 Ck11
Ida ◻ SP 195 Nb45
Idabato ◻ CAM 188 Lc43
Idabel ◻ USA 238 Fc29
Idabo ◻ ETH 192 Na42
Idaho ◻ USA 228 Cc22
Idaho ◻ WAN 188 Lb42
Idaho Falls ◻ USA 232 Ee24
Idah ◻ WAN 188 Lc42
Idalia N.P. ◻ AUS 149 Sc58
Idaere ◻ WAN 188 Ld42
Ida-Oumarkt ◻ MA 174 Kf31
Idar-Oberstein ◻ D 59 Lh41
Ida Valley ◻ AUS 144 Ra60
Ida al-Ghanam ◻ SUD 184 Mc40
Ideles ◻ DZ 182 Lc34
Idenao ◻ CAM 188 Lc43
Idgaon ◻ BD 120 Pg35
Idgarh ◻ IND 120 Pg35
Idi ◻ RI 126 Pj43
Iditole ◻ ETH 195 Nb43
Idini ◻ RI 91 Na27
Idiofa ◻ RDC 199 Lk48
Id-Kah-Mosque ◻ CHN 100 Oj25
Idkole ◻ EAT 196 Mg48
Idku ◻ WAN 188 Lc42
Idkom ◻ WAN 188 Lc42
Idoma ◻ EAT 194 Mh47
Idomu ◻ WAN 188 Lc41
Idongo ◻ RCA 190 Ma42
Idongo ◻ EAT 196 Mh49
Idonongo ◻ RDC 190 Lk45
Idoo ◻ EAK 194 Mj46
Idorodu ◻ WAN 188 Lb42
Idra ◻ GR 71 Md53
Idracowra ◻ AUS 148 Rg58
Idre ◻ S 40 Ln29
Idrefjäll ◻ S 40 Ln29
Idrija ◻ SLO 66 Lp44
Idstein ◻ D 59 Lj40
Idumba ◻ RDC 199 Ma47
Idutywa ◻ ZA 205 Me62
Idvor ◻ SRB 68 Ma45
Iecava ◻ LV 45 Me34
Ie-jima ◻ J 113 Rd32
Iepe ◻ BR 274 He57
Ieper ◻ B 51 Lc40
Ierápetra ◻ GR 71 Mf55
Ierissós ◻ GR 69 Md50
Iernut ◻ RO 67 Me44
Ifakara ◻ EAT 197 Mj50
Ifaki ◻ WAN 188 Lc42
Ifanadiana ◻ RM 207 Nd56
Ifanirea ◻ RM 207 Nd57
Ife ◻ WAN 188 Lc42
Iferouâne ◻ RN 182 Le36
Ifetedo ◻ WAN 188 Lc42
Ifetesene ◻ DZ 176 Lc33
Iffezheim ◻ D 59 Lj42
Ifjord ◻ N 39 Mh20
Ifon ◻ WAN 188 Lc42
Ifrane ◻ MA 175 Kh29
Ifumbo ◻ EAT 196 Mg49
Iga ◻ WAN 188 Ld40
Igalukila ◻ EAT 196 Mg48
Igalulu ◻ EAT 196 Mg48
Iganga ◻ EAU 194 Mg45
Igangan ◻ WAN 188 Lb42
Igara ◻ BR 273 Ja48
Igapora ◻ BR 275 Hh53
Igaporã ◻ BR 275 Hh53
Igapó-Açú ◻ BR 270 Gj48
Igara ◻ RUS 88 Pd05
Igarapava ◻ BR 275 Hg56
Igarapé-Açú ◻ BR 267 Hg46
Igarapé Capana, T.I. ◻ BR 270 Gf50
Igarapé Grande ◻ BR 272 Hh48
Igarapé Lourdes, T.I. ◻ BR 270 Gh51
Igarapé Mirim ◻ BR 267 Hf46
Igarka ◻ RUS 88 Pb05
Igatpuri ◻ IND 116 Og36
Igawa ◻ EAT 196 Mh50
Igbanke ◻ WAN 188 Lc42
Igbgoor ◻ WAN 188 Lc42
Igboho ◻ WAN 188 Lb42
Igbo-Oro ◻ WAN 188 Lb42
Igbor ◻ WAN 188 Ld42
Igbor ◻ TR 91 Nc26
Igdir ◻ MA 174 Kf30
Igel ◻ BR 273 Hj51

Igusule ◻ EAT 194 Mg47
Iharana ◻ RM 206 Ne52
Iharosberény ◻ H 66 Ls44
Iheret ◻ EAK 194 Mj47
Iherir ◻ DZ 176 Lc33
Iheya ◻ J 113 Rd32
Iheya-jima ◻ J 113 Rd32
Ihiala ◻ WAN 188 Lc43
Ihlara ◻ TR 90 Mh26
Ihode ◻ FIN 44 Mc30
Ihosy ◻ RM 207 Nd57
Ihu ◻ PNG 155 Sc49
Ihugh ◻ WAN 188 Ld42
Ihumbu ◻ EAT 197 Mh49
Iho ◻ WAN 188 Ld43
Iida ◻ J 113 Rj28
Iidaan ◻ SP 193 Ne42
Iide-san ◻ J 111 Rk27
Iittala ◻ FIN 44 Me29
Iisalmi ◻ FIN 44 Mg28
Ijatëne ◻ RMM 181 Kf35
Ijara ◻ EAK 195 Nd46
Ijebu-Igbo ◻ WAN 188 Lb42
Ijebu-Ode ◻ WAN 188 Lb42
Ijen-Merapi Maelang Reserves ◻ RI 129 Qh50
Ijevan ◻ ARM 91 Nc25
IJmuiden ◻ NL 51 Le38
Ijoubban ◻ RIM 181 Kg34
Ijoukak ◻ MA 175 Kf30
IJssel ◻ NL 51 Lg38
IJsselmeer ◻ NL 51 Lf38
IJsselstein ◻ NL 51 Lf38
Ijui ◻ BR 276 Hd60
Ikaalinen ◻ FIN 44 Md29
Ikalamavony ◻ RM 207 Nd56
Ikali ◻ RDC 199 La47
Ikaito Monastery ◻ GE 91 Nc25
Ikanbujimal ◻ CHN 101 Pe26
Ikanda ◻ RDC 199 Ma47
Ikang ◻ WAN 188 Le43
Ikanga ◻ EAK 194 Mk46
Ikare ◻ WAN 188 Lc42
Ikaría ◻ GR 71 Mg53
Ikast ◻ DK 42 Lk34
Ikauna ◻ IND 117 Pa32
Ikebe ◻ WAN 188 Lc42
Ikeda ◻ J 111 Sb24
Ikeja ◻ WAN 188 Lb42
Ikela ◻ RDC 199 Lk46
Ikeda ◻ J 111 Rk27
Ikere ◻ WAN 188 Lc42
Ikh Bogd Uul ◻ MNG 104 Qc23
Ikh Bogd Uul ◻ MNG 104 Pk23
Ikh Bulag ◻ MNG 104 Qd24
Ikh Gazaryn Chuluu ◻ MNG 104 Qd23
Ikh'Khyrkhan ◻ MNG 104 Qc22
Ikh Khenteyn Nuruu ◻ MNG 104 Qd22
Ikh Nuuruudyn Khotgor ◻ MNG 101 Ph21
Ikhsüüj ◻ MNG 104 Qd21
Ikiala ◻ J 113 Re29
Ikiak ◻ USA 229 Cc10
Ikire ◻ WAN 188 Lc42
Ikirun ◻ WAN 188 Lc42
Iki-Tsushima Q.N.P. ◻ J 113 Re28
Ikiztepe ◻ TR 90 Mj25
Ikola ◻ EAT 196 Mf49
Ikom ◻ WAN 188 Ld42
Ikom ◻ WAN 188 La42
Ikoma ◻ EAT 194 Mh47
Ikomu ◻ WAN 188 La41
Ikongo ◻ EAT 196 Mh49
Ikonongo ◻ RDC 190 Lk45
Ikoo ◻ EAK 194 Mj46
Ikorodu ◻ WAN 188 Lb42
Ikot Ekpene ◻ WAN 188 Ld43
Ikoto ◻ SUD 194 Mg43
Ikskile ◻ LV 45 Me34
Ikuba ◻ EAT 196 Mf49
Ikungi ◻ EAT 196 Mh48
Ikutha ◻ EAK 194 Mk47
Ilaga ◻ RI 154 Rg47
Ilagan ◻ RP 124 Ra37
Ilaiyankudi ◻ IND 118 Ok41
Ilaji ◻ WAN 188 Lb42
Ilaka Afovoany ◻ RM 207 Nc56
Ilakka ◻ RMM 207 Nc57
Ilam ◻ IR 91 Nd29
Ilam ◻ NEP 117 Pd32
Ilangali ◻ EAT 196 Mh49
Ilara ◻ WAN 188 Lc42
Ilaro ◻ WAN 188 Lb42
Ilaura ◻ PNG 155 Sd49
Ilaut ◻ EAK 194 Mj45
Ilave ◻ PE 278 Gf54
Ilawa ◻ PL 65 Lu37
Ilbilbie ◻ AUS 149 Se58
Ilbisil ◻ EAK 194 Mj47
Ilchester ◻ GB 49 Ks40
Ildir ◻ TR 71 Mg52
Ile ◻ KZ 100 Oj23
Île-à-la-Crosse ◻ CDN 231 Eg18
Ile-Alatau N.P. ◻ KS 97 Og26
Île Aoba ◻ VU 158 Td53
Île Aride ◻ SY 195 Nh48
Île Art ◻ F 158 Td55
Ilebo ◻ RDC 199 Ma48
Île Brion ◻ CDN 240 Gj22
Île Chesterfield ◻ F 206 Nb54
Île d'Ambre ◻ MS 207 Nj56
Île d'Anticosti ◻ CDN 240 Gj21
Île de France ◻ E 51 Lc41
Île de Gorée ◻ SN 180 Kb38
Île de Jerba ◻ TN 176 Lf29
Île de la Gonâve ◻ RH 250 Gd36
Île de la Tortue ◻ RH 250 Gd35
Île Denis ◻ SY 195 Nh47
Île d'Entree ◻ CDN 240 Gk22
Îles de Geneviers ◻ CDN 240 Ha20
Île des Pins ◻ F 158 Td57
Îles de Tiagba ◻ CI 187 Kh43
Île de Tumba ◻ RDC 199 La47
Îles d'Or ◻ F 53 Lg47
Île d'Oriane ◻ CDN 240 Gj21
Île du Nord ◻ SY 195 Nh47
Île du Nord ◻ SY 206 Nf51
Île du Petit Mécantina ◻ CDN 240 Ha20
Îles du Salut ◻ F 266 Hd43
Île d'Yeu ◻ F 52 Ks44
Île Europa ◻ F 203 Na57
Île Joinville ◻ 286 Ha32
Île Kótomo ◻ F 158 Td57
Île Maré ◻ F 158 Td56
Île Ouen ◻ F 158 Td57
Îles Belep ◻ F 158 Tb55
Îles Chausey ◻ F 52 Ks42
Îles de Glénan ◻ F 50 Kr43
Île de la Madeleine ◻ CDN 240 Ha20
Îles de la Madeleine, P.N. ◻ SN 180 Ka38
Îles de Los ◻ RG 186 Kd41
Îles des Saintes ◻ F 251 Gk38

Illimo Túcume ◻ PE 268 Ga49
Illiniza, Volcán ◻ EC 268 Ga46
Illizi ◻ DZ 176 Ld32
Ilkirch-Graffenstaden ◻ F 51 Lh42
Illueca ◻ E 56 Kt49
Illzach ◻ F 53 Lh43
Ilm ◻ D 58 Ln39
Ilmajoki ◻ FIN 41 Mc28
Ilmenau ◻ D 59 Ll40
Ilminster ◻ GB 49 Ks40
Ilnik ◻ USA 228 Ca17
Ilo ◻ PE 269 Ge54
Iłobu ◻ WAN 188 Lc42
Iloca ◻ RCH 280 Gd63
Ilog ◻ RP 124 Rb40
Iloilo ◻ RP 124 Ra40
Ilok ◻ HR 68 Lu45
Ilomantsi ◻ FIN 44 Mi28
Ilorin ◻ WAN 188 Lc41
Îlots Nosy Faho et Nosy Longo ◻ RM 206 Nd53
Ilphoten ◻ D 59 Ll41
Ilüka ◻ AUS 149 Sg60
Ilükste ◻ LV 45 Mg35
Ilulissat = Jakobshavn ◻ DK 227 Hc05
Ilupu ◻ IND 120 Ph31
Ilūr ◻ RI 131 Rf48
Ilushi ◻ WAN 188 Ld42
Ilva Mare ◻ RO 67 Me43
Ilwaki ◻ RI 131 Re49
Ilwendo ◻ Z 201 Mc54
Ilža ◻ PL 65 Mb39
Imabari ◻ J 113 Rg28
Imaculada ◻ BR 273 Jb49
Imágo ◻ J 113 Rj28
Imakane ◻ J 111 Rk27
Imala ◻ MEX 244 Eg33
Imala ◻ MOC 203 Mk53
Imam al Hamzah ◻ IRQ 93 Nc30
Imamganj ◻ IND 117 Pc33
Imamoğlu ◻ TR 90 Mj27
Imamzadeh Qolam Rasull ◻ IR 98 Oa33
Imamzadeh Jafar ◻ IR 91 Nf28
Imanombo ◻ RM 207 Nc58
Imari ◻ J 113 Re29
Imarui ◻ BR 277 Hf60
Imasa ◻ SUD 185 Mj36
Imasgo ◻ BF 187 Kj39
Imatong Mountains ◻ SUD 194 Mg43
Imatra ◻ FIN 44 Mj29
Imatrankoski ◻ FIN 44 Mj29
Imavere ◻ EST 44 Mf32
Imbarie ◻ BR 277 He58
Imbert ◻ DOM 250 Ge36
Imbituba ◻ BR 277 Hf59
Imbituva ◻ BR 277 He58
Imboden ◻ USA 239 Fe27
Imbwae ◻ Z 201 Mc54
Imeni-maraqandoso S ◻ RM 207 Nc57
Imerimandroso ◻ RM 207 Nd54
Imese ◻ RDC 190 La44
Imi ◻ ETH 192 Nd42
Imi-n-Ifri ◻ MA 175 Kg30
Imi-n-Ouasiif ◻ MA 175 Kg30
Imi-n-Tanoute ◻ MA 174 Kf30
Imishli ◻ AZ 91 Ne26
Imla ◻ DARS 180 Kc34
Immenstaat ◻ D 59 Lt43
Immingham ◻ GB 49 Ku37
Immokalee ◻ USA 243 Fk32
Imola ◻ I 60 Lm46
Imoschi ◻ HR 61 Ls47
Imotski ◻ HR 61 Ls47
Imouzzér-des-Ida-Outanane ◻ MA 174 Kf30
Imouzzér-Kandar ◻ MA 175 Kh29
Impasugong ◻ RP 125 Rc41
Imperatriz ◻ BR 272 Hf48
Impéria ◻ I 60 Lj47
Impéria ◻ CDN 233 Ek25
Imperial Mills ◻ CDN 231 Ee18
Imperial Palace ◻ CHN 107 Qj25
Imperieuse Reef ◻ AUS 142 Qk54
Impfondo ◻ RCB 190 Lk45
Imphal ◻ IND 120 Ph34
Imphy ◻ F 53 Ld44
Impuo ◻ ANG 200 Lh52
Imrali Adasi ◻ TR 89 Mj50
Imran ◻ YE 94 Nc39
Imroz ◻ TR 69 Mf50
Imst ◻ A 60 Ll43
Imuris ◻ MEX 244 Ee30
Imusho ◻ Z 201 Mb54
Imvouba ◻ RCB 198 Lh47
Ina ◻ J 113 Rj28
Inaafrmadow ◻ SP 193 Nc41
Ina-Abanghart ◻ RN 182 Le37
Inácio ◻ BR 274 Ht55
Inácio Martins ◻ BR 277 He58
I-n-Adiattafene ◻ RMM 181 Kj38
In Afellahh ◻ DZ 182 Le34
Inagua N.P. ◻ BS 250 Gd35
In Akamil ◻ DZ 176 Le31
In Akeouet ◻ DZ 176 Le32
I-n-Akhmed ◻ RMM 181 Kk36
I-n-Alei ◻ RMM 181 Kj37
I-n-Azaoua ◻ RN 182 Ld35
In-Belbel ◻ DZ 175 La32
Inca, Cerro del ◻ BOL/RCH 279 Gf56
Inca da Maloca ◻ BR
Incahuasi ◻ BOL 278 Gh56
Incahuasi ◻ RA/RCH 279 Gf58
Incahuasi ◻ RA 279 Gg58
Incahuasi ◻ PE 269 Gc52
Incallajta ◻ BOL 278 Gg54
Incebel Dağlari ◻ TR 90 Mj26
Ince Burun ◻ TR 69 Mh50
Ince Burun ◻ TR 90 Mg27
Incekum Burnu ◻ TR 90 Mg27
Incense Route → KSA 92 Mk34
Incense Route → YE 94 Nd38
Inchadén ◻ RMM 181 Kk37
Inch'on → ROK 112 Rd27
Incline ◻ MOC 202 Mg53
Incline Village ◻ USA 234 Ea26
Incomáti ◻ MOC 202 Mg56
Indaial ◻ BR 277 Hf59
Indaiabira ◻ BR 275 Hj53
Indaiatuba ◻ BR 275 Hg57
Indalsälven ◻ S 41 Lq27
Indalstø ◻ N 42 Lg29
Indaw ◻ MYA 120 Pj35

Jakunvara ◎ RUS 44 Mm28
Jakutsk ◎ RUS 89 Rb06
Jal ◎ USA 238 Ej29
Jalaid Qi ◎ CHN 105 Rb22
Jalai Nur ◎ CHN 105 Qj21
Jalalabad ◎ AFG 99 Of28
Jalalabad ◎ IND 115 Ok32
Jalal-Abad ◎ KS 97 Og25
Jalalpur ◎ IND 117 Pb32
Jalalpur ◎ PK 99 Oh29
Jalama ◣ USA 234 Dk28
Jalance ◎ E 57 Kt51
Jalandhar ◎ IND 114 Oh30
Jalang ◎ RI 130 Ra48
Jalangi ◎ IND 120 Pe33
Jalapa ◎ GCA 248 Ff38
Jalapa = Xalapa ⦿ MEX 246 Fb36
Jalapa ◎ MEX 247 Fd37
Jalasjärvi ◎ FIN 41 Mc28
Jalaun ◎ IND 117 Ok32
Jalawla ◎ IRQ 91 Nc28
Jaldag ◎ AFG 99 Od30
Jaldiyan ◎ IR 91 Nc27
Jales ◎ BR 274 He56
Jalesar ◎ IND 115 Ok32
Jaleshwar ◎ IND 117 Pd35
Jalez ◎ AFG 99 Oe28
Jalgaon ◎ IND 116 Oh35
Jalgaon ◎ IND 116 Oh36
Jalgaon ◎ IND 116 Oj35
Jali ◎ MW 203 Mh53
Jalibah ◎ IRQ 93 Nd30
Jalingo ◎ WAN 189 Lf41
Jalisco ⊡ MEX 246 Eh36
Jallo Park ♣ PK 99 Oh30
Jalna ◎ IND 116 Oh36
Jalnagar ◎ IND 117 Pb34
Jalor ◎ IND 116 Og33
Jalostotitlán ◎ MEX 246 Ej35
Jalpa ◎ MEX 245 Ek33
Jalpa ◎ MEX 246 Ej35
Jalpaiguri ◎ IND 120 Pe32
Jalpan de Serra ◎ □ ⛪ MEX 246 Fa35
Jalu ◎ LAR 177 Ma31
Jalu Oasis ✿ LAR 177 Ma31
Jama ◎ EC 268 Fk46
Jamaame ◎ SP 195 Nb45
Jamaame ◎ SP 195 Nb45
Jamaica ◎ C 250 Gc35
Jamaica ■ JA 250 Ga37
Jamaica Channel ≋ JA 250 Gc37
Jamal ◎ C 250 Gc35
Jamalpur ◎ BD 120 Pe33
Jamalwal ◎ PK 99 Oe30
Jama Masjid ☪ IND 117 Ok33
Jamari ◎ BR 270 Gj51
Jamari ◎ WAN 189 Lf40
Jamarovka ◎ RUS 104 Qf20
Jamb ◎ IND 117 Ok35
Jamba ◎ ANG 200 Lj53
Jambahal ◎ IND 117 Pc34
Jambi ◎ RI 127 Qb46
Jambo ◎ GH 187 La41
Jambol ◎ BG 69 Mg48
Jambongan ▲ MAL 128 Qj42
Jambongan ◎ MAL 128 Qj42
Jambusar ◎ IND 116 Og34
Jamda ◎ IND 117 Pc34
Jame Mosque ☪ IR 91 Nf28
Jame Mosque ☪ IR 93 Ne29
Jame Mosque ☪ IR 96 Nh27
Jame Mosque ☪ IR 98 Ng29
Jameos del Agua ◣ E 174 Kd31
Jamesabad ◎ PK 99 Oe33
James Bay ≋ CDN 227 Fd08
James Cook Museum 🏛 AUS 147 Sc53
James Corner = Nyororo ◎ EAT 196 Mh50
James Craik ◎ RA 281 Gj62
James Dalton Highway ⛟ USA 229 Ce12
James Island □ ♜ WAG 186 Kb39
James Range ▲ AUS 143 Rg58
Jamestown ◎ AUS 150 Rk62
Jamestown ◎ USA 236 Fa22
Jamestown ◎ USA 237 Ga24
Jamestown ◎ USA 239 Fh27
Jamestown ◎ USA 242 Ga29
Jamestown ◎ ZA 205 Md61
Jämijärvi ◎ FIN 44 Mc29
Jaminawá Arara do Rio Bage, T.I. ⌂ BR 269 Gd50
Jaminawá do Igarapé Preto, T.I. ⌂ BR 268 Gd49
Jamindan ◎ RP 124 Rb40
Jäminkipohja ◎ FIN 44 Me29
Jämjö ◎ S 43 Lq34
Jam Jodhpur ◎ IND 116 Of35
Jamkhandi ◎ IND 116 Oh37
Jamkhed ◎ IND 116 Oh36
Jamkino ◎ RUS 45 Mk33
Jammalamadugu ◎ IND 119 Ok38
Jammerbugten ⛱ ⚑ DK 42 Lk33
Jammersdrif ◎ ZA 205 Md60
Jam, Minaret of □ ☪ AFG 99 Oc28
Jammu ◎ 114 Oh29
Jammu and Kashmir ⊡ IND 115 Oj28
Jamnagar ◎ IND 116 Of34
Jamnagar Fort ♜ IND 116 Of34
Jamnice ◎ CZ 66 Lq41
Jampil' ◎ UA 73 Me21
Jampur ◎ PK 99 Of31
Jämsä ◎ FIN 44 Mf29
Jämsänkoski ◎ FIN 44 Mf29
Jamshedpur ◎ IND 117 Pd34
Jamtara ◎ IND 117 Pd34
Jamtari ◎ WAN 189 Lf42
Jämtland ▲ S 41 Lp27
Jamu ◎ ETH 192 Mh42
Jamui ◎ IND 117 Pd33
Jamuna Bridge ⛟ BD 120 Pe33
Jamundi ◎ CO 264 Gb44
Jamunkira ◎ IND 117 Pc35
Jana ▲ KSA 93 Ne32
Jana ≋ RUS 89 Rd05
Janakpur ◎ ♖ Ψ NEP 115 Pc32
Janan ◎ IND 116 Of34
Janannah ▲ UAE 95 Ng33
Janauba ◎ BR 275 Hj53
Jand ◎ PK 99 Og29
Jandaq ◎ IR 98 Nh28
Jandola ◎ PK 99 Of29
Jandowae ◎ AUS 149 Sf59
Janesville ◎ USA 237 Ff24
Jang ◎ GH 187 Kj41
Jang ◎ IND 120 Pf32
Janga ◎ GH 187 Kk40
Jangada ◎ BR 274 Hb53
Jangamo ◎ MOC 203 Mh58
Jangaon ◎ IND 117 Ok37
Jangipur ◎ IND 120 Pe33
Jangjay ◎ AFG 99 Od29
Jangkar ◎ RI 129 Qh49
Jangra ◎ IND 117 Pc35
Janja ◎ BIH 68 Lu46
Janjina ◎ HR 61 Ls48
Janjira ♜ IND 116 Og36
Jan Kempdorp ◎ ZA 205 Mc59
Jan Lake ◎ CDN 233 Ej18
Jan Mayen ▲ N 26 Kb02
Jan Mayen ▲ N 26 Kb02
Jano-Indigirskaja nizmennost' ▲ RUS 89 Sa04
Janos ◎ MEX 244 Ef30
Jánoshalma ◎ H 67 Lu44
Jánosháza ◎ H 66 Ls43
Jánossomorja ◎ H 66 Ls43
Janów ◎ PL 65 Lu40
Janów ◎ PL 65 Md37
Janów Lubelski ◎ PL 65 Mc40
Janowo ◎ PL 65 Ma37
Janów Podlaski ◎ PL 65 Md38
Jansenville ◎ ZA 205 Mc62
Janskij zaliv ≋ RUS 89 Rd04
Janskoe ploskogor'e ▲ RUS 89 Rc05
Jantan ◎ RI 154 Rh47
Jantarnyj ◎ RUS 45 Lu36
Jantia Hills ▲ IND 120 Pg33
Jantingue ◎ MOC 205 Mg58
Jantra ◎ BG 69 Mf47
Januária ◎ BR 275 Hh53
Janville ◎ F 51 Lb42
Janzé ◎ F 50 Kt43
Japan ■ J 77 Sa06
Japan Basin ▿ 111 Rh24
Japanese World War II Bunker ⊠ RI 154 Rg48
Japanese World War II Headquarter 🏛 RI 125 Rd45
Japan Trench ▿ J 76 Sa06
Japaratinga ◎ BR 273 Jc50
Japaratuba ◎ BR 273 Jb51
Japerica ◎ BR 267 Hg46
Japonvar ◎ BR 275 Hh54
Jäppilä ◎ FIN 44 Mh28
Japuira, T.I. ⌂ BR 271 Ha51
Japur ◎ IR 98 Nj30
Japura ◎ BR 270 Gg46
Japurá ≋ BR 270 Gh47
Japura ◎ RI 127 Qb46
Japvo ▲ IND 120 Ph33
Jaqué ◎ PA 249 Ga42
Jaquiri, T.I. ⌂ BR 270 Gh47
Jarabacoa ◎ DOM 250 Ge36
Jarablos ◎ SYR 90 Mj27
Jaraguá ◎ BR 274 Hf53
Jaraguá do Sul ◎ BR 277 Hf59
Jaragua, P.N. ✦ DOM 250 Ge37
Jarahueca ◎ C 243 Ga34
Jaraicejo ◎ E 55 Kp51
Jaraiz de la Vera ◎ E 55 Kp50
Jaral de Berrios ◎ MEX 246 Ek35
Jaramillo ◎ RA 282 Gg69
Ja'ranah ◎ KSA 92 Mk35
Jarandilla de la Vera ◎ ♜ E 55 Kp50
Jaraniyo ◎ ETH 192 Mk40
Jaransk ◎ RUS 72 Nd17
Jaranwala ◎ PK 99 Og30
Jarara, T.I. ⌂ BR 274 Hc57
Jarawara Jamamadi Kanamati, T.I. ⌂ BR 270 Gh49
Jarbridge ◎ USA 234 Ec25
Jarcevo ◎ RUS 72 Mg18
Jardim ◎ BR 273 Ja49
Jardim ◎ BR 274 Hb56
Jardim Alegre ◎ BR 276 He58
Jardim do Serido ◎ BR 273 Jb49
Jardinah ◎ LAR 177 Ma30
Jardín América ◎ RA 276 Hc59
Jardine River N.P. ⛺ AUS 147 Sb51
Jard-sur-Mer ◎ F 52 Kt44
Jaredi ◎ WAN 188 Lc39
Jaremča ⛲ UA 67 Me42
Jaremča ◎ UA 67 Me42
Jargalant ◎ MNG 101 Pf22
Jargalant ◎ MNG 101 Pj23
Jargalant ◎ MNG 104 Qa22
Jargalant ◎ MNG 104 Qc20
Jargalant ◎ MNG 104 Qc21
Jargalant ◎ MNG 104 Qc21
Jargalant Uul ▲ MNG 101 Pj23
Jargaltkhaan ◎ MNG 104 Qe22
Jargeau ◎ F 53 Lc43
Jarha ◎ IND 117 Pa34
Jari ≋ BR 271 Hd46
Järlåsa ◎ S 43 Ls31
Jarlshof Π GB 48 Kt31
Jarmen ◎ D 58 Lo37
Jarmolynci ◎ UA 73 Md21
Järna ◎ S 43 Lp30
Järna ◎ S 43 Ls31
Jarnac ◎ F 52 Ku45
Jarny ◎ F 51 Lf41
Jarn Yaphour ◎ UAE 95 Nh33
Jaro ◎ RP 124 Rc40
Jarocin ◎ PL 64 Ls39
Jaroměř ◎ CZ 66 Lq40
Jaroměřice ♜ CZ 66 Lq41
Jaroměřice nad Rokytnou ◎ CZ 66 Lq41
Jaroslavl' ◎ RUS 72 Mk17
Jarosław ◎ PL 65 Mc40
Jarosławiec ◎ PL 64 Lr36
Järpen ◎ ✚ S 40 Lo27
Jarqo'rg'on ◎ UZ 97 Od27
Jarrahdale ◎ AUS 144 Qj62
Jarrar ◎ KSA 92 Nb33
Järsnäs ◎ S 43 Lp33
Jarso ◎ ETH 192 Mh41
Jartai ◎ CHN 106 Qc26
Jaru ◎ BR 270 Gj51
Jarub ◎ YE 95 Ng37
Jarud Qi ◎ CHN 105 Ra23
Järva-Jaani ◎ EST 44 Mf31
Järvakandi ◎ EST 44 Me32
Järvelä ◎ FIN 44 Mf30
Järvenpää ◎ FIN 44 Mf30
Järvsö ◎ S 41 Lr29
Jasaan ◎ RP 125 Rc41
Jasanova ◎ AL 68 Lu48
Jasa Tornič ◎ SRB 68 Ma45
Jasenice ◎ HR 61 Lq46
Jasenskaja ◎ RUS 73 Mk22
Jashpurnagar ◎ IND 117 Pc34
Jasienica ◎ PL 64 Lp39
Jasiira Guiba ▲ SP 195 Nb46
Jasiira Jula ▲ SP 195 Nb46
Jasiira Koiama ▲ SP 195 Nb46
Jasiksan ◎ GH 187 La42
Jasinja ◎ UA 67 Me42
Jašiūnai ◎ LT 45 Mf36
Jask ◎ IR 95 Nj33
Jasło ◎ PL 65 Mb41
Jasmund, N.P. ⛺ D 58 Lo36
Jasná ◎ ⛷ SK 67 Lu42
Jasnaja ◎ RUS 105 Qh20
Jasna Poljana ◎ BG 69 Mh48
Jasnoe ◎ RUS 45 Mb35
Jasnogorsk ◎ RUS 72 Mj18
Jasnomorskij ◎ RUS 111 Sa22
Jasov ◎ SK 67 Ma42
Jasper ◎ CDN 232 Ea19
Jasper ◎ USA 238 Fd27
Jasper ◎ USA 238 Fd30
Jasper ◎ USA 239 Fg26
Jasper ◎ USA 239 Fg29
Jasper ◎ USA 241 Gb24
Jasper ◎ USA 242 Fj30
Jasper ◎ USA 239 Fh28
Jasper Lake ≋ CDN 232 Ea19
Jasper N.P. ■ ✦ ⛺ CDN 232 Eb19
Jasper ◎ USA 239 Fh28
Jasper Tramway ⛷ CDN 232 Eb19
Jasrana ◎ IND 115 Ok32
Jassan ◎ IRQ 93 Nc29
Jassira ◎ ⛱ SP 195 Nc45
Jastarnia ◎ ⛱ PL 64 Lt36
Jastrebarsko ◎ HR 61 Lq45
Jastrowie ◎ PL 64 Lr37
Jastrząbka ◎ PL 65 Mb37
Jastrzębia Gora ◎ ⛱ PL 64 Lt36
Jastrzębie-Zdrój ◎ PL 64 Lt41
Jasubibeteri ◎ YV 265 Gh44
Jasynuvata ◎ UA 73 Mj21
Jászalsószentgyörgy ◎ H 67 Ma43
Jászapáti ◎ H 67 Ma43
Jászárokszállás ◎ H 67 Lu43
Jászberény ◎ H 67 Lu43
Jataí ◎ BR 274 He54
Jath ◎ IND 116 Oh37
Jati ◎ PK 99 Oe33
Jatibarang ◎ RI 129 Qe49
Jatibonico ◎ C 243 Ga35
Jatijajar Cave ◣ RI 129 Qe49
Jatiraga ◎ RI 129 Qf49
Jatiwangi ◎ RI 129 Qe49
Jatni ◎ IND 117 Pc35
Jatobá ◎ BR 271 Hd48
Jatobá ◎ BR 273 Hj48
Jatoba ◎ BR 274 Hc52
Jatoba do Piauí ◎ BR 273 Hk48
Jatoi ◎ PK 99 Of31
Jättendal ◎ S 41 Ls29
Jatuarana ◎ BR 271 Ha47
Jatuarana, T.I. ⌂ BR 271 Gk47
Jaú ◎ BR 274 Hf57
Jauarauá ◎ BR 270 Gh47
Jáua-Sarisariñama, P.N. ⛺ YV 265 Gh43
Jauco ◎ C 250 Gc35
Jauja ◎ PE 269 Gc51
Jaumave ◎ MEX 246 Fa34
Jaungulbene ◎ LV 45 Mg33
Jaunkalsnava ◎ LV 45 Mf34
Jaunpiebalga ◎ LV 45 Mg33
Jaunpils ◎ LV 45 Md34
Jaunpur ◎ ☪ IND 117 Pb33
Jaupaci ◎ BR 274 He54
Jauru ◎ BR 274 Hc55
Jauru ◎ BR 278 Ha53
Java ▲ RI 129 Qe49
Java ◎ SME 266 Hc43
Javalambre ▲ E 57 Kt50
Javand ◎ AFG 99 Oc28
Javanrub ◎ IR 91 Nd28
Javari ◎ BR 268 Ge48
Javari ≋ BR 271 Hd46
Javartkhoshuu ◎ MNG 104 Qg21
Java Sea ≋ RI 129 Qf48
Java Trench ▿ 76 Pb10
Jávea = Xàbia ◎ ⛱ ♖ E 57 La52
Javi ◎ BR 272 Hj52
Javkhlant ◎ MNG 104 Qf21
Javkhlant ◎ MNG 104 Qg22
Javoriv ◎ UA 67 Md41
Javorivskyj N.P. ♣ UA 67 Md41
Javorník ◎ CZ 66 Ls40
Jaw ◎ BRN 93 Nf33
Jawan Tomb ⚱ KSA 93 Ne32
Jawatha Mosque ☪ KSA 93 Ne33
Jawhar ◎ IND 116 Og36
Jawi ◎ RI 129 Qe46
Jawor ◎ □ ⛪ PL 64 Lr39
Jawor Solecki ◎ PL 65 Mb39
Jaworzno ◎ PL 65 Lu40
Jawoyn A.L. ◸ AUS 146 Rg53
Jay ◎ USA 238 Fc27
Jayanca ◎ PE 268 Ga49
Jayapatna ◎ IND 117 Pb36
Jayapura ◎ RI 155 Sa47
Jaynagar ◎ IND 117 Pd32
Jayton ◎ USA 238 Ek29
Jaza'ir al Zubayr ▲ YE 94 Nb38
Jaza'ir Farasan ▲ KSA 94 Na37
Jazirah ◎ KSA 94 Nb36
Jazirat Al Batinah ▲ KSA 93 Ne32
Jazirat Antufash ▲ YE 94 Nb38
Jazirat at Tarfah ▲ YE 94 Nb38
Jazirat Djebel Zuqar ▲ YE 94 Nb38
Jazireh-ye Abu Musa ▲ IR 98 Nh33
Jazireh-ye Forur ▲ IR 98 Nh32
Jazireh-ye Hendorabi ▲ IR 98 Ng32
Jazireh-ye Hengam ▲ IR 98 Nh32
Jazireh-ye Hormoz ▲ IR 98 Nj32
Jazireh-ye Jabrin ▲ IR 93 Nf32
Jazireh-ye Khark ⛴ IR 93 Nf31
Jazireh-ye Kish ▲ IR 98 Ng32
Jazireh-ye Larak ▲ IR 98 Nj32
Jazireh-ye Lavan ▲ IR 98 Ng32
Jazireh-ye Qeshm ▲ IR 98 Nj32
Jazireh-ye Sirri ▲ IR 98 Nh33
Jazireh-ye Tonb-e Bozorg ▲ IR 98 Nh32
Jazminal ◎ MEX 245 Ek33
Jazna ◎ BY 45 Mj35
Jdiriya ◎ DARS 174 Ke32
Jeanerette ◎ USA 239 Fe31
Jean Marie River ◎ CDN 231 Dk15
Jean Rabel ◎ RH 250 Gd36
Jebba ◎ WAN 188 Lc41
Jebel ◎ RO 68 Mb45
Jebri ◎ PK 99 Oc32
Jebus ◎ RI 127 Qc46
Jedburgh ◎ GB 48 Ks35
Jedlińsk ◎ PL 65 Mb39
Jednorożec ◎ PL 65 Mb37
Jędrzejów ◎ PL 65 Ma40
Jedwabne ◎ PL 65 Mc37
Jedwabno ◎ PL 65 Ma37
Jeedamya ◎ AUS 144 Ra60
Jefawa ◎ SUD 184 Mb40
Jefferson ◎ USA 237 Ff24
Jefferson ◎ USA 238 Fc29
Jefferson ◎ USA 242 Fk27
Jefferson City ⦿ USA 238 Fd26
Jefferson Davis Mon. ♙ USA 239 Fg27
Jefferson, Mount ▲ USA 232 Dk23
Jefferson, Mount ▲ USA 234 Eb26
Jeffersontown ◎ USA 239 Fh26
Jeffersonville ◎ USA 239 Fh26
Jeffersonville ◎ USA 242 Fj29
Jeffrey City ◎ USA 235 Eg24
Jeffrey's Bay ◎ ⛱ ⚑ ZA 205 Mc63
Jef-Jef el Kébir ▲ TCH 184 Ma35
Jega ◎ WAN 188 Lc39
Jege ◎ WAN 188 Lc41
Jehanabad ◎ IND 117 Pc33
Jeinemeni, Cerro ▲ RCH 282 Gd69
Jejevo ◎ SOL 157 Sk50
Jeju ◎ ROK 112 Rd29
Jeju Do ■ ⛴ ▲ ROK 112 Rd29
Jēkabpils ◎ LV 45 Mf34
Jelanec' ◎ UA 73 Mf22
Jelbart Ice Shelf ≋ 286 Kd33
Jelcz-Laskowice ◎ PL 64 Ls39
Jelekangphu Gang ▲ IND 102 Pe31
Jelenia Góra ◎ ♨ PL 64 Lq40
Jelenino ◎ PL 64 Lr37
Jelgava ◎ LV 45 Md34
Jeli ◎ MAL 126 Qa43
Jellicoe ◎ CDN 237 Fg21
Jelling ◎ DK 42 Lk35
Jelmusibak ◎ RI 129 Qh46
Jelovac ◎ SRB 68 Mb46
Jeløy ▲ N 42 Ll31
Jelsa ◎ N 42 Lg31
Jelutung ◎ RI 129 Qd47
Jema ◎ GH 187 Kk42
Jemaa Ida Oussemlal ◎ MA 174 Kf31
Jemâa-Sahi ◎ MA 175 Kf29
Jemaja ▲ RI 126 Qc44
Jemaluang ◎ MAL 126 Qb44
Jember ◎ RI 129 Qg50
Jemberem ◎ GNB 186 Kc40
Jemez Ind. Res. ⌂ USA 235 Eg28
Jemez Pueblo ◎ USA 235 Eg28
Jemielno ◎ PL 64 Lr39
Jeminay ◎ CHN 101 Pc22
Jemma ◎ WAN 188 Le40
Jemma ◎ WAN 188 Le41
Jempara ◎ RI 129 Qh47
Jen ◎ WAN 189 Lf41
Jena ◎ D 58 Lm40
Jena ◎ USA 239 Fd30
Jenakijeve ◎ UA 73 Mk21
Jenbach ◎ A 60 Lm43
Jenda ◎ MW 196 Mg52
Jendarata ◎ MAL 126 Qa44
Jendouba ◎ TN 176 Le27
Jengish Chokusu ▲ KS 100 Pa24
Jenin ◎ IL 90 Mh29
Jenipapo ◎ BR 271 Gk48
Jenipapo ◎ BR 272 Hf49
Jenluise Bank ▿ 287 Qb31
Jenner ◎ CDN 233 Ee20
Jenner ◎ USA 234 Dj26
Jennersdorf ◎ A 61 Lr44
Jennings ◎ USA 239 Fd30
Jenny ◎ SME 266 Hc43
Jepara ◎ ⛱ RI 129 Qf49
Jeppener ◎ RA 281 Ha63
Jepua ◎ FIN 41 Mc27
Jequeri ◎ BR 275 Hj56
Jequiá ◎ BR 273 Jb51
Jequié ◎ BR 273 Hk52
Jequitaí ◎ BR 275 Hh54
Jequitibá ◎ BR 275 Hj55
Jequitinhonha ◎ BR 275 Hk54
Jerada ◎ MA 175 Kj28
Jeramungup ◎ AUS 144 Qk62
Jerangle ◎ AUS 151 Se63
Jerantut ◎ MAL 126 Qb44
Jerash ◎ Π JOR 90 Mh29
Jerbar ◎ SUD 194 Mf43
Jerdera ◎ RI 154 Rh49
Jerécuaro ◎ MEX 246 Ek35
Jereh ◎ IR 93 Nf31
Jérémie ◎ RH 250 Gc36
Jeremoabo ◎ BR 273 Ja51
Jereweh ◎ RI 130 Qj50
Jerez ◎ MEX 246 Ej34
Jerez de la Frontera ◎ E 55 Ko54
Jerez de los Caballeros ◎ E 55 Ko52
Jergucat ◎ AL 70 Ma51
Jericho ◎ AUS 149 Sd57
Jericho ◎ IL 92 Mh30
Jerichow ◎ D 58 Ln38
Jericoacoara, P.N. de ⛺ BR 273 Hk47
Jerigu ◎ GH 187 Kk41
Jerilderie ◎ AUS 151 Sc63
Jerka ◎ PL 64 Lr39
Jerkoh ◎ MAL 126 Qa43
Jerko La ⌒ CHN 102 Pa30
Jerome ◎ USA 232 Ec24
Jerori ◎ BOL 278 Gh53
Jersey ⛴ GB 50 Ks41
Jersey City ◎ USA 241 Gc25
Jerseyville ◎ USA 239 Fe26
Jersey Zoo 🐾 GB 50 Ks41
Jertih ◎ MAL 126 Qb43
Jerudong Park ♣ BRU 128 Qh43
Jerumal ◎ BR 273 Hk50
Jerumenha ◎ BR 273 Hj49
Jerusalem ● □ ♖ IL 92 Mh30
Jeruzalem ⛪ SLO 66 Lr44
Jervis Bay ◎ ⛵ ⛱ AUS 151 Sf63
Jervois Range ▲ AUS 148 Rh57
Jerzens ◎ ⛷ A 60 Ll43
Jerzu ◎ I 62 Lk51
Jesenice ◎ CZ 66 Lp41
Jesenice ◎ SLO 66 Lp44
Jeseník ◎ CZ 66 Ls40
Jesi ◎ I 61 Lo47
Jesmond ◎ CDN 232 Dj20
Jésolo ◎ I 61 Ln45
Jessen ◎ D 58 Ln39
Jesse Owens Mem. Park 🏛 USA 239 Fg28
Jesser Point ▲ ZA 205 Mg59
Jessheim ◎ N 42 Lm30
Jessore ◎ BD 120 Pe34
Jesuitas ◎ BR 276 Hd58
Jesuit Missions of the Chiquitanía □ ⛪ BOL 278 Gk54
Jesup ◎ USA 242 Fk30
Jesús ◎ PE 269 Gb51
Jesús ◎ PY 276 Hc59
Jesús Carranza ◎ MEX 247 Fc37
Jesús del Tavarangué □ ⛪ PY 276 Hc59
Jesús de Machaca ◎ BOL 278 Gf54
Jesús María ◎ MEX 245 Eh34
Jesús María ◎ MEX 246 Ej35
Jesús María ◎ RA 280 Gh61
Jesús Menéndez ◎ C 243 Gb35
Jetavana Dagoba □ ⛪ CL 119 Pa41
Jeti-Öghüz ◎ ♨ KS 100 Ok24
Jetmore ◎ USA 238 Fa26
Jetpur ◎ IND 116 Of35
Jeumont ◎ F 51 Le40
Jeuram ◎ RI 126 Pj43
Jevargi ◎ IND 116 Oj37
Jever ◎ D 58 Lh37
Jevnaker ◎ N 42 Ll30
Jevpatorija ◎ UA 73 Mg23
Jewar ◎ IND 115 Oj31
Jewels Cave Nat. Mon. ◣ USA 233 Ej24
Jewish Autonomous Region ⊡ RUS 89 Rc09
Jew Town ✡ IND 118 Oj41
Jeypur ◎ IND 117 Pb36
Jeziorany ◎ PL 65 Ma37
Jezioro Bukowo ≋ PL 64 Lr36
Jezioro Jamno ≋ PL 64 Lr36
Jezioro Jeziorak ≋ PL 65 Lu37
Jezioro Jeziorsko ≋ PL 64 Lt39
Jezioro Kopan ≋ PL 64 Lr36
Jezioro Łebsko ≋ PL 64 Ls36
Jezioro Mamry ⛵ ✚ PL 65 Mb36
Jezioro Śniardwy ⛵ ✚ PL 65 Mb37
Jezioro Wicko ≋ PL 64 Lr36
Jezioro Zegrzyńskie ≋ PL 65 Mb38
Jeżów ◎ PL 65 Lu39
Jeżowe ◎ PL 65 Mc40
Jezzine ◎ RL 90 Mh29
Jhabua ◎ IND 116 Oh34
Jhajha ◎ IND 117 Pd33
Jhajjar ◎ IND 114 Oj31
Jhal ◎ PK 99 Od31
Jhalakati ◎ BD 120 Pf34
Jhalawar ◎ IND 116 Oj33
Jhalida ◎ IND 117 Pc34
Jhalod ◎ IND 116 Oh34
Jhang ◎ PK 99 Og30
Jhanjharpur ◎ IND 117 Pd32
Jhansi ◎ ♜ IND 117 Ok33
Jhansi Fort ♜ IND 117 Ok33
Jhanzi ◎ IND 120 Ph32
Jhargram ◎ IND 117 Pd34
Jharkhand ⊡ IND 117 Pc34
Jharol ◎ IND 116 Og33
Jharsuguda ◎ IND 117 Pc35
Jhatpat ◎ PK 99 Oe31
Jhelum ◎ PK 99 Og29
Jhenaidah ◎ BD 120 Pe34
Jhenida ◎ BD 120 Pe34
Jhimpir ◎ PK 99 Od33
Jhudo ◎ PK 99 Oe33
Jhunjhunun ◎ IND 114 Oh31
Jiachuan ◎ CHN 106 Qd29
Jiading ◎ CHN 112 Ra30
Jiahe ◎ CHN 108 Qg33
Jiajiang ◎ CHN 108 Qb31
Jiamusi ◎ CHN 110 Rf22
Ji'an ◎ CHN 109 Qh32
Ji'an ◎ CHN 110 Rd25
Jian ◎ IR 98 Ng30
Jianchang ◎ CHN 107 Qk25
Jianchaxi ◎ CHN 108 Qe31
Jianchi ◎ CHN 108 Qe30
Jianchuan ◎ CHN 121 Pk32
Jiande ◎ CHN 109 Qk31
Jiang ■ ♖ CHN 108 Qd31
Jiang'an ◎ CHN 108 Qc31
Jiangbei ◎ CHN 108 Qd31
Jiangcheng ◎ CHN 121 Qa34
Jiangchuan ◎ CHN 121 Qb33
Jiangdi ◎ CHN 121 Qb32
Jiangdu ◎ CHN 112 Qk29
Jiange ◎ CHN 106 Qc29
Jianggjin ◎ CHN 108 Qd31
Jianghong ◎ CHN 108 Qe35
Jianghua ◎ CHN 108 Qf33
Jiangjunmiao ◎ ☉ CHN 101 Pf23
Jiangkou ◎ CHN 108 Qe30
Jiangkou ◎ CHN 108 Qe32
Jiangling ◎ ♜ CHN 108 Qg30
Jiangluo ◎ CHN 106 Qc29
Jiangmen ◎ CHN 109 Qg34
Jiangshan ◎ CHN 109 Qk31
Jiangshan ◎ CHN 109 Ra31
Jiangsu ⊡ CHN 112 Qk29
Jiangxi ⊡ CHN 109 Qh32
Jiangyin ◎ CHN 112 Ra30
Jiangyong ◎ CHN 108 Qf33
Jiangyou ◎ CHN 106 Qc30
Jianhe ◎ CHN 108 Qe32
Jianhu ◎ CHN 112 Qk29
Jianle ◎ CHN 109 Qj32
Jianli ◎ CHN 109 Qg31
Jianmen Path ⛩ CHN 106 Qc29
Jianning ◎ CHN 109 Qj32
Jian'ou ◎ CHN 109 Qk32
Jianping ◎ CHN 107 Qk25
Jianshui ◎ ♖ CHN 121 Qb34
Jianyang ◎ CHN 108 Qc30
Jianyang ◎ CHN 109 Qk32
Jiaode ◎ CHN 121 Qc34
Jiaohe ◎ CHN 110 Rd24
Jiaohe Gucheng ▲ CHN 101 Pe24
Jiaojiang ◎ CHN 109 Ra31
Jiaokou ◎ CHN 106 Qf27
Jiaoling ◎ CHN 109 Qj33
Jiaonan ◎ CHN 112 Qk28
Jiaotelo ◎ CHN 102 Pd31
Jiaozhou ◎ CHN 107 Ra27
Jiaozuo ◎ CHN 107 Qg28
Jiasa ◎ CHN 121 Qa33
Jiashan ◎ CHN 112 Qj29
Jiashan ◎ CHN 112 Ra30
Jiashi ◎ CHN 100 Oj26
Jia Xian ◎ CHN 106 Qf26
Jia Xian ◎ CHN 107 Qg29
Jiaxing ◎ CHN 112 Ra30
Jiayin ◎ CHN 110 Rf21
Jiayu ◎ CHN 109 Qg31
Jiayu G. ♜ ⛩ CHN 103 Pk26
Jiayuguan ◎ CHN 103 Pk26
Jibert ◎ RO 67 Mf45
Jiberu ◎ WAN 189 Lg41
Jibiya ◎ WAN 182 Ld39
Jibjaat ◎ OM 95 Nh37
Jibla ◎ ♖ YE 94 Nc39
Jibóia ◎ BR 265 Gf45
Jibou ◎ RO 67 Md43
Jicarilla Apache Ind. Res. ⌂ USA 235 Eg27
Jícaro Galán ◎ HN 248 Fg39
Jichang ◎ CHN 108 Qd33
Jichang ◎ CHN 121 Qc32
Jičín ◎ CZ 66 Lq40
Jiddah ◎ ☪ ⛱ KSA 92 Mk35
Jiddat al-Harasis ▲ OM 95 Nh36
Jiele Golden Pagoda ▲ CHN 120 Pj33
Jielong ◎ CHN 108 Qd31
Jieshi ◎ CHN 109 Qh34
Jieshou ◎ CHN 107 Qh29
Jiexi ◎ CHN 109 Qh34
Jiexiu ◎ CHN 106 Qf27
Jieyang ◎ CHN 109 Qj34
Jieznas ◎ LT 45 Me36
Jiggalong ◎ AUS 142 Ra57
Jiggalong Aboriginal Reserve ◸ AUS 142 Ra57
Jiggs ◎ USA 234 Ec25
Jigme Dorji N.P. ⛺ BHT 120 Pe32
Jigongshan ⛰ CHN 107 Qh30
Jiguaní ◎ C 243 Gb35
Jihanah ◎ YE 94 Nc38
Jihlava ◎ ♖ CZ 66 Lq41
Jihua Dao ⛱ CHN 110 Ra25
Jiigley ◎ SP 195 Nc43
Jijel ◎ DZ 176 Lc27
Jijie ◎ CHN 121 Qb34
Jijiga ◎ ETH 193 Nb41
Jijona = Xixona ◎ E 57 Ku52
Jijü ◎ CHN 121 Qa31
Jilamo ◎ HN 248 Fg38
Jilan ◎ IR 96 Nh27
Jilava ◎ RO 69 Mg46
Jilavele ◎ RO 69 Mg46
Jilbadji Nature Reserve ♣ AUS 144 Qk61
Jilib ◎ SP 195 Nb45
Jilin ◎ ▲ ⛪ CHN 110 Rd24
Jilin ⊡ CHN 110 Rd24
Jilin Hada Ling ▲ CHN 110 Rc24
Jima ◎ ⁂ ETH 192 Mj42
Jim Abad ◎ IR 96 Nk27
Jimani ◎ DOM 250 Ge36
Jimata ◎ ETH 192 Mj41
Jimbe ◎ ANG 201 Mb51
Jimbolia ◎ RO 68 Ma45
Jimda ◎ CHN 103 Pg31
Jimei ◎ CHN 109 Qk33
Jimena de la Frontera ◎ E 55 Kp54
Jiménez ◎ MEX 245 Eh32
Jiménez ◎ MEX 245 Ek31
Jimenez ◎ RP 125 Rb41
Jiménez del Téul ◎ MEX 246 Ej34
Jimenoa Waterfall ⛲ DOM 250 Ge36
Jimeta ◎ WAN 189 Lg41
Jim Jim Falls ⛲ AUS 146 Rg52
Jimmy Carter N.H.S. 🏛 USA 239 Fh29
Jimo ◎ CHN 107 Ra27
Jimsar ◎ CHN 101 Pe24
Jimulco ◎ MEX 245 Ej33
Jinan ⦿ CHN 107 Qj27
Jinchai ◎ CHN 108 Qe33
Jinchang ◎ CHN 106 Qb26
Jincheng ◎ CHN 107 Qg28
Jincheng ◎ CHN 121 Qb33
Jinchuan ◎ CHN 106 Qb30
Jinci Si ▲ ⛩ CHN 106 Qg27
Jind ◎ IND 114 Oj31
Jindabyne ◎ AUS 151 Se64
Jindare ◎ AUS 146 Rf53
Jindian ▲ CHN 121 Qb33
Jindřichov ◎ CZ 66 Ls40
Jindřichův Hradec ◎ CZ 66 Lq41
Jinfo Shan ▲ CHN 108 Qd31
Jing'an ◎ CHN 109 Qh31
Jingbian ◎ CHN 106 Qe27
Jingchuan ◎ CHN 106 Qd28
Jingde ◎ CHN 112 Qk30
Jingdezhen ◎ CHN 109 Qj31
Jingdong ◎ CHN 121 Qa33
Jingellic ◎ AUS 151 Sd63
Jingemarra ◎ AUS 144 Qj59
Jinggangshan ◎ CHN 109 Qh32
Jinggangshan ⛰ CHN 109 Qh32
Jinggu Daizu ◎ CHN 121 Qa34
Jinghe ◎ CHN 100 Pb23
Jinghong ◎ CHN 121 Qa34
Jingjiang ◎ CHN 112 Ra29
Jingle ◎ CHN 106 Qf26
Jingmen ◎ CHN 108 Qg30
Jingning ◎ CHN 106 Qc28
Jingpo ◎ CHN 110 Re24
Jingshan ◎ CHN 109 Qg30
Jingtai ◎ CHN 106 Qc27
Jingtie Shan ▲ CHN 103 Pj26
Jingtieshan ◎ CHN 103 Pj26
Jingxi ◎ CHN 108 Qd34
Jing Xian ◎ CHN 112 Qk30
Jingxiang ◎ CHN 112 Qj28
Jingxing ◎ CHN 105 Rb22
Jingxing ◎ CHN 107 Qh27
Jingyu ◎ CHN 110 Rd24
Jingyuan ◎ CHN 106 Qc27
Jingyu Nao ▲ CHN 106 Qe29
Jingzhou ◎ CHN 108 Qe32
Jinhe ◎ CHN 105 Ra20
Jinhe ◎ CHN 121 Qa32
Jinhua ◎ CHN 109 Qk31
Jinín ◎ EC 268 Fk46
Jining ◎ CHN 107 Qg25
Jining ◎ CHN 112 Qj28
Jinja ◎ EAU 194 Mg45
Jinja War Cemetery ⚱ EAU 194 Mg45
Jinjiang ◎ CHN 121 Qa32
Jinjiang = Panzhihua ◎ CHN 121 Qa32
Jinka ◎ 🏛 ⁂ ETH 194 Mj43
Jinkou ◎ CHN 109 Qh30
Jinning ◎ CHN 121 Qb33
Jinniu ◎ CHN 109 Qh31
Jinotega ◎ NIC 248 Fh39
Jinotepe ◎ NIC 248 Fg40
Jinping ◎ CHN 108 Qe32
Jinping ◎ CHN 121 Qb34
Jinsha ◎ CHN 108 Qd32
Jinsha ◎ CHN 112 Ra29
Jinsha Jiang ⛵ CHN 121 Qb32
Jinshan ◎ CHN 112 Ra30
Jinshanlin ♜ CHN 107 Qj25
Jinshatan ◎ CHN 107 Qg26
Jinshi ◎ CHN 108 Qf31
Jinshiqiao ◎ CHN 108 Qf32
Jinta ◎ CHN 103 Pk26
Jintan ◎ CHN 112 Qk30
Jintololo Island ▲ RP 124 Rb40
Jintotolo Channel ≋ RP 124 Rb40
Jintur ◎ IND 116 Oj36
Jinxi ◎ CHN 109 Qj32
Jinxi ◎ CHN 110 Ra25
Jinxian ◎ CHN 109 Qj31
Jinyang ◎ CHN 121 Qb32
Jinyun ◎ CHN 109 Ra31
Jinzhou ◎ CHN 107 Ra26
Jinzhou ◎ CHN 110 Ra25
Ji-Paraná ◎ BR 270 Gk51
Jipijapa ◎ EC 268 Fk46
Jiqui ◎ C 243 Ga35
Jiquilillo ◎ NIC 248 Fg39
Jiquilpan de Juárez ◎ MEX 246 Ej35
Jiquiriçá ◎ BR 273 Ja52
Jiqzhi ◎ CHN 106 Qa29
Jirampal ◎ IND 117 Pa36
Jirga Alem ◎ ETH 192 Mk42
Jiri ◎ NEP 115 Pd32
Jirkov ◎ CZ 66 Lo40
Jiroft ◎ IR 98 Nj31
Jirriban ◎ SP 193 Ne42
Jirwan ◎ KSA 95 Nf34
Jishan ◎ CHN 106 Qf28
Jishou ◎ CHN 108 Qe31
Jishu ◎ CHN 110 Rd23
Jishui ◎ CHN 109 Qh32
Jitarning ◎ AUS 144 Qj62
Jitia ◎ RO 69 Mg45
Jitian ◎ CHN 108 Qc30
Jitra ◎ MAL 126 Qa42
Jitzamuri ◎ MEX 244 Ef32
Jiucai Ling ▲ CHN 108 Qf33
Jiuchang ◎ CHN 108 Qd32
Jiuhuajie ◎ CHN 112 Qj30
Jiuhuashan ♖ CHN 112 Qj30
Jiujiang ◎ CHN 109 Qj31
Jiuling Shan ▲ CHN 109 Qh31
Jiulong = Kowloon ◎ ♖ CHN 109 Qh34
Jiulong Shan ▲ CHN 109 Qk31
Jiulong Waterfall Group ◎ CHN 121 Qc33
Jiuquan ◎ CHN 103 Pk26
Jiurongcheng ◎ CHN 107 Rb27
Jiusuo ◎ CHN 109 Qe36
Jiutai ◎ CHN 110 Rc23
Jiuxu ◎ CHN 108 Qd33
Jiuyishan ⛰ CHN 108 Qg33
Jiuzhaigou ◎ CHN 106 Qb29
Jiuzhaigou □ ✦ ♣ CHN 106 Qb29
Jiuzhan ◎ CHN 105 Rc20
Jiuzhou ◎ CHN 121 Qc33
Jivundu ◎ Z 201 Mc52
Jiwani ◎ PK 98 Oa33
Jiwen ◎ CHN 105 Rb20
Jiwika ◎ RI 154 Rk47
Jixi ◎ CHN 110 Rf23
Jixi ◎ CHN 112 Qk30
Ji Xian ◎ CHN 106 Qf27
Ji Xian ◎ CHN 107 Qj25
Jixian ◎ CHN 110 Re22
Jixian ◎ CHN 110 Rf22
Jiyang ◎ CHN 107 Qj27
Jiyuan ◎ CHN 107 Qg28
Jizan ◎ KSA 94 Nb37
Jizzax ◎ UZ 97 Od25
Joaçaba ◎ BR 276 He59
Joachimsthal ◎ D 58 Lo38
Joaíma ◎ BR 275 Hk54
Joal-Fadiout ◎ ⛱ SN 180 Kb38
João Arregui ◎ BR 276 Hb60
João Câmara ◎ BR 273 Jc48
João Chagas ◎ ANG 201 Mb51
João Farias ◎ BR 266 Ha46
João Lisboa ◎ BR 272 Hg48
João Monlevade ◎ BR 275 Hj55
João Neiva ◎ BR 275 Hk55
Joáo Pataço ◎ MOC 203 Mh55
João Pessoa ⦿ ⛱ ⛩ BR 273 Jc49
João Pinheiro ◎ BR 275 Hg54
Joaquim Pires ◎ BR 273 Hj47
Joaquín V.González ◎ RA 279 Gh58
Joara ◎ IND 116 Oh34
Jobabo ◎ C 243 Gb35
Jobat ◎ IND 116 Oh34
Jobele ◎ WAN 188 Lb42
Jocoli ◎ RA 280 Gf62
Jocotepec ◎ MEX 246 Ej35
Jódar ◎ E 55 Kr53
Jodensavanna ◎ SME 266 Hc43
Jodhpur ◎ IND 114 Og32
Jodiya ◎ IND 116 Of34
Jodlo ◎ RI 131 Rf46
Jodoigne ◎ B 51 Le40
Joe Batt's Arm ◎ CDN 241 Hc21
Joensuu ◎ ♫ FIN 44 Mk28
Joes ◎ USA 238 Ej26
Joetsu ◎ J 111 Rk27
Jofane ◎ MOC 202 Mh56
Jôf di Montásio ▲ I 61 Lo44
Joffre, Mount ▲ CDN 232 Ec20
Jofre ◎ MEX 246 Ek35
Jogana ◎ WAN 188 Le39
Jogbani ◎ IND 117 Pd32
Jõgeva ◎ EST 44 Mg32
Jog Falls ⛲ IND 118 Oh38
Joghara ◎ IND 117 Pc32
Jogidan ◎ IR 98 Nj32
Jogindar Nagar ◎ IND 115 Oj29
Jogoli ◎ GH 187 La41
Jogues ◎ CDN 237 Fj21
Johan ◎ PK 99 Od31
Johanna Beach ⛱ ⚑ AUS 151 Sb65
Johannesburg ◎ USA 234 Eb28
Johannesburg ⦿ ▦ ◉ ZA 205 Md59
Johanngeorgenstadt ◎ D 59 Ln40
Johi ◎ GUY 266 Ha45
Johi ◎ PK 99 Od32
John Day ≋ USA 232 Dk23
John Day Fossil Beds Nat. Mon. Clarno Unit ♖ ☉ USA 232 Dk23
John Day Fossil Beds Nat. Mon. Painted Hills Unit ♖ ☉ USA 232 Dk23
John Day Fossil Beds Nat. Mon. Sheep Rock Unit ♖ ☉ USA 232 Ea23
John Deere H.S. 🏛 USA 237 Ff24
John Deere Pavilion 🏛 USA 236 Fe25
Johndibli ◎ LB 186 Kf42
John D'Or Prairie ◎ CDN 231 Ec16
John d'Or Prairie Ind. Res. ⌂ CDN 231 Ec16
John Fitzgerald Kennedy Hyannis Museum 🏛 USA 241 Ge25
John Flynn Memorial ♙ ⛪ AUS 146 Rh55
John Henry Statue ♙ USA 242 Fk27
John Hopkins Glacier ❄ USA 230 Db16
John o'Groats ◎ GB 48 Kr32
John Pennekamp Coral Reef S.P. ≋ USA 243 Fk33
Johnson City ◎ USA 238 Ek27
Johnson City ◎ USA 238 Fa30
Johnson City ◎ USA 241 Gb24
Johnson City ◎ USA 242 Fj27
Johnson N.H.P. 🏛 USA 238 Fa30
Johnson River ≋ CDN 231 Dh14
Johnsons ◎ USA 232 Dj25
Johnsons Crossing ◎ CDN 230 Dd15
Johnson Space Center 🏛 USA 238 Fc31
Johnstone ◎ AUS 147 Sd54
Johnstone ◎ AUS 149 Se60
Johnstone ◎ GB 48 Kq35
Johnstown ◎ USA 237 Ga25
Johnstown ◎ USA 241 Gc24
Johnstown Flood Nat. Mon. ♙ USA 237 Ga25
Johnsville ◎ USA 239 Fe29
John W. Kyle S.P. ♣ USA 239 Ff28
Johor Bahru ◎ MAL 127 Qb45
Jõhvi ◎ EST 44 Mh31
Joigny ◎ F 53 Ld43
Joinville ◎ BR 277 Hf59
Joinville ◎ F 51 Lf42
Joița ◎ RO 69 Mf46
Jokau ◎ SUD 192 Mg41
Jokhang ▲ CHN 103 Pf31
Jokina Čuprija ◎ SRB 68 Lu47
Jokkmokk ◎ S 38 Lu24
Jökulgilstindar ▲ IS 46 Kf26
Jökulsárlón ❄ ⛵ IS 46 Kd26
Jolfa ◎ IR 91 Nc26
Joliet ◎ USA 237 Ff25
Joliette ◎ CDN 240 Gd22
Jolo ◎ RP 125 Ra42
Jolo Group ▲ RP 125 Ra43
Jolo Island ▲ RP 125 Ra42
Jomala ◎ FIN 44 Lu30
Jombang ◎ RI 129 Qg49
Jomboy ◎ UZ 97 Od26
Jomda ◎ CHN 103 Pk30
Jomu ◎ EAT 194 Mg47
Jonai Bazar ◎ IND 120 Ph32
Jonava ◎ LT 45 Me35
Jondal ◎ N 42 Lg30
Jonê ◎ CHN 106 Qb28
Jones ◎ CDN 236 Fc21
Jones ◎ RP 124 Ra37
Jonesboro ◎ USA 238 Fb30
Jonesboro ◎ USA 239 Fd29
Jonesboro ◎ USA 239 Fe28
Jones Islands ▲ USA 229 Cf10
Jones Mountains ▲ 286 Fb33
Jonesport ◎ USA 240 Gg23
Jones Sound ≋ CDN 227 Fc03
Jonesville ◎ USA 242 Fj27
Jongeldi ◎ UZ 96 Ob25
Jonggol ◎ RI 129 Qd49
Jongling ◎ CHN 110 Rc25
Jongmyo Shrine □ ⛩ ROK 112 Rd27
Joniškis ◎ LT 45 Md34
Joniškėlis ◎ LT 45 Me34
Jönköping ◎ S 43 Lp33
Jonquière ◎ CDN 240 Ge21
Jonquières ◎ F 53 Le46
Jonuta ◎ MEX 247 Fd36
Jonzac ◎ F 52 Ku45
Joowhar ◎ SP 195 Nc44
Joplin ◎ USA 238 Fc27
Jora ◎ IND 117 Oj32
Jordan ≋ IL 90 Mh29
Jordan ■ JOR 92 Mj30
Jordan ◎ RP 124 Rb40
Jordan ◎ USA 233 Eg22
Jordânia ◎ BR 275 Hk53
Jordanów ◎ PL 65 Lu41
Jordańow Śląski ◎ PL 64 Lr40
Jordan Valley ◎ USA 232 Eb24
Jordbro ◎ S 43 Lt31
Jorf ◎ MA 175 Kh30
Jorhat ◎ IND 120 Ph32
Joriapani ◎ NEP 115 Pa31
Jorigam ◎ IND 117 Pb36
Jorm ◎ AFG 97 Of27
Jörn ◎ S 41 Ma25
Joroinen ◎ FIN 44 Mh28
Jørpeland ◎ N 42 Lg31
Joru ◎ WAL 186 Ke42
Jos ◎ ⁂ ◣ WAN 188 Le41
Jošanica ◎ SRB 68 Mb47
Jošanička Banja ◎ SRB 68 Ma47
Jose Abad Santos ◎ RP 125 Rc43
José Batlle y Ordóñez ◎ ROU 276 Hc62
José Bonifacio ◎ BR 274 Hf56
José Cardel ◎ MEX 247 Fb36
José de Freitas ◎ BR 273 Hj48
José del Carmen Ramírez, P.N. ♣ DOM 250 Ge36
José de San Martín ◎ RA 282 Ge68
José Enrique Rodó ◎ ROU 276 Hb62
Joselândia ◎ BR 272 Hh48
Joselândia ◎ BR 274 Hb54
José Luís Tamayo ◎ EC 268 Fk47
Josenii Bârgăului ◎ RO 67 Me43
Jose Panganiban ◎ RP 124 Rb38
José Paso ◎ RA 281 Gj63
José Pedro Varela ◎ ROU 276 Hc62
Joseph Bonaparte Gulf ≋ AUS 143 Re53
Josephstaal ◎ PNG 155 Sc48
José Rodrigues ◎ BR 272 He48
Joshimat ◎ IND 115 Ok30
Joshin Etsu Kogen N.P. ⛺ J 111 Rk27
Joshipur ◎ IND 117 Pd35
Joshua Tree N.P. ⛺ USA 234 Eb29
Josipdol ◎ HR 61 Lq45
Joškar-Ola ⦿ RUS 72 Nd17
Jos Plateau ▲ WAN 188 Le41
Josselin ◎ ♜ F 50 Ks43
Jostedalsbreen ❄ N 40 Lg29
Jostedalsbreen n.p. ⛺ N 40 Lg29
Jotunheimen n.p. ⛺ N 40 Lj29
Joubertberge ▲ NAM 200 Lg55
Joubertina ◎ ZA 204 Mb62
Joulter Cays ▲ BS 243 Ga33
Joungs Cove ◎ CDN 240 Gh23
Jourdanton ◎ USA 245 Fa31
Joure ◎ NL 51 Lf38
Joutel ◎ CDN 237 Ga21
Joutsa ◎ FIN 44 Mg29
Joutseno ◎ FIN 44 Mj29
Jovellanos ◎ C 243 Fk34
Joviânia ◎ BR 274 Hf54
Jovsa ◎ SK 67 Mc42
Jowai ◎ IND 120 Pg33
Jowsam ◎ IR 98 Nh30
Joyabaj ◎ GCA 248 Fe38
Joya de Cerén □ Π ES 248 Ff39
Joyag ◎ BD 120 Pf34
Joyce, Mount ▲ 286 Sd34
Jozani-Chwaka Bay Conservation Area ♣ EAT 197 Mk49
Józefów ◎ PL 65 Mb38
Józefów ◎ PL 65 Mb39
Józefów ◎ PL 65 Md40
Jozini ◎ ZA 205 Mg59
Jreïda ◎ RIM 180 Kb36
Jreïf ◎ RIM 180 Kd37
Jri ◎ ROK 112 Rd28
Juabesu ◎ GH 187 Kj42
Juan Aldama ◎ MEX 245 Ej33
Juan B.Alberdi ◎ RA 279 Gh59
Juan Bautista Alberdi ◎ PY 276 Ha59
Juan de Ayolas ◎ PY 276 Hb59
Juan de Fuca Strait ≋ CDN/USA 232 Dj21
Juan de Nova ▲ F 203 Nb54
Juan Dolio ◎ ⛱ DOM 250 Gf36
Juan E.Barra ◎ RA 281 Gk64
Juan E.Estigarribia ◎ PY 276 Hc58
Juangcheng ◎ CHN 107 Qh28
Juangriego ◎ YV 265 Gj40
Juan Guerra ◎ PE 268 Gb49
Juani Island ▲ EAT 197 Mk49
Juan Island ▲ USA 232 Dj21
Juan Jorba ◎ RA 280 Gh62
Juan José Castelli ◎ RA 279 Gk58
Juán José Perez ◎ BOL 278 Gf53
Juanjui ◎ PE 268 Gb49
Juan L.Lacaze ◎ ROU 281 Hb63
Juan N.Fernández ◎ RA 281 Ha65
Juan W.Gez ◎ RA 280 Gg62
Juapon ◎ GH 187 La42
Juara ◎ BR 271 Hb51
Juárez ◎ MEX 244 Ef30
Juárez ◎ MEX 245 Ek32
Juari ≋ BR 272 He49
Juazeirinho ◎ BR 273 Jb49
Juàzeiro ◎ BR 273 Hk50
Juàzeiro do Norte ◎ ⛪ BR 273 Ja49
Juazohn ◎ LB 186 Kf43
Juba ≋ SP 195 Nb44
Juba ◎ ⚑ SUD 194 Mf43
Jubail al Sinaiyah ◎ KSA 93 Ne32
Juban ◎ YE 94 Nc38
Jubany ◎ ANT 286 Ha31
Jubbah ◎ KSA 92 Na31
Jübek ◎ D 58 Lk36
Jubilee Lake ≋ AUS 145 Rd60
Juçara ◎ BR 274 He53
Juçara ◎ GUY 266 Ha42
Jucás ◎ BR 273 Ja49
Juchavičy ◎ BY 45 Mj34
Juchipila ◎ MEX 246 Ej35
Juchitán de Zaragoza ◎ MEX 247 Fc37
Juchnowiec Dolny ◎ PL 65 Md38
Jucuri ◎ BR 273 Jb48
Jucurutu ◎ BR 273 Jb49
Judah ◎ KSA 93 Ne33
Judaiat al Hamir ◎ IRQ 92 Na30
Judayyidat 'Ar'ar ◎ KSA 92 Na30
Judenburg ◎ A 61 Lp43
Judian ◎ CHN 121 Pk32
Judibana ◎ YV 264 Ge40
Judin ◎ RUS 72 Na21
Juelsminde ◎ DK 42 Ll35
Juglong ◎ AUS 151 Se63
Jugorskij Poluostrov ▲ RUS 88 Oa05
Juh ◎ CHN 106 Qe27
Juhnov ◎ RUS 72 Mh18
Juigalpa ◎ NIC 248 Fh39
Juillac ◎ F 52 Lb45
Juína ◎ BR 271 Ha51
Juininha, T.I. ⌂ BR 278 Ha53
Juist ⛱ D 58 Lg37
Juiz de Fora ◎ BR 275 Hj56
Jujun ◎ RI 127 Qa47
Jujuy ⊡ RA 279 Gg57
Jukagirskoe ploskogor'e ▲ RUS 89 Sc05
Jukkasjärvi ◎ ⛪ S 38 Ma23
Jukongjukong ◎ RI 129 Qh49
Julaca ◎ BOL 278 Gg56
Julau ◎ MAL 128 Qf44
Julcán ◎ PE 268 Ga50
Julcul ◎ PE 269 Gb51
Juldessa ▲ ETH 195 Mk44
Julesburg ◎ USA 238 Ej25
Juli ◎ ⁂ PE 278 Gf54
Júlia ◎ BR 270 Gf46
Juliaca ◎ PE 269 Ge53
Julia Creek ◎ AUS 147 Sa56
Julianadorp ◎ NL 51 Le38
Julianatop ▲ SME 266 Hb44
Julianehåb = Quaqortoq ◎ DK 227 Hc06
Julia Pfeiffer S.P. ⛱ ⚑ USA 234 Dk27
Juliasdale ◎ ZW 202 Mg55
Jülich ◎ D 58 Lg40
Julijske Alpe ▲ SLO 66 Lo44
Julimes ◎ MEX 245 Eh31
Julio Borges ◎ BR 272 Hh51
Júlio de Castilhos ◎ BR 276 Hd60
Julio D.Otaño ◎ PY 276 Hc59
Júlio Mesquita ◎ BR 274 Hf57
Julong Shan ▲ CHN 106 Qf30
Julwania ◎ IND 116 Oh35
Juma ◎ UZ 97 Od26
Jumalig Island ▲ RP 124 Rb38
Jumba la Mtwana Π EAK 195 Mk47
Jumbe Foume ◎ EAT 197 Mj51
Jumbe Salims ◎ EAT 197 Mj51
Jumbilla ◎ PE 268 Gb48
Jumboo ◎ SP 195 Nb46
Jumeaux ◎ F 53 Ld45
Jumentos Cays ▲ BS 250 Gc34
Jumilla ◎ E 57 Kt52
Jumina, T.I. ⌂ BR 267 He43
Jumi Pozo ◎ RA 279 Gh60
Jumla ◎ NEP 115 Pb31
Jumma Masjid (Gulbarga) ☪ IND 116 Oj37
Jumurda ◎ LV 45 Mf34
Jun Abad ◎ IR 98 Oa31
Juna Downs ◎ AUS 142 Qk57
Junagadh ◎ IND 116 Of35
Junagarh ◎ IND 117 Pb36
Junan ◎ CHN 112 Qk28
Juncal, Cerro ▲ RA/RCH 280 Gf62
Junction ◎ USA 235 Ed26
Junction ◎ USA 238 Fa30
Junction Bay ≋ AUS 146 Rg51
Junction City ◎ USA 232 Dj23
Junction City ◎ USA 238 Fb26
Junction City ◎ USA 238 Fd29
Junction, Mount ▲ AUS 143 Re55
Jundah ◎ AUS 148 Sb58
Jundee ◎ AUS 144 Ra59
Jundiaí ◎ BR 275 Hg57
Juneau ⦿ USA 230 Dc16
Junee ◎ AUS 149 Se57
Jung ◎ S 42 Lo32
Jungar Qi ◎ CHN 106 Qf26
Jungfrau ▲ CH 60 Lh44
Jungfraubahn ⛟ CH 60 Lh44
Jungoley Canal ≋ SUD 191 Mf41
Jungshahi ◎ PK 99 Od33
Jungue ◎ ANG 200 Lh51
Junín ◎ CO 264 Ga45
Junín ◎ PE 269 Gc51
Junín ◎ RA 281 Gk63
Junín de los Andes ◎ RA 280 Ge65
Juniper Dunes Wilderness ♣ USA 232 Ea22
Juniper Forests ♣ PK 99 Od30
Juniyah ◎ RL 90 Mh29
Junleri ◎ WAN 189 Lf41
Junlian ◎ CHN 108 Qc31
Junnar ◎ IND 116 Og36
Juno ◎ USA 238 Ek30
Junqoley ◎ SUD 191 Mf42
Junsele ◎ S 41 Lr27
Juntas ◎ CR 249 Fh40
Juntas ◎ RCH 279 Gf60
Juntura ◎ USA 232 Ea24
Juodkrantė ◎ LT 45 Mb35
Jupaguá ◎ BR 272 Hh51
Jupiter ◎ USA 243 Fk32
Juquiá ◎ BR 277 Hg58
Jur ≋ SUD 191 Me41
Jura ▲ F 53 Lg43
Jura ▲ GB 48 Kp35
Juraciški ◎ BY 45 Mf36
Jurado ◎ CO 264 Gb42
Jurado ◎ CO 264 Gb42
Juramento ◎ BR 275 Hj54
Jurbarkas ◎ LT 45 Mc35
Jur'evec ◎ RUS 72 Nb17
Jur'ev-Pol'skij ◎ RUS 72 Mk17
Jüri ◎ EST 44 Me31
Juribela ◎ NEP 117 Pc32
Jurien ◎ AUS 144 Qh61
Jurilovca ◎ RO 69 Mj46
Juring ◎ RI 154 Rh49
Jurjev monastyr ⛪ RUS 72 Mf16
Jur'jivka ◎ UA 73 Mj21
Jūrkalne ◎ LV 45 Mb33
Jūrmala ◎ ⛱ LV 45 Md34
Jurmo ▲ FIN 44 Mb31
Jurong ◎ CHN 112 Qk30
Jurovo ◎ RUS 72 Nb17
Jurua ◎ BR 270 Gg47
Juruá ≋ BR 270 Gh47
Juruena ≋ BR 271 Ha50
Juruena ◎ BR 271 Ha51
Juruti ◎ BR 271 Hb47
Jurva ◎ FIN 41 Mb28
Juscimeira ◎ BR 274 Hc54
Jusepín ◎ YV 265 Gj41
Juškino ◎ RUS 44 Mh32
Jussey ◎ F 53 Lf43
Jussiape ◎ BR 273 Hk52
Jussura ◎ BR 273 Hk51
Justiniano Posse ◎ RA 281 Gj62
Justo Daract ◎ RA 280 Gh62
Juszkowy Gród ◎ PL 65 Md38
Jutaí ◎ BR 270 Gg47
Jutaí ◎ BR 273 Hk50
Jutai Grande ◎ BR 270 Gh46
Jüterbog ◎ D 58 Lo39
Juti ◎ BR 274 Hc57
Jutiapa ◎ HN 248 Fg38
Juticalpa ◎ HN 248 Fg38
Jutila ◎ Z 201 Md52
Jutland ▲ DK 42 Lj34
Juupoajoki ◎ FIN 44 Me29
Juva ◎ FIN 44 Mh29
Ju Xian ◎ CHN 112 Qk28
Juxtlahuaca ◣ MEX 246 Fa37
Juža ◎ RUS 72 Nb17
Južno-Aličurskij hrebet ▲ TJ 97 Og27
Južno-Kamyšovyj hrebet ▲ RUS 111 Sb22
Južno-Kuril'sk ◎ RUS 111 Sc23
Južno-Sahalinsk ◎ RUS 111 Sb22
Južnoukrajins'k ◎ UA 73 Mf22
Južnyj ◎ RUS 45 Ma36
Juzufova ◎ BY 45 Mh36
Juzzak ◎ PK 98 Oa31
Jwalamukhi Temple Ψ IND 115 Oj29
Jwaneng ◎ RB 205 Mc58
Jyderup ◎ DK 42 Lm35
Jylland Bank ▿ 42 Lh34
Jyväskylä ◎ FIN 44 Mf28

K

Kaaba ☪ KSA 92 Mk35
Kaabong ◎ EAU 194 Mh44
Kaaimanston ◎ SME 266 Hb43
Kaala ▲ F 158 Tc56
Kaamanen ◎ FIN 39 Mh21
Kaansoo ◎ EST 44 Mf32
Kaap Agulhas ⚑ ZA 204 Ma63
Kaap Dernburg ▲ NAM 204 Lh59
Kaapmuiden ◎ ZA 205 Mf58
Kaapstad ● ♖ ⚓ ZA 204 Lk62
Kaaresuvanto ◎ FIN 39 Mc22
Kaarina ◎ FIN 44 Mc30
Kaashidhoo ▲ MV 118 Og43
Kaavi ◎ FIN 44 Mj28
Kabaena ▲ RI 130 Ra48
Kabaga ◎ G 198 Lg46
Kabah Π MEX 247 Ff35
Kabakly ◎ TM 96 Ob26
Kabala ◎ WAL 186 Ke41
Kabale ◎ EAU 191 Me46
Kabalebo-stuwmeer(projected) ≋ SME 266 Hb43
Kabalega Falls N.P. = Murchison Falls N.P. ⛺ ✦ EAU 194 Mf44
Kabalı ◎ TR 90 Mh25
Kabalo ◎ RDC 196 Md49
Kabambare ◎ RDC 196 Md48
Kabanbai ◎ KZ 100 Pa23
Kabanbai ◎ KZ 100 Pb22
Kabanga ◎ RDC 199 Lk49
Kabanga ◎ Z 202 Md54
Kabango ◎ RDC 196 Md49
Kabangu ◎ RDC 199 Mb51
Kabanjahe ◎ ♖ RI 127 Pk44
Kabankalan ◎ RP 124 Rb41
Kabanpe ◎ GH 187 Kj41
Kabanza ◎ Z 202 Md54
Kabao ◎ LAR 176 Lf30
Kabara ▲ FJI 159 Ua55
Kabardino-Balkaria ⊡ RUS 91 Nb24
Kabardino-Balkarskij zapovednik ♣ RUS 91 Nb24
Kabare ◎ RDC 196 Me47
Kabarei ◎ RI 131 Rf46
Kabarnet ◎ EAK 194 Mh45
Kabasalan ◎ RP 125 Rb42
Kabatepe ◎ TR 69 Mg50
Kabau ◎ RI 131 Rc47
Kabba ◎ WAN 188 Ld42
Kåbdalis ◎ S 38 Ma24
Kabe ◎ WAN 188 Lc40
Kabelvåg ◎ N 38 Lp22
Kaberamaido ◎ EAU 194 Mg45
Kabetan ▲ RI 125 Ra45
Kabeya ◎ RDC 199 Mb49
Kabi ◎ ETH 192 Mk40
Kabile ◎ LV 45 Mc34
Kabinburi ◎ THA 123 Qa38
Kabinda ◎ RDC 199 Mc49
Kabir ◎ RI 131 Rc50
Kabirizi ◎ EAU 191 Me45

Karmé □ TCH 189 Lh39
Karmøy ▲ N 42 Lf31
Karnak ☒ ET 179 Mg33
Karnal □ IND 115 Oj31
Kanali River Rafting ☒ NEP 115 Pa31
Karnapu ▲ TCH 183 Lj35
Karnaprayag □ IND 115 Ok30
Kärnare □ BG 69 Me48
Karnes City □ USA 245 Fb31
Karnezéika ☒ GR 71 Md55
Karnischer Alpen ▲ A 61 Ln44
Karnisar □ IND 114 Og31
Karnobat □ BG 69 Mg48
Karoi □ ZW 202 Me54
Karokh ☒ AFG 98 Ob28
Karong □ IND 120 Ph33
Karonga □ MW 196 Mg50
Karonie □ AUS 145 Rb61
Karoola □ AUS 151 Sa62
Karoonda □ AUS 150 Rk63
Karor N.P. ☒ ZA 204 Mb62
Karor □ PK 99 Of30
Karora □ RI 130 Qa45
Karouassas □ RMM 181 Kk37
Karpackie Góry ▲ PL 65 Md37
Kärpänkylä □ FIN 39 Mh35
Kárpathos ▲ GR 71 Mh55
Kárpathos ☒ GR 71 Mh55
Karpaty kyj nacionalnyj park ☒ UA 67 Md42
Karpenísi □ GR 71 Mb52
Karpuzlu □ TR 69 Mg50
Karra □ IND 117 Ok34
Karratha □ AUS 142 Qj56
Karreedouw □ ZA 205 Mc62
Karridale □ AUS 144 Qh63
Kars □ TR 91 Nb25
Kársava □ LV 45 Mh34
Karsí □ WAN 188 Ld41
Karsta □ S 43 Lj31
Karstädt □ D 58 Lm37
Kärstula □ FIN 44 Me38
Kartabu □ GUY 266 Ha42
Kartal □ TR 69 Mb50
Kartangaruru, Walpiri & Walmajert A.L. ☒ AUS 143 Re55
Karterés □ GR 68 Md50
Karthago □ ☒ TN 176 Lf27
Karthala ▲ COM 206 Nb51
Karú □ PL 64 Lt36
Karul □ PNG 156 Sg47
Karumba □ AUS 151 Sf62
Karúbaga □ RI 154 Rk47
Karubwe □ Z 202 Me52
Karufa □ RI 154 Rg47
Karuia rahvuspark ☒ EST 45 Mg33
Karuma Game Reserve ☒ EAU 194 Mf44
Karumai □ J 111 Sa25
Karumba □ AUS 147 Sa54
Karumbhar Island ▲ IND 116 Oe34
Karumwa □ EAT 194 Mg47
Karungi □ S 39 Md24
Karungu □ EAK 194 Mh46
Karup □ DK 42 Lk34
Kárur □ IND 118 Ok40
Karvia □ FIN 41 Mc38
Karvina □ CZ 66 Lt41
Karvio □ FIN 44 Mj28
Karwar □ IND 117 Pa34
Karwi □ IND 116 Oh38
Karwendelgebirge ▲ A 60 Lm43
Karwi □ IND 117 Pa33
Karymskoe □ RUS 105 Qh20
Karynzharyk ☒ KZ 96 Ng24
Kas ☒ SUD 184 Mc39
Kaš □ TR 90 Mg27
Kasa □ RDC 199 Lk46
Kasaba Bay □ Z 196 Mf50
Kasabonika □ CDN 227 Fc08
Kasai □ J 113 Rh28
Kasai Khurd □ IND 116 Og36
Kasalu □ Z 202 Md53
Kasama □ Z 196 Mf51
Kasamule □ RDC 196 Md47
Kasan □ IR 91 Nf29
Kasane □ ☒ RB 201 Mc54
Kasanga □ EAT 196 Mf50
Kasangulu □ RDC 198 Lh48
Kasanka N.P. □ Z 196 Mf52
Kasanza □ RDC 199 Mb49
Kasaragod □ IND 118 Oh39
Kasauz □ J 113 Re31
Kasary □ RUS 72 Na21
Kasaai □ WAL 186 Ke41
Kasaai □ IND 115 Oj30
Kasbah de Bizerte ☒ TN 176 Le27
Kasbah de Fès ▲ MA 175 Kh28
Kasba Tadla □ MA 175 Kg29
Kascjanevici □ BY 45 Mh36
Kascjukoviči □ BY 72 Mg19
Kascjukovka □ BY 72 Mf19
Kasdir □ DZ 175 Kh29
Kasdol □ IND 117 Pb35
Kasberga □ S 43 Lg35
Kaseda □ J 113 Rf30
Kasempa □ Z 201 Mc52
Kasenga □ RDC 196 Me51
Kasenye □ RDC 194 Mf46
Kasese □ EAU 194 Mf45
Kasese □ RDC 191 Mf46
Kasenye □ RDC 198 Lh48
Kasanka N.P. □ Z 196 Mf52
Kasaragod □ IND 118 Oh39
Kasganj □ IND 115 Oj32
Kashabowie □ CDN 236 Fe21
Kashangani □ ZW 202 Ma56
Kashechewan □ CDN 227 Fd08
Kashi □ CHN 100 Oh26
Kashiji Plain ▲ Z 201 Mb52
Kashima □ J 113 Sa28
Kashipur □ IND 115 Oj33
Kashipur □ IND 117 Pb36
Kashiwa □ J 113 Sa28
Kashiwazaki □ J 111 Rk27
Kashmar □ IR 98 Nk28
Kashmor □ PK 99 Oe31
Kashwal □ SUD 191 Me42
Kasia □ IND 117 Pb32
Kasia □ LAO 121 Qb36
Kasimov □ RUS 72 Na18
Kasin □ RUS 72 Mj17
Kasinje □ MW 203 Mh53
Kasiruta ▲ RI 131 Rd46
Kaskas □ SN 180 Kc37

Koobi Fora ⬚ EAK 194 Mj43
Kookynie ⬚ AUS 144 Ra60
Koolan Island ⬚ AUS 142 Rb54
Kooline ⬚ AUS 147 Sb53
Kooline ⬚ AUS 142 Qj57
Koolpinyah ⬚ AUS 146 Rf52
Koomboolombah ⬚ AUS 147 Sc54
Koonalda ⬚ AUS 145 Re61
Koondoo ⬚ AUS 149 Sc58
Koonga Park ⬚ AUS 143 Rd55
Kooniba ⬚ AUS 148 Rg61
Koonmarra ⬚ AUS 144 Qa59
Koopan Sud ⬚ ZA 204 Ma59
Koopmansfontein ⬚ ZA 205 Mc60
Koo Puay Noi ▲ THA 123 Qb38
Koor ⬚ RI 154 Rg46
Koorawatha ⬚ AUS 151 Se63
Koorda ⬚ AUS 144 Qj51
Koosa ⬚ EST 44 Mf32
Kooskia ⬚ USA 232 Ec22
Kootenay Bay ⬚ CDN 232 Eb21
Kootenay N. Res. IA CDN 232 Ea21
Kootenay Lake ⬚ CDN 232 Eb21
Kootenay N.P. ⬚ CDN 232 Eb20
Kootenay River ⬚ USA 232 Ec21
Kootjieskolk ⬚ ZA 204 Ma61
Kopa ⬚ KZ 100 Oh24
Kopa ⬚ Z 196 Mf51
Kopargo ⬚ DY 188 La41
Kopasker ⬚ IS 46 Kd24
Kopavogur ⬚ IS 46 Jt26
Ko Payang ▲ THA 122 Pj41
Kopbirlik ⬚ KZ 100 Oj22
Kopejsk ⬚ RUS 88 Oa07
Koper ⬚ SLO 66 Lo45
Kopervik ⬚ N 42 Lf31
Ko Pha Yam ▲ THA 122 Pk41
Ko Phi ▲ THA 122 Pk42
Ko Phuket ⬚⬚▲ THA 122 Pk42
Kopiago ⬚ PNG 155 Sb48
Kopidino ⬚ CZ 66 Lo42
Köping ⬚ S 43 Lq31
Kopingue ⬚ CI 187 Kj41
Koplik i Poshtëm ⬚ AL 68 Lu48
Kopmanholmen ⬚ S 41 Lt27
Kopor'e ⬚ RUS 44 Mk31
Koporokenitè-Na ⬚ RMM 181 Kj38
Koppa ⬚ IND 118 Oh39
Koppal ⬚ IND 116 Oh39
Koppang ⬚ N 40 Lm29
Kopparberg ⬚ S 42 Lp31
Kopparstenarne ⬚ S 43 Lu32
Koppe Dag ▲ IR/TM 96 Nj27
Kopperå ⬚ N 40 Lm29
Koppom ⬚ S 42 Ln31
Ko Prah Thong ▲ THA 122 Pk41
Koprivna ⬚ BIH 68 Lt46
Koprivnica ⬚ HR 68 Lt46
Koprivnice ⬚ CZ 66 Lt41
Koprivštica ⬚ BG 69 Me48
Köprübaşı ⬚ TR 71 Mj52
Köprülü Kanyon Milli Parkı ⬚▲ TR 90 Mf27
Köpu ⬚ EST 44 Mc32
Koputh ⬚ EAU 194 Mh44
Kopýčynci ⬚ UA 67 Mf41
Kora ⬚ IND 117 Pd33
Ko Ra ▲ THA 122 Pk41
Korab ▲ SRB/AL 68 Ma49
Korablino ⬚ RUS 72 Mk19
Ko Racha Noi ▲ THA 122 Pk42
Ko Racha Yai ▲ THA 122 Pk42
Koral ⬚ AZ 100 Og24
Ko'rahe ⬚ ETH 193 Nc42
Korand ⬚ IR 96 Nh27
Korangal ⬚ IND 116 Oj37
Korannaberg ▲ ZA 204 Mb59
Kora N.P. ⬚ EAK 195 Mk46
Koraput ⬚ IND 117 Pb36
Korasa ⬚ SOL 157 Sj49
Karatagere ⬚ IND 118 Oj39
Ko Rawi ▲ THA 122 Pk42
Korba ⬚ IND 117 Pb34
Korba ⬚ TN 176 Lf27
Korbach ⬚ D 58 Lj39
Korbol ⬚ TCH 190 Lj41
Korbous ⬚ TN 176 Lf27
Korçe ⬚ AL 70 Ma50
Korčevka ⬚ RUS 72 Nd18
Korčula ▲ HR 61 Ls48
Kordila ⬚ KZ 100 Oh24
Kordkuy ⬚ IR 96 Nh27
Korea Bay ⬚ 107 Rb26
Korean Folk Village ⬚ ROK 112 Rd27
Korea Strait ⬚ 113 Re29
Korec' ⬚ UA 73 Md20
Koregaon ⬚ IND 116 Oh37
Korem ⬚ ETH 192 Mk39
Kore Maïroua ⬚ RN 182 Lb39
Korenevo ⬚ RUS 72 Mh20
Korenica ⬚ HR 61 Lq46
Korenovsk ⬚ RUS 73 Mk21
Korèra-Koré ⬚ RMM 180 Kf38
Korf ⬚ RUS 89 Tb06
Korfantów ⬚ PL 64 Lt40
Korff Ice Rise ⬚ 286 Gb34
Korgas ⬚ KZ 100 Pa23
Korgen ⬚ N 38 Lo24
Korgom ⬚ RN 182 Le39
Korhogo ⬚ CI 187 Kh41
Koria ⬚ FIN 44 Mg30
Koribundu ⬚ WAL 186 Ke42
Korientzé ⬚▲ RMM 181 Kj38
Koriñasi ⬚ GR 70 Mb53
Korim ⬚ RI 154 Rj46
Korinós ⬚ GR 70 Mc50
Kórinthos ⬚ GR 70 Mc53
Korioumè ⬚ RMM 181 Kj37
Koripobi ⬚ PNG 157 Sh49
Korita ⬚ BIH 68 Lt47
Koriyama ⬚ J 111 Sa27
Korjaksaja Sopka, vulkan ▲ RUS 89 Sd08
Korjukivka ⬚ UA 72 Mg20
Korjuteli ⬚ TR 90 Mf27
Korla ⬚ CHN 101 Pd25
Körmend ⬚ H 66 Lr43
Kornaka ⬚ RN 182 Ld38
Kornat ▲ HR 61 Lq47
Kornati, N.P. ⬚⬚▲ HR 61 Lq47
Korneuburg ⬚ A 66 Lr42
Kórnik ⬚ PL 64 Ls39
Kornofolia ⬚ GR 69 Mg49
Kornwestheim ⬚ D 59 Lk42
Koro ⬚ CI 187 Kg41
Koro ▲ FJI 159 Tk54
Koroba ⬚ PNG 155 Sb48
Korobo ⬚ CDN 187 Kk42
Korod ⬚ EAT 197 Md48
Korodzība ⬚ RMM 182 Lc40
Köroğlu Dağları ▲ TR 90 Mf25
Korogwe ⬚ EAT 197 Mk48
Korocha ⬚ RUS 72 Mj19
Korohuita ⬚ CI 187 Kj41
Korolevu ⬚ FJI 159 Tj55
Kooli Desert ⬚ EAK 194 Mj44
Koromačno ⬚ HR 61 Lp46
Koronadal ⬚ RP 125 Rc42
Korondougou ⬚ RMM 187 Kg41
Koroneia ⬚ GR 70 Mb54
Koronowo ⬚ PL 64 Ls37
Korop ⬚ UA 72 Mg20
Koror ⬚ PAL 124 Rh42
Koro Sea ⬚ FJI 159 Tk54
Körösladány ⬚ H 67 Mb44
Körös-Maros N.P. ⬚⬚ H 67 Ma43
Korosten' ⬚ UA 72 Me20
Korostyšiv ⬚ UA 73 Me20
Korovin Island ▲ USA 228 Bk18
Korovniki ▲ RUS 72 Mk17

Korovou ⬚ FJI 159 Tk54
Korovou ⬚ SOL 157 Sh49
Koroyanitu N.P. ⬚▲ FJI 159 Tj54
Korpilahti ⬚ FIN 44 Mf28
Korpiselka ⬚ RUS 44 Mm28
Korpo = Korppoo ⬚ FIN 44 Mb30
Korppoo = Korpo ⬚ FIN 44 Mb30
Korreh ⬚ IR 98 Ng39
Korsakow ⬚ RUS 111 Sb22
Korsberga ⬚ S 43 Lg33
Korsimoro ⬚ BF 187 Kk39
Korsnäs ⬚ FIN 41 Mb28
Korsør ⬚ DK 42 Lm35
Korsun-Ševčenkivs'kyj ⬚ UA 73 Mf21
Korsze ⬚ PL 65 Mb36
Kortel ⬚ SUD 185 Mf39
Korten ⬚ BG 69 Mf48
Kortesjärvi ⬚ FIN 44 Mc28
Kortrijk ⬚ B 57 Ld40
Koruca ⬚ TR 71 Mh51
Korup, P.N. de ⬚▲ CAM 188 Le43
Koruyeh ⬚ IR 97 Nh30
Korwa Autonomous District ⬚ RUS 89 Rb06
Korýčany ⬚ CZ 66 Ls41
Korycin ⬚ PL 65 Md37
Korzybie ⬚ PL 64 Lr36
Kós ⬚ GR 71 Mh54
Kós ▲ GR 71 Mh54
Kosai ⬚ ETH 192 Mj42
Kós-Agaç ⬚ RUS 101 Pe21
Kosaja Gora ⬚ RUS 72 Mj18
Ko Samet N.P. ⬚▲ THA 123 Qa39
Kosanica ⬚ MNE 68 Lu47
Košarovce ⬚ SK 67 Mb41
Kosava ⬚ BY 65 Mf38
Koscian ⬚ PL 64 Lr38
Kościelec ⬚ PL 64 Lt38
Kościerzyna ⬚ PL 64 Ls36
Kościół Mariacki ⬚ PL 64 Lr36
Kościół Sytersów ⬚ PL 64 Lr40
Kosciusko ⬚ USA 239 Ff29
Kosciuszko, Mount ▲ AUS 151 Se64
Kosciuszko N.P. ⬚ AUS 151 Se63
Koš-Döbö ⬚ KS 100 Oh25
Kose ⬚ EST 44 Mf31
Kose ⬚ TR 91 Mk25
Ko Sèe Daglan ▲ TR 90 Mj25
Kosgi ⬚ IND 116 Oj37
Kosha ⬚ SUD 185 Mf35
Koshi ⬚ RDC 199 Lk48
Koshikijima-retto ▲ J 113 Re30
Kosh-k ⬚ AFG 98 Nz28
Koshok-k Kohneh ⬚ AFG 98 Od28
Koshoba ⬚ TM 96 Nh25
Ko Si ▲ THA 122 Pk42
Kosi Bay Nature Reserve ⬚▲ ZA 205 Mg59
Kosikköy ⬚ SK 67 Ma42
Košicka Belá ⬚ SK 67 Mb42
Košihovce ⬚ SK 67 Lu42
Ko Similan ▲ THA 122 Pj41
Ko Similan N.P. ⬚▲ THA 122 Pj41
Kosingne ⬚ SRB 68 Lu46
Koska ⬚ HR 61 Lt45
Koskenpää ⬚ FIN 44 Mf28
Koskue ⬚ FIN 44 Mc28
Kosmás ⬚ GR 70 Mc53
Koson ⬚ UZ 97 Oc26
Kosong ⬚ PRK 112 Re26
Kosonsoy ⬚ UZ 97 Of25
Kosovska Mitrovica ⬚ KSV 68 Ma48
Kosów Lacki ⬚ PL 65 Mc38
Kosrayl ⬚ IR 91 Nc28
Kosse ⬚ USA 238 Fb30
Kosso ⬚ CI 187 Kh43
Kossol Reef ⬚ PAL 124 Rh42
Kossuth-Múzeum ⬚ H 67 Lu43
Kosta ⬚ S 43 Lq34
Kostanaj ⬚ KZ 88 Oa08
Kostanjevica na Krki ⬚▲ SLO 66 Lq45
Kostelec nad Černými Lesy ⬚ CZ 66 Lq41
Kostelec na Hané ⬚ CZ 66 Ls41
Kostenec ⬚ BG 69 Me48
Kosterøarna ▲ S 42 Lm32
Kostinbrod ⬚ BG 68 Md48
Kostjantynivka ⬚ UA 73 Mj21
Kostomłoty ⬚ PL 64 Lr39
Kostopil' ⬚ UA 65 Mg40
Kostroma ⬚ RUS 72 Na17
Kostryna ⬚ UA 67 Mc42
Kostrzyn ⬚ PL 64 Lg38
Kosubuke ⬚ WAN 188 Ld41
Kosubuke ⬚ RDC 199 Mb48
Koûroudjél ▲ RIM 180 Kd38
Koûroukoto ⬚ RMM 186 Ke39
Kouroussa ⬚ RG 186 Kf40
Kourosh Palace ⬚ IR 93 Nf31
Koursys ⬚ RMM 183 Lg37
Koussanar ⬚ SN 186 Kc39
Koussané ⬚ RMM 186 Ke38
Koussédï ⬚ CAM 189 Lh39
Kousseri ⬚ CAM 189 Lh39
Koussoundou ⬚ TG 187 La41
Koutaba ⬚ CAM 188 Le43
Koutaïlas ⬚ GR 71 Me53
Koutammakou ⬚▲ TG 187 La40
Koutia Gaïdi ⬚ SN 180 Kc38
Koutiala ⬚ RMM 187 Kh40
Kouto ⬚ CI 187 Kg41
Koutougou ⬚ TG 187 La40
Kouvola ⬚ FIN 44 Mg30
Kovačevci ⬚ SRB 68 Ma48
Kovacevac ⬚ SRB 68 Ma45
Kovada Gölü Milli Parkı ⬚▲ TR 90 Mf27
Kovalam ⬚ IND 118 Oj41
Kovalam Beach ⬚▲ IND 118 Oj41
Kovancılar ⬚ TR 91 Mk26
Kov-Ata ⬚ TM 96 Nj26
Kovdor ⬚ RUS 39 Mf23
Kovernino ⬚ RUS 72 Nb17
Kovero ⬚ FIN 44 Mf28
Kovilpatti ⬚ IND 118 Oj41
Kovrov ⬚ RUS 72 Na17
Kovvur ⬚ IND 117 Pa37
Kovylkino ⬚ RUS 72 Nb18
Kowal ⬚ PL 65 Lu38
Kowale Oleckie ⬚ PL 65 Mc36
Kowangge ⬚ RI 130 Qk50
Kowanyama ⬚ AUS 147 Sc54
Kowary ⬚ PL 64 Lq40
Kowloon ⬚ CHN 109 Qh34
Kowon ⬚ PRK 110 Rd26
Koxlax ⬚ WAN 182 Ld39
Koya ⬚ SUD 186 Kd39
Ko Yao Yai ▲ THA 122 Pk42
Koyasan sacred site (Koya) ⬚▲ J 113 Rf28
Köycegïz ⬚ TR 71 Mj54
Koyukuk ⬚ USA 229 Bk13
Koyukuk ⬚ USA 229 Ca13
Koyukuk National Wildlife Refuge ⬚ USA 229 Cb13
Koyulhisar ⬚ TR 91 Mj26
Koyyuru ⬚ IND 117 Pb37
Kotongoru II ⬚ TCH 190 Lk41
Koton-Karfi ⬚ WAN 188 Ld40
Koton-Koro ⬚ WAN 188 Lc40
Kotor Katedrala ⬚ MNE 68 Lt48
Kotoriba ⬚ HR 61 Lr44
Kotor Varoš ⬚ BIH 61 Lt46
Kotovsk ⬚ RUS 72 Na19
Kotovsk ⬚ UA 73 Me42
Kötschach ⬚ A 61 Lo44

Kottagudem ⬚ IND 117 Pa37
Kottai Malai ▲ IND 118 Oj41
Kottampatti ⬚ IND 118 Ok40
Kottappatti ⬚ IND 119 Oj41
Kottarakara ⬚ IND 118 Oj41
Kottayam ⬚ IND 118 Oj41
Kotto ⬚ RCA 190 Ma43
Kottur ⬚ IND 118 Oj38
Kotuj ⬚ RUS 89 Qa05
Koturdepe ⬚ TM 96 Ng26
Kotwa ⬚ ZW 202 Mg54
Kotzebue ⬚ USA 229 Bj12
Kotzebue Sound ⬚ USA 229 Bj12
Kötzting ⬚ D 59 Ln41
Kouadio-Prikro ⬚ CI 187 Kh42
Kouakourou ⬚ RMM 181 Kh38
Kouande ⬚ DY 187 La40
Kouango ⬚ RCA 190 Ma43
Kouankan ⬚ RG 186 Kf41
Kouassikro ⬚ CI 187 Kj42
Kouba Olanga ⬚ TCH 183 Lk38
Koubia ⬚ RG 186 Ke40
Koubo Abou Azraq ⬚ TCH 184 Ma40
Kouéré ⬚ BF 187 Kh40
Koufalia ⬚ GR 70 Mc50
Koufey ⬚ RN 183 Lg38
Koufonisi ▲ GR 71 Mh54
Kougaberge ▲ ZA 204 Mb62
Kougnohou ⬚ TG 187 La42
Kougoulou ⬚ TG 187 La42
Kouhezi ⬚ CHN 110 Ra24
Kouibli ⬚ CI 187 Kg42
Kouka ⬚ BF 187 Kh40
Kouki ⬚ RCA 190 Lj42
Koukia = Bentia ⬚ RMM 181 La38
Koukou ⬚ TCH 184 Mb40
Koukourou ⬚ RCA 190 Ma42
Koula ⬚ RMM 187 Kh39
Koulbo ⬚ TCH 184 Ma39
Koulbous ⬚ SUD 184 Mb38
Koulé ⬚ RG 186 Kf41
Koulé Ekou ⬚ DY 188 Lb41
Koulikoro ▲ RMM 187 Kg39
Kouloura ⬚ RN 188 Lb39
Kouloua ⬚ CI 186 Kg42
Koum ⬚ CAM 189 Lh42
Koumac ⬚ F 158 Tc56
Koumaïra ⬚ RMM 181 Kj38
Koumala ⬚ AUS 149 Sd57
Koumameyong ⬚ G 198 Ld45
Koumantou ⬚ RMM 187 Kg40
Koumbal ⬚ RCA 190 Mb41
Koumbala ⬚ CI 187 Kh41
Koumbala ⬚ RCA 190 Ma41
Koumbia ⬚ BF 187 Kh40
Koumbia ⬚ RG 186 Ke40
Koumbili ⬚ BF 187 Kk40
Koumbi Saleh ⬚ RIM 181 Kf38
Koumbri ⬚ BF 187 Kj39
Koumia ⬚ RMM 187 Kh39
Koumogo ⬚ TCH 190 Lk41
Koumpentoum ⬚ SN 180 Kc38
Koumra ⬚ TCH 190 Lj41
Kounahiri ⬚ CI 187 Kh42
Kounávi ⬚ GR 71 Mf55
Koundara ⬚ RG 186 Kd39
Koundé ⬚ RCA 190 Lj42
Koundessong ⬚ CAM 189 Lg44
Koundian ⬚ RG 186 Ke40
Koundian ⬚ RMM 186 Ke39
Koundijourou ⬚ TCH 183 Lk39
Koundougou ⬚ BF 187 Kh40
Kounen-Fao ⬚ CI 187 Kj42
Koungheul ⬚ SN 186 Kc39
Koungji ⬚ BF 187 Kj39
Koungouri ⬚ TCH 189 Lk40
Kouniana ⬚ RMM 187 Kh39
Kounoune ⬚ SN 186 Kc39
Kounoupitsa ⬚ GR 69 Md53
Kounsitel ⬚ RG 186 Kd40
Kountze ⬚ USA 238 Fc30
Kouoro ⬚ RMM 187 Kh39
Koup ⬚ ZA 204 Ma61
Kouragué ⬚ BF 187 Ke39
Kouragué ⬚ RMM 186 Ke39
Kouré ⬚ RN 182 Lb39
Kourémale ⬚ RMM 186 Kf40
Kourgou ⬚ TCH 189 Lg41
Kouri ⬚ BF 187 Kj39
Kouri ⬚ RMM 187 Kh39
Kouri Kouri ⬚ TCH 183 Lj39
Kourion ⬚ CY 90 Mg28
Kourkéto ⬚ RMM 180 Ke38
Kourou ⬚ F 266 Hd43
Kourou ⬚ CI 186 Kg41
Kourouba ⬚ RMM 186 Kf39
Kouroukoto ⬚ RMM 186 Ke39
Kourouma ⬚ BF 187 Kh40
Kourouninkoto ⬚ RMM 186 Ke39
Kouroussa ⬚ RG 186 Kf40

Kozłów ⬚ PL 65 Lu40
Kozlu ⬚ TR 90 Mf25
Kozluk ⬚ TR 91 Na26
Kozlupınar ⬚ TR 91 Mk26
Koźmin ⬚ PL 64 Lt39
Koźminek ⬚ PL 64 Lt39
Kozmiec ⬚ PL 64 Lq39
Kozu-jima ▲ J 113 Rk28
Kozyn ⬚ UA 65 Mf40
Kpagto ⬚ GH 187 Kk41
Kpalbusi ⬚ GH 187 Kk41
Kpalimé ⬚ TG 187 La42
Kpando ⬚ GH 187 La42
Kparigu ⬚ GH 187 Kk40
Kpaso ⬚ GH 187 La42
Kpassagon ⬚ DY 188 Lb42
Kpatawe Falls ⬚ LB 186 Kf42
Kpatinga ⬚ GH 187 Kk41
Kpéssi ⬚ TG 187 La41
Kpetoe ⬚ GH 187 La42
Kpetuo ⬚ LB 186 Kf42
Kraankuil ⬚ ZA 205 Mc60
Krabi ⬚ THA 122 Pk41
Kra Buri ⬚ THA 122 Pk40
Krafla ▲ IS 46 Kd25
Kragenæs ⬚ DK 42 Lm35
Kragerø ⬚ N 42 Lk32
Kraguievac ⬚ SRB 68 Ma46
Krajiste ⬚ SRB 68 Lu48
Krajnovka ⬚ RUS 91 Nd24
Krakatau Island = Rakata ▲ RI 127 Qc49
Krakatau Volcano ▲ RI 127 Qc49
Kráke ⬚ DY 188 Ls42
Kräklingbo ⬚ S 43 Lt33
Krakorum ⬚ GH 187 Kj42
Krakovec' ⬚ UA 67 Mc41
Krakow am See ⬚ D 58 Ln37
Kralendijk ⬚ NL 265 Gf38
Králicky Sneźnik ▲ PL 64 Lr40
Kraljevica ⬚ HR 61 Lp45
Kraljevo ⬚ SRB 68 Ma47
Kralovice ⬚ CZ 66 Lo41
Král'ovský Chlmec ⬚ SK 67 Mb42
Kralupy nad Vltavou ⬚ CZ 66 Lp40
Kramators'k ⬚ UA 73 Mj21
Kramfors ⬚ S 41 Ls28
Kramjanica ⬚ BY 65 Me37
Kranidi ⬚ GR 69 Mcd53
Kranj ⬚ SLO 66 Lq44
Kranjska Gora ⬚ SLO 66 Lo44
Kranovo ⬚ BG 69 Mg48
Kranovodskoye plato ▲ TM 96 Ng25
Kransfontein ⬚ ZA 205 Me60
Kranskop ⬚ ZA 205 Mf60
Kranuan ⬚ THA 123 Qa38
Kraolandia ⬚ BR 272 Hg50
Kraolândia, T.I. ⬚ BR 272 Hg50
Krapina ⬚ HR 61 Lq44
Krapinske Toplice ⬚ HR 61 Lq44
Krapkowice ⬚ PL 64 Ls40
Krasaesin ⬚ THA 122 Qa42
Kras-navina ⬚ RUS 10 Rf24
Krasilava ⬚ LV 45 Mh35
Krasilice ⬚ CZ 66 Ln40
Krasnae ⬚ BY 45 Mh36
Krása Hôrka ▲ SK 67 Ma42
Krasnaja Gora ⬚ RUS 72 Mh20
Krasnaja Gorbatka ⬚ RUS 72 Na18
Krasnaja Jaruga ⬚ RUS 72 Mj20
Krásna nad Hornádom ⬚ SK 67 Mb42
Krasnik ⬚ PL 65 Mc40
Krasnoarmejsk ⬚ RUS 72 Mk17
Krasnoarmijs'k ⬚ UA 73 Mj21
Krasnobród ⬚ PL 65 Md40
Krasnodar ⬚ RUS 73 Mk22
Krasnodarskoe Vodohranilišče ⬚ RUS 73 Mk23
Krasnodon ⬚ UA 73 Mk21
Krasnogvardijs'ke ⬚ UA 73 Mh23
Krasnojarovo ⬚ RUS 105 Re20
Krasnojarsk ⬚ RUS 88 Pc07
Krasnojil's'k ⬚ UA 67 Mf42
Krasnokamensk ⬚ RUS 105 Qk20
Krasnokuts'k ⬚ UA 72 Mh20
Krasnomajskij ⬚ RUS 72 Mj17
Krasnopavlivka ⬚ UA 73 Mj21
Krasnoperekops'k ⬚ UA 73 Mg23
Krasnopillja ⬚ UA 72 Mh20
Krasnopołesc ⬚ PL 65 Mb37
Krasnoslobodsk ⬚ RUS 72 Nb18
Krasnotorovka ⬚ RUS 45 Lu36
Krasnovolja ⬚ UA 65 Mf39
Krasnoye Znamya ⬚ TM 96 Ob27
Krasnoznamensk ⬚ RUS 45 Mc36
Krasnyé Baki ⬚ RUS 72 Nc17
Krasnyj Holm ⬚ RUS 72 Mj16
Krasnyj Luč ⬚ UA 73 Mk21
Krasnyj Manyč ⬚ RUS 73 Na22
Kraste ⬚ AL 68 Ma49
Krasti ⬚ LV 45 Me34
Krasyliv ⬚ UA 73 Md21
Krathing Falls ⬚ THA 123 Qb40
Kratie ⬚ K 123 Qd39
Kratke Range ▲ PNG 155 Sc49
Kratovo ⬚ MK 68 Mb48
Krau ⬚ RI 155 Sa47
Kraziai ⬚ LT 45 Mc35
Kréva ⬚ BY 45 Mg36
Kreb Bekaïl el Bâss ▲ RMM 182 La35
Kreb Sefid ⬚ RMM 181 Kj38
Kregbé ⬚ CI 187 Kj42
Krek ⬚ K 123 Qc40
Krekanava ⬚ LT 45 Me35
Kremenčuk ⬚ UA 73 Mg21
Kremenec' ⬚ UA 65 Mf40
Kremikovci ⬚ BG 68 Md48
Kreml ⬚ RUS 72 Mj17
Kreml Novgorod ▲ RUS 72 Mf16
Kremmen ⬚ D 58 Ln38
Kremmling ⬚ USA 235 Eg25
Kremna ▲ SRB 68 Lu47
Kremnicky hrad ⬚ SK 67 Lu42
Krems ⬚ A 61 Lo44
Krems ⬚ A 66 Lq42
Krepoljin ⬚ SRB 68 Mb46
Krepsko ⬚ PL 64 Lr37
Kresevo ⬚ BIH 68 Lt47
Kresk-Królowa ⬚ PL 65 Mc38
Kresna ⬚ BG 68 Md49
Krestcy ⬚ RUS 72 Mg16
Krestena ⬚ GR 70 Mb53
Kretinga ⬚ LT 45 Mb35
Kreuzeck ▲ A 61 Lo44
Kreuzenstein ▲ A 66 Lr42
Kreuztal ⬚ D 58 Lj40
Kriátisi ⬚ GR 70 Mc52
Kribi ⬚ CAM 188 Le44
Krieglach ⬚ A 61 Lq43
Krieldrif ⬚ ZA 205 Me59
Krikelos ⬚ GR 70 Mb52
Krim-Krim ⬚ TCH 190 Lh41
Krimmler Fälle ⬚ A 61 Ln43
Krims ⬚ GR 70 Mc49
Krinides ⬚ GR 69 Me49
Krishna ⬚ IND 117 Ok37
Krishnagiri ⬚ IND 118 Ok39
Krishnai ⬚ IND 120 Pk33
Krishnanagar ⬚ IND 120 Pg33
Krisuvik ⬚ IS 46 Jt26
Kristdala ⬚ S 43 Lr33
Kristianscend ⬚ N 40 Lf27
Kristiankaupunki = Kristinestad ⬚ FIN 41 Mb28
Kristinehamn ⬚ S 42 Lp31
Kristinestad = Kristiinankaupunki ⬚ FIN 41 Mb28
Kriva Feja ⬚ SRB 68 Mb48
Kriva Palanka ⬚ MK 68 Mc48

Krivodol ⬚ BG 68 Md47
Krivolak ⬚ MK 68 Mc49
Krivorož'e ⬚ RUS 72 Na21
Krk ⬚ HR 61 Lp45
Krk ▲ HR 61 Lp45
Krížanov ⬚ CZ 66 Lr41
Križevci ⬚ HR 61 Lr44
Križpolje ⬚ HR 61 Lq46
krjaž Čekanovskogo ▲ RUS 89 Ra04
Krk ⬚ HR 61 Lp46
Krka, N.P. ⬚ HR 61 Lq47
Krkonošský N.P. ⬚ CZ 66 Lq40
Krn ▲ SLO 66 Lo44
Krnja ⬚ MNE 68 Lu48
Krnov ⬚ CZ 66 Ls40
Krobia ⬚ PL 64 Lr39
Krøderen ⬚ N 42 Lk30
Krokek ⬚ S 43 Lr32
Krokilio ⬚ GR 70 Mc52
Krokom ⬚ S 41 Lp27
Kroměříž ⬚ CZ 66 Ls41
Krolevec' ⬚ UA 72 Mg20
Kromdraai ⬚▲ ZA 205 Md59
Kroměříž ⬚ CZ 66 Ls41
Kromy ⬚ RUS 72 Mh19
Kronach ⬚ D 59 Lm40
Kronacur ⬚ LV 45 Md34
Kronborg ⬚ DK 42 Ln34
Kronoby ⬚ FIN 44 Mc28
Kronotskij Zapovednik ⬚ RUS 89 Sd09
Kronoprins Olav kyst ⬚ 286 Na32
Kronshagen ⬚ D 58 Ll36
Kronstadt ⬚ RUS 44 Mk31
Kroonstad ⬚ ZA 205 Md59
Kröpelin ⬚ D 58 Lm36
Kropotkin ⬚ RUS 73 Na23
Krośniewice ⬚ PL 65 Lu38
Krosno ⬚ PL 65 Mb41
Krosno Odrzańskie ⬚ PL 64 Lq38
Kross ▲ IS 46 Ju27
Krotoszyn ⬚ PL 64 Ls39
Krotz Springs ⬚ USA 239 Fe30
Krško ⬚ SLO 66 Lq45
Krstac ⬚ MNE 68 Lt48
Krueng Raya ⬚ RI 126 Ph43
Krupa na Vrbasu ⬚ BIH 61 Ls46
Krupanj ⬚ SRB 68 Lu46
Krupinska planina ▲ SK 67 Lu42
Krušari ⬚ BG 69 Mh47
Kruševac ⬚ SRB 68 Lu45
Kruševo ⬚ MK 68 Mb49
Krušné hory ▲ D/CZ 59 Ln40
Krušovica ⬚ BG 69 Me47
Krustpils ▲ LV 45 Mf34
Kruszwica ⬚ PL 65 Lu39
Kruszyna ⬚ PL 65 Lu38
Kruzwyz ▲ PL 64 Lt38
Kruzof Island ▲ USA 230 Dc17
Krynica ⬚ PL 65 Ma41
Kryms'ky hory ▲ UA 73 Mh23
Krynica ⬚ PL 65 Ma41
Kryve Ozero ⬚ UA 73 Mf22
Kryvyj Rih ⬚ UA 73 Mg22
Kryzopil' ⬚ UA 73 Me21
Krzeszów ⬚ PL 65 Mc40
Krzeszyce ⬚ PL 64 Lq38
Krzywa ⬚ PL 64 Lq39
Ksabi ⬚ DZ 175 Kk31
Ksan Ind. Village ▲ CDN 230 Dg18
Ksar El Barka ▲ RIM 180 Kd36
Ksar el Boukhari ⬚ DZ 176 Lb28
Ksar el-Hallouf ⬚ TN 176 Lf28
Ksar El Hirane ⬚ DZ 176 Lb29
Ksar-el-Kebir ⬚ MA 175 Kg26
Ksar-es-Seghir ⬚ MA 175 Kh26
Ksar Ghilane ⬚ TN 176 Lf29
Ksar Lamsa ⬚ TN 176 Le27
Ksar Ouled Soltane ▲ TN 176 Lf29
Ksar, Oued ⬚ RIM 180 Kd35
Ksenskij ⬚ RUS 72 Mk20
Kšiěžpol ⬚ PL 65 Mc40
Ksour Essaf ⬚ TN 176 Lf28
Kstovo ⬚ RUS 72 Nb17
KTHI-TV Tower ⬚ USA 236 Fb22
Ktismata ⬚ GR 70 Ma51
Kuah ⬚ MAL 126 Pk42
Kuaidjin ⬚ BD 120 Pf35
Kuala ⬚ RI 126 Pk44
Kualabali ⬚ RI 126 Pj44
Kuala Batee ⬚ RI 126 Ph44
Kuala Berang ⬚ MAL 126 Qb43
Kuala Besut ⬚ MAL 126 Qb43
Kualabetara ⬚ RI 127 Qb46
Kuala Dua Beach ⬚ RI 126 Qb44
Kuala Dungun ⬚ MAL 126 Qb44
Kuala Kangsar ⬚ MAL 126 Qa44
Kualakapuas ⬚ RI 129 Qh47
Kuala Kedah ⬚ MAL 126 Qa43
Kuala Krai ⬚ MAL 126 Qb43
Kuala Kubu Baharu ⬚ MAL 126 Qa44
Kualalangsa ⬚ RI 126 Ph43
Kuala Lipis ⬚ MAL 126 Qb44
Kuala Lumpur ⬚⬚ MAL 126 Qa44
Kualapembuang ⬚ RI 129 Qg47
Kuala Perlis ⬚ MAL 126 Qa43
Kualapesaguan ⬚ RI 129 Qf46
Kuala Pilah ⬚ MAL 126 Qb44
Kuala Rompin ⬚ MAL 126 Qb44
Kualasimpang ⬚ RI 126 Ph43
Kuala Tatau ⬚ MAL 128 Qg44
Kualatungkal ⬚ RI 127 Qc46
Kuala Tungkal ⬚ RI 127 Qb46
Kuamut ⬚ MAL 129 Qj44
Kuancheng ⬚ CHN 110 Qc25
Kuandian ⬚ CHN 110 Rb26
Kuantan ⬚ MAL 126 Qb44
Kuaotunu ⬚ NZ 152 Th64
Kuba ⬚ SUD 184 Mc39
Kubang ⬚ RI 129 Qf46
Kubango ▲ ANG 200 Lh52
Kubar ⬚ SUD 185 Me40
Kubbum ⬚ SUD 184 Mb40
Kubli Tunnel ⬚ J 111 Sa28
Kubu ⬚ RI 129 Qj49
Kubumesaai ⬚ RI 128 Qh45
Kuçada German ⬚ BIH 61 Lt46
Kuçova ⬚ AL 68 Lu50
Kučurgan ⬚ MD 73 Mf22

Kuchary ⬚ PL 64 Ls39
Kucheh ⬚ IR 98 Nk30
Kuchino-Erabu-jima ▲ J 113 Rf30
Kuchino-jima ▲ J 113 Re31
Kuchits'ka Volja ⬚ UA 65 Mf39
Kučiste ⬚ KSV 68 Ma48
Kücükbahce ⬚ TR 71 Mg52
Kücükçekmece ⬚ TR 71 Mg51
Kücükkuyu ⬚ TR 71 Mg52
Kücükoba ⬚ TR 90 Mj26
Kumbach ⬚ D 59 Lm40
Kulob ⬚ TJ 97 Oe27
Kulp ⬚ TR 91 Na26
Kulpara ⬚ AUS 150 Rk63
Kulpi ⬚ IND 120 Pe34
Kulshabi ⬚ SUD 184 Me40
Kulsubai ▲ IND 116 Oh37
Kultamuseo ⬚ FIN 39 Mh22
Kulti ⬚ IND 117 Pd34
Kultuk ⬚ RUS 104 Qb20
Kuldayn ⬚ SUD 185 Mf36
Kudene ⬚ RI 154 Rh49
Kudiakor Is. ▲ USA 228 Bj18
Kudi-Boma ⬚ RDC 198 Lf49
Kudirkos Naumiestis ⬚ LT 45 Mc36
Kudjip ⬚ PNG 155 Sc48
Kudlig ⬚ IND 118 Oj38
Kudnu ▲ IND 118 Oj38
Kudowa-Zdroj ⬚ PL 64 Lr40
Kudremukh ▲ IND 118 Oh39
Kudu ⬚ WAN 188 Lc41
Kudus ⬚ RI 129 Qf49
Kuélab ⬚ PE 268 Gb49
Kutew ⬚ PL 65 Mb38
Kufstein ▲ A 61 Ln43
Kugey ⬚ RUS 73 Mk22
Kugitang Caves ▲ TM 97 Od27
Kugluktuk ⬚ CDN 226 Ea05
Kuha ⬚ IR 98 Oa30
Kuhak ⬚ IR 99 Oc32
Kuhak ▲ IR 99 Oc32
Kuhbanan ⬚ IR 98 Nj30
Kuhdasht ⬚ IR 91 Nd29
Kuh-e Aladagh ▲ IR 96 Nj27
Kuh-e Alijuq ▲ IR 93 Nf31
Kuh-e Baba ▲ AFG 99 Oc28
Kuh-e Bageran ▲ IR 98 Nk29
Kuh-e Baradar-e Sah ▲ IR 91 Nd27
Kuh-e Baran ▲ IR 98 Oa29
Kuh-e Bazman ▲ IR 98 Nk31
Kuh-e Binalud ▲ IR 96 Na27
Kuh-e Birg ▲ IR 99 Oa32
Kuh-e Buhan ▲ IR 98 Nj32
Kuh-e Chah Shirin ▲ IR 98 Nh28
Kuh-e Chehel Abdoli ▲ AFG 99 Ob29
Kuh-e Damavand ▲ IR 96 Ng28
Kuh-e Dinar ▲ IR 93 Nf30
Kuh-e Dom ▲ IR 98 Ng29
Kuh-e Esger ▲ IR 98 Nk28
Kuh-e Garbos ▲ IR 91 Ne29
Kuh-e Garin ▲ IR 91 Ne29
Kuh-e Gebal Barez ▲ IR 98 Nk31
Kuh-e Hage ▲ IR 98 Oa30
Kuh-e Hezar ▲ IR 98 Nj30
Kuh-e Hogalak ▲ IR 91 Nd28
Kuh-e Huran ▲ IR 98 Nk32
Kuh-e Joghatay ▲ IR 96 Nj27
Kuh-e Kalar ▲ IR 93 Nf30
Kuh-e Kalur ▲ IR 91 Nd29
Kuh-e Kheybar ▲ IR 98 Nj31
Kuh-e Khorunaq ▲ IR 98 Nh29
Kuh-e Lalezar ▲ IR 98 Nj31
Kuh-e Mamand ▲ AFG 99 Ob29
Kuh-e Momenabad ▲ IR 98 Nk29
Kuh-e Nakhochay ▲ IR 91 Nd28
Kuh-e Nokhoch ▲ IR 98 Oa32
Kuh-e Palangan ▲ IR 98 Oa30
Kuh-e Sabalan ▲ IR 91 Nd26
Kuh-e Safidar ▲ IR 98 Ng31
Kuh-e Safid Hers ▲ AFG 97 Of27
Kuh-e Sahand ▲ IR 91 Nd28
Kuh-e Sayyad ▲ AFG 97 Of27
Kuh-e Shah Jahan ▲ IR 96 Nj27
Kuh-e Sheh Jahan ▲ IR 96 Nj27
Kuh-e Sorkh ▲ IR 98 Nj28
Kuh-e Sorkh ▲ IR 96 Nh28
Kuh-e Taftan ▲ IR 99 Oa31
Kuh-e Vakhan ▲ AFG 97 Of27
Kuh-e Zardeh ▲ IR 91 Ne29
Kuhha-ye Bashagerd ▲ IR 98 Nk32
Kuhha-ye Kuhpaye ▲ IR 98 Nh29
Kuhha-ye Qohrud ▲ IR 98 Ng29
Kuhl Arnawad ▲ TJ 97 Of26
Kuhlungsborn ⬚ D 58 Lm36
Kuhmalahti ⬚ FIN 44 Me29
Kuhmo ⬚ FIN 39 Mh25
Kuhmoinen ⬚ FIN 44 Me29
Kuhpayeh ⬚ IR 98 Nh29
Kuhrang ⬚ IR 93 Nf30
Kuhtorin Lug ⬚ RUS 105 Re19
Kui ⬚ PNG 155 Sd49
Kui Buri ⬚ THA 122 Pk39
Kuinetsa ⬚ EAT 44 Mj31
Kuis ⬚ NAM 204 Lg58
Kuiseabfgrond ⬚ NAM 204 Lh57
Kuiseb Canyon ▲ NAM 204 Lh57
Kuisebpas ▲ NAM 204 Lh57
Kuitan ⬚ CHN 109 Qh34
Kuito ⬚ ANG 200 Lj52
Kuiu Island ▲ USA 230 Dc17
Kuivaniemi ⬚ FIN 39 Md25
Kuivastu ⬚ EST 44 Md32
Kujama ⬚ WAN 188 Ld40
Kuji ⬚ J 111 Sa25
Kujie ▲ J 111 Sa25
Kujoor-e ⬚ IR 96 Ng28
Kukan ⬚ IND 117 Pd33
Kukawa ⬚ WAN 189 Lg39
Kuke ⬚ RB 201 Mb56
Kukerin ⬚ AUS 144 Qk62
Kukës ⬚ AL 68 Ma48
Kukkolaforsen ⬚ FIN 41 Mc25
Kukmor ⬚ RUS 72 Nd17
Kuknur ⬚ IND 116 Oh38
Kuknuru ⬚ IND 117 Pa37
Kukës ⬚ AL 68 Ma48
Kukulje ⬚ BIH 61 Ls46
Kukup ⬚ MAL 127 Qb46
Kula ⬚ BG 68 Mc47
Kula ⬚ SRB 68 Lu45
Kula ⬚ TR 71 Mj52
Kulachi ⬚ PK 99 Of30
Kula-ombo ⬚ Z 201 Mb53
Kulandy ⬚ KZ 96 Nk22
Kulang ⬚ RI 129 Qg46
Kulanu de Medio Juruá, T.I. ⬚ BR 268 Ge49
Kulina do Rio Envira, T.I. ⬚ BR 269 Ge50

Kuling ⬚ RI 129 Qg46
Kulito ⬚ ETH 192 Mk42
Kulittalai ⬚ IND 118 Ok40
Kulukpalli ⬚ IND 116 Ok37
Kullen ⬚ S 42 Ln34
Kullu ⬚ IND 115 Oj30
Kulmac Dağları ▲ TR 90 Mj26
Kulob ⬚ TJ 97 Oe27
Kulp ⬚ TR 91 Na26
Kulpara ⬚ AUS 150 Rk63
Kulpi ⬚ IND 120 Pe34
Kulshabi ⬚ SUD 184 Me40
Kulsubai ▲ IND 116 Oh37
Kultamuseo ⬚ FIN 39 Mh22
Kulti ⬚ IND 117 Pd34
Kultuk ⬚ RUS 104 Qb20
Kulu ⬚ TR 90 Mg26
Kulubi ⬚ ETH 192 Na41
Kulukak ⬚ PNG 156 Sg50
Kulundinskaja ravnina ⬚▲ RUS 88 Od08
Kulungu ⬚ RDC 198 Lj46
Kuma ⬚ RI 155 Rf44
Kumagaya ⬚ J 111 Rk27
Kumai ⬚ RI 129 Qf47
Kumamoto ⬚ J 113 Re30
Kumano ⬚ CL 119 Pa42
Kumano ⬚ J 113 Rf29
Kumano sacred site ⬚▲ J 113 Rf29
Kumanovo ⬚ MK 68 Mb48
Kumara Junction ⬚ NZ 153 Tf67
Kumarghat ⬚ IND 120 Pg33
Kumari Amman Temple ⬚▲ IND 118 Oj41
Kumarina ⬚ AUS 144 Qk58
Kumasi ⬚ J 111 Rk24
Kumasi ⬚ GH 187 Kk42
Kumba ⬚ CAM 188 Le43
Kumba ⬚ EAT 196 Mg50
Kumba ⬚ RDC 199 Md49
Kumbakonam ⬚ IND 119 Ok40
Kumbanikesa ⬚ SOL 157 Sj49
Kumbarilla ⬚ AUS 149 Sf59
Kumbe ⬚ RI 155 Sa50
Kumbe ⬚ TR 90 Mf26
Kumbhagiri ⬚ IND 120 Pg33
Kumbh Mela (Allahabad) ⬚▲ IND 117 Pa33
Kumbia ⬚ AUS 149 Sf59
Kumbo ⬚ CAM 188 Le43
Kumbum-Stupa ⬚ CHN 102 Pe31
Kume-jima ▲ J 113 Rd32
Kumertau ⬚ RUS 88 Nd08
Kumhari ⬚ IND 117 Pa34
Kumi ⬚ EAU 194 Mg45
Kumielsk ⬚ PL 65 Mb37
Kumkale ⬚ TR 71 Mg51
Kumköy ▲ TR 71 Mh49
Kumla ⬚ S 43 Lq31
Kumlinge ▲ FIN 44 Ma30
Kumluca ⬚ TR 90 Mf28
Kümmersee ⬚ D 58 Ln37
Kumo ⬚ WAN 189 Lh40
Kumphawapi ▲ THA 123 Qb37
Kumsong ⬚ ROK 112 Rd28
Kumta ⬚ IND 118 Oh38
Kumu ⬚ RDC 191 Mb44
Kümüx ⬚ CHN 101 Pd24
Kumzar ⬚ OM 98 Nj32
Kuna ⬚ USA 232 Eb24
Kuna Cave ⬚ USA 232 Eb24
Kunakanmulam ⬚ IND 118 Oj40
Kunatata Hill ▲ WAN 188 L42
Kunavaram ⬚ IND 117 Pa37
Kuncauzcyna ⬚ BY 45 Mh37
Kunda ⬚ EST 44 Mg31
Kundalila Falls ⬚ Z 196 Md51
Kundam ⬚ IND 117 Pd33
Kundelungu ▲ RDC 196 Md50
Kundelungu, P.N. des ⬚ RDC 196 Md51
Kundian ⬚ PK 99 Of29
Kundiawa ⬚ PNG 155 Sc49
Kundla ⬚ SOL 157 Sj50
Kunduk ⬚ CI 187 Mh49
Kunduz ⬚ AFG 97 Od27
Kunduran ⬚ RI 129 Qf49
Kundy ⬚ RUS 91 Nd24
Kunene ⬚ NAM 200 Lg54
Kunene ⬚ NAM 200 Lh54
Kunga ⬚ S 42 Ln33
Kunghit Island ▲ CDN 230 De19
Kungila ⬚ SUD 185 Mg40
Kunggi Ala-Too ▲ KS 100 Oj24
Kungsäter ⬚ S 42 Lr33
Kungshamn ⬚ S 42 Lm32
Kungsör ⬚ S 43 Lr31
Kungurtug ⬚ RUS 101 Pj20
Kungwe ⬚ RDC 199 Mc47
Kunhegyes ⬚ H 67 Ma43
Kuni Muktar Nyala Sanctuary ⬚ ETH 192 Na41
Kunigal ⬚ IND 118 Oj39

Kurawar ⬚ IND 116 Oj34
Kurayoshi ⬚ J 113 Rg28
Kurdamir ⬚ AZ 91 Ne25
Kurdeg ⬚ IND 117 Pc34
Kurdistan ▲ TR 91 Nb27
Kurdufan ⬚ SUD 184 Me39
Kurduna ⬚ PK 99 Od30
Kurdzinovo ⬚ RUS 91 Na24
Küre Dağlan ▲ TR 90 Mg25
Kuremäe ⬚ EST 44 Mh31
Küre Dağları ▲ EST 45 Mc32
Kurfi ⬚ WAN 188 Ld39
Kurgan ⬚ RUS 88 Ob07
Kurganinsk ⬚ RUS 73 Na23
Kurghaldzhino Nature Reserve ⬚ KZ 96 Ng22
Kurgolovo ⬚ RUS 44 Mj31
Kuria Muria Islands ▲ OM 95 Nh37
Kuridala ⬚ AUS 148 Sa56
Kurigan ⬚ IR 91 Ne28
Kurigram ⬚ BD 120 Pe33
Kurik ⬚ RI 155 Rk50
Kurikka ⬚ FIN 44 Mb28
Kurikoma O.N.P. ⬚ J 111 Sa26
Kuril Islands ▲ RUS 89 Sb09
Kuril'sk ⬚ RUS 111 Sd23
Kuril Trench ⬚ RUS 89 Sb10
Kufim ⬚ IND 116 Oj34
Kurim ⬚ CZ 66 Lr41
Kurin ⬚ F 158 Te56
Ku-Ring-Gai Chase N.P. ⬚ AUS 151 Sf62
Kurinjippadi ⬚ IND 119 Ok40
Kurpapango ⬚ NZ 153 Tj65
Kurparkan kansallispuisto ⬚▲ FIN 44 Mc30
Kurkhera ⬚ IND 117 Pa35
Kurkijoki ⬚ RUS 44 Mk29
Kurkur ⬚ AFG 97 Oe27
Kurlovskij ⬚ RUS 72 Na18
Kurmuk ⬚ SUD 185 Mh40
Kurnool ⬚ IND 116 Ok38
Kuroiso ⬚ J 111 Sa27
Kuro-jima ▲ J 113 Re30
Kurort ⬚ CDN 233 Ej20
Kuromatsunai ⬚ J 111 Sa26
Kurovskoe ⬚ RUS 72 Mk18
Kurów ⬚ PL 65 Mc39
Kurri Kurri ⬚ AUS 151 Sf62
Kurseong ⬚ IND 120 Pe32
Kurshim ⬚ KZ 101 Pb21
Kursiu n.p. ⬚▲ LT 45 Mb35
Kursk ⬚ RUS 72 Mj20
Kursmov ⬚ RUS 72 Mk20
Kurskaja kosa N ⬚ RUS/LT 45 Ma35
Kuršumlija ⬚ SRB 68 Ma47
Kuršunlu ⬚ TR 90 Mg25
Kurtalan ⬚ TR 91 Na27
Kuruba ⬚ IND 116 Oj35
Kuru ⬚ FIN 44 Md29
Kuru ⬚ IND 117 Pc34
Kurubonla ⬚ WAL 186 Ke41
Kurukkuchalai ⬚ IND 118 Ok41
Kuruktag ▲ CHN 101 Pd25
Kuruman ⬚ ZA 204 Mb59
Kuruman Hills ▲ ZA 204 Mb59
Kurume ⬚ J 113 Rf29
Kurunegala ⬚ CL 119 Pa42
Kurupukari ⬚ GUY 266 Ha43
Kuryk ⬚ KZ 96 Ng24
Kuryavdčy ⬚ BY 65 Me37
Kuşadası ⬚ TR 71 Mh53
Kuşadası Körfezi ⬚ TR 71 Mh53
Kusagaki-gunto ▲ J 113 Re30
Kuşcenneti Milli Parkı ⬚ TR 69 Mh50
Kuşcenneti Milli Parkı ⬚ IND 117 Pa37
Kuševska ⬚ RUS 73 Mk22
Kusel ⬚ D 59 Lh41
Kušėla ⬚ RUS 44 Mj31
Kushalnagar ⬚ IND 118 Oj39
Kusheriki ⬚ WAN 188 Ld40
Kushikino ⬚ J 113 Rf30
Kushimoto ⬚ J 113 Rf29
Kushiro ⬚ J 111 Sc24
Kushiro-cho N.P. ⬚ J 111 Sc24
Kushiro-Shitsugen N.P. ⬚ J 111 Sc24
Kushiva ⬚ TM 96 Nh26
Kushmurun ⬚ KZ 88 Oa08
Kushtia ⬚ BD 120 Pe34
Kusiwagiasi, Mount ▲ PNG 155 Sa48
Kuskokwim River ⬚ USA 228 Bj15
Kuskokwim Mountains ▲ USA 228 Cb14
Kuskokwim Bay ⬚ USA 228 Bj16
Kusma ⬚ NEP 115 Pb31
Kusnacht ⬚ CH 61 Lj43
Kusong ⬚ PRK 110 Rc25
Kustanay ⬚ KZ 88 Oa08
Kustavi ▲ FIN 44 Mb30
Kustendil ⬚ D 58 Ln37
Kutcharo-ko ⬚ J 111 Sc24
Kutna Hora ⬚ CZ 66 Lq41
Kutno ⬚ PL 65 Lu38
Kutootsu ⬚ J 111 Pb36
Kutu ⬚ RDC 190 Lk46
Kutubdia Island ▲ BD 120 Pf35
Kuty ⬚ UA 67 Mf42
Kutyaba ⬚ RUS 44 Mj31
Kuujjua ⬚ CDN 227 Gc07
Kuusamo ⬚ FIN 39 Mh24
Kuusankoski ⬚ FIN 44 Mg30
Kuutse Mägi ▲ EST 45 Mh33
Kuvasvesi ⬚ FIN 44 Mg28
Kuvango ⬚ ANG 200 Lj53
Kuwait ⬚ KWT 93 Nd31
Kuwae ⬚ VU 158 Td53
Kuwait ■ KWT 93 Nd31
Kuwana ⬚ J 113 Rf28
Kuyanat ⬚ UZ 97 Oe25
Kuybyshev Reservoir ⬚ RUS 72 Nd17
Kuytun ⬚ CHN 100 Pc23
Kuyucak ⬚ TR 71 Mj53
Kuyuwini Landing ⬚ GUY 266 Ha44
Kuzbass ⬚ RUS 88 Pe07
Kuzey Anadolu Dağları ▲ TR 90 Mh25
Kuzneckij Alatau ▲ RUS 88 Pe07
Kuznecovs'k ⬚ UA 65 Mf39
Kuznecovo ⬚ RUS 111 Sa22
Kuznecovo ⬚ RUS 72 Mj17
Kuźnica ⬚ PL 65 Md37
Kvål ⬚ N 40 Ll27
Kvalsund ⬚ N 39 Mc21
Kvändrup ⬚ DK 42 Ll35
Kvalpynten ⬚ N 38 Ma07

Logone ≋ CAM/TCH 189 Lh40
Logone Birni ◎ CAM 189 Lh40
Logone Gana ◎ TCH 189 Lh40
Lógos ◎ GR 70 Mc52
Logozohe ◎ DY 188 Lb42
Logroño ⊙ ■ E 56 Ks48
Logrosán ◎ E 55 Kp51
Løgstør ◎ DK 42 Lk34
Løgumkloster ◎ DK 42 Lj35
Lohaghat ◎ IND 115 Pa31
Lohals ◎ DK 42 Ll35
Lohara ◎ IND 117 Pa35
Lohardaga ◎ IND 117 Pc34
Lohatanjona Angadoka ▲ RM 206 Nd52
Lohatanjona Maromony ▲ RM 206 Nd53
Lohawat ◎ IND 114 Og32
Lohikoski ◎ FIN 44 Mj29
Lohja ◎ FIN 44 Me30
Lohmar ◎ D 58 Lh40
Lohne ◎ D 58 Lj38
Lohr ◎ D 59 Lk40
Loi ◎ PNG 156 Sd47
Loibltunnel ▲ A/SLO 61 Lp44
Loiborsoit ◎ EAT 197 Mj48
Loi, Gunung ▲ RI 128 Qg45
Loi-kaw ◎ MYA 120 Pj36
Loikisale ◎ EAT 194 Mj47
Loi-lawm ◎ MYA 120 Pj34
Loimaa ◎ FIN 44 Md30
Loima Hills ▲ EAK 194 Mh44
Loir ≋ F 50 Ku43
Loire □ ■ F 52 Ku43
Loire ≋ F 52 Lb43
Loiro Poco ◎ BR 265 Gf45
Loi Sang ▲ MYA 120 Pj35
Loi Song ▲ MYA 120 Pj34
Loi Tawngkyaw ▲ MYA 120 Pj34
Loitz ◎ D 58 Lo37
Loiyangalani ◎ ■ EAK 194 Mj44
Loja ◎ E 55 Kq53
Loja ◎ EC 268 Ga47
Lojanice ◎ SRB 68 Lu46
Lojsthajd ▲ S 43 Lt33
Lokači ◎ UA 65 Me40
Lokalema ◎ RDC 190 Mb45
Lokandu ◎ RDC 199 Mc47
Lokapur ◎ IND 116 Oh37
Lokata ◎ RI 131 Rf46
Lökbetan ◎ AZ 91 Ne25
Løken ◎ N 42 Lm31
Lokeren ◎ B 51 Ld39
Loket ■ CZ 66 Ln40
Lokgwabe ◎ RB 204 Ma58
Lokichar ◎ EAK 194 Mh44
Lokichar ◎ EAU 194 Mh44
Lokitanyaly ◎ EAK 194 Mh44
Lo Kitaung ◎ EAK 194 Mh43
Loknja ◎ RUS 72 Mf17
Loko ◎ WAN 188 Ld41
Lokofe ◎ RDC 199 Mb46
Lokoja ◎ WAN 188 Ld42
Lokolama ◎ RDC 199 Lk47
Lokolia ◎ RDC 199 Ma46
Lokomby ◎ RM 207 Nd57
Lokomo ◎ CAM 189 Lh44
Lokon ■ RI 125 Rc45
Lokono ◎ PNG 156 Sf47
Lokori ◎ EAK 194 Mj45
Lőkösháza ◎ H 67 Mb44
Lokossa ◎ DY 188 La42
Lokot' ◎ RUS 72 Mh19
Lokoti ◎ CAM 189 Lh42
Loksa ◎ EST 44 Mf31
Loksado ■ RI 129 Qh47
Lokutu ◎ RDC 191 Mb45
Lol ≋ SUD 191 Md41
Lol ◎ SUD 191 Me42
Lola ◎ ANG 200 Lg53
Lola ◎ RG 186 Kf42
Lolela ◎ USA 232 Dh25
Lolengi ◎ RDC 190 Ma45
Lolgorien ◎ EAK 194 Mh46
Loliondo ◎ EAT 194 Mh47
Lolland ▲ DK 42 Lm36
Lollar ◎ D 58 Lj40
Lolo ◎ USA 232 Ec22
Loloata Resort ■ PNG 155 Sd50
Lolobau Island ▲ PNG 156 Sf48
Lolodorf ◎ CAM 188 Lf44
Lolo Hot Springs ◎ USA 232 Ec22
Lolokadan ◎ IR 98 Oa31
Lolui Island ▲ EAU 194 Mg46
Lolwane ◎ ZA 205 Mb59
Lolworth ◎ AUS 147 Sc56
Lom ◎ BG 68 Md47
Lom ◎ ■ N 40 Lj29
Loma ◎ ETH 192 Mj42
Loma ◎ USA 233 Ee22
Loma Alta ◎ USA 245 Ek31
Loma Bonita ◎ MEX 247 Fc36
Loma de Cabrera ◎ DOM 250 Ge36
Lomaloma ◎ FJI 159 Ua54
Lomami ≋ RDC 191 Mc45
Lomami ◎ RDC 199 Mb46
Loma Mountains Forest Reserve ■ WAL 186 Ke41
Lomas ◎ PE 269 Gc53
Lomas Coloradas ▲ RA 282 Gg67
Lomas de Arena ■ BOL 278 Gj54
Lomas de Arena ◎ MEX 245 Eh30
Lomas del Real ◎ MEX 246 Fb34
Lomas de Zamora ◎ RA 281 Ha63
Lomaum ◎ ANG 200 Lh52
Lombadina ◎ AUS 142 Rb54
Lombadina Point ▲ AUS 142 Rb54
Lombardía ◎ MEX 246 Ej36
Lombardy □ I 60 Lk45
Lombe ◎ ANG 198 Lj50
Lombe ◎ RI 130 Rb48
Lombez ◎ F 52 La47
Lomblen ▲ RI 131 Rb50
Lombok ▲ RI 130 Qj50
Lombol ◎ SN 180 Kb38
Lombolo ◎ RCB 198 Lh48
Lomci ◎ BG 69 Mg47
Lomé ● ■ ≋ TG 187 La42
Lomela ≋ RDC 199 Ma46
Lomela ◎ RDC 199 Mb47
Łomianki ◎ PL 65 Ma38
Lomié ◎ CAM 189 Lg44
Loming ◎ SUD 194 Mg43
Lomma ◎ S 42 Lo35
Lommel ◎ B 51 Lf39
Lom nad Rimavicou ◎ SK 67 Lu42
Lomond ◎ CDN 233 Ed20
Lomonosov ◎ RUS 44 Mk31
Lomonosov Ridge ■ 286 Hb01
Lomo Plata ◎ PY 279 Ha57
Lomphat ◎ K 123 Qd39
Lomphat W.S. ■ K 123 Qd39
Lompobatang, Gunung ▲ RI 130 Ra48
Lompoc ◎ USA 234 Dk28
Lom Sak ◎ THA 122 Qa37
Łomża ◎ PL 65 Mc37
Lonand ◎ IND 116 Oh36
Lonar ◎ IND 116 Oj36
Lonavala ◎ IND 116 Og36
Lonavala Hill Resort ■ IND 116 Og36
Lončakovo ◎ RUS 110 Rh22
Loncoche ◎ RCH 280 Gd65
Loncopue ◎ RA 280 Ge65
Londa ◎ IND 116 Oh38
Londa Tana-Toraja ■ RI 130 Qk47
Londela-Kayes ◎ RCB 198 Lg48
Londengo ◎ ANG 200 Lg52
Londiani ◎ EAK 194 Mh46
Londolovit ◎ PNG 156 Sg47
London ◎ CDN 237 Fk24
London ● ■ ■ GB 49 Ku39
London ◎ USA 239 Fh27
Londonderry ◎ ■ GB 47 Kn36
London Reefs ▲ 128 Qg41
Londres ◎ RA 279 Gg59
Londrina ◎ BR 274 He57
Lone Butte ◎ CDN 232 Dk20
Lone Pine ◎ USA 234 Ea27
Lone Pine Ind. Res. ■ USA 234 Eb27
Lone Star Park ■ USA 238 Fb29
Lone ton ◎ MYA 120 Pj33
Lone Tree ◎ RB 204 Mb57
Long ◎ THA 121 Pk36
Longa ◎ ANG 200 Lk53
Longadambau ◎ RI 128 Qh45
Long'an ◎ CHN 106 Qe27
Long'an ◎ CHN 108 Qd34
Longana ◎ VU 158 Td53
Long'anqiao ◎ CHN 110 Rc22
Longarone ◎ I 60 Ln44
Longavi, Nevado de ▲ RCH 280 Ge64
Longbawan ◎ RI 128 Qh44
Long Bay Beach ■ GB 251 Gh36
Long Bay Beach ≋ JA 250 Gb36
Long Beach ◎ USA 234 Ea29
Long Beach ◎ USA 239 Ff30
Long Beach ◎ USA 241 Gc26
Long Beach ◎ USA 241 Gd25
Long Beach ◎ USA 242 Ga29
Long Beach Pen. ≋ USA 232 Dh22
Long Branch ◎ USA 241 Gc25
Long Branch S.P. ■ USA 238 Fd26
Long Cay ▲ BH 248 Fg37
Longchamp ■ F 51 Lc42
Longchang ◎ CHN 108 Qc31
Longchang ◎ CHN 108 Qd32
Longchuan ◎ CHN 109 Qh33
Longchuan ◎ CHN 121 Pk33
Long Cove ◎ CDN 241 Hd22
Long Creek ◎ USA 232 Ea23
Long Dat ◎ VN 123 Qd40
Longeau ◎ F 53 Lf43
Longfellow ◎ USA 245 Ej30
Longfellow, Mount ▲ NZ 153 Tg67
Longford ◎ AUS 151 Sd66
Longford ◎ IRL 47 Kn37
Long Gaij ◎ RI 128 Qh45
Longgang ◎ CHN 108 Qc31
Longgang Shan ▲ CHN 110 Rd24
Longgong Cave ■ CHN 121 Qc32
Longgun ◎ CHN 109 Qf36
Long Hai Beach ■ VN 123 Qd40
Longhe ◎ CHN 105 Rb19
Longhua ◎ CHN 107 Qj25
Longhui ◎ CHN 108 Qf32
Longhurst, Mount ▲ 286 Sd34
Longido ◎ EAT 194 Mj47
Longikis ◎ RI 129 Qj46
Longiram ◎ RI 129 Qh46
Long Island ▲ AUS 142 Qh56
Long Island ▲ AUS 149 Se57
Long Island ■ BS 250 Gc34
Long Island ▲ CDN 240 Gg23
Long Island ▲ ■ PNG 155 Sd48
Long Island ■ ≋ ■ USA 241 Gd25
Longjiang ◎ CHN 105 Rb22
Longjing ◎ CHN 110 Re24
Longkou ◎ CHN 107 Ra27
Longku ◎ IND 120 Pg33
Longlac ◎ CDN 237 Fg21
Long Lake ◎ USA 241 Gc24
Long Lake Ind. Res. ■ CDN 237 Fg21
Long Lake N.W.R. ■ USA 236 Fa22
Long Lama ◎ MAL 128 Qh44
Longleat House ■ GB 49 Ks39
Long Lellang ◎ MAL 128 Qh44
Longli ◎ CHN 108 Qd32
Longlin ◎ CHN 121 Qc33
Longling ◎ CHN 121 Pk33
Longlinjie ◎ CHN 108 Qd34
Longmen ◎ CHN 108 Qf35
Longmen ◎ CHN 109 Qh34
Longmen Shan ▲ CHN 106 Qb30
Longmen Shiku □ ▲ ■ CHN 107 Qg28
Long Men Xia ■ CHN 108 Qe30
Longmont ◎ USA 235 Eh25
Longnah ◎ RI 128 Qj45
Longnan ◎ CHN 109 Qh33
Longnawang ◎ RI 128 Qh45
Longo ◎ CI 187 Kh41
Longo ◎ G 198 Lg46
Longo ◎ RCB 190 Lj45
Longobucco ◎ I 63 Lr51
Longonjo ◎ ANG 200 Lh52
Longotea ◎ PE 268 Gb49
Longozabe ◎ RM 207 Ne55
Long Palai ◎ MAL 128 Qh44
Long Point ▲ CDN 236 Fa19
Long Point ◎ CDN 237 Fk24
Long Point ▲ CDN 241 Ha21
Long Point Prov. Park ■ ■ CDN 237 Fk24
Long Prairie ◎ USA 236 Fc23
Long Preston ◎ GB 49 Ks36
Longquan ◎ CHN 108 Qd32
Longquan ◎ CHN 109 Qk31
Long Range Mountains ▲ CDN 241 Hb21
Longreach ◎ AUS 149 Sc57
Longs Creek ◎ CDN 240 Gg23
Long Seridan ◎ MAL 128 Qh43
Long Shan ▲ CHN 106 Qa26
Longshan ◎ CHN 108 Qe31
Longshan ◎ CHN 109 Qg34
Long Shan Si ■ CHN 109 Qk33
Longsheng ◎ CHN 108 Qf33
Longtanshan Park ■ CHN 110 Rd24
Long Thanh ◎ VN 123 Qd40
Longtian ◎ CHN 109 Qk33
Long Tompas ■ ZA 205 Mf58
Longton ◎ AUS 147 Sc56
Longtown ◎ GB 48 Ks35
Longué-Jumelles ◎ F 52 Ku43
Longueuil ◎ CDN 241 Gd23
Longuyon ◎ F 51 Lf41
Long Valley ◎ USA 236 Ek24
Long Valley Junction ◎ USA 235 Ed27
Longview ◎ CDN 233 Ec20
Longview ◎ USA 232 Dj22
Longview ◎ USA 238 Fc29
Longwa ◎ EAT 197 Mj48
Longwangmiao ◎ CHN 110 Rg23
Longwarry ◎ AUS 151 Sc65
Longwy ◎ F 51 Lf41
Longxi ◎ CHN 106 Qc28
Long Xian ◎ CHN 106 Qd28
Longxing Temple ■ CHN 107 Qh26
Long Xuyen ◎ VN 123 Qc40
Longyan ◎ CHN 109 Qj33
Longyao ◎ CHN 107 Qh27
Longyearbyen ◎ ■ N 38 Lh06
Longyou ◎ CHN 109 Qk31
Longzhen ◎ CHN 105 Rd21
Longzhou ◎ CHN 108 Qd34
Löningen ◎ D 58 Lh38
Łoniów ◎ PL 65 Mb40
Lonkintsy ◎ RM 207 Ne54
Lonoke ◎ USA 239 Fe28
Lonquimay ◎ RA 281 Gj64
Lonquimay ◎ RCH 280 Ge65
Lonquimay, Volcán ▲ RCH 280 Ge65
Lonrong ◎ RI 130 Ra48
Lönsboda ◎ S 43 Lp34
Lons-le-Saunier ◎ F 53 Lf44
Lontar ◎ ■ ■ RI 131 Re48
Lontar ▲ RI 131 Rf48
Lontou ◎ RMM 180 Ke38
Lontra ◎ BR 272 He48
Lontué ◎ RCH 280 Ge63
Loogootee ◎ USA 239 Fg26
Lookout Mount ▲ USA 229 Cd12
Lookout Ridge ▲ USA 229 Ca11
Loolmalassin ▲ EAT 194 Mj47
Looma ◎ AUS 143 Rc55
Loon ◎ RP 124 Rb41
Loongana ◎ AUS 145 Rd61
Loon Lake ◎ CDN 233 Ef18
Loonse en Drunense Duinen, N.P. ■ NL 51 Lf39
Loop Head ▲ IRL 47 Kl38
Loosdrechtse Plassen ■ NL 51 Lf38
Lop ◎ CHN 102 Pa27
Lopar ◎ HR 61 Lp46
Lopary ◎ RM 207 Nd57
Lopătari ◎ RO 69 Mg45
Lopatovo ◎ RUS 45 Mj33
Lopatyn ◎ UA 65 Me40
Lop Buri ◎ THA 122 Qa38
Lopé, P.N. de la ■ ■ ■ G 198 Lf46
Lopez ◎ CO 264 Gb44
Lopez ◎ RP 124 Rb39
Lop Nur ≋ CHN 101 Pf25
Lop Nur = Yuli ◎ CHN 101 Pd25
Lopori ≋ RDC 190 Ma45
Lopou ◎ CI 187 Kh43
Loppi ◎ FIN 44 Me30
Lopuhinka ◎ RUS 44 Mk31
Lora del Río ◎ E 55 Kp53
Lorain ◎ USA 237 Fj25
Loralai ◎ PK 99 Oe30
Lorca ◎ E 57 Kt53
Lorch ◎ D 59 Lh40
Lordegan ◎ IR 93 Nf30
Lord Howe Island ▲ AUS 134 Sb13
Lord Howe Rise ■ 134 Ta12
Lord Howe Seamounts ■ 134 Sb12
Lord Loughborough Island ▲ MYA 122 Pj40
Lordsburg ◎ USA 235 Ef29
Lore ◎ TLS 131 Rd50
Lore Lindu N.P. ■ RI 130 Ra46
Lorena ◎ BR 268 Ge49
Lorena ◎ BR 277 Hh57
Lorengau ◎ PNG 156 Sd47
Lorentz ≋ RI 154 Rk48
Lorentz N.P. □ ■ ■ RI 154 Rj48
Lorenzo Geyres ◎ ROU 276 Hb62
Loreto ◎ BOL 278 Gh53
Loreto ◎ BR 271 Ha51
Loreto ◎ CO 268 Ge47
Loreto ◎ EC 268 Gb46
Loreto ◎ I 61 Lo47
Loreto ◎ ▲ ■ MEX 244 Ee32
Loreto ◎ MEX 246 Ek34
Loreto ◎ RA 276 Hb59
Loreto ◎ RP 124 Rc40
Loreto Aprutino ◎ I 61 Lo48
Lorgues ◎ F 53 Lg47
Lorica ◎ CO 264 Gc41
Lorient ◎ ■ F 50 Kr43
Lőrinci ◎ H 67 Lu43
Loring ◎ USA 233 Eg21
Loriol-sur-Drôme ◎ F 53 Le46
Loris ◎ USA 242 Ga29
Lorlie ◎ CDN 233 Ej20
Lormes ◎ F 53 Ld43
Lormi ◎ IND 117 Pa34
Lorna Glen ◎ AUS 144 Ra59
Lorne ◎ AUS 151 Sb65
Lorneville ◎ CDN 240 Gg23
Loronyo ◎ SUD 194 Mg43
Loropéni ◎ BF 187 Kj40
Lörrach ◎ D 59 Lh43
Lorraine ◎ AUS 147 Rk55
Lorraine ▲ F 51 Lf41
Lorraine □ F 51 Lf42
Lorris ◎ F 53 Lc43
Loruk ◎ EAK 194 Mj45
Lorzot ◎ TN 176 Lf30
Los ◎ S 41 Lq29
Losai N.P. ■ ■ EAK 194 Mj45
Los Aldamos ◎ MEX 245 Fa32
Los Alerces, P.N. ■ ■ RA 282 Ge67
Los Almos ◎ USA 235 Eg28
Los Altos ◎ RA 279 Gh60
Los Americanos ◎ MEX 245 Ej32
Los Amores ◎ RA 276 Ha60
Los Andes = Sotomayor ◎ CO 264 Gb45
Los Andes ◎ RCH 280 Ge62
Los Angeles ◎ RCH 280 Gd64
Los Angeles ◎ ■ USA 234 Ea28
Los Ánimas ◎ MEX 244 Eg31
Los Antiguos ◎ RA 282 Ge69
Los Arcos ◎ E 56 Ks48
Losari ◎ RI 129 Qe49
Los Arrieros ◎ MEX 244 Ee31
Los Asientos ◎ PA 249 Fk42
Los Azabaches ◎ MEX 244 Ee33
Los Baldecitas ◎ RA 279 Gg61
Los Banos ◎ USA 234 Dk27
Los Barrancos ◎ YV 265 Gj41
Los Barriles ◎ MEX 244 Ef34
Los Barrios ◎ E 55 Kp54
Los Berros ◎ RA 280 Gf61
Los Blancos ◎ RA 279 Gj57
Los Caracas ◎ YV 265 Gg40
Los Cardones, P.N. ■ ■ RA 279 Gg58
Los Caribes ◎ YV 265 Gk43
Los Chiles ◎ CR 249 Fh40
Los Chiriguanos ◎ RA 279 Gk58
Los Chuchumatanes, P.N. ■ GCA 248 Fe38
Los Cocos ■ YV 265 Gg40
Los Cocos ■ YV 265 Gg40
Los Colorados ◎ RA 279 Gg60
Los Colorados, P.N. ■ CO 264 Gc40
Los Conquistadores ◎ RA 276 Ha61
Los Corozos ◎ YV 265 Gg42
Los Corrales de Buelna ◎ E 54 Kq47
Los Cortijos de Arriba ◎ E 55 Kq51
Los Cristianos ◎ ≋ ■ E 174 Kb31
Losesia ◎ EAK 194 Mj45
Los Flamencos ■ CO 264 Gd40
Los Frailes ◎ MEX 244 Eg33
Los Frentones ◎ RA 279 Gk59
Los Gatuzos ■ NIC 249 Fh40
Los Glaciares, P.N. ■ ■ RA 282 Gd70
Los Güires ◎ YV 265 Gk41
Los Haïtises, P.N. ■ DOM 250 Gf36
Losheim ◎ D 59 Lg41
Los Hoyos ◎ GCA 248 Fe38
Los Hoyos ◎ MEX 244 Ef30
Łosice ◎ PL 65 Mc38
Los Indios ◎ C 250 Gc35
Lošinj ▲ HR 61 Lp46
Losiny ostrov N.P. ■ RUS 72 Mj18
Los Jobillos ◎ DOM 250 Ge36
Los Juríes ◎ RA 279 Gj60
Los Katíos, P.N. ■ ■ CO 264 Gb42
Loskop Dam Nature Reserve ■ ■ ZA 205 Me58
Los Lagos ◎ RCH 280 Gd65
Los Limones ◎ HN 248 Fg38
Los Llanos de Aridane ◎ ■ E 174 Kb31
Los Lunas ◎ USA 235 Eg28
Los Mármoles, P.N. ■ MEX 246 Fa35
Los Médanos ◎ MEX 244 Ee32
Los Menucos ◎ RA 280 Gf66
Los Mochis ◎ MEX 244 Ef33
Los Molles ◎ ■ RCH 280 Ge62
Los Monasterios de Suso y Yuso □ ■ E 56 Ks48
Los Monos ◎ RA 282 Gf69
Los Muermos ◎ RCH 280 Gd66
Los Navalmorales ◎ E 55 Kq51
Los Negrones ◎ YV 264 Ge40
los Nevados, P.N. ■ CO 264 Gc43
Løsning ◎ DK 42 Lk35
Losogonoi Plateau ▲ EAT 197 Mj48
Los Ojitos ◎ MEX 244 Ef32
Losomba ◎ RDC 199 Mc47
Los Osos ◎ USA 234 Dk28
Los Palacios y Villafranca ◎ E 55 Kp53
Los Palos ◎ RH 250 Ge36
Los Patos ◎ BOL 279 Gj56
Lospatos ◎ TLS 131 Rd50
Los Patricios ◎ CO 268 Ge46
Los Pedales ◎ YV 264 Gd40
Los Penitentes ■ RA 280 Gf62
Los Picos ◎ MEX 245 Ej31
Los Pijiguaos ◎ YV 265 Gg42
Los Pinos ◎ C 243 Fj34
Los Pinos ■ MEX 244 Eg34
Los Puentes ◎ MEX 244 Eg33
Los Reyes de Salgado ◎ MEX 246 Ej36
Los Santos ◎ PA 249 Fk42
Los Sauces ◎ RCH 280 Gd64
Lossiemouth ◎ GB 48 Kr33
Los Tajitos ◎ MEX 244 Ed30
Los Tamariscos ◎ RA 282 Gf68
Los Taques ◎ YV 264 Ge40
Los Telares ◎ RA 279 Gj60
Los Teques ◎ YV 265 Gg40
Lost Maples S.N.A. ■ USA 245 Fa31
Los Toriles ■ MEX 246 Eh35
Lost River ◎ USA 228 Bg13
Lost River Range ▲ USA 232 Ed23
Los Troncones ◎ MEX 244 Eg33
Los Troncos ◎ BOL 278 Gj54
Lostwithiel ◎ GB 49 Kq40
Losuia ◎ PNG 156 Sf50
Los Valles ◎ PA 249 Fk41
Los Vientos ◎ PE 279 Gf58
Los Yébenes ◎ E 55 Kr51
Lota ◎ RCH 280 Gd64
Lote 15, Cerro ▲ RA 282 Ge68
Lothair ◎ USA 233 Ee21
Lothair ◎ ZA 205 Mf59
Lotia ◎ IND 117 Ok34
Lotiki Plain ▲ EAK 194 Mh43
Loto ◎ RDC 199 Mb47
Lotošino ◎ RUS 72 Mh17
Lottigna ◎ CH 60 Lj44
Löttorp ◎ S 43 Lr33
Lotugadda ◎ IND 117 Pb37
Lotuke ▲ SUD 194 Mg43
Lotung ▲ MAL 128 Qj43
Lotyń ◎ PL 64 Lr37
Loubomo ◎ G 198 Lf47
Loubomo ◎ ■ ■ RCB 198 Lg48
Loudéac ◎ F 50 Ks42
Loudi ◎ CHN 108 Qf32
Loudima ◎ RCB 198 Lg48
Loudon ◎ MW 196 Mg52
Loudun ◎ F 52 La44
Loué ◎ F 50 Ku43
Louga ◎ SN 180 Kb38
Lough Allen ≋ IRL 47 Km36
Lough Boderg ≋ IRL 47 Km37
Loughborough ◎ GB 49 Kt38
Lough Conn ≋ IRL 47 Kl36
Lough Corrib ≋ IRL 47 Kl37
Lough Derg ≋ IRL 47 Km38
Lough Ennel ≋ IRL 47 Kn37
Lough Foyle ≋ IRL/GB 47 Kn35
Lough Gill ≋ IRL 47 Km36
Lough Gowna ≋ IRL 47 Kn37
Lough Leane ≋ IRL 47 Kl38
Lough Mask ≋ IRL 47 Kl37
Lough Melvin ≋ IRL 47 Km36
Lough Neagh ≋ GB 47 Ko36
Lough Oughter ≋ IRL 47 Kn37
Lough Owel ≋ IRL 47 Kn37
Loughrea ◎ IRL 47 Km37
Lough Ree ≋ IRL 47 Kn37
Lough Sheelin ≋ IRL 47 Kn37
Lough Swilly ≋ IRL 47 Kn35
Lougou ◎ DY 188 Lb40
Louhans ◎ F 53 Lf44
Louingui ◎ RCB 198 Lh48
Louisa ◎ USA 239 Fj26
Louisa Downs ◎ AUS 143 Rd55
Louisa Reef ▲ 128 Qg42
Louisbourg ◎ CDN 240 Gk23
Louisburg ◎ USA 242 Ga27
Louisburgh ◎ ≋ IRL 47 Kl37
Louisdale ◎ CDN 240 Gk23
Louise Island ▲ CDN 230 De19
Louiseville ◎ CDN 240 Gd22
Louisiade Archipelago ▲ PNG 156 Sg51
Louisiana ■ DK 42 Ln35
Louisiana □ USA 238 Fd30
Louisiana Downs ■ USA 238 Fd29
Louisiana State Arboretum ■ USA 239 Fd30
Lou Island ▲ PNG 156 Sd47
Louis Trichardt ◎ ■ ■ ZA 202 Me57
Louisvale ◎ ZA 204 Ma60
Louisville ◎ USA 235 Eh26
Louisville ◎ USA 239 Ff29
Louisville ◎ USA 239 Fh26
Louisville ◎ USA 242 Fj29
Loukíssia ◎ GR 69 Md52
Loukoléla ◎ RCB 198 Lj46
Loukouo ◎ RCB 198 Lh47
Loulan Gucheng ■ ▲ CHN 101 Pe25
Loulé ◎ ■ P 55 Kn53
Loulouni ◎ RMM 187 Kh40
Lou Lou Park ◎ AUS 149 Sd57
Loum ◎ CAM 188 Le43
Loumbi ◎ SN 180 Kd38
Loumou ◎ RCB 198 Lh48
Louny ◎ CZ 66 Lo40
Loup City ◎ USA 236 Fa25
Lourdes ◎ ■ F 52 Ku47
Lourenço ◎ BR 267 He44
Loures ◎ P 55 Kl52
Lour-Escale ◎ SN 180 Kc38
Lourinhã ◎ P 55 Kl51
Louta ◎ BF 187 Kj39
Louth ◎ AUS 149 Sc61
Louth ◎ GB 49 La37
Louth ◎ RIM 180 Kd37
Loutrá ◎ GR 71 Me53
Loutrá Edipsoú ◎ GR 68 Md52
Loutrá Eleftherón ◎ GR 69 Me50
Loutráki ◎ GR 68 Md53
Loutráki ◎ GR 70 Mb52
Loutropigí ◎ GR 70 Mc51
Loutros ◎ GR 69 Mg50
Louvakou ◎ RCB 198 Lg47
Louverné ◎ F 50 Ku42
Louvicaurt ◎ CDN 237 Gb21
Louvie-Juzon ◎ F 52 Ku47
Louviers ◎ F 51 Lb41
Louvigné-du-Désert ◎ F 50 Kt42
Louvre □ ■ F 51 Lc42
Louwsburg ◎ ■ ■ ZA 205 Mf59
Louxo ◎ CHN 108 Qe34
Lövånger ◎ S 41 Mb26
Lovčen, N.P. ■ MNE 68 Lt48
Love ◎ CDN 233 Eh19
Loveč ◎ ■ ■ BG 69 Me47
Loveland ◎ USA 235 Eh25
Loveland ◎ USA 239 Fh26
Lovell ◎ USA 233 Ef23
Lovelock ◎ USA 234 Ea25
Lóvere ◎ I 60 Ll45
Loverna ◎ CDN 233 Ef20
Lover's Leap ■ JA 250 Gb37
Lovi ◎ GH 187 Kk41
Loviisa = Lovisa ◎ FIN 44 Mg30
Lovina Beach ■ RI 129 Qh50
Loving ◎ USA 238 Fa29
Lovington ◎ USA 238 Ej29
Lovisa = Loviisa ◎ FIN 44 Mg30
Lovište ◎ HR 61 Ls47
Lövő ◎ H 66 Lr43
Lovosice ◎ CZ 66 Lp40
Lovran ◎ HR 61 Lp45
Lovreć ◎ HR 61 Lr47
Lovrin ◎ RO 68 Ma45
Lövstabruk ◎ S 43 Ls30
Lóvua ◎ ANG 199 Ma49
Lóvua ◎ ANG 201 Mb51
Lowalang ◎ IND 117 Pc33
Low Cape ▲ USA 228 Cc17
Lowell ◎ USA 232 Ec22
Lowell ◎ USA 241 Ge24
Lowelli ◎ SUD 194 Mg43
Löwenberg ◎ D 58 Lo38
Lower ◎ ZA 205 Me60
Lower Brule Ind. Res. ■ USA 236 Fa23
Lower Fort Garry N.H.S. ■ CDN 236 Fa20
Lower Glenelg N.P. ■ AUS 150 Sa65
Lower Guinea ▲ 162 Lb09
Lower Hatchie N.W.R. ■ USA 239 Ff28
Lower Hutt ◎ NZ 153 Th66
Lower Lough Erne ■ GB 47 Kn36
Lower-Normandie □ F 50 Ku42
Lower Peninsula ▲ USA 237 Fh24
Lower Post ◎ CDN 230 Df16
Lower Sabie ◎ ■ ZA 205 Mf58
Lower Sackville ◎ CDN 240 Gj23
Lower Sioux Ind. Res. ■ USA 236 Fc23
Lower Valley of the Awash □ ■ ETH 192 Na40
Lower Valley of the Omo □ ■ ETH 194 Mh43
Lower Zambezi N.P. ■ ■ Z 202 Me53
Lowestoft ◎ GB 49 Lb38
Lowest Point in U.S. ≋ USA 234 Eb27
Łowicz ◎ ■ PL 65 Lu38
Lowkhi ◎ AFG 98 Ob30
Lowman ◎ USA 232 Ec23
Lowood ◎ AUS 149 Sg59
Low Rocky Point ▲ AUS 151 Sc67
Lowry Ind. Ruins ■ USA 235 Ef27
Lowville ◎ USA 241 Gc24
Loxstedt ◎ D 58 Lj37
Loxton ◎ AUS 150 Sa63
Loxton ◎ ZA 204 Mb61
Loyada ◎ DJI 193 Nb40
Loyengo ◎ SD 205 Mf59
Loyish ◎ UZ 97 Od26
Loyore ◎ EAU 194 Mh44
Lož ◎ SLO 66 Lp45
Loznica ◎ BG 69 Mg47
Loznica ◎ SRB 68 Lu46
Ložnikovo ◎ RUS 105 Qj20
Lozova ◎ UA 73 Mj21
Lozoyuela ◎ E 55 Kr50
Ltyentye Apurte A.L. ■ AUS 148 Rh58
Luabo ◎ MOC 203 Mj55
Luabo ◎ RDC 199 Mc50
Luacano ◎ ANG 201 Ma51
Luachimo ◎ ANG 199 Ma49
Luaco ◎ ANG 199 Ma49
Luali ◎ RDC 198 Lg48
Luama ≋ RDC 196 Me48
Luambe N.P. ■ Z 196 Mg52
Luampa ◎ Z 201 Mc53
Luampa Kuta ◎ Z 201 Mc53
Lu'an ◎ CHN 112 Qj30
Luanchuan ◎ CHN 106 Qf29
Luanco ◎ E 54 Kp47
Luanda ● ■ ■ ANG 198 Lg50
Luanda ◎ BR 274 Hd57
Luando ◎ ANG 200 Lk51
Luang Nam Tha ◎ LAO 121 Qa35
Luango ≋ ANG 198 Lg48
Luang Pho Phra Chai ■ THA 121 Qb37
Luang Prabang ◎ □ ■ LAO 121 Qb36
Luang Prabang Range ▲ LAO 121 Qa36
Luangue ◎ ANG 199 Lk50
Luangue ≋ ANG 199 Lk50
Luangwa ≋ Z 196 Mg51
Luangwa ◎ Z 202 Mf53
Luanheca ◎ ANG 200 Lj53
Luanjing ◎ CHN 106 Qc27
Luano ◎ RDC 199 Lk48
Luanping ◎ CHN 107 Qj25
Luanshya ◎ Z 196 Me52
Luan Toro ◎ RA 280 Gh64
Luan Xian ◎ CHN 107 Qk26
Luanza ◎ RDC 196 Me50
Luarca ◎ E 54 Ko47
Luashi ◎ RDC 201 Mb51
Luatamba ◎ ANG 201 Ma52
Luau ◎ ANG 201 Mb51
Luba ◎ ≋ GQ 188 Le44
Lubaanbajo ◎ RI 130 Qk50
Lubaantun ■ BH 248 Ff37
Lubaczów ◎ PL 65 Md40
Lubamba ◎ RDC 199 Mc48
Lubań ◎ PL 64 Lq39
Lubāna ◎ LV 45 Mg34
Lubang ◎ RP 124 Ra39
Lubang Island ▲ RP 124 Ra39
Lubango ◎ ANG 200 Lg53
Lubanza ◎ RDC 199 Ma48
Lubao ◎ RDC 199 Mc48
Lubartów ◎ PL 65 Mc39
Lubawa ◎ PL 65 Lu37
Lübbecke ◎ D 58 Lj38
Lübbenau (Spreewald) ◎ D 58 Lo39
Lübben (Spreewald) ◎ D 58 Lo39
Lubbock ◎ USA 238 Ek29
Lubec ◎ USA 240 Gg23
Lübeck ◎ □ ■ D 58 Ll37
Lübecker Bucht ≋ D 58 Lm36
Lubefu ≋ RDC 199 Mb48
Lubefu ◎ RDC 199 Mc48
Lubero ◎ RDC 191 Me46
Lubersac ◎ F 52 Lb45
Lubiąż ◎ PL 64 Lr39
Lubień Kujawski ◎ PL 65 Lu38
Lubimbi ◎ ZW 202 Md55
Lubin ◎ PL 64 Lr39
Lubjaniki ◎ RUS 72 Na18
Lublin ◎ ■ PL 65 Mc39
Lubliniec ◎ PL 64 Lt40
Lubniewice ◎ PL 64 Lq38
Lubny ◎ UA 73 Mg21
Lubok Antu ◎ MAL 128 Qf45
Lubomino ◎ PL 65 Ma36
Lubompo ◎ Z 202 Md53
Luboń ◎ PL 64 Lr38
L'ubotín ◎ SK 67 Ma41
Lubsko ◎ PL 64 Lp39
Lubu ◎ RI 130 Rb46
Lubuczewo ◎ PL 64 Ls36
Lubudi ◎ RDC 199 Mc50
Lubukalung ◎ RI 127 Qa46
Lubukbargalung ◎ RI 127 Qa46
Lubukbesar ◎ RI 127 Qb46
Lubukbesar ◎ RI 129 Qd47
Lubuklinggau ◎ RI 127 Qb47
Lubukmalaka ◎ RI 127 Qa46
Lubukpakam ◎ RI 126 Pk44
Lubukpinang ◎ RI 127 Qa47
Lubuksikaping ◎ RI 127 Qa45
Lubuktapi ◎ RI 127 Qb48
Lubumba ◎ RDC 196 Me47
Lubumbashi ◎ RDC 196 Md51
Lubungu ◎ Z 202 Md53
Lubutu ◎ RDC 191 Md46
Lubwe ◎ Z 196 Me51
Lubycza Królewska ◎ PL 65 Md40
Lübz ◎ D 58 Ln37
Luca Cernii de Jos ◎ RO 68 Mc45
Lucala ◎ ANG 198 Lh50
Lucanas ◎ PE 269 Gc53
Lucapa ◎ ANG 199 Ma50
Lucas ◎ USA 236 Fd25
Lucas do Rio Verde ◎ BR 274 Hc52
Lucas González ◎ RA 276 Ha62
Lucaya ◎ BS 243 Ga32
Lucca ◎ ■ ■ I 60 Ll47
Lucea ◎ JA 250 Ga36
Lucedale ◎ USA 239 Ff30
Lučegorsk ◎ RUS 111 Rh22
Lucena ◎ E 55 Kq53
Lucena ◎ RP 124 Ra39
Luc-en-Diois ◎ F 53 Lf46
Lučenec ◎ SK 67 Lu42
Lucera ◎ I 63 Lq49
Lucerna ◎ PE 278 Gf52
Lucero ◎ MEX 245 Fb33
Lucheng ◎ CHN 107 Qg27
Lucheng ◎ CHN 108 Qd33
Luchenza ◎ MW 203 Mh53
Luchima ◎ MOC 203 Mh53
Lüchow ◎ D 58 Lm38
Luchuan ◎ CHN 108 Qf34
Lüchun ◎ CHN 121 Qb34
Lucia ◎ USA 234 Dk28
Lučica ◎ SRB 68 Mb46
Lucin ◎ USA 235 Ed25
Lucindale ◎ AUS 150 Sa64
Lucio Blanco ◎ MEX 245 Fa33
Lucira ◎ ANG 200 Lg52
Luc'k ◎ ■ UA 65 Mf40
Luckau ◎ D 58 Lo39
Luckenwalde ◎ D 58 Lo38
Luckhoff ◎ ZA 205 Mc60
Lucknow ◎ AUS 148 Sa57
Lucknow ⊙ IND 117 Pa32
Lucky Lake ◎ CDN 233 Eg20
Lucma ◎ PE 268 Ga49
Lucma ◎ PE 269 Gd52
Lu Coddu Vecchiu ■ I 62 Lk49
Luçon ◎ F 52 Kt44
Lucongpo ◎ CHN 108 Qf30
Lucossa ◎ ANG 198 Lh48
Lucre ◎ PE 269 Ge52
Luc-sur-Mer ◎ F 50 Ku41
Lucunde ◎ ANG 200 Lh52
Lucunga ◎ ANG 198 Lh49
Lucusse ◎ ANG 201 Ma52
Lüda ◎ ■ ≋ CHN 107 Ra26
Ludbreg ◎ HR 61 Lr44
Ludden ◎ USA 236 Fa22
Lüdenscheid ◎ D 58 Lh39
Lüderitz ◎ ■ ■ NAM 204 Lh59
Lüderitz Bay ≋ NAM 204 Lh59
Lüderitz Shark Island Resort ■ ■ NAM 204 Lh59
Ludesar ◎ IND 114 Oh31
Ludhiana ◎ IND 114 Oh30
Ludian ◎ CHN 121 Qb32
Luding ◎ CHN 108 Qb31
Lüdinghausen ◎ D 58 Lh39
Ludington ◎ USA 237 Fg24
Ludlow ◎ GB 49 Ks38
Ludlow ◎ USA 233 Ej23
Ludlow ◎ USA 234 Eb28
Ludlow ◎ USA 235 Eh27
Ludomy ◎ PL 64 Lr38
Ludowici ◎ USA 242 Fk30
Luduș ◎ RO 67 Me44
Ludvika ◎ S 43 Lq30
Ludwigsburg ◎ D 59 Lk42
Ludwigsfelde ◎ D 58 Lo38
Ludwigshafen ◎ D 59 Lj41
Ludwigslust ◎ D 58 Lm37
Ludwigstadt ◎ D 59 Lm40
Ludza ◎ LV 45 Mh34
Luebo ◎ RDC 199 Ma48
Lueki ◎ RDC 199 Mc47
Luemba ◎ RDC 196 Me47
Luena ◎ ANG 200 Lk51
Luena ≋ ANG 201 Mb52
Luena ◎ RDC 199 Mc50
Luena ◎ Z 196 Mf51
Luena ≋ Z 201 Mc53
Luena Flats ▲ Z 201 Mb53
Luengué ◎ ANG 201 Ma54
Lueta ◎ RDC 199 Mb49
Lüeyang ◎ CHN 106 Qd29
Lufeng ◎ CHN 109 Qh34
Lufico ◎ ANG 198 Lg49
Lufkin ◎ USA 238 Fc30
Lug ◎ HR 61 Lt45
Luga ◎ RUS 44 Mk32
Lugano ◎ CH 60 Lj45
Luganville ◎ VU 158 Td53
Lugazi ◎ EAU 194 Mg45
Lugela ◎ ■ MOC 203 Mj54
Lughaye ◎ SP 193 Nb40
Lugo ◎ E 54 Kn48
Lugo ◎ I 60 Lm46
Lugoj ◎ RO 68 Mb45
Lugovoi ◎ KZ 100 Og24
Lugu ◎ CHN 102 Pc29
Lugu ◎ CHN 108 Qb31
Lugus Island ▲ RP 125 Ra43
Luh ◎ RUS 72 Nb17
Luhamaa ◎ EST 45 Mh33
Luhanka ◎ FIN 44 Mf29
Luhans'k ◎ UA 73 Mk21
Luhe ◎ CHN 109 Qh34
Luhe ◎ CHN 112 Qk29
Luhovicy ◎ RUS 72 Mk18
Luhuo ◎ CHN 103 Qa30
Luia ◎ ANG 199 Ma50
Luiana ◎ ANG 201 Mb54
Luiana ≋ RB 201 Mb54
Luico V.Mansilla ◎ RA 279 Gh60
Luidja ◎ EST 44 Mc32
Luikonlahti ◎ FIN 44 Mj28
Luilaka ≋ RDC 199 Ma47
Luilu ≋ RDC 199 Mb49
Luimbale ◎ ANG 200 Lh52
Luinga ◎ ANG 198 Lh50
Luino ◎ I 60 Lj45
Luiro ◎ MOC 203 Na52
Luís Correia ◎ BR 273 Hk47
Luis Domingues ◎ BR 267 Hh46
Luishia ◎ RDC 196 Md51
Luislândia ◎ BR 275 Hh54
Luislândia do Oeste ◎ BR 275 Hh54
Luiza ◎ RDC 199 Mb49
Luizi ◎ RDC 196 Md49
Luiz Viana ◎ BR 273 Hk50
Luján ◎ RA 280 Gh62
Luján ◎ RA 281 Ha63
Lujan de Cuyo ◎ RA 280 Gf62
Lujiang ◎ CHN 112 Qj30
Luka ◎ BIH 68 Lt47
Luka ◎ SRB 68 Mc46
Luka ◎ UA 67 Me41
Lukafu ◎ RDC 196 Md51
Lukojanov ◎ RUS 72 Nc18
Lukang Folk Arts Festival ■ RC 109 Ra34
Lukasu ◎ RDC 199 Mc50
Luka Telašćica ■ HR 61 Lq47
Lukatini ◎ EAT 196 Mg49
Lukavac ◎ BIH 68 Lt46
Lukaya ◎ EAU 194 Mf46
Luke, Mount ▲ AUS 144 Qj59
Lukengo ◎ RDC 196 Me48
Lukenie ≋ RDC 199 Lk47
Lukeville ◎ USA 235 Ed30
Lukiv ◎ UA 65 Me39
Lukole ◎ EAT 197 Mk49
Lukolela ◎ RDC 199 Lj46
Lukolela ◎ RDC 199 Mc48
Lukonzolwa ◎ RDC 196 Me50
Lukovit ◎ BG 69 Me47
Lukovnikovo ◎ RUS 72 Mh17
Lukovo ◎ HR 61 Lp46
Lukovo ◎ MK 68 Ma49
Łuków ◎ PL 65 Mc39
Luksagu ◎ RI 131 Rb46
Łukta ◎ PL 65 Ma37
Lukula ◎ RDC 196 Md49
Lukula ◎ RDC 198 Lg48
Lukuliro ◎ EAT 197 Mk50
Lukulu ◎ Z 201 Mb53
Lukumburu ◎ EAT 196 Mh50
Lukuni ◎ RDC 198 Lj48
Lukusuzi N.P. ■ ■ Z 196 Mg52
Lukwasa ◎ IND 116 Oj33
Lukwika ◎ EAT 197 Mk51
Lula ◎ USA 239 Fe28
Luleå ◎ □ ■ S 41 Mc25
Luleälven ≋ S 38 Ma24
Lüleburgaz ◎ TR 69 Mh49
Luliang ◎ CHN 121 Qb33
Lüliang Shan ▲ CHN 106 Qf27
Lulimba ◎ RDC 196 Me48
Luling ◎ USA 245 Fb31
Lulong ◎ CHN 107 Qk26
Lulonga ◎ RDC 190 Lk45
Lulonga ≋ RDC 190 Lk45
Lulua ≋ RDC 199 Mb48
Lulúti ◎ MOC 203 Mk53
Lulworth, Mount ▲ AUS 144 Qj59
Luma ◎ WAN 188 Lc40
Luma Cassai ◎ ANG 200 Lk51
Lumaco ◎ RCH 280 Gd65
Lumajang ◎ RI 129 Qg50
Lumaku, Gunung ▲ MAL 128 Qh43
Lumangwe Falls ■ Z 196 Me50
Lumar ◎ IR 91 Nd29
Lumata ◎ RDC 201 Md52
Lumba ◎ RDC 190 Lk43
Lumbala ◎ ANG 201 Mb52
Lumbala N'guimbo ◎ ANG 201 Ma53
Lumbaquí ◎ EC 268 Gb45
Lumberman's Museum ■ USA 240 Gf22
Lumbermen's Mon. ■ USA 237 Fj23
Lumberton ◎ USA 238 Fc30
Lumberton ◎ USA 242 Ga28
Lumbier ◎ E 56 Kt48
Lumbini ◎ □ ▲ NEP 115 Pb32
Lumbo ◎ MOC 203 Na53
Lumbrales ◎ E 54 Ko50
Lumbreras ◎ RA 279 Gh58
Lumby ◎ CDN 232 Ea20
Lumding ◎ IND 120 Pg33
Lumeje ◎ ANG 201 Ma51
Lumeta ◎ ANG 200 Ma54
Lumezzane ◎ I 60 Ll45
Lumholtz N.P. □ ■ AUS 147 Sc55
Lumi ◎ PNG 155 Sb47
Lumimba ◎ Z 196 Mg52
Lumimba ◎ Z 196 Mg52
Lumino ◎ Z 201 Mc54
Lumona ◎ Z 202 Md53
Lumparland ▲ FIN 44 Ma30
Lumpkin ◎ USA 239 Fh30
Lumsden ◎ CDN 233 Eh20
Lumsden ◎ NZ 153 Te68
Lumuna ◎ RDC 196 Md47
Lumut ◎ BRU 128 Qh43
Lumut ▲ MAL 126 Qa44
Lumutan ▲ MAL 128 Qj43
Lumut, Gunung ▲ RI 129 Qh46
Lumwana ◎ Z 201 Mc51
Lün ◎ MNG 104 Qc22
Luna ◎ RP 124 Ra36
Luna ◎ RP 124 Ra37
Luna ◎ USA 235 Ef29
Lunahuana ◎ PE 269 Gb52
Lunan ◎ CHN 121 Qb33
Lunan Shan ▲ CHN 121 Qb32
Lunar Crater ■ USA 234 Ec26
Lunavada ◎ IND 116 Og34
Lunawanna ◎ AUS 151 Sd67
Lunca Corbului ◎ RO 69 Me46
Lunca de Jos ◎ RO 67 Mf44
Luncani □ ■ RO 68 Md45
Lund ◎ CDN 232 Dh21
Lund ◎ ■ S 42 Lo35
Lund ◎ USA 235 Ed27
Lunda ◎ MOC 202 Mh54
Lundazi ◎ Z 196 Mg52
Lunde ◎ N 42 Lk31
Lunder ◎ DK 42 Lk35
Lunderskov ◎ DK 42 Lk35
Lundu ◎ EAT 196 Mh51
Lundu ◎ Z 196 Mg51
Lundy Island ▲ GB 49 Kq39
Lüneburg ◎ ■ D 58 Ll37
Lüneburger Heide ▲ D 58 Lk37
Lunel ◎ F 53 Le47
Lünen ◎ D 58 Lh39
Lunenburg ◎ □ ■ CDN 240 Gh23
Lunenburg ◎ USA 242 Ga27
Lunéville ◎ F 51 Lg42
Lunga ◎ MOC 203 Na53
Lunga ≋ Z 202 Md53
Lunga Lunga ◎ EAK 197 Mk48
Lunge ◎ ANG 200 Lj52
Lungé-Bungo ≋ ANG 200 Lk52
Lunggar ◎ CHN 102 Pb30
Lungharigi ◎ VU 158 Td52
Lungi ◎ WAL 186 Kd41
Lungi Lol ◎ WAL 186 Kd41
Lunglei ◎ IND 120 Pg34
Lungshan Temple ▲ RC 109 Ra33
Lungthung ◎ IND 120 Pf34
Lungungu ◎ RDC 196 Md47
Lungwebungu ◎ Z 201 Mb52
Lunin ◎ BY 65 Mg38
Luninec ◎ BY 65 Mg38
Luning ◎ USA 234 Ea26
Lunino ◎ RUS 72 Nc19
Lunkaransar ◎ IND 114 Og31
Lunna ◎ BY 65 Me37
Lunsar ◎ WAL 186 Kd41
Lunsemfwa ◎ Z 202 Me53
Lunsemfwa Falls ■ Z 202 Me53
Luntai ◎ CHN 100 Pc25
Lunyuk ◎ RI 130 Qj50
Lunyuk Beach ■ RI 130 Qj50
Lunzu ◎ MW 203 Mh53
Lunzua ◎ Z 196 Mf50
Lunzua Falls ■ Z 196 Mf50
Luobai ◎ CHN 108 Qd34
Luobei ◎ CHN 110 Rf22
Luobuzhuang ◎ CHN 101 Pe26
Luochuan ◎ CHN 106 Qe28
Luodian ◎ CHN 108 Qd33
Luoding ◎ CHN 108 Qf34
Luofu ◎ RDC 191 Me46
Luofushan ■ ▲ CHN 109 Qh34
Luohe ◎ CHN 107 Qh29
Luonan ◎ CHN 106 Qf28
Luoning ◎ CHN 106 Qf28
Luoping ◎ CHN 121 Qc33
Luopioinen ◎ FIN 44 Me29
Luoshan ◎ CHN 107 Qh29
Luotian ◎ CHN 109 Qh30
Luotuoquanzi ◎ CHN 101 Ph24
Luoxiao Shan ▲ CHN 109 Qg32
Luoyang ◎ CHN 107 Qg28
Luoyuan ◎ CHN 109 Qk32
Luozi ◎ RDC 198 Lh48
Lupahira ◎ EAT 196 Mh50
Lupa Market ◎ EAT 196 Mg50
Lupambela ◎ EAT 196 Mg49
Lupana ◎ PE 268 Gd47
Lupane ◎ ZW 202 Md55
Lupaso ◎ EAT 197 Mk51
Lupembe ◎ EAT 196 Mh50
Lupéron ◎ DOM 250 Ge36
Lupiro ◎ EAT 197 Mj50
Lupon ◎ RP 125 Rd42
Lupton Conservation Park ■ AUS 144 Qj62
Lupuka ◎ Z 201 Mb54
Lupula ◎ ANG 200 Lj53
Luputa ◎ RDC 199 Mb49
Luqiao ◎ CHN 109 Ra31
Luqiao ◎ CHN 112 Qj29
Luqu ◎ CHN 106 Qb28
Luquan Yizu ◎ CHN 121 Qb33
Luque ◎ PY 276 Hb58
Luquembo ◎ ANG 200 Lj51
Lurcy-Lévis ◎ F 53 Lc44
Lure ◎ F 53 Lg43
Lurgan ◎ GB 47 Ko36
Luri ◎ RI 129 Qj47
Luribay ◎ BOL 278 Gg54
Lurín ◎ PE 269 Gb52
Lúrio ◎ MOC 203 Mj53
Lurnfeld ◎ A 61 Lo44
Luruguma ◎ EAK 194 Mh44
Lusahanga ◎ EAT 194 Mf47
Lusaka ◎ RDC 199 Mc49
Lusaka ● ■ ■ Z 202 Me53
Lusako ◎ RDC 196 Md48
Lusalira ◎ EAU 194 Mf45
Lusamba ◎ RDC 199 Mc48
Lusambo ◎ RDC 199 Mb48
Lusancay Islands ■ PNG 156 Sf50
Lusanga ◎ RDC 199 Lk48
Lusangi ◎ RDC 196 Md48
Lusenga Plain N.P. ■ ■ Z 196 Me50
Lushan ◎ CHN 107 Qg29
Lushan ▲ CHN 107 Qk27
Lushan ◎ CHN 108 Qd32
Lushan □ ■ ▲ CHN 109 Qj31
Lushi ◎ CHN 106 Qf28
Lushimba Rest Camp ◎ Z 201 Mc53
Lushnjë ◎ AL 70 Lu50
Lushoto ◎ EAT 197 Mk48
Lushui ■ CHN 109 Qg31
Lushui ◎ CHN 121 Pk33
Lushuihe ◎ CHN 110 Rd24
Lüshun ◎ CHN 107 Ra26
Lusiba ◎ Z 201 Mc54
Lusignan ◎ F 52 La44
Lusignan ◎ GUY 266 Ha42
Lusigny-sur-Barse ◎ F 51 Le42
Lusikisik ◎ ZA 205 Me61
Lusinga ◎ RDC 196 Md50
Lusitania ◎ CO 264 Gc44
Lusiwasi ◎ Z 196 Mf52
Lusk ◎ USA 235 Eh24
Luso ◎ P 54 Km50
Luss ◎ GB 48 Kq34
Lussac-les-Châteaux ◎ F 52 La44
Lussan ◎ F 53 Le46
Lussenga ◎ ANG 198 Lg49
Lussusso ◎ ANG 198 Lh51
Lusu ◎ Z 201 Mc54
Lusulu ◎ ZW 202 Md55
Luswaka ◎ RDC 196 Md50
Lutao ▲ RC 109 Ra34
Lutembo ◎ ANG 201 Ma52
Lütfiye ◎ TR 71 Mh52
Luth ◎ SUD 191 Mf42
Luthergedenkstätte Eisleben □ ■ D 58 Lm39
Luthergedenkstätte Wittenberg □ ■ D 58 Ln39
Lutherstadt Eisleben ◎ D 58 Lm39
Lutherstadt Wittenberg ◎ D 58 Ln39
Luti ◎ SOL 157 Sj49
Lütjenburg ◎ D 58 Ll36
Lutlut ◎ MYA 122 Pk39
Luton ◎ GB 49 Ku39
Lutong ◎ MAL 128 Qh43
Lútselk'e = Snowdrift ◎ CDN 231 Ee14
Lutshima ◎ RDC 199 Lk48
Lutuai ◎ ANG 200 Ma52
Lutuhyne ◎ UA 73 Mk21
Lutunguru ◎ RDC 191 Me46
Lututów ◎ PL 64 Lt39
Lutzputs ◎ ZA 204 Ma60
Luuk ◎ RP 125 Ra43
Luumäki ◎ FIN 44 Mh30
Luuq ◎ SP 195 Nb44
Luverne ◎ USA 236 Fb24
Luverne ◎ USA 239 Fg30
Luvia ◎ FIN 44 Mb29
Luvo ◎ ANG 198 Lh48
Luvu ◎ RDC 198 Lg48
Luvua ≋ ANG 201 Mb51
Luvua ≋ RDC 196 Md49
Luvuei ◎ ANG 201 Ma52
Luwawa ◎ MW 196 Mg52
Luwembe ◎ Z 202 Mf53
Luwero ◎ EAU 194 Mg45
Luwingu ◎ Z 196 Me51
Luwo ◎ CHN 108 Qe34
Luwuk ◎ RI 130 Rb46
Luxembourg ■ L 51 Lg41
Luxembourg ● □ ■ L 51 Lg41
Luxemburg ◎ USA 236 Fe24
Luxeuil-les-Bains ◎ F 53 Lg43
Luxi ◎ CHN 108 Qf31
Luxi ◎ CHN 121 Pk33
Luxi ◎ CHN 121 Qb33
Lüxia ◎ CHN 109 Ra32
Luxikegongba ◎ CHN 102 Pd30
Luxor ◎ ET 179 Mg33
Luxor □ ■ ET 179 Mg33
Luyando ◎ PE 269 Gc50
Luyi ◎ CHN 107 Qh29
Luz ◎ BR 275 Hh55
Lužajka ◎ RUS 44 Mj30
Luz-Ardiden ■ F 52 Ku48
Luzern ◎ ■ CH 60 Lj43
Luzhai ◎ CHN 108 Qe33
Luzhi ◎ CHN 121 Qc32
Luzhou ◎ CHN 108 Qc31
Luzi ◎ ANG 201 Ma52
Luzi ◎ RDC 199 Lk48
Luziâna ◎ BR 275 Hg54
Luzilândia ◎ BR 273 Hj47
Luzino ◎ PL 64 Lt36
Lužki ◎ BY 45 Mh35
Luzon ▲ RP 124 Ra38
Luzon Strait ≋ 76 Ra08
Luz-Saint-Sauveur ◎ F 52 Ku48
Lužskaja guba ≋ RUS 44 Mj31
Luzy ◎ F 53 Ld44
L'viv ◎ □ ■ UA 67 Md41
Lwakhaka ◎ EAK 194 Mh45
Lwela ◎ Z 196 Me51
Lwówek Śląski ◎ PL 64 Lq39
Lyall, Mount ▲ NZ 153 Td68
Lyantonde ◎ EAU 194 Mf46
Lycan ◎ USA 238 Ej27
Lychen ◎ D 58 Lo37
Lycksele ◎ S 41 Lt26
Lydenburg ◎ ■ ZA 205 Mf58
Lydia ◎ USA 238 Ek26
Lydney ◎ GB 49 Ks39
Lyell Island ▲ CDN 230 De19
Lykso ◎ ZA 205 Mc59
Lyle ◎ USA 232 Dk23
Lyman ◎ UA 72 Mj21
Lyme Bay ≋ GB 49 Kr40
Lyme Regis ◎ GB 49 Ks40
Lymington ◎ GB 49 Kt40
Lynchburg ◎ USA 239 Fg28
Lynchburg ◎ USA 242 Fk28
Lynchburg ◎ USA 242 Ga27
Lynden ◎ USA 232 Dj21
Lyndhurst ◎ AUS 147 Sc55
Lyndhurst ◎ AUS 148 Rk61
Lyndon ◎ AUS 144 Qh57
Lyndonville ◎ USA 241 Gd23
Lyngdal ◎ N 42 Lh32
Lyngør ■ N 42 Lk32
Lyngseidet ◎ ■ N 38 Ma21
Lynn ◎ USA 235 Ed25
Lynn ◎ USA 241 Ge24
Lynndyl ◎ USA 235 Ed26
Lynn Haven ◎ USA 239 Fh30
Lynton ◎ GB 49 Kr39
Lyntupy ◎ BY 45 Mg35
Lyon ⊙ □ ■ F 53 Le45
Lyon Mountain ◎ USA 241 Gd23
Lyons ◎ USA 238 Fa26
Lyons ◎ USA 241 Gb24
Lyons ◎ USA 242 Fj29
Lyons Falls ◎ USA 241 Gc24
Lyons-la-Forêt ◎ F 51 Lb41
Lypci ◎ UA 72 Mj20
Lypova Dolyna ◎ UA 72 Mg20
Lyra Reef ▲ PNG 156 Sg46
Łyse ◎ PL 65 Mb37
Lysefjorden ■ N 42 Lg32
Lysekil ◎ ■ S 42 Lm32
Lyskovo ◎ RUS 72 Nc17
Lysøysundet ◎ N 40 Lk27
Lyss ◎ CH 60 Lh43
Lystrup ◎ DK 42 Ll34
Lysvik ◎ S 42 Lo31
Lysyčans'k ◎ UA 73 Mk21
Lytham Saint Anne's ◎ GB 49 Ks37
Lyton ◎ AUS 144 Qh60
Lytton ◎ CDN 232 Dk20
Lyubimets ◎ BG 69 Mg49

M

Ma ◎ CAM 188 Lf42
Maala ◎ Z 202 Md53
Ma'alaea Bay ≋ ■ USA 234 Cb35
Maalahti ◎ FIN 44 Mb28
Maalhosmadulu North = Raa Atoll ▲ MV 118 Og43
Maalhosmadulu South = Baa Atoll ▲ MV 118 Og43
Maamba ◎ Z 202 Md54
Maam Cross ◎ IRL 47 Kl37
Ma'an ◎ CAM 188 Lf44
Ma'an ◎ JOR 92 Mh30
Maanit ◎ MNG 104 Qb21
Maanit ◎ MNG 104 Qd22
Ma'an, Mount ■ CHN 121 Pk33
Maanselkä ▲ FIN 39 Mj23
Ma'anshan ◎ ■ CHN 112 Qk30
Maardu ◎ EST 44 Mf31
Ma'aret Mokhouz ◎ SYR 90 Mj28
Maarianhamina = Mariehamn ◎ FIN 44 Lu30
Maarja ◎ EST 44 Mg32
Ma'arrat an-Nu'man ◎ SYR 90 Mj28
Maas ≋ NL 51 Lg39
Maasai Mara National Reserve ■ ■ EAK 194 Mh46
Maasbracht ◎ NL 51 Lf39
Maaseik ◎ B 51 Lf39
Maasim ◎ RP 125 Rc43
Maasin ◎ RP 124 Rc40
Maasmechelen ◎ B 51 Lf40
Maasstroom ◎ ZA 202 Me57
Maastricht ◎ ■ ■ NL 51 Lf40
Maatsuyker Islands ▲ AUS 151 Sd67
Maazaplateau ▲ ET 179 Mf32
Mâaziz ◎ MA 175 Kg29
Maba ◎ RI 125 Re45
Mababe Depression ▲ RB 201 Mc55
Ma'bad ◎ IR 96 Nh28
Mabaduam ◎ PNG 155 Sa49
Mabaia ◎ ANG 198 Lh49
Mabaké ◎ SN 180 Kc38
Mabalacat ◎ RP 124 Ra38
Mabalane ◎ MOC 202 Mg57
Mabana ◎ RDC 191 Me45
Mabanda ◎ BU 196 Me48
Ma'bar ◎ YE 94 Nc38
Mabating ◎ CHN 121 Pk31
Mabdeitikra ◎ IND 117 Pb34
Mabein ◎ MYA 120 Pj34
Mabel Creek ◎ AUS 148 Rh60
Mabélé ◎ CAM 189 Lg42
Mabeleapudi ◎ RB 202 Md57
Mabelle ◎ USA 238 Fa29
Mabenga ◎ RDC 199 Lk47
Mabenge ◎ RDC 191 Mc43
Mabian ◎ CHN 108 Qb31
Mabinay ◎ RP 124 Rb41
Mablethorpe ◎ GB 49 La37
Mabo ◎ SN 186 Kc39
Mabokweni ◎ EAT 197 Mk48
Maboleni ◎ ZW 202 Me55
Mabopane ◎ ZA 205 Me58
Mabote ◎ MOC 202 Mh57
Mabou ◎ CDN 240 Gk22
Mabroûk ◎ RMM 181 Kk36
Mabrous ◎ RN 183 Lg35
Mabruk ◎ LAR 177 Lj30
Mabton ◎ USA 232 Dk22
Mabuasehube Game Reserve ■ RB 204 Mb58
Mabuhay ◎ RP 125 Rb42
Mabuiag Island ▲ AUS 147 Sb50
Mabuki ◎ EAT 194 Mg47
Mabura ◎ GUY 266 Ha43
Mabuto ◎ WAN 188 Lc40
Mabutsane ◎ RB 204 Mb58
Macache ◎ EC 268 Ga46
Macachin ◎ RA 281 Gj64
Macaé ◎ BR 275 Hk57
Macaena ◎ MOC 205 Mg58
Macaíba ◎ BR 273 Jc48
Macajuba ◎ BR 273 Hk52
Macanda ◎ MOC 203 Mh54
Macandze ◎ MOC 202 Mg57
Macane ◎ MOC 202 Mg56
Macao ⊙ □ ■ CHN 109 Qg34
Macao □ CHN 109 Qg35
Macapá ⊙ ■ BR 267 He45
Macará ◎ EC 268 Ga48
Macara ◎ RP 124 Ra36
Macaracas ◎ PA 249 Fk42
Macarani ◎ BR 275 Hk53
Macarí ◎ PE 269 Ge53
Maçaroca ◎ BR 273 Hk50
Macaroni ◎ AUS 147 Sa54
Macarrão, T.I. ■ BR 270 Gg47
Macarrtane ◎ MOC 205 Mg58

Macarthur – Maneroo

Macarthur ⊙ AUS 150 Sb65
Macas ⊙ EC 268 Ga47
Macatanja ⊙ MOC 203 Mj54
Macaú ⊡ BR 273 Jb48
Macauari ⊙ BR 266 Ha46
Macaúba ⊙ BR 272 Hg48
Macaúbas ⊙ BR 273 Hj52
Macauley Island ▲ NZ 152 Lo61
Maceió ◉ BR 272 Jg49
Macclenny ⊙ USA 242 Fj30
Macclesfield ⊙ GB 49 Ks37
Macdiarmid ⊙ CDN 237 Fd21
Macdonald Downs ⊙ AUS 148 Rh57
Macdonald, Mount ▲ VU 158 Te54
Macdonnell Ranges ▲ AUS 143 Rg57
Macea ⊙ RO 67 Md44
Maceda ⊡ E 54 Kn48
Macedo de Cavaleiros ⊙ P 54 Ko49
Macedonia ▣ MK 68 Mb49
Macenta ⊙ RG 186 Kf41
Macerata ⊙ I 61 Lo47
MacGrath ⊙ USA 229 Cc14
Mach ⊙ PK 99 Od31
Macha ⊙ BOL 279 Gg55
Macha ⊙ Z 202 Md54
Machacalis ⊙ BR 273 Hh54
Machacamarca ⊙ BOL 278 Gg55
Machachi ⊙ EC 266 Ga46
Machachuta ⊙ ZW 202 Me56
Machadinho ⊙ BR 270 Gj50
Machado ⊙ BR 275 Hh56
Machadodorp ⊙ ZA 205 Mf58
Machagai ⊙ RA 279 Gk59
Machaila ⊙ MOC 203 Mf57
Machakos ⊙ EAK 194 Mj46
Machala ⊙ EC 268 Ga47
Machali ⊙ RCH 280 Ge63
Machalilla ⊙ EC 268 Fk46
Machalilla, P.N. ⊞ EC 268 Fk46
Machanbew ⊙ MYA 120 Pj32
Machaneng ⊙ RB 202 Md57
Machanga ⊙ MOC 203 Mh56
Macheault ⊡ F 51 Le41
Machecoul ⊙ F 52 Kt44
Macheke ⊙ ZW 202 Mf56
Machemmarunies ▲ EAT 202 Me57
Machemma Ruines ▲ ZA 202 Me57
Macheng ⊙ CHN 109 Qh30
Macherla ⊙ IND 117 Oc37
Machesse ⊙ MOC 203 Mh55
Machgaon ⊙ IND 117 Pd35
Machhapuchare ▲ NEP 115 Pb31
Machias ⊙ USA 240 Gg23
Machico ⊙ P 174 Kb29
Machilipatnam ⊙ IND 117 Pa35
Machilla Kuta ⊡ BOL 278 Gf55
Machina ⊙ WAN 182 Lf39
Machingamkop ▲ MA 203 Mh53
Machiques ⊙ YV 266 Gd40
Machu Picchu ⊞▲ PE 269 Gd52
Machynlleth ⊙ GB 49 Kg38
Macia ⊙ MOC 205 Mg58
Maciana Marina ⊡ I 60 Ll48
Maciejowice ⊡ PL 65 Mb39
Mácin ⊙ RO 69 Mj45
Macinaggio ⊡ F 60 Lk48
Mackay ⊙ AUS 149 Se56
Mackay ⊙ USA 232 Ed24
MacKay Lake ⊡ CDN 231 Ee14
Mackenzie ⊡ CDN 226 Dd06
Mackenzie ⊡ CDN 230 Dj18
Mackenzie Bay ⊡ CDN 226 Da05
Mackenzie Bison Sanctuary ⊞ CDN 231 Eb15
Mackenzie Highway ⊡ CDN 231 Dj14
Mackenzie King Island ⊡ CDN 226 Ec03
Mackenzie Mountains ▲ CDN 230 Df14
Mackinac S.P. ⊞ USA 237 Fh23
Mackinaw City ⊙ USA 237 Fh23
Mackinnon Road ⊙ EAK 195 Mk47
Macklin ⊡ CDN 233 Ef19
Macks Inn ⊙ USA 233 Ee23
Macksville ⊙ AUS 149 Sf60
Maclean ⊙ AUS 149 Sf60
Macleantown ⊡ ZA 205 Md62
Maclear ⊙ ZA 205 Me61
Macmillan Pass ⊡ CDN 230 Df14
Macmillan Plateau ▲ CDN 230 Dd14
Maco ⊙ RP 125 Rc42
Macobere ⊙ MOC 202 Mf56
Macocola ⊙ ANG 198 Lj49
Macomb ⊙ USA 239 Fe25
Macomer ⊡ I 62 Lj50
Mâcon ◉ F 53 Le44
Macon ⊙ USA 238 Fz26
Macon ⊙ USA 239 Ft29
Macon ⊙ USA 242 Fj29
Macondo ⊙ ANG 201 Mb52
Macossa ⊙ MOC 203 Mh56
Macquarie Harbour ⊡ AUS 151 Sc67
Macquarie Islands ⊡ 134 Sd54
Macquarie Ridge ⊡ 134 Sb15
Mac Robertson Land ▲ 287 Nd33
Macroom ⊙ IRL 47 Kn39
Macrorie ⊡ CDN 233 Eg20
Mactaris ▲ TN 176 Le28
Mactún ⊡ MEX 247 Fe37
Macucauá ⊙ BR 268 Ge49
Macuira, P.N. ⊞ CO 264 Ge39
Macuje ⊙ CO 268 Gd47
Macumba ⊡ AUS 148 Rh59
Macururé ⊙ BR 273 Ja50
Macusani ⊙ PE 269 Ge53
Macuspana ⊙ MEX 247 Fd37
Macuze ⊙ MOC 203 Mj54
Macwahok ⊙ USA 240 Gf23
Madá ⊡ MOC 203 Mh56
Madadeni ⊙ ZA 205 Mf59
Madadi ⊙ JOR 92 Mh30
Madadi ⊙ TCH 190 Mb43
Madazdi ⊙ ZW 202 Me54
Madaoua ⊙ RN 182 Le39
Madagascar ▣ 162 Na12
Madagascar ⊡ 163 Na11
Madagascar Basin ⊡ 162 Na12
Madagascar Ridge ⊡ 162 Na13
Madagali ⊙ WAN 188 La42
Madain Salah ⊞ KSA 92 Mj42
Madakasira ⊙ IND 116 Oj39
Madalena ⊙ BR 273 Ja48
Madama ⊡ RN 183 Lg40
Madampa ⊙ RP 125 Rc42
Madampa ⊙ CL 119 Ok42
Madan ⊙ BG 69 Me47
Madana ⊙ TCH 190 Lj41
Madanapalle ⊙ IND 119 Ok39
Madang ◉ PNG 155 Sc48
Madang Reso ⊞ EAT 197 Mk49
Madäng Resort ⊡ AUS 151 Sc48
Mädängsholm ⊡ S 43 Lo32
Madan Mahal Fort ▲ IND 117 Pa34
Madaoua ⊙ IND 117 Ok33
Madaoua ⊙ RN 182 Le39
Madaouros ▲ DZ 176 Lf27
Madaripur ⊙ BD 120 Pf34
Madarka ⊙ IND 117 Pd35
Madaripur ⊙ RN 182 Ld39
Madawaska ⊙ PNG 156 Sg51
Madba ⊙ USA 240 Gf22
Madbar ⊡ SUD 194 Mf42
Madd Island ⊙ PNG 156 Sg50
Maddalena ⊙ I 163 Lp49
Madded ⊙ IND 117 Pa36
Maddela ⊙ RP 124 Ra37
Maddhupur ⊡ IND 119 Ok38
Maddur ⊙ IND 117 Oj39
Madeir ⊡ SUD 190 Me42
Madeira ⊡ BR 271 Ha48
Madeira ⊡ 163 Ka05
Madeira ⊡ P 162 Ka05
Madeira Rise ⊡ 162 Ka06
Maden ⊙ TR 91 Md27
Madeng ⊙ CHN 121 Pk32
Madenlyet ⊙ KZ 100 Od32
Madera ⊙ MEX 244 Ef31
Madésimo ⊡ I 60 Lk44
Madgaon = Margao ⊙ IND 116 Oh37
Madgoul ⊙ DJI 192 Nb39
Madh ⊙ IND 116 Oh35

Madha ⊙ KSA 94 Nb36
Madh adh Dhahab ⊙ KSA 94 Na34
Madhav N.P. ⊞ IND 117 Oj33
Madhav Vilas Palace ⊞ IND 116 Oj33
Madhipura ⊙ IND 117 Pd32
Madhubani ⊙ IND 117 Pd32
Madhugiri ⊙ IND 116 Oj38
Madhupur Jungle N.P. ⊞ BD 120 Pf33
Madhya Pradesh ▣ IND 116 Oh34
Madibogo ⊙ ZA 205 Mc59
Madidi, P.N. ⊞ BOL 278 Gf53
Madikeri ⊙ IND 116 Oj38
Madina ⊙ BOL 270 Gg51
Madina ⊙ GNB 186 Kc40
Madina ⊡ KSA 94 Na34
Madina ⊙ C 187 Kg41
Madina ⊙ RIM 180 Kd38
Madina ⊙ RMM 187 Kg40
Madinani ⊙ CI 187 Kg41
Madina-Gao ⊙ RMM 187 Kg40
Madina-Sako ⊡ RMM 187 Kg40
Madina-Salambande ⊙ RG 186 Ke40
Madinat al Abyar ⊙ LAR 177 Ma29
Madinat al 'bid ⊙ YE 94 Nc39
Madingou ⊙ RCB 198 Lg48
Madingrin ⊙ CAM 189 Lh41
Madi Opei ⊙ EAU 194 Mg44
Madirovalo ⊙ RM 206 Nd54
Madison ⊙ USA 236 Fd23
Madison ⊙ USA 236 Fb24
Madison ⊙ USA 238 Fb25
Madison ⊙ USA 237 Ff24
Madison ⊙ USA 239 Fg28
Madison ⊙ USA 239 Fh26
Madison ⊙ USA 241 Gd23
Madison ⊙ USA 242 Fj30
Madison Canyon Earthquake Area ⊞ USA 233 Ee23
Madisonville ⊙ USA 238 Fc30
Madisonville ⊙ USA 239 Fg27
Madjun ⊙ RI 129 Qf49
Madja ⊙ RCA 189 Lk42
Madjingo ⊙ G 190 Lh45
Madley, Mount ▲ AUS 143 Rb58
Mado Gashi ⊙ EAK 195 Mk45
Madona ⊙ LV 45 Mf34
Madonna del Sasso ⊞ CH 60 Lj44
Madonna di Campiglio ⊡ I 60 Ll44
Madonna Downs ⊙ AUS 145 Rb61
Madouille ⊙ DF 96 Mj36
Madrakah ⊙ KSA 94 Na35
Madras = Chennai ◉ IND 119 Pa39
Madras ⊙ USA 232 Dk23
Madrasat Qasr Abu Hadi ⊙ LAR 177 Lj32
Mâdrec ⊡ BG 69 Mg48
Madre de Deus de Minas ⊙ BR 275 Hh56
Madre de Dios ⊡ CO 268 Gg50
Madre de Dios ⊡ PE 269 Ge52
Madrejón ⊙ RA 279 Gj57
Madrid ◉ E 55 Kr50
Madrid ⊙ USA 239 Fe25
Madrid ⊡ RP 124 Rc41
Madridejos ⊙ E 55 Kr51
Madrigal ⊙ PE 269 Ge53
Madrigal de las Altas Torres ⊙ E 54 Kq49
Madqalejo ⊙ E 55 Kp51
Madrona ⊙ BG 69 Mg48
Madroñera ⊙ E 55 Kp51
Madu ⊙ RI 130 Ra49
Madu ⊙ SUD 184 Md38
Madugula Kondas ▲ IND 117 Pb37
Madula ⊙ RDC 191 Mc45
Madura ⊙ AUS 145 Rd61
Madura ⊙ RI 129 Qg49
Madurai ◉ IND 118 Ok41
Madurantakam ⊙ IND 119 Ok39
Madwa ⊡ EAT 194 Mh47
Madyan ⊙ PK 99 Od30
Madyo ⊙ EAT 196 Mh49
Madziwadzido ⊙ ZW 202 Md56
Madziwa Mine ⊙ ZW 202 Me54
Madzure ⊙ RDC 194 Mf44
Maebashi ◉ J 111 Rk27
Mae Chai ⊡ THA 121 Pk36
Mae Chan ⊡ THA 121 Pk36
Mae Charim ⊡ THA 121 Pj36
Mae Hong Son ⊡ THA 121 Pj36
Mae Khachan ⊡ THA 121 Pk36
Mae La Na ⊡ THA 121 Pj36
Mae La Noi ⊡ THA 121 Pj36
Maél-Carhaix ⊡ F 50 Kr42
Maelia ⊡ E 57 La49
Mâe Malai ⊡ THA 121 Pk36
Mâe Maria, T.I. ⊞ BR 272 Hf48
Mae Phrik ⊡ THA 122 Pk37
Mae Pok ⊡ THA 121 Pk37
Mae Ramat ⊡ THA 121 Pj37
Mae Rim ⊡ THA 121 Pk36
Mae Sai ⊡ THA 121 Pk36
Mae Sariang ⊡ THA 121 Pj36
Maes Howe ▲ GB 48 Kr31
Mae Sot ⊡ THA 122 Pj37
Maestra de Campo Island ⊡ RP 124 Ra39
Mae Su ⊡ THA 121 Pj36
Mae Suai ⊡ THA 121 Pk36
Mae Suya ⊡ THA 121 Pj36
Mae Taeng ⊡ THA 121 Pk36
Mae Tub Reservoir ⊡ THA 121 Pk37
Mae Tun ⊡ THA 122 Pj37
Mae Wong N.P. ⊞ THA 122 Pk38
Mae Yom N.P. ⊞ THA 121 Qa38
Mafa ⊡ RP 125 Rd45
Mafa ⊡ WAN 189 Lg40
Mafeng ⊡ C 187 Kj43
Mafeteng ⊙ LS 205 Md60
Mafeteng Rock Paintings ⊞ LS 205 Md60
Maffin ⊙ RI 154 Rk46
Maffra ⊙ AUS 151 Sd64
Mafia Channel ⊡ EAT 197 Mk49
Mafia Island ⊡ EAT 197 Mk49
Mafia Marine Park ⊞ EAT 197 Mk50
Mafikeng ⊙ ZA 205 Mc58
Mafili ⊙ RCH 280 Gd65
Mafou ⊙ EAT 197 Mj50
Mafouné ⊙ RMM 187 Kh39
Mafra ⊙ BR 277 Hf58
Mafra ⊙ P 55 Kl52
Mafraq ⊡ JOR 90 Mj29
Mafuiane ⊙ RP 125 Rb41
Mafwegogho ⊙ ZW 202 Me55
Magadan ◉ RUS 89 Sc07
Magados Island ⊡ RP 125 Qk43
Magallanes, Cerro ▲ EC 268 Ef50
Magangue ⊙ CO 264 Gc41
Maganik ▲ MNE 68 Lu48
Maganoy ⊙ RP 125 Rc43
Maganza ⊙ RDC 198 Lk47
Magao ⊙ TCH 189 Lh40
Magaria ⊙ RN 182 Le39
Magaria ⊙ PNG 156 Se51
Magba ⊙ CAM 189 Lh43
Magbakele ⊙ RDC 190 Lk45
Magburaka ⊙ WAL 186 Ke41

Mahidasht ⊙ IR 91 Nd28
Mahien ⊙ SYR 90 Mj28
Mahila ⊙ RDC 196 Me49
Mahilëv ⊡ BY 72 Mf19
Mahina ⊙ WAN 188 Lc42
Mahina ⊙ RMM 186 Ke39
Mahirija ⊙ MA 175 Kg29
Mahisama ⊙ IND 116 Ok37
Mahitsy ⊡ RM 207 Nd55
Mahjub ⊙ AZ 91 Nd28
Mahlaing ⊙ MYA 120 Ph35
Mahmiya ⊙ SUD 185 Mg37
Mahmudabad ⊙ IND 115 Pa32
Mahmud Abad ⊙ IR 96 Nf29
Mahmud-e Eraqi ⊙ AFG 99 Oe28
Mahmud Jiq ⊙ IR 91 Nd27
Mahnar Bazar ⊙ IND 117 Pc33
Mahneh ⊙ IR 98 Nk28
Mahnesan ⊙ IR 91 Nd27
Mahnomen ⊙ USA 236 Fb22
Mahoba ⊙ IND 117 Ok35
Mahóba ⊙ IND 115 Pa32
Mahora ⊡ E 57 Kt51
Mahora ⊙ IR 91 Nd27
Mahou ⊙ RMM 187 Kh39
Mahoua ⊙ TCH 190 Lh42
Mahrauni ⊙ IND 117 Ok33
Mahrès ⊙ TN 176 Lf28
Mahri ⊙ PK 99 Od32
Mahuamaeroe ⊙ PNG 156 Sg47
Mahuta ⊙ WAN 188 Lc40
Mahur Island ▲ PNG 156 Sg47
Mahura ⊙ UA 67 Md42
Mahur ⊙ IND 120 Ph35
Mahuva ⊙ IND 116 Og35
Mahwa ⊙ IND 116 Oj33
Maia ⊙ E 57 La49
Maiaia ⊙ BR 267 Hf46
Maiauata ⊙ BR 267 Hf46
Maibo ⊙ TCH 190 Lk41
Maicao ⊙ CO 264 Ge40
Mai Chau ⊙ VN 121 Qc35
Maiche ⊡ F 53 Lg43
Maici ⊡ BR 270 Gg49
Maidanshar = Kowt-e Ashrow ⊙ AFG 99 Oe28
Maidenhead ⊙ GB 49 Ku39
Maiden, Mount ▲ AUS 144 Rb59
Maidi ⊙ IR 91 Nd28
Maidstone ⊙ CDN 233 Ef19
Maidstone ⊙ GB 49 La39
Maidugur ⊡ WAN 189 Lg40
Maidukuru ⊙ IND 119 Ok38
Maie ⊙ RDC 194 Mf44
Maiella, P.N.della ⊞ I 63 Lp48
Maierus ⊙ RO 69 Mf45
Maigatari ⊙ WAN 188 Lc39
Maihar ⊙ IND 117 Pa33
Maiinchi ⊙ WAN 188 Ld39
Maijishan Shiku ⊞ CHN 106 Qc28
Maikala Range ▲ IND 117 Pa34
Maikapshagai ⊙ KZ 101 Pc22
Maikona ⊙ EAK 194 Mj44
Maikoro ⊙ TCH 190 Lj41
Mailani ⊙ IND 115 Pa31
Maille-le-Camp ⊡ F 51 Le42
Maïlsi ⊙ PK 99 Og31
Maimana = Meymaneh ⊙ AFG 97 Oc28
Maimón ⊙ DOM 250 Ge36
Main ⊡ D 59 Lk41
Main-Donau-Kanal ⊡ D 59 Lm42
Mainali ⊙ BD 120 Pf34
Main Brook ⊙ CDN 241 Hb20
Main Camp ⊙ ZW 202 Md55
Maindargi ⊙ IND 119 Ok37
Mainé-Soroa ⊙ RN 183 Lg39
Maing Kwan ⊙ MYA 120 Pj32
Mainland ⊙ GB 48 Kr31
Mainland ▲ GB 48 Kt31
Mainling ⊙ CHN 103 Pk31
Mainoru ⊙ AUS 146 Rh53
Mainpuri ⊙ IND 115 Ok33
Main Range N.P. ⊞ AUS 149 Sf59
Maintenon ⊡ F 51 Lb42
Maintirano ⊙ RM 207 Nc55
Maio ⊡ CV 186 Jh38
Maiovka ⊙ YV 265 Gk42
Maipo, Volcán ▲ RCH/RA 280 Gf63
Maipú ⊙ RA 281 Ha64
Maiquetía ⊙ YV 265 Gg40
Maisaca ⊡ IND 115 Sh48
Mairi ⊙ RCH 280 Gd65
Maisanda ⊙ IND 116 Oj36
Maisi ⊙ C 250 Gc35
Maisiaigala ⊙ LT 45 Mf36
Maisome Island ⊡ EAT 194 Mg47
Maison Carrée de Nimes ⊞ F 57 Le44
Maisons de Champagne d'Épernay ⊞ F 51 Le41
Maitabi, Mount ▲ SOL 157 Sj49
Maitbhanga ⊙ BD 120 Pf34
Maitencillo ⊙ RCH 280 Gd62
Maitioukoulou ⊙ RCA 190 Lj42
Maitland ⊙ AUS 147 Se60
Maitland ⊙ AUS 151 St62
Maitland Range ⊡ AUS 143 Rd58
Maitri ⊡ RI 130 Ra47
Maivel ⊙ RI 130 Ra47
Maja ⊙ RUS 89 Rd07
Majadahonda ⊙ E 55 Kr50
Majagual ⊙ CO 264 Gc41
Majene ⊙ RI 130 Qk46
Majagua ⊙ C 250 Ga35
Majahual ⊙ MEX 247 Fe36
Majalengka ⊙ RI 129 Qe49
Majalgaon ⊙ IND 116 Oj35
Majamai ⊙ CHN 106 Qc27
Majene ⊙ RI 130 Qk46
Majete Game Reserve ⊞ MW 203 Mh53
Majevica ▲ BIH 68 Lt46
Majgaon ⊙ IND 117 Pb34
Majhgawan ⊙ IND 117 Pb33
Majhioli ⊙ IND 117 Pb33
Majhoul ⊙ IR 91 Nd28
Majie ⊙ CHN 121 Qb33
Maji ⊙ ETH 194 Mg43
Majiaxian ⊙ CHN 106 Qc27
Maji-Saj ⊙ KS 97 Og25
Majkain ⊙ KZ 101 Ob21
Majors Place ⊙ USA 234 Ec26
Majskij ⊙ RUS 91 Nc24
Majskoe ⊙ RUS 105 Re19
Majuba ⊙ YE 94 Nd37
Maka ⊙ SN 186 Kd37
Maka ⊙ CB 190 Lj44
Makabana ⊙ RCB 198 Lg47
Makada ⊙ RCB 198 Lg47
Makak ⊙ CAM 189 Lh44
Makalondi ⊙ RN 182 La39

Makanda ⊙ RCB 198 Lg47
Makanjila ⊙ MW 203 Mh52
Makanshy ⊙ KZ 100 Pd22
Makantaka ⊙ NIC 249 Fh39
Makapan Valley ⊞ RI 130 Qk49
Makaranangang ⊙ RI 130 Qk49
Makarewoj ⊡ SUD 185 Mf39
Makari ⊙ WAN 188 Lg40
Makari ⊙ CAM 189 Lh39
Makaroa ⊙ NZ 153 Te68
Makarov Basin ⊡ 286 Ed01
Makarova ⊡ RDC 72 Nb19
Makaraka ⊙ IR HR 61 Ls47
Makaza ⊡ 196 Mf50
Makassar ⊙ RI 130 Qk48
Makassar Strait ⊡ RI 130 Qj47
Makaw ⊙ MYA 121 Rc50
Makay ⊡ RA 280 Ga60
Makaybalay ⊙ RP 125 Rc41
Makayeva ⊙ NEP 115 Pa31
Makdai ⊙ CHN 101 Od32
Makedeon ⊙ MK 68 Mb49
Makedonias ▣ MK 68 Mb49
Makekeda ⊙ RDC 191 Md44
Makekeda ⊙ RDC 191 Md44
Makeni ⊙ WAL 186 Ke41
Makgadikgadi Pans ⊡ RB 201 Mc56
Makgadikgadi Pans N.P. ⊞ RB 201 Mc56
Makhdumnagar ⊙ IND 117 Pb32
Makhfar ⊡ IR 91 Nd28
Makhmur ⊙ IND 116 Oj37
Makhu ⊙ IND 114 Oh30
Maki ⊙ ETH 192 Mk42
Maki ⊙ RI 154 Rh47
Makikeng ⊙ ZA 205 Mc58
Makikiwa ⊙ UA 73 Mk21
Makindu ⊙ EAK 195 Mj47
Makingeny Cave ▲ EAK 194 Mh45
Makira ▲ SOL 157 Ta51
Makirankobe ⊡ BR 272 Hf48
Makkah ⊙ KSA 94 Na35
Mako ⊙ SN 186 Kd39
Mako ⊙ EAT 196 Mj46
Makoli ⊙ Z 201 Md52
Makoli ⊙ Z 202 Mc54
Makonde Plateau ▲ EAT 197 Mk51
Makongo ⊙ CAM 187 Kk41
Makongolosi ⊙ EAT 196 Mg50
Makopong ⊙ RB 204 Mb58
Makorako ▲ NZ 153 Tf65
Makotipoko ⊙ RCB 198 Lj46
Makou ⊙ CHN 109 Qg30
Makoua ⊙ RCB 198 Lj46
Makovo ⊙ MK 68 Mb49
Makow Mazowiecki ⊙ PL 64 Ls37
Makow Mazowiecki ⊙ PL 65 Mb38
Makran Coast Range ▲ PK 99 Ob33
Makrany ⊙ BY 65 Me39
Makrihisar ⊙ GR 68 Md51
Makrihisar ▲ GR 68 Md51
Makronisi ▲ GR 71 Mf53
Maksatiha ⊙ RUS 72 Mh17
Maksudangarh ⊙ IND 116 Oj33
Maktau ⊙ EAK 194 Mh47
Maktar ⊙ TN 176 Le29
Maku ⊙ IR 91 Nc26
Makuende ⊙ RDC 196 Mf50
Makumbako ⊙ EAT 196 Mg50
Makumbi ⊙ RDC 199 Ma48
Makumo ⊙ ZW 202 Md54
Makunda ⊙ RB 200 Ma57
Makunduchi ⊙ EAT 197 Mk49
Makurdi ◉ WAN 188 Ld41
Makurdi ⊙ WAN 188 Ld41
Makushin ⊙ USA 244 Cp19
Makurazaki ⊙ J 113 Rf30
Makutano ⊙ EAK 194 Mh45
Makuyuni ⊙ EAT 194 Mj47
Makwa ⊙ RDC 196 Me49
Makwate ⊙ RB 202 Md57
Makwiro ⊙ ZW 202 Me55
Makwyak ⊙ RB 204 Mb58
Mala ⊙ PE 269 Gb52
Mala ⊡ RI 131 Rf46
Mala ⊙ RCB 198 Lh47
Mala A.L. ⊙ AUS 143 Rf56
Mala A.L. ⊡ AUS 143 Re54
Malabang ⊙ RP 125 Rc43
Malabo ◉ GQ 188 Ld44
Malabar Coast ⊡ IND 118 Oj40
Malabar, Gunung ▲ RI 129 Qe49
Malabrigo ⊙ PE 268 Ga50
Malabuyoc ⊙ RP 125 Rb42
Malacca ⊙ MAL 122 Pg41
Malacacheta ⊙ BR 275 Hj54
Malacacheta ⊡ BR 266 Gk44
Malacky ⊙ SK 66 Lr42
Maladzeczna ⊡ BY 45 Mg36
Malá Fatra, N.P. ⊞ SK 67 Lu41
Málaga ⊙ CO 264 Gd42
Málaga ⊙ E 55 Kq54
Málaga ⊙ USA 235 En29
Malaga Beach Resort ⊡ PNG 156 Sd47
Malagarasi ⊡ EAT 196 Mf48
Malagón ⊡ E 55 Kr51
Malaha ⊙ CHN 101 Od32
Majenke ⊙ RI 129 Qf49
Majdanpek ⊡ SRB 68 Mb46
Majela ⊡ BR 267 Hf46
Majestic Castle ▲ IRL 47 Kn37
Mājkōvó ⊙ IND 116 Oj33
Majkain ⊙ KZ 101 Ob21
Malakand ⊙ PK 99 Oe29
Malakanagiri ⊙ IND 117 Pb36
Malakula ▲ VU 158 Td53
Malakwal ⊙ PK 99 Og29
Malala ⊙ EAT 196 Mh48
Malalaua ⊙ PNG 155 Sd50
Malalamai ⊙ PNG 155 Sc48
Malalbergo ⊡ I 60 Ll45
Malalhue ⊙ RCH 280 Gd65
Mala Mari N.P. ⊞ EAK 195 Na43
Malamfashi ⊙ WAN 188 Ld40
Mala Mari N.P. ⊞ EAK 195 Na43
Malang ⊙ RI 129 Qg49
Malang A.L. ⊙ AUS 143 Re54
Malangen ⊡ N 38 Lu21
Malanje ⊙ ANG 198 Lj50
Malanville ⊙ DY 188 Lb40
Malappuram ⊙ IND 118 Oj40
Mala Serdoba ⊙ RUS 72 Nc19
Malargüe ⊙ RA 280 Gf63

Malarrif ⊙ IS 46 Jr26
Malaryta ⊡ BY 65 Me39
Malasait ⊙ PNG 156 Sf48
Malaspina Glacier ▲ USA 230 Ck16
Malatya ⊙ TR 90 Mk28
Malavi ⊙ IR 93 Nd29
Malavi ⊙ IR 93 Nd29
Malawali ⊙ IND 118 Oj39
Malawi ▣ MW 203 Mh52
Malawi, Lake ⊡ MW 203 Mh52
Malax ⊙ FIN 43 Mc28
Malax ⊙ FIN 43 Mc28
Malay ⊙ RP 124 Ra40
Malaybalay ⊙ RP 125 Rc41
Malayer ⊙ IR 91 Nd28
Malaysia ▣ MAL 77 Qa09
Malazgirt ⊙ TR 91 Md27
Malbaza ⊙ RN 182 Le39
Malbork ⊙ PL 64 Lo36
Malborn ⊡ D 59 Lh41
Malbran ⊡ RA 279 Gj60
Malbuisson ⊡ F 53 Lg44
Malca Rie ⊙ SP 195 Na44
Malcésine ⊡ I 60 Ll45
Malchin ⊙ D 58 Lo37
Malchow ⊙ D 58 Ln37
Malchow ⊙ AUS 144 Ra60
Maldegem ⊙ B 51 Ld39
Malden ⊙ GB 49 Kn36
Maldives ▣ MV 76 Ob09
Maldives ▣ MV 76 Ob09
Maldonado ⊙ EC 268 Ga45
Maldonado ⊙ ROU 281 Hc63
Maldybaj ⊙ KZ 100 Od24
Maldyty ⊙ PL 65 Lp36
Male ⊡ IR 91 Nd28
Male ◉ MV 118 Oj39
Malè ⊡ I 60 Ll44
Malea, Gunung ▲ RI 127 Pk45
Maleatis ⊙ GR 71 Md53
Malebo ⊙ RDC 198 Lh47
Maledegme ⊙ B 51 Ld39
Malegaon ⊙ IND 116 Oh35
Malegaon Jahagir ⊙ IND 116 Oj35
Malei ⊙ SUD 191 Md41
Malei ⊙ SUD 191 Md41
Malek ⊙ SUD 191 Md42
Malekan ⊙ IR 91 Nd27
Malek Karpaty ▲ CZ 66 Ls42
Malele ⊙ RCB 198 Lg48
Malema ⊙ MOC 203 Mj53
Malema-Nkulu ⊙ RDC 196 Me50
Malemba-Nkulu ⊙ RDC 196 Me50
Malème-Hodar ⊙ SN 180 Kc38
Malendok Island ▲ PNG 156 Sg47
Malesa ⊙ RP 125 Rd43
Malesherbes ⊡ F 51 Lc42
Malestan ⊙ AFG 99 Oe29
Malestroit ⊡ F 50 Ks43
Maleta ⊙ RUS 104 Qb21
Maletsunyane Falls ▲ LS 205 Me60
Malgobek ⊙ RUS 91 Nc24
Malgrat de Mar ⊙ E 57 Ld49
Malha ⊙ SUD 184 Md38
Malhada ⊙ BR 275 Hj53
Malhat ⊡ IRQ 91 Nd28
Malheur ⊡ USA 232 Eb24
Malheur Nat. Wildlife Refuge ⊞ USA 232 Ea24
Malhia ⊙ YV 265 Gj43
Mali ▣ 187 Kh39
Mali ⊙ RDC 196 Me49
Mali ⊡ 163 Kd08
Mali ⊡ GR 71 Md55
Maliau ⊙ MAL 126 Qj43
Mali Iyosin ⊡ HR 61 Lp46
Mali Island ▲ MYA 122 Pk49
Malili ⊙ RI 130 Ra47
Malilla ⊙ S 43 Lq33
Malimalim ⊙ SN 186 Kc39
Malimba de Arriba ⊙ RDC 196 Me50
Malinaundi ⊡ RDC 194 Mf44
Malindang, Mount ▲ MV 118 Oq42
Malindi ◉ EAK 195 Na47
Malindi ⊙ EAK 195 Na47
Malindi Marine N.P. ⊞ EAK 195 Na47
Malinalco ⊙ MEX 246 Fa36
Malines ⊙ B 51 Le39
Malinga ⊙ G 198 Lg47
Malin Head ▲ IRL 47 Ko35
Malinke ⊙ SN 186 Kc39
Malini ⊙ RDC 196 Me49
Malino ⊙ RI 130 Ra46
Malinska ⊡ HR 61 Lp45
Malipaoro ⊙ RI 130 Ra46
Malinyi ⊙ EAT 197 Mj50
Malipari ⊙ IND 117 Pd33
Maliq ⊙ AL 70 Ma50
Mal i Shpatit ⊙ AL 68 Ma49
Mali Vrh ⊡ RP 125 Rc42
Malia ⊙ IND 116 Of34
Malibamat'so ⊡ LS 205 Md60
Malidjama ⊙ AUS 149 Sg60
Malini ⊙ RDC 196 Me49
Malkapur ⊙ IND 116 Oj35
Malkara ⊙ TR 69 Mg49
Malko Tarnovo ⊙ BG 69 Mg48
Mal'kovo ⊙ RUS 104 Qd20
Mali Lošinj ⊡ HR 61 Lp46
Malko Tarnovo ⊙ BG 69 Mg48
Malkangiri ⊙ IND 117 Pb36
Malkara ⊙ TR 69 Mg49
Mallaig ⊙ GB 48 Kp33
Mallanganee ⊙ AUS 149 Sg60
Mallari ⊡ TR 69 Mf49
Mallawi ⊙ ET 179 Mf32
Mallawi ⊙ ET 179 Mf32
Malle Cliffs N.P. ⊞ AUS 151 Sb63
Malli ⊙ RG 186 Ke40
Mallorca ⊡ E 57 Ld51
Mallorytown ⊙ CDN 240 Ga23
Mallow ⊙ IRL 47 Kn38
Mallwyd ⊙ GB 49 Kr38
Malm ⊡ N 38 Ll25
Malmbäck ⊙ S 43 Lp33
Malmedy ⊙ B 51 Lg40
Malmesbury ⊙ GB 49 Ks39
Malmköping ⊙ S 43 Lq31
Malmö ◉ S 43 Lo35
Malmyž ⊙ RUS 88 Nh07
Malnitz ⊡ A 61 Lo43
Maloarhangel'sk ⊙ RUS 72 Mj19
Maloca ⊙ BR 267 He45
Maloca do Gonçalo ⊙ BR 271 Hb49
Malokurir'skoe ⊙ RUS 111 Sd24
Malolo ⊡ FJI 159 Tj54
Malolo Plantation Lodge ⊡ PNG 155 Sc48
Malolos ⊙ RP 124 Ra38
Malolotja Nature Reserve ⊞ SD 205 Mf59
Malong ⊙ PNG 156 Sf47
Malonda ⊙ RDC 199 Mc50
Malone ⊙ USA 241 Gc23
Malong ⊙ CHN 121 Qb33
Malonga ⊙ RDC 199 Mb51
Malopolska ▣ PL 65 Ma40
Malorita ⊙ RDC 196 Md51
Malosa ⊙ S 43 Lc30
Malouzini ⊡ RDC 196 Md51
Malpas Hut ⊙ AUS 147 Sb55
Malpica de Bergantiños ⊡ E 54 Km47
Malpaso ⊙ MEX 246 Ej34
Málpils ⊙ LV 45 Me34
Malpura ⊙ IND 116 Oj33
Mals im Vinschgau = Mâlles Venosta ⊙ I 60 Ll44
Malta ⊡ I 63 Lp55
Malta ⊙ LV 45 Mh34
Malta ⊡ M 63 Lp55
Malta ⊙ USA 233 Eg21
Malta ⊙ USA 234 Eg28
Maltahöhe ⊙ NAM 204 Lj58
Maltam ⊙ CAM 189 Lh39
Maltahat ▲ 61 Lo44
Maltur ⊙ AUS 150 Rg62
Malton ⊙ GB 49 Ku36
Maluera ⊙ MOC 202 Mf53
Malu ⊙ CHN 108 Qd35
Malumfashi ⊙ WAN 188 Ld40
Malum Islands ▲ PNG 157 Sh47
Malundu ⊙ RI 130 Qk47
Malung ⊙ S 43 Lo30
Malungindi ⊙ RDC 196 Md51
Maluso ⊙ RP 125 Ra42
Maluszyn ⊙ PL 65 Lu40
Malut ⊙ SUD 185 Mf39
Maluti ⊙ LS 205 Md60
Maluti ▲ SUD 157 Ta50
Malvas ⊙ PE 269 Gb50
Malvern ⊙ USA 238 Fd28
Malwal ⊙ SUD 191 Md41
Malya ⊙ EAT 194 Mg47
Malyj Curásevo ⊙ RUS 72 Nd18
Malyj Enisej ⊡ RUS 105 Qj20
Malyj Naryn ⊡ KS 100 Oj25
Malyn ⊙ UA 72 Na18
Malyševa ⊙ RUS 105 Od23
Malyševo ⊙ RUS 72 Na18
Mały Płock ⊙ PL 65 Mb38
Mama ⊡ RUS 104 Qb19
Mâme Ana ⊡ BR 271 Hb48
Mama Hatun Türbesi ▲ TR 91 Na26
Mamalia ⊡ RN 280 Ga62
Mamalluapuram ⊙ IND 119 Ok39
Mamallapuram Beach ⊡ IND 119 Ok39
Mamana Island = Rum Cay ▲ BS 250 Gc34
Mamanguape ⊙ BR 273 Jc49
Mamanuca Group ⊡ FJI 159 Tj54
Mâmari ⊙ SN 180 Kd38
Mamasa ⊙ RI 130 Qk47
Mamase ⊙ EAT 196 Mh48
Mamba ⊙ EAT 196 Mh48
Mamberamo ⊡ RI 154 Rk46
Mamberamo Delta ⊡ RI 154 Rk46
Mamberamo-Foja Mountains-Routfaer Reserves ⊞ RI 154 Rk47
Mambi ⊙ YV 265 Gj43
Mambia ⊙ RG 186 Kd41
Mambili Mountains ▲ CAM/WAN 189 Lg42
Mambili Mountains ▲ CAM/WAN 189 Lg42
Mambima Falls ⊡ Z 196 Me51
Mambolo ⊙ WAL 186 Ke41
Mambore ⊙ BR 275 He57
Mambova ⊙ Z 201 Mc54
Mamburao ⊙ RP 124 Ra39
Mamburao ⊙ RP 124 Ra40
Mamewe ⊙ Z 196 Me51
Mamfe ⊙ CAM 188 Le43
Mami A.L. ⊙ WAN 201 Mb52
Mamia ⊙ IR 93 Ne30
Mamili N.P. ⊞ NAM 201 Mb54
Mamiru ⊡ EAT 197 Mk49
Mamiru ⊙ RDC 72 Nb19
Mamit ⊙ IND 120 Pg34
Mamit ⊙ IND 120 Pg34
Mamma Koz ⊙ IR 91 Nd28
Mamfe ⊙ RI 154 Rj47
Mamfe ⊙ CAM 188 Le43
Mamit ⊙ IND 120 Pg34
Mamit ⊙ IND 120 Pg34
Mamfe ⊙ CAM 188 Le43
Mamou ⊙ RG 186 Kd40
Mamoudzou ◉ F 206 Nc52
Mampikony ⊙ RM 206 Nd54
Mampode ⊙ Z 54 Kp47
Mampong ⊙ GH 187 Kk42
Mampong Range ▲ GH 187 Kk42
Mamshit ⊞ IL 92 Mh30
Mamu ⊙ WAN 188 Ld42
Mamudo ⊙ MOC 197 Na52
Mamue Choique ⊙ RA 280 Gf66
Mamul Malal, P. ⊞ RA/RCH 280 Ge65
Mamuju ⊙ RI 130 Qk47
Mamulique ⊙ MEX 245 Ek32
Mamun ⊙ RB 200 Ma57
Mamur Kalesi ▲ TR 90 Mg27
Mamurya Rock Paintings ⊞ IND 116 Oj33
Mamvu ⊙ RDC 191 Md45
Man ⊙ CI 187 Kg42
Man ⊙ IND 116 Oj36
Mana ⊙ USA 234 Ce29
Mâna ⊡ F 267 He43
Mana ⊙ USA 234 Ce29
Mana Camp ⊙ ZW 202 Me53
Manacapuru ⊙ BR 270 Gh48
Manacor ⊙ E 57 Ld51
Manado ◉ RI 131 Rb45
Manados ⊙ NIC 248 Fg39
Managua ◉ NIC 248 Fg39
Manaha ⊡ OM 95 Ne36
Manaíra ⊙ BR 273 Jb49
Manaira ⊙ BR 273 Ja49
Manajav ⊙ UA 67 Md42
Manak Chowk and Havelis (Jaisalmer) ⊞ IND 116 Of32
Manakara ⊙ RM 207 Ne56
Manambolosy ⊙ RM 206 Nd54
Manambondro ⊙ RM 207 Nd57
Manamensalo ⊡ FIN 39 Mh24

Manami ⊙ RI 154 Rh47
Manam Island ▲ PNG 155 Sc48
Manamoc Island ▲ RP 124 Ra40
Mananara Avaratra ⊙ RM 206 Ne54
Manandona ⊡ RM 207 Nd56
Manangatang ⊙ AUS 151 Sb63
Manangoora ⊙ AUS 146 Rj53
Mananjary ⊙ RM 207 Ne56
Manankoro ⊙ RMM 187 Kg40
Manantali ⊙ RMM 186 Ke39
Manantenina ⊡ RM 207 Nd58
Manantody ⊡ IND 118 Oj40
Manapari ⊙ IND 116 Oj40
Mana Pass ⊡ CHN/IND 102 Ok30
Manapiri ⊙ PE 269 Ge52
Manaquiri ⊙ BR 270 Gh48
Manarantsandry ⊡ RM 206 Nc54
Manaria ▲ BR 270 Gg48
Manari ⊙ PNG 155 Sd50
Manariá ⊙ BR 270 Gg48
Manasa ⊙ IND 116 Oj34
Manas He ⊡ CHN 101 Pc23
Manas Hu ⊡ CHN 101 Pc23
Manasarowar = Mapam Yumco ⊡ CHN 102 Pa30
Manasiquim ⊙ RUS 89 Nd31
Manaskent ⊙ RUS 91 Nf25
Manaslu ▲ NEP 115 Pc31
Manassas ⊙ USA 241 Ga26
Manas Tiger Reserve ⊞ IND 120 Pf32
Manas Tiger Reserve ⊞ IND 120 Pf32
Manastir Dečani ⊞▲ KSV 68 Ma48
Manastir Đurđevi Stupovi ⊞ MNE 68 Lu48
Mänästirea ▲ RO 69 Mj46
Mänästirea Cocoş ▲ RO 67 Me45
Mânästirea Curtea ▲ RO 67 Me45
Mänästirea Hurezi ▲ RO 68 Md46
Mänästirea Sinaia ▲ RO 69 Mf45
Manastirea Snagov ▲ RO 69 Mf46
Manastir Gracanica ⊞▲ KSV 68 Mb48
Manastir Kalenic ⊞ SRB 68 Ma47
Manastir Ljubostinja ⊞ SRB 68 Mb47
Manastir Manasija ⊞ SRB 68 Mb47
Manastir Mileseva ⊞ SRB 68 Lu47
Manastir Ostrog ⊞ MNE 68 Lu48
Manastir Ravanica ⊞ SRB 68 Mb47
Manastir Savina ⊞ MNE 68 Lt48
Manastir Sopoćani ⊞▲ SRB 68 Ma47
Manastir Studenica ⊞▲ SRB 68 Ma47
Manastir Žiča ▲ SRB 68 Ma47
Manati ⊡ KZ 101 Pb21
Manati ⊙ C 243 Ga34
Manatial ⊙ BOL 278 Gj55
Manatuto ⊙ TLS 131 Rc50
Manau ⊙ PNG 155 Sd50
Man'aung ⊙ MYA 120 Pg36
Manaure ⊙ CO 264 Gd40
Manaus ◉ BR 270 Gh48
Manavgat ⊙ TR 90 Mf27
Manawar ⊙ IND 116 Oh34
Manawoka ▲ RI 131 Rd48
Manay ⊙ RP 125 Rd42
Manayana Rock Paintings ⊞ RB 205 Mc58
Manba ⊙ CHN 121 Qa34
Manbazar ⊙ IND 117 Pd34
Manbij ⊙ SYR 90 Mj27
Mancha Khiri ⊙ THA 123 Qb37
Mancha Real ⊙ E 55 Kr53
Mancheng Hanmu Tombs ▲ CHN 107 Qh26
Manchester ⊙ GB 49 Ks37
Manchester ⊙ USA 236 Fe24
Manchester ⊙ USA 241 Gd25
Manchester ⊙ USA 241 Gd25
Manchester ⊙ USA 242 Fj27
Manchester Center ⊙ USA 241 Gd22
Manchhar Lake ⊡ PK 99 Od33
Manchilrayal ⊙ IND 117 Pa34
Manchok ⊙ WAN 188 Le41
Manchuria ⊡ CHN 76 Ra05
Manciano ⊡ I 60 Lm48
Mancos ⊙ USA 235 Ef27
Manda ⊙ PK 98 Ob32
Manda ⊙ RM 206 Nc54
Manda ⊙ IND 117 Pb35
Manda ⊙ TCH 190 Lk41
Manda ⊙ EAT 196 Mh51
Manda ▲ EAT 196 Mg50
Mandagadde Bird Sanctuary ⊞ IND 116 Oj38
Mandaguari ⊙ BR 274 He57
Mandai ⊙ PK 99 Oa34
Mandai ⊙ EAK 194 Mk47
Mandal ⊙ MNG 104 Qd21
Mandal ⊙ N 42 Lj32
Mandal ⊙ MYA 120 Pj34
Mandala, Puncak ▲ RI 239 Rk47
Mandalay ⊙ MNG 104 Qd23
Mandalgovi ⊙ MNG 107 Qf23
Mandali ⊙ IRQ 91 Nc29
Mandamari ⊙ IND 117 Pa34
Mandamabgwe ⊙ ZW 202 Md56
Mandan ⊙ USA 236 Fa22
Mandapam ⊙ IND 118 Ok41
Mandaqui ⊡ BR 274 He57
Mandar ⊙ RI 130 Qk47
Mandal ⊙ MNG 105 Qg22
Mandawela ⊡ CI 187 Kh42
Mandas ⊙ I 62 Lk51
Mandel ⊙ AFG 98 Oa29
Mandela ⊙ TCH 189 Lh40
Mandera ⊙ EAK 195 Na44
Manderscheid ⊙ D 59 Lh41
Mandeville ⊙ JA 250 Ga36
Mandheera ⊙ SP 193 Nc41
Mandi ⊙ IND 114 Oj30
Mandiacaze ⊙ MOC 203 Mh58
Mandiakuy ⊙ RMM 187 Kh39
Mandian ⊙ RMM 187 Kh39
Mandiana ⊙ RG 186 Kf40
Mandi Bahauddin ⊙ PK 99 Og29
Mandiba ⊙ BR 274 Hf57
Mandié ⊙ MOC 202 Mf54
Mandié ⊙ MOC 203 Mj54
Mandiji = Sangala ⊙ G 198 Lh46
Mandinga ⊙ PA 249 Ga41
Mandio ⊙ MOC 203 Mh53
Mandla ⊙ IND 117 Pa34
Mandor ⊙ RI 127 Qe45
Mandla ⊙ IND 117 Pa34
Mandoto ⊙ RM 207 Nd56
Mandoudi ⊙ GR 71 Me52
Mandra ⊙ GR 71 Me53
Mandra ⊙ RO 69 Me45
Mandraka ⊡ RM 207 Nd55
Mandritsara ⊙ RM 206 Ne54
Mandrosonoro ⊙ RM 207 Nd56
Mandú ⊙ IND 116 Oh34
Mandu ⊙ IND 117 Pc34
Mandurah ⊙ AUS 144 Qj61
Mandúria ⊙ I 63 Lt50
Mandvi ⊙ IND 116 Of34
Mandwa Beach ⊡ IND 116 Og36
Mandya ⊙ IND 117 Oj38
Maneadero ⊙ MEX 244 Eb31
Manegaon ⊙ IND 117 Ok34
Manchanbery ⊙ AUS 143 Rc56
Maneromango ⊙ EAT 197 Mk49
Maneroo ⊙ AUS 149 Sb57

Manevyči – Matsuzaka

Manevyči UA 65 Mf39
Manfalût ET 179 Mf32
Manfeilong CHN 121 Qa35
Manfred AUS 144 Qj59
Manfred Downs AUS 147 Sa56
Manfredónia I 63 Lq49
Manga BF 187 Kk40
Manga BR 275 Hj53
Manga CAM 189 Lg42
Manga PNG 156 Sg48
Mangada RDC 191 Md44
Mangada RDC 191 Me44
Manga Grande ANG 198 Lg49
Mangai EAK 195 Na46
Mangai PNG 156 Sf47
Mangai RDC 199 Lk48
Mangaïzé RN 182 La38
Mangalagiri IND 117 Pa37
Mangalia RO 69 Mj47
Mangalmé TCH 189 Lk39
Mangalore AUS 149 Sd59
Mangalore AUS 151 Sc64
Mangalore IND 118 Oh39
Mangalvedha IND 116 Oh37
Mangamaunu NZ 153 Tg67
Mangamila RM 207 Nd55
Mangango Z 201 Mc53
Manganti RI 127 Qa46
Mangaon IND 116 Og36
Mangarwar IND 116 Oh33
Mangawah IND 117 Pa33
Mangaweka NZ 153 Th65
Mangaweka NZ 153 Tj65
Mangchang CHN 108 Qd33
Mangdangshan CHN 112 Qj28
Mange PNG 155 Sd49
Mange WAL 186 Kd41
Mangen N 42 Lm31
Manggar RI 129 Qe47
Manggasi RI 154 Rj47
Manggopoh RI 127 Qa46
Mangho Pir PK 99 Od33
Manghystau KZ 96 Nf24
Manghystau shyghanaghy KZ 96 Nf23
Manghystau üstirti KZ 96 Ng24
Mangial IND 116 Oj36
Mangindrano RM 206 Ne53
Mang'it UZ 96 Oa24
Mangkururrpa A.L. AUS 143 Re56
Manglaralto EC 268 Fk46
Manglares CO 264 Gb43
Manglar Zapoton MEX 247 Fd38
Mangnai CHN 103 Pf27
Mangnai Zhen CHN 103 Pf26
Mangoaka RM 206 Ne52
Mangochi MW 203 Mh53
Mango Creek BH 248 Ff37
Mango Creek BH 248 Ff37
Mangoky RM 207 Nc56
Mangole RI 131 Rc46
Mangom CAM 189 Lg42
Mangombe RDC 191 Md46
Mangonui NZ 152 Tg63
Mangoudara BF 187 Kh41
Mangral IND 116 Of35
Mangrove Cay BS 243 Ga32
Mangrove Cay BS 243 Gb33
Mangrul Pir IND 116 Oj35
Mangshan CHN 107 Qg28
Mangualde P 54 Kn50
Manguchar PK 99 Od31
Mangueigne TCH 184 Ma40
Mangueira, T.I. BR 265 Gk44
Mangueirinha BR 276 Hd58
Manguel Creek AUS 142 Rb54
Mangui CHN 105 Rb19
Manguito C 243 Fk34
Mangum USA 238 Fa28
Mangungu RDC 198 Lj48
Mangunza Z 202 Md54
Mangut RUS 104 Qg21
Mangwe ZW 202 Mf55
Manhamade MOC 203 Mj54
Manhao CHN 121 Qb34
Manhattan USA 233 Ee23
Manhattan USA 238 Fb26
Manhica MOC 205 Mg58
Manhuaçu BR 275 Hj56
Manhumirim BR 275 Hk56
Manhup Kale UA 73 Mg23
Mani CO 264 Gd43
Máni GR 70 Mc54
Mani RDC 199 Mc49
Mani TCH 189 Lh39
Mani WAN 188 Ld39
Mania RM 207 Nd56
Maniago I 61 Ln44
Mania-Muna RDC 199 Mb50
Maniapure YV 265 Gg42
Manicaland ZW 202 Mf55
Manicani Island RP 124 Rc40
Manicoré BR 270 Gk48
Manicouagan CDN 240 Gf20
Manifah KSA 93 Ne32
Maniganggo CHN 103 Pk30
Manigotagan CDN 236 Fb20
Manihari IND 117 Pd33
Manika IND 117 Pc34
Manika RDC 201 Mc51
Manikganj BD 120 Pe34
Manikpur IND 117 Pa33
Manila RP 124 Ra38
Manila USA 235 Ef25
Manila Bay RP 124 Ra38
Manilaid EST 45 Me32
Manildra AUS 151 Se62
Manilla AUS 149 Sf61
Maningrida AUS 146 Rh52
Maninjau RI 127 Qa46
Manipa RI 131 Rd47
Manipur IND 120 Pg33
Manisa TR 71 Mh52
Manises E 57 Ku51
Manistee USA 237 Fg23
Manistique USA 237 Fg23
Manitisque Lake USA 237 Fh22
Manitoba CDN 227 Fa08
Manitou CDN 236 Fa21
Manitou CDN 240 Gh20
Manitou USA 238 Fa28
Manitou Lake CDN 236 Fd21
Manitoulin Island CDN 237 Fj23
Manitou Springs USA 235 Eh26
Manitouwadge CDN 237 Fh21
Manitowaning Lodge CDN 237 Fk23
Manitowish USA 236 Fe22
Manitowoc USA 237 Fg23
Manitsoq = Sukkertoppen DK 227 Hb05
Maniwaki CDN 241 Gc22
Maniwaki Ind. Res. CDN 237 Gb22
Maniwori RI 154 Rh47
Manizales CO 264 Gc43
Manja RM 207 Nc56
Manjakandriana RM 207 Nd55
Manjamba MOC 196 Mh52
Manjar Sumba IND 116 Oh36
Manjeri IND 118 Oj40
Manjhand PK 99 Oe33
Manjira Wildlife Sanctuary IND 117 Ok36
Manjira W.S. IND 116 Ok37
Manjlegaon IND 116 Oj36
Manjo CAM 188 Le43
Manjola ZW 202 Md54
Manjou CAM 189 Lg43
Mankachar IND 120 Pe33
Mankanza RDC 190 Lk45
Månkarbo S 43 Ls30
Man Kat MYA 121 Pk35
Mankato USA 236 Fd23
Mankato USA 238 Fa26
Mankera PK 99 Of30
Mankhan MNG 104 Qa20
Mankhan Nature Reserve MNG 101 Pg22
Manki CAM 189 Lf43
Mankim CAM 189 Lg43
Mankono CI 187 Kg41
Mankpan GH 187 Kk41
Mankrangso GH 187 Kk42
Mankulam CL 119 Pa41
Manley Hot Springs USA 229 Ce13
Man Li MYA 120 Pj34
Manlleu E 57 Lc49
Manmad IND 116 Oh35
Manna RI 127 Qb48
Manna Hill AUS 150 Rk62
Man-Namlet MYA 121 Pk34
Mannar CL 119 Ok41
Mannemkonda IND 117 Pa36
Manners Creek AUS 148 Rj57
Mannheim D 59 Lj41
Manni CHN 102 Pd28
Manning CDN 231 Eb17
Manning USA 233 Ej22
Manning USA 242 Fk29
Manning Prov. Park CDN 232 Dk21
Manning Range, Mount AUS 144 Qk60
Manningtree GB 49 Lb39
Mann Ranges AUS 145 Re58
Mannum AUS 150 Rk63
Mannville CDN 233 Ee19
Mano WAL 186 Kd41
Manoá Pium, T.I. BR 266 Gk44
Manogongu LB 186 Ke42
Manohardi BD 120 Pf33
Manokwari RI 154 Rh46
Manokwari RI 154 Rh47
Manole BG 69 Me48
Manolo Fortich RP 125 Rc41
Manombo Atsimo RM 207 Nb57
Manometimay RM 207 Nc56
Manompana RM 207 Ne54
Manono RDC 196 Md49
Manonwa RDC 199 Mc48
Manor IND 116 Og36
Manorhamilton IRL 47 Km36
Manori Beach IND 116 Og36
Manosque F 53 Lf47
Manou RCA 190 Ma41
Manouane CDN 240 Gc22
Manova WAL 186 Ke41
Manp'o PRK 110 Rd25
Manpur IND 117 Pa35
Manqabâd ET 179 Mf32
Manresa E 57 Lb49
Mansa IND 114 Oh31
Mansa Z 196 Me51
Mansabá GNB 186 Kc39
Mansa Konko WAG 186 Kc39
Mansalay RP 124 Ra39
Man Sam MYA 120 Pj34
Mansar IND 117 Ok35
Mansehra PK 99 Og28
Mansel Island CDN 227 Fd06
Mansfeld D 58 Lm39
Mansfield AUS 151 Sd64
Mansfield GB 49 Kt37
Mansfield USA 237 Fj25
Mansfield USA 238 Fc28
Mansfield USA 241 Gb25
Mansfield Jetty USA 245 Fb32
Mansfiled USA 238 Fd30
Mansi MYA 120 Ph33
Mansiari IND 115 Pa30
Mansidão BR 272 Hh51
Mansilla E 56 Kr48
Mansilla E 56 Ks48
Mansilla de las Mulas E 54 Kp48
Mansinha BR 272 Hg50
Mansión CR 249 Fh40
Mansle F 52 La45
Mansôa GNB 186 Kc39
Manson Creek CDN 230 Dh18
Manso-Nkwanta GH 187 Kk42
Mansoura DZ 176 Lc27
Mansourah DZ 175 Kk28
Mansur Abad IR 98 Ng31
Mansur Abad IR 98 Nk29
Mansura Ruins PK 99 Oe33
Manta DY 187 La40
Manta EC 268 Fk46
Mantadia-Andasibe, P.N.de RM 207 Ne55
Mantalinga RI 130 Ra47
Mantalingajan, Mount RP 128 Qj41
Mantamádos GR 71 Mg51
Mantanai Besar MAL 128 Qj42
Mantare EAT 194 Mg47
Mantasoa RM 207 Nd55
Mantawa RI 130 Rb46
Manteca USA 234 Dk27
Mantecal YV 265 Gf42
Mantecal YV 265 Gh42
Mantehage RI 125 Rc45
Mantena BR 275 Hk55
Mantes-la-Jolie F 51 Lb42
Mantes-la-Ville F 51 Lb42
Manthani IND 117 Ok36
Manthiréa GR 70 Mc53
Manti USA 235 Ee26
Manticao RP 125 Rc41
Manto HN 248 Fg38
Manto PE 269 Gd52
Mantorp S 43 Lq32
Mantos Blancos RCH 279 Ge57
Mántova I 60 Ll45
Mantralayam IND 116 Oj38
Mäntsälä FIN 44 Mf30
Mänttä FIN 44 Me28
Mantua C 243 Fh34
Mantuan Downs AUS 149 Sd58
Mantung AUS 150 Sa63
Mantup RI 129 Qg49
Mäntyharju FIN 44 Mg29
Mäntyluoto FIN 44 Mb29
Manu IND 120 Pg34
Manú PE 269 Ge52
Manu WAN 182 Lc39
Manubepium RI 154 Rh46
Manuel MEX 246 Fa34
Manuel Antonio, P.N. CR 249 Fh41
Manuel Benavides MEX 245 Ej31
Manuel Díaz ROU 276 Hc61
Manuel Emídio BR 272 Hj49
Manuel J.Cobo RA 281 Hb63
Manuel Ribas BR 276 He58
Manuel Tames C 250 Gc35
Manuel Urbano BR 270 Gf50
Manuel Vitorino BR 275 Hk53
Manui RI 131 Rb47
Manuk RI 131 Rf48
Manukan RP 125 Rb41
Manukau NZ 152 Th64
Manunda AUS 150 Rk62
Manunga Z 196 Me50
Manunui NZ 153 Th65
Manú, P.N. PE 269 Ge52
Manur IND 116 Oh36
Manusela RI 131 Re47
Manusela N.P. RI 131 Re47
Manus Island PNG 156 Sd46
Manvi IND 116 Oj38
Manville USA 235 Eh24
Manweng MYA 120 Pj34
Many USA 238 Fd30
Manyallaluk A.L. AUS 146 Rg53
Manyani EAK 195 Mk47
Manyapadu IND 116 Oj38
Manyas TR 69 Mh50
Manyberries CDN 233 Ee21
Manych Depression RUS 26 Na05
Manyelanong Game Reserve RB 205 Mc58
Manyeleti Game Reserve ZA 205 Mf58
Manyémen CAM 188 Le43
Many Farms USA 235 Ef27
Manyikeni MOC 203 Mh57
Manyinga Z 201 Mc52
Manyo EAT 196 Mf49
Manyoni EAT 196 Mh48
Manypeaks AUS 144 Qk63
Manzai PK 99 Oe30
Manzai PK 99 Of29
Manzanares CO 264 Gc43
Manzanares E 55 Kr52
Manzanilla Beach TT 251 Gk40
Manzanillo C 243 Gb35
Manzanillo MEX 246 Eh36
Manzengele RDC 199 Lj49
Manzhouli CHN 105 Qj21
Manzil PK 99 Ob31
Manzini SD 205 Mf59
Manzshir Monastery MNG 104 Qd22
Manzurka RUS 104 Qd19
Mao DOM 250 Ge36
Maó E 57 Le51
Mao EAT 196 Mf50
Mao TCH 183 Lh38
Maocaojie CHN 108 Qg31
Mao'ershan CHN 110 Rd23
Maogong CHN 108 Qe32
Maohutang CHN 108 Qf30
Maojing CHN 106 Qd27
Maokeng ZA 205 Md59
Mao Ling CHN 106 Qe28
Maoming CHN 108 Qf35
Maope RB 202 Md57
Maopora RI 131 Rd49
Mao Xian CHN 106 Qb30
Mapagoro EAT 196 Mg50
Mapai MOC 202 Mf57
Mapamoiwa PNG 156 Sf50
Mapam Yumco CHN 102 Pa30
Mapanda RDC 199 Mc50
Mapane RI 130 Ra46
Mapangu RDC 199 Ma48
Mapanza Z 202 Md54
Mapastepec MEX 247 Fd38
Mapat RI 128 Qj44
Mapati RCB 198 Lg47
Mapé RCA 190 Mb43
Mapelane Nature Reserve ZA 205 Mg60
Maphisa ZW 202 Me56
Mapi RI 154 Rk49
Mapili RI 130 Qk47
Mapinhane MOC 203 Mh57
Mapire YV 265 Gh42
Mapiri BOL 278 Gf53
Mapiripán CO 264 Gd44
Maple Creek CDN 233 Ef21
Maple Ridge CDN 232 Dj21
Maplesville USA 239 Fg29
Mapleton USA 236 Fc24
Mapoon AUS 147 Sa52
Mapoon A.L. AUS 147 Sb51
Mapor RI 127 Qc45
Mapor Beach RI 127 Qc45
Mapuera BR 266 Hb46
Mapulanguene MOC 205 Mg58
Mapunga Z 201 Md52
Mapungubwe ZA 202 Me57
Mapungubwe (Vhembe-Dongola) N.P. ZA 202 Me57
Mapusa IND 116 Og38
Maputi RI 125 Qk45
Maputo MOC 205 Mg58
Maqên CHN 106 Qa28
Maqna KSA 92 Mh31
Maqrat YE 95 Nf38
Maqteïr RIM 180 Ke35
Maqu CHN 106 Qb29
Maquecha MOC 202 Mg56
Maqueda E 55 Kq50
Maquela do Zombo ANG 198 Lh49
Maqueze MOC 205 Mg58
Maquinchao RA 280 Gf66
Maquinista Levet RA 280 Gg62
Maquoketa USA 236 Fe24
Mara GUY 266 Hb42
Mara IND 117 Pb34
Mara ZA 202 Me57
Maraã BR 270 Gh46
Maraa Urubaxi, T.I. BR 270 Gh46
Marabá BR 272 Hf48
Marabadiassa CI 187 Kh41
Marabahan RI 129 Qh47
Marabidiyah IRQ 91 Nb29
Marabitanas BR 265 Gg45
Marabout Moulay Hassan DZ 182 Lc33
Marabouts TN 176 Ld29
Maracá BR 267 He44
Maracaçumé BR 267 Hh47
Maracaí BR 274 He57
Maracaibo YV 264 Ge40
Maracaju BR 274 Hc56
Maracanã BR 267 Hg46
Maracanã BR 267 Hj47
Maracanã BR 271 Ha49
Maracanaú BR 273 Ja47
Maracás BR 273 Hk52
Maracas Beach TT 251 Gk40
Maracay YV 265 Gg40
Maracoa CO 265 Gf44
Maradah LAR 177 Lk31
Maradankadawala CL 119 Pa41
Maradi RN 182 Ld39
Maradun WAN 188 Ld39
Marafa EAK 195 Mk47
Marafa Depression (Hell's Kitchen) EAK 195 Mk47
Maragheh IR 91 Nd27
Maragogi BR 273 Jc50
Maragogipe BR 273 Ja52
Marah KSA 93 Nc33
Marahoue, P.N.de la CI 187 Kg42
Marais Poitevin F 52 Kt44
Marais Salants F 50 Ks43
Marais Vernier F 50 La41
Maraiwatsede, T.I. BR 272 He51
Marajai, T.I. BR 270 Gh47
Maraka RN 182 Ld39
Marakabei LS 205 Me60
Marakele N.P. ZA 205 Md58
Marakesa RDC 191 Md45
Marakhayy YE 95 Nf38
Marakkanam IND 119 Ok39
Maraku WAN 188 Le40
Maralal EAK 194 Mj45
Maralal Nature Sanctuary EAK 194 Mj45
Maraldy KZ 101 Pc21
Marale HN 248 Fg38
Marali RCA 190 Lk42
Maralinga AUS 145 Rf61
Maralinga Tjarutja A.L. AUS 145 Rf60
Maramag RP 125 Rc42
Maramasike SOL 157 Ta50
Marambio 287 Ha31
Maran MAL 126 Qb44
Marana USA 235 Ee29
Maranalgo AUS 144 Qj60
Marand IR 91 Nc26
Marandala CI 187 Kh41
Marandet RN 182 Ld37
Maranello I 60 Ll46
Marang MAL 126 Qb43
Marango AUS 149 Sd59
Maranguape BR 273 Ja47
Maranhão BR 271 Hb47
Maranhão BR 274 Hf53
Maranhão BR 255 Hb10
Maranhoto BR 270 Gj47
Marañón PE 268 Gc48
Marans F 52 Ku44
Maranura PE 269 Gd52
Marapanim BR 267 Hg46
Marapi BR 266 Hb45
Mara Rosa BR 272 Hf52
Marasende RI 130 Qk48
Mărășești RO 73 Md23
Mărașu RO 69 Mh46
Marat UZ 97 Oc24
Marataízes BR 275 Hk56
Maratea I 63 Lq50
Marathon AUS 147 Sb56
Marathon CDN 237 Fg21
Marathon USA 243 Fk33
Marathon USA 245 Ej30
Marathónas GR 69 Md52
Maratua RI 125 Qk44
Maraú BR 275 Ja53
Marau BR 276 Hd60
Maraudeur F 266 Hd44
Maravatío de Ocampo MEX 246 Ek36
Maravilha BR 271 Gk47
Maravilha BR 276 Hd59
Maravilhas BR 275 Hh55
Maravilla BOL 270 Gg51
Marawah LAR 177 Ma29
Marawaka PNG 155 Sc49
Marawi RP 125 Rc41
Marawi SUD 185 Mf36
Maraxo Patá BR 266 Hb45
Marayes RA 280 Gg61
Marayoun RL 90 Mh29
Mar'ayt YE 95 Nf37
Marazion GB 49 Kp40
Marbach D 59 Lk42
Marbella E 55 Kq54
Marble Bar AUS 142 Qk56
Marble Bar Road AUS 142 Ra56
Marble Canyon USA 235 Ee27
Marble Hall ZA 205 Me58
Marble Hill USA 239 Ff27
Marble Point 287 Tb34
Marburg D 58 Lj40
Marcabelí EC 268 Ga47
Marcala HN 248 Fg38
Marcali H 66 Ls44
Marcaltő H 66 Ls43
Marčana HR 61 Lo46
Marcapata PE 269 Ge52
Marcapomacocha PE 269 Gb51
Marcelândia BR 271 Hc51
Marcelino BR 265 Gg45
Marcelino BR 270 Gg46
Marcell USA 236 Fd22
Marcelo BR 267 He47
March GB 49 La38
Marchagee AUS 144 Qj61
Marche I 61 Lo47
Marche-en-Famenne B 51 Lf40
Marchena E 55 Kp53
Marchenoir F 52 Lb43
Marchinbar Island AUS 146 Rj51
Marciac F 52 La47
Marcigny F 53 Le44
Marcilla RP 124 Ra39
Marcillac-la-Croisille F 52 Lc45
Marcinkonys LT 45 Me36
Marcinkowice PL 65 Ma41
Marcionílio Sousa BR 273 Hk52
Marck F 51 Lb40
Marco USA 243 Fk33
Marco de Canaveses P 54 Km49
Marconi N.H.S. CDN 240 Ha22
Marco Rondon BR 278 Gk52
Marcos Juárez RA 281 Gj62
Marcos Parente BR 272 Hj49
Marcoux USA 236 Fb22
Marcus Baker, Mount USA 229 Cg15
Mard Abad IR 91 Nf28
Mardan PK 99 Og28
Mar de Ajó RA 281 Hb64
Mar de Espanha BR 275 Hj56
Mar del Plata RA 281 Hb65
Mardie AUS 142 Qh56
Mardie Island AUS 142 Qh56
Mardin TR 91 Na27
Mardin Dağları TR 91 Na27
Maré F 158 Te56
Mare RI 130 Ra48
Marea del Portillo C 243 Gb36
Mare aux Crocodiles de Dounkou BF 187 Kj39
Mare aux Crocodiles de Sabou BF 187 Kj39
Marechal Cândido Rondon BR 276 Hc58
Marechal Deodoro BR 273 Jc50
Maree AUS 148 Rk60
Mareeba AUS 147 Sc54
Mareeq SP 195 Nd44
Maremma I 60 Lm48
Maréna RMM 180 Ke38
Marenge RDC 196 Me48
Marengo USA 236 Fd25
Marengo Cave USA 239 Fg26
Marennes F 52 Kt45
Marerano RM 207 Nc56
Mareth TN 176 Lf29
Mareuil-sur-Lay F 52 Kt44
Marevo RUS 72 Mg17
Marfa M 63 Lp55
Marfa USA 245 Eh30
Margao IND 116 Og38
Margaree Forks CDN 240 Gk22
Margaret AUS 148 Sb59
Margareteville USA 241 Gc24
Margaret, Mount AUS 142 Qj57
Margaret River AUS 144 Qh62
Margarida BR 274 Hb56
Margarima PNG 155 Sb49
Margaríti GR 70 Ma51
Margaritove RUS 73 Mk22
Margasari RI 129 Qh47
Margate GB 49 Lb39
Margate ZA 205 Mf61
Mărgău RO 67 Mc44
Margecany SK 67 Mb42
Margherita IND 120 Ph32
Margherita di Savóia I 63 Lr49
Marghita RO 67 Mc43
Margiana TM 96 Oa26
Marg'ilon UZ 97 Of25
Margone I 60 Lh45
Margonin PL 64 Ls38
Margosatubig RP 125 Rb42
Marguerite CDN 232 Dj19
Margyang CHN 102 Pe31
Marhamat UZ 97 Og25
Marhanec' UA 73 Mh22
Marhoum DZ 175 Kk28
Mari BR 270 Gh49
Mari PNG 155 Sa50
Mari SYR 91 Na28
Maria BR 267 Hf46
Maria MOC 203 Mj54
Maria PE 268 Gb49
Maria Aurora RP 124 Ra38
María Elena RCH 279 Gf57
María Eugenia RA 279 Gk61
Mariager DK 42 Lk34
Mariahan IND 117 Pb33
María Ignacia RA 281 Ha64
Maria Island AUS 146 Rh53
Maria Island N.P. AUS 151 Se67
Mariakani EAK 195 Mk47
Maria Laach D 59 Lh40
Mariala N.P. AUS 149 Sc59
Marialva P 54 Kn50
Maria, Mount GB 283 Ha71
Marian AUS 149 Se56
Mariana BOL 278 Gj55
Mariana BR 275 Hj56
Mariana Islands 134 Sa08
Mariana Trench 134 Sa08
Mariani IND 120 Ph32
Marianna USA 239 Fe28
Marianna USA 239 Fh30
Mariannelund S 43 Lq33
Mariano I.Loza RA 276 Ha60
Marianópolis BR 272 Hh48
Mariánské Lázně CZ 66 Ln41
Mariarano RM 206 Nd53
Maria Saal A 61 Lp44
Maria Teresa ANG 198 Lh50
María Teresa RA 281 Gk63
Mariazell A 61 Lq43
Ma'rib YE 94 Nc38
Maribo DK 42 Lm36
Maribor SLO 66 Lq44
Maribou Mountains CDN 231 Eb16
Maricá BR 277 Hj57
Maricaban Island RP 124 Ra39
Marical Caceres PE 269 Gc52
Maricao USA 251 Gg36
Maridi SUD 191 Me43
Marie Byrd Land ANT 287 Ed34
Mariefred S 43 Ls31
Marie-Galante F 251 Gk38
Mariehamn = Maarianhamina FIN 44 Lu30
Mariel C 243 Fj34
Mari-El RUS 72 Ne17
Marielyst DK 42 Lm36
Marienberg D 59 Lo40
Mariental NAM 204 Lj58
Mariés GR 69 Me50
Mariestad S 43 Lo32
Marieta YV 265 Gg43
Marietta USA 239 Fh29
Marietta USA 239 Fk26
Mariga WAN 188 Lc40
Marigat EAK 194 Mh45
Marignane F 53 Lf47
Marigot F 251 Gj36
Marigot RH 250 Gd36
Marigot WD 251 Gk38
Marihatag RP 125 Rd41
Marija Bistrica HR 61 Lr44
Marijampolė LT 45 Md36
Marikal IND 116 Oj37
Marikina RP 124 Ra38
Marília BR 274 Hf57
Marimba ANG 198 Lj50
Marín E 54 Km48
Marina di Belvedere I 63 Lq51
Marina di Carrara I 60 Ll46
Marina di Cetraro I 63 Lq51
Marina di Grosseto I 60 Ll48
Marina di Léuca I 63 Lt51
Marina di Pisa I 60 Ll47
Marina di Ragusa I 63 Lp54
Marina di Ravenna I 60 Ln46
Marina Plains AUS 147 Sb53
Mariñas E 54 Kn47
Marinduque Island RP 124 Ra39
Marine de Sisco F 60 Lk48
Marineland USA 242 Fk31
Marineland of Florida USA 242 Fk31
Marinella I 62 Ln53
Marineo I 62 Lo53
Mariner Glacier 287 Tb33
Marinette USA 237 Fg23
Maringá BR 274 He57
Maringa RDC 190 Ma45
Maringué MOC 203 Mh54
Maringues F 53 Ld45
Marinha Grande P 55 Km51
Marinho de Fernando de Noronha, P.N. BR 273 Jd47
Marinho dos Abrolhos, P.N. BR 275 Ja55
Marinka BG 69 Mh48
Marino de Punta Francés-Punta Pedernales, P.N. C 243 Fj35
Marino de Vallarta, P.N. MEX 246 Eh35
Marino Golfo de Chiriquí, P.N. PA 249 Fj41
Marino Isla Bastimentos, P.N. PA 249 Fk41
Marino Las Baulas, P.N. CR 248 Fh40
Marion USA 236 Fe24
Marion USA 237 Fh25
Marion USA 237 Fj25
Marion USA 238 Fb26
Marion USA 239 Fe28
Marion USA 239 Ff27
Marion USA 239 Ff27
Marion USA 239 Fg29
Marion USA 242 Fk27
Marion USA 242 Fk28
Marion USA 242 Ga28
Marion Downs AUS 148 Rk57
Maripasoula F 266 Hd44
Maripipi Island RP 124 Rc40
Mariposa USA 234 Ea27
Mariposa Monarca MEX 246 Ek36
Mariquita CO 264 Gc43
Marisa RI 125 Ra45
Mariscala ROU 281 Hc63
Mariscal José Félix Estigarribia PY 279 Gk56
Mariscos GCA 248 Ff38
Marita Downs AUS 149 Sb57
Maritime Alps F 53 Lg46
Maritime Museum (Geraldton) AUS 144 Qh60
Mariupol' UA 73 Mj22
Mariusa, P.N. YV 265 Gj41
Marivan IR 91 Nd28
Mariveles RP 124 Ra38
Mariveles Reef 128 Qg42
Märjamaa EST 44 Me32
Marka SP 195 Nc45
Markabougou RMM 187 Kg39
Markabygd N 40 Lm27
Markakasa IND 117 Pa35
Markakol Nature Reserve KZ 101 Pc21
Markala RMM 187 Kg39
Markapur IND 117 Ok38
Markaryd S 43 Lo34
Marken ZA 202 Me57
Markermeer NL 51 Lf38
Market Drayton GB 49 Ks38
Market Harborough GB 49 Ku38
Market Rasen GB 49 Ku37
Market Weighton GB 49 Ku37
Markham CDN 237 Ga24
Markham, Mount 287 Tb35
Markhun PK 114 Oh27
Marki PL 65 Mb38
Markik IND 116 Ok37
Markit CHN 100 Oj26
Markivka UA 72 Mk21
Markkleeberg D 58 Ln39
Markópoulo GR 69 Md53
Markounda RCA 190 Lj42
Markovo BG 69 Mh47
Markoy BF 181 Kk38
Marks USA 239 Fe28
Marksewo PL 65 Mb37
Marksville USA 239 Fe30
Marktheidenfeld D 59 Lk41
Markt Indersdorf D 59 Lm42
Marktoberdorf D 59 Ll43
Marktredwitz D 59 Ln40
Mark Twain Birthplace S.H.S USA 238 Fd26
Mark Twain Boyhood Home & Museum USA 239 Fe26
Mark Twain National Forest USA 239 Fe27
Mark Twain N.W.R. USA 239 Fe25
Mark Twain N.W.R. USA 239 Fe26
Mark Twain S.P. USA 239 Fe26
Markundi SUD 184 Mb40
Markwassie ZA 205 Md59
Marl D 58 Lh39
Marla AUS 148 Rg59
Marlborough AUS 149 Se57
Marlborough GB 49 Kt39
Marlborough GUY 266 Ha42
Marlborough Sounds NZ 153 Th66
Marle F 51 Ld41
Marlin USA 238 Fb30
Marlinton USA 239 Fk26
Marl Island PNG 155 Sc46
Marlo AUS 151 Se64
Marloth Nature Reserve ZA 204 Ma62
Marlow GB 49 Ku39
Marlow USA 238 Fb28
Marma S 43 Ls30
Marmande F 52 La46
Marmara TR 69 Mh50
Marmara Adası TR 69 Mh50
Marmaraereglisi TR 69 Mh50
Marmara Gölü TR 71 Mj52
Marmaris TR 71 Mj54
Mármaro GR 71 Mg52
Mar Menor E 57 Ku53
Mármol MEX 244 Eg34
Marmolada I 60 Lm44
Marmot Island USA 228 Ce16
Marmul OM 95 Nh36
Marnay F 53 Lf43
Marne D 58 Lk37
Marneuli GE 91 Nc25
Marniu IND 120 Ph32
Maro TCH 190 Lk41
Maroa YV 265 Gg44
Maroantsetra RM 206 Ne53
Marobi Raghza PK 99 Oe29
Marod IND 117 Pa35
Maroda IND 117 Pa36
Marofandilia RM 207 Nc56
Maroharatra RM 207 Nd56
Marojejy, P.N.de RM 206 Ne53
Marol 115 Oj28
Marolambo RM 207 Ne56
Maromandia RM 206 Ne53
Maromandia RM 206 Nf53
Maromokotro RM 206 Ne53
Marondera ZW 202 Mf55
Maronga AUS 149 Se59
Marongora ZW 202 Me54
Maroni F 266 Hc43
Maroochydore AUS 149 Sg59
Maroona AUS 151 Sb64
Maroonah AUS 142 Qh57
Maropaika RM 207 Nd57
Maros RI 130 Ra48
Maroseranana RM 207 Ne55
Marotandrano RM 206 Ne54
Marotolana RM 206 Ne53
Marotta I 61 Lo47
Maroua CAM 189 Lh40
Marova BR 270 Gj46
Marovac SRB 68 Mb48
Marovato RM 206 Ne52
Marovato RM 206 Ne53
Marovato RM 207 Nc58
Marovoay RM 206 Nd54
Marowo RI 130 Ra46
Marqadeh Gharbiyeh SYR 91 Na28
Marqua AUS 148 Rj57
Marquard ZA 205 Md60
Marquelia MEX 246 Fa37
Marquesas Keys USA 243 Fj33
Marquette USA 237 Fg22
Marquez USA 238 Fb30
Marquise F 51 Lb40
Marquq SUD 191 Mf41
Marra A.L. AUS 146 Rh53
Marracua MOC 203 Mj54
Marracuene MOC 205 Mg58
Marradi I 60 Lm46
Marradong AUS 144 Qj62
Marrak KSA 94 Na37
Marrakech MA 175 Kf30
Marrakush MA 175 Kf30
Marrawah AUS 151 Sc66
Marrecão BR 270 Gg49
Marrecas, T.I. BR 276 He58
Marrero USA 239 Fe31
Marromeu MOC 203 Mh55
Marron AUS 144 Qh58
Marrupa MOC 197 Mj52
Marsa Alam ET 179 Mh33
Marsa-Ben-Mehidi DZ 175 Kj28
Marsabit EAK 194 Mj44
Marsabit National Reserve EAK 194 Mk44
Marsa Darur SUD 185 Mj36
Marsa Delwein SUD 179 Mj35
Marsala I 62 Ln53
Marsa Matruh ET 178 Md30
Marsa Mubârak ET 179 Mh33
Marsa Salak SUD 185 Mj35
Marsa Shin'ab SUD 179 Mj35
Marsassoum SN 186 Kc39
Maršavicy RUS 45 Mj33
Mars Bay BS 243 Gb34
Marsberg D 58 Lj39
Marsciano I 60 Ln48
Marsden AUS 151 Sd62
Marseille F 53 Lf47
Marseille-en-Beauvaisis F 51 Lb41
Marsella CO 264 Gc43
Marsella PE 268 Gc47
Marsga al Burayqah LAR 177 Lk30
Marshall LB 186 Ke42
Marshall USA 228 Bj15
Marshall USA 236 Fc23
Marshall USA 237 Fh24
Marshall USA 238 Fc29
Marshall USA 238 Fd26
Marshall USA 238 Fd28
Marshall USA 242 Fj28
Marshall Islands 134 Ta08
Marshall Islands 135 Ta08
Marshalltown USA 236 Fd24
Marshfield USA 236 Fe23
Marshfield USA 238 Fd27
Marsh Harbour BS 243 Gb32
Mars Hill USA 240 Gg22
Marsh Island USA 239 Fe31
Mársico Nuovo I 63 Lq50
Marsoui CDN 240 Gg21
Märsta S 43 Ls31
Marstal DK 42 Ll36
Marstrand S 42 Lm33
Martaban MYA 122 Pj37
Martap CAM 189 Lg42
Martapura RI 127 Qc48
Martapura RI 129 Qh47
Marte WAN 189 Lg39
Martelange B 51 Lf41
Marten River CDN 237 Ga22
Martensøya N 38 Ma05
Martfű H 67 Ma43
Mártha GR 71 Mf55
Martha's Vineyard USA 241 Ge25
Martigné-Ferchaud F 50 Kt43
Martigny CH 60 Lh44
Martigues F 53 Lf47
Martil MA 175 Kh28
Martilla FIN 44 Mc30
Martin SK 67 Lt41
Martin USA 236 Ek24
Martin USA 239 Ff27
Martina Franca I 63 Ls50
Martinborough NZ 153 Th66
Martinésia BR 274 Hf55
Martínez de la Torre MEX 246 Fb35
Martinho Campos BR 275 Hh55
Martinique F 251 Gk38
Martinique Channel 251 Gk38
Martinópole BR 273 Hk47
Martinópolis BR 274 He57
Martinsburg USA 241 Ga26
Martinšćica HR 61 Lp46
Martin's Drift RB 202 Md57
Martinsicuro I 61 Lo48
Martinsville USA 239 Fg26
Martinsville USA 242 Ga27
Martins Well AUS 148 Rk61
Martna EST 44 Md32
Marton NZ 153 Th66
Martorell E 57 Lb49
Martos E 55 Kr53
Martti FIN 39 Mj23
Martuni ARM 91 Nc25
Maru IND 122 Pg41
Maru RI 131 Rf49
Maru WAN 188 Ld39
Maruanum BR 267 He45
Marudá BR 267 Hg46
Marudi MAL 128 Qh43
Maruf AFG 99 Od30
Marulan AUS 151 Se63
Marum, Mount VU 158 Te54
Marungu EAT 196 Mf48
Marungua EAK 194 Mj46
Maru'ura SOL 157 Ta50
Marvanthe Beach IND 118 Oh39
Marvão P 55 Kn51
Marv Dasht IR 98 Ng31
Marve Beach IND 116 Og36
Marvejols F 53 Ld46
Marvell USA 239 Fe28
Marvik N 42 Lg31
Marvine, Mount USA 235 Ee26
Marvo Lagoon SOL 157 Sk50
Marvyn USA 239 Fh29
Marwah AFG 98 Ob28
Marwan KSA 94 Nd34
Marwayne CDN 233 Ee19
Marwick Head GB 48 Kr31
Mary TM 96 Oa27
Maryal Bai SUD 191 Md41
Mary Anne Group AUS 142 Qh56
Mary Anne Passage AUS 142 Qh56
Maryborough AUS 149 Sg58
Maryborough AUS 151 Sb64
Marydale ZA 204 Mb60
Maryhill USA 232 Dk23
Mary Kathleen uranium deposit AUS 147 Rk56
Maryland USA 241 Gb26
Mary Moffat's Museum ZA 204 Mb60
Maryport GB 48 Kr36
Marystown CDN 241 Hc22
Marysville USA 234 Dk26
Marysville USA 237 Fj25
Marysville USA 238 Fb26
Maryvale AUS 147 Sc55
Maryvale AUS 148 Rh58
Maryville USA 242 Fj28
Marzad MNG 104 Qb23
Marzagão BR 274 Hf54
Marzan Abad IR 91 Nf27
Marzuq LAR 177 Lg33
Masagua GCA 248 Fe38
Masa guara HN 248 Fg38
Masahunga EAT 194 Mg47
Masai-Mbia RDC 198 Lj47
Masai Steppe EAT 197 Mj48
Masaka EAU 194 Mf46
Masaki EAT 197 Mk49
Masalembo besar RI 129 Qh48
Masalembo kecil RI 129 Qh48
Masalima RI 130 Qj48
Masalli AZ 91 Ne26
Masamba RI 130 Ra47
Masan ROK 113 Re28
Masanga RDC 199 Mb46
Masanjor IND 117 Pd33
Masapi RI 130 Ra46
Masapun RI 131 Rd49
Masara EAK 194 Mh46
Masasi EAT 197 Mk51
Masaurhi IND 117 Pc33
Masawa RI 130 Qk47
Masaya NIC 248 Fg40
Masaya, P.N., Volcán NIC 248 Fg39
Masbate RP 124 Rb39
Masbate RP 124 Rb39
Mascara DZ 175 La28
Mascarene Basin 162 Nb11
Mascarene Islands 207 Nh56
Mascarene Plain 162 Nb12
Mascareños MEX 246 Fb35
Masconi RA 281 Gk63
Mascota MEX 246 Eh35
Mas de las Matas E 57 Ku50
Masegoso de Tajuña E 57 Ks50
Masela RI 131 Re50
Masenberg A 61 Lq43
Maseru LS 205 Md60
Mashabih KSA 92 Mj33
Mashala RDC 199 Mb48
Mashan CHN 108 Qe34
Mashar SUD 191 Md41
Mashatu Game Reserve RB 202 Me57
Mashava ZW 202 Mf56
Mashhad IR 96 Nk27
Mashhad IR 96 Oa27
Mashi CHN 108 Qf31
Mashi ETH 192 Mh42
Mashike J 111 Sa24
Mashki Chah PK 98 Ob31
Mashonaland East ZW 202 Mf55
Mashonaland Central ZW 202 Mf54
Mashonaland West ZW 202 Me54
Mashra' ar-Raqq SUD 191 Me41
Masia RDC 198 Lj47
Masiaca MEX 244 Ef32
Masiaka WAL 186 Kd41
Masian RI 154 Rh49
Masigo EAT 196 Mf49
Masi-Manimba RDC 199 Lj48
Masimbu RI 130 Qk46
Masin RI 130 Rb48
Masindi EAU 194 Mf45
Masindi Port EAU 194 Mg45
Masinga Reservoir EAK 194 Mj46
Masingbi WAL 186 Ke41
Masinloc RP 124 Qk38
Masirah OM 95 Nk35
Masirah Channel OM 95 Nk35
Masiri IR 93 Nf30
Masis ARM 91 Nc25
Masisea PE 269 Gc50
Masisi RDC 191 Me46
Masisi ZA 202 Mf57
Masjed-e-Abolfazi IR 98 Nk31
Masjed Negar AFG 99 Oc28
Masjed Soleyman IR 93 Ne30
Masjid Basar RI 126 Pk44
Masjid-e-Jame IR 91 Nc26
Masjid-e-Jami IR 93 Nf29
Masjid-i-Jami (Herat) AFG 98 Ob28
Masjid Zahir MAL 126 Qa42
Maskall BH 248 Ff37
Maskall BH 248 Ff37
Maskana Minaret SYR 90 Mk28
Maski IND 116 Oj38
Masku FIN 44 Mc30
Masmak Fort KSA 93 Nd33
Masoala, P.N.d' RM 206 Nf53
Masoarivo RM 207 Nc55
Masokut RI 127 Pk46
Masomeloka RM 207 Ne56
Mason USA 237 Fh24
Mason USA 238 Fa30
Mason City USA 236 Fd24
Masoni RI 131 Rc46
Maspalomas E 174 Kc32
Masparrito YV 264 Ge41
Masqat OM 95 Nk34
Masrakh IND 117 Pc32
Massa I 60 Ll46
Massaango ANG 198 Lj50
Massachusetts USA 241 Gd24
Massachusetts Bay USA 241 Ge24
Massacre Canyon Mon. USA 238 Ek25
Massada IL 92 Mh30
Massafra I 63 Ls50
Massaguet TCH 189 Lh39
Massakory TCH 189 Lh39
Massala CI 187 Kg42
Massala G 198 Lf47
Massalassef TCH 189 Lj40
Massama WAN 188 Ld39
Massa Marittima I 60 Ll47
Massamba MOC 202 Mg53
Massambará BR 276 Hb60
Massangam CAM 189 Lf43
Massangano ANG 198 Lh50
Massangena MOC 202 Mg56
Massangulo MOC 203 Mh52
Massano MOC 203 Mh53
Massantola RMM 187 Kg39
Massapê BR 273 Hk47
Massaranduba BR 277 Hf59
Massat F 52 Lb48
Massau ANG 198 Lj49
Massawa ER 192 Mk38
Massena USA 241 Gc23
Massenya TCH 189 Lj40
Masset CDN 230 Dd18
Masseube F 52 La47
Massey CDN 237 Fj22
Massiac F 53 Ld45
Massibi ANG 201 Mb51
Massif Central F 53 Ld45
Massif d'Abo TCH 183 Lh35
Massif d'Atafi RN 183 Lh34
Massif de Dahra DZ 176 La27
Massif de l' Adamaoua CAM 189 Lh42
Massif de l'Adrar DZ 182 Ld33
Massif de l'Adrar RIM 180 Ke35
Massif de l'Aurès DZ 176 Ld28
Massif de la Vanoise F 53 Lg45
Massif de l'Esterel F 53 Lg47
Massif de l'Ouarsenis DZ 176 La28
Massif des Maures F 53 Lg47
Massif de Taghouaji RN 182 Le37
Massif de Tchingou F 158 Tc56
Massif de Termit RN 183 Lf37
Massif du Humboldt F 158 Td56
Massif du Kapka TCH 184 Ma38
Massif du Manengouba CAM 188 Le43
Massif du Sud ou de la Hotte RH 250 Gc36
Massif du Tamqué RG 186 Kd39
Massif du Yadé RCA 190 Lh42
Massif Tabulaire F 266 Hd44
Massigui RMM 187 Kg40
Massillon USA 237 Fk25
Massin RP 124 Rb40
Massina RMM 181 Kh38
Massina RMM 181 Kh38
Massinga MOC 203 Mh57
Massingir MOC 202 Mg57
Massosse ANG 200 Lj53
Mastabah KSA 92 Mk35
Masterton NZ 153 Th66
Mastic Beach USA 241 Gd25
Mastic Point BS 243 Gb33
Mastihári GR 71 Mh54
Mastuj PK 97 Og27
Mastung PK 99 Od31
Masturah KSA 92 Mk34
Masty BY 65 Me37
Masuda J 113 Rf28
Masud Palace AFG 99 Oe29
Masugnsbyn S 39 Mc23
Masuguru EAT 197 Mk51
Masuika RDC 199 Mb49
Mašuki BY 65 Mg38
Masuleh IR 91 Ne27
Masulipatnam IND 117 Pa37
Masurai, Gunung RI 127 Qa47
Masuria PL 65 Ma37
Masvingo ZW 202 Mf56
Masvingo ZW 202 Mf56
Maswa Game Reserve EAT 194 Mh47
Mata RDC 199 Ma49
Matabaie RDC 199 Mb49
Matabeleland North ZW 202 Md55
Matabeleland South ZW 202 Me56
Matabele Plain Z 201 Mb54
Mata Bia, Gunung TLS 131 Rd50
Matabis ZW 202 Mf56
Mataca MOC 197 Mj52
Matachewan CDN 237 Fk22
Matacú BOL 278 Gj54
Mata de Palma YV 264 Ge42
Mata de São João BR 273 Ja52
Matadi RDC 198 Lg48
Mata do Buçaco P 54 Km50
Matador USA 238 Ek28
Mataga ZW 202 Mf56
Matagalpa NIC 248 Fh39
Matagami CDN 237 Gb21
Matagorda USA 245 Fb31
Matagorda USA 245 Fc31
Matagorda Island USA 245 Fb31
Matagorda Peninsula USA 245 Fc31
Matagorda S.P. USA 245 Fc31
Mata Grande BR 273 Jb50
Matagua C 243 Fk34
Mataj KZ 100 Ok23
Matak RI 126 Qd44
Matakana Island NZ 152 Tj64
Matakaoa Point NZ 152 Tk64
Matakawa NZ 152 Th64
Matakohe NZ 152 Th64
Matala ANG 200 Lh53
Mátala GR 71 Me56
Matalam RP 125 Rc42
Mata Lama EAK 195 Mk44
Matalaque PE 269 Ge54
Matale CL 119 Pa42
Matam SN 180 Kd38
Matamagallanes RA 282 Gf68
Matamala de Almazán E 56 Ks49
Matamata BR 270 Gg48
Mata Mata ZA 204 Ma58
Matambo EAT 197 Mj49
Matamey RN 182 Le39
Matamoros MEX 245 Ej33
Matamoros MEX 245 Fb33
Mat'an KSA 94 Nb37
Matanana EAT 196 Mh50
Matanao RP 125 Rc42
Ma'tan as Sarah LAR 178 Ma35
Ma'tan Bishrah LAR 178 Mb34
Matanda Z 196 Me51
Matandu EAT 197 Mj50
Matane CDN 240 Gg21
Mata Negra YV 265 Gj41
Matanga RI 131 Rb46
Matanga RM 207 Nd57
Matanhi PK 99 Of29
Mataniko Falls SOL 157 Ta50
Matankari RN 182 Lc39
Matanuska Glacier USA 229 Cg15
Matanzas C 243 Fk34
Matanzas YV 265 Gj41
Matão BR 274 Hf56
Mataoleo RI 131 Rb48
Matapédia CDN 240 Gg22
Matara CL 119 Pa43
Matara ER 192 Mk38
Matará RA 279 Gj60
Mataraca BR 273 Jc49
Mataral BOL 278 Gh55
Mataram RI 130 Qj50
Mataranka AUS 146 Rg53
Mata Redonda MEX 246 Fb36
Mataró E 57 Lc49
Mata Roma BR 273 Hj47
Matarombeo Mountains RI 130 Ra47
Matassi EAT 197 Mj49
Matatiele ZA 205 Me61
Mataupa PNG 156 Sf50
Matausu RI 130 Ra48
Mata-Uta F 135 Ba11
Mataveni CO 265 Gg43
Matawai NZ 153 Tj65
Matây ET 179 Mf31
Matayaya DOM 250 Ge36
Matching Green GB 49 La39
Matechai ANG 200 Ma51
Mated IND 117 Ok37
Mategua BOL 278 Gj52
Matehuala MEX 246 Ek34
Mateiros BR 272 Hg51
Matélica I 61 Lo47
Matelot TT 251 Gk40
Matema EAT 196 Mh50
Matema MOC 202 Mg53
Matera I 63 Lr50
Matéri DY 187 La40
Mátészalka H 67 Mc43
Matete RDC 191 Md45
Matetsi ZW 201 Mc55
Mateur TN 176 Le27
Matewar RI 154 Rk46
Matha F 52 Ku45
Mathahaw Pt. CDN 232 Dg21
Matheniko Game Reserve EAU 194 Mh44
Matheson CDN 237 Fk21
Mathews Range EAK 194 Mj45
Mathilde RA 281 Gk61
Mathis USA 245 Fb31
Mathiston USA 239 Ff29
Mathoura AUS 151 Sc63
Mathráki GR 70 Lu51
Mathura IND 115 Oj32
Mati RP 125 Rd42
Matiakoali BF 187 La39
Matiari PK 99 Oe33
Matías Cardoso BR 275 Hj53
Matias Olímpio BR 273 Hj47
Matías Romero MEX 247 Fc37
Matibane MOC 203 Na53
Matienzo 287 Ha32
Matima RB 201 Mc56
Matina CR 249 Fj40
Matinha BR 267 Hh47
Matinhos BR 277 Hf58
Matīši LV 45 Mf33
Matisi Shiku CHN 103 Pk26
Matjiesfontein ZA 204 Ma62
Matkasel'kja RUS 44 Ml29
Matkuli IND 117 Ok34
Matlapaneng RB 201 Mb55
Matli PK 99 Oe33
Matlock GB 49 Kt37
Matmata RIM 180 Kd36
Matmata TN 176 Le29
Matna SUD 185 Mh39
Matnog RP 124 Rc39
Matobo Hills ZW 202 Me56
Matobo N.P. (Rhodes Matopos N.P.) ZW 202 Me56
Matões BR 273 Hj48
Mato Grosso BR 255 Ha11
Mato Grosso do Sul BR 255 Ha11
Matola MOC 205 Mg58
Matomondo EAT 196 Mh51
Matondo MOC 203 Mh55
Matongo EAT 196 Mh48
Matope MW 203 Mh53
Matopos ZW 202 Me56
Matosinhos P 54 Km49
Matou CHN 109 Qh31
Matoury F 267 Hd43
Mato Verde BR 275 Hj53
Mátra H 67 Lu43
Matraca CO 265 Gf44
Mátraháza H 67 Lu43
Matras Beach RI 129 Qd46
Matrei A 61 Ln44
Matroosberg ZA 204 Lk62
Matrouha TN 176 Ld29
Matru WAL 186 Kd42
Matrubah LAR 178 Mb29
Matsai ZW 202 Mf56
Matsanga RCB 198 Lg46
Matsari CAM 189 Lg43
Matsieng Footprints RB 205 Mc58
Matsoandakana RM 206 Ne53
Matsue J 113 Rg28
Matsu Lietao RC 109 Ra32
Matsumae J 111 Sa25
Matsumoto J 113 Rj27
Matsu Temple RC 109 Ra34
Matsuyama J 113 Rg29
Matsuzaka J 113 Rj28

Midnapore ◻ IND 117 Pd34
Midongy Atsimo ◻ RM 207 Nd57
Midsayap ◻ RP 125 Rc42
Midsund ◻ N 40 Lg28
Midu ◻ CHN 121 Qa33
Midutura ◻ IND 116 Ok38
Midway ◻ CDN 232 Ea21
Midway ◻ USA 235 Eh29
Midway ◻ USA 239 Fg30
Midway Islands ▲ USA 135 Ba07
Midway Range ▲ CDN 232 Ea21
Midwest ◻ USA 233 Eg24
Midwest City ◻ USA 238 Fb28
Midyat ◻ TR 91 Na27
Midyobo ◻ GQ 188 Lf45
Miechów ◻ PL 65 Ma40
Miedźno ◻ PL 64 Lt40
Międzychód ◻ PL 64 Lq38
Międzylesie ◻ PL 64 Lr40
Międzyrzec Podlaski ◻ PL 65 Mc39
Międzyrzecz ◻ PL 64 Lq38
Międzywodzie ◻ ≋ PL 64 Lp36
Międzyzdroje ◻ PL 64 Lp37
Miehikkälä ◻ FIN 44 Mh30
Miélan ◻ F 52 La47
Mielec ◻ PL 65 Mb40
Miélékouka ◻ RCB 190 Lh45
Miena ◻ AUS 151 Sd66
Mier ◻ MEX 245 Fa32
Miercurea-Ciuc ◻ RO 73 Mc22
Miercurea Sibiului ◻ RO 68 Md45
Mieres ◻ E 54 Kp47
Mierzeja Helska ▲ ≋ PL 64 Lt36
Mierzeja Wiślana ★ PL/RUS 65 Lu36
Miesbach ◻ D 59 Lm43
Mieszków ◻ PL 64 Ls38
Mieszkowice ◻ PL 64 Lp38
Mietoinen ◻ FIN 44 Mb30
Miette Hot Springs ◻ CDN 232 Eb19
Mifol ◻ AL 70 Lu50
Mifulu ◻ EAT 196 Mf48
Migdol ◻ ZA 205 Mc59
Migennes ◻ F 53 Ld43
Miging ◻ IND 120 Ph31
Migliónico ◻ I 63 Lr50
Mi Gong Ci ★ CHN 107 Qg30
Migori ◻ EAK 194 Mh46
Migre ◻ SUD 185 Mh38
Migriño ◻ MEX 244 Ee34
Miguasha, P.N. de ■ ★ CDN 240 Gg21
Miguel Alves ◻ BR 273 Hj48
Miguel Calmon ◻ BR 273 Hk51
Miguel Cané ◻ RA 281 Gj64
Miguelópolis ◻ BR 274 Hf56
Miguel Riglos ◻ RA 281 Gj64
Mihăeşti ◻ RO 69 Me46
Mihail Kogălniceanu ◻ RO 69 Mj46
Mihajlov ◻ RUS 72 Mk18
Mihajlovka ◻ RUS 72 Nb20
Mihajlovka ◻ RUS 104 Qc20
Mihajlovka ◻ RUS 110 Rg24
Mihajlovo ◻ BG 68 Md47
Mihajlovo ◻ BG 69 Mf48
Mihalkovo ◻ BG 69 Me49
Miheşu de Câmpie ◻ RO 67 Me44
Mihintale ◻ ▲ CL 119 Pa41
Mihnevo ◻ RUS 72 Mj18
Mihona ◻ IND 117 Ok32
Mijdahah ◻ YE 94 Ne38
Mijek ◻ DARS 180 Kd34
Mi-jima ▲ J 113 Rf28
Mikamiene ◻ EAT 197 Mk48
Mikasa ◻ J 111 Sa24
Mikaševičy ◻ BY 72 Md19
Mikaszówka ◻ PL 65 Md37
Mikata ◻ EAT 197 Mj49
Miķeltornis ◻ LV 45 Mc33
Mikindani ◻ EAT 197 Na51
Mikir Hills ▲ IND 120 Pg32
Mikkeli ◻ FIN 44 Mh29
Miknas ◻ ☐ ★ MA 175 Kh29
Mikołajki ◻ PL 65 Mb37
Mikolongo ◻ MW 203 Mh54
Mikołów ◻ PL 65 Lt40
Míkonos ≋ ★ ★ GR 71 Mf53
Míkonos ◻ ★ GR 71 Mf53
Mikouyi ◻ G 198 Lg46
Mikre ◻ BG 69 Me47
Mikulčice ★ CZ 66 Ls42
Mikulov ◻ ★ CZ 66 Lr42
Mikumi ◻ EAT 197 Mj49
Mikumi N.P. ★ EAT 197 Mj49
Mikum-sanmyaku ▲ J 111 Rk27
Mikuni ◻ J 113 Rj27
Mikura-jima ▲ J 113 Rk29
Mila ◻ DZ 176 Ld27
Milaca ◻ USA 236 Fd23
Miladinovci ◻ MK 68 Mb49
Milagres ◻ BR 273 Ja49
Milagres ◻ BR 273 Ja52
Milagro ◻ E 56 Kt48
Milagro ◻ EC 268 Ga47
Milagro ◻ RA 280 Gh61
Milagros ◻ RP 124 Rb39
Miłakowo ◻ PL 65 Ma36
Milala ◻ EAT 197 Mk50
Milam ◻ USA 238 Fd30
Milam Glacier ★ IND 115 Pa30
Milam Glacier ★ IND 115 Pa30
Milan ◉ ★ ★ I 60 Lk45
Milan ◻ USA 238 Fd25
Milan ◻ USA 239 Ff28
Milando ◻ ANG 199 Lj50
Milang ◻ AUS 150 Rk63
Milange ◻ MOC 203 Mh54
Milange ◻ RDC 196 Md47
Milano ◻ USA 238 Fb30
Milanoa ◻ RM 206 Ne52
Milanówek ◻ PL 65 Ma38
Milas ◻ TR 71 Mh53
Milavidy ◻ BY 65 Mf38
Milazzo ◻ I 63 Lq52
Milbana ◻ MOC 203 Mk53
Milbank ◻ USA 236 Fb23
Milden ◻ CDN 233 Eg20
Mildred ◻ USA 233 Eh22
Mildura ◻ AUS 150 Sb63
Mile ◻ CHN 121 Qb33
Mile ◻ ETH 192 Na40
Miléa ◻ GR 70 Mb51
Milepa ◻ MOC 197 Mj51
Miles ◻ AUS 149 Sf59
Miles City ◻ USA 233 Eh22
Mile Serdo Reserve ★ ETH 192 Na40
Mileševo ◻ SRB 68 Lu45
Mi'leso ◻ ETH 192 Na41
Milestone ◻ CDN 233 Eh20
Milestone ◻ IRL 47 Km38
Milet ★ TR 71 Mh53
Mileto ◻ I 63 Lr52
Mileura ◻ AUS 144 Qj59
Milevsko ◻ CZ 66 Lp41
Milford ◻ GB 49 Ku39
Milford ◻ USA 235 Ed26
Milford ◻ USA 241 Gc26
Milford ◻ USA 241 Gd25
Milford Haven ◻ GB 49 Kp39
Milford Sound ★ NZ 153 Td68
Milford Sound ◻ NZ 153 Td68
Milgarra ◻ AUS 147 Sa55
Milgun ◻ AUS 144 Qk58
Miliana ◻ DZ 176 Lb27
Milići ◻ BIH 68 Lu46
Milicz ◻ PL 64 Ls39
Milikapiti ◻ AUS 146 Rf51
Milín ◻ CZ 66 Lp41
Miling ◻ AUS 144 Qj61
Milingimbi ◻ AUS 146 Rh52
Militello ◻ ☐ ★ I 63 Lp53
Milítsa ◻ GR 70 Mb54
Milla Milla ◻ AUS 147 Sc54
Milla Milla Falls ★ AUS 147 Sc54
Millaroo ◻ AUS 147 Sd56
Millas ◻ F 52 Lc48
Millau ◻ F 53 Ld46
Mill City ◻ USA 232 Dj23
Milledgeville ◻ USA 242 Fj29
Millen ◻ USA 242 Fk29
Miller ◻ USA 236 Fa23
Miller ◻ USA 238 Fa25
Miller ◻ ZA 205 Mb62
Miller, Mount ▲ USA 230 Cj15
Miller, Mount ▲ 287 Tb35
Millerovo ◻ RUS 72 Na21
Millersburg ◻ USA 237 Fk25
Millerton ◻ USA 238 Fc29
Millerton ◻ USA 241 Gd25
Millertown ◻ CDN 241 Hb21
Millican ◻ USA 232 Dk24
Millicent ◻ AUS 150 Sa64
Milligan Hills ▲ CDN 231 Dk17
Millijiddie A.L. ★ AUS 143 Rc55
Millington ◻ USA 239 Ff28
Millinocket ◻ USA 240 Gf23
Million Dollar Point ★ VU 158 Td53
Millmerran ◻ AUS 149 Sf59
Millom ◻ GB 49 Kr36
Millport ◻ USA 239 Ff29
Millrose ◻ AUS 144 Ra59
Mills Lake ◻ CDN 231 Ea15
Millstätter See ★ A 61 Lo44
Millstone ◻ USA 239 Fk26
Millstream-Chichester N.P. ★ ★ ★ AUS 142 Qj56
Milltown ◻ CDN 241 Hc22
Milltown Malbay ◻ IRL 47 Kl38
Millungera ◻ AUS 147 Sa55
Millville ◻ USA 241 Gc26
Millwood S.P. ★ USA 238 Fd29
Milly Milly ◻ AUS 144 Qj59
Milmersdorf ◻ D 58 Lo37
Milna ◻ HR 61 Lr47
Milnerton ◻ ZA 204 Lk62
Milnesand ◻ USA 238 Ej29
Milo ≈ RG 186 Kf40
Milos ★ ★ GR 71 Me54
Milos ◻ ★ GR 71 Me54
Milot ◻ AL 68 Lu49
Milot ◻ RH 250 Gd36
Milówka ◻ PL 65 Lu41
Milparinka ◻ AUS 148 Sa60
Milpillas de la Sierra ◻ MEX 246 Ej34
Milpitas ◻ USA 234 Dk27
Miltenberg ◻ D 59 Lk41
Milton ◻ CDN 240 Gh23
Milton ◻ NZ 153 Te69
Milton ◻ USA 239 Fg30
Milton Brandão ◻ BR 273 Hk48
Milton Freewater ◻ USA 232 Ea23
Milton Keynes ◻ GB 49 Ku38
Miltou ◻ TCH 189 Lj40
Miluo ◻ CHN 109 Qg31
Milwaukee ◻ USA 237 Fg24
Milwaukee deep ★ 251 Gg36
Milwaukie ◻ USA 232 Dj23
Mimbelly ◻ RCB 190 Lj44
Mimili ◻ AUS 145 Rg59
Mimizan ◻ F 52 Kt46
Mimoň ◻ CZ 66 Lp40
Mimongo ◻ G 198 Lf46
Mimosa Rocks N.P. ★ AUS 151 Se64
Mimoso ◻ BR 274 Hd56
Mimoso do Oeste ◻ BR 272 Hb52
Mimpoutou ◻ RCB 190 Lj44
Mimyj ◻ RUS 89 Qc06
Mina, Cerro ▲ CO 264 Gd41
Mina ◻ MEX 245 Ek33
Mina ◻ USA 234 Ea26
Mina Ahmadi ◻ KWT 93 Ne31
Mina Algarrobo ◻ RCH 279 Ge60
Minab ◻ IR 98 Nj32
Mina Carbón Peket ◻ RCH 282 Ge72
Mina Clavero ◻ RA 280 Gh61
Minaçu ◻ BR 272 Hf52
Mina de São Domingos ◻ P 55 Kn53
Mina Djebel Ali ◻ UAE 95 Nh33
Minahasa ▲ RI 125 Rb45
Mina Incahuasi ◻ RA 279 Gg58
Minaki ◻ CDN 236 Fc21
Mina la Casualidad ◻ RA 279 Gf58
Minami Alps N.P. ★ J 113 Rk28
Minamikayabe ◻ J 111 Sa25
Minami-Tane ◻ J 113 Rf30
Minamurra ★ AUS 151 Sf63
Mina Pirquitas ◻ RA 279 Gg57
Minaret Mosque ★ RI 129 Qf49
Minaret of Jam ☐ ★ AFG 99 Oc28
Minas ◻ C 243 Gb35
Minas ◻ RI 127 Qa45
Minas ◻ ROU 281 Hc63
Mina Saud ◻ KWT 93 Ne31
Minas de Barroterán ◻ MEX 245 Ek32
Minas de Corrales ◻ ROU 276 Hc61
Minas de Matahambre ◻ C 243 Fh34
Minas Gerais ★ BR 255 Hb11
Minas Novas ◻ BR 275 Hj54
Minatitlán ◻ MEX 246 Eh36
Minatitlán ◻ MEX 247 Fc37
Minaya ◻ E 57 Ks51
Minbu ◻ MYA 120 Ph35
Min Buri ◻ THA 122 Qa39
Minbyar ◻ MYA 120 Pg35
Minchika ◻ WAN 189 Lg40
Minchinabad ◻ PK 99 Og30
Mincivan ◻ AZ 91 Nd26
Mindanao ▲ RP 125 Rd42
Mindanao Sea ≈ RP 124 Rc41
Mindelheim ◻ D 59 Ll42
Mindelo ◻ ★ ★ CV 186 Jh37
Minden ◻ D 58 Lj38
Minden ◻ USA 238 Fa25
Minden ◻ USA 238 Fd29
Minderoo ◻ AUS 142 Qh56
Mindif ◻ CAM 189 Lh40
Mindik ◻ PNG 155 Sd49
Mindiptana ◻ RI 155 Sa48
Mindjik ◻ TCH 184 Ma40
Mindo ◻ EC 268 Ga46
Mindon ◻ MYA 120 Ph36
Mindoro ▲ RP 124 Ra39
Mindoro Strait ≈ RP 124 Ra39
Mindouli ◻ RCB 198 Lh48
Mindourou ◻ CAM 189 Lg44
Minduri ◻ BR 275 Hh56
Mine ◻ J 113 Re28
Mine ◻ J 113 Rf28
Mine Center ◻ CDN 236 Fd21
Minehead ◻ GB 49 Kr39
Mine Head ▲ IRL 47 Kn39
Mineiros ◻ BR 274 Hd54
Mineral ◻ USA 234 Dk25
Mineral de Cucharas ◻ MEX 245 Eh34
Mineral del Chico ◻ MEX 246 Fa35
Mineral de Pozos ◻ MEX 246 Ek35
Mineral Hot Springs ◻ USA 235 Eh26
Mineral'nye Vody ◻ RUS 91 Nb23
Mineral Springs ★ ZA 202 Mf57
Mineral Water Spring ★ MNG 104 Qc22
Mineral Water Springs ★ MNG 104 Qe23
Mineral Wells ◻ USA 238 Fa29
Miners' Memorial ★ ZA 204 Lj60
Miners' Mus. ★ CDN 240 Gh23
Minersville ◻ USA 235 Ed26
Minervino Murge ◻ I 63 Lr49
Minfeng ◻ CHN 102 Pb27
Minga ◻ RDC 196 Md51
Minga ◻ Z 202 Mf53
Mingala ◻ RCA 190 Ma43
Mingan ◻ CDN 240 Gh20
Minganja ◻ ANG 200 Ma52
Mingao ◻ CO 265 Gg44
Mingary ◻ AUS 150 Sa62
Mingbuloq ◻ UZ 96 Ob24
Mingbuloq botig'i ≈ UZ 96 Ob24
Mingeçevir ◻ AZ 91 Nd25
Mingela ◻ AUS 147 Sd55
Mingenew ◻ AUS 144 Qh60
Minggang ◻ CHN 107 Qh29
Minghoshan ◻ CHN 101 Ph25
Mingin ◻ MYA 120 Ph34
Mingin Taung ▲ MYA 120 Ph33
Minglanilla ◻ E 57 Kt51
Ming Ming ◻ PNG 155 Sd48
Mingo N.W.R. ★ USA 239 Fe27
Mingora ◻ PK 97 Og28
Mingorria ◻ E 55 Kq50
Mingoyo ◻ EAT 197 Mk51
Mingshashan ★ CHN 103 Ph26
Mingshui ◻ CHN 110 Rc22
Ming Tombs ☐ ★ CHN 107 Qj25
Mingue ◻ CAM 189 Lg43
Mingulay ▲ GB 48 Kn34
Minguri = Nacala Velha ◻ MOC 203 Na53
Mingxi ◻ CHN 109 Qj32
Minhe Huizu Tuzu Zizhixian ◻ CHN 106 Qb27
Minhla ◻ MYA 120 Ph36
Minhla ◻ MYA 122 Ph37
Minho ▲ P 54 Km49
Miničevo ◻ SRB 68 Mc47
Minicoy Island ★ ★ ★ IND 118 Og41
Minidoka ◻ USA 232 Ed24
Minignan ◻ CI 186 Kg41
Minilya Roadhouse ◻ AUS 144 Qh57
Minimarg ◻ 114 Oh28
Mining Hall of Fame (Kalgoorlie) ★ AUS 144 Ra61
Mining Hall of Fame (Tennant Creek) ★ AUS 146 Rh55
Miniota ◻ CDN 236 Ek20
Mini Park ★ RI 129 Qd49
Ministro Ramos Mexia ◻ RA 280 Gg66
Minjilang ◻ AUS 146 Rg51
Minkébé, P.N.de ★ ★ G 189 Lg45
Minlaton ◻ AUS 150 Rj63
Minle ◻ CHN 106 Qa26
Minmaya ◻ J 111 Sa25
Minna ◻ WAN 188 Ld41
Minna Bluff ▲ 287 Tc34
Minneapolis ◻ USA 236 Fd23
Minneapolis ◻ USA 238 Fb26
Minnedosa ◻ CDN 236 Fa20
Minneola ◻ USA 238 Fa27
Minnesota ◻ USA 236 Fb22
Minnewaukan ◻ USA 236 Fa21
Minnie Downs ◻ AUS 149 Sc58
Minnies ◻ AUS 147 Sb54
Minnipa ◻ AUS 150 Rh62
Minong ◻ USA 236 Fe22
Minority Village ★ CHN 121 Qb33
Minot ◻ USA 236 Ek21
Minqin ◻ CHN 106 Qb26
Minqing ◻ CHN 109 Qk32
Minquan ◻ CHN 107 Qh28
Min Shan ▲ CHN 106 Qb29
Minsk ● BY 45 Mh37
Mińsk Mazowiecki ◻ PL 65 Mb38
Minta ◻ CAM 189 Lg43
Mintable ◻ AUS 148 Rg59
Mintaqat Umm Khuwayt ▲ LAR 178 Mb30
Minter City ◻ USA 239 Fe29
Mintlaw ◻ GB 48 Ks33
Minto ◻ CDN 230 Db14
Minto ◻ CDN 236 Ek21
Mintom II ◻ CAM 189 Lg44
Minto, Mount ▲ 287 Tc33
Minton ◻ CDN 233 Eh21
Minturno ◻ I 62 Lo49
Minu Dašt ◻ IR 96 Nh27
Minvoul ◻ G 189 Lg44
Minwakh ◻ YE 94 Ne37
Min Xian ◻ CHN 106 Qb28
Mio ◻ USA 237 Fh23
Miomo ◻ F 60 Lk48
Mionica ◻ SRB 68 Ma46
Mioveni ◻ RO 69 Me46
Miquelon ◻ CDN 237 Gb21
Miquelon ◻ F 241 Hb22
Miquihuana ◻ MEX 246 Fa34
Mira ◻ E 57 Kt51
Mira ◻ I 60 Ln45
Mira ◻ P 54 Km50
Mir Abad ◻ IR 98 Oa31
Mirabel ◻ CDN 241 Gc23
Mirabela ◻ BR 275 Hh54
Miracatu ◻ BR 277 Hg58
Miracema ◻ BR 275 Hj56
Miracema do Tocantins ◻ BR 272 Hf50
Miracosta ◻ PE 268 Ga49
Mirador ◻ BR 268 Gd48
Mirador ◻ BR 272 Hh49
Mirador- Dos Lagunas- Río Azul, P.N. ★ GCA 247 Ff37
Mirador, P.N. de ★ BR 272 Hh49
Mira Estrela ◻ BR 274 He55
Miraflores ◻ BR 270 Gh47
Miraflores ◻ CO 264 Gd43
Miraflores ◻ CO 264 Ge45
Miraflores ◻ RA 279 Gk58
Miragoâne ◻ RH 250 Gd36
Miraí ◻ BR 275 Hj56
Miraj ◻ IND 116 Oh37
Miramar ◻ BR 271 Gk48
Miramar ◻ MEX 246 Eh36
Miramar ◻ ★ RA 281 Gj61
Miramar ◻ ★ ★ RA 281 Hb65
Miramas ◻ F 53 Le47
Mirambeau ◻ F 52 Ku45
Miramichi ◻ CDN 240 Gh22
Miramichi Bay ≈ CDN 240 Gh22
Miramont-de-Guyenne ◻ F 52 La46
Miram Shah ◻ PK 99 Oe29
Miran ◻ ▲ CHN 101 Pe26
Miran ◻ PK 99 Of30
Miranda ◻ BR 274 Hb56
Miranda ◻ MOC 196 Mh52
Miranda de Ebro ◻ E 56 Ks48
Miranda do Douro ◻ P 54 Ko49
Miranda do Norte ◻ BR 272 Hh47
Miranda Downs ◻ AUS 147 Sa54
Mirande ◻ F 52 La47
Mirandela ◻ P 54 Kn49
Mirandiba ◻ BR 273 Ja50
Mirándola ◻ I 60 Lm46
Mirandópolis ◻ BR 274 He56
Mirandópolis ◻ BR 275 Hk53
Mirani ◻ AUS 149 Se56
Mirani ★ OM 95 Nk34
Miranle da Sura ◻ BR 270 Gj51
Mirano ◻ I 60 Ln45
Miranorte ◻ BR 272 Hf50
Mirante ◻ BR 275 Hk53
Mirante do Paranapanema ◻ BR 274 Hd57
Mirapo ◻ PNG 155 Sd50
Miraporanga ◻ BR 274 Hf55
Mira-por-vos Cays ▲ BS 250 Gc34
Mira-por-vos Passage ≈ BS 250 Gc34
Mirassol ◻ BR 274 Hf56
Mirassol d'Oeste ◻ BR 278 Ha53
Miratu, T.I. ★ BR 270 Gh47
Miravalles ▲ E 54 Ko48
Mir Bachech Kowt ◻ AFG 99 Oe28
Mirbat ◻ OM 95 Nh37
Mircze ◻ PL 65 Md40
Mirebalais ◻ RH 250 Gd36
Mirebeau ◻ F 52 La44
Mirebeau-sur-Bèze ◻ F 53 Lf43
Mirecourt ◻ F 51 Lg42
Mirepoix ◻ F 52 Lb47
Mirgani ◻ IND 117 Pc32
Miri ◻ MAL 128 Qg43
Miria ◻ RN 182 Le39
Mirialguda ◻ IND 117 Ok37
Miriam Vale ◻ AUS 149 Sf58
Mirikata ◻ AUS 148 Rh60
Mirima National Park ★ AUS 143 Re53
Mirina ◻ ★ GR 71 Mf51
Mirina Kástro ★ GR 71 Mf51
Mirinzal ◻ BR 267 Hh47
Mir Javeh ◻ IR 98 Oa31
Mirleft ◻ ★ ★ MA 174 Ke31
Mir Mövsum Ağa ★ AZ 91 Ne26
Mirnyj ◻ 287 Pc32
Miroč ▲ SRB 68 Mc46
Mirogi ◻ EAK 194 Mh46
Mirong ◻ CHN 121 Qb34
Mirool ◻ AUS 151 Sd63
Mirosławiec ◻ PL 64 Lr37
Mirotice ◻ CZ 66 Lp41
Mirovice ◻ CZ 66 Lp41
Mirow ◻ D 58 Ln37
Mirpur Batoro ◻ PK 99 Oe33
Mirpur Khas ◻ PK 99 Oe33
Mirpur Mathelo ◻ PK 99 Oe31
Mirpur Sakro ◻ PK 99 Od33
Mirrote ◻ MOC 203 Mk52
Mirrow ◻ CDN 233 Ed19
Mirsale ◻ SP 195 Nd43
Mirski zamak ☐ ★ BY 65 Mg37
Mirtna ◻ AUS 149 Sd56
Mirtóon Sea ≈ GR 71 Md53
Mirtos ◻ GR 71 Mf55
Miruro ◻ MOC 202 Mf53
Mirzapur ◻ IND 117 Pb33
Mirzapur Hills ▲ IND 117 Pb33
Misahualli ◻ EC 268 Gb46
Misaki ◻ EAT 196 Mh48
Misaki ◻ J 113 Rg29
Misaki ◻ J 113 Rh28
Misantla ◻ MEX 246 Fb36
Misau ◻ WAN 188 Lf40
Misawa ◻ J 111 Sa25
Mischii ◻ RO 68 Md46
Miscou Centre ◻ CDN 240 Gh22
Misele ◻ RDC 199 Lj48
Misery, Mount ▲ NZ 153 Tf67
Mishaleyi ◻ CHN 100 Pa26
Mishamo ◻ EAT 196 Mf48
Mishan ◻ CHN 110 Rf23
Mishan ◻ IR 93 Nf30
Mishkeegogamang Indian Reserve ▲ CDN 236 Fe20
Misiki ◻ PNG 155 Sb49
Misima ◻ EAT 197 Mk48
Misima Island ▲ PNG 156 Sg51
Misinchinka Ranges ▲ CDN 230 Dj18
Misiones ◻ RA 276 Hc59
Misión Platanal ◻ YV 265 Gh44
Misión San Fernando de Velicatá ▲ MEX 244 Ec31
Misión San Francisco de Borja Adac ▲ MEX 244 Ed31
Misión Santa Gertrudis ◻ MEX 244 Ed31
Misión Santa María de los Angeles ▲ MEX 244 Ec31
Miskah ◻ KSA 92 Nb33
Miski ◻ SUD 184 Mc38
Miskolc ◻ H 67 Ma42
Mismar ◻ SUD 185 Mh36
Mišnjak ◻ HR 61 Lp46
Misole ◻ EAT 196 Mg48
Misool ▲ RI 131 Re47
Misoumin ◻ CI 187 Kj42
Misratah ◻ ≋ LAR 177 Lh29
Misrikh ◻ IND 115 Pa32
Missanabie ◻ ★ CDN 237 Fh21
Missão Assunção ◻ BR 265 Gg45
Missão Pari Cachoeira ◻ BR 270 Gf45
Missão Velha ◻ BR 273 Ja49
Missara ◻ SN 186 Ke39
Misséni ◻ RMM 187 Kg40
Missinaibi Lake ≈ CDN 237 Fj21
Missinaibi Lake Prov. Park ★ CDN 237 Fj21
Missinaibi River ≈ CDN 237 Fj20
Missinipe ◻ CDN 231 Eh18
Mission ◻ CDN 232 Dj21
Mission ◻ USA 236 Ek24
Mission Beach ◻ AUS 147 Sd54
Mission Ridge ◻ USA 236 Ek23
Mission San Buenaventura ▲ USA 234 Ea28
Mission San Juan Capistrano ▲ USA 234 Eb29
Mission San Luis Obispo ▲ USA 234 Dk28
Mission Santa Barbara ▲ USA 234 Ea28
Mission San Xavier del Bac ▲ USA 235 Ee29
Missira ◻ SN 186 Kd39
Mississauga ◻ CDN 237 Ga24
Mississippi ★ USA 239 Fe28
Mississippi ◻ USA 239 Fe29
Mississippi Cruises ★ USA 239 Fe29
Mississippi Delta ★ USA 239 Ff31
Misso ◻ EST 45 Mh33
Missoula ◻ USA 232 Ed22
Missour ◻ MA 175 Kj29
Missouri ≈ USA 236 Ek23
Missouri ◻ USA 238 Fd27
Missouri Breaks Wild and Scenic River ★ USA 233 Ef22
Missouri City ◻ USA 238 Fc31
Missouri Valley ◻ USA 238 Fc25
Mistawasis Ind. Res. ▲ CDN 233 Eg19
Mistelbach ◻ A 66 Lr42
Misterbianco ◻ I 63 Lp53
Misterei ◻ SUD 184 Mb39
Misterhult ◻ S 43 Lr33
Misti, Volcán ▲ PE 269 Ge54
Mistletoe S.P. ★ USA 242 Fj29
Mistrás ☐ ★ GR 70 Mc53
Mistretta ◻ I 63 Lp53
Misty Fjords Nat. Mon. ★ ★ USA 230 De18
Misumba ◻ RDC 199 Ma48
Misumi ◻ J 113 Rf29
Mita-Mirim ◻ BR 270 Gh46
Mita Mita ◻ AUS 151 Sd64
Mitan ◻ OM 95 Ng36
Mitatib ◻ SUD 185 Mj37
Mitchell ◻ AUS 149 Sd59
Mitchell ◻ USA 232 Dk23
Mitchell ◻ USA 235 Ej25
Mitchell ◻ USA 236 Fa24
Mitchell ◻ USA 236 Fb24
Mitchell and Alice Rivers N.P. ★ AUS 147 Sb53
Mitchell Falls ★ AUS 143 Rc53
Mitchell Highway (New South Wales) ★ AUS 149 Sd61
Mitchell Highway (Queensland) ★ AUS 149 Sd59
Mitchell, Mount ▲ USA 242 Fj28
Mitchell River ◻ AUS 143 Rc53
Mitchell River ≈ AUS 147 Sb53
Mitchell River N.P. ★ AUS 143 Rc53
Mitchelstown ◻ IRL 47 Km38
Miteja ◻ EAT 197 Mk50
Mithankot ◻ PK 99 Of31
Mitha Tiwana ◻ PK 99 Og29
Mithi ◻ ★ PK 99 Oe33
Mithimna ◻ GR 71 Mg51
Mitiamo ◻ AUS 151 Sc64
Mitikas ◻ GR 70 Ma52
Mitkof Island ▲ USA 230 Dd17
Mitla ★ MEX 247 Fb37
Mito ◻ J 111 Sa27
Mitoko ◻ RDC 190 Ma44
Mitole ◻ EAT 197 Mk50
Mitomoni ◻ EAT 196 Mh51
Mitrašinci ◻ MK 68 Mc49
Mitrofania Island ▲ USA 228 Ca18
Mitrofanovka ◻ RUS 72 Mk21
Mitrovo ◻ SRB 68 Ma47
Mitsamiouli ◻ ★ COM 206 Nb51
Mitsinjo ◻ RM 206 Nc53
Mitsuishi ◻ J 111 Sb24
Mitsushima ◻ J 113 Re28
Mittellandkanal ≈ D 58 Lh38
Mittelrheintal ☐ ★ D 59 Lh40
Mittenwald ◻ ★ D 59 Lm43
Mittersill ◻ A 60 Ln43
Mitterteich ◻ D 59 Ln41
Mittweida ◻ D 58 Ln40
Mitu ◻ CO 264 Ge45
Mitundu ◻ MW 202 Mg53
Mitunguu ◻ EAK 194 Mj46
Mitwaba ◻ RDC 196 Md50
Mityana ◻ EAU 194 Mg45
Mitzic ◻ G 198 Lf45
Miura-hanto ▲ J 113 Rk28
Miuri ◻ EAT 197 Mk50
Mixco ◻ GCA 248 Fe38
Mixtlán ◻ MEX 246 Eh35
Miya ◻ WAN 188 Le40
Miyake-jima ▲ J 113 Rk28
Miyako ◻ J 111 Sa26
Miyako Jima ▲ J 113 Rc33
Miyakonojo ◻ J 113 Rf30
Miyandoab ◻ IR 91 Nd27
Miyaneh ◻ IR 91 Nd27
Miyanoura-dake ▲ J 113 Rf30
Miyazaki ◻ J 113 Rf30
Miyazu ◻ J 113 Rh28
Miyun ◻ CHN 107 Qj25
Mizan Teferi ◻ ETH 192 Mh42
Mizdah ◻ LAR 177 Lg30
Mizen Head ▲ IRL 47 Kl39
Miževičy ◻ BY 65 Mf38
Mizhi ◻ CHN 106 Qf27
Mizil ◻ RO 69 Mg45
Mizoč ◻ UA 65 Mg40
Mizoram ◻ IND 120 Pg34
Mizpah ◻ USA 233 Eh22
Mizpé Ramon ◻ IL 92 Mh30
Mizque ◻ BOL 278 Gh54
Mizuho ◻ 287 Nb32
Mizur ◻ RUS 91 Nc24
Mizusawa ◻ J 111 Sa26
Mjadzel ◻ BY 45 Mg36
Mjaksa ◻ RUS 72 Mk16
Mjanji ◻ EAU 194 Mg45
Mjetë ▲ AL 70 Ma50
Mjölby ◻ S 43 Lq32
Mjönäs ◻ S 43 Lo31
Mjøndalen ◻ N 42 Lk31
Mkalamo ◻ EAT 197 Mk48
Mkambati Nature Reserve ★ ★ ZA 205 Me61
Mkanga ◻ EAT 196 Mg49
Mkangira ◻ EAT 197 Mj50
Mkarangama ◻ EAT 197 Mk49
Mkasi ◻ Z 196 Mg50
Mkata ◻ EAT 197 Mk48
Mkharram Foqani ◻ SYR 90 Mj28
Mkhaya Nature Reserve ★ SD 205 Mf59
Mkhota ◻ MW 196 Mg52
Mkoani ◻ EAT 197 Mk48
Mkokotoni ◻ EAT 197 Mk48
Mkomazi ◻ EAT 197 Mk48
Mkomazi Game Reserve ★ EAT 194 Mj47
Mkombe ◻ EAT 196 Mf49
Mkuchika ◻ EAT 197 Mk51
Mkushi Boma ◻ Z 196 Me52
Mkushi River ◻ Z 196 Me52
Mkuze ◻ ZA 205 Mg59
Mkuze Game Reserve ★ ★ ZA 205 Mg59
Mkwaja ◻ EAT 197 Mk48
Mkwasine ◻ ZW 202 Mf56
Mladá Boleslav ◻ CZ 66 Lp40
Mladá Vožice ◻ CZ 66 Lp41
Mladenovac ◻ SRB 68 Ma46
Mlandizi ◻ EAT 197 Mj49
Mlandizi ◻ EAT 197 Mk49
M'Lang ◻ RP 125 Rc42
Mława ◻ PL 65 Ma37
Mlawula Nature Reserve ★ ★ SD 205 Mf59
Mlilwane Wildlife Sanctuary ★ SD 205 Mf59
Mliniště ◻ BIH 61 Lr46
Mljet ▲ HR 61 Ls48
Mljet, N.P. ★ ★ HR 61 Ls48
Młodasko ◻ PL 64 Lr38
Młogoszyn ◻ PL 65 Lu38
Mloka ◻ EAT 197 Mk49
Młynary ◻ PL 65 Lu36
Młynarze ◻ PL 65 Mb38
Mlyniv ◻ UA 65 Mf40
Mmabatho ◉ ZA 205 Mc58
Mmadinare ◻ RB 202 Md56
Mmamabula ◻ RB 202 Md57
Mmashoro ◻ RB 202 Md56
Mmathethe ◻ RB 205 Mc58
Mmatshumo ◻ RB 201 Mc56
Mnarani Ruins ★ EAK 195 Mk47
Mnero ◻ EAT 197 Mk51
Mníšek nad Hnilcom ◻ SK 67 Ma42
Mnyani ◻ EAT 196 Mh49
Mo ◻ N 42 Lm30
Moa ≈ BR 268 Gd49
Moa ◻ C 250 Gc35
Moa ◻ EAT 197 Mk48
Moa ▲ RI 130 Ra46
Moa ▲ RI 131 Re50
Moa ≈ WAL 186 Ke42
Moab ◻ USA 235 Ef26
Moacşa ◻ RO 69 Mf45
Moai ▲ RCH 269 Gc54
Moa Island ▲ AUS 147 Sb51
Moala ▲ FJI 159 Tk55
Mo'alleman ◻ IR 98 Nh28
Mo'allem Kalayeh ◻ IR 91 Nf27
Moama ◻ AUS 149 Sc61
Moamba ◻ MOC 205 Mg58
Moanda ◻ G 198 Lg46
Moapa R. Ind. Res. ▲ USA 234 Ec27
Moara Vlăsiei ◻ RO 69 Mg46
Moate ◻ IRL 47 Kn37
Moatize ◻ MOC 202 Mg54
Moba ◻ RDC 196 Me49
Mobara ◻ J 113 Sa28
Mobaye ◻ RCA 190 Ma43
Mobayi-Mbongi ◻ RDC 190 Ma43
Mobdoua ◻ RIM 181 Kg38
Mobena ◻ RDC 190 Lk45
Moberly ◻ USA 238 Fd26
Mobile ◻ USA 239 Fg30
Moble ◻ AUS 149 Sc59
Mobridge ◻ USA 236 Ek23
Moca ◻ DOM 250 Ge36
Moca ◻ GQ 188 Le44
Mocajuba ◻ BR 267 Hf47
Mocambinho ◻ BR 275 Hh53
Moçambique ◻ ☐ ★ MOC 203 Na53
Mocambo ◻ BR 273 Hk52
Moccasin ◻ USA 233 Ef22
Moccasin ◻ USA 234 Dk27
Moc Chau ◻ VN 121 Qc35
Moce ▲ FJI 159 Ua55
Mocha ◻ ★ YE 94 Nb39
Moche Pirámides ★ PE 269 Ga50
Moche Pirámides (Túcume) ★ PE 268 Ga49
Mochima, P.N. ★ ★ YV 265 Gh40
Moc Hoa ◻ VN 123 Qc40
Mochong ◻ CHN 108 Qd32
Mochudi ◉ RB 205 Md58
Mochumí ◻ PE 268 Ga49
Mochy ◻ PL 64 Lr38
Mocimboa da Praia ◻ ★ ★ MOC 197 Na51
Mocimboa do Rovuma ◻ MOC 197 Mk51
Mociu ◻ RO 67 Me44
Möckern ◻ D 58 Lm38
Mockfjärd ◻ S 43 Lp30
Môco ▲ ANG 200 Lh52
Mocoa ◻ CO 264 Gb45
Mococa ◻ BR 275 Hg56
Mocoduene ◻ MOC 203 Mh57
Mocomoco ◻ BOL 278 Gf53
Mocorito ◻ MEX 244 Eg33
Mocorón ◻ HN 249 Fh38
Moctezuma ◻ MEX 244 Ef31
Moctezuma ◻ MEX 246 Ek34
Mocuba ◻ MOC 203 Mj54
Mocupe ◻ PE 268 Ga49
Modahtou ◻ DJI 192 Na40
Modan ◻ RI 154 Rg47
Modane ◻ F 53 Lg45
Modăr ▲ BG 69 Me49
Modasa ◻ IND 116 Og34
Modderpoort San Rock Paintings ★ ZA 205 Md60
Model ◻ USA 235 Eh27
Módena ◻ ☐ ★ I 60 Ll46
Modena ◻ USA 235 Ed27
Modesto ◻ USA 234 Dk27
Modesto Méndez ◻ GCA 248 Ff38
Modest Town ◻ USA 241 Gc27
Modhera Sun Temple ★ IND 116 Og34
Módica ◻ ☐ ★ I 63 Lp54
Modigliana ◻ I 60 Lm46
Modinagar ◻ IND 115 Oj31
Modjigo ▲ RN 183 Lg37
Modliborzyce ◻ PL 65 Mc40
Mödling ◻ A 66 Lr42
Modong ◻ RI 127 Qc47
Modot ◻ MNG 104 Qe22
Modra špilja ★ HR 61 Lr48
Modriča ◻ BIH 68 Lt46
Möðrudalur ▲ IS 46 Ke25
Modugno ◻ I 63 Lr49
Moe ◻ AUS 151 Sd65
Moebase ◻ MOC 203 Mk54
Moelv ◻ N 40 Ll30
Moengo ◻ SME 266 Hc43
Moeraki Boulders ★ NZ 153 Tf68
Moerkesung ◻ CHN 102 Pc30
Moers ◻ D 58 Lg39
Moffat ◻ GB 48 Kr35
Moffen ▲ N 38 Lh05
Moffet Pt. ▲ USA 228 Bj18
Moffit ◻ USA 236 Ek22
Moftin ◻ RO 67 Mc43
Mofu ◻ Z 196 Mf51
Moga ◻ IND 114 Oh30
Moga ◻ RDC 196 Md47
Mogadishu ● ★ ★ SP 195 Nc44
Mogadouro ◻ P 54 Ko49
Mogalu ◻ RDC 190 Lk44
Moganshan ★ CHN 112 Qk30
Mogao Ku ☐ ▲ ★ CHN 101 Ph25
Mogapinyana ◻ RB 202 Md57
Mogaung ◻ MYA 120 Pj33
Mogee Bli ◻ LB 186 Kf43
Moghar ◻ IR 98 Ng29
Moghrar ◻ DZ 175 Kk29
Mogila ▲ EAK 194 Mh43
Mogili ◻ RUS 45 Mj34
Mogilno ◻ PL 64 Ls38
Mogincual ◻ MOC 203 Na53
Mogliano Véneto ◻ I 60 Ln45
Mogna ◻ RA 279 Gf61
Mogoča ◻ RUS 89 Ra08
Mogojtuj ◉ RUS 105 Qh20
Mogok ◻ MYA 120 Pj34
Mogorjelo ★ BIH 61 Ls47
Mogoşoaia ★ RO 69 Mf46
Mogosoaia ◻ RO 69 Mg46
Mogotio ◻ EAK 194 Mh45
Mogpog ◻ RP 124 Ra39
Mogroum ◻ TCH 189 Lh40
Moguer ◻ E 55 Ko53
Mogumber ◻ AUS 144 Qj61
Mogwase ◻ ZA 205 Md58
Mogzon ◻ RUS 104 Qg20
Mohács ◻ H 67 Lt44
Mohács ★ H 67 Lt45
Mohala ◻ IND 117 Pa35
Mohale's Hoek ◻ LS 205 Md61
Mohall ◻ USA 236 Ek21
Mohammadabad ◻ IR 98 Oa30
Mohammad Abad ◻ IR 98 Ng29
Mohammad Abad ◻ IR 98 Nh31
Mohammad Abad ◻ IR 98 Nj31
Mohammad Agha ◻ AFG 99 Oe28
Mohammad Hasan Khaan Bridge ★ IR 96 Ng27
Mohammadia ◻ DZ 175 La28
Mohammedia ◻ ★ ★ MA 175 Kg29
Mohana ◻ IND 117 Pc36
Mohanganj ◻ BD 120 Pf33
Mohania ◻ IND 117 Pb33
Mohanlalganj ◻ IND 117 Pa32
Mohanpur ◻ NEP 117 Pd32
Moharli ◻ IND 117 Ok35
Mohdra ◻ IND 117 Ok33
Mohe ◻ CHN 105 Rb19
Mohe ◻ CHN 105 Rb19
Mohean ◻ IND 122 Pg42
Moheda ◻ S 43 Lp34
Mohéli = Mwali ★ ★ COM 206 Nb52
Mohelnice ◻ CZ 66 Lr41
Mohen ◻ FSM 135 Sb09
Mohenjo Daro ☐ ★ PK 99 Oe32
Mohgaon ◻ IND 117 Pa34
Möhne ≈ D 58 Lj39
Möhnesee ◻ D 58 Lj39
Mohnyin ◻ MYA 120 Pj33
Moho ◻ PE 278 Gf53
Mohoda ◻ IND 116 Ok35
Mohol ◻ IND 116 Oh37
Mohora ◻ H 67 Lu43
Mohoro ◻ EAT 197 Mk50
Mohyliv-Podil's'kyj ◻ UA 73 Md21
Moi ◻ N 42 Lg32
Moiben ◻ EAK 194 Mh45
Moi Hoa Binh Pagoda ▲ VN 123 Qc41
Moila Point ▲ PNG 157 Sh49
Moimba ◻ ANG 200 Lg54
Moincêr ◻ CHN 102 Pa30
Moinsi Hills ▲ GH 187 Kk42
Mo i Rana ◻ N 38 Lp24
Mõisaküla ◻ EST 45 Mf32
Moises Ville ◻ RA 279 Gk61
Moisie ◻ CDN 240 Gg20
Moissac ◻ ▲ F 52 Lb46
Moïssala ◻ TCH 190 Lj41
Moitaco ◻ YV 265 Gh41
Möja ▲ S 43 Lt31
Mojácar ◻ E 57 Kt53
Mojados ◻ E 54 Kq49
Mojave ◻ USA 234 Ea28
Mojave Desert ▲ USA 234 Eb28
Mojave National Preserve ★ USA 234 Ec28
Mojiang ◻ CHN 121 Qa34
Moji das Cruzes ◻ BR 277 Hg57
Moji-Guaçu ◻ BR 275 Hg57
Moji-Mirim ◻ BR 275 Hg57
Mojiquiçaba ◻ BR 275 Ja54
Mojo ◻ ETH 192 Mk41
Mojokerto ◻ RI 129 Qg49
Mojosari ◻ RI 129 Qg49
Mojynkum ▲ KZ 97 Oe23
Mojynty ◻ KZ 100 Og22
Moka ◻ DY 188 Lb42
Moka ◻ IND 118 Oj38
Moka ◻ J 111 Sa27
Mokalsar ◻ IND 116 Og33
Mokambo ◻ RDC 196 Me52
Mokameh ◻ IND 117 Pc33
Mokhotlong ◻ LS 205 Me60
Mokhpal ◻ IND 117 Pa36
Möklinta ◻ S 43 Lr30
Moknine ◻ TN 176 Lf28
Moko ◻ RN 182 Lb39
Mokobody ◻ PL 65 Mc38
Mokokchung ◻ IND 120 Ph32
Mokolo ◻ CAM 189 Lg40
Mokolodi Nature Reserve ★ RB 205 Mc58
Mo Ko Phi Phi N.P. ★ THA 122 Pk42
Mokoreta ◻ NZ 153 Te69
Mokowe ◻ EAK 195 Na47
Mokp'o ◻ ROK 112 Rd28
Mokre ◻ PL 64 Ls37
Mokren ◻ BG 69 Mg48
Mokšan ◻ RUS 72 Nc19
Mokuti ◻ ★ NAM 200 Lj55
Mokwa ◻ WAN 188 Lc41
Mol ◻ B 51 Lf39
Mola di Bari ◻ I 63 Ls49
Molalatau ◻ RB 202 Me57
Mo'lali botig'i ▲ UZ 97 Oc25
Molaly ◻ KZ 100 Ok23
Molaman ◻ IND 114 Og31
Molas ◻ MEX 247 Fg35
Molat ▲ HR 61 Lp46
Mold ◻ GB 49 Kr37
Moldava nad Bodvou ◻ SK 67 Mb42
Molde ◻ ★ N 40 Lh28
Moldo-Too ▲ KS 100 Oh25
Moldova ■ MD 73 Me22
Moldoveanu ▲ RO 67 Me45
Molecreek ◻ AUS 151 Sd66
Molegbe ◻ RDC 190 Ma43
Molem N.P. ★ IND 116 Oh38
Mole N.P. ★ ★ GH 187 Kk41
Molepolole ◉ ★ RB 205 Mc58
Môle-SaintNicolas ◻ RH 250 Gd36
Molesworth ◻ AUS 148 Sb60
Molėtai ◻ LT 45 Mf35
Molfetta ◻ ★ I 63 Lr49
Molibagu ◻ RI 125 Rb45
Moliden ◻ S 44 Lt27
Molières ◻ F 52 Lb46
Molina ◻ E 57 Kt50
Molina ◻ RCH 280 Ge63
Molina de Segura ◻ E 57 Kt52
Moline ◻ USA 236 Fe25
Moline ◻ USA 238 Fb27
Molinella ◻ I 60 Lm46
Molinggapoto ◻ RI 125 Rb45
Molinos ◻ RA 279 Gg58
Moliro ◻ RDC 196 Mf50
Molise ◻ I 63 Lp49
Molkom ◻ S 43 Lo31
Mollafeneri ◻ TR 69 Mk50
Mollendo ◻ ★ ★ PE 269 Gd54
Mollerussa ◻ E 57 La49
Mollisfossen ★ N 38 Mb21
Mölln ◻ D 58 Ll37
Mölltorp ◻ S 43 Lp32
Molo ◻ MYA 120 Pj34
Molobala ◻ RMM 187 Kh39
Molobog ◻ RI 125 Rc45
Molocopote ◻ BR 266 Hc45
Molodežnaja ◻ 287 Na33
Molodi ◻ RUS 44 Mj32
Molodo ◻ RMM 181 Kg38
Molokai ▲ USA 234 Cb35
Molong ◻ AUS 151 Se62
Molong ◻ IND 120 Pg33
Molopo ≈ RB/ZA 205 Mc58
Moloporivier ◻ ZA 205 Mc58
Mólos ◻ GR 70 Mc52
Moloskovicy ◻ RUS 44 Mk31
Moloundou ◻ CAM 189 Lh44
Molsheim ◻ F 51 Lh42
Molteno ◻ ZA 205 Md61
Molu ▲ RI 131 Rf49
Molucca Islands ▲ RI 134 Ra10
Molucca Sea ≈ RI 131 Rc46
Molumbo ◻ MOC 203 Mj53
Molunat ◻ HR 61 Lt48
Molwe ◻ RDC 201 Mc51
Moma ◻ MOC 203 Mk54
Moma ◻ RDC 199 Mb49
Momaligi ◻ WAL 186 Kd42
Momba ◻ AUS 148 Sb61
Mombaça ◻ BR 273 Ja48
Mombasa ◻ ★ ★ EAK 197 Mk48
Mombasa Marine N.P. ★ ★ EAK 197 Mk48
Mombenzélé ◻ RCB 190 Lj45
Mombetsu ◻ J 111 Sb23
Mombetsu ◻ J 111 Sb24
Mombo Camp ◻ ★ RB 201 Mb55
Mombongo ◻ RDC 190 Mb45
Mombongo ◻ RDC 191 Mc45
Mombuey ◻ E 54 Ko48
Mombum ◻ RI 154 Rk50
Momčilgrad ◻ BG 69 Mf49
Mommark ◻ DK 42 Ll36
Momote ◻ ★ PNG 156 Sd47
Momotombo, Volcán ▲ NIC 248 Fg39
Mompiche ★ EC 268 Fk45
Mompono ◻ RDC 190 Ma45
Momskij hrebet ▲ RUS 89 Sb05
Møn ▲ DK 42 Ln35
Mon ◻ IND 120 Ph32
Monach Islands ▲ GB 48 Kn33
Monaco ● ★ ★ MC 53 Lh47
Monaghan ◻ IRL 47 Ko36
Monahans ◻ USA 245 Ej30
Mona Passage ≈ DOM/USA 250 Gf36
Monapo ◻ MOC 203 Na53
Mona Quimbundo ◻ ANG 199 Lk50
Monarch Mtn. ▲ CDN 232 Dh20
Monari ◻ AFG 99 Oe29
Monasterace Marina ◻ I 63 Lr52
Monasterio de Guadalupe ☐ ▲ E 55 Kp51
Monasterio de Leyre ▲ E 56 Kt48
Monasterio de Piedra ▲ E 57 Kt49
Monasterio de San Juan de la Peña ▲ E 56 Ku48
Monasterio de Veruela ▲ E 56 Kt49
Monasterio de Yuste ▲ E 55 Kp50
Monastero di Sabiona = Kloster Säben ▲ I 60 Lm44
Monastery of Saint Anthony ▲ ET 179 Mg31
Monastery of Saint Catherine ☐ ▲ ET 179 Mg31
Monastery of Saint Paul ▲ ET 179 Mg31
Monastery of Saint Simeon ▲ ET 179 Mg33
Monastir ◻ I 62 Lk51
Monastir ◻ TN 176 Lf28
Monastyrščina ◻ RUS 72 Mf18
Monastyrysče ◻ UA 73 Me21
Monastyrys'ka ◻ UA 67 Mf41
Monatélé ◻ CAM 189 Lf43
Monboré ◻ CAM 189 Lh41
Moncada ◻ E 57 Ku51
Moncalieri ◻ I 60 Lh45
Moncalvo ▲ E 54 Ko48
Moncalvo ◻ I 60 Lj45
Monção ◻ BR 272 Hh47
Monção ◻ E 54 Km48
Mončegorsk ◻ RUS 39 Mn23
Mönchengladbach ◻ D 58 Lg39
Monchique ◻ ★ P 55 Km53
Monchy ◻ CDN 233 Eg21
Moncks Corner ◻ USA 242 Fk29
Monclova ◻ MEX 245 Ek32
Moncontour ◻ F 50 Ks42
Moncton ◻ CDN 240 Gh22
Mondaí ◻ BR 276 Hd59
Mondéjar ◻ E 55 Kr50
Mondello ◻ I 62 Lo52
Mon Desir ◻ NAM 200 Lh55
Mondim de Basto ◻ P 54 Kn49
Mondjamboli ◻ RDC 190 Mb44
Mondjuku ◻ RDC 199 Ma46
Mondo ◻ EAT 197 Mh48
Mondo ◻ TCH 183 Lh39
Mondocino ◻ USA 234 Dj26
Mondolfo ◻ I 61 Lo47
Mondombe ◻ RDC 199 Mb46
Mondomo ◻ CO 264 Gb44
Mondoñedo ◻ E 54 Kn47
Mondoro ◻ CI 187 Kg41
Mondoro ◻ RMM 181 Kk38
Mondoubleau ◻ F 50 La43
Mondovì ◻ I 60 Lh46
Mondovi ◻ USA 236 Fe23
Mondragone ◻ I 62 Lo49
Mondrian Island ▲ AUS 145 Rb63
Mondriz ◻ E 54 Kn47
Mondsee ◻ A 61 Lo43
Mondy ◻ RUS 104 Qa20
Moneague ◻ JA 250 Gb36
Moneasa ◻ ★ RO 67 Mc44
Monein ◻ F 52 Ku47
Monemvassiá ◻ ★ ★ GR 69 Md54
Monemvassiá Kástro ★ GR 69 Md54
Monesterio ◻ E 55 Ko52
Monestir de Montserrat ▲ E 57 Lb49
Monestir de Sant Cugat ▲ E 57 Lc49
Monestir Santes Creus ▲ E 57 Lb49
Moneta ◻ USA 233 Eg24
Monett ◻ USA 238 Fd27
Moneyingyi Wetland Wildlife Sanctuary ★ MYA 122 Pj37
Moneymore ◻ GB 47 Ko36
Monfalcone ◻ ★ I 61 Lo45
Monforte ◻ P 55 Kn51
Mongo ◻ RDC 190 Mb43
Mongalla ◻ SUD 194 Mf43
Mongalla Game Reserve ★ SUD 194 Mf43
Mongbwalu ◻ RDC 194 Mf45
Mong Cai ◻ VN 121 Qd35
Mongemputu ◻ RDC 199 Ma47
Mongeri ◻ WAL 186 Ke41
Mongge ◻ RI 154 Rg46
Monggui ◻ RI 154 Rh46
Möng Hpayak ◻ MYA 121 Pk35
Möng Hsat ◻ MYA 121 Pk35
Möng Hsu ◻ MYA 121 Pk34
Mongkaing ◻ MYA 120 Pj35
Mongla ◻ BD 120 Pe34
Möng Long ◻ MYA 120 Pj34
Möng Mit ◻ MYA 120 Pj34
Mongne ◻ MYA 120 Pj35
Mongo ◻ TCH 189 Lk39
Mongol Dagurian Nature Reserve ★ MNG 105 Qh21
Mongol Els ▲ MNG 101 Ph22
Mongolia ■ MNG 77 Pb05
Mongomo ◻ GQ 189 Lf45
Mongonu ◻ WAN 189 Lg39
Mongororo ◻ TCH 184 Mb39
Mongotong ◻ CHN 103 Pk31
Mongoumba ◻ RCA 190 Lk44
Möng Pan ◻ MYA 121 Pk35
Möng Ping ◻ MYA 121 Pk35
Möng Ton ◻ MYA 121 Pk35
Mongu ◻ Z 201 Mb53
Mongua ◻ ANG 200 Lh54
Monguel ◻ RIM 180 Kd37
Möng Yai ◻ MYA 121 Pk34
Möng Yang ◻ MYA 121 Pk35
Möng Yawng ◻ MYA 121 Qa35
Möng Yu ◻ MYA 120 Pk34
Monheim ◻ D 59 Ll42
Mönh Hajrhan ▲ MNG 101 Pf22
Moni ◻ RI 130 Ra50
Moni Ágios Ioanni Theologou ☐ ▲ GR 71 Mg53
Moni Arkádi ▲ GR 71 Me55
Monico ◻ USA 237 Ff23
Monida ◻ USA 233 Ed23
Moni Dochiariu ▲ GR 69 Me50
Monimpébougou ◻ RMM 181 Kh38
Moni Simonos Pétras ▲ GR 69 Me50
Mõniste ◻ EST 45 Mg33
Monistrol-d'Allier ◻ F 53 Ld46
Monistrol-sur-Loire ◻ F 53 Le45
Moni Timiou Prodromou ▲ GR 69 Md49
Monitor ◻ CDN 233 Ee19
Monitor Range ▲ USA 234 Eb26
Monitos ◻ CO 264 Gb41
Monje ◻ RA 281 Gk62
Monkaringa ◻ GH 187 Kk40
Monkayo ◻ RP 125 Rd42
Monkey Bay ◻ ★ ★ MW 203 Mh53
Monkey Mia ◻ AUS 144 Qg58
Mönkhbulag ◻ MNG 104 Qb22
Mońki ◻ PL 65 Mc37
Monkira ◻ AUS 148 Sa58
Monkoto ◻ RDC 199 Ma46
Monmouth ◻ GB 49 Ks39
Monmouth Park ★ USA 241 Gc25
Monnow Bridge ★ GB 49 Ks39
Monobamba ◻ PE 269 Gc51
Mono Lake ★ USA 234 Ea26
Monolíthio ◻ GR 70 Mb51
Monólithos ◻ GR 71 Mh54
Monolon ◻ AUS 148 Sb61
Monopamba ◻ CO 268 Gb45
Monópoli ◻ I 63 Ls50
Monou ◻ TCH 184 Mb37
Monóvar ◻ E 57 Ku52
Monowai ◻ NZ 153 Td68
Monreal del Campo ◻ E 57 Kt50
Monreale ◻ ▲ I 62 Lo52
Mon Repos Conservation Park ★ AUS 149 Sg58
Monroe ◻ USA 232 Dj23
Monroe ◻ USA 232 Dk22
Monroe ◻ USA 235 Ed26
Monroe ◻ USA 237 Ff24
Monroe ◻ USA 237 Fj25
Monroe ◻ USA 239 Fd29
Monroe ◻ USA 241 Gc25
Monroe ◻ USA 242 Fj29
Monroe ◻ USA 242 Fk28
Monroe City ◻ USA 239 Fe26
Monroeville ◻ USA 239 Fg30
Monrou ◻ DY 188 Lb40
Monrovia ● ★ ★ LB 186 Ke42
Monroy ◻ E 55 Ko51
Monroyo ◻ E 57 Ku50
Mons ◻ ☐ ★ B 51 Ld40
Monsanto ◻ P 55 Kn50
Monsaraz ◻ P 55 Kn52
Monschau ◻ ★ D 58 Lg40
Monsèlice ◻ I 60 Lm45
Monsenhor Gil ◻ BR 273 Hj48
Møns Klint ★ DK 42 Ln36
Mönsterås ◻ S 43 Lr33
Montagnac ◻ F 53 Ld47
Montagnana ◻ ★ I 60 Lm45
Montagne Azul Paulista ◻ BR 274 Hf56
Montagne d'Ambre, P.N.de la ★ ★ RM 206 Ne52
Montagne de Lure ▲ F 53 Lf46
Montagne de Nganha ▲ CAM 189 Lh42
Montagne du Lubéron ▲ F 53 Lf47
Montagne Noire ▲ F 52 Lc47
Montagnes Arawa ▲ F 266 Hd44
Montagnes Trinité ▲ F 266 Hd43
Mont Agou ▲ TG 187 La42
Montagu ◻ ★ ZA 204 Ma62
Montague ◻ CDN 240 Gj22
Montague Island ★ ★ AUS 151 Sf64
Montague Island ▲ USA 229 Cg16
Mont Aigoual ▲ F 53 Ld46
Montaigu ◻ F 52 Kt44
Montaitas ◻ KZ 97 Oe24
Montalbán ◻ E 57 Ku50
Montalcino ◻ I 60 Lm47
Montalegre ◻ ANG 198 Lj50
Montalegre ◻ P 54 Kn49
Montalivet-les-Bains ◻ F 52 Kt45
Montalto ▲ I 63 Lq52
Montalto di Castro ◻ I 60 Lm48
Montalto Uffogo ◻ I 63 Lr51
Montalvânia ◻ BR 275 Hh53
Montalvo ◻ EC 268 Ga46
Montalvo ◻ EC 268 Gb47
Montamarta ◻ E 54 Kp49
Montana ◻ BG 68 Md47
Montana ◻ USA 233 Ee22
Montaña de Celaque ▲ HN 248 Ff38
Montaña de Comayagua ▲ HN 248 Fg38
Montaña Punta Piedra ▲ HN 248 Fh38
Montañas de Colón ▲ HN 249 Fh38
Montañas de Comayagua ▲ HN 248 Fg38
Montañas de Convento ▲ EC 268 Ga46
Montañas del Norte de Chiapas ▲ MEX 247 Fd37
Montañas de Onzole ▲ EC 268 Ga45
Montañas de Patuca ▲ HN 248 Fh38
Moñtanas de Yoro ▲ HN 248 Fg38
Montañas de Yoro ▲ HN 248 Fg38
Montanha ◻ BR 275 Hk55
Montargil ◻ P 55 Km51
Montargis ◻ F 53 Lc43
Montashee Mtns. ▲ CDN 232 Ea20
Montauban ◻ F 52 Lb47
Montauban-de-Bretagne ◻ F 50 Ks42
Montauk ◻ USA 241 Gd25
Montbard ◻ F 53 Le43
Mont Bata ◻ RCA 190 Lh43
Montbazillac ★ F 52 La46
Montbazon ◻ F 52 La43
Montbéliard ◻ F 53 Lg43
Mont Bellevue de l'Inini ▲ F 266 Hd44
Mont Bélo ◻ RCB 198 Lg48
Mont Birougou ▲ ▲ G 198 Lg46
Mont Birougou, P.N.de ★ ★ G 198 Lg46
Montblanc ◻ ★ E 57 Lb49
Mont Blanc ▲ F/I 53 Lg45
Montbrison ◻ F 53 Le45
Montbron ◻ F 52 La45
Montceau-les-Mines ◻ F 53 Le44
Montchanin ◻ F 53 Le44
Mont Cottica ▲ F 266 Hc43
Montcuq ◻ F 52 Lb46
Mont-de-Marsan ◻ F 52 Ku47
Mont de Niangbo ▲ CI 187 Kh41
Montdidier ◻ F 51 Lc41
Mont-Dore ◻ F 158 Td57
Mont Douan ▲ CI 186 Kg42
Monteagle ◻ AUS 149 Sd57
Monteagudo ◻ BOL 278 Gj55
Monte Alban ☐ ★ MEX 246 Fb37
Monte Albo ▲ I 62 Lk50
Monte Alegre ◻ BR 266 Hc46
Monte Alegre de Goiás ◻ BR 272 Hg52
Montealegre del Castillo ◻ E 57 Kt52
Monte Alegre de Minas ◻ BR 274 Hf55
Monte Alén, P.N.de ★ ★ GQ 188 Lf45
Monte Amaro ▲ I 63 Lp48
Monte Amiata ▲ I 60 Lm48
Monte Argentário ▲ I 60 Lm48
Monte Argentário-Porto San Stéfano ◻ I 60 Lm48
Monte Azul ◻ BR 275 Hj53
Montebello Islands ▲ AUS 142 Qh56
Montebelluna ◻ I 60 Ln45
Monte Belo ◻ ANG 200 Lh52
Monte Binga ▲ MOC/ZW 202 Mg55
Monte Botte Donato ▲ I 63 Lr51
Monte Buckland ▲ RA 283 Gh73
Monte Burney ▲ RCH 282 Gd72
Monte Calvo ▲ I 63 Lq49
Monte Campana ▲ RA 282 Gh73
Montecarlo ◻ RA 276 Hc59
Monte Carmelo ◻ BR 275 Hg55
Monte Caseros ◻ RA 276 Hb61
Montecatini Terme ◻ I 60 Ll47
Montecchio Emilia ◻ I 60 Ll46
Montecchio Maggiore ◻ I 60 Lm45
Monte Cervati ▲ I 63 Lq50
Montech ◻ F 52 Lb47
Monte Christo ◻ ZA 202 Md57
Monte Cimone ▲ I 60 Ll46
Monte Cinto ▲ F 60 Lk48
Monte Comán ◻ RA 280 Gg63
Monte Creek ◻ CDN 232 Ea20
Monte Cristi ◻ DOM 250 Ge36
Montecristi ◻ EC 268 Fk46
Monte Cristi, P.N. ★ RH 250 Ge36
Monte Cristo ◻ BR 270 Gg48
Montecristo, P.N. ★ ES 248 Ff38
Monte d'Accoddi ★ I 62 Lj50
Monte Darwin ▲ RCH 282 Gf73
Monte die Sette Fratelli ▲ I 62 Lk51
Monte Dinero ◻ RA 282 Gf72
Monte di Prunu ▲ F 60 Lk48
Monte Dourado ◻ BR 271 Hd46
Montefalco ◻ I 60 Lm48

Ngwale ☐ EAT 197 Mj51
Ngwedaung ☐ MYA 120 Pj36
Ngwena ☐ ZW 202 Me55
Ngweze Pool ☒ CAM 201 Mb54
Ngwo ☐ CAM 188 Le42
Nhachengue ☐ MOC 203 Mh57
Nhacoà ☐ GNB 186 Kc40
Nhacra ☐ GNB 186 Kc40
Nhamasonge ☐ MOC 202 Mg54
Nhamatanda ☐ MOC 202 Mg54
Nhamayabué ☐ MOC 203 Mh54
Nhamundá ☐ BR 271 Hb47
Nhamundá Mapuera, T.I. ☐ BR 266 Ha46
Nhandeara ☐ BR 274 He56
Nharea ☐ ANG 200 Lj51
Nha Trang ☐ VN 123 Qe39
Nhemba ☐ MOC 202 Mg53
Nhill ☐ AUS 150 Sa64
Nhlangano ☐ SD 205 Mf59
Nho Quan ☐ VN 122 Qd37
Nhulunbuy ☐ AUS 146 Rj52
Niablé ☐ CI 187 Kj42
Niada ☐ RCA 190 Ma43
Niafounké ☐ RMM 181 Kh38
Niagara Falls ☐ USA 236 Fb22
Niagara Falls ☐ CDN 237 Ga24
Niagara Falls ☐ USA 237 Ga24
Niagara Falls ☐ USA/CDN 237 Ga24
Niague ☐ CI 187 Kg43
Niah ☐ MAL 128 Qg44
Niah Caves ☆ MAL 128 Qg44
Niah N.P. ☒ MAL 128 Qg44
Niakaramandougou ☐ CI 187 Kh41
Niakhar ☐ SN 180 Kb38
Nialaha'u Point ☐ SOL 157 Ta50
Niambézaria ☐ CI 187 Kh43
Niamey ● ☒ RN 182 Lb39
Niamina ☐ RMM 187 Kg39
Niamtougou ☐ TG 187 La41
Niamvoudou ☐ CAM 189 Lg43
Niandankoro ☐ RG 186 Kf40
Nianfissa ☐ CI 187 Kg41
Niangara ☐ RDC 191 Md44
Niangara ☐ RDC 191 Md44
Niangoloko ☐ BF 187 Kh40
Nianio ☐ CI 187 Kg43
Nia-Nia ☐ RDC 191 Md45
Nianing ☐ SN 180 Kb38
Niantanina ☐ RMM 186 Kf40
Nianyu ☐ IND 120 Ph32
Nianzishan ☐ CHN 105 Rb22
Niao Dao ☒ CHN 103 Pk27
Niaoshu Shan ▲ CHN 106 Qc28
Niapu ☐ RDC 191 Md44
Niapu ☐ RDC 191 Md44
Niaro ☐ SUD 185 Mf40
Nias ▲ RI 127 Pj45
Niasar fire temple ☆ IR 91 Nf28
Nibe ☐ DK 42 Lj34
Nibong Tebal ☐ MAL 126 Qa43
Nicagé ☐ MOC 197 Mk52
Nicaj-Shalë ☐ AL 68 Lu44
Nicaragua ■ 248 Fj39
Nicasio ☐ PE 269 Ge53
Niceville ☐ USA 239 Fg30
Nicgale ☐ LV 45 Mg34
Nichinan ☐ J 113 Rf30
Nichlaul ☐ IND 117 Pb32
Nicholasville ☐ USA 239 Fh27
Nicholls ☐ BD 120 Pk33
Nicholson ☐ AUS 143 Re55
Nicholson, Mount ▲ AUS 149 Se58
Nicholson Range ▲ AUS 144 Qj59
Nicholson ☐ AUS 146 Rk54
Nichols Town ☐ BS 243 Ga33
Nicman ☐ CDN 240 Gg20
Nicobar Islands ▲ IND 122 Pj41
Nicola Mameet Ind. Res. ☐ CDN 232 Dk20
Nicolás Bruzzone ☐ RA 280 Gh63
Nicosia ● CY 90 Mg28
Nicosia ☐ I 63 Lp53
Nicotera ☐ I 63 Lp53
Nicoya ☐ CR 248 Fh40
Nictau ☐ CDN 240 Gg22
Nicuadala ☐ MOC 203 Mj54
Niculitel ☐ RO 69 Mj45
Nicupa ☐ MOC 203 Na53
Nidadavole ☐ IND 117 Pa37
Nidda ☐ D 59 Lk40
Nidderau ☐ D 59 Lj40
Nidri ☐ GR 70 Ma52
Niebore ☐ RG 186 Ke40
Niebüll ☐ D 58 Lj36
Niedalino ☐ PL 64 Lq38
Niederaula ☐ D 58 Lk40
Niederbronn-les-Bains ☐ F 51 La42
Nieder Tauern ▲ A 61 Lp43
Niederlausitz ▲ D 58 Lo39
Niedersachsen ☐ D 58 Lj38
Niedersächsisches Wattenmeer, N.P. ☒ D 58 Lh37
Niedrzwica Duża ☐ PL 65 Mc39
Niefang ☐ GQ 188 Lf45
Niéga ☐ BF 187 Kk39
Niégo ☐ BF 187 Kj40
Niekerkshoop ☐ ZA 204 Mb60
Nielisz ☐ PL 65 Mc39
Niellé ☐ CI 187 Kh40
Niem ☐ RCA 190 Lh42
Niemba ☐ RDC 196 Md48
Niemce ☐ PL 65 Mc39
Niemelanke ☐ RMM 180 Ke36
Niemisel ☐ S 39 Mb24
Niena ☐ RMM 187 Kg40
Nienburg ☐ D 58 Lk38
Nierstein ☐ D 59 Lj41
Niesen ▲ CH 60 Lh44
Niesky ☐ D 58 Lp39
Nieu-Bethesda ☐ ZA 205 Mc61
Nieuw Amsterdam ☐ SME 266 Hc43
Nieuwegein ☐ NL 51 Lf38
Nieuw Nickerie ☐ SME 266 Hb43
Nieuwoudtville ☐ ZA 204 Lk61
Nieuwpoort ☐ B 51 Lc39
Nieuwpoort ☐ NL 265 Gf39
Nieweglosz ☐ PL 65 Mc39
Niezabyszewo ☐ PL 64 Ls36
Nifi ☐ KSA 93 Nb33
Niğde ☐ TR 90 Mh27
Nigel ☐ ZA 205 Me59
Niger ■ WAN 182 La08
Niger ☐ 163 La09
Niger Delta ☒ WAN 188 Lc43
Niger Fan ☒ 162 La09
Nigeria ■ 163 La09
Nighasan ☐ IND 115 Pa31
Nightmote ☐ USA 228 Bh15
Nigrandé ☐ EAT 197 Mj50
Nigrita ☐ GR 68 Md50
Nigua ☒ 250 Ge36
Niha Caves ☆ RL 90 Mh29
Nihada ☐ OM 95 Nj34
Nihessiue ☐ MOC 203 Mk53
Nihing ☐ PK 99 Oc31
Nihoa ▲ USA 234 Bk34
Nihonmatsu ☐ J 111 Sa27
Niigata ☐ J 111 Rk27
Niihama ☐ J 113 Rg29
Niihau ▲ USA 234 Bk35
Niimi ☐ J 113 Rh28
Niitsu ☐ J 111 Rk27
Nijar ☐ E 55 Ks44
Nijiao ☐ CHN 121 Qb33
Nijkerk ☐ NL 51 Lf38
Nij Jaluk ☐ IND 120 Pg32
Nijmegen ☐ NL 51 Lf39
Nijverdal ☐ NL 51 Lg38
Nikea ☐ GR 70 Mc51
Nikel' ☐ RUS 39 Na01
Nikiforos ☐ GR 69 Me49
Nikitskij monastyr' ☆ RUS 72 Mk17
Nikkaluokta ☐ S 38 Lu23
Nikki ☐ DY 188 La41
Nikkö ☐ J 111 Rk27
Nikkōemon ☐ CAM 189 Lf44
Nikolaevsk-na-Amure ☐ RUS 89 Sa08
Nikolo-L'vovskoe ☐ RUS 110 Rf24

Nikol'sk ☐ RUS 72 Nd19
Nikopol ☐ BG 69 Me47
Nikopol' ☐ UA 73 Mh22
Nikópoli ☐ GR 70 Ma51
Nikópoli ☐ GR 70 Ma51
Nikopolis ad Istrum ☆ BG 69 Mf47
Niksar ☐ TR 90 Mj26
Nikšić ☐ MNE 68 Lt48
Nilanga ☐ IND 116 Oj36
Nilaveli Beach ☐ CL 119 Pa41
Nile ☐ ET 162 Mb07
Nile ☐ SUD 185 Mg36
Nile Delta ☒ ET 179 Mf30
Niles ☐ USA 237 Fg25
Nilgiri ☐ IND 117 Pd35
Nilgiri Mtn. Railway ☒ ☆ IND 118 Oj42
Nili ☐ AFG 99 Od29
Nilka ☐ CHN 100 Pb24
Nilpass ☐ AFG 99 Od28
Nilphamari ☐ BD 120 Pe33
Nilt ☐ 114 Oh27
Nimach ☐ IND 116 Oj33
Nimbin ☐ AUS 149 Sg60
Nimboto ☐ RI 155 Sa47
Nîmes ☐ F 53 Le47
Nimjat ☐ RIM 180 Kc37
Nim Ka Khera ☐ IND 116 Oh33
Nimmitabel ☐ AUS 151 Se64
Nimrud ☆ IRQ 91 Nc27
Nimule ☐ SUD 194 Mg44
Nimule N.P. ☒ SUD 194 Mg44
Nina ☐ NAM 204 Lk57
Ninat ☐ RIM 180 Ka37
Nindigully ☐ AUS 149 Se60
Nine Degree Channel ☒ IND 118 Og41
Ninette ☐ CDN 236 Fa21
Ninette ☐ NAM 200 Lk57
Ninety Mile Beach ☒ AUS 151 Sd65
Ninety Mile Beach ☒ NZ 152 Tg53
Ningaloo ☒ ☆ AUS 142 Qg57
Ningaloo Reef Marine Park ☒ ☆ AUS 142 Qg57
Ning'an ☐ CHN 110 Re23
Ningari ☐ RMM 181 Kj38
Ningau Island ▲ PNG 156 Sd48
Ningbo ☐ CHN 109 Ra31
Ningcheng ☐ CHN 107 Qk25
Ningde ☐ CHN 109 Qk32
Ningde ☐ CHN 109 Qh32
Ningde ☐ CHN 109 Ra31
Ningduo ☐ CHN 107 Qg26
Ninghai ☐ CHN 109 Ra31
Ningming ☐ CHN 108 Qd34
Ningnan ☐ CHN 121 Qb32
Ningqiang ☐ CHN 106 Qd29
Ningshan ☐ CHN 106 Qe29
Ningwu ☐ CHN 106 Qg26
Ningxia Huizu Zizhiqu ☐ CHN 106 Qd27
Ning Xian ☐ CHN 106 Qe28
Ningxiang ☐ CHN 108 Qg31
Ninh Binh ☐ VN 121 Qc35
Ninh Hoa ☐ VN 123 Qe39
Ninh Son ☐ VN 123 Qe40
Ninia ☐ RI 154 Rk48
Ninigo Group ▲ PNG 155 Sc46
Ninilchik ☐ USA 228 Ce15
Ninive ☆ IRQ 91 Nc27
Ninjin ☐ CHN 107 Qg23
Ninohe ☐ J 111 Sa25
Ninole ☐ USA 234 Cc36
Niños Héroes ☐ MEX 244 Ef32
Ninotsminda ☐ GE 91 Nb25
Ninove ☐ B 51 Ld40
Nioaque ☐ BR 274 Hc56
Nioaque, T.I. ☐ BR 274 Hc56
Niobrara ☐ USA 236 Ek24
Niobrara ☒ USA 236 Fa24
Niodior ☐ SN 186 Kb39
Niofoin ☐ CI 187 Kg41
Nioka ☐ RDC 194 Mf44
Nioki ☐ RDC 199 Lj47
Niokolo-Koba ☐ SN 186 Kd39
Niokolo-Koba, P.N.du ☒ SN 186 Kd39
Niono ☐ RMM 181 Kh38
Nioro du Rip ☐ SN 186 Kc39
Nioro du Sahel ☐ RMM 180 Kf38
Niort ☐ F 52 Ku44
Nioul ☐ BF 187 Kk39
Niout ☐ RIM 181 Kg37
Nipa ☐ PNG 155 Sb49
Niphanjang ☐ RI 127 Qc46
Nipani ☐ IND 116 Oh37
Nipawin ☐ CDN 233 Eh19
Nipawin Prov. Park ☒ CDN 233 Eh19
Nipepe ☐ MOC 203 Mj52
Niphad ☐ IND 116 Oh35
Nipigon ☐ CDN 237 Ff21
Nipigon Bay ☒ CDN 237 Ff21
Nipišiš ☐ CDN 241 Ha21
Nipomo ☐ USA 234 Dk28
Nippur ☆ IRQ 93 Nc29
Niquelândia ☐ BR 274 Hf53
Niquero ☐ C 243 Gb35
Nir ☐ IR 91 Nd26
Nira ☐ IND 116 Oh36
Nirgua ☐ YV 265 Gf41
Nirmal ☐ IND 116 Ok36
Nirwana Beach ☒ RI 130 Rb48
Niš ☐ SRB 68 Mb47
Nisa ☐ P 60 Kn51
Nisa ▲ TM 96 Nk27
Nisab ☐ KSA 91 Nc30
Nisab ☐ YE 94 Nd38
Nisäat ☐ RI 130 Qk50
Nisciemi ☐ I 63 Lp53
Nishapur ☐ IR 96 Nj27
Nishino-shima ▲ J 113 Re28
Nishino-Omote ☐ J 113 Rf30
Nishi-Okoppe ☐ J 111 Sb23
Nishi-Sonogi-hanto ▲ J 113 Re29
Nishon ☐ UZ 97 Oc26
Nisiá Petalií ▲ GR 71 Me53
Nisio Strofádhes ▲ GR 70 Ma53
Niskibi ☐ CDN 237 Fg20
Nisko ☐ PL 65 Mc40
Nisporeni ☐ MD 73 Me22
Nissedal ☐ N 42 Li31
Nisséko ☐ BF 187 Kh40
Nissi ☐ EST 44 Me31
Nissi Ioaninon ☆ GR 70 Ma51
Nissiros ▲ GR 71 Mh54
Nissum Fjord ☒ DK 42 Lh34
Nisut Plateau ☒ CDN 230 De15
Nita'a ☐ KSA 93 Na32
Nita Downs ☐ AUS 142 Ra55
Niterói ☐ BR 277 Hj57
Nitinat ☐ CDN 232 Dj21
Nit Pass ☒ CHN/IND 102 Ok30
Nitmiluk N.P. ☒ ☆ AUS 146 Rg53
Nitra ☐ SK 66 Lt42
Nitra ☒ SK 66 Lt42
Nitrianske Pravno ☐ SK 67 Lt42
Nitriansky hrad ☆ SK 66 Lt42
Nittambuwa ☐ CL 119 Pa41
Nittedal ☐ N 42 Lk31
Niuchang ☐ CHN 108 Qd31
Niuchang ☐ CHN 121 Qc34
Niue ☒ NZ 134 Bb11
Niumi N.P. ☒ WAG 186 Kb39
Niur, Gunung ▲ RI 130 Qk50
Niutoushan ☐ CHN 121 Qh34
Niuzhuang ☐ CHN 110 Rb25
Nivano ☐ PK 98 Ob32
Nivala ☐ FIN 41 Me27
Nivelles ☐ B 51 Ld40

Nivenskoe ☐ RUS 45 Ma36
Nivernais ▲ F 53 Ld43
Niveri ☐ IND 114 Oh27
Niwas ☐ IND 117 Pa34
Nixi ☐ CHN 121 Pk32
Nixon ☐ USA 234 Ea26
Niya = Minfeng ☐ CHN 102 Pb27
Nizamabad ☐ IND 116 Ok36
Nizamabad Temple ☆ IND 116 Ok36
Nizamghat ☐ IND 120 Ph31
Nizampatam ☐ IND 117 Pa38
Nizina Wielkopolska ☒ PL 64 Lq39
Nizip ☐ TR 90 Mj27
Nizke Tatry ▲ SK 67 Lu42
Nizke Tatry, N.P. ☒ SK 67 Lu42
Nizna Boca ☐ SK 67 Lu42
Nižnaja Lomov ☐ RUS 72 Nb19
Nižnevartovsk ☐ RUS 88 Ob06
Niznij Casučej ☐ RUS 105 Qh20
Niznij Pjandž ☐ TJ 97 Oe27
Nizniy Tagil ☐ RUS 88 Nd07
Nižnaja Tunguska ☒ RUS 88 Pc05
Nizwa ☐ OM 95 Nj34
Nižyn ☐ UA 72 Mf20
Nizza Monferrato ☐ I 60 Lj46
Njazidja ☐ IL 92 Mh30
Njegoš ☆ RUS 88 Ob06
Njinjo ☐ EAT 197 Mk51
Njivice ☐ HR 61 Lp45
Njombe ☐ EAT 196 Mh50
Njombe ☐ EAT 196 Mh50
Njupeskär ☒ S 40 Lr29
Njurba ☐ RUS 89 Qd06
Nkalagu ☐ WAN 188 Ld42
Nkambe ☐ CAM 188 Lf42
Nkawkaw ☐ GH 187 Kk42
Nkayi ☐ RCB 198 Lh47
Nkayi ☐ ZW 202 Me55
Nkhamenya ☐ MW 196 Mg52
Nkhata Bay ☐ MW 196 Mh51
Nkhotakota ☐ MW 196 Mg52
Nkhotakota Game Reserve ☒ MW 196 Mg52
Nko ☐ RCB 198 Lh47
Nkoambang ☐ CAM 189 Lg43
Nkolabona ☐ G 189 Lf45
Nkole ☐ Z 196 Mf51
Nkolmengbunga ☐ G 189 Lf44
Nkolmetet ☐ CAM 188 Lf44
Nkome ☐ EAT 194 Mf47
Nkomfap ☐ WAN 188 Le43
Nkondwe ☐ EAT 196 Mf49
Nkongjok ☐ CAM 188 Lf44
Nkongsamba ☐ CAM 188 Le43
Nkon Ngok ☐ CAM 189 Lf43
Nkoteng ☐ CAM 189 Lg43
Nkoué ☐ RCB 198 Lh47
Nkourala ☐ RMM 187 Kg40
Nkula Falls ☐ MW 203 Mh53
Nkundi ☐ EAT 196 Mh49
Nkungulu ☐ MW 203 Mh53
Nkurenkuru ☐ NAM 200 Lk54
Nkwalini ☐ ZA 205 Mf60
Nkwanta ☐ GH 187 Kj43
Nkwanta ☐ GH 187 La41
Nnewi ☐ WAN 188 Ld42
No.24 Well ☐ AUS 143 Rb57
No.35 Well ☐ AUS 143 Rc57
Noailles ☐ F 51 Lc41
Noakhali ☐ BD 120 Pf34
Noanama ☐ CO 264 Gb44
Noatak ☐ USA 229 Bj12
Noatak National Preserve ☒ USA 229 Bk11
Nobadeer (Nantucket) ☒ USA 241 Gf25
Nobeoka ☐ J 113 Rf30
Nobere ☐ BF 187 Kk40
Nobles Nob Mine ☆ AUS 146 Rh55
Nobokwe ☐ ZA 205 Md61
Nobol ☐ EC 268 Fk46
Noboribetsu ☐ J 111 Sa24
Nobres ☐ BR 274 Hc53
Nochi-katsuura ☐ J 113 Rh29
Noci ☐ I 63 Ls50
Nockatunga ☐ AUS 148 Sb59
Nockberge, N.P. ☒ A 61 Lo44
Nocochea ☐ AUS 149 Sc60
Nocona ☐ USA 238 Fb29
Noda ☐ J 111 Sa25
Nodeland ☐ N 42 Li32
Nöding-Nol ☐ S 42 Lh33
Nodwengu ▲ ZA 205 Mf60
Noel ☐ CDN 240 Gj23
Noel Kempff, P.N. ☒ BOL 278 Ha53
Noenieput ☐ ZA 204 Ma59
Noépé ☐ TG 187 La42
Noetinger ☐ RA 281 Gj62
Nœux-les-Mines ☐ F 51 Lc41
Nogales ☐ USA 235 Ee30
Nogales ☐ MEX 235 Ee30
Nogales ☐ MEX 244 Ef32
Nogara ☐ I 61 Ll45
Nogat ☐ I 60 Lj45
Nogal Valley ☒ SP 193 Nd41
Nogamut ☐ USA 228 Cb15
Nogarejas ☐ E 54 Kp39
Nogata ☐ J 113 Rf29
Nogent ☐ F 53 Lf42
Nogent-le-Roi ☐ F 51 Lb42
Nogent-le-Rotrou ☐ F 50 La42
Nogent-sur-Seine ☐ F 51 Ld42
Noginsk ☐ RUS 72 Mk18
Nogoya ▲ RA 276 Ha62
Noguera ☐ E 57 Kr41
Nohalal ☐ MEX 247 Fc36
Nohar ☐ IND 114 Oh31
Noheji ☐ J 111 Sa25
Nohfelden ☐ D 59 Lh41
Noia ☐ E 54 Km48
Noirétable ☐ F 52 Ks44
Noirmoutier ☐ F 52 Ks44
Noirmoutier-en-l'Île ☐ F 52 Ks44
Nojack ☐ CDN 233 Ec19
Nojima-saki ▲ J 113 Rk28
Nokaneng ☐ RB 201 Mb55
Nokha ☐ IND 114 Og32
Nokja ☐ IR 98 Oa32
Nok Kundi ☐ PK 98 Ob31
Nokomis ☐ CDN 233 Eb20
Nokou ☐ TCH 183 Lh38
Nokuku ☐ VU 158 Td53
Nola ☐ I 63 Lp50
Nola ☐ RCA 190 Lj44
Nolay ☐ F 53 Le44
Nolhivaranfaru ☐ MV 118 Og42
Noli ☐ EAT 197 Mk51
Noli ☐ I 60 Lj46
Noma misaki ▲ J 113 Rf30
Nomane ☐ PNG 155 Sc49
Nombre de Dios ☐ MEX 246 Eh34
Nomeny ☐ F 51 Lg42
Nomgon ☐ MNG 104 Qb21
Nomhon ☐ CHN 103 Pj27
Nomitsis ☐ GR 70 Mb53
Nomoi ☐ 134 Ta09
Nomrog Nature Reserve ☒ MNG 105 Qk22
Nomtsas ☐ NAM 204 Lj58
Nonacho Lake ☒ CDN 231 Ef15
Nonancourt ☐ F 51 Lb42
Nonántola ☐ I 60 Lm46
Non Champa ☐ THA 123 Qd37
Nondalton ☐ USA 228 Cc15
Nong'an ☐ CHN 110 Rc23
Nong Bua ☐ THA 122 Qa38
Nong Bua Daeng ☐ THA 123 Qb38
Nong Bua Khok ☐ THA 123 Qc38
Nong Bua Lam Phu ☐ THA 123 Qb37
Nong Bua Rahaeo ☐ THA 123 Qa38

Nongchang ☐ CHN 106 Qe27
Nong Chang ☐ THA 122 Pk38
Nong Haet ☐ LAO 121 Qb36
Nong Han ☐ THA 123 Qb37
Nong Khai ☐ THA 122 Qa38
Nong Khi ☐ THA 123 Qb37
Nongoma ☐ ZA 205 Mf59
Nongowa ☐ RG 186 Ke41
Nong Phai ☐ THA 122 Qa38
Nong Phok ☐ THA 123 Qc37
Nong Phu ☐ THA 123 Qc38
Nong Rua ☐ THA 123 Qb37
Nongqai Fort ☆ ZA 205 Mf60
Nongsa Beach ☒ RI 127 Qc45
Nongstoin ☐ IND 120 Pf33
Nong Yai ☐ THA 123 Qa39
Nonning ☐ AUS 150 Rj62
Nonoai ☐ BR 276 Hd59
Nonoava ☐ MEX 244 Eg34
Nonogasta ☐ RA 279 Gg60
Non Thai ☐ THA 123 Qc38
Nontron ☐ F 52 La45
Nonza ☐ F 60 Lk48
Nooleeye ☐ SP 195 Nd44
Noonamaan ☐ AUS 146 Rd52
Noondonnia ☐ AUS 145 Rb62
Noonkanbah A.L. ☐ AUS 143 Rc58
Noonu Atoll ▲ MV 118 Og43
Noordoewer ☐ ❋ NAM 204 Lj60
Noordoostpolder ▲ NL 51 Lf38
Noordwijk aan Zee ☐ NL 51 Le38
Noormarkku ☐ FIN 44 Mb29
Noosa ☐ AUS 229 Bk12
Nootka Island ▲ CDN 232 Dh21
Nooyeah Downs ☐ AUS 148 Sb60
Nopiloa ☆ MEX 246 Fb35
Nopoming Prov. Park ☒ CDN 236 Fc20
Nóqui ☐ ANG 198 Lg48
Nora ☒ I 62 Lj52
Nora ▲ S 43 Lq31
Noralee ☐ CDN 230 Dg19
Noralup ☐ AUS 144 Qj63
Norassoba ☐ RG 186 Kf40
Norbote ☐ S 43 Lq30
Norberto de la Riestra ☐ RA 281 Ha63
Nórcia ☐ I 61 Lo48
Nordagutu ☐ N 42 Lk31
Nordaustlandet ▲ N 38 Ma06
Nordborg ☐ DK 42 Lj35
Nordby ☐ DK 42 Lj35
Nordby ▲ DK 42 Lj35
Nordøyar ▲ DK 46 Ko28
Nordegg ☐ CDN 232 Ec19
Norden ☐ D 58 Lh37
Nordenham ☐ D 58 Lj37
Nordens Ark ☒ N 42 Lm32
Nordenskiöld Land ▲ N 38 Lh07
Norderney ☐ D 58 Lh37
Norderstedt ☐ D 58 Lk37
Nordeste ☐ ANG 199 Ma49
Nordfold ☐ N 38 Lq23
Nordhausen ☐ D 58 Ll39
Nordholz ☐ D 58 Lj37
Nordhorn ☐ D 58 Lh38
Nordkjosbotn ☐ N 38 Lu21
Nördlingen ☐ D 59 Ll42
Nordmaling ☐ S 41 Lu27
Nordman ☐ USA 232 Eb21
Nordmark ☐ S 43 Lq31
Nord-Osen ☐ N 42 Ll30
Nordreisa ☐ N 38 Ma20
Nord-Ostsee-Kanal ☒ D 58 Lk36
Nordoyane ☒ N 40 Lg28
Nordrhein-Westfalen ☐ D 58 Lh39
Nordsee ☒ 26 La04
Noresund ☐ N 42 Lk30
Norfolk ☐ USA 236 Fb24
Norfolk ☐ USA 242 Gb27
Norfolk Broads ☒ GB 49 Lb38
Norfolk Island ▲ AUS 134 Ta12
Norfolk Island ▲ AUS 134 Ta12
Norfolk Ridge ☒ 134 Ta12
Norheimsund ☐ N 42 Lg30
Noriega ▲ USA 234 Dj27
Norik ▲ RUS 88 Pb05
Noring, Gunung ▲ MAL 126 Qa43
Normal ☐ USA 239 Ff25
Norman ☐ USA 238 Fb28
Normanby Island ▲ PNG 156 Sf51
Normandia ☐ BR 266 Ha44
Normandien ☐ ZA 205 Me60
Normandin ☐ CDN 240 Gg21
Normangee ☐ USA 238 Fb30
Norman's Cay ▲ BS 243 Gb33
Normanton ☐ AUS 147 Sa54
Normanville ☐ AUS 150 Rk63
Norman Wells ☐ CDN 226 Dc05
Normétal ☐ CDN 237 Ga21
Norotshama River Resort ☒ ❋ NAM 204 Lj60
Norquay ☐ CDN 233 Ej20
Norquinco ☐ RA 280 Ge66
Norråker ☒ S 41 Lq27
Norra Kvills n.p. ☒ S 43 Lq33
Norrbärke ☐ S 43 Lq30
Norra Aaby ☐ DK 42 Lj35
Norre Alslev ☐ DK 42 Lm36
Nørre Nebel ☐ DK 42 Lj35
Nørre Vorupør ☐ DK 42 Lh34
Norrhult ☐ S 43 Lq33
Norris ☐ USA 233 Ee23
Norris Point ☐ CDN 241 Ha21
Norrköping ☐ S 43 Lr32
Norrsundet ☐ S 43 Lr30
Norrtälje ☐ S 43 Ls31
Nors ☐ DK 42 Lh33
Norsk ☐ RUS 105 Re19
Norsup ☐ VU 158 Td54
Norte, Cerro ▲ RA 282 Gd67
Norte ☐ BR 274 Hb53
Nortelândia ☐ BR 274 Hc53
Nortfoji ☐ J 111 Sa25
Norton ▲ J 113 Rf30
Norton ☐ USA 236 Ek26
Norton ☐ USA 238 Fd27
Norton ☐ ZW 202 Mf54
Norton Shores ☐ USA 237 Fg24
Norton Sound ☒ USA 228 Bh14

North Downs ☒ GB 49 La39
North East ☐ RB 202 Md56
Northeast Cape ▲ USA 228 Bf14
Northeast Coast National Scenic Area ☒ RC 109 Ra33
North East Islands ▲ AUS 146 Rj52
Northeast Point ▲ BS 250 Gc33
Northeast Point ▲ BS 250 Gd34
Northeast Point ▲ BS 250 Gd35
Northeast Point ▲ CDN 241 Hc20
Northeast Point ▲ AUS 228 Bf17
Northeast Providence Channel ☒ BS 243 Gb32
Northern ☐ D 58 Lk39
Northern Cape ☐ ZA 204 Lk60
Northern Cay ▲ BH 248 Fg37
Northern Cheyenne Ind. Res. ☐ USA 233 Eg22
Northern Hot Springs Park ☒ ☆ CHN 108 Qd31
Northern Indian Lake ☒ CDN 227 Fa07
Northern Ireland ☐ GB 47 Kn36
Northern Lau Group ▲ FJI 159 Ua54
Northern Mariana Islands ☐ USA 135 Sa08
Northern Sporades ▲ GR 71 Me51
Northern Territory ☐ AUS 135 Rb12
Northfield ☐ USA 236 Fd23
North Fiji Basin ☒ 134 Tb11
North Foreland ▲ GB 49 Lb39
North Fork Kuskokwim River ☒ USA 229 Cc14
North Frisian Islands ▲ D 58 Lj36
North Goulburn Island ▲ AUS 146 Rg51
Northhaam ☐ ZA 205 Md58
Northhampton ☐ AUS 144 Qh60
North Head ☐ AUS 147 Sb55
North Head ▲ NZ 152 Tf64
Northhome ☐ USA 236 Fc22
North Horr ☐ EAK 194 Mj44
North Island ▲ AUS 144 Qg60
North Island ▲ AUS 144 Qg60
North Island ▲ NZ 152 Tj64
North Kessock ☐ GB 48 Kq33
North Komelik ☐ USA 235 Ee29
North Korea ■ PRK 77 Ra05
North Lakhimpur ☐ IND 120 Ph32
North Las Vegas ☐ USA 234 Ec27
Northleach ☐ GB 49 Kt39
North Little Rock ☐ USA 239 Fd28
North Luangwa N.P. ☒ Z 196 Mg51
North Luconia Shoals ☒ 128 Qd42
North Male Atoll ▲ MV 118 Og43
North Mankato ☐ USA 236 Fc23
North Miladhunmadulu Atoll = Shaviyani Atoll ▲ MV 118 Og42
North Nilandhoo Atoll = Faafu Atoll ▲ MV 118 Og42
North Ossetia ☐ RUS 91 Nc24
North Pen. ▲ CDN 236 Ff20
North Peron Island ▲ AUS 143 Re52
North Platte ☐ USA 235 Ej25
North Platte ☒ USA 236 Ek25
North Point ▲ AUS 228 Bf17
North Point ▲ WAN 188 Lc43
North Pole ▲ 286 La01
North Ronaldsay ▲ GB 48 Ks31
North Portal ☐ CDN 233 Eg21
North Rim ☐ USA 235 Ed27
North Ronaldsay ▲ GB 48 Ks31
North Salmara ☐ IND 120 Pf33
North Saskatchewan River ☒ CDN 233 Ef19
North Sea ☒ 26 La04
North Sentinel Island ▲ IND 122 Pg40
North Siberian Lowland ☒ RUS 88 Pb04
North Star ☐ AUS 149 Sf60
North Stradbroke Island ▲ AUS 149 Sg59
North Taranaki Bight ☒ NZ 153 Th65
North Thiladhunmathee Atoll = Haa-Alifu Atoll ▲ MV 118 Og42
North Tonawanda ☐ USA 237 Ga24
North Trap ▲ NZ 153 Td69
North Ubian Island ▲ RP 129 Ra42
North Uist ▲ GB 48 Kn33
Northumberland Islands ▲ AUS 149 Se56
North Vancouver ☐ CDN 232 Dj21
North Vernon ☐ USA 239 Fh26
Northville ☐ USA 236 Fa23
North Walsham ☐ GB 49 Lb38
North West ☐ ZA 204 Mb59
North West Basin ▲ AUS 144 Qh57
Northwest Bay ☐ CDN 236 Fa22
North West Cape ☒ AUS 142 Qf57
North West Cape ▲ AUS 228 Be14
Northwest Coastal Highway ☒ AUS 144 Qh59
Northwest Point ▲ BS 250 Gd35
Northwest Providence Channel ☒ BS 243 Ga32
Northwest River ☐ CDN 241 Ha21
Northwest Territories ☐ CDN 226 Dc06
North Windham ☐ USA 241 Ge24
North York Moors N.P. ☒ GB 49 Kt36
Northwood ☐ USA 236 Fb22
North York Basin ☒ BR 273 Jb51
Norton Sound ☒ USA 228 Bh14
Nortonville ☐ USA 239 Fh27
North America ☒ 210 Eb04
Northam ☐ AUS 144 Qj61
Nortalla ☐ BR 273 Hk48
Norwalk ☐ USA 237 Fj25
Norwalk ☐ USA 241 Gd25
Norway ■ N 27 La31
Norway House ☐ CDN 227 Fb03
Norwegian Basin ☒ 26 Kb03
Norwegian Sea ☒ 26 Kb02
Norwegian Trench ☒ 42 Lf32
Norwich ☐ GB 49 Lb38
Norwich ☐ USA 241 Gd25
Norwood ☐ USA 235 Eg26
Norwood ☐ USA 241 Gd25
Nosappu-misaki ▲ J 111 Sc24
Nosara ☐ CR 248 Fh41
Nosairie ☐ RM 206 Nf53
Nosbe ☐ RM 206 Ne52
nos Kaliakra ▲ BG 69 Mj47
Nosovo ☐ RUS 45 Mh33
Nossa Senhora Aparecida ☆ BR 277 Hh50
Nossa Senhora da Glória ☐ BR 273 Jb51
Nossa Senhora das Dores ☐ BR 273 Jb51
Nossa Senhora da Victoria ☆ ANG 198 Lg50
Nossa Senhora do Socorro ☐ BR 273 Jb51
Nossebro ☐ S 42 Ln32
Nossen ☐ D 58 Ln39
Nossombougou ☐ RMM 187 Kg39
Nosy Be ▲ RM 206 Ne52
Nosy Berafia ▲ RM 206 Ne52
Nosy Boraha ▲ RM 206 Nf53
Nosy Faly ▲ RM 206 Ne52
Nosy Komba ▲ RM 206 Ne52
Nosy Lava ▲ RM 206 Nd53

Nosy Mitsio ▲ RM 206 Ne52
Nosy Radama ▲ RM 206 Ne53
Nosy Sainte-Marie ▲ RM 207 Ne54
Nosy Varika ☐ RM 207 Ne56
Noszolop ☐ H 66 Ls43
Notia Pindos ▲ GR 70 Mb52
Notintsila ☐ ZA 205 Me61
Nótio Stenó Kerkiras ☒ GR 70 Ma51
Nötö ▲ FIN 44 Mb31
Noto ☐ I 63 Lq54
Notocote ☐ MOC 203 Mk54
Notodden ☐ N 42 Lk31
Noto Gouye Diama ☐ SN 180 Kb38
Noto-hanto ▲ J 111 Rj27
Noto-jima ▲ J 111 Rj27
Notre Dame Bay ☒ CDN 241 Hc21
Notre-Dame-de-Haut ☆ F 53 Lf47
Notre-Dame de la Paix ☐ CI 187 Kh42
Notre-Dame-de-la-Garde ☆ F 53 Lf47
Notre-Dame de l'Épine ☆ F 51 Le41
Notre-Dame de Rouen ☆ F 51 La41
Notre-Dame de Saint-Omer ☆ F 51 Lc40
Notre-Damedu-Nord ☐ CDN 237 Ga22
Notre Dame Junction ☐ CDN 241 Hc21
Notsé ☐ TG 187 La42
Notsé ☐ TG 187 La42
Nottingham ☐ GB 49 Kt38
Nottingham Downs ☐ AUS 149 Sb56
Nottingham Road ☐ ZA 205 Me60
Nott, Mount ▲ AUS 150 Rh62
Nottoway ☒ USA 242 Ga27
Nottuln ☐ D 58 Lh39
Noual, Sabkhet en ☒ TN 178 Lf29
Nouâdhibou ☐ RIM 180 Kb35
Nouakchott ● ☒ RIM 180 Kb36
Nouâmghâr ☐ RIM 180 Kb36
Nouméa ● ❋ F 158 Td57
Noumoukiédougou ☐ CI 187 Kh41
Nouna ☐ BF 187 Kj39
Noupoort ☐ ZA 205 Mc61
Nourlangie Rock ☆ AUS 146 Rg52
Nouvelle ☐ CDN 240 Gj21
Nouzaïd ☐ AFG 99 Oc29
Növa ☐ EST 44 Md31
Nova Alvorada do Sul ☐ BR 274 Hc56
Nova Andradina ☐ BR 274 Hd57
Nova Apua ☐ BR 270 Gh50
Nova Aurora ☐ BR 274 Hh55
Nova Borowa ☐ UA 73 Me20
Nova Brasilândia ☐ BR 270 Gj51
Nova Brasilândia ☐ BR 274 Hc53
Nova Bystřice ☐ CZ 66 Lp42
Nova Caipemba ☐ ANG 198 Lh49
Nova Canaã do Norte ☐ BR 271 Hc51
Novačene ☐ RUS 88 Ob06
Novaci ☐ MK 68 Mb49
Novaci ☐ RO 68 Md45
Nova Coimbra ☐ MOC 196 Mh53
Nova Crnja ☐ SRB 68 Ma45
Nova Cruz ☐ BR 273 Jc49
Nova Esperança ☐ ANG 198 Lh49
Nova Esperança ☐ BR 274 Hd57
Nova Friburgo ☐ BR 277 Hj57
Nova Gaia ☐ ANG 199 Lj51
Nova Golega ☐ MOC 202 Mg56
Nova Gorica ☐ SLO 60 Lo45
Nova Gradiška ☐ HR 61 Ls45
Nova Granada ☐ BR 277 Hf56
Nova Independência ☐ BR 274 He56
Novaja Derevnja ☐ RUS 45 Mb36
Novaja Pahost ☐ BY 45 Mh35
Novaja Ruda ☐ BY 65 Me37
Nová Jičín ☐ CZ 66 Lt41
Novajorque ☐ BR 273 Hk49
Novalja ☐ HR 61 Lp46
Nova Londrina ☐ BR 274 Hd57
Nova Lusitânia ☐ MOC 203 Mh55
Nova Mambone ☐ MOC 203 Mh56
Nova Nabúri ☐ MOC 203 Mk54
Nova Odesa ☐ UA 73 Mf22
Nova Olímpia ☐ BR 274 Hc54
Nova Olinda ☐ BR 273 Hk49
Nova Olinda do Norte ☐ BR 271 Ha47
Nova Paraíso ☐ BR 266 Gk45
Nova Petrópolis ☐ BR 276 He60
Nova Ponte ☐ BR 277 Hg55
Nova Roma ☐ BR 275 Hh52
Nova Russas ☐ BR 273 Hk48
Nova Santarém ☐ MOC 203 Mh52
Nova Scotia ☐ CDN 227 Gg10
Nova Serrana ☐ BR 275 Hh55
Nova Sofala ☐ MOC 203 Mh55
Nova Soure ☐ BR 273 Jb51
Novato ☐ USA 234 Dj26
Nova Topola ☐ BIH 61 Ls45
Nova Ušycja ☐ UA 73 Me21
Nova Varoš ☐ SRB 68 Lu47
Nova Venécia ☐ BR 275 Hk55
Nova Viçosa ☐ BR 275 Hk55
Nova Viseu ☐ MOC 197 Mj52
Nova Vodolaha ☐ UA 72 Mj21
Nova Xavantina ☐ BR 274 He53
Novaya Zemlya ▲ RUS 76 Nb02
Nova Zagora ☐ BG 69 Mg48
Nove de Julho, T.I. ☐ BR 270 Gj49
Nové Hrady ☐ CZ 66 Lp42
Nové Mesto na Moravě ☐ CZ 66 Lq41
Nové Mesto nad Metují ☐ CZ 66 Lr40
Nové Mesto nad Váhom ☐ SK 66 Ls42
Nové Zámky ☐ SK 66 Lt43
Novgorodka ☐ RUS 45 Mj33
Novgorodka ☐ UA 73 Mg21
Novhorod-Sivers'kyj ☐ UA 72 Mg19
Novhorod-Volyns'kyj ☐ UA 73 Md20
Novi Bečej ☐ SRB 68 Ma45
Novi Bilokorovyči ☐ UA 72 Me20
Novi Grad ☐ BIH 61 Ls45
Novi Iskăr ☐ BG 68 Md48
Novi Kneževac ☐ SRB 68 Ma44
Novi Ligure ☐ I 60 Lj46
Novion-Porcien ☐ F 51 Le41
Novi Pazar ☐ BG 69 Mh47
Novi Pazar ☐ SRB 68 Ma47
Novi Sad ☐ SRB 68 Lu45
Novi Sanžary ☐ UA 73 Mh21
Novi Strilyšča ☐ UA 66 Md41
Novi Troyany ☐ UA 69 Mj45
Novi Vinodolski ☐ HR 61 Lp45
Novo ☐ RI 154 Rj45
Novo Acre ☐ BR 275 Hk53
Novo Acordo ☐ BR 275 Hg51
Novo Airão ☐ BR 270 Gk48
Novo Alegre ☐ BR 275 Hj53
Novoaleksejevka ☐ UA 73 Mh22
Novoaleksandrovsk ☐ RUS 90 Na23
Novoanninskij ☐ RUS 73 Nb21
Novoazovs'k ☐ UA 73 Mk22
Novobod ☐ TJ 97 Oe26
Novočeboksarsk ☐ RUS 72 Nd18
Novocimljanskaja ☐ RUS 73 Nb22
Novo Cruzeiro ☐ BR 275 Hj54
Novočuguevka ☐ RUS 111 Rg23
Novodevičij monastyr' ☆ RUS 72 Mj18
Novofedorivka ☐ UA 73 Mg22
Novohrad-Volyns'kyj ☐ UA 73 Md20
Novohrodivka ☐ UA 73 Mj21
Novoil'inovka ☐ UA 73 Mk21
Novojavorivs'ke ☐ UA 66 Mc41
Novo Jardim ☐ BR 275 Hh52
Novokačalinsk ☐ RUS 110 Rf23

Novokievskij Uval ☐ RUS 105 Re20
Novokuzneck ☐ RUS 88 Pb08
Novolazarevskaja ☒ 287 Lc33
Novo Lino ☐ BR 273 Jc50
Novo Mesto ☐ SLO 66 Lq45
Novomičurinsk ☐ RUS 72 Mk18
Novomihajlovskij ☐ RUS 73 Mk23
Novomoskovs'k ☐ UA 73 Mh21
Novo Mundo ☐ BR 272 He52
Novomykolajivka ☐ UA 73 Mg22
Novonikolaevskij ☐ RUS 72 Nb20
Novomyrhorod ☐ UA 73 Mf21
Novonikolaevskij ☐ RUS 72 Nb20
Novooleksijivka ☐ UA 73 Mh22
Novo Oriente ☐ BR 270 Gf50
Novo Oriente ☐ BR 273 Hk48
Novo Oriente de Minas ☐ BR 275 Hk54
Novo Paraná ☐ BR 271 Hb51
Novo Pensamento ☐ BR 270 Gj46
Novopokrovskaja ☐ RUS 111 Rh23
Novopokrovskij ☐ RUS 73 Mk24
Novopokrovskaja ☐ RUS 73 Na23
Novopskov ☐ UA 73 Mk21
Novorossijsk ☐ RUS 73 Mk23
Novorzev ☐ RUS 72 Me17
Novoselov ☐ RUS 88 Pa07
Nové Sedlo ☐ CZ 66 Ln40
Novoselivka ☐ UA 73 Mg21
Novoselovo ☐ RUS 45 Mj33
Novoselyci ☐ UA 73 Mg23
Novo Selo ☐ BG 68 Mc46
Novo Selo ☐ BG 69 Mg48
Novo Selo ☐ BIH 61 Ls45
Novo Selo ☐ MK 68 Mc49
Novosel'e ☐ RUS 45 Mj32
Novosibirsk ☐ RUS 88 Pa07
Novosibirskie Ostrova ▲ RUS 89 Ra02
Novosibirskoe vodohranilišče ☒ RUS 88 Pa08
Novosokol'niki ☐ RUS 72 Mf17
Novotroick ☐ RUS 88 Nd08
Novotroickoe ☐ RUS 105 Rd20
Novotroickoe ☐ RUS 110 Rf21
Novotrojic'ke ☐ UA 73 Mh22
Novoukrajinka ☐ UA 73 Mf21
Novovolyns'k ☐ UA 66 Mc40
Novovoskresenovka ☐ RUS 105 Rd19
Novska ☐ HR 61 Ls45
Novy Bor ☐ CZ 66 Lp40
Novyj Bug ☐ UA 73 Mg22
Novyj Dvor ☐ BY 65 Me37
Novyj Dvor ☐ BY 65 Me38
Novyj Oskol ☐ RUS 72 Mj20
Novyj Port ☐ RUS 88 Oc05
Novyj Rozdil ☐ UA 67 Me41
Novyj Urengoj ☐ RUS 88 Od05
Novy Jičín ☐ CZ 66 Lt41
Novyj Jarylyč ☐ UA 67 Mf41
Novyj Port ☐ RUS 88 Oc05
Nowa Dęba ☐ PL 65 Mb40
Nowa Gaia ☐ ANG 199 Lj51
Nowa Karczma ☐ PL 64 Ls36
Nowa Ruda ☐ PL 64 Lr40
Nowa Słupia ☐ PL 65 Mb40
Nowa Sól ☐ PL 64 Lq39
Nowa Wieś ☐ USA 238 Fc27
Nowa Wieś ☐ PL 65 Mb37
Nowa Wieś Ełcka ☐ PL 65 Mc37
Nowa Wieś Lęborska ☐ PL 64 Ls36
Nowa Wieś Lęborska ☐ PL 64 Ls36
Nowe Miasteczko ☐ PL 64 Lq39
Nowe Miasto nad Pilicą ☐ PL 65 Ma39
Nowen ☐ CDN 236 Fa22
Nowendoc ☐ AUS 149 Sf61
Nowe Warpno ☐ PL 64 Lp37
Nowgong ☐ IND 117 Pa36
Nowinka ☐ PL 65 Mc37
Nowitna National Wildlife Refuge ☒ USA 229 Cc13
Nowogard ☐ PL 64 Lq37
Nowogród ☐ PL 65 Mb38
Nowogród Bobrzański ☐ PL 64 Lq39
Nowogrodziec ☐ PL 64 Lq39
Nowo Miasto nad Warta ☐ PL 64 Lr38
Nowoleksandrivka ☐ UA 73 Mk22
Nowowesolsk ☐ PL 65 Ma40
Nowra ☐ AUS 151 Sf63
Nowshera ☐ PK 99 Of29
Nowsud ☐ IR 91 Nd28
Nowy Duninów ☐ PL 65 Lu38
Nowy Dwór ☐ PL 65 Mc37
Nowy Dwór Gdański ☐ PL 65 Lu36
Nowy Dwór Mazowiecki ☐ PL 65 Ma38
Nowy Korczyn ☐ PL 65 Mb40
Nowy Sącz ☐ PL 65 Ma41
Nowy Staw ☐ PL 64 Lt36
Nowy Targ ☐ PL 65 Ma41
Nowy Tomyśl ☐ PL 64 Lr38
Nowy Wiśnicz ☐ PL 65 Ma41
Nowy Żmigród ☐ PL 65 Mb41
Noxon ☐ USA 232 Ec22
Noxubee N.W.R. ☒ USA 239 Fe29
Noyant ☐ F 52 La43
Noyers ☐ F 53 Le43
Noyes Island ▲ USA 230 Dc18
Noyon ☐ F 51 Lc41
Noyon ☐ MNG 104 Qb22
Nozay ☐ F 50 Kt43
Nrusinghanath Temple ☆ IND 117 Pc35
Nsadzu = Cassacatiza ☐ MOC 202 Mg53
Nsalu Cave ☆ Z 196 Mf51
Nsanje ☐ MW 203 Mh54
Nsawam ☐ GH 187 Kk43
Nsawkaw ☐ GH 187 Kj42
Nsefu ☐ Z 196 Mg51
Nselema ☐ MW 203 Mh53
Nsoc ☐ GQ 189 Lg44
Nsok ☐ GQ 189 Lf44
Nsombo ☐ Z 196 Mf50
Nsongeczi ☐ EAU 194 Mf46
Nsontin ☐ RDC 199 Lk47
Nsopzup ☐ MYA 120 Pj33
Nsukka ☐ WAN 188 Ld42
Nsumbu N.P. ☒ Z 196 Mf50
Nswatugi and Pomongwe Caves ☆ ZW 202 Me56
Ntadembele ☐ RDC 198 Lj47
Ntamou ☐ Z 201 Mc52
Ntatrat ☐ RIM 181 Kj37
Ntcheu ☐ MW 203 Mh53
Ntemwa ☐ Z 202 Md53
Ntibane ☐ ZA 205 Me61
Ntionla ☐ TCH 183 Lk38
Ntoroko ☐ EAU 194 Mf45
Ntomba ☐ RDC 198 Lk46
Ntonyane ☐ ZA 205 Me62
Ntoum ☐ G 189 Le44
Ntsotso ☐ RCB 198 Lh46
Ntui ☐ CAM 189 Lf43
Ntungamo ☐ EAU 194 Mf46
Ntuntu ☐ EAT 196 Mg48
Ntusi ☐ EAU 194 Mf45
Ntwetwe Pan ☒ RB 201 Mb55
Nuageux, Mont ▲ F 158 Td57
Nuanetsi ☒ ZW 202 Mf56
Nuangola ☐ USA 241 Gc25
Nuasjärvi ☒ FIN 41 Mh26
Nubia ☒ SUD 185 Mg33
Nubian Desert ☒ SUD 185 Mg33
Nubieber ☐ USA 234 Dk25
Nubledo ☐ E 54 Kp38
Nüden ☐ MNG 104 Qd21
Nudo Ausangate ▲ PE 269 Ge52
Nudo Coropuna ▲ PE 269 Gd53
Nudo de Apolobamba ▲ PE 269 Gf53
Nudo de Sunipari ▲ PE 269 Ge53
Nudo Tres Cruces ▲ PE 269 Ge53

Nueva Alejandría ☐ PE 268 Gd48
Nueva Armenia ☐ HN 248 Fg39
Nueva Asunción ☐ PY 278 Gk56
Nueva California ☐ RA 280 Gf62
Nueva Concepción ☐ ES 248 Fg38
Nueva Constitución ☐ RA 280 Gg63
Nueva Esperanza ☐ RA 279 Gj59
Nueva Esperanza ☐ YV 265 Gj42
Nueva Florida ☐ YV 265 Gf41
Nueva Fortuna ☐ YV 265 Gj42
Nueva Galia ☐ RA 280 Gg62
Nueva Germania ☐ PY 274 Hb57
Nueva Gerona ☐ C 243 Ga34
Nueva Guinea ☐ NIC 249 Fh40
Nueva Helvecia ☐ ROU 281 Hb63
Nueva Imperial ☐ RCH 280 Gd65
Nueva Italia ☐ RA 279 Gk61
Nueva Italia de Ruiz ☐ MEX 246 Eh36
Nueva Lubeka ☐ RA 282 Ge68
Nueva Ocotepeque ☐ HN 248 Fg38
Nueva Palmira ☐ ROU 276 Ha62
Nueva Patria ☐ MEX 245 Ej33
Nueva Pompeya ☐ RA 279 Gk58
Nueva Rosita ☐ MEX 245 Ej33
Nueva San Salvador ☐ ES 248 Fg39
Nueva Villa de Padilla ☐ MEX 245 Fa33
Nuevitas ☐ C 243 Gb35
Nuevo Berlín ☐ ROU 276 Ha62
Nuevo Berlín ☐ ROU 276 Ha62
Nuevo Campechito ☐ MEX 247 Fc36
Nuevo Casas Grandes ☐ MEX 244 Eg30
Nuevo Coahuila ☐ MEX 247 Fc37
Nuevo Esperanza ☐ PE 268 Gd46
Nuevo Ideal ☐ MEX 245 Eh33
Nuevo Laredo ☐ MEX 245 Fa32
Nuevo León ☐ MEX 245 Ek32
Nuevo Leon ☐ MEX 244 Ej31
Nuevo Milagro ☐ MEX 245 Ej31
Nuevo Mundo ☐ CO 264 Ge43
Nuevo Palomas ☐ MEX 244 Eg31
Nuevo Porvenir ☐ MEX 245 Eh31
Nuevo Progreso ☐ PE 269 Gb50
Nuevo Progreso ☐ MEX 246 Fb34
Nuevo Torino ☐ RA 281 Gk61
Nufáru ☐ RO 69 Mj45
Nugget Point ▲ NZ 153 Te69
Nugtat bulgis al Habgilgiyah ☐ LAR 176 Lj29
Nugyo ☒ BR 273 Hk51
Nuguria Islands ▲ PNG 157 Sh47
Nuhaka ☐ NZ 153 Tj65
Nuiqsut ☐ USA 229 Ce10
Nui Than ☐ VN 123 Qe37
Nuits-Saint-Georges ☐ F 53 Le43
Nukhayla ☐ SUD 184 Md36
Nukini, T.I. ☐ BR 268 Gd50
Nuku'alofa ● ☒ TO 135 Ba11
Nukufetau Atoll ▲ TUV 135 Sb47
Nuku Hiva ▲ F 133 Cb10
Nukumanu Atoll = Tasman Islands ▲ PNG 157 Sh48
Nukus ☐ UZ 96 Nk24
Nulavik ☐ USA 228 Ca13
Nulato ☐ USA 229 Cb10
Nulbear ☐ AUS 149 Sc59
Nules ☐ E 57 Ku51
Nullabor ▲ USA 145 Rf61
Nullarbor N.P. ☒ AUS 145 Re61
Nullarbor Plain ☒ AUS 145 Rf61
Nullarbor Regional Reserve ☒ AUS 145 Re61
Nullawa ☐ AUS 149 Sd60
Nulti ☐ CHN 202 Mf57
Num ▲ RI 154 Rh46
Numagalong ☐ AUS 143 Rg56
Numaligarh ☐ IND 120 Pg33
Numan ☐ WAN 188 Lg41
Numata ☐ J 111 Rk27
Numata ☐ J 111 Sa24
Numazu ☐ J 113 Rk28
Numbulwar ☐ AUS 146 Rh53
Numedalen ▲ N 42 Lj30
Numfoor ▲ RI 154 Rh46
Nummi ☐ FIN 44 Md30
Nummela ☐ FIN 44 Md30
Nummi ☐ FIN 44 Md30
Nummi-Pusula ☐ FIN 44 Md30
Nummijärvi ☐ FIN 44 Mc28
Nunavut ☐ CDN 226 Eb06
Nundroo ☐ AUS 145 Rg61
Nuneaton ☐ GB 49 Kt38
Nungarin ☐ AUS 144 Qj61
Nungba ☐ IND 120 Pg34
Nungo ☐ MOC 197 Mj52
Nungwe ☐ EAT 194 Mg47
Nunivak Island ▲ USA 228 Bg15
Nunkun ▲ IND 114 Oj28
Nunpuzo ☐ USA 228 Bj14
Nunukan ▲ RI 128 Qj45
Núpsstaður ☆ IS 46 Kc27
Nur ☐ IR 96 Nf27
Nur Abad ☐ IR 91 Ne28
Nur Abad ☐ IR 93 Nf30
Nur Gama ☐ PK 99 Of28
Nuraghe Santa Barbara ☆ I 62 Lj50
Nuraghe Santa Cristina ☆ I 62 Lj50
Nuraghe Sant'Antine ☆ I 62 Lj50
Nuraghe Santa Sabina ☆ I 62 Lj50
Nuratau N.P. ☒ UZ 97 Od27
Nürburgring ☆ D 59 Lh40
Nurdağlar ☐ TR 90 Mj27
Nurek ☐ TJ 97 Oe27
Nurek Dam ☆ TJ 97 Oe27
Nurete ☐ SUD 184 Mb39
Nurhak ☐ TR 90 Mj27
Nurlat ☐ RUS 72 Ne18
Nurmo ☐ FIN 44 Mc28
Nürnberg ☐ D 59 Ll41
Nurota ☐ UZ 97 Oc26
Nurota tizmasi ▲ UZ 97 Od25
Nürtingen ☐ D 59 Lk42
Nusa Dua ☐ RI 129 Qh50
Nusa Penida ▲ RI 129 Qh50
Nušawiplan ☐ RI 154 Rg48
Nushki ☐ PK 99 Ob31
Nush Abad ☆ IR 91 Nf28
Nushagak Peninsula ▲ USA 228 Ca16
Nutwood Downs ☐ AUS 146 Rh53
Nuuk = Godthåb ● DK 227 Hb06
Nuukuulaaq susiqatsika ☆ FIN 44 Me30
Nuwara Eliya ☐ CL 119 Pb41
Nuweiba ☐ ET 179 Mg31
Nuwejaarspoort ☐ NAM 204 Lk60
Nuweveldberge ▲ ZA 204 Mb61
Nuxis ☐ I 62 Lj51
Nuy ☐ ZA 204 Lk62
Nuzvid ☐ IND 117 Pa37
Nwanedi Game Reserve ☒ ZA 202 Mf57
Nwanetsi ☐ ZA 205 Mf58
Nwoya = EAU 194 Mf44
Nxai Pan ☐ RB 201 Mb55
Nxai Pan N.P. ☒ RB 201 Mb55
Nyabing ☐ AUS 144 Qj62

Nyagassola ⊡ RG 186 Kf39
Nyahanga ⊡ EAT 194 Mg47
Nyahururu ⊡ EAK 194 Mj45
Nyainqêntanglha Feng ▲ CHN 103 Pf30
Nyainqêntanglha Shan ▲ CHN 102 Pe31
Nyaimrong ⊡ CHN 103 Pg29
Nyakahra ⊡ EAT 194 Mj47
Nyakanazi ⊡ EAT 194 Mg47
Nyakitasi ⊡ EAT 197 Mk50
Nyala ⊡ SUD 184 Mc39
Nyâlesund ⊡ N 38 Lf06
Nyali ⊡ Q 198 Lf47
Nyalikungu ⊡ EAT 194 Mg47
Nyama ⊡ Z 202 Me53
Nyamandhlovu ⊡ ZW 202 Me55
Nyamapanda ⊡ ZW 202 Mg54
Nyamassila ⊡ TG 187 Laa2
Nyamayeropa ⊡ ZW 202 Mg54
Nyamgalika ⊡ EAT 196 Mf48
Nyamirembe ⊡ EAT 194 Mf47
Nyamlell ⊡ SUD 191 Md41
Nyamok ⊡ CAM 189 Lh42
Nyamtumbo ⊡ EAT 197 Mj51
Nyamuswa ⊡ EAT 194 Mh46
Nyanga ⊡ Q 198 Lf47
Nyanga ⊡ RCB 198 Lf47
Nyanga ⊡ ZW 202 Mg55
Nyanga ⊡ NAM 201 Ma55
Nyanga N.P. ⊡ ZW 202 Mg55
Nyang'olo ⊡ EAT 197 Mh47
Nyantwiga ⊡ EAT 194 Mf47
Nyanza ⊡ RWA 196 Me47
Nyanza-Lac ⊡ BU 196 Me48
Nyararanda ⊡ EAT 196 Me48
Nyaru ⊡ EAK 194 Mh45
Nyarweyo ⊡ EAU 194 Mf45
Nyasa ⊡ RDC 196 Md48
Nyassar ⊡ CAM 189 Lh42
Nyaungkhashe ⊡ MYA 122 Pj37
Nyaunglebin ⊡ MYA 120 Pj36
Nyaungshwe ⊡ MYA 120 Pj35
Nyaung-U ⊡ MYA 120 Ph35
Nyazura ⊡ ZW 202 Mg55
Nybergsund ⊡ N 40 Ln29
Nyborg ⊡ DK 42 Ll35
Nybro ⊡ S 43 Lq34
Nyékládháza ⊡ H 67 Ma43
Nyengedi ⊡ EAT Mk51
Nyergesújfalu ⊡ H 66 Lt43
Nyeri ⊡ EAK 194 Mj46
Nyeru ⊡ EAU/SUD 194 Mf44
Nyero Rockpaintings ⊡ EAU 194 Mg45
Ny-Friesland ▲ N 38 Lj06
Nyhammar ⊡ S 43 Lp30
Nykøbing F ⊡ DK 42 Lm36
Nykøbing M ⊡ DK 42 Lk34
Nykøbing S ⊡ DK 42 Lm35
Nyköping ⊡ S 43 Lr32
Nykroppa ⊡ S 43 Lp31
Nykvarn ⊡ S 43 Ls31
Nylstroom ⊡ ZA 205 Me58
Nylsvlei Nature Reserve ⊡ ZA 205 Me58
Nymagee ⊡ AUS 151 Sg64
Nymboida ⊡ AUS 149 Sg60
Nymboida N.P. ⊡ AUS 149 Sg60
Nymburk ⊡ CZ 66 Lq40
Nymphe Bank ⊞ 47 Kn39
Nynäshamn ⊡ S 43 Ls32
Nyngan ⊡ AUS 149 Sg61
Nyoka ⊡ Z 201 Md52
Nyoma Rap ⊡ 115 Ok29
Nyommalat ⊡ LAO 121 Qc37
Nyons ⊡ F 53 Lf46
Nyororo ⊡ EAT 196 Mh50
Nyřany ⊡ CZ 66 Lo41
Nyrud ⊡ N 39 Me21
Nysa ⊡ PL 64 Ls40
Nysäter ⊡ S 42 Ln31
Nyssa ⊡ USA 71 Wj53
Nystad = Uusikaupunki ⊡ FIN 44 Mb30
Nysted ⊡ DK 42 Lm36
Nyudo-saki ⊡ J 111 Rk25
Nyunzu ⊡ RDC 196 Md48
Nyuruandanga ⊡ EAT 197 Mk49
Nyuts Archipelago ⊞ AUS 150 Rg62
Nyvycl ⊡ UA 65 Me40
Nyžni Sirohozy ⊡ UA 73 Mf22
Nyžni Torhajl ⊡ UA 73 Mf22
Nyžni Vorota ⊡ UA 67 Ma42
Nyžn'ohirs'kyj ⊡ UA 73 Mh23
Nzambi ⊡ RCA 190 Mb43
Nzambi ⊡ RDC 199 Lj46
Nzara ⊡ SUD 191 Md43
Nzaasi ⊡ RCB 198 Lg48
Nzébéla ⊡ RG 186 Kf41
Nzega ⊡ EAT 194 Mg47
Nzérékoré ⊡ RG 186 Kf42
N'Zeto ⊡ ANG 198 Lg49
Nzingu ⊡ EAT 194 Mg47
Nzingu ⊡ RDC 196 Md49
Nzi-Noua ⊡ CI 187 Kg42
Nzo ⊡ RG 186 Kf42
Nzoro ⊡ RCA 190 Lh42
Nzulezu Stilt Settlement ⊡ GH 187 Kj43

O

Oahu ⊡ USA 234 Ca35
Oak Alley Plantation ⊡ USA 239 Fe31
Oakbank ⊡ AUS 150 Sa62
Oakburn ⊡ CDN 236 Ek20
Oakdale ⊡ USA 239 Fd30
Oakes ⊡ USA 236 Fa22
Oakey ⊡ AUS 149 Sf59
Oak Grove ⊡ USA 239 Fe29
Oakham ⊡ GB 49 Ku38
Oak Harbour ⊡ USA 232 Dj21
Oak Hill ⊡ USA 239 Fe27
Oak Hill ⊡ USA 239 Fk26
Oak Hills ⊡ USA 147 Sc55
Oak Lake ⊡ CDN 236 Ek20
Oak Lawn ⊡ USA 237 Fg25
Oakland ⊡ CA 234 Dj27
Oakland ⊡ USA 237 Fd24
Oakland ⊡ USA 241 Ga26
Oakland ⊡ USA 236 Fb25
Oaklands ⊡ AUS 151 Sd63
Oakley ⊡ USA 232 Ed24
Oakley ⊡ USA 238 Fa28
Oakley ⊡ USA 232 Ed24
Oakman ⊡ USA 239 Ff29
Oak Point ⊡ USA 239 Fc30
Oak Ridge ⊡ USA 239 Ff27
Oakville ⊡ CDN 237 Ga24
Oakville ⊡ USA 232 Dj22
Oaky Creek ⊡ AUS 149 Se57
Oamaru ⊡ NZ 153 Tf68
Oaste II ⊡ 287 Ge32
Oates Land ⊡ 287 Sd33
Oatlands ⊡ AUS 151 Sd67
Oaxaca ⊡ USA 236 Fb37
Oaxaca ⊡ MEX 246 Fb37

Ob' ⊡ RUS 88 Ob06
Oba ⊡ CDN 237 Fh21
Oba ⊡ WAN 188 Lc42
Obaa ⊡ RI 154 Rk49
Obaba ⊡ RCB 198 Lg48
Obaha ⊡ PNG 156 Se50
Obaidullagani ⊡ IND 116 Oj34
Obala ⊡ CAM 189 Lg43
Obalapuram ⊡ IND 118 Oj35
Obama ⊡ J 113 Rh28
Oban ⊡ AUS 146 Rk56
Oban ⊡ GB 48 Kp34
Oban ⊡ WAN 188 Le43
Oanazawa ⊡ J 111 Sa26
Oban Hills ⊡ WAN 188 Le43
O Barco ⊡ E 54 Ko48
Obbia = Hobyo ⊡ SP 193 Ne43
Obbnäs = Upinniemi ⊡ FIN 44 Me30
Obehie ⊡ WAN 188 Lc43
Obele ⊡ WAN 188 Lc42
Obeliaí ⊡ LT 45 Mf35
Obelisco di Antinoe ⊡ ER 192 Mk38
Oberá ⊡ RA 276 Hc59
Oberammergau ⊡ D 59 Lm43
Oberes Donautal ⊡ D 59 Lk42
Ober-Gatlinburg Ski Resort ⊡ USA 242 Fj28
Oberhausen ⊡ D 58 Lg39
Oberkirch ⊡ D 59 Lj42
Oberlausitz ⊡ D 59 Lp40
Oberlin ⊡ USA 239 Fd30
Obernai ⊡ F 51 Lh42
Obernburg ⊡ D 59 Lk41
Oberndorf ⊡ A 60 Ln43
Oberndorf ⊡ D 59 Lj42
Oberon ⊡ AUS 151 Se62
Oberpfälzer Wald ▲ D 59 Ln41
Oberpullendorf ⊡ A 61 Lr43
Oberstdorf ⊡ D 59 Ll43
Obertyn ⊡ UA 67 Mf42
Oberwart ⊡ A 61 Lr43
Obi ⊡ RI 131 Rd46
Obi ⊡ WAN 188 Lc42
Obiaruku ⊡ WAN 188 Ld43
Óbidos ⊡ BR 266 Hc46
Óbidos ⊡ P 54 Kn51
Obihiro ⊡ J 112 Sc24
Obilatu ⊡ RI 131 Rd46
Bispo Trejo ⊡ RA 279 Gj61
Ob Luang N.P. ⊡ THA 121 Pk36
Oblučé ⊡ RUS 110 Rf21
Obninsk ⊡ RUS 72 Mj18
Obo ⊡ CHN 106 Qg27
Obo ⊡ RCA 191 Md43
Oboasi ⊡ GH 187 Kk42
Obogoborap ⊡ ZA 204 Ma59
Obock ⊡ DJI 193 Nb39
Obogu ⊡ GH 187 Kk42
Obojan ⊡ RUS 72 Mj20
Obokote ⊡ RDC 196 Md46
Oboli ⊡ RCB 198 Lh46
Obolon' ⊡ UA 73 Mg21
Oborniki ⊡ PL 64 Lr38
Oborniki Śląskie ⊡ PL 64 Lr39
Oborowo ⊡ PL 64 Lt38
Obory ⊡ CZ 66 Lp41
Obrenovac ⊡ SRB 68 Ma46
Obrež ⊡ HR 61 Lq45
O'Brien ⊡ USA 232 Dj24
Obrovac ⊡ HR 61 Lq46
Obruk Yaylası ⊡ TR 90 Mg26
Observatorio El Leoncito ⊡ RA 280 Gf61
Observatorio Calar Alto ⊡ E 55 Ks53
Observatorio de S. Pedro ⊡ MEX 244 Ec30
Observatory Inlet ⊞ CDN 230 Df18
Obskaya Guba ⊞ RUS 88 Oc05
Obsza ⊡ PL 65 Mc40
Obuasi ⊡ GH 187 Kk42
Obubra ⊡ WAN 188 Le42
Obudu ⊡ WAN 188 Le42
Obudu Cattle Ranch ⊡ WAN 188 Le42
Obusa ⊡ RUS 104 Qb19
Obytčina kosa ⊞ UA 73 Mj22
Obzor ⊡ BG 69 Mh48
Ocala ⊡ USA 73 Mf22
Ocala ⊡ USA 242 Fj31
Ocámcîre ⊡ GE 91 Na24
Ocampo ⊡ MEX 244 Ef31
Ocampo ⊡ MEX 244 Eh32
Ocampo ⊡ MEX 245 Ej32
Ocampo ⊡ MEX 246 Ek35
Ocampo ⊡ MEX 244 Fa34
Ocaña ⊡ CO 264 Gd41
Ocaña ⊡ E 55 Kr51
Ocate ⊡ USA 235 Eh27
Ocauçú ⊡ BR 274 Hf57
Occidente ⊡ CO 268 Ga46
Occoneechee S.P. ⊡ USA 242 Ga27
Ocean Cape ⊡ USA 230 Ck16
Ocean City ⊡ USA 241 Gc26
Ocean City ⊡ USA 241 Ga26
Ocean Falls ⊡ CDN 230 Dg19
Oceanopolis ⊡ F 51 Kr42
Ocean Shores ⊡ USA 232 Dh22
Ocean Shores ⊡ USA 232 Dh22
Oceanside ⊡ USA 234 Eb29
Ocean Springs Harbor ⊡ USA 234 Ea29
Ocean Springs ⊡ USA 239 Ff30
Oceretavate ⊡ UA 73 Mh22
Ochero ⊡ EAU 194 Mg45
Ochiai ⊡ J 113 Rg28
O Chiese Ind. Res. ⊡ CDN 233 Ec19
Ochil Hills ▲ GB 48 Kr34
Ochobo ⊡ WAN 188 Ld42
Ochopee ⊡ USA 243 Fk33
Ochsenfurt ⊡ D 59 Ll41
Ochtrup ⊡ D 58 Lh39
Ochtyrka ⊡ UA 72 Mg20
Ocieka ⊡ PL 65 Mb40
Ocilla ⊡ USA 242 Fj30
Ockelbo ⊡ S 41 Lr30
Ocmulgee Nat. Mon. ⊡ USA 242 Fj29
Ocna Mureş ⊡ RO 67 Md44
Ocna Sibiului ⊡ RO 67 Me44
Ocnele Mari ⊡ RO 67 Md44
Ocoliş ⊡ RO 67 Md44
Ocongate ⊡ PE 269 Ge52
Oconomowoc ⊡ USA 237 Ff24
Oconto ⊡ USA 237 Fg23
Ocoruro ⊡ PE 269 Ge53
Ocós ⊡ GCA 247 Fe37
Ocotal ⊡ NIC 248 Fg39
Ocotlán ⊡ MEX 246 Ej35
Ocotlán de Morelos ⊡ MEX 246 Fb37
Ocozocoautla ⊡ MEX 247 Fd37
Ocracoke ⊡ USA 242 Gc28
Ocracoke Lighthouse ⊡ USA
Ocros ⊡ PE 269 Gd51
Ocros ⊡ PE 269 Ge52
Octagonal Pavilion ▲ CHN 121 Qa35
Ocua ⊡ MOC 203 Mk52
Ocumare del Tuy ⊡ YV 265 Gg40
Ocuri ⊡ BOL 278 Gh55
Oda ⊡ J 113 Rf28
Oda ⊡ GH 187 Kk43
Ódáðahraun ▲ IS 46 Kd25
Odadjan ⊡ PRK 110 Rg25
Odaesan N.P. ⊡ ROK 112 Re27
Ôdâkra ⊡ S 42 Lm34
Odan ⊡ NEP 115 Pa31
Odate ⊡ J 111 Sa25
Odawara ⊡ J 113 Rk28
Odda ⊡ N 42 Lg30
Odden Færgehavn ⊡ DK 42 Lm35
Odder ⊡ DK 42 Ll35
Oddsta ⊡ GB 48 Ku30
Oddur = Xuddur ⊡ SP 193 Nb43
Odemira ⊡ P 54 Kn53
Ödemiş ⊡ TR 90 Mh52
Odendaalsrus ⊡ ZA 205 Md59
Odensbacken ⊡ S 43 Lq31
Odense ⊡ DK 42 Ll35

Odepur ⊡ IND 117 Pb35
Oder ⊡ D 58 Lp38
Oderbruch ⊡ D 58 Lp38
Oderzo ⊡ I 60 Ln45
Odessa ⊡ UA 73 Mf22
Odessa ⊡ USA 232 Ea22
Odessa ⊡ USA 238 Ek29
Odessa Meteor Crater ⊡ USA 245 Ej30
Odienne ⊡ CI 187 Kg41
Odighi ⊡ WAN 188 Ld42
Odimba ⊡ G 198 Le48
Odindovo ⊡ RUS 72 Mj18
Odiongan ⊡ RP 124 Ra39
Odjala ⊡ G 198 Lg46
Obo ⊡ CHN 124 Rg28
Odobasca ⊡ RO 69 Mg45
Odolanow ⊡ PL 64 Ls39
Odonkawkrom ⊡ GH 187 Kk42
Odoorn ⊡ NL 51 Lg38
Odorheiu Secuiesc ⊡ RO 67 Mf44
Odra ⊡ PL 64 Ls40
Odrzywół ⊡ PL 65 Ma39
Odumasi ⊡ GH 187 Kk43
Oduponkpehe ⊡ GH 187 Kk43
Odžaci ⊡ SRB 68 Lu45
Odžak ⊡ BIH 68 Lt45
Odzala-Kokoua, P.N.d' ⊡ RCB 190 Lh45
Odzemu ⊡ RCB 198 Lj46
Odzi ⊡ ZW 202 Mg55
Odziba ⊡ RCB 198 Lh47
Oebisfelde ⊡ D 58 Lm38
Oeiras ⊡ BR 273 Hj49
Oeiras do Pará ⊡ BR 267 Hf46
Øekény ⊡ H 67 Lu43
Oekusi ⊡ TLS 131 Rc50
Oelrichs ⊡ USA 233 Ej24
Oelsnitz ⊡ D 59 Ln40
Oelsnitz ⊡ D 59 Ln40
Oeno Island ⊞ 236 Fa24
Oenpelli ⊡ AUS 146 Rg52
Oettingen ⊡ D 59 Ll42
Oetz ⊡ A 60 Ll43
Ofa ⊡ WAN 188 Lc41
Ofahoma ⊡ USA 239 Ff29
Ofcofaco ⊡ ZA 205 Mf58
Ofenpass ⊡ CH 60 Ll44
Ofere ⊡ WAN 188 Lc42
Offenbach ⊡ D 59 Lj40
Offenburg ⊡ D 59 Lh42
Offumpo ⊡ CI 187 Kg42
Oficina Alemania ⊡ PE 279 Gf58
Oficina Chile ⊡ PE 279 Gf58
Oficina Victoria ⊡ RCH 278 Gf56
Ofinso ⊡ GH 187 Kk42
Ofoase ⊡ GH 187 Kk42
Ofugo ⊡ WAN 188 Le42
Ofunato ⊡ J 111 Sa26
Oga ⊡ J 111 Rk26
Ogaden ▲ ETH 193 Nc42
Oga-hanto ⊞ J 111 Rk26
Ogaki ⊡ J 113 Rj28
Ogani ⊡ USA 236 Ek25
Ogani ⊡ WAN 188 Ld43
Ogar ⊡ RI 154 Rg47
Ogba ⊡ WAN 188 Lc42
Ogbomoso ⊡ WAN 188 Lc42
Ogden ⊡ USA 235 Ee25
Ogden ⊡ USA 238 Fa26
Ogdensburg ⊡ USA 241 Gc23
Ogdua ⊡ RI 155 Rd45
Ogea Driki ⊞ FJI 159 Ua55
Ogea Levu ⊞ FJI 159 Ua55
Ogema ⊡ CDN 233 Eh21
Ogema ⊡ USA 237 Fe22
Ogembo ⊡ EAK 194 Mh46
Ogi ⊡ J 111 Rk27
Ogies ⊡ ZA 205 Me59
Ogilvie ⊡ CDN 229 Da13
Ogilvie Mountains ▲ CDN 229 Da13
Oglala ⊡ USA 233 Ej24
Oglala Grassland N.P. ⊡ USA 233 Ej24
Oglanly ⊡ TM 96 Nh26
Oglat Beraberf ⊡ DZ 175 Kj30
Oglat el Faci ⊡ DZ 175 Kk32
Oglat el Faci ⊡ DZ 175 Kk32
Oglat Mariboura ⊡ DZ 175 Kk29
Ogmore ⊡ AUS 149 Se57
Ogoja ⊡ WAN 188 Le42
Ogoki ⊡ CDN 237 Fh20
Ogoki Reservoir ⊞ CDN 236 Ff20
Ogoki River ⊡ CDN 237 Fg20
Ogoste ⊡ SRB 68 Mа48
Ogr ⊡ SUD 184 Mа39
Ogre ⊡ LV 45 Me34
Ogrodniki ⊡ PL 65 Md36
Ogrodzieniec ⊡ PL 65 Lu40
Ogulin ⊡ HR 61 Lq45
Ogun ⊡ WAN 188 Lc43
Ogur ⊡ EAU 194 Mg45
Ôgur ▲ IS 46 Js25
Ogurugu ⊡ WAN 188 Ld42
Ogwashi-Uku ⊡ WAN 188 Ld42
Ohafia ⊡ WAN 188 Le43
Ohakune ⊡ NZ 153 Th65
Ohanet ⊡ DZ 176 La31
Ohangoron ⊡ UZ 97 Oe25
Ohangwena ⊡ NAM 200 Lj54
O'Higgins, Gral.B. ⊡ 287 Ha31
Ohio ⊡ USA 237 Fj25
Ohogamuit ⊡ USA 228 Bk15
Ohotskoe ⊡ RUS 111 Sb22
Ohrid ⊡ MK 68 Ma49
Ohrigstad ⊡ ZA 205 Mf58
Ôhringen ⊡ D 59 Lk41
Ôhura ⊡ NZ 153 Th65
Oiapoque ⊡ BR 267 Hd44
Oiapoque, T.I. ⊡ BR 267 Hd44
Oil City ⊡ USA 237 Ga25
Oil Gathering Station ⊡ LAR 177 Lj31
Oilton ⊡ USA 245 Fa32
Oiseaux du Djoudi, P.N.des ⊡ SN 180 Kb37
Oisemont ⊡ F 51 Lb41
Oita ⊡ J 113 Rf29
Oital ⊡ KZ 100 Og24
Oiyk ⊡ KZ 97 Of24
Ojai ⊡ USA 234 Ea28
Ojcowski P.N. ⊡ PL 65 Lu40
Öje ⊡ S 40 Lo30
Öje ⊡ WAN 188 Ld42
Ojika-jima ⊞ J 113 Re29
Ôjima ⊡ J 113 Rk28
Ojinaga ⊡ MEX 245 Eh31
Ojito de Camellones ⊡ MEX 244 Eg33
Ojiya ⊡ J 111 Rk27
Ojmjakon ⊡ RUS 104 Qj19
Ojojona ⊡ HN 248 Fg39
Ojos Negros ⊡ E 57 Kt50
Ojrzeń ⊡ PL 65 Ma38
Oju ⊡ WAN 188 Ld42
Ojuelos de Jalisco ⊡ MEX 246 Ek35
Oka ⊡ RUS 104 Qa19
Okaba ⊡ RI 154 Rk50
Okahandja ⊡ NAM 200 Lj56
Okalecko ⊡ PL 65 Mc36
Ókéma ⊡ J 113 Rg27
Okěmmelsk ⊡ RUS 89 Ra06
Okanagan Valley ▲ CDN 232 Ea21
Okandjombo ⊡ NAM 200 Lg55
Okankolo ⊡ NAM 200 Lj54
Okanogan Range ▲ CDN 232 Dk19
Okapa ⊡ PNG 155 Sc49
Okara ⊡ PK 99 Og30
Okartowo ⊡ PL 65 Mb37
Ôlenëgorsk ⊡ RUS 39 Mo22
Ôlenëk ⊡ RUS 89 Qc05
Oklěmmskij zaliv ⊞ RUS 89 Qd04
Olengurone ⊡ EAK 194 Mh46
Olenino ⊡ RUS 72 Mg17
Olenivka ⊡ UA 73 Mg23

Okavango ⊡ RB 201 Mb55
Okavango ⊡ RB 201 Mb55
Okavango Delta ▲ RB 201 Mb55
Okavango Swamp ⊞ RB 201 Mb55
Okave ⊡ NAM 200 Lj56
Okaya ⊡ J 113 Rg28
Okazaki ⊡ J 113 Rj28
Okazize ⊡ NAM 200 Lj56
Okeechobee ⊡ USA 243 Fk32
Okeene ⊡ USA 238 Fa27
Okefenokee N.W.R. ⊡ USA 242 Fj31
Okehampton ⊡ GB 49 Kq40
Oke-Iho ⊡ WAN 188 Lc41
Okene ⊡ WAN 188 Ld42
Oke-Odde ⊡ WAN 188 Lc41
Oker ⊡ D 58 Ll38
Oketsew ⊡ GH 187 Kk43
Okha ⊡ IND 116 Oe34
Okha Mathi ⊡ IND 116 Oe34
Okhotsk ⊡ RUS 89 Sa07
Okhi ⊡ RI 131 Rd47
Okia ⊡ RCB 198 Lh46
Okiéné ⊡ RCB 198 Lh47
Okiep ⊡ ZA 204 Lj60
Okigwe ⊡ WAN 188 Ld43
Oki Islands ▲ J 113 Rg27
Okinawa ⊡ J 113 Rd32
Okinawa Islands ▲ J 113 Re33
Okinawa-jima ▲ J 113 Re32
Okinoerabu-jima ▲ J 113 Rg29
Oki-tai-jai ▲ J 113 Rh27
Okitipupa ⊡ WAN 188 Lc42
Okkan ⊡ MYA 122 Ph37
Okla ⊡ CDN 233 Ej19
Oklahoma ⊡ USA 238 Fa28
Oklahoma City ⊡ USA 238 Fb28
Okmulgee ⊡ USA 239 Fc28
Oko ⊡ WAN 188 Lc42
Okola ⊡ CAM 189 Lg43
Okollo ⊡ EAU 194 Mf44
Okondja ⊡ G 198 Lg46
Okondjatu ⊡ NAM 200 Lk56
Okongo ⊡ NAM 200 Lj54
Okongwati ⊡ NAM 200 Lg54
Okonjima ⊡ NAM 200 Lj56
Okonmwé ⊡ RCB 198 Lj47
Okoppe ⊡ J 111 Sb23
Okoro, Mount ▲ WAN 188 Lc42
Okotoks ⊡ CDN 233 Ec20
Okotusu ⊡ NAM 200 Lf54
Okouyo ⊡ RCB 198 Lh46
Okoyo ⊡ RCB 198 Lh47
Okpala-Ngwa ⊡ WAN 188 Ld43
Okrika ⊡ WAN 188 Ld43
Okrzeja ⊡ PL 65 Mc39
Oksapmin ⊡ PNG 155 Sb48
Oksbøl ⊡ DK 42 Lj35
Øksfjord ⊡ N 38 Mа21
Øksibil ⊡ RI 155 Saa48
Okstindane ▲ N 38 Lh06
Oktjabr'sk ⊡ KZ 88 Nd09
Oktwin ⊡ MYA 120 Pk38
Oku ⊡ CAM 188 Lf42
Oku ⊡ J 113 Rg32
Okubie ⊡ WAN 188 Lc43
Okuçani ⊡ HR 61 Ls45
Okuchi ⊡ J 113 Rf29
Okuloka ⊡ RUS 72 Mg16
Okundi ⊡ WAN 188 Le42
Okushiri ⊡ J 111 Rk24
Okushiri-to ▲ J 111 Rk24
Okuta ⊡ WAN 188 Lb41
Olá ⊡ PA 249 Fk41
Óladfjörður ⊡ IS 46 Kc25
Olafsvik ⊡ IS 46 Jr26
Olaf V Land ▲ N 38 Lk06
Ôlaine ⊡ LV 45 Md34
Ôlands norra udde ⊞ S 43 Ls33
Ôlands södra grund ⊞ 43 Lr35
Ôlands södra udde ⊞ S 43 Lr34
Olargues ⊡ F 53 Lc47
Olaria ⊡ BR 273 Hk47
Olary ⊡ AUS 150 Sa62
Olascoaga ⊡ RA 281 Gk63
Olathe ⊡ USA 239 Fc26
Olavarria ⊡ RA 281 Gk64
Olavlinna ⊡ FIN 44 Mg29
Olawa ⊡ PL 64 Ls40
Olbernhau ⊡ D 59 Lo40
Olbia ⊡ I 62 Lk50
Old Bulawayo ⊡ ZW 202 Me56
Old Coralie ⊡ AUS 147 Sa55
Old Cork ⊡ AUS 148 Sa57
Old Crow ⊡ CDN 229 Da12
Old Crow Flats ▲ CDN 229 Ck11
Old Dongola ⊡ SUD 185 Mf38
Old Dongola ⊡ SUD 185 Mf38
Oldeani ⊡ EAT 194 Mh47
Oldenburg ⊡ D 58 Lj37
Oldenburg in Holstein ⊡ D 58 Ll36
Oldenzaal ⊡ NL 51 Lg38
Olderfjord ⊡ N 39 Mf20
Old Faithful Geysir ⊡ USA 233 Ee23
Old Forge ⊡ USA 241 Gc24
Old Fort ⊡ USA 242 Fj28
Old Fort Hays ⊡ USA 238 Fa28
Old Fort Niagara S.H.S. & Fort Niagara L.H. ⊡ USA 237 Ga24
Old Fort William ⊡ USA 237 Gd24
Old Ft. Henry ▲ CDN 237 Ga24
Old Ft. Parker S.H.S. ⊡ USA 238 Fb30
Old Gold Mine ▲ NZ 153 Tf67
Oldham ⊡ GB 49 Ks37
Old Harbor ⊡ USA 228 Cd17
Old Head of Kinsale ⊞ IRL 47 Km39
Old Irontown Ruins ⊡ USA 235 Ed27
Old Man of Hoy ▲ GB 48 Kr32
Old Maswa ⊡ EAT 194 Mg47
Oldmeldrum ⊡ GB 48 Ks33
Old Minto ⊡ USA 229 Cf13
Old Mkushi ⊡ Z 202 Me52
Old Mosque ▲ RI 129 Qi49
Old Numery ⊡ AUS 148 Rh58
Old Perlican ⊡ CDN 241 Hd21
Old Petauke ⊡ Z 202 Mf53
Old Rampart ⊡ USA 229 Ck12
Old Sitka ⊡ USA 230 Dc17
Old Spanish Treasure ▲ USA 238 Fb28
Old Suakin coral stone houses ▲ SUD 185 Mj36
Oldtidsveien ▲ N 42 Lm31
Oldtimer's Mus. (Maple Creek) ▲ CDN 233 Ef21
Old Town ⊡ USA 240 Ge23
Old Village ⊡ USA 228 Cc15
Old wagon bridge ▲ ZA 205 Mc60
Olean ⊡ USA 237 Ga24
Olecko ⊡ PL 65 Mc36
Ôléggio ⊡ I 60 Lj45
Olekma ⊡ RUS 89 Ra06
Ôlëkminsk ⊡ RUS 89 Ra06
Ôlëkminskij Stanovik ▲ RUS 89 Qf08
Oleksandrija ⊡ UA 73 Mj21
Oleksandrija ⊡ UA 73 Mg21
Oleksandrijśka ⊡ UA 73 Mg21
Ôlen ⊡ N 42 Lf31
Ôlenëgorsk ⊡ RUS 39 Mo22

Oléron ▲ F 52 Kk45
Oles'ko ⊡ UA 67 Me41
Olešnica ⊡ PL 64 Ls39
Olesno ⊡ PL 64 Lt40
Oleszno ⊡ PL 65 Md40
Oleszyce ⊡ PL 65 Mc40
Ôlevs'k ⊡ UA 65 Me40
Olevu ⊡ EAU 194 Mf45
Olex ⊡ USA 232 Dk23
Olga ⊡ D 58 Lh39
Ol'ga ⊡ RUS 111 Rh24
Olga, Mount ▲ AUS 145 Rf58
Olgiy ⊡ MNG 101 Pf21
Olhão ⊡ P 54 Kn53
Olho d'Agua das Flores ⊡ BR 273 Jb50
Ol'hi ⊡ RUS 72 Na19
Ol'hovatka ⊡ RUS 72 Mk20
Oli ⊡ WAN 188 Lc42
Olib ▲ HR 61 Lp46
Oliena ⊡ I 62 Lk50
Olifants ⊡ NAM 200 Lh58
Olifants ⊡ ZA 202 Mf57
Olifants Game Reserve ⊡ ZA 205 Mf58
Olifantshoek ⊡ ZA 204 Mb59
Olimje Samostan ▲ SLO 61 Lq44
Olimp ⊡ RO 69 Mh47
Olimpia ⊡ BR 274 Hf56
Olimpiáda ⊡ GR 69 Md50
Ólimpos Beydağları Milli Parkı ⊡ TR 90 Mf27
Olinala ⊡ MEX 246 Fa37
Olinda ⊡ BR 273 Hj48
Olinda ⊡ BR 273 Jc49
Olindina ⊡ BR 273 Ja51
Olinga = Maganja ⊡ MOC 203 Mh52
Olite ⊡ E 57 Kt48
Oliva ⊡ E 57 Ku52
Oliva ⊡ RA 281 Gj62
Oliva de la Frontera ⊡ E 55 Ko52
Olivais ⊡ BR 278 Ge23
Olivca-a-Nova ⊡ ANG 200 Lg53
Oliveira ⊡ BR 274 Hh56
Oliveira de Azeméis ⊡ P 54 Km50
Oliveira do Hospital ⊡ P 54 Kn50
Oliveira dos Brejinhos ⊡ BR 273 Hj52
Olivehurst ⊡ USA 234 Dk26
Olivet ⊡ F 51 Lb43
Olivet ⊡ USA 236 Fb24
Olivia ⊡ USA 236 Fb23
Olivine Range ▲ NZ 153 Te68
Ôljeitu Khudabanda ⊡ IR 91 Ne27
Ôljutorskij zaliv ⊞ RUS 89 Tb07
Ol Kalou ⊡ EAK 194 Mj46
Olkusz ⊡ PL 65 Lu40
Ollague ⊡ RCH 279 Gf56
Ollagüe, Volcán ▲ BOL/RCH 279 Gf56
Ollantaytambo ⊡ PE 269 Gd52
Ollerton ⊡ GB 49 Kt37
Ollombo ⊡ RCB 198 Lh46
Olmedo ⊡ E 54 Kq49
Olmedo ⊡ EC 268 Ga46
Olmeto ⊡ F 62 Lj49
Olmos ⊡ PE 268 Ga48
Olney ⊡ USA 238 Fa29
Olofström ⊡ S 43 Lp34
Oloitti ⊡ USA 165 Kn52
Oloitokitok ⊡ EAK 194 Mj47
Olonec ⊡ RUS 89 Ta05
Olosjki hrebet ▲ RUS 89 Ta05
Olonki ⊡ RUS 104 Qb19
Olongapo ⊡ RP 124 Ra38
Olonkinbyen ⊡ N 248 Fg38
Olorgesailie ▲ EAK 194 Mj47
Oloron-Sainte-Marie ⊡ F 52 Ku47
Olot ⊡ E 53 Lc48
Olovjannaja ⊡ RUS 105 Qh20
Olovo ⊡ BIH 68 Lt46
Olpat ⊡ IND 116 Oj35
Olpe ⊡ D 58 Lh39
Ol'ša ⊡ RUS 72 Mf18
Olsberg ⊡ D 58 Lj39
Olszany ⊡ PL 65 Ma39
Olszanka ⊡ PL 65 Mc37
Olsztyn ⊡ PL 65 Ma37
Olsztyn ⊡ PL 64 Lu40
Olta ⊡ RA 279 Gg61
Oltedal ⊡ N 42 Lg32
Olteniţa ⊡ RO 69 Mh46
Oltina ⊡ RO 69 Mh46
Oltinko'l ⊡ UZ 96 Nh25
Oltu ⊡ TR 91 Na25
Ol Tukai ⊡ EAK 194 Mj47
Oltuş ⊡ BY 65 Md39
Oluan'pi ⊞ RC 109 Ra35
Oluanpi ⊞ RC 109 Ra35
Olukonda National Monument ▲ NAM 200 Lk54
Oluku ⊡ WAN 188 Lc42
Olu Malua = Three Sisters Islands ▲ SOL 157 Tb51
Olumo Rock ▲ WAN 188 Lb42
Olustvere ⊡ EST 44 Mf32
Olutanga Island ▲ RP 125 Ra42
Onyx Cave ⊡ USA 239 Fd28
Olvera ⊡ E 55 Kp53
Olyka ⊡ UA 65 Mf40
Olympia ⊡ USA 232 Dj22
Olympic Mountains ▲ USA 232 Dj22
Olympic N.P. ⊡ USA 232 Dj22
Olympos ⊡ CY 90 Mg28
Olympos ▲ GR 70 Mc50
Olympos N.P. ⊡ GR 70 Mc50
Olympus, Mount ▲ USA 232 Dj22
Olynthos ⊡ GR 68 Md50
Olżziyt ⊡ MNG 104 Qa21
Old Oyo ⊡ WAN 188 Lc41
Old Oyo N.P. ⊡ WAN 188 Lc41

Omdurman ⊡ SUD 185 Mg38
Omega ⊡ I 60 Lj45
Omeo ⊡ AUS 151 Sd64
Ometepec ⊡ MEX 246 Fa37
Om Hajer ⊡ ER 192 Mj38
Omidiyeh ⊡ IR 91 Ne30
Omi-Hachiman ⊡ J 113 Rj28
Omineca Mountains ▲ CDN 230 Dg17
Omirzak ⊡ KZ 96 Nf24
Omiš ⊡ HR 61 Ls47
Omitara ⊡ NAM 200 Lk57
Ômkareshwar ⊡ IND 116 Oj34
Ommen ⊡ NL 51 Lg38
Ômnôgôv' ⊡ MNG 104 Qb24
Omolon ⊡ RUS 89 Ta06
Omolon ⊡ RUS 89 Sd05
Omoloy ⊡ RUS 89 Rd05
Omo Strict Nature Reserve ⊡ WAN 188 Lc42
Omo Valley ▲ ETH 194 Mh43
Ompomoueina ⊡ G 198 Lh46
Ompupa ⊡ ANG 200 Lg54
Omsk ⊡ RUS 88 Oc08
Omu ⊡ J 111 Sb23
Omu-Aran ⊡ WAN 188 Lc41
Omurtag ⊡ BG 69 Mg47
Omusati ⊡ NAM 200 Lh55
Omuta ⊡ J 113 Rf29
Oña ⊡ EC 268 Ga47
Onahama ⊡ J 111 Sa27
Onalaska ⊡ USA 237 Fe24
Onang ⊡ RI 130 Qk47
Onawa ⊡ USA 236 Fb24
Onaway ⊡ USA 237 Fh23
Onbimisan ⊡ TR 90 Mg27
Oncativo ⊡ RA 281 Gj61
Oncocua ⊡ ANG 200 Lg54
Onda ⊡ E 57 Ku51
Ondaw ⊡ MYA 120 Ph34
Onder ⊡ KZ 123 Ra19
Onderstedorings ⊡ ZA 204 Mа61
Ondjiva ⊡ ANG 200 Lh54
Ondo ⊡ WAN 188 Lc42
Ondörhaan ⊡ MNG 104 Qf22
Ondverdarnes ⊞ IS 46 Jq26
One Tree ⊡ AUS 151 Sc63
Onega ⊡ RUS 89 Ta05
Oneata ⊞ FJI 159 Ua55
Onefour ⊡ CDN 233 Ed21
Oneida ⊡ USA 241 Gc24
Onekotan, ostrov ▲ RUS 110 Sc20
Onerata ⊡ RO 73 Mg22
Onetangi ⊡ NZ 152 Th64
One Tree ⊡ AUS 151 Sc63
Onga ⊡ G 198 Lh46
Ongandjera ⊡ NAM 200 Lh54
Ongarue ⊡ NZ 153 Th65
Ongava Lodge ▲ NAM 200 Lh55
Ongeri ⊡ RDC 199 Mc48
Ongnae-ri ⊡ PRK 110 Re25
Ongon ⊡ AUS 144 Qk52
Ongonuol ⊡ RI 155 Rd45
Ongi ⊡ MNG 104 Qf23
Ongiyn Monastery ▲ MNG 104 Qc23
Ôngjin ⊡ PRK 112 Rc27
Ongkwar ⊡ RI 155 Rd45
Ông Lang Beach ⊞ VN 123 Qb40
Ongnul Qi ⊡ CHN 105 Qk24
Ongole ⊡ IND 119 Ok38
Ongonyl ⊡ RCB 198 Lj46
Ongon Gotjanl ⊡ MNG 104 Qd23
Onguday ⊡ RUS 101 Pk20
Oni ⊡ GE 91 Nb24
Onich ⊡ GB 48 Kp34
Onida ⊡ USA 236 Fa23
Onigajo ⊡ J 113 Rj29
Onilahy ⊡ RM 207 Nb57
Onioga ⊡ RI 129 Qh46
Ônjôsel ▲ RI 131 Rd46
Onkel Toms Hutte ▲ D 58 Lo38
Onnang ⊡ RI 129 Qh46
Ôno ⊡ J 113 Rj28
Onofio ⊡ HN 248 Fg39
Onoko ⊡ RI 130 Qh47
Onolimbu ⊡ RI 127 Pj45
Onomichi ⊡ J 113 Rg28
Onon ⊡ MNG 104 Qf21
Onon-Bal'dzinskij hrebet ▲ MNG 104 Qf21
Onondaga Cave S.P. ⊡ USA 239 Fe26
Onondaga Cave S.P. ⊡ USA 239 Fe26
Onoto ⊡ YV 265 Gh41
Onoway ⊡ CDN 233 Eb19
Onseepkans ⊡ NAM 204 Lk60
Ontake-san ▲ J 113 Rj28
Ontar ⊡ VU 158 Td53
Ontario ⊡ CDN 227 Fb08
Ontario ⊡ USA 232 Eb23
Ontario Peninsula ▲ CDN 237 Fk24
Ontario Place ⊡ CDN 237 Ga24
Ontimitta ⊡ IND 119 Ok38
Ontojärvi ⊞ FIN 44 Mh27
Ontometing ⊡ ZA 204 Ma59
Ontong Java Atoll ⊞ SOL 157 Sk48
Ong Lang Beach ⊞ VN 123 Qb40
Ontong Java Rise ⊞ 134 Sb10
Ônuma Q.N.P. ⊡ J 111 Sa27
Ônuskis ⊡ LT 45 Mf34
Onverwacht ⊡ SME 266 Hc43
Onyang ⊡ ROK 112 Rd27
Onza-Lieve-Vrouwekerk ▲ B 51 Ld40
Oobagooma ⊡ AUS 143 Rc54
Oodaadatta ⊡ AUS 148 Rh59
Ôod van Kuruman ▲ ZA 204 Mb59
Oodweyne ⊡ SP 193 Nc41
Ooldea ⊡ AUS 145 Rf61
Oombulgurri A.L. ⊡ AUS 143 Rd53
Oona River ⊡ CDN 230 De18
Oopmyn ⊡ ZA 205 Mc60
Ooratippra ⊡ AUS 148 Rh57
Oori-London ⊡ GB 205 Md62
Oorindi ⊡ AUS 148 Sa56
Oos-Londen = East London ⊡ ZA 205 Md62
Oost-Vlieland ⊡ NL 51 Lf37
Oostburg ⊡ NL 51 Lc39
Oostende ⊡ B 51 Lc39
Oosterhout ⊡ NL 51 Le39
Oosterschelde ⊞ NL 51 Ld39
Oosterscheldedam ⊡ NL 51 Ld39
Oosterwolde ⊡ NL 51 Lg38
Oostkapelle ⊡ NL 51 Lc39
Ootacamund ⊡ IND 118 Oj40
Ootsa Lake ⊞ CDN 230 Dg19
Ooty = Ootacamund ⊡ IND 118 Oj40

Opobo ⊡ WAN 188 Ld43
Opočno ⊡ RUS 45 Mj34
Opoczno ⊡ PL 65 Ma39
Opole ⊡ PL 64 Ls40
Opol'e ⊡ RUS 44 Mj31
Opole Lubelskie ⊡ PL 65 Mb39
Opononi ⊡ NZ ⊡ NAM 200 Lh55
Oppeln = Opole ⊡ PL 64 Ls40
Oppenheim ⊡ D 59 Lj41
Opportunity ⊡ USA 232 Eb22
Opsa ⊡ BY 45 Mg35
Optalmia Range ▲ AUS 142 Qk57
Optic Lake ⊡ CDN 233 Ek18
Optima N.W.R. ⊡ USA 238 Ek27
Opunake ⊡ NZ 153 Tg65
Opuwo ⊡ NAM 200 Lg55
Op Xian ⊡ CHN 108 Qd30
Oqbaytal ⊡ UZ 97 Oc24
Oqtash ⊡ UZ 97 Oc25
Oqtov tizmasi ▲ UZ 97 Oc25
Ora = Auer ⊡ I 60 Lm44
Ora ⊡ PNG 156 Sf48
Oraba ⊡ EAU 194 Mf44
Oracle ⊡ USA 235 Ee29
Orachova ⊡ BIH 61 Ls45
Orahova ⊡ KSV 68 Ma48
Orahovica ⊡ BIH 61 Ls46
Orahovica ⊡ HR 61 Ls45
Orai ⊡ IND 117 Ok33
Oraison ⊡ F 53 Lf47
Oran ⊡ USA 232 Dk22
Oran ⊡ E 88 Nc08
Oran ⊡ DZ 175 Kk28
Oranapai ⊡ GUY 266 Ha42
Orang ⊡ IND 120 Pg32
O Rang ⊡ K 123 Qd38
Orange ⊡ AUS 151 Se62
Orange ⊡ USA 238 Fd30
Orange ⊡ USA 241 Ga26
Orange de Azeméis ⊡ USA 238 Fd30
Orange Cay ▲ BS 243 Ga33
Orange City ⊡ USA 236 Fb24
Orange Creek ⊡ AUS 148 Rg58
Orange Fan ⊞ 162 Lj12
Orangeville ⊡ CDN 237 Ga24
Orange Walk ⊡ BH 247 Ff36
Orange Walk ⊡ BH 247 Ff36
Orani ⊡ RP 124 Ra38
Orania ⊡ ZA 205 Mc60
Oranienburg ⊡ D 58 Lo38
Oranje k'l NAM/ZA 204 Lj60
Oranjegebergte ▲ SME 266 Hc43
Oranjemund ⊡ NAM 204 Lj60
Oranjestad ⊡ NL 251 Gj37
Oranjestad ▲ NL 264 Ge39
Oranjeville ⊡ ZA 205 Me59
Orapa ⊡ RB 201 Mc56
Orăştie ⊡ RO 67 Md45
Oraşu Nou ⊡ RO 67 Md43
Oraţia, Mount ▲ USA 238 Bk16
Oravainen ⊡ FIN 44 Mc27
Oravita ⊡ RO 68 Mb45
Oravská Lesná ⊡ SK 67 Lu41
Oravská Polhora ⊡ SK 67 Lu41
Oravský Podzámok ▲ SK 67 Lu41
Orbec ⊡ F 50 La41
Orbeasca ⊡ RO 69 Mf46
Orbec ⊡ F 50 La41
Orbetello ⊡ I 60 Lm48
Orbost ⊡ AUS 151 Se64
Ôrbyhus ⊡ S 43 Ls30
Orchard City ⊡ USA 235 Ee27
Orchha ⊡ IND 117 Ok33
Orchid Island ⊞ RC 109 Ra35
Orchid Island ⊞ FJI 159 Tk55
Orchowo ⊡ PL 64 Lt38
Orcières ⊡ F 53 Lg46
Orcopampa ⊡ PE 269 Gd53
Ôrcsa ⊡ BY 72 Mf18
Orda ⊡ TCH 183 Lj35
Orda ⊡ KZ 96 Nc24
Ordena di Monte Perdido, P.N.de ⊡ E 56 La48
Ord, Mount ▲ AUS 143 Rc54
Ord River ⊡ AUS 143 Re54
Ôrdu ⊡ TR 90 Mj25
Orduña ⊡ USA 238 Ej26
Ordubad ⊡ AZ 91 Nc26
Ore ⊡ WAN 188 Lc42
Ôrebäck ⊡ S 47 Kt50
Orebić ⊡ HR 61 Ls48
Orebro ⊡ S 43 Lq31
Oredež ⊡ RUS 44 Mj31
Oregon ⊡ USA 237 Fg24
Oregon ⊡ USA 237 Fj25
Oregon ⊡ USA 232 Dk24
Oregon City ⊡ USA 232 Dj23
Oregon Dunes N.R.A. ⊡ USA 232 Dh24
Ôrebro ⊡ S 43 Lq31
Ôrg-to-d-H ⊡ H 66 Lt43
Orehovo-Zuevo ⊡ RUS 72 Mk18
Orel ⊡ RUS 72 Mj19
Orellana ⊡ PE 268 Gb49
Orem ⊡ USA 235 Ee26
Ôren ⊡ TR 90 Mh53
Orenburg ⊡ RUS 88 Nd08
Ôrencik ⊡ TR 90 Mj26
Orense = Ourense ⊡ E 54 Ko48
Oreor ⊡ PAL 156 Rf44
Orestiáda ⊡ GR 69 Mg49
Ôresundsbro ▲ 42 Ln35
Ôrfa ⊡ TR 90 Mk26
Orfeo ⊡ RO 73 Mg22
Orgãos, P.N.dos ⊡ BR 274 Hj57
Ôrgel ⊡ F 53 Lc44
Orgelet ⊡ F 53 Lf44
Orgiva ⊡ E 55 Kr53
Ôrgön ⊡ MNG 104 Qd24
Orhaneli ⊡ TR 90 Mj26
Orhangazi ⊡ TR 90 Mj25
Orhei ▲ MD 73 Me22
Orhei ⊡ MD 73 Me22
Orhomenós ⊡ GR 68 Mc52
Orick ⊡ USA 232 Dh25
Orient ⊡ USA 232 Eb22
Oriental, Cordillera ▲ CO 264 Gc43
Oriente Novo ⊡ BR 270 Gj50
Oriente ⊡ USA 148 Sd60
Orihuela ⊡ E 57 Kt52
Orinoco ⊡ YV 265 Gh42
Orinoco Delta ⊞ YV 265 Gj41
Orio ⊡ GR 71 Me52

Oriolo ⊡ I 63 Lr50
Oriomo ⊡ PNG 155 Sb50
Orissa ⊡ IND 117 Pb36
Orissaare ⊡ EST 45 Md32
Oristano ⊡ I 62 Lj51
Orito ⊡ CO 268 Gb45
Oritupano ⊡ YV 265 Gj41
Orivesi ⊞ FIN 44 Me29
Oriximiná ⊡ BR 266 Hc46
Orizaba ⊡ MEX 246 Fb36
Ôrje ⊡ N 42 Lm31
Orjen ▲ MNE 68 Lt48
Orkanger ⊡ N 40 Lk27
Ôrkelljunga ⊡ S 43 Ln34
Orkney ⊡ ZA 205 Md59
Orkney Islands ⊞ GB 48 Ks33
Orla ⊡ USA 245 Ej30
Orlamünde ▲ D 59 Lm40
Ôrland ⊡ N 40 Lk27
Orlândia ⊡ BR 274 Hg56
Orlândia ⊡ USA 242 Fk31
Orlea ⊡ RO 69 Me47
Orléanais ▲ F 51 Lb43
Orléans ⊡ F 51 Lb43
Orléans ▲ F 51 La42
Orleans ⊡ USA 241 Gd25
Orleans Farms ⊡ USA 245 Rb62
Orlesti ⊡ RO 67 Me45
Orlické hory ▲ CZ 66 Lr40
Orlik ⊡ RUS 104 Pk19
Orlivka ⊡ UA 69 Mj45
Orlja ⊡ BY 65 Me37
Orlovo ⊡ WAN 188 Ld43
Orly ⊡ F 51 Lc42
Orman Reef ⊞ AUS 147 Sb50
Ormara ⊡ PK 99 Oc33
Ormea ⊡ I 60 Lh46
Ormoc ⊡ RP 124 Rc40
Ormond Beach ⊡ USA 242 Fk31
Ormond-by-the-Sea ⊡ USA 242 Fk31
Ormos Panórmou ⊞ GR 71 Mf53
Ormoz ⊡ SLO 66 Lr44
Ôrnsköldsvik ⊡ S 40 Ls28
Ormtjernkampen n.p. ⊡ N 40 Lk29
Ornans ⊡ F 51 Lg44
Orneta ⊡ PL 65 Ma36
Ôrnô ▲ S 43 Lt31
Ôrnsköldsvik ⊡ S 40 Ls28
Orobayaya ⊡ BOL 278 Gj52
Oro Blanco ⊡ PE 268 Gad9
Orocué ⊡ RO 67 Mc44
Orocó ⊡ BR 273 Ja50
Orocue ⊡ CO 264 Ge43
Orocuina ⊡ HN 248 Fg39
Orogrande ⊡ USA 235 Eg29
Oroi ⊡ PNG 155 Sd50
Oroluk ⊞ 132 Sa15
Oromocto ⊡ CDN 240 Gd23
Orondo ⊡ USA 232 Dk22
Oroners ⊡ AUS 147 Sb53
Oronga ⊡ PNG 155 Sc48
Oronkua ⊡ BF 187 Kj40
Orope ⊡ USA 240 Gd23
Oropesa ⊡ PE 269 Ge53
Orpheus Island ▲ AUS 147 Sd55
Orophan ⊡ CHN 105 Ra21
Orr ⊡ USA 236 Fd21
Orrefors ⊡ S 43 Lq34
Orroroo ⊡ AUS 150 Rk62
Orša ⊡ BY 72 Mf18
Orsa ⊡ S 40 Lp29
Orsay ⊡ F 51 Lc42
Ôrsasjön ⊞ S 40 Lp29
Ôrsag N.P. ⊡ H 66 Lr44
Orsk ⊡ RUS 88 Nd08
Orsova ⊡ RO 68 Mc46
Ôrsta ⊡ N 42 Lg28
Ortaca ⊡ TR 90 Mh53
Ortadereesin ⊡ KZ 100 Oh24
Ortahisar ▲ TR 90 Mj26
Ortaklar ⊡ TR 71 Mh53
Ortaköy ⊡ TR 90 Mh26
Ortaköy ⊡ TR 90 Mh26
Ortaköy ⊡ TR 90 Mk25
Orta Nova ⊡ I 63 Lq49
Ôrtala ⊡ S 43 Lt30
Orte ⊡ I 60 Ln48
Ortega ⊡ CO 264 Gc44
Orthez ⊡ F 52 Ku47
Ortigueira ⊡ BR 277 He58
Ortigueira ⊡ E 54 Kn47
Ortisei = Sankt Ulrich ⊡ I 60 Lm44
Ortiz ⊡ MEX 244 Ee31
Ortíz ⊡ YV 265 Gg41
Ortles = Ortles ▲ I 60 Ll44
Ortona ⊡ I 63 Lp48
Ortonville ⊡ USA 236 Fb23
Ortrand ⊡ D 58 Lo39
Ôrum ⊡ DK 42 Lk34
Orumiyeh ⊡ IR 91 Nc27
Orumiyeh Bazaar ▲ IR 91 Nc27
Ôrundu ⊡ EAU 194 Mg45
Orungo ⊡ EAU 194 Mg44
Oruro ⊡ BOL 278 Gg54
Oruzgan ⊡ AFG 99 Oc29
Orvault ⊡ F 52 Kt43
Orvieto ⊡ I 60 Ln48
Orvin Land ▲ N 38 Mc05
Orwin ⊡ USA 241 Gc26
Ôryahovo ⊡ BG 68 Md47
Oržiu ⊡ LT 45 Me34
Oržyca ⊡ UA 73 Mg21
Orzysz ⊡ PL 65 Mb37
Oš ⊡ KS 97 Og25
Ôs ⊡ N 40 Ll26
Osa ⊡ RUS 104 Qb19
Osada prasłowiańska ▲ PL 64 Ls38
Osage ⊡ USA 236 Fc24
Osage City ⊡ USA 238 Fb26
Osage Ind. Res. ⊡ USA 238 Fb28
Ôsaka ⊡ J 113 Rh28
Osawatomie ⊡ USA 238 Fc26
Osborn ⊡ USA 233 Fb24
Osborne ⊡ USA 238 Fa26
Osby ⊡ S 43 Ln34
Oscar Il-Land ▲ N 38 Lg06
Oscar Soto Maynes ⊡ MEX 244 Eg31
Osceola ⊡ USA 236 Fc25
Osceola ⊡ USA 239 Fe28
Osceola ⊡ USA 239 Fe27
Osceola ⊡ USA 236 Fb24
Oschatz ⊡ D 58 Lo39
Oschersleben ⊡ D 58 Lm38
Oschiri ⊡ I 62 Lk50
Osciłki ⊡ PL 65 Md37
Oscoda ⊡ USA 237 Fj23
Osečina ⊡ SRB 68 Lu46
Osen ⊡ N 40 Ll26

Panglao Island – Perico

Panglao Island RP 124 Rb41
Panglong MYA 120 Pj35
Pangnirtung CDN 227 Gc05
Pango PNG 156 Sg47
Pangoa PNG 155 Sa49
Pango Aluquem ANG 198 Lh50
Pangonda RCA 190 Ma42
Pangquangou Z.B. CHN 106 Qf27
Pangrango, Gunung RI 129 Qd49
Pang Sida N.P. THA 123 Qb38
Pangu CHN 105 Rb19
Panguipulli RCH 280 Gd65
Panguitch USA 235 Ed27
Panguma WAL 186 Ke41
Pangururan RI 127 Pk44
Pangutaran Group RP 125 Ra42
Pangutaran Island RP 125 Ra42
Panhala IND 116 Oh37
Panhandle USA 239 Fh30
Paničkovo BG 69 Mf49
Panihati IND 120 Pe34
Panikhar 115 Oj28
Panipat IND 114 Oj31
Paniqui RP 124 Ra38
Panitan RP 124 Rb40
Panitian RP 125 Qk41
Panjab AFG 99 Od28
Panjabungan Tonga RI 127 Pk45
Panjakent TJ 97 Od26
Panjang RI 127 Qc48
Panjang RI 128 Qe44
Panjang RI 131 Rf48
Panjgur PK 99 Oc32
Panji RI 127 Pj44
Panjin CHN 110 Rb25
Panjpai PK 99 Od31
Panjshir-Valley AFG 97 Oe28
Panka BHT 120 Pf32
Pankshin WAN 188 Le41
Pankulam CL 119 Pa41
Panlong CHN 108 Qd30
P'anmunjom ROK 112 Rd27
Panna IND 117 Pa33
Panna N.P. IND 117 Pa33
Pannawonica AUS 142 Qj56
Panngi VU 158 Te53
Panniar IND 114 Oj32
Pannonhalma H 66 Ls43
Panopah RI 129 Qf46
Panorama BR 274 He56
Pánormos GR 71 Mg53
Panrutti IND 119 Ok40
Panshan, Mount CHN 107 Qj25
Panshanu Pass WAN 188 Le41
Panshi CHN 110 Rd24
Panskura IND 117 Pd34
Pantai RI 129 Qj47
Pantai koka RI 130 Rb50
Pantai Remis MAL 126 Qa43
Pantalam IND 118 Oj41
Pantalica I 63 Lq53
Pantanal BR 271 Hb49
Pantanal de Nabileque BR 274 Hb56
Pantanal do Rio Negro BR 274 Hb55
Pantanal do São Lourenço BR 274 Hb54
Pantanal do Taquarí BR 274 Hb55
Pantanal Matogrossense BR 274 Hb54
Pantanal Matogrossense, P.N.do BR 274 Hb54
Pântano do Sul BR 277 Hf59
Pântano Grande BR 276 Hd61
Pantar RI 131 Rc50
Pantekra RI 126 Pj43
Pantelleria I 62 Lm54
Pantemakassar TLS 131 Rc50
Pantha MYA 120 Ph34
Panther Huk NAM 204 Lh59
Panther Swamp N.W.R. USA 239 Fe29
Panti RI 127 Qa45
Panticeu RO 67 Md43
Panticpaeum UA 73 Mj23
Pantijan A.L. AUS 143 Rc54
Pantoja PE 268 Gc46
Pantoloan RI 130 Qk46
Pantu MAL 128 Qf45
Pantukan RP 125 Rc42
Pantzarané CI 187 Kj41
Panu RDC 199 Lk47
Panwari IND 117 Ok33
Panxi CHN 121 Qb33
Panxian CHN 121 Qc33
Panyam WAN 188 Le41
Panzhihua CHN 121 Qa32
Panzi RDC 199 Lj49
Paoay RP 124 Ra38
Páola I 63 Lr51
Paoli USA 239 Fg26
Paomaping CHN 121 Qa32
Paonia USA 235 Eg26
Paonta Sahib IND 115 Oj30
Paopao Island PNG 157 Sh47
Paoua RCA 190 Lj42
Paouignan DY 188 Lb42
Pápa H 66 Ls43
Papagaio BR 272 Hh48
Papagaios BR 275 Hh55
Papago Ind. Res. USA 235 Ed29
Papaikou USA 234 Cc36
Papakura NZ 152 Th64
Papallacta Pass BR 270 Gf46
Papalutla MEX 246 Fa36
Papanasam Beach IND 118 Oj41
Papanduva BR 277 He59
Papantla MEX 246 Fb35
Paparoa N.P. NZ 153 Tf67
Paparoa Range NZ 153 Tf67
Papa Stour GB 48 Kt30
Papa Westray GB 48 Ks31
Papayato RI 125 Ra45
Pape LV 45 Mb34
Papela RI 131 Rb51
Papenburg D 58 Lh37
Papera BR 270 Gh46
Papernja BY 45 Mh36
Papey IS 46 Kf26
Paphos CY 90 Mg28
Papilė LT 45 Mc34
Papillion USA 236 Fb25
Papilys LT 45 Mf34
Papiniseri IND 118 Oh40
Papollo NIC 248 Fg40
Paposo PE 279 Ge58
Pappadahandi IND 117 Pb36
Paprenda IND 117 Pa33
Papua New Guinea PNG 135 Sa10
Papuk HR 61 Ls45
Papulankutja AUS 145 Re58
Papun MYA 120 Pj36
Papunya AUS 143 Rf57
Papuri CO 265 Gf45
Papurí YV 264 Ge40
Paqiu SUD 191 Mf42
Paquera CR 249 Fh41
Paquiçamba BR 272 He47
Paquiçamba, T.I. BR 272 He47
Paquisha EC 268 Ga47
Par IND 120 Pg32
Pará BR 267 Hf46
Pará BR 255 Ha10
Para RI 125 Rc44
Parabubure, T.I. BR 274 Hd53
Paraburdoo AUS 142 Qj57
Paracale RP 124 Rb38
Paracanã, T.I. BR 272 He48
Paračany BY 65 Mf37
Paracas PE 269 Gb52
Paracatu BR 275 Hg54
Parachilna AUS 148 Rk61
Parachinar PK 99 Of29
Paracho MEX 246 Ej36
Paraćin SRB 68 Mb47
Paracuhuba, T.I. BR 271 Ha47
Paracuru BR 273 Ja47
Parada BR 267 He47
Paradela P 54 Kn49
Para de Minas BR 275 Hh55
Paradip IND 117 Pd35
Paradise USA 234 Dk26
Paradise Island BS 243 Gb33
Paradise Valley USA 234 Eb25
Paradísi GR 71 Mj54
Paradísia GR 70 Mc53
Paradji RG 186 Kd40
Parado RI 130 Qk50
Paradonparp Beach THA 122 Pk40
Paragominas BR 272 Hg47
Paragoula USA 239 Fe27
Paraguaçu Paulista BR 274 He57
Paraguai BR 274 Hb56
Paraguaipoa YV 264 Ge40
Paraguarí PY 276 Hb58
Paraguay PY 276 Hb58
Paraguay 255 Ha12
Paraíba BR 273 Jc49
Paraíba BR 255 Ja10
Paraíba do Sul BR 275 Hk56
Paraíba do Sul BR 277 Hj57
Paraibano BR 272 Hj49
Parainen = Pargas FIN 44 Mc30
Paraiso BR 271 Ha49
Paraíso BR 274 Hd55
Paraíso CR 248 Fh40
Paraíso MEX 247 Fd36
Paraíso do Leste BR 274 Hc54
Paraíso do Norte BR 274 Hd57
Paraíso do Tocantins BR 272 Hf51
Paraisópolis BR 277 Hh57
Paraitepui YV 265 Gk43
Paraiyanalankulam CL 119 Pa41
Parajuru BR 273 Jb48
Parakan RI 129 Qf49
Parakou DY 188 Lb41
Parakylia AUS 148 Rj61
Paralía GR 70 Mc52
Paralía Porovítsis GR 70 Mc52
Paralkote IND 117 Pa36
Parama Island PNG 155 Sb50
Paramakudi IND 118 Ok41
Paramaribo SME 266 Hc43
Paramatti IND 118 Oj40
Parambu BR 273 Hk49
Paramillo CO 264 Gc42
Paramillo, P.N. CO 264 Gb42
Paramirim BR 273 Hj52
Paramithiá GR 70 Ma51
Páramo Frontino CO 264 Gb42
Paramonga PE 269 Gb51
Páramos del Angel EC 268 Gb45
Páramos El Batallón y La Negra, P.N. YV 264 Ge41
Paramoti BR 273 Ja48
Paran RI 129 Qh47
Paranã BR 272 Hg52
Paranã BR 272 Hg52
Paraná BR 274 He56
Paraná BR 255 Ha12
Paraná RA 281 Gk61
Paraná do Boa Boa, T.I. BR 270 Gg46
Paraná do Parica, T.I. BR 270 Gg46
Paranaguá BR 277 Hf58
Paranaíba BR 274 He55
Paranaíba BR 274 He55
Paranaiguara BR 274 He55
Paranaita BR 271 Hb50
Paraná Juca BR 265 Gf45
Paranal PE 279 Ge58
Paranal Observatory RCH 279 Ge58
Paranam SME 266 Hc43
Paranapanema BR 274 He57
Paranapanema BR 277 Hf57
Paranapebas BR 272 Hf49
Paranatinga BR 274 Hc53
Paranavaí BR 274 Hd57
Parandak IR 91 Nf28
Paranésti GR 69 Me49
Parang RI 131 Rf47
Parang RP 125 Ra43
Parang RP 125 Rc42
Paranga EAU 194 Mg44
Parangtritis RI 129 Qf50
Paranhos BR 274 Hc57
Paranthan CL 119 Pa41
Parantij IND 116 Og34
Paraopeba BR 275 Hh55
Paraparaumu NZ 153 Th66
Parapuã BR 274 He56
Parasgaon IND 117 Pa36
Parasi NEP 115 Pb32
Parasia IND 117 Ok34
Parasunanpur IND 118 Oj38
Paratebueno CO 264 Gd43
Parateca BR 272 Hj52
Parati BR 277 Hh57
Paratinga BR 273 Hj52
Paratoo AUS 150 Rk62
Paratwada IND 116 Oj35
Părău RO 69 Mf45
Paraúna BR 274 He54
Paraw Bibi Shrine TM 96 Nj26
Paray-le-Monial F 53 Le44
Parazinho BR 273 Jc48
Parbatsar IND 114 Oh32
Parbé BF 187 Kk39
Parbhani IND 116 Oj36
Parc de la Gatineau CDN 241 Gb23
Parc de la Jacques-Cartier CDN 240 Ge22
Parc de la Lékédi G 198 Lg46
Parc des Grands-Jardins CDN 240 Ge22
Parc d'Ivoloina RM 207 Ne55
Parc Güell E 57 Lc49
Parchim D 58 Lm37
Parc marin de Muanda RDC 198 Lg48
Parc national de la Guadeloupe F 251 Gk37
Parc National de l'Île-Bonaventure-et-du-Rocher-Percé CDN 240 Gh21
Parc National du Mont Tremblant CDN 240 Gc22
Parc Natural del Montseny E 57 Lc49
Parc Natural de Montserrat E 57 Lb49
Parc Naturel de Brière F 50 Ks43
Parc Naturel Hautes Fagnes-Eifel B 51 Lg40
Parc Naturel National de Port-Cros F 53 Lg47
Parc Naturel Régional d'Armorique F 50 Kq42
Parc Naturel Régional de Camargue F 53 Le47
Parco PE 269 Gc51
Parcoy PE 268 Gb49
Parc Prov. Baldwin CDN 240 Gg21
Parc Prov. de Forestville CDN 240 Gf21
Parc Provinciala de la Rivière Bleue F 158 Td57
Parc Régional des Volcans d'Auvergne F 53 Lc45
Parczew PL 65 Mc39
Parding CHN 102 Pe29
Pardo BR 274 Hd56
Pardubice CZ 66 Lq40
Pare BY 65 Mg39
Pare RI 129 Qg49
Parečča BY 65 Me37
Parecis BR 274 Hb52
Parecis BR 274 Hb53
Paredes de Nava E 54 Kq48
Pareditas RA 280 Gf62
Paredón MEX 245 Ek33
Paredón MEX 247 Fd37
Parelhas BR 273 Jb49
Parenda IND 116 Oh36
Parent CDN 240 Gc22
Parentis-en-Born F 52 Kt46
Parepare RI 130 Qk47
Paresido Rio Formoso, T.I. BR 274 Ha53
Paresi, T.I. BR 278 Ha53
Párga GR 70 Ma51
Pargarutan RI 127 Pk45
Pargas = Parainen FIN 44 Mc30
Pargi IND 116 Oj37
Pargnyongdo PRK 112 Rc27
Pargolovo RUS 44 Ml30
Pargua RCH 280 Gd66
Parguaza YV 265 Gg42
Parhar TJ 97 Oe27
Paria BOL 278 Gg54
Pariacoto PE 269 Gb50
Pariaguán YV 265 Gh41
Pariaman RI 127 Qa46
Paricatuba BR 270 Gk48
Paricutín, P.N. MEX 246 Ej36
Parigi RI 130 Ra46
Parika GUY 266 Ha42
Parikkala FIN 44 Mk29
Parilla AUS 150 Sa63
Parima-Tapirapecó, P.N. YV 265 Gh44
Parinacota RCH 278 Gf55
Parinacota, Volcán RCH 278 Gf55
Parinari PE 268 Gc48
Paring RI 129 Qh46
Paringa AUS 150 Sa63
Parintins BR 271 Hb47
Paripiranga BR 273 Jb51
Paris F 51 Lc42
Paris USA 235 Ee24
Paris USA 238 Fc29
Paris USA 238 Fd26
Paris USA 238 Fd28
Paris USA 239 Ff27
Paris USA 239 Fg26
Parishan Lake IR 93 Nf31
Paris USA 239 Fh26
Parit MAL 126 Qa43
Parit RI 127 Qa45
Paritsungaiburung RI 127 Qb46
Paritsungainyirih RI 127 Qb45
Parituluh RI 127 Qb46
Park IR 98 Oa33
Parkal IND 117 Ok36
Parkano FIN 44 Md28
Park City USA 238 Fb27
Parkent UZ 97 Oe25
Parker USA 234 Ec28
Parker Island MYA 122 Pk40
Parker, Mount AUS 143 Re54
Parkersburg USA 239 Fk26
Parkers Prairie USA 236 Fc22
Parkes AUS 151 Se62
Park Falls USA 236 Fe23
Park Hill USA 239 Fe27
Park Krajobrazowy Beskidu Śląskiego PL 65 Lt41
Park Krajobrazowy Bory Stobrawskie PL 64 Ls40
Park Krajobrazowy Dolina Baryczy PL 64 Ls39
Park Krajobrazowy Lasy Janowskie PL 65 Mc40
Park Krajobrazowy Mierzeja Wiślana PL 65 Lu36
Park Krajobrazowy Orlich Gniazd PL 65 Lu40
Park Krajobrazowy Pogórza Przemyskiego PL 65 Mc41
Parkman CDN 236 Ek21
Parkman USA 233 Eg23
Park Mużakowski PL 64 Lp39
Park Range USA 235 Eg25
Park Rapids USA 236 Fc22
Park River USA 236 Fb21
Parkston USA 236 Fb24
Parksville CDN 232 Dh21
Parlabian RI 127 Pk45
Parlakimidi IND 117 Pc36
Parlange Plantation USA 239 Fe30
Parli IND 116 Oj36
Parma I 60 Ll46
Parmana YV 265 Gh42
Parnaguá BR 272 Hh51
Parnaíba BR 273 Hj47
Parnaíba BR 273 Hk47
Parnamirim BR 273 Ja50
Parnamirim BR 273 Jc48
Parnarama BR 273 Hj48
Parnassós GR 70 Mc52
Parnassos N.P. GR 70 Mc52
Parnassus NZ 153 Tg67
Parndana AUS 150 Rj63
Párnitha N.P. GR 69 Md52
Pärnjõe EST 44 Me32
Pärnu EST 44 Me32
Pärnu EST 45 Me32
Pärnu-Jaagupi EST 44 Me32
Pärnu laht EST 45 Me32
Paro BHT 120 Pe32
Paroa NZ 152 Tj64
Paro Dzong BHT 120 Pe32
Paro Dzong BHT 120 Pe32
Parola IND 116 Oh35
Paroma, Cerro BOL/RCH 278 Gf56
Paroo AUS 144 Qj59
Paropean RI 130 Qk47
Páros GR 71 Mf53
Páros GR 71 Mf53
Parotáni BOL 278 Gg54
Parowan USA 235 Ed27
Parque Argueológico Vale do Côa P 54 Kn49
Parque Arqueológico San Agustín CO 264 Gb45
Parque Arqueológico Tierradentro CO 264 Gb44
Parque de los Menhires RA 279 Gh59
Parque do Aripuanã BR 271 Ha51
Parque do Tumucumaque BR 266 Hc45
Parque General de Division Omar Torrijos - El Cope PA 249 Fk41
Parque Indígena Araguaia BR 272 He51
Parque Indígena do Xingu BR 271 Hd51
Parque Indígena Yanomami BR 265 Gj45
Parque Int. del Rio Bravo MEX 245 Eh31
Parque Internacional La Amistad CR/PA 249 Fj41
Parque Luro RA 280 Gh64
Parque Nacional Arrecifes de Xcalak MEX 247 Fg36
Parque Nacional Sierra de San Pedro Mártir MEX 244 Ec30
Parque Natural Cabo de Gata E 55 Ks54
Parque Natural da Arrabida P 55 Kl52
Parque Natural da Ria Formosa P 55 Kn54
Parque Natural da Serra da Estrela P 54 Kn50
Parque Natural da Serra de São Mamede P 55 Kn51
Parque Natural das Serras Aire e Candeeiros P 55 Km51
Parque Natural de Albufera E 57 Ku51
Parque Natural de las Dunas de Corralejo E 174 Kc31
Parque Natural del Desierto Central MEX 244 Ec31
Parque Natural de Monfragüe E 55 Ko51
Parque Natural de Montesinho P 54 Kn49
Parque Natural de Sintra-Cascais P 55 Kl52
Parque Natural do Alvão P 54 Kn49
Parque Natural do Douro Internacional P 54 Ko49
Parque Natural do Sudoeste Alentejano e Costa Vicentina P 55 Km53
Parque Natural do Tejo Internacional P 55 Kn51
Parque Natural do Vale do Guadiana P 55 Kn53
Parque Natural Los Novillos MEX 245 Ek31
Parque Natural Presa de la Amistad MEX 245 Ek31
Parque Natural Río Celestún MEX 247 Fe35
Parque Natural Río Lagartos MEX 247 Fg35
Parque Natural San Felipe MEX 247 Ff35
Parque Natural Sierra de la Laguna MEX 244 Ef34
Parque Natural Sierra del Carmen MEX 245 Ek31
Parque Provincial Ischigualasto RA 279 Gg61
Parque Salus ROU 281 Hc63
Parra E 55 Kr51
Parrakie AUS 150 Sa63
Parral RCH 280 Ge64
Parramore Island USA 241 Gc27
Parras de la Fuente MEX 245 Ej33
Parres = Arriondas E 54 Kp47
Parrita CR 249 Fh41
Parrsboro CDN 240 Gh23
Parry I. Ind. Res. CDN 237 Fk23
Parry Islands CDN 226 Ea03
Parry Sound CDN 237 Fk23
Pars Abad IR 91 Nd26
Parsberg D 59 Lm41
Parsons USA 238 Fc27
Parson's Pond CDN 241 Hb20
Parsons Range AUS 146 Rh52
Parsora IND 117 Pc35
Partago DY 188 La41
Partanna I 62 Ln53
Parthenay F 52 Ku44
Partibanur IND 118 Ok41
Partille S 42 Ln33
Partinicio I 62 Lo53
Partizansk RUS 111 Rg24
Partizánske SK 66 Lt42
Partur IND 116 Oj36
Paru AUS 146 Rf51
Paru BR 271 Hd46
Paruna AUS 150 Sa63
Parur IND 118 Oj40
Paruraj IND 117 Pc32
Paruro PE 269 Ge52
Parvareh IR 98 Nj29
Parvatipuram IND 117 Pb36
Părvomaj BG 69 Mf48
Paryang CHN 102 Pb30
Paryčy BY 72 Me19
Påryd S 43 Lq34
Parys ZA 205 Md59
Pasaband AFG 99 Oc29
Pasada Conaf RCH 282 Gd71
Pasadena CDN 241 Hb21
Pasadena USA 234 Ea28
Pasadena USA 238 Fc31
Pasagshak S.R.S. USA 228 Cd17
Pasaje EC 268 Ga47
Pasamayo PE 269 Gb51
Pasanauri GE 91 Nc24
Pasangkayu RI 130 Qk46
Pasapuat RI 127 Qa47
Pasarbantal RI 127 Qa47
Pasarbaru RI 127 Qa46
Pasarbembah RI 127 Qb47
Pasargadae IR 98 Ng30
Pasarkambang RI 127 Qa46
Pasar Maga RI 127 Pk45
Pasarmatango RI 127 Pk45
Pasarseluma RI 127 Qb48
Pasarsibuhuan RI 127 Pk45
Pasawng MYA 120 Pj36
Pasayten W.A. USA 232 Dk21
Pascagoula USA 239 Ff30
Pasco USA 232 Ea22
Pasewalk D 58 Lp37
Pasi RI 130 Ra49
Pasiene LV 45 Mj34
Pasinler TR 91 Na25
Pasirganting RI 127 Qa47
Pasir Mas MAL 126 Qb42
Pasirpengaraian RI 127 Qa45
Pasir Puteh MAL 126 Qb43
Paskalevo BG 69 Mh47
Påskallavik S 43 Lr33
Paškovskij RUS 73 Mk23
Paskuh IR 98 Oa32
Pasłęk PL 65 Lu36
Pašman HR 61 Lq47
Pašman HR 61 Lq47
Pasman RA 281 Gj64
Pasni PK 99 Ob33
Paso Argentino RA 280 Gf62
Paso Cardenal A.Samoré RA/RCH 280 Ge66
Paso Caruachi YV 265 Gj41
Paso de Caballo YV 265 Gg41
Paso de Indios RA 282 Gf67
Paso de Jama RA/RCH 279 Gg57
Paso de la Cruz RA 279 Gh58
Paso del Agua Negro RA 279 Gf61
Paso de la Laguna RA 276 Ha61
Paso de la Patria PY 276 Ha59
Paso de los Algarrobos RA 280 Gg64
Paso de los Indios RA 280 Gf65
Paso de los Libres RA 276 Hb60
Paso de los Toros ROU 276 Hb62
Paso de los Vientos C 250 Gd35
Paso del Planchón RA/RCH 280 Ge63
Paso del Sapo RA 280 Gf67
Paso de Pino Hachado RA/RCH 280 Ge65
Paso de Vacas MEX 246 Ek36
Paso Flores RA 280 Ge66
Paso Hondo MEX 247 Fd38
Paso Maipo RA/RCH 280 Gf63
Paso Maule o Pehuenche RA/RCH 280 Ge64
Paso Real C 243 Fj34
Paso Real CR 249 Fj41
Paso Robles USA 234 Dk28
Paso Rodolfo Roballos RA 282 Ge69
Paso Sico RA/RCH 279 Gg57
Paso Socompa RA/RCH 279 Gf58
Pasqua CDN 233 Eh20
Pasquales MEX 246 Ej36
Pasquia Hills CDN 233 Ej19
Pasrur PK 99 Oh29
Passage de la Déroute F 50 Kt41
Passagem Franca BR 272 Hj49
Passa Tempo BR 275 Hh56
Passau D 59 Lo42
Passaya RG 186 Ke40
Passe d'Amogjâr RIM 180 Kd35
Passe de Djoûk RIM 180 Ke37
Passe de Korizo TCH 183 Lh34
Passe de Salvador RN 183 Lg34
Passe du Vent RH 250 Gd36
Passekudah Beach CL 119 Pa42
Passi RP 124 Rb40
Passi SN 186 Kb39
Passira BR 273 Jc49
Pass Island CDN 241 Hb22
Passo dello Spluga = Splügenpass I/CH 60 Lk44
Passo del San Bernardino CH 60 Lk44
Passo del Tonale I 60 Ll44
Passo di Résia = Reschenpass I 60 Ll44
Passo Fundo BR 276 Hd60
Passos BR 275 Hg56
Pastavy BY 45 Mg35
Pasteur RA 281 Gj63
Pasto CO 264 Gb45
Pastos Bons BR 272 Hh49
Pasto Ventura RA 279 Gg59
Pastrana E 57 Ks50
Pasu 114 Oh27
Pasual RP 124 Ra37
Pasul Bratocea RO 69 Mf45
Pasul Mestecăniș RO 67 Mf43
Pasul Șetref RO 67 Me43
Pasul Valișoara RO 67 Mc44
Pasuruan RI 129 Qg49
Pasvalys LT 45 Me34
Pásztó H 67 Lu43
Pata BOL 278 Gf53
Pata CO 268 Ge46
Pata RCA 190 Ma41
Pata SN 186 Kc39
Patacamaya BOL 278 Gg54
Patag N.P. RP 124 Rb40
Patagonia RA 282 Ge71
Patagonian Shelf 282 Gh70
Pata-Idié CI 187 Kg43
Pata Island RP 125 Ra43
Patamba RDC 199 Lk47
Patamundai IND 117 Pd35
Patan IND 116 Og34
Patan IND 116 Og37
Patan NEP 115 Pc32
Patani WAN 188 Ld43
Patarbar IND 117 Pc34
Pătârlagele RO 69 Mg45
Patas IND 116 Oh36
Pata Temple CHN 107 Qg28
Patchewollock AUS 150 Sb63
Patea NZ 153 Th65
Pategi WAN 188 Lc41
Paté Island EAK 195 Na47
Patemba RDC 199 Mb48
Patensie ZA 205 Mc62
Paternò I 63 Lp53
Paternoster ZA 204 Lj62
Pateros USA 232 Ea21
Paterson USA 232 Ea23
Paterson USA 241 Gc25
Paterson ZA 205 Mc62
Paterson Inlet NZ 153 Te69
Paterson Range AUS 142 Rb56
Patewa IND 117 Pb35
Pathalgaon IND 117 Pb34
Pathalipam IND 120 Ph32
Pathankot IND 114 Oh29
Pathapkandi IND 120 Pg33
Patharghata BD 120 Pe34
Patharkot NEP 117 Pc32
Pathé MEX 246 Fa36
Pathiu THA 122 Pk40
Pathri IND 116 Oj36
Pathrud IND 116 Oh36
Pathum Thani THA 122 Qa38
Pati RI 129 Qf49
Pati RI 131 Rd50
Patia BD 120 Pg34
Patia = El Bordo CO 264 Gb44
Patiala IND 114 Oj30
Patience F 266 Hd44
Patiko EAU 194 Mg44
Patikul RP 125 Ra42
Patillos RCH 278 Ge56
Patio Chiquito CO 264 Ge43
Patiram IND 120 Pe33
Patiriti GR 69 Md51
Patiška MK 68 Mb49
Pativilca PE 269 Gb51
Patkan IR 98 Nj31
Patlong LS 205 Me61
Pátmos GR 71 Mg53
Patna IND 117 Pc33
Patnanongan Island RP 124 Rb38
Patna Sahib IND 117 Pc33
Patnongan RP 124 Rb40
Patnos TR 91 Nb26
Pato Branco BR 276 Hd59
Patoles MEX 244 Eg34
Patomskoe nagor'e RUS 89 Qc07
Patong THA 122 Pk42
Patongo EAU 194 Mg44
Patos BR 273 Jb49
Patos de Minas BR 275 Hg55
Patos do Piauí BR 273 Hk49
Patquia RA 279 Gg61
Pátra GR 70 Mb52
Patratu IND 117 Pc34
Patreksfjörður IS 46 Jr25
Patricia CDN 233 Ee20
Patricia USA 238 Ej29
Patrickswell IRL 47 Km38
Patrimônio BR 274 Hf55
Patrocinio BR 275 Hg55
Patroputtu IND 117 Pb36
Patsul IND 116 Oj35
Pattadakal IND 116 Oh38
Pattalasang RI 130 Ra48
Pattambi IND 118 Oj40
Pattani THA 123 Qa42
Pattaya THA 122 Qa39
Patten USA 240 Gf22
Patterson USA 242 Fj30
Patterson, Mount CDN 229 Dc13
Patti I 63 Lp52
Pattoki PK 99 Og30
Pattukkottai IND 119 Ok40
Patu BR 273 Jb49
Patuakhali BD 120 Pf34
Patuanak CDN 231 Eg18
Pătulele RO 68 Mc46
Patullo, Mount CDN 230 Df17
Patur IND 116 Oj35
Pátzcuaro MEX 246 Ek36
Pau F 52 Ku47
Pau-A-Pique BR 273 Hk50
Paúba BR 277 Hg58
Pau Brasil, P.N.do BR 275 Hg53
Pau Brasil, T.I. BR 275 Hk55
Paucarbamba PE 269 Gc52
Paucartambo PE 269 Ge52
Paú dos Ferros BR 273 Ja49
Pauh RI 127 Qb47
Pauillac F 52 Ku45
Pauk MYA 120 Ph35
Paukkaung MYA 120 Ph36
Paulatuk CDN 226 Dd05
Paul B. Johnson S.P. USA 239 Ff30
Paul Bunyan Center USA 236 Fc22
Paulhaguet F 53 Ld45
Paúliani GR 70 Mc52
Paulina USA 232 Ea23
Paulina Peak USA 232 Dk24
Paulino Neves BR 273 Hj47
Paulista BR 273 Jc49
Paulistana BR 273 Hk50
Paulo Afonso BR 273 Ja50
Paulo de Faria BR 274 Hf55
Paulo Ramos BR 272 Hh48
Paulpietersburg ZA 205 Mf59
Paul Roux ZA 205 Md60
Paul Sauer Bridge ZA 204 Mb63
Pauls Valley USA 238 Fb28
Paumari do Cuniua, T.I. BR 270 Gh49
Paumari do Lago Manissua, T.I. BR 270 Gh48
Paumari do lago Maraha, T.I. BR 270 Gh49
Paumari do Lago Parica, T.I. BR 270 Gh48
Paumari do Rio Ituxi, T.I. BR 270 Gh49
Paungbyin MYA 120 Ph33
Paungdawthi MYA 122 Pj37
Paungde MYA 120 Ph36
Paunini BR 270 Gg49
Paup PNG 155 Sb49
Pausa PE 269 Gd53
Pau Seco BR 275 Ja53
Paute EC 268 Ga47
Pavagada IND 118 Oj38
Pavagadh IND 116 Og34
Pavant Range USA 235 Ed26
Pavão BR 275 Hk54
Paveh IR 91 Nd28
Pavel Banja BG 69 Mf48
Pavia I 60 Lk45
Pavia P 55 Km52
Pavilion CDN 232 Dk20
Pavilly F 51 La41
Pāvilosta LV 45 Mb34
Pavino Polje MNE 68 Lu47
Pavlikeni BG 69 Mf47
Pavlivka UA 65 Me40
Pavlodar KZ 88 Od08
Pavlof Is. USA 228 Bk18
Pavlof Vol. USA 228 Bk18
Pavlohrad UA 73 Mh21
Pavlovo RUS 72 Nb18
Pavlovsk RUS 72 Mf16
Pavlovsk RUS 72 Na20
Pavlovskaja RUS 73 Mk22
Pavlovskij Posad RUS 72 Mk18
Pavlovskoe RUS 72 Na17
Pavlyš UA 73 Mg21
Pavullo nel Frignano I 60 Ll46
Pavuvu Island SOL 157 Sk50
Pawa RDC 191 Md44
Pawa RDC 191 Me44
Pawaia PNG 155 Sc49
Pawapuri IND 117 Pc33
Pawayan IND 115 Pa31
Pawé CAM 189 Lf43
Pawhuska USA 238 Fb27
Pawłów PL 65 Md39
Pawnee Bill Mus. USA 238 Fb27
Pawnee Ind. Village USA 238 Fb26
Pawnee Nat. Grassland USA 235 Eh25
Pawnee Rock S.M. USA 238 Fa26
Pawtucket USA 241 Ge25
Pawu A.L. AUS 143 Rg56
Pawut MYA 122 Pk39
Pawut MYA 122 Pk39
Paxí GR 70 Ma51
Paxson USA 229 Ch14
Paxtakor UZ 97 Od25
Paxtaobod UZ 97 Oe25
Payagyi MYA 122 Pj37
Payaheislam RI 125 Rd45
Payakumbuh RI 127 Qa46
Payang, Gunung RI 128 Qh45
Payar SN 180 Kc38
Payerne CH 60 Lg44
Payette USA 232 Eb23
Paymogo E 55 Kn53
Paynes Find AUS 144 Qj60
Paysandú ROU 276 Ha62
Pays d'Auge F 50 Ku41
Pays de la Loire F 50 Kt43
Payson USA 235 Ee25
Payson USA 235 Ee28
Payún, Cerro RA 280 Gf64
Payung RI 129 Qd47
Payyanur IND 118 Oh39
Paz BR 276 Hd58
Pazar TR 91 Na25
Pazarbası Burnu TR 90 Mf25
Pazarcık TR 90 Mj27
Pazardžik BG 69 Me48
Pazarić BIH 68 Lt47
Pazarköy TR 71 Mh51
Pazarlar TR 71 Mk51
Paz de Ariporo CO 264 Ge43
Paz del Rio CO 264 Gd42
Pazha PK 99 Oe31
Pazin HR 61 Lo45
Pazña BOL 278 Gg55
Pčelarovo BG 69 Mf49
Pčelnik BG 69 Mh47
Pe MYA 122 Pk39
Peace Memorial Hiroshima J 113 Rg28
Peace Point CDN 231 Ed16
Peace River CDN 231 Eb17
Peace River CDN 231 Ed16
Peach Springs USA 235 Ed28
Peach Tree USA 239 Fg30
Peachtree City USA 239 Fh29
Peak Charles N.P. AUS 144 Ra62
Peak District N.P. GB 49 Kt37
Peak Hill AUS 144 Qk58
Peak Hill AUS 151 Se62
Peal de Becerro E 55 Kr53
Peale, Mount USA 235 Ef26
Pearce USA 235 Ef30
Pea Ridge N.M.P. USA 238 Fc27
Pearisburg USA 242 Fk27
Pearl City USA 234 Cb35
Pearl Harbor USA 234 Ca35
Pearl Island MV 118 Og43
Pearl Island NZ 153 Td69
Pearl Mosque PK 99 Of31
Pearl River CHN 108 Qf34
Pearl S. Buck Mus. USA 239 Fk26
Pearsall USA 245 Fa31
Pearson USA 242 Fj30
Pearson Island AUS 150 Rh62
Pearson Reef 128 Qg41
Pearston ZA 205 Mc62
Peary Channel CDN 226 Ed03
Peary Land DK 227 Jb02
Peawanuck CDN 227 Fc07
Pebane MOC 203 Mk54
Pebas PE 268 Ge47
Pebbly Beach AUS 151 Sf63
Peć KSV 68 Ma48
Peçanha BR 275 Hj55
Pecan Island USA 239 Fd31
Pécel H 67 Lu43
Pečenjevce SRB 68 Mb47
Pečerskaja lavra UA 73 Mf20
Pechea RO 69 Mh45
Pecica RO 67 Mb44
Pećka Patrijaršija KSV 68 Ma48
Pečki RUS 45 Mh33
Pečora RUS 88 Nc05
Pečora RUS 88 Nd05
Pečorskoe more RUS 88 Nb04
Pečory RUS 45 Mh33
Pecos USA 235 Eh28
Pecos USA 245 Ej30
Pecos N.H.P. USA 235 Eh28
Pecos Plains USA 235 Eh29
Pécs H 66 Lt44
Pedana IND 117 Pa37
Pedasi PA 249 Fk42
Pedaso I 61 Lo47
Pedda Alavalapadu IND 119 Ok38
Pedda Arikatla IND 119 Ok38
Peddaballe IND 119 Ok39
Peddapalli IND 117 Ok36
Peddie ZA 205 Md62
Pedernales DOM 250 Ge36
Pedernales EC 268 Fk45
Pedernales RCH 279 Gf59
Pedernales YV 265 Gj41
Pederneiras BR 274 Hf57
Pedestal Rocks USA 238 Fd28
Pediwang RI 125 Rd45
Pedra Azul BR 275 Hk53
Pedra Azul BR 275 Hk56
Pedra Badejo CV 186 Jj38
Pedra Branca BR 273 Ja48
Pedra de Lume CV 186 Jj37
Pedra do Feitiço ANG 198 Lg48
Pedrafita do Cebreiro E 54 Kn47
Pedralba E 57 Ku51
Pedra Preta BR 274 Hc54
Pedras de Fogo BR 273 Jc49
Pedras de Maria da Cruz BR 275 Hh53
Pedras Negras ANG 198 Lh50
Pedras Negras BR 278 Gj52
Pedras Salgadas P 54 Kn49
Pedras Tinhosas STP 188 Ld45
Pedraza de la Sierra E 54 Kr49
Pedregal YV 264 Ge40
Pedregosa CO 264 Gd42
Pedregulho BR 275 Hg56
Pedreiras BR 271 Hc48
Pedreiras BR 272 Hh48
Pedrero, Cerro el RA 282 Ge68
Pedriceña MEX 245 Ej33
Pedro Afonso BR 272 Hf50
Pedro Avelino BR 273 Jb48
Pedrobank 250 Ga37
Pedro Betancourt C 243 Fk34
Pedro Canário BR 275 Ja55
Pedro Carbo EC 268 Fk46
Pedro Cays JA 250 Gb37
Pedro de Valdivia RCH 279 Gf57
Pedro Gomes BR 274 Hc55
Pedro II BR 273 Hk48
Pedro Juan Caballero PY 274 Hc57
Pedro Luro RA 281 Gj65
Pedro Muñoz E 57 Ks51
Pedro Vaz CV 186 Jj38
Peebinga AUS 150 Sa63
Peebles GB 48 Kr35
Peel GB 49 Kq36
Peel Sound CDN 227 Fa04
Peene D 58 Lo37
Peerless CDN 233 Ef18
Peerless USA 233 Eh21
Peers CDN 232 Ec19
Peerto Iradier GQ 188 Le45
Péfkos GR 70 Ma50
Pegasus Bay NZ 153 Tg67
Pegatan RI 129 Qg47
Peggys Cove CDN 240 Gj23
Pegnitz D 59 Lm41
Pegnitz D 59 Lm41
Pego E 57 Ku52
Pegu MYA 122 Pj37
Peguis Ind. Res. CDN 236 Fa20
Pegunungan Border RI 155 Sa47
Pegunungan Fakfak RI 154 Rg47
Pegunungan Foja RI 154 Rk47
Pegunungan Gauttier RI 154 Rk47
Pegunungan Hose MAL 128 Qg44
Pegunungan Jayawijaya RI 154 Rk48
Pegunungan Kumafa RI 154 Rg47
Pegunungan Maoke RI 154 Rj48
Pegunungan Tamrau RI 154 Rg46
Pegunungan Tiyo RI 154 Rh48
Pegunungan Van Rees RI 154 Rj47
Pegunungan Wondiwoi RI 154 Rh47
Pehlivanköy TR 69 Mg49
Péhonko DY 188 La40
Pehuajó RA 281 Gk63
Pehuén-Co RA 281 Gk65
Peigan Ind. Res. CDN 233 Ed21
Peili SUD 191 Md42
Peine D 58 Ll38
Peineta, Cerro RA 282 Gd71
Peintures rupestres (Fada) TCH 184 Ma37
Peiting D 59 Ll43
Peitz D 58 Lp39
Peixe BR 272 Hf52
Pei Xian CHN 112 Qj28
Peixoto de Azevedo BR 271 Hc51
Pejantan RI 129 Qd45
Pekabata RI 130 Qk47
Pekalongan RI 129 Qe49
Pekan MAL 126 Qb44
Pekanbaru RI 127 Qa45
Pekan Jabi MAL 126 Qb44
Pekin RI 128 Qj44
Pekin USA 236 Fa22
Pekin USA 239 Ff25
Peking CHN 107 Qj26
Pekinga DY 188 Lb39
Peking Man = Zhoukoudian CHN 107 Qh26
Péla RG 186 Kf42
Pelabuhan Ratu RI 129 Qd49
Pelabun Kelang MAL 126 Qa44
Pelaihari RI 129 Qh47
Pelapis RI 129 Qe46
Pelau Island SOL 157 Sk48
Pelawan RI 127 Qb47
Pélébina DY 188 La41
Pelechua CO 264 Gd40
Pelechuco BOL 278 Gf53
Pelegonia MK 68 Mb49
Pelejo PE 268 Gc49
Pelekech EAK 194 Mh44
Peleliu PAL 124 Rh42
Peleng RI 131 Rb46
Pelenge RDC 199 Mb47
Pèlerinage des Gitans F 53 Le47
Peletá GR 70 Mc53
Pélézi CI 187 Kg42
Pelham AUS 147 Sb55
Pelhřimov CZ 66 Lq41
Pelican USA 230 Db17
Pelican Mtns. CDN 231 Ec18
Pelican Rapids CDN 233 Ek19
Pelican Rapids USA 236 Fb22
Pelileo EC 268 Ga46
Pelion USA 242 Fk29
Pelister, N.P. MK 68 Mb49
Pelješac HR 61 Ls48
Pelkosenniemi FIN 39 Mh23
Pélla GR 70 Mc50
Pella JOR 90 Mh29
Pelland USA 236 Fd21
Pellegrini RA 281 Gj64
Pellinge = Pellinki FIN 44 Mf30
Pellinki = Pellinge FIN 44 Mf30
Pello FIN 39 Me24
Pellworm D 58 Lj36
Pelly Mountains CDN 230 Dd15
Pelly Plateau CDN 230 De14
Pelokang RI 130 Qk49
Peloponnesus GR 70 Mb53
Pelotas BR 276 Hd61
Pelotas BR 277 He60
Pelplin PL 64 Lt37
Pelsart Island AUS 144 Qg60
Pelsor USA 238 Fd28
Pélussin F 53 Le45
Pem PNG 156 Se50
Pemalang RI 129 Qe49
Pemanggil MAL 126 Qc44
Pematangkaras RI 127 Qc47
Pematang Purba RI 127 Pk44
Pematang Siantar RI 127 Pk44
Pemba MOC 197 Na52
Pemba Z 202 Md54
Pemba Channel EAT 197 Mk48
Pemba Island EAT 197 Mk48
Pemberton AUS 144 Qj63
Pemberton CDN 232 Dj20
Pembroke AUS 149 Se59
Pembroke CDN 241 Gb23
Pembroke GB 49 Kq39
Pembroke USA 242 Fk29
Pembroke Dock GB 49 Kq39
Pembrokeshire Coast N.P. GB 49 Kp39
Pembuanghulu RI 129 Qg47
Pemuco RCH 280 Gd64
Pen IND 116 Og36
Peña Blanca PE 268 Gd47
Peña Blanca RCH 279 Ge59
Peñacerrada E 56 Ks48
Peñafiel E 54 Kq49
Penafiel P 54 Km49
Peñaflor RCH 280 Ge62
Penajam RI 129 Qj46
Penal Colony PA 249 Fk42
Peñalén E 57 Ks50
Penalva BR 272 Hh47
Penamacor P 55 Kn50
Penambulai RI 154 Rh49
Peña Mira E 54 Ko49
Penampang MAL 128 Qj43
Penang MAL 126 Qa43
Penápolis BR 274 He56
Peña Prieta E 54 Kq48
Peñaranda de Bracamonte E 54 Kp50
Peñaranda de Duero E 54 Kr49
Penaron RI 126 Pj43
Peñarroya-Pueblonuevo E 55 Kp52
Penarth GB 49 Kr39
Peñas de San Pedro E 55 Ks52
Peñas Negras YV 265 Gh42
Peña Ubiña E 54 Kp48
Peñausende E 54 Kp49
Pench N.P. IND 117 Ok35
Pendanga BR 272 Hj50
Pendé RCA 190 Lj42
Pendembu WAL 186 Kd41
Pendembu WAL 186 Ke41
Pendências BR 273 Jb48
Pendeng RI 126 Pj43
Pender Bay A.L. AUS 142 Rb54
Pendjari, P.N.de la DY 187 La40
Pendleton USA 232 Ea23
Pendolo RI 130 Ra47
Pendopo RI 127 Qb47
Pendra Road IND 117 Pa34
Pendurti IND 117 Pb37
Penebangan RI 129 Qe46
Peneda-Gerês, P.N.da P 54 Km49
Penedo BR 268 Ge49
Penedo BR 273 Jb51
Pene-Katamba RDC 199 Mc46
Pene-Mende RDC 196 Me48
Peneri Tacaquiri, T.I. BR 270 Gg49
Pénéssoulou DY 188 La41
Pengalengan RI 129 Qd49
Peng'an CHN 108 Qd30
Penganak RI 127 Qc46
Pengchia Yü RC 109 Rb33
Penge RDC 191 Md44
Penge RDC 191 Me44
Penge RDC 199 Mc48
Penge ZA 205 Mf58
Penghu Islands RC 109 Qk34
Pengkou CHN 109 Qj33
Penglai CHN 107 Ra27
Penglai CHN 109 Qf36
Penglai Ge CHN 107 Ra27
Penglaizhen CHN 108 Qc30
Pengshan CHN 108 Qb30
Pengshui CHN 108 Qe31
Penguin AUS 151 Sd66
Penguin Island CDN 241 Hb22
Pengxi CHN 108 Qc30
Pengze CHN 109 Qj31
Pengzhou CHN 108 Qb30
Penhalonga ZW 202 Mg55
Péni BF 187 Kh40
Peniche P 55 Kl51
Penicuik GB 48 Kr35
Penida RI 129 Qh49
Peninjai RI 127 Qa46
Península Brunswick RCH 282 Ge72
Península de Araya YV 265 Gj40
Península de Azuero PA 249 Ga41
Península de la Guajira CO 264 Ge39
Península de Nicoya CR 248 Fh41
Península de Osa CR 249 Fj41
Península de Paracas PE 269 Gb52
Península de Paraguaná YV 264 Ge39
Península de Paría YV 265 Gj40
Península de Paría, P.N. YV 265 Gj40
Península de Taitao RCH 282 Gc69
Península de Zapata C 243 Fk34
Península dos Tigres ANG 200 Lf54
Península Dumas RCH 282 Gf73
Península Ferrol PE 269 Ga50
Península Hardy RCH 282 Gf73
Peninsula Mitre RA 282 Gh73
Península Muñoz Gamero RCH 282 Gd72
Peninsula Quevado MEX 244 Eg33
Peninsula San Martín RCH 282 Gc70
Península Siscuelan RCH 282 Gd69
Península Skiring RCH 282 Gc68
Península Sta. Elena CR 248 Fg40
Península Staines RCH 282 Gd71
Península Tres Montes RCH 282 Gc69
Península Valdés RA 281 Gj67
Península Valiente PA 249 Fk41
Península Wharton RCH 282 Gc70
Península Wilcock RCH 282 Gd71
Péninsule de Gaspésie CDN 240 Gh21
Péninsule d'Ungava CDN 227 Gb06
Peñiscola E 57 La50
Penisola Salentina I 63 Ls50
Pénjamo MEX 246 Ek35
Penjawan RI 128 Qg45
Penjwin IRQ 91 Nc28
Penkun D 58 Lp37
Penmarc'h F 50 Kq43
Penna Ahobilam IND 118 Oj38
Pennagaram IND 118 Oj39
Pennant CDN 233 Ef20
Penne I 61 Lo48
Penne-d'Agenais F 52 La46
Pennell Coast 287 Tb33
Penneshaw AUS 150 Rj63
Penn Hills USA 237 Ga25
Pennines GB 26 Kb05
Pennsylvania USA 241 Ga25
Penny CDN 230 Dk19
Penn Yan USA 241 Gb24
Pennyroyal Plateau USA 239 Fh27
Penny Strait CDN 227 Fa03
Peno RUS 72 Mg17
Penobscot Bay USA 241 Gf23
Penobscot River USA 240 Gf23
Penola AUS 150 Sa64
Peñón Blanco MEX 245 Eh33
Penong AUS 148 Rg61
Penonomé PA 249 Fk41
Penot, Mount VU 158 Td54
Penrith AUS 151 Sf62
Penrith GB 49 Ks36
Penryn GB 49 Kp40
Pensa BF 187 Kk39
Pensacola USA 239 Fg30
Pensacola Mountains 287 Hb35
Penshurst AUS 150 Sb64
Penshurst CR 249 Fj41
Pensiangan MAL 128 Qj43
Penta IND 117 Pa36
Pentakota IND 117 Pb37
Pentálofos GR 70 Mb50
Pentápoli GR 69 Md49
Pentecost Downs AUS 143 Rd54
Pentecostes BR 273 Ja47
Pentecost Island VU 158 Te53
Penteleu RO 69 Mg45
Penticton CDN 232 Ea21
Penticton Ind. Res. CDN 232 Ea21
Pentland AUS 147 Sc56
Pentland Hills GB 48 Kr35
Peñuelas MEX 246 Ej35
Penukonda IND 118 Oj38
Penwegon MYA 120 Pj36
Penyal d'Ifac E 57 La52
Penza RUS 72 Nc19
Penzance GB 49 Kp40
Penzberg D 59 Lm43
Penzele RDC 199 Lk46
Penžinskaja guba RUS 89 Ta06
Penzlin D 58 Lo37
Peoria USA 235 Ed29
Peoria USA 239 Ff25
Pepa RDC 196 Me49
Pepeekeo USA 234 Cc36
Pepel WAL 186 Kd41
Pepple Island GB 283 Ha71
Peqin AL 68 Lu49
Peque CO 264 Gc42
Pequizal, T.I. BR 278 Ha53
Perabumulih RI 127 Qc47
Perälä FIN 44 Mb28
Peraleda del Zaucejo E 55 Kp52
Perales del Alfambra E 57 Ku50
Pérama GR 70 Ma51
Pérama GR 70 Ma51
Perambalur IND 119 Ok40
Perämeren kansallispuisto FIN 41 Me25
Peramiho EAT 196 Mh51
Peranka FIN 39 Mk25
Peranzanes E 54 Ko48
Peräseinäjoki FIN 44 Md28
Perbulan RI 127 Pk44
Percé CDN 240 Gh21
Percival Lakes AUS 143 Rc56
Percy Islands AUS 149 Sf56
Percy Quin S.P. USA 239 Fe30
Perdagangan RI 126 Pk44
Perdala IND 118 Oh39
Perđamajski BY 65 Mf37
Perdasdefogu I 62 Lk51
Perdekop ZA 205 Me59
Perdigão P 55 Kn51
Perdizes BR 275 Hg55
Perdões BR 275 Hh56
Perečyn UA 67 Mc42
Perehins'ke UA 67 Me42
Pereira CO 264 Gc43
Pereira Barreto BR 274 He56
Pereirinha BR 271 Hb50
Pereiro BR 273 Ja49
Perejaslav-Chmel'nyc'kyj UA 73 Mf20
Perejaslavka RUS 111 Rh22
Perelešinskij RUS 72 Na20
Pere Marquette S.P. USA 239 Fe26
Perembahan RI 127 Qc47
Peremyšljany UA 67 Me41
Perenjori AUS 144 Qj60
Péréré DY 188 Lb41
Pereščepyne UA 73 Mh21
Pereslavl'-Zalesskij RUS 72 Mk17
Pereslavsky N.P. RUS 72 Mk17
Perespa UA 65 Mf40
Peret AUS 147 Sa52
Pereval Akbajtal TJ 97 Og26
Pereval Anzob TJ 97 Oe26
pereval Čyjyrčyk KS 97 Og25
pereval Durbet Daba MNG/RUS 101 Pe21
Pereval Harami RUS 91 Nd24
Pereval Kajtezek TJ 97 Og27
Pereval Krestovyi GE 91 Nc24
pereval Kyzyl-Art TJ/KS 97 Og26
Pereval Mamisonski RUS/GE 91 Nb24
Perevalovo RUS 45 Mb36
pereval Taldyk KS 97 Og26
pereval Vyškivs'kyj UA 67 Md42
Perevoz RUS 72 Nc18
Perez RA 281 Gk62
Perez USA 232 Dk25
PérezRosales , P.N. RCH 280 Gd6
Perfume Pagoda = Huong Pagoda VN 121 Qc35
Pergamino RA 281 Gk62
Pergamon Akropolis TR 71 Mh51
Perge TR 90 Mf27
Pérgine Valsugana I 60 Lm44
Pérgola I 61 Ln47
Perguiça CV 186 Jh37
Perhentian MAL 126 Qb43
Perho FIN 44 Me27
Periam RO 67 Ma44
Péribonka CDN 240 Gd21
Perico RA 279 Gh58

Quincy – Reserva Nacional Estricta San Antonio

Quincy USA 241 Ge24
Quincy Hills USA 239 Fe26
Quindanning AUS 144 Qj62
Quines RA 280 Gh62
Quinga MOC 203 Na53
Quingenge ANG 200 Lh52
Quingey F 53 Lf43
Quinhagak USA 228 Bk16
Quinhámel GNB 186 Kf40
Qui Nhon VN 123 Qe39
Quiniluban Group RP 124 Ra40
Quiniluban Island RP 124 Ra40
Quinlan and Regional Cultural Centre (Laura) AUS 147 Sc53
Quinta BR 276 Hd62
Quintana de Castillo E 54 Ko48
Quintana del Puente E 54 Kq48
Quintanar de la Orden E 55 Kr51
Quintanar del Rey E 57 Kt51
Quintana Roo MEX 247 Fe36
Quintero F 56 Ks42
Quintin F 52 Kd41
Quinto E 57 Ku49
Quinzau ANG 198 Lh49
Quinzau ANG 198 Lg42
Quionga MOC 197 Na51
Quiongua ANG 200 Lh53
Quiotepec MEX 246 Fb37
Quipapá BR 273 Jb50
Quipeio ANG 200 Lh52
Quiriego MEX 244 Ef32
Quirigua GCA 248 Ff38
Quiriguá GCA 248 Ff38
Quirima RCH 280 Gd64
Quirima ANG 200 Lk51
Quirindi AUS 149 Sf61
Quirinópolis BR 274 He55
Quiriquire YV 265 Gj41
Quiriza BOL 279 Gh56
Quiroga E 54 Kn48
Quiroga MEX 246 Ek36
Quiroga RA 281 Gk63
Quirós RA 279 Gd60
Quiroz YV 264 Ge40
Quiruvilca PE 268 Ga49
Quissamã MOC 197 Na52
Quissanga BR 275 Hk57
Quissico MOC 203 Mh58
Quitandinha BR 277 Hf58
Quitapa ANG 200 Lh53
Quiterajo MOC 197 Na51
Quiteve ANG 200 Lr44
Quitexe ANG 198 Lh49
Quitman USA 238 Fc29
Quitman USA 239 Ff29
Quivira N.W.R. USA 238 Fa26
Quivolgo RCH 280 Gd64
Quixabá BR 273 Hj51
Quixadá BR 270 Gg50
Quixadá BR 273 Ja48
Quixaxe MOC 203 Na53
Quixeramobim BR 273 Ja48
Quixeré BR 273 Jb48
Quizenga ANG 198 Lh50
Qujiang CHN 109 Qg33
Qujing CHN 107 Qd33
Qulban Layyah IRQ 93 Nd31
Quljuqtov togi lar UZ 96 Og25
Qullai Kommunizm TJ 97 Og26
Qumar Heyan CHN 103 Pd28
Qumarlêb CHN 103 Ph28
Qumnah KSA 94 Na37
Qundao CHN 107 Ra26
Quneitra SYR 90 Mh29
Qunfudh YE 94 Ne37
Qungqiang CHN 106 Qa29
Qungtag CHN 102 Pd31
Qungtag CHN 102 Pd31
Quobba AUS 144 Qg58
Quoin Island AUS 143 Re53
Quorn AUS 150 Rk62
Qurayat OM 95 Nk34
Qurayd SUD 185 Mf40
Qurdud SUD 185 Me40
Qureida SUD 184 Mc40
Qurghonteppa TJ 97 Oe27
Qurrasa SUD 185 Mg38
Qûs ET 179 Mg33
Qusar AZ 91 Nd26
Qusay'ir YE 95 Nf36
Quss Abu Sa'id ET 178 Md32
Qusum CHN 103 Pg31
Qutang CHN 108 Qe30
Qutub Minar IND 114 Oj31
Quwarah JOR 92 Mh31
Quwu Shan CHN 106 Qc27
Qu Xian CHN 108 Qe30
Quxu CHN 102 Pf31
Quyang CHN 107 Qh26
Quynh Luu VN 121 Qc36
Quzhou CHN 109 Qk31
Quzhou CHN 109 Qk31
Qyrqqyz-Qala UZ 96 Oa25

R

Raa Atoll MV 118 Og43
Raab A 61 Lq43
Raabs A 66 Lq42
Raahe FIN 41 Me26
Rääkkylä FIN 39 Me24
Raanujärvi FIN 39 Me24
Raas RI 129 Qh49
Raasay GB 48 Ko33
Raas Binna SP 193 Nf40
Raas Caluula SP 193 Nf40
Raas Caseyr SP 193 Nf41
Raas Ilig SP 193 Ne42
Raas Khansiir SP 193 Nc40
Raas Macbar SP 193 Nf41
Raas Maskan SP 193 Nf40
Raas Surud SP 193 Nf40
Raas Xaafuun SP 193 Ng40
Rab HR 61 Lp46
Rab HR 61 Lp45
Raba RI 129 Qk50
Rabaable SP 193 Ne41
Rabac HR 61 Lp45
Râbâfûzes H 66 Lr44
Rabak WAN 182 Lc39
Rabahidvég H 66 Lr43
Rabak SUD 185 Mg40
Rabat RI 154 Rh49
Rabaraba PNG 156 Se51
Rabat M 63 Lp55
Rabat MT 63 Lp55
Rabaul PNG 156 Sd48
Rabba WAN 188 Lc41
Rabdure SP 195 Nb43
Rabia RI 131 Rf46
Rabida IRQ 91 Nb27
Rabigh KSA 92 Mk34
Rabka-Zdroj PL 65 Lu41
Rābniţa MD 73 Me22
Rabodalo RI 155 Rd45
Rabo da Onça BR 270 Gh46
Rabor IR 93 Nh31
Rabwah PK 99 Of30
Rabyannah LAR 178 Mb33
Rača SRB 68 Mb47
Racalmuto I 62 Lo53
Raccon Cay BS 243 Gb34
Racconigi I 60 Lh46
Raceland USA 239 Fe31
Rachal USA 245 Fa32
Rachel USA 234 Ec27
Rachid RIM 180 Ka36
Rachiv UA 67 Md42
Rachogba 115 Oj29
Raciaz PL 65 Ma38
Racibórz PL 64 Lt40
Racky SK 67 Ma42
Racine USA 237 Ff25
Racķa Vas HR 61 Lp45
Rackla Range CDN 229 Dd13
Rada YE 94 Nc38
Radakowice PL 64 Ls40
Radalj SRB 68 Lu46

Radaškovíčy BY 45 Mh36
Radaškovíčy BY 45 Mh36
Rada Tilly RA 282 Gg69
Rada Tilly RA 282 Gg69
Rădăuţi RO 73 Md22
Radcliff USA 239 Fh27
Radde RUS 110 Rf21
Radeberg D 59 Ln40
Radebeul D 58 Lo39
Radeburg D 58 Lo39
Radechiv UA 65 Md39
Radechiv UA 65 Md39
Rademachersmedjorna S 43 Lr31
Radenci SLO 66 Lr44
Radenthein A 61 Lo44
Radeveliv UA 65 Mf40
Radford USA 239 Fe28
Radhanpur IND 116 Of34
Radijovce MK 68 Mb49
Radilovo BG 69 Me45
Radimlja BIH 61 Ls47
Radin IND 117 Pb36
Radiostation (Varberg) S 42 Ln33
Radisson CDN 233 Eg19
Radisson USA 236 Fe23
Radium Hot Springs CDN 232 Eb20
Radkan IR 96 Nk27
Radlje ob Dravi SLO 66 Lq44
Radnor Forest GB 49 Kr38
Radolfzell D 59 Lj43
Radom PL 65 Mb39
Radomicko PL 64 Lq38
Radomir BG 68 Md48
Radomko PL 64 Lq38
Radomský UA 73 Me42
Radomysl nad Sanem PL 65 Mb40
Radomyśl Wielki PL 65 Mb40
Radovan RO 68 Md46
Radovec BG 69 Mg49
Radoviš MK 68 Mc49
Radovljica SLO 66 Lp44
Radstadt A 61 Lo43
Radun' BY 45 Mf36
Radvilišķis LT 45 Md35
Radzanów PL 65 Ma38
Radzi CHN 103 Pk30
Radziejów PL 64 Lt38
Radzyń Chełmiński PL 64 Lt37
Radzyń Podlaski PL 65 Mc39
Rae-Bareli IND 117 Pa32
Raetihi NZ 153 Tf65
Rafaela RA 281 Gk61
Rafael Freyre C 243 Gb35
Rafah IL 92 Mf31
Rafaïlovka UA 65 Mg39
Raffingora ZW 202 Mf54
Raffin Kada WAN 188 Le42
Rafha KSA 93 Nb31
Rafiganj IND 117 Pc33
Rafina GR 71 Me52
Rafin Cabas WAN 188 Le41
Rafin Dinga WAN 188 Ld42
Rafsanjan IR 98 Nh30
Raft Mountains USA 235 Ed25
Raftspoulo USA 70 Md51
Raga SUD 191 Mc41
Ragaciems LV 45 Md33
Ragaing Yoma MYA 120 Ph36
Ragang, Mount RP 125 Rc42
Ragged Island Range BS 250 Ga34
Ragged Islands BS 243 Gb34
Raghopur IND 117 Pd33
Raglan NZ 152 Tf64
Ragland USA 238 Ff30
Ragley USA 238 Fd30
Rage n.p. N 38 Lg23
Ragueneau CDN 240 Gf21
Ragusa I 63 Lp54
Raha RI 130 Ra48
Rahačov BY 72 Mf19
Rahad Canal SUD 184 Mb40
Rahad Canal SUD 185 Mh38
Rahad Game Reserve SUD 185 Mh39
Rahama WAN 188 Le40
Rahatgarh IND 117 Ok34
Rahatpoulo USA 70 Md51
Raheste EST 45 Md32
Rahib SUD 184 Md37
Rahimabad IND 120 Pe32
Rahim ki Bazar PK 99 Oe33
Rahimyar Khan PK 99 Of31
Rahole National Reserve EAK 195 Mk45
Rahouia DZ 175 La28
Rahu IND 116 Oj35
Rahuri IND 116 Oh36
Raichur IND 116 Oj37
Raidin IND 117 Pc34
Raiganj IND 120 Pe33
Raigarh IND 117 Pb35
Raigarh IND 117 Pb35
Raijua RI 130 Ra51
Raikal IND 117 Ok36
Raikera IND 117 Pb34
Raikova Pecina SRB 68 Mb46
Railroad Valley USA 234 Ec27
Railway Mus. CDN 232 Ea20
Raimundo, T.I. BR 265 Gk44
Raimundo BR 274 He55
Rain D 59 Ll42
Rainbow USA 229 Cf15
Rainbow Beach AUS 149 Sg58
Rainbow Bridge Nat. Mon. USA 235 Ee27
Rainbow City USA 239 Fh29
Rainbow Warrior Wreck Diving NZ 152 Th53
Rainier N.P., Mount USA 232 Dc22
Rainis RI 125 Rd43
Rainsville USA 239 Fh28
Rainy River CDN 236 Fc21
Raippaluoto FIN 44 Mb27
Raipur IND 117 Pa34
Raipur IND 116 Oh33
Raipur IND 117 Pa35
Raipura IND 117 Ok34
Rairangpur IND 117 Pc34
Raisdorf D 58 Ll36
Raisen IND 116 Oj34
Raisinghnagar IND 114 Og31
Raisio FIN 44 Mc30
Raiskoto Praskalo BG 69 Me48
Raith CDN 236 Ff21
Raivala FIN 44 Mc29
Rai Valley NZ 153 Tg66
Raiz BR 267 Hj47
Rajagaon IND 117 Pa36
Rajahmundry IND 117 Pa37
Rajaji N.P. IND 114 Oj31
Raja-Jooseppi FIN 39 Mg22
Rajakhera IND 116 Oj33
Rajampet IND 119 Ok38
Rajanpur PK 99 Of31
Rajapalaiyam IND 118 Oj41
Rajapur IND 116 Oj37
Rajapur IND 117 Pa33
Rajashnawar IND 116 Oj37
Rajasthan IND 114 Og32
Rajauli IND 117 Pc33
Rajawada (Indore) IND 116 Oh34
Rajbari BD 120 Pf34
Rajec-Jestrebi CZ 66 Lr41
Rajec Poduchowny PL 65 Mb39
Rajegaon IND 117 Pb35
Raj Gangpur IND 117 Pc34
Rajgarh IND 114 Oh31
Rajgarh IND 116 Oj33
Rajgir IND 117 Pc33
Rajgrod PL 65 Mc37
Rajhara Jharandalli IND 117 Pa35
Rajin PRK 110 Rf24
Rajka H 66 Ls43
Rajkot IND 116 Of34

Rajmahal IND 117 Pd33
Rajmahal Hills IND 117 Pd33
Raj Nandgaon IND 117 Pa35
Rajoda IND 117 Pb36
Rajpipla IND 116 Og35
Rajpur IND 120 Pe34
Rajpura IND 114 Oj30
Rajsamand IND 116 Og34
Rajshahi BD 120 Pe33
Raka CHN 102 Pc31
Rakaca H 67 Ma42
Rakaia NZ 153 Qb39
Rakaposhi IND 114 Oh27
Rakata RI 127 Qc49
Rakaunui NZ 153 Tj66
Rakav BY 45 Mf37
Rakaye BF 187 Kk40
Rakhman-Kainary KZ 101 Pd21
Rakhne PK 99 Oa35
Rakhyut OM 95 Ng37
Rakiraki FJI 159 Tk54
Rakit RI 129 Qh48
Rakitone RUS 111 Rh23
Rakkestad N 42 Lm31
Rákóczi H 67 Mb42
Rakonshi J 111 Sa24
Rakops RB 201 Mc56
Rakovica SP 193 Ne41
Rakovica HR 61 Lq46
Rakovice CZ 66 Lq41
Rakovski BG 69 Me46
Rakushechnyi müyis KZ 96 Nh25
Rakvere EST 44 Mg31
Ralco RCH 280 Ge64
Ralegaon IND 117 Ok35
Ralik Chain 134 Ta09
Ralls USA 238 Ek29
Ralston USA 238 Fb27
Ralún RCH 280 Gd66
Ram BIH 61 Ls47
Rama NIC 249 Fh39
Ramabhadrapuram IND 117 Pb36
Ramah Navajo Ind. Res. USA 235 Ef28
Ramak AFG 99 Oe29
Ramalingasvara Temple IND 119 Ok41
Ramallah IL 92 Mh30
Ramanagaram IND 118 Oj40
Ramanathapuram IND 119 Ok41
Ramanathaswamy Temple (Rameswaram) IND 118 Ok41
Ramanuj Ganj IND 117 Pb34
Ramapuram IND 118 Oh38
Ramardori RI 154 Rh46
Ramaredi IND 116 Ok36
Ramatlabama ZA 205 Mc58
Ramavaram IND 117 Pa37
Rambai IND 129 Qf46
Rambat IND 127 Qc46
Rambervillers F 51 Lg42
Ramboullet F 51 Lc42
Rambre MYA 120 Pg36
Rambrè MYA 120 Pg36
Rambutyo Islands PNG 156 Sd47
Ramea CDN 241 Hb22
Ramelau, Mount TLS 131 Rc50
Rameski RUS 72 Mj17
Rameswaram IND 119 Ok41
Ramganj BD 120 Pf34
Ramgarh IND 116 Oj35
Ramgarh IND 117 Pc33
Ramgarh IND 114 Of32
Ramgarh IND 116 Of34
Ramgarh IND 117 Pb34
Ramhormoz IR 93 Ne30
Ramingining AUS 146 Rh52
Ramisi EAK 195 Mk46
Ramkam IR 98 Nj32
Ramkanhaeng N.P. THA 122 Pk37
Ramlat al Sab'atayn YE 94 Nd38
Ramlat al-Wahíbah OM 95 Nk35
Ramlat ar-Rabkha OM 95 Nj35
Ramlat Dahm YE 94 Nc37
Ramlat Ghafah 95 Nh35
Ramlat Umm al-Hait OM 95 Nj36
Ramlat Zallaf LAR 177 Lg32
Ramle ER/ETH 192 Na39
Ramnagar IND 115 Ok31
Ramnagar IND 117 Pa33
Ramnagar IND 117 Pb33
Ramnäs S 43 Lr31
Ramnicelu RO 69 Mh45
Râmnicu Sărat RO 69 Mh45
Râmnicu Vâlcea RO 67 Me45
Ramo ETH 192 Na42
Ramon RF 124 Ra37
Ramona USA 234 Ea29
Ramón Castilla PE 270 Gf48
Ramón Corona MEX 245 Ej33
Ramos BR 271 Hd46
Ramos Arizpe MEX 245 Ek33
Ramos Island RP 128 Qj41
Ramotswa RB 205 Mc58
Rampa ANG 198 Lr51
Rampart USA 229 Ce13
Rampart USA 229 Cf15
Rampur IND 115 Oj30
Rampur IND 116 Ok31
Rampur IND 115 Ok31
Rampur IND 116 Ok31
Rampur IND 117 Ok34
Rampur IND 117 Pa34
Rampur IND 117 Pd34
Rampur Hat IND 117 Pd33
Rampura IND 116 Oj36
Ramree = Rambre MYA 120 Pg36
Ramree Island = Rambrè MYA 120 Pg36
Ram Sanehighat IND 117 Pa32
Ramsar IR 91 Nf27
Ramsele S 41 Lq27
Ramsey GB 49 Kq36
Ramsey Island GB 49 Kp39
Ramshir IR 93 Ne30
Ramsjö S 43 Lq29
Ramstein D 59 Lh41
Ramu IND 120 Pg34
Ramu J 93 Nj30
Ramumbuoso PNG 156 Sg51
Ramu River PNG 155 Sc48
Ramygala LT 45 Me35
Ran USA 189 Lj39
Ranaghat IND 120 Pe34
Ranai RI 127 Qb45
Ranai, Mount RI 128 Qa43
Ranaka RB 205 Mc58
Ranakah, Gunung RI 130 Ra50
Ranakpur IND 116 Og34
Ranau MAL 128 Qj43
Rancagua RCH 280 Gd63
Ranchi IND 117 Pc34
Rancho Cordova USA 234 Dk26
Rancho Alegre MEX 244 Ej34
Rancho Nuevo MEX 244 Eg33
Rancho Queimado BR 277 He58
Rancho Veloz C 243 Fk34
Rancul RA 281 Gh63
Randado USA 245 Fa32

Randalstown GB 47 Ko36
Randangan Panua Reserve RI 125 Ra45
Randazzo I 63 Lp53
Randeggi WAN 188 Ld40
Randers DK 42 Ll34
Randfontein ZA 205 Md59
Randolph USA 233 Pk30
Randle USA 232 Dc22
Randowaya RI 154 Rj46
Ranfurly CDN 233 Ee19
Ranfurly NZ 153 Tf68
Rangae THA 123 Qa42
Rangamati BD 120 Pg34
Rangampet IND 116 Ok37
Ranganathaswamy Temple IND 119 Ok40
Rangaon IND 120 Pe34
Rangeley USA 241 Gg25
Rangely USA 235 Ek26
Ranger USA 149 Sc57
Ranger uranium mine AUS 146 Rg52
Ranges Valley AUS 148 Sa56
Rangia IND 120 Pf32
Ranginui NZ 153 Th65
Rangkasbitung RI 129 Qd49
Rangium PRK 110 Rd25
Rangoon MYA 120 Ph37
Rangpur BD 120 Pe33
Rangsang RI 127 Qb45
Rangtag CHN 106 Qc29
Ranguana Cay BH 248 Ff37
Ranibennur IND 118 Oh38
Raniganj IND 117 Pb32
Raniganj IND 120 Pe33
Raniganj IND 117 Pd34
Ranik Chain IND 117 Pc34
Raniguda IND 117 Pb36
Ranikhet IND 115 Ok31
Ranikot Fort PK 99 Oe33
Ranipur IND 119 Ok39
Ranipur IND 116 Ok34
Ranipur PK 99 Oe32
Ranipur Jharial IND 117 Pb35
Ranital IND 114 Oj29
Ranital IND 117 Pb33
Ranken Store AUS 146 Rj55
Rankin USA 238 Ek30
Rankin Springs AUS 151 Sd62
Rankwell A 59 Lj43
Rannes AUS 149 Sf58
Rannoch Station GB 48 Kq34
Rann of Kachchh IND 116 Oe34
Rano WAN 188 Le40
Ranohira RM 207 Nc57
Ranomafana RM 207 Nd56
Ranomafana RM 207 Nc57
Ranomafana, P.N.de RM 207 Nd56
Ranomena RM 207 Nd57
Ranong THA 122 Pk41
Ranongga SOL 157 Sj50
Ranot THA 122 Qa40
Ranotsara Avaratra RM 207 Nd57
Ranquil del Norte RA 280 Gf64
Ranski RI 154 Rh46
Ransta S 43 Lr31
Rantabe RM 206 Ne53
Rantai IND 117 Ok35
Rantasalmi FIN 44 Mj28
Rantau RI 129 Qh47
Rantau Abang MAL 126 Qb43
Rantauates RI 127 Qa46
Rantaubulan RI 127 Qa46
Rantaubinuang RI 127 Qa46
Rantaupanjang RI 127 Qd46
Rantauparangin RI 127 Qa45
Rantauprapat RI 127 Pk44
Rantemario, Gunung RI 130 Ra47
Rantepao RI 130 Qk47
Ranthambore N.P. IND 116 Oj32
Rantop VU 158 Te55
Rantoul USA 239 Ff25
Ranua FIN 39 Mg25
Ranya IRQ 91 Nc27
Rao SN 180 Kd38
Raohe CHN 110 Rg22
Raoli IND 115 Oj29
Ra'oen-l'Étape F 53 Lg42
Raoping CHN 109 Qj34
Raoul Island NZ 132 Ua60
Rapale MOC 203 Mk53
Rapallo I 60 Lh46
Rapang RI 130 Qk47
Rapa Nui, P.N. RCH 269 Gc54
Rapar IND 116 Of34
Rapel USA 233 Ej33
Rapid Bay AUS 150 Rk63
Rapid City USA 236 Ej24
RapideBlancStation CDN 240 Gd22
Rapides de Gembele RDC 190 Mb44
Rapides de Koudo DY 188 Ld40
Rapides de l'Éléphant RDC 190 Lk43
Rapides de Nyanga G 198 Lf44
Rapides du Congo RCB/RDC 198 Lh46
Rapid River USA 237 Ff23
Rapina EST 45 Mg32
Rapla EST 45 Md32
Rappahannock USA 241 Gb27
Rapperswil CH 60 Lj43
Rappottenstein A 66 Lq42
Rapu Rapu Island RP 124 Rc39
Raqchi PE 269 Ge53
Raqdalin LAR 177 Lf29
Raqqa SYR 90 Mk28
Raragala Island AUS 146 Rj51
Rara N.P. NEP 115 Pb31
Râs Abu 'Ali KSA 93 Ne32
Râs Abu Gallum Reserve ET 179 Mh31
Râs Abu Madd KSA 92 Mj33
Râs Abu Rasas OM 95 Nk35
Râs Abu Sawmah ET 179 Mh32
Râs Abu Shagara SUD 185 Mj35
Râs Abu Urayqit KSA 93 Nf33
Rasa Island RP 124 Qk41
Ras Al-'Ain SYR 91 Na27
Rasa Norte RA 281 Gj66
Râs al Askar KSA 94 Na36
Râs al Gunaiz OM 95 Nk34
Râs al-Hadd OM 95 Nk34
Râs al-Hadd OM 95 Nk34
Râs al Hasan KSA 94 Na36
Râs al Hilal LAR 178 Mb31
Ra's al Khafji KSA 93 Nd31
Ras al Khaimah UAE 95 Nh33
Râs al Madd KSA 92 Mj33
Râs al Tanaqib KSA 93 Nd32
Râs an Naqab JOR 92 Mh31
Râs Attabii SUD 185 Mh35
Ras at Tarfa KSA 94 Nb37
Rasawi RI 131 Rf46
Râs az Zawr KSA 93 Ne32
Râs Banas ET 179 Mh33
Râs Barîdî KSA 92 Mj33
Rascani MD 73 Md22
Rasdhoo Atoll MV 118 Og43
Râs Dujm OM 95 Nj36
Râs el-Barr ET 179 Mf30
Râs Faste IR 98 Oa33

Rás Gârib ET 179 Mg31
Ras Ghemeis UAE 95 Nf33
Rasha CHN 103 Pk30
Rashaant MNG 101 Pt22
Rashad SUD 185 Mf39
Râs Hatîbah KSA 92 Mk35
Rasheiden SYR 90 Mj29
Rashid ET 179 Mf30
Rashid IR 91 Ne27
Rashshah YE 94 Nd38
Rasht IR 91 Ne27
Rasi Salai THA 123 Qc38
Ras Jaddi PK 99 Oa33
Ras Jiwani PK 98 Oa33
Ras Karkuma KSA 92 Mj33
Ras Kebdana MA 175 Ks30
Ras Koh PK 99 Oc31
Ra's Laffan Q 93 Nf33
Ras Lanuf LAR 177 Lk31
Ras Madrakah OM 95 Nj36
Ras Mastirah OM 95 Nk35
Ras Matârimah ET 179 Mg31
Ras Momi YE 95 Ng39
Ras Muari PK 99 Od33
Ras Muhammad ET 179 Mh32
Râs Muhammad N.P. ET 179 Ma33
Ras Nouâdhibou RIM 180 Ka35
Râs Nuss OM 95 Nh37
Ras da Catarina BR 273 Ja50
Rasol IND 117 Pc34
Ras Ormara PK 99 Oc33
Rasova RO 69 Mh46
Rasovo BG 68 Md47
Râs Qabr al Hindi OM 95 Nj32
Ra's Rakan Q 93 Nf32
Râs Rasib KSA 94 Na37
Rasra IND 117 Pb33
Ra's Rakan Q 93 Nf32
Râs Sajir OM 95 Nh37
Ras Sarkan OM 98 Nj32
Ra's Shaikh ET 192 Na38
Ras Sharbithat OM 95 Ng37
Ra's Shu'ab YE 95 Ng39
Rass Kabouabia TN 176 Lf28
Rasskazovo RUS 72 Na19
Ras Suqrah OM 95 Nj36
Râs Tannurah KSA 93 Nf32
Rastatt D 59 Lj42
Rasteð D 58 Lj37
Râs Tirmirat RIM 180 Kq36
Ra's Warfallah LAR 177 Lh31
Ratak Chain 134 Ta08
Ratan S 41 Lp28
Rati Gatta IND 116 Oh35
Ratíškovice CZ 66 Ls42
Ratlam IND 116 Oh34
Ratnagiri IND 116 Og37
Ratnapura CL 119 Pa42
Ratne UA 65 Md39
Ratodero PK 99 Oe32
Raton USA 235 Ek27
Ratta RUS 100 Pb17
Rattanburi THA 123 Qc38
Ratten A 61 Lq43
Rattaphum THA 122 Pk40
Ratua IND 117 Pd33
Ratu IND 117 Pc34
Ratzeburg D 58 Ll37
Ratz, Mount CDN 230 Dd17
Rau RI 155 Rc45
Rau RI 127 Qd45
Raubling D 59 Lm43
Rauch RA 281 Ha64
Raudales MEX 247 Fc37
Rauha FIN 44 Mj28
Rauland N 42 Lj31
Raukumara Range NZ 152 Tj65
Rauma FIN 44 Mb29
Raung, Gunung RI 129 Qg50
Rautjärvi FIN 44 Mj28
Ravansar IR 91 Nb28
Ravar IR 98 Nj31
Ravalli USA 232 Ec22
Ravand IR 91 Nf28
Ravanusa I 62 Lo53
Ravar IR 98 Nj31
Ravat KS 97 Of26
Ravelo BOL 278 Gh55
Ravena USA 234 Dk25
Ravenna I 60 Lm46
Ravenna USA 238 Fa25
Ravensburg D 59 Lk43
Ravensthorpe AUS 144 Ra62
Ravenswood AUS 147 Sd56
Ravenswood USA 247 Sd56
Ravensworth AUS 147 Sd56
Ravi PK 99 Of30
Ravna Gora HR 61 Lp45
Ravne na Koroškem SLO 66 Lp44
Ravnina TM 96 Ob27
Rawa MAL 126 Qc44
Rawaindi PK 99 Og29
Rawa Aopa Watumohae N.P. RI 130 Ra48
Rawalpindi PK 99 Og29
Rawal Kot PK 99 Og29
Rawa Mazowiecka PL 65 Ma39
Rawandoz IRQ 91 Nc27
Rawapindi IND 116 Oe34
Rawas RI 127 Qc46
Rawene NZ 152 Tf63
Rawi IND 115 Oj31
Rawicz PL 64 Ls39
Rawlinna AUS 145 Rc61
Rawlins USA 235 Eh25
Rawlinson Range AUS 143 Rd58
Rawson RA 282 Gh67
Rawson CDN 233 Ej21
Rawu CHN 102 Ph31
Rawwah IRQ 91 Na28
Ray CDN 236 Fb21
Raya, Gunung RI 127 Qd46
Rayachoti IND 119 Ok39
Rayadrug IND 118 Oj39
Rayagada IND 117 Pb36
Raychikhinsk RUS 110 Rd21
Raydah YE 94 Nc37
Rayevskiy RUS 72 Nk19
Rayleigh GB 49 La39
Raymond CDN 233 Ee21
Raymond USA 239 Fe30
Raymond USA 232 Dc22
Raymondville USA 245 Fa33
Raymond Terrace AUS 149 Sf62
Rayner Roland DZ 175 Fb32
Raynesford USA 233 Ef22
Ray Mountains USA 229 Ce13
Rayón MEX 244 Ee31
Rayo Cortado RA 279 Gj61

Rayón MEX 244 Ee31
Rayón MEX 246 Fa35
Rayón MEX 246 Fa35
Rayong THA 122 Qa39
Raysut OM 95 Ng37
Rayis KSA 92 Mk35
Razan IR 91 Ne28
Razanka BY 65 Mf37
Razav-sea
Razbojna SRB 68 Mb47
Razdol BG 68 Md49
Razdol'noe RUS 110 Rf24
Razgrad BG 69 Mg47
Razi IR 91 Ne27
Razlog BG 68 Md49
Razmak PK 99 Oe29
Rea CDN 231 Ec14
Reach Falls JA 250 Gb37
Reader Railroad USA 238 Fc20
Reading GB 49 Ku39
Reading USA 241 Gc25
Real de Catorce MEX 246 Ek34
Realeza BR 275 Hj56
Réalmont F 52 Lc47
Ream N.P. – Preah Sihanouk National Park K 123 Qd40
Reata 176 La30
Rebecca, Mount AUS 144 Qh59
Rebiana Sand Sea LAR 178 Ma33
Rebild Bakker, Nationalpark DK 42 Lk34
Reboledo de Sama BOL 279 Gh56
Reboliera E 55 Ks52
Rebouças BR 277 He58
Rebun-tō J 111 Sa23
Reburi J 111 Sa23
Recanati I 61 Ln47
Recea RO 68 Mf45
Recife BR 273 Ka49
Recife da Silva BR 267 Hh46
Recife Manuel Luis BR 267 Hh44
Récif Petrie F 158 Tc55
Récif des l'Astrolabe F 158 Tc55
Récifs de l'Entrecasteaux F 158 Tb55
Recklinghausen D 58 Lh39
Reclining Buddha CHN 121 Pk33
Recoaro Terme I 60 Lm45
Reconquista RA 281 Gk60
Recreio São Felix, T.I. BR 271 Ha47
Recuay PE 269 Gb50
Recyca BY 72 Mf19
Recz PL 64 Lq37
Redang MAL 126 Qb43
Redange-sur-Attert L 51 Lf41
Redbank AUS 151 Se64
Red Bank CDN 240 Gj21
Red Bay CDN 241 Hb20
Red Bay USA 239 Fg29
Red Bluff AUS 144 Qg58
Red Bluff USA 234 Dj25
Redcar GB 49 Kt36
Redcliff ZW 202 Me55
Redcliffe AUS 149 Sg59
Red Cliff Ind. Res. USA 236 Fe22
Red Cloud USA 238 Fa25
Red Deer CDN 233 Ed19
Red Deer Valley Badlands CDN 233 Ed20
Redding USA 234 Dj25
Redditch GB 49 Kt38
Redea RO 68 Me46
Red Earth CDN 233 Ee18
Redeyef TN 176 Le29
Redfield USA 236 Fa24
Redkino RUS 72 Mj17
Red Lake CDN 236 Fc20
Red Lake Ind. Res. USA 236 Fb22
Red Lake Road CDN 236 Fd20
Redlands USA 234 Eb29
Red Lion USA 241 Gb26
Red Lodge USA 233 Ef23
Reno USA 234 Ea26
Redmond USA 232 Dd23
Redon F 52 Kk42
Red Oak USA 236 Fb25
Redonda AG 251 Gj37
Redondela E 54 Km48
Redondo USA 234 Ea28
Redoubt Flatters RN 182 Ld35
Red River USA 235 Ek27
Red River CDN 236 Fb21
Red River VN 121 Qc34
Red River Delta VN 121 Qd35
Red Rock CDN 230 Dj19
Red Sea 76 Mb07
Redvers CDN 236 Ej21
Red Volta GH/BF 187 Kk40
Redwater CDN 233 Ee19
Red Wing USA 236 Fc24
Redwood USA 230 Ch15
Redwood City USA 234 Dj27
Redwood N.P. USA 234 Dh25
Redwood Valley USA 234 Dj27
Rędziny PL 65 Lu40
Rędzikowo PL 64 Ls36
Reed USA 234 Ec27
Reed Bingham S.H.S. USA 242 Fj30
Reedley USA 234 Ea27
Reedsburg USA 236 Fe24
Reedsport USA 232 Dg24
Reedy Creek AUS 149 Se59
Reef Fort (Delhi) IND 115 Oj31
Reef Road USA 243 Gg42
Reefton NZ 153 Tf67
Reese 157 Sj51
Refahiye TR 91 Mk26
Reform USA 239 Fg29
Reftele S 43 Lp33
Refugio USA 245 Fa31
Refugio de Fauna Laguna Castillos ROU 282 Hc63
Regaïa MA 175 Kt28

Regalbuto I 63 Lp53
Regen D 59 Ln41
Regen D 59 Lo42
Regência BR 275 Ja55
Regência BR 275 Ja55
Regeneração BR 273 Hf49
Regensburg D 59 Ln41
Regenstauf D 59 Ln41
Regente Feijó BR 274 He57
Regestan AFG 99 Oc30
Reggane DZ 175 La32
Reggio di Calábria I 63 Lq53
Réggio nell'Emília I 60 Ll46
Reghin RO 67 Me44
Reghinópolis BR 274 Hf56
Reginópolis BR 274 Hf56
Registro BR 277 Hf58
Regnitz D 59 Lm41
Regozero RUS 40 Mh26
Reguengos de Monsaraz P 55 Kn52
Regway CDN 233 Eh21
Rehau D 59 Ln41
Rehburg-Loccum D 58 Lk38
Rehoboth NAM 204 Lj57
Rehoboth USA 235 Ef28
Rehoboth Beach USA 241 Gc26
Rehovot IL 92 Mh30
Reial Monestir de Poblet E 57 Lc49
Reichenau D 59 Lk43
Reichenbach D 59 Ln40
Reichshoffen F 51 Lh42
Reid Reef FJI 159 Ua54
Reidsville USA 242 Fj28
Reidsville USA 242 Fj29
Reigate GB 49 Ku39
Re'im IL 92 Mh30
Reims F 53 Le41
Reinach CH 60 Lh43
Reinbek D 58 Ll37
Reinberg D 58 Lo36
Reindeer Island CDN 236 Fa19
Reindeer Lake CDN 236 Ee07
Reindeer Station CDN 229 Db13
Reinheim D 59 Lj41
Reinosa E 54 Kq48
Reipholtsfjöll IS 46 Js25
Reisa n.p. N 39 Mc21
Reisjärvi FIN 39 Md26
Reitz ZA 205 Md59
Reivilo ZA 205 Mc59
Rejaf SUD 194 Mf43
Rejdovo RUS 111 Se23
Rejmyre S 43 Lq32
Rejštejn CZ 66 Lo41
Rekacice BIH 61 Ls46
Reken D 58 Lh39
Reliance CDN 231 Ef14
Relizane DZ 175 La28
Remada TN 176 Lf29
Remagen D 58 Lh40
Remanso BR 270 Hf49
Remanso BR 273 Hj50
Remarkable, Mount AUS 143 Rd54
Remarkable, Mount AUS 147 Sk56
Rembang RI 129 Qf49
Remda RUS 44 Mh32
Remedios C 243 Ga34
Remel el Abiod TN 176 Le30
Remeghje Pass NAM 204 Lj58
Remígio BR 273 Jb49
Rémire SY 195 Na48
Remiremont F 53 Lg42
Rémon-Montjoly F 267 Ha43
Remolino CO 264 Gc40
Remparts d'Aigues-Mortes F 53 Le47
Rems D 59 Lk42
Remscheid D 58 Lh39
Rencēni LV 45 Mf33
Renda LV 45 Mc33
Rendina GR 69 Md50
Rendova SOL 157 Sj50
Rendsburg D 58 Lk36
Rene Brunelle Prov. Park CDN 237 Fj21
Renfrew CDN 241 Gb23
Rengali IND 117 Pc35
Rengat RI 127 Qb46
Rengma Hills IND 120 Pg32
Rengo RCH 280 Gd63
Renheji CHN 109 Qg30
Renhua CHN 109 Qg33
Reni UA 69 Mj45
Renigunta IND 119 Ok39
Renland GRØ 227 Jc05
Renmark AUS 151 Sb62
Rennel Island SOL 157 Ta51
Rennerod D 58 Lj40
Rennes F 52 Kk42
Renningen D 59 Lj42
Reno USA 234 Ea26
Renous CDN 240 Gj22
Renqiu CHN 108 Qh26
Renshou CHN 108 Qc31
Rensselaer USA 237 Fg25
Renton USA 232 Dc22
Renukot IND 117 Pa33
Renville USA 236 Fb23
Renwez F 51 Le41
Renwick NZ 153 Tg66
Reo BF 187 Kk40
Reo RI 130 Ra50
Reola EST 45 Mg32
Reotipur IND 117 Pb33
Repalle IND 117 Pa38
Repartimento BR 271 Hd47
Repedea RO 67 Md43
Repetek Desert Reserve TM 96 Oc26
Reposaari FIN 44 Mb29
Repovesi kansallispuisto FIN 44 Mg29
Repvåg N 38 Mc05
Represa Agua Vermelha BR 274 Hd56
Represa Barra Bonita BR 277 He57
Represa Cachoeira Dourada BR 274 Hd55
Represa Camargos BR 275 Hf57
Represa Capivara BR 274 Hd57
Represa de Acaray PY 276 Hc58
Represa de Balbina BR 266 Ha46
Represa de Boa Esperança BR 272 Hh50
Represa de Chavantes BR 277 He57
Represa de Foz do Areia BR 277 He58
Represa de Furnas BR 275 Hf56
Represa de Itaipu BR 276 Hc58
Represa de Nova Ponte BR 275 He55
Represa de Paraibuna BR 277 Hf57
Represa de Salto Grande ROU/RA 276 Hb60
Represa de Samuel BR 271 Gj49
Represa de Tucuruí BR 272 Hd48
Represa Emborcação BR 275 He55
Represa Ilha Grande BR 276 Hd57
Represa Ilha Solteira BR 274 Hd56
Represa Jupiá BR 274 Hd56
Represa Peixoto BR 275 Hf56
Represa Porto Primavera BR 274 Hd56

Represa Promissão BR 274 Hf56
Represa Salto Osório BR 276 Hd58
Represa Salto Santiago BR 276
Represa Três Irmãos BR 274 Hd56
Represa Três Marias BR 275 Hh55
Reptielsporen ZA 202 Me57
Reptile Footprints ZA 202 Me57
Republic USA 232 Ea21
Republic USA 238 Fc27
Repulse Bay CDN 227 Fc05
Reque PE 268 Ga48
Requena E 57 Kt51
Requena PE 268 Gd48
Requena YV 265 Gh42
Resadiye TR 71 Mh54
Resadiye TR 90 Mj25
Reşadiye Yarımadası TR 71 Mh54
Resas CO 268 Gd46
Reschenpass – Passo di Resia I 60 Lj44
Resen MK 68 Mc49
Resende BR 277 Hf57
Reserva CO 268 Gd46
Reserva BR 277 He58
Reserva CO 268 Gd46
Reserva RA 281 Gk64
Reserva Biológica Atol das Rocas BR 273 Jd47
Reserva Biológica Augusto Ruschi BR 275
Reserva Biológica Cordillera de Sama BOL 279 Gh56
Reserva Biológica da Pedra Talhada BR 273 Jb50
Reserva Biológica da Serra Negra BR 273 Ja50
Reserva Biológica de Córrego Grande BR 275 Ja55
Reserva Biológica de Saltinho BR 273 Jc50
Reserva Biológica de Santa Isabel BR 273 Jc51
Reserva Biológica de Sooretama BR 275 Ja55
Reserva Biológica de Una BR 275 Ja53
Reserva Biológica do Abufari BR 270 Gj48
Reserva Biológica do Comboios BR 275 Hk55
Reserva Biológica do Córrego do Veado BR 275 Hk55
Reserva Biológica do Guaporé BR 278 Gj52
Reserva Biológica do Gurupi BR 272 Hg47
Reserva Biológica do Jaru BR 270 Gk50
Reserva Biológica do Lago Piratuba BR 266 Hd45
Reserva Biológica do Poço das Antas BR 277 Hj57
Reserva Biológica do Rio Trombetas BR 266 Hb46
Reserva Biológica do Tapirapé BR 272 He48
Reserva Biológica do Tingua BR 277 Hj57
Reserva Biológica do Uatumã BR 266 Ha46
Reserva Biológica Guaribas BR 273 Jc49
Reserva Biológica Marinha do Arvoredo BR 277 Hf59
Reserva Biológica União BR 277 Hj57
Reserva Biósfera Isla San Pedro Martir MEX 244 Ec32
Reserva Biósfera Sierra del Rosario C 243 Fj34
Reserva de Ambriz ANG 198 Lg49
Reserva de la Biósfera Menorca E 57 Le50
Reserva de la Biósfera Calakmul MEX 247 Ff36
Reserva de la Biósfera de Rio Plátano HN 249 Fh38
Reserva de la Biósfera S. de las Californias MEX 244 Ed31
Reserva de la Biósfera el Vizcaino MEX 244 Ec32
Reserva de la Biósfera Estación Biológica del Beni BOL 278 Gg53
Reserva de la Biósfera Maya GCA 247 Fe37
Reserva de la Biósfera Montes Azules MEX 247 Fd37
Reserva de la Biósfera Pantanos de Centla MEX 247 Fd36
Reserva de la Biósfera Península de Guanahacabibes C 243 Fh35
Reserva de la Biósfera Pilón Lajas BOL 278 Gg53
Reserva de la Biósfera Sian Ka'an MEX 247 Fg36
Reserva de las Biósfera Bosawas NIC 249 Fh38
Reserva de la Biósfera Pinacate y Gran Desierto de Altar MEX 244 Ed30
Reserva de Maputo MOC 205 Mg61
Reserva de Marromeu MOC 203 Mh55
Reserva de Namibe ANG 200 Lg53
Reserva de Prod. Faunística Cuyabeno EC 268 Gb46
Reserva do Cabo Pomene MOC 203 Mh57
Reserva do Gilé MOC 203 Mk54
Reserva do Niassa MOC 197 Mj52
Reserva do Sanga MOC 196 Mh53
Reserva Ecológica El Angel EC 268 Ga45
Reserva Ecológica Juami-Japurá BR 270 Gg47
Reserva Ecológica Jutaí-Solimões BR 270 Gg47
Reserva Especial de la Biósfera Isla del Golfo de California MEX 244 Ed31
Reserva Especial de la Biósfera Isla del Golfo de California MEX 244 Ed31
Reserva Especial de la Biósfera Isla Tiburón MEX 244 Ed31
Reserva Especial do Milando ANG 198 Lj50
Reserva Forestal do Rio Negro BR 265 Gk45
Reserva Forestal Mundurucânia BR 271 Ha49
Reserva Forestal Sipapo YV 265 Gg43
Reserva Marina Galápagos, P.N. EC 269 Fe45
Reserva Nacional Alacalufes RCH 282 Gc72
Reserva Nacional Alto Bío Bío RCH 280 Ge65
Reserva Nacional Amazónia BR
Reserva Nacional Manuripi Heath BOL 270 Gg51
Reserva Nacional de las Guaitecas RCH 282 Gc68
Reserva Nacional Cerro Castillo RCH 282 Gd68
Reserva Nacional Coihaique RCH
Reserva Nacional de Fauna Andina Eduardo Avaroa BOL 279 Gg57
Reserva Nacional de Muela BOL 279 Gh56
Reserva Nacional de Paracas PE 269 Ga54
Reserva Nacional Estricta Colonia Benítez RA
Reserva Nacional Estricta El Leoncito RA 280 Gf61
Reserva Nacional Estricta San Antonio RA 276 Hd58

Reserva Nacional Federico Albert – Rosica

Reserva Nacional Federico Albert RCH 280 Gd63
Reserva Nacional Formosa RA 279 Gk58
Reserva Nacional Gil del Vilches RCH 280 Ge63
Reserva Nacional Hernando de Magallanes RCH 282 Gd72
Reserva Nacional Junín PE 269 Gc51
Reserva Nacional Kalatalixar RCH 282 Gc70
Reserva Nacional Lachay PE 269 Gb51
Reserva Nacional Lago Carlota RCH 282 Ge68
Reserva Nacional Lago Cochrane RCH 282 Gd69
Reserva Nacional Lago las Torres RCH 282 Gd68
Reserva Nacional Lago Palena RCH 282 Ge67
Reserva Nacional Lago Penuelas RCH 280 Ge62
Reserva Nacional Lago Rosselot RCH 282 Gd68
Reserva Nacional Laguna Torca RCH 280 Ge63
Reserva Nacional Laguna Varillar RCH 282 Ge72
Reserva Nacional Las Chinchillas RCH 280 Ge61
Reserva Nacional Las Vicuñas RCH 278 Gf55
Reserva Nacional L.General Carrera RCH 282 Gd69
Reserva Nacional Los Flamencos RCH 279 Gg57
Reserva Nacional Los Ruiles RCH 280 Gd63
Reserva Nacional Malalcahuello RCH 280 Ge65
Reserva Nacional Malleco RCH 280 Ge65
Reserva Nacional Nalcas RCH 280 Ge65
Reserva Nacional Natural Nukak CO 264 Ge44
Reserva Nacional Natural Puinawai CO 265 Gf44
Reserva Nacional Nuble RCH 280 Ge64
Reserva Nacional Otamendi RA 281 Ha63
Reserva Nacional Pacaya-Samiria PE 268 Gc48
Reserva Nacional Pampa del Tamarugal RCH 278 Gf56
Reserva Nacional Pampa Galeras PE 269 Gc53
Reserva Nacional Paposo RCH 279 Ge58
Reserva Nacional Radal Siete Tazas RCH 280 Ge63
Reserva Nacional Ralco RCH 280 Ge64
Reserva Nacional Río Blanco RCH 280 Ge62
Reserva Nacional Río Clarillo RCH 280 Ge62
Reserva Nacional Río de los Cipreses RCH 280 Ge63
Reserva Nacional Salinas-Aguada Blanca PE 269 Ge54
Reserva Nacional Tariquia BOL 279 Gh56
Reserva Nacional Titicaca PE 278 Gf53
Reserva Nacional Valdiva RCH 280 Gd66
Reserva Natural do Ilhéu dos Pássaros ANG 198 Lg50
Reserva Natural Integral do Luando ANG 200 Lj51
Reserva parcial do Bufalo ANG 200 Lg52
Reservas Marinas HN 248 Fg37
Reserve CDN 233 Ej19
Reserve USA 235 Ef29
Réserve communautaire de Lac Télé RCB 190 Lj45
Réserve de Bay RMM 187 Kj39
Réserve de Biosphère Arganeraie MA 174 Kf31
Réserve de Biosphère des Oasis du Sud Marocain MA 175 Kh30
Réserve de Biosphère Mare aux Hippopotames BF 187 Kh40
Réserve de Campo CAM 188 Le44
Réserve de Douala-Edéa CAM 188 Le44
Réserve de Douentza RMM 181 Kj38
Réserve de faune à Okapi RDC 191 Me45
Réserve de faune Bomu Occidentale RDC 191 Mc43
Réserve de faune Bomu Orientale RDC 191 Mc43
Réserve de Faune d'Abdoulaye TG 187 La41
Réserve de Faune d'Arli BF 187 La40
Réserve de faune de Bahr Salamat TCH 189 Lk40
Réserve de faune de Binder-Léré TCH 190 Lh41
Réserve de Faune de Bontioli BF 187 Kj40
Réserve de Faune de Dimonika RCB 198 Lg47
Réserve de faune de Fada Archei TCH 184 Ma37
Réserve de Faune de Kourtiagou BF 188 La40
Réserve de Faune de Kpèssi TG 187 La41
Réserve de faune de l'Abou-Telfane TCH 189 Lk39
Réserve de faune de la Ouandjia-Vakaga RCA 190 Mb41
Réserve de faune de l'Aouk-Aoukale RCA 190 Ma41
Réserve de faune de la Yata-Ngaya RCA 190 Mb41
Réserve de Faune de l'Oti TG 187 La40
Réserve de faune de Mandélia TCH 189 Lh40
Réserve de Faune de Mont Fouari RCB 198 Lf47
Réserve de Faune de Ndiael SN 180 Kb37
Réserve de Faune de Nyanga-Nord RCB 198 Lg47
Réserve de Faune de Pama BF 187 La40
Réserve de faune de Pangar et Djérem CAM 189 Lg43
Réserve de faune de Siniaka-Minia TCH 189 Lk40
Réserve de Faune de Tsoulou RCB 198 Lg47
Réserve de faune de Zemongo RCA 191 Mc42
Réserve de faune du Bas Chari TCH 189 Lh39
Réserve de faune du Dzanga-Sangha RCA 190 Lj44
Réserve de Faune du Ferlo Nord SN 180 Kc38
Réserve de Faune du Ferlo Sud SN 180 Kc38
Réserve de faune du Gribingui-Bamingui RCA 190 Lk42
Réserve de faune du Koukourou-Bamingui RCA 190 Ma42
Réserve de faune du N'Zo CI 187 Kg42
Réserve de Faune du Sahel BF 181 Kk38
Réserve de Faune du Singou BF 187 La40
Réserve de faune Ouadi Rimï-Ouadi Achim TCH 183 Lh36
Réserve de Fina RMM 186 Kf39
Réserve de Gourma RMM 181 Kj38
Réserve de Kalfou CAM 189 Lh40
Réserve de Kéniébaoulé RMM 186 Kf39
Réserve de Kongassambougou RMM 186 Kf39
Réserve de la Faune de la Léfini RCB 198 Lh47
Réserve de la Montagne des Sources F 158 Td57
Réserve de la Nana Barya RCA 190 Lj42
Réserve de Rabi-Ndogo G 198 Le47
Réserve de Wonga-Wongué G 198 Le46
Réserve du Badinko RMM 186 Kf39
Réserve du Bafing Makana RMM 186 Ke39
Réserve du Bassin inférieur de l'Ogooué G 198 Le46
Réserve Duchénier CDN 240 Gf21
Réserve du Dja CAM 189 Lg44
Réserve Faunique Ashuapmushuan CDN 240 Gd21
Réserve faunique Assinica et des Lacs Albanel-Mistissini- et-Waconichi CDN 240 Gc20
Réserve Faunique de Matane et Dunière CDN 240 Gg21
Réserve Faunique de Papineau-Labelle CDN 241 Gc22
Réserve faunique de Port-Cartier / Sept-Îles CDN 240 Gg20
Réserve Faunique de Rimouski CDN 240 Gf21
Réserve Faunique des Chic-Chocs CDN 240 Gh21
Réserve Faunique des Laurentides CDN 240 Ge22
Réserve Faunique La Vérendrye CDN 237 Gb22
Réserve Faunique Mastigouche CDN 240 Gd22
Réserve Faunique Portneuf CDN 240 Gd22
Réserve Faunique Rouge-Matawin CDN 240 Gc22
Réserve Faunique St-Maurice CDN 240 Gd22
Réserve floristique de Yangambi RDC 191 Mc45
Réserve forestière de Luki RDC 198 Lg48
Reserve (Hagar Nish Plateau) ER 185 Mj37
Réserve Manicouagan CDN 240 Gf20
Réserve Naturelle de Scandola F 60 Lj48
Réserve Naturelle Intégrale Dite Sanctuaire des Addax RN 182 Le36
Réserve naturelle intégrale du Mont Nimba CI/RG 186 Kf42
Réserve Partielle de Faune d'Ansongo-Menaka RMM 182 La38
Réserve Partielle de Faune de Dosso RN 188 Lb39
Réserves des Girafes de Kouré RN 182 Lb39
Réserves Naturelles Nationales de l'Aïr et du Ténéré RN 182 Le36
Réserve Spéciale d'Andranomena RM 207 Ne54
Réserve Spéciale d'Ankarana RM 206 Ne52
Réserve totale de Faune de Tamou RN 188 Lb39
Réserve Totale de Faune du Tadrés RN 182 Ld38
Réservoir de La Grande Quatre CDN 240 Gd18
Réservoir de LG Deux CDN 227 Ga08
Réservoir Gouin CDN 240 Gc21
Réservoir Manicouagan CDN 240 Gf20
Rešetylivka UA 73 Mh21
Residenz Ansbach D 59 Ll41
Residenz in Kempten D 59 Ll43
Residenz in Würzburg D 59 Lk41
Resistencia RA 276 Ha59
Reşiţa RO 68 Mb45
Resolute CDN 227 Fa04
Resolution Island NZ 153 Td68
Resplendor BR 275 Hk55
Restauração BR 266 Gk45
Restinga de Jurubatiba, P.N.do BR 275 Hk57
Restinga de Marambaia BR 277 Hj57
Restinga Seca BR 276 Hd60
Reszel PL 65 Mb36
Retalhuleu GCA 248 Fe38
Retén Atalaya RCH 280 Ge62
Retezat RO 68 Mc45
Retezat, P.N. RO 68 Mc45
Retford GB 49 Ku37
Rethel F 51 Le41
Rethem D 58 Lk38
Réthimno GR 71 Me55
Reti PK 99 Oe31
Reti RDC 194 Mf44
Retiers F 50 Kt43
Retiro BR 274 Hd52
Retreat AUS 148 Sb58
Retretti FIN 44 Mk29
Rétság H 67 Lu43
Rettarfoss IS 46 Kd25
Retuerta del Bullaque E 55 Kq51
Return Islands USA 229 Cf10
Retz A 66 Lq42
Reungeut RI 126 Pj43
Réunion F 207 Nh56
Réunion 163 Nb12
Reus E 57 Lb49
Reuterstadt Stavenhagen D 58 Ln37
Reutlingen D 59 Lk42
Reutte A 60 Ll43
Reva USA 233 Ej23
Revdar IND 116 Og33
Revel F 52 Lb47
Revelganj IND 117 Pc33
Revelstoke CDN 232 Ea20
Reventador, Volcán EC 268 Gb46
Revfülöp H 66 Ls44
Révia = Cassembe MOC 197 Mj52
Revigny-sur-Ornain F 51 Le42
Revillagigedo Channel USA 230 De18
Revillagigedo Island USA 230 De18
Revin F 51 Le41
Řevnice CZ 66 Lp41
Revolución Mexicana MEX 247 Fd37
Revtangen N 42 Lf32
Revúca SK 67 Ma42
Rewa IND 117 Pa33
Rewalsar IND 115 Oj30
Réwane SN 180 Kc38
Rewari IND 114 Oj31
Rexburg USA 233 Ee24
Rey IR 96 Nf28
Rey Abad IR 96 Nh27
Rey Bouba CAM 189 Lh41
Reyðarfjörður IS 46 Kf25
Reyes BOL 278 Gg53
Reyhanlı TR 90 Mj27
Reykhólar IS 46 Js25
Reykholt IS 46 Jt26
Reykholt IS 46 Ju26
Reykjadiskur IS 46 Ka25
Reykjafjörður IS 46 Jr25
Reykjahlíð IS 46 Kd25
Reykjanes IS 46 Js25
Reykjanes Ridge 227 Jc06
Reykjanestá IS 46 Js27
Reykjavík IS 46 Jt26
Reynaga MEX 246 Eh36
Reynoldsburg USA 237 Fj26
Reynolds Range AUS 143 Rg57
Reynosa MEX 245 Fa32
Rezé F 52 Kt43
Rēzekne LV 45 Mh34
Rezekne LV 45 Mh34
Rezina MD 73 Me22
Rezovo BG 69 Mj49
Rezvan IR 96 Nh27
Rezvan Shahr IR 91 Ne27
Rgotina SRB 68 Mc46
Rhafsai MA 175 Kh28
Rharb MA 175 Kg28
Rhayader GB 49 Kr38
Rheda-Wiedenbrück D 58 Lj39
Rhein CH 60 Lk44
Rheinau D 59 Lh42
Rheine D 58 Lh38
Rheinfall CH 60 Lj43
Rheinfelden D 59 Lh43
Rheinland-Pfalz D 59 Lg40
Rheinsberg D 58 Ln37
Rheinstetten D 59 Lj42
Rhemilès DZ 175 Kh31
Rhiconich GB 48 Kq32
Rhin D 58 Ln37
Rhine 26 La05
Rhinelander USA 236 Ff23
Rhino Camp EAU 194 Mf44
Rhinow D 58 Ln38
Rho I 60 Lk45
Rhode Island USA 241 Ge25
Rhodes GR 71 Mj54
Rhodes GR 71 Mj54
Rhododendron USA 232 Dk23
Rhodope Mountains BG/GR 68 Md49
Rhön D 59 Lk40
Rhondda GB 49 Kr39
Rhône F 53 Le45
Rhône-Alpes F 53 Le45
Rhônegletscher CH 60 Lj44
Rhoufi DZ 176 Ld28
Rhourd-el-Baguel DZ 176 Ld30
Rhume D 58 Ll39
Rhumsiki CAM 189 Lg40
Rhyolite Ghost Town USA 234 Eb27
Riaba GQ 188 Le44
Riachão BR 272 Hg49
Riachão das Neves BR 272 Hh51
Riachão do Jacuípe BR 273 Ja51
Riachinho BR 275 Hh54
Riacho de Santana BR 273 Hj52
Riacho dos Machados BR 275 Hj53
Riacho He-He RA 276 Ha58
Riacho Seco BR 273 Ja50
Ria de Aveiro P 54 Km50
Riákia GR 70 Mc50
Riala S 43 Lt31
Rianápolis BR 274 Hf53
Riangdo IND 120 Pf33
Riangnom SUD 191 Mf41
Riaño E 54 Kq48
Rians F 53 Lf47
Rías Altas E 54 Km47
Rías Baixas = Rías Bajas E 54 Kl48
Rías Bajas = Rías Baixas E 54 Kl48
Rías Gallegas E 54 Kl47
Riaza E 54 Kr49
Ribadavia E 54 Km48
Ribadelago E 54 Ko48
Ribadeo E 54 Kn47
Ribadesella E 54 Kp47
Ribah WAN 188 Lc40
Ribamar Fiquené BR 272 Hg48
Ribarica BG 69 Me48
Ribarska Banja SRB 68 Mb47
Ribas do Rio Pardo BR 274 Hd56
Ribat TN 176 Lf28
Ribatejo P 55 Km51
Ribat-el-Kheir MA 175 Kh29
Ribaué MOC 203 Mk53
Ribe DK 42 Lj35
Ribécourt F 51 Lc41
Ribeira = Santa Eugenia E 54 Km48
Ribeira da Cruz CV 186 Jh37
Ribeira Grande CV 186 Jh37
Ribeirão Branco BR 277 Hf58
Ribeirão do Pinhal BR 274 He57
Ribeirão Preto BR 275 Hg56
Ribera I 62 Lo53
Ribérac F 52 La45
Ribera Cascalheira BR 272 He52
Ribera das Néves BR 275 Hh55
Riberalta BOL 270 Gg51
Riberão BR 273 Jc50
Ribnica BIH 68 Lt46
Ribnica SLO 66 Lp45
Ribnitz-Damgarten D 58 Ln36
Ribo Escale SN 180 Kc38
Říčany CZ 66 Lp41
Ricardo Flores Magón MEX 244 Eg31
Ricardo Palma PE 269 Gb51
Ricaute CO 264 Gc44
Riccarton Park NZ 153 Tg67
Ríccia I 63 Lp49
Riccione I 61 Ln46
Rice USA 234 Ec28
Rice Bowls USA 234 Cb35
Rice Lake USA 236 Fe23
Rice Lake N.W.R. USA 236 Fd22
Rich MA 175 Kh29
Richardsbaai ZA 205 Mg60
Richards Bay ZA 205 Mg60
Richards Bay Nature Reserve ZA 205 Mg60
Richardson USA 229 Cg13
Richardson USA 238 Fb29
Richardson Highway USA 229 Ch14
Richardson Island CDN 231 Ea13
Richardson Mountains CDN 229 Dc12
Richard Toll SN 180 Kc37
Richdale CDN 233 Ee20
Richelieu F 52 La44
Richey USA 233 Eh22
Richfield USA 232 Ec24
Richfield USA 235 Ed26
Richfield USA 242 Fk28
Richibucto CDN 240 Gh22
Rich Lake CDN 233 Ee18
Richland USA 232 Ea22
Richland USA 232 Eb23
Richland Center USA 236 Fe24
Richlands USA 242 Fk27
Richmond AUS 147 Sb56
Richmond AUS 151 Sf62
Richmond CDN 232 Dj21
Richmond CDN 240 Gd23
Richmond GB 49 Kt36
Richmond GB 49 Ku39
Richmond USA 234 Dj27
Richmond USA 238 Fd26
Richmond USA 239 Fh26
Richmond USA 239 Fh27
Richmond USA 241 Gb27
Richmond ZA 205 Mb61
Richmond Hill AUS 149 Sc57
Richmond Hill CDN 237 Ga24
Richmond Hill USA 242 Fk30
Richmond International Raceway USA 241 Gb27
Richmont ZA 205 Mf60
Richtersveld N.P. ZA 204 Lj60
Richton USA 239 Ff30
Richwood USA 239 Fk26
Ricobayo E 54 Kp49
Ricrán PE 269 Gc51
Ridderkerk NL 51 Le39
Riddle USA 232 Eb24
Rideau Canal CDN 241 Gb23
Rideau Hills CDN 241 Gb23
Ridgecrest USA 234 Eb28
Ridgeland USA 242 Fk29
Ridgeway USA 242 Fk28
Riding Mountain CDN 236 Ek20
Riding Mountain N.P. CDN 236 Ek20
Riebeekkasteel ZA 204 Lk62
Riebeekstaad ZA 205 Md59
Riebook Oos ZA 205 Md62
Riecito YV 265 Gf40
Ried D 59 Lk43
Ried im Innkreis A 66 Lo42
Riedlingen D 59 Lk42
Riegersburg A 61 Lq43
Riesa D 58 Lo39
Riesi I 63 Lp53
Rietavas LT 45 Mb35
Rietbron ZA 204 Mb62
Rietfontain ZA 204 Ma59
Rietfontein NAM 201 Ma56
Rieti I 62 Ln48
Rietschen D 58 Lp39
Rietveld Schröderhuis NL 51 Lf38
Rietvlei ZA 205 Mf60
Rieumes F 52 Lb47
Rieupeyroux F 52 Lc46
Riez F 53 Lg47
Rifle USA 235 Eg26
Rifleman Bank 128 Qf42
Rift Valley EAT/EAK 194 Mj47
Rīga LV 45 Me34
Rigacikun WAN 188 Ld40
Rigan IR 98 Nk31
Rigby USA 233 Ee24
Riggins USA 232 Eb23
Rignac F 52 Lc46
Rig Rig TCH 183 Lh38
Riguldi EST 44 Md31
Riihikoski FIN 44 Mc30
Riihimäki FIN 44 Me30
Riiser-Larsen Ice Shelf 287 Ka33
Riisitunturin kansallispuisto FIN 39 Mj24
Riito MEX 244 Ec29
Rijal 'Alma KSA 94 Nb36
Rijau WAN 188 Lc40
Rijeka HR 61 Lp45
Rijksmuseum NL 51 Le38
Rijssen NL 51 Lg38
Rikbaktsa, T.I. BR 271 Ha51
Rikubetsu J 111 Sb24
Rikuchu-Kaigan N.P. J 111 Sb26
Rila BG 68 Md48
Rila BG 68 Md48
Rila, N.P. BG 68 Md48
Riley USA 232 Ea24
Rilou CHN 103 Qa31
Rilski manastir BG 68 Md48
Rimavská Sobota SK 67 Ma42
Rimba Panti Nature Reserve RI 127 Pk45
Rimbey CDN 233 Ec19
Rimbo S 43 Lt31
Rimforsa S 43 Lq32
Rímini I 61 Ln46
Rímnio GR 70 Mb50
Rimouski CDN 240 Gf21
Rimrock USA 232 Dk22
Rinaré BR 273 Ja48
Rinbung CHN 102 Pe31
Rinca RI 130 Qk50
Rinção BR 274 Hf56
Rincón CR 249 Fj41
Rincón, Cerro RA/RCH 279 Gg58
Rincon USA 234 Ea28
Rincón USA 251 Gg36
Rincón Beach USA 251 Gg36
Rincón Blanco RA 279 Gf60
Rincón de Guayabitos MEX 246 Eh35
Rincón del Atuel RA 280 Gf63
Rincón de la Vieja, P.N. CR 248 Fh40
Rincón del Guanal C 243 Fj35
Rincón de los Sauces RA 280 Gf64
Rincón de Romos MEX 246 Ej34
Rindal N 40 Lk27
Ringamåla S 43 Lp34
Ringarum S 43 Lr32
Ringaskiddy IRL 47 Km39
Ringe DK 42 Ll35
Ringgi SOL 157 Sj50
Ringgold USA 238 Fd29
Ringgold Isles FJI 159 Ua54
Ringim WAN 188 Le39
Ringkøbing DK 42 Lj34
Ringkøbing Fjord DK 42 Lj35
Ringling Museum of Art USA 243 Fj32
Ring of Kerry IRL 47 Kk39
Ringoma ANG 200 Lj52
Ringsted DK 42 Lm35
Ringvassøy N 38 Lu21
Ringwood GB 49 Kt40
Rínia GR 71 Mf53
Rínia GR 71 Mf53
Rinihue RCH 280 Gd65
Riniquiari CO 264 Ge44
Rinjani, Gunung RI 130 Qj50
Rinjim Mukur WAN 188 Le40
Rinns Point GB 48 Ko35
Rinópolis BR 274 He56
Rintala RUS 44 Mk29
Rinteln D 58 Lk38
Río GR 70 Mb52
Río Abiseo, P.N. PE 268 Gb49
Río-Andírio-Bridge GR 70 Mb52
Río Aragón E 56 Kt48
Rio Areia, T.I. BR 276 He58
Rio Ariapo BR 265 Gh45
Río Azul GCA 247 Ff37
Riobamba EC 268 Ga46
Rio Bananal BR 275 Hk55
Río Bec MEX 247 Ff36
Rio Benito GQ 188 Le45
Rio-Biá, T.I. BR 270 Gg48
Río Blanco BOL 278 Gj52
Río Blanco CO 264 Gb44
Ríoblanco CO 264 Gc44
Río Blanco NIC 249 Fh39
Río Blanco PE 268 Gd48
Río Blanco RA 279 Gf60
Rio Blanco USA 235 Eg26
Rio Bonito BR 277 Hj57
Rio Branco BR 266 Gk45
Rio Branco BR 268 Ge48
Rio Branco BR 270 Gg50
Rio Branco BR 270 Gh50
Rio Branco BR 270 Gj51
Rio Branco BR 270 Gk51
Rio Branco BR 271 Ha51
Rio Branco BR 272 Hh51
Rio Branco BR 274 Ha53
Río Branco PE 270 Gf51
Río Branco ROU 276 Hd62
Rio Branco do Sul BR 277 Hf58
Rio Branco, T.I. BR 278 Gj52
Rio Bravo MEX 245 Fa33
Río Bravo del Norte MEX 245 Ej31
Rio Brilhante BR 274 Hc56
Rio Bueno JA 250 Gb36
Río Bueno RCH 280 Gd66
Río Cahncalá MEX 247 Fe37
Río Caribe YV 265 Gj40
Rio Casca BR 275 Hj56
Río Cauto C 243 Gb35
Río Cebullos RA 280 Gh61
Río Chico YV 265 Gh40
Río Cico RA 282 Gf70
Rio Claro BR 275 Hg57
Río Claro CR 249 Fj41
Río Colorado RA 280 Gh65
Rio Conchas BR 274 Hc53
Río Corrientes EC 268 Gb47
Río Cuarto RA 280 Gh62
Rio das Cobras, T.I. BR 276 Hd58
Rio das Ostras BR 275 Hk57
Rio das Pedras MOC 203 Mh57
Rio de Janeiro BR 277 Hj57
Rio de Janeiro BR 255 Hb12
Río de la Plata RA/ROU 281 Hb63
Río de los Sauces RA 280 Gh62
Río de Oro CO 264 Gd41
Rio do Antônio BR 275 Hk53
Rio do Pires BR 273 Hj52
Rio do Prado BR 275 Hk54
Rio dos Pardos, T.I. BR 277 He59
Rio do Sul BR 277 Hf59
Rio Douro P 54 Kn49
Río Duero E 54 Kp49
Río Dulce, P.N. GCA 248 Ff38
Rio Ebro E 57 Ku49
Río Frias RA 282 Ge68
Rio Frio P 54 Ko49
Rio Frio Cave BH 248 Ff37
Río Gállego E 56 Ku48
Río Gallegos RA 282 Gf71
Río Grande BOL 278 Gg56
Río Grande BOL 278 Gj55
Rio Grande BR 272 Hj51
Rio Grande BR 274 Hf56
Rio Grande BR 276 Hd62
Río Grande MEX 246 Ej34
Río Grande MEX 246 Fb37
Rio Grande NIC 248 Fg39
Río Grande NIC 249 Fj39
Rio Grande PE 269 Gc53
Río Grande RA 280 Gf64
Río Grande RA 282 Gf72
Río Grande RA 282 Gg72
Río Grande RCH 280 Ge61
Rio Grande USA 245 Ej31
Rio Grande USA 251 Gh36
Río Grande YV 265 Gk41
Río Grande YV 265 Gk41
Rio Grande City USA 245 Fa32
Río Grande de Tarija BOL/RA 279 Gh57
Rio Grande do Norte BR 255 Ja10
Rio Grande do Piauí BR 273 Hj49
Rio Grande do Sul BR 255 Ha13
Rio Grande Gorge USA 235 Eh27
Rio Grande Plateau 254 Ja13
Rio Gregorio, T.I. BR 268 Ge50
Río Guadalquivir E 55 Ko54
Rio Guadiana P 55 Kn53
Rio Guaporé, T.I. BR 278 Gh51
Riohacha CO 264 Gd40
Río Hato PA 249 Fk41
Río Hondo GCA 248 Ff38
Rio Ichilo BOL 278 Gh54
Rioja PE 268 Gb49
Río Jarama E 55 Kr50
Rio Jaú, P.N. do BR 270 Gj47
Río Júcar E 57 Ku51
Río Lagartos MEX 247 Ff35
Rio Largo BR 273 Jc50
Río Lindo HN 248 Ff38
Riom F 53 Ld45
Rio Maina BR 277 Hf60
Rio Maior P 55 Km51
Río Mayo RA 282 Ge68
Rio Mequens, T.I. BR 278 Gk52
Riom-ès-Montagnes F 53 Lc45
Río Miño E/P 54 Km48
Río Mulato BOL 278 Gg55
Rio Negrinho BR 277 Hf59
Río Negro BOL 270 Gh51
Rio Negro BR 270 Gj46
Rio Negro BR 274 Hc55
Rio Negro BR 277 Hf59
Rionegro CO 264 Gd42
Río Negro PY 276 Hb58
Río Negro RA 276 Ha59
Río Negro RA 280 Gg65
Rio Negro RA 280 Gf66
Río Negro RCH 280 Gd66
Río Negro ROU 276 Hb62
Rio Negro Ocaía, T.I. BR 270 Gh51
Río Negro, P.N.de ROU 276 Ha62
Rionero in Vúlture I 63 Lq50
Rio Nexpa MEX 246 Ej37
Rio Novo BR 275 Hj56
Rio Paranaíba BR 275 Hg55
Rio Pardo BR 276 Hd60
Rio Pardo das Minas BR 275 Hj53
Rio Paru d'Este, T.I. BR 266 Hc45
Río Pico RA 282 Ge68
Río Pilcomayo, P.N. RA 276 Ha58
Rio Pindaré, T.I. BR 272 Hh47
Río Platano HN 249 Fh38
Rio Pomba BR 275 Hj56
Rio Preto da Eva BR 271 Ha47
Río Primero RA 281 Gj61
Rio Quente BR 274 Hf54
Rio Rancho USA 235 Eg28
Rio Real BR 273 Jb51
Río Seco YV 264 Ge40
Río Segundo RA 279 Gj61
Río Segura E 55 Ks52
Río Sereno PA 249 Fj41
Río Sil E 54 Kn48
Río Simpson, P.N. RCH 282 Gd68
Rio Sono BR 272 Hg50
Rio SouthJuan DOM 250 Ge36
Riosucio CO 264 Gb42
Riosucio CO 264 Gc43
Río Tajo E 55 Kr50
Rio Teá, T.I. BR 270 Gg46
Río Tercero RA 280 Gh62
Río Tígre EC 268 Gb47
Rio Tinto BR 273 Jc49
Río Tocuyo YV 265 Gf40
Rio Tuba RP 128 Qj41
Rioug RIM 180 Ke37
Rio Verde BR 274 He54
Rio Verde EC 268 Ga45
Ríoverde MEX 246 Ek35
Río Verde MEX 247 Ff36
Rio Verde de Mato Grosso BR 274 Hc55
Rio Vermelho BR 275 Hj55
Río Viejo, P.N. YV 264 Ge42
Río Villegas RA 280 Ge66
Rio Vista USA 234 Dk26
Rioz F 53 Lg43
Rio Zêzere P 55 Kn51
Río Zújar E 55 Kp52
Ripač BIH 61 Lq46
Ripanj SRB 68 Ma46
Ripky UA 72 Mf20
Ripley USA 239 Ff28
Ripley USA 239 Ff28
Ripley USA 239 Fk26
Ripoll E 56 Lc48
Ripon GB 49 Kt36
Riponpet IND 118 Oh39
Riposto I 63 Lq53
Ripplebrook USA 232 Dj23
Riquewihr F 53 Lh42
Rireibo do Pombal BR 273 Ja51
Risalpur PK 99 Og28
Risbäck S 41 Lq26
Riscal de Cataviña MEX 244 Ec31
Riscle F 52 Ku47
Rishikesh IND 115 Ok30
Rishiri J 111 Sa23
Rishirifuji J 111 Sa23
Rishiri-Rebun-Sarobetsu N.P. J 111 Sa23
Rishiri-to J 111 Sa23
Rishton UZ 97 Of25
Rising Star USA 238 Fa29
Risin & Kellingin DK 46 Kn28
Riska N 42 Lf32
Riske Creek CDN 232 Dj20
Risnes N 42 Lg32
Risnjak, N.P. HR 61 Lp45
Rison USA 239 Fd29
Risør N 42 Lk32
Risoul 1850 F 53 Lg46
Rissani MA 175 Kh30
Risti EST 44 Me32
Ristiina FIN 44 Mh29
Ristilä FIN 44 Mg28
Ristna neem EST 44 Mc32
Rita Blanca National Grassland USA 238 Ej27
Ritchie ZA 205 Mc60
Rithi IND 117 Pa34
Ritlite BG 68 Md47
Rito ANG 200 Lk54
Rito Gompar CHN 103 Pg31
Ritsem S 38 Ls23
Ritter USA 232 Ea23
Ritter Hot Springs USA 232 Ea23
Ritterhude D 58 Lj37
Ritzville USA 232 Ea22
Riumar E 57 La50
Rivadavia RA 279 Gj58
Rivadavia RA 280 Gf61
Rivadavia RA 281 Gj63
Rivadavia RCH 279 Ge60
Riva del Garda I 60 Ll45
Rivas CR 249 Fj41
Rivas NIC 248 Fh40
Rive-de-Gier F 53 Le45
Rivera EC 268 Ga47
Rivera RA 281 Gj64
Rivera ROU 276 Hc61
Riverboat Cruises (Murray River) AUS 150 Sb63
River Cess LB 186 Kf43
River Falls USA 236 Fd23
River Gambia N.P. WAG 186 Kc39
Riverhead USA 241 Gd25
Riverina AUS 144 Ra60
River Jordan CDN 232 Dh21
River Kwai Bridge THA 122 Pk38
River Rafting (Devaprayag) IND 115 Ok30
River Rafting (Tanakpur) IND 115 Pa31
Rivers CDN 236 Ek20
Riversdal ZA 204 Ma63
Riversdale BH 248 Ff37
Riversdale NZ 153 Te68
Riversdale ZA 204 Ma63
Riversdale Beach NZ 153 Tj66
Riverside AUS 149 Se56
Riverside USA 232 Ea24
Riverside USA 234 Eb29
Riverside USA 235 Eg25
Riverside USA 235 Eh29
Riversleigh AUS 146 Rk55
Riverton CDN 236 Fb20
Riverton NZ 153 Td69
Riverton USA 233 Ef24
Riverview CDN 240 Gh22
Rivesaltes F 53 Lc48
Riviera USA 245 Fb32
Riviera di Levante I 60 Lk46
Riviera di Ponente I 60 Lj47
Rivièrea-Pièrre CDN 240 Gd22
Rivière-au-Renard CDN 240 Gh21
Rivière-au-Tonnerre CDN 240 Gh20
Rivière-aux-Graines CDN 240 Gh20
Rivière aux Sables CDN 240 Ge21
Rivière-auxSaumons CDN 240 Gj21
Rivière Bleue CDN 240 Gf22
Rivière-du-Loup CDN 240 Gf22
Rivière-Héva CDN 237 Ga21
Rivière Manicouagan CDN 240 Gf21
Rivière Pentecôte CDN 240 Gg21
Rivière-Pilote F 251 Gk38
Rivière Saint-Jean CDN 240 Gh20
RivièreSaint Jean CDN 240 Gh20
Rivière Saint-Maurice CDN 240 Gd21
Rivière Sud-Est MS 207 Nj56
Riviersonderend ZA 204 Lk63
Rivne UA 65 Mg40
Rivne UA 73 Mf21
Rívoli I 60 Lh45
Rivungo ANG 201 Ma54
Riwat PK 99 Og29
Riwoqê CHN 103 Pj30
Riyadh KSA 93 Nd33
Riyadh al Khabra KSA 93 Nb32
Rizal RP 124 Ra37
Rizal RP 124 Ra39
Rize TR 91 Na25
Rizhao CHN 112 Qk28
Rizokarpaso = Dipkarpaz CY 90 Mh28
Rjabovskij RUS 72 Na20
Rjazan' RUS 72 Mk18
Rjazanka RUS 72 Nb19
Rjažsk RUS 72 Na19
Rjukan N 42 Lj31
Rkîz RIM 180 Kc37
Roa E 54 Kr49
Roa N 42 Ll30
Road Town GB 251 Gh36
Roan Cliffs USA 235 Ef26
Roanne F 53 Le44
Roanoke USA 239 Fh29
Roanoke USA 242 Ga27
Roanoke Rapids USA 242 Gb27
Roans Prairie USA 238 Fc30
Roastbeef Island NAM 204 Lh59
Robat IR 98 Nj30
Robat-e Ja'li AFG 98 Oa31
Robat-e-Khoshab IR 98 Nj29
Robat-e Khoshk Aveh AFG 98 Ob29
Robat-e-Posht Badam IR 98 Nh29
Robat-e-Qarah Bil IR 96 Nj27
Robatkarim IR 91 Nf28
Robat Khan IR 98 Nj29
Robat Kur IR 98 Nj29
Robat Sang IR 98 Nk28
Robb CDN 232 Eb19
Robben Island ZA 204 Lk62
Robbies Pass NAM 200 Lg55
Robbins Island AUS 151 Sc66
Robbinsville USA 242 Fj28
Robe AUS 150 Rk64
Robe ETH 192 Na42
Röbel D 58 Ln37
Robe, Mount AUS 148 Sa61
Robert Lee USA 238 Ek30
Robert's Arm CDN 241 Hc21
Roberts Creek Mtn. USA 234 Eb26
Robertsfors S 41 Ma26
Robertsganj IND 117 Pb33
Robertson ZA 204 Lk62
Robertsport LB 186 Ke42
Robertstown AUS 150 Rk62
Roberval CDN 240 Gd21
Robi ETH 192 Mk42
Robinhood AUS 147 Sb55
Robins Camp ZW 201 Mc55
Robinson USA 239 Fg26
Robinson, Mount AUS 142 Qk57
Robinson Range AUS 144 Qk58
Robinson River AUS 146 Rj54
Robinson River PNG 156 Se51
Robledo E 55 Ks52
Robles La Paz CO 264 Gd40
Roblin CDN 236 Ek20
Röblingen D 58 Lm39
Robooksibia RI 154 Rh46
Roboré BOL 278 Ha55
Robsart CDN 233 Ef21
Robson, Mount CDN 232 Ea19
Robstown USA 245 Fb32
Roby USA 238 Ek29
Roca Bruja CR 248 Fg40
Rocafuerte EC 268 Fk46
Rocamadour F 52 Lb46
Rocanville CDN 236 Ek20
Roca Redonda EC 269 Fe45
Roça Tapirapé BR 272 He50
Roccadáspide I 63 Lq50
Rocca Imperiale I 63 Lr50
Roccamena I 62 Lo53
Roccaraso I 63 Lp49
Roccastrada I 60 Lm47
Roccella Iónica I 63 Lr52
Rocha ROU 281 Hc63
Rochdale GB 49 Ks37
Roche Cabrit F 266 Hd43
Rochechouart F 52 La45
Rochedo BR 274 Hc55
Rochefort B 51 Lf40
Rochefort F 52 Ku45
Rochelle USA 237 Ff25
Rocher Ako'akas CAM 189 Lf44
Rocher Corneille F 53 Ld46
Rocher d'Ifandana RM 207 Nd56
Rocher du Mézessé CAM 189 Lg44
Rocher River CDN 231 Ed15
Rocheservière F 52 Kt44
Rochester GB 49 La39
Rochester USA 236 Fd23
Rochester USA 237 Fg25
Rochester USA 241 Gb24
Rochester USA 241 Ge24
Roche Tado F 266 Hd43
Rochlitz D 58 Ln39
Rockall Plateau 26 Ka04
Rockall Trough 26 Ka04
Rock Creek CDN 229 Da13
Rock Creek CDN 232 Ea21
Rockdale USA 238 Fb30
Rockdale USA 239 Fg28
Rockefeller Plateau 287 Da34
Rock Engravings NAM 204 Lk59
Rock Engravings ZA 205 Mc59
Rock Falls USA 237 Ff25
Rockford USA 237 Ff24
Rockford USA 239 Fg29
Rock Fort Temple (Trichy) IND 118 Ok40
Rockglen CDN 233 Eh21
Rockhampton AUS 149 Sf57
Rockhampton Downs AUS 146 Rh55
Rock Hill USA 242 Fk28
Rockingham AUS 144 Qh62
Rockingham USA 242 Ga28
Rockingham Bay AUS 147 Sd55
Rocklake USA 236 Fa21
Rockland CDN 241 Gc23
Rockland USA 241 Gf23
Rock 'n' Roll Hall of Fame (Cleveland) USA 237 Fk25
Rock of Cashel IRL 47 Kn38
Rock Paintings LS 205 Me61
Rock Paintings RB 205 Mc58
Rock Paintings ZA 204 Ma61
Rockport USA 232 Dk21
Rock Port USA 238 Fc25
Rockport USA 245 Fb31
Rock Rapids USA 236 Fb24
Rock River USA 235 Eh25
Rock Sound BS 243 Gb33
Rock Springs USA 233 Eg22
Rock Springs USA 235 Ef25
Rocksprings USA 245 Ek31
Rockstone GUY 266 Ha42
Rockton AUS 151 Se64
Rockville USA 239 Fg26
Rockville USA 241 Gb26
Rockwood USA 239 Fh28
Rockwood USA 241 Gf23
Rocky Boy USA 233 Ef21
Rocky Boy Ind. Res. USA 233 Ef21
Rocky Ford USA 238 Ej26
Rocky Gully AUS 144 Qj63
Rocky Island ET 179 Mj34
Rocky Mount USA 242 Ga27
Rocky Mount USA 242 Gb28
Rocky Mountain House CDN 233 Ec19
Rocky Mountain N.P. USA 235 Eh25
Rocky Mountains CDN/USA 210 Db04
Rocky Mountains Forest Reserve CDN 233 Ec20
Rocky Mtn. House N.H.S. CDN 233 Ec19
Rocky Mtns. Forest Reserve CDN 232 Eb19
Rocky Point USA 228 Bj13
Ročov CZ 66 Lo40
Rocroi F 51 Le41
Roda Velha BR 272 Hh52
Rødberg N 42 Lj30
Rødbyhavn DK 42 Lm36
Roddickton CDN 241 Hb20
Rödeby S 43 Lq34
Rødekro DK 42 Lk35
Rodel GB 48 Ko33
Roden NL 51 Lg37
Rodeo RA 279 Gf61
Rodeo USA 235 Ef30
Rodez F 53 Lc46
Rodi Gargánico I 63 Lq49
Rodina Mat UA 73 Mf20
Roding D 59 Ln41
Rodna RO 67 Me43
Rodna, P.N. RO 67 Me43
Rodniki RUS 72 Na17
Rodolívos GR 69 Md50
Ródos GR 71 Mj54
Rodovia Perimetral Norte BR 266 Hb45
Rødvig DK 42 Ln35
Roebourne AUS 142 Qj56
Roebuck Plains AUS 142 Rb54
Roedtan ZA 205 Me58
Roela EST 44 Mg31
Roermond NL 51 Lg39
Roeselare B 51 Ld40
Roeseveltpiek SME 266 Hc44
Roeşti RO 68 Me46
Roetgen D 58 Lg40
Rofia WAN 188 Lc40
Rogač HR 61 Lr47
Rogačevka RUS 72 Mk20
Rogačica SRB 68 Lu46
Rogaguado BOL 278 Gh52
Rogaliński Park Krajobrazowy PL 64 Lr38
Rogaška Slatina SLO 66 Lq44
Rogatica BIH 68 Lu47
Rogers USA 238 Fc27
Rogers City USA 237 Fj23
Rogerson USA 232 Ec24
Rogers Pass CDN 232 Eb20
Rogersville CDN 240 Gh22
Roggeveen Basin 254 Fa12
Roggeveldberge ZA 204 Ma62
Rogliano I 63 Lr51
Rogo WAN 188 Ld40
Rogone MOC 203 Mj53
Rogovo RUS 45 Mj33
Rogowo PL 64 Ls38
Rogoz RO 67 Md43
Rogoźniczka PL 65 Mc38
Rogoźno PL 64 Lr38
Rogun WAN 188 Lc41
Rohan F 50 Ks42
Rohat IND 116 Og33
Rohatyn UA 67 Me41
Rohožník SK 66 Ls42
Rohrbach A 66 Lo42
Rohrbach-lès-Bitche F 51 Lh41
Rohri PK 99 Oe32
Rohru IND 115 Oj30
Rohtak IND 114 Oj31
Rohtas IND 117 Pb33
Rohtas Fort PK 99 Og29
Rohuküla EST 44 Md32
Rohuneeme EST 44 Me31
Roi Et THA 123 Qb37
Roismala FIN 44 Mc29
Roissy F 51 Lc42
Roja LV 45 Mc33
Rojão P 54 Km50
Rojas RA 281 Gk63
Röjdåfors S 42 Ln30
Rojhan PK 99 Oe31
Roka EAK 195 Mk47
Rokan RI 127 Qa45
Rokeby AUS 147 Sb52
Rokeby N.P. AUS 147 Sb52
Rokewood AUS 151 Sb64
Rokiciny PL 65 Lu39
Rokiškis LT 45 Mf35
Rokkasho J 111 Sa25
Rokom SUD 194 Mf43
Rokoroko RI 131 Rb48
Rokycany CZ 66 Lo41
Rokytne UA 72 Md20
Roland CDN 236 Fb21
Rolândia BR 274 He57
Roland in Bremen D 58 Lj37
Røldal N 42 Lg31
Roldan RA 281 Gk62
Rolde NL 51 Lg38
Rolfstorp S 42 Ln33
Rolim de Moura BR 270 Gk51
Roll USA 238 Fa28
Rolla USA 236 Fa21
Rolla USA 239 Fe27
Rolleston AUS 149 Se58
Rollet CDN 237 Ga22
Rolleville BS 250 Gc34
Rolling Fork USA 239 Fe29
Rolling Hills CDN 233 Ee20
Rolling R. Ind. Res. CDN 236 Ek20
Rollingstone AUS 147 Sd55
Rollo BF 187 Kk39
Roluos Group K 123 Qc39
Roma AUS 149 Se59
Roma LS 205 Md60
Roma S 43 Lt33
Roma USA 245 Fa32
Romaine CDN 240 Gk20
Romallo RA 281 Gk62
Roman BG 69 Md47
Roman RO 73 Md22
Roman Baths GB 49 Ks39
Romang RA 276 Ha60
Romang RI 131 Rd49
Romania RO 27 Ma05
Romanovka RUS 104 Qg19
Romanshorn CH 60 Lk43
Romans-sur-Isère F 53 Lf45
Romantische Straße D 59 Lk41
Romanzof Mountains USA 229 Ch11
Romaria BR 275 Hg55
Romblon RP 124 Rb39
Romblon Island RP 124 Rb39
Romblon Strait RP 124 Rb39
Rome I 62 Ln49
Rome USA 239 Fh28
Rome USA 241 Gc24
Romilly-sur-Seine F 51 Ld42
Romiton UZ 97 Oc26
Romlott-vár H 66 Ls44
Rommani MA 175 Kg29
Romney USA 241 Ga26
Romny RUS 105 Re20
Romny UA 72 Mg20
Rømø DK 42 Lj35
Romo RI 128 Qe45
Romodan UA 73 Mg21
Romorantin-Lanthenay F 53 Lb43
Rømø Sommerland DK 42 Lj35
Romsdalen N 40 Lh28
Romsey GB 49 Kt40
Rómulo Calzada MEX 247 Fd37
Ron IND 116 Oh38
Ronan USA 232 Ec22
Roncador BR 276 Hd58
Roncador Reef SOL 157 Sk49
Roncesvalles E 56 Kt47
Ronchamp F 53 Lg43
Ronciglione I 62 Ln48
Ronda E 55 Kp54
Ronda Alta BR 276 Hd59
Rondane n.p. N 40 Lk29
Rønde DK 42 Ll34
Ronde WG 251 Gk39
Rondeador, T.I. BR 272 Hh48
Rondeau Prov. Park CDN 237 Fk24
Rondon BR 274 Hd57
Rondon do Pará BR 272 Hf48
Rondônia BR 255 Gb11
Rondonópolis BR 274 Hc54
Rond-Point de Gaulle TCH 183 Lj36
Ronehamn S 43 Lt33
Rongai EAK 194 Mh46
Rong'an CHN 108 Qe33
Rongbon Cave THA 123 Qa39
Rongbuk Monastery CHN 102 Pd31
Rongcheng CHN 107 Rb27
Rongjenj IND 120 Pf33
Rong Kat THA 121 Pk36
Rongkop RI 129 Qf50
Rong Kwang THA 121 Qa36
Rongo EAK 194 Mh46
Rongshui CHN 108 Qe33
Rõngu EST 45 Mg32
Rong Xian CHN 108 Qc31
Rong Xian CHN 108 Qf34
Ronien Daun Sam K 123 Qb39
Ron Morel Mus. CDN 237 Fj21
Rønne DK 43 Lp35
Ronneby S 43 Lq34
Ronne Ice Shelf ANT 287 Gd34
Ronnenberg D 58 Lk38
Rönnöfors S 40 Lo27
Ron Phibun THA 122 Pk41
Ronse B 51 Ld40
Roodeport ZA 205 Md59
Rooiberge LS 205 Me60
Rooibokkraal ZA 205 Md58
Rooikop NAM 204 Lh57
Rooikraal ZA 205 Me58
Rooin RI 154 Rh47
Rooirand NAM 204 Lj58
Roorkee IND 115 Oj31
Roosendaal NL 51 Le39
Roosevelt BR 271 Gk50
Roosevelt USA 235 Ef25
Roosevelt Campobello Internat. Park CDN 240 Gg23
Roosevelt, Mount CDN 230 Dh16
Roosevelt N.P. Nth. Unit USA 233 Ej22
Roosevelt N.P. Sth. Unit USA 233 Ej22
Roosevelt, T.I. BR 271 Gk51
Roossenekal ZA 205 Me58
Roosville CDN 232 Ec21
Root Lake CDN 233 Ek18
Ropar IND 114 Oj30
Ropczyce PL 65 Mb40
Roper Bar AUS 146 Rh53
Roper River AUS 146 Rh53
Roper Valley AUS 146 Rh53
Ropotovo MK 68 Mb49
Roquefort F 52 Ku46
Roque Gonzales BR 276 Hc60
Roque Pérez RA 281 Ha63
Roquesteron F 53 Lh47
Roquetaillade F 52 Ku46
Roquetas de Mar E 55 Ks54
Roquetes E 57 La50
Roraima BR 255 Gb09
Roraima, Mount GUY/YV 266 Gk43
Rore BIH 61 Lr46
Rori IND 114 Oh31
Rori RI 154 Rj46
Rorke's Drift ZA 205 Mf60
Røros N 40 Lm28
Rorschach CH 60 Lk43
Rørvik N 40 Lm26
Ros' BY 65 Me37
Rošal' RUS 72 Mk18
Rosal de la Frontera E 55 Kn53
Rosales RP 124 Ra38
Rosalia USA 232 Eb22
Rosalindbank 249 Fk37
Rosamorada MEX 245 Eh34
Rosana BR 274 Hd57
Rosans F 53 Lf46
Rosário BR 267 Hh47
Rosario DOM 250 Ge36
Rosario MEX 244 Ef32
Rosario PE 279 Ge58
Rosario PY 276 Hb58
Rosario RA 281 Gk62
Rosario ROU 281 Hb63
Rosario RP 124 Ra37
Rosario RP 124 Ra39
Rosario YV 264 Gd40
Rosario de la Frontera RA 279 Gh58
Rosario de Lerma RA 279 Gh58
Rosario del Tala RA 276 Ha62
Rosário do Sul BR 276 Hc61
Rosario Izapa MEX 247 Fd38
Rosario Oeste BR 274 Hb53
Rosarito MEX 244 Eb29
Rosarito MEX 244 Ec31
Rosarito MEX 244 Ee32
Rosarno I 63 Lq52
Rosa Seamount 244 Ec32
Rosa Zárate EC 268 Ga45
Rosburg USA 232 Dj22
Roscales E 54 Kq48
Roščino RUS 44 Mk30
Roscoff F 50 Kr42
Roscommon IRL 47 Km37
Roscrea IRL 47 Kn38
Rose MNE 68 Lt48
Rose USA 236 Fa24
Roseau USA 236 Fc21
Roseau WD 251 Gk38
Rose BlacheHarbour Le Cou CDN 241 Ha22
Rosebud AUS 151 Sc65
Rosebud USA 236 Ek24
Rosebud Ind. Res. USA 236 Ek24
Roseburg USA 232 Dj24
Rosecrans Memorial Airport (Saint Joseph) USA 238 Fc26
Rosedale AUS 149 Sd57
Rosedale USA 239 Fe29
Rosedown Plantation USA 239 Fe30
Rose Harbour CDN 230 De19
Rose Hill = Beau-Bassin MS 207 Nj56
Rosehill Gardens AUS 151 Sf62
Rosemont Plantation USA 239 Fe30
Rosenberg USA 238 Fc31
Rosendal N 42 Lg31
Rosendal ZA 205 Md60
Rosengarten D 58 Lk37
Rosenheim D 59 Ln43
Rose Point CDN 230 De18
Rose Prairie CDN 231 Dk17
Roses E 56 Ld48
Roseto degli Abruzzi I 61 Lp48
Rosetown CDN 233 Eg20
Rosetta ET 179 Mf30
Rose Valley CDN 233 Ej19
Rosewood AUS 143 Re54
Rosh Pinah NAM 204 Lj59
Roshtkhar IR 98 Nk28
Roşia RO 67 Mc44
Roşia de Secaş RO 67 Md44
Roşia Nouă RO 67 Mc44
Rosica BG 69 Mh47

Rosice CZ 66 Lr41
Rosignano Marittimo I 60 Ll47
Rosignano Solvay I 60 Ll47
Rosignol GUY 266 Hb42
Roşiori RO 67 Md43
Roşiori de Vede RO 69 Me46
Roskilde DK 42 Ll35
Roskilde Rockfestival DK 42 Ln35
Roslagen S 43 Lt30
Roslavl' RUS 72 Mg19
Rosman USA 242 Fj28
Rosmead ZA 205 Mc61
Rosolini I 63 Lj54
Rosoman MK 68 Mb49
Rosporden F 50 Kr43
Rossano I 63 Lr51
Rossan Point IRL 47 Km36
Rossarden AUS 151 Sd66
Ross Bay Jtn. CDN 240 Gg19
Ross-Bethio SN 188 Kf40
Ross Ice Shelf ANT 287 Bd35
Rössing NAM 200 Lh57
Rössing Uranium Mine NAM 200 Lh57
Rosslare IRL 47 Ko38
Rosslare Harbour IRL 47 Ko38
Rosslau D 58 Ln39
Rosso RIM 180 Kc37
Ross-on-Wye GB 49 Ks39
Rossoš' RUS 72 Mk20
Rossport CDN 237 Fg21
Ross River CDN 230 Dd15
Ross Sea ANT 287 Bd33
Rosston USA 238 Fd29
Rossville AUS 147 Sc53
Rosswood CDN 230 Dt18
Rosswood Plantation USA 238 Fe30
Røst N 38 Lr23
Rostaq AFG 97 Oe27
Rostaq IR 96 Nh29
Rostkala TJ 97 Of27
Rostock D 58 Ln36
Rostov RUS 72 Mk17
Rostov-na-Donu RUS 73 Na22
Rostrenen F 50 Kr42
Rosvik N 38 Lq23
Roswell USA 235 En29
Roswell USA 239 Fh28
Rota E 55 Ko54
Rot am See D 58 Ll39
Rotenburg D 58 Lk39
Rotenburg (Wümme) D 58 Lk37
Roth D 59 Lm41
Rothbury GB 49 Ks36
Rothenburg (Tauber) D 59 Ll41
Rothera 287 Gc32
Rotherham GB 48 Ks38
Rothesay GB 48 Kp36
Rothschild USA 236 Ff23
Rothwell GB 49 Kt37
Roti RI 131 Rb51
Roti RI 131 Rb51
Rotifunk WAL 186 Kd41
Rotondella I 63 Lr50
Rotorua NZ 152 Tj66
Rotsskildery ZA 204 Ma61
Rotsskildery RB 205 Mc58
Rott D 59 Ln42
Rotten CH 60 Lk44
Rottenburg D 59 Lm42
Rottenburg D 59 Lm42
Rotterdam NL 51 Lf39
Rottne S 43 Lp33
Rottnest Island AUS 144 Qh61
Rottumeroog NL 51 Lg37
Rottumerplaat NL 51 Lg37
Rottweil D 59 Lk42
Rotuma FJI 159 Tj52
Rötz D 59 Ln41
Roualist Bank 123 Qc41
Roubaix F 51 Ld40
Roudnice nad Labe CZ 66 Lp40
Rouen F 51 Lb41
Rougemont F 53 Lg43
Rough Rock USA 235 Er27
Rouillac F 52 Ku46
Roulans F 53 Lg43
Round Mountain AUS 149 Sg61
Round Mountain USA 238 Fa30
Round Rock USA 235 Ep29
Round Rock USA 239 Fb30
Roundup USA 233 Ef22
Round Valley Ind. Res. USA 234 Dj26
Rousay GB 267 Hd43
Roussaj F 53 Lg43
Roussillon F 53 Le45
Roussillon F 53 Lf47
Route 62 ZA 204 Lk62
Route 66 USA 239 Ff26
Route 66 (Missouri) USA 238 Fd27
Route 66 (New Mexico) USA 235 Eh28
Route 66 (New Mexico) USA 235 Eh28
Route des Crêtes F 53 Lg43
Route des Grandes Alpes F 53 Lg46
Route des Kasbahs MA 175 Kg30
Route Napoléon F 53 Lg46
Route transsaharienne DZ/RN 182 Lc35
Rouxville ZA 205 Md61
Rouyn-Noranda CDN 237 Ga21
Rova d'Antongona RM 207 Na55
Rovaniemi FIN 44 Mc24
Rovato I 60 Lk45
Roven' SK 66 Ma39
Roven'ki RUS 72 Mk21
Rovereto I 60 Ll45
Rovigo I 60 Lm45
Rovinari RO 68 Md46
Rovine di Roselle I 60 Lm48
Rovinj HR 61 Ln45
Row PL 64 Lq38
Rowena AUS 149 Se60
Rowley Shoals AUS 142 Qk54
Rowy PL 64 Lq36
Roxas RP 124 Qk40
Roxas RP 124 Ra37
Roxas RP 124 Ra39
Roxas RP 64 Rb40
Roxboro USA 242 Ga27
Roxborough Downs AUS 148 Rk57
Roxby Downs AUS 148 Rj61
Roy USA 235 Eg25
Roy USA 235 Ed25
Roy USA 235 Ed28
Royal Bardia N.P. NEP 115 Pa31
Royal Botanic Gardens GB 49 Kt39
Royal Chitwan N.P. NEP 115 Pc32
Royal Citadel (Polonnaruwa) CL 119 Pd42
Royal City USA 232 Ea22
Royal Exhibition Building and Carlton Gardens AUS 151 Sc64
Royal Gorge USA 235 Eh26
Royal Manas N.P. BHT 120 Pf32
Royal N.P. AUS 151 Sf63
Royal Palm Beach USA 243 Fk32
Royal Pavilion GB 49 Ku40
Royal Sukla Phanta N.P. NEP 115 Pa31
Royan F 51 Kt46
Roy Hill AUS 142 Qk57
Røykfossen N 38 Mb21
Röyttä FIN 44 Mc24
Royston GB 49 Ku38

Royston USA 242 Fj28
Roza BG 69 Mg48
Rozafa AL 68 Lu48
Rozay-en-Brie F 51 Lc42
Rożan PL 65 Mb38
Rozdil'na UA 73 Mg23
Rozdol'ne UA 73 Mg23
Roženovo RUS 105 Re20
Rozengain RI 131 Rd48
Roztensji manastir BG 68 Md49
Rozivka UA 73 Mj23
Rožmitál pod Třemšínem CZ
Rožňava SK 67 Ma42
Rozogi PL 65 Mb37
Rożok RUS 72 Na18
Rozoy-sur-Serre F 51 Le41
Rozvadov CZ 66 Ln41
Rozžyšče UA 65 Mf40
Rrogozhinë AL 68 Lu49
Rtiščevo RUS 72 Na18
Rt Kamenjak HR 61 Lo46
Rt Ploča HR 61 Lq47
Ruacana NAM 200 Lh54
Ruacana Falls NAM 200 Lh54
Ruahine N.P. NZ 153 Tj66
Ruahine Range NZ 153 Tj66
Ruang RI 131 Rd44
Ruangwa EAT 197 Mk51
Ruapehu, Mount NZ 153 Th65
Ruapuke Island NZ 153 Te69
Ruba BY 72 Mf18
Rubafu EAT 194 Mf46
Rubbestadneset N 42 Lf31
Rubcovsk RUS 88 Pa08
Rubeho Mountains EAT 197 Mj49
Rubeshibe J 111 Sb34
Rubi D 59 Lf41
Rubondo N.P. EAT 194 Mf47
Rubuga EAT 196 Mg48
Ruby USA 229 Cc13
Ruby USA 234 Ec25
Ruby Mts. Scenic Area USA 234 Ec25
Ruby Range CDN 230 Da15
Rubys Inn USA 235 Ed27
Rubyvale AUS 149 Sd57
Ruby Valley USA 234 Ec25
Rucachoroi, Cerro RA 280 Ge65
Rucăr RO 69 Me45
Rucava LV 45 Mb34
Rucheng CHN 109 Qg33
Ruciane-Nida PL 65 Mb37
Rud IR 98 Oa28
Ruda S 43 Lq33
Rudall USA 149 Sd57
Rudall River N.P. AUS 142 Rb57
Rudarpur IND 117 Pb32
Ruda Śląska PL 65 Lt40
Rudauli IND 117 Pa33
Rudbar AFG 98 Ob30
Rudbar IR 96 Nh28
Rudersberg D 59 Lf41
Rüdersdorf D 58 Lo38
Rüdesheim D 59 Lh41
Rudhauli IND 117 Pb32
Rudilla E 57 Kt50
Rudinka HR 61 Lq46
Rüdnikes LT 45 Me36
Rudky UA 67 Mf39
Rudkøbing DK 42 Ll36
Rudky UA 67 Ma41
Ruda Glava SRB 68 Mc46
Rudnaja Pristan' RUS 111 Rh23
Rudnichnyj KZ 100 Ok23
Rudnik BG 69 Mh45
Rudnik SRB 68 Ma46
Rudnja PL 64 Ld33
Rudnja RUS 72 Mf18
Rudnyj KZ 88 Od08
Rudo BIH 68 Lu47
Rudolstadt D 58 Lm40
Rudong CHN 112 Ra29
Rudrapur IND 115 Ok31
Rud Sar IR 91 Nf27
Rue F 51 Lb40
Rueda E 54 Kq49
Ruelle F 52 Ku46
Ruente Nacional CO 264 Gd43
Rufa'a SD 184 Mg38
Ruffec F 52 La44
Rufiji EAT 197 Mk50
Rufino RA 281 Gj63
Rufisque SN 188 Kd39
Rufunsa Z 202 Me53
Rugãji LV 45 Mh33
Ruganga EAT 196 Mh50
Rugao CHN 112 Ra29
Rugby GB 49 Kt38
Rugeley GB 49 Ks38
Rugheiwa SUD 185 Mf37
Rugles F 52 La42
Rugombo BU 196 Me47
Rugovska klisura KSV 68 Ma48
Rugozi EAT 194 Mg47
Rugui RUS 72 Mg19
Ruhan' RUS 72 Mg19
Ruhnu saar EST 45 Md33
Ruhr D 58 Lh39
Rui'an CHN 109 Ra32
Ruicheng CHN 109 Qd31
Ruidera E 55 Ks52
Ruidosa USA 238 Ek30
Ruidoso USA 235 Eh29
Ruijin CHN 120 Pj33
Ruiru EAT 194 Mg46
Ruisbrokos P.N. USA 182 Ld36
Ruines d'Assodé RN 182 Le36
Ruines de Loropéni BF 187 Kj40
Ruines d'Empúries E 57 Ld48
Ruines de Gouraya DZ 177 Ld34
Ruines d'Aksum ETH 184 Ma38
Ruins of Fort Craig USA 238 Ek28
Ruins of Sambor K 123 Qc39
Ruins of Windsor USA 239 Fe30
Ruiru EAT 194 Mg46
Rujbersbos P.N. ZA 204 Mb62
Ruiz MEX 244 Ef33
Rūjiena LV 45 Mf33
Rukanga EAT 195 Mk47
Rukube EAT 194 Mg47
Rukenge EAT 194 Mf47

Rumeila SUD 185 Mh39
Rumia PL 64 Lr36
Rumilly F 53 Lf45
Rumphi MW 196 Mg51
Rumpi Hills CAM 188 Le43
Rumšiškes LT 45 Me36
Run RI 131 Re48
Runcorn GB 49 Kr37
Rundu NAM 200 Lk54
Runestensen DK 42 Lj35
Rungsted DK 42 Lm35
Rungu RDC 191 Md44
Rungu RDC 191 Me44
Rungwa EAT 196 Mh49
Rungwa EAT 196 Mg49
Rungwa Game Reserve EAT 196 Mh49
Rungwe EAT 196 Mg50
Runiz IR 98 Ng31
Runmarö S 43 Lt31
Runtuna S 43 Ls32
Runzewe EAT 194 Mf47
Ruokojärvi FIN 39 Me23
Ruokolahti FIN 44 Me29
Ruoqiang CHN 103 Pe26
Ruovesi FIN 44 Mc29
Rupanyup AUS 151 Sb64
Rupat RI 127 Qa45
Rupawati IND 116 Og34
Rupea RO 69 Me45
Rupert USA 232 Ec28
Rupia RI 127 Pc33
Rupia RI 127 Pc33
Ruppert Coast 287 Cd34
Rupsa ZW 202 Mg55
Rura IND 117 Ok32
Rurópolis Presidente Medici BR 271 Hc44
Rurrenabaque BOL 278 Gd53
Rurum WAN 188 Le40
Ruskan TJ 97 Of27
Rusape ZW 202 Mg55
Rusera IND 117 Pd33
Rushan CHN 107 Ra27
Rushden GB 49 Ku38
Rushinga ZW 202 Mg54
Rushungi EAT 197 Mk50
Rushville USA 234 Ec25
Rusizi, P.N.de RDC 196 Me47
Ruskeala FIN 44 Mf29
Rusné LT 45 Mb35
Ruso USA 234 Ek22
Rusovce SK 66 Lr42
Russell NZ 152 Th63
Russell USA 238 Fb26
Russell Islands SOL 157 Sk50
Russell, Mount USA 229 Ce14
Russell Springs USA 238 Ex26
Russellville USA 238 Fd28
Russel Range AUS 146 Rd63
Rüsselsheim D 59 Lj41
Russenegg USA 234 Ed25
Russia RUS 77 Oa03
Russkinskije USA 239 Fg27
Rust A 61 Lq43
Rustavi GE 91 Nc25
Rust de Winter ZA 205 Me58
Rust de Winter Nature Reserve ZA 205 Me58
Rusterfjelbma N 39 Mj20
Ruston USA 239 Fd29
Rusumu EAT 194 Mf47
Rusumu Falls EAT 194 Mf47
Rutana BU 196 Me47
Rute E 55 Kq53
Ruteng RI 131 Qk49
Rutenga ZW 202 Mf56
Rutete EAT 194 Mf47
Ruth USA 234 Ec26
Rutherfordton USA 242 Fj28
Ruti PNG 155 Sc48
Rutigliano I 63 Lr49
Rutka-Tartak PL 65 Mc36
Rutland Island IND 122 Pg43
Rutland Plains AUS 147 Sa53
Rutledalen N 40 Lf29
Rutog CHN 102 Ok29
Rutshuru RDC 191 Me46
Rutul RUS 91 Nd25
Ruvo di Puglia I 63 Lr49
Ruvu EAT 197 Mk48
Ruvuma, P.N.de la BU 196 Mf47
Ruvuma EAT/MOC 197 Mj51
Ruvu Rest EAT 197 Mk48
Ruweis UAE 95 Ng33
Ruwenzori RDC/EAU 191 Me45
Ruwenzori Mountains N.P. EAU 191 Me45
Ru-ye Sang AFG 97 Oe28
Rügen D 58 Lo36
Ruyuan CHN 109 Qg33
Ruza RUS 72 Mj18
Ruzaevka RUS 72 Nc18
Růžencin PL 65 Mb38
Ružomberok SK 67 Lu41
Rwanda R 163 Ma10
Rwindi RDC 191 Me46
Ry DK 42 Lk34
Ryan, Mount AUS 151 Se62
Rybachye KZ 45 Ma35
Rybačij PL 65 Mc36
Rybczewice PL 65 Mc39
Rybinsk RUS 72 Mk16
Rybinsk Reservoir RUS 72 Mk16
Rybnik PL 64 Lt40
Rybnik PL 65 Ld37
Rybnoe RUS 72 Mk18
Rychłocice PL 64 Lt39
Rychnal PL 64 Lt39
Rychnov CHN 120 Pj33
Ryd S 43 Lp34
Rydaholm S 43 Lp34
Rydberg Peninsula 287 Ga33
Rydboholm S 43 Lp34
Ryde GB 49 Kt40
Rydet S 42 Lm33
Rydsnäs S 43 Lp33
Rydułtowy PL 65 Lt40
Rydzewo PL 65 Mb37
Rye GB 49 La40
Ryegate USA 233 Ef22
Ryki PL 65 Mb39
Ryl'sk RUS 72 Mh20
Rymań PL 64 Lq37
Rymanów PL 65 Mb41
Rymanov-Zdrój PL 65 Mb41
Rymättylä FIN 44 Mb30
Ryn PL 65 Mb37
Ryōhakusanchi J 113 Rj27
Ryongchong Temple PRK 112 Rd26
Ryotsu J 111 Rk26
Rypin PL 65 Lu37
Rysjö BOL 278 Gf55
Ryssby S 43 Lp34
Rytterknægten DK 43 Lp35
Ryukyu Islands J 76 Ra07
Ryukyu Trench J 107 Ra07
Rzasnik PL 65 Mb38
Rzeczenica PL 64 Lr37
Rzepin PL 64 Lp38
Rzeszów PL 65 Mb40
Řžev RUS 72 Mh17
Ržyščiv UA 73 Mf21

S

Sa PNG 155 Sc48
Sa NL 131 Kh38
Saa CAM 189 Lh43
Sa'a SOL 157 Ta50
Saacow = Jilib SP 195 Nb45
Saadani National Park EAT 197 Mk48
Saaintontein ZA 204 Ma61
Sääksjärvi FIN 44 Md27
Saalbach A 61 Ln43
Saalburg D 59 Lj40
Saale D 59 Lm40
Saalfeld D 59 Lm40
Saalfelden am Steinernen Meer A 61 Ln43
Saam NL 251 Gj37
Saan SYR 90 Mj28
Saanich CDN 232 Dj21
Saar D 59 Lg41
Saarbrücken D 59 Lg41
Saarburg D 59 Lg41
Sääre EST 45 Mc33
Saaremaa EST 45 Mc33
Saarijärvi FIN 44 Md28
Saarijärvi FIN 56 Mf38
Saaristomeren kansallispuisto = Skärgårdshavets n.p. FIN 44 Mb31
Saarland D 59 Lg41
Saarschleife D 59 Lg41
Šaartuz TJ 97 Oe27
Saatli AZ 91 Ne26
Saba NL 251 Gj37
Šabac SRB 68 Lu46
Sabadell E 57 Lc49
Sabah MAL 128 Qj43
Sabaiya SUD 191 Md42
Sabak MAL 126 Qa44
Sabalana RI 130 Qk49
Sabalgarh IND 116 Oj32
Sabalpanth IND 116 Oj32
Saba Marine Park NL 251 Gj37
Sabana CO 268 Gd46
Sabana de Cardona YV 265 Gg42
Sabana de la Mar DOM 250 Gf36
Sabana Grande YV 264 Gf40
Sabanalarga CO 264 Gd42
Sabanalarga CO 264 Gd43
Sabanalarga CO 264 Gd43
Sabana San Francisco BR 247 Ff36
Sabancaya, Volcán PE 269 Gc53
Sabanca MEX 247 Fe36
Sabaneta CO 264 Gd42
Sabaneta YV 265 Gf41
Sabang RI 125 Qk45
Sabang RP 124 Qk40
Sabanözü TR 90 Me26
Sabaoth ETH 192 Mk41
Sabar BR 275 Hg53
Sabarei EAK 194 Mj43
Sabari RI 187 La41
Sabati RI 127 Pk46
Saboudia I 62 Ln49
Sabaya BOL 278 Gf55
Sabbioneta I 60 Ll45
Saba No Nat THA 124 Qa42
Sabberi RI 126 Qa44
Sabha LAR 174 Ld31
Sabiñánigo E 56 Ku48
Sabinas MEX 245 Ek32
Sabine N.W.R. USA 238 Fd31
Sabine Peninsula CDN 226 Eb03
Sabinópolis BR 275 Hj55
Sabinosa E 174 Ka32
Sabirabad AZ 91 Ne26
Sabká THA 124 Qa42
Sablayan RP 124 Qk40
Sable Island CDN 240 Gk24
Sablé-sur-Sarthe F 50 Ku43
Sabon Birni WAN 188 Ld40
Sabongari WAN 188 Lb39
Sabon Kafi WAN 182 Le40
Saborna crkva SRB 68 Ma46
Sabou BF 187 Kj40
Sabratha LAR 174 Lc29
Sabrina Coast 287 Ra32
Sabtang Island RP 109 Ra35
Sabuda RI 131 Rf47
Sabugal P 54 Kn50
Sabulubbek RI 127 Pk46
Saby S 43 Lp33
Saça RO 67 Md39
Saçama ANG 201 Ma52
Saccolongo I 60 Lm45
Saccorbo E 57 Ks50
Sacedón E 57 Ks50
Šaček BY 72 Md19
Šack RUS 72 Na18
Šac'k UA 65 Md39
Sacks USA 239 Fh29
Šac'kyj pryrodnyj n. p. UA 65 Md39
Saco CDN 233 Eg22
Saco USA 233 Eg22
Sacol Island MEX 245 Rb42
Sacoşu Turcesc RO 68 Mb45
Sacramento BR 275 Hg55
Sacramento, T.I. BR 271 Ha49
Sacramento USA 234 Dk26
Sacro Monte di Ghiffa I 60 Lj45
Sacro Monte di Oropa I 60 Lj45
Sacro Monte di Serralunga di Crea I 60 Lj45
Sacro Monte di Soccorso I 60 Ls45
Sacro Monte di Valperga Canavese I 60 Lh45
Săcueni RO 67 Mc43
Sacuunda ANG 201 Mb53
Sada ZA 205 Mb62
Sada E 56 Kn48
Sadaba E 57 Ks48
Sadabad RM 207 Nd55
Sadad SYR 90 Mj28
Sadai RI 129 Qd47
Sadani RI 131 Sd48
Sadam RI 129 Nj34
Sādāt City E 177 Mf30
Sadani EAT 197 Mk49
Sadao THA 122 Qa42
Sadao THA 122 Qa42
Sadd-e Eskandar IR 96 Nh27
Saddle L., Ind. Res. CDN 233 Ed18
Saddle Mount AUS 144 Qj55
Saddle Peak IND 122 Pg43
Saddle-Peaks VU 158 Te56
Sadd Malky KSA 94 Nb37
Sa Dec VN 123 Qc40
Sa Ngam J 111 La44
Sainsoutou SN 186 Ke39
Sadiola RMM 186 Ke39
Sadich IR 98 Nk33
Sadio SN 180 Kc38
Sadiola IND 116 Og34
Sadovo BG 69 Me48
Sadovoe RUS 73 Nc21
Saelices E 57 Ks51
Saentausa S 46 Ke25
Saeera de São Domingos BR 275 Hg53
Safaha SUD 191 Md41
Safahr BF 187 Kj39
Safara P 54 Ko52
Safed Koh AFG 97 Oc28
Safford USA 235 Ef29
Safi MA 174 Kf29
Safi TCH 183 Lj38
Safia PNG 156 Se50
Safid IND 117 Pa32
Safir YE 94 Nc37
Safita SYR 90 Mj28
Safonovo RUS 72 Mg18
Safranbolu TR 90 Mg25
Safwan IRQ 93 Nd30
Sâg RO 67 Mc43
Saga CHN 102 Pc31
Saga J 113 Rf29
Sagabari RMM 186 Kf39
Sagadi SUD 185 Mg39
Sagae J 111 Sa26
Sagaing MYA 120 Ph34
Sagala RMM 187 Kg39
Sagallou DJI 193 Nb40
Sagamu WAN 188 La42
Sagan EAK 194 Mh45
Sagar IND 117 Ok34
Sagar IND 118 Oj37
Saganthit Kyun MYA 122 Pk40
Sagaranten RI 129 Qd49
Sagaria BD 120 Pf34
Sagarmatha = Mount Everest NEP/CHN 115 Pd31
Sagarpara IND 120 Pe33
Sagastyr RUS 89 Rb04
Sagata SN 180 Kb38
Sagauli IND 117 Pc32
Sagay RP 124 Ra40
Sag Harbor USA 241 Gd25
Saginaw USA 237 Fj24
Saginaw Bay USA 237 Fj24
Saglek Bay CDN 227 Gd07
Sagleipie LB 186 Kf42
Sagne RIM 180 Kd38
Sagone F 62 Lj48
Sagra E 57 Ks53
Sagrada Familia E 57 Lc49
Sagres P 55 Km54
Sagsag PNG 156 Sf48
Sagu MYA 120 Ph35
Saguache USA 235 Eh26
Sagua la Grande C 250 Gc35
Sagua deTánamo C 250 Gd36
Saguaro N.P. USA 235 Ef29
Saguaro N.P. USA 235 Ee29
Sagunt E 57 Ku51
Saguto E 57 Ku51
Sagure ETH 192 Mk42
Sagvåg N 42 Lf31
Sagwon USA 229 Cf11
Sagwon USA 229 Ch11
Sa'gya CHN 102 Pc31
Sahagún CO 264 Gd42
Sahagún E 54 Kq48
Sahara City = Medinet Sahara ET 174 Ld32
Sahara Surt LAR 177 Ld30
Saharanpur IND 117 Oj31
Saharsa IND 117 Pd33
Sahaswan IND 115 Ok32
Sahavato RM 207 Nd56
Sahbaz IR 96 Ne27
Sah Chida BD 120 Pf33
Sahel 162 Kb38
Sahibganj IND 117 Pd33
Sahiwal PK 99 Og30
Sahiwal PK 99 Og30
Sah Kuh IR 96 Nh29
Sahl al Matran SUD 185 Mg37
Sahneh IR 91 Nd28
Sahra City = Medinet Sahara ET
Sah Soltan IR 98 Nk29
Sahara Surt LAR 177 Lg30

Šahr-e-Suhte IR 98 Oa30
Sahristan TJ 97 Oe26
Šahty RUS 73 Na22
Sahuaripa MEX 244 Ef31
Sahuaro de J.Ma. Morelos MEX
Sahuayo de J.Ma. Morelos MEX
Sai J 111 La25
Saibai Island AUS 147 Sb50
Sai Buri THA 122 Qa42
Sai-Cinza, T.I. BR 271 Ha49
Saida RM 275 Hg55
Saïda DZ 175 La28
Saidapuram IND 119 Ok38
Saidia MA 175 Kj28
Saïdor PNG 155 Sd48
Saidpur BD 120 Pf33
Saidu Sharif PK 97 Og28
Saidu stupas PK 97 Og28
Saigō J 113 Rg27
Saigon VN 123 Qd40
Saihan Toroi CHN 106 Qa25
Sai Island Temple SUD 185 Mf35
Saikanosy Ampasindava RM 206 Nd52
Saikanosy Masoala RM 206 Nf53
Saikhoa Ghat IND 120 Ph33
Saiki J 113 Rf29
Saillans F 53 Lf46
Saillans F 53 Lf46
Sailu IND 117 Ok35
Saimaa FIN 44 Mf29
Saimen kanal FIN/RUS 44 Mj29
Sain Alto MEX 246 Ej34
Sai Ngam J 111 La44
Sainshand CHN 106 Qc24
Saint Abb's Head GB 48 Ks36
Saint Adolphe CDN 236 Fb21
Saint Affrique F 53 Le46
Saint-Agrève F 53 Le46
Saint-Aignan F 52 La43
Saint Albans GB 49 Ku39
Saint Albans USA 241 Gc25
Saint Albert CDN 233 Ed18
Saint Albert Dome PNG 155 Sb48
Saint-Alexandre F 53 Lf46
Saint-Amand-en-Puisaye F 53 Ld43
Saint-Amand-les-Eaux F 51 Ld40
Saint-Amand-Montrond F 53 Lc44
Saint-Ambroise CDN 240 Gc21
Saint-Ambroix F 53 Lf46
Saint-André-de-Cubzac F 52 Ku46
Saint-André-de-l'Eure F 51 La42
Saint Andrews GB 48 Ks35
Saint Andrew's USA 242 Fj31
Saint Andrews CDN 241 Ha22
Saint Anne GB 50 Ks41
Saint Anthony USA 233 Ee24
Saint-Antoine F 52 Lb44
Saint Arnaud AUS 151 Sb64
Saint Arnaud NZ 153 Te68
Saint-Aubin-d'Aubigné F 50 Kt42
Saint-Aubin-du-Cormier F 50 Kt42
Saint Augustine CDN 240 Ha20
Saint Augustine USA 242 Fk31
Saint Augustine USA 242 Fk31
Saint Austell GB 49 Kq40
Saint-Autremontine d'Issoire F 53 Ld45
Saint-Avold F 51 Lg41
Saint Barbe CDN 241 Hb20
Saint-Barthélemy F 251 Gj37
Saint-Barthélemy N 42 153 Te68
Saint-Béat F 52 La47
Saint Bees AUS 149 Se56
Saint Bees Islands AUS 149 Se56
Saint Benedict F 207 Nh56
Saint-Benoit-du-Sault F 52 Lb44
Saint Bernard F 267 Hd44
Saint-Bertrand-de-Comminges F 52 La47
Saint-Bonnet F 53 Lg46
Saint Brendan's CDN 241 Hd21
Saint-Brévin-les-Pins F 52 Ks43
Saint-Brice-en-Coglès F 50 Kt42
Saint Bride's Bay GB 49 Kp39
Saint Bride's Bay CDN 241 Hc22
Saint-Brieuc F 50 Ks42
Saint-Brieuc CDN 236 Fd19
Saint-Calais F 52 La43
Saint-Cast-le-Guildo F 50 Ks42
Saint Catharines CDN 237 Ga24
Saint Catherine's Point GB 49 Kt40
Saint-Céré F 53 Lc45
Saint-Chamond F 53 Lf45
Saint Charles USA 239 Fe28
Saint Charles USA 236 Fc23
Saint Charles CDN 236 Fb21
Saint-Chély-d'Apcher F 53 Le46
Saint-Chinian F 53 Le47
Saint-Claud F 52 La45
Saint Clears GB 49 Kp39
Saint Cloud F 51 Lc42
Saint Cloud USA 236 Fc23
Saint Croix USA 251 Gh36
Saint Croix USA 234 Dj26
Saint Croix USA 251 Gh37
Saint Croix N.S.R. USA 236 Fd23
Saint David's GB 49 Ko39
Saint David's Head GB 49 Ko39
Saint-Denis F 51 Lc42
Saint-Denis RE 207 Nh56
Saint-Dié-des-Vosges F 53 Lg42
Saint-Dizier F 51 Le42
Saint-Doulchard F 53 Lc43
Saint-Élie F 267 Hd43
Saint-Livrade-sur-Lot F 52 La46
Saint-Eloy-les-Mines F 53 Ld44
Saint-Égrève F 53 Lf45
Saint Elias Mountains CDN 230 Da15
Saint Kilda F 47 Km33
Saint Kitts and Nevis 251 Gj37
Saint-Laurent-du-Maroni F 266 Hc43
Saint Lawrence AUS 149 Se57
Saint Lawrence Island USA 228 Be14
Saint Léonard CDN 236 Ekzo
Saint-Léonard-de-Noblat F 52 Lb45
Saint Leu F 207 Nh56
Saint Louis CDN 236 Eh19
Saint Louis SN 180 Kc38
Saint Louis USA 239 Fe26
Saint Louis RE 207 Nh56
Saint Louis USA 235 Eg25
Saint Lucia WL 251 Kg39
Saint-Étienne F 53 Lf45
Saint Lucia ZA 205 Mg60

Saint Lucia 251 Kg39
Saint-Étienne-de-Saint-Geoirs F 53 Lf45
Saint-Étienne-du-Rouvray F 51 La41
Saint Magnus Bay GB 48 Kt30
Saint-Maixent-l'École F 52 Ku44
Saint-Malo F 50 Ks42
Saint-Marcellin F 53 Lf45
Saint Margaret Bay USA 232 Ee22
Saint Marks USA 242 Fj31
Saint Marks USA 239 Fb33
Saint Mary CDN 240 Gd21
Saint-Martin-de-Candigou F 52 Lc48
Saint Martins USA 240 Gh23
Saint-Martin-Vésubie F 53 Lh46
Saint-Flour F 53 Ld45
Saint-Fort-sur-Gironde F 52 Ku45
Saint Francis Bay USA 236 Mc63
Saint Francis Islands AUS 150 Rg62
Saint Francisville USA 239 Fe30
Saint Francois Mountains USA 239 Fe27
Saint-Gabriel CDN 240 Gd22
Saint-Gaudens F 52 La47
Saint-Geniez-d'Olt F 53 Lc46
Saint-Genix-sur-Guiers F 53 Lf45
Saint George AUS 149 Se60
Saint George CDN 241 Ha22
Saint George USA 235 Ed27
Saint George USA 242 Fj30
Saint George USA 243 Fk30
Saint George, Cape PNG 156 Sg48
Saint George Island USA 228 Bf17
Saint George's 251 Gk39
Saint George's CDN 241 Ha21
Saint George's F 267 Hd44
Saint George's Bay GB 49 Kp39
Saint George's Bay (NFL) CDN 241 Ha21
Saint George's Bay (NS) CDN 240 Gk23
Saint George's Castle GH 187 Kk43
Saint George's Channel IND 122 Pg42
Saint George's Channel PNG 156 Sg48
Saint George's Channel 47 Ko39
Saint-Georges-de-Didonne F 52 Ku45
Saint-Germain-du-Bois F 53 Lf44
Saint-Germain-en-Laye F 51 Lc42
Saint-Germain-Laval F 53 Le44
Saint-Gervais-d'Auvergne F 53 Ld44
Saint-Gervais-les-Bains F 53 Lg45
Saint-Gildas-des-Bois F 50 Ks43
Saint-Gilles-Croix-de-Vie F 52 Kt44
Saint-Girons F 52 Lb48
Saint-Girons-en-Marensin F 52 Kt46
Saint Govan's Head GB 49 Ko39
Saint Gregory, Mount 241 Ha21
Saint-Guénolé F 50 Kr43
Saint-Guilhem-le-Désert F 53 Le46
Saint Helena 163 Kb11
Saint Helena Bay ZA 204 Lk62
Saint Helens AUS 151 Se66
Saint Helens USA 232 Dj23
Saint Helens, Mount Volcanic Mon. USA 232 Fk31
Saint Helens Point AUS 151 Se66
Saint Helier GB 50 Ks41
Saint-Hilaire/Lange, P.N.de BR 277 Hf58
Saint-Hilaire-le-Grand de Poitiers F 52 La44
Saint-Hippolyte F 53 Lg43
Saint-Hippolyte-du-Fort F 53 Le46
Saint-Honoré-les-Bains F 53 Ld44
Saint-Hubert F 51 Lf40
Saint-Hyacinthe CDN 240 Gd22
Saint Ignace USA 237 Fh23
Saint-Ignace-des-Saults CDN 240 Gd22
Saint Ignace CDN 237 Fg21
Saint-Imier CH 60 Lg43
Saint Ives GB 49 Ko40
Saint Ives GB 49 Ku38
Saint James USA 236 Fc24
Saint James CDN 236 Fd19
Saint-Jean F 207 Nh56
Saint-Jean-Brévelay F 50 Ks43
Saint-Jeande-Dieu CDN 240 Gd22
Saint-Jean-de-Luz F 52 Kt47
Saint-Jean-de-Monts F 52 Ks44
Saint-Jean-Pied-de-Port F 52 Kt47
Saint-Jean-Port-Joli CDN 240 Gd22
Saint-Jean-Pouigo F 52 La47
Saint-Jean-surRichelieu CDN 241 Gd23
Saint John CDN 241 Ha22
Saint John GB 251 Gh36
Saint John USA 238 Fb27
Saint Joe USA 232 Eb22
Saint John's USA 235 Ef28
Saint John Island USA 251 Gh36
Saint John's AUS 251 Gk37
Saint John's CDN 241 Hd21
Saint Johns USA 235 Ef28
Saint Johnsbury USA 241 Gd24
Saint John's Island F 179 Mj34
Saint John's Town of Dalry GB 48 Kq36
Saint Jorge de Limpopo MOC 202 Mg57
Saint Joseph CDN 236 Fb21
Saint Joseph USA 238 Fc26
Saint Joseph USA 238 Fc26
Saint Joseph F 207 Nh56
Saint Joseph USA 239 Fd31
Saint Joseph's CDN 241 Hd22
Saint Joseph USA 239 Fe30
Saint Jovite CDN 240 Gc22
Saint-Julien-de-Genevois F 53 Lf45
Sainte-Eulalie F 53 Le46
Sainte-Foy-la-Grande F 52 La46
Sainte-Hedwidge CDN 240 Gc21
Sainte-Justine CDN 240 Gd22
Saint Kilda F 47 Km33
Saint Kitts and Nevis 251 Gj37
Saint-Laurent-du-Maroni F 266 Hc43
Saint Lawrence AUS 149 Se57
Saint Lawrence Island USA 228 Be14
Saint-Léonard CDN 236 Ek20
Saint-Léonard-de-Noblat F 52 Lb45
Saint Leu F 207 Nh56
Saint Louis CDN 236 Eh19
Saint Louis SN 180 Kc38
Saint Louis USA 239 Fe26
Saint Louis RE 207 Nh56
Saint Louis USA 235 Eg25
Saint-Maixent CDN 240 Gc22
Saint-Mammès F 51 Lc42
Saint-Mandrier-sur-Mer F 53 Lg47
Saint Mary USA 233 Ee21
Saint Mary's GB 49 Kn41
Saint Mary's AUS 151 Se66
Saint Matthias Group PNG 156 Sa46
Saint Mary's USA 233 Fd29
Saint Mary's USA 242 Fk30
Saint Mary's Bay CDN 241 Hd22
Saint Mary's Peak AUS 148 Rj61
Saint Mathieu F 52 Lb45
Saint Matthew Island USA 228 Bd15
Saint Matthews USA 242 Fk29
Saint-Maximin-la-Sainte-Baume F 53 Lf47
Saint-Médard-en-Jalles F 52 Ku46
Saint-Méen-le-Grand F 50 Ks42
Saint Michael USA 228 Bj14
Saint Michaels USA 235 Ef28
Saint Michael's Mount GB 49 Kp40
Saint-Michel F 51 Le41
Saint-Michel-de-l'Attalaye RH 250 Gd36
Saint-Mihiel F 51 Lf42
Saint Mungo GB 48 Kq35
Saint-Nazaire F 52 Ks43
Saint Neots GB 49 Ku38
Saint-Nicolas-de-Port F 51 Lg42
Saint-Omer F 51 Lc40
Saintonge F 52 Ku45
Saint-Pamphile CDN 240 Gf22
Saint-Pascal CDN 240 Gf22
Saint-Paul F 53 Lc47
Saint-Paul F 207 Nh56
Saint Paul USA 236 Fc23
Saint Paul USA 236 Fa25
Saint-Paul-de-Fenouillet F 52 Lc48
Saint-Paulien F 53 Le45
Saint-Paul-Île CDN 240 Gk22
Saint Paul Island USA 228 Bf17
Saint-Paul-lès-Dax F 52 Kt46
Saint Paul's Cathedral RP 124 Ra38
Saint Paul's Subterranean N.P. RP 124 Qj41
Saint-Péray F 53 Lf46
Saint-Père-en-Retz F 52 Ks43
Saint Peter CDN 240 Gk23
Saint Peter USA 236 Fc23
Saint Peter Island AUS 150 Rg62
Saint-Pol-de-Léon F 50 Kr42
Saint-Pol-sur-Mer F 51 Lc39
Saint-Pol-sur-Ternoise F 51 Lc40
Saint-Pons-de-Thomières F 53 Lc47
Saint-Pourçain-sur-Sioule F 53 Ld44
Saint-Priest F 53 Lf45
Saint-Privat F 53 Lc45
Saint-Quay-Portrieux F 50 Ks42
Saint-Quentin F 51 Ld41
Saint-Raphaël F 53 Lg47
Saint-Raymond CDN 240 Gd22
Saint-Rémy-de-Provence F 53 Lf47
Saint-Renan F 50 Kq42
Saint-Saëns F 51 Lb41
Saint-Sauveur-en-Puisaye F 53 Ld43
Saint-Sauveur-le-Vicomte F 50 Kt41
Saint-Sauveur-sur-Tinée F 53 Lh46
Saint-Savin F 52 La45
Saint-Seine-l'Abbaye F 53 Lf43
Saint-Sernin F 52 La47
Saint-Sever F 52 Kt46
Saint Shotts CDN 241 Hd22
Saint-Siméon CDN 240 Gf22
Saint Simons Island USA 242 Fk30
Saint Stephen CDN 240 Gg23
Saint-Sulpice F 53 Lb47
Saint-Théophone F 52 Kr42
Saint Thomas CDN 237 Fk24
Saint Thomas USA 251 Gh36
Saint-Tite CDN 240 Gd22
Saint-Tropez F 53 Lg47
Saint Urbain CDN 240 Gf22
Saint-Ursanne CH 60 Lh43
Saint-Vaast-la-Hougue F 50 Kt41
Saint-Valéry-en-Caux F 50 La41
Saint-Valéry-sur-Somme F 51 Lb40
Saint-Vallier F 53 Lf45
Saint Victor's Petroglyphs Prov.H.S. CDN 233 Eg21
Saint Vincent F 53 Le45
Saint Vincent WV 251 Gk39
Saint Vincent and the Grenadines 251 Gk39
Saint Vincent N.W.R. USA 239 Fh31
Saint Vincent Passage 251 Gk39
Saint-Vith F 51 Lg40
Saint Walburg CDN 233 Eh19
Saint-Xavier USA 233 Eh22
Saint-Yorre F 53 Le44
Saint-Yrieix-la-Perche F 52 Lb45
Saint-Zénon CDN 240 Gc22
Sainyabuli LAO 121 Qb36
Saïotesh KZ 91 Nc23
Saioua CI 187 Kh42
Saipal NEP 115 Pa31
Saïpina BOL 278 Gh55
Sai Ree Beach THA 122 Pk40
Saisombun LAO 121 Qb36
Saïssac F 53 Lc47
Saitama J 113 Rk28
Sai Thong N.P. THA 122 Qa38
Saïwa Swamp N.P. EAK 194 Mh45
Saïyala SUD 185 Mg37
Saïyid PK 99 Og29
Sai Yok THA 122 Pk39
Sai Yok Noï Waterfall THA 122 Pk39
Sai Yok Yaï N.P. THA 122 Pk39
Sajam RI 154 Rg46
Sajama, Nevado de BOL 278 Gf55
Sajama, P.N. BOL 278 Gf55
Šajkaš SRB 68 Ma45
Sajószentpéter H 67 Ma42
Šajmak TJ 97 Oh27
Sajósvámos H 67 Ma42

Saka – San Pascual

Saka ETH 192 Mj41
Saka LV 45 Mb34
Saka MA 175 Kj28
Sakabinda RDC 201 Mc51
Sakaeo THA 123 Qb39
Sakai GH 187 Kj40
Sakai J 113 Rh28
Sakaide J 113 Rg28
Sakaiminato J 113 Rg28
Sakai N.P. J 113 Re29
Sakakah KSA 92 Na30
Sakakemang RI 127 Qb47
Sakala kõrgustik EST 45 Mf32
Sakania RDC 196 Me52
Sakar TM 97 Ob26
Sakaraha RM 207 Nc57
Sakar Dağı TR 71 Mh51
Sakar Island PNG 156 Se48
Sakartvelo = Georgia GE 91 Nb25
Sakarya TR 90 Mf25
Sakarya = Adapazarı TR 90 Mf25
Sakassou CI 187 Kh42
Sakata J 111 Rk26
Sakbayeme CAM 188 Lf43
Saké RDC 191 Me46
Sakété DY 188 Lb42
Saketi RI 129 Qd49
Sakha RUS 89 Qc05
Sakhalin RUS 89 Sa08
Sakhi Gopal IND 117 Pc36
Sakhon Nakhon THA 123 Qc37
Saki WAN 188 Lb41
Šakiai LT 45 Md36
Sakiet Eddaïr TN 176 Lf28
Sakiet Sidi Youssef TN 176 Le27
Säkilahti FIN 44 Mk29
Sakiramke RI 155 Sa50
Sakju PRK 110 Rc25
Sakkara ET 179 Mf31
Sakke IND 117 Pa34
Sak Lek THA 122 Qa37
Sakleshpur IND 118 Oh39
Sakoamadinika RM 207 Ne54
Sakone SN 186 Kb39
Sakony RUS 72 Nb18
Sakrand PK 99 Oe32
Sakré Déléb TCH 190 Lk41
Sakri IND 116 Oh35
Sakri IND 117 Pd32
Sakrivier ZA 204 Ma61
Sakskøbing DK 42 Lm36
Saku J 111 Rk27
Saky UA 73 Mg23
Sakya Monastery CHN 102 Pe31
Säkylä FIN 44 Mc29
Sala EAK 195 Mk47
Sala S 43 Lr31
Šaľa SK 66 Ls42
Salaberry-deValleyfield CDN 241 Gc23
Salacgrīva LV 45 Me33
Sala Consilina I 63 Lq50
Saladas RA 276 Ha60
Saladero M.Cabal RA 281 Gk61
Saladillo RA 281 Ha63
Salado RA 279 Gj59
Saladougou RG 186 Kf40
Salaga GH 187 Kk41
Salagle SP 195 Nb45
Salahly SP 193 Nc41
Salaiman Range PK 99 Oe31
Salajwe RB 205 Mc57
Salakas LT 45 Mg35
Salal TCH 183 Lj38
Salala LB 186 Ke42
Salala SUD 179 Mj35
Salalah OM 95 Nh37
Salama EAK 194 Mj46
Salamá GCA 248 Fe38
Salamá HN 248 Fg38
Salamajärven kansallispuisto FIN 44 Me27
Salamanca E 54 Kp50
Salamanca MEX 246 Ek35
Salamanca PA 249 Ga41
Salamanca RCH 280 Ge61
Salamanca USA 237 Ga24
Salamanga MOC 205 Mg59
Salamaua PNG 155 Sd49
Salamey IR 98 Nk28
Salamina CO 264 Gc40
Salamina CO 264 Gc43
Salamina GR 69 Md53
Salamína GR 69 Md53
Salamiyyeh SYR 90 Mj28
Salamo PNG 156 Sf50
Salang-Tunnel AFG 97 Oe28
Salantai LT 45 Mb34
Salar de Aguilar RCH 279 Gf58
Salar de Antofalla RA 279 Gg58
Salar de Arizaro RA 279 Gg58
Salar de Atacama RCH 279 Gf57
Salar de Cauchari RA 279 Gg57
Salar de Chiguana BOL 279 Gg56
Salar de Coipasa BOL 278 Gf55
Salar de Empexa BOL 278 Gf56
Salar de la Mina RA 279 Gg59
Salar del Hombre Muerto RA 279 Gg58
Salar de Llamara RCH 279 Gf56
Salar de Pajonales RCH 279 Gf58
Salar de Pedernales RCH 279 Gf59
Salar de Pintados RCH 278 Gf56
Salar de Pipanaco RA 279 Gg60
Salar de Pocitos RA 279 Gg58
Salar de Uyuni BOL 278 Gg56
Salar Pocitos RA 279 Gg58
Salar Punta Negra RCH 279 Gf58
Salas E 54 Ko47
Salas PE 268 Ga49
Salas de los Infantes E 56 Kr48
Salasil KSA 93 Ne32
Salaspils LV 45 Me34
Salatiga RI 129 Qf49
Sălătrucu RO 67 Me45
Salavan LAO 123 Qd38
Salavat IR 91 Nd26
Salavat RUS 88 Nd08
Salavat Abad IR 91 Nd28
Sala Vichey K 123 Qc39
Salawati RI 131 Rf46
Salawin N.P. THA 121 Pj36
Sala-y-Gomez-Fracture Zone 254 Fa12
Salayie LB 186 Kf42
Salazar RA 281 Gj64
Salbris F 53 Lc43
Salcabamba PE 269 Gc52
Salcantay, Nevado PE 269 Gd52
Salcedo EC 268 Ga46
Salcia RO 68 Mc46
Salcia RO 68 Mc46
Salcia RO 69 Me47
Salcia RO 69 Me47
Šalčininkai LT 45 Mf36
Saldaña CO 264 Gc44
Saldaña E 54 Kq48
Saldanha ZA 204 Lj62
Saldanhabaai ZA 204 Lj62
Saldanha Bay ZA 204 Lj62
Saldé SN 180 Kd37
Saldungaray RA 281 Gk65
Saldus LV 45 Mc34
Sale AUS 151 Sd65
Salé MA 175 Kg28
Sale MYA 120 Ph35
Salebhatta IND 117 Pb35
Saleé RIM 180 Kf36
Saleh Abad IR 91 Ne28
Salehan AFG 98 Oa30
Salem IND 118 Ok40
Salem USA 232 Dj23
Salem USA 236 Fb24
Salem USA 239 Fe27
Salem USA 239 Fg26
Salem USA 241 Gc26
Salem USA 242 Fk27
Salem ZA 205 Md62
Salémata SN 186 Kd39
Salemi I 62 Ln53
Salem Plateau USA 239 Fe27
Sälenfjällen S 40 Lo29
Salerno I 63 Lp50
Salers F 53 Lc45
Sales BR 274 Hf56
Salesópolis BR 277 Hg57
Salewara IND 117 Pa35
Saleye CI 187 Kj41
Salgado BR 273 Jb51
S'Algar E 57 Le51
Salgótarján H 67 Lu42
Sälgrund FIN 44 Mb28
Salgueiro BR 273 Ja50
Salher IND 116 Og35
Sali DZ 175 Kk32
Sali HR 61 Lq47
Šali RUS 91 Nc24
Salibabu RI 125 Rd44
Salibabu RI 125 Rd44
Salida USA 235 Eh26
Saliente Alto E 55 Ks53
Saligbé TG 187 La42
Salihler TR 71 Mg51
Salihli TR 71 Mj52
Salihorsk BY 72 Md19
Salikene WAG 186 Kc39
Salikénié SN 186 Kc39
Salima MOC 197 Mj52
Salima MW 203 Mh52
Salima SUD 179 Me35
Salimgarh IND 116 Oh34
Salimi IND 117 Pb36
Salin MYA 120 Ph35
Salina USA 235 Ee26
Salina USA 238 Fb26
Salina Cruz MEX 247 Fc37
Salina Point BS 250 Gc34
Salinas BR 275 Hj54
Salinas EC 268 Fk47
Salinas MEX 244 Eg32
Salinas MEX 247 Fc36
Salinas PE 268 Fk49
Salinas USA 234 Dk27
Salinas de Garci Mendoza BOL 278 Gg55
Salinas de Hidalgo MEX 246 Ek34
Salinas Peak USA 235 Eg29
Salinas Pueblo Missions Nat. Mon. USA 235 Eg28
Salinau RI 129 Qj47
Saline Royale F 53 Lf43
Salinópolis BR 267 Hg46
Salins-les-Bains F 53 Lf44
Salira Indah Beach RI 129 Qd48
Salisbury CDN 240 Gh22
Salisbury GB 49 Kt39
Salisbury USA 241 Gc26
Salisbury USA 242 Fk28
Salisbury Plain GB 49 Kt39
Salispuedas MEX 244 Eb30
Săliște RO 68 Md45
Salistral YV 265 Gh41
Salitral PE 268 Ga48
Salitre BR 273 Hk49
Salitre EC 268 Ga46
Salitrillo MEX 246 Fb36
Salka WAN 188 Lc40
Šalkar KZ 88 Nd09
Salkhad SYR 90 Mj29
Sallanches F 53 Lg45
Sallent E 57 Lb49
Salling DK 42 Lj34
Salliquelo RA 281 Gj64
Sallisaw USA 238 Fc28
Sallisbury Island AUS 145 Rb63
Sallom SUD 185 Mj36
Sallum ET 178 Mc30
Salmana ET 179 Mg30
Salmas IR 91 Nc26
Salme EST 45 Mc32
Salmenkylä FIN 44 Me28
Salmerón E 57 Ks50
Salmiya KWT 93 Ne31
Salmo CDN 232 Eb21
Salmon USA 232 Ed23
Salmon Arm CDN 232 Ea20
Salmon Fork USA/CDN 229 Ck12
Salmon Gums AUS 145 Ra62
Salmon River Mountains USA 232 Ec23
Salmossi BF 181 Kk38
Salo FIN 44 Md30
Salò I 60 Ll45
Salo RCA 190 Lj44
Salon IND 117 Pa32
Salon-de-Provence F 53 Lf47
Salonga Nord, P.N.de la RDC 199 Ma46
Salonga Sud, P.N.de la RDC 199 Ma47
Salonica GR 70 Mc50
Salonta RO 67 Mb44
Salpausselkä FIN 44 Mf29
Sal Rei CV 186 Jj37
Salsacate RA 280 Gh61
Salsbruket N 40 Lm26
Salses-le-Château F 53 Lc48
Salsomaggiore Terme I 60 Lk46
Salta RA 279 Gh58
Salta RA 279 Gg58
Saltaire GB 49 Kt37
Saltash GB 49 Kq40
Saltburn-by-the-Sea GB 49 Ku36
Salt Cay GB 250 Ge35
Saltcoats CDN 233 Ej20
Salt Desert IR 98 Ng28
Saltee Islands IRL 47 Ko38
Saltery Bay CDN 232 Dh21
Saltfjellet-Svartisen n.p. N 38 Lp24
Saltholm DK 42 Ln35
Saltillo MEX 245 Ek33
Salt Lake City USA 235 Ee25
Salto BR 277 Hg57
Salto I 62 Ln48
Salto MEX 244 Eg33
Salto RA 281 Gk63
Salto ROU 276 Hb61
Salto Angel YV 265 Gj42
Salto da Divisa BR 275 Ja54
Salto de Agua MEX 247 Fd37
Salto de Cavalo ANG 198 Lh50
Salto de Eqipantla MEX 247 Fc36
Salto de Las Rosas RA 280 Gf63
Salto del Guairá PY 276 Hc58
Salto del Laja RCH 280 Gd64
Salto de Pirapora BR 277 Hg57
Salto do Jacuí BR 276 Hd60
Salto Hacha YV 265 Gj42
Salton Sea USA 234 Ec29
Salt Plains N.W.R. USA 238 Fa27
Salt Range PK 99 Og29
Salt River Canyon USA 235 Ee29
Salt Springs USA 242 Fk31
Saltstraumen N 38 Lp23
Saltvik FIN 44 Ma30
Saltwater Hot Springs RC 109 Ra34
Salua RI 130 Qk46
Saluda USA 242 Fk29
SalueBesar RI 131 Rb46
Salue Kecil RI 131 Rb47
Salug RP 125 Rb41
Salugan RI 125 Ra45
Salumbar IND 116 Oh33
Salumpaga RI 125 Ra45
Salur IND 117 Pb36
Saluzzo I 60 Lh46
Salvador BR 273 Ja52
Salvaterra BR 267 Hf46
Salvatierra MEX 246 Ek35
Salvatierra-Agurain E 56 Ks48
Salvatierra de los Barros E 55 Ko52
Salween 121 Pk36
Salyan AZ 91 Ne26
Salyersville USA 242 Fj27
Šalyhyne UA 72 Mh20
Salza A 61 Lq43
Salzach A 61 Ln43
Salzach D 59 Ln42
Salzbergwerk A 61 Lo43
Salzburg A 61 Lo43
Salzgitter D 58 Ll38
Salzkotten D 58 Lj39
Salzwedel D 58 Lm38
Sam G 198 Lf45
Sam IND 114 Of32
Sama PE 269 Ge54
Samachique MEX 244 Eg32
Samachvalavičy BY 45 Mh37
Samad OM 95 Nk34
Samad Abag IR 98 Nk29
Samagaltaj RUS 101 Ph20
Sama Grande PE 269 Ge54
Samah KSA 93 Nc31
Samail OM 95 Nj34
Samaipata BOL 278 Gj55
Samakhiali IND 116 Of34
Samako RI 130 Rb46
Samakona CI 187 Kg41
Samakoulou RMM 186 Kf39
Samakro CI 187 Kj43
Samal RP 125 Rc42
Samalayuca MEX 244 Eg30
Samales Group RP 125 Ra43
Samal Island RP 125 Rc42
Samalkot IND 117 Pb37
Samâlût ET 179 Mf31
Samama RI 125 Qk44
Saman PNG 156 Sh51
Samaná DOM 250 Gf36
Samana Cay BS 250 Gd34
Samanco PE 269 Ga50
Samanda IND 120 Pf33
Samandağ TR 90 Mh27
Samangan = Aybak AFG 97 Oe27
Samanlı Dağları TR 69 Mk50
Samar RP 124 Rc40
Sámara CR 248 Fh41
Samarga RUS 111 Rk22
Samari PNG 155 Sb50
Samaria N.P. GR 71 Me55
Samariapo YV 265 Gg43
Samarina GR 70 Mb50
Samarinda RI 129 Qj46
Samarqand UZ 97 Od26
Samarra IRQ 91 Nb28
Samarra IRQ 91 Nb28
Samarskoye KZ 101 Pb21
Samaru WAN 188 Ld40
Samaruma IND 117 Pb34
Samastipur IND 117 Pc33
Samasuma Island PNG 155 Sc46
Samate RI 131 Rf46
Samatiguila CI 187 Kg41
Samatwa EAT 197 Mj48
Samaúma BR 270 Gj46
Şamaxı AZ 91 Ne25
Samba BF 187 Kj39
Samba RCA 190 Lj43
Samba RDC 190 Ma45
Samba RDC 196 Md48
Samba 114 Oh29
Samba Caju ANG 198 Lh50
Sambailo RG 186 Kd39
Sambalgou BF 187 La39
Sambaliung Mountains RI 128 Qj45
Sambalpur IND 117 Pb35
Sambas RI 128 Qe45
Sâmbăta RO 67 Mc44
Sambau RI 127 Qc46
Sambava RM 206 Nf53
Sambhal IND 115 Ok31
Sambhar IND 114 Oh32
Sambialgou BF 187 La39
Sambir UA 67 Md41
Sambo ANG 200 Lj52
Samboja RI 129 Qj46
Samborondón EC 268 Ga46
Sâmbra Oilor RO 67 Md43
Sambro CDN 240 Gj23
Sambuca di Sicilia I 62 Lo53
Samburu EAK 195 Mk47
Samburu National Reserve EAK 194 Mj45
Sambusu NAM 200 Lk54
Sambwa EAT 197 Mj48
Samch'ok ROK 113 Re27
Samch'onp'o ROK 113 Re28
Samding Monastery CHN 102 Pf31
Same EAT 197 Mj48
Samé RMM 180 Ke38
Samen IR 91 Ne28
Samer F 51 Lb40
Samford AUS 149 Sg59
Samfya Z 196 Me51
Samhah YE 95 Ng39
Samharam OM 95 Nh37
Sämi EST 44 Mg31
Sámi GR 70 Ma52
Sami IND 116 Of34
Sami PK 99 Ob32
Sămica BG 69 Me49
Samirah KSA 92 Nb32
Samitah KSA 94 Nb37
Samjiyon PRK 110 Re25
Samka MYA 120 Pj35
Şamkir AZ 91 Nc25
Samlaut W.S. K 123 Qb39
Şamlı TR 71 Mh51
Sammallahdenmäki FIN 44 Mb29
Samnapur IND 117 Pa34
Sam Ngao THA 122 Pk37
Samnu LAR 177 Lh32
Samo PNG 156 Sg47
Samoa ANG 199 Ma50
Samoa 135 Ba11
Samoa Islands WS/USA 134 Ba11
Samobor HR 61 Lq45
Samoeng THA 121 Pk36
Samoëns F 53 Lg44
Samohaji = Vasco da Gama IND 116 Og38
Samokov BG 68 Md48
Samolva RUS 45 Mh32
Samorogouan BF 187 Kh40
Sámos GR 71 Mg53
Sámos GR 71 Mg53
Samos SRB 68 Ma45
Samosir RI 127 Pk44
Samostan Stična SLO 66 Lp45
Samothrake GR 69 Mf50
Samothráki GR 69 Mf50
Samothráki GR 69 Mf50
Samoyé RG 186 Kf42
Sampa GH 187 Kj42
Sampaga RI 130 Qk47
Sampaka RI 125 Rb45
Sampanahan RI 129 Qj47
Sampang RI 129 Qg49
Sampano RI 130 Ra47
Sampelga BF 187 La39
Samphamit Falls K/LAO 123 Qc38
Sampit RI 129 Qg47
Sampun PNG 156 Sg48
Sampwe RDC 196 Md50
Samrala IND 114 Oj30
Samraong K 123 Qb38
Samreboi GH 187 Kj43
Samro RUS 44 Mj32
Samsang CHN 102 Pb30
Samsø DK 42 Ll35
Samson USA 239 Fh30
Sam Son VN 121 Qc36
Samsong Temple PRK 112 Rc26
Samson Ind. Res. CDN 233 Ed19
Samsu TR 91 Nb26
Samsun TR 90 Mj25
Samtens D 58 Lo36
Samthar IND 117 Ok33
Samtredia GE 91 Nb24
Samucumbi ANG 200 Lk52
Samuda RI 129 Qg47
Samuhú RA 279 Gk59
Samulondo RDC 199 Mb50
Samundri PK 99 Og30
Samur AFG 98 Oa30
Samurai Houses J 111 Sa26
Samut Prakan THA 122 Qa39
Samut Sakhon THA 122 Qa39
Samut Songkhram THA 122 Qa39
Samye Monastery CHN 103 Pf31
San RMM 187 Kh39
Sanaa YE 94 Nc38
Sanaba BF 187 Kj39
Sanabria CO 264 Gb44
Sanadinovo BG 69 Me47
SANAE IV 287 Kd33
Sanaga CAM 188 Lf44
San Agustin YV 265 Gg42
San Agustín de Valle Fértil RA 280 Gg61
Sanak USA 228 Bj18
Sanak Island USA 228 Bj18
Sanak Islands USA 228 Bj18
San Alberto PY 276 Hc58
San Alejandro PE 269 Gc50
Sanam Abu Dom SUD 185 Mf36
Sanamxai LAO 123 Qd38
Sanana RI 131 Rd47
Sanana RI 131 Rd47
Sanand IND 116 Og34
Sanandağ IR 91 Nd28
Sanando RMM 187 Kg39
Sânandrei RO 68 Mb45
San Andrés C 243 Gb35
San Andrés CO 249 Fk39
San Andrés CO 249 Fk39
San Andrés E 174 Kb31
San Andrés GCA 247 Ff37
San Andres RP 124 Rb39
San Andres RP 124 Rc39
San Andrés de Giles RA 281 Ha63
San Andrés Tuxtla MEX 247 Fc36
Sananduva BR 276 He59
San Angelo USA 238 Ek30
Sanankoroba RMM 187 Kg39
San Antón PE 269 Ge53
San Antonio BH 248 Ff37
San Antonio C 243 Ga35
San Antonio CO 264 Ga45
San Antonio MEX 244 Ef34
San Antonio MEX 244 Eg30
San Antonio MEX 245 Fa33
San Antonio RA 279 Gh60
San Antonio RA 280 Gg62
San Antonio RCH 280 Ge62
San Antonio USA 235 Eg29
San Antonio USA 245 Fa31
San Antonio YV 265 Gg44
San Antonio YV 265 Gj42
San Antonio de Areco RA 281 Ha63
San Antonio de Caparo YV 264 Ge42
San Antonio de Esquilache PE 269 Ge54
San Antonio de Getucha CO 264 Gc45
San Antonio del Mar MEX 244 Eb30
San Antonio de los Cobres RA 279 Gg58
San Antonio del Parapeti BOL 278 Gj55
San Antonio del Sur C 250 Gc35
San Antonio de Táchira YV 264 Gd42
San Antonio de Tamanaco YV 265 Gg41
San Antonio Mts. USA 235 Eh29
San Antonio Oeste RA 280 Gh66
San Antonio Rayon MEX 246 Fa34
Sanarate GCA 248 Fe38
Sanare YV 265 Gf40
Sanaré YV 265 Gf41
Sanaroa Island PNG 156 Sf50
Sanary-sur-Mer F 53 Lf47
Sanasombun LAO 123 Qc38
San Augustin CO 264 Gb44
San Augustin MEX 244 Ec31
San Augustin RP 124 Rb39
San Augustine USA 238 Fc30
Sanaw OM 95 Nj34
Sanaw YE 95 Nf37
Sanawad IND 116 Oj34
San Bartolo BOL 278 Gg53
San Bartolo MEX 246 Ek34
San Bartolo PA 249 Fk41
San Bartolo PE 269 Gb52
San Bartolomé de la Torre E 55 Kn53
San Bartolomé de Tirajana E 174 Kc32
San Bartolomeo in Galdo I 63 Lq49
San Bautista ROU 281 Hc63
Sanbei Yangshan CHN 106 Qd26
San Benedetto del Tronto I 61 Lo48
San Benedetto Po I 60 Ll45
San Benito NIC 248 Fg39
San Benito USA 245 Fb32
San Benito Abad CO 264 Gc41
San Benito Mtn. USA 234 Dk27
San Bernado RA 281 Gk64
San Bernardino USA 234 Eb28
San Bernardino de Milpillas Chico MEX 245 Eh34
San Bernard N.W.R. USA 245 Fc31
San Bernardo MEX 244 Ef32
San Bernardo MEX 245 Eh32
San Bernardo RA 279 Gk59
San Bernardo del Viento CO 264 Gc41
San Blas MEX 244 Ef32
San Blas MEX 245 Ek32
San Blas MEX 246 Eh35
San Borja BOL 278 Gg53
San Borjitas MEX 244 Ed32
San Buenaventura MEX 245 Ek32
Sanca CDN 232 Eb21
Sancak TR 91 Na26
San Carlos CR 249 Fh40
San Carlos GQ 188 Le44
San Carlos MEX 244 Ec31
San Carlos MEX 244 Ed33
San Carlos MEX 244 Ee32
San Carlos MEX 245 Ek31
San Carlos NIC 249 Fh40
San Carlos PA 249 Ga41
San Carlos PY 274 Hb57
San Carlos RA 276 Hc59
San Carlos RA 279 Gh58
San Carlos RA 280 Gf62
San Carlos RCH 280 Ge64
San Carlos ROU 281 Hc63
San Carlos RP 124 Ra38
San Carlos RP 124 Rb40
San Carlos USA 235 Ee29
San Carlos YV 265 Gf41
San Carlos de Bariloche RA 280 Ge66
San Carlos de Bolívar RA 281 Gk64
San Carlos de Guaroa CO 264 Gd44
San Carlos del Zulia YV 264 Ge41
San Carlos de Río Negro YV 265 Gg45
San Carlos Ind. Res. USA 235 Ee29
San Carlos Park USA 243 Fk32
San Cataldo I 62 Lo53
San Cataldo I 63 Lt50
San Cayetano CO 264 Gc43
San Cayetano RA 281 Ha65
Sancerre F 53 Lc43
Sancha CHN 106 Qf26
Sancha CHN 108 Qe33
Sanchahe CHN 110 Rc23
Sanchakou CHN 100 Ok26
Sánchez DOM 250 Gf36
Sánchez, Cerro RA 282 Gf71
Sanchi IND 116 Oj34
Sanchi IND 116 Oj34
Sanchidrián E 54 Kq50
Sanchor IND 116 Of33
San Christobal DOM 250 Ge36
San Christoval Range CDN 230 De19
San Cirilo, Cerro PE 268 Ga49
San Ciro de Acosta MEX 246 Fa35
San Clemente E 57 Ks51
San Clemente RCH 280 Ge63
San Clemente = Cerro San Valentín RCH 282 Gd69
San Clemente USA 234 Eb29
San Clemente del Tuyú RA 281 Hb64
San Clemente Island USA 234 Ea29
Sanclerlândia BR 274 He54
Sancoins F 53 Lc44
Sancos PE 269 Gd53
San Cosme y Damián PY 276 Hb59
San Cristóbal BOL 278 Gg56
San Cristóbal RA 279 Gk61
San Cristóbal RCH 279 Gf57
San Cristóbal YV 264 Gd42
San Cristóbal de Entreviñas E 54 Kp48
San Cristóbal de la Barranca MEX 246 Ej35
San Cristóbal de las Casas MEX 247 Fd37
Sancti Spíritu RA 281 Gj63
Sancti-Spíritus C 243 Ga35
Sancti-Spíritus E 54 Ko50
Sanctuaire de Mont Iboundji G 198 Lf46
Sančursk RUS 72 Nd17
Sand N 42 Lg31
Sand N 42 Lm30
Sanda FIN 44 Ma30
Sandai RI 129 Qf46
Sandakan MAL 125 Qk43
Sandal EAK 194 Mh45
Sandama RMM 186 Kf39
Sandan K 123 Qd39
Sandando ANG 201 Ma51
Sandane N 40 Lg29
San Daniele di Friuli I 61 Lo44
Sandanski BG 68 Md49
Sandaré RMM 180 Ke38
Sanday GB 48 Ks31
Sandbach GB 49 Ks37
Sandbanks Prov. Park CDN 241 Gb23
Sandberg ZA 204 Lk62
Sande D 58 Lj37
Sandefjord N 42 Ll31
Sandégué CI 187 Kj42
Sandema GH 187 Kk40
Sanderao IND 116 Og33
Sandercock Nunataks 287 Nc32
Sanderk IR 98 Nj32
Sanders USA 235 Ef28
Sanderson USA 245 Ej30
Sandersville USA 242 Fj29
Sandfire Flat AUS 142 Ra55
Sandgerði IS 46 Js26
Sandhammeren S 43 Lp35
Sand Hill BH 248 Ff37
Sandhill USA 239 Ff29
Sand Hills GUY 266 Ha42
Sand Hills USA 236 Ek24
Sandi SUD 185 Mg37
Sandia PE 278 Gf53
San Diego USA 234 Eb29
San Diego USA 245 Fa32
San Diego de Alcalá MEX 245 Eh31
San Diego de Cabrutica YV 265 Gh41
San Diego de la Unión MEX 246 Ek35
Sandıklı TR 90 Mf26
Sandila IND 117 Pa32
Sandilands Prov. Forest CDN 236 Fb21
Sandiman, Mount AUS 144 Qh58
Sanding RI 127 Qa47
Sandino C 243 Fh34
Sand in Taufers = Campo Túres I 60 Lm44
San Dionisio RP 109 Ra36
Sandl A 66 Lq42
Sandnes N 42 Lf32
Sandnessjøen N 38 Ln24
Sando MOC 203 Mh54
Sandoa RDC 199 Mb50
Sandoméri GR 70 Mb53
Sandomierz PL 65 Mb40
Sandön FIN 44 Mb27
San Donà di Piave I 61 Ln45
Sandougou CI 187 Kh42
Sandovo RUS 72 Mj16
Sandoway MYA 120 Ph36
Sandoy DK 46 Ko29
Sandøysund N 42 Ll31
Sandpit CDN 230 De19
Sand Point USA 228 Bk18
Sandpoint USA 232 Eb21
Sandrakatsy RM 206 Ne54
Sandrandahy RM 207 Nd56
Sandray GB 48 Kn34
Sandringham AUS 148 Rk58
Šandrivka UA 73 Mh21
Sand Springs USA 233 Eg22
Sand Springs USA 238 Fb27
Sandstad N 40 Lk27
Sandstone AUS 144 Qj59
Sandur IND 118 Oj38
Sandusky USA 237 Fj24
Sandusky USA 237 Fj25
Sandu Suizu CHN 108 Qd32
Sandveld Nature Reserve ZA 205 Mc59
Sandverhaar NAM 204 Lj59
Sandvik S 43 Lr33
Sandvika N 40 Lo26
Sandviken S 43 Lr30
Sandvikvåg N 42 Lf31
Sandwich GB 49 Lb39
Sandwich USA 237 Ff25
Sandwich Bay NAM 204 Lh57
Sandwich Harbour NAM 204 Lh57
Sandwip Island BD 120 Pf34
Sandy GB 49 Ku38
Sandy USA 235 Ee25
Sandy Bar CDN 236 Fb19
Sandy Bay NZ 152 Th63
Sandy Bay Ind. Res. CDN 236 Fa20
Sandy Bight AUS 145 Rb62
Sandy Cape AUS 149 Sg58
Sandy Cape AUS 151 Sc66
Sandy Cove CDN 241 Hb20
Sandy Desert PK 99 Ob31
Sandy Hills USA 238 Fc29
Sandykachi TM 96 Ob27
Sandy Lake CDN 227 Fb08
Sandy Lake CDN 231 Ed18
Sandy Lake CDN 241 Hb21
Sandy Point BS 243 Gb32
Sandy Point GB 250 Gd35
Sandy Point IND 122 Pg40
Sandy's Beach USA 234 Cb35
Sané RMM 181 Kk37
San Estanislao CO 264 Gc40
San Estanislao PY 276 Hb58
San Esteban HN 248 Fh38
San Esteban de Gormaz E 54 Kr49
San Evaristo MEX 244 Ee33
San Faustino MEX 244 Eb29
San Felipe CO 264 Gc40
San Felipe CO 265 Gg45
San Felipe MEX 244 Ec30
San Felipe MEX 246 Ek35
San Felipe RCH 280 Ge62
San Felipe YV 265 Gf40
San Felipe de Jesús MEX 244 Eg32
San Felipe de Vichayal PE 268 Fk48
San Felipe Jalapa de Díaz MEX 246 Fb36
San Felipe Nuevo Mercurio MEX 245 Ej33
San Félix RCH 279 Ge60
San Félix ROU 276 Ha62
San Félix YV 264 Ge40
San Ferdinando di Púglia I 63 Lq49
Sanfermines E 56 Kt48
San Fermin MEX 245 Eh32
San Fernando E 55 Ko54
San Fernando MEX 245 Fa33
San Fernando RCH 280 Ge63
San Fernando RP 124 Ra37
San Fernando RP 124 Ra38
San Fernando TT 251 Gk40
San Fernando de Apure YV 265 Gg42
San Fernando de Atabapo YV 265 Gg43
San Fernando del Valle de Catamarca RA 279 Gh60
Sånfjällets n.p. S 40 Lo28
Sanford CDN 236 Fb21
Sanford USA 241 Ge24
Sanford USA 242 Fk31
Sanford USA 242 Ga28
Sanford, Mount USA 229 Ch14
San Francesco d'Arezzo I 60 Lm47
San Francisco BOL 278 Gh53
San Francisco BOL 278 Gh54
San Francisco MEX 245 Eh32
San Francisco PA 249 Fk41
San Francisco PE 269 Gd52
San Francisco RA 279 Gj61
San Francisco RP 124 Rb39
San Francisco RP 125 Rc41
San Francisco USA 234 Dj27
San Francisco YV 265 Gk43
San Francisco de Becerra HN 248 Fg38
San Francisco de Bellocq RA 281 Gk65
San Francisco de Borja MEX 244 Eg32
San Francisco de la Paz HN 248 Fg38
San Francisco del Chañar RA 279 Gj60
San Francisco del Laishi RA 276 Ha59
San Francisco del Monte de Oro RA 280 Gg62
San Francisco del Rincón MEX 246 Ek35
San Francisco de Mostazal RCH 280 Ge62
San Francisco Gotera ES 248 Ff39
San Francisquito MEX 244 Ed31
San Fratello I 63 Lp52
Sang GH 187 Kk41
Sanga ANG 200 Lh51
Sanga BF 187 La40
Sanga = Makaloge MOC 196 Mh52
Sanga RMM 181 Kj38
San Gabriel EC 268 Gb45
San Gabriel Mts. USA 234 Ea28
Sangala G 198 Lf46
San Galgano I 60 Lm47
Sangali IND 119 Ok38
San Gallan PE 269 Gb52
Sangam (Allahabad) IND 117 Pa33
Sangameshwar IND 116 Og37
Sangamner IND 116 Oh36
Sangan IR 98 Oa28
Sanganeb Atoll Marine N.P. SUD 185 Mj36
Sangar IR 91 Ne27
Sangar RUS 89 Rb06
Sangarafa RIM 180 Kd37
Sangardo RG 186 Ke41
Sangareddi IND 116 Oj37
Sangarhi IND 117 Pa35
Sangasanga RI 129 Qj46
Sangaste EST 45 Mg33
Sangatanga G 198 Le46
San Gavino Monreale I 62 Lj51
Sangay, P.N. EC 268 Ga46
Sangay, Volcán EC 268 Ga47
Sangazi TR 90 Me25
Sangbé CAM 189 Lg42
Sangbor AFG 98 Ob28
Sangcharak = Tokzar AFG 97 Od28
Sang Chom THA 121 Qb36
Sange RDC 196 Me49
Sangeang RI 130 Qk50
San Genaro Norte RA 281 Gk62
Sangenjo = Sanxenxo E 54 Km48
Sângeorgiu de Pădure RO 67 Me44
Sângeorz-Băi RO 67 Me43
Sanger USA 234 Ea27
Sângerei MD 73 Me22
Sangerfield USA 241 Gc24
San Gergorio RA 281 Gj63
Sangerhausen D 58 Lm39
San Germán USA 251 Gg36
Sângeru RO 69 Mg45
Sanggau RI 129 Qf45
Sanghar PK 99 Oe32
Sangihe RI 125 Rc44
San Gil CO 264 Gd42
San Gimignano I 60 Lm47
Sangin AFG 99 Oc29
San Giovanni I 60 Ll48
San Giovanni di Sinis I 62 Lj51
San Giovanni in Fiore I 63 Lr51
San Giovanni in Persiceto I 60 Lm46
San Giovanni Rotondo I 63 Lq49
San Giovanni Valdarno I 60 Lm47
Sangiran RI 129 Qf49
San Giuliano Terme I 60 Ll47
San Giusto di Trieste I 61 Lo45
Sangiyn Dalay MNG 101 Pj23
Sangiyn Dalay MNG 104 Qc22
Sangkhla Buri THA 122 Pk38
Sangkulirang RI 128 Qj45
Sangkum Andet K 123 Qd39
Sangla EST 45 Mg32
Sanglang CHN 108 Qd33
Sangli IND 116 Oh37
Sanglia Dol RI 131 Rf49
Sangmelima CAM 189 Lg44
Sango ZW 202 Mf56
Sangod IND 116 Oj33
Sangola IND 116 Oh37
Sangolqui EC 268 Ga46
Sangoshe RB 201 Mb55
Sangouani CI 187 Kg41
Sangouiné CI 186 Kg42
Sangowo RI 125 Re44
Sangradouro Volta Grande, T.I. BR 274 Hd53
Sangre de Christo Mts. USA 235 Eh27
Sangre de Cristo Mts. USA 235 Eh27
San Gregorio PE 269 Gd50
San Gregorio Carrio ROU 276 Hb62
San Gregorio de Polanco ROU 276 Hc62
Sangre Grande TT 251 Gk40
Sangrur IND 114 Oh30
Sangsang CHN 102 Pd31
Sangsit RI 129 Qh50
Sangüesa E 56 Kt48
Sanguéya RG 186 Kc40
Sanguiana RG 186 Ke40
San Guillermo, P.N. RA 279 Gf60
Sanguily C 243 Ga35
Sangun IR 93 Nf30
Sangwali NAM 201 Mb55
Sangzhi CHN 108 Qf31
Sanhe CHN 105 Ra20
Sanhe CHN 108 Qd32
Sanhuizhen CHN 108 Qd30
Sâni RIM 180 Ke37
Sanibel USA 243 Fj32
Sanibel Island USA 243 Fj32
San Ignacio BH 248 Ff37
San Ignacio CR 249 Fh41
San Ignacio MEX 244 Ed32
San Ignacio MEX 244 Ef33
San Ignacio MEX 244 Eg34
San Ignacio MEX 245 Fa32
San Ignacio MEX 246 Ek34
San Ignacio PE 268 Ga48
San Ignacio de Moxos BOL 278 Gh53
San Ignacio de Velasco BOL 278 Gk54
San Ignacio Guazú PY 276 Hb59
San Ignacio Mini RA 276 Hc59
San Ignacio Mini RA 276 Hc59
San Ignacio Rio Muerto MEX 244 Ee32
San'in-kaigan N.P. J 113 Rh28
Sanipah RI 129 Qj47
Sani Pass LS/ZA 205 Me60
San Isidro NIC 248 Fg39
San Isidro RA 279 Gh60
San Isidro RA 281 Ha63
San Isidro RP 124 Rc39
San Isidro RP 125 Rd42
San Isidro de El General CR 249 Fj41
San Isidro del Curuguaty PY 276 Hc58
Sanitz D 58 Ln36
Saniyat ad Daffah LAR 178 Mc30
San Jacinto PE 268 Fk47
San Jacinto PE 268 Fk48
San Jacinto RP 124 Rb39
San Jaime de la Frontera RA 276 Ha61
San Javier BOL 278 Gh53
San Javier E 57 Ku53
San Javier MEX 244 Ee33
San Javier MEX 247 Fe37
San Javier RA 276 Ha61
San Javier RA 276 Hc59
San Javier RCH 280 Ge63
San Javier ROU 276 Ha62
Sanjay Gandhi N.P. IND 116 Og36
San Jerónimo MEX 245 Ej33
San Jerónimo MEX 246 Fb35
Sanjia CHN 108 Qf35
Sanjiang CHN 108 Qe33
Sanjiangkou CHN 121 Qa32
Sanjiaotang CHN 109 Ra31
Sanjo J 111 Rk27
San Joaquim BR 267 Hf46
San Joaquín BOL 278 Gh52
San Joaquín, Cerro EC 269 Ff46
San Joaquín MEX 246 Fa35
San Joaquín RP 124 Rb40
San Joaquin Valley USA 234 Ea27
San Jorge CO 265 Gf42
San Jorge NIC 248 Fh40
San Jorge RA 281 Gk61
San Jorge ROU 276 Hc62
San Jorge Island SOL 157 Sk50
San José CO 264 Gb45
San José CR 249 Fh41
San José E 55 Ks54
San José HN 248 Fg38
San José PY 276 Hb58
San José RA 276 Hc59
San José RA 279 Gg59
San José RA 279 Gh60
San Jose RP 124 Ra37
San Jose RP 124 Ra38
San Jose RP 124 Ra39
San Jose RP 124 Rb39
San Jose USA 234 Dk27
San José YV 265 Gf42
San Jose de Buenavista RP 124 Ra40
San José de Buja YV 265 Gj41
San José de Chimbo EC 268 Ga46
San José de Chiquitos BOL 278 Gk54
San José de Comondú MEX 244 Ee32
San José de Feliciano RA 276 Ha61
San José de Gracia MEX 244 Ed32
San José de Guaribe YV 265 Gh41
San José de Jáchal RA 279 Gf61
San José de la Costa YV 265 Gf40
San José de la Dormida RA 279 Gj61
San José de la Esquina RA 281 Gk62
San José de La Mariquina RCH 280 Gd65
San José de la Piedra MEX 244 Ec31
San José de las Lajas C 243 Fj34
San José de las Palomas MEX 244 Ec31
San José de las Salinas RA 279 Gh60
San José del Bocay NIC 248 Fh39
San José del Cabo MEX 244 Ef34
San José del Guaviare CO 264 Gd44
San José del Monte RP 124 Ra38
San José del Morro RA 280 Gh62
San José de los Molinos PE 269 Gc52
San José de Lourdes PE 268 Ga48
San José del Palmar CO 264 Gb43
San José del Progreso MEX 246 Fb37
San José de Maipo RCH 280 Ge62
San José de Mayo ROU 281 Hb63
San José de Moradillas MEX 244 Ee31
San José de Ocoa DOM 250 Ge36
San José de Pimas MEX 244 Ee31
San José de Quero PE 269 Gc52
San José de Tiznados YV 265 Gg41
San Jose Island USA 245 Fb32
San José, Volcán RA/RCH 280 Gf62
San Juán CR/NIC 249 Fh40
San Juan DOM 250 Ge36
San Juan PE 269 Gc53
San Juan RA 280 Gf61
San Juan RA 280 Gf61
San Juan RCH 279 Gf57
San Juan RP 124 Rb39
San Juan USA 229 Cf15
San Juan USA 251 Gg36
San Juan YV 264 Gd40
San Juan Batista RCH 269 Ga62
San Juan Bautista PY 276 Hb59
San Juán de Arama CO 264 Gd44
San Juán de Flores HN 248 Fg38
San Juan de Guadalupe MEX 245 Ej33
San Juán del César CO 264 Gd40
San Juán de Limay NIC 248 Fg39
San Juán de los Cayos YV 265 Gf40
San Juan de los Lagos MEX 244 Ec30
San Juan de los Lagos MEX 246 Ej35
San Juán de los Morros YV 265 Gg41
San Juan del Río MEX 244 Ef30
San Juan del Río MEX 245 Eh33
San Juan del Río MEX 246 Fa35
San Juan del Sur NIC 248 Fh40
San Juan de Manapiare YV 265 Gg43
San Juán de Payara YV 265 Gg42
San Juán de Urabá CO 264 Gb41
San Juán de Yanac PE 269 Gc52
San Juan Evangelista MEX 247 Fc37
San Juanico MEX 244 Ed32
San Juanito MEX 244 Eg32
San Juan Ixcaquixtla MEX 246 Fb36
San Juan Mts. USA 235 Eg27
San Juán Nepomuceno CO 264 Gc41
San Juan Nepomuceno PY 276 Hc59
San Juan N.H.P. USA 232 Dj21
San Juan y Martinez C 243 Fj34
San Justo RA 279 Gk61
San Justo RA 281 Ha63
Sankadiokro CI 187 Kj42
Sankanbiaiwa, Mount WAL 186 Ke41
Sankarayinarkovil IND 118 Oj41
Sankaridrug IND 118 Oj40
Sankeshwar IND 116 Oh37
Sankha THA 123 Qb38
Sankosh BHT 120 Pf32
Sankra IND 114 Of32
Sankt Andrä A 61 Lp44
Sankt Anna S 43 Lr32
Sankt Annen in Annaberg-Buchholz D 59 Ln40
Sankt Anton A 60 Ll43
Sankt Brigitta FIN 41 Mc27
Sankt Efrasinnia monastyr BY 72 Me18
Sankt Elisabeth in Marburg D 58 Lj40
Sankt Florian A 66 Lp42
Sankt Gallen CH 60 Lk43
Sankt Georgen D 59 Lj42
Sankt Georg in Wiener Neustadt A 61 Lr43
Sankt Gilgen A 61 Lo43
Sankt Goar D 59 Lh40
Sankt Gotthard CH 60 Lj44
Sankt Ingbert D 59 Lh41
Sankt Jakob A 60 Ln44
Sankt Johann A 60 Ln43
Sankt Johann A 61 Lo43
Sankt Leon-Rot D 59 Lj41
Sankt Margrethen CH 60 Lk43
Sankt Martin CH 60 Lk44
Sankt Michael BY 72 Md19
Sankt Michaelisdonn D 58 Lk36
Sankt Moritz CH 60 Lk44
Sankt Peter-Ording D 58 Lj36
Sankt Pölten A 66 Lq42
Sankt Sophia BY 72 Me18
Sankt Ulrich = Ortisei I 60 Lm44
Sankt Valentin A 66 Lp42
Sankt Veit an der Glan A 61 Lp44
Sankt Vika S 43 Ls32
Sankt Wendel D 59 Lh41
Sankuru RDC 199 Ma48
San Leo I 60 Ln47
San Leonardo de Yagüe E 54 Kr49
Sanlifan CHN 109 Qh30
Şanlıurfa TR 90 Mk27
San Lorenzo BOL 278 Ha54
San Lorenzo EC 268 Fk46
San Lorenzo EC 268 Ga45
San Lorenzo HN 248 Fg39
San Lorenzo Tenochtitlan MEX 247 Fc37
San Lorenzo, Cerro PE 268 Ga49
San Lorenzo PE 270 Gf51
San Lorenzo PY 276 Hb58
San Lorenzo RA 276 Ha60
San Lorenzo RA 281 Gk62
San Lorenzo de Calatrava E 55 Kr52
San Lorenzo de El Escorial E 55 Kq50
San Lorenzo de El Escorial E 55 Kq50
San Lorenzo de la Parrilla E 57 Ks51
San Lourdes BOL 270 Gf51
Sanlúcar de Barrameda E 55 Ko54
Sanlúcar de Guadiana E 55 Kn53
San Lucas BOL 278 Gh56
San Lucas MEX 244 Ef34
San Lucas USA 234 Dk27
San Lucas de Abajo MEX 245 Ej33
San Lúcido I 63 Lr51
San Luis C 250 Gc35
San Luis CO 264 Gc42
San Luis GCA 247 Ff37
San Luis MEX 244 Ec31
San Luis PE 269 Gb50
San Luis RA 280 Gg62
San Luis RA 280 Gg63
San Luis RCH 279 Gf59
San Luis USA 234 Ec29
San Luis USA 235 Eh27
San Luis al Medio ROU 276 Hd62
San Luis de la Loma MEX 246 Ek37
San Luis de la Paz MEX 246 Ek35
San Luis del Cordero MEX 245 Eh33
San Luis de Montagnes Belos BR 274 He54
San Luis de Palmar RA 276 Ha59
San Luis de Shuaro PE 269 Gc51
San Luis Gonzaga MEX 244 Ee33
San Luis Obispo USA 234 Dk28
San Luis Potosí MEX 246 Ek34
San Luis Potosí MEX 246 Ek34
San Luis Río Colorado MEX 244 Ec29
San Luis Valley USA 235 Eh27
Sanluri I 62 Lj51
San Manuel USA 235 Ee29
San Marcelino RP 124 Ra38
San Marco I 60 Ln45
San Marco MEX 247 Fe37
San Marco in Lámis I 63 Lq49
San Marcos BR 267 Hf46
San Marcos CO 264 Gc41
San Marcos MEX 246 Fa37
San Marcos MEX 246 Fa37
San Marcos PE 268 Ga49
San Marcos USA 245 Fb31
San Mariano RP 124 Rb37
San Marino AUS 148 Rh60
San Marino RSM 60 Ln47
San Marino RSM 60 Ln47
San Martín BOL 278 Gj52
San Martín RA 279 Gh60
San Martín RA 280 Gf62
San Martín 287 Gc32
San Martín 1 RA 276 Ha58
San Martín 2 RA 276 Ha58
San Martín de Frómista E 54 Kq48
San Martín de los Andes RA 280 Ge66
San Martín del Pimpollar E 55 Kp50
San Martín de Montalbán E 55 Kq51
San Martín de Valdeiglesias E 55 Kq50
San Martino di Castrozza I 60 Lm44
San Martín Texmelucan MEX 246 Fa36
San Mateo CR 249 Fh41
San Mateo EC 268 Fk46
San Mateo USA 234 Dj27
San Mateo USA 235 Eg28
San Mateo YV 265 Gh41
San Mateo Ixtatán GCA 248 Fe38
San Matías BOL 278 Ha54
Sanmaur CDN 240 Gd22
Sanmen CHN 109 Ra31
Sanmenxia CHN 106 Qf28
San Miguel BOL 278 Gk54
San Miguel CO 268 Gb45
San Miguel CO 268 Ge45
San Miguel CO/EC 268 Gb45
San Miguel ES 248 Ff39
San Miguel MEX 245 Ej31
San Miguel MEX 246 Ej35
San Miguel PA 249 Ga41
San Miguel PE 268 Ga49
San Miguel PE 269 Gd52
San Miguel RA 276 Hb59
San Miguel RA 280 Gg62
San Miguel RA 281 Ha63
San Miguel RP 124 Ra38
San Miguel RP 124 Rd41
San Miguel USA 234 Dk28
San Miguel USA 235 Ee30
San Miguel de Allende MEX 246 Ek35
San Miguel de Azapa RCH 278 Ge55
San Miguel de Baga C 243 Gb35
San Miguel de Huachi BOL 278 Gg53
San Miguel del Cantil MEX 244 Eg33
San Miguel del Monte RA 281 Ha63
San Miguel de Salinas E 57 Ku53
San Miguel de Temoaya MEX 245 Eh34
San Miguel de Tucumán RA 279 Gh59
San Miguel do Araguaia BR 272 He52
San Miguelito HN 248 Ff38
San Miguelito MEX 244 Ef30
San Miguelito NIC 249 Fh40
San Miguelito PA 249 Ga41
San Miguel Palmas MEX 246 Fa35
San Miguel Suchixtepec MEX 247 Fb37
Sânmihaiu de Câmpie RO 67 Me44
Sanming CHN 109 Qj32
San Miniato I 60 Ll47
Sänna EST 45 Mg33
Sanna IND 117 Pb34
San Narciso RP 124 Rb39
Sannaspos ZA 205 Md60
San Nicandro Gargánico I 63 Lq49
San Nicolás BOL 278 Gh53
San Nicolás MEX 244 Ef31
San Nicolás de la Joya MEX 244 Eg32
San Nicolás de los Arrocos RA 281 Gk62
San Nicolás de los Garza MEX 245 Ek33
San Nicolas Island USA 234 Ea29
Sânnicolau Mare RO 67 Ma44
Sannieshof ZA 205 Mc59
Sanniki PL 65 Lu38
Sannohe J 111 Sa25
Sannou RG 186 Kd40
Sanok PL 65 Mc41
Sanokwelle LB 186 Kf42
San Onofre CO 264 Gc41
San Onofre USA 234 Eb29
Šanovo BG 69 Mf48
Sanoyie LB 186 Kf42
San Pablo CO 264 Gb45
San Pablo CO 264 Gd42
San Pablo EC 268 Ga46
San Pablo PE 268 Ga49
San Pablo RP 124 Ra38
San Pablo YV 265 Gg42
San Pablo de Huacareta BOL 278 Gj56
San Pablo de Lipez BOL 279 Gg56
San Paolo fuori le Mura I 62 Ln49
San Pascual RP 124 Rb39

San Pedro ◻ BH 248 Fg37
San Pédro ◻ CI 187 Kg43
San Pedro ◻ E 55 Ka52
San Pedro ◻ MEX 244 Ed31
San Pedro ◻ PA 269 Ge51
San Pedro ◻ RA 276 Hc59
San Pedro ◻ RA 279 Gh58
San Pedro ◻ RA 279 Gh59
San Pedro ◻ RCH 280 Gd64
San Pedro ◻ YV 265 Gg43
San Pedro Amuzgos ◻ MEX 246 Fa37
San Pedro de Atacama ◻ RCH 279 Gf57
San Pedro de Buena Vista ◻ BOL 278 Gh55
San Pedro de Cachí ◻ PE 269 Gc52
San Pedro de Colalao ◻ RA 279 Gh59
San Pedro de Coris ◻ PE 269 Gc52
San Pedro de la Roca Castle = El Morro ◻ ◻ C 250 Gc35
San Pedro de las Colonias ◻ MEX 245 Ej33
San Pedro de la Soledad ◻ MEX 244 Ef34
San Pedro de Lloc ◻ PE 268 Ga49
San Pedro del Norte ◻ NIC 249 Fh39
San Pedro del Paraná ◻ PY 276 Hb59
San Pedro del Pinatar ◻ E 57 Ku53
San Pedro de Quemez ◻ BOL 278 Gf56
San Pedro de Ycuamandiyú ◻ PY 276 Hb58
San Pedro d.M. ◻ DOM 250 Gf36
San Pedro Juchatengo ◻ MEX 246 Fb37
San Pedro Norte ◻ RA 279 Gh61
San Pedro Sula ◻ HN 248 Ff38
San Pedro Tapanatepec ◻ MEX 247 Fc37
San Pedro Totolapan ◻ MEX 247 Fb37
San Pedro, Volcán ◻ RCH 279 Gf56
Sanpoku ◻ J 111 Rk26
San Policarpio ◻ RP 124 Rc39
Sanqiao ◻ CHN 108 Qd31
Sanquhar ◻ GB 48 Kr35
Sansanné, P.N. ◻ CO 264 Ga44
San Quintin ◻ MEX 244 Ec30
San Quintin ◻ MEX 247 Fe37
San Quirico d'Orcia ◻ I 60 Lm47
San Rafael ◻ BOL 278 Gf52
San Rafael ◻ BOL 278 Gh54
San Rafael ◻ ◻ BOL 278 Gb54
San Rafael ◻ CO 265 Gg46
San Rafael ◻ CR 249 Fh40
San Rafael ◻ EC 268 Gb46
San Rafael ◻ MEX 245 Ek33
San Rafael ◻ PE 269 Gb51
San Rafael ◻ RA 280 Gf63
San Rafael ◻ YV 264 Ge40
San Rafael de Atamaica ◻ YV 265 Gg42
San Rafael de Canagua ◻ YV 264 Ge41
San Rafael de Imataca ◻ YV 265 Gk42
San Rafael Desert ◻ USA 235 Ee26
San Rafael Glacier ◻ RCH 282 Gd69
San Rafael Knob ◻ USA 235 Ee26
San Ramón ◻ BOL 278 Gh52
San Ramón ◻ BOL 278 Gj53
San Ramón ◻ C 243 Gb35
San Ramón ◻ CR 249 Fh40
San Ramón ◻ MEX 247 Ft35
San Ramón ◻ PE 268 Gb48
San Ramón ◻ PE 269 Gc51
San Ramón ◻ RA 279 Gg61
San Ramón ◻ ROU 281 He57
San Ramón ◻ RP 125 Ra42
San Ramon de la Nueva Orán ◻ RA 279 Gh57
San Remigio ◻ RP 124 Rb40
San Remo ◻ AUS 151 Sc65
San Remo ◻ I 60 Lh47
San Rolando ◻ E 55 Kp54
San Roque ◻ RP 124 Rc39
Sans Souci, Citadelle/ ◻ ◻ RH 250 Gd36
San Saba ◻ USA 238 Fa30
Sansalé ◻ RG 186 Kc40
San Salvador ◻ BS 250 Gc33
San Salvador ◻ ◻ ES 248 Ff39
San Salvador ◻ PE 268 Gd47
San Salvador ◻ RA 276 Ha61
San Salvador de Jujuy ◻ RA 279 Gh58
San Salvador El Seco ◻ MEX 246 Fb36
San Salvo ◻ I 63 Lq48
Sansanding ◻ RMM 187 Kh39
Sansanne-Mango ◻ TG 187 La40
Sansanpur ◻ IND 115 Pa31
San Sebastián = Donostia ◻ E 56 Ks47
San Sebastián ◻ MEX 246 Eh35
San Sebastián ◻ MEX 246 Fa35
San Sebastián ◻ MEX 282 Gf72
San Sebastián ◻ USA 251 Gg36
San Sebastián de la Gomera ◻ E 174 Kb31
San Sebastián de los Reyes ◻ E 55 Kr50
San Sebastián Zinacatepec ◻ MEX 246 Fb36
Sansepolcro ◻ I 60 Ln47
San Severino Marche ◻ I 60 Ln47
San Severo ◻ I 63 Lq49
Sanshui ◻ CHN 109 Qg34
Sanshul ◻ CHN 109 Qg34
San Silvestre ◻ BOL 270 Gf51
San Silvestre ◻ YV 264 Ge41
Sanski Most ◻ BIH 61 Lr46
Sanso ◻ RMM 187 Kg40
San Stéfano di Camastra ◻ I 63 Lp52
Sansul ◻ CHN 108 Qc32
Sansundi ◻ RI 154 Rh46
Sansu-ri ◻ PRK 110 Rd25
Santa ◻ PE 269 Gb50
Santa ◻ USA 232 Eb22
Santa Amalia ◻ E 55 Ko51
Santa Ana ◻ BOL 278 Ge51
Santa Ana ◻ ◻ BOL 278 Gk54
Santa Ana ◻ BOL 279 Gh56
Santa Ana ◻ C 243 Gb35
Santa Ana ◻ EC 268 Ga46
Santa Ana ◻ EC 268 Ga47
Santa Ana ◻ ES 248 Ff38
Santa Ana ◻ MEX 244 Ee30
Santa Ana ◻ PE 268 Gd48
Santa Ana ◻ RA 276 Hc59
Santa Ana ◻ RA 279 Gg57
Santa Ana ◻ USA 234 Eb29
Santa Ana ◻ YV 265 Gh41
Santa Anita ◻ MEX 244 Et34
Santa Anita ◻ MEX 245 Ej31
Santa Anita Park ◻ USA 234 Eb28
Santa Bárbara ◻ BR 270 Gg48
Santa Bárbara ◻ CO 264 Gc43
Santa Bárbara ◻ E 55 Ks53
Santa Bárbara ◻ HN 248 Ff38
Santa Bárbara ◻ MEX 244 Eh32
Santa Bárbara ◻ RCH 280 Gd64
Santa Bárbara ◻ USA 234 Ea28
Santa Bárbara ◻ YV 264 Ge42
Santa Bárbara ◻ YV 265 Gg44
Santa Barbara Channel ◻ USA 234 Dk28
Santa Bárbara de Casa ◻ E 55 Kn53
Santa Bárbara d'Oeste ◻ BR 275 Hg57
Santa Barbara Island ◻ USA 234 Ea29
Santa Birgitta Kapell ◻ S 43 Lr34
Santa Brígida ◻ BR

Santa Catalina ◻ CO 264 Gc40
Santa Catalina ◻ PA 249 Fk42
Santa Catalina ◻ PE 268 Ga49
Santa Catalina ◻ PE 268 Gc49
Santa Catalina ◻ RA 279 Gg56
Santa Catalina ◻ RA 279 Gh60
Santa Catalina ◻ RP 125 Rb41
Santa Catalina ◻ YV 265 Gf42
Santa Catalina ◻ YV 265 Gk41
Santa Catalina Island ◻ USA 234 Ea29
Santa Catarina ◻ BR 255 Hb12
Santa Catarina ◻ MEX 244 Ec31
Santa Catarina ◻ MEX 245 Ek33
Santa Cecilia ◻ BR 277 He59
Santa Cecilia ◻ CR 248 Fh40
Santa Cesarea Terme ◻ I 63 Lt50
Santa Clara ◻ ◻ C 243 Gb34
Santa Clara ◻ BR 267 Ha46
Santa Clara ◻ C 243 Ga34
Santa Clara ◻ RA 279 Gh58
Santa Clara ◻ USA 234 Dk28
Santa Clara ◻ YV 265 Gh41
Santa Clara-a-Velha ◻ P 55 Km53
Santa Clara de Olimar ◻ ROU 276 Hc62
Santa Clara do Ingai ◻ BR 276 Hd60
Santa Clara Ind. Res. ◻ USA 235 Ea28
Santa Clotilde ◻ PE 268 Gd47
Santa Coloma de Queralt ◻ E 57 Lb49
Santa Comba ◻ E 54 Km47
Santa Croce Camerina ◻ I 63 Lp54
Santa Cruz ◻ BOL 278 Gf53
Santa Cruz ◻ BR 270 Gj50
Santa Cruz ◻ BR 271 Hd47
Santa Cruz ◻ BR 271 Hd47
Santa Cruz ◻ BR 273 Hk50
Santa Cruz ◻ BR 273 Ja49
Santa Cruz ◻ BR 275 Hk55
Santa Cruz ◻ BR 275 Hk55
Santa Cruz ◻ MEX 246 Eh35
Santa Cruz ◻ MEX 246 Eh35
Santa Cruz ◻ PE 268 Gc48
Santa Cruz ◻ PE 269 Gb51
Santa Cruz ◻ RA 282 Ge69
Santa Cruz ◻ RCH 280 Gd63
Santa Cruz ◻ RP 124 Qk38
Santa Cruz ◻ RP 124 Ra38
Santa Cruz ◻ RP 124 Ra39
Santa Cruz ◻ RP 125 Ra39
Santa Cruz ◻ RP 125 Rc42
Santa Cruz ◻ USA 234 Dj27
Santa Cruz ◻ YV 265 Gh42
Santa Cruz Cabrália ◻ BR 275 Ja54
Santa Cruz das Palmeiras ◻ BR 275 Hg56
Santa Cruz de Bucaral ◻ YV 265 Gf40
Santa Cruz de Campezo ◻ E 56 Ks48
Santa Cruz de la Palma ◻ E 174 Kb31
Santa Cruz de la Sierra ◻ BOL 278 Gj54
Santa Cruz del Norte ◻ C 243 Fk34
Santa Cruz del Quiché ◻ GCA 248 Fe38
Santa Cruz del Sur ◻ C 243 Gd35
Santa Cruz de Mompox ◻ CO 264 Gc41
Santa Cruz de Mudela ◻ E 55 Kr52
Santa Cruz de Succhabamba ◻ PE 268 Ga49
Santa Cruz de Tenerife ◻ ◻ E 174 Kb31
Santa Cruz d.J.R. ◻ MEX 246 Ek35
Santa Cruz do Capibaribe ◻ BR 267 Hf46
Santa Cruz do Rio Pardo ◻ BR 275 Hf56
Santa Cruz dos Milagres ◻ BR 273 Hj48
Santa Cruz Island ◻ USA 234 Ea29
Santa Cruz Islands ◻ SOL 134 Ta10
Santa Cruz Verapaz ◻ GCA 248 Fe38
Santadi ◻ I 62 Lj51
Santa Edwiges ◻ BR 273 Ja49
Santa Elena ◻ EC 268 Fk47
Santa Elena ◻ MEX 245 Ej32
Santa Elena ◻ RA 276 Ha61
Santa Elena, Cabo ◻ RA 282 Gh68
Santa Elena ◻ RP 124 Rb38
Santa Elena ◻ YV 265 Gj41
Santa Elena de Uairén ◻ YV 265 Gk43
Santa Eleodora ◻ RA 281 Gj63
Santa Eufémia ◻ E 55 Kq52
Santa Eugenia ◻ E 54 Km48
Santa Eulália ◻ BR 271 Gk48
Santa Eulália ◻ MEX 245 Ej31
Santa Eulària des Riu ◻ E 57 Lb52
Santa Fé ◻ BR 268 Gd48
Santa Fé ◻ ◻ C 243 Fj34
Santa Fé ◻ CO 264 Ge42
Santa Fé ◻ E 55 Kr53
Santa Fé ◻ MEX 244 Ee33
Santa Fé ◻ MEX 245 Ej31
Santa Fé ◻ PA 249 Fk41
Santa Fé ◻ PA 249 Ga41
Santa Fé ◻ RA 281 Gk61
Santa Fé ◻ RA 281 Hb59
Santa Fe ◻ RP 124 Rb39
Santa Fe de Antioquia ◻ CO 264 Gc42
Santa Fé de Minas ◻ BR 275 Hh54
Santa Fé do Sul ◻ BR 274 He56
Santa Filomena ◻ BR 272 Hh50
Santa Filomena ◻ BR 273 Hk50
Sant'Ágata di Militello ◻ I 63 Lp52
Santa Helena ◻ BR 267 Hh47
Santa Helena ◻ BR 269 Ge50
Santa Helena ◻ BR 272 Hd49
Santa Helena de Cusima ◻ CO 264 Gd43
Santa Helena de Goiás ◻ BR 274 Hd55
Santai ◻ CHN 108 Qc30
Santa Inés ◻ BR 269 Hd47
Santa Inés ◻ BR 273 Ja52
Santa Inés ◻ YV 265 Gf40
Santa Inez, T.I. ◻ BR 266 Gk43
Santa Isabel ◻ EC 268 Ga47
Santa Isabel ◻ MEX 246 Ek34
Santa Isabel ◻ MEX 248 Fh40
Santa Isabel ◻ PE 268 Gd48
Santa Isabel ◻ RA 280 Gf63
Santa Isabel ◻ SOL 157 Sk49
Santa Isabel do Araguaia ◻ BR 272 Hf49
Santa Isabel do Rio Negro ◻ BR 270 Gh46
Santa Isabella ◻ RA 280 Gg64
Santa Juana ◻ RCH 280 Gd64
Santa Juana ◻ YV 265 Gg42
Santa Juana ◻ YV 265 Gg42
Santa Lucia ◻ BR 271 Ga48
Santa Lucia ◻ C 243 Fh34
Santa Lucia ◻ C 243 Gb35
Santa Lucia ◻ EC 268 Ga46
Santa Lucia ◻ PE 269 Gc53
Santa Lucia ◻ YV 264 Gd41
Santa Lucia ◻ YV 265 Gh41
Santa Lucia ◻ ROU 281 Hb63
Santa Lucia ◻ ROU 276 Hc62
Santa Lucía do Piauí ◻ BR 267 Hh47
Santa Lucia Range ◻ USA 234 Dk28
Santa Luz ◻ BR 272 Hh50
Santa Luzia ◻ BR 267 Hg46
Santa Luzia ◻ BR 273 Hj49
Santa Luzia ◻ BR 275 Hj55
Santa Luzia ◻ CV 186 Jh38
Santa Magdalena ◻ RA 281 Gk61
Santa Margherita ◻ I
Santa Margherita ◻ ANG 200 Lg52
Santa Maria ◻ BR 267 Hd46
Santa María ◻ BR 271 Ga48
Santa Maria ◻ BR 274 Hd56

Santa Maria ◻ ◻ CV 186 Jj37
Santa Maria ◻ HN 248 Fg38
Santa Maria ◻ MEX 244 Ec30
Santa Maria ◻ MEX 244 Ee31
Santa Maria ◻ RA 279 Gh60
Santa Maria ◻ RP 125 Ra42
Santa Maria ◻ YV 265 Gf42
Santa Maria ◻ YV 265 Gk41
Santa Maria Island ◻ BR 234 Ea25
Santa Maria ◻ YV 264 Ge41
Santa Maria Asunción Tlaxiaco ◻ MEX 246 Fb37
Santa Maria Ayoquezco ◻ MEX 246 Fb37
Santa Maria Cápua Vétere ◻ I 63 Lp49
Santa Maria da Boa Vista ◻ BR 273 Ja50
Santa Maria da Vitória ◻ BR 272 Hh52
Santa Maria de Ipire ◻ YV 265 Gh41
Santa Maria de Jetibá ◻ BR 275 Hk56
Santa Maria de la Peña ◻ E 56 Ku48
Santa Maria del Azogue ◻ MEX 244 Ea47
Santa Maria del Camí ◻ E 57 Lc51
Santa Maria delle Grazie ◻ ◻ I
Santa Maria del Oro ◻ MEX 245 Eh33
Santa Maria del Oro ◻ MEX 246 Eh35
Santa Maria de Los Guaicas ◻ YV 265 Gh44
Santa Maria del Páramo ◻ E 54 Kp48
Santa Maria del Regno ◻ I 62 Lj50
Santa Maria del Río ◻ MEX 246 Ek35
Santa Maria de Nieva ◻ PE 268 Gb48
Santa Maria do Oeste ◻ BR 275 He58
Santa María do Suaçuí ◻ BR 275 Hj55
Santa Maria do Tocantins ◻ BR 272 Hg50
Santa María Ecatepec ◻ MEX 247 Fc37
Santa Maria Huatulco ◻ MEX 247 Fb38
Santa Maria Huazolotitlán ◻ MEX 246 Fb37
Santa Maria Island ◻ VU 158 Td53
Santa Maria la Real de Nieva ◻ E 54 Kq49
Santa Marinella ◻ I 62 Lm48
Santa Marta ◻ ANG 200 Lg52
Santa Marta ◻ CO 264 Gc40
Santa Martha ◻ BR 273 Hh55
Santa Martha ◻ MEX 244 Ed33
Santa Martha ◻ MEX 246 Fa36
Santa Mónica ◻ MEX 245 Ek31
Santa Mónica ◻ USA 234 Ea28
Santan ◻ RI 128 Qj46
Santan ◻ BR 267 He45
Santan ◻ BR 267 He45
Santana ◻ BR 272 Gg50
Santana ◻ BR 272 Hh52
Santana ◻ CO 264 Gd42
Santana ◻ P 174 Kb29
Santana da Boa Vista ◻ BR 276 Hd61
Santana da Serra ◻ P 55 Km53
Santana de Pirapama ◻ BR 275 Hh55
Santana do Acaraú ◻ BR 273 He47
Santana do Araguaia ◻ BR 272 He50
Santana do Cariri ◻ BR 273 Ja49
Santana do Ipanema ◻ BR 273 Jb50
Santana do Livramento ◻ BR 274 Hc61
Santana do Livramento ◻ BR 276 Hd61
Santana, T.I. ◻ BR 274 Ha53
Santander ◻ E 56 Kr47
Santander ◻ RP 124 Ra41
Santander Jiménez ◻ MEX 245 Fa33
Sant'Andrea Frius ◻ I 62 Lk51
Sant' Ángelo dei Lombardi ◻ I 63 Lq50
Sant'Ángelo Lodigia ◻ I 60 Lk49
Sant' Antíoco ◻ I 62 Lj51
Sant' Antíoco de Portmany ◻ E 57 Lb52
Sant' Antoni de Portmany ◻ E 57 Lb52
Santanyí ◻ E 57 Ld52
Santa Olalla del Cala ◻ E 55 Ko53
Santa Pau ◻ E 57 Lc48
Santa Paula ◻ USA 234 Ea28
Santa Pola ◻ E 57 Ku52
Sant' Apollinare Nuovo di Ravenna ◻ I 60 Lm46
Santa Quitéria do Maranhão ◻ BR 273 Hj47
Sant' Arcángelo ◻ I 63 Lr50
Santarcángelo di Romagna ◻ I 60 Lm46
Santarém ◻ BR 271 Hc47
Santarém ◻ P 55 Km51
Santarém Novo ◻ BR 267 Hg46
Santaren Channel ◻ BS 243 Ga33
Santa Rita ◻ BR 267 Hh47
Santa Rita ◻ BR 270 Gf47
Santa Rita ◻ BR 273 Jd49
Santa Rita ◻ CO 268 Gd45
Santa Rita ◻ HN 248 Fg38
Santa Rita ◻ MEX 244 Ea33
Santa Rita ◻ YV 264 Gd40
Santa Rita ◻ YV 265 Gg41
Santa Rita de Cássia ◻ BR 272 Hh51
Santa Rita de Catuna ◻ RA 280 Gg61
Santa Rita do Araguaia ◻ BR 274 Hd54
Santa Rita do Pardo ◻ BR 274 Hd56
Santa Rita do Passa Quatro ◻ BR 275 Hg56
Santa Rita do Sapucaí ◻ BR 275 Hh57
Santa Rosa ◻ BOL 278 Gg53
Santa Rosa ◻ BR 265 Gj44
Santa Rosa ◻ BR 272 Hf51
Santa Rosa ◻ BR 276 Hc59
Santa Rosa ◻ BR 276 Hd61
Santa Rosa ◻ EC 268 Ga47
Santa Rosa ◻ MEX 244 Ef31
Santa Rosa ◻ NIC 249 Fh39
Santa Rosa ◻ PE 269 Ge50
Santa Rosa ◻ USA 234 Dj26
Santa Rosa ◻ USA 235 Dj26
Santa Rosa ◻ USA 238 Eh28
Santa Rosa ◻ YV 264 Ge42
Santa Rosa ◻ YV 265 Gf42
Santa Rosa ◻ YV 265 Gh41
Santa Rosa Beach ◻ USA 239 Fj30
Santa Rosa da Vigia ◻ BR 267 Hf46
Santa Rosa de Amonadona ◻ YV 265 Gg45
Santa Rosa de Copán ◻ HN 248 Ff38
Santa Rosa de las Minas ◻ PY 276 Hb59
Santa Rosa del Conlara ◻ RA 280 Gg62
Santa Rosa del Lima ◻ BR 277 Hf60
Santa Rosa del Monday ◻ PY 276 Hb58
Santa Rosa de Ocopa ◻ PE 269 Gc51
Santa Rosa de Osos ◻ CO 269 Gb51
Santa Rosa de Viterbo ◻ BR 275 Hg56

Santa Rosa Island ◻ USA 234 Dk29
Santa Rosa Island ◻ USA 239 Fg30
Santa Rosalia ◻ YV 265 Gh42
Santa Rosalía ◻ MEX 244 Ed32
Santa Rosalía ◻ MEX 247 Fe36
Santa Rosa, P.N. ◻ CR 248 Fh40
Santarskie ostrova ◻ RUS 89 Rd07
Severa ◻ F 60 Lk48
Santa Sylvina ◻ RA 279 Ga59
Santa Teresa ◻ MEX 244 Eb30
Santa Teresa ◻ MEX 245 Fa33
Santo Tomás ◻ MEX 244 Eb30
Santo Tomás ◻ NIC 249 Fh39
Santa Teresa ◻ PE 269 Gd53
Santa Teresa ◻ PE 268 Gc48
Santa Teresa ◻ BR 275 Hk55
Santa Teresa ◻ BR 281 Gk62
Santa Teresa ◻ YV 265 Gg40
Santa Teresa Cápua Vétere ◻ I 63 Lp49
Santa Teresa de Goiás ◻ BR 272 Hf52
Santa Teresa di Riva ◻ I 63 Lq53
Santa Teresa do Tocantins ◻ BR 272 Hg51
Santa Teresa Gallura ◻ I 62 Lk49
Santa Teresa, P.N. ◻ ROU 276 Hd62
Santa Teresinha de Goiás ◻ BR 274 Hf53
Santa Teresita ◻ RA 281 Hb64
Santa Theresa ◻ AUS 148 Rh58
Santa Victoria ◻ RA 279 Gh57
Santa Victoria ◻ BR 274 He55
Santa Vitória ◻ BR 274 He55
Santa Vitória do Palmar ◻ BR 276 Hd62
Santa Yriex ◻ BR 275 Hj55
Santa Yolanda ◻ F 60 Lk48
Santerno ◻ I 60 Lm46
Santo Amaro ◻ BR 268 Ga49
Santo Amaro ◻ BR 273 Ja52
Santo Amaro ◻ BR 274 Hd53
Santo André ◻ ANG 200 Lh52
Santo André ◻ BR 277 Hg57
Santo Ângelo ◻ BR 276 Hd60
Santo Antônio ◻ BR 266 Hb46
Santo Antônio ◻ BR 267 Hd46
Santo Antônio ◻ BR 271 Gk47
Santo Antônio ◻ BR 272 Hh52
Santo Antônio da Barra ◻ BR 274 He53
Santo Antônio da Platina ◻ BR 274 He57
Santo Antônio do Içá ◻ BR 270 Gg47
Santo Antônio do Jacinto ◻ BR 275 Hk54
Santo Antônio do Sudoeste ◻ BR 276 Hd59
Santo Augusto ◻ BR 276 Hd60
Santo Corazón ◻ BOL 278 Ha54
Santo Cristo ◻ BR 276 Hd60
Santo Domingo ◻ C 243 Fk34
Santo Domingo ◻ ◻ DOM 250 Gf36
Santo Domingo ◻ MEX 244 Ec31
Santo Domingo ◻ MEX 244 Ee33
Santo Domingo ◻ MEX 245 Ek33
Santo Domingo ◻ RA 280 Gf63
Santo Domingo de Acobamba ◻ PE 269 Gc51
Santo Domingo de la Calzada ◻ E 56 Ks48
Santo Domingo de los Colorados ◻ EC 268 Ga46
Santo Domingo de Silos ◻ E 54 Kr49
Santo Domingo Pueblo ◻ USA 235 Eg28
Santo Domingo Tehuantepec ◻ MEX 247 Fc37
Santo Estêvão ◻ BR 273 Jb52
Santo Expedito ◻ BR 273 Ja52
Santo Inácio ◻ BR 273 Hd49
Santo Inácio ◻ BR 274 He57
Santo Tomé ◻ YV 265 Gh42
Santoña ◻ E 56 Kr47
Santo Tomás ◻ I 266 Hd43
São Gonçalo do Amárante ◻ BR 273 Ja47

Santos ◻ AUS 148 Sa60
Santos ◻ BR 277 Hg57
Santos Dumont ◻ BR 275 Hj56
Santos Lugares ◻ RA 279 Gj59
Sao Hill ◻ EAT 196 Mh50
São Ifigênia de Minas ◻ BR 275 He51
São Jerônimo ◻ BR 276 He60
São Jerônimo, T.I. ◻ BR 274 He57
São João ◻ BR 231 Gk48
São João ◻ BR 276 Hd58
São João Batista ◻ BR 267 Hh47
São João da Barra ◻ BR 277 Hh56
São João da Boa Vista ◻ BR 275 Hg56
São João d'Aliança ◻ BR 275 Hg53
São João da Madeira ◻ P 54 Km50
São João da Ponte ◻ BR 275 Hh53
São João de Pirabas ◻ BR 267 He46
São João de Rio Pardo ◻ BR 275 Hg56
São João do Caiuá ◻ BR 274 Hd57
São João do Paraíso ◻ BR 275 Hk53
São João do Paraná ◻ BR 271 Gh50
São João do Piauí ◻ BR 273 Hj50
São João dos Patos ◻ BR 272 Hj49
São João dos Poleiros ◻ BR 272 Hj48
São João do Tigre ◻ BR 273 Jb50
São João do Triunfo ◻ BR 275 He58
São João Evangelista ◻ BR 275 Hj55
São Joaquim ◻ BR 270 Gg45
São Joaquim ◻ BR 277 Hf60
São Joaquim da Barra ◻ BR 275 Hg56
São Joaquim, P.N.de ◻ BR 277 Hf60
São José ◻ BR 267 Hf47
São José ◻ BR 270 Gf50
São José ◻ ◻ I 111 Sa24
São José ◻ BR 276 Hd58
São José ◻ BR 271 He47
São José ◻ BR 277 Hf59
São José da Tapera ◻ BR 273 Jb50
São José de Anaua ◻ BR 265 Gk45
São José de Belmonte ◻ BR 273 Ja49
São José de Mipibu ◻ BR 273 Jd49
São José de Piranhas ◻ BR 273 Ja49
São José de Ribamar ◻ BR 267 Hh47
São José do Caciporé ◻ BR 267 He44
São José do Cerrito ◻ BR 277 He59
São José do Egito ◻ BR 273 Ja49
São José do Norte ◻ BR 276 Hd61
São José do Peixe ◻ BR 273 Hj49
São José do Piriá ◻ BR 267 Hg46
São José do Rio Claro ◻ BR 271 Hb52
São José do Rio Preto ◻ BR 274 He56
São José dos Ausentes ◻ BR 276 Hd59
São José dos Campos ◻ BR 277 Hh57
São José dos Martírios ◻ BR 272 Hf50
São José dos Pinhais ◻ BR 277 Hf58
São José do Xingu ◻ BR 271 Hd51
São Leopoldo ◻ BR 276 He60
São Leopoldo, T.I. ◻ BR 270 Gh48
São Lourenço ◻ BR 275 Hh57
São Lourenço do Oeste ◻ BR 276 Hd59
São Lourenço do Sul ◻ BR 276 He61
São Lucas ◻ ANG 200 Lj51
São Luís ◻ BR 266 Gk45
São Luís ◻ ◻ BR 267 Hh47
São Luís Gonzaga ◻ BR 276 Hd60
São Luís de Quitunde ◻ BR 273 Jc50
São Luís do Quitunde ◻ BR 273 Jc50
São Luís Gonzaga ◻ BR 276 Hd60
São Luiza do Oeste ◻ BR 270 Gf51
São Luzia do Pacuí ◻ BR 267 He45
São Manuel ◻ BR 274 He57
São Manuel ◻ BR 274 Hf57
São Manuel ou Teles Pires ◻ BR 271 Hb50
São Marcos ◻ BR 276 He60
São Marcos da Serra ◻ P 55 Km53
São Marcos, T.I. ◻ BR 265 Gk44
São Marcos, T.I. ◻ BR 272 Hd48
São Martinho de Angueira ◻ P 54 Ko49
São Mateus ◻ BR 275 Ja55
São Mateus do Maranhão ◻ BR 272 Hh48
São Mateus do Sul ◻ BR 277 He58
São Miguel ◻ BR 273 Ja49
São Miguel ◻ BR 277 Hf59
São Miguel Arcanjo ◻ BR 277 Hf57
São Miguel das Missões ◻ ◻ BR 276 Hc60
São Miguel das Missões ◻ BR 276 Hc60
São Miguel d'Oeste ◻ BR 276 Hd59
São Miguel do Guamá ◻ BR 267 Hg46
São Miguel do Iguaçu ◻ BR 276 Hc58
São Miguel dos Campos ◻ BR 273 Jb50
São Miguel dos Macacos ◻ BR 267 He46
São Nicolau ◻ ANG 200 Lg53
São Nicolau ◻ IND 117 Ok35
São Paio ◻ BR 255 Hb12
São Paulo ◻ BR 277 Hg57
São Paulo de Olivença ◻ BR 270 Gf47
São Pedro ◻ BR 267 He47
São Pedro ◻ BR 270 Gg46
São Pedro ◻ BR 273 Ja49
São Pedro ◻ BR 276 He59
São Pedro da Aldeia ◻ BR 277 Hj57
São Pedro do Piauí ◻ BR 273 Hj48
São Pedro dos Crentes ◻ BR 272 Hg49
São Pedro do Sul ◻ BR 276 Hd60
São Pedro, T.I. ◻ BR 271 Ha47
São Pedro do Quilemba ◻ ANG 198 Lh50
São Rafael ◻ BR 273 Ja48
São Raimundo das Mangabeiras ◻ BR 272 Hh49
São Raimundo Nonato ◻ BR 273 Hj50
São Romão ◻ BR 275 Hg53
São Romão ◻ BR 277 Hf57
São Roque de Minas ◻ BR 275 Hg56
São Sebastião ◻ BR 210 Ga06
São Sebastião ◻ BR 273 Hj50
São Sebastião ◻ BR 277 Hh57
São Sebastião da Amoreira ◻ BR 274 He57
São Sebastião da Boa Vista ◻ BR 267 He46
São Sebastião do Paraíso ◻ BR 275 Hg56
São Sebastião do Tocantins ◻ BR 272 Hg50
São Sebastião do Oeste ◻ BR 275 Hh56
São Sebastião do Uatumã ◻ BR 271 Ha47
São Sepé ◻ BR 276 Hd61
São Simão ◻ BR 274 He55
São Simão ◻ BR 275 Hg56
São Simão ◻ BR 276 He59

São Gonçalo dos Campos ◻ BR 273 Ja52
São Tomé ◻ BR 267 He66
São Tomé ◻ BR 267 Hd46
São Tomé ◻ ◻ STP 188 Ld45
São Tomé ◻ ◻ STP 188 Ld45
São Tomé and Principe ◻ ◻ 163 La09
São Valentim ◻ BR 276 Hd60
São Vendelino ◻ BR 276 He60
São Vicente ◻ BR 268 Gc48
São Vicente ◻ BR 274 He53
São Vicente ◻ BR 277 Hg57
São Vicente do Sul ◻ BR 276 Hc60
São Vicente Ferrer ◻ BR 267 Hh47
Sápai ◻ GR 69 Mf49
Sapanca ◻ F 266 Hd43
Sapanjang ◻ RI 129 Qh49
Sapari ◻ YV 265 Gf42
Sápat ◻ RI 127 Qb46
Sápé ◻ BR 273 Hk48
São Gonçalo da Serra ◻ BR 273 Hk48
Sapele ◻ WAN 188 Lc43
Sapelo Island National Estuarine Research Reserve ◻ USA 242 Fk50
Sapernoe ◻ RUS 44 Mk30
Sapidan ◻ IR 93 Nf30
Sapiénza ◻ GR 70 Mb54
Sapinero ◻ USA 235 Eg26
Sapiranga ◻ BR 276 He60
Sapi Safari Area ◻ ◻ ZW 202 Me53
Sápmi ◻ N 39 Lc42
São Gonçalo do Caiuá ◻ BR 274 Hd57
Sapo, N.P. ◻ LB 186 Kf43
Sapoa ◻ RDC 199 Mb48
Saposoa ◻ PE 268 Gb49
Sapouí ◻ BF 187 Kk40
Sapožok ◻ RUS 72 Na19
Sapphire Mts. ◻ USA 232 Ed22
Sapporo ◻ ◻ J 111 Sa24
Sapri ◻ I 63 Lq50
Sapucaia ◻ BR 271 Hd47
Sapucaia ◻ BR 276 Hd60
Sapucaia do Sul ◻ BR 276 Hd60
Sápudi ◻ USA 238 Fb28
Sapulu ◻ RI 129 Qk49
Saputul ◻ MAL 128 Qj43
Saqqara ◻ ◻ IRQ 91 Nd27
Saqqez ◻ IR 91 Nd27
Saquisilí ◻ EC 268 Ga46
Sara ◻ BF 187 Kj40
Sara ◻ TG 187 La41
Sara ◻ RI 154 Mc28
Sarab ◻ IR 91 Nd27
Sarab Dowreh ◻ IR 91 Ne29
Sarab-e Jahangir ◻ IR 93 Nd29
Sarabit el Khádim ◻ ET 179 Mg31
Sarafand ◻ THA 122 Qa38
Sarafchegan ◻ IR 91 Nf28
Saraf Doungous ◻ TCH 189 Lk39
Sarafud ◻ RUS 72 Na19
Saragt ◻ TM 96 Oa27
Sara Hahan ◻ SP 193 Nd40
Saraí ◻ IND 117 Pa34
Sarai Gambila ◻ PK 99 Of29
Sar'ain ◻ IR 91 Nd26
Saraiu ◻ RO 69 Mj46
Sarajevo ◻ ◻ BIH 68 Lt47
Sara-Kawa ◻ TG 187 La41
Sarakhs ◻ IR 96 Oa27
Sarakiná ◻ GR 70 Mb51
Saraktaš ◻ RUS 72 Nh20
Sara Koyra ◻ RN 182 La38
Saramati ◻ MYA 120 Pj33
Sarameroza ◻ PE 268 Gb48
Sarandê, T.I. ◻ BR 271 Ha47
Sarandi ◻ BR 276 Hd58
Sarandí ◻ BR 274 He57
Sarandi Grande ◻ ROU 276 Hb62
Sarangani Islands ◻ RP 125 Rc43
Sarangani ◻ IND 117 Pb35
Sarangpur ◻ IND 116 Oj34
Saran, Gunung ◻ RI 129 Qf46
Saranac Lake ◻ USA 241 Gc23
Sarandë ◻ AL 70 Ma51
Sárándi ◻ H 67 Mb43
Sarandí ◻ BR 274 He57
Sarangpur ◻ IND 117 Pb35
Saran ◻ RUS 85 Nc07
Sarayakha ◻ KZ 97 Od25
Sarayköy ◻ TR 71 Mj53
Sarbaz ◻ IR 96 Oa32
Sarbinowo ◻ PL 64 Lq36
Sar Bisheh ◻ IR 98 Nk29
Sarbogárd ◻ H 67 Lt44
Sardárn ◻ IND 114 Oh31
Sardasht ◻ IR 93 Nf30
Sardégna = Sardinia ◻ I 62 Lj50
Sardinata ◻ CO 264 Gd41
Sardinha ◻ BR 274 He57
Sardinia = Sardégna ◻ I 62 Lj50
Sardīs ◻ TR 71 Mj52
Sardo ◻ ETH 193 Nc41
Sardoal ◻ P 55 Km51
Sárdobod ◻ UZ 96 Ob25
Sárdobod ◻ UZ 97 Od27
Sarhad ◻ AFG 99 Og28
Sarhala ◻ CI 186 Kf42
Sárhorog ◻ IR 96 Ob33
Sari ◻ IR 92 Nh27
Sária ◻ GR 71 Mh54
Sária ◻ RI 128 Qf46
Sariba Island ◻ PNG 156 Sf51
Sarich, Mys ◻ UA 73 Md47
Sarıçam ◻ TR 90 Mg26
Sárida ◻ CO 264 Gd43
Sarigan ◻ USA 138 Sa10
São Gonçalo do Amárante ◻ BR 273 Ja47

Sarıgöl ◻ TR 71 Mj52
Sarikamış ◻ TR 91 Na25
Sarika Falls ◻ THA 122 Qa38
Sarikamış ◻ TR 91 Nb25
Sarıkaya ◻ TR 90 Mf26
Sariko'l ◻ UZ 97 Oc26
Sarikorla ◻ RMM 187 Kg39
Sarıköy ◻ TR 69 Mh50
Sarimoy ◻ UZ 96 Oa25
Sarimoy ◻ UZ 96 Ob25
Sarina ◻ AUS 148 Sc65
Sariñena ◻ E 56 Ku49
Sáripul ◻ TR 91 Nb44
Sáripol ◻ RI 129 Qh46
Sariq ◻ UZ 97 Od27
Sarir al Qattusah ◻ LAR 177 Lh32
Sariri ◻ PNG 156 Se50
Sarir Kalanshiyū ◻ LAR 177 Ma32
Sariri ◻ PNG 156 Se50
Sarir Tibesti ◻ LAR 183 Lj34
Sarir Umm ◻ LAR 177 Lh32
Sariska Tiger Reserve ◻ IND 114 Oj32
Sariska Tiger Reserve ◻ IND 114 Oj32
Sarisský hrad ◻ SK 67 Mb41
Sarita ◻ USA 255 Fb32
Sariwŏn ◻ PRK 110 Rc26
Saríyer ◻ TR 69 Mk49
Sarja ◻ RUS 72 Mg16
Sarkadkeresztúr ◻ H 67 Mb43
Sarkala ◻ IND 116 Of35
Sarkan ◻ KZ 100 Ok23
Sárkikvčyna ◻ BY 45 Mh35
Sarkikaragac ◻ TR 90 Md26
Sarkikuduk ◻ WAN 188 Le41
Sarkişla ◻ TR 90 Mj26
Sarlanga ◻ USA 72 Md20
Sarlat-la-Canéda ◻ F 52 Lb46
Sármága ◻ RO 67 Md43
Sarmetie ◻ VU 158 Td54
Sarmi ◻ RI 154 Sa46
Sarmiento ◻ RA 280 Gh61
Sarmiento ◻ RA 282 Ge68
Sarmizegetusa Regia ◻ RO 68 Md45
Sarnai ◻ S 40 Lo29
Sarnaki ◻ PL 65 Mc38
Sarnano ◻ I 60 Ln47
Sarnath ◻ IND 117 Pb33
Sarnen ◻ CH 60 Lj44
Sarner See ◻ CH 60 Lj44
Sárnevo ◻ BG 69 Mf48
Sárnico ◻ I 60 Lk45
Sarny ◻ UA 72 Me20
Saroako ◻ RI 130 Ra47
Saróland ◻ CDN 237 Fj24
Saroma ◻ J 111 Sb23
Saromoana ◻ RM 206 Ne54
Saronida ◻ GR 69 Md53
Saronikós Kólpos ◻ GR 69 Md53
Saronno ◻ I 60 Lj45
Sárosd ◻ H 67 Lt43
Saros Körfezi ◻ TR 69 Mg50
Sarospatak ◻ H 67 Mb42
Sarowbi ◻ AFG 99 Oe29
Sár Planina ◻ MK/KSV 68 Ma48
Sarpsborg ◻ N 42 Li31
Sarrabe ◻ F 51 Lh42
Sarrapio ◻ YV 265 Gh42
Sarrebourg ◻ F 51 Lh42
Sarre-Union ◻ F 51 Lh42
Sarrguemines ◻ F 51 Lh41
Sarria ◻ RMM 187 Kh39
Sarstoon R. ◻ BH 248 Ff38
Sartam ◻ IND 120 Pd31
Sartène ◻ F 62 Lj49
Sartèl ◻ GR 69 Md50
Sarti ◻ GR 69 Md50
Saruhanli ◻ TR 71 Mj52
Sarulla ◻ RI 127 Pk45
Sarumatinggi ◻ RI 127 Pk44
Saruqi ◻ IR 91 Ne28
Saruwaged Range ◻ PNG 155 Sd49
Sárvár ◻ H 66 Lr43
Sarvestan ◻ IR 93 Nf30
Sarwar ◻ IND 116 Oh34
Saryagash ◻ KZ 97 Oe26
Sary-Bulak ◻ KS 100 Oj25
Saryesik-Atyrau ◻ KZ 100 Oj23
Saryozek ◻ KZ 100 Oj23
Saryshagan ◻ KZ 100 Og22
Sárvas ◻ H 67 Md43
Sary-Taš ◻ KS 99 Og27
Saraya ◻ SN 186 Kc39
Sarez p.Łagój ◻ P 55 Kn51
Sárzedas ◻ P 55 Kn51
Saratoga Racetrack ◻ USA 241 Gd24
Saratoga Springs ◻ USA 241 Gd24
Saravan ◻ IR 91 Ne27
Sara Pathar ◻ IND 120 Pe32

Sarangul ◻ TR 71 Mj52
Sarikamiş ◻ TR 91 Na25
Saramula ◻ GR 96 Mba30
Sar Planina, N.P. ◻ KSV 68 Mb48
Saronno ◻ I 60 Lj45
Sarpan ◻ IND 120 Pe32
Sarangpur ◻ IND 116 Oj34
Saranac Lake ◻ USA 241 Gc23
Sarangani ◻ RP 125 Rc43
Saranpur ◻ IND 116 Oj34
Saran ◻ RUS 85 Nc07
Saran, Gunung ◻ RI 129 Qf46
Saratov ◻ RUS 72 Nd20
Saratak ◻ RUS 72 Nh20
Saraykeye ◻ TR 90 Md26
Saraykyi ◻ TR 71 Mj53
Sarbaz ◻ IR 96 Oa32
Sar-e Pol ◻ AFG 97 Od28
Sare Nyaye ◻ SN 186 Kc39
Sar-e Pol-e-Sahab ◻ IR 91 Nc28
Sáréyamou ◻ RMM 181 Kj37
Sarfeyt ◻ OM 95 Ng37
Sargodha ◻ PK 99 Of29
Sargur ◻ IND 118 Oj40
Sardougou ◻ RMM 181 Kj37
Sardougou ◻ RMM 181 Kj37
Sari-i Sang ◻ AFG 99 Og27
Saricanak ◻ RI 128 Qf46
Sarigol ◻ TR 71 Mj52
Sarıkışla ◻ TR 90 Mj26
Saríyer ◻ TR 69 Mk49
Sarmi ◻ RI 154 Sa46
Sarmiento ◻ RA 280 Gh61
Sarno ◻ I 63 Lp50
Sarny ◻ UA 72 Me20
Sarólea ◻ J 111 Sb23
Saror ◻ IR 91 Ne28
Sar-e Rachal ◻ IR 91 Ne28
Saroni ◻ GR 69 Md53
Sarwar ◻ IND 116 Oh34
Saryagash ◻ KZ 97 Oe26
Saryshagan ◻ KZ 100 Og22
Saskatchewan ◻ CDN 232 Ej13
Saskatchewan Landing Prov. Park ◻ CDN 233 Ei20
Saskatchewan River Crossing ◻ CDN 232 Eb19
Saskatoon ◻ CDN 233 Eg19
Saskylach ◻ RUS 79 Qf30
Sasolburg ◻ ZA 205 Md59
Sasoma ◻ IND 115 Oj28
Sasovo ◻ RUS 72 Na18
Sassafras ◻ AUS 147 Sb55
Sassandra ◻ CI 186 Kf43
Sassari ◻ I 62 Lj50
Sassel ◻ I 60 Lk46
Sasso Marconi ◻ I 60 Lm46
Sassuolo ◻ I 60 Ll46
S'Arenal ◻ E 57 Lc51
Saré Ndiaye ◻ SN 186 Kc39
Sassenheim ◻ NL 51 Lf38
Sátao ◻ P 54 Kn50
Satara ◻ IND 118 Og38
Satara ◻ ZA 205 Mf57
Satawan Atoll ◻ FSM 13 Sc09
Satengar ◻ RI 129 Qj49
Satevó ◻ MEX 244 Eg32
Satellite Beach ◻ USA 243 Fk32
Sätenäs ◻ S 42 Ln32
Sâtara ◻ RO 69 Mj44
Sat'er ◻ ETH 194 Nc43
Satara ◻ IND 118 Og38
Sathing Phra ◻ THA 123 Qa42
Sátila ◻ S 42 Lj33
Sätila ◻ S 42 Lj33
Satkhira ◻ BD 117 Pd34
Satmala Hills ◻ IND 118 Og36
Satna ◻ IND 117 Pa33
Sátoraljaújhely ◻ H 67 Mb42
Satpura Range ◻ IND 116 Og35
Satu Mare ◻ RO 67 Mc43
Satun ◻ THA 122 Qa42
Saturnina ◻ BR 270 Ha51
Saubara ◻ BR 273 Ja52
Saúde ◻ BR 273 Ja51
Saudi Arabia ◻ SA 94 Nc34
Sauer ◻ L 51 Lg41
Sauðárkrókur ◻ IS 38 Kb25
Sauerland ◻ D 59 Lh39
Saugues ◻ F 53 Le46
Sauherad ◻ N 42 Lh31
Saujon ◻ F 52 La45
Sauk Centre ◻ USA 236 Fc22
Saul ◻ F 266 Hb44
Saulieu ◻ F 53 Lf44
Saulkrasti ◻ LV 45 Md33
Sault Sainte Marie ◻ CDN 237 Fh22
Sault Sainte Marie ◻ USA 237 Fh22
Saumalköl ◻ KZ 85 Nk08
Saumarez Reefs ◻ AUS 149 Se57
Saumlaki ◻ RI 131 Rd49
Saumur ◻ F 52 La44
Saúna ◻ BR 271 Ha50
Sauðafell ◻ IS 38 Jk26
Saurimo ◻ ANG 200 Lk50
Sava ◻ HN 248 Fg38
Sava ◻ HR/SRB 68 Lt46
Savá ◻ HN 248 Fg38
Savage River ◻ AUS 150 Sb66
Savai'i ◻ WS 160 Ba11
Savalou ◻ BJ 187 La42
Savannah ◻ USA 238 Fc28
Savannah ◻ USA 242 Fk29
Savannah ◻ USA 243 Fk29
Savannah River ◻ USA 242 Fk29
Savannakhet ◻ LAO 121 Qc37
Save ◻ BJ 187 La41
Savé ◻ BJ 187 La41
Save R. ◻ MOC 202 Mf56
Saveh ◻ IR 92 Nf28
Savelugu ◻ GH 187 Kk41
Savona ◻ I 60 Lj46
Savonlinna ◻ FIN 41 Me29
Savran' ◻ UA 73 Me21
Savu Sea = Sawu, Laut ◻ RI 131 Ra50
Savukoski ◻ FIN 39 Mf25
Sawahlunto ◻ RI 127 Qa46
Sawai Madhopur ◻ IND 116 Oh33
Sawankhalok ◻ THA 120 Pk37
Sawara ◻ J 111 Sa28
Sawknah ◻ LAR 177 Lh31
Sawmills ◻ ZW 202 Md55
Sawu, Laut = Savu Sea ◻ RI 131 Ra50
Satevó ◻ MEX 244 Eg32

Siota – South Sandwich Islands

Siota RI 131 Rd50
Siota SOL 157 Ta50
Sioux Center USA 236 Fb24
Sioux City USA 236 Fb24
Sioux Falls USA 236 Fb24
Sioux Ind. Mus. USA 236 Ek24
Sioux Lookout CDN 236 Fe20
Sioux Narrows CDN 236 Fc21
Sipacate GCA 248 Fe39
Sipacate Naranjo, P.N. GCA 248 Fe39
Sipadan MAL 125 Qk43
Sipahutas RI 127 Pk44
Sipai PNG 157 Sh48
Sipalay RP 124 Rb41
Sipaliwini SME 266 Hb44
Šipan HR 61 Ls48
Sipán PE 268 Ga49
Siparia TT 251 Gk40
Šipčenski Prohod BG 69 Mf48
Si Phang-Nga N.P. THA 122 Pk41
Sipi CO 264 Gb43
Sipi Falls EAU 194 Mh45
Sipilou CI 186 Kf42
Siping CHN 108 Qb31
Siping CHN 110 Rc24
Sipiongot RI 127 Pk45
Sipirok RI 127 Pk45
Sipisopiso Waterfall RI 127 Pk44
Sipitang MAL 128 Qh43
Šipka BG 69 Mf48
Siple Dome 287 Cc35
Siple, Mount 287 Dc33
Sipocot RP 124 Rb39
Sipoo = Sibbo FIN 44 Mf30
Sipot RI 126 Pj43
Šipovo BIH 61 Ls46
Sippola FIN 44 Mh30
Sipura RI 127 Pk47
Siqu CHN 109 Qh34
Siquia NIC 249 Fh39
Siquijor RP 125 Rb41
Siquijor Island RP 125 Rb41
Siquisique YV 265 Gf40
Sir IND 117 Pb32
Sira IND 118 Oj39
Sira N 42 Lg32
Siracha THA 122 Qa39
Siracusa I 63 Lq53
Siraikoppa IND 118 Oh38
Sirakoro RMM 186 Kf39
Sirakoro RMM 187 Kg40
Siramana RG 186 Kf40
Şiran TR 91 Mk25
Sirana CI 186 Kg41
Sirasso CI 187 Kg41
Sirathu IND 117 Pa33
Sirattana THA 123 Qc38
Siraway RP 125 Rb42
Sir Bani Yas UAE 95 Ng33
Sir Bu Nu'air UAE 95 Nh33
Sirch IR 98 Nj30
Sirdaryo UZ 97 Oe25
Sire ETH 192 Mj41
Sire ETH 192 Mk41
Sir Edward Pellew Group AUS 146 Rj53
Siref TCH 184 Ma39
Siren USA 236 Fd23
Siret RO 73 Md22
Sirevåg N 42 Lf32
Sirgiri IND 117 Pb35
Sirheni Bushveld Camp ZA 202 Mf57
Siria RO 67 Mb44
Siriganj BD 120 Pe33
Sirikit Reservoir THA 121 Qa37
Sirinat N.P. THA 122 Pk41
Sirinhaém BR 273 Jc50
Sirinum Lake PNG 155 Sd50
Siriu RO 69 Mg45
Siriworra RI 154 Rg47
Sir James MacBrien, Mount CDN 230 Dg14
Sirjan IR 98 Nh31
Sir Joseph Banks Group AUS 150 Rj63
Sirkazhi IND 119 Ok40
Sirmione I 60 Ll45
Sírna GR 71 Mg54
Şırnak TR 91 Nb27
Sirohi IND 116 Og33
Sirok H 67 Ma43
Široka lăka BG 69 Me49
Široké SK 67 Ma41
Široki Brijeg BIH 61 Ls47
Sirombu RI 127 Pj45
Sironcha IND 117 Ok36
Sirong CHN 108 Qe33
Sirong RI 131 Rb46
Sironj IND 116 Oj33
Sironko EAU 194 Mh45
Síros GR 71 Me53
Sirrayn KSA 94 Na36
Sir Robert Campell Island MYA 122 Pk40
Sirsa IND 114 Oh31
Sirsa IND 117 Pb33
Sirsi IND 118 Oh38
Sirsilla IND 117 Ok36
Sirsiri SUD 194 Mf43
Sirsirtara HN 249 Fh38
Sirsova Ridge RUS 89 Tc07
Siruguppa IND 116 Oj38
Sirur IND 116 Oh36
Sirur Tajband IND 116 Oj36
Širvintos LT 45 Me35
Sirwa YE 94 Nc38
Sirwar IND 116 Oj37
Sisa PE 268 Gb49
Sisai IND 117 Pc34
Sisak HR 61 Lr45
Si Saket THA 123 Qc38
Sisal MEX 247 Fe35
Si Samrong THA 122 Pk37
Sisante E 57 Ks51
Si Satchanalai THA 122 Pk37
Si Satchanalai Historical Park THA 122 Pk37
Si Satchanalai N.P. THA 122 Pk37
Si Sawat THA 122 Pk38
Sishen ZA 204 Mb59
Sishilang CHN 106 Qe26
Sishui CHN 112 Qj28
Sisian ARM 91 Nc26
Sisimiut = Holsteinsborg DK 227 Hb05
Siskiyou Mts. USA 232 Dj25
Sison RP 124 Ra37
Si Songkhram THA 121 Qc37
Sisophon K 123 Qb39
Sissano PNG 155 Sb47
Sissédougou CI 187 Kg41
Sisseton USA 236 Fb23
Sissi TCH 189 Lk40
Sissonne F 51 Ld41
Sistan TM 98 Oa30
Siştărovaţ RO 67 Mb44
Sistema Ibérico E 56 Ks48
Sisteron F 53 Lf46
Sisters USA 232 Dk23
Siswali IND 116 Oj33
Sitakund BD 120 Pf34
Sitalike EAT 196 Mf49
Sitamarhi IND 117 Pc32
Sitampiky RM 207 Nd54
Sitang CHN 106 Qa27
Sitapur IND 115 Pa32
Sitar IND 120 Pe32
Sites archéologiques de la Dépression de l'Upemba RDC 196 Md50
Sites d'extraction de fer de Kindiba BF 187 Kj39
Sites funéraires de Morondava RM 207 Nc56
Sitges E 57 Lb49
Si That THA 123 Qb37
Si Thep THA 122 Qa38
Si Thep Historical Park THA 122 Qa38
Sithobela SD 205 Mf59
Sithonia GR 69 Me50
Sithra IND 117 Pb34
Sitía GR 71 Mg55
Sitiecito C 243 Fk34
Sitila MOC 203 Mh57
Sitin CHN 121 Qc34
Sitio d'Abadia BR 275 Hg53
Sitio do Mato BR 272 Hj52
Sitio Novo BR 272 Hg48
Sitio Novo do Tocantins BR 272 Hg48
Sitka USA 230 Dc17
Sitohóri GR 69 Md50
Sitona ER 192 Mj38
Sitotio Z 201 Mb54
Sittard NL 51 Lf40
Sittingbourne GB 49 La39
Sitting Bull Monument USA 236 Ek23
Sittwe MYA 120 Pg35
Situbondo RI 129 Qh49
Sitwa EAT 196 Mf49
Sitwe Z 196 Mg51
Si-u MYA 120 Pj34
Siulakderas RI 127 Qa46
Siumbatu RI 130 Rb47
Siumpu RI 130 Rb48
Siuna NIC 249 Fh39
Siuna RI 130 Rb46
Siuri IND 117 Pd34
Sivac SRB 68 Lu45
Šivačevo BG 69 Mg48
Sivaganga IND 119 Ok41
Sivakasi IND 118 Oj41
Sivaki RUS 105 Rd19
Sivaram Wildlife Sanctuary IND 117 Ok36
Sivaram W.S. IND 117 Ok36
Sivas TR 90 Mj26
Sivé RIM 180 Kd38
Siverek TR 91 Mk27
Siverskij RUS 44 Ml31
Sivrihisar TR 90 Mf26
Siwa ET 178 Mc31
Siwa RI 130 Ra47
Siwa Z 201 Mb53
Siwa Lima Museum RI 131 Re47
Siwan IND 117 Pc32
Siwa Oasis ET 178 Mc31
Sixes USA 232 Dh24
Six Flags B 51 Le40
Six Flags Astroworld USA 238 Fc31
Six Flags Great America USA 237 Ff24
Six-Fours-les-Plages F 53 Lf47
Si Xing CHN 112 Qj29
Six Miles MOC 203 Mh55
Six Nations Ind. Res. CDN 237 Fk24
Sixth Cataract SUD 185 Mg37
Siyabuswa ZA 205 Me58
Siyahcheshmeh IR 91 Nc26
Siyambalanduwa CL 119 Pa42
Siyana IND 115 Ok31
Siyand IR 98 Ng30
Siyang CHN 112 Qk29
Siyezen AZ 91 Ne25
Siyu Fort EAK 195 Na47
Sızır TR 90 Mh26
Siziwang Qi CHN 106 Qf25
Sizun F 50 Kq42
Sjælland DK 42 Lm35
Sjain RUS 111 Rh22
Sjanno BY 72 Me18
Sjaunja naturreservat S 38 Lu23
Sjenica SRB 68 Lu47
Sjerogošte MNE 68 Lu48
Sjeverni Velebit, N.P. HR 61 Lq46
Sjeverodonec'k UA 72 Mk21
Sjøasen N 40 Lm26
Sjöbo S 43 Lo35
Sjøholt N 40 Lg28
Sjötofta S 42 Lo33
Sjötorp S 43 Lo32
Sjøvegan N 38 Ls22
Sjuntorp S 42 Ln32
Sjuøyane N 38 Ma05
Sju søstre N 40 Ln25
Sjuvjaoro RUS 44 Mk29
Skabro SYR 90 Mk27
Skadarsko jezero, N.P. MNE 68 Lu48
Skadovs'k UA 73 Mg22
Skælskør DK 42 Lm35
Skærbæk DK 42 Lj35
Skaftung FIN 44 Mb28
Skagafjörður IS 46 Ka25
Skagaströnd IS 46 Ju25
Skagatá IS 46 Ju24
Skagen DK 42 Ll33
Skagens museum DK 42 Ll33
Skagerrak 42 Lj33
Skagi IS 46 Ju24
Skagit Prov. Park CDN 232 Dk21
Skagshamn S 44 Lt27
Skagway USA 230 Dc16
Skaill GB 48 Ks32
Skaistgirys LT 45 Md34
Skaistkalne LV 45 Me34
Skála GR 70 Mc54
Skála GR 71 Mg53
Skała PL 65 Lu40
Skála Eressú GR 71 Mf51
Skálafellsjökull IS 46 Ke26
Skála Marión GR 69 Me50
Skála Oropoú GR 69 Md52
Skala-Podil's'ka UA 73 Md21
Skálavík DK 46 Ko29
Skálholt IS 46 Ju26
Skalica BG 69 Mg48
Skalica SK 66 Ls42
Skalotí GR 69 Me49
Skandáli GR 71 Mf51
Skandawa PL 65 Mb36
Skanderborg DK 42 Lk34
Skåne S 43 Lo35
Skånevik N 42 Lf31
Skänninge S 43 Lq32
Skara S 43 Lo32
Skara Brae GB 48 Kr31
Skarberget N 38 Lr22
Skärblacka S 43 Lq32
Skarðsheiði IS 46 Jt26
Skardu 115 Oh28
Skare N 42 Lg31
Skåre S 43 Lo31
Skärgårdshavets n.p. = Saaristomeren kansallispuisto FIN 44 Mb31
Skärhamn S 42 Lm33
Skarness N 42 Lm30
Skärplinge S 43 Ls30
Skaryszew PL 65 Mb39
Skarżysko-Kamienna PL 65 Ma39
Skattkärr S 43 Lo31
Skattungbyn S 41 Lp29
Skaudvilė LT 45 Mc35
Skawina PL 65 Lu41
Skaymat DARS 174 Kc33
Skazar AFG 97 Of27
Skeby S 43 Lo32
Skeda S 43 Lq32
Skedshult S 43 Lr32
Skee S 42 Lm32
Skeena Mountains CDN 230 Df17
Skegness GB 49 La37
Skei N 40 Lg29
Skei N 40 Lj28
Skeiðarársandur IS 46 Kc27
Skeldon GUY 266 Hb43
Skeleton Coast NAM 200 Lf54
Skeleton Coast N.P. NAM 200 Lg55
Skellefteå S 41 Ma26
Skelleftehamn S 41 Mb26
Skellig Michael IRL 47 Kk39
Skender Vakuf BIH 61 Ls46
Skene S 42 Ln33
Skepastí GR 71 Me55
Skerries IRL 47 Ko37
Skhira TN 176 Lf28
Skhirat MA 175 Kg29
Skhour-Rehamna MA 175 Kg29
Ski N 42 Ll31
Ski Area Cairngorm Mountains GB 48 Kr33
Ski Area Nevis Range GB 48 Kp34
Skiáthos GR 69 Md51
Skiáthos GR 69 Md51
Skibbereen IRL 47 Kl39
Skibladner N 42 Lm30
Skibotn N 38 Ma21
Skidal' BY 65 Me37
Skidegate CDN 230 Dd19
Skidmore USA 245 Fb31
Skien N 42 Lk31
Skierbieszów PL 65 Md40
Skierniewice PL 65 Ma39
Skikda DZ 176 Ld27
Skillingaryd S 43 Lp33
Skinnastaður IS 46 Kd24
Skinnskatteberg S 43 Lq31
Skipton AUS 151 Sb64
Skipton GB 49 Ks37
Skirmantiškė LT 45 Md35
Skirmish Point AUS 146 Rh51
Skiropoula GR 71 Me52
Skiros GR 71 Me52
Skive DK 42 Lk34
Ski World USA 239 Fg26
Skjaldbreiður IS 46 Ju26
Skjern DK 42 Lj35
Skjernøy N 42 Lh33
Skjervøy N 38 Ma20
Skjolden N 40 Lh29
Skjønhaug N 42 Lm31
Sklop BIH 61 Lr46
Šklov BY 72 Mf18
Šklyv UA 65 Mf40
Škocjanske jame SLO 66 Lp45
Skoczów PL 65 Lt41
Škofja Loka SLO 66 Lp44
Škofljica SLO 66 Lp45
Skógafoss IS 46 Ka27
Skógar IS 46 Ka27
Skoghall S 43 Lo31
Skogskyrkogården S 43 Lt31
Skoki PL 64 Ls38
Skokloster S 43 Ls31
Skole UA 67 Md41
Skolivs'ki Beskydy N.P. UA 67 Mc42
Skollenborg N 42 Lk31
Skópelos GR 69 Md51
Skópelos GR 69 Md51
Skopiá GR 70 Mc51
Skopin RUS 72 Mk19
Skopje MK 68 Mb48
Skopsko Kale MK 68 Mb48
Skopun DK 46 Ko29
Skórcz PL 64 Lt37
Skorków PL 65 Ma40
Skorodnoe RUS 72 Mj20
Skorogoszcz PL 64 Ls40
Skoroszyce PL 64 Ls40
Skorovatn N 40 Lo26
Skørping DK 42 Lk34
Skortsinós GR 70 Mc53
Skosai RI 155 Sa47
Skotterud N 42 Ln31
Skoulikariá GR 70 Mb51
Skoura MA 175 Kg30
Skoúrta GR 69 Md52
Skövde S 43 Lo32
Skovorodino RUS 89 Ra08
Skowhegan USA 241 Gf23
Skownan CDN 236 Fa20
Skoyo 114 Oh28
Skra GR 68 Mc49
Skrad HR 61 Lp45
Skradin HR 61 Lq47
Skradinski buk HR 61 Lq47
Skreia N 42 Lm30
Skrekken N 42 Lh30
Škrip HR 61 Lr47
Skrīveri LV 45 Mf34
Skrunda LV 45 Mc34
Skudeneshavn N 42 Lf31
Skukuza ZA 205 Mf58
Skule S 44 Lt27
Skuleskogens n.p. S 44 Lt27
Skulgam N 38 Lu21
Skull Valley Ind. Res. USA 235 Ed25
Skulsk PL 64 Lt38
Skulte LV 45 Me33
Skultorp S 43 Lo32
Skultuna S 43 Lr31
Skuodas LT 45 Mb34
Skuon K 123 Qc39
Skurup S 43 Lo35
Skurv S 43 Lq34
Skutari = Shkodër AL 68 Lu48
Skutskär S 43 Ls30
Skútustaðir IS 46 Kc25
Skúvoy DK 46 Ko29
Skverbai LT 45 Me35
Skvyra UA 73 Me21
Skwierzyna PL 64 Lq38
Sky Blu 287 Gb33
Skye GB 48 Ko33
Skykomish USA 232 Dk22
Skyline Caverns USA 241 Ga26
Skytrain Ice Rise 287 Ga34
Skyttorp S 43 Ls30
Slade Point AUS 147 Sb51
Slagelse DK 42 Lm35
Slamet, Gunung RI 129 Qe49
Slana USA 229 Cj14
Slănčev Briag BG 69 Mh48
Slancy RUS 44 Mj31
Slane IRL 47 Ko37
Slănic RO 69 Mf45
Slano HR 61 Ls48
Slaný CZ 66 Lp40
Śląskie PL 64 Lq39
Slate Falls CDN 236 Fe20
Slate Island CDN 237 Fg21
Slatina BIH 61 Ls46
Slatina HR 61 Ls45
Slatina RO 69 Me46
Slatina SRB 68 Lu46
Slatina-Timiş RO 68 Mc45
Slaton USA 238 Ek29
Slattum N 42 Ll31
Slaukava BY 65 Mg37
Slave Coast DY/WAN 188 Lb42
Slave Lake CDN 231 Ec18
Slave Point CDN 231 Ec15
Slavharad BY 72 Mf19
Slavic bazaar BY 72 Mf18
Slavičín CZ 66 Ls41
Slavikai LT 45 Mc36
Slavinja SRB 68 Mc47
Slav'janka RUS 110 Rf24
Slavjansk na-Kubani RUS 73 Mk23
Slavkoviči RUS 45 Mk33
Slavnoe RUS 111 Se23
Slavonice CZ 66 Lq42
Slavonija HR 61 Ls45
Slavonski Brod HR 61 Lt45
Slavonski Šamac HR 61 Lt45
Slavsk RUS 45 Mb35
Slavs'ke UA 67 Md42
Slavuta UA 73 Md20
Sławatycze PL 65 Md39
Slawi RI 129 Qe49
Sławno PL 64 Lr36
Slayton USA 236 Fc24
Sleaford GB 49 Ku38
Slea Head IRL 47 Kk38
Sleeping Bear Dunes Nat. Lakeshore USA 237 Fg23
Sleeping Giant Prov. Park CDN 237 Ff21
Sleepy Eye USA 236 Fc23
Ślesin PL 64 Lt38
Slidell USA 239 Ff30
Sliema M 63 Lp55
Slieve Bloom Mountains IRL 47 Kn37
Slieve League IRL 47 Km36
Sligachan GB 48 Ko33
Sligo IRL 47 Km36
Sligo Bay IRL 47 Km36
Slim DZ 176 Lb28
Slisenvaara RUS 44 Mk29
Slite S 43 Lt33
Slivata BG 68 Md47
Sliven BG 69 Mg48
Slivnica BG 68 Md48
Slivo Pole BG 69 Mg47
Śliwice PL 64 Lt37
Sljudjanka RUS 104 Qb20
Sloboda LV 45 Mh34
Slobozia RO 69 Mh46
Slobozia Mare MD 69 Mj45
Slocan CDN 232 Eb21
Słomniki PL 65 Ma40
Slonim BY 65 Mf37
Slough GB 49 Ku39
Slovakia SK 67 Lu42
Slovenia SLO 66 Lp45
Slovenj Gradec SLO 66 Lq44
Slovenská Bistrica SLO 66 Lq44
Slovenská L'upča SK 67 Lu42
Slovenský raj, N.P. SK 67 Ma42
Slov'jans'k UA 73 Mj21
Słowiński P.N. PL 64 Ls36
Słubice PL 64 Lp38
Sluck BY 72 Md19
Slunj HR 61 Lq45
Słupca PL 64 Ls38
Słupia PL 65 Mb40
Słupno PL 65 Lu38
Słupsk PL 64 Lr36
Slurry ZA 205 Mc58
Slussfors S 41 Lr25
Slyne Head IRL 47 Kk37
Småland S 43 Lp33
Smålandsstenar S 43 Lo33
Smalininkai LT 45 Mc35
Smaljanica BY 65 Me38
Smaljavičy BY 72 Me18
Small Malaita = Maramasike SOL 157 Ta50
Smallwood Reservoir CDN 227 Gd08
Smara DARS 174 Ke32
Smârdioasa RO 69 Mf47
Smarhon' BY 45 Mg36
Šmarje pri Jelšah SLO 66 Lq44
Smeaton CDN 233 Eh19
Smeberg S 42 Lm32
Smedby S 43 Lr34
Smederevo SRB 68 Ma46
Smedjebacken S 43 Lq30
Smethport USA 237 Ga25
Smidovič RUS 110 Rg21
Śmierdnica PL 64 Lp37
Śmigiel PL 64 Lr38
Smila UA 73 Mf21
Smilec BG 69 Me48
Smiley CDN 233 Ef20
Smiltene LV 45 Mf33
Smith CDN 231 Ed18
Smith Bay CDN 227 Ga03
Smith Bay USA 229 Cc10
Smith Center USA 238 Fa26
Smithers CDN 230 Dg18
Smith Ferry USA 232 Eb23
Smithfield USA 242 Ga28
Smithfield ZA 205 Md61
Smith Group, Sir J. AUS 147 Se56
Smith Island IND 122 Pg39
Smith Island USA 242 Gb29
Smith Point AUS 146 Rg51
Smith River CDN 230 Dg16
Smith's Knoll 49 Lc38
Smithton AUS 151 Sc66
Smithtown AUS 149 Sg61
Smithville USA 239 Fh28
Smithville USA 239 Fk26
Smithville House AUS 148 Sa61
Smjadovo BG 69 Mh47
Smjörfjöll IS 46 Kf25
Smogulec PL 64 Ls37
Smojlovo RUS 45 Mj33
Smoke Creek Desert USA 234 Ea25
Smoke Hole Caverns USA 241 Ga26
Smoky Falls CDN 237 Fj20
Smoky Falls CDN 237 Fk20
Smoky Hills USA 238 Fa26
Smoky Lake CDN 231 Ed18
Smoky River CDN 231 Ea18
Smøla N 40 Lh27
Smołdzino PL 64 Ls36
Smolenice SK 66 Ls42
Smolensk RUS 72 Mg18
Smolensko-Moskovskaja vozyšennost' RUS 72 Mg18
Smoljan BG 69 Me49
Smoljaninovo' RUS 110 Rg24
Smolnik PL 65 Mc41
Smolsko BG 69 Md48
Smooth Rock Falls CDN 237 Fk21
Smože UA 67 Md42
Smygehamn S 43 Lo35
Smygehuk S 43 Lo35
Smyha UA 65 Mf40
Smyley Island 287 Ga33
Smyrna USA 239 Fh29
Smyrna USA 241 Gc26
Snabai RI 154 Rh46
Snaefell GB 49 Kq36
Snæfell IS 46 Ke26
Snæfellsnes IS 46 Js26
Snækollur IS 46 Ka26
Snake and Manjang Caverns ROK 112 Rd29
Snake Indian River CDN 232 Ea19
Snake Island AUS 151 Sd65
Snake River CDN 229 Dd13
Snake River USA 232 Eb23
Snake River Canyon USA 232 Eb22
Snake River Plains USA 232 Ed24
Snaran Jogizai PK 99 Oe30
Snare Lakes CDN 231 Ec13
Snåsa N 40 Ln26
Snedsted DK 42 Lj34
Sneek NL 51 Lf37
Sneekermeer NL 51 Lf37
Sneem IRL 47 Kl39
Sneeuberg ZA 205 Mc61
Snežnaja RUS 104 Qc20
Sniebal IND 120 Pg34
Śnieżka PL 64 Lq40
Śnieżnik Kłodzki PL 64 Lr40
Snihurivka UA 73 Mg22
Snina SK 67 Mc42
Snjatyn UA 67 Mf42
Snježna Marija HR 61 Lr45
Snøhetta N 40 Lk28
Snøhuten N 42 Lg31
Snoqualmie Pass USA 232 Dk22
Snøtoppen N 38 Lk05
Snou BY 65 Mg37
Snoul K 123 Qd39
Snoul W.S. K 123 Qd39
Snowdon GB 49 Kq37
Snowdonia N.P. GB 49 Kr38
Snowdrift CDN 231 Ee14
Snowflake CDN 236 Fa21
Snowflake USA 235 Ee28
Snow Hill USA 241 Gc26
Snow Lake CDN 233 Ek18
Snow Lake USA 239 Fe28
Snow Mount USA 234 Dj26
Snowshoe Peak USA 232 Ec21
Snowtown AUS 150 Rk62
Snowville USA 235 Ed25
Snowy Mountains AUS 151 Se64
Snowy River AUS 151 Se64
Snowy River N.P. AUS 151 Se64
Snug Corner BS 250 Gd34
Snyder USA 238 Ek29
So BF 181 Kk38
Soacha CO 264 Gc43
Soahany RM 207 Nc55
Soalala RM 206 Nc54
Soalara RM 207 Nb57
Soaloka RM 207 Nc55
Soamanonga RM 207 Nc57
Soanierana-Ivongo RM 207 Ne54
Soanindrarivy RM 207 Nd55
Soap Lake USA 232 Ea22
Soaserana RM 207 Nc56
Soata CO 264 Gd42
Soave I 60 Lm45
Soavina RM 207 Nd56
Soavina RM 207 Ne56
Soavinandriana RM 207 Nd55
Soba WAN 188 Le40
Sobaek Sanmaek ROK 112 Rd28
Sobaeksan N.P. ROK 112 Re27
Sobat SUD 191 Mg41
Soberania, P.N. PA 249 Ga41
Sobibór PL 65 Md39
Sobinka RUS 72 Na18
Sobo-Katamuki Q.N.P. J 113 Rf29
Sobolevo RUS 72 Na18
Sobótka PL 65 Mb40
Sobra HR 61 Ls48
Sobradinho BR 273 Hk50
Sobradinho BR 275 Hg53
Sobradinho BR 276 Hd60
Sobrado BR 272 Hg52
Sobral BR 269 Ge50
Sobral BR 273 Hk47
Sobrance SK 67 Mc42
Søby DK 42 Ll36
Socaire RCH 279 Gg57
Socastee USA 242 Ga29
Socavão BR 277 Hf58
Sochaczew PL 65 Ma38
Sochinsky nacional'nyj park RUS 73 Mk23
Soči RUS 73 Mk24
Society Hill USA 242 Ga28
Socodor RO 67 Mb44
Socompa PE 279 Gf58
Socompa RA 279 Gf58
Socompa, Volcán RCH/RA 279 Gf58
Socorro BR 275 Hg57
Socorro BR 276 He58
Socorro CO 264 Gd42
Socorro RP 124 Rc41
Socorro USA 235 Eg28
Socorro USA 235 Eg30
Socota CO 264 Gd42
Socota PE 268 Ga49
Socotra YE 95 Nh39
Soc Trang VN 123 Qc41
Socuéllamos E 57 Ks51
Soda Creek CDN 232 Dj19
Sodakor IND 114 Of32
Sodankylä FIN 39 Mg23
Soda Springs USA 233 Ee24
Söderåkra S 43 Lr34
Söderarm S 43 Lu31
Söderåsens n.p. S 42 Lo35
Söderbärke S 43 Lq30
Söderfors S 43 Ls30
Söderhamn S 41 Ls29
Söderköping S 43 Lq32
Södermanland S 43 Lr31
Södertälje S 43 Ls31
Södertörn S 43 Ls31
Södervik S 43 Lt31
Sodi RI 130 Qk46
Sodiri SUD 184 Me38
Sodium ZA 204 Mb61
Sodo ETH 192 Mj42
Sodore ETH 192 Mk41
Södra Midsjöbanken 43 Ls35
Södra Ölands odlingslandskap S 43 Lr34
Södra Vi S 43 Lq33
Sodwana Bay N.P. ZA 205 Mg59
Soe RI 131 Rc50
Soekmekaar ZA 202 Me57
Soeng San THA 123 Qb38
Soesdyke GUY 266 Ha42
Soest D 58 Lj39
Soetdoring Nature Reserve ZA 205 Md60
Sofádes GR 70 Mc51
Sofara RMM 181 Kh38
Sofia BG 68 Md48
Sofijivka UA 73 Mg21
Sofijskij sobor RUS 72 Mf16
Sofiysky sobor UA 72 Mf20
Sof Omar Caves ETH 192 Na42
Sofporog RUS 39 Mm25
Sogakofe GH 187 La42
Sogamoso CO 264 Gd43
Sögel D 58 Lh38
Sogeri PNG 155 Sd50
Sogndal N 40 Lh29
Sognefjorden N 40 Lf29
Sogod RP 124 Rc40
Sogolle TCH 183 Lh38
Sogoot MNG 104 Pk21
Sogossagasso BF 187 Kh40
Soguip'o ROK 112 Rd29
Soğukpınar TR 69 Mk50
Soğuksu Milli Parkı TR 90 Mg25
Söğüt TR 90 Me27
Söğütlü TR 91 Na26
Sog Xian CHN 103 Pg30
Sohâg ET 179 Mf32
Sohagi IND 117 Pa33
Sohar OM 95 Nj33
Sohela IND 117 Pb35
Sohey IR 98 Ng29
Sohna IND 114 Oj31
Sohós GR 68 Md50
Sohuksan Do ROK 112 Rc28
Soignies B 51 Le40
Soila IND 114 Og32
Şoimi RO 67 Mc44
Soin BF 187 Kj39
Soini FIN 56 Me28
Sointula CDN 232 Dg20
Soissons F 51 Ld41
Soja J 113 Rg28
Sojat IND 116 Og33
Sojol RI 125 Ra45
Sojoton Point RP 124 Rb41
Sojuz 287 Gc33
Sokal' UA 65 Me40
Sokch'o ROK 112 Re26
Söke TR 71 Mh53
Sokele RDC 199 Mc50
Sokhumi GE 91 Na24
Sokhumi GE 91 Na24
Sokna N 42 Lk30
Soko CI 187 Kj42
Soko Banja SRB 68 Mb47
Sokodé TG 187 La41
Sokoiyo RI 130 Ra47
Sokolac BIH 68 Lt47
Sokoliv UA 67 Mf41
Sokółka PL 65 Md37
Sokollu Camii TR 69 Mh49
Sokolo RMM 181 Kg38
Sokolov CZ 66 Ln40
Sokołów Małopolski PL 65 Mc40
Sokołów Podlaski PL 65 Mc38
Sokolski manastir BG 69 Mf48
Sokoły PL 65 Mc38
Sokorbey RN 182 Lb39
Sokoto WAN 182 Lc39
Sokoto WAN 188 Lc40
Sokoulama RG 186 Kf41
Sokoura RMM 187 Kj39
Soksok RN 182 Ld38
Sola C 243 Gb35
Sola N 42 Lf32
Sola VU 158 Td52
Sola de Vega MEX 246 Fb37
Solahpet IND 116 Oj37
Solan IND 115 Oj30
Solana RP 124 Ra37
Solana USA 243 Fk32
Solana del Pino E 55 Kq52
Solander Island NZ 153 Td69
Solânea BR 273 Jc49
Solano RP 124 Ra37
Solano YV 265 Gg45
Solar de Mateus P 54 Kn49
Solares E 56 Kr47
Solat RI 125 Rd45
Solberg S 41 Ls27
Sol'cy RUS 72 Mf16
Soldado Monge EC 268 Gb47
Sol de Julio RA 279 Gj60
Sol de Mañana BOL 279 Gg57
Sölden A 60 Lm44
Soldotna USA 228 Ce15
Solé BF 181 Kj38
Soleb Temple SUD 185 Mf35
Solec Kujawski PL 64 Lt37
Soledad CO 264 Gc40
Soledad USA 234 Dk27
Soledad YV 265 Gj41
Soledad de Doblado MEX 246 Fb36
Soledad de G. Sánchez MEX 246 Ek34
Soledade BR 273 Jb49
Soledade BR 276 Hd60
Solemar BR 277 Hg58
Solenzara F 62 Lk49
Solenzo BF 187 Kh39
Sole Pit 49 Lb37
Solh Abad IR 98 Nj28
Solhan TR 91 Na26
Soli RN 182 Ld38
Solihull GB 49 Kt38
Solikamsk RUS 88 Nd07
Soliman TN 176 Lf27
Solimões = Amazon BR 270 Gj47
Solingen D 58 Lh39
Solís de Mataojo ROU 281 Hc63
Solita CO 264 Gc45
Solitaire NAM 204 Lj57
Sölktäler A 61 Lo43
Sollebrunn S 42 Ln32
Sollefteå S 41 Ls27
Sollentuna S 43 Ls31
Sóller E 57 Lc51
Solliden S 43 Lr34
Sollihøgda N 42 Ll31
Solna BF 187 La39
Solncevo RUS 72 Mj20
Solnečnogorsk RUS 72 Mj17
Solnice CZ 66 Lr40
Solo RI 129 Qf49
Šolohovskij RUS 73 Na21
Solok RI 127 Qa46
Sololo EAK 195 Mk44
Soloma GCA 248 Fe38
Solomon Islands 135 Ta10
Solomon Islands 157 Sj48
Solomon Sea PNG 156 Sf49
Solomon's Wall RB 202 Me57
Solon CHN 105 Ra22
solonchakovyye vpadiny Unguz TM 96 Nk26
Solone UA 73 Mh21
Solongtyn davaa MNG 104 Pk21
Solonópole BR 273 Ja48
Solor RI 131 Rb50
Solothurn CH 60 Lh43
Solotvyn UA 67 Me42
Solotvyna UA 67 Md43
Solov'evsk RUS 105 Qh21
Solsona E 56 Lb49
Solsvik N 40 Le30
Solt H 67 Lu44
Šolta HR 61 Lr47
Soltan Abad IR 96 Nj27
Soltan Bagh AFG 99 Oe29
Soltaniyeh IR 91 Ne27
Soltau D 58 Lk38
Solti-lapály H 67 Lu44
Soltvadkert H 67 Lu44
Solusi ZW 202 Me56
Solvang USA 234 Dk28
Solvarbo S 43 Lq30
Sölvesborg S 43 Lp34
Solway Firth GB 48 Kr36
Solwezi Z 201 Md52
Soly BY 45 Mg36
Solymar ROU 281 Hc63
Sol y Nieve E 55 Kr53
Som IND 116 Og33
Soma J 111 Sa27
Soma TR 71 Mh51
Somabhula ZW 202 Me55
Somadougou RMM 181 Kh38
Somaén E 57 Ks49
Somain F 51 Ld40
Somalia 163 Na09
Somali Plateau ETH 192 Na41
Somalomo CAM 189 Lg44
Somavaram IND 117 Pb37
Somba RI 130 Qk47
Sómbak'e = Yellowknife CDN 231 Ec14
Sombo ANG 199 Ma50
Sombor SRB 68 Lu45
Sombrerete MEX 246 Ej34
Sombrero KNA 251 Gj36
Sombrero RCH 282 Gf72
Sombrero Channel IND 122 Pg42
Sombrero Negro RA 279 Gk57
Sombrio BR 277 Hf60
Şomcuta Mare RO 67 Md43
Somdet THA 123 Qb37
Somero FIN 44 Md30
Somers AUS 151 Sc65
Somerset AUS 147 Sb51
Somerset AUS 151 Sc66
Somerset CDN 236 Fa21
Somerset USA 239 Fh27
Somerset USA 241 Ga26
Somerset-East ZA 205 Mc62
Somerset Island CDN 227 Fb04
Somerset Oos ZA 205 Mc62
Somerset West ZA 204 Lk63
Somerton AUS 149 Sf61
Somianki PL 65 Mb38
Somil ANG 201 Ma53
Somina BIH 68 Lt48
Somina MNE 68 Lt48
Sömmerda D 58 Lm39
Sommerdown NAM 200 Lk56
Sommesous F 51 Le42
Sommières F 53 Le47
Somo RMM 187 Kh39
Somogyvár H 66 Ls44
Somonino PL 64 Lt36
Somosomo FJI 159 Ua54
Somotillo NIC 248 Fg39
Sompeta IND 117 Pc36
Som Poi THA 123 Qb38
Sompolno PL 64 Lt38
Somra MYA 120 Ph33
Soná PA 249 Fk41
Sonaco GNB 186 Kc39
Sonagiri IND 117 Ok33
Sonai-Rupa N.P. IND 120 Pg32
Sonamukhi BD 120 Pe33
Sonamukhi IND 117 Pd34
Sonapur IND 117 Pb35
Sonari IND 120 Ph32
Sonarigaon IND 120 Ph32
Sonbong PRK 110 Rf24
Sonch'on PRK 110 Rc26
Soncillo E 56 Kr48
Sonda PK 99 Oe33
Sóndalo I 60 Ll44
Søndeled N 42 Lk32
Sønderborg DK 42 Lk36
Sønder Nissum DK 42 Lj34
Sønder Omme DK 42 Lj35
Sondershausen D 58 Ll39
Søndersø DK 42 Ll35
Søndervig DK 42 Lj34
Sondi RI 127 Pk44
Sondo IND 117 Ok36
Son Dong VN 121 Qd35
Søndrestrømfjord = Kangerlussuaq DK 227 Hb05
Sóndrio I 60 Lk44
Sondu EAK 194 Mh46
Son en Breugel NL 51 Lf39
Sonepat IND 114 Oj31
Song MAL 128 Qg45
Song THA 121 Qa36
Song WAN 189 Lg41
Songa MOC 202 Mg53
Songa RDC 199 Mc50
Songa RI 131 Rd46
Songbu CHN 109 Qh30
Song Cau VN 123 Qe39
Songea EAT 196 Mh51
Songgwangsa Temple ROK 112 Rd28
Songhua Hu CHN 110 Rd24
Songijang CHN 112 Ra30
Songir IND 116 Og34
Songir IND 116 Oh35
Songjiang CHN 110 Re24
Songjianghe CHN 110 Rd24
Songkan CHN 108 Qd31
Songkhla THA 123 Qa42
Songkhon LAO 123 Qc37
Song Khwae THA 121 Qa36
Song-Köl KS 100 Oh25
Songkou CHN 109 Qk33
Songling CHN 105 Ra22
Song Ling CHN 107 Qk25
Song Luy VN 123 Qe40
Songmen CHN 109 Ra31
Songming CHN 121 Qb33
Songnim PRK 112 Rc26
Songnisan N.P. ROK 112 Rd27
Songo ANG 198 Lh49
Songo SUD 191 Mc41
Songo-lolo RDC 198 Lh48
Songo Mnara EAT 197 Mk50
Songpan CHN 106 Qb29
Song Phinong THA 122 Qa38
Songsha CHN 102 Pa30
Song Shan CHN 107 Qg28
Songshan Z.B. CHN 107 Qh25
Songtao CHN 108 Qe31
Songxi CHN 109 Qk32
Song Xian CHN 106 Qg28
Songyang CHN 109 Qk31
Songyu ROK 113 Re27
Songyuan CHN 110 Rc23
Songzanlin Monastery CHN 121 Pk32
Songzi CHN 108 Qf30
Sonhat IND 117 Pb34
Son Hiep VN 123 Qe39
Son Hoa VN 123 Qe39
Sonid Youqi CHN 104 Qg24
Sonid Zuoqi CHN 105 Qg24
Sonjo EAT 194 Mh47
Sonkovo RUS 72 Mj17
Sonkwale Mountains WAN 188 Le42
Son La VN 121 Qb35
Son Mbong CAM 188 Lf44
Sonmiani PK 99 Od33
Sonneberg D 59 Lm40
Sonoita USA 235 Ee30
Sonoma Range USA 234 Eb25
Sonora BR 274 Hc54
Sonora MEX 244 Ee31
Sonora USA 234 Dk27
Sonora USA 238 Ek30
Sonoran Desert USA 234 Ec29
Sonora Pass USA 234 Ea26
Sonoumom DY 188 Lb41
Sonoyta MEX 244 Ed30
Sonozo CI 187 Kg41
Sonpar Hills IND 117 Pb33
Sonpuri IND 116 Of35
Sonqor IR 91 Nd28
Sonseca E 55 Kr51
Sonsón CO 264 Gc43
Sonsonate ES 248 Ff39
Sonsorol Islands PAL 124 Rg43
Sonstraal ZA 204 Mb59
Sonta RDC 196 Me51
Sontang RI 127 Qa45
Son Tay VN 121 Qc35
Sonthofen D 59 Ll43
Sontra D 58 Lk39
Soomaa rahvuspark EST 45 Mf32
Sooya SP 195 Nb45
Sopachuy BOL 278 Gh55
Sopchoppy USA 239 Fh30
Soperton USA 242 Fj29
Sophie F 266 Hd43
Sop Huai THA 121 Pk36
Sopianae H 66 Lt44
Sopinusa RI 154 Rg47
Soplin PE 268 Gb47
Sop Moei THA 122 Pj37
Sopore 114 Oh28
Sopot PL 64 Lt36
Sopot SRB 68 Ma46
Sopotnica MK 68 Mb49
Sop Prap THA 121 Pk37
Sopron H 66 Lr43
Soprtrán CO 264 Gc42
Soputan RI 125 Rc45
Sora I 62 Lo49
Sorab IND 118 Oh38
Sorada IND 117 Pc36
Sorah PK 99 Oe32
Soraksan ROK 112 Re26
Soraksan N.P. ROK 112 Re26
Sora Mboum CAM 189 Lh42
Sorano I 60 Lm48
Sorapa PE 278 Gf54
sor Arys KZ 97 Od23
sor Ashchkol KZ 97 Od23
Sorata BOL 278 Gf53
Sorau WAN 189 Lg41
Søraust-Svalbard naturreservat N 38 Ma07
Sorbas E 55 Ks53
Sore F 52 Ku46
Sorel CDN 240 Gd22
Sorell AUS 151 Sd67
Soresina I 60 Lk45
Sør-Flatanger N 40 Ll26
Sórgono I 62 Lk50
Sorgues-l'Ouvèze F 53 Le46
Sorgun TR 90 Mh26
Sør-Gutvika N 40 Lm25
Sori DY 188 Lb40
Soria E 56 Ks49
Soriano ROU 276 Ha62
sor Kajdak KZ 96 Ng23
Sørkappøya N 38 Lj07
Sorkh Ab AFG 98 Ob29
Sørland N 42 Lg32
Sor Laspur PK 97 Og27
Sørli N 40 Lo26
Sornac F 53 Lc45
Sorø DK 42 Lm35
Soro IND 117 Pd35
Soro PK 99 Od30
Soro = Bahr el Ghazal TCH 183 Lj38
Sorobango CI 187 Kj41
Soroca MD 73 Me21
Sorocaba BR 277 Hg57
sor Oli Kultyk KZ 96 Ng23
Sorombéo CAM 189 Lh41
Sorondideri RI 154 Rh46
Sorong RI 131 Rf46
Sororó, T.I. BR 272 Hf48
Soroti EAU 194 Mg45
Sorrento CDN 232 Ea20
Sorrento I 63 Lp50
Sorriso BR 274 Hc52
Sorsakoski FIN 44 Mh28
Sorsan Grasslands IND 116 Oj33
Sorsele S 41 Ls25
Sorso I 62 Lj50
Sorsogon RP 124 Rc39
Sør-Spitsbergen n.p. N 38 Lj07
Sørstraumen N 38 Mb21
Sort E 56 Lb48
Sortavala RUS 44 Ml29
Sortland N 38 Lq22
Sørumsand N 42 Lm31
Sørvågen N 38 Lo23
Sørvágur DK 46 Kn28
Sosan ROK 112 Rd27
Sosan Haean N.P. ROK 112 Rd27
Sösdala S 43 Lo34
Sos del Rey Católico E 56 Kt48
Sosedka RUS 72 Nb19
Sosneado, Cerro RA 280 Gf63
Sosnenskij RUS 72 Mj19
Sosnicy RUS 44 Mk31
Sosnogorsk RUS 88 Nc06
Sosnove UA 73 Md20
Sosnovka RUS 72 Na19
Sosnovo RUS 44 Ml30
Sosnovo-Ozërskoe RUS 104 Qf19
Sosnovyj Bor RUS 44 Mk31
Sosnowica PL 65 Md39
Sosnowiec PL 65 Lu40
Sosolo SOL 157 Sj49
Sosonpal IND 117 Pa36
Sospel F 53 Lh47
Sosso RCA 190 Lh44
Sossobé RMM 181 Kh38
Sossusvlei NAM 204 Lh58
Sossusvlei Lodge NAM 204 Lh58
Sossusvlei Pan NAM 204 Lh58
Šoštanj SLO 66 Lq44
Šostka UA 72 Mg20
Sosúa DOM 250 Ge36
Sošyčne UA 65 Me39
Sotara, Volcán CO 264 Gb44
Soteapan MEX 247 Fc36
Sotian RMM 187 Kg40
Sotik EAK 194 Mh46
Sotillo de la Adrada E 55 Kq50
Soto RA 280 Gh61
Soto del Barco E 54 Ko47
Sotogrande E 55 Kp54
Sotok RI 129 Qf45
Soto La Marina MEX 246 Fa34
Sotomayor CO 264 Gb45
Sotouboua TG 187 La41
Sotra N 42 Lf30
Sottunga FIN 44 Ma30
Sottunga FIN 44 Ma30
Sotuta MEX 247 Ff35
Souanké RCB 189 Lh44
Souassi TN 176 Lf28
Soubakaniédogou BF 187 Kh40
Soubakpérou DY 188 La41
Soubané RG 186 Kc40
Soubéira BF 187 Kk39
Soubré CI 187 Kg43
Souchang CHN 109 Qk31
Soudan AUS 146 Rj56
Soudougui BF 187 La40
Souf DZ 176 Ld29
Soufflenheim F 51 Lh42
Soufli GR 69 Mg49
Soufrière WL 251 Gk39
Sougueur DZ 176 La28
Souhoulé RG 186 Kf42
Souillac F 52 Lb46
Souillac MS 207 Nj56
Souilly F 51 Lf41
Souk-Ahras DZ 176 Ld27
Souk-el-Arba-des-Beni-Hassan MA 175 Kh28
Souk-el-Arba-du-Rharb MA 175 Kg28
Souk-Jemâa-de-Oulad-Abbou MA 175 Kg29
Soukoukoutane RN 182 Lb38
Souk Tenadjeleline RMM 182 La36
Soul ROK 112 Rd27
Soulabali SN 186 Kc39
Soulac-sur-Mer F 52 Kt45
Soúli GR 70 Mc53
Soulíou GR 70 Ma51
Soulópoulo GR 70 Ma51
Sound of Barra IRL 48 Kn33
Sound of Harris GB 48 Kn33
Sound of Jura GB 48 Kp35
Sound of Monach GB 48 Kn33
Sound of Mull GB 48 Kp34
Sound of Sleat GB 48 Kp33
Sounds of Starlight Theatre AUS 148 Rg57
Soungrougrou SN 186 Kc39
Souq al-Milh YE 94 Nc38
Source Bleu de Meski MA 175 Kh30
Source chaude de Déssikou RCA 190 Lk42
Source chaude de Soborom TCH 183 Lj35
Source du Nil BU 196 Me47
Sour-el-Ghozlane DZ 176 Lb27
Souris CDN 236 Ek21
Souris CDN 240 Gj22
Souroukaha CI 187 Kh41
Sourountouna RMM 187 Kh39
Sourpi GR 70 Mc51
Sousa BR 273 Ja49
Sousceyrac F 52 Lc46
Sousel P 55 Kn52
Sous-Massa, P.N. MA 174 Kf30
Sousse TN 176 Lf28
Soustons F 52 Kt47
South Africa 163 Ma13
Southampton GB 49 Kt40
Southampton USA 241 Gd25
Southampton Island CDN 227 Fd06
South Andaman IND 122 Pg39
South Australia AUS 135 Rb13
South Australian Basin 134 Ra14
Southaven USA 239 Ff28
South Banda Basin RI 131 Rd49
South Banggi Strait MAL 128 Qj42
Southbank CDN 230 Dh18
South Bay CDN 236 Fd20
South Bay USA 243 Fk32
South Baymouth CDN 237 Fj23
South Bend USA 237 Fg25
South Bimini BS 243 Ga33
South Boston USA 242 Ga27
South Brahmaputra Hills IND 120 Pg33
South Branch CDN 241 Ha22
Southbridge NZ 153 Tg67
South Brook CDN 241 Hb21
South Brookfield CDN 240 Gh23
South Bruny Island AUS 151 Sd67
South Bruny N.P. AUS 151 Sd67
South Carolina USA 242 Fk28
South Cay CO 249 Fk38
South Channel RP 124 Ra38
South China Mountains CHN 108 Qd33
South China Sea 76 Qb08
South Coast Highway AUS 144 Ra62
South Dakota USA 236 Ek23
South Downs GB 49 Ku40
South East RB 205 Mc58
South East Aru Marine Reserve RI 154 Rh49
South East Cape AUS 151 Sd67
Southeast Cape USA 228 Bf14
Southeast Forests N.P. AUS 151 Se64
Southeast Indian Ridge 134 Qa14
South East Pacific Basin 254 Ea14
South East Point AUS 151 Sd65
Southeast Point BS 250 Gd35
Southend-on-Sea GB 49 La39
Southerland Falls NZ 153 Td68
Southern Alps NZ 153 Te68
Southern Altay Gobi Nature Reserve MNG 101 Pj24
Southern Central Reserve A.L. AUS 145 Rc59
Southern Cross AUS 144 Qk61
Southern Indian Lake CDN 227 Fa07
Southern Laos Cruise LAO/K 123 Qc38
Southern N.P. SUD 191 Me42
Southern Pines USA 242 Ga28
Southern Sporades GR 71 Mf52
Southern Uplands GB 48 Kq35
Southey CDN 233 Eh20
South Fiji Basin 134 Tb12
South Foreland GB 49 Lb39
South Fork USA 235 Eg27
SouthFrancisco de Macoris DOM 250 Ge36
South Galway AUS 148 Sb58
South Georgia GB 254 Ja15
South Georgia GB 255 Ja15
South Goulburn Island AUS 146 Rg51
South Gut Saint Ann's CDN 240 Gk22
South Harbour CDN 240 Gk22
South Hatia Island BD 120 Pf34
South Haven USA 237 Fg24
South Hill USA 242 Ga27
South Horr EAK 194 Mj45
South Island AUS 149 Sf56
South Island EAK 194 Mj44
South Island NZ 153 Te67
South Island N.P. EAK 194 Mj44
South Junction CDN 236 Fc21
South Kinangop EAK 194 Mj46
South Kitui National Reserve EAK 195 Mk46
South Korea ROK 77 Ra06
South Lake Tahoe USA 234 Ea26
South Luangwa N.P. Z 196 Mf52
South Luconia Shoals 128 Qg43
South Male Atoll MV 118 Og44
South Miladhunmadulu Atoll = Noonu Atoll MV 118 Og43
South Molton GB 49 Kr39
South Mtn. USA 232 Eb24
South Nahanni River CDN 230 Dh15
South Nilandhoo Atoll = Dhaalu Atoll MV 118 Og44
Southold USA 241 Gd25
South Orkney Islands GB 254 Hb14
South Orkney Islands GB 255 Hb15
South Ossetia GE 91 Nc24
South Padre Island USA 245 Fb32
South Padre Island USA 245 Fb32
South Pass City USA 235 Ef24
South Pole ANT 287 Ga36
South Porcupine CDN 237 Fk21
Southport AUS 149 Sg59
Southport AUS 151 Sd67
Southport CDN 241 Hd21
Southport GB 49 Kr37
Southport USA 242 Ga29
South Prince of Wales Wilderness USA 230 Dd18
South Pt. BS 250 Gc34
South Point = Ka Lae USA 234 Cc36
South Ronaldsay GB 48 Ks32
South Salmara IND 120 Pf33
South Sandwich Islands GB 254 Jb15
South Sandwich Islands GB 255 Jb15

South Sandwich Trench 254 Jb15
South Saskatchewan River CDN 233 El20
South Scotia Ridge 287 Hb31
South Shetland Islands ANT 287 Ha31
South Shields GB 48 Kt36
South Sioux City USA 236 Fb24
South Solomon Trench 157 Ta51
South Stradbroke Island AUS 149 Sg59
South Taranaki Bight NZ 153 Th66
South Tasman Rise 134 Sa14
South Tucson USA 235 Ee29
South Turkana National Reserve EAK 194 Mh45
South Uist GB 48 Kn33
Southwest Cape AUS 151 Sc67
Southwest Cape NZ 153 Td69
Southwest N.P. AUS 151 Sd67
Southwold GB 49 Lh38
South Yandaminta AUS 148 Sa60
Souto Soares BR 273 Hk52
Soutpan ZA 205 Md60
Soutpansberg ZA 202 Me57
Souvigny F 63 Lf42
Sovata RO 67 Mf44
Soverato I 63 Lr52
Sovereign Hill AUS 151 Sb64
Sovetsk RUS 45 Mb35
Sovetskaja RUS 72 Nb21
Sovetskaja 287 Pb34
Sovetskij RUS 44 Nh30
Sovetskoe RUS 91 Nb24
Sowa Pan RB 201 Mc56
Sowczyce PL 64 Lt40
Soweto ZA 205 Md59
Sowia Góra PL 64 Lg38
Sowma'eh Sara IR 91 Ne27
Soy EAK 194 Mh45
Soyaló MEX 247 Fd37
Soya-misaki J 111 Sb23
Soyo ANG 198 Lg49
Sozak KZ 97 Oe23
Sozopol BG 69 Mh48
Sozu J 111 Rj27
Spa B 57 Lh40
Spain E 27 Kb06
Spalding AUS 150 Rk62
Spalding GB 49 Ku38
Spálené Poříčí CZ 66 Lo41
Spaniard's Bay CDN 241 Hd22
Spanish Fork USA 235 Ee25
Spanish Head GB 49 Kp36
Spanish Town JA 250 Gb37
Spanwerk ZA 205 Md58
Sparks USA 234 Ea26
Sparreholm S 43 Lr31
Sparta USA 234 Ea26
Sparta USA 239 Ft28
Sparta USA 242 Fc29
Sparta USA 237 Fd24
Spartanburg USA 242 Fk28
Spárti GR 70 Mc53
Sparwood CDN 232 Ea21
Spas-Klepiki RUS 72 Na18
Spaso-Jakovlenskij monastyr' RUS 72 Mk17
Spasovo BG 69 Mj47
Spassk-Dal'nij RUS 110 Rg23
Spassk-Rjazanskij RUS 72 Na18
Spatsizi Plateau CDN 230 Df17
Spatsizi Plateau Wilderness Prov. Park CDN 230 Df17
Spean Bridge GB 48 Kq34
Spearfish USA 233 Ej23
Spearman USA 238 Ea27
Speculator USA 241 Gc24
Speedwell Island AUS 283 Ha72
Speightstown BDS 251 Ha39
Spello I 61 Ln47
Spencer USA 236 Fa24
Spencer USA 239 Fh26
Spencer USA 236 Fd25
Spencer USA 239 Fj28
Spencer USA 239 Ft28
Spencer Bay NAM 204 Lh58
Spencer Gulf AUS 150 Rj63
Spentrup DK 42 Ll34
Speos of Horemheb ET 179 Mg33
Sperrin Mountains GB 47 Kn36
Spessart D 59 Lk41
Spétses GR 69 Md53
Spétses GR 69 Md53
Speyer D 59 Lj41
Speyside Beach TT 251 Gk40
Spezand PK 99 Od30
Spezzano Albanese I 63 Lr51
Spezzano della Sila I 63 Lr51
Spiddle IRL 47 Kl37
Spiekeroog D 58 Lh37
Spielcasino Baden-Baden D 59 Lj42
Spijkenisse NL 51 Le39
Špilberk CZ 66 Lq40
Spileon Dirou GR 70 Mc54
Spileo Stalaktiton GR 71 Mf53
Spillimbergo I 61 Ln44
Spiljani KSV 68 Ma48
Spilsby GB 49 La37
Spinazzola I 63 Lr50
Spin Buldak AFG 99 Od30
Spindlerův Mlýn CZ 66 Lq40
Spioenkop ZA 205 Me59
Spirit Lake USA 236 Fc24
Spirit Lake Ind. Res. USA 236 Fa22
Spirit River CDN 231 Ea18
Spiritwood CDN 233 Eg19
Spirovo RUS 72 Mh17
Spišská Belá SK 67 Ma41
Spišský hrad SK 67 Ma42
Spitak ARM 91 Nc25
Spitsbergen N 26 Lb02
Spitskopvlei ZA 205 Mc61
Spittal an der Drau A 61 Lo44
Spitz A 66 Lq42
Spitzkoppe NAM 204 Lh58
Spitzkoppe Rock Paintings NAM 200 Lh56
Spiveys Corner USA 242 Ga28
Split HR 61 Lr47
Split HR 61 Lr47
Splügenpass = Passo dello Spluga I/CH 60 Lk44
Spodsbjerg DK 42 Ll36
Spofford USA 245 Ek31
Spoggies AUS 150 Rg62
Spogi LV 45 Mg34
Spokane USA 232 Eb22
Spokane Ind. Res. USA 232 Eb22
Špola UA 73 Mf21
Spoleto I 61 Ln48
Spook Cave USA 236 Fe24
Spookmyndorp NAM 204 Lh59
Spooner USA 236 Fe23
Spotorno I 60 Lj46
Spotted House USA 233 Eh23
Spottrup DK 42 Lj34
Spratly Islands 128 Qh40
Spray USA 232 Ea23
Spree D 58 Lp39
Spreewald D 58 Lp39
Spremberg D 58 Lp39
Sprengisandur IS 46 Kc26
Spring USA 238 Fc30
Springbok ZA 204 Lj60
Springdale CDN 241 Hd21
Springdale USA 238 Fc26
Springe D 58 Lk38
Springerville USA 235 Eh28
Springfield USA 232 Dj23
Springfield USA 239 Fe26
Springfield USA 238 Fd27

Springfield USA 239 Ff26
Springfield USA 239 Fg27
Springfield USA 239 Fh27
Springfield USA 238 Fa28
Springfield USA 241 Gd24
Springfield USA 242 Fk29
Springfield Plateau USA 238 Fd27
Springfontein ZA 205 Mc61
Spring Garden GUY 266 Ha42
Spring Hill USA 243 Fj31
Springrale USA 148 Sa57
Spring Ridge AUS 149 Sf61
Springs Junction NZ 153 Tg67
Springsure AUS 149 Se60
Springvale AUS 143 Rd54
Springvale USA 241 Gd24
Springvale Homestead AUS 146 Rg53
Spring Valley ZA 205 Md62
Springview USA 236 Fa24
Springville USA 235 Ee25
Springville USA 237 Ga24
Springwater CDN 236 Fj22
Sproge S 43 Lt33
Spruce Grove CDN 233 Ed19
Spruce Home CDN 233 Eh19
Spruce Island USA 228 Cd17
Spruce Meadows CDN 233 Ec20
Spruce Pine USA 242 Fj28
Spruce Woods Prov. Park CDN 236 Fa21
Spur USA 238 Ek29
Spurn Head GB 49 La37
Spuž MNE 68 Lu48
Squamish CDN 232 Dj21
Squaw Creek N.W.R. USA 238 Fc25
Squaw Lake USA 236 Fc22
Squaw Valley USA 234 Dk26
Squillace I 63 Lr52
Squinzano I 63 Lt50
Squires Mem. Prov. Park CDN 241 Hb21
Sragen RI 129 Qf49
Sravanabelgola IND 118 Oj39
Sravasti IND 117 Pb32
Srb HR 61 Lr46
Srbac BIH 61 Ls45
Srbobran SRB 68 Lu45
Srbovac KSV 68 Ma48
Srdiečko SK 67 Lu42
Sre Ambel K 123 Qd40
Srebárna BG 69 Mh46
Srebárna Nature Reserve BG 69 Mg47
Srebrenica BIH 68 Lu46
Srebrenik BIH 68 Lt45
Sredec BG 69 Mh48
Sredec BG 69 Mg48
Srednnyj hrebet RUS 89 Ta07
Sredna Gora BG 69 Me48
Sredneljala RUS 105 Re20
Srednerusskaja vozvyšennost' RUS 72 Mj19
Sre Koki K 123 Qd39
Šrem PL 64 Ls39
Sremska Mitrovica SRB 68 Lu46
Sremski Karlovci SRB 68 Lu45
Sre Noy K 123 Qc39
Sre Peang K 123 Qb39
Sretensk RUS 105 Qj19
Sribawono RI 127 Qc48
Sribne UA 73 Mg20
Sri Dungargarh IND 114 Oh31
Srigiripadu IND 117 Ok37
Sri Jayewardenepura CL 119 Ok42
Srikakulam IND 117 Ok39
Sri Karanpur IND 114 Og31
Sri Krishna Mutt (Udupi) IND 118 Oh39
Srimangal BD 120 Pf33
Sri Mohangarh IND 114 Of32
Srinagar IND 118 Oj39
Srinagar IND 114 Oh28
Srinakarin N.P. THA 122 Pk38
Srinakarin Reservoir THA 122 Pk38
Sringeri IND 118 Oh39
Srinivaspur IND 118 Oj38
Srirangam IND 119 Ok40
Srirangapatna IND 118 Oj39
Srisailam IND 116 Oj37
Srivilliputtur IND 118 Oj41
Środa Wielkopolska PL 64 Ls38
Srokowo PL 65 Mb36
Sr'reenshamali SYR 90 Mk27
Staaten River N.P. AUS 147 Sd54
Stabbursdalen n.p. N 39 Me20
Stachanov UA 73 Mk21
Stachy CZ 66 Lo41
Stack Skerry GB 48 Kq31
Stad N 40 Lf28
Staðarfell USA 148 Js25
Staðarhóll IS 46 Jt25
Staðarhraun IS 46 Jr25
Stade D 58 Lk37
Staderton ZA 205 Me59
Stadskanaal NL 51 Lh38
Stadthagen D 58 Lk38
Stadtlohn D 58 Lh39
Staffa GB 48 Kn34
Staffelberg D 59 Lm40
Stafford GB 48 Kq33
Staffanstorp S 42 Lo35
Stafford GB 49 Kt38
Stagira GR 69 Md50
Stahnsdorf D 58 Lo38
Staicele LV 45 Me33
Stajki BY 65 Mg14
Staked Plains = Llano Estacado USA 238 Ej29
Stakliškés LT 45 Me36
Stalbe LV 45 Mf33
Stalker Castle GB 48 Kp34
Stalldalen S 43 Lp31
Staller Sattel I/A 60 Ln44
Stalowa Wola PL 64 Mc40
Stambolijski BG 69 Me48
Stamford GB 49 Ku38
Stamford USA 238 Fa29
Stamford USA 241 Gd25
Stamford Bridge GB 49 Ku37
Stampriet NAM 204 Lk58
Stamsund N 38 Lm22
Stáncení RO 67 Mf44
Standing Rock Ind. Res. USA 236 Ek23
Standing Stone USA 239 Fh27
Stanford USA 237 Fj24
Stanford USA 233 Ee22
Stanford USA 232 Ee22
Stånga S 43 Lt33
Stanhope AUS 151 Sc64
Stanhope AUS 149 Sf60
Stanisic SRB 68 Lu45
Staňkov CZ 66 Lo41
Stanley AUS 151 Sc66
Stanley GB 283 Hb71
Stanley USA 233 Eh22
Stanley USA 232 Eb23
Stanley Mission CDN 231 Eh18
Stanley, Mount EAU/RDC 194 Mf45
Stanley Reservoir IND 118 Oj40
Stanovoj nagor'e RUS 89 Qc07
Stanovoy Khrebet RUS 89 Ra07
Stans CH 60 Lj44
Stansbury AUS 150 Rj63
Stanthorpe AUS 149 Sf60
Stanton USA 238 Ej29
Stanwell Park AUS 151 Sf63
Stanwood USA 232 Dj21
Stanyčno-Luhans'ke UA 72 Mk21
Staphorst NL 51 Lg38

Stapleford ZW 202 Mg55
Staples USA 236 Fc22
Stapleton USA 236 Ek25
Staporków PL 65 Ma39
Stara PL 65 Lt39
Starachowice PL 65 Mb39
Staraja Russa RUS 72 Mf17
Stara Kiszewa PL 64 Lt36
Stara Moravica SRB 68 Lu45
Stara Novalja HR 61 Lp46
Stara Pazova SRB 68 Ma46
Stara Reka BG 69 Mg47
Stara Zagora BG 69 Mf48
Star City USA 239 Fe29
Stare Dolistovo PL 65 Mc37
Stare Jeżewo PL 65 Mc37
Stare Kiełbonki PL 65 Mb37
Stargard Szczeciński PL 64 Lq37
Starica RUS 72 Mh17
Starica RUS 72 Mf19
Starigrad HR 61 Lr47
Stari grad Mostar BIH 61 Ls47
Stari grad Sarajevo BIH 68 Lt47
Stari Ras SRB 68 Ma47
Starke USA 242 Fj31
Starkville USA 239 Ff29
Starkweather USA 236 Fa22
Starnberg D 59 Lm42
Starnberger See D 59 Lm43
Starobil's'k UA 72 Mk21
Starobin BY 72 Md19
Starodub RUS 72 Mg19
Starogard PL 64 Lq37
Starogard Gdański PL 64 Lt37
Starojur'evo RUS 72 Na19
Starokostjantyniv UA 73 Md21
Starominskaja RUS 73 Mk22
Staro Nagoričane MK 68 Mb48
Staro Petrovo Selo HR 61 Ls45
Starosel BG 69 Me48
Staro Selo BG 69 Mg47
Starotitarovskaja RUS 73 Mj23
Starozilovo RUS 72 Mk18
Start Point GB 49 Kr40
Stary Dvor RUS 72 Na17
Stary Dzierzgoń PL 65 Lu37
Stary Oskol RUS 72 Mj20
Stary Melk SK 67 Lu42
Stary Sambir UA 67 Mc41
Stary Smokovec SK 67 Ma41
Staßfurt D 58 Lm39
Staszów PL 65 Mb40
State College USA 241 Gb25
State Line USA 239 Ff30
State Mosque MAL 126 Qa44
Statenville USA 242 Fj31
Statesboro USA 242 Fk29
Statesville USA 242 Fk28
Stathelle N 42 Lk31
Station de capture d'Epulu RDC 191 Md45
Statue of Liberty USA 241 Gd25
Stäucteni MD 73 Me22
Staunton USA 241 Ga26
Staunton River S.P. USA 242 Ga27
Stavanger N 42 Lf31
Stave SRB 68 Lu46
Stavelot B 51 Lf40
Stavre S 41 Lp26
Stavrodromi GR 70 Mb53
Stavrós GR 69 Md50
Stavroskiádi GR 70 Ma50
Stavroúpoli GR 69 Me49
Stawiski PL 65 Mc37
St-CharlesGarnier CDN 240 Gf21
Steamboat USA 238 Fa28
Steamboat Springs USA 235 Eg25
Stebbins USA 228 Bj14
Stebnyk UA 67 Md41
Steele USA 236 Fa23
Steele USA 239 Fe27
Steele, Mount CDN 230 Ck15
Steelpoort ZA 205 Mf58
Steelville USA 239 Fe26
Steenbergen NL 51 Le39
Steen River CDN 231 Eb16
Steenvoorde B 51 Lc40
Steenwijk NL 51 Lg38
Steep Point AUS 144 Qg59
Steese Highway USA 229 Ch13
Stefan Karadža BG 69 Mg47
Stefánsson Island CDN 226 Ec04
Steffen, Cerro RA/RCH 282 Ge68
Steffisburg CH 60 Lh44
Stege DK 42 Lm36
Stegna PL 64 Lu36
Stei RO 67 Mc44
Steillopsbrug ZA 202 Me57
Steilrandberge NAM 200 Lh56
Stein D 59 Lm41
Steinach D 59 Lm40
Stein am Rhein CH 60 Lj43
Steinau D 59 Lk40
Steinbach CDN 236 Fb21
Steine N 38 Lm22
Steinfeld D 58 Lj38
Steinfort L 57 Lg41
Steinhagen D 58 Lj38
Steinhatchee USA 242 Fj31
Steinhausen NAM 201 Lk56
Steinheim D 58 Lk39
Steinhuder Meer D 58 Lk38
Steinkjer N 40 Lm26
Steinkopf ZA 204 Lj60
Steinsdalfossen N 42 Lg30
Steins Ghost Town USA 235 Eh29
Steinsdalsfossen N 42 Lg30
Steki LT 45 Mg34
Stella Maris BS 250 Gc34
Stellanton CDN 240 Gj23
Stellenbosch ZA 204 Lk62
Stelling van Amsterdam NL 51 Le38
Stelmužė LT 45 Mg35
Stelvio, P.N.delle = Stilfser Joch, N.P. I 60 Ll44
Stená Foúrkas GR 70 Mc52
Stenay F 51 Lf41
Stendal D 58 Lm38
Stende LV 45 Mc33
Stenen CDN 233 Ej20
Stenhouse AUS 150 Rj63
Steni Dikithira GR 69 Md53
Steni Kimolou Sifnou GR 71 Me54
Stenó Kéas GR 71 Me53
Stenó Kithíra GR 71 Me54
Stenó Koufonísi GR 71 Mg54
Stenó Kithnou GR 71 Me53
Stenó Petási GR 69 Md53
Stenó Poliegou Folégandrou GR 71 Me54
Stenó Serífou GR 71 Me53
Stenó Sífnou GR 71 Me53
Stenshuvuds n.p. S 43 Lp35
Stenstorp S 43 Lp32
Stenungsund S 42 Ln32
Stepan UA 65 Mg39
Step'anavan ARM 91 Nc25
Stepanci MK 68 Mb49
Stephanie Wildlife Reserve ETH 194 Mj43
Stephenville CDN 241 Ha21
Stephenville USA 238 Fa29
Stephenville Crossing CDN 241 Ha21
Stepnica PL 64 Lq37
Stepnoe RUS 89 Qc08
Stepojevac SRB 68 Ma46
Stepp Rock CDN 236 Fb21
Sterdyň-Osada PL 65 Mc38
Sterkfontein ZA 205 Md59

Sterkfontein Dam Nature Reserve ZA 205 Me60
Sterkspruit ZA 205 Md61
Sterkstroom ZA 205 Md61
Stérna GR 69 Mf50
Sterling City USA 238 Ek30
Sterling Highway USA 228 Ce16
Sterling Hts. USA 237 Fj24
Sterling Landing USA 229 Cc14
Sterlitamak RUS 88 Nd08
Sternberg D 58 Lm37
Šternberk CZ 66 Ls41
Sterling = Vipiteno I 60 Lm44
Stęszew PL 64 Lr38
Stettin Lagoon PL/D 64 Lp37
Stettler CDN 233 Ed19
Steubenville USA 237 Fk25
Stevenage GB 49 Ku39
Stevenson Peak AUS 145 Rf58
Stevens Pass USA 232 Dk22
Stevens Point USA 236 Ff23
Stevens Village USA 229 Cf12
Stevensville USA 232 Ec22
Stevns Klint DK 42 Ln35
Stewart CDN 230 Df18
Stewart Crossing CDN 230 Ck14
Stewart Island NZ 153 Te69
Stewart Island NZ 153 Te69
Stewart Islands SOL 157 Tb50
Stewart Plateau CDN 229 Dc14
Stewarts Point USA 234 Dj26
Stewart Valley CDN 233 Eg20
Stewartville USA 236 Fd24
Steynsburg ZA 205 Mc61
Steynsrus ZA 205 Md59
Steyr A 66 Lp42
Steytlerville ZA 205 Mc62
Stężyca PL 64 Lt36
Stiegler's Gorge EAT 197 Mk49
Stift Altenburg A 66 Lq42
Stift Göttweig A 66 Lq42
Stift Klosterneuburg A 66 Lr42
Stift Kremsmünster A 66 Lp42
Stift Melk A 66 Lq42
Stift Sankt Paul A 61 Lp44
Stift Seckau A 61 Lp43
Stiftskirche Innichen I 60 Ln44
Stift Zwettl A 66 Lq42
Stigen S 42 Ln32
Stigliano I 63 Lr50
Stigliano I 63 Lr50
Stigtomta S 43 Lr32
Stika GR 70 Mc52
Stilida GR 70 Mc52
Stillwater USA 234 Ea26
Stillwater USA 238 Fb27
Štímlje KSV 68 Mb48
Stinápari RO 68 Mb46
Stinear, Mount 287 Ob33
Stinnett USA 238 Ek28
Štip MK 68 Mc49
Stira GR 71 Me52
Štirovača HR 61 Lq46
Stirling AUS 147 Sa54
Stirling AUS 148 Rg56
Stirling CDN 233 Ee21
Stirling Castle GB 48 Kr34
Stirling North AUS 150 Rj62
Stirling Range N.P. AUS 144 Qk63
Štítary CZ 66 Lq42
Štíty CZ 66 Lr41
Stob BG 68 Md48
Stobi MK 68 Mb49
Stockach D 59 Lk43
Stockaryd S 43 Lp33
Stockbridge GB 49 Kt39
Stockbridge Ind. Res. USA 237 Ff23
Stockdale USA 245 Fb31
Stockerau A 66 Lr42
Stockholm S 43 Ls31
Stockholm S 43 Ls31
Stockman's Hall of Fame AUS 149 Sc57
Stockport GB 49 Ks37
Stockport ZA 202 Md57
Stockton USA 234 Dk27
Stockton USA 238 Fa26
Stockton-on-Tees GB 49 Kt36
Stockton Plateau USA 245 Ej30
Stockton S.P. USA 238 Fd26
Stoczek Łukowski PL 65 Mb39
Stöðvarfjörður IS 46 Ke26
Stoffberg ZA 205 Me58
Stoke-on-Trent GB 49 Ks38
Stokes N.P. AUS 144 Ra62
Stokes Point AUS 151 Sb65
Stokksnjell's IS 46 Jt27
Stokksnes N 38 Lo24
Stokmarknes N 38 Lm22
Stolac BIH 61 Ls47
Stolin BY 72 Md20
Stolkerbsijver SME 266 Hc43
Stollberg D 58 Ln40
Stöllet S 43 Lo30
Stómio GR 70 Mc51
Stone GB 49 Ks38
Stoneham USA 235 Eh25
Stonehenge AUS 148 Sb58
Stonehenge GB 49 Kt39
Stone Ind. Res. CDN 232 Dj19
Stone Mtn. Prov. Park CDN 231 Dh17
Stone Mtn. N.P. USA 242 Fj29
Stone Rondavel NAM 204 Lk59
Stonewall CDN 236 Fb21
Stone-walled ruins RB 202 Md57
Stöng IS 46 Kb26
Stonglandet N 38 Lj22
Stonehouse SME 266 Hc44
Stony Creek Ind. Res. CDN 230 Dh19
Stony Plain CDN 233 Ec20
Stony Rapids CDN 226 Ee07
Stony River USA 228 Ca14
Stopnica PL 65 Ma40
Stör D 58 Lk37
Stora Alvaret S 43 Lr34
Stora Askö S 43 Lr33
Stora Sjöfallets n.p. S 38 Lc23
Storby FIN 44 Lu30
Storebælt DK 42 Ll35
Storebæltsbro DK 42 Ll35
Storebro S 43 Lq33
Støre Heddinge DK 42 Lm35
Stor mosse n.p. S 43 Lp33
Storå S 43 Lp31
Storavan S 41 Lt24
Store Koldewey N 39 Lk07
Storfjorden N 38 Lk07
Storforsen S 41 Ma25
Storfors S 43 Lp31
Storjord N 38 Me05
Storkow D 58 Lo38

Storožynec' UA 67 Mf42
Storsjön S 41 Lp28
Storsjön S 43 Ls33
Storsudret S 43 Lt33
Storuman S 41 Lo25
Storvorde DK 42 Ll34
Storvreta S 43 Ls31
Story USA 233 Eh23
Story City USA 236 Fd24
Stoughton CDN 233 Ej21
Stoughton USA 237 Fg24
Stourhead GB 49 Ks39
Stovbcy BY 65 Mg37
Stovbcy BY 65 Mg37
Støvring DK 42 Lk34
Stow-on-the-Wold GB 49 Kt39
Strabane GB 47 Kn36
Stradella I 60 Lk45
Straelen D 58 Lg39
Straßwalchen A 61 Lo43
Strahan AUS 151 Sc67
Strait of Belle Isle CDN 227 Ha08
Strait of Canso CDN 240 Gk23
Strait of Dover 51 Lb40
Strait of Gibraltar 55 Kp55
Strait of Hormuz IR 96 Nj32
Strait of Jubal ET 179 Mg32
Strait of Jubal ET 179 Mg32
Strait of Magellan RA 282 Ge72
Strait of Malacca MAL/RI 126 Pk43
Strait of Messina I 63 Lq52
Strait of Otranto I/AL 63 Lt50
Straits of Florida 243 Fk34
Strakonice CZ 66 Lo41
Straldža BG 69 Mg48
Stralki BY 45 Mj35
Stralsund D 58 Lo36
Strámbino I 60 Lh45
Strâmtura RO 67 Me43
Strand ZA 204 Lk63
Stranda N 40 Lg28
Strandkirkja IS 46 Jt27
Strandby DK 42 Ll33
Strandebarm N 42 Lg30
Strangford GB 47 Kp36
Strängnäs S 43 Lr31
Strängsjö S 43 Lr32
Stranraer GB 47 Kp36
Strasbourg CDN 233 Eh20
Strasbourg F 51 Lh42
Strasburg USA 236 Fa23
Strašeni MD 73 Me22
Strășeni MD 73 Me22
Strasswalchen A 61 Lo43
Stratford CDN 237 Fk24
Stratford NZ 153 Tf65
Stratford USA 238 Ek28
Stratford-upon-Avon GB 49 Kt38
Strathalbyn AUS 150 Rk63
Strathburn AUS 147 Sd53
Strathcona Prov. Park CDN 232 Dh21
Strathgordon AUS 148 Sb57
Strathgordon AUS 151 Sc67
Strathhaven AUS 147 Sb53
Strathmay AUS 147 Sb53
Strathmore AUS 151 Sc63
Strathmore AUS 147 Sc55
Strathmore AUS 149 Sc57
Strathroy CDN 237 Fk24
Strathroy CDN 237 Fk24
Stratinista GR 70 Ma51
Stratinska BIH 61 Lr46
Stratoni GR 69 Md50
Stratonikeia TR 71 Mj53
Strátos GR 70 Mb52
Stratton USA 241 Ge23
Stratton USA 235 Ej26
Straubing D 59 Ln42
Straumnes IS 46 Jr25
Strausberg D 58 Lo38
Strawberry Mountain USA 232 Eb23
Stražica BG 69 Mf47
Strážný CZ 66 Lo42
Štrba SK 67 Ma41
Štrbské Pleso SK 67 Ma41
Streaky Bay AUS 150 Rh62
Streaky Bay AUS 150 Rh62
Streator USA 237 Ff25
Strečno SK 67 Lt41
Streeter USA 236 Fa23
Strehaia RO 68 Mc46
Strelcha BG 69 Me48
Strelka RUS 72 Nd18
Strelki RUS 72 Nd18
Strelna RUS 44 Mh27
Strenči LV 45 Mf33
Stresa I 60 Lj45
Strešer SRB 68 Mb48
Strevell USA 235 Ed24
Strezimirovci SRB 68 Mb48
Strezovci KSV 68 Mb48
Stříbro CZ 66 Ln41
Strilky UA 67 Mc41
Strimonikó GR 68 Md49
Strimica MK 68 Mb49
Stroeder RA 281 Gj66
Strofilia GR 69 Md53
Strogonof Point USA 228 Ca17
Strokkur IS 46 Jt26
Strömfors FIN 44 Mf29
Stromeferry GB 48 Kp33
Stromiec PL 65 Mb39
Stromness GB 48 Kr31
Strömsnäsbruk S 43 Lo34
Stroud GB 49 Ks39
Strömstad S 42 Lm31
Strong, Mount PNG 155 Sd49
Strongoli I 63 Ls51
Stronsay GB 48 Ks31
Strontian GB 48 Kp34
Stropkov SK 67 Mb41
Strošinci SRB 68 Lu46
Stroud AUS 151 Sf62
Stroud GB 49 Ks39
Strougi-Krasnye RUS 45 Mh31 (Strugi-Krasnye)
Struisbaai ZA 204 Ma63
Struma BG/MK 68 Md49
Strumešnica BY 65 Mh37
Strumica MK 68 Mc49
Struer DK 42 Lj34
Struga MK 68 Ma49
Strugi-Krasnye RUS 45 Mh31
Struisbaai ZA 204 Ma63
Struma BG 68 Md48
Struve Geodetic Arc BY 65 Me37
Struve Geodetic Arc EST 45 Mg32
Struve Geodetic Arc FIN 44 Mg00
Struve Geodetic Arc LV 45 Mf34
Struve Geodetic Arc RUS 72 Mh18
Struve Geodetic Arc S 39 Md24
Struve Geodetic Arc UA 73 Md21
Strydenburg ZA 204 Mb60
Strydpoortberge ZA 205 Me58
Stryi UA 67 Mc41
Stryj UA 67 Md41
Stryków PL 64 Lt39
Stryn N 40 Lg28
Strzegom PL 64 Lr40
Strzelce Krajeńskie PL 64 Lq38
Strzelce Opolskie PL 64 Lt40
Strzelecki National Park AUS 151 Se66
Strzelecki Regional Reserve AUS 148 Sa60
Strzelecki River AUS 148 Sa59
Strzelin PL 64 Ls40
Strzelno PL 64 Lt38
Stuart USA 239 Fc25
Stuart USA 242 Fj27
Stuart Bluff Range AUS 143 Rg57
Stuart Highway (Northern Territory) AUS 145 Rg56
Stuart Highway (South Australia) AUS 148 Rk60
Stuart Island USA 228 Bj14
Stuart Lake CDN 230 Dh18
Stuart Range AUS 148 Rj60
Stuart Valley AUS 148 Rj60
Stuarts Point AUS 149 Sg60
Stubai Alpen A 60 Lm43
Stubbekøbing DK 42 Ln36
Stubbenkammer D 58 Lo36

Stubičke Toplice HR 61 Lq45
Stubline SRB 68 Ma46
Studenci HR 61 Ls47
Studénka CZ 66 Lt41
Studina RO 69 Me47
Studzieniczna PL 65 Md37
Stugun S 41 Lp27
Stuhr D 58 Lj37
Stuibenfall A 60 Ll43
Stuie CDN 230 Dg19
Stung Treng K 123 Qd39
Stupava SK 66 Lq42
Stupino RUS 72 Mk18
Stupnik HR 61 Lq45
Sturgeon Bay USA 237 Ff23
Sturgeon Falls CDN 237 Ga22
Sturgeon L. Ind. Res. CDN 231 Eb18
Sturgeon River CDN 233 Eg19
Sturgis CDN 233 Ej23
Sturgis USA 233 Eh23
Sturko S 43 Lq34
Sturovo SK 67 Lt43
Sturt Creek AUS 143 Re55
Sturt Highway (New South Wales) AUS 151 Sb63
Stutterheim ZA 205 Md62
Stuttgart D 59 Lk42
Stuttgart USA 239 Fe28
Stuyahok USA 228 Bk14
Stykkishólmur IS 46 Js25
Suai TLS 131 Rc50
Suakin SUD 188 Mj38
Suam EAK 194 Mh45
Suan Phung THA 122 Pk39
Suapi BOL 278 Gg53
Suaqui Grande MEX 244 Ef31
Suardi RA 279 Gk61
Suarmar IND 114 Oh30
Sua-Sua YV 265 Gk42
Suatá YV 266 Gd41
Suay Rieng K 123 Qd40
Subah RI 129 Qe49
Subanburung RI 127 Qb47
Subarnagiri IND 117 Pb36
Subei CHN 100 Pk25
Subiaco I 62 Lo49
Subi Besar RI 128 Qe44
Subic RP 124 Ra38
Subi Kecil RI 128 Qe44
Subiyah KWT 93 Ne31
Sublett USA 232 Ed24
Sublette USA 238 Ek27
Subotica SRB 68 Lu44
Subrahmanya IND 118 Oh39
Subtenente Perin RA 279 Gk61
Subway Caves USA 234 Dk25
Sucatinga BR 273 Ja48
Suceava RO 73 Me22
Suchan PL 64 Lq37
Suchedniów PL 65 Ma39
Suchitoto ES 248 Fh39
Suchowola PL 65 Md37
Suchý Río MEX 246 Ej34
Suchumi GE 91 Na24
Sucio CO 264 Gc42
Sucre BOL 278 Gh55
Sucre CO 264 Gc41
Sucre USA 268 Fk46
Sucuba, T.I. BR 265 Gk44
Sucuiu RO 69 Mg45
Sucupira do Norte BR 272 Hh49
Sucurú BR 273 Ja49
Sud SUD 191 Md41
Súdavík IS 46 Jr26
Sudak UA 73 Mh23
Sudan SUD 163 Ma08
Sudan USA 238 Ej28
Sudbury CDN 237 Fk22
Sudbury GB 49 Lb39
Sudd SUD 191 Md41
Süderbrarup D 58 Lk36
Sudest Island PNG 156 Sg51
Sudislavl' RUS 72 Na17
Sudogda RUS 72 Na18
Sudova Vyšnja UA 67 Mc41
Sudureyri IS 46 Jr24
Suduroy FO 48 Kn29
Sudža RUS 72 Mh20
Sué SUD 191 Md43
Sueca E 57 Ku51
Suemez Island USA 230 Dd18
Sueng's Stone USA 238 Kr33 (?)
Suez ET 179 Mg31
Suez Bay ET 179 Mg31
Suez Canal ET 179 Mg30
Sufaynah KSA 94 Na34
Suffield CDN 233 Ee20
Suffolk USA 242 Gd27
Sufiyan IR 91 Nc26
Sugag IND 116 Oj35
Sugar burn USA 232 Kr33 (?)
Sugarloaf Mtn. USA 228 Cb16
Sugauli IND 117 Pc32
Sughizao RI 130 Ra48
Sugoy RUS 89 Sa06
Sugu WAN 189 Lg40
Sugun CHN 100 Oj26
Suhai IND 117 Pb36
Suhindol BG 69 Mf47
Suhl D 59 Ll40
Sühläh RUS 72 Mh18
Suia-Missu BR 271 Hd51
Suica BIH 61 Ls47
Suichang CHN 109 Qk33
Suichuan CHN 109 Qj32
Sui Xian CHN 107 Qf28
Suifen RUS 110 Re24
Suifenhe CHN 110 Re23
Suihua CHN 105 Rd22
Suileng CHN 110 Rd22
Suining CHN 108 Qd30
Suining CHN 109 Qh32
Suippes F 51 Le41
Suir IRL 47 Kn38
Suixi CHN 109 Qj30
Suixian CHN 108 Qf29
Suiyang CHN 105 Rd22
Suiyang CHN 108 Qe31
Suizhou CHN 109 Qg30
Sujangarh IND 114 Oh32

Sujawal PK 99 Oe33
Sukabumi RI 129 Qd49
Sukadana RI 127 Qd46
Sukadana RI 129 Qe46
Sukagawa J 111 Sa27
Sukajadi RI 127 Pk44
Sukanegara RI 129 Qd50
Sukamara RI 127 Qd47
Sukamenang RI 127 Qb47
Sukau MAL 126 Qk44
Sukenegara RI 129 Qd49
Sukhbaatar MNG 104 Qd20
Sükhbaatar MNG 104 Qd20
Sukhothai THA 122 Pk37
Sukhothai Historical Park THA 122 Pk37
Sukhuma LAO 123 Qc38
Suki PNG 155 Sa50
Sukkertoppen = Manitsoq DK 227 Hb05
Sukkur PK 99 Oe32
Sukma IND 117 Pa36
Sukna SYR 90 Mk28
Sukorejo RI 129 Qe49
Sukria SUD 188 Mj39
Sukromny RUS 72 Mk16
Sukses NAM 200 Lj56
Sukumo J 113 Rg29
Sukur Cultural Landscape WAN 189 Lg40
Sula = Sunija Stijena MNE 68 Lu47
Sulagiri IND 118 Oj39
Sulaiyimah KSA 94 Ne35
Sulawesi RI 76 Ra10
Sulecin PL 64 Lq38
Sulęcin PL 64 Lq38
Sulęczyno PL 64 Ls36
Sulejów WAN 188 Ld41
Sulejówek PL 65 Mb38
Sulen, Mount PNG 155 Sb47
Sule Skerry GB 48 Kq31
Sulechów RUS 91 Nd24
Sulia RDC 191 Md46
Suliki RI 127 Qa46
Sulima WAL 186 Ke42
Sulingen D 58 Lj38
Sulislawice PL 64 Lq37
Suliszewo PL 64 Lq37
Sulitjelma N 38 Lc23
Sulitjelma N/S 38 Lc23
Sułkowice PL 64 Lt41
Sullana PE 268 Fk48
Sullivan USA 239 Fe26
Sullivan USA 239 Ff26
Sullivan Bay CDN 232 Dg20
Sullivan, Mount AUS 146 Rf54
Sully-sur-Loire F 53 Lc43
Sulmierzyce PL 64 Ls39
Sulphur USA 238 Fb29
Sulphur USA 238 Fd30
Sulphur Springs USA 238 Fc29
Sultan CDN 237 Fj22
Sultan LAR 177 Ma30
Sultan-e-Bakwah AFG 98 Ob29
Sultanhani TR 90 Mg27
Sultan Hamud EAK 194 Mj47
Sultanhani TR 90 Mg27
Sultanhani TR 90 Mg27
Sultanica Caravanserai TR
Sultani Mosque TR 96 Ng28 (?)
Sultan Kudarat RP 125 Rc42
Sultanpur IND 117 Pb33
Sultan's Palace BRU 128 Qk43
Sultan's Palace MAL 126 Qa42
Sultan's Palace N 176 Le30
Sultan's Palace TM 96 Nk24
Sultan Tekesh TM 96 Nk24
Sulu CO 264 Gc41
Sulu RDC 199 Mc48
Suluan Island RP 124 Rd40
Suluq LAR 177 Ma30
Sulu Sea RP 124 Ra40
Sulutöbe KZ 97 Od23
Sulya IND 118 Oh39
Sulzbach-Rosenberg D 59 Lm41
Sumaco E EC 268 Ga46
Sumaco, N.P. EC 268 Ga46
Sumadija SRB 68 Ma46
Sumalacu CHN 105 Rd21
Sumampa RA 279 Gj60
Sumar RUS 88 Ng07
Sumar IR 91 Nc29
Sumare BR 275 Hg57
Sumatra USA 232 Ec22
Sumatra RI 76 Pb09
Sumava, N.P. CZ 66 Lo41
Sumba RI 130 Qk51
Sumba Strait RI 130 Qk50
Sumbawa RI 130 Qk50
Sumbawa Besar RI 130 Qj50
Sumbawanga EAT 196 Mg48
Sumbe ANG 198 Lh51
Sumber KZ 100 Pa26
Sumba H 187 Kk42
Sumbing RI 129 Qf45
Sumburgh Head GB 48 Kt31
Sumdo CHN 100 Qa31
Sumé BR 273 Jb49
Sumedang RI 129 Qd49
Sumedho LAO 123 Qc38
Sumeih SUD 191 Mc41
Sumeïha TR 91 Mh25
Sumenep RI 129 Qh49
Sumgait AZ 91 Ne25
Šumiaci RUS 72 Mg18
Šumihovo RI 129 Qd49 (?)
Sumiswald CH 60 Lh43
Sumiyin Bulag MNG 104 Qc20
Summerford CDN 241 Hc21
Summerland USA 232 Ea22
Summer Palace CHN 107 Qj26
Summerside CDN 240 Gj22
Summerstrand ZA 205 Md62
Summersville USA 242 Fk26
Summerville USA 239 Fh28
Summit Lake CDN 230 Dh18
Summit Lake CDN 230 Dj18
Summit Lake Ind. Res. CDN 231 Dg18
Sumpango GCA 248 Fg38
Sumperk CZ 66 Lr41
Sumprabum MYA 120 Pj32
Sumter USA 242 Fk29
Sumur IND 115 Oh29
Sumy UA 72 Mh20
Sumzom CHN 103 Pj31

Sunag IND 116 Oh37
Sunah YE 94 Ne38
Sunakhalla IND 117 Pb35
Sunam IND 114 Oh30
Sunan CHN 100 Pk25
Sunan PRK 112 Rc26
Sunbay Beach USA 251 Gh36
Sunbura AUS 151 Sc64
Sunburst USA 233 Ee21
Sunbury AUS 241 Gb25
Sunbury USA 242 Gd27
Sunchales RA 281 Gk61
Suncho Corral RA 279 Gj59
Sunch'on PRK 110 Rc26
Sunch'on ROK 112 Rd28
Sun City USA 234 Eb29
Sun City USA 238 Ek27
Sun City ZA 205 Md58
Sun City Center USA 243 Fj32
Sundaargarh IND 117 Pb34
Sundance USA 233 Eh23
Sundarban National Park IND/BD 120 Pe34
Sundarbans National Park IND 120 Pe34
Sundargarh IND 115 Oj30
Sunda Shelf RI 129 Qd49
Sunda Strait RI 127 Qa48
Sunday Strait AUS 143 Rb54
Sundborn S 43 Lq30
Sundby DK 42 Lj34
Sunde N 42 Lf31
Sunderland GB 49 Kt36
Sundern D 58 Lj39
Sundown Daglan TR 90 Mf26
Sunde-Lutete RDC 198 Lh48
Sundown N.P. AUS 149 Sf60
Sundre CDN 233 Ec20
Sundsvall S 41 Ls28
Sungaiapus RI 129 Qf45
Sungaibali RI 129 Qj47
Sungaibamban RI 126 Pk44
Sungaibeliah RI 127 Qb46
Sungaibengkali RI 127 Qb46
Sungaibuluh RI 127 Qc46
Sungaidareh RI 127 Qa46
Sungaiguntung RI 127 Qb45
Sungai Kolok THA 123 Qa42
Sungailiat RI 127 Qc46
Sungailurus RI 127 Qd46
Sungaipenuh RI 127 Qa46
Sungaipinang RI 127 Qb45
Sungai Petani MAL 126 Qa43
Sungaiselesan RI 127 Qb46
Sungai Sinput MAL 126 Qa43
Sungguminasa RI 130 Ra48
Sungikai SUD 188 Md39
Sung Noen THA 123 Qa38
Sungo MOC 202 Mg54
Sungsang RI 127 Qb47
Sungurlu TR 90 Mg25
Suni I 62 Lh50
Sunizona USA 235 Eh30
Sunja HR 61 Lr45
Sun Kosi NEP 117 Pd32
Sun Kosi Reservoir NEP 117 Pd32
Sun Kosi River Rafting NEP 117 Pd32
Sunland USA 234 Eb28
Sunndalsøra N 40 Lh27
Sunne S 43 Lo31
Sunnemo S 43 Lo31
Sunnersberg S 42 Lo32
Sunndal N 40 Lg28
Sunne S 43 Lo31
Sunnyside USA 232 Ea22
Sunnyside USA 232 Eb22
Sunnyvale USA 234 Dk27
Suntai WAN 188 Lf42
Suntaż LV 45 Me34
Sun Temple (Konark) IND 117 Pc35
Suntar RUS 89 Qd06
Suntsar PK 96 Oa33
Suntu ETH 192 Mj41
Sun Valley USA 232 Ec24
Sunwi-do PRK 112 Rc27
Sunwu CHN 105 Rd21
Sunyani GH 187 Kk42
Suoche CHN 100 Oh27
Suomenlinna FIN 44 Me30
Suomusjärvi FIN 44 Md30
Suomussalmi FIN 41 Mh25
Suonenjoki FIN 44 Mh28
Suong K 123 Qd40
Suoqiao CHN 108 Qb30
Supaul BR 278 Ge54
Supaul IND 117 Pd33
Supe ETH 192 Mh41
Superagüi, P.N.do BR 277 Hf58
Superbagneres F 52 La48
Superior USA 232 Ec22
Superior USA 235 Eg28
Superior USA 236 Fe22
Super Tubes USA 234 Dk23 (?)
Supia CO 264 Gc43
Supikovce UA 67 Me41
Supljja IND 116 Of34
Supply USA 242 Gb28
Support Force Glacier 287 Hd35
Supru PL 65 Md37
Supsa GE 91 Na25
Supung CHN 110 Rd26
Suq al Ahad KSA 94 Nb36
Suqian CHN 108 Qk28
Suq ash Shuyukh IRQ 93 Nd30
Suqutra YE 95 Nh39
Surabaya RI 129 Qh49
Surahammar S 43 Lr31
Surallah RP 125 Rc42
Suran SYR 90 Mj28
Surany SK 66 Lt42
Surat IND 116 Og35
Surat Thani THA 122 Pk41
Suratgarh IND 114 Og31
Suraz PL 65 Mc38
Surazh BY 72 Mf17
Surazh RUS 72 Mg19
Surbiton ROK 112 Rd27
Surdila-Greci RO 69 Mh45
Surdulica SRB 68 Mb48
Sure D 57 Lg41
Surendranagar IND 116 Og34
Suretka CR 249 Fk41
Surf City USA 234 Eb29
Surf City USA 242 Gd28
Surfers Paradise AUS 149 Sg60
Surfing Beaches AUS 144 Qk63

Taptugay ▲ RUS 105 Ra19
Tapul ◻ RP 125 Ra43
Tapul Group ▲ RP 125 Ra43
Tapul Island ▲ RP 125 Ra43
Tapun ◻ IND 120 Pj32
Taqah ◻ OM 95 Nh37
Taqtaq ◻ IRQ 91 Nc28
Taquara ▲ BR 277 He60
Taquara ◻ BR 273 Jb50
Taquari ◻ BR 274 Hf59
Taquarituba ◻ BR 277 Hf57
Tara ◻ AUS 149 Sf59
Tara ◻ RUS 88 Oc07
Tara ▲ LM ▲ MNE 68 Lu41
Tarabuco ▲ BOL 278 Gh55
Tarabulus → ◻ LAR 177 Lg29
Taraclia ◻ MD 73 Me22
Taraco ◻ PE 278 Gf53
Taradale ◻ IND 117 Ok34
Taraghin ◻ LAR 177 Lh33
Taragma ◻ SUD 185 Mg37
Tarago ◻ AUS 151 Se63
Tarajim ◻ WAN 189 Lf40
Tarakan ◻ RI 125 Qj44
Tarakan ▲ RI 128 Qj44
Tarakbits ◻ PNG 155 Sa48
Tarakeswar ◻ IND 120 Pe34
Tarakom ▲ AFG 98 Oa30
Taralga ◻ AUS 151 Se63
Tarama Jima ▲ J 113 Rc33
Taramangalam ◻ IND 118 Oj40
Taran ◻ IR 91 Nd27
Taranaki, Mount ▲ NZ 153 Th65
Tarancón ◻ E 57 Ks50
Tara ▲ LM ▲ NR 92 Mh27
Tarangire N.P. ◻ EAT 197 Mj48
Tara, N.P. ◻ SRB 68 Lu47
Taransay ◻ GB 48 Kn33
Taranto ◻ I 63 La50
Tarapaca ◻ CO 270 Gf47
Tarapoa ◻ EC 268 Gd48
Tarapoto ▲ PE 268 Gd49
Taraq an Na'jah ◻ SYR 90 Mk28
Taraquá ◻ BR 270 Gh46
Tarara ◻ PNG 157 Sh49
Tarare ◻ F 53 Le45
Tarariras ◻ ROU 281 Hb63
Tararua Range ▲ NZ 153 Th65
Tarasá ◻ IND 122 Pg41
Tarašča ◻ UA 73 Mf21
Tarascon-sur-Ariège ◻ F 52 Lb48
Tarat ◻ DZ 176 Le32
Tarata ◻ PE 269 Ge54
Tarauacá ◻ BR 268 Ge50
Tarauz ◻ KZ 97 Of24
Tarazona de la Mancha ◻ E 57 Kt51
Tarbagataj ◻ RUS 104 Qd20
Tarbagataj Žotasy ▲ KZ 102 Pg22
Tarbaghatai ◻ KZ 100 Pa22
Tarbela ◻ PK 99 Og28
Tarbela Reservoir ◻ PK 99 Og28
Tarbert ◻ GB 48 Kp33
Tarbert ◻ GB 48 Kp35
Tarbert ◻ GB 48 Kn33
Tarbert ◻ IRL 47 Kl38
Tarbes ◻ F 52 La47
Tarbrax ◻ AUS 147 Sb56
Tarcento ◻ I 61 Lo44
Tarcoola ◻ AUS 148 Rh61
Tarczyn ◻ PL 65 Ma39
Tardun ◻ AUS 144 Qh60
Taree ◻ AUS 149 Sg61
Taren Tanri ◻ IND 114 Oh30
Tarfaya ◻ MA 174 Kd32
Târgovişte ◻ BG 69 Mg47
Târgovişte ◻ RO 69 Mf46
Târgu Cărbuneşti ◻ RO 68 Md46
Targuist ◻ MA 175 Ks28
Târgu Jiu ◻ RO 69 Md43
Târgu Lăpuş ◻ RO 67 Md43
Târgu Mureş ◻ RO 67 Me44
Târgu-Neamţ ◻ RO 73 Md22
Târgu Ocna ◻ RO 73 Md23
Târgu Secuiesc ◻ RO 73 Md23
Targusor ◻ RO 69 Mh46
Tarhaouhaout ▲ DZ 182 Lc34
Tarhunah ◻ LAR 177 Lg29
Tari ◻ PNG 155 Sd48
Tarica ◻ PE 269 Gb50
Tarif ◻ UAE 95 Ng33
Tarifa ◻ E 55 Kp55
Tarija ◻ BOL 279 Gh56
Tarikere ◻ IND 118 Oh38
Tarikhana Mosque ◻ IR 96 Nh27
Tarim ◻ YE 94 Ne37
Tari Mashen ◻ IND 115 Na45
Tarin Basin ▲ CHN 100 Pa26
Tarime ◻ EAT 194 Mh46
Tarin He ◻ CHN 100 Pa25
Taring ◻ RI 126 Pj44
Tarin Kowt ◻ AFG 99 Oc29
Tarira ◻ BR 270 Gh45
Tarïatu ◻ IND 129 Qj46
Taritip ◻ RI 129 Qj46
Tarka La ▲ IND 120 Pe32
Tarkastad ◻ ZA 205 Md62
Tarkio ◻ USA 232 Ec22
Tarkwa ◻ GH 187 Kk43
Târlişua ◻ RO 67 Me43
Tari River N.P. ◻ AUS 151 Sf63
Tarlton Downs ◻ AUS 148 Rh57
Tarm ◻ DK 42 Lj35
Tarma ◻ PE 269 Gc51
Tarmaber Pass ▲ ETH 192 Mk41
Tarn ◻ F 52 Lc47
Tarnaleksz ◻ H 67 Ma42
Tarna Mare ◻ RO 67 Md42
Tărnăveni ◻ RO 67 Md43
Tarnobrzeg ◻ PL 65 Mb40
Tarnogród ◻ PL 65 Mc40
Tarnów ◻ SK 67 Mb41
Tarnova ◻ RO 67 Mc44
Tarnów ◻ PL 65 Ma40
Tarnowskie Góry ◻ PL 65 Lt40
Tärnsjö ◻ S 43 Lr30
Taroa ◻ CO 264 Ge39
Tarok ◻ PNG 156 St48
Tarokehn ◻ LB 186 Kg43
Taroko ◻ RC 109 Ra33
Taroko N.P. ◻ RC 109 Ra33
Taroom ◻ AUS 149 Se58
Tarouant ◻ MA 174 Kf30
Taroum ◻ RN 182 Lb38
Tarourirt ◻ MA 175 Kj28
Tarpon Springs ◻ USA 243 Fj31
Tarporley ◻ GB 49 Ks37
Tarqa ◻ I 62 Lm48
Tarra-Bulga National Park ◻ AUS 151 Sd65
Tárraco romana ◻ E 57 Lb49
Tarrafal ◻ CV 186 Jh37
Tarrafal ◻ CV 186 Jh37
Tarragona ◻ E 57 Lb49
Tarragona ◻ RP 125 Rd42
Tarraleah ◻ AUS 151 Sd67
Tars L'DX 42 Lh36
Tars ▲ DK 42 Lh36
Tarsa Khurd ◻ IND 117 Ok36
Tarso Emissi ▲ TCH 183 Lj35
Tarso Lango ▲ TCH 183 Lk35
Tarso Voon ▲ TCH 183 Lj35
Tarsus ◻ TR 90 Mj27
Tartagal ◻ RA 279 Gh57
Tartagal ◻ RA 279 Gi56
Tartagal ◻ RA 267 He45
Tartarugalzinho ◻ BR 271 Hd45
Tartu ◻ EST 45 Me31
Tartus ◻ SYR 90 Mj28
Tarucumi-zan ▲ J 111 Sa24
Tarumae-zan ▲ J 111 Sa24
Tarumirim ◻ BR 275 Hk55
Tarusa ◻ RUS 72 Mh18
Tarut ◻ KSA 93 Nf32
Tarut Castle ◻ KSA 93 Nf32
Tarutung ◻ RI 127 Pk44
Tarvin ◻ GB 49 Ks37
Tárvisio ◻ I 61 Lo44
Tarxien ◻ M 63 Lp55
Tasajera ◻ RUS 10 Pe21
Tasboget ◻ KZ 97 Oc23
Táscates ◻ MEX 244 Eg32
Taşeli Yaylası ▲ TR 90 Mg27
Tasgaon ◻ IND 116 Oh37
Tash Gozar ◻ AFG 99 Oc27
Tashihunpho Monastery ▲ CHN 102 Pe31
Tashir ◻ AR 91 Nc25
Tashk ◻ IR 98 Ng31
Tashkent → ◻ UZ 97 Oe25
Tash-Kumyr ◻ KS 97 Og26
Tasik Chini ◻ MAL 126 Qb44
Tasikmalaya ◻ RI 129 Qe44
Tasiu ◻ RI 130 Qi47
Tasker ◻ RN 183 Lf38
Taskesken ◻ KZ 100 Pa22
Taşköprü ◻ TR 90 Mh25
Tasman ◻ PNG 156 Sf47
Tasman Basin ▲ 134 Sa43
Tasman Bay ◻ NZ 153 Tg66
Tasman Head ▲ AUS 151 Sd67
Tasmania ◻ AUS 135 Sa14
Tasmanian Wilderness World Heritage Area ◻ AUS 151 Sc67
Tasman Islands ▲ PNG 157 Sk48
Tasman Mountains ▲ NZ 153 Tg66
Tasman Peninsula ◻ AUS 151 Se67
Tasman Point ▲ AUS 146 Rj53
Tasman Sea ▲ 134 Sb13
Tašovy ◻ RN 182 Le37
Tasova ◻ TR 90 Mj25
Tassara ◻ RN 182 Lc37
Tassa Takorat ◻ RN 182 Lc37
Tasserest ◻ RMM 182 Lb38
Tassili du Hoggar ▲ DZ 182 Lc35
Tassili n'Ajjer ◻ DZ 176 Le33
Tassili n'Ajjer, P.N.du ◻ DZ 176 Le33
Tasso Fragoso ◻ BR 272 Hh50
Tasuj ◻ IR 91 Nb26
Tasuki ◻ IR 98 Oa30
Tata ◻ H 66 Lt43
Tatabánya ◻ H 66 Lt43
Ta Ta Creek ◻ CDN 232 Ec21
Tata de Samory ◻ RG 186 Kf41
Tátádrăştii de Jos ◻ RO 69 Mf46
Tataháza ◻ H 67 Lu44
Tatajachuna, Cerro ▲ RCH 278 Gf55
Tatali ◻ GH 187 La41
Tata Mailau, Gunung = Mount Ramelau ▲ TLS 131 Rc50
Tatamá, P.N. ◻ CO 264 Gb43
Tataouine ◻ TN 176 Lf29
Tatar Pazardzhik → ◻ BG 69 Me47
Tatarbunary ◻ UA 73 Me23
Tatarskij Proliv ▲ RUS 89 Sa08
Tatarstan ◻ RUS 27 Nb04
Tătăruşi ◻ RO 73 Md22
Tatau ◻ MAL 128 Qh43
Tatau Island ▲ PNG 156 Sf47
Tatav monastery ▲ ARM 91 Nc25
Taté-yama ▲ J 111 Rj27
Tatéma ◻ RG 186 Kd41
Tate-yama ▲ J 111 Rj27
Tateyama ▲ J 113 Rk28
Tathlith ◻ KSA 94 Nb36
Tathra N.P. ◻ AUS 144 Qh60
Tatichería ◻ IND 119 Ok38
Tatitlek ◻ USA 229 Cg15
Tat Kha ◻ THA 124 Qb37
Tatla Lake ◻ CDN 230 Dg17
Tatlatui Prov. Park ◻ CDN 230 Dg17
Tato ◻ IND 120 Ph31
Tatokotu ◻ RN 182 Le38
Tatopani ◻ NEP 115 Pb31
Tatra Mountains ◻ PL/SK 67 Lu41
Tatrang ◻ CHN 102 Pc36
Tatransky národny park ◻ SK 67 Lu41
Tatrzanski P.N. ◻ PL 65 Ma41
Tatshenshini-Alsek Wilderness Prov. Park ◻ CDN 230 Db16
Tattakarai ◻ IND 118 Oj40
Tatti ◻ KZ 100 Og24
Tatuanui ◻ NZ 152 Th64
Tatum ◻ USA 238 Eg27
Tatum ◻ USA 235 Ec29
Tatvan ◻ TR 91 Nb26
Tau ▲ N 42 Lf31
Tau ◻ USA 273 Ha48
Ta Uan Xe ◻ VN 123 Qe38
Taubaté ◻ BR 277 Hh57
Tauber ◻ D 59 La41
Tauberbischofsheim ◻ D 59 La41
Tauca ◻ PE 269 Gb50
Tauere ◻ D 58 Ln39
Taufkira ◻ CHN 102 Oj34
Taufkirchen ◻ D 59 Ln42
Taukum ▲ KZ 100 Oh23
Taulabé ◻ HN 248 Fg38
Taulov ◻ DK 42 Lk35
Taumarunui ◻ NZ 153 Th65
Taumaturgo ◻ BR 269 Gd50
Tau Munly ▲ KZ 100 Of22
Taunay/Ipegue, T.I. ◻ BR 274 Hb56
Taung ◻ ZA 205 Mc59
Taungbyu ◻ MYA 120 Ph34
Taungdwin ◻ MYA 120 Ph35
Taunggyi ◻ MYA 120 Ph35
Taung Skull Fossil Site ◻ ZA 205 Mc59
Taungthar ◻ MYA 120 Ph35
Taungthonlon ▲ MYA 120 Ph33
Taunsa ◻ PK 99 Of30
Taunton ◻ GB 49 Kr39
Taunton ◻ USA 241 Ge25
Taunus ◻ D 59 La40
Taupo ◻ NZ 153 Tj65
Tauramena ◻ CO 264 Gc43
Tauranga ◻ NZ 152 Tj64
Taurianova ◻ I 63 Lr52
Taurisano ◻ I 63 Lr52
Taurus Point ▲ NZ 152 Tg63
Taurus Mountains ▲ TR 90 Mf27
Taushyk ◻ KZ 96 Na24
Tauste ◻ E 56 Kt49
Tauta ◻ PNG 155 Sc48
Tauu Islands ▲ PNG 157 Sk48
Tavai ◻ PY 276 Hc59
Travakli İskelesi ◻ TR 71 Mg51
Tavan Bogd ▲ MNG 101 Pg21
Tavares ◻ USA 242 Fk31
Tavas ◻ TR 90 Me27
Tavau ▲ FIJI 159 Tj54
Tavernes de la Valldigna ◻ E 57 Ku51
Taveta ◻ EAK 194 Mj47
Taveta ◻ EAK 196 Mh50
Taveuni ▲ FJI 159 Tj54
Tavira ◻ P 55 Ko53
Tavistock ◻ GB 49 Kq40
Tavoliere ◻ I 63 Lq49
Tavoy ◻ MYA 122 Pk39
Tavrichanka ◻ RUS 110 Rf24

Tavşanlı ◻ TR 71 Mk51
Tavua ▲ FJI 159 Tj53
Tavuki ▲ FJI 159 Tk55
Tavurvur ▲ PNG 156 Sg48
Tawa ◻ RI 131 Re46
Tawai ◻ RI 130 Qk46
Tawali ◻ RI 130 Qi47
Tawaliah ◻ AUS 146 Rh54
Tawali ◻ IND 120 Pj32
Tawangmangu ▲ RI 129 Qf49
Tawa Reservoir ◻ IND 117 Ok34
Tawargin ◻ IND 120 Pj32
Tawas City ◻ USA 237 Fj23
Ta Haroto ◻ NZ 153 Tj65
Tawau ◻ MAL 128 Qk44
Tawau Hills N.P. ◻ MAL 128 Qk43
Tawilah ◻ SUD 184 Mc39
Tawilah ◻ SUD 184 Mc39
Tawitawi ◻ IND 120 Pg34
Tawi-Tawi Island ▲ RP 125 Qk43
Tawu ◻ RC 109 Ra34
Tawum Bum ▲ MYA 120 Pj32
Tawurgha ◻ LAR 177 Lg29
Taxco ◻ MEX 246 Ej36
Taxi ◻ CHN 105 Rd21
Taxiatosh ◻ UZ 96 Nk34
Taxila ◻ PK 99 Og29
Taxisco ◻ GCA 248 Fe38
Taxkorgan ◻ CHN 100 Oh37
Taxtako'pir ◻ UZ 96 Oa24
Tayabamba ◻ PE 269 Gd50
Tayabas Bay ▲ RP 124 Ra39
Tayan ◻ RI 129 Qf46
Tayandu ◻ RI 154 Rd48
Tayan Uul ▲ MNG 101 Ph23
Tayfur ◻ TR 89 Mg50
Tayganggong ◻ SP 196 Nc43
Te Kaha ◻ NZ 152 Tj64
Tekamah ◻ USA 236 Fb25
Tékane ▲ RIM 186 Kc38
Tekax ◻ MEX 247 Ff35
Tekax ◻ TR 69 Mk49
Tekeim ◻ SUD 185 Mf40
Tekeli ◻ KZ 100 Oh24
Tekeli ◻ KZ 100 Oh24
Tekirdağ ◻ TR 69 Mh50
Tekit ◻ MEX 247 Ff35
Tekkali ◻ IND 117 Pc36
Tekke ◻ TR 90 Mh26
Tekman ◻ TR 91 Na26
Tekovník ◻ RO 68 Md45
Tekax ◻ RA 280 Ge64
Tekirghene ◻ DZ 176 Ld27
Teles ◻ I 63 Lp49
Telfer ◻ AUS 142 Rb56
Telford ◻ GB 49 Ks38
Telfs ◻ A 60 Lm43
Telgte ◻ D 58 Lh39
Telhan Kalesi ▲ TR 91 Na27
Teli ◻ RDC 191 Me44
Telica ◻ NIC 248 Fg38
Télimélé ◻ RG 186 Kd40
Telkwa ◻ CDN 230 De17
Tell Abyad ◻ SYR 90 Mk27
Tellamura ◻ IND 120 Pf34
Tell As'samn ◻ SYR 90 Mk28
Tell el-Amārna ▲ ET 179 Mf32
Tell oukheda ◻ IND 118 Oh40
Tellicherry = Thalasseri ◻ IND 118 Oh40
Tellier ◻ RA 282 Gg69
Tellis ◻ TCH 183 Lj38
Tell Tamir ◻ SYR 91 Na27
Telluride ◻ USA 234 Eb27
Telluride Ski Area ◻ USA 235 Eg27
Tel'manove ◻ UA 73 Mj22
Telmessos ▲ TR 90 Me27
Telo ◻ RI 127 Pk46
Telok Brunei ◻ MAL 128 Qh43
Telok Kimanis ◻ MAL 128 Qj43
Telok Labuk ◻ MAL 128 Qj43
Telok Lahad Datu ◻ MAL 125 Qk43
Telok Loak ◻ MAL 128 Qg43
Teloloapan ◻ MEX 246 Ej36
Telpani ◻ NEP 115 Pa31
Telsang ◻ IND 116 Oh37
Telšiai ◻ LT 45 Mc35
Telтеn nuur ◻ MNG 101 Pg21
Teltow ◻ D 59 Lo38
Teluk Adang ◻ RI 129 Qj47
Teluk Airhitam ◻ RI 129 Qd47
Telukbatang ◻ RI 129 Qe46
Telukbayur ◻ RI 127 Qa45
Teluk Bengkolan ◻ RI 129 Qa46
Teluk Berau ▲ RI 154 Rg47
Teluk Bintuni ◻ RI 154 Rg47
Telukbutun ◻ RI 128 Qd43
Teluk Cenderawasih ▲ RI 154 Rh47
Teluk Chempedak Beach ◻ MAL 126 Qb44
Telukdalam ◻ RI 127 Pj45
Teluk Datu ◻ MAL 128 Qf44
Teluk Gelintin ◻ RI 130 Rb50
Teluk Intan ◻ MAL 126 Qa43
Teluk Kabui ◻ RI 154 Rf46
Teluk Kampa ◻ RI 127 Qc46
Teluk Kamrau ▲ RI 154 Rg47
Teluk Klabat ◻ RI 127 Qc46
Teluk Kotawaringin ◻ RI 129 Qf47
Teluk Kumai ▲ RI 129 Qf47
Teluk Langsa ▲ RI 127 Pj44
Teluk Langsa ◻ RI 127 Pj44
Telukkinibung ◻ RI 126 Pk44
Teluk Nuri ◻ RI 129 Qe46
Teluk Painan ◻ RI 127 Qa46
Teluk Saleh ▲ RI 130 Qj50
Teluk Sebakung ◻ RI 129 Qj47
Teluk Sebuku ▲ RI 128 Qk44
Teluk Sekatak ◻ RI 128 Qj44
Teluk Sempit ◻ RI 129 Qd46
Teluk Sibolga ▲ RI 127 Pk45
Teluk Sindeh ◻ RI 130 Ra50
Teluk Sukadana ◻ RI 129 Qe46
Teluk Telaga ◻ RI 127 Pj44
Teluk Triton ▲ RI 154 Rg47
Teluk Weda ◻ RI 125 Rd45
Teluk Windu ◻ RI 131 Rb50
Tema ▲ GH 187 Kk43
Temacine ◻ DZ 176 Ld29
Temagami ◻ CDN 237 Ga22
Temaju ◻ RI 129 Qd46
Temanggung ◻ RI 129 Qf49
Témate ◻ MEX 247 Ff35
Tembaga ◻ RI 131 Re47

Tefeer ◻ MA 175 Kh28
Tefé ◻ WAL 186 Ka41
Tegada ◻ IND 117 Pa36
Tegal ◻ RI 129 Qe49
Tegalbuleud ◻ RI 129 Qd49
Tegernsee ◻ D 59 Lm43
Teghra ◻ IND 117 Pc33
Tegina ◻ WAN 188 Lc41
Tegineneng ◻ RI 127 Qc48
Tegua ▲ VU 158 Td52
Tegucigalpa ◻ HN 248 Fg38
Teguidda-n-Tessoumt ◻ RN 182 Ld37
Tehachapi Mts. ▲ USA 234 Ea28
Te Haroto ◻ NZ 153 Tj65
Tehini ◻ CI 187 Kj41
Tehoru ◻ RI 131 Re47
Tehuacán ◻ MEX 246 Fb36
Teide, P.N.del ◻ E 174 Kb31
Teignmouth ◻ GB 49 Kr40
Teilta ◻ SUD 185 Mg37
Teimoori Tomb ◻ IR 96 Nj27
Teimur ▲ IR 98 Oa34
Teixeira ◻ BR 273 Jb49
Teixeira de Freitas ◻ BR 275 Ja54
Teixeiras ◻ BR 275 Hj56
Tejakula ◻ RI 129 Qf49
Teji ◻ ETH 192 Mk41
Tejira ◻ RN 182 Le38
Tejkovo ◻ RUS 72 Na17
Tejoruco ◻ MEX 246 Fa37
Tejucupapo ◻ BR 273 Jd49
Tejupilco de Hidalgo ◻ MEX 246 Ek36
Te Teko ◻ NZ 153 Tj64
Tekane ▲ RIM 186 Kc38

Tembagapura ◻ RI 154 Rj48
Tembe Elephant Reserve ◻ ZA 205 Mg56
Tembe, T.I. ◻ BR 267 Hf47
Tembilahan ◻ RI 127 Qb46
Tembilahan ◻ RI 127 Qb46
Tembisa ◻ ZA 205 Me58
Tembladera ◻ PE 268 Ga49
Temblador ◻ YV 265 Gj41
Tembo ◻ RDC 199 Lj49
Tembo ◻ RDC 199 Lj49
Temecula ◻ USA 234 Eb29
Temelon ◻ GQ 188 Lf45
Temerin ◻ SRB 68 Lu45
Temirlan ◻ KS 100 Ok24
Temiang ▲ RI 127 Qb46
Teminabuan ◻ RI 131 Rf46
Temirlan ◻ KZ 97 Of35
Temirtau ◻ KZ 99 Oe21
Témiris ◻ MEX 244 Ef32
Temiscaming ◻ CDN 237 Ga22
Temlej ◻ TCH 189 Lc40
Temmu-gu ◻ IND 118 Oj40
Temora ◻ AUS 151 Sd63
Temomozis ◻ MEX 244 Ef32
Temoris ◻ MEX 244 Ef32
Temosachic ◻ MEX 244 Eg32
Temozón ◻ MEX 247 Ff35
Tempe ◻ USA 235 Ee29
Tempeh ◻ RI 129 Qf49
Tempestad ◻ PE 268 Gc46
Tempio di Giove Anxur ◻ I 62 Lo49
Tempio di Hera Lacinia ◻ I 63 Ls51
Tempio Malatestiano di Rimini ◻ I 61 Lo46
Tempio Pausania ◻ I 62 Lk50
Tempio Tavole Palatine ◻ I 63 Lq50
Tempio d'Auguste et de Livie ◻ F 53 Le45
Temple of Amun ◻ ET 179 Mg33
Temple of Hatshepsut ◻ ET 179 Mg33
Temple of Haven ◻ CHN 107 Qj25
Temple of Hibis ◻ ET 179 Mf33
Temple of Horus ◻ ET 179 Mf33
Temple of Kawa ◻ SUD 185 Mf36
Temple of Khnum ◻ ET 179 Mf33
Temple of Kôm Ombo ◻ ET 179 Mg33
Temple of Luxor ◻ ET 179 Mg33
Temple of Nadura ◻ ET 179 Mf33
Temple of Philae ◻ ET 179 Mg33
Temple of Poseidon ◻ GR 71 Me53
Temple of Sebeus ◻ SUD 185 Mf35
Temples of Naqa ◻ SUD 185 Mg37
Temples of Sesebi ◻ SUD 185 Mf35
Templeton ◻ D 58 Lo37
Templin ◻ D 59 Ln38
Tempoal de Sánchez ◻ MEX 246 Fa35
Tempué ◻ ANG 200 Lk52
Temrjuk ◻ RUS 73 Mj23
Temu ◻ RCH 280 Gd67
Temuco ◻ RCH 280 Gd66
Temuka ◻ NZ 153 Tf68
Tena ◻ EC 268 Gc48
Tenakee Springs ◻ USA 230 Dc17
Tenala = Tenhola ◻ FIN 44 Md30
Tenali ◻ IND 117 Pa37
Tenancingo, Gunung ▲ RI 130 Ra46
Tenancingo de Degollado ◻ MEX 246 Fa36
Tenasserim ◻ MYA 122 Pk39
Tenasserim = Taninthari ◻ MYA 122 Pk39
Tenasserim Island ▲ MYA 122 Pj39
Tenby ◻ GB 49 Kp39
Tench Island ▲ PNG 156 Sf46
Tendaho ◻ ETH 192 Na40
Ten Degree Channel ▲ IND 122 Pg41
Tendelti ◻ SUD 185 Mg38
Tendrara ◻ MA 175 Kq29
Tenébrio ◻ BR 271 Hf48
Ténékou ◻ RMM 181 Kh38
Ténente Portela ◻ BR 276 Hd59
Ténentou ◻ RMM 181 Kh38
Tenerapa ◻ MEX 245 Eh33
Ténéré ◻ RN 183 Lf36
Ténéré (Long Island) ◻ USA 241 Ge25
Tenerife ◻ E 174 Kb31
Tengahdai ◻ RI 130 Rb50
Tenggol ▲ MAL 126 Qb43
Tenggarong ◻ RI 129 Qj46
Tenggol ▲ MAL 126 Qb43
Tengkis ◻ RI 127 Qc46
Tengréla ◻ CI 187 Kh41
Tengzhou ◻ CHN 108 Qk27
Te-n-Guembo ◻ RIM 180 Kf37
Teng Xian ◻ CHN 108 Qf34
Tengzhou ◻ CHN 112 Qj28
Tenharim Marmelos, T.I. ◻ BR 270 Gi48
Tenia ◻ IND 118 Oj40
Teniente Agripino Enciso, P.N. ◻ PY 278 Gf56
Teniente Luis Carvajal ◻ RA 282 Gc32
Teniente Maza ◻ RA 280 Gf64
Teniente Pinglo ◻ PE 268 Gb48
Tenille ◻ USA 242 Fj33
Tenindewa ◻ AUS 144 Qh60
Tenkasi ◻ IND 118 Oj41
Tenke ◻ RDC 196 Md51
Tenkodogo ◻ BF 187 Kk40
Tenisra ◻ MEX 245 Eh33
Ten Mile Lake ◻ CDN 231 Ga18
Tennant Creek ◻ AUS 146 Rh55
Tennessee ◻ USA 233 Ed24
Tennessee N.W.R. ◻ USA 243 Ff27
Tennessee N.W.R. ◻ USA 239 Fj27
Tenom ◻ MAL 128 Qj43
Tenosique ◻ MEX 247 Ff37
Tensas River N.W.R. ◻ USA 239 Fe29
Ten Sleep ◻ USA 233 Eg22
Tenstrike ◻ USA 236 Fc21
Tentano ◻ IND 130 Ra46
Tenterfield ◻ AUS 149 Sf60
Ten Thousand Islands N.W.R. ◻ USA 243 Fk33
Tentolomatinan, Gunung ▲ RI 125 Rb45
Tentra ◻ IND 116 Oj32
Tenya ◻ IND 116 Oj32
Tenzug ◻ GH 187 Kk40
Teotlite ◻ MEX 246 Ej35
Teotl, Cerro al ▲ OQ/YV 264 Gd40
Teotihuacán ◻ MEX 246 Fa36
Teotl ◻ MEX 247 Ff37
Teófilo Otoni ◻ BR 275 Hj55
Teofilândia ◻ BR 273 Ja51
Teocuitla ◻ MEX 244 Eh34
Teófilo Otoni ◻ BR 275 Hj55
Teonimanu Island ▲ RP 125 Ra42
Teos ◻ TR 71 Mg52
Teotihuacán ◻ MEX 246 Fa36
Teotitlán del Valle ◻ MEX 246 Fb37
Teotilán de Flores Magón ◻ MEX 246 Fb36
Tepa ◻ GH 187 Kj42
Tepache ◻ MEX 244 Eg32

Tepalcatepec ◻ MEX 246 Ej36
Tepalcingo ◻ MEX 246 Fa36
Tepatitlán de Morelos ◻ MEX 246 Ej35
Tepeguajes ◻ MEX 246 Fb34
Tepeji ◻ BG 69 Mg47
Tepekede ◻ AL 70 Lu50
Tepelenë ◻ AL 70 Lu50
Tepelou ◻ RI 125 Re45
Tepere ◻ MOC 203 Mk52
Tepexi de Rodriguez ◻ MEX 246 Fb36
Tepic ◻ MEX 246 Eh35
Tepir ◻ MEX 247 Ff35
Tepla ◻ CZ 66 Ln41
Teplice ◻ CZ 66 Lm40
Teploe ◻ RUS 72 Mj19
Tepozteco ◻ MEX 246 Fa36
Tepoztlán ◻ MEX 246 Fa36
Te Puke ◻ NZ 152 Tj64
Tequila ◻ MEX 246 Ej35
Tequisquiapan ◻ MEX 246 Fa35
Téra ◻ RN 181 La38
Teradomari ◻ J 111 Rj27
Terakeka ◻ SUD 194 Mf43
Terälahti ◻ FIN 44 Md29
Téramo ◻ I 61 Lo48
Teran ◻ CO 264 Ga45
Terang ◻ AUS 151 Sb65
Te Rapa Racecourse ◻ NZ 152 Th64
Ter Apel ◻ NL 51 Lh38
Terapo ◻ PNG 155 Sd50
Terara ▲ RCH 279 Gi56
Terbuny ◻ RUS 72 Mk19
Tercan ◻ TR 91 Na26
Terceira Aliança ◻ BR 274 Hc56
Terenos ◻ BR 274 Hb55
Terepaima, P.N. ◻ YV 265 Gf41
Teresa ◻ RCH 279 Gf56
Teresina ◻ BR 273 Hj48
Teresópolis ◻ BR 277 Hj57
Terezinha de Goiás ◻ BR 272 Hg52
Tergiste ◻ F 51 Ld41
Terjit ◻ RIM 180 Kd35
Terling ◻ MYA 120 Pj34
Terme ◻ TR 90 Mj25
Terme di Lurisia ◻ I 60 Lh46
Termessos ◻ TR 90 Mf27
Termez ◻ UZ 99 Oc27
Termini Imerese ◻ I 62 Lp52
Terrak ◻ N 40 Lo25
Terraba ◻ I 62 Lk51
Terme di Cauquenes ◻ RCH 280 Gd63
Termoli ◻ I 63 Lp49
Termoli ◻ I 63 Lq49
Ternate ▲ RI 125 Rd45
Ternej ◻ RUS 111 Rj23
Terneuzen ◻ NL 51 Lg39
Terni ◻ I 61 Lo48
Ternopil' ◻ UA 66 Md41
Terowie ◻ AUS 150 Rk62
Terpai ◻ RDC 191 Me43
Terpsa ◻ CHN 105 Rd21
Terrace ◻ CDN 230 Df18
Terrace Bay ◻ CDN 237 Fg21
Terra ▲ NAM 200 Lg55
Terracina ◻ I 62 Lo49
TerracottaArmy ◻ CHN 106 Qd28
Terrak ◻ N 40 Lo25
Terralba ◻ I 62 Lk51
Terra Mítica ◻ E 57 Ku52
Terra Nova ◻ BR 273 Ja50
Terra Nova ◻ BR 273 Ja50
Terra Nova N.P. ◻ CDN 241 Hd21
Terra Preta ◻ BR 271 Ha49
Terra Preta ◻ BR 271 Ha49
Terra Rica ◻ BR 276 Hd57
Terra Verhelma, T.I. ◻ BR 270 Gj48
Terre Adelie ▲ 287 Rd32
Terre Haute ◻ USA 239 Fg26
Terrebonne ◻ CDN 241 Gd23
Terre Clarie ▲ 287 Rc32
Terreiros ◻ MEX 245 Ek31
Terreton ◻ USA 233 Ed24
Terry ◻ USA 233 Eg22
Terry Hie Hie ◻ AUS 149 Sf60
Terschelling ▲ NL 51 Lf37
Tersef ◻ TCH 189 Lg39
Tertenia ◻ I 62 Ll51
Teruel ◻ CO 264 Gb45
Teruel ◻ E 57 Kt50
Terutao ▲ THA 122 Qa39
Terutao N.P. ◻ THA 122 Qa39
Te루지 ◻ RI 127 Qd47
Terusan ◻ RI 127 Qd47
Tervakoski ◻ FIN 44 Md30
Tervel ◻ BG 69 Mh47
Tervo ◻ FIN 56 Mg28
Tervola ◻ FIN 39 Me26
Tervuren ◻ B 51 Lf40
Terwood ◻ AUS 147 Sc54
Tesaliа ◻ CO 264 Gc44
Teşanj ◻ BIH 68 Lt46
Teseney ◻ ER 192 Mk38
Teshi ◻ EAK 194 Mg46
Teshio ◻ J 111 Sb23
Teshikaga ◻ J 111 Sc24
Tešica ◻ SRB 68 Mb46
Teslic ◻ BIH 68 Lt46
Teslin ◻ CDN 230 Dc15
Tesno ◻ RI 130 Ra46
Tesovo ◻ RUS 44 Mf31
Tessalit ◻ RMM 182 La35
Tessaoua ◻ RN 182 Ld38
Tesséroukane ◻ RN 182 Ld38
Tessier ◻ CDN 231 Ef19
Testel del Gargano ◻ I 63 Lr49
Testour ◻ TN 177 Lf28
Tét ◻ F 52 Lc48
Tetanga ◻ RI 130 Ra50
Tetas, Punta ▲ RCH 278 Ge56
Tété ◻ BR 272 Hg47
Tete ◻ MOC 202 Mg54
Tetepare Island ▲ SOL 157 Sj49
Teteringen ◻ NL 51 Lg39
Teterow ◻ D 59 Ln37
Tetiev ◻ UA 73 Me21
Tetijiv ◻ UA 73 Me21

Tétini ◻ RG 186 Kf41
Tetlin Junction ◻ USA 229 Cj14
Tetlin National Wildlife Refuge ◻ USA 229 Cj14
Tétouan ◻ MA 175 Kh28
Tetovo ◻ BG 69 Mg47
Tetovo ◻ MK 68 Ma48
Tettnang ◻ D 59 La43
Teuchern ◻ D 58 Ln39
Teuchitla ◻ MEX 177 Ma29
Teulada-Moraira ◻ E 57 La52
Teulon ◻ CDN 236 Fa20
Teun ▲ RI 131 Re49
Teunom ◻ RI 126 Ph43
Teuri-to ▲ J 111 Sa23
Teutoburger Wald ▲ D 58 Lj38
Teutonia ◻ BR 276 He60
Teuva ◻ FIN 44 Mb28
Teverya ◻ IL 90 Mh29
Tewa ◻ CDN 196 Qb28
Te Wahipounamu ◻ NZ 153 Td68
Tewantin-Noosa ◻ AUS 149 Sg59
Tewukkou N.W.R. ◻ USA 236 Fb22
Tewkesbury ◻ GB 49 Ks39
Texada Island ▲ CDN 232 Dh1
Texarkana ◻ USA 238 Fc29
Texas ◻ AUS 149 Sf60
Texas ◻ USA 238 Fz29
Texas Motor Speedway ◻ USA 238 Fb29
Texas Rangers Hall of Fame ◻ USA 238 Fb30
Texel ▲ NL 51 Le38
Teyateyaneng ◻ LS 205 Md60
Teywarah ◻ AFG 99 Oc29
Tezfortain ◻ MEX 246 Fb34
Tezpur ◻ IND 120 Pg32
Tezu ◻ IND 120 Ph32
Tha ◻ IND 120 Ph32
The Alley ◻ CAN 150 Rf59
The Olgas ▲ AUS 145 Rf58
Theologos ◻ GR 68 Mb52
The Overland ▲ AUS 150 Sa64
Thepa ◻ THA 123 Qa42
The Pas ◻ CDN 233 Ek19
The Pennines ◻ GB 49 Ks36
The Pride of Africa ◻ M 202 Md54
The Sa Thit ◻ THA 123 Qa38
Théra ◻ GR 71 Mf54
The Registan ◻ UZ 97 Od26
Theri ◻ IND 115 Ok30
Thermes de Migloky ◻ RM 206 Ne52
Thermes de Vichy ◻ F 71 Mg51
Thermo ◻ GR 70 Ma52
Thermopolis ◻ USA 233 Ef24
The Rock ◻ AUS 151 Sd64
Theron Mountains ▲ 287 Jc34
The Royal Brierl ◻ IND 114 Oh32
The Sands ◻ GUY 266 Gk43
The Slot = New Georgia Sound ◻ SOL 157 Sj49
The Sound ◻ DK 42 Ln35
Thesprotikó ◻ GR 70 Ma51
Thessalon ◻ CDN 237 Fj22
The Steppe ▲ KZ 88 Oa09
Thetford ◻ GB 49 La38
Thetford Mines ◻ CDN 240 Gd22
Thet ke gyin ◻ MYA 120 Ph34
The Twins ▲ AUS 144 Rh56
Theunissen ◻ ZA 205 Md60
The Valley ◻ GB 49 Ks37
Thevenard Island ▲ AUS 142 Qh56
The Village ◻ USA 238 Fb29
The Wash ▲ GB 49 La37
The Wedge ▲ USA 234 Eb29
The Whitsundays ◻ AUS 149 Se58
The Woodlands ◻ USA 238 Fc30
Thialf ◻ NL 51 Lg38
Thiba ◻ EAK 194 Mj46
Thiboudaux ◻ USA 239 Fe31
Thief River Falls ◻ USA 236 Fb21
Thiene ◻ I 60 Lm45
Thierachern ◻ F 51 Ld41
Thiers ◻ F 52 Lc45
Thiès ◻ SN 180 Ka38
Thiesi ◻ I 62 Lj50
Thika ◻ EAK 194 Mj46
Thikombia ▲ FIJI 159 Tk53
Thillot ◻ Butokkar ◻ SN 180 Kc17
Thimád al Fata'im ◻ LAR 177 Lk30
Thimlich Ohinga ◻ EAK 194 Mh46
Thimphu ● BHT 120 Pe32
Thingsaii ◻ IND 122 Pg42
Thionville ◻ F 51 Lg41
Thira ◻ GR 71 Mf54
Thira = Santorini ◻ GR 71 Mf54
Thira ▲ GR 71 Mf54
Third Cataract ▲ SUD 184 Me34
Thirukkovilur ◻ IND 119 Ok40
Thiruvananthapuram ◻ IND 119 Ok40
Thisted ◻ DK 42 Lj34
Thisvi ◻ GR 71 Me52
Thistle Island ◻ AUS 150 Rj63
Thitani ◻ EAK 194 Mj46
Thiva ◻ GR 71 Me52
Thiviers ◻ F 52 La45
Thizy ◻ F 53 Le44
Tho ◻ K 123 Qb39
Thnal Bek ◻ K 123 Qd40
Thoen ◻ THA 122 Qa38
Thoeng ◻ THA 121 Qa38
Thohoyandou ◻ ZA 202 Mf57
Tholaria ◻ GR 71 Mg54
Thomas Mann Haus ◻ LT 45 Mb35
Thomaston ◻ USA 239 Fh29
Thomasten Corner ◻ CDN 240 Gg23
Thomasville ◻ USA 239 Fj29
Thomasville ◻ USA 242 Fh30
Than Uyen ◻ VN 121 Qb35
Thanwin Myit ◻ MYA 121 Pk35
Thomonde ◻ RH 250 Ge36
Thompson ◻ CDN 227 Fa07
Thompson Landing ◻ CDN 231 Ee14
Thompson Pass ◻ USA 229 Ch15
Thompson Falls ◻ USA 232 Ec22
Thompson's ● Falls ▲ CDN 230 Dj16
Thomson River ◻ AUS 148 Sb57
Thomson's Falls = Nyahururu ◻ EAK 194 Mj45
Thong Pha Phum ◻ THA 122 Pk38
Thong Sala ◻ THA 122 Pj41
Thongwa ◻ MYA 122 Pj38
Thon Hai ◻ VN 123 Qd37
Thon Kiang ◻ THA 122 Pk41
Thonon-les-Bains ◻ F 53 Lg44
Thoreau ◻ USA 235 Ef28
Thornhill ◻ GB 49 Ks35
Thorntonia ◻ AUS 146 Rk55
Thorshavnheane ▲ 287 Mc33
Thorsminde ◻ DK 42 Lh34
Thorton Beach ◻ AUS 147 Sc54
Thot Not ◻ VN 123 Qc40
Thouars ◻ F 52 Ku44
Thoubal ◻ IND 120 Ph33
Thowada Goemba ◻ BHT 120 Pf32
Thowada Goemba ▲ BHT 120 Pf32
Thowak ◻ GB/TH 69 Mf49
Thrapston ◻ GB 49 Ku38
Thredbo Village ◻ AUS 151 Se64
Three Forks ◻ USA 233 Ee23
Three Gorges Dam ◻ CHN 108 Qf28
Three Gorges of Wuyang R. ◻ CHN 108 Qd29
Three Hills ◻ CDN 233 Ed20
Three Kings Islands ▲ NZ 152 Tg63
Three Pagodas Pass ◻ THA 122 Pk38
Three Parallel Rivers of Yunnan Protected Areas ◻ ◻ CHN 121 Pk32
Three Rivers ◻ AUS 144 Qk58
Three Rivers ◻ USA 235 Ef29
Three Rivers ◻ USA 237 Fh25
Three Rivers ◻ USA 245 Fa31

Three Sisters – Traben-Trarbach

Three Sisters AUS 148 Sa58
Three Sisters AUS 151 Sf62
Three Sisters USA 232 Dk23
Three Sisters ZA 204 Mb61
Three Sisters Islands SOL 157 Tb51
Three Springs AUS 144 Qh60
Three Way Roadhouse AUS 146 Rh55
Thrissur IND 118 Oj40
Throckmorton USA 238 Fa29
Throssell Range AUS 142 Ra57
Thrumching La N.P. BHT 120 Pf32
Thrushton N.P. AUS 149 Sd59
Thuburbo Majus TN 176 Le27
Thu Dau Mot VN 123 Qd40
Thud Point AUS 147 Sa52
Thueyts F 53 Le46
Thuillier, Mount IND 122 Pg42
Thuir F 52 Lc48
Thul PK 99 Oe31
Thula YE 94 Nb38
Thulamela ZA 202 Mf57
Thule = Qaanaaq DK 227 Gc03
Thuli ZW 202 Me56
Thun CH 60 Lh44
Thunda AUS 148 Sb58
Thundelarra AUS 144 Qj60
Thunder Bay CDN 236 Ff21
Thuner See CH 60 Lh44
Thung Hua Chang THA 121 Pk36
Thung Muang THA 121 Qa36
Thung Nao THA 121 Qa36
Thung Salaeng Luang N.P. THA 122 Qa37
Thung Song THA 122 Pk41
Thung Tako THA 122 Pk40
Thung Wa THA 122 Pk42
Thung Wua Laen Beach THA 122 Pk40
Thung Yai THA 122 Pk41
Thungyai-Huai Kha Kaeng Wildlife Sanctuaries THA 122 Pk38
Thurayban KSA 94 Na36
Thüringen D 58 Ll40
Thüringer Wald D 58 Ll40
Thurles IRL 47 Kn38
Thurlga AUS 150 Rh62
Thurloo Downs AUS 148 Sb60
Thursby GB 48 Kr36
Thursday Island AUS 147 Sb51
Thurso GB 48 Kr32
Thury-Harcourt F 50 Ku42
Thusis CH 60 Lk44
Thyborøn DK 42 Lj34
Thylungra AUS 148 Sb59
Thymania AUS 148 Sb57
Thyolo MW 203 Mh54
Thysville = Mbanza-Ngungu RDC 198 Lh48
Tiabge CI 187 Kh43
Tiadiaye SN 180 Kb38
Tiago BR 266 Hb46
Tiahuanaco BOL 278 Gf54
Tiahuanacu BOL 278 Gf54
Tianbanjie CHN 109 Qj31
Tianchang CHN 112 Qk29
Tian Chi CHN 101 Pd24
Tiandeng CHN 108 Qd34
Tiandong CHN 108 Qd34
Tian'e CHN 108 Qd33
Tianeti GE 91 Nc24
Tianguá BR 273 Hk47
Tianguel-Bori RG 186 Kd40
Tianjin CHN 107 Qj26
Tianjin Shi CHN 107 Qj26
Tianjun CHN 103 Pk27
Tiankoura BF 187 Kj40
Tianlin CHN 108 Qd33
Tianmen CHN 109 Qg30
Tianmu Shan CHN 112 Qk30
Tianmushan Z.B. CHN 112 Qk30
Tianqiaoling CHN 110 Re24
Tian-Shan' CHN 100 Pa24
Tianshui CHN 106 Qc28
Tianshuihai 102 Ok28
Tiantai CHN 109 Ra31
Tiantaishan CHN 109 Ra32
Tiantong Si CHN 109 Ra32
Tiantoubarak RN 182 Ld38
Tian Ya Hai Jiao CHN 109 Qe36
Tianyang CHN 108 Qd34
Tianyi Ge CHN 109 Ra32
Tianzhen CHN 107 Qh25
Tianzhou Jiaotang CHN 107 Ra27
Tianzhu CHN 106 Qb27
Tianzhu CHN 108 Qe32
Tianzhushan CHN 112 Qj30
Tiaret DZ 176 La28
Tiaro AUS 149 Sg58
Tiassalé CI 187 Kh43
Tibagi BR 277 He58
Tibana CO 264 Gd43
Tibana RO 73 Md22
Tibati CAM 189 Lg42
Tibaú BR 273 Jb48
Tibau, Gunung RI 128 Qh45
Tibel'ti RUS 104 Qb20
Tiber I 62 Ln48
Tiberghamine DZ 175 La31
Tibesti TCH 183 Lj35
Tibet CHN 77 Pa07
Tibilisi GE 91 Nc25
Tibiri RN 182 Lb39
Tibiri RN 182 Ld39
Tibo BF 181 Kj38
Tibo RDC 191 Md44
Tibo RDC 191 Me44
Tibo RI 130 Qk47
Tibooburra AUS 148 Sb60
Tibro S 43 Lp32
Tibú CO 264 Gd41
Tiburon RH 250 Gc36
Tiča BG 69 Mg48
Tica MOC 203 Mh55
Ticao Island RP 124 Rb39
Tica Tica BOL 278 Gg56
Tichet RMM 181 La36
Tichit RIM 180 Kf36
Tichla DARS 180 Kc35
Ticho ETH 192 Mk42
Ticino CH 60 Lj44
Tickalara AUS 148 Sb60
Ticonderoga USA 241 Gd24
Ticsani, Volcán PE 269 Ge54
Ticul MEX 247 Ff35
Tidaholm S 43 Lo32
Tidal River AUS 151 Sd65
Tidan S 43 Lp32
Tidarmène RMM 182 Lb37
Tiddim MYA 120 Pg34
Tiddis DZ 176 Ld27
Tidi Dunes RN 183 Lh35
Tidjikja RIM 180 Ke36
Tidore RI 125 Rd45
Tiébissou CI 187 Kh42
Tiéblé BF 187 Kk40
Tiebl'gahl SYR 91 Na28
Tiéboro TCH 183 Lj35
Tiefa CHN 110 Rb24
Tiéfala RMM 187 Kg40
Tiéfora BF 187 Kh40
Tiel NL 51 Lf39
Tiel SN 180 Kc38
Tieli CHN 110 Re22
Tieling CHN 110 Rb24
Tielong 102 Ok28
Tielt B 51 Ld40
Tiémé CI 187 Kg41
Tié-Ndiékro CI 187 Kh42
Tienen B 51 Le40
Tiéningboué CI 187 Kh41
Tienko CI 187 Kg40
Tienko CI 187 Kg41
Tien Yen VN 121 Qd35
Tiera BF 187 Kh40
Tiéré RMM 187 Kh40
Tierfontein ZA 205 Md60
Tierir AUS 149 Se57
Tierp S 43 Ls30
Tierra Amarilla RCH 279 Ge59
Tierra Amarilla USA 235 Eg27
Tierra Blanca MEX 247 Fb36
Tierra Colorada MEX 246 Fa37
Tierra de Campos E 54 Kp49
Tierra del Fuego RA 282 Gf72
Tierra del Fuego RA 282 Gg73
Tierra del Fuego, P.N. RA 282 Gg73
Tierra del Vino E 54 Kp49
Tierralta CO 264 Gb41
Tierranueva MEX 246 Ek35
Tierras Blancas RCH 279 Ge61
Tierras de Sayago E 54 Ko49
Tiesa E 55 Kp53
Tie Siding USA 235 Eh25
Tie Ta CHN 107 Qh28
Tietê BR 274 He56
Tietê BR 277 Hg57
Tieyon AUS 148 Rg59
Tiffin USA 237 Fj25
Tiflèt MA 175 Kg29
Tifore RI 125 Rd45
Tifrirt RIM 180 Kd35
Tifton USA 242 Fj30
Tifu RI 131 Rd47
Tiga F 158 Td56
Tiga MAL 128 Qh43
Tigaon RP 124 Rb39
Tigapulan Mountains RI 127 Qb46
Tigbauan RP 124 Rb40
Tiger USA 232 Eb21
Tiger Island GUY 266 Ha42
Tigharry GB 48 Kn33
Tighenif DZ 175 La28
Tighina MD 73 Me22
Tignère CAM 189 Lg42
Tigniré RIM 180 Kc36
Tignish CDN 240 Gh22
Tigoumatene RMM 181 Kh37
Tigre PE 268 Gc47
Tigre RA 281 Ha63
Tigre YV 265 Gj41
Tigris IRQ 91 Nb27
Tigrovaya Balka zapovednik TJ 97 Oe27
Tiguelguemine DZ 176 Lb32
Tiguent RIM 180 Kb37
Tiguentourine DZ 176 Le32
Tiguézéfene RN 182 Lb38
Tigui TCH 183 Lk36
Tiguili TCH 189 Lk40
Tigzirt DZ 176 Lc27
Tihamat YE 94 Nb37
Tihany H 66 Ls44
Tiholop MEX 247 Ff35
Tihoreck RUS 73 Na23
Tihosuco MEX 247 Ff35
Tihvin RUS 72 Mg16
Tihvinskaja grjada RUS 72 Mh16
Tijara IND 114 Oj32
Tiji LAR 176 Lf29
Tijuana MEX 244 Eb29
Tijuca, P.N.da BR 277 Hj57
Tijucas BR 277 Hf59
Tika CDN 240 Gh20
Tikal GCA 247 Ff37
Tikal GCA 247 Ff37
Tikal, P.N. GCA 247 Ff37
Tikamgarh IND 117 Ok33
Tikanlik CHN 101 Pd25
Tikaré BF 187 Kk39
Tikarpara IND 117 Pb35
Tikarpara IND 117 Pc35
Tikem TCH 190 Lh41
Tikitiki NZ 152 Tk64
Tikkaballi IND 117 Pc35
Tikkakoski FIN 44 Mf28
Tiko CAM 188 Le43
Tikokino NZ 153 Tj65
Tikopia SOL 158 Te52
Tikota IND 116 Oh37
Tikrit IRQ 91 Nb28
Tiku RI 127 Pk46
Tikuna de Feijoal, T.I. BR 270 Gf48
Tikus RI 127 Qb47
Tila MEX 247 Fd37
Tiladru IND 117 Pa37
Tilaj H 66 Ls44
Tilal an-Nuba SUD 185 Mf39
Tilama RCH 280 Ge62
Tilamuta RI 125 Rb45
Tilbooroo AUS 149 Sc59
Tilburg NL 51 Lf39
Tilbury GB 49 La39
Tilcara RA 279 Gh57
Tilcha AUS 148 Sa60
Til-Châtel F 53 Lf43
Tilda IND 117 Pa35
Tildega IND 117 Pb34
Tilden USA 245 Fa31
Tileagd RO 67 Mc43
Tilemsen MA 174 Ke31
Tilemsès RN 182 Lc38
Tilemsi RMM 181 La36
Tilemsi = Lerneb RMM 181 Kh37
Tilisaro RA 280 Gh62
Tiliviche RCH 278 Gf55
Tillabéri RN 182 La38
Tillamook USA 232 Dj23
Tillamook Bay USA 232 Dh23
Tillanchang Dwip IND 122 Pg41
Tillberga S 43 Lr31
Tillia RN 182 Lc37
Tillsonburg CDN 237 Fk24
Tiloa RN 182 Lb38
Tilopozo RCH 279 Gf57
Tílos GR 71 Mh54
Tilpa AUS 149 Sc61
Tilrhempt DZ 176 Lb29
Tiltagoonah AUS 149 Sc61
Tilža LV 45 Mh34
Tim RUS 72 Mj20
Tim UZ 97 Oc26
Tima ET 179 Mf32
Timahdite MA 175 Kh29
Timampu RI 130 Ra47
Timanfaya, P.N.de E 174 Kd31
Timare RI 154 Rj48
Timargarha PK 97 Of28
Timaru NZ 153 Tf68
Timaševsk RUS 73 Mk23
Timau EAK 194 Mj45
Timba CO 264 Gb44
Timbalier Bay USA 239 Fe31
Timbauba BR 273 Jc49
Timbavati Game Reserve ZA 205 Mf58
Timbedgha RIM 181 Kf37
Timber Creek AUS 146 Rf53
Timber Lake USA 236 Ek23
Timberline Lodge Ski Area USA 232 Dk23
Timber Mill AUS 146 Rg51
Timber Mtn. USA 234 Ec26
Timbiras BR 272 Hj48
Timbó BR 277 Hf59
Timbo LB 186 Kf43
Timbo RG 186 Ke40
Timbó Grande BR 277 He59
Timboroa EAK 194 Mh45
Timbulun RI 127 Qa46
Timbunke PNG 155 Sb48
Timbun Mata MAL 125 Qk43
Timé BF 181 Kk38
Timellouline DZ 176 Le31
Timétrine RMM 181 Kk36
Timfristós GR 70 Mb52
Timgad DZ 176 Ld28
Timia RN 182 Le36
Timiaouine DZ 182 La35
Timika RI 154 Rj48
Timimoun DZ 175 La31
Timișoara RO 68 Mb45
Timissa RMM 187 Kh39
Timmele S 43 Lo33
Timmelsjoch A/I 60 Lm44
Timmerkpuk Mt. USA 229 Bj11
Timmins CDN 237 Fk21
Tim-Missao DZ 182 Lb35
Timna YE 94 Nc38
Timna Park IL 92 Mh31
Timon BR 273 Hj48
Timor TLS 131 Rc50
Timor Museum RI 131 Rb51
Timor Sea 131 Rd51
Timor Trough 131 Rc51
Timote RA 281 Gj63
Timoteo BR 275 Hj55
Timotes YV 264 Ge41
Timoudi DZ 175 Kk31
Timpanogos Cave Nat. Mon. USA 235 Ee25
Timpas USA 238 Ej27
Timpaus RI 131 Rb46
Timrå S 41 Ls28
Timun RI 127 Qb45
Timurni IND 116 Oj34
Tinaco YV 265 Gf41
Tinaga Island RP 124 Rb38
Ti-n-Aguelhaj RMM 181 Kj37
Ti-n-Akof BF 181 Kk38
Tin Alkoum DZ 183 Lf33
Tinambac RP 124 Rb39
Tinambung RI 130 Qk47
Tinaquillo YV 265 Gf41
Ti-n-Azabo RMM 181 La37
Ti-n-Bessaïs RIM 181 Kf34
Ti-n-Brahim RIM 180 Kc36
Tin Can Bay AUS 149 Sg58
Tindangou BF 187 La40
Tindari I 63 Lq52
Tindila RG 186 Kf40
Tindivanam IND 119 Ok39
Tindouf DZ 174 Kf32
Tiné SUD 184 Mb38
Tinejdad MA 175 Kh30
Tineo E 54 Ko47
Tinerhir MA 175 Kh30
Ti-n-Essako RMM 182 Lb36
Tinfouchy DZ 175 Kh31
Tin Fouye DZ 176 Ld31
Tinfunqué, P.N. PY 279 Ha57
Tinga GH 187 Kj41
Tingal SUD 185 Mf40
Tinggi MAL 126 Qc44
Tinglayan RP 124 Ra37
Tinglev DK 42 Lk36
Tingmiarmiut Fjord DK 227 Hd06
Tingo Maria PE 269 Gb50
Tingo María, P.N. PE 269 Gb50
Tingong CHN 108 Qe33
Tingri CHN 102 Pd31
Tingsryd S 43 Lp34
Tingstäde S 43 Lt33
Tinguipaya BOL 278 Gh55
Tinguiririca, Volcán RCH 280 Ge63
Tingvoll N 40 Lj28
Tingwon Group PNG 156 Se47
Tingya SUD 185 Mg40
Tinh Gia VN 121 Qc36
Tinhoa CI 186 Kf42
Tinigrat RIM 181 Kf36
Tinigua, P.N. CO 264 Gc44
Tiniroto NZ 153 Tj65
Tinjil RI 127 Qc49
Ti-n-Kâr = Timétrine RMM 181 Kk36
Tinlot B 51 Lf40
Ti-n-Medjouf RIM 180 Kc36
Tin Merzouga DZ 183 Lf34
Tinnenburra AUS 149 Sc60
Tinobu RI 130 Rb47
Tinogasta RA 279 Gg60
Tinombo RI 125 Ra45
Tinompo RI 130 Ra47
Tínos GR 71 Mf53
Tínos GR 71 Mf53
Tinputz PNG 157 Sh48
Tinqueux F 51 Ld41
Tin Rerchoch DZ 182 Lc35
Tinsukia IND 120 Ph32
Tintâne RIM 180 Ke37
Tintang RI 128 Qj45
Tin Tarabine DZ 182 Ld34
Ti-n-Tehoun RMM 181 Kj37
Tinténiac F 50 Kt42
Tinterhert DZ 182 Le33
Tintern Abbey GB 49 Ks39
Ti-n-Tijot' RMM 181 Kh37
Tintina RA 279 Gj59
Tintinara AUS 150 Sa63
Tintioulen RG 186 Kf40
Tinui NZ 153 Tj66
Tinūži LV 45 Me34
Ti-n-Zaouâtene RMM 182 Lb36
Tinzouline MA 175 Kg30
Tioga USA 233 Ej21
Tioman MAL 126 Qc44
Tione di Trento I 60 Ll44
Tioneste USA 237 Ga25
Tionk Essil SN 186 Kb39
Tioor RI 131 Rf48
Tiop RI 127 Qa47
Tiorobougou RMM 187 Kf39
Tioroniaradougou CI 187 Kh41
Tiou BF 187 Kj39
Tiou BF 187 Kj40
Tiouilit RIM 180 Kb36
Tipaza DZ 176 Lb27
Tipón PE 269 Ge52
Tipparti IND 117 Ok37
Tipperary AUS 146 Rf52
Tipperary IRL 47 Km38
Tipton, Mount USA 234 Ec28
Tip Tree, Mount AUS 147 Sc54
Tiptur IND 118 Oj39
Tipuru GUY 266 Ha43
Tiputini EC 268 Gc46
Tiquimul MEX 247 Fe36
Tiradentes BR 275 Hh56
Tiranë AL 68 Lu49
Tirangole SUD 194 Mg43
Tirano I 60 Ll44
Tiran & Sanâfir Islands Reserve ET 179 Mh32
Tiraouene RN 182 Ld36
Tiraque BOL 278 Gh54
Tirasberge NAM 204 Lj58
Tiraspol MD 73 Me22
Tirau NZ 152 Th64
Tire TR 71 Mh52
Tirebolu TR 91 Mk25
Tirecatinga, T.I. BR 278 Ha52
Tiree AUS 149 Sc56
Tiree GB 48 Ko34
Tirgaran AFG 97 Of27
Tirgua, P.N. YV 265 Gf41
Tirhatimine DZ 176 Lb33
Tirich Mir PK 97 Of27
Tiriri EAU 194 Mg45
Tirkšliai LT 45 Mc34
Tirlta AUS 148 Sb61
Tirmalgiri IND 117 Ok37
Tirmini RN 182 Le39
Tírnavos GR 70 Mc51
Tiro RG 186 Ke41
Tirol = Tirolo I 60 Lm44
Tirolo = Tirol I 60 Lm44
Tirora IND 117 Pa35
Tiros BR 275 Hh55
Tiroungoulou RCA 190 Mb41
Tirrénia I 60 Ll47
Tirschenreuth D 59 Ln41
Tirthahalli IND 118 Oh39
Tirth Raj Prayag IND 117 Pa33
Tirúa RCH 280 Gd65
Tiruchendur IND 118 Ok41
Tiruchengodu IND 118 Oj40
Tiruchirapalli IND 119 Ok40
Tirumala IND 119 Ok39
Tirumangalam IND 118 Oj41
Tirumayam IND 118 Ok40
Tirunelveli IND 118 Oj41
Tirupati IND 119 Ok39
Tirupatur IND 119 Ok39
Tiruppattur IND 118 Ok40
Tiruppur IND 118 Oj40
Tirután PE 268 Gc49
Tiruvannamalai IND 119 Ok39
Tiruvarur IND 119 Ok40
Tiruvellore IND 119 Ok39
Tiruvettipuram IND 119 Ok39
Tiruvottiyur IND 119 Pa39
Tiruvuru IND 117 Pa37
Tiryns GR 70 Mc53
Tis IR 98 Oa33
Tišća BIH 68 Lt46
Tisdale CDN 233 Eh19
Tisgaon IND 116 Oh36
Tisgui-Remz MA 174 Kf31
Tishomingo USA 238 Fb28
Tishomingo N.W.R. USA 238 Fb28
Tis Isat Falls ETH 192 Mj40
Tiškevičiu rūmai LT 45 Mb35
Tišnov CZ 66 Lr41
Tisovec SK 67 Lu42
Tissemsilt DZ 176 La28
Tisvildeleje DK 42 Ln34
Tiszabecs H 67 Mc42
Tiszacsege H 67 Mb43
Tiszacsermely H 67 Mb42
Tiszadada H 67 Mb42
Tiszaföldvár H 67 Ma44
Tiszafüred H 67 Ma43
Tiszakécske H 67 Ma44
Tiszalúc H 67 Mb42
Tiszaújváros H 67 Mb43
Tiszavasvári H 67 Mb43
Tit DZ 175 La32
Tit DZ 182 Lc34
Titalya IND 120 Pe32
Titan Dome 287 Tb36
Titao BF 187 Kj39
Titay RP 125 Rb42
Tite GNB 186 Kc40
Titigading RI 127 Qa45
Titiklut USA 229 Cb10
Titisee-Neustadt D 59 Lj43
Titiwaifuru RI 154 Rk47
Titlagarh IND 117 Pb35
Titlis CH 60 Lj44
Tit-Mellil MA 175 Kg29
Titran N 40 Lj27
Ti Tree AUS 147 Sa53
Ti-Tree AUS 148 Rg57
Titu RO 69 Mf46
Titule RDC 191 Mc44
Titusville USA 237 Ga25
Titusville USA 242 Fk31
Tiumpan Head GB 48 Ko32
Tivaouane SN 180 Kb38
Tivat MNE 68 Lt48
Tiveden S 43 Lp32
Tivedens n.p. S 43 Lp32
Tiverton GB 49 Kr40
Tivoli DK 42 Ln35
Tívoli I 62 Ln49
Tivoli USA 245 Fb31
Tiwai Island Wildlife Sanctuary WAL 186 Ke42
Tiwi EAK 197 Mk48
Tiwi OM 95 Nk34
Tiwi Aboriginal Reserve AUS 146 Rf51
Tixmul MEX 247 Ff36
Tixtla de Guerrero MEX 246 Fa37
Tiya ETH 192 Mk41
Tiyama J 111 Rk27
Tiyo ER 192 Na38
Tizayuca MEX 246 Fa36
Tizimín MEX 247 Ff35
Tizi-n-Bachkoum MA 175 Kg30
Tizi-n-Tairhemt MA 175 Kh29
Tizi-n-Tarhatine MA 175 Kg30
Tizi-n-Test MA 175 Kg30
Tizi-n-Tichka MA 175 Kg30
Tizi-n-Tinifift MA 175 Kg30
Tizi Ouzou DZ 176 Lc27
Tiznit MA 174 Kf31
Tižtiž IR 91 Nd28
Tizzano F 62 Lj49
Tjačiv UA 67 Md42
Tjæreborg DK 42 Lj35
Tjällmo S 43 Lq32
Tjaneni SD 205 Mf59
Tjan'-šan' KS 97 Of24
Tjapukai Aboriginal Cultural Centre AUS 147 Sc54
Tjatino RUS 111 Sd23
Tjatja, vulkan RUS 111 Sd23
Tjentište BIH 68 Lt47
Tjibaou Cultural Centre F 158 Td57
Tjøme N 42 Ll31
Tjörn S 42 Lm33
Tjörnes IS 46 Kc24
Tjøtta N 40 Ln25
Tjumen' RUS 88 Ob07
Tkhinvali GE 91 Nc24
Tlacoapa MEX 246 Fa37
Tlacolula de Matamoros MEX 247 Fb37
Tlacotalpan MEX 247 Fc36
Tlahualilo de Zaragoza MEX 245 Ej32
Tlaltenango de Sánchez Román MEX 246 Ej35
Tlapacoyan MEX 246 Fb36
Tlapa de Comonfort MEX 246 Fa37
Tlapehuala MEX 246 Ek36
Tlaquepaque MEX 246 Ej35
Tlaxcala MEX 246 Fa36
Tlaxcala MEX 246 Fa36
Tlaxco MEX 246 Fa36
Tlell CDN 230 De19
Tlemcen DZ 175 Kk28
Tlemcen, P.N.de DZ 175 Kk28
Tleta-Akhssass MA 174 Kf31
Tleta-Henchane MA 174 Kf30
Tlisan LAR 177 Lj31
Tloh RUS 91 Nd24
Tlokoeng LS 205 Me60
Tłuchowo PL 65 Lu38
Tłuszcz PL 65 Mb38
Tmassah LAR 177 Lh32
Tmeïmichât RIM 180 Kc35
Tnaot K 123 Qc39
Tô BF 187 Kj40
Toamasina RM 207 Ne55
To Awai SUD 185 Mh35
Toay RA 280 Gh64
Toba CHN 103 Pj30
Toba J 113 Rj28
Toba RMM 187 Kg40
Tobacco Range BH 248 Fg37
Tobago TT 251 Gk40
Tobago Rain Forest Reserve TT 251 Gk40
Toba Inlet CDN 232 Dh20
Toba Kakar Range PK 99 Od30
Tobalai RI 131 Re46
Tobar Donoso EC 268 Ga45
Tobarra E 57 Kt52
Toba Tek Singh PK 99 Og30
Tobeatic Wildlife Management Area CDN 240 Gh23
Tobelo RI 125 Rd45
Tobercurry IRL 47 Km36
Tobermore AUS 148 Rj57
Tobermory AUS 149 Sb59
Tobermory CDN 237 Fk23
Tobermory GB 48 Ko34
Tobias Barreto BR 273 Jb51
Tobias Fornier RP 124 Ra40
Tobijima J 111 Rk26
Tobin Lake CDN 233 Ej19
Tobin, Mount USA 234 Eb25
Toblach = Dobbiaco I 60 Ln44
Tobli LB 186 Kf42
Toboali RI 129 Qd47
Tobol RUS 88 Ob07
Toboli RI 130 Ra46
Tobol'sk RUS 88 Ob07
Tobré DY 188 Lb40
Toca CO 264 Gd43
Tocache Nuevo PE 268 Gb50
Tocaia BR 273 Hj48
Tocaima CO 264 Gc43
Tocancipa CO 264 Gd43
Tocantinia BR 272 Hf50
Tocantinópolis BR 272 Hg49
Tocantins BR 272 Hf50
Tocantins BR 255 Hb11
Tocata RA 280 Gf61
Toccoa USA 242 Fj28
Toch'o Do ROK 112 Rd28
Töcksfors S 42 Lm31
Toco ANG 200 Lg53
Toco TT 251 Gk40
Tocoa HN 248 Fh38
Tocopilla RCH 279 Ge57
Tocopuri, Cerro de BOL 279 Gg57
Tocra = Teuchira LAR 177 Ma29
Tocumwal AUS 151 Sc63
Tócura CO 264 Gb42
Tocuyito YV 265 Gf40
Tocuyo de la Costa YV 265 Gf40
Tod ET 179 Mg33
Toda-saki J 111 Sa26
Todeli RI 131 Rc46
Tödi CH 60 Lj44
Todi I 60 Ln48
Todmorden AUS 148 Rh59
Todorići BIH 61 Ls46
Todos Santos BOL 278 Gh54
Todos Santos MEX 244 Ee34
Todtnau D 59 Lh43
Todupulai IND 118 Oj41
Toéguen BF 187 Kk39
Toéni BF 187 Kj39
Toéssé BF 187 Kk40
Toez CO 264 Gb44
Toffa DY 188 Lb42
Tofield CDN 233 Ed19
Tofino CDN 232 Dh21
Töfsingdalens n.p. S 40 Ln28
Toft GB 48 Kt30
Tofta S 42 Ln33
Tofta S 43 Lt33
Tofte N 42 Ll31
Töftedal S 42 Lm32
Toftir DK 46 Ko28
Toftlund DK 42 Lk35
Tog ETH 193 Nb41
Toga VU 158 Td52
Toganaly AZ 91 Nd25
Togarakunta IND 118 Oj38
Togba RIM 180 Ke37
Togbo RCA 190 Ma43
Togi J 111 Rj27
Togiak USA 228 Bk16
Togiak National Wildlife Refuge USA 228 Bk16
Togian RI 130 Ra46
tog'lari Aččitov UZ 96 Oa24
Togni SUD 185 Mh36
Togo CDN 236 Ek20
Togo PNG 155 Sb50
Togo RMM 187 Kh39
Togo USA 236 Fd22
Togo 163 La09
Togobala RG 186 Kg41
Togo Hills GH 187 La42
Togoroma CO 264 Gb43
Togou RMM 187 Kh39
Togoville TG 187 La42
Tögrög MNG 101 Pg22
Tögrög MNG 101 Ph23
Togton CHN 106 Qf25
Toguéré-Koumbé RMM 181 Kh38
Tohamiyam SUD 185 Mj36
Tohana IND 114 Oh31
Tohddoo Atoll MV 118 Og43
Tohmajärvi FIN 44 Ml28
Toho RI 129 Qe45
Tohoku Shinkansen J 111 Sa26
Toholampi FIN 41 Me27
Tohoun TG 187 La42
Toibalewe IND 122 Pg40
Toijala FIN 44 Md29
Toili RI 130 Rb46
Toineke RI 131 Rc51
Toivakka FIN 44 Mg28
Toivala FIN 44 Mh28
To-jima J 113 Rk28
Tojo J 113 Rg28
Toka GUY 266 Ha43
Tokachi-dake J 111 Sb24
Tokaido Shinkansen J 113 Rk28
Tokaj H 67 Mb42
Tokaj-Hegyalja H 67 Mb42
Tokamachi J 111 Rk27
Tokapalle IND 117 Ok38
Tokar SUD 185 Mj36
Tokara Islands J 113 Re31
Tokara Strait J 113 Rf30
Tokarevka RUS 72 Na19
Tokarnia PL 65 Mc41
Tokár-tető H 67 Mb42
Tokat TR 90 Mj25
Tokatoka NZ 152 Th64
Tokchokto Do ROK 112 Rd27
Tokch'on PRK 110 Rd26
Tok Do ROK 113 Rf27
Tokelau Islands NZ 134 Ba10
Tökhöm MNG 104 Qe23
Toki TCH 190 Lj41
Tok Junction USA 229 Cj14
Tokmak KS 100 Oh24
Tokmak UA 73 Mh22
Toko BOL 278 Gh54
Tokomaru Bay NZ 152 Tk65
Tokoro J 111 Sc23
Tokoroa NZ 152 Th65
Tokouno RG 186 Kf41
Toksovo RUS 44 Ml30
Toksum CHN 101 Pe24
Toktogul KS 97 Og25
Tokuno-jima J 113 Re32
Tokunoshima J 113 Re32
Tokushima J 113 Rh28
Tokuyama J 113 Rf28
Tokyo J 113 Rk28
Tokyo-Disneyland J 113 Rk28
Tokysan N.P. ROK 112 Rd28
Tokzar AFG 97 Od28
Tol PNG 156 Sg48
Tolaga Bay NZ 153 Tk65
Tolala RI 130 Ra47
Tôlanaro RM 207 Nd58
Tolandona RI 130 Rb48
Tolbo MNG 101 Pf21
Tolbuzino RUS 105 Rc19
Toldo Chimbangue, T.I. BR 276 Hd59
Tolé RCA 190 Lh42
Tole Bi KZ 100 Og24
Toledo BOL 278 Gg55
Toledo BR 276 Hd58
Toledo E 55 Kq51
Toledo RP 124 Rb40
Toledo USA 232 Dj22
Toledo USA 232 Dj23
Toledo USA 237 Fj25
Toledo Bend Reservoir USA 238 Fd30
Tolentino I 61 Lo47
Tolfa I 62 Lm48
Tolga DZ 176 Lc28
Tolga N 40 Ll28
Tolgskij monastyr RUS 72 Na17
Tolhuaca, P.N. RCH 280 Ge65
Toli CHN 100 Pb23
Toliara RM 207 Nb57
Tolima, Nevado de CO 264 Gc43
Tolitoli RI 125 Ra45
Tollarp S 43 Lo35
Tollensesee D 58 Lo37
Tollimarjon UZ 97 Oc26
Tolmezzo I 61 Lo44
Tolmin SLO 66 Lo44
Tolo RDC 199 Lk47
Tolofu RI 125 Rd45
Tolo Humma IND 117 Pc36
Tolokiwa Island PNG 155 Sd48
Tolon GH 187 Kk41
Tolongoina RM 207 Nd56
Tolosa E 56 Ks47
Tolsan Do ROK 113 Rd28
Toltén RCH 280 Gd65
Toltrele de la Prut MD 73 Md21
Tolú CO 264 Gc41
Toluca MEX 246 Fa36
Toludur IND 119 Ok40
Toluk KS 97 Og25
Toluviejo CO 264 Gc41
Toma BF 187 Kj39
Tomah USA 236 Fe24
Tomahawk USA 236 Ff23
Tomakivka UA 73 Mh22
Tomakomai J 111 Sa24
Tomanggong MAL 125 Qk43
Tomani MAL 128 Qh43
Tomaniivi FJI 159 Tk54
Tomar BR 270 Gj46
Tomar KZ 100 Oh22
Tomar P 55 Km51
Tomarovka RUS 72 Mj20
Tomarza TR 90 Mh26
Tomás PE 269 Gc52
Tomás de Borlanga EC 269 Fe46
Tomaševac SRB 68 Ma45
Tomás Garrido MEX 247 Ff36
Tomašpil' UA 73 Me21
Tomas Romero Pereira PY 276 Hc59
Tomaszów Lubelski PL 65 Md40
Tomaszów Mazowiecki PL 65 Lu39
Tomat SUD 184 Md40
Tomata RI 130 Ra46
Tomatlán MEX 246 Eh36
Tombe ANG 200 Lj52
Tombeau des Askia RMM 181 Kk37
Tombeaux de Rois Sakalava RM 206 Nd53
Tombeaux Mahafaly RM 207 Nc58
Tombeaux royaux Antemoro d'Ivato RM 207 Nd57
Tombeaux royaux d'Antananarivo RM 207 Nd55
Tombeaux Royaux de Mahabo RM 207 Nc56
Tombeaux (Tiéboro) TCH 183 Lj35
Tombe du Camerounais TCH 183 Lj36
Tombel CAM 188 Le43
Tomboco ANG 198 Lg49
Tomb of Sultan Hasanuddin RI 130 Qk48
Tombokro CI 187 Kh42
Tombolo RI 130 Ra48
Tombos BR 275 Hj56
Tombouctou RMM 181 Kj37
Tombs of Buganda Kings EAU 194 Mg45
Tombs of the Nobles ET 179 Mg33
Tombstone USA 235 Ee30
Tombstone Courthouse S.H.P. USA 235 Ee30
Tombua ANG 200 Lf53
Tombul-džamija BG 69 Mg47
Tom Burke ZA 202 Me57
Tomdibuloq UZ 97 Oc25
Tomé RCH 280 Gd64
Tomea RI 131 Rb48
Tomé-Açu BR 267 Hf47
Tomelilla S 43 Lo35
Tomelloso E 55 Kr51
Tomești RO 68 Mc45
Tomești RO 73 Md22
Tomina BOL 278 Gh55
Tomingley AUS 151 Se62
Tomini RI 125 Ra45
Tominian RMM 187 Kh39
Tomintoul GB 48 Kr33
Tomioka J 111 Rk27
Tomislavgrad BIH 61 Ls47
Tomkinson Ranges AUS 145 Re59
Tomma N 38 Ln24
Tomochic MEX 244 Eg31
Tomohon RI 125 Rc45
Tomori RCA 190 Lh44
Tomorlog CHN 103 Pf26
Tomortei CHN 107 Qg25
Tompa H 67 Lu44
Tompe RI 130 Qk46
Tompet RI 127 Pk45
Tompira RI 130 Ra47
Tompi Seleka ZA 205 Me58
Tompkinsville USA 239 Fh27
Tom Price AUS 142 Qj57
Tomsk RUS 88 Pb07
Toms River USA 241 Gc26
Tomtabacken S 43 Lp33
Tomtor RUS 89 Sa06
Tomu RI 154 Rg47
Tom White, Mount USA 229 Cj15
Tom Yawkey Wildlife Center USA 242 Ga29
Tónachic MEX 244 Eg31
Tonalá MEX 246 Ej35
Tonalá MEX 247 Fc36
Tonami J 111 Rj27
Tonantins BR 270 Gg47
Tonara I 62 Lk50
Tonate F 266 Hd43
Tonbridge GB 49 La39
Tonda PNG 155 Sa50
Tondano RI 125 Rc45
Tondela P 54 Km50
Tønder DK 42 Lj36
Tondi IND 119 Ok41
Tondibi RMM 181 Kk37
Tondidarou RMM 181 Kh37
Tondi Kiwindi RN 182 La38
Tondon RG 186 Kd40
Toné BF 187 Kj40
Tonekabon IR 91 Nf27
Tone Nga Chang Falls THA 122 Qa42
Tone Wai Town LB 186 Kf43
Tong SUD 191 Me42
Tonga AUS 149 Sb61
Tonga CAM 188 Lf43
Tonga SUD 191 Mf41
Tonga 135 Ba11
Tongaat ZA 205 Mf60
Tonga Islands 134 Ba11
Tong'an CHN 109 Qk33
Tongariro N.P. NZ 153 Th65
Tonga Trench TO 134 Ba12
Tongbai CHN 107 Qg29
Tongbai Shan CHN 107 Qg29
Tongcheng CHN 109 Qg31
Tongcheng CHN 112 Qj30
Tongchon PRK 112 Rd26
Tongchuan CHN 106 Qe28
Tongdao CHN 108 Qe32
Tongde CHN 106 Qa28
Tongehatan Point RP 125 Ra43
Tongeren B 51 Lf40
Tonggu CHN 109 Qh31
Tong'guan CHN 106 Qf28
Tongguan CHN 121 Qa34
Tongguzbasti CHN 100 Pa26
Tonggu Zhang CHN 109 Qj33
Tonghae ROK 113 Re27
Tonghai CHN 121 Qb33
Tonghaikou CHN 109 Qg30
Tonghe CHN 110 Re23
Tonghua CHN 110 Rc25
Tongi BD 120 Pf34
Tongjiang CHN 106 Qd30
Tongjiang CHN 110 Rg22
Tongliao CHN 110 Rb24
Tongling CHN 112 Qj30
Tonglu CHN 109 Qk31
Tongnan CHN 108 Qc30
Tongoa VU 158 Te54
Tongobory RM 207 Nc57
Tongomayél BF 181 Kk38
Tongoni Ruins EAT 197 Mk48
Tongoy RCH 279 Ge61
Tongren CHN 106 Qa28
Tongren CHN 108 Qe32
Tongshan CHN 109 Qh31
Tongshi CHN 109 Qe36
Tongue GB 48 Kq32
Tongue of the Ocean BS 243 Gb33
Tongwe EAT 197 Mk48
Tong Xian CHN 107 Qj26
Tongxiang CHN 112 Ra30
Tongxin CHN 106 Qc27
Tongxu CHN 107 Qh28
Tongyu CHN 105 Rb23
Tongyu CHN 107 Qg27
Tongzi CHN 108 Qd31
Tonhe MYA 120 Ph33
Tonichi MEX 244 Ef31
Tonina CO 265 Gg44
Toniná MEX 247 Fe37
Tonk IND 114 Oh32
Tonka RMM 181 Kj37
Tonki C. USA 228 Ce16
Tonkoro AUS 148 Sb57
Tonlé Sap K 123 Qc39
Tonle Sap Biosphere Reserve K 123 Qc39
Tonnay-Boutonne F 52 Ku45
Tonnay-Charente F 52 Ku45
Tonneins F 52 La46
Tonnerre F 53 Ld43
Tönning D 58 Lj36
Tono J 111 Sa26
Tonopah USA 234 Eb26
Tonosi PA 249 Fk42
Tonosoyo J 113 Rh28
Tonotha RB 202 Md56
Tonquil Island RP 125 Ra42
Tonsaket USA 232 Ea21
Tønsberg N 42 Ll31
Tonsina USA 229 Ch15
Tonstad N 42 Lh32
Ton Tae Falls THA 122 Pk42
Tontelbos ZA 204 Ma61
Tonto Nat. Mon. USA 235 Ee29
Tonusu RI 130 Ra46
Tonya TR 91 Mk25
Toobanna AUS 147 Sd55
Toobeah AUS 149 Se60
Toodyay AUS 144 Qj61
Tooele USA 235 Ed25
To'Okona PNG 155 Sd49
Toolbec AUS 148 Sa57
Tooligie AUS 150 Rh62
Toolondo AUS 150 Sa64
Toombs House S.H.S. USA 242 Fj29
Toompine AUS 149 Sc59
Toomula AUS 147 Sd55
Toora AUS 151 Sd65
Toorale AUS 149 Sc61
Tooraweenah AUS 149 Se61
Tooromt MNG 101 Pg20
Toowoomba AUS 149 Sf59
Tooxin SP 193 Nf40
Topar KZ 100 Oh23
Topaz Lake USA 234 Ea26
Topčii BG 69 Mg47
Topczewo PL 65 Mc38
Tope de Coroa CV 186 Jh37
Topeka USA 238 Fc26
Topkapı Saray TR 69 Mk49
Toplet RO 68 Mc46
Topley CDN 230 Dg18
Topli Do SRB 68 Mc47
Toplița RO 67 Mf44
Topohaé MEX 244 Ee31
Topola SRB 68 Ma46
Topolčani MK 68 Mb49
Topol'čany SK 66 Lt42
Topoli RDC 191 Md44
Topoli RDC 191 Me44
Topolobampo MEX 244 Ef33
Topolog RO 69 Mj46
Topoloveni RO 69 Mf46
Topolovgrad BG 69 Mg48
Topolovo BG 69 Mf49
Toponica SRB 68 Ma47
Toporu RO 69 Mf46
Toppenish USA 232 Dk22
Toppur IND 118 Ok40
Topraq-Qala UZ 96 Oa25
Topsfield USA 240 Gg23
Tops, Mount AUS 148 Rg56
Top Springs AUS 146 Rf54
Topura PNG 156 Sf51
Topusko HR 61 Lr45
Tor ETH 192 Mg42
Torà E 57 Lb49
Toramarkog CHN 103 Pj29
To'raqo'rg'on UZ 97 Of25
Torata PE 269 Ge54
Torbalı TR 71 Mh52
Torbantea AUS 149 Sg58
Torbat-e-Heydariyeh IR 98 Nk28
Torbat-e Jam IR 98 Oa28
Torbay CDN 241 Hd22
Torčyn UA 65 Me40
Tordesillas E 54 Kp49
Töre S 41 Mc25
Töreboda S 43 Lp32
Torekov S 42 Ln34
Torelló E 57 Lc48
Toreno E 54 Ko48
Torfjanovka RUS 44 Mh30
Torfufell IS 46 Kb25
Torgau D 58 Ln39
Torgelow D 58 Lp37
Torhout B 51 Ld39
Tori IND 117 Pc34
Tori RMM 187 Kj39
Toribio CO 264 Gb44
Tori-Bossito DY 188 Lb42
Torigni-sur-Vire F 50 Kt41
Torija E 55 Kr50
Tori-jima J 113 Re32
Toril E 57 Kt50
Torit SUD 194 Mg43
Torkaman IR 91 Nd27
Tormabum WAL 186 Ke42
Tormac RO 68 Mb45
Torna IND 116 Og36
Tornado Mount CDN 233 Ec21
Tornal'a SK 67 Ma42
Torndirrup N.P. AUS 144 Qj63
Torneälven S 38 Mb23
Torneträsk S 38 Lu22
Torneträsk S 38 Lu22
Tornio FIN 41 Me25
Tornjoš SRB 68 Lu45
Tornquist RA 281 Gj65
Toro E 54 Kp49
Toro, Cerro del RA/RCH 279 Gf60
Torö S 43 Ls32
Torobi RI 131 Re46
Torobulu RI 130 Rb48
Torodi RN 182 La39
Toro Doum TCH 183 Lj37
Toro Game Reserve = Semliki Wildlife Reserve EAU 194 Mf45
Törökbalint H 67 Lt43
Torokina PNG 157 Sh49
Toro Kinkéné CI 187 Kh41
Törökszentmiklós H 67 Ma43
Toroli RMM 187 Kj39
Toro Negro Forest USA 251 Gg36
Toronto CDN 237 Ga24
Torony H 66 Lr43
Toropec RUS 72 Mf17
Tororo EAU 194 Mh45
Torošino RUS 45 Mj33
Toro Toro, P.N. BOL 278 Gh55
Torpathar IND 117 Pb34
Torpo N 40 Lj30
Torpshammar S 41 Lr28
Torqabeh IR 96 Nk27
Torquay AUS 151 Sc65
Torquay GB 49 Kr40
Torra Bay NAM 200 Lg56
Torrance USA 234 Ea29
Torrão P 55 Km52
Torre Annunziata I 63 Lp50
Torrebeleña E 55 Kr50
Torreblanca E 57 La50
Torrecampo E 55 Kq52
Torrecilla en Cameros E 56 Ks48
Torre de Belém P 55 Kl52
Torre de Bujaco E 55 Ko51
Torre de la Higuera E 55 Ko53
Torre del Greco I 63 Lp50
Torre de Moncorvo P 54 Kn49
Torre de'Pàsseri I 62 Lo48
Torredonjimeno E 55 Kr53
Torrejón de Ardoz E 55 Kr50
Torrelaguna E 55 Kr50
Torrelavega E 54 Kq47
Torremaggiore I 63 Lq49
Torremolinos E 55 Kq54
Torremormojón E 54 Kq49
Torrens Creek AUS 147 Sc56
Torrent E 57 Ku51
Torreón MEX 245 Ej33
Torre-Pacheco E 57 Kt53
Torre Péllice I 60 Lh46
Torrequemada E 55 Ko51
Torres BR 277 Hf60
Torres-de-Alcalá MA 175 Kh28
Torres del Paine, P.N. RCH 282 Gd71
Torres Islands VU 158 Td52
Torres mudéjares de Teruel E 57 Kt50
Torres Novas P 55 Km51
Torres Strait AUS/PNG 147 Sa50
Torres Vedras P 55 Kl51
Torrevieja E 57 Ku53
Torrey USA 235 Ee26
Torricelli Mountains PNG 155 Sb47
Torri del Benaco I 60 Ll45
Torríglia I 60 Lk46
Torrijas E 57 Ku50
Torrijos E 55 Kq51
Torrijos RP 124 Rb39
Tørring DK 42 Lk35
Tørring N 40 Lm26
Torrington GB 49 Kq40
Torrington USA 235 Eh24
Torrock TCH 190 Lh41
Torroella de Montgrí E 57 Ld48
Torronsuon kansallispuisto FIN 44 Md30
Torsåker S 43 Lr30
Torsås S 43 Lq34
Torsby S 42 Ln30
Torshälla S 43 Lr31
Tórshavn DK 46 Ko28
Torsö S 43 Lo32
Tortel RCH 282 Gd69
Történeti Emlékpark H 67 Ma44
Tortiya CI 187 Kh41
Tortkol KZ 97 Oe24
To'rtko'l UZ 96 Oa25
Tortola GB 251 Gh36
Tórtoles de Esgueva E 54 Kq49
Tortolì I 62 Lk51
Tortona I 60 Lj46
Tortorici I 63 Lp52
Tortosa E 57 La50
Tortuguero, P.N. NIC 249 Fj40
Torud IR 98 Nh28
Torue RI 130 Ra46
Torugart KS 100 Oh25
Torul TR 91 Mk25
Toruń PL 64 Lt37
Torup S 42 Lo34
Tõrva EST 45 Mf32
Tory RUS 104 Qb20
Tory Island IRL 47 Km35
Toržkovskaja grjada RUS 72 Mh17
Toržok RUS 72 Mh17
Torzym PL 64 Lq38
Tosagua EC 268 Fk46
Tosanachic MEX 244 Eg31
Tosa-shimizu J 113 Rg29
Tosbara IND 114 Oh31
Tosbotn N 40 Ln25
Tosca ZA 205 Mb58
Toshka Project (Southern Valley Development Project) ET 179 Mf34
Tosi SUD 185 Mf40
Tosno RUS 72 Mf16
Tosonchengel MNG 104 Pk21
Tostado RA 279 Gk60
Tõstamaa EST 45 Md32
Tostedt D 58 Lk37
Tosya TR 90 Mh25
Tószeg H 67 Ma43
Tot EAK 194 Mh45
Totana E 57 Kt53
Totata LB 186 Kf42
Totatiche MEX 246 Ej35
Totebo S 43 Lr33
Toteng RB 201 Mb56
Tôtes F 51 Lb41
Totiyas SP 195 Nb44
Tótkomlós H 67 Ma44
Tøtlandsvik N 42 Lg31
Totnes GB 49 Kr40
Totness SME 266 Hb43
Toto ANG 198 Lh49
Toto WAN 188 Ld41
Totok RI 125 Rc45
Totonicapán GCA 248 Fe38
Totontepec MEX 246 Fb37
Totora BOL 278 Gf54
Totora BOL 278 Gh54
Totoral RCH 279 Ge59
Totoralejos RA 279 Gh60
Totora Palca BOL 278 Gh55
Totoras RA 281 Gk62
Totoya FJI 159 Ua55
Tottenham AUS 151 Sd62
Tottori J 113 Rh28
Totumito YV 264 Ge42
Totutla MEX 246 Fb36
Tou BF 187 Kj39
Touâjîl RIM 180 Kd34
Touâret RN 182 Ld35
Touat DZ 175 Kk32
Touba CI 187 Kg41
Touba SN 180 Kc38
Toubakouta SN 186 Kb39
Toubéré Bafal SN 180 Kd38
Toubkal, P.N.du MA 175 Kf30
Touboro CAM 189 Lh42
Toucy F 53 Ld43
Touérât RMM 181 Kj37
Tougan BF 187 Kj39
Tougé RG 186 Ke40
Touggourt DZ 176 Ld29
Tougnifili RG 186 Kc40
Tougouri BF 187 Kk39
Tougoutaou RN 182 Ld38
Touho F 158 Tc56
Touijînet RIM 181 Kf36
Touil RIM 180 Ke38
Toukoroba RMM 187 Kg39
Toukoto RMM 186 Kf39
Toul F 51 Lf42
Toulépleu CI 186 Kf42
Touli RC 109 Ra34
Toulon F 53 Lf47
Toulon-sur-Arroux F 53 Le44
Toulounga TCH 189 Lk40
Toulouse F 52 Lb47
Toumbélaga RN 182 Ld38
Toumkous RN 182 La38
Toumodi CI 187 Kh42
Toumoundjila RG 186 Kf40
Touna RMM 187 Kh39
Tounfafi RN 182 Lc38
Toungo WAN 189 Lg41
Toungoo MYA 120 Pj36
Toungour TCH 183 Lk37
Toura DY 188 Lb40
Tourassine RIM 174 Ke33
Tourba TCH 189 Lh39
Tourcoing F 51 Ld40
Tour Eiffel F 51 Lc42
Tourîne RIM 180 Ke34
Tourlaville F 50 Kt41
Tournai B 51 Ld40
Tournavista PE 269 Gc50
Tourni BF 187 Kh40
Tournon-d'Agenais F 52 Lb46
Tournon-sur-Rhône F 53 Le45
Tournus F 53 Le44
Touros BR 273 Jc48
Tourouа CAM 189 Lg41
Touroug MA 175 Kh30
Touroukoro BF 187 Kh40
Touroungoumbé RMM 180 Kf38
Tours F 52 La43
Toury F 51 Lb42
Tousséguéla RMM 187 Kg40
Toussiana BF 187 Kh40
Toutes Aides CDN 236 Fa20
Toutoukro CI 187 Kh42
Toutswemogala Hill RB 202 Md56
Touws River ZA 204 Ma62
Töv MNG 104 Qc22
Tovar YV 264 Ge41
Tovar YV 265 Gg40
Tovarankurichchi IND 118 Ok40
Tovarkovskij RUS 72 Mk19
Tovarnik HR 61 Lu45
Tovste UA 67 Mf42
Tovuz AZ 91 Nc25
Tow USA 238 Fa30
Towada J 111 Sa25
Towada-Hachimantai N.P. J 111 Sa26
Towai LB 186 Kf42
Towakaima GUY 266 Ha42
Towale RI 130 Qk46
Towanda USA 241 Gb25
Towari RI 130 Ra48
Towcester GB 49 Ku38
Tower = Isla Genovesa EC 269 Ff45
Tower USA 236 Fd22
Towera AUS 142 Qh57
Tower of London GB 49 Ku39
Tower of Silence IR 98 Nh30
Tower Peak AUS 145 Rb62
Towi RI 130 Ra46
Towla ZW 202 Me56
Towle ZA 202 Me57
Towner USA 236 Ek21
Towner USA 238 Ej26
Townsend USA 233 Ee22
Townshend Island AUS 149 Sf57
Townsville AUS 147 Sd55
Towot SUD 192 Mh42
Towraghondi AFG 98 Ob28
Towrana AUS 144 Qh58
Towr Ham AFG 99 Of28
Towson USA 241 Gb26
Toyama J 111 Rj27
Toyo J 113 Rh29
Toyohashi J 113 Rj28
Toyokawa J 113 Rj28
Toyooka J 113 Rh28
Toyós HN 248 Fg38
Toyota J 113 Rj28
Toyotomi J 111 Sa23
Toypapkeh RI 129 Qh50
Töysä FIN 44 Md28
To'ytepa UZ 97 Oe25
Tozeur TN 176 Le29
Tqibuli GE 91 Nb24
Tqvarčeli GE 91 Na24
Trabanca E 54 Ko49
Traben-Trarbach D 59 Lh41

Trablous ⌂ RL 90 Mh28
Tra Bong ⌂ VN 123 Qe38
Trabzon ⌂ TR 91 Mh25
Tracadie ⌂ CDN 240 Gh22
Tra Co Beach ≋ VN 121 Qd35
Tracy ⌂ USA 234 Dz27
Tracy City ⌂ USA 239 Fh28
Traditional war-dances ✦ RI 127 Pj45
Trælleborg ⌂ DK 42 Lh36
Trafalgar ⌂ USA 151 Sd65
Tragacete ⌂ E 57 Kt50
Tragoncillo ⌂ E 55 Ks52
Trahia ⌂ GR 69 Md53
Traiguén ⌂ RCH 280 Gd65
Trail ⌂ CDN 232 Eb21
Traipu ⌂ BR 273 Ja47
Traiskirchen ⌂ A 59 Ln38
Trakai ⌂ LT 45 Me35
Trakan Phut Phon ⌂ THA 123 Qc38
Tra Kieu Citadel ✦ VN 123 Qe38
Trakis istorinis n.p. ✿ LT 45 Me35
Tralee ⌂ IRL 47 Kl38
Tralee Bay ≋ IRL 47 Kl38
Tramandai ⌂ BR 277 He61
Tramore ⌂ IRL 47 Kn38
Tra My ⌂ VN 123 Qe38
Tran ⌂ BG 68 Mc48
Tranås ⌂ S 43 Lp32
Trancas ⌂ RA 279 Gb59
Trancoso ⌂ BR 275 Ja54
Tranent ⌂ GB 48 Ks35
Trang ⌂ THA 123 Pk42
Trangan ⌂ RI 154 Rh49
Trang Bang ⌂ VN 123 Qd40
Trang Dinh ⌂ VN 123 Qd36
Tranì ⌂ I 61 Lr49
Tranomaro ⌂ RM 207 Nd58
Tranoroa ⌂ RM 207 Nc58
Tran Phu ⌂ VN 123 Qd40
Tranqueras ⌂ ROU 276 Hc61
Transkei ⌂ 91 Nd27
Transamazônica ═ BR 271 Hd47
Transantarctic Mountains ▲ ANT 287 Jc35
Trans-Canada Highway (British Columbia) ═ CDN 232 Dk21
Trans-Canada Highway (Alberta) ═ CDN 233 Eh19/Eg20
Trans-Canada Highway (Manitoba) ═ CDN 236 Ek20
Trans-Canada Highway (New Brunswick) ═ CDN 240 Gg22
Trans-Canada Highway (Newfoundland) ═ CDN 241 Hd21
Trans-Canada Highway (Nova Scotia) ═ CDN 240 Gj23
Trans-Canada Highway (Ontario) ═ CDN 237 Fh21/Fk21
Trans-Canada Highway (Quebec) ═ CDN 240 Gg22
Trans-Canada Highway (Saskatchewan) ═ CDN 233 Ej19/Eg22
Transhimalaya ▲ 76 Pa06
Transpantanera ═ BR 274 Hb54
Transsib ⌂ RUS 72 Na16
Transsib ⌂ RUS 105 Qh20
Trans-Sumatra-Highway ═ RI 127 Qa45
Transua ⌂ CI 187 Kj42
Transylvania ▲ RO 67 Md44
Transylvanian Alps ▲ RO 68 Md45
Tra On ⌂ VN 123 Qc41
Trapalco, Cerro ▲ RA 280 Gd65
Trápani ⌂ I 62 Ln52
Trappetangetsforsarna ≋ S 41 Lp24
Traralgon ⌂ AUS 151 Sd65
Trarza ⌂ RIM 180 Kc37
Trasacco ⌂ I 62 Lo49
Trashigang ⌂ BHT 120 Pf32
Trâs os Montes ▲ P 54 Kn49
Trat ⌂ THA 123 Qb40
Traun ⌂ A 66 Lp42
Traunreut ⌂ D 59 Ln43
Traunstein ⌂ D 59 Ln43
Travellers Village ⌂ AUS 145 Re61
Travernünde ⌂ D 58 Ll37
Traverse City ⌂ USA 237 Fh23
Traverse Peak ▲ USA 229 Ca13
Travesia de Tunuyán ⌂ RA 280 Gg62
Travesia Puntana ▲ RA 280 Gg63
Tra Vinh ⌂ VN 123 Qd41
Travnik ▲ BIH 61 Ls46
Travo ⌂ F 62 Lk49
Trawas ⌂ RI 127 Qb47
Trawniki ⌂ PL 65 Mc39
Trayning ⌂ AUS 144 Qj61
Trbovlje ⌂ SLO 66 Lq44
Treasure Beach ⌂ JA 246 Gb35
Treasury Islands ▲ SOL 157 Sh49
Trebbin ⌂ D 58 Ln38
Trebel ⌂ D 58 Ln36
Trebíč ⌂ CZ 66 Lq41
Trebinje ⌂ BIH 68 Lt48
Trebisacce ⌂ I 63 Lr51
Trebišov ⌂ SK 67 Mb42
Treblinka ⌂ PL 65 Mb38
Trebnje ⌂ SLO 66 Lq41
Trebonne ⌂ AUS 147 Sd55
Trecate ⌂ I 60 Lj45
Tre Cime ▲ I 60 Ln44
Treene ⌂ D 58 Lk36
Treffurt ⌂ D 58 Ll39
Tregaron ⌂ GB 49 Kr38
Trégastel-Plage ⌂ F 50 Kr42
Tregozo ⌂ USA 232 Ec21
Tregrosse ⌂ 152 Te59
Tréguier ⌂ F 50 Kr42
Trehörna ⌂ 236 Fa21
Treherbovy Gorez ▲ RUS 104 Qd19
Treignac ⌂ F 52 Lb45
Treinta y Tres ⌂ ROU 276 Hc62
Treis-Karden ⌂ D 59 Lh40
Treja ⌂ MEX 246 Ez47
Trekkopje ⌂ NAM 200 Lh57
Trekljano ⌂ BG 68 Mc48
Tre Kroner ▲ N 38 Lg06
Trélazé ⌂ F 52 La43
Trelew ⌂ RA 282 Gh67
Trelleborg ⌂ S 42 Lo35
Trementina ⌂ USA 235 Ek26
Tremen, Volcán ▲ RA 280 Gd64
Tremezzo ⌂ I 60 Lk45
Tremiti ⌂ I 61 Lq48
Trenary ⌂ USA 237 Fg22
Trenčiansky hrad ▲ SK 66 Lt42
Trenčín ⌂ SK 66 Lt42
Trenel ⌂ RA 280 Gd63
Trenggalek ⌂ RI 129 Qf50
Tenino Verde ▲ 62 Ls51
Trenque Lauquen ⌂ RA 281 Gj63
Trentham ⌂ AUS 151 Sb64
Trentham Gardens ✿ NZ 153 Th66
Trentino-Alto Adige ⌂ I 60 Lm44
Trento ⌂ I 60 Lm44
Trenton ⌂ RP 125 Rd41
Trenton ⌂ CO 264 Gb45
Trenton ⌂ USA 238 Fd25
Trenton ⌂ USA 237 Fk28
Trenton ⌂ USA 241 Gc25
Trenton ⌂ USA 242 Fj31
Trephina Gorge N.P. ✿ AUS 148 Rh57
Tres Altitos, Cerro ▲ RA 280 Gf62
Trés Arroios ⌂ BR 276 Hd59
Trés Arroyos ⌂ RA 281 Gk65
Trés Barras ⌂ BR 277 Hf59
Trés Bocas ⌂ RA 279 Gk62
Três Bocas ⌂ RA 280 Gd61
Três Casas ⌂ BR 270 Gj49
Trés Cerros ⌂ RA 282 Gf66
Três Corações ⌂ BR 275 Hh56
Trés Cruces, Cerro ▲ MEX 247 Fd38
Trés Cruces ⌂ BR 279 Gf57
Trés Cruces, Nevado ▲ RA/RCH 279 Gf59
Tres Isletas ⌂ RA 279 Gh59

Três Lagoas ⌂ BR 274 He56
Tres Lagos ⌂ BR 282 Ge70
Tres Lomas ⌂ RA 281 Gj64
Três Mapejos ⌂ BOL 270 Gh51
Três Marias ⌂ BR 275 Hh55
Tres Morros ⌂ RA 279 Gh57
Tres Passos ⌂ BR 276 Hd59
Três Picos ⌂ BR 275 Ja56
Três Picos, Cerro ▲ RA 281 Gj65
Três Piedras ⌂ USA 235 Eh27
Três Pinheiros ⌂ BR 276 Hh59
Três Pontas ⌂ BR 275 Hh56
Três Praias ⌂ BR 270 Gg50
Três Rios ⌂ BR 275 Hj56
Tressillian ⌂ AUS 149 Sd57
Tresticklans n.p. ✿ S 42 Lm31
Três Unidos ⌂ BR 270 Gf49
Tretten ⌂ N 40 Ll29
Treuchtlingen ⌂ D 59 Ll42
Treuenbrietzen ⌂ D 58 Ln38
Trevelin ⌂ RA 282 Ge67
Trevi ⌂ I 61 Ln48
Treviglio ⌂ I 60 Lk45
Treviso ⌂ I 60 Ln45
Trevor ⌂ CDN 237 Fz22
Tri ⌂ SK 66 Lt42
Tribeč ▲ SK 66 Lt42
Tri City ⌂ USA 232 Dj24
Tribal ⌂ AUS 151 Sc62
Tribunj ⌂ HR 61 Lq47
Tricase ⌂ I 63 Lt51
Trichy = Thrissur ⌂ IND 118 Oj40
Trichy = Tiruchirapalli ⌂ IND 119
Trici ⌂ BR 273 Hk48
Tri City ⌂ USA 232 Dj24
Trida ⌂ AUS 151 Sc62
Trieste ⌂ I 60 Ln45
Trie-sur-Baïse ⌂ F 52 La47
Triglav ▲ SLO 66 Lo44
Triglavski narodni park ✿ SLO 66 Lo44
Trigiac ⌂ F 52 La43
Trigono ⌂ GR 70 Mb50
Trikala ⌂ GR 70 Mb51
Trikéri ⌂ GR 68 Md51
Trikkandimadu ⌂ CL 119 Pa42
Trikkandiyur ⌂ IND 118 Oh40
Trikora Beach ≋ RI 127 Qc45
Trilbar ⌂ AUS 144 Qj58
Trill ⌂ RA 281 Gj63
Trillo ⌂ E 57 Ks50
Trimouille Islands ▲ AUS 142 Qh56
Trincheira Bacajá, T.I. ▲ BR 272 He48
Trincheira, T.I. ▲ BR 271 Ha47
Trincheras ⌂ MEX 244 Ee30
Trincomalee ⌂ CL 119 Pa41
Trindade ⌂ BR 273 Hk49
Trindade ⌂ BR 274 Hf54
Třinec ⌂ CZ 66 Lt41
Trinidad ⌂ AUS 149 Sb58
Trinidad ⌂ BOL 278 Gh53
Trinidad ⌂ BR 274 Hk35
Trinidad ⌂ CO 264 Ge43
Trinidad ⌂ PY 276 Hb59
Trinidad ⌂ ROU 276 Hb62
Trinidad ⌂ TT 251 Gk40
Trinidad ⌂ USA 232 Dn25
Trinidad and Tobago ■ TT 251 Gk40
Trinidad del Paraná ✦ PY 276 Hc59
Trinidade ⌂ BR 267 Hf47
Trinitápoli ⌂ I 61 Lr49
Trinity ⌂ USA 234 Dj25
Trinity ⌂ USA 238 Fd29
Trinity ⌂ USA 238 Fc30
Trinity Bay ≋ AUS 147 Sc53
Trinity East ⌂ CDN 241 Hd21
Trinity Peninsula ▲ ANT 287 Ha31
Trinity Site ✦ USA 235 Ea25
Trinity Site ✦ USA 235 Eg29
Trino ⌂ I 60 Lj45
Triora ⌂ I 60 Lh46
Trios ⌂ BR 266 Hc44
Trípoli ⌂ GR 70 Mc53
Tripoli ● LAR 177 Lg29
Tripoli ⌂ RL 90 Mh28
Tripolitania ▲ LAR 177 Lg30
Tripunithura ⌂ IND 118 Oj41
Tripura ⌂ IND 120 Pf34
Tristan da Cunha ▲ GB 163 Ka13
Tristeza, Cerro ▲ RA 282 Ge70
Trisul ▲ IND 115 Ok30
Trisuli River Rafting ✦ NEP 115 Pc32
Tri Ton ⌂ VN 123 Qc41
Triunvirato ⌂ RA 281 Gk63
Trivandrum = Thiruvananthapuram ● IND 118 Oj41
Trivento ⌂ I 63 Lq49
Troick ⌂ RUS 88 Oa08
Troickaja ⌂ RUS 73 Ma43
Troisdorf ⌂ D 58 Lh40
Trois-Pistoles ⌂ CDN 240 Gf21
Trois Rivières ⌂ CDN 240 Gg22
Trois Sauts ⌂ F 266 Hd44
Troize-Sergieva Lavra ✦ RUS 72 Mk17
Troiznij monastyr ✦ RUS 72 Na18
Trojaci ⌂ MK 68 Mb49
Trojan ⌂ BG 69 Me48
Trojanski manastir ✦ BG 69 Me48
Trolla ⌂ TCH 183 Lh38
Trollaskagi ▲ IS 46 Jr26
Trollåkirkje ▲ IS 46 Jr26
Trollåskagi ▲ IS 46 Kb25
Trollhättan ⌂ S 42 Lm32
Trollhätte kanal ⌂ S 42 Lm32
Trollstigen ▲ N 40 Ln28
Trombetas ⌂ BR 266 Hb44
Tromostovje ✦ SLO 66 Lp44
Tromoya ⌂ N 42 Lj32
Trompsburg ⌂ ZA 205 Mc61
Tromsø ⌂ N 38 Lu17
Tronador, Cerro ▲ RA/RCH 280 Ge66
Troncones ⌂ MEX 246 Ek36
Troncoso ⌂ MEX 246 Ez37
Trøndelag ▲ N 40 Ll28
Trondheim ⌂ N 40 Lj27
Troodos Mountains ▲ CY 90 Mg28

Troutbeck ⌂ ZW 202 Mg55
Trout Creek ⌂ CDN 237 Ga23
Trout Creek ⌂ USA 232 Dz22
Trout Lake ⌂ USA 231 Dk15
Trout Lake ⌂ USA 232 Dz23
Trout River ⌂ CDN 241 Ha21
Trouville-sur-Mer ⌂ F 50 La41
Trowbridge ⌂ GB 49 Ks39
Trowutta ⌂ AUS 151 Sc66
Troy ⌂ TR 71 Mg51
Troy ⌂ USA 232 Ec21
Troy ⌂ USA 238 Ez28
Troy ⌂ USA 238 Fh30
Troy ⌂ USA 238 Fc26
Troy ⌂ USA 241 Gd25
Troy ⌂ USA 242 Fd28
Troyes ⌂ F 51 Le42
Troyitsko monastyr ✦ UA 72 Mf20
Troy Peak ▲ USA 234 Ec26
Troyya ⌂ 198 Lg45
Trsat ⌂ HR 61 Lp45
Trstat ⌂ HR 61 Lp45
Trstena ⌂ SK 67 Lu41
Trstenik ⌂ SRB 68 Ma48
Truant Island ▲ AUS 146 Rj51
Truaru, T.I. ▲ BR 265 Gk44
Trubčevsk ⌂ RUS 72 Mg19
Trubetčino ⌂ RUS 72 Mk19
Truch ⌂ CDN 230 Dj17
Truckee ⌂ USA 234 Dk26
Trud ⌂ BG 264 Gb43
Tribune ⌂ USA 238 Ez26
Tribunj ⌂ HR 61 Lq47
Trujillo ● HN 248 Fg38
Trujillo ⌂ E 55 Kp51
Trujillo ⌂ PE 269 Ga50
Trujillo ⌂ YV 264 Ge41
Trujillo ⌂ FSM 134 Sb09
Trulli di Alberobello ✦ I 63 Ls50
Trumann ⌂ USA 239 Fe28
Trumbull, Mount ▲ USA 235 Ed27
Trumieje ⌂ PL 65 Lt37
Trumon ⌂ RI 127 Pj44
Trundle ⌂ AUS 151 Sd62
Trunkey ⌂ AUS 151 Sd62
Truro ⌂ GB 49 Kp40
Truro ⌂ CDN 240 Gh23
Trusan ⌂ MAL 128 Qh43
Trusc Madi, Gunung ▲ MAL 128 Qj43
Trussville ⌂ USA 239 Fz29
Trustrup ⌂ DK 42 Ll34
Truth or Consequences ⌂ USA
Trutnov ⌂ CZ 66 Lq40
Tryon ⌂ USA 236 Fz25
Tryphena ⌂ NZ 152 Th64
Tryškiai ⌂ LT 45 Mc34
Tržac ⌂ BIH 61 Lq46
Trzcianka ⌂ PL 64 Lq38
Trzcinna ⌂ PL 64 Lp38
Trzciel ⌂ PL 64 Lp38
Trzcińsko-Zdrój ⌂ PL 64 Lp38
Trzebiatów ⌂ PL 64 Lp37
Trzebiez ⌂ PL 64 Lo38
Trzebinia ⌂ PL 65 Lu40
Trzebnica ⌂ PL 64 Ls39
Trzemeszno ⌂ PL 64 Ls38
Trzydnik Duży ⌂ PL 65 Mb39
Tsabit ⌂ DZ 180 Lb31
Tsadu ⌂ RUS 72 Ma18
Tsagaan Agui Cave ✦ MNG 104 Qa23
Tsagaan Chuluta ⌂ CHN 103 Pj26
Tsagaandörvölj ⌂ MNG 104 Qa23
Tsagaannuur ⌂ MNG 101 Pe21
Tsagaan-Olom ⌂ MNG 104 Qa23
Tsagaan-Ovoo ⌂ MNG 104 Qa23
Tsagaan Shiveet Uul Nature Reserve ✿ MNG 101 Ua23
Tsagaan Tsavyn ▲ MNG 104 Qa23
Tsagaan-Ûûr ⌂ MNG 104 Qa23
Tsagen ⌂ GZ 91 Nj24
Tsalka ⌂ GE 91 Nh27
Tsama ⌂ RCB 198 Lh46
Tsamia ⌂ RN 182 Le38
Tsandi ⌂ NAM 200 Lh54
Tsanyawa ⌂ WAN 203 Mh53
Tsant ⌂ MNG 104 Qa22
Tsanyawa ⌂ WAN 188 Le40
Tsaobis Leopard Nature Park ✿ NAM 200 Lh57
Tsarahonenana ⌂ RM 206 Ne53
Tsaramandroso ⌂ RM 206 Nd53
Tsaratanana ▲ RM 207 Nd54
Tsaratanana ⌂ RM 207 Nd54
Tsaravinany ⌂ RM 207 Ne55
Tsarisshoogte Pass ▲ NAM 204 Lj58
Tsast Uul ▲ MNG 101 Pg21
Tsatsu ⌂ RI 205 Mc58
Tsau ⌂ RB 201 Mb56
Tsavdan ⌂ MNG 101 Pk21
Tsavo ⌂ EAK 195 Mk47
Tsavo East N.P. ✿ EAK 195 Mk47
Tsavo West N.P. ✿ EAK 194 Mk47
Sawah ⌂ LAR 177 Lg32
Tseepantee Lake ⌂ CDN 231 Dk14
Tseikuru ⌂ EAK 194 Mk46
Tsembo ⌂ RCB 198 Lg47
Tsengel ⌂ MNG 101 Pg21
Tsentral'nyye Karakumy ⌂ TM 96 Nc26
Tsepélovo ⌂ GR 70 Ma51
Tses ⌂ NAM 204 Lk58
Tseteng ⌂ RB 204 Mb57
Tsévié ⌂ TG 187 La42
Tshabong ⌂ RB 204 Mb59
Tshako ⌂ RDC 199 Mb50
Tshala ⌂ RDC 198 Lg48
Tshela ⌂ RDC 198 Lg48
Tsheseheb ⌂ RB 202 Md56
Tshibala ⌂ RDC 199 Mb48
Tshibamba ⌂ RDC 199 Mb48
Tshibuka ⌂ RDC 196 Me47
Tshibuka ⌂ RDC 199 Mb49
Tshidilamolomo ⌂ ZA 205 Mc58
Tshie ⌂ RDC 199 Mb49
Tshikapa ⌂ RDC 199 Mb49
Tshilenge ⌂ RDC 199 Mb49
Tshimbalanga ⌂ RDC 199 Mb50
Tshimbo ⌂ RDC 199 Mb49
Tshimbulu ⌂ RDC 199 Mb49
Tshintsenda ⌂ RDC 201 Mb52
Tshintshanku ⌂ RDC 199 Mb49
Tshipise ⌂ ZA 202 Mf57
Tshisenge ⌂ RDC 199 Ma49
Tshitadi ⌂ RDC 199 Ma49
Tshofa ⌂ RDC 199 Mc48
Tsholotsho ⌂ ZW 202 Md55
Tshongwe ⌂ RDC 199 Ma57
Tshootsha ⌂ RB 201 Ma57
Tshuapa ⌂ RDC 199 La46
Tshuau ⌂ GUY 266 Ga47
Tshwane = Pretoria ● ZA
Tsiaki ⌂ RUS 198 Lg47
Tsiatosotra ⌂ RM 207 Nc56
Tsimafana ⌂ RM 207 Nc56
Tsimanampetsotsa, P.N.de ✿ RM 207 Nb58
Tsimazava ⌂ RM 206 Nd53
Tsimipa ⌂ RM 207 Nc56
Tsingtao ⌂ CHN 107 Ra27
Tsingy de Bemaraha, P.N.des ✿ RM 207 Nc55
Tsinjoarivo ⌂ RM 207 Nd55
Tsintsabis ⌂ NAM 200 Lj55
Tsintombe ⌂ RM 207 Nc56
Tsiroanomandidy ⌂ RM 207 Nd55
Tsitondroina ⌂ RM 207 Nd56
Tsitsikamma N.P. ✿ ZA 204 Mb63
Tsivory ⌂ RM 207 Nd57
Tsodilo ⌂ RB 201 Ma56

Tsodilo Hills ✦ RB 201 Ma55
Tsoe ⌂ RB 201 Mc56
Tsogstsalu ⌂ 101 CHN
Tsolo ⌂ ZA 205 Me61
Tsomo ⌂ ZA 205 Md61
Tsoohyn Dhuluu ⌂ MNG 104 Qf23
Tsqaltubo ⌂ GE 91 Nh26
Tsu ⌂ J 113 Rj28
Tsubata ⌂ J 111 Rj27
Tsuchiura ⌂ J 111 Rk28
Tsugaru Q.N.P. ✿ J 111 Sa25
Tsugaru Strait ≋ J 111 Sa25
Tsujima ⌂ J 113 Rd28
Tsuli ⌂ ZW 202 Md55
Tsumbiri ⌂ RDC 198 Lh47
Tsumeb ● NAM 200 Lj55
Tsumis Park ⌂ NAM 204 Lj57
Tsunzhudale ⌂ NAM 200 Lh54
Tsuruga ⌂ J 113 Rj28
Tsurugi-san ▲ J 113 Rh29
Tsurui ⌂ J 111 Sc24
Tsuruoka ⌂ J 111 Rk26
Tsuwano ⌂ BR 273 Rg28
Tswalu Private Desert Reserve ✿ ZA 204 Mb59
Tswapong Hills ▲ RB 202 Md57
T-Tree Bay ≋ AUS 149 Sg59
Tual ⌂ RI 154 Rg48
Tua Marine National Park = Bunaken-Manado Tua Marine National Park ✿ RI 125 Rc45
Tuaran ⌂ MAL 128 Qh47
Tuan Giao ⌂ VN 121 Qb35
Tuangku ⌂ RI 127 Pj44
Tuao ⌂ RP 124 Ra37
Tuapse ⌂ RUS 73 Mk23
Tuatapere ⌂ NZ 165 Tc68
Tuba City ⌂ USA 235 Ee27
Tuban ⌂ RI 129 Qg49
Tubarão ⌂ BR 277 Hf60
Tubarão Latunde, T.I. ▲ BR 278 Gk52
Tubarjal ⌂ KSA 90 Mk30
Tubbataha Reef National Marine Park ✿ ● RP 125 Qk41
Tubbergen ⌂ NL 51 Lh38
Tubeya ⌂ RDC 199 Mb49
Tubigon ⌂ RP 124 Rb41
Tubisbyrmita ⌂ RI 154 Rg46
Tubize ⌂ B 51 Le40
Tubod ⌂ RP 125 Rb41
Tubruq ⌂ LAR 178 Mb29
Tubtaraka ⌂ RUS 72 Mg19
Tubu ⌂ RB 201 Mb55
Tuburan ⌂ RP 124 Ra40
Tubutama ⌂ MEX 244 Ee30
Tucacas ⌂ YV 265 Gf40
Tucano ⌂ BR 273 Ja46
Tuchan ⌂ F 52 Lc48
Tucheng ⌂ CHN 121 Qc32
Tuchitua ⌂ CDN 230 Df15
Tuchola ⌂ PL 64 Ls38
Tucholski Park Krajobrazowy ✿ PL 64 Ls37
Tuchów ⌂ PL 65 Mb41
Tuckanarra ⌂ AUS 144 Qj59
Tucker Glacier ⌂ ANT 287
Tucson ⌂ RUS 72 Mj18
Tucson ⌂ USA 235 Ez29
Tucumán ⌂ RA 279 Gg59
Tucumá ⌂ BR 272 He49
Tucumán ⌂ RA 272 He49
Tucumcari ⌂ USA 238 Ej28
Tucumé ✦ PE 268 Ga49
Tucunaré ⌂ BR 270 Gk52
Tucunaré ⌂ BR 270 Gh45
Tucupido ⌂ YV 265 Gg41
Tucupita ⌂ YV 265 Gj41
Tucuruba ⌂ BR 271 Ha48
Tucuruí ⌂ BR 272 He47
Tucu-Tucu ⌂ RA 282 Ge70
Tuczna ⌂ PL 65 Mc38
Tuczno ⌂ PL 64 Lq38
Tudela ⌂ E 56 Kt49
Tudela de Duero ⌂ E 54 Kq49
Tudun Wada ⌂ WAN 188 Le40
Tuéjar ⌂ E 57 Kt51
Tufanbeyli ⌂ TR 90 Mh26
Tufej ⌂ RO 69 Me46
Tufi Dive Resort ✦ PNG 156 Se50
Tug ⌂ CHN 106 Qf25
Tugela Ferry ⌂ ZA 205 Mf60
Tughyl ⌂ KZ 101 Pd22
Tugidak Island ▲ USA 228 Cc17
Tugu ⌂ GH 187 Kk41
Tuguegarao ⌂ RP 124 Ra37
Tuhala ⌂ EST 44 Me31
Tuham, Gunung ▲ RI 128 Qg45
Tui ⌂ E 54 Kn48
Tui ⌂ RCA
Tuillbigeal ⌂ AUS 151 Sd62
Tuimaada ⌂ RUS 73 Mk19
Tuina ⌂ RCH 279 Gf57
Tuineje ⌂ E 174 Kc31
Tuiuiue ⌂ BR 274 Hb54
Tujuwe ⌂ RI 130 Ra48
Tujuk ⌂ KZ 100 Ok24
Tújle ⌂ U 45 Me33
Tujuwe ⌂ RI 130 Rs48
Tukayel ⌂ ETH 193 Nc41
Túkh ⌂ ET 179 Mf30
Tuki ⌂ SOL 157 Sj49
Tukola Tolha ⌂ CHN 103 Pj29
Tukosmera ⌂ VU 158 Te55
Tukrah ⌂ LAR 178 Mb29
Tuktoyaktuk ⌂ CDN 226 Dc08
Tukums ⌂ LV 45 Md34
Tukuna Porto Espiritinal, T.I. ▲ BR 270 Gf48
Tukuna Umariaçu, T.I. ▲ BR 270 Gf48
Tukuyu ⌂ EAT 196 Mg50
Tula ⌂ EAK 195 Mk46
Tula ⌂ MEX 246 Fa35
Tula ⌂ MEX 246 Fa35
Tula ⌂ RUS 72 Mj18
Tula de Allende ✦ MEX 246 Fa35
Tulak ⌂ AFG 99 Ob29
Tulameen ⌂ CDN 232 Dz21
Tulancingo ⌂ MEX 246 Fa35
Tulare ⌂ SRB 68 Mb48
Tulare ⌂ USA 234 Ea27
Tulare ⌂ USA 234 Ea27
Tularosa ⌂ USA 235 Eg29
Tulate ⌂ GCA 248 Fe38
Tulayhah ⌂ SYR 91 Na29
Tula Yiri ⌂ WAN 189 La41
Tulbagh ⌂ ZA 204 Lk62
Tulcán ⌂ EC 268 Gb47
Tulcea ⌂ RO 69 Mj45
Tul'čyn ⌂ UA 72 Me21
Tüledy araldary ⌂ KZ 96 Nz23
Tulehu ⌂ RI 131 Re47
Tulga ⌂ SUD 185 Sb57
Tul Block ⌂ RB 205 Md58
Tuléar = Toliara ⌂ RM 207 Nc57
Tuliszków ⌂ PL 64 Ls38
Tuliszków ⌂ PL 64 Ls38
Tulit'a = Fort Norman ⌂ CDN 230 De13
Tuljapur ⌂ IND 116 Oj37
Tulla ⌂ AUS 151 Sc66
Tullahoma ⌂ USA 239 Fg28
Tullamore ⌂ AUS 151 Sd62
Tullamore ⌂ IRL 47 Km37
Tulle ⌂ F 52 Lb45
Tullibigeal ⌂ AUS 151 Sd62
Tullins ⌂ F 53 Lf45
Tulln ⌂ 66 Lr42
Tullos ⌂ USA 239 Fd30
Tullus ⌂ SUD 185 Ma39
Tulltorpsåsen ⌂ S 43 Lq34
Tulsa ⌂ USA 238 Fb26
Tulsipur ⌂ IND 117 Pd33
Tulsipur ⌂ NEP 115 Pb31

Tulsk ⌂ IRL 47 Km37
Two Hills ⌂ CDN 233 Ee19
Tuluá ⌂ CO 264 Gb43
Tuluca ⌂ BR 275 Hj54
Tuluksak ⌂ USA 228 Bk15
Tulul Al Ashaqif ▲ JOR 90 Mj29
Tulum ● MEX 247 Fg35
Tulum ⌂ MEX 247 Fg35
Tulum, Parque Nacional ✿ ● MEX 247 Fg35
Tulume ⌂ RDC 198 Mh49
Tuluran ⌂ RP 125 Rc41
Tulyčiv ⌂ UA 65 Md39
Tumaco ⌂ CO 264 Ga45
Tumaini ⌂ RDC 199 Mb49
Tumba ⌂ RDC 199 Mb49
Tumba ⌂ WAN 189 Lg40
Tumbangiri ⌂ RI 129 Qf46
Tumbangkiran ⌂ RI 129 Qf46
Tumbangmirih ⌂ RI 129 Qf46
Tumbangsamba ⌂ RI 129 Qf46
Tumbangtalaken ⌂ RI 129 Qf46
Tumbarumba ⌂ AUS 151 Sd63
Tumbes ⌂ PE 268 Fk47
Tumbiscato de Ruiz ⌂ MEX 246 Ek36
Tumbler Ridge ⌂ CDN 230 Dk18
Tumbukut ⌂ MYA 120 Pj33
Tumbuw ⌂ RDC 196 Md51
Tumby Bay ⌂ AUS 150 Rj63
Tumd Youqi ⌂ CHN 106 Qf25
Tumd Zuoqi ⌂ CHN 106 Qf25
Tumen ⌂ CHN 110 Re24
Tumeremo ⌂ YV 265 Gk42
Tumgaon ⌂ IND 117 Pc35
Tumia, T.I. ▲ BR 270 Gg49
Tumindao Island ▲ RP 125 Qk43
Tumkur ⌂ IND 118 Oj39
Tumner ⌂ SUD 190 Mf40
Tumpat ⌂ MAL 126 Qa42
Tumpat ⌂ CHN 109 Qh35
Tumsar ⌂ IND 117 Pc34
Tumu ⌂ GH 187 Kk40
Tumucumaque, P.N. do ✿ ▲ BR 266 Hd45
Tumupasa ⌂ BOL 278 Gf53
Tumut ⌂ AUS 151 Sd63
Tuna ⌂ IND 116 Of34
Tuna Gain ⌂ RI 129 Qf46
Tunapa, Cerro ▲ BOL 278 Gg55
Tunapuna ⌂ TT 251 Gk40
Tunari, P.N. ✿ BOL 278 Gg54
Tunas de Zaza ⌂ C 243 Ga35
Tunaydiba ⌂ SUD 185 Mh39
Tuncbilek ⌂ TR 71 Mh51
Tunceli ⌂ TR 91 Na26
Tunchang ⌂ CHN 109 Qf36
Tuncurry ⌂ AUS 151 Sf62
Tunduma ⌂ EAT 196 Mg50
Tunduru ⌂ EAT 197 Mj51
Tuneiro ⌂ BR 273 Hk47
Tundla ⌂ IND 116 Oj33
Tungabhadra ⌂ IND 118 Oj38
Tungabhadra Reservoir ⌂ IND 116 Oj38
Tungaru ⌂ SUD 185 Mf40
Tungaztarim ⌂ CHN 102 Pb27
Tungho ⌂ RC 109 Ra34
Tungnaa ⌂ IS 46 Ka26
Tungokočen ⌂ RUS 105 Qh19
Tungshih ⌂ RC 109 Ra34
Tungsten ⌂ CDN 230 Df15
Tungting Lake ⌂ CHN 108 Qg31
Tungua ⌂ 137 Tb10
Tunguragua, Volcán ▲ EC 268 Ga46
Tunguwatu ⌂ RI 154 Rh49
Tungur ⌂ SUD 185 Ma39
Tunguska ⌂ RUS 104 Qd19
Tuni ⌂ IND 117 Pb37
Tunia ⌂ CO 264 Gb43
Tunica ⌂ USA 239 Fe28
Tunis ■ TN 176 Lf27
Tunisia ■ TN 163 La08
Tunja ● CO 264 Gd43
Tunka La ▲ IND 120 Pf32
Tunkas ⌂ MEX 247 Ff35
Tünkhel ⌂ MNG 104 Qc22
Tunku Abdul Rahman Park ✿ ● MAL
Tunnel Creek N.P. ✿ AUS 143 Rc54
Tunnel de Tende ⌂ F/I 53 Lh46
Tunnel du Fréjus ⌂ F 53 Lg45
Tunnel du M Blanc ⌂ F 53 Lg45
Tunas las Raíces ⌂ RCH 280 Ge65
Tunneis ⌂ USA 234 Qa33
Tunquén ⌂ RCH 280 Ge62
Tunstall ⌂ GB 49 Ks36
Tunta Topocalma ⌂ RCH 280 Gd63
Tuntum ⌂ BR 272 Hh48
Tuntutuliak ⌂ USA 228 Bj15
Tunungua ⌂ BR 270 Gk47
Tunuyán ⌂ RA 280 Gf62
Tunzam ⌂ MYA 120 Pg33
Tuolo ⌂ CHN 108 Qa34
Tuol Tol ⌂ K 123 Qb39
Tuol Totoeng ⌂ K 123 Qb39
Tuong Duong ⌂ VN 121 Qc36
Tuotuo Heyan ⌂ CHN 103 Pg28
Tüp ⌂ KS 100 Ok24
Tupaciguara ⌂ BR 274 Hf55
Tupaciretã ⌂ BR 276 Hd60
Tupanatinga ⌂ BR 273 Ja46
Tupanciretã ⌂ BR 276 Hd60
Tupelo ⌂ USA 239 Fz28
Tupi ⌂ RP 125 Rc42
Tupik ⌂ RUS 105 Qh19
Tupilco ⌂ MEX 247 Fd36
Tupinambá Paulista ▲ BR 274 He56
Tupirantins ⌂ BR 272 Hf50
Tupitsa ⌂ BOL 278 Gg57
Tupper Lake ⌂ USA 241 Gc23
Tupper Lake ⌂ USA 241 Gc23
Tupungato, Cerro ▲ RA/RCH 280 Gf62
Tuquan ⌂ CHN 105 Ra23
Túquerres ⌂ CO 264 Gb45
Tura ⌂ CHN 102 Pd27
Tura ⌂ IND 120 Pf33
Tura ⌂ RUS 88 Qd08
Turabah ⌂ KSA 93 Nb31
Turabah ⌂ KSA 93 Nb31
Turagua, Cerro ▲ YV 265 Gh42
Turaiza ⌂ IND 118 Oh40
Turaiyur ⌂ IND 118 Oj40
Turan ⌂ RUS 104 Qc20
Turana ▲ RUS 105 Rc20
Turangi ⌂ NZ 153 Th65
Turan Lowland ⌂ UZ 96 Ne24
Turar ⌂ KZ 97 Oz24
Turayf ⌂ KSA 90 Mk30
Turbaco ⌂ CO 264 Gz40
Turbah ⌂ YE 94 Nb39
Turbat ⌂ PK 99 Ob32
Turbe ⌂ BIH 61 Ls46
Turbeville ⌂ USA 242 Ga29
Turbio ⌂ EC 264 Gb46
Turbo ⌂ CO 264 Gb42
Turčianske Teplice ⌂ SK 67 Lt42
Turco ⌂ BOL 278 Gf55
Turda ⌂ CDN 231 Dk13
Turda ⌂ RO 68 Md44
Turégano ⌂ E 54 Kq50
Turek ⌂ PL 64 Ls38
Turen ⌂ YV 265 Gf41
Tureni ⌂ RO 67 Md44
Tureng Tepe ✦ IR 95 Nc28
Turfan Depression ⌂ CHN 102 Pd26
Turgaj ⌂ KZ 96 Nj23
Turgayskoe plato ⌂ 76 Oa04
Turgen ⌂ MNG 101 Pg21
Turgi ⌂ CH 59 Lj43
Turgot ⌂ WAN 188 Lf41
Turgutlu ⌂ TR 71 Mg52
Turgutreis ⌂ TR 71 Mg53
Turhal ⌂ TR 90 Mj25

Turiaçu ⌂ BR 267 Hh46
Turija'k ⌂ UA 65 Mg39
Turijs'k ⌂ UA 65 Md39
Turilari ⌂ BR 279 Gg59
Turin ⌂ CDN 233 Ee21
Turin ⌂ CO 264 Gf45
Turiris ⌂ E 57 Kt51
Turiščevo ⌂ RUS 72 Mh19
Turjak ⌂ KSV 68 Ma48
Türkeli ⌂ TR 69 Mh50
Türkeve ⌂ H 67 Ma43
Turkey ■ TR 77 Mb06
Turkey Creek ⌂ AUS 143 Re54
Turkistan ⌂ KZ 97 Oz24
Turkmenabat ⌂ TM 96 Nd26
Turkmenbashi ⌂ TM 96 Mz26
Turkmengala ⌂ TM 96 Nz27
Turkmenistan ■ TM 96 Ne27
Turkmenskij zaliv ≋ TM 96 Mz26
Türkoğlu ⌂ TR 90 Mj27
Turks and Caicos Islands ⌂ GB 250 Ge35
Turks Islands ⌂ GB 250 Ge35
Turku → Abo ⌂ FIN 44 Mc30
Turkwel Gorge Reservoir ⌂ EAK 194 Mh45
Turlock ⌂ USA 234 Dk27
Turmalina ⌂ BR 275 Hj54
Turnagain Arm ≋ USA 229 Ce15
Turneffe Islands ▲ BH 248 Fg37
Turner ⌂ AUS 143 Re54
Turner ⌂ USA 232 Ef21
Turner Falls Park ✦ USA 238 Fb27
Turner Lake ⌂ CDN 233 Ef17
Turner Peninsula ▲ WAL 186 Kz42
Turnhout ⌂ B 51 Le39
Türnitz ⌂ A 61 Lq43
Turnor Lake ⌂ CDN 231 Eh17
Turnu Măgurele ⌂ RO 69 Me46
Turnu Roşu ⌂ RO 69 Me45
Turoš ⌂ 87
Turpan ⌂ CHN 101 Pd26
Turrialba ⌂ CR 249 Fj41
Turriff ⌂ GB 48 Ks35
Tursaq ⌂ IRQ 91 Nc29
Tursunzade ⌂ TJ 97 Oe26
Turt ⌂ MNG 104 Qz19
Turtel ⌂ MK 68 Mb49
Turtle Beach ≋ YE 95 Ng39
Turtle Islands ▲ RP 125 Qk43
Turtle Harbour ≋ HN 248 Fg37
Turtle Islands ▲ WAL 186 Kz42
Turtle Islands Marine Park ✿ ● RP 125 Qk43
Turtle Lake ⌂ CDN 233 Ef19
Turtle Lake ⌂ USA 236 Fd23
Turuépano, P.N. ✿ YV 265 Gj40
Turuhansk ⌂ RUS 88 Pb05
Turu/Mariquita, T.I. ▲ BR 267 Hf47
Turun ⌂ 273 Jaa7
Turuvanür ⌂ IND 118 Oj39
Turvânia ⌂ BR 274 Hf54
Turvo ⌂ BR 276 Hf59
Turvo ⌂ BR 277 Hf60
Turzovka ⌂ SK 66 Lt41
Tus ⌂ IR 95 Nc28
Tusaqualla ⌂ BR 279 Gg57
Tuscaloosa ⌂ USA 239 Fg29
Tuscánia ⌂ I 60 Ln48
Tuscany ⌂ I 60 Lm47
Tuscumbia ⌂ USA 239 Fg28
Tusenøyane ▲ N 38
Tusenøyane ⌂ 134
Tusenøane ⌂ M 37 Ma05
Tuskegee ⌂ USA 239 Fh29
Tušnica ▲ BIH 61 Ls47
Tustumena Lake ⌂ USA 228 Cc16
Tütaev ⌂ RUS 72 Mk17
Tutak ⌂ TR 91 Nb26
Tuticorin ⌂ IND 118 Oj41
Tutóia ⌂ BR 272 Hj46
Tutira ⌂ NZ 153 Tj65
Tutoko, Mount ▲ NZ 152 Te68
Tutrakan ⌂ BG 69 Mh46
Tuttlingen ⌂ D 59 Lj43
Tutuala ⌂ TLS 131 Rd50
Tutuila ▲ USA 158
Tutupaca, Volcán ▲ PE 269 Ge54
Tutwiler ⌂ USA 239 Fe28
Tuulos ⌂ FIN 44 Me29
Tuupovaara ⌂ FIN 44 Mj28
Tuusniemi ⌂ FIN 44 Mh30
Tuusula ⌂ FIN 44 Me30
Tuva ⌂ RUS 88 Pd08
Tuval ⌂ 135 Tb10
Tuvalu Islands ▲ TUV 134 Tb10
Tuwan-eyane ⌂ N 37 Ma05
Tuwayq ⌂ KSA 92 Nz33
Tuwwal ⌂ KSA 92 Mk34
Tuxcueca ⌂ MEX 246 Ej35
Tuxford ⌂ CDN 233 Ee21
Tuxpan ⌂ MEX 246 Ez36
Tuxpan ⌂ MEX 246 Fb35
Tuxpan = Tuxpam ✦ ● MEX 246 Fb35
Tuxtepec ⌂ MEX 247 Fc36
Tuxtla Gutiérrez ● MEX 247 Fd37
Túy Duc ⌂ VN 123 Qd39
Tuyen Quang ⌂ VN 121 Qc35
Tuy Hoa ⌂ VN 123 Qe39
Tuy Phong ⌂ VN 123 Qe40
Tuyserkān ⌂ IR 95 Nz29
Tuz Gölü ⌂ TR 90 Mg26
Tuzi ⌂ MNE 68 Lu48
Tüzigoot Nat. Mon. ✿ USA 235 Ee28
Tuz Khurmatu ⌂ IRQ 91 Nc29
Tuzla ⌂ BIH 68 Lt46
Tuzluca ⌂ TR 91 Nb25
Tuzule ⌂ RDC 199 Mb51
Tvärdica ⌂ BG 69 Mf48
Tvärdogôra ⌂ PL 64 Ls39
Tveitsund ⌂ N 42 Lj31
Tver ⌂ RUS 72 Mh17
Tving ⌂ S 43 Lq34
Tvrdava ⌂ SRB 61 Ls46
Tvrdoš ✦ BIH 68 Lt48
Tvrdošin ⌂ SK 67 Lu41
Tweed ⌂ GB 48 Ks35
Tweed Heads ⌂ AUS 151 Sg61
Tweedsmuir Prov. Park ✿ CDN
Tweefontein ⌂ ZA 204 Lk62
Tweeling ⌂ ZA 205 Me59
Twee Rivieren ⌂ NAM 204 Lk58
Tweespruit ⌂ ZA 205 Md60
Twello ⌂ NL 51 Lg38
Twelve Apostles ✦ AUS 151 Sb65
Twelve Foot Davis Prov. Hist. Site ✦ CDN 233 Ez17
Twentynine Palms ⌂ USA 234 Ec28
Twifo-Praso ⌂ GH 187 Kk43
Twin Falls ⌂ USA 146 Rg52
Twin Falls Gorge ✦ CDN 231 Eb15
Twin Islands ▲ CDN 237 Ga19
Twin Lakes ⌂ CDN 239 Cj15
Twin Mount ⌂ USA 236 Fa22
Twin Peaks ▲ USA 234 Ez26
Twin Ring Motegi ✦ J 111 Sa27
Twin Wells ⌂ AUS 150 Sa62
Twistringen ⌂ D 58 Lj38

Twizel ⌂ NZ 153 Tf68
Two Harbors ⌂ USA 236 Fe22
Two Hills ⌂ CDN 233 Ee19
Two Rivers ⌂ USA 237 Fg23
Two Rocks ⌂ AUS 144 Qh61
Two Wells ⌂ AUS 150 Rk63
Twyfelfontein Rock Engraving ✦ ● NAM 200 Lh56
Twyford ⌂ GB 49 Ks39
Tychowo ⌂ PL 64 Lr37
Tychy ⌂ PL 65 Lu40
Tyczyn ⌂ PL 65 Mz41
Tygda ⌂ RUS 105 Rz20
Tyfors ⌂ S 43 Lo30
Tyhee ⌂ LV 45 Mc33
Tykë ⌂ LV 45 Mc33
Tylawa ⌂ PL 65 Mb41
Tyler ⌂ USA 238 Fc29
Tylertown ⌂ USA 239 Fe30
Týlôsand ⌂ S 43 Lo33
Tyndall ⌂ USA 236 Fb24
Tyndrum ⌂ GB 48 Kr34
Tynemouth ⌂ GB 48 Kt35
Tyniste nad Orlici ⌂ CZ 66 Lr40
Tynset ⌂ N 40 Ll28
Tyôpye Kiyuchi ▲ KS 100 Oh24
Tyre ⌂ RL 90 Mh29
Tyrell Falls ✦ CDN 231 Ef14
Tyresta n.p. ✿ S 43 Ls31
Tyringe ⌂ S 43 Lo34
Tyringe ⌂ S 43 Lo34
Tyristrand ⌂ N 42 Lj30
Tyrnyauz ⌂ RUS 91 Na24
Tyrol Basin Ski Area ✦ USA 236 Ff24
Tyrrell Lake ⌂ CDN 231 Ef14
Tyrrhenian Sea ≋ 62 Lb06
Tyškivka ⌂ UA 72 Mf21
Tysnes ▲ N 42 Lf30
Tyssedal ⌂ N 42 Lg30
Tystberga ⌂ S 43 Ls31
Tyszowce ⌂ PL 65 Md40
Tytuvénai ⌂ LT 45 Md34
Tywyn ⌂ GB 49 Kq38
Tzaneen ⌂ ZA 202 Mf57
Tzazar ⌂ 115 Qj29
Tzermiádo ⌂ GR 71 Mf55
Tzintzuntzan ✦ MEX 246 Ek36
Tziscao ⌂ MEX 247 Fd37
Tzucacab ⌂ MEX 247 Ff35

U

Uaçá, T.I. ▲ BR 267 He44
Uaco Cungo ⌂ ANG 200 Lh51
Uamba ⌂ ANG 198 Lj49
Uanda ⌂ AUS 149 Sc56
Uanle Uen = Wankaawayn ⌂ SP 195 Nc44
Uape ⌂ MOC 203 Mk54
Uar Addol ⌂ SP 195 Na44
Uarges ⌂ EAK 194 Mj45
Uar Igarore ⌂ SP 195 Nb45
Uari, T.I. ▲ BR 270 Qh47
Uatâ-Paraná, T.I. ▲ BR 270 Gg47
Uatumã ⌂ BR 271 Ha47
Uauá ⌂ BR 273 Hk48
Uauaretê ⌂ BR 265 Gf45
Uaxactún ✦ GCA 247 Fg37
Ub ⌂ SRB 68 Lu47
Uba ⌂ BR 275 Hj56
Ubaí ⌂ BR 275 Hh54
Ubaíra ⌂ BR 275 Hh54
Ubaitaba ⌂ BR 275 Ja54
Ubaji ⌂ 135 Tb10
Ubajara ⌂ BR 273 Hj47
Ubaji ⌂ OM 95 Nj34
Ubangi ⌂ RCB/RDC 190 Lj45
Ubangi ⌂ RDC 199 Mb50
Ubaté ⌂ CO 264 Gc43
Ubatuba ⌂ BR 277 Hh57
Ubauro ⌂ PK 99 Oe31
Ubberup ⌂ DK 42 Ll35
Ube ⌂ J 113 Rf29
Ubeda ⌂ E 55 Kr52
Ubehebe Crater ✦ USA 234 Eb27
Uberaba ⌂ BR 275 Hg55
Uberaba ⌂ BOL 278 Gk54
Überlingen ⌂ D 59 Lj43
Uberlândia ⌂ BR 274 Hf55
Ubia, Gunung ▲ RI 154 Rj48
Ubiarco ⌂ E 54 Kr48
Ubirr Rock ✦ AUS 146 Rg52
Ubiratã ⌂ BR 276 Hd58
Ubl ⌂ MNE 68 Lt48
Ubombo ⌂ ZA 205 Mg59
Ubon Ratchathani ⌂ THA 123 Qc38
Ubombo ⌂ ZA 205 Mg59
Ubon Rois ⌂ RUS 111 Rh23
Ubovka ⌂ RUS 111 Rh23
Ubundu ⌂ RDC 199 Mc46
Ucacha ⌂ RA 281 Gj62
Ucapinima ⌂ CO 265 Gf45
Ucayali ⌂ PE 269 Gc49
Ucayali ⌂ PE 266 Gc49
Uçès ⌂ BY 65 Mf38
Uch ⌂ PK 99 Of31
Uch-Adzhi ⌂ TM 96 Nz26
Uchkuduk ⌂ UZ 96 Nz24
Uchami ⌂ RUS 105 Qh25
Ucharonidge ⌂ AUS 146 Rh54
Uchiza ⌂ PE 269 Gb50
Uchqudug ⌂ UZ 96 Oz24
Uchsay ⌂ UZ 96 Nd24
Ucluelet ⌂ CDN 232 Dh21
Uckermark ⌂ D 58 Lo37
Uckfield ⌂ GB 49 Lz40
Ucluelet ⌂ CDN 232 Dh21
Ucross ⌂ USA 233 Eg23
Ucú ⌂ ANG 198 Lg49
Uda ⌂ RUS 89 Qc05
Udachnyj ⌂ IND 117 Pd35
Udaipur ⌂ IND 116 Of34
Udaipur ⌂ IND 116 Of34
Udaipur ⌂ IND 117 Pd34
Udala ⌂ IND 117 Pd35
Udanti ⌂ IND 117 Pd35
Udayagiri ⌂ IND 116 Oj34
Udayagiri Caves ✦ IND 116 Oj34
Udayagiri ⌂ IND 117 Pc35
Udayavar ⌂ SUD 185 Mh38
Udayt ⌂ SUD 185 Mh38
Udbina ⌂ HR 61 Lq46
Uddevalla ⌂ S 42 Lm32
Uddheden ⌂ S 42 Ln31
Uddiyana ⌂ IND 115 Ok30
Udgir ⌂ IND 116 Oj36
Udine ⌂ I 60 Ln44
Udmalaippettai ⌂ IND 118 Oj40
Udomlja ⌂ RUS 72 Mh17
Udon Thani ⌂ THA 122 Qb37
Udong ⌂ K 123 Qb39
Udoru ⌂ J 111 Ok28
Udskoe ⌂ RUS 105 Rc19
Udu Point ▲ FIJ 159 Tj54
Udumalpet ⌂ IND 118 Oj40
Udupi ⌂ IND 118 Oh39
Udzungwa Mountains N.P. ✿ ● EAT 197 Mj51
Ueckermünde ⌂ D 58 Lo37
Uedem ⌂ D 51 Lg39
Uege = Waqid ⌂ SP 195 Nb44
Uehling ⌂ USA 236 Fb24
Uel'en ⌂ RUS 191 Mb50
Uelzen ⌂ D 58 Ll38
Ueno ⌂ J 113 Rj28

Uetersen ⌂ D 58 Lk37
Uetze ⌂ D 58 Ll38
Ufa ⌂ RUS 88 Nd08
Ufeyn ⌂ SP 193 Ne40
Ugab Rock Finger ✦ ● NAM 200 Lh56
Ugab Vingerklip ✦ ● NAM 200 Lh56
Ugále ⌂ LV 45 Mc33
Ugalla ⌂ EAT 196 Mf48
Ugalla River Game Reserve ✿ EAT 196 Mf48
Uganda ■ ⌂ 163 Mb09
Uganik Island ▲ USA 228 Cd16
Ugao ⌂ SRB 68 Ma47
Ugarcin ⌂ BG 69 Me47
Ugarit ✦ SYR 90 Mh28
Ugashik Bay ≋ USA 228 Ca17
Ugashik Lake ⌂ USA 228 Cb15
Ugba ⌂ WAN 188 Le42
Ugep ⌂ WAN 188 Le43
Ughelli ⌂ WAN 188 Ld43
Ugie ⌂ ZA 205 Me61
Ugijar ⌂ E 55 Kr53
Uglegorsk ⌂ RUS 111 Rg22
Uglekamensk ⌂ RUS 111 Rg24
Ugljić ⌂ RUS 72 Mk17
Uglovka ⌂ RUS 72 Mh17
Ugljan ▲ HR 61 Lq46
Ugljane ⌂ HR 61 Lq46
Uglovoe ⌂ RUS 105 Qk20
Ugo ⌂ WAN 188 Lq42
Ugol'noye Kopi ⌂ RUS 89 Td06
Ugoofaaru ⌂ MV 118 Og42
Ugra ⌂ RUS 72 Mh18
Ugumji ⌂ WAN 188 Le42
Uğurlu ⌂ TR 90 Mf27
Uhaymir ⌂ SUD 185 Mg48
Uhekera ⌂ EAT 196 Mg48
Uherské Hradište ✦ CZ 66 Ls41
Uherský Brod ⌂ CZ 66 Ls41
Uhl ⌂ WAN 188 Le42
Uhiere ⌂ WAN 188 Ld42
Uhlenhorst ⌂ NAM 204 Lj57
Uhniv ⌂ UA 65 Md39
Uhrichsville ⌂ USA 237 Fk25
Uibai ⌂ BR 273 Hj51
Uige ⌂ ANG 198 Lj49
Uijongbu ⌂ ROK 112 Rd27
Uiju ⌂ PRK 110 Rc25
Uintah and Ouray Ind. Res. ⌂ USA 235 Ee25
Uinta Mountains ▲ USA 235 Ee25
Uirapuru ⌂ BR 278 Ha53
Uiraúna ⌂ BR 273 Ja49
Uiseb Caves ✦ NAM 200 Lj55
Uis Myn ⌂ NAM 200 Lh56
Uísong ⌂ ROK 113 Re27
Uithoorn ⌂ NL 51 Lq38
Uithuizen ⌂ NL 51 Lg37
Uitkyk ⌂ ZA 204 Lk60
Uitsitngin (Fish River Canyon) ✿ ● NAM 204 Lj59
Ujaly ⌂ KZ 96 Nh23
Ujanmas ⌂ RI 127 Qa47
Ujar ⌂ RUS 105 Qj20
Ujjain ⌂ IND 116 Oj34
Ujście ⌂ PL 64 Lq38
Ujězdziec Maly ⌂ PL 64 Ls39
Ujherbtó ⌂ H 67 Mb43
Uji ⌂ J 113 Rh28
Uji-gunto ▲ J 113 Re30
Uji ⌂ 154 Rh48
Ujohbilang ⌂ RI 128 Qh45
Ujscie ⌂ PL 64 Lr37
Ujungkulon N.P. ✿ RI 127 Qa49
Ujung Pandang = ⌂
Ukata ⌂ WAN 188 Lc40
Ukerewe ⌂ EAT 196 Mg47
Ukerewe Island ▲ EAT 196 Mg47
Ukhia ⌂ BD 120 Pg35
Uki Ni Masi Island ▲ SOL 157 Ta51
Ukmergè ⌂ LT 45 Me35
Ukraine ■ UA 77 Mb05
Ukraine Cultural Heritage Village ✦ CDN 233 Ed19
Ukta ⌂ PL 65 Mz37
Ukui ⌂ RI 127 Qa46
Ukwa ⌂ WAN 188 Le42
Ula ⌂ TR 71 Mh53
Ulaan-Ereg ⌂ MNG 104 Qc22
Ulaan-Eleg ⌂ MNG 105 Qj22
Ulaanbaatar ● MNG 104 Qc22
Ulaangom ⌂ MNG 101 Pg21
Ulaan-Uul ⌂ MNG 104 Qa22
Ulaan Tayga ▲ MNG/RUS 104 Pk20
Ulaanzirem ⌂ MNG 104 Qb23
Ulan Bator = ● MNG
Ulanhot ⌂ CHN 110 Ra23
Ulan-Hua ⌂ CHN 106 Qf25
Ulan Tohoi ⌂ CHN 106 Qb25
Ulan-Udè ● RUS 104 Qd20
Ulapara ⌂ BD 120 Pf34
Ularbemban ⌂ RI 127 Qb45
Ulastay ⌂ MNG 101 Pj21
Ulawa ⌂ EAT 197 Mj50
Ulawa ⌂ SOL 157 Ta50
Ulaya ⌂ EAT 197 Mj49
Ulbroka ⌂ LV 45 Me34
Ulcinj ⌂ MNE 68 Lu49
Uldz ⌂ MNG 104 Qe21
Ulefoss ⌂ N 42 Lj31
Uleila del Campo ⌂ E 55 Ks53
Ulete ⌂ EAT 197 Mj49
Ulfborg ⌂ DK 42 Lj34
Ulhasnagar ⌂ IND 116 Of36
Uljanik ⌂ HR 61 Lr45
Uljanovsk ⌂ RUS 73 Nz18
Uljanovo ⌂ RUS 105 Qj20
Uljma ⌂ SRB 68 Ma46
Ulladulla ⌂ AUS 151 Se63
Ullal ⌂ IND 118 Oh39
Ullal Beach ≋ IND 118 Oh39
Ullapool ⌂ GB 48 Kq33
Ullared ⌂ S 42 Ln33
Ullastret ✦ E 55 Ln49
Ullsfjorden ⌂ N 38 Ma06
Ulldecona ⌂ E 57 Kt51
Uljanik ⌂ HR 61 Lr45
Ullóa ⌂ BOL 278 Ee53
Ulu ⌂ RUS 89 Rz06
Ullung-do ▲ ROK 113 Rf27
Ulm ⌂ D 59 Lj42

Ulmara ▣ AUS 149 Sg60	Unango ▣ MOC 196 Mh52	Urganlı ▣ TR 71 Mh52	Usuki ▣ J 113 Rf29	Vaiden ▣ USA 239 Ff29
Ulmu ▣ D 59 Lg40	Unari ▣ FIN 39 Mf23	Urgench = Urganch ▣ UZ 96 Oa25	Usulutan ▣ ES 248 Ff39	Vaihingen (Enz) ▣ D 59 Lj42
Ulmu ▣ RO 69 Mk46	Unauna ▣ RI 130 Ra46	Urgoma Mountains ▲ ETH 192 Mk42	Usumacinta ➤ GCA/MEX 247 Fe37	Vai Isaka ▣ PNG 155 Sc47
Ulongwe ▣ MOC 203 Mh53	Unawari ▣ RI 154 Rh47	Ürgüp ▣ TR 90 Mh26	Usur ▣ IND 117 Pa36	Vaikam ▣ IND 118 Oj41
Irika ▣ S 43 Lq32	Unawatuna Beach ≋ CL 119 Pa43	Urho ▣ UZ 97 Od26	Usva ▣ RUS 72 Mk19	Väike-Pakri ▲ EST 44 Md31
Iriceham ▣ S 43 Lo33	Unazah ▣ KSA 93 Nb32	Urho ▣ CHN 101 Pc22	Usvjaty ▣ RUS 72 Mg17	Vaikuntha Perumal Temple ⌂ IND
Irika ▣ S 43 Lq32	Uncastillo ▣ E 56 Kf48	Urho Kekkosen kansallispuisto ⌂ FIN	Uta ▣ RI 154 Rj48	119 Ok39
Ilsan ▣ ROK 113 Re28	Uncompahgre Plateau ▲ USA	39 Mg31	Utakter ▣ N 42 Lf31	Vail ▣ USA 235 Eg26
Ilster ▣ D 58 Lk40	235 Ef26	Uria ▣ RO 67 Me43	Utah Lake ▣ USA 235 Ed25	Vailly-sur-Sauldre ▣ F 53 Lc43
Ilster ▣ IRL/GB 47 Kn36	Undara Volcanic N.P. ⬟ AUS 147 Sc55	Uribe ▣ CO 264 Gb44	Utah Lake ▣ USA 235 Ed25	Vainikkala ▣ FIN 44 Mg30
Ilitima ▣ AUS 151 Sb63	Undaunda ▣ Z 202 Me53	Uribe ▣ CO 264 Gb44	Utakter ▣ N 42 Lf31	Vainode ▣ LV 45 Mb31
Ilu ▣ MYA 122 Pk40	Undenäs ▣ S 43 Lq32	Uribia ▣ CO 264 Gd40	Utangala ▣ RI 125 Rb45	Vaison-la-Romaine ▣ F 53 Lf46
Ilu ▣ RI 125 Rc44	Underberg ▣ ZA 205 Me60	Uribicha ▣ BOL 278 Gg53	Utanljö ▣ S 41 Ls28	Vaison-la-Romaine ▣ F 53 Lf46
Ilus 89 Rb06	Undersåker ▣ S 40 Lo27	Urica ▣ YV 265 Gh41	Utena ▣ LT 45 Mf35	Vajkfebir ▣ TR 91 Mk25
Ilu SUD 185 Mg40	Underwater Caves ≋ BS 243 Gb33	Uri Hauchab Mountains ▲ NAM	Utegi ▣ EAT 194 Mh46	Vajszló ▣ H 66 Ls45

Verchnjadzvinsk ○ BY 45 Mh35
Verchnje Syn'ovydne ○ UA 67 Md41
Verchn'odniprovs'k ○ UA 73 Mh21
Verdalsøra ○ N 40 Lm27
Verde ▲ MEX 244 Eg32
Verde Island ○ RP 124 Ra39
Verden (Aller) ○ D 58 Lk38
Verdigre ○ USA 236 Fa24
Verdun ○ F 51 Lf41
Verdún ○ ROU 276 Hc62
Vereeniging ○ ZA 205 Md59
Verena ○ ZA 205 Me58
Verenal ○ CO 264 Gb44
Vergara ○ ROU 276 Hd62
Vergeleë ○ ZA 205 Mc58
Vergemort ○ AUS 148 Sb57
Vergennes ○ USA 241 Gd23
Vergina ○ GR 70 Mc50
Vergt ○ F 52 La46
Verhneimbatsk ○ RUS 88 Pb06
Verhnezejskaja ravnina ▲ RUS 89 Rb08
Vernhie Osel'ki ○ RUS 44 Ml30
Vernhie Usugh ○ RUS 105 Qh19
Véria ○ N 38 Lj05
Verín ○ BG 68 Md48
Verín ○ E 54 Kn49
Verinsko ○ BG 68 Mf48
Veriora ○ CH 60 Lj43
Verkehrshaus ○ CH 60 Lj43
Verkhoyanskiy Mountains ▲ RUS 89 Rb05
Verkykerskop ○ ZA 205 Me59
Verl ○ D 58 Lj39
Verla ○ FIN 44 Mg29
Verlegenhuken ▲ N 38 Lj05
Vermand ○ F 51 Ld41
Vermenton ○ F 53 Ld44
Vermilion ○ CDN 233 Ee19
Vermilion Bay ○ CDN 236 Fd21
Vermilion ○ USA 236 Fb24
Vermont ○ USA 241 Gd23
Vernadsky ○ 287 Gc32
Vernal ○ USA 235 Ef25
Verazza ○ I 60 Lk46
Verne ○ RO 69 Mg45
Verneuil-sur-Avre ○ F 52 La42
Vernoe ○ RUS 105 Re20
Vernon ○ CDN 232 Ea20
Vernon ○ F 51 Lb41
Vernon ○ USA 235 Ed25
Vernon ○ USA 238 Fa28
Vernon Islands ▲ AUS 146 Rf52
Vero ○ F 62 Lk48
Vero Beach ○ USA 243 Fk32
Verona ○ I 60 Lm45
Véronica ○ RA 281 Hb43
Ver-o-Peso (Belém) ▲ BR 267 Hf46
Versailles ○ F 51 Lc42
Versailles ○ USA 238 Fd23
Versailles ○ USA 239 Fh26
Versailles ○ USA 239 Fh26
Versalles ○ CO 264 Gd43
Veršino-Darasunskij ○ RUS 105 Qh19
Versmold ○ D 58 Lj38
Vertelim ○ RUS 72 Nc18
Vertentes ○ BR 273 Jc49
Vertijivka ○ UA 72 Mf20
Vertintes ○ I 243 Ga35
Vertisko ▲ GR 68 Md50
Vértiz ○ RA 280 Gg43
Verviers ○ F 51 Le42
Verulam ○ ZA 205 Mf60
Verviers ○ B 51 Lf41
Vervins ○ F 51 Ld41
Vesanka ○ FIN 44 Mf28
Ves'egonsk ○ RUS 72 Mj16
Veselí nad Lužnicí ○ CZ 66 Lp41
Veselí nad Moravou ○ CZ 66 Ls42
Veseloe ▲ RUS 45 Lu36
Veselovskoe Vodohranilišče ○ RUS 73 Na22
Veselynove ○ UA 73 Mf22
Vesenskaja ○ RUS 72 Na21
Vesoul ○ F 53 Lg43
Vespaciano ○ BR 275 Hj55
Vessigebro ○ S 42 Ln34
Veste Coburg ○ D 59 Ll40
Vesterålen ○ N 38 Lp22
Vesterli ○ N 38 Lg21
Vestero Havn ○ DK 42 Ll33
Vesterøy ▲ N 42 Ll31
Vestfirðir ○ IS 46 Jo24
Vestfjorden ○ N 38 Ln23
Vestiges préhistoriques et Peintures rupestres ▲ RN 182 Le35
Vestmanna ○ DK 46 Kn28
Vestmannaeyjar ○ IS 46 Ju27
Vestnes ○ N 40 Lh28
Vestvågøy ▲ N 38 Ln22
Vesúvio ▲ I 63 Lp50
Veszprém ○ H 66 Ls43
Vetel ○ RO 68 Mc45
Vetlanda ○ S 43 Lq33
Vetluga ○ RUS 72 Nc17
Vétrny Jeníkov ○ CZ 66 Lq41
Veulettes-sur-Mer ○ F 50 La41
Veurne ○ B 51 Lc39
Vevelstad = Forvika ○ N 40 Ln25
Vevey ○ CH 60 Lg44
Vévi ▲ GR 70 Mb50
Veymandhoo ○ MV 118 Og44
Veynes ○ F 53 Lf46
Vezelay ○ F 53 Ld44
Vezirköprü ○ TR 90 Mh25
V. Guerrero ▲ MEX 244 Ed24
V. Guerrero ▲ MEX 246 Ej24
Ví ○ S 41 Ls28
Via Appia ○ I 62 Ln49
Viacha ○ BOL 278 Gf54
Viadana ○ I 60 Ll46
Viaduc-de-Garabit ○ F 53 Ld46
Viaducto la Polvorilla ○ RA 279 Gg58
Viadutos ○ BR 276 Hd59
Vialadougou ○ CI 187 Kg41
Viale ○ RA 276 Ha61
Via Lemovicensis ○ F 52 La45
Via Mala ○ CH 60 Lk44
Viamonte ○ RA 281 Gj62
Viana ○ ANG 198 Lg50
Viana ○ BR 267 He46
Viana ○ BR 267 Hd47
Viana ○ BR 273 Jh51
Viana ○ E 56 Ks48
Viana de Bolo ○ E 54 Kn48
Viana do Alentejo ○ P 55 Kn52
Viana do Castelo ○ P 54 Km49
Vianden ○ L 51 Lg41
Vianen ○ NL 51 Lf39
Viangchan ○ LAO 120 Qb36
Vianópolis ○ BR 274 Hf54
Via Podiensis ○ F 52 Lb46
Via Tolosana ○ F 52 Lb47
Viareggio ○ I 60 Ll47
Viate ○ G 198 Ll45
Via Turonensis ○ F 52 La44
Vibble ○ S 43 Lt33
Vibo Valentia ○ I 63 Lr52
Vibraye ○ F 50 La42
Vic ○ E 57 Lc49
Vícam ○ MEX 244 Ee32
Vicdessos ○ F 52 Lb48
Vic-en-Bigorre ○ F 52 La47
Vicente Guerrero ▲ MEX 244 Ec30
Vicente Guerrero ▲ MEX 246 Ej34
Vicentinópolis ○ BR 274 Hf54
Vicenza ○ I 60 Lm45
Vichada ○ CO 265 Gf43
Vichadero ○ ROU 276 Hc61
Vichy ○ F 53 Ld44
Vichy-Bellerive ○ F 53 Ld44
Vici ○ USA 238 Fa27
Vicksburg ○ USA 239 Fe29
Vic-le-Comte ○ F 53 Ld45
Vic-le-Fesq ○ F 53 Le47
Vico ○ F 60 Lj48
Viçosa ○ BR 273 Jb50

Viçosa ○ BR 275 Hj56
Viçosa do Ceará ○ BR 273 Hk47
Vic-sur-Cère ○ F 53 Lc46
Victor ○ USA 233 Ea14
Victor Harbour ○ AUS 150 Rk63
Victoria ○ CAM 188 Le43
Victoria ○ CDN 232 Dj21
Victoria ○ CO 264 Gc43
Victoria ▲ M 63 Lp54
Victoria ○ RA 281 Gk62
Victoria ○ RCH 280 Gd65
Victoria ○ RP 124 Ra39
Victoria ▲ SY 195 Nh48
Victoria ○ USA 245 Fb31
Victoria Beach ○ CDN 236 Fb20
Victoria Bryant S.P. ○ USA 242 Fj28
Victoria Falls ▲ Z/ZW 201 Mc54
Victoria Falls ○ Z 201 Mc54
Victoria Falls ○ ZW 201 Mc54
Victoria Highway ○ AUS 143 Re53
Victoria Lake ○ CDN 241 Hb21
Victoria Land ▲ ANT 287 Tb33
Victoria Memorial ▲ IND 120 Pe34
Victoria, Mount ▲ MYA 120 Pg35
Victoria, Mount ▲ PNG 155 Tg67
Victoria Nile ○ EAU 194 Mf43
Victoria Nile ○ EAU 194 Mf44
Victoria Park Racecourse ▲ AUS 150 Rk63
Victoria River ○ AUS 146 Rf53
Victoria River ○ AUS 241 Hb21
Victoria River Downs ○ AUS 146 Rf54
Victorias ○ RP 124 Rb40
Victoria Strait ○ CDN 226 Ed05
Victoriaville ○ CDN 240 Gc22
Victoria West ○ ZA 204 Mb61
Victor, Mount ▲ 287 Jf34
Victor Rosales ○ MEX 246 Ej34
Victorville ○ USA 234 Ec28
Vícúga ○ RUS 72 Na17
Vicuna ○ RCH 279 Ge61
Vícuga Mackenna ○ RA 280 Gh62
Vicus ○ PE 268 Fk48
Vida ○ USA 232 Dj23
Vida ○ USA 233 Eg23
Vidal ○ PE 268 Gd47
Vidal Junction ○ USA 234 Ec28
Vidal Junction ○ USA 234 Ec28
Vidalia ○ S 41 Ma25
Vidauban ○ F 53 Lg47
Videbæk ○ DK 42 Lj34
Videira ○ BR 276 Hd59
Videle ○ RO 69 Mf46
Viðigelmir ▲ IS 46 Ju26
Vidin ○ CZ 66 Ln41
Vidigueira ○ P 55 Kn52
Vidisha ○ IND 117 Oj34
Vidiskiai ○ LT 45 Me35
Vidneva ○ RY 45 Mg36
Vidra ○ RO 73 Md23
Vidsel ○ S 41 Ma25
Vidua ▲ BIH 68 Lt46
Vidvik ○ N 46 Kd25
Vidzeme ▲ LV 45 Mg33
Vidzy ○ BY 45 Mg35
Viechtach ○ D 59 Ln41
Viedgesville ○ ZA 205 Me61
Viedma, Volcán ▲ RA 282 Gj66
Vielha ○ E 56 La48
Vielsalm ○ B 51 Lf41
Vienenburg ○ D 58 Ll39
Vieng Kham ○ LAO 121 Qb35
Vieng Phukha ○ LAO 121 Qa35
Vieng Thong ○ LAO 121 Qb35
Vieng Xai ○ LAO 121 Qc35
Vienna ○ A 66 Ls42
Vienna ○ USA 239 Fe26
Vienna ○ USA 239 Ff27
Vienna ○ USA 264 Gd43
Vienne ○ F 53 Le45
Vientiane = Viangchan ● LAO 121 Qb36
Vieques ○ USA 251 Gh36
Viernheim ○ D 59 Lj41
Vierwaldstätter See ○ CH 60 Lj44
Vierzehnheiligen ○ D 59 Lm40
Vierzon ○ F 53 Lc43
Viesca ○ MEX 245 Ej33
Viesīte ○ LV 45 Mf34
Vietas ○ S 38 Lt23
Vietnam ○ VN 77 Qa08
Viet Tri ○ VN 121 Qc35
Vieux Bordeaux ○ F 52 Ku46
Vieux-Fort ○ CDN 241 Hb20
View Point (Fish River Canyon) ○ NAM 204 Lj59
Vif ○ F 53 Lf45
Viga ○ RP 124 Rc39
Vigeland ○ N 42 Lh32
Vigévano ○ I 60 Lj45
Vigia ○ BR 267 Hf46
Vigia Chico ○ MEX 247 Fg36
Vignola ○ I 60 Ll46
Vigrestad ○ N 42 Lg32
Vihari ○ PK 99 Og33
Vihiers ○ F 52 Ku43
Vihorlat ○ RM 207 Ne54
Vihtari ○ FIN 44 Mh29
Vihti ○ FIN 44 Me30
Viiala ○ FIN 44 Md29
Viira ○ EST 45 Md32
Viisarimäki ○ FIN 44 Mg28
Viitasaari ○ FIN 44 Mf27
Viitna ○ EST 44 Mg31
Vijayapuri North ○ IND 117 Ok37
Vijayawada ○ IND 117 Pa37
Vijayadurg ○ IND 116 Og37
Vijayadurg Beach ○ IND 116 Og37
Vik ○ IS 46 Ka27
Vik ○ N 40 Lh28
Vik ○ S 43 Lp35
Vikajärvi ○ FIN 38 Mf24
Vikarabad ○ IND 116 Oj37
Vikedal ○ N 42 Lg31
Vikeke ○ TLS 131 Rd50
Viken ○ S 42 Ln34
Vikenara Point ○ SOL 157 Sk50
Vikenará ○ N 40 Lj27
Vikevåg ○ N 42 Lg31
Vikindu ○ EAT 197 Mk49
Viking ○ CDN 233 Ee19
Vikna ○ N 40 Ll26
Vikos-Aoos N.P. ▲ GR 70 Ma51
Vikram ○ N 38 Lt21
Viksøyri ○ N 40 Lg29
Vikulovo ○ RUS 88 Oc07
Vila Bela da São Trinidade ○ BR 278 Ha53
Vila Capixabas ○ BR 270 Gg51
Vila Conceição ○ BR 272 Gg61
Vila de Manica ○ MOC 202 Mg55
Vila de Rei ○ P 55 Km51
Vila de Sena ○ MOC 203 Mh54
Vila dos Remédios ○ BR 273 Jd47
Vila Flor ○ ANG 200 Lh52

Vilakalaka ○ VU 158 Td53
Vilalba = Villalba ○ E 54 Kn47
Vila Martins ○ BR 270 Gf49
Vila Meriti ○ BR 271 Ha48
Vila Mouzinho ○ MOC 203 Mh53
Vila Nazaré ○ BR 270 Gh47
Vilāni ○ LV 45 Mg34
Vilankulo ○ MOC 203 Mj56
Vila Nova ○ ANG 200 Lj52
Vila Nova da Fronteira ○ MOC 203 Mh54
Vila Nova de Cerveira ○ P 54 Km49
Vila Nova de Famalição ○ P 54 Km49
Vila Nova de Foz Côa ○ P 54 Kn49
Vila Nova de Milfontes ○ P 55 Km53
Vila Nova de Paiva ○ P 54 Kn50
Vila Nova do Piauí ○ BR 273 Ja49
Vila Nova do Seles ○ ANG 200 Lh51
Vilanova i la Geltrú ○ E 57 Lc50
Vila Nova Sintra ○ CV 186 Jh38
Vila Palestina ○ BR 272 Hg48
Vila Porto Franco ○ BR 271 Ha49
Vila Pouca de Aguiar ○ P 54 Kn49
Vila-real ○ E 57 Ku51
Vila Real ○ P 54 Kn49
Vila Real de Santo Antonio ○ P 55 Kn53
Vilar Formoso ○ P 54 Kn50
Vila Rica ○ BR 272 He51
Vila Rica ○ PY 276 Ha59
Vilarinho do Monte ○ BR 271 Hd46
Vila Tugendhat ○ CZ 66 Lr41
Vila Valério ○ BR 275 Hk55
Vila Velha ○ BR 267 He44
Vila Velha ○ BR 275 Hk56
Vila Velha ○ BR 277 He58
Vila Velha de Ródão ○ P 55 Kn51
Vila Verde de Ficalho ○ P 55 Kn53
Vila Viçosa ○ P 55 Kn52
Vilcabamba ○ EC 268 Ga48
Vilcabamba Viejo ▲ PE 269 Gd52
Vilcas Huaman ▲ PE 269 Gd52
Vilcashuamán ▲ PE 269 Gd52
Vilches ○ E 56 Kr52
Vilcún ○ RCH 280 Gd65
Vildbjerg ○ DK 42 Lj34
Vilejka ○ BY 45 Mg36
Vilelas ○ RA 279 Gj59
Vilhelmina ○ S 41 Lr26
Vilhena ○ BR 278 Gk52
Viljandi ○ EST 45 Mf32
Viljoenskroon ○ ZA 205 Md59
Viljui ○ RUS 89 Ra06
Viljujsk ○ RUS 89 Ra06
Viljujskoe plato ▲ RUS 89 Qc05
Viljujskoe vodohranilišče ○ RUS 88 Qb07
Vilkaviškis ○ LT 45 Md36
Vilkija ○ LT 45 Md35
Vilkitskogo, proliv ○ RUS 89 Qb02
Villa Abecia ○ BOL 278 Gh56
Villa Adriana ○ I 62 Ln49
Villa Ahumada ○ MEX 244 Eg30
Villa Alegre ○ RCH 280 Ge63
Villa Alemana ○ RCH 280 Ge62
Villa Alhué ○ RCH 280 Ge62
Villa Amengual ○ RA 276 Ha60
Villa Angela ○ RA 279 Gh59
Villa Atamisqui ○ RA 279 Gg60
Villa Atuel ○ RA 280 Gg63
Villa Azueta ○ MEX 247 Fc36
Villaba ○ RP 124 Rc40
Villa Berthet ○ RA 279 Gh59
Villablino ○ E 54 Kn48
Villa Bruzual ○ YV 265 Gf41
Villa Bustos ○ RA 279 Gg60
Villacañas ○ E 55 Kr51
Villa Cañas ○ RA 281 Gk63
Villacarrillo ○ E 56 Kr52
Villacarriedo ○ E 56 Kr47
Villach ○ A 66 Lo44
Villacidro ○ I 62 Lj51
Villa Constitución ○ RA 281 Gk62
Villada ○ E 54 Kq48
Villadama ○ MEX 245 Ek32
Villa de Arista ○ MEX 246 Ek34
Villa de Cura ○ YV 265 Gg40
Villa de Guadelupe ○ MEX 247 Fe36
Villa del Carmen ○ ROU 276 Hb62
Villa del Rosario ○ RA 281 Gj61
Villa del Totoral ○ RA 279 Gj60
Villa de Reyes ○ MEX 246 Ek35
Villa d'Este ○ I 62 Ln49
Villa de Zaachila ○ MEX 246 Fb37
Villadiego ○ E 54 Kq48
Villa Dolores ○ RA 280 Gh61
Villa Dos Trece ○ RA 276 Ha59
Villa El Chocón ○ RA 280 Gf64
Villa Elisa ○ RA 276 Ha62
Villa Escalante ○ MEX 246 Ej36
Villa Figueroa ○ RA 279 Gj59
Villaflores ○ MEX 247 Fd37
Villa Florida ○ PY 276 Ha59
Villa Foscari ○ I 61 Lm45
Villafranca del Bierzo ○ E 54 Kn48
Villafranca de los Barros ○ E 55 Ko52
Villafranca de los Caballeros ○ E 55 Kr51
Villafranca di Verona ○ I 60 Ll45
Villafranca del Guadalquivir ○ E 55 Ko52
Villa General Belgrano ○ RA 280 Gh62
Villa General Güemes ○ RA 276 Ha58
Villa General M.Belgrano ○ RA 276 Ha58
Villa General Roca ○ RA 280 Gg62
Villages de Pygmés ▲ RDC 191 Me45
Villa Gesell ○ RA 281 Hb64
Vilhata ○ FIN 44 Md29
Vila Gobernador Gálvez ○ RA 281 Gk62
Villa González Ortega ○ MEX 246 Ek34
Villa Guadalupe ○ MEX 244 Ed30
Villaguay ○ RA 276 Ha61
Villa Guillermina ○ RA 276 Ha60
Villahermosa ○ E 55 Ks52
Villa Hermosa ○ MEX 247 Fd36
Villahermosa ○ MEX 247 Fd37
Villa Hidalgo ○ MEX 246 Ej35
Villahoz ○ E 56 Kr48
Villa Huidobro ○ RA 280 Gh63
Villa Insurgentes ○ MEX 244 Ed33
Villa Iris ○ RA 281 Gj64
Villa Jesús María ○ MEX 244 Eb31
Villa Jovis ○ I 63 Lp50
Villajoyosa = La Vila Joiosa ○ E 57 Ku52
Villa Juárez ○ MEX 244 Ef32
Villa Juárez ○ MEX 246 Ej34
Villalba = Villalba ○ E 54 Kn47
Villa Lola ○ YV 265 Gj42
Villalón de Campos ○ E 54 Kq48
Villalonga ○ RA 281 Gj65
Villalpando ○ E 54 Kq49
Villa Madero ○ MEX 247 Fd36
Villa Mainero ○ MEX 245 Fa33
Villamanán ○ E 54 Kp48
Villa María ○ RA 281 Gj62
Villa Mazán ○ RA 279 Gg60

Villa Media Agua ○ RA 280 Gf61
Villa Mercedes ○ RA 280 Gg62
Villa Minetti ○ RA 276 Ha60
Villa M.Moreno ○ RA 279 Gh59
Villa Montes ○ BOL 278 Gj56
Villa Nazaré ○ BR 270 Gh47
Villanca ○ MK 68 Mc49
Viniste ○ RO 238 Fc27
Villanueva ○ BOL 270 Gh51
Villanueva ○ CO 264 Gd40
Villanueva ○ HN 248 Fg38
Villanueva ○ MEX 246 Ej34
Villanueva ○ NIC 248 Fg39
Villanueva ○ RA 280 Gf62
Villanueva de Alcorón ○ E 57 Ks50
Villanueva de Argaño ○ E 56 Kr48
Villanueva de Córdoba ○ E 55 Kq52
Villanueva de Gállego ○ E 56 Ku49
Villanueva de la Fuente ○ E 55 Ks52
Villanueva de la Jara ○ E 57 Kt51
Villanueva de la Serena ○ E 55 Kp52
Villanueva de la Sierra ○ E 55 Ko50
Villanueva de las Torres ○ E 55 Kr53
Villanueva del Campo ○ E 54 Kp49
Villanueva del Fresno ○ E 55 Kn52
Villanueva del Huerva ○ E 57 Kt49
Villanueva de los Castillejos ○ E 55 Kn53
Villanueva del Rio y Minas ○ E 55 Kp53
Villa Ocampo ○ RA 276 Ha60
Villa O'Higgins ○ RCH 282 Gd67
Villa Ojo de Agua ○ RA 279 Gj60
Villa Ortega ○ RCH 282 Ga68
Villapalacios ○ E 56 Ks52
Villa Paranacito ○ RA 276 Ha62
Villapinzón ○ CO 264 Gd43
Villaputzu ○ I 62 Lk51
Villard ○ RH 250 Gd36
Villard-de-Lans ○ F 53 Lf45
Villaret ○ S 43 Lp31
Villares del Saz ○ E 55 Ks51
Villarejo de Fuentes ○ E 57 Ks51
Villarejo de Salvanés ○ E 55 Kr50
Villarmayor ○ E 54 Kp50
Villa Romana del Casale □ ... I 63 Lp53
Villarpando ○ DOM 250 Ge36
Villarrica ○ PY 276 Hb58
Villarrica ○ RCH 280 Gd65
Villarrica, P.N. ▲ RCH 280 Ge65
Villarrobledo ○ E 57 Ks51
Villarroya de la Sierra ○ E 56 Kt49
Villarubia de los Ojos ○ E 55 Kr51
Villars-les-Dombes ○ F 53 Lf45
Villarta de los Montes ○ E 55 Kq51
Villatobas ○ E 55 Kr51
Villasana de Mena ○ E 56 Kr47
Villa Sánchez Magalanes ○ MEX 247 Fd36
Villa San Giovanni ○ I 63 Lq52
Villa San José de Vinchina ○ RA 279 Gg60
Villa San Martín = Ciudad de Loreto ○ RA 279 Gh60
Villa Santa María ○ I 63 Lp49
Villa Serano ○ BOL 278 Gh55
Villasimius ○ I 62 Lk51
Villa Trinidad ○ RA 279 Gk61
Villa Tunari ○ BOL 278 Gh54
Villa Unión ○ MEX 244 Eg34
Villa Unión ○ MEX 246 Ek34
Villa Unión ○ RA 279 Gf60
Villa Valeria ○ RA 280 Gh63
Villa Vásquez ○ DOM 250 Ge36
Villaviciosa ○ CO 264 Gd43
Villaviciosa ○ E 54 Kp47
Villaviciosa de Córdoba ○ E 55 Kp52
Villa Viscarra ○ BOL 278 Gh54
Villa Ygatimi ○ PY 276 Hb58
Villazón ○ BOL 279 Gh57
Villedieu-les-Poêles ○ F 50 Ku42
Villedieu-sur-Indre ○ F 52 Lb44
Villefort ○ F 53 Le46
Villefranche-de-Conflent ○ F 52 Lc48
Villefranche-de-Lauragais ○ F 52 Lb47
Villefranche-de-Rouergue ○ F 53 Lc46
Villefranche-du-Périgord ○ F 52 La46
Villefranche-sur-Cher ○ F 53 Lb43
Villefranche-sur-Mer ○ F 53 Lh47
Villefranche-sur-Saône ○ F 53 Le45
Villena ○ E 57 Ku52
Villeneuve-les-Avignon ○ F 53 Le47
Villeneuve-sur-Lot ○ F 52 La46
Villeneuve-sur-Yonne ○ F 51 Ld42
Ville Platte ○ USA 239 Fd30
Villeréal ○ F 52 La46
Villers-Bocage ○ F 50 Ku41
Villers-Bocage ○ F 51 Lc41
Villers-Bretonneux ○ F 51 Lc41
Villers-Cotterêts ○ F 51 Ld41
Villersexel ○ F 53 Lg43
Villers-sur-Mer ○ F 50 La41
Villeurbanne ○ F 53 Le45
Villiers ○ ZA 205 Me59
Villiers-Saint-Georges ○ F 51 Ld42
Villingen-Schwenningen ○ D 59 Lj42
Villupuram ○ IND 119 Ok38
Vilnius ● LT 45 Mf36
Vilsandi rahvuspark ▲ EST 45 Mb32
Vil'šany ○ UA 73 Mh20
Vilsbiburg ○ D 59 Ln42
Vilshofen ○ D 59 Lo42
Vimão ○ BR 276 Hd45
Vimianzo ○ E 54 Kl47
Vimieiro ○ P 55 Kn52
Vimioso ○ P 54 Ko49
Vimmerby ○ S 43 Lq33
Vimoutiers ○ F 50 La42
Vimpeli ○ FIN 44 Md27
Vinac ○ BIH 61 Ls46
Viña del Mar ○ RCH 280 Ge62
Vinanivao ○ RM 203 Nd53
Vinaròs ○ E 57 La50
Vinay ○ F 53 Lf45
Vincennes ○ USA 239 Fg26
Vincennes Bay ○ 287 Qb32
Vincente Noble ○ DOM 250 Ge36
Vinces ○ EC 268 Ga46
Vinderup ○ DK 42 Lj34
Vindhya Aono H.A. ○ S 43 Lj31
Vindhya Range ▲ IND 116 Oj34
Vineland ○ USA 235 Ea26
Vineland ○ USA 241 Gc26
Vineyard Sound ○ USA 241 Ge25
Vingåker ○ S 43 Lq31
Vinh ○ VN 121 Qc36
Vinh Cam Ranh ○ VN 123 Qe40
Vinh Chao ○ VN 123 Qd41
Vinh Hy ○ VN 123 Qe40
Vinh Loc ○ VN 121 Qc36

Vinh Long ○ VN 123 Qd40
Vinh Moc Tunnel ○ VN 121 Qd37
Vinh Phan Ri ○ VN 123 Qe40
Vinh Phan Thiet ○ VN 123 Qe40
Vinh Rach Gia ○ VN 123 Qc41
Vinh Son ○ VN 123 Qe38
Vinh Trang Pagoda ▲ VN 123 Qd40
Vinh Van Phong ○ VN 123 Qe39
Vinica ○ MK 68 Mc49
Viniste ○ RO 238 Fc27
Vinkovci ○ HR 61 Lt45
Vinnycja ○ UA 73 Me21
Vinograd ○ BG 69 Mh17
Viñón ○ S 43 Lq31
Viñon-sur-Verdon ○ F 53 Lf47
Vinstra ○ N 40 Lk29
Vinson Massif ▲ 287 Fd34
Vintar ○ RP 124 Ra36
Vintermarknad ▲ S 38 Lu24
Vinukonda ○ IND 117 Ok37
Viöca ○ RCB 198 Lh47
Violet Town ○ AUS 151 Sd64
Violet Valley A.L. ▲ AUS 143 Rd54
Viooisdrif ○ ZA 204 Lj60
Vipingo Mountains ▲ MW 196 Mg51
Vipiteno = Sterzing ○ I 60 Lm44
Vir ○ HR 61 Lq46
Virachey N.P. ▲ K 123 Qd38
Virac ○ RP 124 Rc39
Virachey N.P. ▲ K 123 Qd38
Virarajendrapet ○ IND 118 Oh39
Virawah ○ PK 99 Of33
Virazon ▲ RA 281 Ha65
Virbalis ○ LT 45 Md36
Virden ○ CDN 236 Fa20
Vire ○ F 50 Ku42
Virei ○ ANG 200 Lg53
Viresi ○ LV 45 Mg33
Virf Cindrel ▲ RO 68 Md45
Virf Fâncelul ▲ RO 67 Mf44
Virf Pietros ▲ RO 67 Me44
Virf Svinecea ▲ RO 68 Mc46
Virgem da Lapa ○ BR 275 Hj54
Virgin Gorda ▲ GB 251 Gh36
Virginia ○ IRL 47 Kn37
Virginia ○ USA 236 Fd22
Virginia ○ ZA 205 Md60
Virginia Beach ○ USA 242 Ga27
Virginia City ○ USA 233 Ea23
Virginia City ○ USA 233 Eg23
Virgin Islands ○ GB 251 Gh36
Virgin Islands ○ GB/USA 251 Gh36
Virgin Is, N.P. ▲ USA 251 Gh36
Virginia ○ BR 275 Hj55
Virgin Passage ○ USA 251 Gh36
Virihaure ○ S 38 Lq23
Virkby = Virkkala ○ FIN 44 Md30
Virkkala = Virkby ○ FIN 44 Md30
Virôchey ○ K 123 Qd38
Virojoki ○ FIN 44 Mh30
Viroinhden ○ FIN 44 Mh30
Viroqua ○ USA 236 Fe24
Virovitica ○ HR 61 Ls45
Virpazar ○ MNE 68 La48
Virrat ○ FIN 44 Md28
Virserum ○ S 43 Lq33
Virtasalmi ○ FIN 44 Mh28
Virton ○ B 51 Lf41
Virtsu ○ EST 44 Me30
Virttaa ○ FIN 44 Mc30
Viru ○ 287 Gd64
Virudhunagar ○ IND 118 Oj40
Virunga, P.N.des ▲ RDC 191 Me46
Vis ○ HR 61 Lr46
Vis ▲ HR 61 Lr47
Visaginas ○ LT 45 Mg35
Visalauke ○ LT 45 Mf35
Visalia ○ USA 234 Ea27
Visarvari ○ IND 116 Oh35
Visby ○ S 43 Lt33
Vischering ○ D 58 Lh39
Visconde do Rio Branco ○ BR 275 Hj56
Viscount Melville Sound ○ CDN 226 Ec04
Visé ○ B 51 Lf40
Viségrad ○ BIH 68 Lu47
Viseisei ○ FJI 159 Tj54
Viseu ○ BR 267 Hg46
Viseu ○ P 54 Kn50
Viseu de Sus ○ RO 67 Me43
Vișegorodok ○ RUS 45 Mj33
Vishakhapatnam ○ IND 117 Pd34
Vishalla Village ○ IND 116 Og34
Vishnupur ○ IND 120 Pe34
Vishwa Shanti Stupa ▲ IND 117 Pc33
Visina ○ RO 69 Mf46
Visingö ▲ S 43 Lp32
Visita ○ BR 271 Ha49
Visafjørs ○ LV 45 Lp33
Viskafors ○ S 43 Ln33
Viskoča ○ HR 61 Lp45
Visočica ▲ BIH 61 Lt47
Visoki Dečani ▲ KSV 68 Ma48
Visoko ○ BIH 61 Lt47
Vísola ○ CO 264 Gc43
Vistrier ○ ZA 205 Mc61
Visseggård ○ S 43 Lq34
Visselhövede ○ D 58 Lk38
Vista Alegre ○ BR 272 Gh61
Vista Alegre ○ BR 270 Gh46
Vistabella del Maestrat ○ E 57 Ku50
Viste Alegre ▲ ANG 198 Lh50
Vistula ○ PL 65 Lu38
Vistula Lagoon ○ PL/RUS 65 Lu36
Vistýtis ○ LT 45 Mc36
Visun Lanius ▲ RCH 280 Gd65
Visuvisu Point ○ SOL 157 Sj49
Vita ○ IND 116 Oh37
Vitalo ○ BR 266 Hd44
Vitebsk ○ BY 72 Mf18
Viterbo ○ I 62 Ln49
Viteze ○ BIH 61 Ls46
Viti ○ Thanh ○ VN 123 Qc41
Vítichi ○ BOL 278 Gh56
Vitigudino ○ E 54 Ko50
Viti Levu ▲ FJI 159 Tj54
Vitim ○ RUS 89 Qc08
Vitina ○ KSV 68 Mb48
Vitolište ○ MK 68 Mb49
Vítor ○ PE 269 Gd54
Vitória ○ BR 271 Hd47
Vitória ▲ BR 275 Hk56
Vitória da Conquista ○ BR 273 Hk53
Vitória de Santo Antão ○ BR 273 Jc50
Vitória do Mearim ○ BR 272 Hh47
Vitória-Gasteiz ○ E 56 Kr48
Vitorino Freire ○ BR 272 Hh48
Vitosa, N.P. ▲ BG 68 Md48
Vitré ○ F 50 Ku42
Vitrolles ○ F 53 Lf47
Vitry-le-François ○ F 51 Le42
Vitshumbi ○ RDC 191 Me46
Vitteaux ○ F 53 Le43
Vittel ○ F 53 Lf42
Vittangi ○ S 38 Ma23
Vittoria ○ I 63 Lp53
Vittorio Veneto ○ I 60 Ln45
Viù ○ I 60 Lh45
Viù ○ I 60 Lh45
Vivario ○ F 62 Lk48
Viveiro ○ E 54 Kn47
Vivian ○ USA 236 Fb19
Vivian ○ USA 239 Fc29
Vivo ○ ZA 202 Me57

Vivonne ○ F 52 La44
Viwa ▲ FJI 159 Tj54
Vizcaíno ▲ MEX 244 Ed32
Vize ○ TR 69 Mh49
Vizianagaram ○ IND 117 Pb36
Vizille ○ F 53 Lf45
Vizinga ○ RUS 72 Na19
Vizovice ○ CZ 66 Ls42
Vižovce ○ I 63 Lp53
Vla.Cucavčíy ○ BY 65 Mg38
Vjalikije Matykaly ○ BY 65 Mf38
Vjatsija ○ RUS 72 Na17
Vjatskoe ○ RUS 72 Na17
Vjazemskij ○ RUS 111 Rh22
Vjaz'ma ○ RUS 72 Mh18
Vjaznikí ○ RUS 72 Nb17
Vladikavkaz ○ RUS 91 Nc24
Vladimir ○ MNE 68 Lu48
Vladimir ○ RUS 72 Na17
Vladimirci ○ SRB 68 Lu46
Vladikovska ○ 287 Qb32
Vladivostok ○ RUS 110 Rf24
Vladslo ○ BG 68 Mf47
Vlagtwedde ○ NL 51 Lg38
Vlahata ○ GR 70 Ma52
Vlaháva ○ GR 70 Mb51
Vlahiá ○ GR 69 Md52
Vlaming Head Lighthouse ▲ AUS
Vlasenica ○ BIH 61 Lt46
Vlasim ○ CZ 66 Lq41
Vlaşin ○ RO 69 Mf46
Vlasotince ○ SRB 68 Mc48
Vlissingen ○ NL 51 Ld39
Vlkolínec □ ... SK 67 Lu41
Vloré ○ AL 70 Lu50
Vlotho ○ D 58 Lj38
Völs ○ A 60 Lm44
Vöcklabruck ○ A 66 Lo42
Vodice ○ HR 61 Lq47
Vodil ○ UZ 97 Of25
Vodňany ○ CZ 66 Lp41
vodní nádrž Hracholusky □ ... CZ 66 Lp41
vodní nádrž Lipno ○ CZ 66 Lp42
Vodlozero ○ HR 61 Lo46
Vodskov ○ DK 42 Ll33
Voerde ○ D 58 Lg39
Vogan ○ TG 187 La42
Vogatako ○ GR 70 Mb50
Vogelkop ▲ RI 131 Rf46
Vogelsberg ▲ D 59 Lk40
Vogelweide ○ NAM 204 Lk58
Voghera ○ I 60 Lk46
Voh ○ F 158 Tc56
Vohburg ○ D 59 Lm42
Vohemar = Iharana ○ RM 206 Ne52
Vohenstrauß ○ D 59 Ln41
Vohidiala ○ RM 207 Ne54
Vohilengo ○ RM 207 Ne53
Vohimasina ○ RM 207 Ne54
Vohipeno ○ RM 207 Nd57
Vohitrandro ○ RM 207 Ne54
Vöhma ○ EST 45 Mc32
Vohpa ○ FIN 44 Mg29
Voiandren ○ FIN 44 Mh30
Viroqua ○ USA 236 Fe24
Voikoski ○ FIN 44 Mg29
Voineasa ○ RO 68 Md45
Voinjama ○ LB 186 Ke41
Voiron ○ F 53 Lf45
Vöiste ○ EST 44 Mf31
Voiteg ○ RO 68 Mb45
Virtsu ○ EST 44 Me30
Viru ○ B 51 Lf41
Voivodina ▲ SRB 68 Lu45
Vojčice ○ DK 42 Lk35
Vojnika ○ UA 73 Mg23
Vojnic ○ HR 61 Lq45
Vojnika ○ BG 69 Mg48
Vojvodino ○ BG 69 Mj47
Vojvodina ▲ SRB 68 Lu45
Vokeo Island ▲ PNG 155 Sc47
Volary ○ CZ 66 Lo42
Volborg ○ USA 233 Eg23
Volcán ○ RA 279 Gh58
Volcán Alcedo ▲ EC 268 Ga46
Volcán Altar ▲ EC 268 Ga46
Volcán Antisana ▲ EC 268 Ga46
Volcán Arhuela ▲ RA 279 Gg58
Volcán Antuco ▲ RCH 280 Ge64
Volcán Aracar ▲ RA 279 Gg58
Volcán Arenal, P.N. ▲ CR 249 Fj41
Volcán Atitlán ▲ GCA 248 Ff38
Volcán Calbuco ▲ RCH 280 Ge66
Volcán Cayambe ▲ EC 268 Ga45
Volcán Chachani ▲ PE 269 Gd54
Volcán Chiguana ▲ BOL 278 Gg56
Volcán Chimborazo ▲ EC 268 Ga46
Volcán Chonhuenco ▲ RCH 280 Ge65
Volcán Concepción ▲ NIC 248 Fh40
Volcán Copahue ▲ RA/RCH 280 Ge64
Volcán Copiapó ▲ RCH 279 Gf59
Volcán Corcovado ▲ RCH 282 Gd67
Volcán Cotopaxi ▲ EC 268 Ga46
Volcán Coulon ○ CO 264 Gd45
Volcán Darwin ▲ EC 268 Fk46
Volcán de Colima ▲ MEX 246 Ej36
Volcán de Fuego ▲ GCA 248 Ff38
Volcán Domuyo ▲ RA 280 Ge64
Volcán Galeras ▲ CO 264 Gc44
Volcán Guagua Pichincha ▲ EC 268 Ga46
Volcán Gualtatiri ▲ RCH 278 Gf55
Volcán Huequi ▲ RCH 280 Gd67
Volcán Iliniza ▲ EC 268 Ga46
Volcán Ipala ▲ HN 248 Ff38
Volcán Isluga ▲ RCH 278 Gf55
Volcán Isluga, P.N. ▲ RCH 278 Gf56
Volcán Lanius ▲ RCH 280 Gd65
Volcán Lascar ▲ RCH 279 Gg57
Volcán Lastarria ▲ RCH/RA 279 Gf58
Volcán Las Vírgenes ▲ MEX 244 Ed32
Volcán Licancábur ▲ RCH 279 Gg57
Volcán Llaima ▲ RCH 280 Gd65
Volcán Llullaillaco ▲ RCH/RA 279 Gf58
Volcán Lonquimay ▲ RCH 280 Ge64
Volcán Maipo ▲ RCH/RA 280 Gf63
Volcán Masaya, P.N. ▲ NIC 248 Fg39
Volcán Michimahuida ▲ RCH 282 Gd67
Volcán Misti ▲ PE 269 Gd54
Volcán Momotombo ▲ NIC 248 Fg39
Volcán Ollague ▲ BOL/RCH
Volcano Mayon ▲ RP 124 Rb39
Volcán Osorno ▲ RCH 280 Ge66
Volcán Parinacota ▲ RCH 278 Gf55
Volcán Pico de Orizaba ▲ MEX

Volcán Poás, P.N. ▲ CR 249 Fj40
Volcán Puracé ▲ CO 264 Gc44
Volcán San José ▲ RA/RCH 280 Gf62
Volcán Sangay ▲ EC 268 Ga46
Volcán San Pedro ▲ RCH 279 Gg57
Volcán Socompa ▲ RCH/RA 279 Gf58
Volcán Sotara ▲ CO 264 Gc44
Volcán Sumaco ▲ EC 268 Gb46
Volcán Tacora ▲ GCA/MEX 247 Fd38
Volcán Tacora ▲ RCH 278 Gf55
Volcán Tajumulco ▲ GCA 248 Ff38
Volcán Tenorio, P.N. ▲ CR 249 Fj40
Volcán Ticsani ▲ PE 269 Ge54
Volcán Tolima ▲ CO 264 Gc44
Volcán Tres ○ RDC 191 Me46
Volcán Tupungato ▲ RA 280 Gf62
Volcán Tutupaca ▲ PE 269 Ge54
Volcán Viedma ▲ RA 282 Gd70
Volcán Viejo ▲ NIC 248 Fg39
Volcán Villarrica ▲ RCH 280 Gd65
Volcán Wolf ▲ EC 268 Fk45
Volcán ○ RO 69 Mh45
Vulcănesti ○ MD 73 Me23
Volčanec ○ MD 73 Me23
Volčansk ○ RUS 72 Mk17
Volda ○ N 40 Lh28
Volga ▲ RUS 26 Na04
Volga Upland ▲ RUS 27 Na05
Volga ○ USA 236 Fa23
Volgodonsk ○ RUS 73 Na21
Volgograd ○ RUS 73 Na20
Vólissós ○ GR 71 Mf52
Volkach ○ D 59 Ll41
Völkermarkt ○ A 61 Lp44
Völkerschlachtdenkmal ○ D 58 Lo39
Völklinger Hütte □ ... D 59 Lg41
Volkov ○ RUS 45 Mh33
Volkspelmonument ○ ZA 205 Mc60
Volksrust ○ ZA 205 Me59
Vollsjö ○ S 43 Lo35
Volnovacha ○ UA 73 Mj22
Volnovakha ○ UA 73 Mj22
Volodarka ○ UA 73 Me21
Volodarsk ○ RUS 72 Nb17
Volodymyrec' ○ UA 65 Mg39
Volodymyr-Volyns'kyj ○ UA 65 Me40
Volokolamsk ○ RUS 72 Mh17
Volokonovka ○ RUS 72 Mj20
Volop ○ ZA 204 Mb60
Vólos ○ GR 70 Mc51
Vološca ○ UA 67 Md41
Volosjanka ○ UA 67 Mc42
Volosovo ○ RUS 44 Mh31
Volotovo ○ RUS 72 Mk20
Volovec' ○ UA 67 Mc42
Völs ○ A 60 Lm44
Volstruisleegte ○ ZA 204 Mb62
Volta Redonda ○ BR 277 Hh57
Volterra ○ I 60 Ll47
Voltri ○ I 60 Lj46
Volturno ○ I 63 Lp49
Volubilis □ ... MA 175 Kh28
Volyně ○ CZ 66 Lp41
Volyně ○ CZ 66 Lp41
Volyns'ka vysočyna ▲ UA 65 Me40
Vom ○ WAN 188 Le41
Von Bachspanningsoord ○ NAM 200 Lj57
Vondrove ○ RM 207 Nc56
Vondrozo ○ RM 207 Nd57
Vonešta Voda ○ BG 69 Mf48
Von François Fort ○ NAM 200 Lj57
Von Frank Mount ▲ USA 229 Cc14
Vónitsa ○ GR 70 Ma51
Vönnu ○ EST 45 Mh32
Von Otteroyane ▲ N 38 Ma06
Voortrekker fort ▲ ZA 205 Mf59
Vopnafjörður ○ IS 46 Kf25
Voranava ○ BY 45 Mf36
Vorbasse ○ DK 42 Lk35
Vordingborg ○ DK 42 Lm35
Vorey ○ F 53 Ld45
Voria Pindos ▲ GR 70 Ma50
Vøringsfossen ▲ N 42 Lh30
Vorjing ▲ IND 120 Ph31
Vorkuta ○ RUS 88 Nd05
Vormsi ▲ EST 44 Md31
Vorochta ○ UA 67 Me42
Voronet □ ... RO 73 Mc22
Voronez ○ RUS 72 Mk19
Voronovo ○ RUS 44 Mf31
Vorotynec ○ RUS 72 Nc17
Vorožba ○ UA 72 Mh20
Vorpommersche Boddenlandschaft, N.P. ○ D 58 Ln36
Vorsterhoop ○ ZA 204 Mb58
Võrtsjärv ○ EST 45 Mf32
Võru ○ EST 45 Mh33
Vosburg ○ ZA 204 Mb61
Vose ○ F 97 Oe27
Vosges ▲ F 53 Lg43
Voskopojë ▲ AL 70 Ma50
Voskresensk ○ RUS 72 Mk18
Voskresenskoe ○ RUS 72 Nc17
Voskresenskoe ○ RUS 105 Re20
Vostok ○ RUS 111 Rh22
Vostok ○ 287 Qb32
Võsu ○ EST 44 Mf31
Vota do Jurem ○ BR 273 Hk47
Votorantim ○ BR 277 Hg57
Votuporanga ○ BR 274 Hf56
Voúdia ○ GR 71 Me54
Vouga ○ ANG 200 Lj52
Vouillé ○ F 52 La44
Vouliagmeni ○ GR 69 Md53
Vourkari ○ GR 71 Me53
Vouziers ○ F 51 Le41
Vovčans'k ○ UA 177 Lj31
Vovčans'k ○ UA 72 Mj20
Voyageurs National Park ○ USA 236 Fd21
Voyri ○ FIN 44 Mc27
vozera Narač ○ BY 45 Mg36
vozera Svir' ○ BY 73 Mf22
Voznesenskoe ○ RUS 72 Nb18
Vozrodenija otasi ▲ UZ 96 Nb23
vozvyšennost' Karabil ▲ TM 96 Ob27
vpadinni Akchakaya ▲ TM 96 Nk25
Vráble ○ SK 66 Lt42
Vraca ○ BG 68 Md47
Vračanski Balkan, N.P. ▲ BG 68 Md47
Vrådal ○ N 42 Lj31
Vradievka ○ UA 73 Mf22
Vrangfoss sluse ○ N 42 Lk31
Vranje ○ SRB 68 Mb48
Vranov ○ CZ 66 Lq42
Vranov nad Topľou ○ SK 67 Mb42
Vrapce Polje ○ MNE 68 Lu47
Vratenice ○ BR 270 Gg51
Vratnica ○ MK 68 Mb48
Vrazji prolaz ▲ HR 61 Lp45
Vrbanja ○ BIH 61 Ls46
Vrbanja ○ HR 61 Lt46
Vrbovec ○ HR 61 Lr45
Vrbovsko ○ HR 61 Lq45
Vrchlabi ○ CZ 66 Lq40
Vrede ○ ZA 205 Me59
Vredefort ○ ZA 205 Md59
Vredefort Dome □ ... ZA 205 Md59
Vredenburg ○ ZA 204 Lk62
Vredendal ○ ZA 204 Lk61
Vreed en Hoop ○ GUY 266 Ha42
Vresse ○ B 51 Le41
Vrgorac ○ HR 61 Ls47
Vrhnika ○ SLO 61 Lp45
Vrhopolje ○ BIH 61 Lr46
Vrín Tisdale ○ SRB 68 Mb48
Vrisses ○ GR 71 Me55
Vrissohóri ○ GR 70 Ma50
Vrontádos ○ GR 71 Mf52
Vrontoú ○ GR 70 Mc50
Vršac ○ SRB 68 Mb45
Vrsar ○ HR 61 Lo46
Vrtoče ○ BIH 61 Lr46
Vrutky ○ SK 67 Lt41
Vrulja ○ MNE 68 Lu47
Vryburg ○ ZA 205 Mc59
Vryheid ○ ZA 205 Mf59
Vsetín ○ CZ 66 Ls41
V-shaped Stone ▲ ... WAG 186 Kc39
Vuaqava ▲ FJI 159 Ua55
Vučitrn ○ KSV 68 Mb48
Vujatići ○ MNE 68 Lu47

W

Wa ○ CI 186 Kf42
Wa ○ GH 187 Kj40
Wafbrzych ○ PL 64 Lr40
Waaclye ○ SP 193 Nd49
Waajid ○ SP 193 Nd44
Waal ○ NL 51 Lf39
Waala ○ F 158 Tb55
Waalre ○ NL 51 Lf39
Waalwijk ○ NL 51 Lf39
Waanyi Garawa A.L. ▲ AUS 146 Rj54
Waar ○ RI 154 Rh47
Waat ○ SUD 191 Mg41
Wabag ○ PNG 155 Sb48
Wabakimi Prov. Park ○ CDN 236 Fd19
Wabasca-Desmarais ○ CDN 231 Ed18
Wabash ○ USA 237 Fh25
Wabasha ○ USA 236 Fd23
Wabe Shebele Wenz ○ ETH 195 Nb43
Wabo ○ PNG 155 Sc49
Wąbrzeźno ○ PL 64 Lt37
Wabuska ○ USA 234 Eb25
Wachapreague ○ USA 242 Gc27
Wachau □ ... A 66 Lq42
Wachille ○ ETH 195 Mk43
Wächtersbach ○ D 59 Lk40
Wacker ○ USA 230 De18
Waco ○ CDN 240 Gd20
Waco ○ USA 238 Fb30
Wad ○ PK 99 Od32
Wada'ah ○ SUD 184 Mc39
Wadalei ○ PNG 156 Sf50
Wadagni N.P. ○ J 113 Rh28
Wad Banda ○ SUD 184 Md39
Wad Ban Naqa □ ... SUD 185 Mg37
Wadbilliga N.P. ○ AUS 151 Se64
Waddell ○ USA 177 Lj31
Waddeneilanden ▲ NL 51 Lf38
Waddenzee ○ NL 51 Lf38
Waddington, Mount ▲ CDN 232 Dh18
Waddy Point ○ AUS 149 Sg58
Wadebridge ○ GB 49 Kq40
Wadena ○ CDN 233 Eh19
Wadena ○ USA 236 Fc22
Wad el Haddad ○ SUD 185 Mg39
Wadern ○ D 59 Lg41
Wad en Nail ○ SUD 185 Mj38
Wadesboro ○ USA 242 Fk28
Wad Hassib ○ SUD 184 Md40
Wadhwan ○ IND 116 Of34
Wadi al-Hayat ○ LAR 177 Lg32
Wādī al-Hitan (Whale Valley) □ ... ET 179 Me30
Wadi al-Milk ○ SUD 184 Me38
Wadi al-Warriya ○ UAE 95 Nj33
Wadi ar Ru'ays ○ LAR 177 Lk32
Wadi as Sulaymaniyah ○ KSA
Wadi Hadramawt ○ YE 94 Nd37
Wadi Halfa ○ SUD 179 Mf35
Wadi Howar ○ SUD 184 Mc37
Wadi Huwar ○ SUD 184 Mc37
Wadi Mathendous ○ LAR 176 Lg33
Wadi Mujib ○ JOR 92 Mj30
Wadi Muqaddam ○ SUD 185 Mf38
Wadi Musa ○ JOR 92 Mj31
Wadi Rum ○ IL 92 Mj31
Wadi Tarhūnah ○ LAR 176 Lf33
Wadi Tathlith ○ KSA 94 Nb35
Wadlew ○ PL 65 Lu39
Wad Madani ○ SUD 185 Mg38
Wadomari ○ J 113 Re32
Wadowice ○ PL 65 Lu41
Wad Rawa ○ SUD 185 Mg38
Wadwani ○ IND 116 Oj35
Waeng ○ THA 123 Qa43
Wafangdian ○ CHN 107 Ra26
Wafra ○ KWT 93 Nd31
Wagait Aboriginal Reserve ▲ AUS 146 Rf52
Wagau ○ PNG 155 Sd49
Wagdhari ○ IND 116 Oj36
Wager Bay ○ CDN 227 Fc06
Wageningen ○ NL 51 Lf39
Wageningen ○ SME 266 Ha43
Wagga Wagga ○ AUS 151 Sd63
Waghausel ○ D 59 Lj41
Wagin ○ AUS 144 Qk62
Wagina ▲ SOL 157 Sj49
Waginger See ○ D 59 Ln43
Wagner ○ CDN 230 De18
Wagner ○ USA 236 Fa24
Wagoner ○ USA 238 Fc27
Wagon Mound ○ USA 235 Ej27
Wagontire ○ USA 232 Ea24
Wagrain ○ A 61 Lo43

Vuka ○ HR 61 Lt45
Vukovar ○ HR 61 Lt45
Vulavu ○ SOL 157 Sk50
Vulcan ○ CDN 233 Ed20
Vulcan ○ RO 68 Md45
Vulcan ○ RO 69 Mh45
Vulcǎnesti ○ MD 73 Me23
vulkan Ključevskaja Sopka ▲ RUS 89 Ta07
vulkan Korjakskaja Sopka ▲ RUS 89 SU08
vulkan Tjatja ▲ RUS 111 Sd23
Vulturení ○ RO 67 Md44
Vulturu ○ RO 69 Mh45
Vumba Mountains ▲ ZW 202 Mg55
Vumba Rock Paintings ▲ MOC 202 Mg55
Vumbwe ○ MW 196 Mg52
Vung Tau ○ VN 123 Qd40
Vuntut National Park ○ CDN 229 Cc13
Vuollerim ○ S 38 Ma24
Vuottas ○ S 39 Mb24
Vurnary ○ RUS 72 Nc18
Vuyyuru ○ IND 117 Pa37
Vwawa ○ EAT 196 Mf49
Vyapartla ○ IND 116 Ok37
Vyara ○ IND 116 Og35
Vybor ○ RUS 72 Mj17
Vyborg ○ RUS 44 Mh29
Vyčegda ○ RUS 88 Nb06
Vydrino ○ RUS 104 Qc20
Vydryči ○ UA 65 Mg39
Vygoniči ○ RUS 72 Mh19
Vyksa ○ RUS 72 Nb18
Vylkove ○ UA 69 Mk45
Vynnyky ○ UA 67 Md42
Vynohradiv ○ UA 67 Mc42
Vypolzovo ○ RUS 72 Mj17
Vyrica ○ RUS 72 Mh16
Vysgorodok ○ RUS 45 Mj33
Výškov ○ CZ 66 Ls41
Výšne Nemecké ○ SK 67 Ma41
Výšnie Ružbachy ○ SK 67 Ma41
Vyšnij Volosek ○ RUS 72 Mh17
Vyšnivec' ○ UA 67 Me41
Vysock ○ RUS 44 Mh29
Vysokaje ○ BY 65 Md38
Vysoké Mýto ○ CZ 66 Lr41
Vysokovsk ○ RUS 72 Mj17
Vysší Brod ○ CZ 66 Lp42
Vytthiri ○ IND 118 Oj40
Vyžnycja ○ UA 67 Me42
Vyžnyc'kyj N.P. ○ UA 67 Me42

Wągrowiec PL 64 Ls38
Vaha RI 131 Rb48
Vahai RI 131 Re47
Vahala TG 187 La42
Vahala al Jufra LAR 177 Lj31
Vahat Salima SUD 179 Me35
Vahe Cantonment PK 99 Qg29
Vahiawa USA 234 Cb35
Vahibah Sands OM 95 Nk35
Vahlbergeya N 38 Lk06
Vahoo USA 236 Fb22
Vahpeton USA 236 Fb22
Vahrooga AUS 144 Qh58
Vai IND 116 Og37
Vaialua USA 234 Ca35
Vaiaia USA 234 Cb35
Vaiapi, T.I. BR 266 Hd45
Vaiblingen D 59 Lk42
Vaibula PNG 156 Sf50
Vaidhan IND 117 Pb33
Vaidhaus D 59 Ln41
Vaier de an Thaya A 66 Lq42
Vaidhofen an der Ybbs A 61 Lp43
Vaigama RI 131 Re46
Vaigeo RI 131 Rf45
Vaikabubak NZ 152 Tj64
Vaihi NZ 152 Tn64
Vaikaia NZ 153 Te68
Vaikanae NZ 153 Th66
Vaikaremoana NZ 153 Tj65
Vaikelo NZ 153 Te69
Vaikerie AUS 150 Sa63
Vaikiki USA 234 Cb35
Vaikouaiti NZ 153 Tf68
Vailapa VU 158 Td53
Vailuku USA 234 Cb35
Vaimarama NZ 153 Tj65
Vaimate NZ 153 Tf68
Vaimea USA 234 Ca35
Vaimea Bay USA 234 Ca35
Vaimiri Atroari, T.I. BR 271 Gk46
Vaingapu RI 130 Ra50
Vaini NZ 153 Tk65
Vainwright CDN 233 Ee19
Vainwright RI 130 Qk30
Vainwright Inlet USA 229 Bk10
Vaiotapu NZ 152 Tj65
Vaiouru NZ 153 Th65
Vaipara NZ 153 Te67
Vaipara NZ 153 Tg67
Vaipawa NZ 153 Tj65
Vaipoua Kauri Forest NZ 152 Tg63
Vaipukang RI 131 Rb50
Vaipukurau NZ 153 Tj66
Vairoa NZ 153 Tj65
Vairoa RI 131 Rf46
Vaisai RI 131 Rf46
Vaitangi National Reserve NZ 152 Th63
Vaitara NZ 153 Th65
Vaitomo Caves NZ 153 Th65
Vaitpinga Beach AUS 150 Rk63
Vaitsburg USA 232 Ea22
Vaiwa PNG 156 Se50
Vajai GUY 266 Ha45
Vajir EAK 195 Na45
Vajir Bor EAK 195 Na45
Vaka RI 131 Rf47
Vaka RDC 190 Ma45
Vakaf Tapai MAL 126 Qb43
Vakamoek RI 131 Rf46
Vaka, P.N.de la P. 198 Lf46
Vakasawan Q.N.P. J 113 Rh28
Vakatin RI 131 Rd47
Vakatobi Marine N.P. RI 130 Rb48
Vakaw CDN 233 Eh19
Vakayama J 113 Rh24
Vakeeny USA 135 Ta08
Vakefield A 51 Lk38
Vakeeny USA 69 Kf37
Vake Forest USA 242 Ga28
Vakinosawa J 111 Sa25
Vakkerstrom ZA 205 Mf59
Vaklarok USA 238 Cb34
Vako PNG 156 Se49
Vakomata Lake CDN 237 Fj22
Vakool AUS 151 Sc63
Vakulla Sprs. S.P. USA 239 Fh30
Vakool AUS 151 Sc63
Valachia RO 68 Mo46
Valaghonya Aboriginal Reserve AUS 142 Ra57
Valamba Z 196 Me52
Valandi IND 116 Oj36
Val Athiang SUD 191 Me42
Valbundrie AUS 151 Sd63
Valburton River AUS 148 Rk59
Valcha USA 149 Sf61
Valcheren NL 51 Lc39
Valcott PL 64 Lt37
Valdfoil D 58 Ln40
Valdburg AUS 144 Qj58
Valdburg Range AUS 144 Qj58
Valdeck D 58 Lj38
Valdegrave Island AUS 150 Rh62
Valdkirch D 59 Ln42
Valdkirchen D 59 Lo42
Valdport USA 232 Dh21
Valdron USA 238 Fc28
Valdshut-Tiengen D 59 Lj43
Valdviertel A 66 Lq42
Valeabahi RI 130 Rb46
Valeakodi RI 130 Rb46
Valembele GH 187 Kk40
Valembele CH 60 Lk43
Vales GB 49 Kg38
Vales USA 228 Bt13
Valewale GH 187 Kk40
Valgett AUS 149 Se61
Valgoolan AUS 144 Qk61
Valgreen AUS 148 Rk56
Valgreen Coast 287 Ed33
Valhalla I D 59 Ln41
Valhalla USA 236 Fb21
Valhalla USA 242 Fj28
Valhalla RDC 191 Me46
Valikale Plantation Resort PNG 156 Sf48
Valir RI 154 Rg48
Valis Island PNG 155 Sb47
Val diving (Caicos Islands) GB 250 Gd35
Wall Doxey S.P. USA 239 Fd28
Walldürn D 59 Lk41
Walled City of Ma'in YE 94 Nc37
Wallekraal ZA 204 Lj61
Wallenfels D 59 Lm40

Wallennbeen AUS 151 Se63
Wallingford GB 49 Kf39
Walling Rock AUS 144 Ra60
Wallis and Futuna F 135 Tb11
Wall of Gengis Khan MNG 105 Qg21
Wallowa Mountains USA 232 Eb23
Walls GB 48 Kt30
Walls of China AUS 151 Sb62
Wallumbilla AUS 149 Se59
Walney Island GB 49 Kf36
Walnut USA 234 Dj27
Walnut USA 239 Ff28
Walnut Canyon Nat. Mon. USA 235 Ee28
Walnut Grove USA 236 Fc23
Walnut Ridge USA 239 Fe27
Walong IND 120 Pj31
Walosi RI 130 Rb48
Walpole AUS 144 Qj63
Walpole-Nornalup N.P. AUS 144 Qj63
Walrus Is. USA 228 Bk16
Walrus Island USA 228 Bf17
Walsall GB 49 Kt38
Walsenburg USA 235 Eh27
Walsh USA 238 Ej27
Walsrode D 58 Lk38
Waltair IND 117 Pb37
Walterboro USA 242 Fk29
Walters USA 238 Fa28
Waltham CDN 241 Gb23
Waltman USA 233 Eg24
Walton CDN 240 Gj23
Walton, Mount AUS 144 Qk61
Walton-on-the-Naze GB 49 Lb39
Waltzing Matilda Center AUS 148 Sb57
Walu Besa RI 131 Rd47
Walungu RDC 196 Me47
Walunguru AUS 143 Re57
Walvis Bay NAM 204 Lh57
Walvis Bay NAM 204 Lj57
Walvis Bay Nature Reserve NAM 204 Lh57
Walvis Ridge 162 La12
Waly Chrobrego PL 64 Lg37
Wamal RI 154 Rk50
Wamanfo GH 187 Kj42
Wamar RI 154 Rh48
Wamaza RDC 196 Md48
Wamba USA 194 Mj45
Wamba RDC 198 La38
Wamba WAN 188 Lo41
Wamba Luadi RDC 199 Lj49
Wambiana AUS 147 Sd56
Wamboin AUS 149 Sd61
Wamego USA 238 Fb26
Wamena RI 154 Rk48
Wamis LAR 177 Lg30
Wampana-Karlantijpa A.L. AUS 146 Rf54
Wampaya Aboriginal Reserve AUS 146 Rf54
Wamsutter USA 235 Eg25
Wana PK 99 Oe29
Wanaaring AUS 149 Sc60
Wanadou TG 186 Kf41
Wanaka NZ 153 Te68
Wanasabari RI 131 Re48
Wanau RI 154 Rg48
Wanblee USA 236 Ek24
Wanda RA 276 Hc58
Wandai RI 154 Rj47
Wandammen Peninsula RI 154 Rh47
Wandammen / Wondiwoi Mountains Reserve RI 154 Rh47
Wanda Shan CHN 110 Rf23
Wandering AUS 144 Qj62
Wanderlândia BR 272 Hg49
Wando PNG 155 Sa50
Wando ROK 112 Rd28
Wandoan AUS 149 Se59
Waneroo AUS 144 Qh61
Wanesabe RI 130 Qj50
Wang PL 64 Lq40
Wang PNG 156 Sg47
Wangamana AUS 149 Sc60
Wanga Mountains WAN 188 Lf42
Wanganui NZ 153 Th65
Wangaratta AUS 151 Sd64
Wangary AUS 150 Rh63
Wangasi-Turu GH 187 Kk41
Wangben CDN 110 Rb24
Wangcang CHN 106 Qd29
Wangcheng CHN 108 Qg31
Wang Chin THA 121 Qa37
Wang Chomphu THA 122 Qa37
Wangdue Phodrang BHT 120 Pe32
Wangen D 59 Lk43
Wangerooge D 58 Lh37
Wanggamet, Gunung RI 130 Ra51
Wanggar CHN 108 Qf33
Wanggar RI 154 Rh47
Wangi Falls AUS 146 Rf52
Wangiwangi RI 131 Rb48
Wangijang CHN 112 Qj30
Wanglang CHN 110 Rd22
Wangmo CHN 108 Qd33
Wang Nam Yen THA 123 Qb39
Wang Nua THA 121 Pk36
Wangqing CHN 110 Re24
Wang Sam Mo THA 122 Qb37
Wang Saphung THA 122 Qa37
Wang Thong THA 122 Qa37
Wang Wiset THA 122 Pk42
Wang Zhaojun CHN 106 Qf25
Wangziguan CHN 106 Qc29
Wanham CDN 231 Ea18
Wan Hsa-la MYA 121 Pk35
Wanhuayan CHN 109 Qg33
Wani IND 117 Ok35
Wanie-Rukula RDC 191 Mc45
Wanigela PNG 156 Se50
Wanimiyn A.L. AUS 146 Rf53
Wanjarri Nature Reserve AUS 144 Ra59
Wanjiabu CHN 109 Qh31
Wankaner IND 116 Og34
Wankavayn SP 195 Nd44
Wan Kongmöng MYA 121 Pk35
Wan Long MYA 121 Pk34
Wanna AUS 144 Qj57
Wannaska USA 236 Fc21
Wannian CHN 109 Qj31
Wanning CHN 108 Qf36
Wanparti MYA 121 Pk35
Wan Pong MYA 121 Pk35
Wanquan CHN 107 Qh25
Wanshan Qundao CHN 109 Qh35
Wansheng CHN 108 Qd31
Wansra RI 154 Rh48
Wantage GB 49 Kf39
Wantoat PNG 155 Sd49
Wanuskewin Heritage P. CDN 233 Eg19

Waratah AUS 151 Sc66
Wara Wara Mountains WAL 186 Ke41
Warbreccan AUS 148 Sb58
Warburg D 58 Lk39
Warburton A.L. AUS 145 Rd59
Warburton Range AUS 145 Rd59
Ward NZ 153 Th66
Wardang Islands AUS 150 Rj63
Wardé RMM 181 Kg38
Warden CDN 205 Mc58
Wardenburg D 58 Lj37
Wardha USA 239 Ff28
Warden IND 120 Pj31
Wardha IND 117 Ok35
Wardo RI 154 Rh46
Ware CDN 230 Dh17
Waregem B 51 Ld40
Wareham GB 49 Kf40
Waren D 58 Ln38
Warendorf D 58 Lj39
Warenbayne AUS 149 Sf59
Warenda AUS 148 Sa57
Warendorf D 58 Lj39
Warga USA 149 Sf59
Wargaadhi SP 195 Nd44
Warialda AUS 149 Sd59
Warin Chamrap THA 123 Qc38
Waring Mountains USA 229 Ca12
Warintchaphum THA 122 Qb37
Warka PL 65 Mb39
Warkopi RI 154 Rh46
Warkworth NZ 152 Th64
Warlubie PL 64 Lt37
Warman CDN 233 Eg19
Warmandi RI 154 Rg46
Warmbad ZA 205 Mb59
Warmbad NAM 204 Lk60
Warmbad Hot Springs NAM 204 Lk60
Warmbad Warmwaterbronne NAM 204 Lk60
War Memorial I NAM 200 Lj56
Warmfontein NAM 204 Lj57
Warminster GB 49 Ks39
Warmquelle NAM 200 Lg55
Warmquelle Hot Springs NAM 200 Lg55
Warm Springs USA 232 Dk23
Warm Springs USA 234 Eb26
Warm Springs USA 241 Ga26
Warm Springs Ind. Res. USA 232 Dk23
Warnemünde D 58 Ln36
Warner CDN 233 Ef20
Warner Bros.Park E 55 Kr50
Warner Range USA 234 Ea25
Warner Robins USA 242 Fj29
Warnes BOL 278 Gj54
Warnice PL 64 Lp38
Warning, Mount AUS 149 Sg60
Warooka AUS 150 Rj63
Waroona AUS 144 Qh62
Waropko RI 155 Sa48
Warora IND 117 Ok35
Warra AUS 149 Sf59
Warracknabeal AUS 150 Sb64
Warragul AUS 151 Sc65
Warramboo AUS 150 Rh62
Warrego Highway AUS 149 Se59
Warrego River AUS 149 Sc59
Warren AUS 149 Sd61
Warren CDN 236 Fb20
Warren USA 233 Ef23
Warren USA 234 Dk25
Warren USA 237 Fj24
Warren USA 237 Fk25
Warren USA 242 Ga25
Warren USA 239 Fe27
Warrendale USA 241 Gc24
Warren Vale USA 147 Sa55
Warrick WAN 188 Lc41
Warriedar AUS 144 Qj60
Warrington GB 49 Ks37
Warrinilla AUS 149 Se58
Warrior Reefs AUS 147 Sb50
Warrnambool AUS 150 Sb65
Warroad USA 236 Fc21
Warroora AUS 144 Qg57
Warrumbungle N.P. AUS 149 Se61
Warsa RI 154 Rg48
Warsaw AFG 97 Oe27
Warsaw PL 65 Mb38
Warsaw USA 237 Fh25
Warsaw USA 237 Ga24
Warsaw USA 241 Gb27
Warsaw IND 116 Oj36
Warshiikh SP 195 Nc44
Warstein D 58 Lj39
Warszkowo PL 64 Lr36
Wart LB 186 Ke42
Warta PL 65 Lt39
Wartburg AUS 147 Sb55
Wartburg D 58 Ll40
Wartburg USA 239 Fh27
Wartburton ZA 205 Mf59
Wartkowice PL 65 Lt39
Waru AUS 144 Qj46
Waru RI 131 Rd47
Waru RI 131 Rf47
Warud IND 117 Ok35
Waruga Stone Graves RI 125 Rc45
Warumungu A.L. AUS 146 Rh55
Warwick AUS 149 Sg60
Warwick GB 49 Kt38
Warwick Channel AUS 146 Rj52
Warwick Downs AUS 148 Rk56
Wasa 287 Kb33
Wasaga Beach CDN 237 Fk23
Watzmann 160 Ln44
Wau PNG 155 Sd49
Wau RI 154 Rh48
Wau SUD 191 Md42
Waubay N.W.R. USA 236 Fb23
Waubra AUS 151 Sc64
Wauchope AUS 146 Rh56
Wauchope AUS 149 Sg61
Wauchula USA 243 Fk32
Waukaringa AUS 150 Rk62
Waukegan USA 237 Ff24
Waukegan USA 237 Ff24
Waukesha USA 237 Ff24
Waupaca USA 237 Ff23
Waupun USA 237 Ff24
Waurika USA 238 Fb28
Wausau USA 237 Fe23
Wausaukee USA 237 Fg23
Wautoma USA 237 Fe23
Wauwatosa USA 237 Ff24
Waveland USA 239 Ff30
Waverley AUS 236 Fd24
Waverly USA 237 Fd25
Waverly USA 239 Fg27
Waverly Downs USA 149 Sd60
Waverly Plantation USA 239 Ff29
Wave Rock AUS 144 Qk62
Waves USA 242 Gc28
Wawa RI 131 Rd47
Wawa CDN 237 Fh22
Wawa SUD 185 Mf35
Wawa al Kabir LAR 177 Lj32
Wawa el Namus LAR 178 Lj33
Wawanesa CDN 236 Fa21
Wawota CDN 233 Ek20
Wawota CDN 233 Ek20

Wasir RI 154 Rh48
Wasit IRQ 93 Nd29
Wasjabo SME 266 Hb43
Waskaganish = Fort Rupert CDN 237 Ga20
Waskesiu Lake CDN 233 Eg19
Waslatan RI 131 Rf49
Wayne USA 236 Fb24
Wassadou SN 186 Kc39
Wassamu J 111 Sb23
Wassatch Plateau USA 235 Ee26
Wassaw N.W.R. USA 242 Fk30
Wassenaar NL 51 Le38
Wasser NAM 204 Lk59
Wasserbung D 59 Ln42
Wasserkuppe D 58 L40
Wasserschloss Glücksburg D 58 Lk36
Wassou RG 186 Kd40
Waswanipi Ind. Res. CDN 240 Gd21
Watagan AUS 149 Sg58
Watam PNG 155 Sc49
Watam RI 125 Re45
Watambayoli RI 130 Ra46
Watampone RI 130 Ra48
Watamu Marine N.P. EAK 195 Na47
Wat Analayo THA 121 Qa36
Watanaka PNG 155 Sd49
Watarrka N.P. AUS 143 Rf58
Watawa RI 131 Rd47
Wat Chang Hai THA 123 Qa42
Watee SOL 157 Tb51
Waterberg NAM 205 Md58
Waterberg NAM 200 Lj56
Waterberg Plateau Park NAM 200 Lj56
Waterbury USA 241 Gd23
Waterbury USA 241 Gd25
Water Cay BS 243 Ga32
Water Cay BS 250 Gc34
Waterford AUS 144 Ra60
Waterford IRL 47 Kb38
Waterford USA 205 Mc62
Waterford Harbour IRL 47 Ko38
Waterhen CDN 236 Fa20
Waterloo B 51 Le40
Waterloo SME 266 Hb43
Waterloo USA 236 Fd24
Waterloo USA 239 Fe26
Waterloo WAL 186 Kd41
Watermeule ZA 204 Mb62
Wat Mill ZA 204 Mb62
Waterport USA 241 Gc23
Watersmeet USA 236 Fe22
Waterton Lakes N.P. CDN 232 Ec21
Waterton Park CDN 233 Ed21
Watertown USA 236 Fb23
Watertown USA 237 Ff24
Watertown USA 241 Gc22
Waterval-Boven ZA 205 Mf58
Waterville USA 241 Gd24
Waterville IRL 47 Kk39
Wat Hin Mak Peng THA 122 Qb37
Wathroo AUS 144 Qj61
Watino CDN 231 Eb18
Wat Khuhaphimuk THA 123 Qa42
Watkins Glen USA 241 Gc24
Wat Luang Temple LAO 123 Qc38
Watmuri RI 131 Rf49
Watom Island PNG 156 Sg48
Watonga USA 238 Fa27
Wat Photihian MAL 126 Qb42
Watroad USA 236 Fc21
Watrooora USA 144 Qg57
Warrumbungle N.P. AUS 149 Se61
Warsa RI 154 Rg48
Watsomba ZW 202 Mg55
Watson AUS 145 Rf61
Watson CDN 233 Eh19
Watson USA 239 Fe29
Watson Lake CDN 230 Df15
Watsonville USA 234 Dk27
Wat Suthon Wararam Woravihan THA 122 Qa38
Watt CDN 231 Eb18
Watten GB 49 Ks31
Wat Tham Mankhon THA 122 Pk39
Watthana Nakhon THA 123 Qb39
Wattwil CH 60 Lk43
Wat Udon THA 123 Qb37
Watutau RI 130 Ra46
Wat Xieng Thong LAO 120 Qk36
Wat Yan Sangwararam THA 122 Qa39
Watzmann 160 Ln44

Wayao CHN 121 Pk33
Waycross USA 242 Fj30
Wayerton CDN 240 Gh22
Waykadal RI 131 Rc46
Way Kambas National Park RI 127 Qc48
Waykilo RI 131 Rc46
Wayne USA 236 Fb24
Wayne USA 239 Fj26
Wayne USA 239 Fj26
Waynesboro USA 239 Ff30
Waynesboro USA 241 Gb25
Waynesboro USA 241 Ga26
Waynesboro USA 237 Fk26
Waynesville USA 242 Fh28
Waynesville USA 242 Fj27
Waynoka USA 238 Fa27
Wayongon MYA 120 Ph34
Wayu EAK 195 Mk46
Waza CAM 189 Lh40
Waza, P.N.de CAM 189 Lh40
Wazah AFG 99 Oe29
Wazirabad PK 99 Oh29
W du Niger, P.N.du DY 188 Lb39
Wé CAM 188 Lf42
Wé F 158 Td60
Waswanipi Ind. Res. CDN 240 Gc21
Weano Gorge AUS 142 Qk57
Wearhead GB 49 Ks36
Weatherford USA 238 Fa28
Weatherford USA 238 Fb29
Weaverville USA 234 Dj25
Weatherford USA 238 Fa28
Webb NZ 153 Te66
Weber Basin USA RI 131 Re49
Webi Shebele SP 195 Nb45
Webster USA 236 Fb23
Webster USA 239 Fk26
Webster City USA 236 Fd24
Webuye EAK 194 Mh45
Wechadlów PL 65 Ma40
Wechselburg D 58 Ln40
Weddell Island GB 283 Gk71
Weddell Sea ANT 287 Hb33
Weddin AUS 151 Sd61
Wedel D 58 Lk37
Wedel-Jarisberg-Land N 38 Lh07
Wednesday Island AUS 147 Sb51
Wedowee USA 239 Fg29
Wedweil SUD 191 Md41
Weebo AUS 144 Ra60
Weed USA 234 Dj25
Weedarah AUS 144 Qh58
Weeim RI 131 Rf46
Weeki Wachee USA 243 Fj31
Weemelah AUS 149 Se60
Weenen ZA 205 Mf60
Weenen Nature Reserve ZA 205 Mf60
Weener D 58 Lh37
Weert NL 51 Lf39
Weethalle AUS 151 Sd62
Wee Waa AUS 149 Se60
Wegdraai ZA 204 Mad60
Weglieniec PL 64 Lq39
Wegorzewo PL 65 Mb36
Wegrów PL 65 Mc38
Weh RI 120 Ph34
Wehni ETH 192 Mj39
Weichang CHN 107 Qj25
Weida D 58 Ln40
Weiden D 59 Ln41
Weifang CHN 107 Qk27
Weihe CHN 107 Rb27
Weihui CHN 110 Re23
Weihui CHN 107 Qh28
Weikersheim D 59 Lk41
Weil am Rhein D 59 Lh43
Weilburg D 59 Lj40
Weilheim D 59 Lm43
Weilmoringle AUS 149 Sd60
Weimar D 58 Lm40
Weinan CHN 106 Qe28
Weingarten D 59 Lk43
Weiningen AUS 147 Sa52
Weipa AUS 147 Sa52
Weippe USA 237 Fd25
Weirton USA 237 Fj25
Weiser USA 232 Eb23
Weishan CHN 112 Qj28
Weishan Yizu CHN 121 Qa33
Weishi CHN 107 Qh28
Weiße Elster D 58 Ln39
Weißenburg D 59 Ll41
Weißenburg D 59 Lm39
Weißenfels D 58 Lm39
Weißwasser D 58 Lp39
Weitchpec USA 234 Dj25
Weixi CHN 109 Qj33
Weitra A 66 Lp42
Weiwera NZ 152 Th64
Weixi CHN 121 Pk32
Wei Xian CHN 107 Qh27
Weixin CHN 108 Qc32
Weiyuan CHN 101 Ph25
Weiyuan CHN 108 Qc31
Weiz A 61 Lq43
Weizhou Dao CHN 108 Qe35
Weko RDC 191 Mc45
Wekusko CDN 233 Fa18
Wekweti = Snare Lakes CDN 231 Ec13
Welab RI 154 Rk50
Welatale MYA 121 Pk43
Welbourn Hill AUS 148 Rh59
Welch USA 242 Fk27
Welch USA 242 Fk27
Weldiya ETH 192 Mk40
Weld Range AUS 144 Qj59
Weleri RI 131 Qd48
Welford N.P. AUS 148 Sb58
Weligama CL 119 Pa42
Welkite ETH 192 Mj41
Welkom ZA 205 Md59
Wellawaya CL 119 Pa42
Wellesley Basin CDN 229 Da14
Wellesley Islands AUS 147 Rk54
Wellingborough GB 49 Ku38
Wellington AUS 151 Se62
Wellington AUS 146 Rj53
Wellington NZ 153 Th66
Wellington GB 49 Ks40
Wellington USA 235 Eh25
Wellington USA 235 Eh25
Wellington USA 238 Fb27
Wellington WAL 186 Kd41
Wellington AUS 151 Se62
Wellington Caves AUS 151 Se62
Wellington Channel CDN 227 Fb03
Wells GB 49 Ks39
Wells USA 234 Ec24
Wellsboro USA 241 Gb25
Wellsford NZ 152 Th64
Wells Gray Prov. Park CDN 232 Dk19
Wells, Mount USA 143 Rd54
Wells-next-the-Sea GB 49 La38
Wellsville USA 241 Gb24
Welna PL 64 Ls38
Welo ETH 192 Mk40
Welsford CDN 240 Gg23
Welshpool GB 49 Ks38
Welski Park Krajobrazowy PL 65 Lu37
Welton USA 235 Ec29
Welutu RI 131 Rd49
Welver D 58 Lj39
Welwel ETH 193 Nc42
Welwitschia Plain NAM 200 Lh56
Wema RDC 191 Mb46
Wemen AUS 150 Sb63
Wemindji CDN 237 Ga20
Wemmershoek ZA 204 Lk62
Wemyss Bay GB 48 Kg36
Wen SUD 191 Md41
Wenago ETH 192 Mk42
Wenatchee USA 232 Dk22
Wenatchee Mtns. USA 232 Dk22
Wenceslau Braz BR 277 Hf57
Wenchang CHN 106 Qd30
Wenchi CHN 109 Qh36

Wencheng CHN 109 Ra32
Wenchi GH 187 Kj42
Wenchuan CHN 106 Qb30
Wenden USA 235 Ed29
Wendeng CHN 107 Rb27
Wendo ETH 192 Mk42
Wendo Genet Hot Springs ETH 192 Mk42
Wendover USA 235 Ed25
Wendover USA 235 Ed25
Wenfang CHN 107 Qh27
Wenga RDC 190 Lk45
Weng'an CHN 108 Qd32
Wenge RDC 191 Mc45
Wenjie CDN 240 Gj24
Wenjie EAK 195 Na46
Wenling CHN 109 Ra31
Wenlock AUS 147 Sb52
Wen Miao CHN 108 Qf33
Wenou DY 188 Lb41
Wenquan CHN 103 Pa23
Wenquan CHN 100 Pa29
Wenquanzhen CHN 109 Qh31
Wenshan CHN 121 Qc34
Wen Shang CHN 112 Qj28
Wenshui CHN 106 Qg27
Wentworth AUS 150 Sb62
Wentworth CDN 240 Gj23
Wentworth Falls AUS 151 Sf62
Wenxi CHN 106 Qf28
Wen Xian CHN 106 Qc29
Wenzhen CHN 109 Qj31
Wenzhou CHN 109 Ra32
Weott USA 234 Dj25
Wepener ZA 205 Md60
Wequan GB 49 Ku39
Wera EAU 194 Mg45
Weragantota CL 119 Pa42
Werbomont B 51 Lf40
Werda ZA 204 Mb60
Werdau D 58 Ln40
Werdohl D 58 Lj39
Were Ilu ETH 192 Mk40
Wereldend ZA 204 Ma58
Werinama RI 131 Re47
Weringa Downs AUS 149 Se59
Werl D 58 Lh39
Werneck D 59 Ll41
Werner Lake CDN 236 Fc20
Wernigerode D 58 Ll39
Wer Ping SUD 191 Me41
Werribee AUS 151 Sc64
Werri Creek AUS 149 Sf61
Werrikimbe N.P. AUS 149 Sg61
Wertheim D 59 Lk41
Werther D 58 Lj39
Werwaru RI 131 Re50
Weser D 58 Lj39
Weserbergland D 58 Lk39
Weskus N.P. ZA 204 Lj61
Wesley USA 240 Gj23
Wesleyville CDN 241 Ho21
Wesola PL 65 Ma38
Wessel Islands AUS 146 Rj51
Wesselsbron ZA 205 Md59
Wessington Springs USA 236 Fa23
West Antarctica ANT 287 Ec34
West Bank IL 92 Mh30
West Bay GB 243 Fk36
West Bend CDN 233 Ej20
West Bend USA 237 Ff24
West Bengal IND 117 Pd34
Westbourne CDN 236 Fa20
West Branch USA 237 Fh23
West Breaker CO 249 Ga38
Westbrook USA 241 Gd24
West Burra GB 48 Kt30
Westbury AUS 149 Sc57
Westby USA 233 Eh22
Westby USA 237 Fe24
West Caicos GB 250 Gd35
West Caroline Basin 134 Rb09
West Coast N.P. ZA 204 Lk62
West Des Moines USA 236 Fd25
Western Australia AUS 135 Qb12
Western Cape ZA 204 Ma62
Western Caucasus RUS 73 Mk23
Western Desert ET 178 Md31
Westerhever Leuchtturm D 58 Lj36
Westerland D 58 Lj36
Westerly USA 241 Ge25
Western Port AUS 151 Sc65
Western Sahara MA/DARS 174 Kd33
Western Sayan Mountains RUS 88 Pc08
Western Tannu-Ola Range RUS 101 Pf20
Western Thebes ET 179 Mg33
Westernschelde NL 51 Lc39
Westerstede D 58 Lh37
Westerville USA 237 Fj25
Westerwald D 58 Lh40
West Falkland GB 283 Gk71
West Fargo USA 236 Fb22
Westfield USA 237 Ga24
Westfield USA 239 Fh26
West Frisian Islands NL 51 Le37
Westgate AUS 149 Sd59
Westgate CDN 233 Fa19
West Glacier USA 232 Ed21
West Group AUS 145 Rd63
West Ice Shelf 287 Pa32
West Indies 250 Gd38
West Island AUS 146 Rj53
West Macdonnell N.P. AUS 143 Rg57
West Monroe USA 239 Fd29
West Nicholson ZW 201 Me56
West Nicholson ZW 241 Gb26
Wetwil USA 149 Sf61
Westhoff USA 238 Fb31
Whitchurch GB 49 Ks38
Whitby GB 49 Ku36
White Bay CDN 241 Hp20
Whitebourne CDN 241 Hq22
White Cape Mount USA 240 Gf23
White City (Tel Aviv) IL 90 Mh29
White Cliff AUS 250 Gd34
White Cliffs AUS 149 Sc61
Westby AUS 148 Sb61
White Cloud USA 237 Fh24
Whitecourt CDN 231 Ec18
White crowned pigeons BS
White Desert ET 179 Me32
Whitedog CDN 236 Fc21
White Earth Ind. Res. USA 236 Fc22
Whitefish Bay CDN/USA 237 Fh22
Whitefish Lake CDN 236 Fe20
Whitehall USA 232 Ec21
Whitehall USA 232 Ec23
Whitehall USA 241 Gd24
White Hall USA 239 Fe26
White Hall USA 239 Fe26
White Haven USA 241 Gc24
Whitehorse CDN 230 Dc15
White Horse USA 236 Ek23
White Island NZ 152 Tj64
White Lady Painting NAM 200 Lh56
White Lake CDN 242 Ga26
Whites-barre USA 241 Gc24
Whiteman Range PNG 156 Se48
Whitemark AUS 151 Se66
White Mesa Natural Bridge USA 235 Eg27
Whites Ice Shelf 287 Ed33
White Mountains USA 241 Gd23
White Mountains USA 228 Bj13
White Mountains USA 229 Cg13
White Mountains USA 234 Eb26
White Mountains USA 235 Ef29
White Mountains N.P. AUS 147 Sc56
Whitemouth USA CDN 236 Fb21
Whitney, Mount USA 234 Ea27
Whitianga NZ 152 Th64
Whitsunday Group AUS 147 Sd56
Whitsunday Islands N.P. AUS 147 Se56
Whitsunday Passage AUS 147 Sd56
Whittier USA 229 Cc15
Whittier USA 234 Ec27
Whittlesea ZA 205 Md61
Whittlesea AUS 151 Sc64
Whyalla AUS 150 Rj62
Whyalla Maritime Museum AUS 150 Rj62
Why USA 235 Ed29
Whycocomagh CDN 240 Gk23
Whycocomagh Ind. Res. CDN 240 Gk22

West Union USA 236 Fe24
West Union USA 234 Fb24
West Valley City USA 235 Ed25
West Virginia USA 239 Fk26
West Wendover USA 235 Ec25
Westwood AUS 149 Sf57
Westwood USA 234 Dk25
West Wyalong AUS 151 Sd62
West Yellowstone USA 233 Ee23
Wetan RI 131 Re49
Wetar RI 131 Rd49
Wetaskiwin CDN 233 Ed19
Wete EAT 197 Mk48
Wete RDC 199 Mc48
Wetherby GB 49 Kt37
Wetlina PL 67 Mc41
Weto WAN 188 Ld42
Wetora ETH 192 Mj40
Wetteren B 51 Ld40
Wettsteingebirge A 60 Lm43
Wetumka USA 238 Fb28
Wetumpka USA 239 Fg29
Wetzikon CH 60 Lj43
Wevoh USA 229 Bg11
Wewahitchka USA 239 Fh30
Wewak PNG 155 Sb49
Wewoka USA 238 Fb28
Wexford USA 238 Fb28
Wexford Harbour IRL 47 Ko38
Weyakwin USA 233 Eh18
Weybridge GB 49 Ku39
Weyburn CDN 233 Ej21
Weyer Markt A 61 Lp43
Weyla SP 193 Ne41
Weyweg CDN 240 Gb23
Weymouth GB 49 Ks40
Whakamaru NZ 153 Th65
Whakapara NZ 152 Th63
Whakatane NZ 152 Tj64
Whale Bay MYA 122 Pk40
Whalebone USA 242 Gc28
Whale Cay BS 243 Gb33
Whale Sanctuary MEX 244 Cc32
Whale Valley = Wadi Al-Hitan ET 179 Me30
Whale Watching (Fraser Island) AUS 149 Sg58
Whaley Bridge GB 49 Kt37
Whalsay GB 48 Ku30
Whananaki NZ 152 Th64
Whangamata NZ 152 Th64
Whanganui N.P. NZ 153 Th65
Whangarei NZ 153 Tk65
Wharton USA 245 Fb31
Wharton, Mount 287 Ta35
Wha T. = Lac la Matre CDN 231 Eb14
Wheatland USA 235 Eh24
Wheaton USA 236 Fb23
Wheaton USA 238 Ek28
Wheeler Peak USA 235 Ec26
Wheeler USA 237 Fe25
Whim Creek USA 142 Qk56
Whiskey Trail GB 48 Ks33
Whitby GB 49 Ku36
White Bay CDN 241 Hp20
Whitebourne CDN 241 Hq22
Whitecourt CDN 231 Ec18
White crowned pigeons BS
White Desert ET 179 Me32
Whitedog CDN 236 Fc21
White Earth Ind. Res. USA 236 Fc22
Whitefish Bay CDN/USA 237 Fh22
Whitefish Lake CDN 236 Fe20
Whitehall USA 232 Ec21
Whitehall USA 232 Ec23
Whitehall USA 241 Gd24
White Hall USA 239 Fe26
White Hall USA 239 Fe26
White Haven USA 241 Gc24
Whitehorse CDN 230 Dc15
White Horse USA 236 Ek23
White Island NZ 152 Tj64
White Lady Painting NAM 200 Lh56
White Lake CDN 242 Ga26
Whites-barre USA 241 Gc24
Whiteman Range PNG 156 Se48
Whitemark AUS 151 Se66
White Mesa Natural Bridge USA 235 Eg27
Whites Ice Shelf 287 Ed33
White Mountains USA 241 Gd23
White Mountains USA 228 Bj13
White Mountains USA 229 Cg13
White Mountains USA 234 Eb26
White Mountains USA 235 Ef29
White Mountains N.P. AUS 147 Sc56
Whitemouth USA CDN 236 Fb21
White Nile SUD 162 Mb08
White Nile SUD 185 Mg40
White Owl USA 236 Ek23
White River ZA 205 Mf58
White River CDN 237 Fh21
White River USA 236 Ek24
White River Junction USA 241 Gd24
White River N.W.R. USA 239 Fe28
White Rock NZ 153 Th66
White Salmon USA 232 Dk22
White Sands National Monument USA 235 Eg29
White Sands Missile Range Museum USA 235 Eg29
White Sands Space Harbor USA 235 Eg29
White Sea RUS 86 Mb03
Whiteshell Prov. Park CDN 236 Fb21
White Sulphur Springs USA 233 Ee22
Whiteville USA 239 Ff28
Whiteville USA 242 Ga28
White Volta GH 187 Kk41
Whitewater USA 237 Ff24
Whitewater USA 235 Ee27
White Wells AUS 144 Qj60
Whitianga NZ 152 Th64
Whitney, Mount USA 234 Ea27
Whitsunday Group AUS 147 Sd56
Whitsunday Islands N.P. AUS 147 Se56
Whitsunday Passage AUS 147 Sd56
Whittier USA 229 Cc15
Whittier USA 234 Ec27
Whittlesea ZA 205 Md61
Whittlesea AUS 151 Sc64
Whyalla AUS 150 Rj62
Whyalla Maritime Museum AUS 150 Rj62
Why USA 235 Ed29

Wiang Ko Sai N.P. THA 121 Pk37
Wiang Sa THA 121 Qa36
Wiawer EAU 194 Mg44
Wiawso GH 187 Kj42
Wiązów PL 64 Ls40
Wibaux USA 233 Eh22
Wich'ale ETH 192 Mk40
Wichita USA 238 Fb27
Wichita Falls USA 238 Fa28
Wichita Mts. USA 238 Fa28
Wichita Mts. N.W.R. USA 238 Fa28
Wick GB 48 Kr32
Wickede D 58 Lh39
Wickenburg USA 235 Ed29
Wickersham Dom USA 229 Cf13
Wickham AUS 142 Qj56
Wicklow IRL 47 Ko38
Wicklow Head IRL 47 Ko38
Wicklow Mountains IRL 47 Kn38
Wicklow Mountains N.P. IRL 47 Ko37
Wi'da PL 64 Ls36
Widgee Mountain AUS 149 Sg59
Widgiemooltha AUS 144 Ra61
Widminy PL 65 Mc37
Wi Do ROK 117 Qd22
Widuchowa PL 64 Lp37
Wiecbork PL 64 Ls37
Wiedenbrück, Rheda- D 58 Lj39
Wiehengebirge D 58 Lj39
Wiehl D 58 Lh40
Wielbark PL 65 Ma41
Wieleń PL 64 Lr38
Wieliczka PL 65 Ma41
Wielkopolski P.N. PL 64 Lr38
Wielun PL 64 Lt39
Wiener Neustadt A 61 Lr43
Wienerwald A 66 Lq42
Wieniawa PL 65 Mb39
Wierden NL 51 Lg38
Wieruszów PL 64 Lt39
Wierzbica PL 65 Mb39
Wierzchowo PL 64 Lr37
Wierzchucino PL 64 Ls36
Wierzchy PL 64 Lt39
Wiesbaden D 59 Lj40
Wieselburg A 66 Lq42
Wiesenburg D 58 Ln39
Wiesentheid D 59 Ll41
Wiesloch D 59 Lj41
Wiesmoor D 58 Lh37
Wiesua LB 186 Ke42
Wietzer Berg D 58 Lk38
Wigan GB 49 Ks37
Wiggins USA 239 Ff30
Wigierski P.N. PL 65 Md36
Wigston GB 49 Kt38
Wigton GB 49 Kr36
Wijchen NL 51 Lf39
Wikki Warm Springs WAN 188 Lf41
Wik'ro ETH 192 Mk39
Wikrowo PL 65 Mb36
Wikwemikong Ind. Res. CDN 237 Fk23
Wil CH 60 Lk43
Wilbarger AUS 145 Rb58
Wilberforce AUS 151 Sf62
Wilbert USA 233 Eh19
Wilbrunga Range AUS 143 Re56
Wilbur USA 232 Ea22
Wilburton USA 238 Fc28
Wilcannia AUS 149 Sc61
Wilchta PL 65 Mb39
Wilczęta PL 65 Ma41
Wildalpen A 61 Lp43
Wildcat Hill CDN 233 Ej19
Wildcat Hill Prov. Park CDN 233 Ej19
Wilderness USA 251 Gg36
Wilderness N.P. ZA 204 Mb63
Wildeshausen D 58 Lj38
Wild Horse CDN 233 Ee21
Wild Horse USA 241 Gd26
Wildlife Sanctuary (Western Australia) AUS 145 Rc62
Wildspitze A 60 Ll44
Wildwood USA 241 Gc26
Wiluja Mia Ochre Mine AUS 144 Qj59
Wilgena AUS 148 Rh61
Wilhelm II Land 287 Pj42
Wilheminagebergte SME 266 Hb44
Wilhelm, Mount PNG 155 Sc48
Wilhelmsøya N 38 Ma06
Wilhelmstal NAM 200 Lj56
Wilkes-Barre USA 241 Gc24
Wilkesboro USA 242 Fk27
Wilkes Land ANT 287 Rc32
Wilkie CDN 233 Ef19
Wilkins Ice Shelf 287 Gd33
Wilków PL 65 Ma39
Willandra Lakes World Heritage AUS 151 Sb62
Willapa Bay USA 232 Dh22
Willard USA 235 Ef28
Willard Bridge USA 142 Rb54
Willcox USA 235 Ef29
Willem Pretorius Nature Reserve ZA 205 Md60
Willem CDN 236 Gf22
Willey USA 241 Ga21
Williambury AUS 144 Qh57
William Creek AUS 148 Rk59
Williams Peninsula PNG 156 Se48
Williams AUS 144 Qj62
Williams Lake CDN 232 Dj19
Williamsport USA 241 Gb24
Williamston USA 242 Gb28
Williamstown USA 237 Fj25
Williamstown USA 251 Gf39
Willington ZA 204 Mb61
Willis Island AUS BS 243 Ga33
Williston USA 233 Eg22
Williston USA 243 Fj31
Williston Lake CDN 230 Dj18
Willmar USA 236 Fc23
Willmore Wilderness Prov. Park CDN 231 Ea19
Wilmington USA 241 Gc25
Wilmington USA 237 Fg25
Wilson Creek USA 232 Ea22
Wilson Hills 287 Sa32
Wilson Inlet AUS 144 Qj63
Wilson Island AUS 147 Sf57

Wilson Island – Yesan

Picture credits

This edition is published on behalf of APA Publications GmbH & Co. Verlag KG, Singapore Branch, Singapore by Verlag Wolfgang Kunth GmbH & Co KG, Munich, Germany

Distribution of this edition:

GeoCenter International Ltd
Meridian House, Churchill Way West
Basingstoke, Hampshire RG21 6YR
Great Britain
Tel.: (44) 1256 817 987
Fax: (44) 1256 817 988
sales@geocenter.co.uk
www.insightguides.com

Original edition:
© 2008 Verlag Wolfgang Kunth GmbH & Co. KG, Munich
Königinstr. 11
80539 Munich
Ph: +49.89.45 80 20-0
Fax: +49.89.45 80 20-21
www.kunth-verlag.de

English edition:
Copyright © 2008 Verlag Wolfgang Kunth GmbH & Co. KG
© Cartography: GeoGraphic Publishers GmbH & Co. KG

Terrain imaging: Produced using SRTM data from Heiner Newe, GeoKarta, Altensteig.

Text: Heike Barnitzke, Gesa Bock, Dirk Brietzke, Michael Kaiser, Wolfgang Kunth, Michael Elser, Ursula Klocker, Norbert Pautner
Translation/Revision: Verlag Wolfgang Kunth GmbH & Co. KG, Munich | JMS Books LLP

Printed in Slovakia

The information and facts presented in this book have been extensively researched and edited for accuracy. The publishers, authors, and editors, cannot, however, guarantee that all of the information in the book is entirely accurate or up to date at the time of publication. The publishers are grateful for any suggestions or corrections that would improve the content of this book.